MW01011632

# Fulbright: A biography

# Fulbright
## A biography

RANDALL BENNETT WOODS

Published by the Press Syndicate of the University of Cambridge
The Pitt Building, Trumpington Street, Cambridge CB2 1RP
40 West 20th Street, New York, NY 10011-4211, USA
10 Stamford Road, Oakleigh, Melbourne 3166, Australia



First published 1995

Printed in the United States of America

*Library of Congress Cataloging-in-Publication Data*
Woods, Randall Bennett, 1944–
Fulbright : a biography / Randall Bennett Woods.
p. cm.
ISBN 0-521-48262-3
1. Fulbright, J. William (James William), 1905–1995 2. Legislators – United States – Biography. 3. United States. Congress. Senate – Biography. 4. United States – Foreign relations – 1945–1989. I. Title.
E748.F88W66 1995
973.9′092 – dc20
[B] 94–46347
CIP

A catalog record for this book is available from the British Library

ISBN 0-521-48262-3 hardback

*Illustration credits*
Photographs courtesy of Walter J. Lemke Papers, Special Collections Division, University of Arkansas Libraries, Fayetteville: Figs. 1–12, 15–18
Cartoon by Ranan Lurie (Fig. 13) © 1976, courtesy of the *New York Times*
Cartoon by George Fisher (Fig. 14) © 1976, courtesy of the *Arkansas Democrat-Gazette*

*For Rhoda*

# Contents

# *Preface*

The idea for a life-and-times biography of J. William Fulbright occurred to me some nine years ago when John Cooper of the University of Wisconsin suggested that I do a short biography of the junior senator from Arkansas for a series he was editing. Upon investigation, I found that there was no up-to-date biography of Fulbright. Both Haynes Johnson and Bernard Gwertzman's balanced, reliable study and Tristram Coffin's uncritically admiring work stop in 1966. William C. Berman's fine book on Fulbright and Vietnam was still two years away. Seth Tillman, the senator's speechwriter and intellectual alter ego during the 1960s, was and is researching a biography, but he had not yet reached the manuscript stage. I informed Cooper that I could turn out a brief biography based on newspaper accounts and a quick perusal of Fulbright's papers, but that it would be superseded when a full-fledged biography appeared. We both agreed that Fulbright deserved a comprehensive study, and I subsequently decided to proceed with the long-term project instead of writing the abbreviated account for Cooper. My thanks to him for deferring to my and, I think, Fulbright's interests.

Biography is, as all who read and write know, different from analytical and narrative history and, ideally, from fiction. I attempted to come to grips with the art form by reading biographies that I admire as well as biographers on biography. Both of these exercises were useful, but, as I soon discovered, were no substitute for time – a great deal of time – spent with the secondary literature, relevant archives, the subject, his staff, his family, his admirers, and his detractors. For me the process of learning who Fulbright was, how and why he changed, and how he related to the times in which he lived has proved to be exhausting, all-consuming, and exhilarating. Walking the fine line between empathy and critical analysis proved difficult, as it does for all biographers, but I think that this was particularly true in the case of Fulbright whom I found to be, despite his obvious shortcomings and errors, a quite compelling personality.

*Fulbright* is not an authorized biography. The senator and his family and staff proved cooperative, but no one even suggested that they be allowed to exercise control over the material. I have reason to believe that family and staff have withheld some letters and records from me, but I have concluded, after dozens of interviews and more than two years of research in the senator's papers at Fayetteville, that such material has far more to do with their lives and business dealings than with his. Fulbright himself proved to be most forthcoming. In the fall of 1988 I spent eleven days – consecutive except for a weekend – with him in Washington; we averaged six hours a day. He was then eighty-four and had suffered two minor strokes. I sat as he reminisced and dozed; occasionally he repeated himself; frequently his recollections were taken straight out of articles and books written about him; but for at least an hour each day Fulbright achieved complete lucidity – the fog cleared from his brain and he remembered remarkable and insightful things about himself, his father, Lyndon Johnson, Vietnam, and a host of other incidents, relationships, and personalities. In the years that followed, I interviewed Fulbright several more times, but he was never able to achieve the same level of introspection and remembrance. Fulbright, like his daughters, Betsy and Bosey, was a fairly private person. I found him ready to talk about public events and policy but reticent about his private life. Most of the information on his personal habits, his relationship with Betty, and other such matters was gleaned from interviews with other family members and staff.

This book is based on a survey of the eleven hundred linear feet of material that comprise the Fulbright papers at the University of Arkansas and research in the Truman, Eisenhower, Kennedy, and Johnson papers as well as the Nixon Presidential Papers Project. Carl Marcy's papers housed in the National Archives proved invaluable, as did the manuscript holdings of the Library of Congress. I conducted some sixty-three interviews with people ranging from the Fulbrights' maid to Robert McNamara. I attempted many more. Some of Fulbright's staff were honest and forthcoming, others guarded and almost deceitful in their effort to protect what they believe to be Fulbright's correct image. I am particularly indebted to Walter Pincus, John Erickson, and Jack Yingling for their forthrightness and to Lee Williams for allowing me to see a portion of his papers. Members of the Johnson administration from McGeorge Bundy to Harry McPherson to George Ball were wonderfully cooperative and granted extended interviews. Despite bitter encounters with Fulbright over Vietnam, they came across as interested in him, in the historical record, in the whole project. With few exceptions, members of the Nixon administration proved to be indifferent. William Rogers was interested and gave me a moderately helpful interview as did John Ehrlichman, who was kind but not interested. Henry Kissinger made and broke three separate appointments for interviews. It became clear that, despite his famous feud with Johnson, Fulbright was culturally and intellectually rooted in the Kennedy–Johnson administration and, despite his cooperation with Rogers and Kissinger, completely alien to the Nixon regime. The two groups, it seems to me, hold a completely different and most revealing attitude toward history.

My indebtedness to persons and institutions for help in this undertaking is huge. The University of Arkansas and particularly the College of Arts and Sciences contributed resources, time, and unstinting encouragement. I benefited from grants extended by the Harry S. Truman Library, Lyndon B. Johnson Library, the Arkansas Council on the Humanities, the Dirksen Congressional Center, and the American Philosophical Society. Colleagues who read the manuscript and offered invaluable advice were LeRoy Ashby, William C. Berman, John M. Cooper, Robert Divine, Willard Gatewood, George Herring, Walter LaFeber, and Robert McMahon. Michael Dabrishius, Betty Austin, and Andrea Cantrell of Special Collections in Mullins Library at the University of Arkansas were unstintingly cooperative and helpful in guiding me through the Fulbright papers. Elizabeth Skinner patiently reproduced a dozen revisions for readers and press. April Brown and Michael Gnat provided invaluable editorial assistance. Although temporarily resident in India at the time, Sivagami Natesan compiled an excellent index. From the beginning of his contact with this project Frank Smith has been enthusiastic and expeditious. I will always be grateful to him for his faith in this biography.

My wife, Rhoda, has borne the emotional brunt of this decade-long labor, and if there is merit in it, she deserves much of the credit. My children, Nicole, Jeffrey, Thomas, and Andrea, have lent much-needed uncritical support. It must be said, of course, that all judgments and all errors in this book are mine and mine alone.

1. Fulbright *(front, right)* as a member of the combined Oxford–Cambridge lacrosse team.

2. Fulbright with his wife, Betty, and his mother, Roberta, shortly after Bill and Betty's return to Arkansas.

3. Bill, Betty, Betsey, and Bosey Fulbright at Rabbit's Foot Lodge.

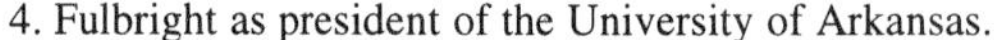

4. Fulbright as president of the University of Arkansas.

5. *(right)* Fulbright, Harry Truman, and William Benton at the signing of the legislation creating the Fulbright Exchange Program in 1946.

6. *(below)* Fulbright, Hubert Humphrey, U Thant, and Nikita Khrushchev at the signing of the Limited Test Ban Treaty in 1963.

7. Fulbright and Lyndon Johnson at a White House briefing on Vietnam early in the war.

8. Fulbright and Johnson aboard Air Force One three weeks after the Kennedy assassination. This photo was inscribed "To J. William Fulbright – Than whom there is no better – Lyndon Johnson."

9. Fulbright, Johnson, McGeorge Bundy, and Mike Mansfield in the Oval Office after Fulbright began questioning American foreign policy. This photo was inscribed "To Bill Fulbright – who listens – maybe – perhaps – Lyndon Johnson." This and the previous inscribed picture hung on Fulbright's office wall.

10. Senate Foreign Relations Committee hearings on Vietnam make front-page news.

The New York Times.

LATE CITY EDITION

NEW YORK, FRIDAY, FEBRUARY 18, 1966.

Senate Panel Hears General Taylor and Some Sharp Questions Follow

Senator J. W. Fulbright, left, Arkansas Democrat who is chairman of the Foreign Relations Committee, and Senator Wayne Morse, center, Oregon Democrat, listen to Gen. Maxwell D. Taylor, right, as he explains Administration's policy in Vietnam. Senator Morse, a severe critic of the policy, engaged in sharp exchange with General Taylor.

Lindsay Modifies His Transit Plan

By SYDNEY H. SCHANBERG

BUILDING TRADES BAR U.S. EFFORTS TO CURB PAY RISES

Wirtz's Peace Plan Scored —Mine Union Also Refuses to Accept Guideposts

By DAMON STETSON

DECISION ON TAXES HELD UP BY MAYOR

Plan May Not Be Disclosed for a Week or Longer—Blow to Borrowing Seen

By ROBERT ALDEN

TAYLOR ASSERTS A 'LIMITED' WAR IS INTENT OF U.S.

Ex-Chairman of Joint Chiefs Refuses to Describe Scope of Vietnam Commitment

TESTIMONY IS TELEVISED

General Tells Senate Panel Troop Needs Are Not an 'Endless Requirement'

By E. W. KENWORTHY

U.S. GRANTS INDIA $100-MILLION LOAN

De Gaulle Note to Johnson On War Is Reported Harsh

BIG ALLIED SWEEP ENDING IN VIETNAM

11. Bill and Betty at a Fulbright family gathering.

12. Fulbright campaigning in Arkansas in 1968.

13. From 1966 on Fulbright was seen as the State Department's principal public adversary – an ironic portrayal given his long-standing support of the Foreign Service and the department vis-à-vis other governmental agencies.

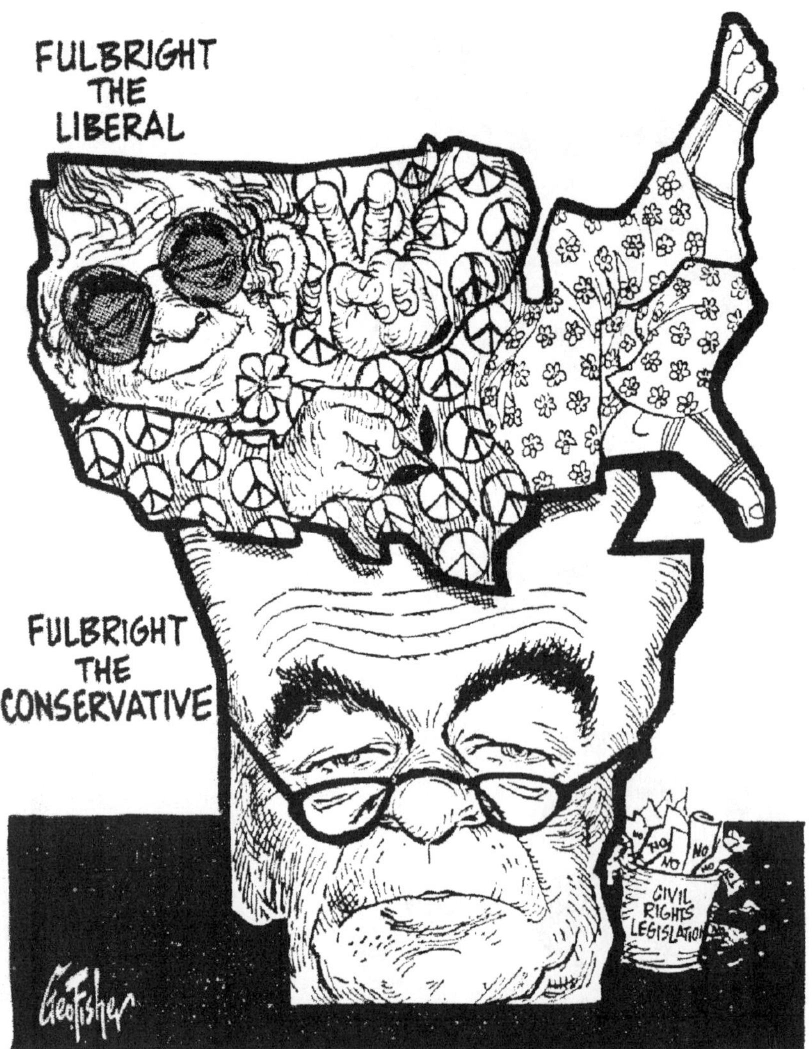


14. Political cartoonist George Fisher portrays the conventional wisdom concerning Fulbright's allegedly dichotomous political life.

15. Fulbright with George Wallace after the latter had recovered from the attempt on his life in Maryland during the 1972 presidential campaign.

16. Kissinger, Fulbright, and Mansfield.

17. William Jefferson Clinton and Fulbright at Boys (State) Nation in Washington in 1963.

18. Fulbright and his second wife, Harriet, in 1989 shortly after their marriage.

# 1

# *Of poets, Prussians, and plutocrats*

In 1850 a young Virginia couple decided to seek their fortune in the trans-Mississippi West. Thomas Edward Waugh studied dentistry at Johns Hopkins University in Baltimore, and in 1848, following his graduation, married Lucy Jones the daughter of a well-to-do Baptist minister, M. L. Jones. The American West beckoned not just to those on the economic and social margin, but lured as well individuals who dreamed of parlaying their modest educations and means into a business or agricultural empire. Just such people were Thomas and Lucy. The young Virginian and his bride arrived in St. Louis full of anticipation and apprehension. Missouri had a generation of statehood under its belt; there were no hostile Indians with which to contend, the Cherokee having been removed to the Indian Territory by congressional order. Nevertheless, compared to the environs of Waugh's Ferry, Virginia, the state and its inhabitants were raw and uncivilized. Thomas and Lucy traveled north on a course that paralleled the majestic Mississippi, and then turned west at Hannibal. The broad, flat alluvial plain, long since claimed for cultivation by frontier farmers moving west from Virginia and the Carolinas, gave way to the rolling prairie, untilled bottoms, and wooded ridges of north-central Missouri.

Thomas and Lucy Waugh were not typical log-cabin pioneers. Thomas brought with him a profession and a modest degree of personal wealth. Unlike the impoverished farmers, the land-hungry veterans of the Mexican War, and the avaricious land speculators who were flocking into Texas or attempting the perilous trek to Oregon and California, the young dentist did not need to squat on cheap federal land or pan for gold. He could set up a practice and use his resources to buy improved land. The couple decided to stop and make their fortune in the village of Rothville. Despite the spring mud and winter cold, the Waughs stayed, prospered, and produced ten children. Thomas's practice was successful enough to allow him to purchase a large tract of land north of the settlement. There he did his best to re-create the horse and cattle farm on which he had grown up in Virginia.

The same year Thomas and Lucy settled, John A. Stratton, another Virginian, arrived in Rothville with his wife, Julia, and numerous children. Both

Strattons could trace their lineage back to Revolutionary War heroes and both came from Virginia plantation backgrounds. John bought a large farm north of town and, together with his small contingent of slaves, began working the Missouri soil. The tobacco seed he had brought with him from his native state prospered, and soon the Strattons took their place among the tiny group of landed gentry around Rothville just as Thomas Waugh was solidifying his position within the town's professional class.

Though the Waughs and Strattons lived in the northern reaches of a border state, both families were Confederate sympathizers. Both tried to conceal their preferences, but their Virginia accents alone were enough to cause suspicion among Union military authorities in the area. More than vocal inflections were involved, however: Those Waugh and Stratton sons who bore arms in the Civil War fought for the Confederacy, and more than likely both of the patriarchs lent material as well as moral aid to rebel guerrilla bands in the area. In 1864 the Union commander arrested and imprisoned Thomas Waugh in nearby Brookfield. Upon his release, Thomas fled southward and took refuge in Texas until after the war was over. John Stratton was not as lucky. One night in mid-July 1864 he was dragged from his home and shot by a marauding band of Union sympathizers angry because of his refusal to contribute $500 to their cause.[1]

Following Grant and Lee's famous meeting at Appomattox Courthouse, Thomas Waugh returned to Rothville to resume his business and family life. Sometime in 1871 or 1872, during the waning days of Reconstruction, their second son married Martha (Pattie) Stratton, the fourth of John and Julia's ten children. The first and most remarkable issue of this union was Roberta, who was born in Rothville in 1874. Like her mother, she would marry a local boy, Jay, the oldest of William and Ida Fulbright's children.

The patriarch of the Fulbright clan was Johan Vilhelm Volbrecht, who had immigrated to America from Germany in the mid-eighteenth century. Sometime during the Civil War Johan's great grandson William had left Indiana, together with his wife Ida, and bought a farm in Chariton County, Missouri, near Rothville. "Old Bill" Fulbright was a frontier farmer, hard-driving, hard-drinking, intense, impatient, and a relentless disciplinarian regarding his four children. One of his grandchildren remembered him as "a tyrant."[2] The transplanted Hoosier quickly earned a reputation around Rothville as an industrious but aggressive German farmer who moved about his property and the county at high speed, in a veritable "cloud of dust."

On September 9, 1866, Jay Fulbright was born to Bill and Ida. He was the eldest of four and the only male. As the sole son in a farming family, young Jay learned the rigors of agriculture early and well. With chores from sunup

1 Allan Gilbert, *A Fulbright Chronicle* (Fayetteville, 1980), 15.

2 Ibid., 28.

to sundown and an unrelenting, insensitive taskmaster for a father, Jay's childhood was anything but idyllic. He would later come to appreciate the fact that his father had taught him discipline, perseverance, and mental toughness, but would throughout his life feel robbed of his childhood.

Jay's mother, Ida, was a quiet woman, but a person of moral and spiritual strength. She frequently served as a buffer between her restive son and her abrasive husband. It quickly became clear to her that Jay was not cut out for farm life, and she consequently encouraged him in his studies.

Jay Fulbright was a serious, ambitious young man. "Mr. Fulbright was not a person you could get to know easily," a Fayetteville business associate later observed of him.[3] His father's strong hand hardened him; he was not foolish enough to rebel openly, but he had enough strength of character to want to make a life of his own. Even as a college student Jay Fulbright let it be known that he had little time for small talk or fools.

Roberta Waugh, his future wife, was no fool. Lucy and her clan were readers and talkers. Some said they read primarily so that they could share their knowledge with others – whether the recipient liked it or not. The Waughs would argue endlessly and heatedly about anything and everything. According to a family historian, Lucy's male offspring "have chosen intelligent, strong-willed wives, who have tended to dominate the family" much as Lucy and her mother, Sophia, dominated theirs.[4]

Roberta's childhood was comfortable and uneventful. Although the family had to draw its own water and cut its own firewood, there were rugs on the floor and quilts on the bed of their spacious, well-built house. Forever etched in Sis's memory were images of trundle beds and hitching posts; long riding skirts and gaily colored blouses; taffy pulls, spelling bees, and corn huskings. Her mother, Roberta recalled, did not do heavy physical labor; after all, her father, James Waugh, was a Virginian by heritage and did not believe in such things.

Determined to get off and stay off of the farm, Jay attended Rothville's public schools and spent one year at a small military academy at Chillicothe. His grades were good enough to gain him entry to the University of Missouri, where he majored in business. Jay was able to combine a variety of campus activities with good grades. He joined the Sigma Alpha Epsilon fraternity, played several intramural sports, and, somewhat surprisingly, joined the drama club. Though his acting career was limited to a handful of university performances, Jay in succeeding years showed keen interest in any and all types of cultural enrichment activities. In perceiving "culture" as an ingredient in economic progress, he would become something of a local pioneer in Fayetteville.

[3] Ibid., 30. [4] Ibid., 75, 10.

Roberta, who was Jay's junior by eight years, did not depart for Columbia and college until her future husband had graduated and been back a year. Homesick to the point of illness at first, the female pride of Rothville persevered and quickly fell in love with college life. She was a good if somewhat uneven student, tending like so many to excel in those subjects, particularly history and English, that interested her. She joined the Kappa Kappa Gamma sorority and soaked up all the exhibits, recitals, and lectures that her schedule would accommodate. Roberta was noted throughout her life for the catholicity of her interests; she took her exposure to the liberal arts at the University of Missouri seriously. A lecture by Walter Williams, who was to found Missouri's famed school of journalism, impressed her especially. Though she decided to concentrate on education, earning her two-year teaching certificate, Roberta retained a life-long passion for journalism.

In October of 1894 Jay Fulbright, 28, and Roberta Waugh, 20, married. The ceremony not only marked the consolidation of Rothville manners and customs in the union of two of its leading families, but the mixture of two very powerful and different personalities. The joining of the Waughs and Fulbrights would produce a family that was capable of intellectual brilliance, stubbornness to the point of stupidity, intense loyalty, intolerance, graciousness, dark anger, complete failure, and stunning achievement. It was a clan whose history was punctuated by an unusual number of triumphs and tragedies.

"Poppa," said Jay Fulbright's oldest daughter, "had had enough of farming" by the time he had had a chance to go off to school. Nonetheless, the young couple started married life on the farm, although it was clear that Jay regarded the land as a means to an end rather than an end in itself. Bill and Ida Fulbright gave each of their children a wedding gift of $10,000. In Jay's case the endowment took the form of a farm with a mortgage on it. One day in the summer of 1897 Jay came in, hung up his hat, and told Roberta, "Ol' Lady [his term of endearment for his wife], pack up; we're moving to town. I just bought the Bank of Sumner [a nearby community]."[5] Roberta was very comfortable with the routine of farm life and had no desire to change. She cried a bit and then dutifully began packing. The break was final, however; Jay Fulbright would own many farms in his life, but never again one that he would work.

In Sumner the couple rented a modest two-story frame house a few blocks from the bank. Frances Lucille, the eldest of their children, had been born on the farm in 1896. Town life seemed to be good for Jay and Roberta's sex life: Anna Waugh entered the world in March 1898 and Jay, Jr. (Jack), the following year. The Fulbrights moved twice more before settling in a steepled, red gingerbread house at the head of Sumner's main street. On April 9, 1905,

[5] Ibid., 32, 38.

Roberta bore the couple's fourth child, James William. All of the Fulbright children were born at home, of course, delivered by the family doctor in Jay and Roberta's bed.

Jay proved to be a natural banker. He had drive and ambition; more important he had judgment and instinct. He had bought the Bank of Sumner in 1897, when the country was still recovering from the Panic of 1893, the worst depression America had experienced up to that time. The young businessman could judge the intrinsic and potential value of property and the reliability of human beings; and he was willing to take chances in a treacherous economy. Jay quickly surmised that the economic opportunities in Sumner were quite limited. He needed to move and he needed collateral. The panic had led to large-scale farm mortgage foreclosures in the West, especially in Kansas. As agricultural prices plummeted, literally thousands of farmers lost their land. Banking, in the unregulated climate of the late nineteenth and early twentieth centuries, included taking advantage of other people's calamities. Jay proved a sheer genius at doing that. Borrowing a sizable sum from the Waughs, he purchased several extensive tracts in Kansas, determined to hold them until the price appreciated – which, of course, it did. As he had hoped, his ventures provided him with the means of testing his skills in an arena larger than Chariton County.

The year that young Bill Fulbright was born and Jay decided to search for greener pastures seemed to many Americans to mark the dawning of a new, more hopeful era. Theodore Roosevelt had been elected to a full term as president the year before. His buoyancy and self-confidence, coupled with the economic boom that was sweeping the nation in the wake of the depression decade of the 1890s, instilled a spirit of hopeful expectation in the breast of many Americans, especially white, male ones. Industry was booming; between 1860 and 1914 the United States advanced from fourth to first among the manufacturing nations of the world. Roosevelt's brand of progressivism promised to regulate big business in the public interest without destroying it. The Pure Food and Drug Act, the Hepburn Act and other measures, the progressive majority assumed, would protect consumers from product and price abuse without cutting off their abundant supply of cheap and high-quality products. Small businessmen were encouraged by the Rough Rider's trust-busting campaign while the denizens of Wall Street continued to prosper despite the president's broadsides. Meanwhile, agricultural prices soared to unprecedented heights: When Congress later translated the concept of parity into legislation during the New Deal, it used the peak years of 1909–14 as the standard for measuring farm prosperity. Finally, as a result of the Spanish–American War the United States had acquired an overseas empire, the badge of great power status at the turn of the century. Bitter labor–management conflicts such as the Pullman and Homestead strikes, financial crashes such as the Panic of 1893, and the politics of polarization associated with the free-silver movement and the election of 1896 seemed part of the distant past. There were still deep and abiding pockets of poverty; educational levels among urban immigrants were abysmally low; blacks were invisible; and women could not yet vote in national elections. For white, middle-class America, however, the material millennium seemed just around the corner; and Jay and Roberta Fulbright epitomized white, middle-class America in the age of Theodore Roosevelt.

As he looked around for greener fields, Jay's eyes turned southward to the Mississippi Delta. The South in 1905 closely resembled an impoverished, developing country. Much as America had been for Britain prior to the Revolutionary War, the South was for the North and Midwest a supplier of raw materials and a consumer of manufactured goods. The region was a colony controlled by northern financial moguls who lent their money to cotton, rice, and sugar planters, financed monopolistic railroads that provided southern farmers with their only means of getting their goods to market, and purchased the region's food, fiber, and fuel for distribution throughout America. Memphis, Tennessee, like New Orleans and Atlanta, was a city where northern capital and southern agriculture met. Jay Fulbright was shrewd enough to realize that in such a city there was abundant opportunity for ambitious opportunists, individuals with a little capital and a keen eye who could take advantage of changing land prices, play the commodities market, and invest in local rail construction.

Memphis was Jay's ultimate objective, but his first stop after departing Sumner was Fayetteville, Arkansas. Although the object of his trip south was business, he brought Roberta and the four children – Lucille, Anna, Jack, and Bill – with him. Old Bill and Ida Fulbright had "retired" to Fayetteville to escape the mud and hard winters of northern Missouri. The elder Fulbright kept himself busy working several acres east and south of the town square. In the back of Jay's mind was a plan whereby Roberta and the children might stay the summer in the Ozarks, where the climate, well in advance of the age of air conditioning, would be more agreeable than in Memphis.

In 1906 Fayetteville was a community of some three thousand inhabitants nestled in the foothills of the Ozark Mountain range, an interconnected system of heavily wooded peaks and ridges that sprawled across forty thousand square miles of northern Arkansas and southwest Missouri.[6] To the south of town lay the Boston Mountains, the last westerly outreach of the Ozarks. To

6 Joseph C. Neal, comp., *History of Washington County, Arkansas* (Springdale, Ark., 1989), 1.

the north and west stretched the Ozark Plateau and the states of Oklahoma, Kansas, and Missouri.[7] During the years following the Civil War Fayetteville's white population grew dramatically, whereas its black population did not – a somewhat surprising development in view of the fact that the Boston Mountains and Springfield plateau were Union territories. The descendants of the community's slaves who stayed gathered in a hollow southeast of the square known as Tin Cup. During the twentieth century, the African-American population of Fayetteville never exceeded 2 percent of the whole.

From its inception, the hub of Fayetteville was its "square." Aside from assorted dry-goods stores, hardware concerns, restaurants, two of the community's three banks, and a hotel, the square was the site of the imposing, gothic-style courthouse completed in 1906, the post office, and the county jail. It was here that Fayetteville's politics were argued, its business done, its finest citizens put on display, its festivals held, and its hopes and fears articulated.

In 1871 the state legislature, in response to a generous grant of land from the prosperous McIlroy family and a $100,000 bond issue voted by the town's citizens, opted to locate the University of Arkansas in Fayetteville. A land-grant college, the school would become as well the state's flagship institution and Fayetteville's economic mainstay. In 1906 as the Fulbrights were making their way to the Ozarks, Fayetteville was signing a contract for electric lighting for the city's streets, and the Frisco Railroad was in the process of instituting what it called "a fast mail train" to St. Louis. University of Arkansas President John Clinton Futrall was just returning from a summer trip to the cotton counties of eastern Arkansas.

Totally preoccupied with her four small children, Roberta was ready to settle down at the first opportunity. Fayetteville impressed her. With its college, it seemed a smaller version of Columbia, Missouri. Having relatives in the area made the northwest Arkansas community doubly attractive to the young mother. In later life, no doubt influenced by various popular myths associated with George Washington, Ulysses Grant, and other political luminaries, Roberta recalled an incident that happened shortly after she moved to Fayetteville, one that further endeared the town to her. Having settled in with the elder Fulbrights, Roberta and the children took a tour of the square. Sis had noticed from the local paper that the "Little Russian Queen" was available "to advise on future developments." With offspring in tow, she located the fortune teller and paid the standard fee. To Roberta's delight, the seer placed her hand on Bill's head and declared, "He'll go far!"[8] Throughout her life Ro-

7 Ibid., 3–4. 8 Gilbert, *Fulbright Chronicle*, 39.

berta would believe desperately in two things – fate and Bill. The Russian Queen only confirmed what she already knew.

During his stay in Fayetteville, Jay dutifully called on the local banks. There were three: First National, McIlroy, and Washington County (shortly to become Arkansas National). He liked what he saw. The people were friendly and business was bustling. He soon learned from one of the local banks that a prominent Oklahoman, J. H. Haskell, had decided to sell his imposing summer home in order to devote his energies to the cause of Oklahoma statehood. At a hastily arranged auction Jay outbid all comers. The house was a two-story mansion with double living room and porches around three sides. It would be an ideal retreat if they chose to headquarter in Memphis, he told Roberta. The structure was large enough to accommodate present and future offspring, and any and all relatives that might come from Rothville. Moreover, as the property included several acres of pasture, livestock, and a barn, it would satisfy Roberta's taste for country living.

With Roberta and the children settled in Fayetteville, Jay set out for Memphis, the first of several trips there he was to make during 1906–7. None of them convinced him that he ought to move. He bought some real estate along the riverfront and invested in several other concerns, but the business community and the banks, in particular, resisted his advances. Instead, by the end of 1907 Jay Fulbright had decided to seek his fortune in Fayetteville.

Roberta was delighted. By the time Jay made up his mind she was deeply involved in civic affairs, club work, and church activities. She would have liked to have worked outside the home, and was, in fact, employed for a time by the Bank of Sumner; but Jay believed it his duty to provide for his family, and he expected his wife to be content with managing the household and children. In the fall of 1910 she became pregnant again, much to her and Jay's surprise and somewhat to her discomfiture. She was by then thirty-six years old and, besides, four children seemed sufficient to a turn-of-the-century, upper-middle-class family. Nonetheless, she was not one to complain. The twins, Helen Stratton and Roberta Empson, were born on April 2, 1911.

Although Helen and Bo were chronologically the youngest members of the Fulbright clan, Bill continued to be the baby and the apple of both his mother and father's eye. Lucille was the oldest and was expected to be responsible. She played the role of first sibling to perfection and as a result appeared mature beyond her years. Anna was thoughtful and slow moving like her grandmother Ida.[9] Jack was a large, aggressive child, already showing signs of the black temper and intense impatience that would plague his adolescence and adulthood. Old Bill Fulbright had left his mark.

While the children grew and Roberta entertained and visited, Jay focused his attention on penetrating the banking community. He quickly evaluated

9 Interview with Suzie Zorn, July 23, 1989, Fayetteville, Ark.

each of Fayetteville's three banks as to their potential and their vulnerability. The McIlroy Bank was dominated by James Hayden (Jim) McIlroy, and was patently a family affair. The First National Bank was headed by Arthur Lewis, the scion of another long and well-established Fayetteville clan. That left the Washington County Bank, which had been chartered in 1884. It was the smallest institution in town and the most susceptible to being taken over. Accordingly, Jay sold some of his property in Sumner and bought a sizable chunk of stock.[10] Jay used his banking assets to buy businesses with management or money problems, put them back in working order, and then sell off part of the stock to recover his investment. The budding tycoon took full advantage of those banker's delights, tax defaults and overdue mortgages. "Dad," Bill recalled, "was in the bank constantly." He kept a sharp eye on how businesses around town were doing and on what today would be called their credit rating.[11]

In 1910 Jay invested in J. C. Mitchell and Co., a real estate and insurance business. Two years later he became president and renamed the firm the Guaranty Trust Co. In 1907 Fayetteville's newest and most active entrepreneur went into partnership with two experienced retail grocers, C. C. and Jeff Conner, to open the Ozark Wholesale Grocery. In 1910 Jay organized the Fayetteville Mercantile Co., and located its warehouses in Shulertown, the name Fayettevillians had given to the cluster of businesses that had grown up on Dickson Street around the Frisco depot just southeast of the university. In 1913 the Fayetteville family empire expanded to include the local newspaper, the *Fayetteville Daily Democrat.* Jay was interested in the paper because he recognized it as an important instrument for promoting Fayetteville, and because it would allow Roberta an outlet for her interest in journalism and politics.

If Jay had a weakness, it was a penchant for setting up his family members in business. In 1914 Thomas Waugh, Roberta's favorite brother, moved to Fayetteville and married a local girl; Jay set him up as stockholder and manager of the Crystal (later, Fayetteville) Ice Co. In 1920, despite Jay's reservations, Tom negotiated a soft-drink franchise for northwest Arkansas with the Coca-Cola Bottling Co. of Atlanta, Georgia. The ice and Cokes went together naturally, of course, and at a nickel a bottle, the profit margin was large. The soft-drink franchise would constitute one of the cornerstones of the Fulbright empire throughout the twentieth century.

By the time Jay acquired Crystal Ice, he had gained control of J. H. Phipps Lumber Co. Phipps was the largest industrial concern in northwest Arkansas, employing more than two hundred men at its peak.[12] In 1917 he offered

10 William S. Campbell, *One Hundred Years of Fayetteville, 1828–1928* (Jefferson City, Mo., 1928), 79, 81.

11 Gilbert, *Fulbright Chronicle,* 43.

12 Campbell, *One Hundred Years of Fayetteville,* 40.

to purchase controlling interest in the company in order to prevent his bank from having to foreclose on notes due. Trapped and embittered, J. H. Phipps had no choice but to sell. Jay made James Waugh, the third of the Waugh children and Roberta's junior by thirteen years, manager of the lumber company and its railroad.[13]

Apparently, Jay, like his father before him, was a Republican. Their sympathies, obviously, had nothing to do with the Civil War; rather, they were drawn to the GOP because it was the party of property and business. Jay was a pragmatist. The fact that he was the scion of a Virginia slaveholding family, posed no problem in his adjusting to northwest Arkansas, which had been overwhelmingly Unionist in its sympathies. He was, in fact, a kind of carpetbagger in reverse. Roberta, as it turned out, was a staunch Democrat, and the family paper reflected that prejudice from the date of its purchase by the Fulbrights.

On the eve of the outbreak of World War I, Jay and Roberta decided to move into town. Haskell Heights was relatively far removed from the banks, and Roberta itched to become more intimately involved with the life of the community, to be able to have university people drop in to discuss economics, philosophy, and current events, to dabble in local politics, to pay visits to her friends, and to cease ferrying her children to and from school in the Model T. Jay had had his eye on a row of mansions on Mount Nord, another of Fayetteville's seven hills, located just north of Dickson Street overlooking both the university to the west and the town square to the immediate south. Jay bought the home built by J. E. Mock in 1906, a two-story provincial mansion that ranked for many years as one of Fayetteville's finest residential structures.

The house at Mount Nord, which Roberta was to inhabit for over forty years, was a rectangular two-story structure with a full portico in front supported by a four white columns. Family life, typically, tended to center on the spacious and light-filled living room and the kitchen located immediately to the rear. The lawn sloped sharply front and back, and two rows of cedar bushes outlined the sidewalk that led from Mount Nord Street to the front porch. Exclusive though 5 Mount Nord was, the lot originally included a barn with cow, and a fair-sized garden plot in which Roberta could putter.

The years following World War I were for Roberta among the happiest of her life. She was immensely proud of Jay, one of Fayetteville's most prominent citizens. Her children were healthy and happy. Two of her favorite brothers, Jim and Tom, lived close by. Her new house was filled with a continuous stream of friends and family. Public affairs, which had always fascinated Roberta, constituted a stimulating backdrop for her delicious sense of personal security. The terrible war in Europe was at long last over, and War-

[13] Gilbert, *Fulbright Chronicle*, 44–5.

ren Harding aside, America was about to embark on one of its most interesting and tumultuous decades. Spurred on by the Anti-Saloon League and the Women's Christian Temperance Union, the nation had opted to deny itself alcohol. Women gained the right to vote in 1920, and during the succeeding decade they not only voted but moved out into the work force in droves, finding employment as teachers, secretaries, and nurses. As hemlines skyrocketed, American females demanded not only the right to smoke with men but to frequent speakeasies with them. All across the nation informed citizens discussed the pros and cons of joining the League of Nations. The great debate between William Jennings Bryan and Clarence Darrow over the origins of humankind lay just over the horizon. Though Jay and Roberta lived squarely in the middle of the "boobs, hillbillies, and hayseeds" that H. L. Mencken and other eastern sophisticates so often derided, the couple, as part of Fayetteville's budding aristocracy, kept up with international events, followed national fads, and felt inferior to no one.

To all of his friends and family James William Fulbright was never anything but "Bill." He was an intense, active child with an abundance of physical and psychological energy. Bright, towheaded, adventurous, he made Fayetteville his oyster. He could fish in the White River to the east of town, pick berries on some of his family's farm land, go exploring on Mount Sequoyah, the beautiful wooded hill just east of the square, and watch the trains coming and going in the cut that separated the university from the commercial district. Even as a preschooler he loved the outdoors; he did so in part because indoors he was usually involved in some kind of mischief. "Bill was always picking and poking at the twins . . . every time he'd get near them he'd pull their hair . . . or a toe . . . anything to make a little trouble," Anna recalled.[14]

Jay and Roberta were sticklers for education. Roberta read to the children regularly, and they were expected to read on their own. Her grandchildren remembered that on Christmas or summer trips to Fayetteville, the first thing they would have to do upon arrival was to demonstrate their spelling prowess for Grandma. She would summon them to the living room, pick a word at random out of the newspaper, and insist that they spell it. All of Roberta's children were expected to excel, but she sensed something special in Bill. To that end when it came time for school, she decided to enroll him at the experimental grammar and secondary school conducted by the university's College of Education in the basement of Peabody Hall. Located on the northeastern edge of the campus, Peabody was only four blocks from Mount Nord. One of Bill's classmates, Margueritte Gilstrap, recalled that the teachers at Pea-

[14] Ibid., 42.

body Experimental School were much influenced by the theories of educational pioneer John Dewey. Students were assigned material to master; in class they sat in embarrassed silence until they began to ask questions. The emphasis was on self-reliance and intellectual assertiveness. Gilstrap remembered also that the curriculum departed somewhat though not entirely from the classical. There were heavy doses of sociology, psychology, and political economy to go with language, math, and science. The teachers at Peabody, she remembered, were particularly fond of the writings of Charles Beard.[15]

As had his father before him, Jay expected his children to lend a hand where needed in the family's behalf – partly to learn the businesses and partly because he believed that work was a tried and true teacher of virtue and molder of character. Bill's first summer job, one he held for several years, was at the bottling plant in Shulertown. In those days before the advent of automatic bottling machines, he, along with a dozen other workers, washed and filled the bottles one at a time. One summer during his early adolescence, Bill was packed off to work on one of the Waugh farms in Rothville. His reaction to the agricultural routine was the same as his father's. "Bill was up here most of just one summer," recalled his uncle, Tom Waugh. "After that dose of farmin', I think he decided summer school was a lot easier."[16] In fact Bill attended school on a near-continuous schedule through high school and into college. Nevertheless, at his father's insistence, he still managed to work part time in the summer at the university creamery run by the College of Agriculture or in one of Jay's businesses.

Though Bill Fulbright had more of the Waughs in him than Jack, he was a Fulbright too. That meant he could be tough, stubborn, and imperious. The summer the family packed him off to Missouri, Anna remembered, weeks went by without a word from the youngest son. As school approached, he had still not communicated, to the intense irritation of his mother. Because no one knew when he was arriving, there was no one to meet him at the station. Mount Nord was a considerable trek, all uphill, from the train depot. Despite the fact that it was not their fault, Bill, as soon as he walked in the door, proceeded to scold his mother and siblings for not meeting him.[17]

Like his father, whom he greatly admired and whose approval he craved, Bill Fulbright was self-contained and independent even as an adolescent; and, like Jay, Bill was regarded by his contemporaries as somewhat aloof. He did not run with a crowd but enjoyed the company of a few close friends, particularly Ed Stone – later known to the architectural world as Edward Durell Stone. Indeed, there was Huck Finn in Bill Fulbright as well as Tom Sawyer. Friends and family remember him as moody, at times given to an intro-

15 Interview with Margueritte Gilstrap, June 23, 1989, Washington, D.C.

16 Gilbert, *Fulbright Chronicle,* 54.

17 Zorn interview.

spection that bordered on brooding. He also had a temper and knew how to fight. One of his lifelong acquaintances recalled how "Bill beat the hell out of me with his fists" after they quarreled over a girl;[18] Fulbright was seventeen at the time. There was also his brother, Jack: A family member recalls that the Fulbright boys engaged in endless matches at the university tennis courts, which sat then as they do now on the corner of Cleveland and Leverett at the northwest corner of the campus. These were usually won by Bill, the smaller, who would drive his older brother to distraction by employing a combination of guile and goading. More than one contest ended with a fistfight or a wrestling match.[19]

From an early age athletics were an important part of Bill's life. Jay Fulbright was one of northwest Arkansas's early golf promoters. Interest in amateur golf in the United States – outside of a few of the country's most elite clubs – dated from 1913. In that year a young Boston caddie named Francis Ouimet won the national championship (U.S. Open) in a playoff with noted British professionals Ted Ray and Harry Vardon. The young American's victory touched off a surge of interest in the sport across the country. At the time of Ouimet's much-publicized victory, there were approximately three hundred thousand golfers in the United States; ten years later the number was two million and growing. Jay, who was a careful reader of the daily sports section, caught the fever. He helped form Fayetteville's first golfing club, located on what was then the Washington County Fair Grounds southwest of Fayetteville. He and the boys could walk virtually across the road from Phipps and play on the primitive nine-hole course. In later years, when in Fayetteville, Jack, Bill, and assorted uncles, cousins, and in-laws would play on the eighty-seven-acre Fayetteville Country Club Course situated atop a hill directly south of town.

In addition to golf, Bill continued to play tennis, eventually captaining the university's tennis team; but the realm in which he gained lasting fame, as one might expect in Arkansas, was football. In 1921 Arkansas hired Francis Schmidt away from the University of Tulsa. Known as a tough disciplinarian, Schmidt had beaten Arkansas 63–7 two years earlier. Soon after his arrival he began scouring the campus for likely prospects, a coach's campus defining the limits of his recruiting area in those days. He had heard that Bill Fulbright, though not large (6 ft, 160 lb) was quick and well coordinated. Bill resisted Schmidt's blandishments but finally agreed to come out.[20]

In Schmidt's first football season at Arkansas his team won four games and lost five – an acceptable percentage, particularly since the wins included a

18 Quoted in Haynes Johnson and Bernard M. Gwertzman, *Fulbright: The Dissenter* (New York, 1968), 27.

19 Interview with Allen Gilbert, Oct. 17, 1989, Fayetteville, Ark.

20 Robert Leflar, *The First 100 Years: Centennial History of the University of Arkansas* (Fayetteville, 1972), 303–5.

40–6 victory over Louisiana State at Shreveport and a 9–0 defeat of Southern Methodist at the first officially designated homecoming game in Fayetteville. SMU was a conference and national power, and Arkansas had already lost four games when they met. As game day approached, sportswriters picked SMU by six touchdowns.

When the players walked onto the field, then situated on the southwest corner of the hilltop on which Old Main was located, more than two thousand spectators had gathered to witness the anticipated slaughter. The Arkansas players, some of them wearing leather caps and some bareheaded, were nervous as they went through their calisthenics. Although the SMU players were older, larger, and brimming with confidence, Arkansas's youngsters were tough and well conditioned. The game quickly settled into a defensive struggle. Operating out of the single wing, Bill Fulbright passed for the only touchdown and sealed the victory with a fourth-down field goal late in the game.

During Bill Fulbright's tenure there, the University of Arkansas embodied the term "provincial institution." Its enrollment remained well below a thousand until after the turn of the century. Students could be admitted with only three years of high school, and because there were few publicly funded high schools in the state, even that requirement could be waived. The heart of the institution was its arts and sciences college. Because most of the students came from Arkansas's towns, few though they were, the agriculture college languished with less than fifteen majors up until the eve of World War I. In 1920 President John C. Futrall began moving the university into the twentieth century. With the establishment of a system of specialized agricultural experiment stations, the College of Agriculture grew in prestige and enrollment. A department of philosophy and psychology – with, for a state institution, a first-rate faculty – was formed in 1923. Futrall established a law school in 1924 and, two years later, a College of Business Administration.[21]

Bill never considered going any place other than Arkansas, and nothing in his university experience caused him to regret his choice. He was the archetypal Big Man on Campus. "My first glimpse of him was in the fall of 1924," recalled Eloise Baerg-King, a fellow student from Fort Smith. "I saw this red sports car with the top down and a couple in there and her hair was flying. She was pretty. There were very few cars then; not many students had them so it made a big impression."[22] Indeed, Bill had a passion for automobiles that would stay with him for the rest of his life. His first summer in college he made $75 working at the university dairy slopping hogs. The week after

21 Ibid., 4, 90–3.
22 Interview with Eloise Baerg-King, Oct. 17, 1990, Fayetteville, Ark.

he quit, according to a contemporary, "he took his stripped down Ford to Bella Vista [a village on the Missouri border], let it out a little coming home, and wound up in night court with a $62 fine for speeding."[23] In addition to his athletic and automotive exploits, he was president of Sigma Chi and a member of virtually every other campus organization that counted, including Marble Arch, the "A" Club, the Arkansas Boosters' Club, and the Glee Club. He graduated with a "B" average in the days when a "C" was truly an average grade.

Like Lyndon Johnson, who was then dominating the student body of Southwest Texas State some five hundred miles to the south, Fulbright took an interest in campus politics. Even as a teenager he was able to persuade people to trust him with their interests. So commanding was his presence that his classmates elected him student body president in May 1923. The Associated Student Government had only been in existence since 1922, and in those early years, its scope was limited. Apart from the provisions governing election of officers, the constitution authorized the student government to deal almost exclusively with freshman hazing and with certain practices that were declared to be university "traditions."[24]

Despite his many honors, Bill Fulbright was not a particularly popular student. "Popular isn't the word," recalled T. C. Carlson, who served as Arkansas's athletic manager. "Bill was highly respected . . . moderately sociable, and not particularly approachable."[25] Carlson remembered being surprised at Fulbright's election as student body president. He was not your typical garrulous, back-slapping politician, but he had charisma and the bearing of a self-assured aristocrat.

Even as a junior in college there is little indication that Fulbright was giving serious thought to his future. He spoke vaguely of either teaching or entering the consular service abroad. There was no mention of a political career. To his peers and family, he did not seem overly ambitious. He was not an avid reader, and he made respectable grades because his father and mother expected it of him.

Life, which had been so good to the Fulbright clan, suddenly turned sour in the years following World War I. One calamity followed another until the walls of security with which Roberta had surrounded herself and her family lay in ruins. In 1922 her brother Tom died. Not only had he been witty and engaging, but as manager and part-owner of the ice company, and a stockholder in Fulbright Mercantile, he had been a valuable part of the family busi-

23 Quoted in Gilbert, *Fulbright Chronicle,* 134.
24 Leflar, *First 100 Years,* 142–3, 153.
25 Quoted in Johnson and Gwertzman, *Fulbright: The Dissenter,* 29.

ness empire. Less than a year later, Jay's mother, Ida, took to her sickbed in Keytsville, Missouri, with her final illness. Although he was suffering from a painful tooth infection, Jay made the trip north and was with his mother when she breathed her last. Soon after returning home, he developed a high fever and died mysteriously within a few days on July 23, 1923. Jay Fulbright was fifty-six.[26]

Though all of the family was distressed by Jay's death, Bill and Roberta were genuinely devastated. Indeed, they were the only two people in Jay's life who could be said to have been truly close to him. He was not a likable man: humorless, austere, unaffectionate. His granddaughter recalled that he swore with more vehemence and passion than anyone she had ever met. The words were not particularly profane, but the feeling – fueled, no doubt, by his father's insensitivity and ruthless driving of him – was intense. If for Anna he was distant and unsympathetic, for the twins, Helen and Bo, he was virtually invisible. Jack and Jay were too much alike temperamentally, if not intellectually, to have ever been close; indeed, they clashed repeatedly. Of the children only Bill seemed fond of his father. Jay took his youngest son everywhere with him; Bill enjoyed meeting people and learning about the businesses. Both he and his father had a bent for the practical and mechanical. Jay was intensely competitive about his business enterprises and proud of his successes. Bill empathized with his father and internalized both his competitiveness and his pride. The major reason Bill Fulbright was close to his father, however, was that he was Roberta's husband: If that bright, witty woman who doted on her second son loved Jay Fulbright, that was enough for Bill.

Fortunately or unfortunately, Roberta had little time to grieve for Jay. Naïvely, she assumed that his business associates were also his friends and, hence, also hers. The vulnerability that Jay had so often exploited was now visited on the Fulbright family empire, and his ruthlessness was repaid in spades. Roberta was flooded with lawsuits contesting titles, demanding payments, seeking injunctions, asking forfeitures, and mandating divestments.

Instinctively, the reluctant matriarch began to consolidate in areas where her position was not firm either because of financial reasons or, as with the Arkansas National Bank, because her fellow stockholders were hostile. Reinforcing that instinct was the fact that the family business was not in a good cash position. She quickly decided to trade her Arkansas National Bank stock for ownership of the Washington Hotel, thereby gaining sole control over the largest and finest hostelry in northwest Arkansas. The Washington also acted as landlord to the bank, and within six months Roberta had evicted it. Jay's reputation for business sense and integrity meant that his credit was excellent

26 Interview with J. William Fulbright, Oct. 11–18, 1988, Washington, D.C.

and he could operate his enterprises with a minimum amount of cash. Roberta quickly discovered that credit was largely a masculine affair. Downtown, moreover, her grit was generally interpreted as either a nuisance or a threat.

What Roberta needed was another male to become "head of family." That need became acute when, within a year of Jay's death, the eldest daughter, Lucille, died, leaving her one-year-old son, Allan, in Roberta's care.[27] Quite naturally, she turned to Jack, who was then in his senior year at Harvard College. At his mother's request, he quit school and returned to Fayetteville. It turned out to be a bad decision for both mother and son. Jack Fulbright was a strikingly handsome young man and a superb athlete. He had played football, basketball, and baseball for the Universities of Arkansas and Missouri before transferring to Harvard. Though big and fast and well coordinated, Jack had failed to make the first team at Harvard, primarily, he said, because he lacked the proper East Coast family connections.

Jack Fulbright was a dull child in a clever family. He was too much like his father and grandfather to be compatible with them. The eldest son was intensely jealous of Bill's intelligence and self-control, and particularly of the fact that he was the apple of his parents' eye. As the oldest he felt he had the "right" to familial respect and authority. This was particularly true after his father's death. He was willful, proud, and stubborn to the point of stupidity. Frustration breeds aggression, and it bred in Jack Fulbright an uncontrollable temper. According to his family, his rages were of monumental proportions, so blind and full of energy that they assumed a life of their own. It was as if Jack himself was bewildered by them. At the same time he could be witty, charming, and outgoing. Friends, especially outside Fayetteville, remembered him with great fondness. He was a hard worker, but that trait stemmed in part from his inability to share responsibility for a project. Unfortunately, contact with the Fulbright clan seemed to bring out the worst in him. Jack returned to Fayetteville determined to assume complete control of the family business and to brook neither criticism nor advice.[28] He was twenty-four going on fifteen.

What ensued was a series of bad decisions compounded by bullheadedness that rocked the Fulbright financial empire and rent the family. In addition to lacking tact or business sense, Jack was given to making snap judgments and then presenting them to the family as faits accomplis. At a time when his mother was desperately short of cash Jack decided to build new ice and bottling plants on West Street, which ran north off of Dickson between the university and Mount Nord. Although the family was opposed, Jack pressed ahead and "damned near broke us in the process," according to Bill.[29]

Further alienating Jack from his family was an incident that occurred within months of his return to Fayetteville. On October 31, 1923, city police ar-

27 Zorn interview. 28 Gilbert, *Fulbright Chronicle,* 68. 29 Fulbright interview.

rested the elder Fulbright and charged him with raping a university coed. At Jack's trial in December the jury convicted him of the lesser charge of assault and battery and fined him $200. Not surprisingly, the *Daily Democrat* did not report the incident, but the neighboring *Springdale News* did, with the observation that "much of the evidence submitted is unfit to print." Several years later a political rival of Roberta's charged that she had paid the jury $3,000 to have the charges reduced. She never denied the accusation.[30]

Eventually Jack recognized that there was no future for him in Fayetteville. The same month he was fined for assault and battery, Jack married Madeline MacKeckney, a warm, gracious Texan. Before the decade was out, the couple moved to New Mexico, where Jack attempted (unsuccessfully) to make his fortune as a cattle rancher.

Unfortunately, the breach created by Jack's obstinacy with his family was permanent. Virtually every future visit home included a family discussion of business matters and ended with his blowing up and leaving town – alone. Jack's sibling rivalry with Bill continued throughout the remainder of their lives.[31] Although Roberta at first defended Jack, his compulsiveness and lack of judgment during the years immediately following Jay's death drove her to rely on her younger son in business matters as well as other things.

Indeed, though Jack rushed back to Fayetteville to take charge of the family empire, Roberta thought it necessary to call in her younger son as well. After Jay's sudden death in July 1923, Bill did not return to school in the fall. He was immediately thrown into the fray. Josephine Waugh, Tom's widow and Roberta's sister-in-law, filed suit demanding that Tom's share of the Crystal Ice Co. be sold and she be awarded the proceeds. There was no way to fix an exact value on the company, so the court ordered the firm sold at auction in order to satisfy the claims on Tom and Jay's estates.

On October 24, 1924, Crystal Ice was auctioned by the sheriff on the steps of the courthouse. There were two bidders. One was a proxy of old Jim McIlroy: Jim Waugh. The aging entrepreneur wanted the now prospering ice delivery and bottling plant back; McIlroy authorized Waugh to spend up to $21,000. The other bidder was Bill Fulbright, aged nineteen. When the dust had settled, Bill had reacquired Crystal Ice for $22,000.[32]

Roberta tried to insinuate Bill into various other business activities. She named him president of the Black Mountain and Eastern Railroad, the short line that served Phipps Lumber Co. (making him, according to Ripley's "Believe It or Not," the youngest railroad president in the United States), but Jack shut his sibling (as well as everybody else) out of the decision-making process. Frustrated, Bill returned to school in 1924.

30 Stephen H. Dew, *The New Deal and Fayetteville, Arkansas, 1933–1941* (M.A. thesis, University of Arkansas, 1987), 225–33.

31 Gilbert interview.

32 Gilbert, *Fulbright Chronicle,* 70–3.

# 2

# *Oxford*

Autumn in the Ozarks is truly spectacular. Sometime in mid-October the maples and oaks begin to turn, and the hills blaze with brilliant reds, golds, and oranges made all the more vivid by the lush green backdrop of thousands of evergreens. The first few cold snaps leave the air crystal clear and the landscape shining. On just such a day in the fall of 1924 Bill Fulbright was making his way across campus when he encountered Professor Clark Jordan, dean of the graduate school. Jordan had taught Fulbright in several English classes, and the academic had become a regular at Roberta's soirées on Mount Nord. Jordan stopped his young protégé and informed him that applications for the Rhodes scholarships had just come in. The opportunity seemed tailor-made for him, Jordan declared enthusiastically. The program called for candidates who could exhibit both academic achievement and athletic prowess. What would he have to do, Bill asked? Nothing, Jordan replied. Selections were based on record, letters of recommendation, and an interview.[1]

That evening Bill told Roberta of his conversation with Jordan. She had, of course, heard of Rhodes and of Oxford, and urged him to apply. It was his duty to realize his potential, she insisted. With an Oxford education his opportunities would be unlimited. Bill agreed, and Roberta set about ensuring that her son was in fact the Arkansan who was selected.

Being from Arkansas was a distinct advantage in the Rhodes competition. In 1924 each state of the union was entitled to two scholarships every three years, and the pool of eligible students in rural states like Arkansas was small. The interviews were scheduled for Little Rock in early December. To Roberta's delight, the chair of the selection committee was none other than John C. Futrall, president of the University of Arkansas and a close family friend of the Fulbrights.[2] No doubt Bill would have been an obvious choice, but the first families of Fayetteville left nothing to chance. Roberta regaled Futrall with Bill's accomplishments several times between October and December. In his elegantly self-deprecating way, Fulbright recalled that there were only nine applicants all told, not one of whom, himself included, was

1 Interview with J. William Fulbright, Oct. 11–18, 1988, Washington, D.C.
2 Interview with Eloise Baerg-King, Oct. 17, 1990, Fayetteville, Ark.

particularly outstanding. He attributed his selection to his exploits on the athletic field, "since two or three had better academic records than I."[3] When the Rhodes scholarships were announced on December 14, Bill Fulbright's name was on the list.

Fulbright finished the fall term at the university and graduated in January with a degree in history. He was nineteen. Because his Rhodes did not begin until the following fall, he spent the spring working in the family businesses and taking a course in the law school. As fortune would have it, the course was taught by a young law professor fresh out of Harvard named Claude Pepper. Fulbright found Pepper fascinating, "the most articulate fellow you ever saw."[4] Pepper not only familiarized his young charges with the intricacies of the legal system, he gave them the benefit of his views on the League of Nations, the corruption of Republican politics, and the origin of the species. Fulbright had never met anyone quite like Pepper. In him he caught a glimpse of the person he might become.

Bill and the other American Rhodes scholars departed New York aboard the Cunard liner *Lancastria* after a send-off dinner at the Harvard Club. "At last we are off and out of sight of land," he wrote his mother. "It is a real thrill going out of New York harbor. You must try it sometime."[5] Thus did the young Arkansan begin his voyage of discovery, of destruction and reconstruction. He and the world would be changed because of it.

Fulbright was understandably apprehensive about the prospect of storms and seasickness. His worries proved groundless. "With the exception of two days the ocean has been as smooth as a lake. I have not been sick in the real sense of the word."[6] The stateroom was commodious, the food excellent, and the companionship enjoyable, the twenty-year-old novice traveler wrote his mother.

> I get up rather late and have lunch at one o'clock, then I either read, play bridge or take exercise until 4 o'clock which is tea time. . . . From 4 to 7 I take my bath and read. We then have dinner. After dinner usually there is a bridge game. There are several interesting boys and there is always something to do at this time. They dance every night but the girls are so scarce that I have not indulged in that sport.[7]

[3] Fulbright interview.

[4] Quoted in Haynes Johnson and Bernard M. Gwertzman, *Fulbright: The Dissenter* (New York, 1968), 34.

[5] J. W. Fulbright [hereinafter referred to as JWF] to Roberta Fulbright, undated, 1925, Personal Papers of J. William Fulbright, Mullins Library, University of Arkansas, Fayetteville, Ark. [hereinafter referred to as PPF]. JWF to Roberta, Sept. 26, 1925, PPF.

[6] JWF to Roberta, Oct. 5, 1925, PPF.

[7] JWF to Roberta, undated, PPF.

When the *Lancastria* docked at Plymouth, Fulbright and his classmates disembarked and immediately took the train to London. The ship had made excellent time, and they had arrived before their colleges were ready for them. Besides, none could resist catching a glimpse of one of the world's most famous cities. Bill was impressed but not intimidated. Through their circle of university and banking friends, the Fulbrights knew a number of people who traveled to Europe regularly. Several were then either visiting or living in London in the fall of 1924.

> I saw Vivian Lemon Tuesday evening and took her to dinner. Yesterday she took me to lunch at the Cheshire Cheese, Doctor Johnson's favorite loafing place. It is very old and retains that ancient atmosphere. We had a drive over London and looked in Westminster Abbey, which is truly marvelous. We also saw Saint Paul's, the Old Temple, the Inns of Court, Buckingham Palace and many other beautiful places. Last night I went to Wembley to see the British Empire Exposition and I am sure that a Worlds [*sic*] Fair could not be more interesting.[8]

After two glorious days of sightseeing it was time to depart for Oxford, then the Western world's most prestigious seat of learning.

Cecil Rhodes devoted his life and his fortune to the search for a mechanism to realize his vision of unifying the English-speaking peoples and extending their influence throughout the world – and quite a fortune it was. In 1870 Rhodes's parents sent their seventeen-year-old to South Africa to join his older brother, Herbert. The following year the Rhodes brothers began working in the diamond fields in Kimberly. Between 1873 and 1881 Rhodes alternated seasons between South Africa and Oxford, where he eventually matriculated from Oriel College. By 1877 he had acquired sole interest in DeBeers Mining Company, the largest producer of diamonds in the world. Extracting millions of man-hours from his black workers at virtual slave wages, South Africa's most famous entrepreneur built one of the world's great fortunes. After serving as prime minister of the Cape Colony, Rhodes retired from public life and devoted his efforts to developing Rhodesia and to furthering the cause of a worldwide, English-speaking commonwealth.[9]

Rhodes believed himself to be the complete man: scholar, soldier, businessman, and statesman. He had the classics specially translated for his perusal, and he ostentatiously carried a dog-eared copy of Marcus Aurelius with him wherever he went. His 1902 will, which set up the Rhodes scholarships,

8 JWF to Roberta, Oct. 9, 1925, PPF.

9 Frank Aydelotte, *The American Rhodes Scholarships: A Review of the First Forty Years* (Princeton, N.J., 1946), 1–2.

aimed at doing nothing less than replicating Cecil Rhodes generation after generation in past and present British colonies and in Germany. Rhodes wanted aspiring intellectuals, but also men of "moral character," fond of "manly outdoor sports," with "instincts to lead."[10] He envisioned, correctly enough, that recipients of Rhodes scholarships would become the scions of their communities: presidents, prime ministers, magistrates, general officers. "No student shall be qualified or disqualified for election to a Scholarship on account of his race or religious opinions," his sixth will read.[11]

Rhodes chose Oxford as the training ground for his protégés because it was what he knew, and it was quintessentially English. In an article on Rhodes and the origins of the scholarships, Lord Lothian explained that, in addition, "he believed that the type of education given there, with its outlook on the civilizations of Greece and Rome, its interest in philosophy, history, law and political science, would develop in his scholars those aptitudes which would specially assist them in the discharge of public duties in after life."[12]

The train ride from London to Oxford, situated in the rolling hills of south-central England, took less than half a day. Fulbright arrived in the ancient city excited but not overly apprehensive. He had come to Oxford, he would later say, seeking as any young man will, "exciting experiences, and if convenient, some knowledge."[13] His first sight of Oxford was disappointing; it appeared as he entered its outskirts to be just a midsized, lightly industrialized town; but as he approached the train station he could catch glimpses of several of the university's twenty-five colleges. The quadrangles, spires, and lush green courtyards of that ancient institution[14] took the young Arkansan's breath away.

Bill Fulbright arrived at Oxford at a fortunate time. World War I had wrought great changes on English society and on Oxford. A spirit of egalitarianism prevailed, and Oxford in the early 1920s was crowded with young men and women of the middle as well as the upper ranges of the social strata. As C. E. Mallet wrote in his three-volume history of Oxford,

> In January 1919, the Union Society was debating whether the world ought to be made safe for democracy or not. Undergraduates were returning to their old employments, their games, their clubs, their studies. In October 1919 there were gathered in Oxford more undergraduates than the University had ever seen before. The pressure on space was very great. The estimate of students in residence had risen in 1920 to four thousand, six hundred and fifty.[15]

10 Quoted in Johnson and Gwertzman, *Fulbright: The Dissenter,* 35.
11 Aydelotte, *American Rhodes Scholarships,* 15.
12 Quoted in Johnson and Gwertzman, *Fulbright: The Dissenter,* 36.
13 Quoted in ibid.
14 A. R. Wooley, *The Clarendon Guide to Oxford* (London, 1963), 8–9.
15 Charles Edward Mallett, *A History of the University of Oxford* (London, 1948), 486.

Before he left Arkansas Fulbright was instructed by Oxford to make a list of eight colleges in the order of his preference. Typically, scholarship winners consulted with members of the committee that selected them or with Oxford alumni. With Fayetteville singularly lacking in old Oxonians, Fulbright pored over the literature the university had sent him. Frustrated, he finally picked eight more or less at random; the college that selected him was Pembroke, founded in 1624 and traditionally used by prelaw and law students. The college that was to constitute Bill Fulbright's intellectual and physical environment for the next three years was neither the worst nor the best that Oxford had to offer. It occupied the site of half a dozen medieval halls, the chief of which were Broadgates Hall and Beef Hall. The refectory of Broadgates comprised the college library. The Master's Lodgings, formerly Wolsey's almshouses, faced St. Aldgate's and was a charming example of sixteenth-century domestic architecture.[16]

As soon as Fulbright arrived at Pembroke the college porter assigned him a room. His scout, a personal servant who changed linen, served breakfast and lunch, and ministered to the students' every need, brought a meal. Like every other student at Oxford, Fulbright's rooms were located in a quadrangle, a series of interconnected buildings surrounding a courtyard. In addition to apartments for students and fellows, the college included a common dining hall, library, chapel, and lecture rooms. "Unfortunately I share my rooms with an American Rhodes Scholar . . . you know the one from Kansas named Hower," the freshman from Arkansas wrote his mother. "He is all right but I wanted to get away from Kansas for awhile." Despite this initial disappointment, R. D. Hower, who went on to become a professor of business history at Harvard, and Fulbright would become fast friends.[17]

Fulbright decided early on to attempt an Honors undergraduate degree in history and political science. Under Oxford's tutorial method of study the individual's work was outlined clearly in the Examination Statutes, a list and description of examinations that he had to pass to earn his degree. Candidates for degree prepared themselves for these examinations primarily through their own efforts but also under the direction of a tutor. The tutor acted as "guide, philosopher and friend," but responsibility for the student's studies, he was clearly made to understand, was his and his alone.[18]

Fulbright had the good fortune to be matched with Ronald Buchanan McCallum, a young Scotsman of singular intelligence and absolute commitment to his students. When he and Fulbright met in 1925, McCallum was in his maiden year at Pembroke. The college's newest fellow had spent the previous year on an Empire grant at Princeton and did not exhibit the anti-

16 Wooley, *Clarendon Guide,* 16–17.
17 JWF to Roberta, Oct. 9, 1925, PPF.
18 Aydelotte, *American Rhodes Scholarships,* 68.

Americanism typical of so many of his colleagues. A Scottish Presbyterian and a devoted member of the Liberal Party, McCallum would earn a solid reputation as a scholar and teacher. His specialties were British elections and international organizations. Judging by Fulbright's enduring admiration for British institutions, especially its parliamentary system, McCallum was a sophisticated but unrepentant Whig. He was, not surprisingly, a great admirer of Woodrow Wilson, and throughout his long career would defend the concept of an international collective security organization as both practical and necessary. At twenty-seven, he was only seven years Fulbright's senior. "My tutor is a scotchman and very pleasant," Bill wrote his sister Anne. "He has not yet acquired the academic air."[19] Shortly after their first formal session, McCallum charmed his young charge by having them bicycle to Burford, where they picnicked at the tomb of Speaker William Lenthall of the Long Parliament. "He was a great admirer of Woodrow Wilson and all that," Fulbright recalled. "I absorbed all of that from him. I saw him every week. I thought him a very fine man, a practical scholar."[20] Until the twilight of Fulbright's career and the death of McCallum in May 1973, the two would maintain a close intellectual and personal relationship.

Fulbright's first weeks at Oxford were a blur of lectures, teas, fittings, and athletic practices. As he wrote to Roberta:

> We are attending the first lecture but the lecturer has failed to appear and I think we shall have to wait until tomorrow to hear any learned discourses. I have been shopping this morning. I bought an outfit for Rugby and I ordered a Tuxedo made. . . . Yesterday we rode our bikes out to Blenheim Palace which is about 7 miles. . . . You cannot imagine the grandeur of the park surrounding the massive pile of stone which is the Palace. The old trees are really wonderful and the grass is a beautiful emerald.[21]

If Fulbright was intellectually innocent upon his arrival in Oxford, he quickly became disabused of the notion that he could get by simply by following the study habits he had developed at the University of Arkansas. "It is an entirely different method of study and easily twice as difficult," he confessed to two of his former professors. "I didn't dream that any University could exist and still maintain such a high standard."[22] His first endeavor was a discourse on the nature of the Anglo–Saxon conquest. "These essays are hard as the dickens to write. . . . It has been raining today and I suppose that we are in for a real spell of Oxford weather," he wrote his mother dejectedly.[23] Later: "I went to my first tutorial this morning. I can't help but

19 JWF to Anne Teasdale, Oct. 23, 1925, PPF.
20 Fulbright interview.
21 JWF to Roberta, Fall 1925, PPF.
22 JWF to Prof. and Dr., Nov. 25, 1925, PPF.
23 JWF to Roberta, Oct. 22, 1925, PPF.

feel like a bonehead over here – and of course I am."[24] The commingling of the intellectual, social, and physical that was the trademark of Oxford Fulbright found both stimulating and intimidating. "I am going to the *Beggar's Opera* tonight," he wrote Anne. "There are all sorts of fine entertainments . . . several orchestras, Russian dancers, Shaw, Ibsen, etc. are playing during this term. I am almost afraid to go after discovering the very poor quality of the graduates of American Universities."[25] He never completely overcame his inferiority complex, but like most Americans who survived at Oxford, he learned to cope with it.

As soon as Pembroke's upperclassmen heard that he had played college football, they let Fulbright know that he was expected to go out for rugby. "This afternoon I am to be initiated into the manly game of Rugger," he wrote home in October. "I have not even seen a game but they are putting me on the scrub team to play anyway. I think I shall like the English system of athletics."[26] He proved to be a natural.

> I have played in several games now, and I think it is almost as good a game as our own football. The English take it easy and it doesn't seem to make a great deal of difference whether they win or not. . . . Every time a good play is made everyone claps. It is so different from our roars and guffaws when we make a touchdown.[27]

With the start of intercollegiate competition, things became a bit more serious, however. "We played Worcester College rugby yesterday and it was a very rough game. Two of my fingers are swollen this morning, but the worst of it is I had one of my back teeth broken." He was undaunted, however. "We have had good luck so far and won all four games. I have been rather lucky in most games so you see why I have been playing."[28]

Homesickness was a problem at first and intermittently thereafter, but it was in fact somewhat of a relief to be away from the stressful family situation in Fayetteville. He could continue to advise his mother but do it from afar. Roberta had become emotionally dependent on her youngest son since Jay's death, and during Bill's first months in England, she wrote him long, complaining letters about her precarious financial position and Jack's mismanagement. He was entirely sympathetic. "Do let Jack go [to Florida to investigate a business opportunity for the family] but don't let him borrow and let him understand that that is all he gets for some time. He isn't entitled to unlimited credit," he admonished his mother.[29] "I feel bad enjoying everything so much and leaving you at home to face the music."[30] But by November Jack had

24 JWF to Roberta, undated, PPF.
25 JWF to Anne, Oct. 23, 1925, PPF.
26 JWF to Roberta, Fall 1925, PPF.
27 JWF to Roberta, Nov. 1, 1925, PPF.
28 JWF to Roberta, Nov. 3, 1925, PPF.
29 JWF to Roberta, undated, PPF.
30 JWF to Roberta, Sept. 28, 1925, PPF.

departed, business prospects had begun to improve, and Roberta's outlook had brightened.

Though he remained bitter at Jack – "for goodness sake don't let that idiot . . . Jack(ass) . . . force you into anything which Mr. Gray doesn't fully approve," he advised his mother – Bill began to relax, really for the first time since his father's death. "I have never slept so soundly in my life and the simple food they serve here seems to need no laxative," he reported home.[31]

Six weeks into his first term, Fulbright had settled into a routine of tea, reading, conversation, and cultural entertainment that was the essence of Oxford life, what one wag termed "organized idleness."[32] Despite his academic inferiority complex, the young Arkansan quickly began to make a mark for himself. He was strikingly handsome, six feet tall, a hundred and sixty-five pounds, with dark, wavy hair, a cleft chin, and penetrating blue eyes. His fellow students found him quick and congenial.

> You know that we have to be in college by twelve o'clock. Last evening we all went to see Bernard Shaw's *Misalliance* and afterwards we dropped in Martindale's [a fellow-student] room for a cup of tea and a chat. We stayed a bit too long and when we were still five blocks away Old Tom [Oxford's clock tower bell] began to toll the hour of midnight. Well I started to run as hard as I could and the last stroke sounded when I was only a few feet from the door so when I rapped the porter let me in. It certainly was a narrow escape from a fine.[33]

Though he complained to Roberta that everything in Oxford was dreadfully expensive, he bought a "plus-four suit," and he and Hower began entertaining. "We are having a few men in to tea this afternoon and I must have the scout bring up some cakes and toast," he signed off in a letter to his mother.[34] Like freshmen everywhere, he soon began to feel that his studies were interfering too much with his social life. "I had the idea that there is no pressure about studying," he wrote home. "That certainly isn't true because one hardly dares read a novel or anything except in his subject. Frankly so damn much education rather makes me sick."[35]

The academic year at Oxford was divided into three terms of just over eight weeks each so that approximately one-half of the calendar year was vacation. Typically, the undergraduate enjoyed six weeks off at Christmas and Easter, and four months in the summer. Under this system, term time was used for mapping out work, covering the material to be mastered in a superficial fash-

31 JWF to Roberta, Nov. 1, 1925, PPF.
32 JWF to Anne, Feb. 16, 1926, PPF.
33 JWF to Roberta, Nov. 1, 1925, PPF.
34 JWF to Roberta, Nov. 25, 1925, PPF.
35 JWF to Roberta, Nov. 3, 1925, PPF.

ion, and listening to lectures. The concentrated reading and studying necessary to pass the Honors examinations was done during vacation. Typically, a conscientious undergraduate would choose a town in a continental country, spend half of the day in his chosen line of study and half in seeing the country, learning the language, and studying the people.[36]

That first Christmas Fulbright and Hower decided to follow tradition and venture forth on the Continent. They picked a small town in southern France, Menton, as their primary site because they both wanted to learn French. The region was said to be remarkably cheap, and the weather, they believed, would be warm and sunny, a relief from the drizzle and cold of Oxford. Like most Oxford freshmen they felt compelled to tour Paris before moving on to their permanent winter quarters. Fulbright was dazzled by the ancient city's architectural treasures and social opportunities. The two Americans took rooms on the Rue de l'Université on the Left Bank of the Seine. With its numerous alleys and byways, the street was a traditional habitat for students. Fulbright and Hower read, drank, and feasted for a pittance at a favorite German restaurant. It was Fulbright's good fortune to join up with an upperclassman friend named Ray Jack. Jack was a Rhodes scholar from Alabama and a friend of Claude Pepper's. He was, according to Fulbright, the "most popular boy at Oxford" and an experienced traveler with many contacts on the Continent. He went ice skating with Jack and then took a girl, to whom the Alabaman had introduced him, to the Montmorte. James and Lois Russell, a couple who were friends with Murray Sheehan, one of Fulbright's former teachers at Arkansas, had him to dinner. Jim was the son of J. Towsend Russell, canon of the Episcopal National Cathedral in Washington. The younger Russell was interested in archaeology and, supported by his wealthy family, had settled in Paris to further his studies. Buoyed by the company and the setting, Fulbright boasted to Fayetteville, "I have come to the conclusion that I can live most any place and still have a good time. It all depends on your state of mind and your pocket-book."[37]

His stay in Menton complete, Fulbright returned to Paris for the Christmas holiday. Christmas Eve found him nearly overwhelmed with homesickness. Memories of the house on Mount Nord, the round of parties, the endless conversations with his mother presiding came flooding back. His heart even softened toward Jack, whose wife, Madeline, had just had a child. "Give my love to Anna, Madeline, Jack and the Baby," he wrote his mother, and he spent Christmas eve buying gifts for everyone.[38] Pleading with Roberta to consider a visit in the summer, he opined, "There is nothing that I would rather have than your love and all I ask is that we can have an opportunity to have a good

36 Aydelotte, *American Rhodes Scholarships,* 63, 75.
37 JWF to Roberta, Dec. 16, 1925, PPF.
38 JWF to Roberta, Dec. 28, 1925, PPF.

time again. . . . "[39] He and Hower consoled themselves with a trip to St. Moritz, one of Europe's most famous resorts. "It is beautiful," he reported; "everything in white with the mountains looming suddenly on the side and losing their white tops in the clouds." The town, however, was filled with German vacationers, he complained, "old, fat has-beens." They went skating and waited eagerly for the Oxford ice hockey team to arrive.[40]

Fulbright returned to England to find eight inches of snow on the ground and nothing of academic profit to show for his vacation. The prospect of a fresh round of tutorials with McCallum and his first set of exams momentarily filled with despair. He confessed to his mother that he had gotten virtually no studying done during his sojourn in France – "it will be a miracle if I get through at all."[41] At the same time he was filled with exhilaration by his recent travels. "I certainly have my share of the good things in life," he acknowledged to Roberta, "and I am beginning to realize every day what a fortunate boy I am."[42] He resolved to apply himself to his studies and for several weeks was successful. "At present I am reading Aristotle's *Politics* and political science in general," he reported to Fayetteville. "I am also reading a tremendous novel, *The Brothers Karamazov* by Dostoevsky. . . . In fact I have been having a fine time with books in general. The more I read the more I want to."[43]

Pembroke in the 1920s was an overwhelmingly male preserve, and though not as isolated and claustrophobic as colleges at Cambridge, society was made up almost entirely of "boys." Fulbright did not complain but nevertheless savored those rare opportunities he had to be with women:

> There were two girls, friends of Ray Jack of Philadelphia, visiting here Monday and Tuesday. We had a fine time looking at the Colleges and talking and playing the Vic. I gave a luncheon for six in my room and it was rather nice. My Scout is a peach. We had soup, cold chicken and ham, fruit salad and cream for dessert. Wine for the girls and beer for the boys. . . . One of the girls brought some lovely Jonquils from a flower shop and the room was charming.[44]

Like most Oxford students, Fulbright became an inveterate theatergoer. In late January he and Hower went to see the famous American actress Lucille La Verne starring in *Sun Up*. She was stunning, and the two young men sent a note between acts asking her to dinner. Her secretary emerged to say that

[39] JWF to Roberta, Dec. 16, 1925, PPF.
[40] JWF to Roberta, Dec. 29, 1925, PPF.
[41] JWF to Roberta, Nov. 26, 1925, PPF.
[42] JWF to Roberta, Jan. 16, 1926, PPF.
[43] JWF to Roberta, Jan. 26, 1926, PPF.
[44] JWF to Roberta, Jan. 29, 1926, PPF.

she was already engaged, but she would be pleased to go to tea with them the next day. "We enjoyed talking to her immensely," he wrote.[45]

In February Roberta wrote with the joyous news that she had settled a lawsuit with J. H. Phipps for $36,000. The Rhodes stipend had been increased from £350 to £400 shortly after Fulbright's appointment, but he still worried constantly about money. By the time he went to Oxford, Fulbright was financially semi-independent. His father had left all of his children stock in his companies, though Roberta retained controlling interest. After Jay's death, Bill began paying his own insurance, buying his own clothes, and looking after his own needs; but dividends from the businesses had been small, and it had sometimes been a struggle to make ends meet. At Claude Pepper's suggestion, Bill and the rest of the family had invested in some Florida real estate, but by early 1926 nothing had come of the venture. With the settlement of the Phipps suit, however, Roberta began sending him one to two hundred dollars periodically.[46]

Perhaps already secretly planning a political career for her son, Roberta began urging him to study the law. Bill resisted. "I don't think that I could ever get interested in Law except in one or two phases of it and that wouldn't do for a teacher."[47] Indeed, he had decided that the life of a college professor was for him. "You can't imagine the tranquil life we lead here. I feel as if I would like for it to continue indefinitely."[48] Although he sometimes had doubts, history was his subject. Philosophy and economics seemed too dry; literature was attractive, but its practical applicability escaped him.[49] History was full of interesting personalities and high drama as well as mass movements and abstract ideologies. In addition, he was convinced that it was the discipline most instructive for individual and communal living.

Bill Fulbright was an intensely physical, competitive young man, and the absence of sport in his life for any length of time made him restless. In February in the midst of Hobbes's *Leviathan,* Keyserling's *Travel Diary of a Philosopher,* and Tagore's *Sadhana,* Fulbright decided at Ray Jack's urging to go out for lacrosse. "I have made up my mind to try everything once for one can never tell when the luck is for one," he informed Roberta.[50] He proved even more adept at lacrosse than rugby. The goal of every Oxford athlete was to play for a varsity team and earn his half-blue, the Oxford version of a varsity letter. There was only one spot on the team in 1926, but although he was a freshman and a novice to the game, Fulbright beat out several more experienced players. It was heady stuff. The young American was immediately fitted for a blazer which only half-blues were allowed to wear, and all his friends came round to pay homage; but the honors had just begun.

45 Ibid.
46 JWF to Roberta, Feb. 7, 1926, PPF.
47 Ibid.
48 JWF to Roberta, Jan. 29, 1926, PPF.
49 JWF to Roberta, Feb. 7, 1926, PPF.
50 JWF to Roberta, Nov. 16, 1925, PPF.

In the game against archrival Cambridge, Fulbright's second, Oxford won 17 to 8. The freshman from Arkansas scored five goals, and at a sumptuous dinner that evening the Oxford captain asked him to be part of the combined Oxford–Cambridge team scheduled to tour the northeastern United States during spring vacation. He decided at once to accept. "We shall play several of the eastern teams and travel first class everywhere," he wrote Roberta. "We go over on the *Majestic* and back on the *Aquitania*. I thought perhaps you could come up to New York or Cambridge and see me."[51]

March was a whirl of games and celebrations. The *London Daily Mirror* carried two pictures of young Fulbright in action on the lacrosse pitch.[52] "I am so excited about my good luck that I can hardly contain myself," he confided to Roberta. "The college thinks that I am the berries, as they say, and I am the first of my class to make a blue. . . . Lady Astor is having a dance in London the day after we go down, but I must refuse it. I hate to do it but I can't do everything."[53]

As it turned out, Roberta could not come east. Instead, Bill talked his team captain into letting him depart a week early so that he could take the train from New York to Fayetteville and spend a few days with his family. As the date approached he became more and more excited. He ordered a suit from Bond Street for Jack and made a special trip to Paris to shop for Roberta, Anne, and Madeline. "Be sure and have the car in good shape . . . I want to run one again," he wrote his mother.[54]

After a few delicious days in the Ozarks in the bosom of his family, Fulbright met the Oxford–Cambridge team in New York. The schedule consisted of ten games with various Ivy League schools and West Point, and included a visit at the White House with President Calvin Coolidge. The trip ended in disaster for the young Arkansan. During the match with Yale, he was blindsided. Torn ligaments in both knees forced him to spend a week in the hospital. While the team completed its tour, a disappointed and extremely uncomfortable Fulbright convalesced in New York at the home of James Imbrie, an Oxford classmate and fellow lacrosse team member. The trip left him with semifunctional knees for the rest of his life. What bothered him the most, however, was the fact that it also put him behind in his studies. "I made a mistake," he recalled, "but it seemed very glamorous to be on the Oxford–Cambridge team."[55] The inability to compete, except in golf, would have a marked impact on Fulbright, an intense, physical person. It augmented a natural restlessness and impatience and gave a certain urgency and edge to his subsequent academic and political endeavors.

51 JWF to Roberta, Feb. 22, 1926, PPF.
52 JWF to Roberta, Feb. 25, 1926, PPF.
53 JWF to Roberta, Mar. 21, 1926, PPF.
54 JWF to Roberta, Mar. 1, 1925, PPF.
55 JWF to Roberta, Mar. 21, 1926, PPF.

Though Fulbright enjoyed his first two terms at Oxford, he still felt himself to be an outsider. Most of his friends were Rhodes or Empire scholars from Australia, Jamaica, or Peru. To his surprise and chagrin he found that the anti-Americanism and superpatriotism that one would expect to encounter in the average citizen was characteristic of Oxonians as well. "I went to a show the other night at the George Street Theater and they had their take-off of the American millionaire," he wrote his mother during the first term. "He was the Duke of Chicago, a former pork packer who had bought the title for $5,000,000. They never fail to make America out as a bunch of rich damn fools."[56] Shortly afterward he attended a meeting of the American Club. The guest speaker was a communist Member of Parliament whom Secretary of State Frank Kellogg had barred from entering the United States. In the midst of the speech, a group of drunken students broke into the meeting shouting anti-Bolshevik and anti-American slogans. They demanded that everyone stand and sing "God Save the King," and when some in attendance were slow to respond, they started a fight. The English, young Fulbright reported to Fayetteville, had acted like "ruffians and asses."[57] "Never fear about me becoming anglicized," he wrote Anne. "We all like the country, some of the people and the school very much, but I have yet to see any one ashamed that he is from U.S.A. after he has been here a year. They really aren't so 'hot' after all."[58]

For a time during his first summer vacation Fulbright lived in Paris with his friend Ralph Church, a philosophy student at Oriel College. Unlike Fulbright, Church had traveled widely and made contacts in the literary and artistic world. Church had become acquainted with Gertrude Stein and others in her salon of American expatriates living on the Left Bank; he frequently met with them at the Brasserie Lipp on the Boulevard St. Germain to drink beer and talk. That summer he took his friend from Arkansas along. A special member of the circle in 1926 was Sherwood Anderson, whose books satirizing small-town, middle-class America were then gaining him an international reputation. Fulbright, who had been reading his works, was able to spend several evenings listening to the great man declaim on life, letters, and himself.[59]

Though Fulbright's knees would not allow him back on the rugby or lacrosse pitch, the notoriety he had already won in athletics and his second year status soon brought invitations to join various clubs. Fulbright accepted membership in the Johnson Literary Society, named for Samuel Johnson, once a habitué of Pembroke. The members of the society would meet every fortnight, share a simple supper, and spend the evening critiquing a paper prepared by one of the members. Fulbright was awestruck by his first few

56 Fulbright interview.
57 JWF to Roberta, Nov. 29, 1925, PPF.
58 Ibid.
59 JWF to Anne, July 16, 1926, PPF.

meetings. Oxford was famed for instilling a critical attitude in its students, and the Johnsonians went at each other as if their academic lives depended on the outcome. As the date for his first presentation approached, the American was wracked with anxiety. At Church's suggestion, he selected Sherwood Anderson as his subject. He had read a bit of Mencken, Fitzgerald, Cabell, and Dos Passos (Hemingway then still being relatively unknown), but his ignorance of even American literature was profound. Church's contacts with the Left Bank expatriates and his wide reading proved invaluable, however. Determined not to embarrass himself, he "worked harder than I'd ever worked in my life."[60] His presentation won no accolades but neither was it embarrassing. In his third year Fulbright would be elected president of the Johnson Society.

The fall of 1926 was spent on finishing Aristotle and Hobbes and exploring continental history, principally French, German, and Italian. Though he found Cavour and Bismarck interesting, Fulbright suffered through periods of disillusionment with the scholarly enterprise, particularly its tendency toward what he perceived to be its hypercriticism. The lectures all seemed the same, he wrote his sister. No matter how great the figure, "the Dons spend their time making out that they were all wrong and quite foolish." McCallum was even more solicitous than the previous year but seemed never to be satisfied with his young charge's essays. "Actually and physically they shrink from applying any pressure," he observed of the faculty, "but they seem to know so much that one is quite ashamed of one's own meager and uncertain learning."[61]

Sometime in the midst of his second year at Oxford, Fulbright decided that academia was not for him. "You know that I could never be an extreme scholar," he wrote his mother; "in fact I don't believe it is desirable." He had made up his mind, he said, to obtain as broad an education as possible and then return to Fayetteville and run the family businesses.[62] With the approach of Christmas, Fulbright's spirits began to improve. He was scheduled to spend the holiday in Paris, which had become his favorite place in the world. He performed well on his term exams, and the Teasel Club, the best in Pembroke, invited him to become a member.[63] In Paris he and his friends went to see *Siegfried* at the opera and attended several symphony concerts. The Russells had him to dinner Christmas night. Somewhat to his mother's surprise, Fulbright went to church several times while he was in Paris. The Fulbrights had attended the First Christian Church in Fayetteville, and Roberta dabbled in Christian Science, but Bill had never shown much interest in religion. St. Sulpice was his favorite church in Paris. "It had the most beautiful music I have ever heard. . . . Religion, seems to me, appeals to the senses and

60 Fulbright interview.
61 JWF to Anne, July 16, 1926, PPF.
62 JWF to Roberta, Oct. 16, 1926, PPF.
63 JWF to Roberta, Dec. 8, 1926, PPF.

emotions more than to the intellect, and rightly so."[64] His letters became more compassionate, his feelings more mature that winter. "I have been thinking of you all a great deal and I realize more and more how important you are to me and how much I do love you," he wrote Roberta. "Before I just sort of took everything for granted and didn't think much about it. Being over here brings things into a new light entirely."[65]

While the matriarch of the Fulbright family was extremely proud of her younger son's accomplishments and experiences, which she described for all of Fayetteville in the *Daily Democrat,* she periodically urged him not to assume airs or lose touch with reality. After reading a scathing article by H. L. Mencken in the *American Mercury* on Americans in England, she wrote him a letter full of distress. "You need have no worry about my becoming a 'high brow,'" he wrote back. "I have become more humble if anything, particularly as regards my education." Mencken's portrayal of Americans at Oxford, he advised, was of a cloth with his other essays on America and Americans – pure iconoclasm.[66]

As the third quarter of 1927 approached its end, young Fulbright once again resolved to devote his summer vacation to studying. The task that lay before him was a simple one: to master the economic history of modern England. When he left Oxford, however, he had no firm plans; Grenoble or perhaps Dijon, he told his mother. He went first to London to meet a group of Arkansas travelers led by Dr. John Marinoni, a Fayetteville physician whose family owned a villa in Italy and who led a European tour each year. They persuaded him to rendezvous with them in Montreux in Switzerland and then continue on to Italy. He had another reason for going. While in London Fulbright had received a letter from a young woman whom he had met at a previous Oxford graduation. Marjorie Walker remembered that her handsome young countryman was going to be on the continent. Perhaps, she had decided, they could have just one more dance. She wrote Fulbright, told him she was going to be in Geneva, and asked him to come up. He agreed. By the time he arrived in Switzerland, however, he had decided on another "quite fantastic scheme."[67]

At Tours the American made friends with a young Pole named Josef Ruscinsky. He was a student at Amsterdam University and hailed from Vilnius, a city in northern Poland (Lithuania was then a part of Poland) only forty miles from the Russian border. Fulbright persuaded Ruscinsky to drive up with him to meet Marjorie and the other Americans. On the way the Pole suggested that he spend the summer with his family. The elder Ruscinskys lived in a villa on the edge of a lake north of Vilnius. It was quiet, Josef pointed out, and the Arkansan could study to his heart's content. Fulbright initially per-

64 JWF to Roberta, Dec. 24, 1926, PPF.
65 JWF to Roberta, Dec. 15, 1926, PPF.
66 JWF to Roberta, Feb. 28, 1927, PPF.
67 Fulbright interview.

ceived the offer to be the opportunity of a lifetime, "a grand experience and a trip I could hardly attempt alone."[68]

After entertaining Marjorie for two days, Fulbright and Ruscinsky set off. In addition to his native tongue, the Pole spoke German, Russian, and French. He and Fulbright had to converse with each other solely in French. In Oxford Fulbright had bought a tiny automobile, a ten-horsepower, ragtop Wolseley. The prospect of making the twelve-hundred-mile trip over mountainous and strange territory was frightening but thrilling. Their journey took them through Innsbruck, the Austrian Tyrol, through Vienna, to Cracow and Warsaw, and finally to Vilnius.[69]

The trip was a motoring adventure. Any rain at all thoroughly drenched the two young men, and the roads were often rough to the point of impassability. It was Fulbright's first experience with Germany and Austria. He was charmed:

> You should see the small towns at night; . . . some sort of band plays after a fashion at German opera. Last night they played me to sleep with *Faust.* I have been looking through the register and found only one American had been here about 3 years ago. . . . I believe I am the luckiest of boys to get such unusual chances to see the world.[70]

Poland was a shock. Vilnius was an impoverished community of some two hundred thousand souls. The cobbled main street dissected a cobweb of muddy alleyways and tenements. Poland had only five years earlier recovered Vilnius and its environs from the Bolsheviks who had overrun it following World War I. The city swarmed with police and soldiers who searched for agents of the Comintern and who continually cast anxious glances at the horizon in search of another Soviet invasion. "They are afraid of the Bolsheviks," Fulbright wrote, "but why any country should fight over Poland I can not see. It is very poor, the people are on the whole poverty stricken, and the Jews are thick and dirty." Aside from an intense patriotism, the country had little to recommend it. A tour of the countryside did not improve the national image in Fulbright's mind. "I wish you could just for a moment see the squalid, filthy Jewish villages in Poland," he wrote Roberta. "Truly our animals are better fed, cleaner and probably as intelligent."[71]

After a few days in Vilnius, Josef and his young American companion made their way through impressive pine forests to the Rucinsky villa, which turned out to be a farmhouse on the edge of a small lake. The setting was beautiful, but lonely. Josef's family, though very solicitous of their guest, spoke only Polish. Other than Josef, there was absolutely no one to whom Fulbright could talk. As the weeks stretched ahead of him with nothing to do

68 JWF to Roberta, July 27, 1927, PPF.
69 JWF to Roberta, July 17, 1927, PPF.
70 JWF to Roberta, July 22, 1927, PPF.
71 JWF to Roberta, July 31, 1927, PPF.

but swim and study, he confessed to an intense homesickness. "Not a soul with whom I can talk English and my French, while it is much more fluent, it is not very expressive," he wrote Roberta. "They are very nice and do everything for me, but I need to be near someone I love."[72] After a time, however, the Arkansan accommodated.

As the day for his departure approached, Fulbright scoured the shops of Vilnius for appropriate gifts for his family, but found nothing. Bolshevism, he concluded, had ruined the place. "How any one with intelligence could be a socialist or communist after seeing Vilnus [*sic*] I cannot imagine," he declared. "They [the communists] have nothing and don't want anyone else to have anything." The natives had become lazy and depressed, spending much of their time and money consuming vodka, he reported with disgust.[73]

Several times during his Polish sojourn Fulbright almost flew the coop to Paris, but the prospect of traveling by himself through the wilds of Eastern Europe deterred him. The second week in August he and his host departed. By the twenty-first Fulbright was back to Paris and civilization. Josef Ruscinsky went on to become an official at the World Bank. His Polish summer remained one of Fulbright's most vivid memories.[74]

In anticipation of his graduation from Oxford, Roberta came to visit in the spring of 1928. Bill had acclimatized, to say the least. She found him, she later reported to friends, wearing tweeds and knickers, and smoking a pipe. Mother and son took tea at an estate owned by a relative of Lord Tennyson, inspected a series of Norman churches, and visited Blenheim Palace, the ancestral home of the Dukes of Marlborough (and the birthplace of Winston Churchill) that had so impressed Bill when he was a freshman. He took her to the Pembroke Ball and treated her to dinner at the George Cafe ("cocktails, wine and everything," as she later told her friends). As president of the Teasel Club, he occupied the principal chair at the head table, with Roberta to his right. It was for Roberta the high point of her life. "I am now at Oxford," she wrote on April 24, 1928. "This to me was almost a sacred pilgrimage and Oxford, with my boy, my Mecca. I find great content from being near him, which I can scarcely explain; he seems much like his father and is very easy for me to live with; I lean on him intuitively."[75]

Fulbright graduated from Oxford in June 1928 with a high second in modern history. He became convinced in later years that the university had done for him what Cecil Rhodes intended that it do. He had been stretched intellectually and culturally. Even had he been so inclined, Fulbright would never be able to retreat into a cocoon of complacency. The march of civilizations across history had dazzled him. The complexities of other cultures and the rage of

72 Ibid.
73 JWF to Roberta, Aug. 17, 1927, PPF.
74 Fulbright interview.
75 Quoted in Johnson and Gwertzman, *Fulbright: The Dissenter,* 40.

his tutors and his fellow students to learn about them left an indelible mark. Most important of all, those with whom he associated assumed that they were going to make a difference in the world. In Great Britain Oxbridge alumni dominated Parliament, the press, academia, and big business. Coupled with his mother's belief in public service, Fulbright's years at Pembroke disposed him to seize any and every opportunity to enter public life. His education, however, was not yet complete.

With Roberta, a cousin, and a friend in tow, Fulbright set off for a grand tour of the Continent. They made their way across France and Switzerland to Vienna. After further dazzling his mother with that city's incomparable architecture and café life, Bill moved the party to the German spa of Baden. After several weeks there, Roberta returned home to Arkansas.

At the close of the summer Fulbright settled down to enjoy the warp and woof of Viennese life. He frequented the opera, read, roamed the city, and, of course, spent his evenings in the cafés. Viennese café life was only slightly less brilliant than that of Paris. It attracted writers, painters, actors, and intellectuals of all types. Topics of discussion ranged from the merits of post-impressionist art to the plight of the Weimar Republic under the Treaty of Versailles to the psychoanalytic theories of a Viennese doctor named Sigmund Freud. Significantly, Fulbright spent more and more time at the Café Louvre. The Louvre was situated near the telegraph station and was the favorite hangout of foreign correspondents, who would gather there every evening to gossip and trade information. Just before the telegraph shut down, the gaggle of correspondents would rush off to meet their deadlines.[76] There one could see William L. Shirer, Walter Duranty, Dorothy Thompson, John Gunther, and Frazier Hunt. It was at the Louvre in October that the young American met and made friends with Mikhail Fodor.

Mike Fodor, a stocky, balding, garrulous Hungarian, was then the Balkan correspondent for the *Manchester Guardian* and contributed as well to the *New York Evening Post* and the *Philadelphia Public Ledger*. In addition to being an able reporter, Fodor was an intellectual who could discuss the complex political life of Eastern Europe in depth and place it in historical perspective. Fodor had done postgraduate work in Zurich after earning an engineering degree from Budapest University. He was, in addition, an accomplished linguist and knew most of the leading political figures in Central and Eastern Europe. Fulbright was fascinated. Though Fodor was fifteen years older, the two became friends. The Hungarian was at an age when bright young protégés are extremely flattering.

76 Fulbright interview.

Throughout that wonderful winter Fulbright listened to Fodor harangue his associates. The Arkansan recalled that his friend seemed to know more than all of the other corespondents put together. Indeed, it was not unusual for Fodor's accounts of events of the week to appear some days later under a different byline in the *New York Times Magazine* or some other publication.

That spring, the spring of 1929, Fodor announced that he was going on his yearly tour of the Balkans to take measure of the political scene. Why didn't Fulbright go along as his associate? With a press card the American could accompany the journalist on his interviews. For a month the two visited the chanceries and palaces of Sophia, Belgrade, and Athens. Fulbright met the prime ministers of Hungary, Romania, and Czechoslovakia, and his mentor urged him to consider a career in journalism. Within six months, he promised, Fulbright could be East European correspondent for the *Post.*[77]

Shortly after a Fodor-led tour of the Acropolis in Athens, Fulbright was felled with a severe throat infection. His mentor lingered a few days, but then had to leave to keep appointments he had made in Albania. Fulbright was to catch up, but the fever and inflammation persisted. Finally, exhausted, the young American booked passage for home. The trip from Marseilles to New York was stormy; seasickness aggravated the throat condition. Exhausted and still gravely ill, Bill Fulbright eventually arrived home. His malady succumbed to the ministrations of his mother, and he regained the splendid health that was to bless the rest of his life. His brief tenure with Fodor constituted an education in itself, his introduction to the real world of international politics.

Fulbright arrived back in Fayetteville with no clear plan of action. He had always intended to return, he later claimed, and help his mother with the various family businesses. More than likely, however, it was his illness that forced him to come back. It may well have been that he would have taken Fodor up on his offer, living his life in the cafés and chanceries of Europe as a foreign correspondent; but back he was.

The fall following Bill's return in April – he had just turned twenty-four – the Great Depression struck. For the rest of their lives both Roberta and Bill were convinced that the family's financial fortunes hung by a thread. The Fulbrights no doubt suffered in the aftermath of the crash of 1929. Bill estimated that two-thirds of all the assets his father had amassed were lost in the ensuing depression; but that was an exaggeration. Everybody's assets were devalued, and the Fulbrights were no worse off than anyone else. Moreover, they managed to retain the essential businesses – Fayetteville Ice, the newspaper, Phipps Lumber, and a wide variety of properties, both residential and com-

[77] JWF to Roberta, Mar. 1, 1929, PPF, and Fulbright interview.

mercial. Nevertheless, the sense of impending economic doom that followed Jay's death had returned.

Bill's friends noted with pleasure that he had not acquired the typical fake British accent. He did seem overly fond of tweeds, and he had leather patches sewn on the elbows of his jackets. Still, he seemed, as one man said, "the same old Bill" – friendly but reserved.[78]

In later life Fulbright claimed that circumstance – opportunity, if pressed – played a greater role in his life than any other factor. Though he was fond of invoking the deity – "God damn . . . !" punctuated nearly every other sentence – Bill Fulbright did not believe in an immanent deity. He did not even believe in fate. Chance, yes; fate, no. The object of life, as Jay had taught him, was to be prepared to take advantage of any and every opportunity that presented itself. He seemed to have been ill prepared for Miss Elizabeth Williams of Philadelphia, however.

One of the most pleasant aspects of Fulbright's trips to Paris had been his visits with Jim and Lois Russell. In addition to having him to dinner whenever he was in town, Russell, who was in Paris studying archaeology, took Fulbright on an outing to the Dordogne and to Altamira Cave, where the two young Americans learned firsthand about Cro-Magnon man. It had been interesting but inconsequential to Fulbright. Indeed, he had all but forgotten about Russell until he received a phone call from him in the summer of 1929.[79]

Russell was in a panic. His father, the canon at the National Cathedral, had just died. Both parents were wealthy – his mother was the daughter of a Brooklyn banker – and they had left their son with a healthy trust of "a million or so," as Fulbright recalled; but the estate, which included Beauvoir, a mansion adjacent to the Cathedral, was beset with debt. Although an able cleric, Russell's father was an inept businessman, and his only offspring had inherited that trait. Russell was being hounded by creditors, he complained; could Fulbright please come to Washington and help him? After some discussion, Fulbright agreed to come and arrange a loan so his friend could get back to Europe and his excavations.[80]

Coming out of the Riggs Bank early one afternoon, Bill ran into James Imbrie, the Oxford classmate in whose home he had convalesced after injuring his knees in the Yale game. Imbrie was then in Washington representing one of his father's brokerage houses. Could Fulbright come to dinner Saturday evening, Imbrie inquired? A friend of his wife was in town and they needed a fourth. Fulbright accepted.

78 Quoted in Johnson and Gwertzman, *Fulbright: The Dissenter,* 43.
79 Fulbright interview.
80 Ibid.

Bill arrived late at the Imbrie's Georgetown house. His hosts' friend was Elizabeth Williams from Philadelphia. Betty Williams was a slender, attractive brunette, one of those women people describe as handsome rather than pretty. Her father, Robert W. Williams, had been a wealthy cotton merchant, and Betty had grown up as a member of one of Philadelphia's most prominent Main Line families. That famous strip of bluebloods stretched west of the city and surrounded such exclusive schools as Haverford and Bryn Mawr. Despite the plethora of fine liberal arts institutions in her neighborhood, Betty never attended college. Her parents sent her instead to one of Philadelphia's finishing schools. She was immaculately groomed, poised without being stiff. Bill obviously thought her one of the most self-confident young women he had ever met. "She was an intriguing girl," he later observed with a grin. "She seduced me, I guess you could say. . . . I hadn't had much to do with women. There were none at Oxford and I was susceptible."[81]

What seduced Bill Fulbright, if that was the right word, was not only Betty's wit and charm, but the difficulty of the chase. Fulbright had always been a teaser, and at times he could become aggressive, even offensive. Shortly after the four sat down to dinner in the Imbrie's apartment, Bill allowed as how he had never met anyone from Philadelphia he had liked. Expecting Betty to be flustered and apologetic, allowing him to gain the psychological upper hand, the Arkansan was rudely surprised. "Don't be an ass!" she retorted.[82] An intriguing girl, indeed. He asked her to lunch for the next day; their courtship had begun.

Fulbright mythmakers have made much of the contrast between Betty and Bill: The roughhewn hillbilly from Arkansas wins the hand of the elegant, refined Philadelphian. In reality, they had much in common. His manners and self-confidence were the equal of hers. Her lack of education seemed to neither of them to be a drawback. She never aspired to be an intellectual or even a professional. Her goal, and she believed it to be a worthy one, was to be a wife and a hostess. Both young people were independent and tough-minded. Bill's father had died when he was sixteen and Betty's when she was fifteen. Unlike Bill she had had to endure her father's failing health – he died from a heart condition – for more than a year. It was an anguishing experience. If anything, Betty was more outgoing than Bill. She loved people, conversation, dinner parties. So did Fulbright, but a natural, deep-seated reserve kept him at a certain distance. His fits of garrulousness on various public issues were as much as anything diversions to keep from discussing his emotional and psychological experiences.

In some ways Betty was a relief from Roberta. Fulbright loved his mother deeply, but he found her suffocating at times. Roberta may have aspired to a place for herself and her family in the larger world, but she at the same time

81 Ibid. 82 Quoted in Johnson and Gwertzman, *Fulbright: The Dissenter,* 45.

suffered from the insecurities of the nouveaux riches. Her frequent paeans to Anglo–Saxonism, her soirées, her extolling of "public service" bespoke a deep-seated status anxiety. Betty came from a world to which Roberta could only aspire. She was old wealth, socially comfortable and assured. Bill felt relatively little pressure in the presence of this new and delightful female. By linking with Betty, he could separate from his mother and at the same time please her by marrying into the world of which she dreamed and that he had experienced at Oxford.

Courtship was prolonged and difficult, like a bad labor. So besotted with Betty was Fulbright that he decided to move to Washington and enroll in George Washington Law School. Her mother owned a summer home on Cape May. Every weekend that he could get away, Bill drove up to visit.

The elder Elizabeth Williams was a formal woman with a deep sense of family and place. She had never been west of the Appalachians, and she did not like Bill Fulbright. He was too rough; there was too much she did not know about him and his background. As she watched the relationship grow, Mrs. Williams became alarmed. If the two married, young Fulbright might take Betty back to Arkansas to live. She could be trampled by buffaloes or kidnapped by moonshiners. Mother Williams announced out of the blue that she was sending Betty on a cruise and extended tour of Europe to complete her education. Bill was crushed. Betty accepted the news with resignation. Her mother was a strong disciplinarian, and there was nothing to do but pack her bags. To Mrs. Williams's chagrin, young Fulbright insisted on accompanying them to New York and seeing Betty off on the boat. For six weeks the lovesick Arkansan hung around the city awaiting her return.[83]

When the day at last arrived, Bill dressed as nattily as he could and set off for the docks. Betty's boat arrived on time, but as she stepped down the gangway, his heart sank: She was with another man. Fulbright swallowed the lump in his throat and manfully went to dinner with Betty, her friend, and a delighted Mrs. Williams.

Fulbright was furious. Though the relationship had certainly not been consummated, he felt like a cuckold. After several angry phone calls from Washington to Cape May, Betty asked Bill to come up. Gradually the relationship recovered. With Mrs. Williams's reluctant approval, the two were married on June 15, 1932. Betty Williams knew instinctively how to get and keep Bill's attention. It was a knack that she would never lose during their half century together.

Despite the ups and downs in his love life, Fulbright proved an excellent law student. His Oxford experience and the passing years had seasoned and focused him. He earned all A's at George Washington and finished second in

83 Interview with Roberta and Julia Foote and Elizabeth Winnacker, Sept. 9, 1991, Washington, D.C.

a class of 150.[84] Legal scholarship suited Fulbright. It was intellectually stimulating and at the same time had a practical application – and Bill Fulbright, despite later efforts by his political enemies to portray him as an ivory-tower intellectual, was a practical man. He had no use for utopian schemes. Ideas affected the way men and women lived, but only, he believed, after those ideas had passed through established legal structures and been tempered by democratic processes.

During this period in his life Fulbright took only a passing interest in the events that swirled about him. On the day that Bill and Betty married, Congress was considering the Patman Bonus Bill authorizing the payment of $2.4 million to the millions of World War I veterans impoverished by the Great Depression. A destitute army of fifteen thousand veterans, many of them with their families, had descended on Washington to lobby for the bill's passage. Their journey was for naught. President Herbert Hoover, fearful that the Bonus Bill would unbalance the budget and devalue the currency, successfully pressured Congress into killing the measure. When the veterans, encamped in a tent city at Anacostia Flats, became restive, the president was persuaded by General Douglas MacArthur to send a small army, complete with tanks and machine guns, to clear the area. The nation was subsequently treated to the spectacle of the U.S. Army manhandling thousands of defenseless veterans and burning their meager worldly possessions. That outrage symbolized the political and intellectual bankruptcy of the Hoover administration and set the stage for the electoral triumph of Franklin D. Roosevelt and the coming of the New Deal.

For James William Fulbright these earthshaking events were merely part of the background to the playing out of his life – his courtship, marriage, and the furthering of his education. Some of his early biographers argued that the Depression and the disintegration of the Versailles peace structure were crucial in shaping his worldview. Fulbright always denied that this was so:

> I hate to be disappointing, but I was a very ordinary kind of a fellow. I had no great illusions of playing any great part in the government. I was deeply concerned about my record when I was at George Washington, and then and later with trying to keep our home base perking, I mean, keeping it solvent. I was scared after the depression began that we were going flat broke. I didn't much like the idea of just being completely penniless, you know. I was deeply concerned about that. I wasn't taken up or involved in the great public issues of the day.[85]

In attributing his lack of political activism in the 1920s and 1930s to the hovering specter of poverty, Fulbright exhibited a disingenuousness. There

84 Fulbright interview.
85 Quoted in Johnson and Gwertzman, *Fulbright: The Dissenter,* 46.

was never any chance that the Fulbrights were going broke. In fact, the Arkansan's apathy was due to a mixture of insensitivity, self-centeredness, and practicality. Bill Fulbright might have been from Fayetteville, Arkansas, but he was to the manor born. He did not know about poor people, had not lived among them. The squalor of rural Poland had been a totally new experience. Indeed, the Fulbrights of Fayetteville had not been touched by, and hence were not moved by, society's ills. They believed in the advancement of the general good – Roberta would become a staunch supporter of Franklin Roosevelt and the New Deal – but their liberalism was a product of rational analysis rather than a compelling social conscience. In addition, as a number of Bill Fulbright's associates would later note, he possessed a singular ability to concentrate, to focus, to shut out distractions. To that extent he was self-centered – not selfish, but entirely absorbed in the landscape of his own life. Finally, Fulbright did not concern himself with matters about which he could do nothing. His tasks in the 1920s and 1930s, he believed, were to set his personal life in order and further his education. The inflation-ridden citizens of the Weimar Republic and the refugees from the Dust Bowl would have to take care of themselves.

# 3

# *First family of Fayetteville*

The Washington Fulbrights began their married life in a rented apartment in Georgetown near 31st and N Streets. Georgetown was not then as exclusive as it would become. Rent was a substantial but manageable $85 a month. The attached brick rowhouse was almost too large for the young couple, but both wanted children as soon as practicable, and so they had allowed for growth.

Shortly before he graduated from George Washington, Fulbright ran into Dwight Savage, a former University of Arkansas law professor who was working in the Justice Department. There were several openings in his agency, Savage told Fulbright; why not apply? The New Deal was unfolding, and Justice was an exciting place to be. Fulbright assented, and, degree in hand, he went to work in the antitrust division as a special attorney.

Despite his impressive title, Fulbright's job consisted chiefly of doing legal research for the senior members of the department. He had the good fortune, however, of being assigned to Walter Rice, a talented and aggressive young lawyer who would later become a vice-president of Reynolds Aluminum. It fell to Rice, and indirectly to Fulbright, to defend the constitutionality of the National Industrial Recovery Act (NIRA),[1] a measure that Congress had passed in 1933 at President Franklin D. Roosevelt's request. The act authorized the creation of the National Recovery Administration (NRA), the Public Works Administration, and government–business–labor commissions to set prices, wages, and production quotas for a given industry.

In 1935 the U.S. government charged the A. L. A. Schechter Poultry Corporation, the Schechter Live Poultry Market, Inc., and the four Schechter brothers who operated them with conspiring to violate provisions of the NRA poultry code for New York. The Brooklyn concern had been passing off contaminated chickens to Jewish customers as kosher. This, the "sick chicken" or Schechter case, was everywhere seen to be crucial. In effect, the federal government claimed the right through the NRA to interfere in a local industry on the grounds that it affected interstate commerce. The outcome of the case would confirm or deny its power to do so.

[1] Interview with J. William Fulbright, Oct. 11–18, 1988, Washington, D.C.

The trial was heady stuff for Fulbright. The case, tried in Brooklyn, attracted national attention. For two weeks Rice argued his case. The judge charged the jury on a Wednesday morning; as of midnight it still had not reached a verdict. Sequestered overnight in a hotel, the jurors returned to their deliberations the next morning. A few minutes after noon they filed in. Guilty on all nineteen counts, declared the foreman. Rice, who was almost as competitive as Fulbright, was jubilant. "This is a sweeping victory of immense importance," he told reporters. The verdict, in effect, upheld the constitutionality of the NIRA and the right of the federal government in general to use the commerce clause to regulate and stimulate the economy. "It was like winning the world championship," Fulbright recalled.[2] Their euphoria was short-lived.

The Schechters appealed, and the case soon reached the Supreme Court. Rice lost. The Court ruled that the Brooklyn firm was not engaged in interstate commerce, and, moreover, that Congress had unconstitutionally delegated legislative powers to the code-writing commissions established by the NRA. The upshot of the case was that the NIRA was declared unconstitutional. "We'd have won if the administration had let us handle it," Fulbright later claimed.[3] That, given the fact that the vote was 9 to 0, was doubtful.

Whether discouraged or bored, Fulbright left the Justice Department in early 1935 to accept a position teaching law at George Washington. He claimed he did it for the money. The government had paid him $2,500 a year, and the dean of the law school offered him $3,500. His years at George Washington were uneventful but beneficial. "I learned much more teaching than I did in school," he insisted.[4] Students remember him as well organized and demanding. Even then he began to urge the brightest to consider entering public service. It was their duty, he would tell them, citing his mother: To whom much was given, much was expected. His reading in history and constitutional law had convinced him that a republic could survive only through a combination of just laws and enlightened rulers. If thoughts of running for public office crossed Fulbright's mind during this period, there is no evidence of it. He was not much given to taking his own temperature. Teaching seemed an admirable profession, a form of public service, but as always he was open-minded about his future.

While Bill was withholding himself from public affairs – waiting, perhaps for the right opportunity – Roberta, back in Arkansas, was taking her own advice. A decade of handling the family's business affairs and operating as a woman in a man's world had brought out her ingrained toughness. According

[2] Quoted in Haynes Johnson and Bernard M. Gwertzman, *Fulbright: The Dissenter* (New York, 1968), 48.

[3] Fulbright interview.

[4] Ibid.

to her niece, Suzie Zorn, Roberta's assertiveness and doggedness stemmed from a combination of "confidence and determination" and "necessity." "She had a bunch of brothers," Zorn later observed, "and she was the strongest of all of them. The brothers were all Waughs, artistic and gentle and none of them powerhouses. She was clearly superior."[5] Roberta's toughness and ambition had already had a major impact on Bill Fulbright's life. Her activities during the 1930s not only served as a continuing example to him but laid the political and to some extent philosophical basis for his subsequent career.

As life became more secure for Roberta, she began to take an active role with the *Daily Democrat,* not as an editor but as a writer. She reported on her 1928 trip to Europe to witness Bill's graduation; that same year she began to write a daily column, which she entitled "As I See It." The column dealt with everything from gardening to her family to local and national politics. During the next thirty years Roberta put more than two million words in newsprint. Indeed, by the early 1930s Roberta's daily visits to the *Democrat*'s offices had become the focal point of her life. There, less than a stone's throw from both the town square and the county courthouse, she played hostess to a steady stream of politicos, gadflies, and "concerned citizens." Conversation never strayed far from politics and local civic affairs. Sometime in the fall of 1934 Roberta Fulbright decided to launch a campaign to bring down the local political establishment.

Washington County politics, like Arkansas politics in general, suffered from the maladies that had plagued the South since the Populist uprising in the 1890s. Although the primary purpose of the poll tax when originally enacted in 1892 had been to discourage blacks from voting, it had simultaneously disfranchised large numbers of poor whites as well. In Washington County during the 1930s the percentage of voting-age citizens who did not pay their poll taxes ranged from 58 percent in 1932 to over 72 percent in 1940. Besides severely limiting the number of voters that participated in every state election, the poll tax also could be easily manipulated by those willing to buy votes or cast fraudulent ballots. Because jury members were selected from poll-tax roles, virtually all of the jurors chosen were businessmen and farm owners with close political connections to the county judge and sheriff. Machine politics were not unique to America's big cities, and Fayetteville had its own machine, the "courthouse ring," or as Roberta Fulbright labeled it, "the Ring."[6]

By all accounts the matriarch of the Fayetteville Fulbrights was a natural-born politician. According to family members, she twice considered running for office herself. Henrietta Peck, a lifelong friend, recalled that while on a

5 Interview with Suzanne Zorn, July 23, 1989, Fayetteville, Ark.

6 Stephen H. Dew, *The New Deal and Fayetteville, Arkansas, 1933–1941* (M.A. thesis, University of Arkansas, 1987), 191–3, 197–8.

cruise with her husband, Sam, and Roberta, her friend spent every night, all night, talking shop with a group of Tammany Hall politicos who happened to be on board.[7] In the end, however, she decided that she could best satisfy her ambition through the achievements of her younger son and as a crusading newspaper publisher.

During the New Deal, the most hopeful and reform-minded force within the local Democratic Party in Fayetteville was an alliance of individuals calling themselves the Good Government League (GGL). Established in 1932 in response to evidence of corruption in Washington County's judge's office (in Arkansas the county judgeship is an administrative position), the GGL included politicians desirous of ousting incumbent county officers. In addition, there were several local ministers, some members of the local veterans' association, and a few Republicans who, because Arkansas was a one-party state, had no choice but to ally themselves with reform-minded Democrats. During 1932–4 the GGL was a weak coalition that worked outside the Democratic Party and limited itself to demanding on occasion the resignation of the circuit judge and several other county officials. Then in November 1934 – after several announced candidates for justice of the peace who were opposed to the Ring were left off the ballot – Roberta Fulbright threw the full weight of the *Daily Democrat* behind the GGL in an attempt to influence the upcoming city election.[8] In editorials and in "As I See It," Roberta called on all those interested in good government to join the GGL; she even went so far as to threaten to publish the names of those who did not.

More specifically, the *Daily Democrat* and the GGL demanded an audit of the county's books. Fortunately, the state comptroller in 1935 was a young, ambitious Little Rock attorney named Griffin Smith. Having decided to run for governor in 1936, Smith believed that leadership of a well-publicized reform movement in northwest Arkansas would stand him in good stead with the voters.[9] After Smith issued his report, the Washington County grand jury returned not one but seventy-four separate indictments. Expecting the trial to be a rude comeuppance for the Ring, Roberta awaited its outcome with delicious anticipation. She should have known better. The dominant figure in Washington County's political establishment was Circuit Judge John S. Combs, a Ring leader. He not only issued a directed verdict of not guilty, but instructed the grand jury to return a counterindictment against State Comptroller Smith for impugning the integrity of the county.[10]

In December the *Democrat*–led crusade got a boost when city Police Chief Neal Cruse, City Attorney Rex Perkins, and Homer Christman, a plumbing contractor, were indicted by a federal grand jury for operating a stolen car

7 Interview with Henryetta Peck, May 23, 1990, Little Rock, Ark.
8 Dew, *The New Deal and Fayetteville,* 201–2.
9 Quoted in ibid., 204.
10 Allen Gilbert, *A Fulbright Chronicle* (Fayetteville, 1980), 94–5.

ring in northwest Arkansas. The state's case seemed to be solid. At his arrest Christman surrendered a set of dies used to change motor numbers on stolen automobiles. Certain of a conviction, Roberta seized the bit. In a special front-page editorial on January 17, 1935, the *Daily Democrat* printed a "Declaration of Good Government" that included a pledge to support "law, order and justice" and a demand for a "New Deal for Washington County affairs." Individuals and groups who had not joined the GGL were encouraged to clip, sign, and return the declaration to the newspaper. "He who is not for me is against me," she proclaimed.[11]

The motives that prompted Roberta to chance the dangerous waters of Washington County politics were several. There was, of course, a genuine sense of moral outrage. "To say that politics in Fayetteville and Washington County in the early Thirties was bad was to treat the situation kindly," she later remembered. "Things, literally, were abominable. Malfeasance at the local level involved graft, poll tax fraud, crooked elections, plus . . . [a] stolen car ring; illegal manufacture and sale of alcohol, and . . . [a] 'protection' racket."[12] To make matters worse, the entire crooked system operated under the shelter of a friendly judiciary, she recalled. It was a network of corruption so long established and well entrenched that most county residents took it for granted, like death and taxes. More practically, there was the matter of the lucrative county printing contract. Though the Fulbrights had labored repeatedly during the 1930s to persuade the county judge's office to reward the *Democrat* with that bit of patronage, it had been given year after year to R. M. Scaggs and the Washington County *Progressive Star*. Scaggs, of course, was an integral part of the Ring.[13]

Meanwhile, the long arm of the law was reaching for members of the Ring on another charge: bootlegging. During Prohibition moonshining became almost an institution in the South. It was convenient and cheap, and there were no identifiable victims. Because of these factors, plus the region's ingrained distrust of the federal government, enforcement of the liquor laws was nearly impossible. Indeed, following repeal in 1933, "white lightin'" survived in many regions, including the Ozarks, for another generation. While the moonshiners profited from avoiding payment of federal taxes, political machines survived on the proceeds of the bribes paid them by the traffickers in illegal booze.

In 1933, shortly after American voters rejected the Noble Experiment, a team of federal tax agents raided a small farm near Greenland, just south of Fayetteville. Captured in the raid was a two-thousand-gallon copper still. The agents turned over the evidence to the sheriff for disposal. Two years later al-

11 Dew, *The New Deal and Fayetteville,* 202–3.
12 Quoted in Gilbert, *A Fulbright Chronicle,* 94.
13 Interview with Margueritte Gilstrap, June 23, 1989, Washington, D.C.

cohol and tax agents, in a raid only a mile from the first one, confiscated another large still. Upon inspection, it proved to be the very same one. Incensed, the agents pressed for and obtained indictments against Sheriff Harley Gover. The trial was held in Fort Smith and, to the delight of the GGL, was scheduled on the same docket as the Cruse–Christman case. Roberta and a staff member, Lessie Stringfellow Read, covered the trial for the *Democrat.*

The high point of the Gover trial came with the testimony of a lady bootlegger, Lutie Jack. Mrs. Jack, a stylishly dressed brunette, testified that she had sold bootleg liquor to most of Fayetteville's leading citizens in the parlor of her farmhouse. She also testified that she paid protection money to the sheriff. The jury promptly indicted Gover and company on charges of racketeering and violating the Federal Revenue Act.

For Roberta and the Good Government League, the Gover, Cruse, and Christman trials were just means to an end. The unfavorable publicity, they hoped, would help unseat incumbent members of the Ring in the 1936 elections. In February of that year Sheriff Harley Gover resigned. His conviction was brandished by the *Democrat* and the GGL as a prime example of the corruption that had penetrated city hall and the county courthouse, and as proof that all of the county incumbents needed to be swept out of office. Through the political influence of Roberta Fulbright and other GGL members, Herbert (Buck) Lewis, was appointed sheriff by Governor J. M. Futrell. Young Lewis was then selling dry goods in his father's hardware store on the north side of the square. He subsequently agreed to be the GGL's candidate for sheriff in the upcoming Democratic primary.[14]

Two days before the 1936 primary the Ring's candidate for city attorney, Rex Perkins, distributed a handbill entitled "Candidate for City Attorney Exposes Jury Fixing." The Fulbrights' attacks on the political establishment were pure hypocrisy, he declared. Family representatives had bribed a jury in 1935 to obtain a favorable ruling for Phipps Lumber and had bribed him, Perkins, to keep quiet about the matter. To top it all off, a Fulbright employee had attempted to intimidate the judge in the case. Roberta refused to respond to the charge, and with good reason: It was true. After the election she admitted that payments had indeed been made, but without her knowledge. It all went to prove, she declared, that personnel in city government were indeed corrupt and needed replacing.[15]

The Ring's candidate for sheriff, Henry Walker, lashed out at what he called the "Lewis–Fulbright Money-Powers" by claiming that the kind of government they wanted "was not a Good Government but a Fulbright Government." "'Ma'" Fulbright, he insisted, had paid $3,000 to a jury in 1923 to have the rape charge against her son Jack reduced to simple assault. Throughout the weeks preceding the election anonymous phone calls, obscene letters,

14 Dew, *The New Deal and Fayetteville,* 220–1. 15 Ibid., 208–9.

and threats of physical violence became almost daily occurrences for the Fulbright family. Roberta's driver began carrying a handgun.[16]

When the primary results were in, all of the GGL candidates had won. Two years later, in 1938, Circuit Judge John S. Combs, the heart and soul of the Ring, was soundly defeated by James W. Trimble, a popular young lawyer from Berryville and future Arkansas congressman. Trimble had prosecuted the case against former sheriff Gover.[17]

Roberta's first foray into reform politics was successful, but her family had had to pay a price. During her war with the Ring, the twins, Helen and Bo, were students at the university. They were attractive, popular girls, prominent in their sorority with plenty of money and prestige. Revelations concerning Jack's escapades and their mother's jury bribery exposed them to mounting ridicule. Following one sorority skit poking fun at the Fulbrights, Bo went to her mother in tears and begged to be allowed to withdraw from school. Roberta seemed totally oblivious to their embarrassment and humiliation. Though she remained loyal to them and eventually became dependent on Helen, Roberta sometimes felt the twins to be a nuisance. Anna Fulbright, who had married prominent St. Louis attorney Kenneth Teasdale, had no illusions about her mother. The women in the family, Anna recalled, all had very negative self-images, felt unfulfilled and unattractive.[18] It was not so much that Roberta did not love her daughters, it was that she had become a man in a man's world. As her success in business and politics demonstrated, she had the right stuff, but she had had to sacrifice much of her feminine side. As one family member recalled, there was no nurturer in the Fulbright household after Jay died.

When Roberta did think about the twins, it was with a good deal of anxiety. They were of average intelligence; they certainly were not very tough; and they were women living in the 1930s. Bo was tremendously energetic. She desperately needed an outlet, a career. Aside from the social obstacles all women of her generation had to face, Bo suffered from intense feelings of personal insecurity. Instead of focusing on school or a career, in 1935 she married Gilbert Swanson, the handsome young heir to the Swanson food empire who had come to northwest Arkansas, a primary poultry-producing area, to set up a chicken-processing plant.[19] It was not, as time would prove, a marriage made in heaven.

Two years later the less flamboyant Helen married Hal Douglas. The Douglas family was prominent in Fayetteville without being of the first rank. Nevertheless, Hal was a real catch. He had been captain of the University of Arkansas baseball team and president of his fraternity. Hal was a good-hearted,

16 Gilbert, *A Fulbright Chronicle,* 105.
17 Dew, *The New Deal and Fayetteville,* 220–3.
18 Interview with Susie Zorn, Sept. 23, 1989, Fayetteville, Ark.
19 Gilbert, *A Fulbright Chronicle,* 102.

tactful young man, shrewd without being scholarly. After earning a law degree and a serving a stint with the FBI, Hal returned with Helen to Fayetteville in 1936.[20] He spent the next forty years, with time out for a tour of duty with the U.S. Navy during World War II, serving as legal and financial counsel to the Fulbright family.

A week following his defeat in the primary race for city attorney, Rex Perkins filed a $40,000 libel suit against the Fulbrights and the *Daily Democrat.* When the case came to trial, the paper's attorney asked for a postponement. His team was not complete: Intending to participate in the defense, he said, was J. William Fulbright, whose duties as professor of law at George Washington University in Washington, D.C., prevented him from being on hand until June.

The Perkins suit frightened Roberta. Forty thousand dollars was a lot of money, and Judge Combs was still on the bench. She trusted Clyde Ellis, her attorney in the case; but as always in times of crisis, she reached for family. Never one to underestimate her son's abilities, she was sure that Bill could defeat the provincial dunderheads that Perkins had hired.

For a variety of reasons Bill and Betty were ready to answer Roberta's call. Bill loved and – what was more important given his makeup – respected his mother. It would be very difficult for him to reject her request for help. Moreover, Betty was anxious to get away from the East Coast, at least for a time. Her mother could be dictatorial, even suffocating. Betty was a strong-willed person in her own right, and she longed for the freedom to develop her own life and friends. A daughter, Elizabeth (Betsy) Fulbright, had been born in February; Fayetteville sounded to Betty like a congenial place to raise children. As coincidence would have it, Robert Leflar, an old acquaintance of Fulbright's who taught law at the university, wrote saying that he would be on leave for the 1936–7 term teaching at the University of Missouri. He had talked the matter over with Julian Waterman, Dean of the Law School, and they had decided that Fulbright was just the man to fill in for him.[21]

Bill Fulbright was thirty-one years old when he returned to Fayetteville. The next two years were to be among the most carefree in his life. Aside from knees that occasionally ached, he was in good health and blessed with a devoted wife and brand-new baby girl. He was free of debt (as he would remain for the rest of his life) and back in the bosom of his family.

Fulbright never had a chance to team up with Ellis in the courtroom. Judge Combs directed a verdict of guilty in the Perkins case, but the jury proved unable to settle on the amount of damages. Combs promised to retry the case,

20 Interview with Doug Douglas, Apr. 12, 1993, Fayetteville, Ark.
21 Fulbright interview.

but he left office before he was able to make good on the threat, and Perkins let the matter drop.

Bill, Betty, and Betsy moved into 5 Mount Nord until they could decide on permanent lodging. Bill spent two days a week trying to put the ever-problematical Phipps Lumber Co. on a more profitable basis; another three were consumed teaching constitutional law and equity at the university.

One morning in the early summer of 1937 Dean Waterman asked Fulbright to meet him for lunch at George's Majestic Lounge. Fulbright was a frequent habitué of George's. The scene that greeted him when he came through the door to meet Waterman was a familiar one. The café was comfortably filled with a cross section of Fayetteville, including the crew of a Frisco freight train, a half-dozen girls from the laundry plant next door, a preacher, a traveling salesman, a couple of Chi Omega's, a doctor, a taxi driver, two beauty parlor operators from across the street, and a clutch of faculty members at Table 1. The jukebox played "Into Each Life Some Rain Must Fall" while George Pappas, the Greek-born owner, was deep-frying potatoes in some two-day-old grease.[22]

Julian Waterman pulled out a chair for his guest and quickly got to the point. Leflar had returned, but the university hated to lose Bill's services. In behalf of his colleagues in the law school, he wanted to offer Fulbright a permanent half-time position. His title would be Lecturer. Bill thought only a moment before accepting.

There was more than family connection and local politics in the law school's decision to hire Fulbright. Waterman was a first-rate scholar and administrator, and Leflar would go on to become one of the nation's premier legal scholars. Both thought Fulbright, as Leflar put it, "a cut above – maybe several cuts above – anyone else we might get down here."[23]

Leflar later speculated that teaching law was Fulbright's true vocation. He was a thorough, well-organized lecturer and a penetrating questioner. Although not a scholar himself, he was a great promoter of high academic standards. As he had done at George Washington, Roberta's son urged his best students to consider a career in politics. England, he declared on numerous occasions, had accumulated power and attained greatness because its most gifted lawyers had agreed to participate in and guide the nation's parliamentary democracy.

Every Anglophile dreams of owning a country estate, and Bill Fulbright was no exception. A couple of months after returning to Fayetteville, he and Betty purchased a 150-acre farm several miles northwest of Fayetteville and west of Springdale. In the middle of the spread sat a three-story chinked log

22 *Journalism Newsletter* No. 88, May 12, 1945, BCN 25, F16, Senatorial Papers of J. William Fulbright, Mullins Library, University of Arkansas, Fayetteville, Ark. [hereinafter referred to as SPF].

23 Quoted in Johnson and Gwertzman, *Fulbright: The Dissenter,* 50.

house. Originally built by a local architect who was enchanted with the region's frontier history, Rabbit's Foot Lodge featured a natural stone fireplace, wooden shutters, and a wraparound fireplace. It had been named for a Cherokee Indian chief alleged to have ruled the area in bygone days. The structure sat atop the crest of a hill overlooking a tree-filled pasture that more closely resembled a park than an area for grazing the fifty white-faced Herefords that Bill bought. The house was surrounded by white oaks, magnolias, and catalpa trees. A natural, low stone wall bordered Rabbit's Foot Lodge, and the yard was crisscrossed with flagstone walks. At the bottom of the hill, across the dirt road that divided the house from the main pasture, was a natural spring.

At the time Fulbright purchased Rabbit's Foot Lodge, the farm had been neglected for several years. Moreover, it possessed neither heating nor indoor plumbing. Betty was attracted to the notion of farm life, but bare wooden-plank floors, smoke-stained timber walls, and outhouses were a bit much. For three months she devoted herself completely to bringing her new home into the twentieth century. The living room remained dark paneled, but Betty painted the rest of the interior colonial white to brighten it up. "She decorated in chintz," Bill's niece, Suzie Zorn, recalled.[24] The house may have been rustic, but Betty had meals served on the best china – an English country pattern, of course. The spring-fed stream was dammed up and a small swimming pool built for the family and its visitors. Additional trees were planted, the grounds landscaped, and soon Rabbit's Foot Lodge was transformed into a country showplace. In addition to the cattle, Bill bought hogs and chickens. He was not, however, a "hands-on" farmer; a tenant family lived on the place and performed most of the chores.

There was no hospital as such in northwest Arkansas until the early 1930s. English physician Dr. Frank Rigall moved to Prairie Grove, a small community southwest of Fayetteville, and built a clinic. There, two days after Christmas 1938, Roberta Waugh Fulbright was born. Nicknamed "Bosey," Bill and Betty's youngest would, despite her given name, grow up to be a clone of her mother.

After Hal Douglas's job with the FBI ended in 1937, he and Helen moved in with Roberta at 5 Mount Nord. If the truth be known, Roberta and Helen did not like Betty Williams Fulbright: Though she could wear calico dresses and make homemade preserves, she never let anyone forget that she was Main Line Philadelphia. Betty could be intimidating in her own way; moreover, she was something of a know-it-all, fond of telling any and everyone she met how to do something whether she knew how to do it or not. Susie Zorn remembered her giving a set piece on how to iron a linen tablecloth, when she knew perfectly well Betty had never put hand to iron in her life. The real

24 Zorn interview.

sticking point with Roberta, however, was that Bill now had another woman in his life.[25]

Betty's assertiveness was in part a matter of self-preservation. Zorn recalled that the Fulbright household was a great place to be if you were strong but excruciating if you were not. Conversation at 5 Mount Nord was dominated by discussions of politics, history, and current affairs. The thinly educated Betty protected herself with her manners:

> Betty had the first finger bowls I ever saw. Her standards about how things should be were very exact. Even later I was struck by the contrast in the dinner presentation at her house. It was always careful and austere . . . small precise portions of every dish. Quite in contrast to down here [Fayetteville] where you have a whole bunch of whatever it is. . . . It was genteel.[26]

Eloise Baerg – once a fellow student of Bill's at Arkansas and now a part-time English teacher there – recalled that entertaining was Betty's real profession: "She had dinners and luncheons. It was always very special. I'd buy a new dress. Envious people would say that she enjoyed it here because she could be more important here than she could be in Washington."[27]

It was not that there were any confrontations with Roberta: Betty almost always deferred to her mother-in-law, and Roberta knew that she could be only so rude to Betty. Bill, the prize for which they competed, was also the glue that bound the two women together.

Throughout her married life, Betty schemed and plotted, maneuvered and planned, as she committed herself totally to keeping her husband's affection and protecting her family from the storms of life. She shared her husband's contempt for people who could not control their tempers and their hormones. Indeed, her contemporaries recalled that Betty Fulbright was formidably self-controlled. The center of her life plan and the vehicle of her ambition was Bill. If she and Roberta had anything in common, it was that they both shared a larger vision of Bill's future. An instinctive politician, Betty seemed from the very outset conscious of the need to cultivate people. Her family and friends remember that after a day of meeting people, she would sit down and make a list of the children's names, the kind of curtains in the wife's house (especially if they were homemade), and the husband's latest achievement. For Bill, who was impossible with small talk, Betty was to be a political asset of immense value.

By the summer of 1939 the Fulbright family business interests were as stable and well managed as they had been since Jay's death.[28] At the prompt-

25 Ibid.

26 Ibid.

27 Interview with Eloise Baerg-King, Oct. 17, 1990, Fayetteville, Ark.

28 Gilbert, *A Fulbright Chronicle*, 119–20.

ing of his friend and boss, Julian Waterman, Bill had been considering making the teaching of law a full-time career. After talking the matter over with Betty, Roberta, and Hal Douglas, Bill decided to accept the university's offer to an appointment as associate professor of law. As the summer drew to a close, he busied himself with preparations for the additional classes he would have to teach.

Late on the night of September 12, 1939, the phone rang in the home of Eloise and Bill Baerg. Professor William Baerg was then the distinguished chairman of the university's entomology department. The world's leading expert on the tarantula, he was known to the student body as "the spider man." It had been an unsettling time for Bill and Eloise: Just two weeks earlier Hitler had invaded Poland, plunging Europe into its second general war in a generation. The Baergs, like most liberal intellectuals, believed that the United States would have to come to the aid of the beleaguered European democracies. When the phone rang late on the night of September 12, Eloise half-feared, half-hoped that it was news that the United States had declared war. "My God," she heard her husband declare. "That's terrible. What will we do?" After he hung up, he came into the bedroom. "John Futrall is dead. His car ran head-on into a truck just south of West Fork."[29]

John C. Futrall was a dignified, competent man who had served the university as president since 1913. Although under law Arkansas governors served as ex officio and acting presidents of the university board of trustees, Futrall had managed to a remarkable degree to insulate his institution from state politics. With his sudden death that insulation was gone, and its removal would open doors for J. William Fulbright that would lead ultimately to state and then national office.

Many faculty members at the University of Arkansas took the position that the selection of the president was their prerogative. The governor of Arkansas in 1939, Carl E. Bailey, had different ideas. Arkansas progressives were up in arms in the 1930s over the Democratic Party's practice of nominating candidates for state office through the Democratic state committee. In 1936 Bailey had captured the governor's office by, among other things, promising to install a system of preferential primaries or some other democratic mechanism for selecting nominees for state office. However, Bailey's philosophy – like that of another progressive and his idol, Woodrow Wilson – held only one constant: his ambition. When in the summer of 1937 U.S. Senator and Senate Majority Leader Joe T. Robinson died suddenly, Governor Bailey accepted the state committee's nomination to replace him. Arkansas's two leading newspapers, the *Democrat* and *Gazette,* took Bailey to task for his incon-

29 Baerg-King interview.

sistencies, and he subsequently lost the election to independent John Miller. Determined to run for reelection as governor in 1938, Bailey decided that it had been weaknesses in his political organization, rather than his betrayal of his progressive philosophy, that had been responsible for his 1937 defeat. One of the areas in which he had little support and almost no organization was northwest Arkansas.

During the spring of 1938 Bailey made it his business to get to Fayetteville as often as possible, and he never neglected to drop by the offices of the *Northwest Arkansas Times* (so renamed by the Fulbrights in 1937 to promote subscriptions) to pay his respects. Roberta Fulbright had written more than one editorial railing against the abuses of the Democratic Party nominating system. "It's usually only a choice between two whom you did not choose to begin with," she wrote in 1937. Despite their mutual espousal of electoral reform, Roberta had not supported Carl Bailey in 1936, and she was extremely put off by his race for Robinson's senate seat in 1937, comparing his political contortions to those of a "Jap tumbler."[30] However, like all seasoned politicians, Roberta was susceptible to cultivation and capable of changing her mind. During his visits, the charming and charismatic Bailey soon convinced her that the apostasy of 1937 had been an aberration. By the summer of 1938 Bailey was a regular visitor to "The Cabin" for dinner; "As I See It" was full of first-person accounts of conversations with Governor Bailey;[31] not surprisingly, Roberta came out four-square for him for reelection in 1940. Following his successful bid for a second term, a campaign in which he carried northwest Arkansas handily, the governor set about paying his political debts.[32]

The faculty's leading candidate to replace Futrall was Julian Waterman. The Pine Bluff native had distinguished himself as an economist, legal scholar, and administrator. He was respected for his integrity and judgment. Bailey named Waterman acting president until the board could meet on September 18. According to Fulbright, the trustees did indeed offer the job to Waterman. "The board of trustees asked Dean Waterman would he be president," he recalled. "He said he didn't want to. I believe that he felt that as a Jew he would be subjected to prejudice which was much worse in those days. He said he was willing to be vice-president, but not president. I am told he recommended me."[33] Eloise Baerg gives another version, however. "Mrs. Waterman was almost my closest friend," she recounts. "She was with me in the garden when the trustees were meeting and she paced back and forth and said,

30 Quoted in Mary Lynn Kennedy, "Politics in Academe: Roberta Fulbright's Role in Her Son's University Presidency" (unpublished graduate essay, Department of History, University of Arkansas, 1975), 3, 5.

31 Gilbert, *A Fulbright Chronicle,* 137.

32 Kennedy, "Politics in Academe," 9.

33 Fulbright interview.

'I wish they would select Julian, not so much because I want to be the wife of the president, but he could do so much for the university.' . . . I never really heard that they offered it to him. Mrs. Waterman was quite disappointed."[34] Waterman was crushed.

Everyone in Fayetteville assumed that Roberta had interceded directly with Carl Bailey to have her son named president. The Fulbrights, of course, denied it. According to Hal Douglas, whom Bailey had appointed to the board of trustees, word that Bill was being considered first came from Little Rock. Two days after Futrall's death, Raymond Rebsamen, Little Rock businessman and university trustee, called and told Fulbright that he was under consideration. Fulbright allegedly said that he was not interested and insisted that Waterman was the best candidate. Again according to the official Fulbright family version, when informed later that Waterman would not accept, Fulbright reluctantly agreed to become president.

With Governor Bailey presiding, the full board met on the eighteenth. As soon as the meeting opened, Bailey turned to Hal and said, "Okay, Douglas, have you got your resignation ready?" Hal, who could not serve with his brother-in-law as president, said that he did. "You're excused now. We've got other business to attend to."[35] According to T. C. Carlson, secretary to the board and longtime university treasurer, the board never considered another candidate. Eleven faculty had in fact formally applied; Fulbright was not among that number. Carlson remembered that Fulbright's selection "came as a complete surprise to most of us . . . and he was elected very perfunctorily, I thought."[36] Beloit Taylor, a former president of the Alumni Association who had been appointed by Bailey to the board in 1937, held that Fulbright's appointment was logical and the product of considerable thought: Arkansas could not afford to compete for academic administrators of national reputation; Fulbright's academic credentials were adequate, he would be able to get along with the legislature, and his Fayetteville ties ensured that he would not go questing after another job in a few years.[37]

The university faculty was disgruntled, but there was little organized opposition to Fulbright's election. At the time of his appointment J. William Fulbright was thirty-four, the youngest university president in the United States.

In fact, the faculty was right to have reservations not only about the process by which Fulbright was elected president but about his qualifications as well. Being a Rhodes scholar and lawyer scarcely qualified one as a university president. In the first place, Fulbright possessed no scholarly credentials: He had been a full-time faculty member for only one year, and had produced not a single article or commentary. He had not a whit of administrative expe-

34 Baerg-King interview.
35 Quoted in Gilbert, *A Fulbright Chronicle,* 138.
36 Ibid.
37 Beloit Taylor to J. N. Heiskell, Jan. 11, 1945, BCN 25, F16, SPF.

rience. Perhaps most important, other than campus politics he had had no political experience. Traditionally, the president of the university was the second most powerful political figure in the state. The institution depended for its funding on his influence and powers of persuasion with the legislature. There were weapons at his disposal – the university alumni comprised potentially the most powerful voting block in the state – but it took skill and experience to wield them.

To his credit, Fulbright was acutely aware of his shortcomings. Being president was "a very great strain on me" he recalled.[38] In fact, his ambitious mother had pushed him into a job for which he was not qualified and that he was not sure he wanted. A student at the time remembered that at the beginning of his tenure President Fulbright drove his car right up to the rear basement entrance of the administration building and entered without speaking to student, faculty, or staff member.[39] He was willing, however, to be thrust into the breach in the belief that out of the very process of seizing opportunity only good things could come. In addition, he generally took the advice of the two most significant women in his life.

Though a novice, Fulbright did have a philosophy of education when he became president of the University of Arkansas. The function of the state's leading institution was to prepare the best of Arkansas's youth to govern the state and even the nation; the curriculum best designed to accomplish that goal was a liberal one. "I believe that by the proper emphasis on the right subjects the universities, in the course of time, can make the students realize the importance of a good government, can teach them that politics can be the most honorable of all professions, and can induce the best of them to enter political life as a career," he told the Fort Smith Civic Club in his first address as president.[40] He rejected the notion that the purpose of education was "to turn one's brains into money," as some modern educators were then claiming. Continued concentration on the disciplines of literature, economics, philosophy, and history would make students aware of the value systems, economic theories, political processes, and social institutions that humanity had devised and tested over the course of its history. From this acquired body of knowledge, future leaders could choose what would work best for themselves and their fellow citizens. Like John Dewey, whose philosophy of pragmatism he had learned at the feet of the Peabody Hall experimenters twenty years earlier, Fulbright held to the notion that nothing could be accepted on faith. Each idea or institution was good only as it was proven to have worth for each generation and each individual. He suspected that there were values and institutions that had universal validity – a sense of cultural relativity and parlia-

38 Quoted in Johnson and Gwertzman, *Fulbright: The Dissenter,* 53.
39 Interview with Dr. Edward McClain, July 25, 1993, Fayetteville, Ark.
40 Civic Club Speech, Dec. 10, 1939, Speech File, SPF.

mentary democracy, for example – but he was not certain; only time would tell. However, for an enlightened society with educated individuals, there could be no shortcuts. Each student had to learn the basics and choose.

In his two years as head of the state university, Fulbright sounded several themes that would appear again and again in his future public utterances. He attacked what he would later refer to as "the blight of anti-intellectualism" and the cult of hostility to politics that was so pervasive in America.[41] He also called upon Arkansans to cast down their buckets where they were and realize their immense potential.

J. William Fulbright was a man of considerable self-confidence in a state afflicted with a deep-seated inferiority complex. The frontier farmers who had migrated across the Appalachians from the Carolinas to Tennessee and Kentucky, and thence to Arkansas, had always been ambivalent about progress. As to their lack of it, they were both defensive and proud. If Arkansas was rural and economically underdeveloped, it was also natural and unspoiled. If the population was generally undereducated and unsophisticated, it was, according to popular perceptions, untainted with the corruption and money grubbing that Thomas Jefferson had associated with urban life. Throughout the twentieth century Arkansans insisted on comparing themselves with Texans, those rich, outgoing, vulgar, and incredibly self-confident beings who lived to the southwest. It was a form of masochism, for in their own eyes, Arkansans would always come up short. In education the state's inferiority complex promoted a kind of perverse apathy. As president of the state's leading educational institution, Fulbright labored desperately to transfer his self-confidence and his ever-broadening horizons to his fellow citizens. He noted with dismay in his speeches how many farmers went to Texas or Oklahoma to buy cattle when there were better animals to be had in Arkansas at a lower price, and how the wealthy sent their children to schools out of state because they simply assumed the schools could not be as good in Arkansas. "We have many things to be proud of in Arkansas and we must cultivate that pride, just as they have in Texas and California," he told the state repeatedly.[42]

Formidable though he was, however, Bill Fulbright was never strong enough to imbue his fellow Arkansans with the self-esteem to which he felt they were entitled. For the most part they believed what others thought about them. They were "Arkies" who like the "Okies" to the west had fled to California and Texas during the Depression in dilapidated jalopies with all their worldly possessions jammed to the roof. They were "hillbillies" still wearing overalls, strawhats, and cavorting about in bare feet, the "boobs" that H. L. Mencken was so fond of roasting in the *American Mercury.* They were the semicivilized barbarians discovered by the "Arkansas Traveller" or the hay-

[41] Quoted in Johnson and Gwertzman, *Fulbright: The Dissenter,* 59.
[42] Quoted in ibid., 58.

seed, huckster characters "Lum and Abner." Added to all this was the mentality of a defeated, exploited people common to all states of the former Confederacy.

The most invidious aspect of Arkansas's poor self-image was its tendency to blame its problems on outside forces. Again, like so many other southern states, it traditionally saw itself as victim, as a people acted upon rather than acting. As did their brethren in other parts of Dixie, white Arkansans took on the collective psychological traits of the hundreds of thousands of downtrodden blacks that they had so long exploited. Partially as a result, the state's citizens historically were underachievers. Those politicians who frequented the "fried chicken circuit" were fond of extolling the virtues of the "Wonder State." They would cite statistics showing the great quantities of cotton, rice, oil, and lumber Arkansas produced. Practically all the aluminum in the United States was mined in Arkansas, and it possessed the only diamond mine in North America. There were undeveloped deposits of zinc, antimony, manganese, mercury, and lead. Numerous rivers and streams, if adequately dammed, held out the promise of unlimited electrical power. The delta of southeast Arkansas comprised some of the richest and most productive farm land in the world. Yet in 1940 the per-capita income in the state was $250, the lowest in the nation. There were numerous real handicaps: lack of a skilled labor force coupled with deep-seated antiunion prejudices, a woefully underdeveloped transportation system, an inability to develop or attract capital, and an inadequate educational system.

Perhaps most important, Arkansas had proved uniquely susceptible to manipulation and domination by special interests. At the time Fulbright ventured forth into the wilderness of state politics, the most powerful interest in the state was Arkansas Power and Light. An outspoken opponent of public power, AP&L sat astride the state senate like a booted rider atop a compliant steed. Although a small severance tax on resources taken from the ground would have been sufficient to have given Arkansas the finest educational system in the Union, the state legislature stubbornly refused to pass one.

Nonetheless, the state's greatest handicap remained its self-image. Fulbright called upon his fellow citizens to think positively and to cultivate the New England habits of thrift, industry, and self-reliance; but at the same time he too quickly fell into the trap of blaming outside forces for his and his school's problems. In speeches around the state and in letters to the Arkansas congressional delegation he attacked the great railroads of the Northeast that had manipulated freight rates in such a way as to drain off Arkansas's wealth into their own pockets and prevent indigenous economic development. Influenced by the New Deal, and particularly the activities of the National Youth Administration (NYA) in Arkansas – and unwilling at that point to take on the special interests – Fulbright decided that federal aid was the best method of breaking the old cycle of outside control and endemic poverty. On several occasions he wrote Congressman Clyde Ellis, a family friend and a former student, appealing through him to Congress to restore funding for the NYA. He also made the first of what would be many appeals for massive federal aid to education. Was it fair, he asked in a letter Ellis read on the floor of the House, that Harvard was able to spend $14 million in 1938–9 while the state universities of the South and West, serving millions more students, were held to $1 million or less? If democracy were to survive, Congress would have to subsidize its public institutions of higher learning.[43] Taking the path of least resistance, Fulbright declared Arkansas to be, in effect, a Third World country. The only solution to its chronic socioeconomic problems was a massive, sustained program of foreign aid.

Since his days at Oxford with Robert McCallum and then subsequently his tour with Mike Fodor, Fulbright had taken a keen interest in foreign affairs. The presidency of the University of Arkansas gave him at last a forum for expressing his views. Not surprisingly, he was an outspoken interventionist. He proudly and publicly touted his membership in William Allen White's Committee to Defend America by Aiding the Allies. He readily accepted the notion that Britain and France were fighting to defend Western civilization from the armies of an imperial totalitarianism. A confirmed Atlanticist, Fulbright believed in a community of interest among the Western democracies. As a member of that community, America had an obligation to spend its blood and treasure in defense of the common good. In various statements that would be used by his enemies a generation later to impugn his views on Vietnam, he issued a call to arms. "It is far better to fight for [our freedom] and to lose than meekly to acquiesce," he remarked in 1940. Time and time again he berated and belittled isolationists and isolationism: "Too often today we hear the profound pronouncement by an isolationist senator that this country does not want war. . . . The fact is the world has war and the question is what it should do about it."[44] Immediately following the fall of France in June 1940 Fulbright wrote President Roosevelt urging him to bolder action in support of Britain. The American armed forces were dominated by old, timid men in whom the youth of the nation were quickly losing faith. "We can not expect Congress to be decisive," he declared. "I am convinced that the people of this country, especially the youth, will follow you enthusiastically if you are daring and bold in this crisis."[45]

Meanwhile, Betty's duties as the president's wife were forcing her to spend more and more time in town. Like most college communities, Fayetteville

43 Quoted in ibid., 57.
44 Quoted in ibid., 59.
45 JWF to FDR, June 19, 1940, letter in possession of Prof. Gary Clifford, University of Connecticut.

was in many ways claustrophobic and incestuous. Dividing the community socially as well as geographically was College Avenue, which ran north–south and doubled as the highway connecting Fort Smith with Joplin, Missouri. To the west lay the university, Shulertown, and the square. To the immediate east was situated Fayetteville's principal residential area, a network of elm-, maple-, and oak-lined streets that were a forest of green in the summer and a blaze of reds, yellows, and oranges in the fall. The first families of Fayetteville all lived there in two- and three-story frame and brick houses. Through the heart of the district ran Washington Avenue. For the most part, university people penetrated the area only as boarders, and even then they had to be recommended. Faculty and staff referred to the first families contemptuously as "the Washington Avenue crowd."[46] The only residential area more prestigious was Mount Nord.

As a Fulbright, Betty had no trouble breaking into the Washington Avenue social circle. She became an active member of the country club that Roberta and Jay had helped found. She was immediately asked to join the Modern Literary Club, which was composed of the leading ladies of Fayetteville, both town and gown. At book club she met Gladys Hosford, the wife of the chair of the math department and future president of Southern Methodist University. The two became intimate friends – "soulmates" – according to a mutual acquaintance.[47]

Though he had won two terms as governor, Carl E. Bailey was still something of a political outsider in Arkansas. Having indicted one of Senator Joseph T. Robinson's protégés for fraud, Bailey had had to create his own political organization during his 1936 run for the governorship, and had won in spite of concerted opposition from Robinson's friends. Despite his incumbency and Robinson's death in 1937, Bailey ran scared throughout his first two-year term. In addition to building his own political organizations in northwest Arkansas and other outlying areas, Bailey consolidated his position by compelling a reluctant legislature to create a state civil service system, as well as by ostentatiously extraditing mobster Charles "Lucky" Luciano from Hot Springs.[48]

The 1940 gubernatorial election, to which Fulbright's appointment to the university presidency was so intimately related, was noteworthy because Carl Bailey, in running again, was challenging Arkansas's strict two-term tradition. His chief challenger for the Democratic nomination was Homer E. Adkins, who as Collector of Internal Revenue for Arkansas was the most pow-

46 Baerg-King interview.
47 Ibid.
48 Timothy P. Donovan and Willard B. Gatewood, Jr., eds., *The Governors of Arkansas: Essays in Political Biography* (Fayetteville, 1981), 185–6.

erful federal appointee in the state. Another of Robinson's protégés, he succeeded to the leadership of the senator's machine when the majority leader died in 1936. Adkins, a former member of the Ku Klux Klan, promised to undo everything Bailey had done. Supported by federal officeholders in the state and endorsed by the entire congressional delegation, Adkins successfully exploited the third-term issue and rolled over Bailey in the May primary.[49]

Adkins's election had dire implications for President Fulbright. Among the issues the new governor had utilized to beat Carl Bailey was his alleged politicization of the University. "Take the University out of politics," Adkins had cried at every opportunity during the campaign, promising if elected to remove himself from the board of trustees. "Intimidation of people in educational circles must stop," he'd proclaimed.[50] Some of the faculty, particularly those who resented the way in which Bill Fulbright had been appointed president, were impressed. Roberta had immediately sensed what Adkins's election would mean and had campaigned hard for Bailey. "Don't be fooled," she had implored her readers; "there just ain't no such animal" as a nonpolitical state institution. "In the main," she'd editorialized, "good politics has been its [the university's] portion . . . so rid your mind of getting away from politics and let your mind run to the idea of voting [for] the best available man."[51]

Roberta's misgivings were well founded. Homer Adkins was a Bible-belt demagogue with an inferiority complex and a taste for revenge. He fancied himself as having come up the hard way, and he was more than ready to lay the Fulbrights low not only because they had supported Bailey but also because they appeared to him to be privileged aristocrats. Shortly after his inauguration, the new governor secured the resignation of six members of the university board of trustees and replaced them with a half dozen of his staunchest supporters.

A board meeting in Little Rock on May 17 touched off a storm of speculation in the press. Rumors circulated that Fulbright and several other university officials were slated for immediate firing.[52] In mid-May university students held a large rally to express their concern over the anticipated upheaval at the highest levels of the administration. Both the pro-Fulbright faction and the pro-Adkins group used the slogan, "Keep the University out of politics." The president's supporters denounced anticipated moves to fire him as unwarranted political interference, whereas the Adkins people argued that his dismissal was necessary to rid the institution of the taint of political manipulation. The crowd at the demonstration was pro-Fulbright by a margin of 6 to 1.[53]

49 Ibid., 188–92.
50 Quoted in Kennedy, "Politics in Academe," 11.
51 Ibid.
52 Robert Leflar, *The First 100 Years: Centennial History of the University of Arkansas* (Fayetteville, 1972), 176–7.
53 Kennedy, "Politics in Academe," 15, and Leflar, *First 100 Years,* 177.

Tensions mounted at the approach of the scheduled date for the next board meeting: commencement day, June 9, 1941. The *Arkansas Gazette* and *Arkansas Democrat* speculated daily on who was to get the ax. Roberta was well-nigh beside herself. On the eve of the meeting one of the new board members released an ominous statement to the press. "In recent years certain political influences have caused a political cancer to appear on the surface of the University of Arkansas," it read, "and I believe the board proposes to cut out that cancer."[54]

The board met throughout commencement morning. On a straight factional vote, the trustees decided 6 to 4 to ask Fulbright to resign. Chairman J. G. Ragsdale of El Dorado instructed T. C. Carlson to deliver the news to the president at his office in Old Main. Carlson, a conservative, rather formal man, entered Fulbright's office with some trepidation.

"Mr. Fulbright," he reported, "the board has just passed a resolution requesting that you resign."

"For what cause?" Fulbright asked.

"There is no cause stated."

"You may tell the board that I do not wish to resign," Fulbright answered.[55]

Carlson returned to the board meeting. The president had declined to resign, he announced. Annoyed but unintimidated, the Adkins majority adopted a resolution declaring the post of president vacant at the end of the school year, that is, after the graduation exercises scheduled to be held that very night. They then named Dean A. M. Harding of the College of Agriculture to fill the vacant position. Carlson departed immediately to break the news to Fulbright.

By tradition presidents of the University of Arkansas hosted a formal luncheon for faculty and other distinguished guests on commencement day. Betty had personally redecorated the high-ceilinged, wood-floored ballroom in the student union for the occasion. By 11:30 the several hundred invited guests had assembled. The noon hour came and passed and still no Fulbright. The crowd fairly hummed with speculation. Eloise Baerg recalled the scene:

> People were waiting and waiting for the board of trustees meeting to be over and noon came and a carrier came and said the meeting was still going on. The luncheon couldn't happen until the president and his wife arrived. Somebody came up and played the piano. We had run out of conversation. At last an official rose to announce the arrival of President and Mrs. Fulbright. I wasn't too far from the doorway. I saw Betty Fulbright and her expression said, "I can carry off this scene." She stepped up to Edna Harding, wife

[54] Quoted in Kennedy, "Politics in Academe," 16.

[55] Quoted in Johnson and Gwertzman, *Fulbright: The Dissenter,* 49.

> of the newly named president. Now, they moved in the same social circles and were, in fact, friends. I heard Betty say, "I congratulate you."[56]

Roberta learned of the chain of events almost as soon as they occurred. She had dispatched her best reporter, Jerry Neil, to cover the board meeting, but because the trustees were meeting in executive session, the press was excluded. Undaunted, Neil took up a post in a stall in the men's room with door closed and his feet up so no one would spot him. In time coffee took its toll on various board members, and they filed in and out of the toilet. By the time the meeting broke up the *Times*'s representative had pieced together the story. His account appeared in the evening edition together with Roberta's anti-Adkins editorial entitled, "Our Fuehrer."[57]

The outdoor commencement exercises for the four hundred graduates of the class of 1941 began at 6:45 in a light rain. News of Fulbright's firing had spread quickly, and when he stepped to the lectern to introduce the main speaker, Dr. Edward C. Elliott of Purdue, the students rose spontaneously and applauded for several minutes. Following Elliott's address, Fulbright passed out the diplomas, his last official act as president of the University of Arkansas. He never issued a public statement about the day's events.

Fulbright's dismissal from the university presidency was a humiliating experience for him and his wife. Many of the faculty and townspeople ostracized the couple during the weeks and months that followed. Eloise Baerg remembered one woman saying to her, after she had invited the Fulbrights to a party, "They're not being received these days, Eloise."[58] There were those who remained loyal: the Watermans, the Hosfords, the Leflars, as well as the Baergs; but it was a trying time.

In truth Adkins's maneuver infuriated Fulbright. The summary firing had aroused his competitive instincts. Bill did not quite have Jack's temper, but he had bulldog tenacity that made him a more formidable opponent than his pugnacious elder brother. Egged on by his mother, he was determined to get even with Homer Adkins. Elected officials invariably become vulnerable, the Fulbrights knew, and Adkins's time would come.

56 Baerg-King interview.
57 Gilbert, *A Fulbright Chronicle,* 140.
58 Baerg-King interview.

# 4

# *A political education*

Six months following his dismissal as president of the University of Arkansas Fulbright ran into Clyde Ellis, the lawyer who had represented the Fulbrights in the Perkins libel suit. After practicing law for a number of years in Bentonville, some thirty miles to the north of Fayetteville, Ellis with the help of the GGL and the *Northwest Arkansas Times* had won a seat in Congress from Arkansas's Third Congressional District in 1938. A Bailey-style progressive, Ellis endeared himself to Roberta by his personal attentions and his advocacy of such New Deal programs as rural electrification and regional public power projects. Unopposed in 1940, he decided in 1942 to abandon his House seat and run for the Senate post being vacated by Lloyd Spencer.[1] As Ellis explained his plans to Fulbright, an idea struck him. "Look, I'm going to announce next Saturday and I think you ought to run for my place. I'll give you the names of my friends and you can go and contact them and tell them I'm for you."[2] Fulbright told Ellis that he was not interested.

Several weeks later the Democratic State Committee, which was still controlled by the Bailey forces, asked Fulbright to come to Little Rock to discuss his political future. For three days they tried to convince him to challenge Homer Adkins for the gubernatorial nomination. He told them as diplomatically as he could that it was the wrong time and explained that, anyway, he had decided to enlist in the armed services in the fall. He and Betty returned to Rabbit's Foot Lodge planning to spend a quiet summer before he entered the Army Air Corps. A week later he got another call to come to Little Rock. "Bill was 'agin' the idea," Betty wrote a friend, "but my curiosity got the better of me – so we went." This time the committee proposed that he run for Congress. His knees and his age – he was thirty-seven – would keep him out of combat duty, party leaders pointed out. His time and talents would be wasted in a desk job. He could do more for his country by entering politics. Again Fulbright protested: He had no political experience, and he really should be getting into the armed forces.[3]

1 Stephen H. Dew, *The New Deal and Fayetteville, Arkansas, 1933–1941* (M.A. thesis, University of Arkansas, 1987), 253–6.

2 Interview with J. William Fulbright, Oct. 11–18, 1988, Washington, D.C.

3 Betty to Don, undated, letter in possession of Mrs. Roberta Foote.

Fulbright was outwardly dubious, inwardly intrigued. The Third District included the top tier of northwest Arkansas counties. Fulbright didn't know the names of all and had never even been in six; but, as Ellis reminded him, he had always touted public service to his students. Over the next few days he consulted his two closest friends and advisers, who were also likely to be his two largest financial backers: Betty and Roberta. Both were enthusiastic. "Well, why not?" Fulbright recalled his mother as saying. "You might as well do it. You've had unusual opportunities. You've had a good education, and how do you justify a Rhodes scholarship if you don't intend doing something useful with it?"[4] Inhibited by discouraging remarks from several townspeople he had consulted, Fulbright remained ambivalent, however. Betty's enthusiasm was decisive. Whereas the prospect of campaigning intimidated him, it exhilarated her. She had, moreover, begun to miss the East Coast. Washington society would allow her to show off her social skills and, perhaps more important, to have Bill for herself, away from Roberta. Fulbright informed the State Democratic Committee that he would run, but only on the condition that if he won, the draft board would waive the draft exemption that went with election to federal office.[5]

"Fulbright for Congress" headquarters was located in an upstairs office of one of the many family-owned buildings on the Fayetteville Square. The campaign staff was made up of students, friends, and a few recruits from the ice company and the newspaper. Doug Smith, a journeyman journalist, and Jerry Neil, Roberta's lavatory reporter, helped with strategy and speechwriting. At Fulbright's insistence, the *Times* provided strictly balanced coverage of the campaign, and his mother never mentioned it in "As I See It." He sensed that her advocacy would do more harm than good, and had the courage to say so. Money was a different matter. The campaign wound up costing ten thousand dollars, the entire amount contributed by Bill, Roberta, and Betty.

Fulbright's chief opponent was Karl Greenhaw, a State Supreme Court justice with a reputation as a spellbinding stump speaker. Backed by the Adkins political machine, Greenhaw suffered from an acute case of overconfidence. Until the last days of the race, he stayed in Little Rock and campaigned through newspapers and surrogates who labored to portray Fulbright as a man out of touch with the people, as an overeducated child of privilege who had been tainted by European society, and as a gentleman farmer who knew nothing of cattle and hogs except through a balance sheet.[6] Such populist appeals had been in vogue in Arkansas politics since the rabble-rousing days of former governor Jeff Davis at the turn of the century. Fulbright seemed a per-

4 Quoted in Haynes Johnson and Bernard M. Gwertzman, *Fulbright: The Dissenter* (New York, 1968), 67–8.

5 Betty to Don, undated, letter in possession of Mrs. Roberta Foote.

6 Fulbright interview.

fect target for such rhetoric. Greenhaw reasoned that in the Ozarks money and education were still highly suspicious commodities. Fulbright, as everyone knew, had both in abundance.

Fulbright and his managers, amateurs though they were, realized that the best and only antidote for Greenhaw's tactics was familiarity. Riding in a used Ford that his wife had bought specifically for the campaign, Bill set out to introduce himself to each and every would-be constituent in the mountainous, rural district 175 miles long and 50 miles wide. In this first campaign Allan Gilbert, then a reporter and editor for the *Times,* acted as advance man. The campaign at the outset was very much a matter of trial and error.[7]

During the first weeks of Fulbright's grand tour of the Ozarks, Gilbert recalled, he would arrive in a designated town a few hours before the candidate. After putting up posters and dropping off ads and news releases at the county newspaper offices, he would identify likely speaking spots. His vision was initially beclouded by inexperience. In Cotter, a typical hill country hamlet, Gilbert chose a small roadside park along a bluff overlooking the White River a few blocks from the main business district. It was, he recalled, "just right for contemplating the issues."[8] He spread the word far and wide; candidate Fulbright would speak at 1:30 at the scenic turnout. The appointed hour arrived, but Fulbright and Gilbert were the only human beings in sight. "Maybe we'd better reschedule downtown," the candidate suggested. As Gilbert scurried to oblige, Fulbright spent a profitable hour pressing the flesh on Cotter's main street. The new time was 3:00 in the village square. Still no one showed. The advance man set yet another time. No voters appeared. In frustration the candidate walked up to the top of the hill overlooking the community and finally spotted some people. "If you don't mind," Fulbright said, "I want to discuss some of the issues that I think are important." A few people gathered around and began to listen. This humiliating experience was repeated at Hindsville, Clifty, and Goshen.[9]

Fulbright and his staff soon learned to curry favor with the power structure as well as the common man. Upon his arrival in an Ozark community, the candidate would go first to the courthouse and introduce himself to the county judge and the sheriff. Ellis had given him a good list of, as Gilbert put it, "the guys who had the hammer in each one of these counties."[10] In the smaller towns, Fulbright abandoned formal speechmaking, opting instead for question-and-answer sessions with local citizens in general stores, filling stations, or barber shops. Betty talked to the women about gardening, home remedies, canning, and the weather.

7 Interview with Allen Gilbert, Oct. 17, 1989, Fayetteville, Ark.
8 Allan Gilbert, *A Fulbright Chronicle* (Fayetteville, 1980), 142.
9 Gilbert interview.
10 Ibid.

In the towns where the population was more concentrated and cosmopolitan, like Harrison or Bentonville, campaigning was more conventional. "We had a great old big double amplifier mounted on a '39 Chevy," Gilbert recalled. "We'd turn down the back seat and fill the trunk with a whole bunch of records – John Philip Sousa."[11] Allan would punctuate the mobile concerts with announcements of the time and place where candidate Fulbright would speak. At the appointed hour the car would park near the speaker's platform, as like as not a flatbed trailer, to serve as a public address system. Little by little Fulbright learned to match his remarks to the interests of a given locale, and his early stiffness and formality evolved into a soft-spoken, conversational style.

The Appalachian and Ozark highlands "was a different South, without plantations, many black people, or a palpable Confederate mystique," Jack Temple Kirby has written. Northwestern and north-central Arkansas in 1942 resembled the southern rim of Appalachia. Benton and Washington counties in the extreme northwest enjoyed relative commercial prosperity with their diversified grain–diary–livestock and fruit-based economies. Most of the residents in the remaining eight counties comprising the Third Congressional District lived close to the subsistence level. Newton and Searcy counties were typical. Hill farmers eked out an existence growing cotton in the glades and valleys for cash, and raising vegetables, fruits, and livestock to feed their families. There was almost no industry in the area, most of the sawmills having closed during the Depression.[12]

The campaign trail that Bill and Betty Fulbright followed in 1942 was hot, dusty, and narrow, a maze of hairpin turns amid dense hickory and oak forests. Dotting the wilderness were country stores, farms, blacksmith shops, and rural post offices. People still lived in log cabins, hospitals were nonexistent, and Saturday-night square dancing enlivened with home brew constituted the principal means of entertainment. Evening Shade, Yellville, Berryville, Mountain Home, and Fifty-six were part of the Fulbright itinerary.

Though Bill refused to let Roberta campaign, he made use of the *Northwest Arkansas Times,* albeit in an indirect way. Once a week in the evening after the day's regular paper had been run, Doug Smith and the staff would come in and print a four-page campaign paper called the *Victory News*. A mishmash of folksy propaganda, it pictured the Fulbrights at Rabbit's Foot Lodge.

11 Ibid.
12 Jack Temple Kirby, *Rural Worlds Lost: The American South, 1920–1960* (Baton Rouge, 1987), 97–8, 106–7.

Bill appeared wearing a slouch hat, an old pair of pants, and plaid shirt, checking for grubs on his cattle, chatting with a farmer in a pasture, or sitting casually with his calico-clad wife and daughters by the spring. Over the years, the shirt, plaid or checked, became a Fulbright campaign trademark and eventually a target for those of his enemies who charged him with hypocrisy. The *Victory News* contained jokes, home remedies, recipes, and elaborations on the candidate's campaign promises.

Throughout the campaign Fulbright worked to portray Greenhaw and his political benefactor, Homer Adkins, as unscrupulous, unprincipled machine politicians. In reality, Fulbright ran as much against Adkins as Greenhaw, an approach dictated both by circumstance and personal feeling. During the heat of the campaign the candidate sent advance man Gilbert out to nail posters to every post and barn in the district. When his nephew returned several days later, Fulbright chewed him out: He had made several speeches in the district and had seen not a poster. As it turned out, workers for the State Highway Department – under Adkins's orders, of course – had followed Gilbert and taken down the signs as he put them up.[13] Fulbright spread the story far and wide.

As far as the governor was concerned, nothing ranked higher on his list of priorities than Fulbright's defeat. While Adkins disliked the Fulbrights in general, he detested Bill particularly. Not only had Roberta taken every opportunity since Bill's firing to flay him in the *Northwest Arkansas Times,* but in addition Fulbright seemed everything Adkins was not: sophisticated, cosmopolitan, and connected to the eastern establishment. Moreover, Adkins accurately sensed much condescension in Fulbright's attitude toward him. "I want any of you who have any influence with people in the Third District," he told the members of the State Welfare Commission, "to do all you can to beat Fulbright. It would be the most humiliating thing that ever happened to me if he should be elected."[14]

The initial run for Congress amounted to an introductory, crash course in politics. Fulbright began the campaign with several assets. Because of his mother's political activities, the Fayettevillian's name was known in the western counties of the district. In addition, his firing from the presidency of the University of Arkansas had created a ground swell of sympathy for him among alumni scattered throughout the district. His chief liability was his inexperience. Campaigning was more subtle than he had imagined, Fulbright later admitted. Set speeches on the value of public service did not seem to make an impression. The hardheaded, practical people of the Ozarks were not yet impressed by image.

13 Gilbert, *A Fulbright Chronicle,* 142.
14 Quoted in Johnson and Gwertzman, *Fulbright: The Dissenter,* 95.

Bill Fulbright turned out to be a relentless, aggressive campaigner. He hated the very thought of failure. Betty described for her mother a typical day:

> We left home Saturday afternoon, and after contacting the local big-shots in Berryville and Harrison – went on to Marshall to spend the night. The little hotel there is run by one of the nicest young couples I've ever met. The Ralph Fergusons – both university graduates. They regaled us . . . with delectable steaks and lots of advice on whom to see locally. Sunday afternoon Bill made his speech at Anderson Flats . . . and we "visited" awhile. This morning we started on through the hills – and so far today have done Leslie, Damascus, Bee Branch, Scottland, and Choctaw![15]

Throughout the campaign Betty was there. Some said that she was the candidate's greatest asset. Those who had advised Bill against running had been worried about the ability of the wealthy Junior League socialite from Philadelphia, the college president's wife, to win friends and influence people in rural Arkansas. Their fears were unfounded. There seemed not an ounce of condescension in her, and she could relate to anyone. She proved to Bill's prospective constituents that she was preoccupied with the same essentials they were: homemaking, child rearing, budget control. Unlike her husband, she could make small talk. She reported to Philadelphia:

> Our opponent has been putting out all sorts of lies about us in the past few days. It would be sort of fun, if it didn't make you so darned mad. . . . Over in a strictly rural county he put out that I was high-hat, never wore anything but Paris models, and had an armed guard on the place. Then in another county that is very poor he put out that I was heiress to four million bucks. So I took myself into the counties, went around and visited the farms and canning factories, and as Bill said – let them "see for themselves."[16]

In the Democratic primary, tantamount to election in Arkansas, Fulbright polled 7,428 votes to Greenhaw's 6,053 and Virgil Willis's 3,876. Willis, from Harrison in Boone County, had counted on a sweep of his home county and an even split between his two adversaries. The vote eliminated Willis, however, and in the runoff Fulbright captured the lion's share of his support, for a four-thousand-vote victory over Greenhaw. Ellis lost his bid for a Senate seat to newcomer John McClellan, whose principal source of support was the politically powerful Arkansas Power and Light Company.[17] For the next thirty-six years "Big John" McClellan would serve as the senior senator from Arkansas. Ellis went on to become one of America's leading advocates of public power as head of the Rural Electrification Administration. On Novem-

15 Betty to Mother, undated, PPF.
16 Betty to Mother, Aug. 7, 1942, PPF.
17 Interview with John Erickson, Oct. 13, 1988, Atlanta, Ga.

ber 3, 1942, the general election results confirmed what everyone already knew: J. William Fulbright was the representative of the Third Congressional District of Arkansas and a brand-new member of the Seventy-eighth Congress.

Although her son's election to Congress fulfilled a lifelong dream for Roberta, the children's departure was wrenching. Bill had to sell Rabbit's Foot Lodge; there would be no more idyllic weekends at "the Cabin." Hal Douglas had accepted a position in Naval Intelligence, and he and Helen spent the duration of the war in Memphis, Atlanta, and New Orleans. Further adding to her personal woes was a mild heart attack, which she'd suffered in the spring of 1942. Still, Bill was now in Congress. Roberta had lived vicariously through him before, and she could do it again.

Bill, Betty, Betsey, and Bosey drove the entire distance from Arkansas to Washington in January 1943. They managed as well to avoid the acute anxiety that house-hunting in wartime Washington usually entailed. A friend of Betty's found them a comfortable if cramped sixth-story apartment on Wyoming Avenue, one-half block west of Connecticut. Wyoming bordered the fashionable Kalorama district, which in turn overlooked Rock Creek Park.[18]

Betty Fulbright found a Washington far different than the one she and Bill had left in 1936. There was the congestion, the ugly temporary buildings, the dirt, the uniforms. At night, the lights no longer shone on the marble monuments beside the Potomac; now, there were blackouts and dimouts and air-raid drills, although by 1943 those were being taken less seriously. To Betty's surprise and delight, however, the war seemed to have enhanced rather than inhibited Washington's social life.

"Because America was the only major nation whose capital was far removed from the battlefields," David Brinkley has written, "wartime Washington . . . was socially the most aggressive and most tireless city in the western world."[19] Visitors studied the scene and proclaimed that the nation's capital was actually a royal court, but whereas Louis XIV had entertained his courtiers at Versailles, the Roosevelts had withdrawn from the seat of action and left the courtiers to entertain each other. Actually, there were roughly three social groupings among Washington's white citizens. The nation's capital still considered itself a southern city, and the community's blacks, comprising 40 percent of the population, were strictly segregated. Out Massachusetts Avenue and in the Kalorama neighborhood lived what the social-page editors referred to as the Cave Dwellers: the earliest residents of the city, most of whom possessed excessive amounts of old money. The name Cave

18 Interview with Elizabeth Winnacker, Oct. 3, 1990, Columbia, Mo.
19 David Brinkley, *Washington Goes to War* (New York, 1988), 145.

Dwellers stemmed from the fact that they were largely invisible. These long-time residents lived within restricted neighborhoods, chauffeurs drove their children to private schools, and a rigid social register kept outsiders at bay. The Cave Dwellers detested the second group, newcomers composed of New Deal and war agency bureaucrats. They were, in the view of the Cave Dwellers, energetic, self-confident, abrasive, argumentative, and worst of all, new. Finally, there were the nouveaux riches, the Eleanor "Cissy" Pattersons and the Evelyn Walsh McLeans, people who lent validity to Brinkley's statement that "not many huge fortunes were ever made in Washington, but a great many made elsewhere were spent there."[20] The upshot of this mixture was a cocktail and dinner party circuit without rival in the world. The object of the exercise was not to serve the best liquor and food, but to attract guests with the biggest names.

Though the Fulbrights were not the biggest names, the fact that they had one foot in the eastern establishment through Betty's Main Line origins and Bill's Rhodes scholarship, and another in officialdom through Bill's seat in Congress, gave them some visibility. Betty installed Betsey in the first grade at nearby Holton Arms, a private school, and hired a part-time black maid and housekeeper to help with Bosey, then four.[21] She thereupon made the rounds of the foreign embassies, 90 percent of which were located between Kalorama on Rock Creek Park and DuPont Circle to the south, leaving her card. That produced an unending string of invitations and immediate visibility on the social circuit.

With Betty and the girls safely ensconced in the apartment on Wyoming, it was time for Bill to take his seat in the new Congress. He was duly escorted to the dais and sworn in with other freshmen members, including Clare Booth Luce (R–Connecticut) and Christian Herter (R–Massachusetts). No sooner had he settled in than Franklin Delano Roosevelt made the sixteen-block trip to Capitol Hill to deliver his State of the Union address. Roosevelt's health had not yet deteriorated, and he was in good form. "The 78th Congress assembles in one of the great moments in the history of this nation," the president intoned. "The past year was perhaps the most crucial for modern civilization. The coming year will be filled with violent conflict – yet with a high promise of better things."

He was right; the tide of battle in World War II was beginning to turn. America's first year of war had started with an unbroken string of defeats – Pearl Harbor, Corregidor, New Guinea in the Pacific, Hitler's occupation of the Ukraine and the Caucasus in Europe, and Field Marshal Erwin Rommel's advance on Egypt in North Africa – but the end of 1942 and the beginning of 1943 saw the Allies stop the Axis advance in a series of crucial encounters.

20 Quoted in ibid., 139.
21 Winnacker interview.

A makeshift fleet had destroyed a Japanese task force at the Battle of Midway; British, American, and Canadian troops had established a beachhead in North Africa; and the Red Army had withstood Hitler's blows at Stalingrad, taken the offensive, and begun pushing the Nazis back. As 1943 progressed the Allied armies went on the attack on nearly every front. It was time, many members of Congress believed, to began planning for the peace. Fulbright decided that he was going to be part of that process.

It was common knowledge in Washington that representatives in the House and Senate were only as effective as their top staffers. Many hired individuals who, rather than being from the home state, had long experience on the Hill. Fulbright decided to take a chance on an inexperienced Arkansan. In March 1942 Clyde Ellis telegraphed John Erickson – the son of a friend of his from Rogers, a well-to-do insurance man and apple-farmer – asking him to come to Washington and be his secretary. When Ellis lost and Fulbright won, the new congressman from the Third District asked Erickson, a Phi Beta Kappa journalism graduate from the University of Arkansas, to come with him as his secretary.[22]

As the Seventy-eighth Congress set about its business, Fulbright and Erickson huddled in the House office building to discuss priorities. The first task at hand, as it was for all novice congressmen, was to select an approach that would guarantee perpetual reelection. There were two paths open to them, Fulbright observed. He could, as did 75 percent of those in both houses, concentrate on serving his constituents, "do local things for the local people, run more errands than anybody else." Or, like Speaker of the House Sam Rayburn, Fulbright could focus on national issues and become a national figure. Both types got reelected. "I'd sort of like to go for the national thing," Erickson remembers Fulbright as saying.[23]

During World War II Americans self-consciously studied the lessons of the immediate past. To many it seemed that Hitlerian aggression in the aftermath of the Munich Conference of 1938 proved that appeasement did not work. With some guilt, they concluded that America's refusal after World War I to join the League of Nations so handicapped that organization that collective security never really had a chance. Had only the United States lent its massive economic and military might to the effort to contain fascist expansion, World War II might never have happened.[24]

Like Theodore Roosevelt, who a half century earlier had decided that overseas expansion was an issue whose time had come, Fulbright sensed that

22 Erickson interview.
23 Ibid.
24 See Robert A. Divine, *Second Chance: The Triumph of Internationalism in America during World War II* (New York, 1967).

America was at long last ready for Wilsonian internationalism. Perhaps if he could define and articulate the direction America should take, he could simultaneously advance his own interests and those of his country. There was more than political expediency behind Fulbright's advocacy of collective security, however. His commitment to Wilsonian principles was a natural offshoot of his mother's activist philosophy and his travels abroad, but particularly of his Oxford experience.[25] Fulbright's tutor and friend, Ronald McCallum, was an ardent admirer of both Woodrow Wilson and the Wilsonian vision of an interdependent, peaceful world. In 1944 the Oxford don would publish *Public Opinion and the Lost Peace,* in which he challenged the long-standing view of John Maynard Keynes that the peace structure worked out at the Versailles Conference was predestined to fail. The concept of the League was sound, McCallum argued; the organization had not worked because political figures on both sides of the Atlantic had never been willing to make a true commitment to the principles that underlay it, and had attempted to use it for their own selfish, political purposes. McCallum concluded his book with an appeal to Americans and Britons to rediscover and rededicate themselves to the principles of Wilsonian internationalism.[26] He discussed these and other ideas in a lengthy wartime correspondence with his former student from Arkansas.

While McCallum wrote, J. William Fulbright, the practicing politician, began to develop and promulgate his own version of Wilsonian internationalism. In one remarkable address to the Foreign Policy Association in New York, Fulbright declared that the progress and welfare of modern humanity depended on the simultaneous and synchronized advance of technology and statecraft. While technology had produced machines that could fly above the earth and cruise beneath the sea, and weapons that could destroy whole cities in the blinking of an eye, there had been no new developments in political theory and practice since the American and French revolutions. None, that is, until the advent of Woodrow Wilson and the notion of international collective security. Tragically, America had rejected that vision after World War I; but the great conflict just ending offered America and the world a second chance.[27]

Underlying Fulbright's internationalism were the assumptions that there existed a body of ideas and a constellation of economic and political institutions that together defined Western civilization; that the United States shared in these ideals and institutions; and that it therefore had an obligation to defend them. If it were true, he told Congress, that Americans, Britons, Scandinavians, and Italians had in common "the love of family, the regard for contractual obligation, the abhorrence of torture and persecution, the distrust

25 Fulbright interview.

26 George Herbert Gunn, "The Continuing Friendship of James William Fulbright and Ronald Buchanan McCallum," *South Atlantic Quarterly,* 83(4) (1984), 417–19.

27 *Congressional Record,* Senate, Nov. 2, 1945, A4652–4.

of tyrannical and oppressive government . . . then we should acknowledge them in order that a definite policy based upon sound considerations be firmly adopted."[28] The United States, he lamented, had not been willing in the past to acknowledge its debt to this common culture, much less its obligation to defend it.

Time and again the former Rhodes scholar attempted to demonstrate that isolationism was merely a facet of old-fashioned nationalism. Those of his contemporaries who posed as defenders of the nation's sovereignty were in fact advocating a return to the policies of the interwar period, when the United States refused to acknowledge that its fate was tied up with those of other democracies. The notion that a nation-state could act unilaterally to secure its interests was an illusion, especially in the world of airplanes, submarines, and incendiary bombs. "If it means anything today," he told his colleagues, "sovereignty as applied to a state surely means that a state is sufficiently independent economically, politically, and physically to defend itself and provide for the security and happiness of its own people." In this turbulent world, he asked, "can it be seriously contended that the vast majority of existing states are sovereign powers?"[29]

At first, Fulbright's view of America's proper role in world affairs exhibited some of the same messianic and parochial characteristics that had marred Wilson's missionary diplomacy. In his early congressional speeches, Fulbright argued that America must help other nations develop their own version of democracy. "Oppression and poverty have a way of breeding strong and bold characters who sooner or later seek revenge upon the society that has oppressed them," he told the George Washington Law School in February 1943. "To save our own civilization, I believe that it is necessary to make it possible for these and other peoples to share in the benefits of that civilization. This cannot be accomplished if we have a war every 25 years."[30] Implicit in this view was the assumption that, given the freedom to choose, all people would opt for a society characterized by democracy, individual liberty, and free enterprise. By late 1945, however, Fulbright's sense of cultural relativity had sharpened. He observed to the Senate that capitalism was not "divine and inviolable," something handed down by the Almighty from above. It had worked for America because a particular set of circumstances and material conditions had prevailed at a particular time in history. The peoples of the earth, Fulbright proclaimed, should be free to develop their own economic and political traditions.[31]

Nevertheless, the principle of self-determination, Fulbright acknowledged, would not in and of itself preserve the world from the deadly cycle of aggres-

28 Ibid., Mar. 28, 1945, 2898.
29 Ibid., 2899.
30 *Congressional Record,* House, Feb. 8, 1943, A477.
31 *Congressional Record,* Senate, Mar. 28, 1945, 2899.

sion and war. Something more was needed, namely an international organization that at the same time reflected existing power relationships and provided a mechanism for peaceful change within and among nations. For such an institution to be successful, the United States – sure to be the world's richest and most powerful nation into the foreseeable future – would have to embrace it.

What the freshman congressman had in mind was an authentic international federation run on democratic principles. In a speech to the American Bar Association, Fulbright outlined his ideal institution: a global organization with a collective security mandate and a military force sufficient to enforce that mandate. In agreeing to participate in such an organization, the United States must realize that it would have to surrender a portion of its sovereignty.[32] Once the charter of the new organization was ratified, the U.S president, through his representative, would have the authority – without consulting Congress or anyone else – to commit American troops to military action authorized by the world body. Fulbright urged his countrymen to cooperate while the times were propitious, before would-be aggressors had the opportunity to develop the means of aggression. Was it not better to cultivate and embrace the superpowers of the future, the Soviet Union and China, while they were still relatively weak?[33]

Like most internationalists, Fulbright was reacting to a particular interpretation of the immediate past. He, like Dean Acheson, Walter Lippmann, and others of his generation, accepted what Gaddis Smith has called a "great cycle" theory of history.[34] According to this view, the story of the twentieth century was largely a recurring pattern of American isolation, European aggression, and American intervention. It was up to his generation, Fulbright believed, to break that cycle. It was the nation's duty "to wage a creative war for a creative peace."[35]

With political and ideological agenda in hand, first-term representative J. William Fulbright faced the 1943 congressional session ready to make his mark. The opportunity arose more quickly and turned out more favorably than he had anticipated.

With a very few exceptions, it was impossible for a member of Congress in Washington to create a splash on the national scene without the support and approval of the Roosevelt White House. Indeed, the combination of World War II and the person of Franklin Roosevelt had rendered Congress well-nigh useless both in its own and in the public's eyes. The president demanded and obtained vast powers the legislators did not want him to have.

32 Ibid., Nov. 2, 1945, A4652–3.

33 *Congressional Record,* House, Jan. 26, 1944, A412.

34 See Gaddis Smith, *The American Secretaries of State and Their Diplomacy: Dean Acheson* (New York, 1972).

35 *Congressional Record,* House, Feb. 8, 1943, A477.

By the middle of 1942, the rules had been set: Members of Congress had to support the war, and they had to defer to Roosevelt and his minions; but they did not have to like it. "I'll be goddamned if I'll bow to Roosevelt and stand on a street corner as an air raid warden with a tin hat, flashlight and a bucket of sand," declared Senator Robert Taft (R–Ohio).[36] Thwarted by the war, Republicans and southern Democrats contented themselves with sniping at the president and conserving their strength for the postwar period.

In some respects Fulbright believed that was all to the best. To say the least, the freshman from Arkansas was not overawed by his colleagues. "My first impression is that the intelligence of the Member is in inverse ratio to the amount of speaking he does on the floor of the House," he wrote in his first Arkansas newsletter.[37] In fact, neither the House nor the Senate could claim to be a community of intellectuals. The typical member was a lawyer from a small city, a graduate of his or her state university with a B average, a participant in some sport, a stalwart on the debating team, and an active member of various fraternities, clubs, and political organizations. If the legislator practiced law at all, he or she preferred courtroom work, which satisfied a need to perform in public. The member's first political campaign was likely to have been for some modest local office, with a power base likely comprising the Rotary, Lions, Kiwanis, Eagles, Elks, Red Men, Odd Fellows, Masons, or a combination thereof.[38]

There were, however, deviations from this archetype. Two of the most notable in the incoming freshman class were Fulbright and Clare Booth Luce. Clare Luce came to Washington with a reputation for chic good looks and a rapier-sharp wit. The wife of *Life* publisher and crusading Sinophile Henry Luce, the congresswoman enjoyed a national reputation of her own, earned first as an actress, then as author of the highly successful Broadway play entitled *The Women*. Her politics were ultraconservative. "She was extremely reactionary," Fulbright recalled, "sort of like what you would associate with Louis XVI."[39] The New Deal was an anathema to her, and she regarded herself as spokesperson for all those Americans who referred to Franklin Roosevelt simply and distastefully as "that man."

Eager to make her debut in the theater of politics, Ms. Luce cast aside the unwritten rule that first-term members wait a decent period before delivering their initial speeches. In early February 1943, barely a month into the session, the redoubtable Clare rose to deliver a slashing attack on administration foreign policy. She denounced the Atlantic Charter and charged that the mastermind of the administration's plans for the postwar world was vice-president Henry A. Wallace. The Iowan, she proclaimed, was planning a

36 Quoted in Brinkley, *Washington Goes to War,* 202.
37 Quoted in Johnson and Gwertzman, *Fulbright: The Dissenter,* 77.
38 Brinkley, *Washington Goes to War,* 206.
39 Fulbright interview.

worldwide Works Progress Administration that would bankrupt the United States and destroy free enterprise and individual liberty abroad. "Much of what Mr. Wallace calls his global thinking is, no matter how you slice it, still globaloney," she declared to the amusement of conservative members and the indignation of liberals.[40]

Luce's biting attack on the administration's foreign policy in the midst of a world war produced a spate of self-righteous counterattacks. The congresswoman was a throwback to old-fashioned imperialism, Dorothy Thompson declared. "Are we going in for a peaceful world, or aren't we?" asked Eleanor Roosevelt.[41]

Fulbright decided that he, as a freshman and an internationalist, should be the one to reply to Ms. Luce. Here was a chance to catch the White House's attention and identify his name with the internationalist notions that he sensed were taking root in the public mind. He went to the Democratic leadership – Luther Johnson of Texas, the ranking member of the House Foreign Affairs Committee, and House Majority Leader John McCormack of Massachusetts – and they agreed. Actually, *Arkansas Gazette* columnist Hardy ("Spider") Rowland had accurately guessed the scenario: "Bill's more experienced but less intelligent colleagues wanted no part of Clare. Knowing she has a tongue like an ice pick, everybody was afraid if any attempt were made to administer a verbal paddling she would give them back better than they sent."[42]

On February 16, a week after Luce's blast, with his wife and staff in the galleries, the Arkansan delivered his first congressional speech:

> I am compelled to conclude that the point of this [globaloney] passage was to ridicule the Vice-President of the United States. Her [Luce's] witty and scintillating remarks about Mr. Wallace were quite equal to the sophisticated style of Walter Winchell. The Atlantic Charter . . . is no more of a monumental generality or virtuous platitude than is the preamble of our own Constitution or our own sacred Declaration of Independence.[43]

Fulbright then got down to the meat of the debate. Luce's speech had really been about the role of aviation in the postwar world. Like so many of her contemporaries, she assumed that air power would be to the coming world what sea power had been to the past. Those that controlled the technology of long-range flights and overseas bases would be in a position to rule the world. Luce recognized that because of its virtual monopoly on four-engine aircraft and its physical occupation of choice base sites at war's end, the United States would be in a position to dominate international aviation. She insist-

40 Quoted in Johnson and Gwertzman, *Fulbright: The Dissenter,* 79.
41 Ibid.
42 "Weary-Go-Round," *Arkansas Gazette,* undated, BCN 6, F33, SPF.
43 *Congressional Record,* House, Feb. 16, 1943, 1011–12.

ed that the United States keep its planes, technology, and bases and not share them with other nations under an international agreement, as Wallace, Secretary of State Cordell Hull, and certain other members of the administration were urging. Fulbright vehemently disagreed. "It seems to me a very unwise and dangerous move for us, at this critical time, to adopt a policy of proceeding now to gobble up all the commercial advantages possible . . . our policies will best be served by a policy of freedom of the skies. . . ."[44] In fact, Fulbright concluded, the Committee on Foreign Affairs should at once undertake a thorough study of all proposals for postwar international organizations designed to prevent war, and recommend one to the executive.

As he had hoped, Fulbright's notoriety was instantaneous. He became known as "the man who told off Mrs. Luce," as a *PM* magazine headline later put it.[45] His foray against the spokeswoman for the *Time–Life* empire earned him the respect of eastern liberals and brought him to the notice of the president. Mail poured in from all parts of the country.[46]

Notoriety was one thing, practical politics quite another. To many, the notion that a freshman member of the lower house of a Congress that had been totally ignored by the executive in the formulation of foreign policy could have any impact on an issue as controversial as membership in a postwar collective security organization was absurd. Indeed, his colleagues in the Arkansas delegation considered Fulbright a fool for seeking a seat on the Foreign Affairs Committee in the first place.[47] The choice assignments sought after by the ambitious were Appropriations, Ways and Means, and, for Arkansans and other rural representatives, Agriculture: These committees approved programs and disbursed funds that could keep members of Congress in Washington for a generation. Fulbright was willing to take a chance, however, and he had obtained his appointment to Foreign Affairs.

Those who wanted to get anything through the Foreign Affairs Committee had first to appease or neutralize its powerful but obtuse chairman, Sol Bloom of New York. Child actor, theatrical producer, songwriter, and real estate developer, Bloom, the son of Polish-Jewish immigrants, had in 1939 pooh-poohed the notion that Hitler would attack Western Europe.[48] Although the pince-nez–wearing New Yorker did not fit the political stereotype of the times, he was very much the congressional autocrat. Fulbright thought him "dictatorial and extremely contemptuous of the junior members."[49] But congressional reluctance to move on a resolution endorsing a revived League of

44 Ibid., 1012.
45 Quoted in Johnson and Gwertzman, *Fulbright: The Dissenter,* 66.
46 Erickson interview.
47 Quoted in Johnson and Gwertzman, *Fulbright: The Dissenter,* 82.
48 Brinkley, *Washington Goes to War,* 210.
49 Quoted in Johnson and Gwertzman, *Fulbright: The Dissenter,* 83.

Nations had to do with more than the House pecking order or Sol Bloom's personality.

Throughout the spring of 1943 the Roosevelt administration remained ambivalent about the wisdom of a world peacekeeping organization. The first week in February, Bloom wrote Secretary of State Cordell Hull, an ardent internationalist, asking if the administration had any objections to a congressional resolution urging the president to enter into an agreement with the other members of the anti-Axis alliance to set up a mechanism for the maintenance of peace in the postwar period. Hull replied that the administration would welcome such a move, but he privately warned Bloom not to proceed until the Senate could be brought on board. Under the Constitution all treaties had to have two-thirds approval by the Senate, he declared, and the State Department wanted no repetition of the 1919 fiasco during which Henry Cabot Lodge, William Borah, and their supporters in the Senate had blocked American entry into the League of Nations.[50] In addition, during the first half of 1943, Roosevelt opposed detailed public discussion of how the Allies would organize the peace. He was afraid that an airing of the issue would provoke the isolationists and disrupt the war effort.[51]

By the summer of 1943, however, it began to appear that if the administration did not act, the Republicans would preempt the issue. In April, former presidential candidate Wendell Willkie published *One World,* an account of his travels through the Middle East, Russia, and China and a plea for American cooperation to preserve postwar peace. The book was an instant bestseller, only the third nonfiction work in American history to sell more than a million copies. In July the Republicans announced their intention to draft a statement on postwar foreign policy at a conference scheduled for Mackinac Island the following fall.[52]

Meanwhile, unaware of the administration's ambivalence, and unintimidated by Sol Bloom, Fulbright on April 5 introduced H.R. 200, which put the House on record as favoring "creation of appropriate international machinery with power adequate to prevent future aggression and to maintain lasting peace, and as favoring participation by the United States therein."[53] The resolution was duly referred to the Committee on Foreign Affairs. Nothing happened. Chastened, Fulbright began lobbying his colleagues. Among the most responsive were John M. Vorys of Ohio, a ranking Republican on the committee and a former isolationist, and James W. Wadsworth of New York, a widely respected Republican congressman who had lost his Senate seat over

50 Cordell Hull, *The Memoirs of Cordell Hull,* 2 vols. (New York, 1948), 1261.

51 See Robert Dallek, *Franklin D. Roosevelt and American Foreign Policy* (New York, 1979), 419.

52 Ibid.

53 Frank McNaughton to Bill Johnson, June 17, 1943, Papers of Frank McNaughton, Harry S. Truman Library, Independence, Mo.

the prohibition issue. At their suggestion, he paid a visit to Undersecretary of State (then Acting Secretary) Sumner Welles. Welles was a brilliant career diplomat, the chief architect of the Good Neighbor Policy, and an ardent supporter of the concept of collective security. He also was a former Groton classmate of Roosevelt's, with a direct line to the White House. Unbeknownst to Bloom, the administration had decided to move on the issue of collective security. Welles agreed to give Fulbright a letter for use with the House Committee on Foreign Affairs stating that the State Department approved of the principles contained in the Fulbright resolution.[54]

Buoyed by the knowledge that he had the backing of the administration, Fulbright persuaded Bloom to consider his and other, similar resolutions. For three days in early June the committee met secretly. Bloom was clearly upset at being upstaged by a freshman, but the powerful Wadsworth was on Fulbright's side. In a last-ditch effort to block the Arkansan, Bloom declared that State Department would have to be consulted. Fulbright had been waiting. "I have a letter," he announced, and produced the note from Welles. Bloom wilted. In the end, the committee decided that Fulbright's proposal was the most concise of the several that had been written, and as such least likely to cause controversy. The members voted unanimously to approve H. Con. Res. 24.[55] With both Speaker Sam Rayburn (D–Texas) and Majority Leader McCormack's seal of approval on it, the resolution was assured of passage.

Fulbright was elated. His phone rang constantly in the wake of Bloom's announcement. The Fulbright resolution, *Life* magazine declared, constituted the first step toward a "truly national foreign policy." "Everybody assumes that just because a fellow comes from Arkansas he can't read or write," Fulbright baited the *Life* reporter. "But that's where they're wrong."[56]

The Senate was stunned by the House committee's action. Laden with prima donnas and jealous of its prerogatives in foreign affairs, the upper house would not be easily upstaged. The senator whose lot it was to lead the opposition to the Fulbright resolution was the chairman of the Senate Foreign Relations Committee and veteran Texas legislator, Tom Connally (D–Texas). Sporting a string tie and white linen suit, Connally was one of many self-appointed guardians of the Senate's prerogatives. Though certainly not an intellectual, Connally was experienced, shrewd, and tough. For months he and a hand-picked subcommittee had been sitting on half a dozen postwar resolutions. The Fulbright resolution, Connally commented scornfully after it was referred to his committee, was "cryptic," and he filed it away with the rest.

Frustrated by the Senate's arrogance and Connally's dilatory tactics, the freshman congressman from Arkansas lashed out. The two-thirds rule for

54 Johnson and Gwertzman, *Fulbright: The Dissenter,* 85.
55 Ibid., 85, 87.
56 Quoted in ibid., 88.

confirmation of treaties is an "anachronism that ought to be done away with," he told reporter Frank McNaughton.[57] In a speech given that May in Constitution Hall entitled "The U.N. Today and Tomorrow," he touted his resolution and remarked sarcastically, "In view of the historic caution and timidity of our illustrious Senate with regard to foreign affairs, it is important that it be not frightened with an esoteric or complicated proposal."[58] For a would-be expert on foreign affairs, the Rhodes scholar had much to learn about diplomacy.

Despite his bravado, Fulbright was shrewd enough to realize that he would never be able to get his resolution through the Senate without direct White House intervention. Displaying the cheek that had gotten his mother through so many crises, he wrote President Roosevelt directly and urged him to support his resolution. He had always felt, he declared, that the president's success had been largely due "to your courage in boldly taking the lead on troublesome problems."[59] Here was another opportunity. On June 28 Roosevelt wrote Hull: "What do you think of pushing the resolution of the Foreign Affairs Committee of the House? It seems to me pretty good, and if we can get it through the House it might work in the Senate also."[60] When the secretary of state responded positively, the president wrote Fulbright that he favored his resolution if he could obtain wide backing for it and if no prejudicial amendments were attached.[61]

When the House passed the Fulbright resolution in late September, Hull told reporters that the Senate should swallow its pride and follow the lower chamber's lead. Connally was furious. "God damn it," he confided to a friend, "everybody's running around here like a fellow with a tick in his navel, hollering about postwar resolutions." Fulbright was a rube freshman from Arkansas. What did *he* know? If the House wanted to take the ball on foreign affairs and run with it, let it keep running. It could never cross the goal line without Senate concurrence.[62] Tom Connally was no isolationist, however. He was willing to go along with a congressional resolution on postwar organization as long as he and the Senate got their share of the credit.

When in early September Republican leaders duly endorsed the notion of an international cooperative organization, the stage was set for congressional action. The House debate began on September 20, and the rhetoric was florid. "Mr. Speaker," declared George H. Mahon (D–Texas), "this is an historic

57 McNaughton to Johnson, June 17, 1943, McNaughton Papers.
58 Quoted in Johnson and Gwertzman, *Fulbright: The Dissenter,* 86.
59 Quoted in James McGregor Burns, *Roosevelt: The Soldier of Freedom* (New York, 1970), 427.
60 Hull, *Memoirs,* 1126.
61 Burns, *Roosevelt,* 427.
62 McNaughton to Eleanor Welch, Sept. 26, 1943, McNaughton Papers.

day in the history of our country. Today we propose to pass a resolution which serves notice to the world that when we have won this war we shall try to keep it won. Never before has such action been taken by Congress." Charles A. "Doc" Eaton (R–New Jersey), the former pastor of John D. Rockefeller's Baptist church in Cleveland, was even more dramatic: "I have seven sons. One died of war wounds July 30. Another was killed over Nuremberg August 10. By God, I will vote for . . . [any] measure which carries some hope of the future abolishment of war's wholesale murder."[63]

Soon it was Fulbright's turn; instead of waffling, he confronted the isolationists. The organization would indeed include machinery to keep the peace, he said. It not only envisaged the use of military force, he asserted, "but may also include the power . . . to control the productive capacity of instruments of aggressive warfare." He denied that the organization envisioned, as its critics charged, an American-financed global welfare system. "It is not contemplated that we, the people of the United States, are to give our goods to others, that we are to raise the standards of living of the peoples of the world, or even to give them all a free and democratic government."[64] Collective security promised peace, and peace was not dependent on making the world over in the image of the organization's most powerful member. Seemingly reassured, the House passed the Fulbright resolution 360 to 29.

Press comment was overwhelmingly favorable. Of the major figures in American journalism, only Col. Robert R. (Bertie) McCormick still clung unrepentantly to his prewar isolationist position. The powerful publisher of the *Chicago Tribune* remained convinced that Great Britain continued to manipulate American foreign policy to its own advantage. In allowing itself to be drawn into the war against Hitler, the United States had acted once again to save a British empire that was exploitive, class-ridden, and hegemonic. The day following the Fulbright resolution's passage, he wrote in the *Tribune:* "The measure was introduced by a first-termer from Arkansas, who in his formative years was sent as a Rhodes Scholar to Oxford to learn to betray his country and deprive it of its independence. In this instance, as no doubt in many others, Mr. Rhodes appears to have got his money's worth."[65]

Shortly thereafter, one of America's most prominent citizens paid a visit to Fulbright's House office. John Erickson recalled the scene:

> This guy came in and it was Wendell Wilkie. He had copies of the *Chicago Tribune* in which McCormick had called Fulbright a traitor. . . . Wilkie wanted to represent Fulbright in a suit against the *Chicago Tribune* and Col. McCormick. Fulbright thought about it and told me to research it. So we went to the Library of Congress

63 Quoted in Johnson and Gwertzman, *Fulbright: The Dissenter,* 89, 90.
64 *Congressional Record,* House, Sept. 20, 1943, 7659.
65 Quoted in Johnson and Gwertzman, *Fulbright: The Dissenter,* 90.

> and did some research on libel of public figures. It just didn't seem to be feasible. Fulbright was considering running for the Senate and it would just stir up a lot of stuff that wouldn't be helpful.[66]

In this case, as in so many others, Fulbright was happy to be known by his enemies.

By the end of September public pressure on the Senate to embrace Wilsonian internationalism officially via Fulbright's proposal had become intense. Thousands of letters in support of the Fulbright resolution poured into the offices of the Senate Foreign Relations Committee (SFRC). Dozens of editorials condemned Connally and his colleagues. Columnist Raymond Clapper declared their foot-dragging to be nothing less than a victory for the isolationists and the forces of aggression.

Loath to be cast in the role of laggards in the march of progress, Connally and the Senate decided to act. While Cordell Hull was in Moscow persuading his Russian and British counterparts to endorse the general notion of a world body, the special subcommittee on international organization reported a seventy-five-word resolution to the full SFRC. The Connally resolution, which bore a striking resemblance to Fulbright's, was passed overwhelmingly by both the committee and the Senate.

The Fulbright–Connally resolution brought Bill Fulbright the degree and kind of attention of which he had dreamed. He was the House's leading spokesman on foreign affairs and the darling of the internationalists. Suddenly his days were packed with intense activity. Hearings, the House sessions, and constituent matters occupied him until six or seven every night. Afterward he generally attended lectures or meetings; he heard General Patrick Hurley report on events in China; he debated the collective security issues at the Co-Op forum. He spoke before the Joint Council for International Cooperation in Boston, the Commission to Study the Organization of Peace in New York, and numerous audiences in Washington.[67] It was intoxicating; his dream of becoming a recognized member of the eastern, Anglophile establishment was coming true. Somehow the Arkansas congressman still found time to read. An Associated Press reporter noted that the Fulbright apartment was jammed with the latest books on international affairs.

Inevitably, Fulbright's family life suffered. "It used to be that Bill would drop the children off at school on his way to the office," Betty told the reporter. "Now he leaves so early I have to get out with them and pound the pavement myself."[68] The girls were usually in bed when he got home. A pattern had been set. Although Fulbright later claimed to feel a vague sense of guilt over the sacrifices his family had had to make for his career, his ab-

66 Erickson interview.
67 Johnson and Gwertzman, *Fulbright: The Dissenter,* 83–4.
68 Quoted in ibid., 91.

sences really did not bother him that much. He trusted Betty implicitly and, besides, as Susie Zorn put it, "He wasn't interested in children . . . anybody's children. He wasn't terribly interested in his own. It was hard getting his attention. He liked intelligent conversation" and he did not have much time for those who were not able to engage in it.[69]

It is important to note that Fulbright's plunge into national politics and foreign affairs came at a time when most Americans were naïvely, touchingly optimistic about the possibility of international cooperation. The horrors of World War II – rumors were beginning to circulate concerning the incineration of hundreds of thousands of Jews and Gypsies in Nazi concentration camps – prompted even the uneducated to cast about for a formula that would make future Armageddons impossible. Led by Franklin Roosevelt, Harry Hopkins, and Henry Wallace, Americans were especially optimistic about Soviet–American cooperation in the postwar world. Following the signing of the Moscow Accords in the fall of 1943, the *Wall Street Journal* waxed lyrical: "Figuratively speaking, the conferees succeeded in building a bridge over a wide and turbulent river. . . . It may well prove to be the turning point in man's age-old struggle up from savagery."[70] Indeed, everything Russian, from folk songs to Shostakovich's symphonies, became popular in the United States. Following a tour of the Russian front, World War I aviation hero Captain Eddie Rickenbacker declared that the Soviet Union was definitely headed in the direction of capitalism and democracy.[71]

Although Fulbright had determined to make his mark as a congressional expert in international affairs, John Erickson saw to it that he did not neglect domestic issues of concern to Arkansans. Most citizens of the state, at least those who controlled their own votes, either had small businesses or were independent farmers; like many other Americans during the latter stages of World War II, they were intensely antiunion. At the outset of his career Fulbright acknowledged that one could not win in Arkansas without being "moderate to conservative" on the labor issue.[72] He was more conservative than moderate, however, voting against various minimum-wage bills and for measures designed to allow federal and state governments to restrict union activities.

Fulbright's liberal critics would later charge that it was in his and his family's interests, as businesspeople, to oppose unionization. That his interests and those of the average property-owning Arkansan intersected was coincidental, Fulbright argued. He justified his opposition to the minimum wage on

69 Interview with Suzie Zorn, July 23, 1989, Fayetteville, Ark.
70 Quoted in Johnson and Gwertzman, *Fulbright: The Dissenter,* 92.
71 Ibid.
72 Erickson interview.

the grounds that labor's efforts to achieve a national scale were inimical to the interests of all Arkansans. The state was trying desperately to attract new industry, and one of the few advantages it could offer was lower labor costs. It was easy enough, he often said, for states like Massachusetts to advocate a minimum wage; they already had an established industrial base. "If we had a minimum wage with no industry, how in the hell would you ever get it started? It had nothing to do with being for or against labor. It did the people of Arkansas no good to have a high wage and no job."[73] Actually, Fulbright believed that on the whole the unionization of American labor had been a positive development. In highly industrialized states, it had helped correct an imbalance between business and labor and put an end to the blatant exploitation of unprotected workers.

Fulbright voted for increased acreage allotments and supported measures that benefited farmers generally; however, when as congressman he had to choose between large and small, he generally sided with the latter. In the process, he made some powerful enemies. Commercially successful farmers and large landowners in the state were represented by the American Farm Bureau Federation, a conservative organization dedicated to advancing the interests of agribusiness. Closely allied with the Farm Bureau was the Agricultural Extension Service operated by the University of Arkansas's College of Agriculture. It tended to serve "well-to-do farmers who could best take advantage or advice, while ignoring impoverished farm families that needed help but found it difficult to avail themselves of it."[74] Most county Farm Bureau chapters in Arkansas were formed with the assistance of the county agents. Indeed, extension agents typically shared their office space with Farm Bureau representatives, and agents frequently misled farmers into believing that Farm Bureau membership was necessary to receive benefits from federal farm programs.[75]

The particular bête noire of the Farm Bureau–Extension Service was the Farm Securities Administration. Established in 1935, the FSA had as its overriding goal the abolition of rural poverty by providing long-term, low-interest loans and free scientific farming advice to tenants. Despite the fact that the FSA made farm-purchase loans to only 47,104 tenants out of 1.8 million nonowners in the United States, the agribusiness establishment regarded the agency as a mortal threat to their interests.[76] R. E. Short, president of the Arkansas Farm Bureau Federation, charged the FSA with "building a gigantic bureaucracy under [the] guise of aiding low income farmers to be used as [a]

73 Fulbright interview.

74 Quoted in Donald Holley, *Uncle Sam's Farmers: The New Deal Communities in the Lower Mississippi Valley* (Urbana, Ill., 1975), 196.

75 Dew, *The New Deal and Fayetteville,* 160–5.

76 Kirby, *Rural Worlds Lost,* 57–8.

pressure group in prosecuting the philosophy of state land socialism."[77] Large commercial farmers – many of them businessmen residing in the Midwest or on the East Coast – or insurance companies were busily enclosing huge tracts of Arkansas farmland. Any agency that would enable tenants to become owners was anathema to them.

During his tenure in the House Fulbright infuriated the agribusiness establishment in Arkansas by fighting attempts to abolish the FSA. "Our Washington office informs us that you did a splendid job in support of the FSA," wrote Douglas Bradley of the Arkansas Farmers' Union in the spring of 1943.[78] It should be noted that in supporting an agency that aided impoverished families, Fulbright was not acting entirely out of altruistic motives. Phipps Lumber Co. sold its wagon wheels to the "forty acres and a mule" class of farmers, and there were no plantations in the Third Congressional District.[79]

For Bill Fulbright, 1943 was a politician's dream. His encounter with Clare Luce and the Fulbright resolution had brought him national, international and, more important, statewide attention. At the suggestion of Clyde Ellis, Fulbright's office had mailed twenty-five thousand reprints of the Luce speech to voters in northwest Arkansas. The response had been overwhelmingly positive. Sometime that summer the thought crossed Fulbright's mind that although he was but a first-term congressman, he had established enough name recognition in Arkansas to challenge incumbent Senator Hattie Caraway for her seat in the upper house.

77 R. E. Short to JWF, April 19, 1943, BCN 3, F17, SPF.
78 Douglas Bradley to JWF, April 26, 1943, BCN 3, F17, SPF.
79 Fenner Stice to Walter L. Reynolds, Aug. 17, 1946, BCN 105, F18, SPF.

# 5

# *Taking the stage*

As the 1944 senatorial elections approached, political pundits observed that incumbent Hattie Caraway was, to say the least, vulnerable. "Silent Hattie" had been chosen in November 1931 to fill the unexpired Senate term of her deceased husband, Thaddeus. In 1932 with the help of Governor Huey Long of Louisiana she had become the first woman from Arkansas to be elected to the Senate. The "Kingfish" had never met Mrs. Caraway, but as part of his effort to ingratiate himself with as many southern politicians as possible, he had come into Arkansas with his sound trucks and flatbed trailers and stumped in her behalf.[1] Mrs. Caraway's reelection in 1938 was a tribute to the strength of the one-party system and the political passivity of the state rather than to the incumbent's legislative accomplishments. Allen Drury of the United Press summed up her career: Hattie Caraway, he wrote, was that "quiet little grandmother with the bright red fingernails who wanders in, reads a newspaper or sits solemnly in the presiding chair, and then wanders out again, having won nothing, lost nothing, done nothing."[2]

Fulbright's competition would in fact come not from Caraway, but from his old nemesis, Homer Adkins. In many respects the Adkins administration had been a smashing success. The establishment of war plants, together with increased military spending and a growing demand for Arkansas agricultural products, had enabled the state to recover from the Depression. During Adkins's wartime tenure the state's first workmen's compensation commission was appointed, and Arkansas's treasury surplus rose from $21 million to $45 million. He also managed to step on some powerful toes. A prominent Methodist layman – "Holy Homer," as he was known to his detractors – decided to wage war on the Hot Springs establishment. Hot Springs, site of the state's only pari-mutuel horse track (Oaklawn, which, because of its southern location, traditionally opened the American thoroughbred racing season), was the scene of gambling, prostitution, and other popular sins. In 1942 Governor

1 Timothy P. Donovan and Willard B. Gatewood, Jr., eds., *The Governors of Arkansas: Essays in Political Biography* (Fayetteville, 1981), 170. See also David Malone, *Hattie and Huey: An Arkansas Tour* (Fayetteville, 1989).

2 Quoted in Haynes Johnson and Bernard M. Gwertzman, *Fulbright: The Dissenter* (New York, 1968), 93.

Adkins authorized the state police to seize gambling equipment in Garland County (Hot Springs) and in Little Rock (fifty miles to the east) without benefit of search warrants. If this did not suffice to prevent gambling in Hot Springs, declared Holy Homer, he would consider declaring martial law and sending in the National Guard. When his confiscation order was declared unconstitutional by the state courts, he tried unsuccessfully to persuade the legislature to outlaw betting on horse races at Hot Springs and dog races at West Memphis.

Adkins continued to amass a deplorable record on civil rights, although in the Arkansas of the 1940s his stance in this area earned far more votes than it lost. When the federal government requested permission to establish two Japanese-American relocation centers in Arkansas, Adkins refused to accept the camps – not because he objected to the gross violation of nisei civil liberties, but because he feared racial contamination from the Japanese-American internees. Only when the Department of Defense resorted to a public appeal did he relent. When President Roosevelt issued Executive Order 8802 in 1941 outlawing racial discrimination in federal job-training programs and in employment by industries with federal contracts, Adkins declared that the order violated the states' rights provisions of the Constitution and was therefore unenforceable in Arkansas.

Former governor Carl Bailey – then ensconced on a large farm near Little Rock and comfortably employed as chief lobbyist for the railway brotherhoods – and his old friend from the Ozarks, Roberta Fulbright, decided that the only thing that could save Arkansas from the humiliation of being represented by Homer Adkins in the Senate was for Bill to run against him.[3] Never mind that Roberta and Hattie Caraway were old friends (Fulbright recalled that during his early days in Washington he was a frequent dinner guest at the Caraway's home); blood was thicker than friendship and all was fair in politics and motherhood.[4]

In August 1943 Roberta arranged for Bill to meet in Little Rock with Bailey and several potential backers. Among them was Archie House, a former boyfriend of Anna Fulbright's and a state attorney; he agreed to become Fulbright's campaign treasurer. Also present were two prominent insurance men, William Darby of National Old Line Insurance and Herbert Thomas, president of Pyramid Life. Charles Murphy of Murphy Oil of El Dorado was there as well. The meeting not only resulted in the group agreeing to support Fulbright if he decided to run, but also marked the beginning of a lifelong political and personal association.[5]

Following Bailey's advice and his own instincts, Fulbright toured the state

3 Interview with William J. Smith, May 23, 1990, Little Rock, Ark.

4 Interview with J. William Fulbright, Oct. 11–18, 1988, Washington, D.C.

5 Interview with John Erickson, Oct. 13, 1988, Atlanta, Ga.

during the fall of 1943, meeting with county judges, sheriffs, and civic club leaders. He was afraid that, given the strength of Adkins's machine, he could wind up being nothing more than "a sacrificial goat."[6] He found substantial support in seventy-three out of Arkansas's seventy-five counties, however. Moreover, the temptation to get even with Adkins was compelling. "Here was the fellow that had fired me out of the University," he later recalled. "I would be very unhappy being a congressman with him in the Senate. I figured, hell, I would just as soon go on back home. I don't know whether I really thought I had a chance to win."[7] After winding up his tour, Fulbright announced his candidacy for the United States Senate.

Fulbright's entry into the Senate race touched off one of the bitterest political campaigns in Arkansas history. It would be, until his defeat in 1974, the toughest electoral battle the former Razorback athlete ever waged. It remained the dirtiest.

As the campaign opened, political pundits rated Fulbright third behind Adkins and Caraway, but ahead of two other candidates: David Terry, a former congressman from Little Rock, and J. Rosset Venable, a Little Rock businessman and World War I veteran.

Fulbright believed that he could run on his proven record as an internationalist. According to the first-term congressman, he had during his year and a half in Washington become a principal architect of the Roosevelt foreign policy. For sponsoring the Fulbright resolution, he declared, "I have received praise from the press, from citizens of the forty-eight states, from fellow congressmen, and from many foreign nations." The measure "has given me recognition and prestige throughout the nation and more especially in Washington, which, if properly and sanely used, can be of great benefit to . . . the people of Arkansas."[8]

Fulbright's plan to make internationalism and his prominent place in it the cornerstones of his campaign strategy received a boost in March 1944 when Cordell Hull named him chairman of the American delegation to a conference of Allied ministers of education in London. The State Department envisioned that out of the meeting would come a United Nations organization capable of reconstructing the damaged or nonexistent educational systems in those nations overrun by the Axis powers. As a former Rhodes scholar and university president, Fulbright seemed a logical choice to represent the United States.[9] Though he needed to spend as much time as possible campaigning in Arkansas, Fulbright decided to accept.

[6] Fulbright interview.

[7] Ibid.

[8] Quoted in Johnson and Gwertzman, *Fulbright: The Dissenter,* 95.

[9] Harley Notter, memorandum, Mar. 28, 1944, BCN 31, F36, SPF.

Fulbright, who had not been in England for eighteen years, was stunned by the changes the war had wrought. Entire sections of London had been razed, and there was no end to the destruction in sight. Indeed, he was to experience ten German V-2 attacks during his monthlong stay. He spent a day and a night at a Flying Fortress base watching the American crews take off for their bombing missions over occupied Europe. Interspersed with the grimness, however, were vivid memories of his halcyon days as a Rhodes scholar. Fulbright looked up several old friends from his time at Oxford. Nancy Astor had him to the family estate at Cliveden for a weekend. Amid the whirl of activity, the Arkansas congressman had time to meet and make friends with an American correspondent named Edward R. Murrow.[10]

The Conference of Allied Ministers of Education could not have opened more auspiciously. On recommendation of the Belgian chief of delegation, Fulbright was elected chairman of the meeting. The delegates duly drafted a charter for a United Nations Organization for Educational and Cultural Reconstruction for submission to their respective governments.[11] Fulbright and the other Americans, including the distinguished poet and future assistant secretary of state for cultural affairs, Archibald MacLeish, were impressed with the need to revive educational systems in liberated areas as quickly as possible. Consequently, the American delegation recommended to Washington that the administration commit funds for short-term bilateral aid to war-torn countries. Russia and China, they argued, should receive top priority.[12] The State Department touted the conference as a triumph of "democratic cooperation" and a giant step toward the establishment of a brave new world.

To Fulbright's delight, Prime Minister Winston Churchill and his wife, Clementine, invited him to lunch at 10 Downing Street shortly before the American delegation departed. Churchill was in vintage form, dominating the conversation at every turn. Interspersed with vivid accounts of the Italian campaign and the Big Three meeting at Teheran were whispered orders to his military aides and paeans to Anglo–American solidarity in the postwar period. Liberal quantities of sherry before, wine during, and brandy after lunch seemed to sharpen rather than diminish his mental powers. He told Fulbright that he understood he was going to challenge Senator Caraway – "trying to unseat the sitting hen," as he put it – and he asked several questions about American politics.[13]

10 Nancy Astor to JWF, Apr. 24, 1944, BCN 31, F35, SPF.

11 Department of State press release, May 3, 1944, BCN 5, F48, SPF.

12 Fulbright et al. to G. Howland Shaw, Apr. 27, 1944, BCN 31, F35, SPF. The administration then proceeded to ignore both the conference's draft document for a separate United Nations Organization for Educational and Cultural Rehabilitation and the aid recommendations made by Fulbright and his colleagues.

13 Quoted in Johnson and Gwertzman, *Fulbright: The Dissenter,* 98.

As part of its continuing effort to buoy the nation's spirits and prepare Britons for the sacrifices of the forthcoming cross-channel invasion, Whitehall asked Fulbright to address the nation on a BBC radio hookup. He spoke first of Arkansas. His constituency, he said, was "ninety-eight percent Anglo–Saxon stock." They were rural dwelling and of modest means, but a self-reliant people, mostly farmers and small businessmen. They had much in common with the average English person. He appealed to his listeners to support a postwar international system that would eliminate the causes of war. "No matter how much we have loved the old world before this war," he said, the fact that there was global conflict meant that something was wrong with it – "fascism, democratic decadence, or general ignorance."[14] If the world did not create machinery to eliminate these flaws, history would surely repeat itself. To help in this great cause, he told his British listeners, he was returning home to campaign for a seat in the Senate.

On Saturday evening, July 2, from his campaign headquarters in the Capital Hotel in Little Rock, J. William Fulbright set forth once again upon the uncertain seas of state politics. "The real issue in this summer's campaign," he told Arkansans over a statewide radio hookup, "is the ability of the candidate to do something positive and constructive about a sure and lasting peace and to improve the welfare of Arkansas residents."[15]

The campaign staff that Fulbright gathered around him was small and relatively inexperienced.[16] Erickson was there; Bailey lent some of his people; various family members helped when they could. Former students and Fulbright family employees who were in the neighborhood pitched in. A fifteen-year-old aspiring politico from Princeton, Arkansas, named Norvill Jones volunteered for menial chores;[17] except for a short stint in the service, he would remain on Fulbright's staff for the next thirty years. The brunt of the campaign, however, was borne by Betty and Bill. Betty then and always involved herself intimately in the details of campaign planning. When they were in Little Rock, the Fulbrights would breakfast with staff and then outline the next day's or week's activities. Betty remembered everyone she had met and made notes on their likes and dislikes, their children's names, and the peculiarities of their particular town or county.

As was true of his race for the House, Fulbright determined to make as many personal appearances across the state as possible. Reported Betty to her mother in Philadelphia:

14 Quoted in ibid.

15 Quoted in Johnson and Gwertzman, *Fulbright: The Dissenter,* 99.

16 Betty to Mother, June 24, 1944, PPF.

17 Jones would end his public career as chief of staff of the Senate Foreign Relations Committee some forty years later.

> Came in last night from a week's trip with Bill. We start at eight in the morning, in the sound truck, Bill, driver, and I all in the front seat. We hit towns at 9 – 11:30 – 2:30 – 5 – and 8:30 – visit in the first three, and speak in the late afternoon and evening. It's utterly exhausting and sort of fascinating.[18]

Sometimes these forays were successful and sometimes they were not. Although Betty was always visible, many who attended Fulbright rallies never got to see the candidate. Erickson recalled:

> It went against his grain to ask somebody to vote for him. If there was a cocktail party, Sid McMath [handsome, gregarious future governor of Arkansas] would sweep through the room shaking hands with everyone. Fulbright would go into the same room, get over in a corner, and talk to one guy. What kind of cotton crop he had had and so on. Reticence and intellectual curiosity.[19]

The central problem of the campaign, as the staff saw it, was Adkins's political network and the power that patronage gave him. His camp no less than Fulbright's included formidable special interests, most notably Arkansas, Louisiana Gas, headed by Witt Stephens; but Adkins's control of the state bureaucracy and his identification with issues vital to Arkansans would be the obstacles most difficult for the challenger to overcome.

At the heart of the Fulbright organization were some ten counties solidly in the Fulbright camp, most of them in northwest Arkansas. Following the successful run for Congress in 1942, Herbert Thomas had written Fulbright a letter that made a great impression on him. Remember, Thomas told Fulbright, that of the 40 percent of the people who voted against you many were either related to or obligated to your opponent. They might have voted for you except for these ties. The worst thing you can do if you win 51 percent to 49 percent, Thomas advised, is to assume that the people who were for you will always be for you and the people who were against you will always be against you. Take care of your friends first, but don't forget the others.[20] Fulbright applied that lesson for the rest of his political life. In 1944 most of Karl Greenhaw's people supported him.

If Fulbright were to win a statewide race, however, he would have to project his appeal beyond the Third Congressional District and Carl Bailey's antiestablishment network. Erickson suggested that they do what came naturally – rely on the University of Arkansas alumni community. This was a large, powerful group with representatives in every corner of the state, and it included both genders and all age groups. Most would remember Fulbright as a true intellectual and as the president of their alma mater – an institution that Homer Adkins had done his best to politicize. In many communities University of Arkansas graduates made up the lion's share of the lawyers, doctors,

[18] Betty to Mother, July 9, 1944, PPF. [19] Erickson interview. [20] Ibid.

journalists, and clergy – the opinion makers. Fulbright would take what help he could get from the courthouse cliques, the county judges and sheriffs; but until he became established as a statewide politician, the elite would be the core of his electorate. Erickson and other members of the Fulbright entourage sensed even at this early date that the educated citizenry of the state and those who had any awareness at all of the outside world longed for something to be proud of – and Fulbright was that something. "At that time people were very sensitive about the image of Arkansas," Erickson recalled. "I can't tell you how many letters I've read from soldiers who've said they've gotten in an argument and someone said who the hell ever came from Arkansas that amounted to a damn. Their proud response was 'Fulbright.'"[21]

The president of the Arkansas Alumni Association, John Harrison, grasped Fulbright's proffered hand with enthusiasm. Indeed, during the campaign his organization put out a campaign sheet entitled "Fulbright Facts." There was, however, a core within a core. According to Erickson:

> Over the years there were quite a number of students who went to school and worked part time for the lumber company, Coca-Cola, the Schlitz distributorship. Those people were industrious and intelligent, and they went out over the state and later were supportive of the Senator. That was important in the first election. There were so many people who had gone through school with Fulbright, his sisters, or had an association with the Sigma Chis.[22]

With Bailey's help Fulbright began to add other components to his coalition. Ignoring the congressman's one-time support of the Farm Security Administration, the planters of eastern Arkansas identified with him for class reasons. Men like Hugh Brinkley and Robert E. Lee Wilson sensed that Fulbright was one of them, and recognized that his internationalism meant lower tariffs and abundant foreign markets for their cotton, rice, and soybeans.

Not everyone in Arkansas was a college graduate, cared about the international scene, or was prepared intellectually or emotionally to be proud of a figure like Fulbright. Homer Adkins set about appealing to their fears and prejudices. Fulbright, Adkins told his red-necked, wool-hatted crowds, was a "nigger lover" and a communist sympathizer. "Fulbright only Arkansas Congressman to Vote to Retain Wm. Pickens, Negro, Alleged Communist" read a full-page ad in the *Arkansas Gazette* and *Arkansas Democrat.*[23] The broadside referred to an incident in which Congressman Fulbright had voted to reinstate a suspended black Treasury Department employee named William Pickens. Congressman Martin Dies (D–Texas) and the House Un-American Activities Committee (HUAC) had charged Pickens with being a friend and financial supporter of American Communist Party chief Earl Browder. The charges were never proved, and Fulbright voted in favor of Pickens's re-

21 Ibid. 22 Ibid. 23 Undated advertisement, BCN 6, F39, SPF.

hiring, just as he had voted against renewed appropriations for HUAC.[24] The Adkins ad appealed not only to the voters' racism and anticommunism, but also to the nativist sentiment that had so long been a staple of the American right. In voting to retain "the Communistic Negro, Pickens," the ad declared, Fulbright had been joined by Congressmen Marcantonio, Auchincloss, D'Alesandro, Dilweg, Capozzoli, Monkiewicz, Sadowski, Ploseser, and Schiffler. "There are too many isms and strange philosophies already at work in Washington," Adkins warned. "The campaign is getting dirty, and the going rough," Betty reported to Philadelphia.[25]

Not only had Fulbright coddled communists and advocated racial equality, the Adkins camp charged, but he was a blatant draft dodger as well. A campaign flyer asked:

> Isn't it true that you announced for Congress AFTER Pearl Harbor – when you were only 36 years of age, and when draft age was 21 to 45? Don't you know that at the time there were thousands of fathers of your age, with two or more children, in the Army, volunteering and being drafted – practically all of them without your wealth? Don't you know that there are thousands of fathers of your age now in the Army – and NOT ON DESK JOBS BUT ACTUALLY IN COMBAT IN NORMANDY, ITALY AND THE PACIFIC THEATER?[26]

Finally, the Adkins people attempted to link Fulbright with organized labor in general and the Congress of Industrial Organizations in particular. Spokespersons for the governor declared that the radical labor politicians who ran the CIO had captured control of the Roosevelt administration, and J. W. Fulbright, as he frequently boasted, was one of the President's chief lieutenants. Internationalism, New Dealism, it was all the same.[27]

Adkins's chief allies in the effort to link Congressman Fulbright with the radical labor movement were not Arkansas's businessmen and industrialists, but its agricultural establishment. In retaliation for Fulbright's support of the FSA, Waldo Frazier, Executive Secretary of the Farm Bureau, permitted members of the Christian-American Association to use the bureau's mailing list to send an anonymous circular accusing Fulbright of ties to the CIO.[28] A Houston-based protofascist organization, the Christian-American Association was incorporated in Texas in 1936 "for the promotion of Americanism, religion and righteousness and to combat alien 'isms' designed to destroy faith in God and Jesus Christ, the church, the home and the American system."[29]

24 Fulbright interview.
25 Betty to Mother, July 9, 1944, PPF.
26 Quoted in Johnson and Gwertzman, *Fulbright: The Dissenter,* 100.
27 *Arkansas Labor Journal,* Apr. 26, 1944, BCN 47, F13, SPF.
28 Erickson interview.
29 John L. Fletcher, "Management and Labor to Fight It Out," *Arkansas Gazette,* June 16, 1946.

The circular linking Fulbright to the CIO was mailed from the Agricultural Extension Service mailing room on the University of Arkansas campus and was addressed with its addressograph equipment.[30]

For a time Fulbright attempted to take the high road and ignored Adkins's charges. By midsummer, however, his operatives around the state were advising him to defend himself. First on the agenda was his alleged draft dodging. The staff contacted Price Dickson, a Fayetteville lawyer who was head of the Washington County Draft Board; he agreed to write a letter stating that in mid-1942 Fulbright's file had come before the board for review. To avoid charges of favoritism, Dickson had had the case transferred to Russellville, a town in central Arkansas. It was returned with a "III-A" classification (deferment due to dependents). At no time, he insisted, had Fulbright corresponded with the board. The letter was reprinted in papers throughout the state.[31]

Then, during a late-summer swing through eastern Arkansas, Fulbright responded item by item to the "innuendo and whispering campaign" against him. He supported the working man's right to organize and bargain collectively, he said, but he denounced wartime strikes and denied vehemently that the CIO had endorsed him. He was not a "New Dealer," he assured voters, although he approved of the Securities and Exchange Commission, the Agricultural Adjustment Act, and other "beneficial legislation." Further bureaucratic control and additional agencies were unnecessary. "I am not for Negro participation in our primary elections," Fulbright declared, "and I do not approve of social equality." He was a strict constitutionalist, he declared to crowds in Jonesboro, Helena, and Cotton Plant. "I do not believe that . . . a Socialistic or Communistic State is inevitable or desirable." The only charge that Fulbright did not deny was that he was pro-British. In a deft reversal of the patriotism issue, he declared that those who did not stand with America's gallant British allies – men and women who had "stood undaunted before Hitler's legions" – were closet isolationists.[32]

Erickson and the staff had carefully planned the campaign around Adkins. To their consternation Col. T. H. Barton of El Dorado entered the race at the last minute. Barton had made a fortune as head of Lion Oil Co., and there was no way to know what impact his money would have. The Fulbright campaign, which spent a hundred thousand dollars and relied on the *Northwest Arkansas Times* to print *Victory News* again, could not match Barton's financial resources. The sixty-four-year-old petroleum executive had no political experience, but he had made something of a name for himself promoting the state livestock show. His entry into the race, Fulbright recalled, "muddied

30 H. E. Thompson to JWF, June 28, 1946, BCN 25, F16, SPF.
31 "Here's the Draft Status of Bill Fulbright," Feb. 8, 1944, BCN 6, F39, SPF.
32 1944 Campaign, undated, BCN 6, F39, SPF.

the waters and created a hell of an uncertainty . . . we couldn't estimate what influence he'd have, what he'd take away, where and how."[33]

As it turned out, what Barton's money meant was entertainment. To accompany him through the remote areas of the state, he hired "Uncle Mac" Mackrell accompanied by the Stamps Baxter Melody Boys, a group of local fiddlers and banjo players. For the pleasure of the state's towns and cities, the "Colonel" retained the services of none other than the cast of the Grand Old Opry. The Tennessee Plowboys, Minnie Pearl, Grandpa Jones, and Eddie Arnold made more than sixty appearances across the state at $1,000 a night. "It is going to be a hard race – as that old S.O.B. Barton is apparently prepared to spend any amount," Betty complained to her mother.[34]

Fulbright campaign worker Jack Yingling, whose father was a Bailey protégé from Bentonville, recalled that at one point the Opry and the Fulbrights hit Paris, Arkansas, at the same time. An elderly resident came into the courthouse from the square where both parties were campaigning. A fellow Parisian asked him how he was going to vote. "Well, I was leaning toward Fulbright but I went out there and saw that Minnie Pearl and she really swayed me toward Barton." Yingling went to the window and discovered that in this instance Minnie Pearl was really Betty Fulbright dressed in a gingham dress.[35]

Barton's hiring the crew of the Grand Old Opry was a brilliant stroke. Tens of thousands of Arkansas Baptists and Church of Christ members typically spent Saturday nights studying their Sunday school lessons and listening on their radios to the simple, safe humor and country music coming out of Nashville. The Opry was exciting but comfortable, a reflection of Arkansas folk culture.

Fortunately, Barton did not know how to handle prosperity. As John Erickson recalled:

> I was up in Rogers for one of these things. There must have been 10,000 people there. Eddie Arnold and the rest of the Opry company whipped the crowd into a frenzy. At the appointed moment, Colonel Barton drove up in his chauffeur-driven Cadillac. Donning his pince-nez glasses, he harangued the audience about the vices of Fabian socialism and the virtues of Jeffersonian democracy. If he had just said thanks for coming and remember the colonel on election day, he would no doubt have given Adkins and Fulbright a run for their money.[36]

33 Quoted in Johnson and Gwertzman, *Fulbright: The Dissenter,* 96.
34 Betty to Mother, June 24, 1944, SPF.
35 Interview with Jack Yingling, Oct. 12, 1988, Savannah, Ga.
36 Erickson interview.

The Adkins people kept hammering away right up until the end. Wrote one lawyer to Fulbright that summer:

> I have been in politics up to my neck since I was twenty years old, and I have seen some mean campaigns, but the Adkins campaign is the worst that I ever saw. Some state officials and state employees drove over the county and flooded it with literature . . . proclaiming that you: voted for a "nigger," would not help pass the Soldier Bill [G.I. Bill of Rights] . . . were endorsed by the C.I.O., by fraud escaped the draft, and everything else they could think of.[37]

Adkins reminded every fundamentalist in the state that the Fayetteville Ice Co. was the wholesale beer distributor for Washington, Benton, and Madison counties, and he accused Fulbright of being "in league with every thug and gambler in Hot Springs."[38]

Fulbright's final speech, delivered over a statewide radio hookup, was tinged with self-pity. Politics, he said, should be conducted on a high plane; if it were not, able young men would shun public careers. The best and the brightest should not have to be submitted to the kind of mudslinging to which he had been exposed.[39] Roberta could not have said it better.

The returns from the Democratic primary election exceeded the Fulbright camp's expectations. Their man led all candidates with sixty-two thousand. Adkins trailed with forty-seven thousand, and Barton was a close third with forty thousand. "Silent Hattie" came in fourth with twenty-three thousand. "This has really been the most utterly hectic, mad and exciting three months I've ever had!" Betty wrote her mother. "It has been maddening, thrilling, and then maddening all over again – but never dull! If we had gotten 51% of the votes cast – we'd have had the nomination without a run-off. That elusive 4%!!" Friends of Betty and Bill's asked them to go to Sun Valley for a brief vacation before the runoff race got started. They wisely refused. "Can you see the voters of the Third Congressional District of Arkansas – if they had a picture of their Congressman doing the Conga at Sun Valley?" Betty wrote her mother.[40] In the runoff Caraway's supporters switched en masse to Fulbright, and Barton's votes were split. The college–progressive vote beat the machine–Klan coalition by thirty-two thousand. The official totals were 117,121 for Fulbright and 85,121 for Adkins. He carried fifty-five of the state's seventy-five counties. Self-righteous to the last, Holy Homer blamed his defeat on reaction to the "moral stand" he had taken on a number of issues.[41]

37 Quoted in Johnson and Gwertzman, *Fulbright: The Dissenter*, 101.
38 Homer Adkins to Blanch Riggs, Aug. 5, 1944, BCN 6, F39, SPF.
39 Quoted in Johnson and Gwertzman, *Fulbright: The Dissenter*, 103.
40 Betty to Mother, undated, PPF.
41 Allan Gilbert, *A Fulbright Chronicle* (Fayetteville, 1980), 148.

In the wake of the 1944 election Congress and the Justice Department received dozens of complaints of voter fraud. The Hot Springs racetrack gambling machine had allegedly rigged the Garland County vote. In eastern Arkansas, offended progressives claimed, planters and county machines had voted black tenant farmers en masse. So numerous were the charges that the Senate Committee on Privileges and Elections sent a subcommittee to the state to investigate.[42] Because eight of ten of Fulbright's biggest counties included Garland and various delta counties, rumors began to circulate that the investigation centered on him. Encouraged and guided by John Wells, *Gazette* city editor and Governor Bailey's onetime executive secretary, Arkansas Attorney General Guy Williams did his best to quash the investigation. Williams called in the subcommittee's chief investigator, George Schillitto, and laid down the law, so to speak. "I began talking with him by saying that I was talking officially as Attorney General of the state and that I was also your friend," Williams reported to Fulbright, who had returned to Washington by that time. "If he was down here to attempt to smear you that we would do our utmost to close up his business and run him out of the state." He could not, however, file suit to stop the inquiry, Arkansas's chief lawyer told Fulbright. "I shall do my best to keep everything on an even keel but I want you and John [McClellan] to attend to things at that end of the line." Whether Fulbright exerted any pressure or not is unclear, but the investigation immediately went into low gear. "I wonder if I started this slow down, or if you did it," Williams reported. "No more boxes have been seized today."[43]

The Senate subcommittee eventually certified the election. There was undoubtedly fraud in Hot Springs, and the thousands of blacks in east and south Arkansas voted the way their landlords instructed them. "We carried one precinct in eastern Arkansas by a vote of 65 to 2," John Erickson recalled. "The local politico in charge called to apologize. The two nays were black men who had once worked for Col. Barton. They had come to him and asked permission to vote for their old boss, and he had given it."[44] But the purchase of votes, voter intimidation, and machine politics were a fact of life in Arkansas in the 1940s no less than in other states.

The *Gazette*'s "Spider" Rowland spoke for the majority of Arkansans in his postmortem on the election. Fulbright had won, he wrote, because he had brought the state more favorable attention than any other figure in its history. Despite his money and education, "he was easier to approach than a public towel." He had convinced the people that though he approved certain domestic programs of the Roosevelt administration, he was no "New Dealer." CIO support, which had been forthcoming despite the candidate's antilabor voting

42 *Congressional Record*, Senate, Mar. 1, 1960, 3981.
43 Guy Williams to JWF, Aug. 30, 1944, BCN 5, F31, SPF.
44 Erickson interview.

record, had been an albatross, but Fulbright had made the grade in spite of it. "I believe," Rowland concluded, "that in the next few years, Fulbright will attract more attention in Washington than a two-headed giraffe in the Hotel McGehee lobby."[45]

The outcome of the 1944 senatorial election earned the state plaudits in the national press. The *Atlanta Journal* claimed that Fulbright's triumph meant that "[t]he people, especially we Southern people, are voting more intelligently." To *New York Times* columnist Arthur Krock, it signified that a "higher type of legislator than the South has been sending to Washington in recent years" would be a member of the Senate.[46]

J. William Fulbright's political achievements since his dismissal from the presidency of the University of Arkansas were stunning. With no organization and no practical experience he had defeated two entrenched Arkansas politicos and gained favorable attention from both the national and international media. Roosevelt, Hull, and other administration figures decided that the Arkansan was a southerner with whom the administration could take pride in being associated – for a change. The educated citizenry of Arkansas – liberal, moderate, and conservative – concluded that in Fulbright the state had a man that would possibly bring Arkansas the respect it had so long been denied. The parallels to Woodrow Wilson's symbolic importance to the South were striking. While reassuring voters that he would be mindful of their vested interests, Fulbright had campaigned and won as a "national" legislator. His victory over Homer Adkins reinforced his conviction that it was possible to immerse himself in the great questions of the day and simultaneously to survive as an Arkansas politician.

The United States Senate in 1945 was still living up to its billing as the most exclusive men's club (now that Fulbright had replaced Caraway) in the world. From the red-and-gold hallway lavishly decorated with paintings and frescoes to the cloakroom where last-minute deals were discussed and even to the spittoons, small wastebaskets, and schoolboy desks on the chamber floor, a ponderous sense of tradition hung over the Senate.

Fulbright, who would become one of the seniority system's great beneficiaries and defenders, initially found it frustrating. He did so primarily because it kept him off the Senate Foreign Relations Committee (SFRC). "Needless to say, I was disappointed," he wrote a constituent following his unsuccessful bid, "but with eighteen other applicants, all of which [*sic*] had some seniority, I knew from the start that there was little chance. You know how Senators are about seniority."[47]

45 Hardy Rowland, "Weary-Go-Round," undated, *Arkansas Gazette,* BCN 6, F33, SPF.
46 Quoted in Johnson and Gwertzman, *Fulbright: The Dissenter,* 103.
47 Quoted in ibid., 108.

As the junior senator from Arkansas wrestled with the Senate establishment, Franklin D. Roosevelt and his entourage made their way to the Crimean resort city of Yalta for the climactic conference of World War II. With General George Patton sweeping across western Germany and the Red Army rampaging through Rumania, Czechoslovakia, Poland, Hungary, and Bulgaria, the president could no longer delay discussion of the postwar order. At Yalta he, Churchill, and Stalin divided Germany into occupation zones, committed themselves to holding free elections as soon as possible in areas under their control, and entered into an agreement whereby the Soviet Union would be rewarded with Outer Mongolia, the Kuril Islands, southern Sakhalin Island, and the opportunity to regain control of Manchuria in return for entering the Pacific war after Germany had surrendered. As to the proposed world organization, the Big Three decided that the USSR should have three votes in the General Assembly, that the permanent members of the Security Council would possess a substantive veto, and that the upcoming United Nations Conference on International Organization (UNCIO) in San Francisco should proceed as scheduled.

Like many other Americans Fulbright was disturbed by the apparent direction of U.S foreign policy. To him the Yalta accords seemed nothing more than a dressed-up spheres-of-interest deal, and the all-encompassing veto ensured that the projected world organization would be more of a four-policeman operation rather than a true collective security apparatus wherein each member surrendered a portion of its sovereignty for the common good. The Roosevelt administration, he decided, was not going to retreat from its commitment to internationalism if he could help it. Procedurally, what was needed was a "settled, consistent, recognizable" foreign policy, one that was hammered out with the advice, consent, and participation of both houses of Congress, Fulbright told the Senate the last week in March. Indeed, he saw Congress as an antidote to the State Department and the foreign policy establishment in general: "[I]t is inherent in their background and their position, that they be ultra-conservative and reluctant to commit our people to any change in the status quo or to the assumption of any new responsibilities." Insofar as substance was concerned, "American foreign policy should have two anchors, the Atlantic community [a concept then being touted by Walter Lippmann] and a collective security organization in which all nations were represented."[48]

At this, the very dawn of the cold war, J. William Fulbright saw no reason why the Western democracies and the Soviet Union could not coexist peacefully. The Russians, he said, had given no evidence that they intended to dominate the world through force as the Germans had attempted to do. Let

48 J. W. Fulbright, "American Foreign Policy – International Organization for World Security," Mar. 28, 1945, BCN 24, F36, SPF.

capitalism and communism compete peacefully; the best system would win. Indeed, "the highly emotional attacks upon communism and Russia by some of our public orators is an indication of the weakness of their faith in our system."[49]

Fulbright's initial foreign policy speech received respectable reviews from the national press. More than one Capitol Hill reporter commented on what a striking figure the Arkansas freshman made. At six feet, 175 pounds he still cut an athletic figure. He was a man of chiseled good looks, with his dark hair graying at the temples, a cleft chin, and high cheek bones surmounted by a pair of intense blue eyes. Personally, he was soft-spoken and self-effacing both with his colleagues and the public.

The powers in the Senate seemed intrigued by the Arkansan's impetuosity in advising Congress and the administration on matters of state. Indeed, as he rose to deliver his maiden Senate address, horn-rimmed glasses grasped between thumb and forefinger, more than thirty of his colleagues were gathered around him, including Republicans Arthur Vandenberg of Michigan, Robert Taft of Ohio, Leverett Saltonstall of Massachusetts, and Warren Austin of Vermont. Lister Hill of Alabama, Alben Barkley of Kentucky, and other members of the Democratic leadership were in attendance as well. Though they disagreed with parts of the speech, Fulbright's colleagues were impressed. The address was well crafted and sophisticated. Here was a man of which the club could be proud.

The resounding applause that followed Fulbright's speech stemmed in part from its call for an expanded role for Congress in the peacemaking process. The national legislature had grown restive as Roosevelt and presidential assistant Harry Hopkins, together with the Joint Chiefs, waged global war and discussed the new world order. Both Senate and House felt bypassed, neglected; and as the fighting drew to a close many were determined to redress the balance. War had always turned Congress into a backwater, but President Roosevelt contributed eagerly to the process. He regarded the Senate as a nuisance to be either leapfrogged or manipulated. Blocked in his efforts to purge the House and Senate of anti–New Deal elements in 1938, he nevertheless dominated that body in the years to follow by moving his domestic policy sharply to the right and successfully invoking national security to keep legislators out of the foreign-policymaking process. However, the man who had done more than any of his predecessors to strengthen the presidency proved to be mortal.

In early April 1945 Franklin D. Roosevelt, ravaged by twenty-five years of physical handicap, the Depression, a world war, and more than a dozen years of presidential politics, withdrew to his spa-retreat at Warm Springs, Georgia, for rest and recuperation. He was suffering from high blood pres-

49 Ibid.

sure and an enlarged heart. On the morning of the twelfth, sitting for a portrait, Roosevelt suddenly slumped over. Efforts to revive him proved futile. The president was dead at age sixty-two.

America went into mourning. Although diehard Republicans, Liberty Leaguers, and America Firsters secretly expressed their relief and delight, the majority reacted to Roosevelt's departure with shock and grief. A *New York Times* reporter found Congressman Lyndon Johnson of Texas in a Capitol corridor stunned and teary eyed. "He was always like a Daddy to me," Johnson declared. "I don't know that I'd ever have come to Congress if it hadn't been for him. But I do know I got my first great desire for public office because of him. . . . God, how he could take it for us all."[50]

Fulbright was conspicuously unmoved. He had had no personal ties to Franklin Roosevelt. "I never did have but one pleasant and rather extended meeting with him," he recalled. That had come during a reception at the White House while the Arkansan was still a member of the House. He had been, as he said, "greatly impressed by the old boy's personality."[51] In fact, Fulbright had probably come up with the same appraisal as John Maynard Keynes some ten years earlier; namely, that Roosevelt was an intellectual lightweight, a man with good values, but always with an eye to the main chance. Moreover, the president's failure to join the internationalist movement and lead it to immediate and concrete fruition signified to Fulbright's mind a lack of resolve.

Though he had failed to secure a seat on the SFRC, Fulbright's preoccupation with the future of the United Nations continued. The San Francisco conference was but two weeks away, and like many other Americans, the junior senator from Arkansas had grave doubts about the new president's ability to lead the nation and the world at such a crucial time in its history. No less than Franklin Roosevelt, Harry S. Truman was first and foremost a politician, but without Roosevelt's education or contacts in the eastern establishment. The president had selected the Missourian to be his running mate in 1944 largely because he was acceptable to liberals as well as conservatives. By the time of Roosevelt's death, Harry Truman had earned a reputation for fairness, honesty, and some knowledge of Congress and budgetary matters, but no one would ever accuse him of being an expert on foreign affairs. Roosevelt had contributed to the problem by refusing to take Truman into his confidence and by shutting him out of all discussions concerning war and postwar problems. To Fulbright's dismay, for the next year the new president oscillated between a policy of confrontation and conciliation toward the Soviet Union.[52]

50 Quoted in Johnson and Gwertzman, *Fulbright: The Dissenter,* 113.
51 Quoted in ibid.
52 See JWF to Bernal Seamster, May 26, 1945, BCN 24, F32, SPF.

Fulbright's slim hopes of being named a delegate to the UNCIO were quickly dashed. The delegation, headed by Secretary of State Edward R. Stettinius, Jr., included two members of the Senate, Tom Connally and Arthur Vandenberg, but not Fulbright. Though intensely disappointed, he busied himself with generating support for the charter being fashioned by the delegates in San Francisco.[53] He introduced a bill to repeal the Johnson Act of 1934, which barred credits to nations who had defaulted on their World War I debts to the United States, and embarked on a modest speaking tour in behalf of the collective security concept. He told the graduates of Gettysburg College that "the source of our troubles may be found in our failure to recognize what I have called the essential interdependence of all men and of all nations."[54] From Gettysburg he took the train to Chicago, the heart of isolationist country. He was appalled, he wrote, at "the virulence of the anti-British feeling in that great Metropolis." Anglophobia, as he well knew, was generally accompanied by a deep-seated isolationism. He wrote his friend Archibald MacLeish, then assistant secretary of state for cultural affairs, suggesting that the department send a flying squad of speakers to Chicago and other population centers to counteract "our most dangerous prejudice."[55]

While Fulbright publicly continued to hail the work of the San Francisco conference, he privately expressed acute distress at the proceedings. Adoption of the all-inclusive veto by the Big Three at Yalta had been bad enough, but now he learned that the charter would exempt from the supervision of the organization matters of a purely internal nature, with the individual members apparently empowered to determine what was internal and what was external. Moreover, none other than Arthur Vandenberg had crafted Article 52, which legitimized regional collective security organizations outside the United Nations. Both of these provisions, it seemed to Fulbright, cut away at the very essence of collective security.

Fulbright and liberal journals like the *New Republic* and the *Nation* were particularly disturbed over an incident involving the seating of the Argentine delegation. Shortly after the conference opened, American diplomats provoked a storm of controversy at home and abroad by sponsoring Argentina for full membership. In doing so, Washington supported a country that for two years after U.S. entry into the war had maintained diplomatic ties with the Axis powers, served as a base for German espionage in the Western Hemisphere, and submitted to the rule of two autocratic, militaristic governments. With the backing of the other twenty American republics, the United States outvoted the Soviet Union in an acrimonious showdown over the Argentine issue. Walter Lippmann led a chorus of criticism charging that in their

53 JWF to A. G. Meehan, Apr. 11, 1945, SPF.

54 Quoted in Johnson and Gwertzman, *Fulbright: The Dissenter,* 114.

55 JWF to MacLeish, May 3, 1945, BCN 30, F24, SPF.

first internationalist test American diplomats had engineered a political power play rather than forging a consensus. Fulbright was equally incensed. "I have been very upset about the turn our delegation took at San Francisco," he confided to an acquaintance.[56]

In fact, despite rumors of atrocities being committed by Soviet troops in Eastern Europe and Germany, Fulbright remained convinced that Russia and Stalin were essentially benign. By mid-1945 the Arkansan was receiving a monthly dispatch from his old friend and mentor, Mike Fodor, who was then a war correspondent with the Third Army. Fodor, relying on his language skills, his immense knowledge of the area, and a generous measure of native cunning, moved freely among the Allied occupation zones, interviewing such notables as Eduard Benes, president of Czechoslovakia.

> Out of these confidential talks, the most important lesson I learned was that Russia is basing her policy entirely on defensive and not on an aggressive basis. . . . She may try to create friendly governments in Yugoslavia, Rumania, Hungary, Bulgaria etc., but this is a side issue – a defensive, friendly expansion, without interfering with those countries in an aggressive way as Germans do.[57]

As the year progressed and stories concerning the physical and political brutalities committed by Soviet occupation authorities in Eastern Europe began reaching the West, Fodor stuck to his guns. Stalin, he wrote, favored a policy of moderation and peace with the rest of the world, but his "mutinous" and "rebellious" generals and marshals wanted to expand the boundaries of the Soviet empire even at the risk of a general war with the West. In the struggle between Stalin and the party on the one hand and the Red Army hierarchy on the other, the "non-military generalissimo" had the upper hand. Given the food shortages in Russia, which had reduced daily caloric intake to eight hundred a day, Stalin would have to keep his vast army in Eastern Europe for some time just in order to feed it; but in the long run he meant no harm, and for the present he had the situation under control. He was encouraged by the analysis and agreed with it, Fulbright wrote Fodor, but he feared that reactionaries and novices in the State Department were destroying any hope of continuing Soviet–American solidarity.[58]

Despite his efforts in behalf of an expanded role for the House and Senate in foreign policymaking, Fulbright believed in an active, powerful executive with the ability and will to conduct the nation's foreign relations. The legislative branch should limit itself to consultation and articulation of broad princi-

56 JWF to E. A. Matthews, May 4, 1945, BCN 24, F31, SPF.

57 Fodor, memorandum, July 12, 1945, BCN 67, F24, SPF.

58 Fodor, memorandum, Dec. 9, 1945, BCN 67, F24, SPF, and JWF to Fodor, May 16 and July 26, 1945, BCN 67, F24, SPF.

ples.[59] However, to function properly the system required an enlightened, sophisticated leadership, something America lacked in 1945, the junior senator believed. Fulbright was particularly appalled at Stettinius. "Frankly, I have not been very pleased with the way our Secretary of State is handling the San Francisco Conference," he wrote to a constituent. "I attribute this [the Argentine imbroglio] largely to his own inexperience and lack of knowledge. After all, it is fantastic that our country should be represented in these important and complicated matters by a man with less than a year's experience."[60]

In Fulbright's view, Stettinius was symptomatic of a larger problem. At this crucial juncture in the history of the world, with the god of internationalism standing in the doorway beckoning with a loud voice, and with humanity suspended over the pit of nationalism and war, America was being led by a combination of empty-headed bureaucrats and relics of the ancient regime, who knew only power politics backed by arms and treaties. Fulbright had always claimed that, in a republic, a meritocracy inevitably emerged to lead the nation; but he was beginning to have his doubts. "The greatest weakness of this country is getting brains into our public service," he wrote in May 1945. "I am sure we will continue to make mistakes until we devise some means to attract able men into the government at an early date in order that they may grow up and know what it is all about."[61]

Never bashful, Fulbright considered going public with his criticism, but on the advice of some of his new friends in the Senate, decided against it. He discussed the matter with Carl Hatch (D–New Mexico), who felt much as Fulbright did, but who advised his young colleague that open criticism on the Senate floor would only make matters worse.[62] There was another reason for Fulbright's reticence, however.

For weeks after Truman became president there had been continuing speculation in Washington that he wanted to replace Stettinius as secretary of state. In a radio broadcast at the end of May, Drew Pearson declared that Fulbright was the likely choice. Fulbright apparently took his candidacy seriously. "I confess that I do not know that I should like to give up my seat in the Senate for any appointment," he wrote an Arkansas politician. "I honestly feel that the Senate can be of great importance in the next several years. In any case, we will have to wait developments."[63] The suspense soon ended when, two days after representatives of fifty nations signed the U.N. Charter in San Francisco, the president named James F. Byrnes to succeed Stettinius. Ful-

59 Memorandum on the authority of the U.S. delegate to the Security Council, 1945, BCN 24, F36, SPF.

60 JWF to Charles A. Stick, May 22, 1945, BCN 24, F49, SPF.

61 JWF to E. A. Matthews, May 4, 1945, BCN 24, F31, SPF.

62 Ibid.

63 Quoted in Johnson and Gwertzman, *Fulbright: The Dissenter,* 115.

bright, the Senate, and the nation quickly turned their attention to the task at hand: ratification.

On July 2, 1945, Harry Truman strode down the aisle of the House basking in the applause of the representatives and senators who had gathered in joint session to hear him appeal for their support of the U.N. Charter. The short, bespectacled, nattily dressed figure reminded the legislators of their crucial role in bringing the internationalist movement to fruition. Fulbright stirred "with embarrassed pleasure in his seat" as the president ticked off the Fulbright and Connally resolutions. Do not, Truman appealed to his former colleagues, repeat the mistakes of the past. Collective security would not work without the full and enthusiastic participation of the United States. Opinion polls showed overwhelming support within and without the Senate; but such had been the case in 1919.

J. William Fulbright listened with growing alarm to the congressional debate over the charter that unfolded during late July and early August 1945. There could be no question about his support of U.S. membership in the United Nations. The charter, he declared, "ranks in importance alongside the Declaration of Independence, the Constitution of the United States, the Emancipation Proclamation, and the League of Nations";[64] but the apparent unanimity with which his colleagues seemed ready to approve membership in the U.N. troubled him. Isolationism was not dead. Only weeks earlier there had been active and concerted opposition to renewal of the Reciprocal Trade Agreements Act (RTAA) and to the Bretton Woods Agreements, which created the International Monetary Fund (IMF) and International Bank (IBRD). All three economic mechanisms were crucial, Fulbright believed, to the creation of a new, interdependent world. When at last during the debate on the San Francisco document it came his turn to speak, the Arkansan rose from his seat and asked, "Can it be that the Senators do not recognize that, if we are accepting this charter in good faith, it means a complete departure from our traditional policy in international relations?" Or was it rather that the isolationists believed that they could have their cake and eat it too? From what he had heard, the charter's provision that the United Nations would be an organization of sovereign states was being taken to mean that America would not have to surrender any freedom of action. Be forewarned, he declared grimly, that "the ultimate objective of international cooperation and peace necessarily involves the development of rules of conduct universally accepted and enforceable."[65] Absolute sovereignty had no place in such a system. No one rose to contend with him, but the nagging feeling remained that without the will on the part of its members to sacrifice independence of action, the world

64 JWF to Mrs. Guy E. Williams, May 1, 1945, BCN 24, F30, SPF. Mail from Arkansas, primarily from church groups, professional womens' clubs, etc., ran heavily in favor of approval of the charter.

65 *Congressional Record*, Senate, July 23, 1945, 7962–4.

organization would never be able to keep the peace. On July 28, 1945, the Senate of the United States approved the charter of the United Nations by a vote of 89–2.

On August 6, 1945, the Enola Gay dropped a single atomic device on the Japanese city of Hiroshima. Eighty-five thousand people died in the immediate blast. On the eighth the Soviet Union entered the war in the Pacific. On the ninth the Air Force loosed a second bomb on Nagasaki with equally devastating result. On August 14 Japan surrendered, and World War II officially came to a close.

Newsreels and photos of the bomb and its aftermath appalled Fulbright. Whole neighborhoods atomized, children burned to the bone, an entire generation of survivors threatened with cancer and genetic mutation. Modern technology had rendered Mars an unspeakable monster. "Like primitive man in the darkness of the caves and jungles," he told the Senate, "we too are faced with elemental and infinite forces which we do not understand." How curious it was, he mused, "to find man, *Homo sapiens,* of divine origin, we are told, seriously considering going underground to escape the consequences of his own folly." "It struck me," he said privately, "that it just made war obsolete. No rational person could ever contemplate having a war with these goddamn weapons because it would just wipe everything out."[66]

Once again decrying the absolute veto power given to the Big Five in the U.N. Charter, Fulbright insisted that in the field of armaments, and especially the production of atomic weapons, the world organization must have complete power to inspect and control throughout the world.[67] In calling for internationalization of the atomic bomb Fulbright was joining Secretary of Commerce Henry Wallace and Secretary of War Henry Stimson as well as leading figures in the scientific community. Truman chose to listen instead to Secretary of the Navy James Forrestal and General Leslie Groves, who had headed the Manhattan Project. A year later Bernard Baruch, America's first representative to the Atomic Energy Commission, proposed a plan that provided for surrender of all nuclear weapons to the international authority and comprehensive inspection, but which would maintain the U.S. atomic monopoly through continued American control of fissionable materials. Not surprisingly, the USSR used its veto to block adoption of the Truman administration's plan.[68] "It seems to me that one of the basic defects in the President's attitude toward international relations," Fulbright wrote Henry Canby, "is his assumption of a moral superiority which permits us to act unilaterally, while at

66 Fulbright interview.

67 *Congressional Record*, Senate, Nov. 2, 1945, A4652–4.

68 Gregg Herken, *The Winning Weapon: The Atomic Bomb in the Cold War, 1941–1950* (New York, 1980), 163–71, 190–1.

the same time insisting that every one else must act multilaterally within the UNO."[69]

J. William Fulbright's first year in office had been a tense and difficult one. There was the steady drumfire of criticism from the isolationist heartland. "If you could see the letters and cards that I get from the vicinity of Chicago threatening me with hanging and calling me a traitor," you would be amazed, he wrote an Arkansas supporter.[70] Moreover, he was finding the constituent service he did have to render increasingly onerous. "As I receive the veritable flood of complaints and requests for special favors day after day, I find that I tend to become cynical, to think all people are concerned only with their special advantages," he confided to a group at Chapel Hill. He spoke of living for three years "in the high pressure competitive atmosphere of Washington," of forgetting "all about the real values of life," of struggling for "advantage over one's neighbor or competitor in business or politics."[71] Even from Fayetteville, Roberta was able to sense that her son was losing his balance. "Bill, precious boy," she wrote, "when I consider what a strain you have been under, I am writing to say stop! Look! listen! Do not exceed the speed limit . . . if you are even a little kin to me you will have a tendency to be too hard on yourself. Don't do it."[72] Thus it was that when Columbia University approached Fulbright in October 1945 about becoming its president, he proved willing to listen.

Columbia's presidency was one of America's most prestigious academic posts. Fulbright was hardly first on the school's list. When Nicholas Murray Butler finally tendered his resignation, four names were put forward: Roosevelt's 1940 Republican presidential challenger, Wendell Wilkie, prominent banking figure Leon Fraser, the Carnegie Foundation's Fred Keppel, and an inside candidate. All four died before the board of governors could reach a decision.[73]

News that Columbia was courting Fulbright hit the front pages of the state press the last week of October. "I am deeply puzzled about what is the right thing to do," he wrote a constituent. "The only issue involved, as I see it, is which position offers me the greater opportunity to exercise influence for the good of Arkansas and the country."[74] Perhaps, he mused, he could make a greater impact in behalf of world peace in New York than in Washington; but

69 JWF to Henry S. Canby, Jan. 19, 1946, BCN 24, F49, SPF.
70 JWF to F. K. Buxton, Dec. 8, 1945, BCN 29, F3, SPF.
71 Quoted in Johnson and Gwertzman, *Fulbright: The Dissenter,* 112.
72 Roberta Fulbright to JWF, Dec. 7, 1945, BCN 5, F31, SPF.
73 Leonard Lyons, "Tittle-Tattle from Times Square,"*Washington Post,* Aug. 23, 1945, BCN 32, F16, SPF.
74 JWF to W. C. McClure, Oct. 13, 1945, BCN 29, F6, SPF.

neither he nor Betty wanted to live in New York, Riverside Drive or not. Advice poured in from all sides, but it conflicted. Herbert Bayard Swope, journalist, raconteur, cultural entrepreneur, and promoter of Bernard Baruch, told him to stay in the Senate. "It seems to me that you can become the chief spokesman for democracy, and champion of a new democracy in the South," he pontificated.[75] Most of his Arkansas boosters, including Herbert Thomas, advised him to take the new job. It would assure your future as a national leader, Thomas advised; a stepping-stone to the presidency, another wrote. "Our state is regarded generally throughout the country as being inhabited by illiterate people," wrote Hugh Hart, "and for a native of Arkansas to become the head of our greatest eastern university would be a continual refutation of that libel."[76] His family was confused. "About a week or ten days ago, Mother wrote me that she thought I had better go to Columbia, and my sister, Anne, wrote that she thought I should stay in the Senate . . . ," he wrote Thomas. "Today, I received a letter from Anne, changing her views, and a telegram from Mother, changing hers."[77]

In the end, he decided to stay in the Senate. His contacts in Arkansas assured Fulbright that he would be unopposed for a second term. Were he to leave Congress after such a short time, it might very well create the impression of a superficial job-hopper who lacked the ability to commit and follow through. Moreover, despite Fulbright's complaints about being besieged by narrow-minded constituents, there were issues in the domestic as well as the international sphere about which he cared deeply and that he could best promote as a member of the United States Senate.

In many ways J. William Fulbright was the archtypical American progressive. His views toward labor–management relations, federal control of corporations, public power, a national minimum wage, and the whole range of issues associated with the rise of the welfare state were those of an enlightened, town-dwelling, Anglo–Saxon small-businessperson. He saw traditional American values and institutions simultaneously threatened by self-serving businessmen and powerful vested interests, and by the ignorant and thus untrustworthy masses. As a classicist and an Anglophile Fulbright was devoted to the republican form of government; indeed, he considered democracy in many ways a dangerous experiment. "God has not ordained that our form of government will succeed; nor, is there any evidence from history to support the thesis that democracy is a natural form of society," he once warned.[78] The Arkansan adhered to the Lockean concept of equality popular in America and

75 Swope to JWF, Oct. 18, 1945, BCN 29, F6, SPF.
76 Hugh Hart, Oct. 29, 1945, BCN 29, F6, SPF.
77 JWF to Thomas, Oct. 30, 1945, BCN 29, F6, SPF.
78 *Congressional Record*, Senate, July 9, 1957, 11080.

Britain during the eighteenth century, which held that humans were born with a tabula rasa; that what they became as adults – wise or foolish, good or evil – was a function of time and circumstance, of what they experienced and of what they were taught and learned. Implicit in this assumption was that humankind could be greatly improved by education and by the conscious reorganization of society.[79] "Our form of government is the product of great human effort," the Arkansan asserted. "It was created by our forefathers with the realization that man is potentially good, but also potentially a beast. Wise actions by our people will always be needed to keep the beast from seizing control."[80] Care for the commonweal must reside, he believed, with an enlightened elite that practiced public virtue, that life-giving characteristic of all republics.

Like so many other southern progressives, Fulbright was convinced that Arkansas and the entire region were economic colonies of the North. In an exchange with Senator Jacob Javits (R–New York) he would declare in 1964:

> Where did New York get its many dollars? It did not take the money out of the ground, out of a gold mine. Did it not exploit every other state in the Union because it controlled the federal government for many years? It controlled the interest rate. It collected money from great insurance companies. It paid two percent for money and loaned it at six percent. For many years Mr. Joseph Eastman [New York industrialist and founder of Eastman Kodak] dominated the Interstate Commerce Commission. The Interstate Commerce Commission set up freight rates so that we in the South could not start an industry. . . .[81]

During his years in the House and his first decade in the Senate, the junior senator from Arkansas would devote considerable energy to freeing the South from its perceived economic bondage.

Fulbright did not put much stock in party discipline. He had won in Arkansas without the help of the national Democratic organization, and he welcomed the freedom his independence allowed him. As a progressive and an independent Democrat, as practitioner of republican virtue, as self-appointed guardian of the liberties of the people, and as representative of the interests of his fellow Arkansans, Fulbright believed that it was not only his privilege but duty to pick and choose among New Deal programs.[82]

Although Harry Truman would soon fall out with Henry Wallace and the left wing of the Democratic party over foreign policy and labor–management relations, it seemed at the outset that he was more committed to the New Deal

79 See Forrest McDonald, *Novus Ordo Seclorum: The Intellectual Origins of the Constitution* (Lawrence, Kans., 1985), 53.
80 Draft of unused speech, Apr. 18, 1946, PPF.
81 *Congressional Record*, Senate, Apr. 29, 1964, 9596.
82 JWF to C. N. Bellingrath, Mar. 6, 1945, BCN 43, F34, SPF.

than his predecessor had been during his third and fourth terms. In September 1945 the man from Missouri proposed a sweeping extension of the New Deal, including the expansion of Social Security to cover new categories of workers, an increase in the minimum-wage bill, a national health insurance plan, new regional development projects like the TVA, a full employment bill and, in an effort to curb inflation, an extension of the life of the Office of Price Administration.

Typically, Fulbright resisted appeals from the White House and the Democratic leadership to fall in line and support the entire administration package. "As I have often told you I consider I am neither New Dealer or anti-New Dealer," he wrote C. N. Bellingrath, "and the most sensible course is one between the two extremes. . . . The only thing I hope is that I don't make more than 50% mistakes."[83] As he had in the House, Fulbright consistently voted with the conservative majority to block Truman's minimum-wage bill, which proposed to raise the nation's base pay from forty to seventy-five cents an hour. Actually, he believed wages in Arkansas too low and favored a gradual rise to fifty-five cents, but in the end the choice available to him was all or nothing.[84] However, on one of the most politically charged issues of the day – price controls – the junior senator from Arkansas voted with the administration to the bitter end.[85] This was also true of the controversial Murray–Patman Full Employment bill. Although conservatives denounced the measure for guaranteeing every American a job – "cradle to grave socialism" – it did no such thing. As Fulbright pointed out, the measure, as amended, merely authorized the executive branch to study the prospects for employment for each succeeding year and make recommendations to Congress. Any legislation to fund public works or stimulate private investment would require separate legislation.[86] "In view of the experience we had in 1931 and 1932 as the result of a complete lack of foresight or coordination in our government and industry," he wrote an Arkansas businessman, "I must admit that I feel that someone should use their intelligence to try to prevent the recurrence of any depression of that nature."[87] Finally, Fulbright continued to be a devotee of public power, continually voting to extend the life of the Southwest Power Administration over the outraged protests of Arkansas Power and Light and its powerful chief executive officer, Hamilton Moses.

[83] JWF to Bellingrath, Mar. 6, 1945, BCN 43, F34, SPF.
[84] JWF to R. W. Benson, June 28, 1945, BCN 48, F12; E. A. O'Neal to JWF, Nov. 7, 1945, BCN48, F13; and JWF to P. F. Watzek, Oct. 1, 1945, BCN 48, F12, SPF.
[85] Draft reply to Senator Taft, June 5, 1945, BCN 4, F14, and JWF to Basil Hoag, May 11, 1946, BCN 38, F40, SPF.
[86] JWF to Amos Guthridge, Sept. 6, 1945, BCN 41, F10, SPF.
[87] JWF to Williamson, Sept. 25, 1945, BCN 41, F10, SPF.

Despite his mixed voting record on domestic matters, Fulbright continued to enjoy the adulation of American liberals. Throughout late 1945 and 1946 he spoke forcefully in behalf of collective security and international cooperation at prestigious forums in Chicago, New York, and Boston. Virtually every newspaper and magazine not controlled by William Randolph Hearst or Eleanor "Cissy" Patterson hailed him as a man with an unlimited political future. No less a personage than Dorothy Thompson, one of America's most influential columnists, took the senator by the arm at a large Washington social gathering and announced: "This man is destined for greatness."[88]

88 Quoted in Johnson and Gwertzman, *Fulbright: The Dissenter,* 112. Mike Fodor, who had once proposed to Thompson, had no doubt been touting him, but Thompson did not need to be convinced.

# 6

# *The conscience of a conservative internationalist*

In 1945 internationalists such as Henry Wallace and Eleanor Roosevelt assumed that their creed was based on a tolerance for other races, cultures, and religions. They associated isolationism with parochialism and nativism. Their vision of a "Parliament of man" had no room for distinctions based on ideology, life-style, and particularly skin color. Ignoring the fact that southerners supported internationalism and multilateralism primarily for economic reasons, many northern liberals assumed that Fulbright, given his education and his views on foreign affairs, was one of a small breed of courageous southerners who opposed discrimination against African Americans and who were willing to risk their careers by participating in the burgeoning civil rights movement. Thus did Herbert Swope advise the Arkansan to shun Columbia so that he might lead the movement in the South for equal rights for all men. Swope and his fellow liberals had sadly miscalculated.

In many ways James William Fulbright was the very antithesis of W. J. Cash's "glandular, God obsessed, hedonistic" southerners, people "doomed by their savage ideal," who shunned intellectual discipline and emphasized orgiastic religiosity to the exclusion of reason and progress. Nonetheless he was, in his own distinctive way, very much a southerner. As U.S. senator he had to represent both the Ozarks and the Arkansas Delta. During his upbringing in Fayetteville, Fulbright had had almost no personal contact with the poverty and racism characteristic of so much of the South. As the son of a well-to-do farmer and banker, he had led a sheltered, privileged life. The black population of northwest Arkansas constituted less than 2 percent of the whole, and sharecropping was virtually unknown in the Ozarks.[1] Fulbright was aware intellectually of the South's low living standards, but he had had almost no personal experience of the human suffering that was the wrenching by-product of those statistics.

At the same time, Fulbright exhibited some of the characteristics of a paternalistic patrician. Among his closest friends and strongest supporters were planters, men like Robert E. Lee Wilson and Hugh Brinkley, who owned tens

[1] Quoted in Jack Temple Kirby, *Rural Worlds Lost: The American South, 1920–1960* (Baton Rouge, 1987), 226, 80, 96, 106–7.

of thousands of acres of land in eastern Arkansas. The Anglophilia and internationalism that figured so prominently in Fulbright's philosophy were typical of many southern aristocrats, while his skepticism and individualism were characteristics traditionally exhibited by southern highlanders.

That J. William Fulbright was a racist is indisputable. He would claim throughout his career that his position on civil rights was a matter of political expediency. "There's no mystery why the people from Georgia, Mississippi, and so on have been what they call bigots," he declared. "They inherited an historical situation. You couldn't be elected if you didn't have that view." That was no less true in Arkansas than elsewhere in the region, he insisted. "People in eastern Arkansas . . . couldn't see their daughter going to school with a black," he argued. "They always imagined the black would rape their daughter. This was the worst possible thing. They were scared of them actually."[2] He also justified his segregationist position on the traditional white supremacist grounds that a democracy should not and could not alter local prejudices through legislation. To his mind the blacks he knew were not equal to whites nor could they be made so by legislative decree. Throughout his career he would regard involuntary integration as anathema. Southerners, Fulbright argued, were trapped by their environment and history, and neither he, nor Congress, nor the Supreme Court could change that.

Fulbright, however, was no racist in the Vardaman–Talmadge–Bilbo tradition. He was no more hostile or resentful toward African Americans than he was toward Indonesians. On a personal level he judged people by their manners, personal cleanliness, and education, not by their skin color; but he did not feel compelled by Christian duty or social conscience to use the power of the state to remedy historical wrongs, correct maldistribution of wealth, or legislate equality of opportunity. His racism was a combination of the blindness of the southern highlander who had not experienced black life and culture, and the noblesse oblige of the planting aristocracy. One of his longtime aides recalled that "he shares the class and caste consciousness of his planter friends from eastern Arkansas, but he does not share their fear of 'race-mixing.'"[3]

In fact, Herbert Swope's notion that Fulbright might assume leadership of a movement in the postwar South to ameliorate racial conditions and animosities was not as farfetched as it later might have seemed. In December 1944 a number of New South leaders, including Clayton Fritchey of the New Orleans *Item,* Ralph McGill of the *Atlanta Constitution,* and progressive figures from the worlds of politics and business met to consider a regional strategy for ending the brutal lynchings that marred southern life, abolishing the poll tax, and phasing out segregation in the public schools. When Fritchey sent

2 Interview with J. William Fulbright, Oct. 11–18, 1988, Washington, D.C.
3 Interview with Lee Williams, June 20, 1989, Washington, D.C.

him a report, Fulbright replied, "I think you are quite right in your saying that this is an important matter and well worth watching." He urged Fritchey to draw Governor J. Melville Broughton of North Carolina into the group: "Because of his position I think that he can do a great deal among the people of the South in getting them to see the reasonableness of a more liberal position." He asked the journalist to meet with him the following month in Washington.[4]

Fritchey came, but it soon became clear that the Arkansan was unwilling to challenge institutionalized racism in the South or even to remain neutral. Along with nineteen other southern Democratic senators, Fulbright voted against the nomination of Aubrey Williams, a southern liberal and protégé of Harry Hopkins, to fill a ten-year term as head of the Rural Electrification Administration.[5] Williams, who had formerly directed the National Youth Administration, was a relentless advocate of laws to eliminate discriminatory hiring practices. Fulbright also voted against a 1943 bill sponsored by Representative Vito Marcantonio of New York to outlaw the poll tax.[6]

Congressmen and senators, Fulbright declared in "The Legislator," a 1944 speech delivered at the University of Chicago, must pick and choose their issues. "The average legislator, early in his career, discovers that there are certain interests, or prejudices, of his constituents which are dangerous to trifle with." In matters affecting the national interest, legislators must choose between the fundamental and the superficial; and to his mind, whereas the United Nations was a matter of fundamental importance, the poll tax was not. The tax, he said, was merely "symbolic of conditions which many deplore."[7] "In an issue of this kind which affects a person's children," he later observed, "you have to go along or you can't be in the Senate. They know what their daughter is and they know what the conditions are in their local school." Arkansans might be subject to persuasion on matters of foreign policy, but not on questions of race relations.[8] Obviously at this point in his life, Fulbright considered some Arkansans and some parents more important than others.

Like so many other southerners who wished to avoid being perceived as blatantly racist, Fulbright argued that social attitudes were immune to legislation. "Personally I would like to see the State itself, through the proper constitutional amendment, accomplish this end [abolition of the poll tax]," he wrote a constituent, but it was clearly not a matter for federal action.[9] "I have long noticed that in Kansas City, Chicago, Detroit, New York and Boston

4 JWF to Fritchey, Jan. 1, 1945, BCN 73, F13, SPF.
5 Quoted in Haynes Johnson and Bernard M. Gwertzman, *Fulbright: The Dissenter* (New York, 1968), 109.
6 David Brinkley, *Washington Goes to War* (New York, 1988), 204.
7 *Congressional Record,* Senate, Mar. 12, 1946, A1284.
8 Fulbright interview.
9 JWF to J. Lewis Henderson, June 15, 1945, BCN 50, F18, SPF.

where they have no poll tax," he wrote a Brooklyn critic, "their politics and their racial difficulties are quite as acute as they are in Arkansas. The basic difficulty is one of education and a higher intellectual and moral level among the citizens of the various states."[10] The Aubrey Williams appointment and the poll tax were important issues, but the key battle between civil rights activists and their opponents at the close of World War II was over continuation of the Fair Employment Practices Committee (FEPC).

As had been true following World War I, America in 1945–6 was contorted by racial conflict. African-American leaders, spurred by wartime rhetoric promising freedom and equality of opportunity for all peoples, were particularly assertive. This newfound aggressiveness, together with the sight of thousands of uniformed black soldiers, provoked a wave of race riots and lynchings across the South. Harry Truman, who believed in legal if not social equality, was appalled. He would eventually declare his support for antilynching and anti–poll tax legislation, but his first move in the civil rights field was to throw his support behind a renewal of the FEPC, first created through executive order by President Roosevelt in 1941.[11]

News that the administration was threatening to reestablish the hated agency created a firestorm in the South, including Arkansas. "In my opinion this is a very vicious bill," Walter Trulock, president of the National Bank of Commerce in Pine Bluff, wrote Fulbright. "It would hamper our development by creating racial prejudice and would open the door and encourage many thoughtless and vicious Negroes to demand social equality."[12] "The power to discriminate in all matters is an endowment of the intelligent human being," declared another constituent.[13] C. E. Webb of the Cotton Belt Good Will Club was more emphatic:

> We all believe it would be best for the Southern States to secede from the negro loving yankees . . . if the North insists on this bill being passed. Of course, we can all lay in an extra supply of ammunition for our shot guns and pistols and prevent the enforcement of provisions of the bill – but we hate to be forced to such tactics.[14]

There were certainly voices raised in behalf of the FEPC inside of Arkansas and out. H. L. Mitchell of the Southern Tenant Farmers' Union wrote urging the junior senator to support the measure. As of 1945 there were 52,492 black farmers in Arkansas; 11,469 were independent owners, with ownership increasing almost uniformly as one proceeded from east to west

10 JWF to Rose Stenzler, Aug. 29, 1946, BCN 48, F9, SPF.
11 Donald R. McCoy, *The Presidency of Harry S. Truman* (Lawrence, Kans., 1984), 106.
12 Trulock to JWF, April 28, 1945, BCN 74, F15, SPF.
13 W. N. Stannus to JWF, Jan. 18, 1946, BCN 50, F19, SPF.
14 Webb to JWF, Jan. 27, 1946, BCN 50, F19, SPF.

across the state. The number of independent owners was declining and would continue to decrease sharply among both blacks and whites. While Mitchell and the twenty-five thousand southern farm families who belonged to the STFU struggled against the enclosure movement, they also looked to the FEPC to protect the increasing number of tenants and farm laborers in their dealings with landlords and agricultural employers. A young black woman from Little Rock named Daisy Bates added her voice to those of Mitchell and labor leader Sidney Hillman, and from Dermott, Arkansas, an African-American clergyman who headed the local branch of the NAACP wrote: "The great powers are . . . striving for an equal and just measure of democracy in the age; sure it should be expected that 12 or 15 million Negroes who have been and are now being tested by fire and every acid test" should share in that vision.[15] For Fulbright, however, these were the wrong voices.

Early in 1946 Fulbright, Walter George, and Lister Hill (D–Alabama) held their noses and joined with James Eastland and Theodore Bilbo of Mississippi in a filibuster that lasted off and on throughout the spring. FEPC regulations would have to be administered by men "close to the people," Fulbright wrote in notes for the debate, and enforcement would be extremely difficult. "Do you think," he asked rhetorically, "that you can make people hire those whom they regard as unfit for any reason?" As he had during the poll tax debate, Fulbright attacked the fair employment practices law on the grounds that the administration and so-called liberals in Congress were attempting to alter public morals and mores through legislative decree. "In theory no one approves of discrimination just as no one approves of bad manners or meanness or sin of any kind," but flaws in human nature could not and should be corrected through legislative statute or judicial edict. In a democratic, secular state the government had no business acting in this realm. "I, of course, believe that there is plenty of room for debate AS TO WHICH SIDE IS LIBERAL" in the FEPC matter, he wrote a constituent.[16] In the end, supporters of the FEPC could not gather enough votes, two-thirds of those present and voting, to force cloture, and the FEPC renewal legislation died.

Fulbright's stance on civil rights caused a sharp reaction among liberal admirers of his foreign policy views. Given "the statesmanlike and progressive positions" that Fulbright had taken on other matters coming before the Senate, A. J. Muste of the Fellowship of Reconciliation wrote him, "it was with some surprise that I noted . . . that you . . . had voted . . . against the proposal to take up the bill to establish a permanent FEPC."[17] The Interdenominational Ministers Council was more direct: "[T]he fact of your superior training, previous places of honor which you have occupied, to say nothing

15 Mitchell, to JWF, June 21, 1945, BCN 50, F17, and "Status of Negro Farmers in Arkansas as of 1945," undated, BCN 36, F3, SPF.
16 JWF to Theron Raines, Feb. 1, 1946, F19, SPF.
17 Muste to JWF, Jan. 28, 1946, BCN 50, F19, SPF.

of your Christian professions, led us to believe that you would have been one of the few champions of fair play to all people, regardless of their racial identifications."[18]

But Fulbright saw no contradiction between his views on international affairs and civil rights. Indeed, he was baffled by the slings and arrows sent his way by the leading internationalists of the day. What he favored was cultural autonomy for all peoples. He was an ardent Wilsonian and, like Arthur Link, believed that Wilson's pledge to "make the world safe for democracy" indicated (at least by 1917) not a determination to export American culture and institutions but rather a commitment to the principle of national self-determination. As a southerner with a strong sense of class, kinship, and place, he believed it no less abhorrent that the North should impose its mores and social theories on the South than the United States should force its culture, political institutions, and economic theories on another society.

The debate over the FEPC angered J. William Fulbright in part because he saw it as an effort by hypocritical neoabolitionists to impose their views on a region they knew nothing about, and in part because it delayed congressional action on the British loan, legislation dear to his heart – and to the pocketbooks of some of his most important constituents.

From 1939 through 1941 Great Britain, as it struggled virtually alone against the forces of international fascism, expended its stocks of gold and dollars in purchasing the material and munitions with which to fight. Passage of the Lend–Lease Act in 1941 helped end the massive drain on British finances, but the United Kingdom was never able to recover. As of July 1945 Britain's gold and dollar reserves had fallen to $1.8 billion and its total external liabilities amounted to $13 billion. (At the same time Fort Knox housed more than $21 billion in gold bullion.)[19]

Following the stoppage of Lend–Lease in the summer of 1945, representatives of the British and American governments gathered in Washington and signed the Anglo–American Financial Agreement on December 6. The United States agreed to extend to Great Britain a total credit of $4.4 billion to be repaid in sixty-two annual installments at 2 percent interest. As of December 31, 1946, sterling paid on current account was to be freely convertible into other currencies, and the United Kingdom endorsed the idea of a gradual reduction and elimination of empire preferences within the framework of an

[18] Rev. George N. Collins and Rev. T. J. Griffin to JWF, Feb. 4, 1946, BCN 50, F20, SPF.

[19] Acheson to Winant, Sept. 14, 1945, 740.00119 Council/9-1945, Department of State Decimal File, RG 59, National Archives, Arlington, Va. [hereinafter referred to as NA].

International Trade Organization.[20] Spokesmen for the Truman administration proclaimed the loan agreement to be an integral part of its internationalist program. It would simultaneously rehabilitate the economy of one of America's most important trading partners and induce Great Britain to open up the sterling bloc to trade with all nations.

Some initial sparring between opponents and supporters of the loan took place over the winter, but Congress did not take up the agreement officially until March 1946. Assistant Secretary of State Will Clayton, Secretary of Commerce Henry Wallace, and a score of other loan supporters testified at length before both the House and Senate Banking and Currency Committees, selected because they were thought to be more favorably inclined toward the loan than the SFRC and the House Committee on Foreign Affairs. Once the legislation was out of committee, however, opposition became loud and persistent. Midwestern isolationists such as William Langer (R–South Dakota) charged that the loan was really an Anglo–American alliance in disguise, and before everyone knew it, the United States would once again be pulling British chestnuts out of the fire. Fiscal conservatives maintained that the loan was the golden straw that would break the American camel's back. "There Will Always Be A U.S.A. If We Don't Give It Away" read the title of an antiloan tract widely circulated at the time.[21] A related criticism advanced with special eloquence by Bernard Baruch and Col. McCormick's spokeswoman in the House, Jesse Sumner (R–Illinois), was that the loan would advance the cause of socialism and economic regimentation on both sides of the Atlantic – in Britain because the new Labor government of Clement Attlee would use the proceeds directly to finance their social experiments, and in the United States because bankruptcy would inevitably destroy the free-enterprise system.[22]

J. William Fulbright was one of the reasons that the administration chose the Banking and Currency Committee instead of the SFRC to hear testimony on the loan. Early in 1943 at a cocktail party in Georgetown, Fulbright had met a brilliant Washington lawyer named Oscar Cox. Another one of Harry Hopkins's disciples, Cox had worked for the Treasury and State Departments. He had been the principal draftsman of the Lend–Lease bill. Like others in Washington, Fulbright stood somewhat in awe of Cox's mastery of the law and the legislative process. When subsequently Cox testified at various hearings on the renewal of Lend–Lease, Fulbright was deeply impressed with his arguments that no-strings-attached aid to Britain was necessary not only to win the war but to rehabilitate a nation that was sure to be one of

20 Keynes to Chancellor of the Exchequer, Dec. 6, 1945, FO 371/45713, Records of the British Foreign Office, Public Record Office, Kew, London, United Kingdom.

21 Quoted in Richard P. Hedlund, "Congress and the British Loan, 1945–1946: A Congressional Study" (Ph.D diss., University of Kentucky, 1976), 153.

22 Baruch to Clayton, Nov. 19, 1945, Papers of Bernard Baruch, Mudd Library, Princeton University, and Hedlund, "Congress and the British Loan," 57.

America's principal trading partners in the postwar world. The man who more than any other influenced Fulbright's views on international trade and monetary questions, however, was Will Clayton.

Tall (6 ft, 6 in.), handsome, silver haired, with a reputation for integrity and civility, Clayton was an evangelist in the cause of multilateralism, a system of international trade free of discrimination and artificial – that is, nonmarket – barriers. At the time Roosevelt called the Houston businessman to Washington to be surplus property administrator and subsequently assistant secretary of state for economic affairs, Clayton headed the largest cotton-exporting firm in the world. Throughout American history cotton growers and exporters had advocated a low-tariff policy in order to have an expanded market for their product, of which, it seemed, there was a continual surplus. Typically, cotton farmers, their brokers such as Clayton, and their political representatives such as Fulbright took the position that the high-tariff policy advocated by the Republican Party was designed to keep the price farmers had to pay for their manufactured products high while denying agriculture much-needed foreign outlets for their goods.

Fulbright was well aware of the low-tariff views of his primarily agricultural constituency. It did not take Clayton to convince the junior senator from Arkansas that reduction of trade barriers and economic aid to develop foreign markets would serve the interests of the cotton, soybean, and poultry farmers of the South; but it was Clayton who confirmed for Fulbright that the free-trade theories advocated by Adam Smith, Woodrow Wilson, and R. B. McCallum were as relevant for the post–World War II era as they had been for earlier periods and other countries. Moreover, as chief lobbyist for the British loan, it was Clayton who convinced the Arkansan to join the crusade in its behalf.

Despite his junior status, Fulbright played a leading role in shepherding the Anglo–American Financial Agreement first through the Banking and Currency Committee and then through the Senate as a whole. That the *Chicago Tribune* was its most outspoken opponent made the fight especially delicious. Initially, Fulbright and other administration spokesmen relied on economic arguments to convince nay-sayers. "It is not charity, nor is it a straight commercial loan," he wrote August Engel, publisher of the *Arkansas Democrat.* "It is an effort to preserve for us an opportunity to do some business with other peoples in the world by the free enterprise method."[23]

The argument that the agreement would help rehabilitate Britain in order that it become a bastion protecting Western Europe from communist subversion and Soviet aggression was one that the State Department was initially loath to make because it ran the risk of arousing possibly uncontrollable public passions; but growing doubts concerning the ability of the West to placate

23 JWF to Engel, Dec. 19, 1945, BCN 24, F21, SPF.

the Kremlin, coupled with polls indicating that the loan was in deep difficulty in the Senate, persuaded the White House to play the anticommunist card.

Fulbright's speeches and letters reflected that shift. "Overshadowing the economy [*sic*] aspects of this agreement," he wrote Ben Rowland, "is the great danger that we are now facing from Russia and communism. I am sure you have read in the papers . . . about the many difficulties we are encountering with the Russians."[24] But for Fulbright as for the Truman administration, the move from an economic to a strategic justification was more than just a matter of tactics. Despite Mike Fodor's reports concerning the benignity of Josef Stalin's intentions, East–West relations continued to deteriorate at an alarming rate during the spring of 1946. As the Soviets busied themselves establishing communist puppet regimes in Eastern Europe and pressuring Iran to grant economic and strategic concessions, Winston Churchill journeyed to the United States the first week in March to address the student body of Westminster College in Missouri. An "iron curtain" had descended across Europe stretching from the Adriatic in the south to Lübeck in the north, the former prime minister declared. Behind that curtain Soviet occupation authorities were stamping out individual freedom and crushing political dissent. Not content with what they had, the Soviets were determined to extend their despicable totalitarian system to the rest of Europe if they could. Only the United States and the atomic bomb stood between Western civilization and the Red Terror.

Many in the United States denounced Churchill as a warmonger, but others, including Fulbright, remembered that in the 1930s the Englishman had been a voice crying in the wilderness against the dangers of appeasing international fascism. In fact, during the winter of 1945–6 Fulbright had decided that the Soviet Union did indeed pose a dire threat to the Atlantic community. In April he wrote Fodor in virtually the same words Arthur Vandenberg had used in his famous address to the Senate: "The great question that confronts all of us, is what is Russia up to? By that I mean, how far is she determined to go in her efforts to break up the British Empire, and if she is permitted to go too far, is there any power in the world left able to cope with her?"[25]

Following a prolonged struggle the Senate approved the Anglo–American Financial Agreement by a vote of 46 to 34 on May 10 and the House by a vote of 219 to 155 on July 12. It was the first of many battles the junior senator would wage in behalf of America's infant foreign aid program.

Despite his support of the British loan, Fulbright had by the spring of 1946 become deeply disillusioned with the Truman administration's foreign poli-

24 JWF to Ben Rowland, May 16, 1946, BCN 24, F24, SPF.
25 JWF to Fodor, Apr. 9, 1946, BCN 67, F24, SPF.

cies. The White House and State Department seemed to be confused, distracted, and inept, unwilling or unable either to confront or conciliate the Soviet Union. While Truman lectured Soviet Foreign Minister Vyacheslav Molotov in late 1945 on his country's failure to live up to the Yalta accords and then sponsored Churchill's bellicose speech, he presided over a dramatic weakening of the U.S. military establishment and a diplomatic campaign of conciliation at the various foreign ministers' conferences held during 1946. Decrying a too-rapid demobilization that reduced America's armed forces from eleven to three-and-a-half million in less than a year, Fulbright complained to a friend that "the country does not seem to be willing to support an army and navy sufficient to make us secure in the Middle East and Far East."[26] To make matters worse, the man from Missouri seemed oblivious to the economic and social chaos that reigned throughout war-devastated Western Europe. Foreshadowing the arguments that were put forward in favor of the Marshall Plan, Fulbright told the Canadian Club of Ottawa:

> If western civilization is to play its proper role in the world of the future, it is essential that it be stabilized politically and revitalized economically . . . The balance of power between the democratic west and the Communist east is exceedingly difficult to maintain if some order is not brought into these areas.[27]

Against the advice of his Senate colleagues, his wife, and his chief of staff, the junior senator from Arkansas opened up on the Truman administration the first week in April. American foreign policy was in shambles, he told the Senate. While paying lip service to internationalism, the White House and State Department had crammed Argentina and the Baruch plan down Moscow's throat at the United Nations. At the same time Washington had demanded the right to retain exclusive possession of island bases in the Pacific captured during World War II while denying the right of other nations to do the same. Demobilization and lack of discipline over wages, prices, and labor–management disputes, Fulbright complained, compounded the administration's other mistakes. "Our idleness and confusion at home have drastically limited our ability not only to supply our own needs but also to supply the dire needs of war-torn Europe and Asia."[28] Little wonder that he complained subsequently about being "shunned in the halls."

"The people in the country are very conscious of the lack of direction given to our policy by the President," Fulbright observed to a constituent. "My hope is that with a little prodding here and there, and with a little judicial criticism he may be encouraged to take a direct position and get some better men

26 JWF to Adrian Williamson, Mar. 20, 1946, BCN 24, F29, SPF.
27 *Congressional Record,* Senate, Mar. 5, 1946, A1397–8.
28 Ibid., Apr. 11, 1946, 3508.

to advise him."[29] In the view of the White House, Fulbright's criticism became somewhat less than judicious when, following the election of Republican majorities in both houses of Congress in the fall of 1946, he suggested that President Truman resign.

As Forrest MacDonald points out in *Novus Ordo Seclorum,* devotees of a republican form of government have traditionally divided into classical, or puritan, republicans and modern, or agrarian, republicans. The former believe that the key to preserving any given republic is an educated, virtuous populous – better people – whereas the latter are convinced that the crucial elements are political processes and institutions – better arrangements.[30] Leaving nothing to chance, J. William Fulbright proposed both a moral and a structural solution to what he perceived to be the breakdown of democratic government in America.

Fulbright had long believed that the American Constitution had erred in so dramatically separating the legislative and executive branches of the federal enterprise, giving to one the sole authority to make the laws and the other the power to execute them. The opportunity for stalemate, particularly when one party was in control of the White House and the other of one or both houses of Congress, was too great. At crucial times in the nation's history – in 1918 as Wilson and the Senate prepared to square off over the Treaty of Versailles and in 1930 when Herbert Hoover failed to persuade a Democratic Congress to adopt his methods for combating the Depression – divided government had thwarted the will of the people.[31] The last week in March 1945 the new senator from Arkansas appeared before the Joint Committee on the Organization of Congress to suggest the creation of an executive–legislative cabinet comprising the president's cabinet and the chairpersons of the standing committees of Congress. Most astounding to his colleagues and political pundits in Washington was Fulbright's suggestion that this cabinet have the power to dissolve the government and call general elections when president and Congress deadlocked over an important issue.[32] Unfortunately, such drastic changes would require several years of debate and a constitutional amendment. Fulbright believed that the issues facing postwar America were so momentous that, when another stalemate threatened in late 1946, he was ready with a suggestion that would not involve the cumbersome amending process.

As the midterm congressional elections of 1946 approached, Harry Truman was as unpopular as any American president had ever been. Although it was Congress that had abolished the Office of Price Administration in July, the public blamed Truman for the runaway inflation that ensued. In Septem-

29 JWF to J. Q. Mahaffey, Dec. 1, 1945, BCN 6, F38, SPF.

30 Forrest McDonald, *Novus Ordo Seclorum: The Intellectual Origins of the Constitution* (Lawrence, Kans., 1985), 70–1.

31 *Congressional Record,* Senate, Mar. 12, 1946, A1285.

32 Ibid., A1586.

ber Secretary of Commerce Henry Wallace had delivered a speech at Madison Square Garden calling for continued Soviet–American friendship and attacking those who advocated a get-tough policy. Truman had mistakenly okayed the address without reading it. At his direction Secretary of State James Byrnes was then in Europe assuring the Germans that we would not abandon them to the forces of international communism. Byrnes howled at Wallace's speech, and Truman felt he had no choice but to fire Wallace, a man immensely popular with American liberals. In mid-October the New York *Evening Post* began spreading rumors that Truman was about to resign. *Time* magazine called the president a liar, and the nation's press kept up a constant drumfire about the "incompetents" who were running the government.[33]

Truman's unpopularity accelerated the natural trend in American politics for the party in control of the White House to lose ground in Congress in midterm elections. When the dust had settled from the November 5 balloting, the Republicans had won control of both houses of Congress for the first time in sixteen years. On election day, Fulbright was having lunch in the Senate cafeteria when a reporter for the Associated Press asked him to comment on the political situation. If the Republicans won, as everyone was predicting, a disaster would ensue, Fulbright replied. It would create the stalemate he had feared. What could be done about it in the short run, the reporter asked? Fulbright thought a minute, and then said, "Why, the President ought to resign and allow a prominent Republican to take his place."[34] Obviously the election should be viewed as a referendum on the Democratic Party's leadership. Truman's resignation would unify the government for the great decisions that lay ahead.

The journalist sat silent, stunned. Fulbright was a Democrat and one of the administration's chief supporters in its foreign policy battles, a trenchant foe of the isolationism that was so conspicuous in the backgrounds of those who might possibly succeed Truman. The reporter, Ann Hicks, followed Fulbright back to his office. May I quote you? she asked. No, he said; he did not want to appear to be prophesying a Democratic defeat. What if the Republicans won? responded Hicks. Then she could quote him, Fulbright replied, whereupon he calmly departed for Philadelphia and a speaking engagement.[35]

The next day Fulbright's suggestion made front-page headlines across the nation. The first story was an AP dispatch from Philadelphia: "Senator J. William Fulbright, D–Ark. said today that since the Republicans had captured both houses of Congress 'President Truman should appoint a Republican Secretary of State and resign from office.'"[36] Jack Yingling recalled that the

33 Diary of Charles G. Ross, Oct. 18, 1946, Box 21, Truman Library.
34 Fulbright interview.
35 Interview with Jack Yingling, Oct. 12, 1988, Savannah, Ga.
36 Quoted in Johnson and Gwertzman, *Fulbright: The Dissenter,* 123.

office was deluged with calls asking for clarification. What had Fulbright said, exactly? The staff, dumbfounded, knew nothing of the AP interview.

At that time, the secretary of state followed the vice-president in line of presidential succession, and there was no vice-president in 1946. The first news report was followed by a United Press story quoting Fulbright as naming Senator Arthur Vandenberg of Michigan, sure to be the new chair of the SFRC, as the most logical choice to succeed Truman. Late in the evening of November 6 Fulbright returned to Washington and began explaining.

The now controversial Arkansan gave an interview to the *New York Times* on the seventh and then held a full-scale press conference on November 10. Citing Article II, Section I of the Constitution, he insisted that presidential resignation was fully covered under the law. As to the president's right to name his successor, that was already inherent in the fact that the secretary of state was next in line; but, Fulbright insisted, it would be both politically expedient and in the national interest for Truman to name Vandenberg, Taft, or some other prominent Republican to be secretary of state and president-designate. Our allies and enemies would understand that the U.S. government truly reflected the will of the majority and commanded full public support for its policies, Fulbright explained. In an effort to prove that his suggestion was motivated by principle rather than personal pique, Fulbright publicly proposed a constitutional amendment allowing Congress to call new elections for president in case of a divided government. As in parliamentary systems, members of Congress as well as the president would have to go before the electorate.[37]

There was a smattering of approving editorials in the press. Marshall Field's *Chicago Sun* ran a front-page endorsement. The *Atlanta Constitution* urged the Democratic Party to give Fulbright's suggestion serious consideration. The national media, however, were overwhelmingly critical, even contemptuous. The Arkansan was caving in to the anti-Truman hysteria that seemed to be sweeping the country, the *New York Times* charged, and his proposal violated the spirit if not the letter of the Constitution. Although Fulbright's scenario was both logical and legal, declared the *Christian Science Monitor*, it would elevate to the presidency a man the people had never voted for and thus contravene the trend toward more direct elections. Even the anti-Truman press was scornful: No one whom Truman picked, scoffed the *Washington Post,* could command public support.[38]

Truman, of course, was furious. That "over-educated Oxford S.O.B." he fumed to his staff. "A little more U.S. land grant college education on the U.S. Constitution and what it meant would do Fulbright a lot of good."[39]

37 Lucille Mock, "Truman and Fulbright, the Controversial Proposal for Resignation," Ms. on file, Truman Library.
38 Ibid.
39 Ibid.

Thereafter in private utterances, the president generally referred to the Arkansan as "Senator Halfbright."

The White House and Democratic Party leadership did take Fulbright's proposal seriously enough to mount a counterattack. The redoubtable Bilbo declared that if there was any resigning to be done, Fulbright ought to be the one doing it. James A. Farley, chairman of the Democratic National Committee, termed the proposal "silly." According to Dean Acheson, who helped the president draft an official reply, the notion of resignation was absurd, and those suggesting it could no longer be taken seriously either politically or intellectually.[40] Truman was well aware that Fulbright's plan would, in removing the threat of veto, give the Republicans a free hand in running the country. By staying in office, the president wrote Upton Sinclair, he would be able to confine the achievements of the reactionaries to those things for which they could muster a two-thirds majority.[41] At a news conference on November 11 Truman announced his intention to accept the will of the people and called on Congress to join with him in developing a bipartisan foreign and domestic policy.

Fulbright claimed to have been astounded by the furor his proposal for a presidential resignation had created. At a cocktail party and style show given by the wife of French ambassador Jean Monnet, he told Betty Hynes of the *Washington Times-Herald,* "No one could be more surprised when I realized the excitement my remarks seemed to have created."[42] The remark, subsequently published, caused some consternation. Was the educated junior senator an arrogant, ambitious politician who was just dissembling, or was he really the naïve scholar in politics?

Rumors abounded as to Fulbright's motives. Some insisted that he was acting out of personal pique. He had been out of favor at the White House since his public criticism of the president and his foreign policies, and he was just venting his spleen. Drew Pearson speculated that his proposal was a veiled attempt to get rid of an unofficial "Arkansas brain trust" in the White House.[43] Truman was surrounded at that point by several native Arkansans – Leslie Biffle, secretary of the Senate and one of Truman's closest friends; John Snyder, the Treasury secretary who had spent most of his life as an Arkansas bank teller; and John Steelman, special assistant to the president. Responding to the advice of these men, Truman dispensed patronage in Arkansas through McClellan rather than Fulbright. The junior senator resented it and saw a chance to get even.[44]

40 Interview with William Bundy, July 5, 1990, Princeton, N.J.
41 Mock, "Truman and Fulbright."
42 Quoted in Johnson and Gwertzman, *Fulbright: The Dissenter,* 104.
43 Ibid., 124.
44 Yingling interview.

It was true that Fulbright, despite his protestations to the contrary, did not like Truman. It infuriated him to be snubbed by a man for whom he had no respect. After visiting the White House in the fall of 1945 to urge Truman to be more active in promoting the United Nations, Fulbright remarked scornfully to Alfred Steinberg: "I didn't make a bit of an impression on the President. He didn't know what I was talking about."[45] The junior senator was an impatient young man. He resented not being invited to San Francisco; he believed that the Fulbright resolution, together with his education and intelligence, entitled him to be one of the president's closest advisers on world affairs. Like the temporarily out-of-favor George Patton prior to the Normandy invasion, Fulbright was convinced that destiny had singled him out to play a major role in an obviously crucial juncture in world history. If he had any doubts in this realm, Roberta and Betty constantly assured him that it was so.

In addition, however, J. William Fulbright was genuinely committed to the parliamentary system of government and would remain so with varying degrees of intensity throughout his public career. The system of checks and balances was, as the founding fathers intended, a guard against tyranny, but it rendered the federal government virtually impotent under certain circumstances. Moreover, the system of fixed elections prevailing in the United States invited politicians to obfuscate, vacillate, and seek the lowest common denominator. Nonfixed elections, a legislative–executive cabinet, and question periods similar to those held in the House of Commons would, the Arkansan believed, introduce a much-needed element of responsibility and accountability. More in spite of than in response to the Fulbright proposal, Harry Truman would later press for and secure a change in the succession law ensuring that elected rather than appointed officials assumed the highest office in the land if the president and vice-president could not serve. The Presidential Succession Act of 1947 placed the speaker of the House and the president pro tempore of the Senate ahead of the secretary of state and other cabinet members in the line of presidential succession after the vice-president.

Bill Fulbright was a stubborn man, not easily intimidated or dissuaded from his chosen course. At the same time his plans to strengthen the nation's political leadership through structural and procedural reform were coming to naught, he was working with greater success on a plan that would improve the quality of the people who inhabited the highest offices in the land.

In his letters from San Francisco during the UNCIO, Bernal Seamster, a friend of Fulbright's and a U.S. observer, had denounced Edward Stettinius and other members of the U.S. delegation for their "lack of understanding

45 Alfred Steinberg, *The Man from Missouri: The Life and Times of Harry S. Truman* (New York, 1962), 263.

and knowledge of the conditions other than in their own circle." The solution to the problem, he concluded, "might well be for the federal government to sponsor a major exchange of students from this country to other countries, and from other nations to our own colleges, universities, and trade schools." Seamster suggested a minimum of a hundred thousand students a year.[46] Fulbright's friend had articulated an idea that had been formulating in his own mind, and he responded enthusiastically:

> Your views are in complete agreement with my own. The real trouble is as you have pointed out the quality of our leadership. . . . I think that our country has failed to attract into the government the best quality of man. Your suggestion about the exchange of students is a very appropriate one.[47]

When exactly Fulbright began considering the idea of a foreign exchange program is unclear. He would claim that the atomic bombing of Hiroshima and Nagasaki focused his thoughts. In the new age of mass destruction, world leaders could not afford to miscalculate. He was not ready to abandon internationalism by any means, but over the fall and winter of 1945 he had begun to have doubts about the willingness of the nations of the world to rely on the collective security organization to safeguard their interests. This, coupled with the cold reception given to his efforts to modify the American federal system, had frustrated and disillusioned him a bit. As he confided to a friend:

> I do not think that mere amendments to the Constitution or Charter or any other mechanical step will automatically bring about a system of law and order. While these changes are necessary, they are only part of the picture. The prejudices and misconceptions which exist in every country regarding foreign people are the great barrier to any system of government.[48]

In seeking a solution to the problem of international misunderstanding and ignorance in high places, it was natural for Fulbright to turn to his own background. In his opinion, the Rhodes experience had converted him from a narrow-gauged denizen of the American heartland into a citizen of the world. Why could not a broader version of the Oxford program do the same for the future leaders of the global village? His 1944 trip to England with Archibald MacLeish and the other members of the American delegation to explore the possibility of creating a United Nations cultural and educational organization had exposed the Arkansan to the needs and potential of the educational systems of other nations. Only four days after Roosevelt's death, Fulbright had

[46] Seamster to JWF, May 24, 1945, BCN 24, F32, SPF.
[47] JWF to Seamster, May 26, 1945, BCN 24, F32, SPF.
[48] JWF to George A. Horne, Feb. 6, 1946, BCN 24, F50, SPF.

told a radio audience that the "exchange of students, the exchange of professors, the translation of books . . . can contribute as much to the preservation of peace as the control of violence."[49] But how to fund such a program? Those members of the conservative coalition that dominated Congress who were not xenophobic were fiscal conservatives. There seemed to be little chance Congress would appropriate funds to pay for scholarly exchange.

The last week in September 1945 Fulbright attended a party in honor of the daughter of Mrs. Merriweather Post, one of Washington's wealthiest hostesses. There he encountered Oscar Cox and Herbert Elliston, the editor of the *Washington Post.* Seeing Cox brought an idea to Fulbright's mind. When he and Dean Acheson had presented the Lend–Lease renewal bill to the House Committee on Foreign Affairs, there had been much discussion of what to do with surplus property.[50] At war's end over four million items remained scattered in warehouses and storage depots around the globe, material that had been purchased with Lend–Lease funds but that America's allies had not had a chance to use. The value of these unused items was unclear; estimates varied from $60 million to $105 million. Surplus property included planes, trains, and tanks, as well as food, machine tools, clothing, telephones, and hospitals. The National Association of Manufacturers and other business groups had succeeded in having Congress pass in 1944 a measure prohibiting their repatriation to the United States;[51] the private sector did not want to have these government stockpiles dumped on its postwar market. Under the Lend–Lease Act, however, recipients were required to pay for those items not used. Fulbright, Cox, Hopkins, Clayton, and other internationalists did not want a new war-debts issue to plague international relations as it had in the aftermath of World War I. Perhaps, Mrs. Post's guests decided, proceeds from sale of surplus property could be used to fund Fulbright's exchange program.[52]

The following day, September 27, Fulbright rose on the floor of the Senate. "I ask unanimous consent to introduce a bill . . . authorizing the use of credits established through the sale of surplus properties abroad," he requested of a near-empty Senate chamber, "for the promotion of international good will through the exchange of students in the fields of education, culture, and science."[53] As he had hoped, no one paid the slightest attention to him. His remarks were not even mentioned in the afternoon newspapers. "The bill was potentially controversial," he later observed in a speech at the University of Colorado, "and I decided not to take the risk of an open appeal to the idealism

49 Quoted in Johnson and Gwertzman, *Fulbright: The Dissenter,* 129.
50 Fulbright interview.
51 Harry P. Jeffrey, "Legislative Origins of the Fulbright Program," *Annals of the American Academy of Political and Social Science,* 491 (May 1987), 41.
52 Fulbright interview.
53 Quoted in Johnson and Gwertzman, *Fulbright: The Dissenter,* 128

of my colleagues. . . . It occurred to me that the less attention the matter got the greater would be the chance of victory for idealism."[54]

Although Fulbright was perhaps remarkable for envisioning international exchange as a prerequisite for the proper functioning of any kind of world government, the idea of study abroad as a means of sharing knowledge and breaking down barriers was certainly not original with him. Indeed, the concept was as old as organized society itself. The development of Western civilization, and to a certain extent Eastern, had in large part been a study in the exchange of ideas and technology between cultures. That truth was lost on most Americans, however.

A dominant theme in U.S. history during the nation's first one hundred and fifty years had been isolationism, and an important component of the isolationist impulse was xenophobia. "Young man," Senator Kenneth McKellar of Tennessee would tell Fulbright after his proposal had passed, "that's a very dangerous piece of legislation . . . You're going to take our young boys and girls over there and expose them to those foreign isms."[55] Prior to World War II foreign travel was restricted to a very few categories of Americans. Statesmen, journalists, and political pundits like Walter Lippmann traveled, mostly in Europe, and interpreted the outside world to America and America to the outside world. Members of the East Coast aristocracy went on "grand tours" of the continent, most of them as parochial as the characters in Henry James's *Daisy Miller*. During the 1920s it became fashionable for alienated intellectuals to take up residence on the Left Bank in Paris. American contacts with Third World areas were limited mostly to missionaries and a handful of businessmen. These contacts, in Fulbright's view, had done little to break down the barriers created by prejudice and ignorance. What was needed was a systematic, long-range, permanent mechanism for the exchange of scholars and students. In a democracy like the United States the knowledge and understanding of other cultures would inevitably trickle down through the educational system to those who were not privileged to travel abroad.

With his bill submitted to the Committee on the Military, Fulbright set about lining up executive support. The White House gave its blessing, although the president "didn't know anything" about the bill, according to Fulbright, and did little to support it.[56] There were objections from other quarters, however. Bureau of the Budget (BOB) officials argued initially that the measure was unconstitutional; money received from surplus property sales had to be remitted to the Treasury and could not be earmarked for education without a specific appropriation bill from Congress. The State Department was dubious as well: This was a foreign policy matter, it sniffed, and foreign

54 Ibid., 129–30.
55 Fulbright interview.
56 Jeffrey, "Legislative Origins," 5–6.

policy initiatives should originate with Foggy Bottom. Besides, the Comintern could use the program to infiltrate its agents into the United States.

Fulbright counterattacked. Working through MacLeish and Clayton he convinced the State Department that spreading knowledge about American culture and values to foreign lands was one of the most effective means available for combating communism. He promised the BOB and Treasury that he would amend his bill to satisfy their reservations. Student exchange was going to be the only way the United States could ever realize any gain from its surplus Lend–Lease, he told conservatives.[57]

In November 1945 the Arkansan introduced a second and broader piece of legislation, one that like the first was couched as an amendment to the Surplus Property Act. It made the State Department the sole disposal agency for surplus property located outside the United States and its possessions. Such property could be paid for in foreign currencies or credits. The secretary of state was empowered to sign agreements with foreign governments to finance educational activities for Americans in other countries and foreign nationals in overseas American institutions, and to pay for transportation of visitors from abroad to study in the United States. Funding for the program would come entirely from foreign currency proceeds from the sale of surplus products abroad. His colleagues "didn't mind funny money," as Fulbright put it.[58]

Fortunately for Fulbright, the chair of the Subcommittee on Surplus Property of the Military Affairs Committee was Senator Joseph P. O'Mahoney (D–Wyoming). O'Mahoney was a graduate of Harvard Law School, cultured and intelligent – "very unusual for a Westerner," the Arkansan observed. Fulbright, who would later complain bitterly about his colleagues' refusal to attend SFRC hearings, made sure that when the appointed day for subcommittee hearings came around, only he and O'Mahoney showed up.[59]

At 10:00 A.M. on February 25, 1946, O'Mahoney brought his gavel down in the Public Lands and Survey Committee Room. Fulbright testified at length and submitted a long letter of support for the exchange program from former president Hoover, who in 1920 had helped found the Belgian–American Educational Foundation. The new assistant secretary of state for public and cultural relations, William Benton, appeared in behalf of Fulbright's measure. Benton – who would later serve in the Senate and, following his defeat by McCarthyites, publish the *Encyclopaedia Britannica* – declared that the Veterans Administration had received several thousand letters from former GIs desiring admission to foreign universities. To make the measure more palatable to Congress, Fulbright added amendments giving preference to veterans, requiring representation from all geographical regions of the country, and limiting aggregate spending in any one nation to $20 million. There was no need to include a provision dealing with countries having no surplus property. He

[57] Ibid., 42–3. [58] Fulbright interview. [59] Ibid.

realized, correctly, that once the program got underway and generated a constituency, political pressure would build for the establishment with appropriated funds of programs in nonsurplus countries. The important thing was to get a skeleton program in place. That the measure contained no provision for dollars to pay for operations in the United States was a calculated gamble by Fulbright. He was certain that his conservative and parochial colleagues would object to any proposal to use American tax dollars; somehow, government agencies using existing funds and working with private foundations would just have to see the program through until the political climate was more conducive to federal expenditures for cultural and educational purposes. Finally, Fulbright talked O'Mahoney out of inserting an antidiscrimination clause.[60] It would be best to let sleeping Bilbos lie.

On April 12, 1946, just six weeks after the subcommittee hearing, the Senate unanimously passed the Fulbright proposal with no debate and without a roll call vote. The bill's sponsor had taken great care to secure Republican support. Senator H. Alexander Smith of New Jersey, a Princeton graduate who had been a member of the Belgian Relief Commission, quietly lobbied his colleagues in behalf of the measure. When the appointed day arrived, Fulbright had made sure that only a handful of senators were present and that the irascible McKellar was off the floor. He had also taken care to clear the bill with the majority and minority leaders. At 5:00 in the afternoon he presented his exchange proposal as a routine measure under the unanimous consent calendar.[61]

The major stumbling block in the House was Mississippi Democrat Will Whittington, a high-ranking member of the Committee on Expenditures in the Executive Departments, to which the exchange bill was assigned. Told that Whittington would be a problem, Fulbright paid him a visit. "Well, if there's any money around for education," the Mississippian declared, "we need . . . [it] in Mississippi. . . . We're not interested in educating foreigners." Fulbright tried to explain that there was "a difference between a non-convertible German mark and a dollar that could be used in Mississippi," but Whittington wouldn't listen.[62] Fulbright believed that the real problem was institutional rivalry. "The House felt imposed upon," he recalled. "They all felt senators were too egotistical. He [Whittington] had no time for a goddamn upstart freshman senator."[63] In desperation, Fulbright turned to Will Clayton, who was a longtime political friend of Whittington's; more important, Anderson, Clayton, and Co. did a great deal of business in Whittington's home district. When the congressman subsequently switched his position, the House committee reported the exchange bill out just before the end of the session with a do-pass recommendation.

60 Jeffrey, "Legislative Origins," 44.
61 Ibid., 45.
62 Quoted in ibid.
63 Fulbright interview.

In the original draft of the 1946 legislation, Fulbright made no provision for a supervisory body; while the exchange proposal was under consideration in the House, however, he became convinced that such a capstone was needed in order to protect the program from political interference and short-term policy considerations. He subsequently appeared before the House Committee on Expenditures and offered an amendment providing for a ten-member, presidentially appointed Board of Foreign Scholarships to select participants and to provide general supervision for the exchange program.[64]

Though Fulbright claimed to be uncertain of the outcome, debate on the floor of the House lasted less than ten minutes, and the members passed the Arkansan's proposal unanimously. The Senate quickly approved the House-amended version on August 1, 1946, and as the session was ending, Harry Truman, with Fulbright standing beside him, signed the bill into law as PL 584.

Shortly thereafter, Assistant Secretary Benton announced that the State Department had completed an agreement with Great Britain to provide $20 million from the sale of surplus property for educational exchanges with the United Kingdom and its colonies. At the same time, Washington was negotiating agreements with more than twenty countries around the globe. Fulbright traveled extensively in Europe and Asia during the next two years in an effort to help explain the program to relevant American embassies and foreign governments.[65]

The original Fulbright Act provided for a wide variety of educational activities. The program would make grants to American students to finance the cost of higher education or research in foreign countries. American scholars and teachers could apply for grants to lecture at foreign institutions and conduct research abroad. In turn, foreign students and academicians were eligible to apply for travel grants to study, teach, and conduct research in the United States. As an alternative, they could apply for scholarships to study at American nondenominational institutions overseas, such as Robert College at Istanbul and the American University at Beirut.[66] Although the Fulbright Act vested in the State Department the authority to negotiate executive agreements for exchanges with foreign governments, it was the Board of Foreign Scholarships (BFS) that exercised overall supervisory powers.[67]

The most urgent task facing that first board appointed by President Truman was the establishment of criteria by which preliminary and final selections

64 Ralph H. Vogel, "The Making of the Fulbright Program," *Annals of the American Academy of Political and Social Science,* 491 (May 1987), 15.

65 *Congressional Record,* Senate, Aug. 2, 1946, A4766, and Fulbright interview.

66 Ibid., A4766.

67 Vogel, "Making of the Fulbright Program," 16.

would be made, and to devise ways and means to apply those criteria to the thousands of American and foreign-born individuals who would be applying for grants. Grantees, the board decided, would have to demonstrate excellence in their chosen field, be possessed of a character that would not scandalize the host country or discredit the sponsoring country, and be outgoing enough to establish contact and share knowledge with a maximum number of persons. After an individual student or scholar was selected by means of an open, national competition, the host country and institution would have veto power. Thus, no country or institution would be able to foist unwanted persons on other nations or universities.[68] In each of the foreign countries with which agreements were signed, binational commissions, comprising academics and government officials who were either citizens of that country or who were U.S. citizens living in the host country, were established to perform the functions that the BFS performed in America.

In 1948 the Fulbright Exchange Program got underway when thirty-five students and one professor came to the United States and sixty-five Americans ventured overseas. Two decades later exchange programs had been set up with 110 countries and geographical areas under forty-nine formal exchange agreements. Total cost of the program to the United States during this period was $400 million, mostly in foreign currencies. During 1948–66, 82,585 individuals – 47,950 of them students – received Fulbright scholarships. Twelve million schoolchildren in the United States and abroad were taught by exchange teachers.[69] As of 1987 the program could claim 156,000 alumni in the United States and abroad.[70] In 1945 virtually no university in Europe had taught American history except as part of the history of Europe. Oxford and the University of London boasted endowed chairs in American history, but they were exceptions to the rule. At a time when the United States was emerging as the most powerful and influential nation in the world, little was known of its culture and history. In part because of the Fulbright program, every nation in Western Europe offered American studies by 1964 and many had established chairs in American history, literature, or civilization.

68 Ibid., 17.

69 Over the years the Fulbright program was expanded several times. In 1948 Congress approved the United States Information and Educational Exchange Act, empowering the State Department to seek appropriations to pay some dollar expenses of foreign grantees, as well as to carry out academic exchanges in countries with minimal surplus property sales. In 1953 and 1954 the House and Senate gave permission to use other foreign currencies owed the United States, most notably from surplus agricultural commodity sales abroad, to finance educational exchange. This was an important step because in some countries surplus property proceeds were already exhausted. In the mid-1950s Congress also authorized the extension of exchanges to additional countries, including eight in Latin America, where previously there had been none. Vogel, "Making of the Fulbright Program," 14. Finally, in 1961, the Fulbright–Hays Act brought together the various pieces of legislation affecting educational exchanges.

70 Ibid., 11.

Thus began a program that Fulbright's Oxford tutor would describe as "the largest and most significant movement of scholars across the earth since the fall of Constantinople in 1453."[71]

The exchange program was one of the few things in Fulbright's life about which he felt passionately. In its defense he could become emotional, irrational, vindictive. During the course of his public life he would work assiduously to maintain and increase its funding. Those who wished to hurt him came quickly to realize that the way to do it was by damaging the exchange program. Indeed, international education became something of a religion for a man whom nearly everyone described as nonreligious. To his mind it was a panacea for the world's problems. Its working would produce a kind of international talented tenth that would lead humanity into a new era of cooperation based on mutual understanding. Its products would be public-spirited rationalists who would understand that war is the ultimate folly of *Homo sapiens.*

World War II, the Holocaust, and the atomic bomb spawned an entire generation of men and women who not only dreamed dreams of brave new worlds, but designed mechanisms to give substance to their vision. For John Maynard Keynes it was the IMF and the World Bank, for Winston Churchill a union of the English-speaking peoples, and for J. William Fulbright an educational exchange program. As these architects of hope would soon learn, however, neither World War II nor their creations were sufficient to eradicate the nationalism, prejudice, avarice, and xenophobia that they so feared.

[71] Quoted in Johnson and Gwertzman, *Fulbright: The Dissenter,* 128.

# 7

# *European federation and trickle-down integration*

On March 7 Harry S. Truman addressed a dramatic joint session of Congress. He described the political situation in the eastern Mediterranean, where communist-led guerrillas were threatening the pro-Western monarchy in Greece and the Soviets were pressuring the Greek government to grant it the right to build bases on the Bosporus and other strategic locations. He asked for $400 million in aid to shore up the Greek monarchy in its struggle with the EAS/ELAM and to enable Turkey to resist Soviet aggression. More important, he announced that it would be his administration's policy to aid any nation threatened by internal communist subversion or external communist aggression. Led by the Soviet Union, the forces of international communism had tossed down the gauntlet; only the United States was capable of picking it up. The president's address was of monumental importance: He was asking Congress to support a military and economic aid package that would, for the first time in the nation's history, involve it in Europe's political and military concerns during peacetime. More than that, he was asking America to assume global responsibility for keeping the peace. Truman made it clear that Greece and Turkey were but examples of a broader threat to freedom. In the past, Americans had identified aggression with direct action engaged in by armies that crossed clearly identifiable frontiers. The present danger, he warned, came from "armed minorities" and "outside pressures" that were nearly impossible to trace to national origins. Truman left immediately after the speech to vacation in Key West, Florida, and await the nation's reaction.

During the congressional hearings on what the press quickly dubbed "the Truman Doctrine," the president's proposals came under attack from liberal senators. The Greek government was undemocratic, corrupt, and reactionary, they pointed out, and Turkey was not a democracy and had remained neutral during most of World War II. Why not, these critics asked, let Greece and Turkey pass into the communist world? The two nations would simply be changing one form of undemocratic government for another. The Truman administration could only answer that, with economic help, Greece might gradually embrace democracy, and Turkey was already moving away from the autocratic era of Mustafa Kemal. Under noncommunist regimes, the future was at least hopeful, whereas under communist rule it was sure to be dark indeed. Fulbright agreed.[1]

Let there be no mistake about the seriousness of the threat posed by international communism, the junior senator from Arkansas told the Senate. Russia had "brought to a higher state of perfection than anyone else the technique of infiltration and corruption from within."[2] Only Nazi Germany was comparable in modern history. The United Nations was simply not yet strong enough to maintain the collective security. "Until we can achieve a system of law among nations," he confided, "the ancient principle of balance of power is the only alternative."[3] When doubters in the Senate charged that the Truman Doctrine contravened internationalism, Fulbright observed that "Russia has already used the veto on 10 different occasions and, I have no doubt, would use it against aid to Greece if she were given the opportunity."

On May 22 the House voted to approve the Greek–Turkish aid package by a vote of 287 to 107 in the House and 67 to 23 in the Senate. Not only was the junior senator from Arkansas present at the creation of the containment policy, he was one of its architects.

Despite his vigorous public support for the Truman Doctrine, Fulbright was troubled by the magnitude and open-ended quality of the commitment the United States was assuming. "I admit that we are faced with far greater obligations than we anticipated by reason of the apparent crumbling of the British Empire," he told the Senate.[4] "If we undertake the support of Greece and Turkey, how and when can we stop the lavish outpouring of our resources?" The answer, Fulbright decided, was a supranational federation. On March 21, 1947, he and Senator Elbert Thomas of Utah introduced a concurrent resolution stating that "Congress favors the creation of a United States of Europe within the framework of the United Nations."[5] For the next five years Fulbright would hold up the idea of European federation as an alternative to an anemic internationalism and a perilous and expensive pax Americana.

Fulbright insisted that the continent was a single cultural entity and that the notion of a united Europe dated back at least to Metternich and the Congress of Vienna. For him, however, the most compelling argument for unification was economic. The Arkansan had been deeply impressed by Hanson Baldwin's reports in the *New York Times,* as well as by Fodor's commentaries, on the privation and pestilence that had overtaken Europe since the end of World War II. The continent had never recovered from the devastation of

[1] Fulbright had expressed his views on the situation in the Near East only months after the civil war in Greece began. See JWF to Lee Hall, Jan. 11, 1945, BCN 46, F4, and Fodor to JWF, Jan. 15, 1945, BCN 67, F24, SPF.

[2] *Congressional Record,* Senate, Apr. 7, 1947, 3137.

[3] JWF to George C. Collier, Mar. 27, 1947, BCN 46, F4, SPF.

[4] *Congressional Record,* Senate, Mar. 3, 1947, 1590.

[5] Ibid., Apr. 7, 1947, 3138.

war, and the harshest winter in twenty years coupled with springtime floods had made matters even worse. It was in these conditions that communism flourished, Fulbright argued. Men and women would always be willing to relinquish their freedom in return for promises of social and economic security. America could provide a minimal amount of aid, but if Europe were to attain lasting prosperity, and thus democracy, its national components would have to integrate their economies. Finally, he argued, unification promised to deal with the problem of aggressive nationalism. Within a federation of Europe, the victors of World War II could control Germany, ensuring that it did not use its industrial and technical might in another insane attempt to conquer the world. In turn, with its fears concerning German aggression laid to rest, the Kremlin might cease its expansionist policies and remove its boot from the nape of Eastern Europe's neck. A United States of Europe (USE) would preserve existing power relationships until the Unatied Nations had a chance "to succeed as a voluntary union of peoples" and "assist Russia to develop the self-restraint which is so patently lacking in her present philosophy of government."[6]

Fulbright had been persuaded by Walter Lippmann to avoid portraying the United States of Europe as an overtly anti-Soviet bloc; rather, any such union should have "an open end towards Eastern Europe."[7] As a result, Fulbright proposed that the fourteen noncommunist states of Europe create a political community that any and all European nations could join. As the economic and political advantages of the USE became manifest, the communist satellite states established in the aftermath of World War II might pull away from the Kremlin and join the new coalition.

Fulbright's advocacy first of the United Nations and then of a United States of Europe placed him squarely in the center of the supranationalist movement that culminated during and after World War II. Journalists, clergymen, social activists, and political figures who comprised the movement were essentially realists, not ivory-tower dreamers as the neoisolationists would have had the world believe. In countless speeches and articles Emery Reeves, Clarence Streit, and other world federalists argued that, because of economic interdependence and industrialism's need for a borderless world, the nation-state could no longer ensure prosperity for its citizens; and due to the basic aggressiveness of forces armed with modern weapons and organized into closely competing political units, national governments would prove unable to ensure the physical security of their citizens as well.[8] In short, nation-states were no longer fulfilling the purpose for which they were created. So

6 Ibid.

7 Lippmann to JWF, Apr. 3, 1947, Papers of Hoyt Purvis, Mullins Library, University of Arkansas, Fayetteville, Ark.

8 See Wesley T. Wooley, *Alternatives to Anarchy: American Supranationalism since World War II* (Bloomington, Ind., 1988), 17.

in tune were Fulbright's ideas with those of other members of the supranationalist movement, that he was seriously considered for the presidency of the United World Federalists at its organizational meeting at Asheville, North Carolina, in February 1947.[9]

Rather quickly, however, Fulbright decided that the world was still too culturally, politically, and geographically diverse, that nationalism was still too strong for the notion of an all-encompassing world government to work. "I have long been interested in his [Clarence Streit's] ideas," he wrote a world federalist, "but our experience with the United Nations has been disappointing. There is no question but that the underlying theory of the Federal Union is correct but to make progress toward it as a practical political matter is exceedingly difficult."[10] Shortening his sights, he proposed to apply the principles of world federalism to a particular region, Europe. The onset of the cold war and the threat posed by international communism made it impossible for the Western democracies to wait until the United Nations matured. If Russia were to be contained and Europe rehabilitated without bankrupting America, the Continent would have to federate economically and politically. In time, as passions cooled and suspicions subsided, and as welfare capitalism had a chance to prove its superiority, the other states of Europe could join the federation. Safe and secure within its new community, the Western democracies could afford to wait for Soviet communism to mellow and the United Nations to catch up.

The Truman administration and its cold-war allies in the press were not so much hostile to Fulbright's proposal for a federation of Europe as they were to the timing of it. To their collective mind the situation on the other side of the Atlantic was so critical that the free world could not wait for Europe to write and ratify a constitution that would establish political union. Economic integration was a different matter, however.

The Truman Doctrine, as numerous historians have observed, comprised both America's declaration of cold war and a stratagem for winning that war; but as a policy it had very real limitations. Defense-oriented, the doctrine was designed to enable friendly governments to resist a communist takeover by force, but it did nothing to alleviate the hunger, homelessness, unemployment, and disease that had created conditions favorable to the success of Soviet-backed communist parties in Western Europe.

After conferring with his subordinates in the State Department, Secretary of State Marshall used the occasion of his commencement address at Harvard on June 5, 1947, to call upon Britain and the nations of the Continent to frame an integrated plan for their collective recovery. When it had devised such a scheme, Europe could count on the United States to supply "friendly aid." Fulbright was an enthusiastic supporter of the European Recovery Pro-

9 Ibid., 19, 34. 10 JWF to Edmund Orgill, Dec. 1, 1947, BCN 43, F70, SPF.

gram (ERP), or Marshall Plan as it came to be known; indeed his Senate address in behalf of the Truman Doctrine had anticipated it. As a converted cold warrior, he saw the program as the economic side of the containment policy – although he believed it to be, like the Truman Doctrine, a Band-Aid solution for a major, long-term problem. He was more enthusiastic about the ERP, however, because he hoped that economic integration might smooth the way for political union.

The first week in May, Fulbright took to the floor of the Senate in an effort to persuade his colleagues and the administration that the economic rehabilitation of Europe would be pointless without political unification. Fulbright was convinced that the United States of Europe was an idea that would appeal simultaneously to isolationists and economic nationalists, to cold-war zealots, and to internationalists. He was beginning to doubt, he told conservatives, the wisdom of pouring money into Europe without a long-term plan that would lead to the Continent's economic self-sufficiency. To internationalists he argued that only within a federation could economic interdependence be achieved and Europe's traditional obsession with national sovereignty be redirected. To Russophobes and anticommunists he made the argument that a United States of Europe was necessary to concentrate the economic, military, and cultural energies of the continent for the coming struggle with the Soviet bloc. Time was short: If the West waited until the situation in Europe "stabilized," it would be too late. Led by the United States, proponents of a regional federation should act while the Continent was still in chaos.[11] That address was to be the first of many in behalf of European federation.

On consecutive nights the first week in December Fulbright delivered the Marfleet Lectures at the University of Toronto. The Arkansan was the eighth holder of the prestigious lectureship and followed, among others, William Howard Taft. His address, entitled "The New World Looks at the Old World," surveyed the various justifications for a federation of Europe, but its principal point was that a United States of Europe was the only alternative to a communist takeover of the Western democracies.

> The continent, in its present fragmentary form, is a large power vacuum which Russia is striving to fill. Let us be under no illusions. If Russia obtains control of Western Europe, the control of Africa, the Near East, and the Middle East will fall into her lap like a ripe plum. Russia will then control not only the heartland but the whole world island; and Europe, Asia, and Africa will become the arsenal of the Slavs. It is no longer a question of Europe's ruling or not ruling dependencies and tropical and backward countries. The question now is, will Europe in her turn be ruled?[12]

11 *Congressional Record,* Senate, May 13, 1947, 6248.

12 JWF, "The New World Looks at the Old World," Marfleet Lectures, Dec. 8 and 9, 1947, BCN 73, F8, SPF.

The national passions and jealousies that had plagued Europe for the previous seven hundred years, coupled with the Truman administration's ironclad determination to avoid being labeled imperialists by the Eurocommunists, proved to be insurmountable obstacles to political union, however. While expressing his agreement "in principle" with the idea of a United States of Europe, the powerful, egotistical, and astonishingly limited chairman of the SFRC, Arthur Vandenberg, consistently opposed any concrete action by Congress to pressure either the administration or Europe to form a political union. The Truman administration was no more enthusiastic. A week before Marshall's famous Harvard address, Vandenberg wrote the secretary of state asking his opinion of the Fulbright–Thomas resolution. "I am deeply sympathetic toward the general objective," he replied, but the United States had to make it clear that it did not intend to controvert the hallowed principle of national self-determination.[13] Marshall's response disgusted Fulbright, who derided it as "unduly timid and cautious."[14] Undaunted, the Arkansan offered an amendment to the Economic Cooperation Act, taken up by Congress in March 1948, that encouraged political as well as economic union; but in the face of administration opposition, it got nowhere.[15]

As he would so often in the future, Fulbright attempted to rally support in the press and the eastern establishment for the notion of a United States of Europe. Such journalistic luminaries as Drew Pearson and Walter Lippmann wrote columns endorsing the concept of political unification. In May of 1948 a diverse group including 1924 Democratic presidential candidate John W. Davis, former president Herbert Hoover, former isolationist senators Robert LaFollette and Burton Wheeler, Congressmen Hale Boggs of Louisiana and Christian Herter of Massachusetts, and even Clare Booth Luce came together to form the American Committee for a Free and United Europe. Not surprisingly, they elected J. William Fulbright as their first president.[16] That fall the junior senator from Arkansas toured Western Europe lobbying French, British, and Italian officials in behalf of political unification.[17]

Throughout the winter and spring of 1948–9 Fulbright received report after depressing report on the unwillingness of the European nations to cooperate with each other even in the economic realm. The recipients of Marshall Plan aid submitted nineteen separate requests for aid rather than one integrated plan. Moreover, wrote a Foreign Service officer stationed in Paris, "the

13 JWF to Gene Farmer, Oct. 12, 1948, BCN 119, F21, and Joseph A. Brandt to JWF, Dec. 1, 1948, BCN 73, F6, SPF.

14 *Congressional Record,* Senate, June 13, 1947, 6957.

15 Ibid., Mar. 3, 1948, 2030–41.

16 Ibid., June 11, 1948, 7817, and JWF to Adlai Turner, May 1, 1948, BCN 37, F31, SPF.

17 JWF to Fodor, Mar. 11, 1949, BCN 105, F29, SPF.

various country programs as presented to the OEEC [Organization of European Economic Cooperation] each showed an alarming trend toward economic self-sufficiency and nationalism."[18] Following one of his grand tours of the Continent, Lippmann confided to Fulbright that "Cripps [Sir Stafford Cripps, British chancellor of the exchequer] admitted to me privately that he would much rather go it alone, and not be obligated to make agreements with the other European nations." This was "a major defeat of a declared American purpose" he told Fulbright, and "worthy of a major speech . . . by you."[19]

Although Walter Lippmann was never loath to give advice to anyone, there was no presumption in his suggestion to Fulbright. The two men had become close friends. As America approached midcentury, Lippmann was reaching the height of his power and influence. His column, "Today and Tomorrow," was the most widely syndicated in America. He personified the term "political pundit." Cofounder of the *New Republic*, editor of the New York *World,* and author of more than a dozen books on public life, Lippmann was a man whose intellect and friendships stretched from the moderate left – Learned Hand and Louis Brandeis – to the enlightened right – Thomas Lamont and Wendell Wilkie.[20] He had advised presidents from Wilson to Roosevelt, and had an opinion on everything. Fulbright had first met Lippmann at a Washington social function shortly after his election to the House. Fulbright's education, his conversational skills, his capacity for analysis and criticism – Lippmann's forte – plus Betty's social acumen elicited frequent dinner invitations from the socially active Lippmanns. For the next quarter century Fulbright and Lippmann would nurture each other intellectually and politically.

In January 1949 as the Senate prepared to take up the North Atlantic Treaty and to consider renewing the Economic Cooperation Act, Fulbright and Elbert Thomas again introduced a concurrent resolution putting Congress on record as favoring the political federation of Europe. Opponents insisted that it was the old "Fortress America" argument in disguise. The real motive behind the United States of Europe idea, editorialized the *New York Times,* was a desire to see America avoid any responsibility for the economic, military, or political well-being of Europe. The Arkansan angrily rejected the *Times*'s charge. He sensed that America's willingness to commit funds and troops to Europe was limited and dependent primarily on the continuation of a high level of Russophobia and cold-war hysteria. The sooner the Continent became self-sufficient, the sooner all parties concerned could set about conducting their

18 Hoyt Price to JWF, Jan. 15, 1949, BCN 46, F5, SPF.
19 Lippmann to JWF, Mar. 11, 1949, BCN 46, F6, SPF.
20 See Ronald Steel, *Walter Lippmann and the American Century* (Boston, 1980).

business on a sensible, rational basis. Nevertheless, the Fulbright–Thomas resolution died.[21]

Fulbright's disappointment and frustration at his inability to sell his United States of Europe idea was ameliorated when, with the Democrats' reconquest of Congress in 1948, he was appointed to the Senate Foreign Relations Committee. For the next quarter century he would use it as a forum from which to espouse his ideas on U.S. foreign policy.

Despite the perceived need to protect Western civilization from communism's advancing hordes and his desire to spread the virtues of federalism and republicanism, Bill Fulbright was never too busy to attend to family business affairs. In long, single-spaced letters he advised the Fayetteville managerial corps on every aspect of their enterprises. He looked for markets for their products. He pleaded with suppliers for extra newsprint – in very short supply after the war – for the family's newspaper, and he worked to reduce tariffs on sugar and subsidies for sugar growers so that the Fulbright Coca-Cola plant would have an adequate and cheap supply of the precious stuff.[22]

For the most part, Fulbright's advice was duly noted in Fayetteville and then filed away. The empire already had an overseer, and a quite competent one. Late in 1944 Bill, Roberta, and the family business got a tremendous boost when Hal Douglas, Helen's husband, obtained his release from the Navy. At Roberta's urging Hal decided to return to Fayetteville and act as her surrogate in all matters. Shortly after his arrival, Douglas set up an office in the *Northwest Arkansas Times* building and began establishing his authority. He left Phipps Lumber pretty much on its own and concentrated instead on the more profitable Fayetteville Ice Co. and on the newspaper. His obsession, however, was property. Mixing his money with that of the family corporation, he began buying real estate, office buildings, and investing in newspapers and radio stations across northwest Arkansas. The business quickly became a Hal and Bill show. As Susie Zorn, Anna Fulbright Teasdale's daughter, put it: "The girls weren't included. Hal and Bill did it all. It was traditional. My mother was resentful, but she didn't know what to do. It was a kind of free-floating resentment." Still, until much later Hal was very popular with the family. "I loved Hal from the time I was a little girl," Zorn recalled. "He had charisma. You wanted to please him but he wasn't standoffish. You didn't feel like you'd won something like you did when you got Bill's attention."[23]

21 *Congressional Record,* Senate, Jan. 31, 1949, 703.

22 JWF to George Meade, Mar. 28, 1947, BCN 105, F22, and JWF to Hal Douglas, May 22, 1945, BCN 105, F10, SPF.

23 Interview with Susie Zorn, July 23, 1989, Fayetteville, Ark.

Most important, Hal managed to stay continuously in Roberta's good graces. As soon as he crossed the threshold in the evenings until he went to bed, Hal and his mother-in-law discussed the day's events. Helen cooked and served dinner and put the Douglas kids, Doug and Ann, to bed and then went upstairs to read. She became increasingly depressed. "They treated Helen exactly like she was the hired help," Allan Gilbert recalled. "Hal, too. Paid no attention to her at all. They didn't have friends, play bridge."[24]

In 1950 Roberta was seventy-six years old. Her occasional columns were fitful, irregular, and at times silly. Yet, she still enjoyed herself. There was the same revolving door of guests, university faculty, the Washington Avenue crowd, employees, and local dignitaries. Roberta never learned to drive but loved automobile rides, to which she insisted on being treated at frequent intervals. Driver and passengers were inevitably subjected to long monologues on the world according to Roberta.

Indeed, the matriarch of Mount Nord had become famous for her garrulousness. One Saturday morning an unfortunate youth appeared at her doorstep. He was taking a religious census, he said. What church did she belong to? Four hours later after a complete history of which relative belonged to which church, the shell-shocked census taker managed to extricate himself. On another occasion, Roberta attended an important local church meeting where the faithful had gathered to discuss the pros and cons of a building expansion. In middebate she rose and delivered a thirty-minute discourse on the dangers of overextension. "But Mrs. Fulbright," declared the incredulous presiding elder, "you're not a member of this church!"[25] "It's forever up to me to be telling folks what they should do," she wrote Bill, "and they don't like it."[26]

There was a certain insensitivity to Roberta Fulbright, a self-centeredness that degenerated into narcissism as she grew older. Though these traits were a natural outgrowth of her personality and the life of self-reliance that events imposed upon her, they blinded her to the plight of her children, especially the women. Helen eventually suffered a nervous breakdown that required treatment at the Menninger Clinic in Topeka, Kansas. Roberta, the other twin, played out the life of a spoiled rich woman. Her marriage with hard-driving Gilbert Swanson foundered, and she would die a premature death. In the late 1940s, however, these troubles were only clouds on a distant horizon.

As busy as their Washington life was, Bill, Betty, Betsy, and Bosey didn't miss a Christmas in Fayetteville. "We were great Christmasers," Susie Zorn recalled. Anna, her mother, married to prominent St. Louis attorney Kenneth Teasdale, never felt truly at home anywhere else during the holiday season.

24 Interview with Allen Gilbert, Oct. 17, 1989, Fayetteville, Ark.
25 Zorn interview.
26 Roberta Fulbright to JWF, Dec. 1, 1944, BCN 5, F31, SPF.

Everyone, including Jack and his family, spent at least ten days at Mount Nord, delighting Roberta and exhausting Helen.[27]

Fulbright had repeatedly appealed to his colleagues to let democracy rule, but for a southern senator dedicated to preserving the region's entrenched caste system, democracy could be a two-edged sword. Though not an advocate of integration per se, Harry Truman believed that African Americans were being discriminated against and were entitled to education, welfare, jobs, and ballots. He was certain as well that if the administration continued to countenance these injustices, blacks would desert the New Deal voting coalition that Franklin Roosevelt had forged in 1936. Increasingly, he accepted the need for greater federal action. In December 1946, in the face of appalling violence in the South earlier that year and the Democratic defeat in November, Truman appointed a biracial committee of distinguished Americans to study the race problem and make recommendations. The committee conducted its business in the midst of one of the darkest and most violent periods in American race relations since the white backlash that had followed World War I. The Detroit race riots of 1943 were only four years in the past; it was, as Robert Donovan has put it, "an age of Jim Crow, white supremacy, states' rights, 'we don't serve colored here,' 'separate but equal' but unequal, 'Nigras,' 'niggers,' 'boy,' 'white only,' a revived Ku Klux Klan, indifference, patronization, police brutality, Gerald L. K. Smith, malign neglect."[28]

In its report, *To Secure These Rights,* the committee recommended that the Civil Rights Section of the Justice Department be made a full division and that the president establish a permanent Commission on Civil Rights. Federal antilynching and anti–poll tax laws were essential, the committee insisted, because blacks continued to be systematically terrorized and disfranchised in certain parts of the country. State power was as often used to oppress black citizens as to protect and liberate them. *To Secure These Rights* called for the abolition of de jure and de facto segregation and proposed once again a Fair Employment Practices Commission to eliminate discrimination in private employment. On February 2 Truman stunned and enraged southerners by sending to the Hill a "Special Message to the Congress on Civil Rights" in which he called for legislative enactment of the recommendations set out in *To Secure These Rights.* Truman's message created a breech in the Democratic Party that appeared irreparable.

On February 7, 1948, the Southern Governors' Conference met in Wakull Springs, Florida, and discussion immediately focused on the administration's

27 Zorn interview.

28 Robert Donovan, *Conflict and Crisis: The Presidency of Harry S. Truman, 1945–1948* (New York, 1977), 334.

civil rights proposals. Governor Fielding Wright of Mississippi suggested that the assembled state executives notify Democratic Party leaders that they were unwilling to stand idly by while the party conducted a civil rights campaign, and he called for the convening of "a Southern conference of true Democrats" in Jackson on March 1. The governors adopted a resolution proposed by Governor J. Strom Thurmond of South Carolina denouncing "the spectacle of the political parties of this country engaging in competitive bidding for the votes of small pressure groups by attacking the traditions, customs, and institutions of the section in which we live."[29]

Racial hatred in Arkansas was not as virulent as it was in Mississippi or South Carolina. The state's attorney general, Guy Williams, agreed to come to Washington in 1948 and testify against anti–poll tax legislation, but not the antilynching bill.[30] Nonetheless, the state was hardly ready to embrace Henry Wallace or Aubrey Williams, who from his limited forum as editor of *Southern Farmer* was denouncing the poll tax, Jim Crowism, lynching, and job discrimination as undemocratic and un-Christian.[31] Even such self-styled Arkansas liberals as Harry Ashmore publicly defended aspects of Jim Crow in 1948.[32] The status of Arkansas's African-American population was a reflection of the racial views of the state's white majority, the timidity of liberals, and the persistence of racism.[33]

The number of African Americans voting in the Arkansas Democratic primary had increased from four thousand to forty-seven thousand during the period following World War II,[34] but most of those were bought or otherwise controlled by the local courthouse machines. Statewide, blacks were not in a position to threaten the balance of power. Only nine of the state's seventy-five counties (Chicot, Crittenden, Desha, Jefferson, Lee, Lincoln, Monroe, Phillips, and St. Francis) had a black majority (totaling, however, nearly two hundred thousand people). Over three-quarters of the state's black population were sharecroppers or farm laborers.[35] Although many of these were cash renters or owners, they were denied equal protection under the law, faced almost insurmountable difficulty in obtaining credit, and could not even buy insurance.

On February 9, two days after the Southern Governors' Conference, Strom Thurmond sent Fulbright a copy of his resolution and asked him to partici-

29 Thurmond to JWF, Feb. 17, 1948, BCN 48, F1, SPF.
30 Williams to JWF, Jan. 14, 1948, BCN 48, F1, and JWF to Williams, Mar. 6, 1948, BCN 48, F1, SPF.
31 Williams to Fielding Wright, Feb. 28, 1948, BCN 438, F1, SPF.
32 "Segregation in South Defended by Two Editors," *Arkansas Gazette,* Nov. 10, 1947.
33 See, for example, Woman's Auxiliary to JWF, Apr. 19, 1947, BCN 30, F23, and Margaret Rhinehart to JWF, May 6, 1947, BCN 30, F23, SPF.
34 *Arkansas Gazette,* July 31, 1948.
35 "Total Population and Negro Population," 1940, BCN 74, F15, SPF.

pate in forthcoming strategy sessions. The Arkansan complimented Thurmond on his resolution but refused the invitation.[36] Fulbright believed that the president was "using bad judgment in pushing this kind of issue at this time," as he wrote Suzanne Chalfant Lighton, a Fayetteville attorney and racial moderate, but he had no desire to participate in any kind of organized political rebellion.[37] To Herbert Thomas he wrote:

> It seems to me that the Southern Governors are going too far in their proposals to withdraw. I have a feeling that if their policies are followed that it can only result in the disintegration of our party and that we would be in for a long Republican rule of from ten to twenty years. The South has never had fair treatment under such a regime and there is no reason to believe that we would get any better treatment this time.[38]

Southerners should feel free to oppose Truman for the nomination, Fulbright continued; but once he got it, if he did, they should fall in line.

Throughout 1948 Fulbright vacillated between wanting to lead a counterattack against northern liberals who were pushing civil rights legislation, and wanting to play the role of conciliator and compromiser. Because he represented Arkansas, Fulbright was automatically accorded membership in a group of twenty-one Dixie senators who met regularly in Senator Richard Russell's (D–Georgia) office to devise ways and means to protect the South from civil rights crusaders. While Fulbright was repelled by Bilbo, Eastland, and other extremists who participated in the meetings, he was absolutely charmed by Russell. The "sage of Winder" (Russell's home town just outside of Atlanta) was then the most powerful man in the United States Senate. Courtly, articulate, tireless, this lawyer-bachelor devoted his life to the Senate, his only real diversion being baseball. Steeped in the traditions of the upper house, he was a master of parliamentary procedure and an assiduous compiler of favors. Despite being a virulent racist, he never let his violent prejudices destroy his personal and political relationships with his colleagues. According to William Rogers, who as assistant attorney general in the Eisenhower administration maintained an excellent relationship with southerners in Congress, Russell always fought by the rules and acted in accordance with his stated principles.[39] As he did with other freshmen, Russell took Fulbright under his wing, guided and protected him.

Fulbright was infuriated by the anti-South speeches and editorials that poured out of the North in the wake of publication of *To Secure These*

[36] Thurmond to JWF, Feb. 9, 1948, and JWF to Thurmond, Feb. 17, 1948, BCN 48, F1, SPF.
[37] JWF to Lighton, Feb. 26, 1948, BCN 48, F1, SPF.
[38] JWF to Thomas, Mar. 15, 1948, BCN 48, F1, SPF.
[39] Interview with William P. Rogers, May 3, 1993, Washington, D.C.

*Rights.* He had printed in the *Congressional Record* an article by Hodding Carter entitled "What's Wrong with the North." It was a savage parody of the northern stereotype of the South. Nowhere, Carter argued, was racial and religious hatred more intense than in New York, Boston, and Chicago: Catholic against Jew, black against white, Irish against Italian. The typical northerner was insecure, isolated, threatened daily by crime, strikes, and rampant materialism. Clearly, the region had a monopoly on neurotics, including "dipsomaniacs, abnormal sex delinquents, divorced couples, Communists, and phony artistic faddists." Fulbright gleefully endorsed Carter's solution to the "northern problem": "Scatter the North's industries in a southerly direction, with Mississippi as the focal point, disperse its population in a different direction and end its political domination by reducing New York, Pennsylvania and possibly Massachusetts to territorial status."[40]

Shortly after Harry Truman delivered his "Message on Civil Rights," Fulbright broached a plan with Russell that he had been talking over with his old friend, Herbert Thomas. What the two Fayettevillians proposed was that the South take the initiative in the area of civil rights and insist on federal laws outlawing discrimination based on race, religion, or national origin everywhere. First should come repeal of the immigration quota system. "Why should Boston object to there being a fifty–fifty population of Jews and Irish Catholics?" All restrictions on and qualifications for voting would be abolished. Hotels, clubs, and theaters as well as schools would be open to all races. The president would be required to select a cabinet reflecting the ethnic makeup of the country. Finally, the federal government would levy a special tax on all raw materials removed from the South, the proceeds of which would be used to fund Negro education.[41]

The Fulbright–Thomas plan, which gained Russell's approval, was only partially facetious. The object of the exercise was to put pressure on northern liberals to compromise. In fact, Fulbright and Russell, if not Thurmond and Eastland, believed that an agreement on the poll tax and lynching was both inevitable and necessary.[42] Fulbright operated on the assumption that liberal Democrats and Republicans were strong enough, despite the filibuster, to push through a comprehensive civil rights program at any time they wanted. What he proposed was a trade-off: southern support for anti–poll tax and antilynching legislation in return for northern acquiescence in segregation and discrimination in hiring. If the South counterattacked vigorously and then offered half a loaf, civil rights advocates in Congress were likely to accept.

Meanwhile, the movement within the Democratic Party to dump Truman was growing stronger by the day. Confided Fulbright to Ashmore:

40 *Congressional Record,* Senate, Aug. 10, 1949, A5431.

41 JWF to Thomas, Mar. 15, 1948, and Thomas to JWF, Mar. 10, 1948, BCN 48, F1, SPF.

42 JWF to R. T. Colquette, Mar. 22, 1948, BCN 48, F1, SPF.

> I hear more persistent rumors that the leaders in Chicago and New York feel that with Truman as the candidate not only will the Democrats lose the national election but that they are in grave danger of losing their local battles, I believe there is a growing desire on the part of some of these leaders in the North to try to agree with the southerners on a candidate which could have the effect of keeping the party together.[43]

Alben Barkley from the border state of Kentucky was mentioned as the most likely alternative. Democratic leaders were not sure that they could win with Barkley, however, and as the presidential nominating convention drew near, they desperately courted Dwight Eisenhower.

The Democratic Convention assembled in July in Philadelphia. It was Fulbright's first, and he was appalled. The anticipated fight between the southern Democrats and the Americans for Democratic Action – led by then-Mayor of Minneapolis Hubert Humphrey – materialized instantly. Following a bitter floor fight, the delegates adopted a civil rights plank demanding an FEPC and federal antilynching and anti–poll tax legislation. Finally, the agitated and haggard delegates named Truman to be their standard-bearer in 1948.

Although the Democratic Party split into three factions – the left-wing coalescing around Henry Wallace to form the Progressive Party, the right around Strom Thurmond to create the States Rights Democratic Party (Dixiecrats), and the center remaining with Truman – the president handily defeated his GOP opponent, the progressive but relentlessly cautious Thomas Dewey of New York. The Democrats not only retained the White House in 1948 but recaptured control of Congress as well. This, coupled with the poor showing of the Dixiecrats – Thurmond had polled a million votes and carried only four states of the deep South – persuaded the administration and the party leadership that they could afford to challenge the South over civil rights. The president made it clear that when the new Congress opened, he would once again press for enactment of an anti–poll tax bill, an antilynching law, and an FEPC.

Over the winter of 1948–9 Fulbright and other moderates maneuvered desperately to find a middle ground. The junior senator from Arkansas seemed more interested in avoiding the political fallout that would result from taking a liberal position on the one hand, and the humiliation of being lumped with the "Bilboites" on the other, than in solving the nation's racial problems. The last week in November Herbert Thomas, after consulting with Fulbright, wrote Harry Ashmore urging him to "get together a few of the other southern liberals – editors, members of Congress, or just citizens – to discuss fully the things the South ought to agree to and do." Legislators who attended could "listen in, express themselves only when they felt an idea would not work,

43 JWF to Ashmore, Mar. 27, 1948, BCN 48, F1, SPF.

and by their silence approve the ideas they thought would be workable." Once agreement was reached on a program, the journalists and community leaders could create a groundswell of opinion that would make it easier for southern members of Congress to become moderates.[44] Thomas's plan could not have been further from the Burkean ideal that Fulbright espoused throughout his public career. Even James Madison would have viewed it as a blueprint for pusillanimity.

In late December Ashmore, Mark Ethridge of the *Louisville Courier-Journal*, and several other moderate editors outlined in their editorial pages the civil rights trade-off plan with which Fulbright and other compromisers had been toying. There was a spirit of compromise abroad in the South, as evidenced by the region's rejection of the Dixiecrats, Ashmore argued. Southerners made a distinction between segregation and discrimination; they could accept anti–poll tax and antilynching legislation but "for many years to come will continue to reject anti-segregation and fair employment laws." The South, the moderates concluded, would even be willing to accept an FEPC if it were a mediatory rather than a judicial body.[45]

Although Fulbright remained unwilling to endorse publicly the plan he had helped inspire, he worked behind the scenes to promote it. At the Arkansan's behest, Senator Carl Hayden (D–Arizona) agreed to champion the compromise in the Senate. On February 2, 1949, Brooks Hays (D–Arkansas) presented it to the House, and the Fulbright–Ashmore–Hays proposal on civil rights subsequently became known as "the Arkansas Plan," a point-by-point reiteration of the program Harry Ashmore had outlined in a December 1948 article in the *Gazette*.[46] Despite Hays's eloquence and Fulbright's lobbying, Truman – egged on by Senator Paul Douglas of Illinois and newly elected Senator Hubert Humphrey of Minnesota – rejected the moderate attempt to distinguish between discrimination and segregation.[47] *To Secure These Rights* and the loyalty of black voters during the 1948 election had convinced the president that both practices were part of the fabric of institutionalized prejudice that was suffocating African Americans. When Congress opened in January, the administration once again pressed ahead with its program, undiluted.

Predictably, Richard Russell's clique of Dixie senators, with Fulbright playing a conspicuous role, responded to this new initiative with a monthlong filibuster.[48] When in the spring of 1949 Republicans and northern Democrats

44 Herbert Thomas to Harry Ashmore, Nov. 27, 1948, BCN 48, F2, SPF.

45 "The Area of Compromise," *Arkansas Gazette*, Dec. 29, 1948.

46 "Exerpts from 'The Arkansas Plan,'" *Arkansas Gazette*, Feb. 3, 1949.

47 JWF to John Welton, Aug. 9, 1948, BCN 48, F2, and JWF to Harry Ashmore, Jan. 3, 1949, BCN 48, F2, SPF.

48 Robert Donovan, *Tumultuous Years: The Presidency of Harry S. Truman, 1949–1953* (New York, 1982), 118–19.

introduced an amendment to Senate Rule XXII, the cloture rule, providing that two-thirds of the senators present and voting could cut off debate on a procedural as well as a substantive measure, the Arkansan, quoting liberally from Walter Lippmann's "Today and Tomorrow," declared that the foundations of American constitutional government were under attack. The system established by the founding fathers had clearly been intended to protect the rights of a substantial minority from the tyranny of the majority. The Truman administration had grown tired of democracy, as executives invariably do, and was attempting to use the cloture amendment to impose its will on Congress and the South.[49] Twenty-three Republicans, half of them from the Midwest, joined the southerners in voting 46 to 41 in sustaining the minority's right to unlimited debate.[50] None of the recommendations put forward by *To Secure These Rights* were enacted into law.

During the years immediately following World War II, Fulbright had felt his way through various foreign and domestic issues. Abandoning his calls for Russian–American cooperation and reliance on the United Nations, the Arkansan had taken his place in the front rank of America's cold warriors. Convinced that the Soviet Union posed a dire threat to Western civilization, he had enthusiastically supported the British loan, the Truman Doctrine, and the Marshall Plan. With an eye to the long haul, however, he had touted the concept of a United States of Europe, a federation that would eventually relieve the United States of its massive foreign aid burden and, it was to be hoped, be able to establish a dialogue with the Kremlin and its satellites.

Drawn reluctantly into the acrimonious debates over civil rights, Fulbright attempted to clear a middle ground between liberal Democrats, who were pressing not only for anti–poll tax and antilynching legislation but also integration, and extreme racists, who were determined to preserve the South's caste system in its crudest form. In the process he joined with Brooks Hays and Harry Ashmore to develop the Arkansas Plan, a scheme that would protect blacks from racial violence and ensure their right to vote without guaranteeing equality of economic opportunity or equal access to public facilities. In the end, however, Fulbright did not have the political courage to put his public stamp of approval on even as modest a plan as this. As he joined with his Dixie colleagues in lobbying against various civil rights bills, he fell back on that tried and true conservative panacea for racial problems: education.

Politically Fulbright's first term in the Senate was a mixed bag. He successfully identified those interests, general and specific, that he needed to serve in order to stay in office: farmers and small businessmen, Reynolds

49 *Congressional Record,* Senate, Mar. 4, 1949, 1876.
50 Donovan, *Tumultuous Years,* 119.

Aluminum, Murphy Oil, and Stephens, Inc. At the same time, his work on the oleo bill[51] and various measures to increase international trade, as well as his opposition to the minimum-wage bill, won him the plaudits of business and agribusiness, while his efforts to bring cheap public power to Arkansas and to make the corporate tax structure more equitable helped preserve his image as a progressive. Fulbright's relationship with the national Democratic Party was more problematical. His criticism of Truman, and particularly his suggestion that the president resign following the 1946 midterm elections, had earned him the undying enmity of the president and party stalwarts like Dean Acheson. Whether calculated or not, the Arkansan had already gained a reputation among his admirers as an independent and among his detractors as a maverick. It was an image that events of his second term would enhance.

51 Throughout 1949–50 Fulbright battled the powerful butter lobby in Congress, seeking to have the tax on oleomargarine removed. The tax was so high that oleo, a soybean derivative, could not compete. Fulbright's success paved the way for Arkansas's soybean industry, one of the state's major enterprises.

# 8

# *"Washington's cleanup man"*

Harry Truman had risen through the ranks of Missouri politics with the help of one of the nation's most disciplined and corrupt political machines. While not corrupt himself, Truman had frequently had to look the other way when Big Tom Pendergast's cronies let contracts to those bidders who offered not the lowest price but the largest kickback. The once-powerful boss of the Kansas City Democratic machine died on January 26, 1945, while on parole from federal prison. Truman never disavowed Pendergast or his machine, and as vice-president he had thrown caution to the wind by flying back for his patron's funeral. "He was my friend and I was his,"[1] he subsequently explained to reporters. For Harry Truman friendship, like blood, was thicker than water.

By contrast James William Fulbright had won election to the House and Senate without the help of an established organization. This had been possible because he hailed from a rural state, his family was wealthy and politically influential, and he and his advisers had been shrewd enough to tap into a ready-made political network, the alumni of the University of Arkansas. The former Rhodes scholar wore his independence on his sleeve. "I don't like machines, I don't like party organization, and I don't like patronage," he told *American Magazine.* "I want to be free to vote as I please."[2] This, together with Fulbright's discovery of the political possibilities of the congressional investigating committee, placed him and Harry Truman on a collision course early in 1950.

J. William Fulbright had not been able to follow up on his early legislative successes. The Fulbright resolution had helped move him up from the House to the Senate, where he had endeared himself to liberals and academics in an increasingly conservative America by pushing the exchange program through Congress. The federation of Europe idea had proved a dead end, and his oleo victory was still months away. However important loyal service to constitu-

1 Quoted in Andrew J. Dunar, *The Truman Scandals and the Politics of Morality* (Columbia, Mo., 1984), 1.

2 Jerome Beatty, "Washington's Cleanup Man," *American Magazine,* 26, Box 798, OF 716B, Truman Papers.

ents was, it was not, as Fulbright well knew, the way one got to be a "national senator." The 1950s were to be the heyday of the congressional investigating committee: the Kefauver crime committee, the McClellan labor racketeering committee, Joseph McCarthy's anticommunist witch-hunting committee. It was natural for the junior senator from Arkansas to turn from legislation to investigation while he waited for an opportunity to make a name for himself in foreign affairs.

In the summer of 1949 Fulbright was chairing a routine hearing of the Senate Banking and Currency subcommittee to oversee the Reconstruction Finance Corporation.[3] During questioning of RFC staff, testimony revealed that a witness, John Haggerty, the Boston loan agency manager for the RFC, had accepted a $30,000-a-year job with the Waltham Watch Co. after leaving government service. There was nothing wrong with that except that Haggerty, while with the RFC, had played a major role in ensuring that the then-bankrupt watch company got a $6 million loan.

Not surprisingly, Fulbright thought Haggerty's action was unethical, and subsequently questioned the five RFC directors about its propriety. He learned that another RFC employee had gone to work for a company that also had borrowed money from the agency. Throughout the questioning the directors were vague and evasive. Fulbright began to wonder if the activities of the agency required a full and thorough airing.

The RFC that President Truman inherited in April 1945 boasted a reputation for having helped pull the country out of the Depression and contributing significantly to the winning of the war. Under President Roosevelt the agency had loaned billions of dollars to thousands of businesses and then, after the outbreak of war, had financed public corporations that acquired, stockpiled, and distributed strategic materials. During Truman's tenure in the White House, however, the corporation deteriorated into a scandal-ridden, poorly administered bureaucracy with an ill-defined mission.

The United States Senate did not really know what to do with the RFC following the war. Inflation seemed to obviate the need for such a lending agency, but no one knew whether or not another depression was just around the corner. Moreover, with tensions between the United States and the Soviet Union increasing daily, the possibility of another war seemed very real. The Senate in 1946 and 1947 granted the RFC a one-year extension, and in 1948 passed legislation prolonging the agency's life through 1956. The RFC continued to be an independent body whose five directors were appointed by the president and confirmed by the Senate. It was accountable only to Congress.

By 1950 the principal function of the RFC was to make loans that would be of political profit to the Truman administration. Dictating the Board's ev-

3 Fulbright was appointed chair in January 1949. Maybank to JWF, Jan. 18, 1949, BCN 40, F6, SPF.

ery move was Donald Dawson, a graduate of the University of Missouri who had worked in all of Truman's campaigns and who since 1947 had been director of personnel and chief dispenser of patronage in the White House. With Matt Connelly, Dawson also was a principal liaison between the White House and the Democratic National Committee. The sportily dressed, backslapping Dawson counted among his friends not only RFC officials, like Dunham and Willett, but also many of the principal borrowers from the RFC. His wife, Ava, worked at the RFC as a supervisor of records and files.[4] Dawson was in a position to influence appointments and promotions at the RFC; at the same time he worked through a network of Washington lawyers and influence peddlers who, in return for large retainers and long-term employment agreements, "represented" would-be borrowers. Those who benefited from RFC largesse were expected to make generous contributions to the Democratic Party and to the president's campaign fund. Truman was only dimly aware of these goings-on, as it turned out, but he remained convinced that patronage was meant for friends.[5]

Actually, Fulbright had sought the chairmanship of the RFC subcommittee of Banking and Currency not because he wanted to embarrass the Truman administration – he was in hot water with the White House as it was – but rather to refocus the agency on small businesses that had difficulty obtaining credit.[6]

In June 1949, while questioning director Harvey Gunderson, Fulbright learned that the Lustron Corporation, an Ohio-based manufacturer of prefabricated houses, had obtained a loan of $15.5 million from the RFC two years earlier, another $10 million in July 1948, $7 million in February 1949, and, according to Gunderson, was soon scheduled to get another $3 million. The Arkansan also learned that the prefab housing manufacturer had obtained these loans with a total of $36,000 in assets. When the RFC subcommittee took the Lustron loan request under consideration, the concern had been losing a million dollars a month. It also learned that, throughout this process, Lustron had retained as its Washington representative Herschel Young, whose Jackson County, Missouri, family was close to that of President Truman. In addition, Herschel's brother, Merl, was then employed as an examiner in the RFC and had handled various Lustron applications. Shortly after the second loan, Merl – who wore plaid sports jackets and picked up his wife, a White House stenographer, in a Cadillac convertible – had resigned his $7,193 job

4 Robert J. Donovan, *Tumultuous Years: The Presidency of Harry S. Truman, 1949–1953* (New York, 1982), 335.

5 HST to Charles Henderson, Dec. 13, 1945, RFC File, President's Secretary's File [hereinafter referred to as PSF]–Personal, Truman Papers.

6 "Fulbright Critical of RFC Policies," 7/13/49, BCN 6, F34, SPF.

with RFC to take an $18,000-a-year position with Lustron. As it turned out, Merl Young was also closely associated with William M. Boyle, Jr., executive director of the Democratic National Committee.[7] Though RFC Chairman Harley Hise rejected Fulbright's demand that the loan be canceled, the Arkansan saw that the committee's findings were published in the *Wall Street Journal.*[8]

In the midst of his investigation of the Lustron Corporation, Fulbright moved to take care of his own housing needs. By the time Fulbright won the Democratic primary in Arkansas in 1950, thus assuring himself another six years in Washington, he, Betty, and the girls had lived in the apartment on Wyoming for six years. As Betty reminded him with increasing frequency, it was no longer sufficient. Betsy and Bosey were entering their teens. It was impossible for them or their parents to have any privacy, and entertaining was out of the question.

Betty Fulbright was a great believer in fate. In late 1950 her aunt, Ann Clifford, died and left her her Philadelphia house complete with furnishings. The proceeds, some sixty thousand dollars, were more than enough to buy a house on Belmont Road, an offshoot of Kalorama that backed directly on Rock Creek.

The area was beautiful, its traditional streets lined with aging oaks and elms. Nearby Massachusetts Avenue provided easy access to Du Pont Circle and the city to the south, and the Zoo and National Cathedral to the north. The neighborhood consisted mainly of Washingtonians and embassy personnel; indeed, the area between Kalorama and Du Pont Circle to the west of Massachusetts was known as "embassy row."

The house at 2527 Belmont Road was a red-brick Colonial Revival with green shutters and white trim. The most striking feature of the house, Bill's favorite room, was a huge, screened-in, two-story room that ran the breadth and height of the rear of the structure and looked directly over Rock Creek. The lower section was a sun porch, where the family ate breakfast, and the upper a screened-in sleeping porch that opened out from Bill and Betty's bedroom. Fulbright slept there even when the temperature dipped below freezing. The house was intimate, elegant, and a bit old-fashioned, furnished as it was with Aunt Ann's Victorian furniture. Bill and Betty never thought of living anywhere else.

7 Marquis Childs, "Loans and Influence," *Washington Star,* June 30, 1949.

8 "$125 Million Gamble," *Wall Street Journal,* Sept. 14, 1949, and JWF to George M. Fuller, Oct. 10, 1949, BCN 39, F20, SPF.

The opening weeks of 1950 found Fulbright in a quandary. If he pressed ahead with the RFC investigation, he was sure to embarrass Truman. The Republicans were sharpening their swords for the 1952 campaign, and continuing revelations would only play into their hands. However, Fulbright reasoned, if the president was not forced to clean house, matters would only get worse; and if Truman refused to abandon his corrupt cronies and discipline the RFC, the sooner he was discredited, the better.[9] In fact, the more the Arkansan thought about it, the more he viewed Truman as an albatross that the party could ill afford. His civil rights program had alienated the South, and the Republicans were already successfully portraying him and Dean Acheson as "executioners" of Jiang Jie-shi (Chiang Kai-shek) and the Chinese Nationalists. To the disgust of reformers inside and outside the party, Truman had refused to do anything about the so-called five-percenters, that legion of influence peddlers who obtained government contracts in return for a percentage. Perhaps a full-scale RFC scandal would finish Truman off, paving the way for a Democratic housecleaning and a new face: Richard Russell, Adlai Stevenson, or even Bill Fulbright. The junior senator from Arkansas was taking an immense gamble, but in a sense there was little for him, personally, to lose. He was already persona non grata at the White House. He had won in Arkansas without the aid of the Democratic national organization, and could do it again. Anyway, muckraking came naturally to Roberta's youngest son.

The first week in February 1950, Fulbright introduced a resolution on the floor of the Senate authorizing his subcommittee to conduct a special investigation of the RFC. Fulbright lined up the necessary votes, and the Senate approved an appropriation of $50,000.[10] The first thing he did was to hire Theodore Herz of Price-Waterhouse to be general counsel and chief investigator. Herz was brilliant, nonpartisan, and completely insensitive to the political implications of his task. He also loved headlines.[11]

The subcommittee opened its investigation with a probe of a $15 million loan to the Texmass Petroleum Co. of Dallas. Herz quickly discovered that the corporation was an oil exploration operation that specialized in dry holes. Perpetually in debt, Texmass had turned to the RFC to bail it out.[12] Several weeks into the investigation, with the help of Lyndon Johnson (D–Texas), the Fulbright committee secured the testimony of Ross Bohannan, a Dallas lawyer representing Texmass. According to Bohannan, soon after the corporation had applied to the RFC, he had gone to Washington and, through a third party, solicited the services of Merl Young. Young was amenable but had informed Bohannan that his good offices with the RFC and White House would cost Texmass $10,000 cash and employment for ten years at $7,500

9 Interview with Jack Yingling, Oct. 12, 1988, Savannah, Ga.
10 JWF to Charles H. Porter, Feb. 7, 1950, BCN 39, F12, SPF.
11 Yingling interview.
12 Dunar, *Truman Scandals,* 83.

per annum.[13] Confronted with this sordid tale and with proof of Texmass's insolvency, Chairman Hise remained unrepentant. In mid-April he appeared before the Fulbright Committee and declared that the RFC was final arbiter of the wisdom and priority of its loans; it could not be intimidated. The Texmass loan would proceed.[14] Fulbright retaliated by releasing the interim report on the Texmass affair. He declared it to be a "bailout," and charged that the loan had not been adequately secured and that the directors had been "remiss" in not uncovering the facts in the case.[15]

At this point in the investigation Harry Truman was only mildly irritated. He did not like Fulbright, but it was clear that, at the very least, the RFC was a bureaucratic mess. His answer to the problem was reorganization. On May 9 the White House submitted legislation that would transfer RFC to the Commerce Department, bringing it more directly under his control, so the president's argument went. Fulbright took to the floor of the Senate to object. "If this plan goes into effect, I do not believe that Congress could determine where responsibility lies," he declared. "To say the least, it could easily be passed back and forth between the Board of Directors and the Secretary of Commerce."[16] On July 6, without even the formality of a roll call in the Senate, the transfer proposal lost.[17]

In the wake of the defeat of the administration's reorganization plan, Donald Dawson convinced the president that the arrogant Arkansan and his self-important, vindictive chief investigator were out to get him. There was clearly no need for the special committee, he argued; the Eightieth Congress had already conducted an investigation. Dawson accused Fulbright of seizing Walter Dunham's telephone log and not returning it, and of planting a mole in the RFC to spy on the agency. The committee staff, he complained to an increasingly indignant Truman, had spread the rumor that Ed Willett's marriage was on the rocks, which it was not, and had even gone so far as to tap telephone lines.[18] If Fulbright wanted a fight, he was going to get one, the president declared.

As both the Fulbright committee and the White House knew, the terms of the RFC directors were scheduled to expire on June 30. Dawson moved quickly to ensure that he controlled the process. Of the five directors, Willett and Dunham were closest to him and had proved most responsive to the political interests of the president and the financial interests of Dawson's cro-

13 Transcripts of the RFC Investigation, undated, Box 272, Cong. Hearings–RFC, PSF, Truman Papers.

14 Ibid.

15 Interim Report, Study of Reconstruction Finance Committee, Senate, 81st Cong., 2d sess., Mar. 29, 1950.

16 *Congressional Record,* Senate, July 6, 1950, 9687.

17 Dunar, *Truman Scandals,* 84–5.

18 Dawson to Truman, Dec. 9, 1950, Box 148, RFC, PSF, Truman Papers.

nies; they would return. Hise and Gunderson were expendable: Both were Republicans and both had dared to speak out against the president's scheme to place the RFC in the Commerce Department.[19] At Dawson's urging, Truman decided to submit the names of C. Edward Rowe, W. Elmer Harber, and Walter E. Cosgriff in addition to Willett and Dunham. After obtaining a sixty-day extension, the president sent the five names to the Hill on August 9.

Fulbright was appalled. Willett and Dunham were the most notorious of the original members, nothing more, in his mind, than political hacks and profiteers. He held up the nominations while Herz investigated the new nominees. Harber, a former Democratic National Committeeman, had just been sued for usury. Ed Rowe, a friend of Willett's, came to the RFC from the directorship of a company that had received a large loan from the agency. Walter Cosgriff, in the opinion of the Comptroller of the Currency, had been following unsound banking practices for years.[20]

By September the Arkansan had used these revelations to convince the rest of the subcommittee not only that the president's nominees were unsuitable, but that a fundamental reorganization of the RFC was necessary. What Fulbright wanted was to substitute a single administrator for the five-person board. He privately informed the White House of his thinking and preliminary recommendations, but Truman ignored him. In December, with the press clamoring for a subcommittee report, Fulbright again tried to head off an open clash with the president. He asked for an off-the-record meeting with Truman. On December 12, accompanied by Senators Paul Douglas (D–Illinois) and Charles Tobey (R–New Hampshire), Fulbright called at the White House. As he later recalled:

> We went in the back door. I thought this was big stuff. I think that was the first time I'd ever done it. We went in the southwest gate and saw no reporters or anybody. The President was very congenial and more or less made us feel that he appreciated our telling him about it, and about our recommendations.[21]

The three lawmakers outlined their findings and asked Truman to submit an RFC reorganization plan along the lines recommended in their report. There was no need for embarrassment or apology; the White House could announce the move as one designed to strengthen the administration of the RFC. The meeting ended on a friendly note. Fulbright and his colleagues were encouraged.

19 Dawson to Truman, April 18, 1950, Box 148, RFC, PSF, Truman Papers, and Dunar, *Truman Scandals*, 85.

20 Dawson to Truman, Dec. 9, 1950, Box 148, RFC, PSF, Truman Papers.

21 Quoted in Haynes Johnson and Bernard M. Gwertzman, *Fulbright: The Dissenter* (New York, 1968), 145.

Then, on December 28, without informing Fulbright, Truman announced that he was resubmitting the names of his August 9 nominees. Meanwhile Dawson, working through Senator Burnett Maybank (D–South Carolina), chairman of the Banking and Currency Committee and a strong administration backer, attempted to have funds for the Fulbright committee cut off when Congress reconvened in January. He failed.[22]

By the end of January 1951, Fulbright's patience was at an end. He had been urging the RFC and the White House to clean up their acts for more than four months and had gotten nowhere. Against the advice of staff, he ordered the subcommittee's findings released without giving the White House an advance copy.[23]

The report, provocatively entitled "Favoritism and Influence," was a bombshell. Released to the press on February 2, 1951, it accused the RFC of succumbing to political influence and acting against the public interest, and implied that the White House had looked the other way.[24] Truman responded with his accustomed pugnacity. The report, "was asinine," he told reporters. "I spent ten years in the Senate," he declared, "and I wrote a lot of reports, but I am happy to say I never wrote one like this." He defended the RFC and its directors, and personally accused Fulbright of ducking him – "he left town when he found out I wanted to see him."

From Florida, where he was giving a long-scheduled speech, Fulbright fired back:

> As to whether the report is asinine, I am willing to let [it] speak for itself. According to the press dispatches, the President states that I left town when I found out he wanted to see me. I do not want to seem disrespectful to the President, but this statement of the President is not true.[25]

In response to Truman's taunts, Fulbright went at public hearings with renewed zeal, airing damaging testimony about Dawson, Young, Boyle, and others in an ongoing spectacle that seemed to confirm everything Truman's critics had been saying about his penchant for cronyism. Through all the accusations and denials, it was difficult to judge the exact degree of guilt. Of one thing everyone in the press was sure, however: The junior senator was doing a grand job.

22 Dawson to Truman, Jan. 15, 1951, Central File – RFC, Papers of Eben A. Sayers, Truman Library.
23 Dunar, *Truman Scandals,* 87–8.
24 Franklin N. Parks to HST, Jan. 16, 1953, Box 148, RFC, PSF, Truman Papers, and Donovan, *Tumultuous Years,* 332.
25 Quoted in Johnson and Gwertzman, *Fulbright: The Dissenter,* 145–6.

Wrote a reporter for the *Buffalo Evening News:*

> He has a quiet manner with almost an impish grin. He frequently sums up the apparent meaning and significance of a whole series of answers in one statement and asks the witness if that is the impression he wants to leave with the committee. Thus, brow-beating tactics which so infuriate witnesses and lead them to the belief they have been made the "goat" of by congressional inquiries have been eliminated.[26]

Fulbright's friend Walter Lippmann chimed in, "Senator Fulbright has set an example, all the more impressive because its sincerity has been so effortless, of how a good senator can behave."[27]

Meanwhile, the White House was shrouded in gloom. Truman discussed the "Fulbright problem" one night at Blair House with some of his advisers, including Joseph Short, his new press secretary. When Truman ventured that the stir over the RFC hearings soon would abate, Short observed, "Mr. President, I don't think this business is going to blow over. I think it is making a deep impression around the country."[28]

Some members of Truman's entourage urged the president to get rid of Dawson in order to spare his administration further embarrassment. He steadfastly refused to abandon his friend, however, and in the midst of the Fulbright committee's hearings, the president departed for Florida and a week-long vacation. As one poker game followed another in Key West, charges of corruption flew in Washington.[29] Truman eventually ran up a white flag by submitting a reorganization plan whose principal feature was the reform Fulbright had been requesting for months: replacement of the board of directors by a single administrator. A five-member Loan Policy Board would establish guidelines, but the executive director would be in charge.[30]

With Fulbright's support, Congress approved the White House reorganization plan, and Truman named Missourian Stuart Symington to head the reconstituted RFC. Nonetheless, the political damage had been done. As the RFC matter came to a close, the *Philadelphia Enquirer* was attacking the president on a daily basis for croynism, and the *New York Daily News* drew parallels with the Harding scandals. It would be years before Harry Truman would forgive the Arkansan.

At the same time the RFC hearings were drawing to a close, the nation sat

26 Quoted in ibid., 144.
27 Quoted in ibid.
28 Quoted in Donovan, *Tumultuous Years,* 334.
29 Quoted in ibid., 335.
30 HST to the Congress of the United States, Feb. 19, 1951, Box 148, RFC, PSF, Truman Papers.

transfixed before its radios listening to organized-crime figures taking the Fifth Amendment or testifying contemptuously before the Kefauver crime committee in New York. Corruption and criminality seemed pervasive. Fur coats and Donald Dawson, five-percenters and Harry Vaughn, crowded other news off the front pages. In New York, the sports world was shocked when investigative reporters disclosed that the national champion City College basketball team had been taking bribes of up to $1,500 to rig games. Similar wrongdoing soon surfaced at Bradley, the University of Kentucky, and New York University.[31]

In an effort to bring the RFC hearings to a dignified close, as well as to justify them, Fulbright joined those pundits in press and academia who were proclaiming the decline of American civilization. Things had reached a terrible state, he told the Senate, when Congress and the people had to hold their officials to a legal standard.[32] In the weeks that followed, the man whom one magazine dubbed "Washington's Cleanup Man" spoke out to denounce "win-at-any-cost" pressure from college alumni for starting the chain of corruption that produced the City College and other basketball scandals. These pressures, he proclaimed, led the colleges to "corrupt not only the hired players, but also the entire student body, who learn from their elders the cynical, immoral doctrine that one must win at all costs."[33] In a trailer for the movie *Saturday's Hero,* the Arkansan endorsed the film, an exposé of crooked college athletics. Finally, in October he and Paul Douglas sponsored a joint resolution to create a commission on ethics in government.[34]

Aside from stimulating discussion, Fulbright's muckraking efforts came to naught. They did, however, add to his stature and contributed to speculation about his political future. Paul Douglas said publicly he favored Fulbright as Democratic nominee for president in 1952, assuming Truman did not seek renomination. In Arkansas, Governor Sid McMath, a strong Truman supporter, declared that Fulbright's proposed candidacy was more than the routine "favorite son" exercise.[35]

As Fulbright well knew, there was never a serious chance the nomination would be his. For Truman, Fulbright was more than ever "an over-educated Oxford S.O.B.," and he added the Arkansan to the growing list of people who would gain the Democratic nomination over his, Truman's, dead body.

31 Johnson and Gwertzman, *Fulbright: The Dissenter,* 146.

32 *Congressional Record,* Senate, Mar. 27, 1951, 2904–5.

33 Beatty, "Washington's Cleanup Man," Truman Papers, and "Alumni 'Pressure' a Spur to Game-Fixing," *New York Daily Mirror,* Mar. 28, 1951.

34 "Crystal Gazer," *New York Times,* Aug. 26, 1951, and *Congressional Record,* Senate, Oct. 9, 1951, 12820.

35 Johnson and Gwertzman, *Fulbright: The Dissenter,* 148.

Fulbright frequently complained that his senatorial duties did not leave him enough time to read, but compared to the average politician, the Arkansan was a bookworm. During the crucial period 1947–50, he read everything he could get his hands on pertaining to foreign affairs. Fulbright was particularly impressed with the reasoning and arguments of George Kennan, who as head of the policy planning staff in the State Department had emerged as America's foremost expert on East–West relations.

In the wake of the Berlin blockade of 1948–9 Kennan had put forward three stratagems for maintaining the world balance of power and containing Soviet expansion, short of armed conflict: The United States should shore up those nations threatened by Soviet imperialism through programs of military and economic aid; it should, by exploiting divisions within the communist world, work to reduce Moscow's ability to project its power beyond its own borders; and it should attempt to modify, over time, the Soviet leadership's view of international relations, with an eye to bringing about a negotiated settlement of differences.[36] The breakup of international communism was an irreversible trend, certain to proceed regardless of what the United States did, he believed.

In its defense policy, Kennan pointed out, the United States must match means with ends. Because American resources were limited, the nation could not blindly follow a policy of globalism, regarding communism anywhere and everywhere as an equally dangerous threat to American interests.

Up until the time George Kennan left the State Department at the end of 1949, the Truman administration followed this pragmatic, asymmetrical approach; but with his departure, with the House Un-American Activities Committee (HUAC) whipping up anticommunist sentiment, and with Dean Acheson under daily attack from the Republicans for selling out Jiang Jie-shi to the Chinese communists, the president and his advisers embraced the globalist approach against which Kennan had warned, and accepted the need for a massive American military buildup. In 1949, in the wake of the detonation by the Soviet Union of its first atomic bomb and Truman's authorization of the development of a hydrogen bomb, the president commissioned a comprehensive statement of interests, threats, and possible responses. The task fell to an ad hoc committee of State and Defense Department officials headed by Kennan's successor, Paul H. Nitze.[37]

The policy statement that they fashioned, NSC-68, was a top-secret document whose contents would not be made public until the 1970s. It argued that any extension of the area under Soviet control constituted a threat to the Unit-

36 John Lewis Gaddis, *Strategies of Containment: A Critical Appraisal of Postwar American National Security Policy* (New York, 1982), 36–7.

37 Kennan had been "promoted" to the post of counselor by Dean Acheson, who did not feel the same need for the Kremlinologist's vision as had George Marshall. Ernest R. May, ed., *American Cold War Strategy: Interpreting NSC 68* (New York, 1993), 4–5.

ed States; and because all points along the boundary of the communist world were of equal importance, the United States would have to pursue a symmetrical rather than an asymmetrical strategy. The emphasis would be on perimeter defense. In part, NSC-68 reflected the Truman administration's growing belief that the public and Congress could and would not distinguish between peripheral and vital interests. Moreover, Nitze and his colleagues assumed Washington could not tolerate any change in the balance of power, whether it resulted from military aggression, economic dominance, or loss of credibility. It assumed finally, and most important, that the ultimate deterrent to communist expansion was military force. Indeed, Nitze and his colleagues called for a policy that would ensure clear Western superiority in arms and troops for the duration of the cold war.

The implications of NSC-68 were profound. It posited the existence of a monolithic threat and assumed it was in the interests and within the power of the United States to battle it on all fronts. By the time Truman received NSC-68 in April 1950, Nitze and Acheson had lined up the military services and influential establishment figures, such as Robert Lovett, in behalf of their sweeping proposal; Kennan and other doubters were kept out of the policy-making loop. Ironically, Truman had named as secretary of defense a Missouri politician named Louis Johnson, who, like the president, was committed to the notion of a balanced budget; but by 1950 both were afraid of being accused of being "soft on communism." The administration began implementing NSC-68 policies in June 1950, when it decided to go to war to defend South Korea. As a result, U.S. defense spending tripled. For the next four decades, it would remain two to three times higher, as a percentage of the gross national product, than in any previous peacetime period in the nation's history.[38]

Although he regarded the foreign policies of the Soviet Union as inimical to the interests of the United States, Fulbright never accepted the idea of a monolithic communist threat. Like Kennan he was able and willing to distinguish between communism as a political and economic principle, and Soviet imperialism. To a friend of his mother he wrote:

> We are not fighting communists as a political party but we are actually fighting the Chinese and the Russians. The Russians have adopted the communist doctrine as an instrument to be used in their effort to dominate their fellowman. They use this doctrine much the same way as they might use airplanes or guns and have done so very effectively. In other words, if communists in a country have no connection with the Russians in their efforts to dominate the world, they can then be considered much like any other political party with which one violently disagrees.[39]

38 May, *American Cold War Strategy*, 8–15.
39 JWF to Lessie Read, Jan. 3, 1951, BCN 48, F11, SPF.

Fulbright supported the war in Korea, but he did so unenthusiastically. He believed that communism should be contained, but he opposed the effort to reunify the peninsula. America's resources were limited and its interests specific. "If we are confronted by alternatives which you mentioned," he wrote a constituent, "that is, an all-out effort in Korea or an evacuation, I would prefer the latter."[40] Speaking to his Senate colleagues in December 1951, he ridiculed the suggestion by the China Lobby's Senator William Knowland (R–California) that Jiang Jie-shi be "unleashed" and provided with American aid so that he could attack the mainland. As everyone knew, the Seventh Fleet patrolled the Formosa Straits to protect the Chinese Nationalists, not to restrain them, he declared. "I find very few in Washington who believe that Chiang Kai-Shek's troops are reliable, and that if we arm them and put them ashore that most of them would not turn their arms over to the enemy," he confided to an Arkansas supporter.[41] At any rate, Fulbright told the Senate, Moscow was the primary enemy and Western Europe the chief prize. America could live with the communization of all of Asia, but it could not tolerate Soviet domination of Western Europe.

> Our basic institutions, including the legislative branch of our Government, our religious system, and most of the ancestry of the people of the United States derive from Europe, not from the Far East. . . . The people of Europe understand our system of society much better than do the people of the Far East.[42]

The problem confronting critics of American foreign policy like Fulbright and Kennan was that their criticism of the new globalism played into the hands of neoisolationists such as Senator Robert Taft and former president Herbert Hoover. Late in 1950 Harry Truman announced that under the authority granted to him by the North Atlantic Treaty and his constitutional role as commander-in-chief, he was permanently stationing troops in Europe; Dwight Eisenhower had agreed to come out of retirement and take command. Neoisolationists were appalled: America was not only to have a peacetime standing army, but portions of it were to be stationed abroad. In December of 1950 Hoover issued a public call for the removal of all U.S. ground troops from Europe and Asia. The United States should form a ring of island outposts, including Great Britain, Japan, and the islands of the Pacific, to defend the new "Fortress America." Because it would never be able to match the manpower of Eurasia, Hoover argued, America should rely on its air force and navy to defend its interests.

40 JWF to N. P. Talburt, Dec. 12, 1950, BCN 46, F10, SPF.
41 JWF to F. L. Danford, Jan. 13, 1951, BCN 46, F13, SPF.
42 *Congressional Record,* Senate, Dec. 11, 1950, 16391–4. See also JWF to Richard K. Burke, Dec. 19, 1950, BCN 46, F13, SPF.

Robert Taft, who was trying desperately to hammer out a foreign policy position in anticipation of his run for the presidency in 1952, heartily endorsed Hoover's approach. As soon as Congress convened in early 1951, the Ohioan introduced a resolution calling for the removal of all troops from Europe and asserting that the president did not have the constitutional authority to deploy American forces without the specific approval of Congress.[43]

Fulbright responded by trying to carve out a middle ground between globalism and neoisolationism. Repeating the standard Atlanticist arguments concerning the indivisibility of cultures and the interdependence of economies, he addressed the current debate:

> Broadly speaking, there may be said to be three policies that have been advanced in recent weeks. . . . First, the limitation of our commitments to the defense of the Western Hemisphere with emphasis upon air and sea power. Second, the so-called Truman doctrine of opposing aggression in every area where it appears. Third, participation in the creation of a land army in Western Europe, in addition to the defense of the Western Hemisphere. One may perhaps call this the Truman doctrine with limitations.[44]

Fulbright warned the country not to give in to the temptation to oversimplify. "In a matter as difficult as combating the imperialism of the Russian Politburo," he told the Senate, "there is no simple blueprint for action, and it is a dangerous illusion to accept one even if it is offered." What was certain, however, was that the Hoover–Taft approach would abandon the peoples of Western Europe to "the tender mercies of the Kremlin," a policy "dangerous to our security" and "morally dishonorable." There was nothing that could be done about China. With regard to other crucial strategic areas – Greece, Turkey, and Japan, for example – the United States should provide the arms and material to enable these countries to resist armed aggression, but not commit to send troops.[45] He concluded with a ringing defense of the Kennan asymmetrical approach:

> It is my view that the safest and wisest policy for us to follow is neither the Hoover–[Joseph P.] Kennedy–Taft policy nor the Truman policy. The former is dangerous to our security and is morally wrong. The latter is beyond our capacity to carry out. I firmly believe, however, that by limiting our commitments to Europe and certain additional strategic areas as I have indicated, we can bring about the unity of the free world. . . .[46]

43 *Congressional Record,* Senate, Jan. 5, 1951, 65.
44 *Congressional Record,* Senate, Jan. 22, 1951, 521.
45 Ibid., 520–2.
46 Ibid., 523.

After John Foster Dulles, Thomas Dewey, and the so-called internationalist wing of the Republican Party came out in support of the stationing of troops in Europe, Taft's resolution failed overwhelmingly. As subsequent events would reveal, however, NSC-68 was in place, and the symmetrical rather than the asymmetrical concept would prevail in American defense policy.

Nearly twenty years in power had brought the Democratic Party into a state of frustration, exhaustion, and confusion. By and large the party was run by aging New Dealers and party brokers who were out of ideas and out of fresh faces. Truman was nearing sixty-eight, Barkley was seventy-four. Chief Justice Fred Vinson, Truman's secret choice for the presidential nomination, was sixty-two and in poor health. The fierce political crosscurrents of the postwar period had prevented the emergence of any new, commanding Democratic leader who had both national appeal and an appetite for battle.

Issues pertaining to civil rights, the cold war, and full employment continued to divide the party deeply. Southerners like Russell, Eastland, and Sparkman either would not or could not accept national legislation on lynching, the poll tax, or an FEPC. The party's left wing remained alienated: Henry Wallace's Progressive Citizens of America continued to advocate an advanced civil rights program, nationalization of basic industries, and a policy of conciliation if not friendship with the Soviet Union. The party's liberal center, organized into the Americans for Democratic Action in 1947, stood pragmatically for a mixed economy, federal legislation to end segregation and discrimination, and a foreign policy of confrontation with and containment of the Soviet Union. As liberals and "internationalists," ADA's Hubert Humphrey, David Dubinsky, Eleanor Roosevelt, John Kenneth Galbraith, and Arthur Schlesinger, Jr., felt that they must battle oppression and exploitation abroad as well as at home: To advocate social justice for Americans while condoning totalitarianism and aggression in other parts of the world seemed inconsistent; and, no doubt, in the face of mounting attacks from the Republican right – which was already skillfully linking liberalism with socialism, and socialism with communism – the ADA was desirous of proving its mettle in the global struggle with Soviet imperialism.[47] Nonetheless, by 1952 the Republicans had largely outflanked the Democrats on cold-war issues.

A number of Democratic hopefuls took the field as Truman's popularity declined. Senator Estes Kefauver of Tennessee grabbed the early lead by coming out into open opposition to the administration. Truman finally announced on March 30 that he would not run again and, with Vinson out of the picture due to ill-health, launched a campaign to draft Governor Adlai E. Stevenson

47 Steven Gillon, *Politics and Vision: The ADA and American Liberalism, 1947–1985* (New York, 1987), 16–32.

of Illinois. Stevenson denied that he was a candidate even to the eve of the Democratic National Convention. When the delegates gathered in Chicago, Kefauver redoubled his efforts. Several favorite sons, including Robert Kerr of Oklahoma and Richard Russell of Georgia, waited in the wings hoping for a deadlock; but Kerr's ties to the oil and gas industry and Russell's stand on civil rights hamstrung their candidacies.

Fulbright of Arkansas allowed his name to be placed in nomination, but he did so only because "such a move would enable us to survey the situation and reserve final decision for the moment when it might be most advantageous for us to use our influence."[48] Though he personally favored Russell, he was realistic about his chances. On July 18 he and John Erickson set off for Chicago by automobile.

From beginning to end the Truman forces were in control of the convention. They approached Stevenson once again; this time he gave in and allowed his name to be placed in nomination. Fulbright and the rest of the Arkansas delegation stuck with Russell until it was obvious that Stevenson was going to win. The Democratic platform demanded repeal of the Taft–Hartley Act, enactment of a full civil rights program, maintenance of high price supports for farmers, and continuing efforts to contain communism. At Truman's behest, Stevenson picked Senator John Sparkman of Alabama as his running mate. The Democrats had to have the South, and Sparkman, a reasonable, moderate man on everything except civil rights, seemed the most acceptable southerner available. Fulbright had been in the running up until the last, but his unpopularity with labor, coupled with the president's animosity, doomed him.[49]

Stevenson was a graduate of Choate and Princeton, a lawyer, and a former Navy Department official. A man of refined taste, he was intelligent, polished, sophisticated, literate, and self-deprecating. He was also wealthy, divorced, and cosmopolitan – a thoroughly modern man who was filled with self-doubt. Stevenson was religious without being "churchy." He was determined to do what was morally right, but Stevenson agreed with Reinhold Niebhur and other contemporary moral philosophers that the path to righteousness was not always clearly marked. He was the opposite of Harry Truman, a direct, humorous, tough person who was essentially free of doubts about what was right and what was wrong.[50]

Meanwhile, the Republicans had held their own convention in Chicago. There the eastern, internationalist wing of the Republican Party headed off the Taftites and orchestrated the nomination of General Dwight David Eisenhower, the hero of Normandy and an outspoken advocate of global contain-

48 JWF to J. R. Crocker, June 5, 1952, BCN 78, F23, SPF.
49 Erickson to John Ward, Aug. 7, 1952, BCN 77, F24, SPF.
50 Donovan, *Tumultuous Years,* 395.

ment. As Eisenhower attempted to heal the breach with the nationalist/conservative wing of the party, the convention picked the ardent anticommunist Republican from California, Richard M. Nixon, for vice-president and adopted a moderate platform.[51]

Stevenson had not campaigned for the nomination, and, if he is to be believed, did not want it. During the preconvention period he carefully quashed any attempt to assemble a formal organization, lest he appear to be a hypocrite. As a result, when the campaign began, the Democratic candidate had no organization, whereas Eisenhower was in command of a well-oiled, well-financed machine.[52] The team that Stevenson subsequently assembled in Springfield was amateurish at best. For his personal campaign manager, the Democratic nominee picked Wilson Wyatt, the first chairman of the ADA. Instead of hiring political professionals, Wyatt surrounded himself with a glamorous group of academics and pundits, including Pulitzer Prize–winning journalist Clayton Fritchey, historian Arthur Schlesinger, Jr., and economist John Kenneth Galbraith.

Despite Stevenson's wit and eloquence, his campaign was clearly foundering by mid-August. After huddling with Governor Allen Shivers of Texas, the candidate announced that he favored federal custody of all off-shore oil lands. When one of his aides pointed out in desperation that he had to have Texas to win, Stevenson retorted: "But I don't have to win."[53] In Chicago, before the national American Legion convention, he indirectly attacked Joseph McCarthy (R–Wisconsin), William Jenner (R–Indiana), and the rest of the red-baiting contingent in Congress. At the same time his lukewarm support of a national FEPC dismayed civil rights leaders. Springfield was long on speechwriters but low on fund-raisers, and by late September, Democratic campaign coffers were virtually empty. Stevenson decided to send for his friend, Bill Fulbright.

Stevenson and Fulbright had known each other since the early New Deal days when both had been young government lawyers, Stevenson for the Agricultural Adjustment Administration and Fulbright for the Justice Department. They were both enlightened patricians, both educated men who admired intellectuals. Fulbright shared Stevenson's distaste for entrenched political organizations, and they saw eye to eye on the tidelands issue. Still, Fulbright was not nor had ever been a Stevenson insider. What prompted him to leave his family and Senate duties and go to Springfield?

No doubt guilt played a role. Fulbright had had as much to do with the tarnishing of Harry Truman, and thus the Democratic Party's image, as anyone outside the Republican Party. An extensive study by the University of Michi-

51 Sam M. Wassell to JWF, Oct. 28, 1952, BCN 78, F14, SPF.
52 Porter McKeever, *Adlai Stevenson: His Life and Legacy* (New York, 1989), 202.
53 Quoted in ibid., 213.

gan Survey Research Center found that the public had been strongly affected by the highly publicized revelations of irregularities and favoritism within the Truman administration.[54] Stevenson had established a reputation for integrity and independence; the least Fulbright could do was lend him a hand. Finally, Fulbright had reason to believe that he was Stevenson's top candidate for the post of secretary of state should he win.[55]

Fulbright arrived in Springfield on October 4, moved into the Governor's Mansion, and virtually took over the campaign. At that point the candidate was about to depart for a four-thousand-mile speaking trip, for which virtually no advance work had been done; indeed, the Stevenson camp's idea of advance work was to hire transportation and reserve speaking space. In addition, there had been little effort to focus popular interest on the Democratic standard-bearer. While Republican public relations experts, armed with bags of confetti and railroad flares, focused on Ike's grin, golf swing, and gardening activities, the Stevenson people concentrated on issues and ideas. Photo opportunities and human interest stories seemed beneath them.[56]

Fulbright immediately got on the phone and stirred up local politicos and journalists along Stevenson's campaign route. Most important, he urged Stevenson to take off the gloves. Up to this point the candidate had repeatedly paid homage to Eisenhower as a war hero and a man of integrity; a debate on the issues would suffice, he believed. Wrong, declared Fulbright. Although Eisenhower might be keeping above the fray, his henchmen were hitting below the belt. Led by Jenner and Nixon, Republican spokesmen accused Stevenson variously of "sitting out World War II in a swivel chair in Washington"; of being a man "who could not recognize a Red when he worked with him [Alger Hiss]"; of turning a deaf ear to "the pitiful millions behind Russia's iron curtain"; and "of being more fit for a psychiatrist's couch than a political campaign."[57] Nixon was particularly vitriolic, labeling Stevenson as both a Truman stooge and a communist fellow traveler. In the Senate, Fulbright had studiously avoided contact with Nixon, a man he viewed as beneath contempt; in the context of the election campaign, however, Nixon could not be ignored. Working with Stevenson's sister, Elizabeth "Buffie" Ives, Fulbright decided to prepare a daily summary of Nixon's diatribes to get the candidate's blood stirred up. It was an uphill battle, however. When Mrs. Ives told her brother over lunch that he "would have to start slugging harder now," the governor replied, "Oh dear, really?" When she replied in the affirmative, the governor asked, "All the time?"[58]

54 Ibid., 206.
55 Ogburn to JWF, Oct. 23, 1952, BCN 78, F15, SPF.
56 Sam Brightman to Fritchey and Flanagan, Oct. 6, 1952, BCN 78, F17, SPF.
57 Wyatt memorandum, Oct. 12, 1952, BCN 78, F16, SPF.
58 Robert W. Notti to JWF, Oct. 7, 1952, BCN 77, F29, SPF.

Stevenson did finally agree to stop flattering Eisenhower; and in truth both he and Fulbright had become deeply concerned about the Republican nominee's qualifications.[59] "As a candidate for President, the general fumbled and faltered every time he sought to go beyond the safe limits of campaign platitudes," Fulbright later observed. "The general's awkwardness, I am convinced, reflected his deep uncertainty. He has moved into unfamiliar territory."[60] Reacting to Fulbright's blandishments and to Eisenhower's refusal to defend his old benefactor, General George Marshall, from attacks by Joe McCarthy, Stevenson took to calling his opponent, derisively, "the General."[61]

Fulbright's second priority was to raise some money: Stevenson's chief fund-raiser, Beardsley Ruml, had fallen flat on his face. The Republicans will win by default, Fulbright told the campaign staff, if Stevenson's strongest selling point, his speeches, were not broadcast on television; and airing them would take dollars. Jack Pickens, Witt Stephens, and John Snyder, Truman's secretary of the treasury, primed the pump, and soon the money began coming in.[62]

The third task the Arkansan set for himself was to persuade Harry Byrd, Allen Ellender, Richard Russell, and other southern Democratic leaders to get off their hands. Russell, who came to Springfield, at least allowed himself to be courted; the rest would not even listen. Byrd was "out picking apples," Fulbright was told when he called.[63]

Fulbright worked tirelessly for Adlai Stevenson in 1952. By midmonth he had opened communications with two hundred party officials in all parts of the country. He supervised a special campaign tour for Vice-President Alben Barkley. After consulting with Stevenson, he sent telegrams over his and Sparkman's signatures to every national committeeperson, state chairman, state vice-chairman, Democratic governor, and Democratic candidate for Congress. In between, he managed to deliver more than a dozen speeches himself.[64]

Stevenson's refusal to counterattack was not the only source of frustration for Fulbright during the 1952 campaign, as he would later recall:

> The Governor just ran everybody crazy, including me, over what we called his perfectionism. We thought he did as well impromptu, particularly on those short speeches about anything, but he insisted

59 Fulbright, like Stevenson, had originally thought well of the former Supreme Allied Commander. "If Eisenhower and Russell are the nominees, I think the country stands to get a good man," Fulbright had written Mike Fodor in March. JWF to Fodor, Mar. 21, 1952, BCN 105, F27, SPF.

60 Quoted in Johnson and Gwertzman, *Fulbright: The Dissenter,* 149.

61 McKeever, *Adlai Stevenson,* 232–7.

62 JWF to Pauline Davis, Oct. 10, 1952, and Pickens to JWF, Oct. 9, 1952, BCN 78, F13, SPF.

63 See, for example, Ellender to JWF, Oct. 13, 1952, BCN 78, F13, SPF.

64 JWF to Wilson Wyatt, Oct. 11, 1952, BCN 78, F16, SPF.

> on having something prepared and he would work – well, he would work until three or four o'clock in the morning changing a word. And he was always late. The texts were never available. . . . He rewrote or reworked no matter what it was.[65]

Meanwhile, the Eisenhower steamroller was gaining momentum. After conciliating and winning the support of Taft at a New York meeting in mid-September, the General hammered away at the Korean issue throughout October. He charged that Truman's blundering had helped to cause the conflict, and he promised that, if elected, he would go to Korea personally and end the war. Eisenhower and his campaigners fought hard to avert a last-minute swing to Stevenson. They need not have worried: The Democratic candidate polled twenty-seven million votes to Eisenhower's thirty-three million and carried only North Carolina, West Virginia, Kentucky, South Carolina, Georgia, Alabama, Mississippi, Louisiana, and Arkansas.

Fulbright was convinced that the campaign had not made one bit of difference to the outcome of the election. As soon as Eisenhower the war hero was nominated, the issue had been decided. Perhaps it was for the best: Both Lippmann and Robert McCallum advised him that it was dangerous for America not to undergo a change of government after twenty years. "I feel very badly about Stevenson being defeated," Fulbright wrote Fodor. "However, now that it is over, I am quite prepared to do everything I can to help the General."[66]

The Stevenson campaign experience was not a total loss. Fulbright had greatly strengthened his position with the national party, repairing much of the damage done by the RFC investigation and his criticism of Truman. Moreover, he had met several men who would figure importantly in his future, especially University of Chicago historian Walter Johnson and writer David Cohn.

The Stevenson–Fulbright relationship continued to be close until Stevenson's death in the summer of 1965. The Arkansan later reminisced:

> He was a curious fellow, you know. He was such an eloquent man on the stump and then, privately, when he was talking to you at lunch or something, he had such self-doubts. He always was haunted with the idea what a fool he was to have run in '52; that his timing was absolutely bad; that he should have stayed on as governor. . . . I'm not sure what kind of President he would have made. I know his motives and his intentions would have been, in my view, right. Whether or not he would have been able to maneuver properly and manage this kind of lions' den, snake pit sort of situation we have here, I don't know. This is a pretty tough government.

65 Quoted in Johnson and Gwertzman, *Fulbright: The Dissenter,* 151.
66 JWF to Fodor, Nov. 11, 1952, BCN 105, F27, SPF.

> There are some pretty tough people in it – in all areas of it. Adlai was a gentleman. I don't know whether a gentleman can make this government really operate or not.[67]

In part, Fulbright's mixed feelings over the outcome of the 1952 election stemmed from the sobering thought of the devastation that would have been wreaked on Stevenson as president by the junior senator from Wisconsin, Joseph McCarthy. The Arkansan had been wary of this red-baiting colleague for some time. Indeed, by the time Dwight Eisenhower was elected president, McCarthy had been orchestrating his anticommunist witch-hunt for more than two years.

[67] Quoted in Johnson and Gwertzman, *Fulbright: The Dissenter,* 151–2.

# 9

# *The enemy within*

At a Lincoln's Day address delivered in February 1950 to a Republican Women's Club in Wheeling West Virginia, Senator Joseph McCarthy announced that he had the names of either 205 or 57 communists in the State Department; because of his mumbling no one could be sure. At a subsequent speech he claimed 81 card-carrying members. Unable to come up with any proof, McCarthy asserted that Owen Lattimore, a professor at Johns Hopkins University and an authority on Far Eastern affairs, was a top espionage agent. When the FBI declared that there was no proof, "Tail-gunner Joe" turned on Philip Jessup, U.S. representative to the U.N. General Assembly. While making his indiscriminate charges, McCarthy typically waved files or folders, frequently dyed pink, containing documentation that he alleged proved his charges. Because of their sensitive nature, of course, the incriminating evidence could not be made public.[1]

The feeling that Soviet Russia posed a mortal threat to American values and to the national security was intense and pervasive, especially after the fall of China. The man and woman on the street took Stalin and Molotov's rhetoric at face value. Had not Marx and Lenin called for the overthrow of capitalism everywhere and by any means? Americans came to perceive Russia as a totalitarian state determined to extend its empire throughout the world as it oppressed the peoples under its control. Stalin was Hitler's political heir, and communism fascism's ideological cousin. In the domestic sphere the anticommunist impulse often found expression in the mindless identification of all social change with communism. In foreign affairs, it caused Americans to divide the world into two camps: communist and capitalist, enslaved and free.

Coming as it did hard on the heels of the most terrible war the world had ever seen, the cold war generated widespread anger, frustration, and depression. Despite the Truman administration's embrace of globalism, the Korean War proved that there were definite limits to American power. There seemed no alternative, then, to long years of stalemate made unbearably anxious by

[1] See Robert Griffith, *The Politics of Fear: Joseph R. McCarthy and the Senate* (Amherst, Mass., 1987), 30–1.

the ever-present threat of a nuclear Armageddon. In 1950 a number of Americans were simply unwilling to accept that reality. Given the benignity of American intentions, the purity of its institutions, and the universal longing to emulate its example, the nation's inability to defeat communism must be due to an enemy within. All would be well, they asserted, but for the fact that communists had infiltrated the federal government, the media, the judiciary, and other high places and were destroying the republic by their relentless treachery. One of early television's most popular programs was "I Was a Communist for the FBI," the melodramatic story of Herbert Philbrick, who, as a double agent for the FBI for nine years, had ferreted out Communists. Though the real-life Philbrick denounced McCarthy as an "amateur," the weekly fictionalization of his adventures heightened popular fears and lent credence to McCarthy's charges.[2] It was this juxtaposition of forces that enabled a very ordinary man from Wisconsin to turn the nation into a polarized mass of persecutors and victims.

McCarthy could not have posed the threat he did, however, without the support of the Republican Party. Eighteen years out of power, the Republicans of the Eighty-first Congress were determined to investigate nearly every aspect of the Democratic administration. As McCarthy ranted and raved, unleashing slanderous accusations in every direction, Robert Taft, William Knowland (R–California), and Everett Dirksen (R–Illinois) stood in the wings and cheered him on.

J. William Fulbright hated and feared demagogues. Charismatic figures who claimed divine or other kinds of inspiration and who pretended to embody the public interest in their persons chilled and repelled him. Witness to his brother's terrifying and then humiliating fits of anger, and schooled in self-discipline by both Roberta and Jay, Fulbright preached self-control and rationality as the supreme virtues. For him Joe McCarthy came to incarnate all that was evil in human nature and to personify the ultimate threat to democratic government.

Fulbright's first impression of McCarthy had been unfavorable. His RFC subcommittee investigation into the Lustron Corporation had turned up the fact that McCarthy had accepted $10,000 from Lustron for compiling a pamphlet on housing. This was a clear case of conflict of interest: McCarthy had then been a vice-chairman of the Subcommittee on Housing of the Banking and Currency Committee, the body that had statutory jurisdiction over the RFC.[3] Fulbright had been shocked; it made him believe, as he remarked later, that McCarthy "was a boodler."[4] Nothing came of the incident at the time,

2 "FBI Counter-Spy Calls McCarthy an 'Amateur,'" *Washington Daily News,* January 13, 1954.

3 *Congressional Record,* Senate, July 31, 1954, 12910.

4 Quoted in Haynes Johnson and Bernard M. Gwertzman, *Fulbright: The Dissenter* (New York, 1968), 157.

however: McCarthy had not violated the law, and he, directly, was not the subject of the investigation.

What angered and dismayed Fulbright was not so much the efforts of professional anticommunists to restrict the activities of subversives through legislation, but the habit of some of their number, principally McCarthy, to accuse indiscriminately and to slander the innocent.[5] Reports from Fulbright exchange students and officials living abroad indicated that McCarthyism was beginning to erode support for the United States among its allies. "What our former friends understand least of all," F. G. Friedmann wrote from Rome, "is that in a country that prides itself in democratic and individualistic traditions, so few men have the courage to stand up and point out the dangers of blindly following the prevalent emotional trends."[6] Europeans, he warned Fulbright, saw in McCarthyism the rule of unreason.

In late 1950 McCarthy headed up a sordid campaign to block the nomination of Anna M. Rosenberg for assistant secretary of defense. Mrs. Rosenberg was a well-known New York businesswoman with wide experience in the field of personnel utilization. She had been nominated by President Truman on the recommendation of Secretary of Defense George C. Marshall for the express purpose of helping the Department of Defense meet the Korean emergency. On November 29, 1950, the Senate Armed Services Committee, chaired by Richard Russell, met briefly and recommended her confirmation unanimously. As the Senate prepared to take up the Rosenberg nomination, members of McCarthy's staff conspired with a group of professional anti-Semites headed by the notorious Gerald L. K. Smith, leader of the Christian Nationalist Crusade, to smear her as a fellow traveler. The conspirators arranged to have one Ralph DeSola, a former communist, swear that he had seen Mrs. Rosenberg at a meeting of the John Reed Club in the mid-1930s, and that he had been told she was a communist.[7]

On December 18 Fulbright rose on the floor of the Senate to defend Rosenberg. "For more than a year now," he declared, "we have witnessed in this country an unparalleled campaign of personal vilification, irresponsible and unrestrained." The "evil geniuses of the Kremlin" could not have devised a more clever plan for paralyzing the United States than to have the Congress and executive spend their time "in a frenzied examination of false charges against our own citizens." The most important point to be made, he concluded, was "that to attack the patriotism and character of persons with whom one may disagree, rather than the ideas and policies involved, is unjustifiable and irresponsible, and dangerous to our security."[8]

5 JWF to Kenneth Colegrove, Aug. 2, 1950, BCN 85, F23, SPF.
6 Friedmann to JWF, Oct. 13, 1950, BCN 48, F11, SPF.
7 Griffith, *Politics of Fear,* 136.
8 *Congressional Record,* Senate, Dec. 18, 1950, 16692.

In an effort to head off McCarthy, Russell announced that his committee would reconsider the nomination. Under his skilled leadership, the staff of the Senate Armed Services Committee began to uncover the ties among McCarthy's staff, Gerald Smith, and other prominent anti-Semites. Both the committee and the full Senate unanimously endorsed Rosenberg.[9] McCarthy, however, was not a man easily discouraged: When he found one avenue of attack blocked, he merely opened up a dozen more.

The first week in September 1951, President Truman submitted the name of Phillip Jessup, a professor at Columbia, for consideration as a delegate to the U.N. General Assembly. The nomination was referred to a special subcommittee of the SFRC headed by John Sparkman of Alabama and including Fulbright. Jessup, who had testified as a character witness for Alger Hiss and been involved marginally in the making of Far Eastern policy, had long been a target of Asia-firsters and the radical right. McCarthy showed up at the hearings with a twenty-eight-page brief on Jessup encased in a bright pink folder.[10] He claimed that the U.N. diplomat had been associated with "six communist fronts" and had followed "the Communist line" in opposing aid to Great Britain during the period of "the Hitler–Stalin pact."[11]

Fulbright immediately moved to the attack. "Do you regard Mr. Herbert Hoover as an intelligent American loyal to the American people and to the American system of government?" he asked McCarthy. McCarthy replied that he did. "How do you explain Mr. Hoover's high regard for Mr. Jessup as shown by these letters which I shall read to you?" McCarthy made no reply. "You can put together a number of zeros and still not arrive at the figure one," Fulbright declared.[12]

The proceedings soon degenerated into acrimonious exchanges between Fulbright and McCarthy, punctuated by shouts and poundings of the gavel. When McCarthy attempted to tarnish Jessup by listing organizations he or his wife had joined, Fulbright asked McCarthy: "Don't you think it's hard on a man to hold him responsible for all the organizations his wife may have joined?" Was he a subversive because Betty had joined the Red Cross at a time when it was headed by General George C. Marshall, "that well-known subversive and conspirator, according to your presentation," Fulbright asked sarcastically?[13] McCarthy sneered and made no reply.

Fulbright would later observe:

> This was the first time I realized that there was just no limit to what he'd say and insinuate. As the hearings proceeded, it suddenly oc-

9 Griffith, *Politics of Fear,* 139.
10 "McCarthy Runs Afoul of Fulbright," *Arkansas Gazette,* Sept. 28, 1951.
11 Griffith, *Politics of Fear,* 148.
12 Ibid., and notes for Jessup Hearing, undated, BCN 88, F16, SPF.
13 Quoted in Johnson and Gwertzman, *Fulbright: The Dissenter,* 159.

> curred to me that this fellow would do anything to deceive you to get his way. I was deeply repulsed, repelled, offended by his conduct in those hearings.[14]

By a vote of 3 to 2 the subcommittee declined to approve the Jessup nomination. Sparkman and Fulbright voted for the nomination, and the three Republicans against. The justification put forward by one of the Democrats, Guy Gillette of Iowa, was chilling. While admitting that Jessup was innocent of any wrongdoing, Gillette wrote Fulbright that "a considerable segment of our people . . . lack confidence in Dr. Jessup. . . . When the interest of an individual comes into conflict with the interest of the Nation, I have no hesitancy as to my decision."[15] In addition, of course, Gillette, like so many of his colleagues, was leery of a vote that could label him as "soft on communism." The nomination was held over until the Senate adjourned, allowing Truman to give Jessup a recess appointment. "It is unbelievable that any United States Senator could be as irresponsible as McCarthy," John Erickson wrote a friend.[16]

As long as Fulbright focused on abstractions and spoke in generalities, he proved relatively immune from attack by McCarthyites and red-baiters. Once he challenged McCarthy directly, however, he was fair game. "Dear Comrade," wrote James Tyler of Pomona, "remember what happened to Sen. Pepper, Sen. Graham, Sen. Taylor of Idaho, Sen. Lucas, Sen. Tydings and Ex-Congressman Vito Marcantonio [all had been defeated for reelection by conservative challengers] for taking the same course you are taking in attacking and smearing everyone who makes any attempt to smoke out these dirty traitors who infest our country."[17]

The 1952 election campaign had been a frustrating and stressful experience for Fulbright. The tensions associated with his initial bouts with McCarthy, coupled with the ensuing Springfield fiasco, sapped his resources. To rest and recuperate, he made arrangements to take Betty on a vacation to England in late November. Just as they were preparing to depart for their much-anticipated tour of the Cotswolds, Bill and Betty received word that Roberta had been stricken with a major heart attack. She had suffered from heart trouble for several years, losing weight and experiencing bouts of severe depression in the process. The family quickly realized that this attack could be her last.

14 Quoted in ibid., 158.
15 Gillette to JWF, Oct. 10, 1951, BCN 88, F15, SPF.
16 Erickson to Lt. Col. Paul Anderson, Oct. 3, 1951, BCN 77, F31, SPF.
17 Tyler to JWF, Oct. 3, 1951, BCN 88, F14, SPF.

Fulbright canceled the trip and rushed the family to Fayetteville. Roberta rallied, and he returned to Washington. She sank again. Three times he returned to northwest Arkansas after being told that his mother had only a few hours to live; three times she rallied. Shortly after Christmas, Fulbright departed for Europe for a visit to several of the exchange programs. Three days following his return, on January 11, 1953, Roberta died.[18]

Services were held in the picturesque First Christian Church in Fayetteville. The Reverend John Asbell, who, as part of the GGL, had fought the Ring in the 1930s, paid tribute to her. "She had loved and been loved, respected and been respected," he eulogized. She had made a difference.[19]

Fulbright grieved for his mother, but unlike his father's death, hers was not a shock. She was seventy-nine. Their separation was part of the natural order of things. Her full life had been characterized by hope and optimism rather than regret and reproach. Sometimes foolish, sometimes noble, she had loved Bill unreservedly, and he had known it.

When the Republicans gained control of Congress in 1952, Joe McCarthy became head of the Committee on Government Operations and subsequently placed himself in charge of the Permanent Subcommittee on Investigations. Immediately he struck at the Voice of America, a subsidiary of the United States Information Agency that, with White House approval, had been ordering works by writers of all political persuasions for its libraries. In February 1953 the State Department began withdrawing books the McCarthy committee considered subversive. Unsatisfied, McCarthy dispatched Roy M. Cohn and G. David Schine, two pretentious young red-baiters on his staff, to investigate VOA libraries. To the alternate amusement and anger of U.S. officials, the pair sped across Europe on their highly visible tour and returned to the United States with more grist for their employer's mill.

During the Jessup hearings Fulbright had become friends with Senator William Benton (D–Connecticut). An early and vociferous critic of McCarthy, Benton had been targeted by rabid anticommunists and defeated in 1952.[20] Though out of the Senate, Bill Benton proved unwilling either to forgive or forget the wrongs done him by Joe McCarthy. In late February he wrote Fulbright urging him to take the lead in opposing the Wisconsin demagogue and offering to supply him with ammunition for the fight. "Bill, I want you to know that if you move in on the McCarthy matter you will be surprised at the response you will get from all over the United States," he predicted.[21]

18 Erickson to Willard Hawkins, Dec. 1, 1952, and JWF to Fodor, Jan. 3, 1953, BCN 105, F27, SPF.

19 Quoted in Allen Gilbert, *A Fulbright Chronicle* (Fayetteville, 1980), 153.

20 Griffith, *Politics of Fear,* 157.

21 Benton to JWF, Feb. 25, 1953, BCN 88, F4, SPF.

Fulbright was sympathetic to Benton's plea, but the new, young Democratic minority leader, Senator Lyndon Baines Johnson, was not. Johnson, reiterating as frequently as he could that McCarthy was "a Republican problem," did not want to step into the GOP's "soft on communism" trap. "I will not commit my party," declared the minority leader, "to some high school debate on the subject, 'Resolved, that Communism is good for the United States,' with my party taking affirmative."[22] Initially Fulbright agreed: "For a Democrat to take the lead at this juncture would cause the Republicans to rally around McCarthy. . . . Unless some leading Republican is willing to take the curse of partisanship off the matter, I doubt that it is wise for a Democrat to make the move."[23]

But very quickly Fulbright's patience began to run out. The Eisenhower administration stood idly by while McCarthy terrorized academia, Hollywood, the media, and the federal bureaucracy. McCarthy's attack on the VOA and its parent, the United States Information Agency (USIA), was particularly alarming to Fulbright because at that time the USIA supervised educational exchange programs. He sensed that the Fulbright scholarship program was in danger; and, in fact, in the summer of 1953 the State Department had withdrawn the fellowship of a scholar whose wife would not answer questions concerning her possible membership in the Communist Party.[24] After questioning BFS members and other exchange officials, Fulbright discovered that State Department security officer and McCarthy protégé Scott McLeod was in effect imposing loyalty oaths on prospective Fulbrighters both in the United States and abroad. In countries such as Italy, where membership in the Italian Communist Party was significant, McCarthyism was threatening to destroy the entire program.[25]

Then the Senate Appropriations Committee, of which McCarthy was a member, scheduled at his behest a hearing on the annual appropriation for the USIA. At stake was nothing less than the future of the Fulbright program, for the exchange funds were then part of the USIA appropriation requests. The hearing took place at a time when Fulbright – just recently returned from Oxford, where he was among six men honored at the fiftieth-anniversary ceremonies of the Rhodes scholarships – was publicly identified with educational exchange, an exercise many right-wingers considered subversive by definition.

The McCarthy–Fulbright confrontation took place before TV cameras in the elegant old Supreme Court chamber in the Capitol. As the nineteenth-century home of the House of Representatives, it had been the scene of Rep-

22 Quoted in Griffith, *Politics of Fear,* 206.
23 Quoted in ibid.
24 Barbara Gilder to Eisenhower, June 22, 1953, Fulbright Cross Reference File, Papers of Dwight D. Eisenhower, Eisenhower Library, Abilene, Kans.
25 Interview with Cipriana Scelba, June 17, 1992, Rome, Italy.

resentative John Quincy Adams's attacks on slavery and of the famous Webster–Hayne debates. McCarthy quickly put everyone on notice that he was not going to let the dignity of his surroundings deter him. He was loud, abusive, and disruptive, at one point seizing the gavel, although he was not chairman. He raved against the exchange program and referred to Fulbright as "Halfbright."

> MCCARTHY: Do you know whether the board that selected the students receives a security check?
>
> FULBRIGHT: It does.
>
> MCCARTHY: Not what you heard. Do you know of your own knowledge?
>
> FULBRIGHT: I have not made the check myself, but on the best authority I know of, it does.
>
> MCCARTHY: You say they get State Department security clearance?
>
> FULBRIGHT: It is my understanding they also are checked by the FBI – that is, the members of the Board of Foreign Scholarships.
>
> MCCARTHY: Do you know whether the policy is not to give Communists or Communist sympathizers scholarships or appoint them as lecturers or professors?
>
> FULBRIGHT: I think one of the leading members of the board is Dean McGuire of Catholic University here, who is an original member.
>
> MCCARTHY: Could you answer the question?
>
> FULBRIGHT: I cannot believe that he is interested in giving Communists scholarships. Another is Colonel Anderson of the Veterans Department . . .
>
> MCCARTHY: [*interrupting*] Could you answer the question?
>
> FULBRIGHT: . . . who has been on it since the beginning, and I do not believe he is interested in doing it.

When McCarthy again insisted that he answer his question, Fulbright retorted: "It is an answer. They do not in my opinion for a moment countenance giving scholarships to Communists if they know it."

Later on in the proceedings McCarthy tried to impeach the integrity and independence of the board. "I ask you these questions," he said to Fulbright, "because the program bearing you name – and I assume the board pays some attention to what you say. . . ."

This time it was Fulbright who interrupted. "Your assumption is entirely incorrect," he declared indignantly. "The board does not pay any attention to what I say. I do not tell the board what do to and I would not think of telling the board about anything. It would be the best way I know of to destroy it."

In a last attempt to discredit the exchange program and Fulbright with it, McCarthy insisted that he be allowed to insert into the record statements made by some Fulbright students "condemning the American way of life and praising the Communist form of government."[26]

Nimbly, Fulbright countered. If the junior senator from Wisconsin was allowed to do that, then he should be permitted to insert "other kinds of statements that have been received." As he made clear, he had come prepared to submit thousands of names and many statements by and about former Fulbright scholars that proved their loyalty and worth to their country. When Chairman Homer Ferguson (R–Michigan) ruled that "if we receive one, we will receive the other," McCarthy dropped his line of attack. Never again did he publicly assault the exchange program. Historian Walter Johnson, an original board member, was convinced that Fulbright's defense had prevented the exchange program from becoming another casualty of McCarthyism.

As the Eisenhower administration approached the end of its first year in office, Joe McCarthy appeared to be riding the crest of a wave of public fear and adulation that would never break. At the outset many senators had tended to give him the benefit of the doubt. Hard-line Soviet rhetoric, coupled with revelations concerning the activities of atom spies in Canada and Soviet double agent Klaus Fuchs at Los Alamos, confirmed that there was indeed a security threat. Despite the outrageousness of McCarthy's charges and the transparency of his cases, virtually every member of Congress still believed that to cross McCarthy was to lay oneself open to charges of being soft on communism and to risk political and personal ruin. McCarthy, who had won reelection to the Senate by a hundred and forty thousand votes in 1952, claimed credit for electing no fewer than eight members of the Senate and defeating a like number. Never mind that Eisenhower's popularity and the nation's disgust with the Democratic Party had been more responsible for these outcomes than McCarthy's political clout: It was perceptions that counted. The president, the Senate, and the nation were intimidated.

The authority for the Permanent Subcommittee on Investigations was due to run out on January 31, 1954. Several of McCarthy's opponents initiated a half-hearted attempt to close his mouth by cutting off his investigative arms; but as the date for the vote on renewal of funds for the McCarthy committee approached, senatorial hands grew clammy and resolve weakened. On the final roll call vote only one senator, J. William Fulbright of Arkansas, dared cast his ballot against the appropriation.[27]

Many of his colleagues considered Fulbright's vote an act of political suicide. "I was a very foolish young fellow who's not going to be around here very long," he remembered the consensus as being. Some felt guilty for not

[26] Quoted in Johnson and Gwertzman, *Fulbright: The Dissenter,* 135–6.
[27] Griffith, *Politics of Fear,* 239.

having joined him. Herbert Lehman of New York, who had openly challenged McCarthy during his rise to power, dropped by Fulbright's office and apologized for not voting with him; it would not happen again, he promised.[28] Fulbright was not particularly concerned over the prospect of McCarthy's vengeance. Indeed, on January 30 he appeared on *Face the Nation* and defended his vote. As it turned out, he knew his constituents better than did his colleagues. When, shortly after the McCarthy committee vote, Senator Wayne Morse thanked a crowd of several hundred in Little Rock for electing Bill Fulbright to the Senate, he received a two-minute standing ovation.[29]

In late 1953, with McCarthyism lying over America like a plague, Fulbright began reading J. W. Wheeler-Bennett's *The Nemesis of Power,* an account of Hitler's rise in Germany. The book immediately brought to mind parallels between the techniques that Hitler used to subvert democracy in the Weimar Republic and the "politics of fear" being practiced by McCarthy. Both relied on the "big lie"; both promised to save their societies from Bolshevism; both poisoned the political process with intimidation and hatred. Fulbright wrote R. B. McCallum:

> I fear for the future. McCarthy is an unscrupulous demagogue with many of the characteristics of Hitler. . . . He has come upon the scene just as television is becoming a powerful medium, and we do not know how to evaluate his influence. To me he is completely revolting from every point of view, but I cannot deny that he seems to have a very substantial following.[30]

Like Nazism, McCarthyism was rooted in bigotry, anti-intellectualism, superpatriotism, and tyranny. Both aimed at the establishment of a police state, and both survived with the aid of a secret police.[31]

Indeed, Fulbright and his staff had long suspected that there was a connection between J. Edgar Hoover and Joe McCarthy. During McCarthy's tenure as chairman, the Permanent Subcommittee on Investigations had hired several former agents to conduct "field work." It became common practice for committee staffer Roy Cohn to proclaim in the midst of a hearing that the proceedings were being conducted in accordance with wishes and desires of the FBI. Fulbright had been infuriated by McCarthy's attacks on Charles E. "Chip" Bohlen, Eisenhower's nominee to be ambassador to the Soviet Union.[32] A career Foreign Service officer, Bohlen had not only been present at the Yalta conference, but during his confirmation hearings had defended

28 Interview with Jack Yingling, Oct. 12, 1988, Savannah, Ga.

29 Leland F. Leatherman to JWF, Mar. 4, 1954, BCN 99 F29, SPF.

30 JWF to McCallum, Mar. 13, 1954, BCN 83, F7, SPF.

31 JWF to James T. Farrell, Mar. 1, 1954, BCN 47, F38, and JWF to C. A. Bishop, Jan. 2, 1954, BCN 88, F4, SPF.

32 A. H. Belmont to L. V. Boardman, Mar. 26, 1954, and SAC, Little Rock to Hoover, Sept. 23, 1953, 62-77126-2, FBI Files.

the accords reached there. Encouraged by Hoover, who confided to the administration that Bohlen was a security risk because he consorted with known homosexuals, McCarthy spread the word that the career Foreign Service officer did not lead a normal "family life." The SFRC detailed Senators Robert Taft and John Sparkman to peruse Bohlen's FBI file. Hoover protested vehemently this "violation" of his agency's confidential records, but under pressure from Eisenhower, who was determined to stick by Bohlen, he relented.[33] Taft and Sparkman found nothing, and the Senate voted to confirm.

When the State Department hired former FBI agent and McCarthy protégé Scott McLeod to be its internal security officer, Fulbright became convinced that the Senate's witch-hunters had direct, ongoing access to the agency's raw files.[34] In September 1953 the special agent assigned to Little Rock made the mistake of calling the junior senator in the course of a security check of a prospective VOA employee. The subject, a former State Department official, had given Fulbright's name as a reference. "Is this investigation being conducted at the request of Senator McCarthy," he demanded. "Has Senator McCarthy accused [deleted] of being a pansy?" The agent replied that the VOA had requested the check and that agency intelligence was confidential. "You must not know what's going on in Washington," Fulbright replied. The agent found the senator "extremely sarcastic," his superior reported to Hoover.[35] Soon after that conversation, Fulbright decided to expose the FBI–McCarthy connection at the first opportunity.

Two months later Senator Karl Mundt, an archconservative from South Dakota who was second in seniority to McCarthy on the Government Operations Committee, told the Bonneville Knife and Fork Club of Salt Lake City:

> The FBI will tip off a congressional committee as to a situation where it is convinced American security is endangered. The committee's inquiry makes it possible to bring the case into the open and, with the suspected Communist spy usually taking refuge in the 5th Amendment's protection against incriminating himself, it is possible to eliminate that particular threat.[36]

McCarthy himself had twice tipped his hand during a February 1954 debate with Senator Allen Ellender. During an attack on the United States Army, he termed an FBI report on a particular officer in which his subcommittee was interested as "excellent," and went on to cite the contents of that report. Later he referred to "the names of forty informers" he had gotten from the agency.[37]

33 L. B. Nichols to J. Edgar Hoover, Mar. 16, 1954, 62-77126-2, FBI Files.
34 Deleted to L. V. Boardman, Mar. 15, 1954, 62-77126-2, FBI Files.
35 SAC, Little Rock to Hoover, Sept. 23, 1953, 62-71126-2, FBI Files.
36 J. D. Williams to JWF, Mar. 15, 1954, BCN 88, F19, SPF.
37 JWF to Frank Ahlgreen, Mar. 23, 1954, BCN 87, F9, SPF.

Fulbright decided to mount a direct attack. On March 14, 1954, he told reporters that Hoover's agency was leaking confidential material to McCarthy, and he, for one, was going to stop cooperating with the FBI. With the cold war in full swing and at the height of the second Red Scare, Fulbright's was a dangerous statement. No American, much less a public official, had the right to refuse to cooperate with America's number one crime fighter, declared Fulton Lewis, Paul Harvey, and other right-wing commentators. Attorney General Herbert Brownell insisted that the bureau had "permitted no such thing during my term as attorney general," and McCarthy branded Fulbright's charges as "a vicious attack on the FBI."

The director was appalled by Fulbright's attack: He considered the junior senator a supporter. Hoover had delivered the commencement address at the University of Arkansas in 1943 and had been a guest in Roberta's house. Hal Douglas had stayed on friendly terms with the FBI, and Fulbright had spoken to the Academy's graduating class in 1949. Whatever his motives, Fulbright's public impugning of the integrity of his beloved agency had placed him beyond the pale in the director's eyes. "The statement of Fulbright is shocking," he minuted a subordinate. "He puts politics above security interests of the country."[38]

Though he was furious with McCarthy for risking the good name of the FBI, Hoover himself wasted no time in coming to the Wisconsin senator's defense. While the two vacationed together at a La Jolla seaside hotel, Hoover told reporters that McCarthy was a vigorous individual who was not going to be pushed around. "When one attacks subversives," declared the nation's chief spy-catcher, he is "going to be the victim of the most extremely vicious criticism that can be made."[39]

Like most bullies, however, J. Edgar Hoover was also a coward. Few public officials had ever dared question the integrity of the FBI. Congress had never refused it a nickel of its funding request. The Arkansan's gall intimidated the director. In the wake of Fulbright's announcement of noncooperation, Hoover attempted a public relations counterattack. "I told Senator [deleted] that this statement of Senator Fulbright was particularly vicious because it put an idea into the minds of people that our files are wide open and therefore they should not give information to the FBI," he reported to Clyde Tolson. "I stated this was exactly what the Communists have been urging their members to do." He praised and encouraged Walter Winchell, Paul Harvey, and others who condemned the Arkansan, and tried to link those like columnist Edgar Mowrer, who defended him, to communist-front organiza-

38 FBI Rept., Apr. 8, 1954, 62-71126-2, FBI Files.

39 "FBI Chief Calls McCarthy Man Who Won't Be Pushed Around," *Washington Star*, Aug. 26, 1953.

tions.[40] At the same time, however, Hoover browbeat Karl Mundt into a public retraction and did his best to cut McCarthy off from further access to FBI files.[41] There was no surveillance of Fulbright, no bugs, no probes into his private affairs. All Hoover could do was to order agents to respect the senator's wishes and have no more contact with him. In fact, he was convinced that Fulbright was laying the groundwork for a full-scale investigation of the bureau, and he was terrified by the prospect.[42] For the rest of his public career, the director would do his best to give the Arkansan a wide berth.

In 1954, with McCarthy apparently at the height of his power, a series of events unfolded that revealed the Wisconsin legislator for the demagogue he was and paved the way for his demise. In the spring of that year McCarthy launched an investigation of the U.S. Army, charging that Secretary of the Army Robert Stevens and his subordinates were protecting communists in uniform.

Although Stevens was forced to turn over army files and permit army officers and civilian employees to appear before the Permanent Subcommittee on Investigations, he counterattacked by filing twenty-nine charges against McCarthy, subcommittee counsel Roy Cohn, and others. From April 22 through June 17, 1954, the Senate Committee on Government Operations under Karl Mundt held hearings on McCarthy's relations with the military. To the dismay of McCarthy's staff, Mundt permitted the proceedings to be televised. In the days that followed, the nation witnessed firsthand the cruelty and indiscriminateness of the Wisconsin demagogue's attacks.[43]

Although the Army–McCarthy hearings were dramatic and spectacular, they were inconclusive. McCarthy's survival, indeed his power, was made possible not by the support of the Senate but by its acquiescence. In the aftermath of the hearings, the majority of the upper house still had no stomach for a confrontation with the junior senator from Wisconsin; but Fulbright, an informal network of senators and staffers nicknamed the "Clearing House," and a seventy-eight-year-old conservative Republican from Vermont named Ralph Flanders had no intention of letting the Senate off the hook. On June 1, 1954, Flanders rose and compared McCarthy to Hitler, denouncing him for spreading division and confusion throughout the land. Echoing Fulbright, he declared, "Were the Junior Senator from Wisconsin in the pay of the Communists he could not have done a better job for them."[44] Behind him sat

40 Hoover to Tolson et al., Mar. 15, 1954, and M. A. Jones to L. B. Nichols, June 30, 1954, 62-71126-2, FBI Files.

41 L. B. Nichols to Clyde Tolson, Mar. 24 and Apr. 14, 1954, 62-71126-2, FBI Files.

42 L. B. Nichols to Clyde Tolson, Apr. 14, 1954, 62-71126-2, FBI Files.

43 Griffith, *Politics of Fear,* 259.

44 Quoted in Griffith, *Politics of Fear,* 274.

Majority Leader William F. Knowland, red-faced and angry yet powerless to stop Flanders's indictment. On June 11, after consulting Fulbright, Flanders introduced a resolution of censure.

Fulbright was delighted. At long last the Republican he and Lyndon Johnson had been waiting for had stepped forward. The task that confronted the Arkansan in the weeks-long buildup to the censure vote was to secure the support of southern senators. The key to this group, many believed, was Fulbright's colleague, the senior senator from Arkansas, John McClellan. A dour, burly, insecure man, McClellan was a shrewd politician who could regularly drink himself into a stupor and still pose as the darling of Arkansas's multitudinous Baptists. As the ranking minority member of McCarthy's committee, McClellan was strategically placed.

Suppressing his dislike, Fulbright met throughout the hearings with McClellan and played an important role in stiffening his backbone. He appealed to the senior senator as a fellow constitutional conservative: McCarthy was trampling on the Bill of Rights and, as states' righters, neither one of them could stand for that. Most important of all, he flattered McClellan unmercifully. "I had lunch with him today and I believe he is beginning to get in the spirit of the thing and recognizes that he has a great responsibility and is taking some pleasure in discharging properly, all of which pleases me," Fulbright wrote Harry Ashmore.[45]

With the Republican hierarchy vehemently opposed to the resolution and the Democrats timorous, the anti-McCarthy coalition worked to build support for censure outside the Senate. Flanders, backed by John Sherman Cooper (R–Kentucky), led the Republican charge while Fulbright, aided by John Sparkman, Mike Monroney of Oklahoma, and Herbert Lehman headed up the Democratic effort. Fulbright relied heavily on a report his staff had elicited from Bethesda Naval Hospital. Citing that document, he spread the word that McCarthy was a classic paranoid schizophrenic, complete with delusions of grandeur, a persecution complex, obsession, a tendency to systematic falsification of the past, and repressed homosexuality. Paranoia, Fulbright noted, was virtually impossible to treat. When the victim was not dangerous, he was at the least "a public nuisance because of his suspicions, accusations and petty litigations."[46]

On July 18 Fulbright appeared on "Meet the Press." "Will you vote next week for the Flanders motion to censure Senator McCarthy?" Mae Craig of the Portland, Maine, *Press Herald* asked. "Yes, Mrs. Craig, I'll vote tomorrow, next week, whenever it comes up." To what in particular do you object,

45 JWF to Ashmore, May 12, 1954, BCN 87, F5, SPF.

46 John Erickson had written to a psychiatrist friend of his at Bethesda describing a "friend" who was, of course, Joe McCarthy, and asking for a diagnosis. Erickson to "Phil," July 23, 1954, BCN 77, F28, and "Characteristics and Symptoms of the Form of Insanity Known as Paranoia," 1954, BCN 87, F12, SPF.

she asked. "I object to his methods . . . his complete lack of any respect for the truth in his own statements." New rules would be inadequate; only censure could halt a man like McCarthy.[47]

During the ensuing Senate debate, Fulbright introduced a list of seven particulars, including branding individuals as guilty without according them due process, inciting government employees to violate the law, and interfering with the conduct of foreign affairs.[48] When Flanders added an extended list of his own, the Senate voted to set up a select committee under Arthur V. Watkins of Utah, a Republican, to consider the charges against him.

The anti-McCarthy forces had won a major victory, but Fulbright and his colleagues were still guarded in their optimism. Only three times in 165 years had the Senate voted to censure one of its members. Between the Senate's institutional timidity and McCarthy's total lack of scruple, the battle might yet be lost.

The report of the Watkins committee exceeded Fulbright and Flanders's expectations, however. "When persons in high places fail to set and meet high standards, the people lose faith," it declared. "If our people lose faith, our form of Government cannot long endure." The select committee proclaimed McCarthy's actions to be "contemptuous, contumacious, and denunciatory," and obstructive to the legislative process; for this reason they recommended that he be officially denounced.[49]

The anti-McCarthy activists hoped that the Senate would be called back into session in late September to consider censure. They feared that any delay would offer their prey and his partisans opportunity for delay and diversion. Neither Republicans or Democrats were anxious to meet the issue before the November elections, however, and the leadership decided to wait.

On November 29 final debate began on the resolution of censure. On December 1 the Senate voted 67 to 22 to condemn Joseph McCarthy. Only three senators – McCarthy, John Kennedy, and Alexander Wiley – refused to vote and went unrecorded.[50] At long last the struggle was over.

Joe McCarthy died on May 2, 1957, reputedly of cirrhosis of the liver. He had always been a heavy drinker, and his censure and subsequent isolation only aggravated the problem.

In thinking back on McCarthy and his reign of terror, what struck Fulbright most was the disconcerting lack of sincerity or personal rancor the demagogue had displayed in making his attacks. There seemed to be no connection between either his intellect or his heart and the words he spoke. He was pure

47 *Meet the Press,* July 18, 1954, transcript, Box 115, Fulbright File, White House Central Files, Eisenhower Papers.
48 Reasons for Censuring McCarthy, undated, BCN 1, F25, SPF.
49 Griffith, *Politics of Fear,* 304.
50 Ibid.

political opportunist without ideology or real grievance. For him anticommunism was simply a means to an end.[51]

In the final analysis Fulbright was more frightened by the ism than by the man. There would always be opportunists and demagogues ready to play on the public's fears and prejudices. Historically, Americans, optimistic and pragmatic, had resisted those who practiced the politics of fear; but the atomic age and the confrontation with the Soviet Union seemed to have unbalanced the popular mind. In the midst of the second Red Scare, the Arkansan speculated on its causes. Perhaps it was the anxiety of unresolved conflict, the siege mentality of a nation confronted with an apparently implacable enemy; or, more darkly, the breadth and depth of McCarthyism could reflect a burgeoning know-nothingism. In their frustration, his countrymen seemed ready to condemn any idea that they considered alien. According to McCarthyites, other cultures were by definition evil and potentially contaminating. Ideas and the questioning that produced them were portrayed as hidden avenues by which communism could gain access to America's psyche. During his jousts with McCarthy and his supporters, Fulbright felt compelled more than once to denounce "the swinish blight of anti-intellectualism." Most disturbing, Fulbright sensed that McCarthyism had merely subsided, that it lurked beneath the surface of American life, ready to burst forth in its consuming fury at the next crisis.

Observers of the American scene had early noted a relationship between McCarthyism and isolationism. Indeed, some, including Fulbright, argued that the Taft–Hoover proposal for withdrawal of U.S. troops from Europe and the witch-hunt for domestic communists were two blooms of a single poisonous plant. Both isolationists and antisubversives were seeking escape from a complex, dangerous world in which, it seemed, the best the United States could hope for was a tenuous stalemate. Conservatives such as Taft and Hoover, joined by such professional anticommunists as Jenner and Mundt, declared their resentment at the expenditures required by the Marshall Plan, the Mutual Security Act, and other foreign aid programs. They felt that the sustaining and nurturing of "alien" cultures and political systems was not in the national interest. Yet isolationists and antisubversives, more than any other Americans, viewed communism and Soviet imperialism as an indivisible and a mortal threat to everything for which America stood. It was no coincidence that as McCarthyism peaked, traditional isolationism, in the form of the Bricker amendment, emerged once again to bid for the favor of the American people.

John Bricker, the junior senator from Ohio, was a disciple of Robert Taft. He shared his more famous colleague's political and foreign policy views but

[51] Interview with J. William Fulbright, Oct. 11-18, 1988, Washington D.C.

lacked Taft's compensating intelligence. A former governor of Ohio and Thomas Dewey's running mate in 1944, Bricker quickly aligned himself with the conservative coalition upon his election to the Senate in 1946. He was an outspoken champion of private enterprise and states' rights. To him unemployment, housing, and civil rights were matters best left to states and localities. He quickly became a favorite target for liberals. "Intellectually he is like interstellar space," declared John Gunther in his *Inside U.S.A.*, "– a vast vacuum occasionally crossed by homeless, wandering clichés."[52] In mid-September 1951 the Ohio legislator introduced a constitutional amendment designed, he claimed, to protect the American people from executive tyranny and, more important, from the nefarious influence of foreign ideologies and cultures. The original proposal, complex and confusing, was modified, simplified, and reintroduced as Senate Joint Resolution 1 on January 7, 1953. The Bricker amendment stipulated that executive agreements would become effective only after congressional action; no treaty of any kind, moreover, would become law until accepted by both houses of Congress; that is, they would not be "self-executing." Any treaty provision that contravened the Constitution was to be automatically null and void. No foreign power or agency, proclaimed the Bricker amendment, was to exercise authority over the domestic affairs of the United States.[53]

The Ohioan's proposal to restrict the executive branch's freedom of action in foreign affairs stemmed from a number of specific but related concerns. In the early days of the amendment, the driving force behind it was the American Bar Association, the bulk of whose membership was afraid that liberals at home, in league with socialists and communists abroad, intended to use international conventions to force antilynching, anti–poll tax, and antidiscrimination legislation on the South. They were joined by Bricker and anti–New Deal Republicans concerned about "creeping socialism." The conservative coalition had become convinced that the United Nations, through vehicles such as the Human Rights Declaration of 1948 and the Genocide Convention, was attempting to force America to become a racially integrated welfare state.[54]

Xenophobia, racism, and economic conservatism dovetailed nicely with the politically profitable issues of executive usurpation and Democratic betrayal. Many conservatives, egged on by the Republican leadership, had come to the conclusion that Franklin Roosevelt had "sold out" and "turned over" Eastern Europe and China to the communists in a series of secret agreements at Yalta. Jenner, Knowland, Taft, and other Republicans had so charged throughout the 1952 presidential campaign. Indeed, the myth of the Yalta

52 Quoted in Duane Tananbaum, *The Bricker Amendment Controversy: A Test of Eisenhower's Political Leadership* (Ithaca, N.Y., 1988), 24.
53 Ibid., 68.
54 Ibid., 7–12, 24–9.

betrayal lay at the heart of McCarthyism; and, despite his professed dislike of McCarthy, Dwight Eisenhower was as ready to wield that sword as the junior senator from Wisconsin. Anticipating the famous "captive nations" resolution, the president declared in his first State of the Union message: "I shall ask the Congress at a later date to join in an appropriate resolution, making clear that this government recognizes no kind of commitment contained in secret understandings of the past with foreign governments which permit this kind of enslavement [communist domination of Eastern Europe]."[55] Proponents of the Bricker amendment promised that it would forever preclude such sellouts as the Yalta accords.

Both critics and supporters of the Bricker proposal agreed that if it were enacted, the United States would not be able to participate in many of the routine functions performed by the United Nations, much less adhere to international treaties on such subjects as human rights, a nuclear test ban, or the abolition of weapons of chemical warfare without a specific vote of Congress and the American people. Liberals argued that the amendment contravened existing constitutional provisions that made treaties the supreme law of the land.

The depth and breadth of support for the Bricker amendment indicated that isolationism and the nativistic and xenophobic roots from which it sprang were still powerful forces in American politics and culture at midcentury. The Ohioan managed to secure the cosponsorship of sixty-two other senators, including forty-four of the forty-seven Republicans. The president of the American Bar Association declared his support; so did the U.S. Chamber of Commerce, the Daughters of the American Revolution, the American Medical Association, the American Legion, the Veterans of Foreign Wars, and many other national organizations.[56] For members of the radical right, the Bricker amendment was part of the ongoing crusade to keep America pure. "Many of the most voluble enemies of the Bricker amendment are . . . reluctant to see a gap . . . that now exists in the Constitution, closed to their plans to bring about domestic and international collectivism," proclaimed the right-wing Economic Council.[57]

In early February 1954, with Joe McCarthy still at the height of his power and the Senate of the United States apparently ready to assume direct control of the nation's foreign policy, Fulbright rose to deliver perhaps the most powerful speech of his young career. The Arkansan accused supporters of the Bricker amendment of staging the most "violent attack" on the Constitution that the nation had seen since the 1850s. Their object was nothing less than "an amendment that . . . throttles the President of the United States in his conduct of foreign relations." As with McCarthyism, it was not the Bricker

55 Memorandum on Anti-Enslavement Resolutions, Mar. 4, 1953, BCN 46, F15, SPF.
56 Stephen E. Ambrose, *Eisenhower,* vol. II, *The President* (New York, 1984), 68.
57 Economic Council Letter, N. 327, Jan. 15, 1954.

amendment itself that was of major concern, the Arkansan proclaimed, but rather the mind-set that had spawned it. The attempt to hamstring the executive was the manifestation of a deep-seated desire to escape from the world. The end of World War II and the coming of the cold war had given rise to "a period of inevitable and unpredictable change," the Arkansan acknowledged, but the proper response was neither national hysteria nor collective withdrawal, but a "willingness and ability to look facts in the face, however bitter they may be, to appraise them at their true worth and then to act calmly, judiciously, and determinedly." Peace – indeed, survival – would not happen by itself. "Nature – pitiless in a pitiless universe – is certainly not concerned with the survival of Americans or, for that matter, of any of the two billion people now inhabiting this earth. Hence, our destiny, with the aid of God, remains in our own hands."

Fulbright's oration ended with a ringing endorsement of federal power:

> I do not share the [isolationist's] fears of an ignorant or willful President or Senate, and this faith on my part is not merely an innocent trust in individuals, present and future. It is a faith in the form of government which we have known for 165 years, in the traditions and history of the institutions of the Presidency, the Senate, and the Supreme Court, and in the ability of our people, present and future, to regulate those institutions through the processes of government, as they have in the past.[58]

Nothing Fulbright had done since the Fulbright resolution and the exchange program so endeared him to American liberals and internationalists as the Bricker amendment speech. Coupled with his stand against McCarthy, the address stamped him in their eyes as America's preeminent champion of civil liberties and an enlightened foreign policy. "I was tremendously impressed and stirred, not only by the cogency of your thought but by the felicity of expression," Arthur Rosenbaum of the Brooklyn Jewish Council wrote.[59] The *New York TImes* gave the speech front-page coverage, and Roy Wilkins of the NAACP cabled his congratulations.[60] It should be noted that those American liberals who had broken away from Henry Wallace and his Russophile followers in 1947 to organize the ADA still regarded cold-war activism as the diplomatic manifestation of their commitment to social justice. They, like Fulbright, believed at this point that the Truman Doctrine, Marshall Plan, Mutual Security Program, Voice of America, and other cold-war programs were mechanisms in service to freedom, democracy, and national self-determination. They perceived an activist foreign policy implemented by a dynamic executive not as an aspect of imperialism, but as a means for combat-

58 *Congressional Record,* Senate, Feb. 2, 1954, 1106.
59 Rosenbaum to JWF, Feb. 3, 1954, BCN 47, F37, SPF.
60 Wilkins to JWF, Feb. 4, 1954, BCN 47, F36, SPF.

ing totalitarianism. Over the next year the Senate debated the Bricker amendment and various compromise proposals put forward by Walter George (D–Georgia), William Knowland (R–California), and Homer Ferguson (R–Michigan). A coalition of internationalist Democrats and Eisenhower Republicans managed to defeat each in turn.[61]

Though the Bricker amendment speech would cause Fulbright to be hailed by American liberals as their new messiah, he saw it for what it was: the statement of a constitutional conservative striving to protect the nation from the extremes of the radical right. It marked the beginning of a lifelong mission.

During the first dozen years of its existence the Fulbright Exchange Program suffered acutely from lack of funds both for individual stipends and for new and enlarged programs. "I personally signed a contract for a year's salary of $1900 to maintain myself and my wife," wrote one scholar working in the Netherlands. "Unmarried students signed for $1500. . . . As a result we have been unable to pursue our studies satisfactorily without liberal supplements from private funds – if we were lucky enough to have any."[62] During 1950–4 Fulbright scratched, clawed, plotted, and schemed to force additional funding for the program from private sources, but particularly from the federal government.

So anxious became Fulbright over the survival and adequate financing of the exchange program that he actually sought to portray it as part of America's propaganda war against the Soviet Union and international communism. The centerpieces of the Truman administration's effort to win the hearts and minds of Europeans were the Voice of America and Radio Free Europe. The measure creating those propaganda agencies – the United States Information and Education Exchange Act of 1948 – was the same piece of legislation that had authorized the State Department to seek appropriations to supplement the Fulbright program. Just as the cold war had been used to sell the British loan, the Arkansan perceived, it could also be employed to promote the exchange program. In addition, Fulbright operated on the assumption initially that linking his brain child with various "information" efforts would create a profitable coattail effect.

It quickly became apparent, however, that the Congress was willing to spend only a certain amount of money for overseas propaganda; elements of the program would have to compete with each other for limited funds. Consequently, from 1950 through 1954 Fulbright played the dangerous game of pushing student and faculty exchange while denigrating the activities of VOA

61 Tananbaum, *Bricker Amendment Controversy*, 157–74.
62 Barry to Alexander Wiley, May 30, 1950, BCN 75, F33, SPF.

and RFE. In the summer of 1950 the junior senator from Arkansas rose on the floor of the Senate and denounced America's two overseas networks. "I think the Europeans have an instinctive resistance to official propaganda and that we are wasting our money," he wrote Richard Russell.[63] The focal point of America's effort to spread the word concerning the blessings of its civilization should be the exchange of persons program, Fulbright argued. In the late summer he and Senator Benton introduced a resolution declaring America's overseas program "deficient in every respect."[64]

J. William Fulbright, to the surprise and consternation of his staff and friends, could be incredibly obtuse when it came to bureaucratic and congressional politics. Fulbright and Benton's attacks, together with McCarthy's assaults and the Cohn–Schine tour, prompted the House to cut the information program, including exchange of persons, by $34 million. The campaign against America's mechanisms of cultural warfare was led by Congressman John Rooney, a crusty, pink-faced Irish Catholic from Brooklyn. As chairman of the House Appropriations subcommittee that passed on the budget proposals of the Justice and State Departments, he was in a position to control the fate of the Fulbright program. Unfortunately for those interested in studying abroad, Rooney was as bitter an enemy of Fulbright's and the exchange program as he was a friend to J. Edgar Hoover and the FBI. He regarded scholarly travel overseas as just another State Department "extravagance." A *Saturday Evening Post* article described him as a man with five special loyalties: Brooklyn, the Catholic Church, Ireland, Israel, and the FBI.[65]

Baffled by what he considered the perversity of the lower house, Fulbright led an internationalist counterattack against cuts in the information program, parts of which he had just finished denouncing. He wrote Dorothy Thompson, Marquis Childs, David Lawrence, Arthur Krock, James Reston, and a dozen other columnists he knew, appealing to them to help save the exchange program.[66] Partly as a result of Fulbright's efforts, a House–Senate conference committee pulled the appropriation back up from $63 million to $85 million.[67] Fulbright and the exchange program had not heard the last of John Rooney, however.

Though not directly involved in the formulation or implementation of American foreign policy during these years, Fulbright studied the issues and began

63 JWF to Russell, Aug. 19, 1950, BCN 30, F9, SPF.

64 *Congressional Record,* Senate, Apr. 26, 1950, 5776, 5774.

65 JWF to George A. Carbone, Apr. 6, 1951, BCN 75, F31, SPF, and "J. Rooney Dies; Democrat Served 30 Years on Hill," *Washington Post,* Oct. 28, 1975.

66 JWF to Harry Ashmore et al., Mar. 26, 1951, BCN 75, F31, SPF.

67 JWF to Fodor, Aug. 29, 1951, BCN 105, F28, SPF.

to develop a philosophy to cover diplomatic and defense matters. Influenced by George Kennan, Reinhold Niehbur, and others, he came to advocate a pragmatic approach to the communist menace. The United States, he argued, should reject both globalism and isolationism. Instead of adopting an all-or-nothing strategy, policymakers should identify those areas strategically and economically crucial to the nation's well-being and focus its limited resources accordingly. At the center of the American circle of interest, of course, was the Atlantic community. All other regions should be evaluated – strategically, not intellectually or morally – on the basis of their ability to preserve Western civilization. To thine own culture be true.

McCarthyites and the radical right perceived the greatest threat to American institutions and democratic processes to be disloyal and ideologically impure elements at home. So too did J. William Fulbright; but rather than communists and the left, the Arkansan perceived McCarthyism and the right to be the cancer from within. Fanaticism had always frightened Fulbright. Those who could not control themselves and their passions disgusted him. Extremism in the service of any principle was deplorable. He was a man of boundaries, searching for, if not always finding, the middle way. McCarthy and his ability to enthrall large segments of the population filled him with foreboding. He sensed correctly that many Americans were impatient with democracy, frustrated, ever on the lookout for a scapegoat. The anxieties of the cold war had exacerbated those tendencies. Although McCarthy was now gone, they and the confrontation with the Soviets remained. The radical right, he sensed, with its anti-intellectualism, its love of authority, and its intolerance, would roam the national landscape once again.

# 10

# *The junior senator from Arkansas*

In an effort to appeal to the huge new middle class created by World War II and the economic boom that followed, President Eisenhower and his advisers set about crafting a "New Republicanism" that rejected both the mossbacked conservatism of the earlier GOP and the welfare statism of the New Deal and Fair Deal. For the New Republicans the central reality of the times was the economy of abundance. While intervening when necessary to see that as many as possible shared in that abundance, the federal government should at the same time protect the innovative, expansive, and creative impulses of private enterprise.[1] Between these two poles there was little political maneuvering room for the national Democratic Party or for an ambitious junior senator from Arkansas. In the face of the New Republicanism, Fulbright did what came naturally: He labored to keep alive memories of the Great Depression.

In 1954 the venerable chairman of the Senate Banking and Currency Committee, Burnet Maybank (D–South Carolina), died, making J. William Fulbright holder of that coveted position. Several days after his ascension, the chairman encountered congressional reporter Jack Steele in a Senate corridor. "Senator," he hailed Fulbright, "are you aware of what's going on in the stock market at this time?" (It was booming.) Fulbright replied that he was, and declared that the matter was of deep concern to him. What was the Banking Committee going to do, Steele asked? "I think we'll have a study on it," the new chairman replied.[2]

To head the stock market investigation, Fulbright brought Jack Yingling, his legislative assistant, onto the committee staff and hired Michael Feldman, who was then working for the Securities and Exchange Commission. "We plan no 'investigation' of the market at the present time in the meaning often attached to that term," Fulbright told the press in January of 1955. "I know of no specific frauds, manipulations, or wrongdoings. . . . However, the remarkable rises in market prices over the past fifteen months . . . certainly warrant the committee's concern and study." Given the Kremlin's constant

1 Charles C. Alexander, *Holding the Line: The Eisenhower Era, 1952–1961* (Bloomington, Ind., 1975), 159–60.

2 Interview with Jack Yingling, Oct. 12, 1988, Savannah, Ga.

references to the instability of the capitalistic system, all Americans must work to "minimize violent fluctuations in our economy." What he had in mind, he declared, were public hearings that would educate both Congress and the American people. Though he did not say so, Fulbright's inference was clear enough: Through its laissez-faire, probusiness policies, the administration was preparing the country for another crash.[3]

The White House and its supporters were furious. Fulbright was attempting to refasten the albatross the GOP had been forced to wear since 1932. The country had suffered through a mild recession in 1953, and George Humphrey, Sherman Adams, Arthur Burns, and others of Eisenhower's confidants were hoping that the boom on Wall Street signaled the beginning of a sustained Eisenhower bull market. They denounced the stock market investigation as an unwarranted interference with the private sector by Congress and an activity that would in itself undermine business confidence in the economy.[4]

Through March and early April a stream of prominent businessmen, bureaucrats, and economists paraded before the Senate Banking and Currency panel. Fulbright's most useful and controversial witness was John Kenneth Galbraith, whose *The Great Crash* was scheduled for publication on March 21. By preaching optimism and advocating confidence in the business leadership when such confidence and optimism were not warranted, the Harding and Coolidge administrations and their business supporters had fueled the runaway inflation of stock prices in the 1920s, Galbraith testified. The Eisenhower administration had been guilty of exactly the same thing during the boom of 1954–5. Instead of constantly extolling their own infallibility, Humphrey, Wilson, and company should radiate prudence and caution. In economics it was always best to emphasize the bad news rather than the good and to be prepared for the worst.[5]

Fulbright's conduct of the stock market hearings, like that of his RFC investigation, was low key. Mildly sardonic rather than abrasive, the chairman's soft-spoken though sharp cross-examination embarrassed hostile witnesses without humiliating them. He could be condescending and patronizing toward his less attentive colleagues. There were rumblings in the cloakrooms concerning "the professor's" educational hearings. The hoary Tom Connally

3 Fulbright press release, Jan. 14, 1955, BCN 122, F27, SPF. His motives were almost entirely political. Indeed, the Arkansan subsequently admitted to a friend that he did not believe that anything was seriously wrong with the stock market. JWF to Sam Grundfest, Jan. 17, 1955, BCN 105, F46, SPF.

4 Roger Stefan to Sherman Adams, August 29, 1953; Arthur Burns to Adams, Sept. 23, 1953; George Humphrey to Adams, Sept. 29, 1953; Stefan to Adams, Feb. 8 and Mar. 16, 1954; and Gabriel Hague to Ann Whitman, Jan. 26, 1955, WHOF, Box 569, F115G, Eisenhower Papers.

5 Capehart Statement, Mar. 21, 1955, BCN 122, F26, SPF.

observed from retirement that there was no such thing as "a friendly investigation" of the stock market by a Democrat.[6]

Nevertheless, the hearings were popular at home. A former campaign worker wrote:

> I want to pass on to you the very favorable comments of citizens of Arkansas with whom I talked on my recent visitation to . . . Eastern Arkansas. From filling station operators to attorneys and accountants, I received expressions of very high praise for the outstanding work you are doing on the "friendly" investigation of the stock market, a majority of whom have seen you on television or heard you over the radio.[7]

Following three weeks of public hearings, Fulbright announced that the committee had not found any "major abuses" in the market. There were signs of some false advertising – the prices of securities of "very questionable merit," especially in mining, uranium, and nuclear power, had risen all out of proportion to their value – but nothing massive or illegal. While he saw no need for new legislation or regulations at present, the Arkansan told the press, the committee would continue to keep a watchful eye on the market.[8] Though the Eisenhower administration denounced the hearings as "dangerous meddling" with the market, the Federal Reserve Board did boost margin requirements for its member institutions to 70 percent.[9]

As soon as school was out in June 1955, Betsy, enrolled in college at Bryn Mawr, and Bosey, still in high school at St. Timothy's, set sail for Europe and a brief tour of the Continent. Betty and Bill went as far as New York to see off Bosey and the group of Italian Fulbrighters with whom she was traveling. Bill stayed over to play golf with wealthy retailer David Crystal at the exclusive Westchester Country Club.[10] Fulbright looked forward to any opportunity to golf. He was an excellent player, invariably straight, if not long, off the tee and superb around the green. Though he enjoyed the outdoors, it was the competition that attracted him. He never played without betting, and he wagered on every aspect of the game. Even at this point in his life, the former lacrosse player demanded strokes and harassed his opponent. Fulbright's nephew, Doug Douglas – an excellent golfer in his own right – recalled that

6 "Sen. Fulbright Keeps 'Em Guessing During Investigation of Stock Market," *Chicago Sun-Times,* Mar. 13, 1955.

7 J. H. Culpepper to JWF, Mar. 18, 1955, BCN 122, F27, SPF.

8 Philip Godfrey to JWF, Mar. 29, 1955, BCN 122, F23, and UPI 691, Mar. 24, 1955, BCN 122, F24, SPF.

9 "Fulbright Watches Stock Market," undated, BCN 100, F33, SPF.

10 Crystal to JWF, June 13, 1955, BCN 105, F34, SPF.

family members used to plead with him to let the senator win lest the family reunion be spoiled.[11]

The trip to Europe was part of the traditional eastern upbringing that Betty Fulbright carefully sculpted for her daughters. "We were on the tail end of the Victorian era as far as the way we grew up," Bosey recalled. Everything was to have its place: no hair in the hairbrush, hemline the proper length, dress for dinner every evening. There were rigid rules for dating, prescribed by their mother. One always accepted the first invitation – no waiting around for a favorite, and no going steady. Playing the field broadened a girl, Betty told her daughters, and better prepared her to select a life partner. When they were younger and home from boarding school, Betsy and Bosey spent a good deal of time with children of other legislators or government officials invited over by their mother. "She made us both take dancing lessons," Bosey remembered. "It was part of being a young lady. We didn't know how to cook but, boy, we sure knew how to dance."[12]

Betsy recalled her home environment as somewhat forbiddingly formal and, as a result, she spent much of her time at friends. "It wasn't relaxed at our house," according to Bosey. "You felt you had to come and . . . don't put your glass on the table, it might mark it."[13] Part of the problem was their father. As Bosey rather charitably put it:

> We were intimidated by daddy. He was always concerned that you were doing well. The first thing he would always ask me was "How much do you weigh, are your nails clean, and what are your grades?" He was a big putdowner. . . . You'd be talking about Sri Lanka and he would ask where that was. "You don't know where that is?" he would ask incredulously and you would slink away.[14]

"When I would have my friends over and he would intimidate them, I would be mortified," Betsy confessed. "I would say, 'Mother, you've got to do something. I won't have any friends.'"[15]

Bosey would later observe without bitterness that life with a famous United States senator was "a two-edged thing." Being Fulbright's daughters gave the girls status and provided them entrée into places others only dreamed of. "People would look at you and say 'That's Senator Fulbright's daughter' and pay attention to you." She never forgot attending a White House reception shortly after Jack Kennedy's inauguration and having the handsome young president call her by name. "But you were never yourself," she remembered.

11 Interview with Doug Douglas, Apr. 12, 1993, Fayetteville, Ark.
12 Interview with Elizabeth Winnacker and Roberta Foote, Sept. 9, 1991, Washington, D.C.
13 Ibid. 14 Ibid. 15 Ibid.

"People would always ask me what he thought about this or that and I would purposely, unconsciously not know. It didn't help the ego too much."[16]

Fulbright could help lead the Democratic attack on the Eisenhower administration comfortable in the knowledge that by the end of 1955 he had virtually assured himself of no opposition in his bid for a third term in the Senate. John Erickson, Fulbright's talented administrative assistant, was proud of the fact that his boss never had to actually run for office while he, Erickson, was on board. In fact, Fulbright's smooth sail through the waters of Arkansas politics during the 1950s was very much a product of Erickson's astute management.

"I felt my role ought to be to maintain a relationship with the people in Arkansas, with his constituency," he later recalled. "We always sort of ran a campaign timed to reach a peak in the fall before election year." As soon as public school let out in Washington in the spring of 1955, Erickson and his wife, Sara Lou, packed up the children and headed for Arkansas. They opened an office in the Old Post Office building in Little Rock and set about blocking potential opponents before they could gain any momentum:

> We would try to arrange a series of appearances before the fish farmers or what not when people were trying to decide whether to run or not. We'd try to tie up any of the big money and show our strength. I remember telling him one time that everything in life is a matter of timing, whether its running for office, making money, or making love.[17]

Except for a couple of visits on personal matters, Fulbright had stayed away from the state for virtually all of 1954. Even though he was intensely busy with his work on Banking and Currency, the junior senator from Arkansas spent the entire fall living in New York, where he served as United States delegate to the United Nations – a belated reward from the State Department for his work in winning American acceptance of the world body.[18] As soon as Congress adjourned in July 1955, however, he and Betty headed for home and hit the campaign trail the Ericksons had prepared for them. These brief flying trips to Arkansas were densely packed; in one seven-day period he dedicated dormitories at Arkansas AM&N College in Pine Bluff, attended the Fair Park Livestock Show in Hope, addressed the North Little Rock Rotary Club, harangued the Kiwanis Club in Dardanelle, attended a ral-

16 Ibid.
17 Interview with John Erickson, Oct. 13, 1988, Atlanta, Ga.
18 JWF to Earle C. Clements, Aug. 11, 1954, BCN 77, F40, SPF.

ly at the Ward Hotel in Fort Smith, and held a press conference at the University of Arkansas in Fayetteville.[19]

Fulbright's chief political coup of the 1954–5 precampaign season was perhaps his cementing of the relationship with Witt Stephens, Arkansas politics' deepest pocket. "Mr. Witt," as he later came to be known, had grown up on a hardscrabble farm in Prattsville and, through sheer gall and determination, had gone on to build the tenth-largest investment firm in America, the largest outside Wall Street. Witt was shrewd enough to see the profit potential in good political connections. After unsuccessfully backing Homer Adkins in 1944, "we recognized talent and got strong for Fulbright." Once attaching himself to a candidate, Witt moved heaven and earth to keep challengers out of the field. In an effort to gain another term for Governor Sid McMath in 1952, Stephens offered one of his challengers, Attorney General Ike Murray, $2,500 to stay out of the race. (Murray refused to withdraw.)[20] However, "Mr. Witt" demanded service from those politicos he supported. Fulbright was no exception.

In 1954 the junior senator intervened with the Securities and Exchange Commission in behalf of W. R. Stephens Investment Co. and made possible a midnight takeover of Arkansas, Louisiana Gas (Arkla). The sale cost Stephens $25 million, but Arkla would become the backbone of a billion-dollar empire.[21] Even more important to Stephens and other Arkansas oil and gas producers was Fulbright's cosponsorship, along with Representative Fred Harris of Oklahoma, in 1956 of a bill to exempt the price of natural gas shipped in interstate commerce from regulation by the Federal Power Commission.[22] Unlike the Arkla takeover, however, the gas bill created a national controversy.

The debate that developed over the Fulbright–Harris measure pitted representatives from the gas-producing states against legislators from consuming states, principally those states of the Northeast and Midwest with large urban populations. Leading the attack for the consumers was Fulbright's old friend, Senator Paul Douglas of Illinois. The bill was nothing less than a conspiracy by big oil and gas companies to reap obscene profits at the expense of the nation's urban masses, many of whom were absolutely dependent on natural gas for heating and cooking, he charged.[23]

19 Schedule for Week of Sept. 25, 1955, BCN 32, F21, SPF.

20 Interview with Witt Stephens, May 24, 1990, Little Rock, Ark.

21 Myer Feldman to JWF, May 2, 1956; John Truemper to JWF, Nov. 5, 1954; Stephens to JWF, Nov. 18, 1954; JWF to Stephens, Nov. 20, 1954; Stephens to JWF, Dec. 16, 1954, BCN 122, F2; and Stephens to JWF, Apr. 27, 1955, BCN 47, F15, SPF.

22 Effect of the Supreme Court Decision in the *Phillips* Case, 1955, BCN 1, F5, SPF.

23 Paul H. Douglas, "Federal Regulation of Independent Natural Gas Producers Is Essential," Oct. 13, 1955, BCN 1, F5, SPF.

Excess profits indeed! exploded Fulbright. For years the North and East had exploited the rest of the country through their domination of Congress and the Interstate Commerce Commission.

> The issue is whether or not the rich and powerful North and East should have our natural gas at nominal prices set by the commission which they expect to control, or whether they should pay reasonable prices set by the law of supply and demand. The issue is whether the poorest section of our land shall continue to be exploited as it has been exploited throughout our history, in order to enrich the great urban centers which have the power to impose their will.[24]

Oil and gas magnates rallied to Fulbright's side. The natural gas bill represented the last stand of free enterprise against creeping socialism, declared Robert F. Hurleigh, a Dallas oilman.[25] Aligned against the measure were such powerful organizations as the United Auto Workers, the National Institute of Municipal Law Officers, the National Farmers Union, and the mayor of virtually every big city outside the Southwest and California.

The Eisenhower administration, attracted by the free-enterprise justification put forward in behalf of the Fulbright–Harris bill and desirous of expanding its political beachhead in the Southwest, favored the measure. When, in the wake of congressional approval the second week in February, Majority Leader Lyndon Johnson publicly assured the president that he would introduce and support any legislation the White House thought necessary to protect consumers against price increases, it appeared that Eisenhower would sign.[26] Before he could act, however, the political implications of his approval became apparent. The bulk of the voting population still resided in the Midwest and Northeast. The president's advisers convinced him that votes were more important than ideology, and he subsequently began searching for a reason to veto the Fulbright–Harris bill. During the Senate's deliberations, Republican Francis Case of South Dakota had disclosed that a lawyer for the gas interests had offered him a $2,500 bribe. No one had paid much attention at the time, and the Fulbright–Harris bill had passed the Senate by a wide margin. Citing the Case incident, Eisenhower declared that the Fulbright–Harris bill was the product of "arrogant" lobbying methods and sent the measure back to Congress on February 20 with a stinging veto.[27]

24 *Congressional Record,* Senate, Mar. 29, 1956, 4288.

25 Robert F. Hurleigh Broadcast, Mutual Broadcasting Company, Jan. 20, 1956, BCN 89, F6, SPF.

26 W. H. Francis to Sherman Adams, Feb. 9, 1956, WHGF, Box 16/9, F129D, Eisenhower Papers.

27 Alexander, *Holding the Line,* 163; Erickson to R. C. Hobbs, Feb. 20, 1956; and Gerald Morgan to John McClellan, Aug. 8, 1956, WHGF, Box 1019, F129D, Eisenhower Papers.

Actually, Eisenhower's veto of the natural gas act was probably the best thing that could have happened to Fulbright politically. He received an immense amount of credit from the oil and gas interests in Arkansas and Texas, while avoiding criticism from users both large and small that might have resulted from higher prices brought about by deregulation. In early 1956 Ben Laney approached Ben Wooten, an Arkansan and president of the First National Bank of Dallas, about the possibility of financial backing for a run against Fulbright. First National was the largest bank in the Southwest, with numerous oil and gas interests as clients. Wooten told Laney that "financially speaking" he could expect no help from him. Fulbright was too valuable and, in his opinion, unbeatable.[28]

Although U.S. senators generally maintained the fiction that they did not meddle in their state's politics, they invariably did, for what transpired back home usually affected their fortunes. While developments in Arkansas in the early 1950s had little impact on Fulbright's 1956 reelection bid, they were to have enormous consequences for his 1962 campaign, indeed for his entire political future.

The 1954 governor's race pitted incumbent Francis Cherry against newcomer Orval Eugene Faubus. The Democratic runoff turned out to be as hot as the Arkansas summer. With temperatures reaching record levels throughout the state, the Cherry campaign introduced the sensational charge that Faubus had attended a communist school, the left-leaning Commonwealth College at Mena, Arkansas, in 1935 and had, in fact, been elected president of its student body. After first denying the allegations, Faubus eventually admitted that he had been at Commonwealth a short time, but insisted that he had left the school when he discovered its true character.[29]

"Never, since I have been voting, have I voted with less enthusiasm than I did in the race for governor," C. E. Yingling, Jack's father, wrote Fulbright. "It was a choice between Huey P. Long, represented by Faubus, and Joe McCarthy, represented by Governor Cherry. I took what I regarded as the lesser of the two evils and voted for Faubus."[30] So did a bare majority of the rest of Arkansas's voters. Orval Faubus won the August 10 primary by seven thousand votes.

Though Fulbright, Yingling, and Erickson had their doubts about Orval Faubus, there was nothing in his background or in his policies during his first term in office to indicate that the governor would assume leadership of the white-supremacist backlash that followed in the wake of the 1954 *Brown*

28 W. P. Gulley to JWF, May 2, 1956, BCN 6, F28, SPF.

29 Timothy P. Donovan and Willard B. Gatewood, Jr., eds., *The Governors of Arkansas: Essays in Political Biography* (Fayetteville, 1981), 214.

30 C. E. Yingling to JWF, Aug. 11, 1954, BCN 11, F48, SPF.

decision. Faubus was born at Greasy Creek near the Ozark village of Combs in Madison County, some thirty-five miles east of Fayetteville. His parents, John Samuel and Addie Faubus, had raised their son in an environment characterized by borderline poverty and political radicalism. A disciple of the Socialist Eugene V. Debs (for whom Orval Eugene was named), Faubus's father was charged with sedition during World War I for his antiwar activities. Faubus's only college experience was at Commonwealth in 1935, and his association with this small Highlander-like experiment was brief. Though he was indeed elected president of the student body, Faubus left before he had a chance to enroll. Commonwealth was later declared a communist-front organization by the Justice Department.

At the outbreak of World War II Faubus enlisted in the Army and, serving with George Patton's Third Army, rose to the rank of major. Following his return to Northwest Arkansas Faubus was named postmaster at Huntsville; he used his first six months' salary to buy the Huntsville *Record,* which he quickly built into the third-largest weekly in Arkansas. Faubus skillfully used his paper to portray himself as a toothpick-chewing, barefoot boy from the hills who was of and for the common man. Despite Francis Cherry's lack of political acumen, Faubus's victory in 1954 was regarded as a major political upset; but even the most seasoned pundits did not yet perceive the breadth of Orval Faubus's political skill or the depth of his ambition.[31]

Despite his attempt to insert the race issue into his 1954 campaign, Faubus was classified throughout his first term as a racial moderate in the McMath mold. He appointed several African Americans to the Democratic state committee and resisted pressure from white supremacists to intervene in the controversial desegregation of Hoxie, a small northeastern Arkansas community. Faubus consistently avoided being labeled on the race issue in his early gubernatorial career. He leaned toward segregation when it was politically expedient but refused to embrace extremist positions. In other areas, he seemed very much the progressive. In 1955 he led the fight to regulate Arkansas Power and Light, succeeded in establishing a children's colony for mentally retarded children at Conway, and appointed millionaire Winthrop Rockefeller to head the Arkansas Industrial Development Commission, a state agency designed to attract new businesses to Arkansas.[32]

Fulbright and his staff quickly established a working relationship with Faubus. He, Erickson, and Yingling had quietly supported him in his contest with Cherry. "I think Fulbright kind of liked Sam," Yingling recalled.[33] The governor's office cooperated closely with Fulbright on river development and the natural gas bill.[34] Faubus was appropriately solicitous. "Bill," he wrote

31 Donovan and Gatewood, *Governors of Arkansas,* 215–17.
32 Ibid., 218.
33 Yingling interview.
34 Faubus to Warren Magnuson, May 10, 1955, BCN 105, F34, SPF.

following a 1955 visit to Washington, "you made a very convincing statement to the subcommittee considering the appropriation for the Arkansas River Basin, and I am quite confident that you made a good impression."[35] Of crucial importance was the fact that both Faubus and Fulbright enjoyed the active support of Witt Stephens.[36] Finally, there seemed little difference between the Rhodes scholar and the man from Greasy Creek on the race issue. Throughout the turbulent decade of the 1950s, J. William Fulbright continued to voice public support for the principle of segregation.

At the opening of the decade, an African-American father had sued his local school district seeking admission of his child to the white school system. Every day Linda Brown had to walk past the all-white school in her neighborhood to reach the city's one all-black institution. Lawyers for the NAACP argued that because of inequalities in per-capita expenditures on pupils, books, and buildings, all-black institutions were inevitably inferior. It took three months for the case, *Brown* v. *Board of Education of Topeka, Kansas,* to wind its way through the federal court system and reach the Supreme Court.

Reporters who covered the Supreme Court recalled no particular sense of anticipation when they gathered on May 17, 1954, to hear the weekly announcement of decisions by the high court. Law clerks working for the court were notoriously loose-tongued, but there had been no advance notice of any significant rulings. Then, one hour into the proceedings, Chief Justice Earl Warren began reading, forcefully, the court's opinion in *Brown.* Education, he declared, represented a central experience in life. Those things that children learned in school remained with them for the rest of their days. The critical question, then, in the case before the court was this: "Does segregation of children in public schools solely on the basis of race . . . deprive the children of the minority group of equal educational opportunities?" Answering for the entire court, he declared: "We believe that it does."[37]

Initial response to the *Brown* decision was reasonably temperate, even in the segregated South. Black newspapers hailed the court's action and predicted the quick demise of institutionalized segregation. In Dixie only governors James Byrnes of South Carolina, Herman Talmadge in Georgia, and Hugh White in Mississippi called in outraged and inflammatory rhetoric for massive resistance. Most common were comments regretting the decision but appealing for calm acceptance of its consequences. In Arkansas Francis Cherry told reporters who had gathered on the steps of the state capitol: "Arkansas will obey the law. It always has." "Big Jim" Folsom of Alabama declared: "When

35 Faubus to JWF, May 10, 1955, BCN 105, F43, SPF.
36 Jim Snoddy to SEC, July 18, 1956, BCN 22, F3, SPF.
37 Quoted in William H. Chafe, *The Unfinished Journey: America since World War II,* 2d ed. (New York, 1991), 152.

the Supreme Court speaks that's the law."[38] Cities like Louisville, Kentucky, Greensboro, North Carolina, and Little Rock indicated that they were ready to begin the process of compliance.

Yet the *Brown* decision, like all controversial legal decrees issued in a democracy, ran the risk of being stillborn. The ruling required commitment, leadership, and concrete action if it was to become more than an empty promise. It quickly became apparent that the political will to bring about an end to Jim Crow in the nation's schools was lacking. The Eisenhower administration took no action in early 1956 when University of Alabama officials expelled Autherine Lucy, the first black person admitted to the institution, on the grounds that her presence threatened the public order. The president remained similarly passive when racial disturbances broke out at the opening of school that year in Mansfield, Texas, Arkansas's Hoxie, and Clinton, Tennessee.

Encouraged by the executive branch's temerity, white supremacists in the South rallied and called for a policy of "massive resistance." State governments shifted their attention from how to comply to how to circumvent the *Brown* decision. The Virginia, Alabama, Mississippi, and Georgia legislatures claimed the right, à la John C. Calhoun's nullification initiative of 1828, to "interpose" themselves between the people and the federal government. They declared the Supreme Court's decision "null, void, and of no effect."[39]

Early in 1956 southern senators began meeting once again in Richard Russell's office. The gatherings were stormy. The radical racists – James Eastland (D–Mississippi), Allen Ellender (D–Louisiana), Thurmond, and John Stennis (D–Mississippi), were out for blood. Mob violence had accompanied the University of Alabama's rejection of Autherine Lucy, and passions were running high. Aside from their own personal feelings, the southerners were being pushed by extremists at home to stand up for Dixie, to show the North that white southerners would not be intimidated. The pressure on the junior senator from Arkansas to conform was immense.

The heart and soul of the Dixie faction in the Senate continued to be Richard Russell, Fulbright's friend and mentor. Beginning with the *Brown* decision, the senior senator from Georgia would become increasingly obsessed with civil rights. He was ably assisted by the mild-mannered but thoroughly reactionary Harry Flood Byrd of Virginia. Praising the faithful and icing the wavering, Russell and Byrd continually emphasized that unanimity was the key to the bloc's success, and they made certain there were few defectors. Those who refused to conform risked ostracism and eventual political death.

The notion of a "Southern Manifesto" stemmed from genuine feelings of outrage at the *Brown* decision and from pressure back home, but also from a determination by the Dixie senators to save one of their number. The vener-

38 Quoted in ibid., 153.

39 Quoted in ibid., 158.

able, moderate chairman of the Senate Foreign Relations Committee, Walter George, was then locked in a life-and-death struggle for his Senate seat with Herman ("Huhman") Talmadge, the red-necked, race-baiting son of Eugene "Old Gene" Talmadge, one of the South's original suspender-snapping demagogues. Hard-line senators in the Dixie association sold moderates on the need for a statement in order to save George's seat.[40]

The original manifesto was drafted by intransigent South Carolinian Strom Thurmond. His uncompromising diatribe called for resistance inside or outside the law, whatever the price. That was too much even for the other firebreathers, and they turned to North Carolina's Sam Ervin, an unkempt, deceptively shrewd young lawyer who very much wanted to be reelected to the Senate. His version of the Southern Manifesto held that the Constitution and various federal statutes had given sole charge of the public schools to the several states. In *Plessy* v. *Ferguson* in 1896 and *Lum* v. *Rice* in 1927 the Supreme Court had upheld this interpretation. The *Brown* decision of 1954 was based on neither law nor precedent, Ervin argued, but solely on "psychology and sociology." Given the fact the Warren Court had "usurped and exercised a power denied it by the very instrument it was professing to interpret," its decision was inoperative. "We pledge ourselves," Ervin concluded, "to do all within our power to reverse and set aside this illegal and unconstitutional decision."[41]

There was no doubt that in 1954 J. William Fulbright was a staunch segregationist who believed that the Supreme Court had reversed *Plessy* v. *Ferguson* without any legal or political justification. In 1950 at the height of the Korean War Fulbright had cosponsored an amendment to a military appropriations bill permitting individual soldiers to decide whether or not they would serve in an integrated unit.[42] In 1952 he helped block an Alaska statehood bill out of a conviction that legislators from the new state would support civil rights legislation.[43] The Court, he remained convinced, would never be able to persuade or compel the planters and tenant farmers of eastern Arkansas to send their daughters to school with black people;[44] but the Thurmond and Ervin drafts went too far. The South had long since passed into a status of permanent minority, he reasoned; tradition and law had become the region's principal shields since the Civil War and would remain so. Nullification, interposition, and extralegal resistance were unthinkable. "Under our system of

40 Erickson interview. The eighty-year-old George, abandoned by the Coca-Cola interests, subsequently withdrew from the race and was appointed ambassador to the United Nations.

41 Ervin draft, 1956, Southern Manifesto, Papers of Richard Russell, University of Georgia, Athens, Ga.

42 J. H. Yingling to H. Whittenberg, Nov. 13, 1950, BCN 23, F38, SNP.

43 J. Fred Parish to JWF, Mar. 5, 1952, and JWF to Parish, Mar. 12, 1952, BCN 47, F19, SNP.

44 Fulbright interview.

government," he wrote a Little Rock constituent, "the Supreme Court is specifically given the authority to interpret the Constitution, and no matter how wrong we think they are, there is no appeal from their decision unless you rebel as the South tried to do in 1860."[45]

Perplexed and troubled, Fulbright consulted his staff. Yingling and Erickson told him not to sign even the more moderate Ervin version of the manifesto. "You're doing a disservice to your constituents if you lead them to believe you can do anything about this," Yingling advised him. Still not satisfied, Fulbright turned to his wife, his best friend and confidante, for advice. They got in the car and drove to Mount Vernon and back. The choice of Washington's home was not accidental. Fulbright would have to sign a statement of some sort, he and Betty agreed: It was the ultimate test of loyalty to the Dixie association, and his constituents would expect him to speak out; but both the Thurmond and Ervin positions were too extreme. There seemed to be no alternative, the couple decided, but for Fulbright to take charge and transform the manifesto into what they considered an acceptable document.[46]

Back in Washington, Fulbright immediately got on the phone to Lister Hill, John Sparkman, and Price Daniel (D–Texas); with varying degrees of enthusiasm they agreed to back a milder version. The Arkansan told Yingling to work up a draft. This was the only way moderates like Hill and himself could retain any influence within the Dixie delegation, Fulbright told his despondent aides.

The Fulbright–Hill–Sparkman–Daniel draft was indeed moderate compared to earlier versions. It termed the *Brown* decision "unwarranted" and pledged that the signers would use all lawful means to bring about its reversal. Its other clauses were even more conciliatory. "We recognize that we are a minority of the Senate," the draft read, and therefore could not hope to prevail either through legislation or constitutional amendment. It appealed to "our people not to be provoked by the agitators and troublemakers invading our states and to scrupulously refrain from disorder and lawlessness."[47]

The hard-liners were appalled. Fulbright had denied them their righteous indignation. His version cast southerners in the role of supplicants rather than outraged victims. At the height of the controversy, Fulbright decided not to sign if the extremists prevailed, and drafted a statement explaining why:

> I fear the statement [manifesto] will not appeal to the good sense, understanding and, indeed, compassion of non-Southerners – with whom we have lived in relative peace since Reconstruction days. . . . I fear the statement holds out the false issue to our own South-

45 JWF to Les Gibbs, Mar. 7, 1956, BCN 19, F43, SNP.
46 Yingling interview.
47 Holland–Fulbright–Daniel–Sparkman revision, 1956, Southern Manifesto, Papers of Richard Russell, University of Georgia, Athens, Ga.

> ern people that there is some means by which we can overturn the Supreme Court's decision. Our duty to our people in their hour of travail is one of candor and realism. It is not realistic to say that a decision of the Supreme Court is "illegal and unconstitutional," and to imply, thereby, that it can be overturned by some higher tribunal. . . .
>
> It is a false assumption that the nation will support us in defiance or castigation of the Supreme Court. . . . I fear the statement will give aid and comfort to agitators and troublemakers within and without the South.[48]

In the end, the hard-liners compromised. They had to have Fulbright and Daniel, both of whom absolutely refused to sign the Thurmond–Ervin version. The two Tennessee senators, Albert Gore and Estes Kefauver, had already refused to affix their signatures as a matter of conscience. Lyndon Johnson, claiming that his participation would undermine his effectiveness as majority leader, begged off as well. Fulbright and Daniel's defection would have rendered the notion of a solid South ludicrous; but Thurmond and company had agreed to compromise, not capitulate.

On Monday, March 12, 1956, nineteen senators and seventy-seven representatives, including J. William Fulbright, joined in attacking the Supreme Court of the United States. The Southern Manifesto was angry and defiant. The Court, it declared, had substituted "naked power for established law," had abused its judicial authority, had created chaos and confusion, and had planted racial hatred and suspicion where there had been friendship and understanding. The signatories pledged to resist integration. Although they added the qualifying phrase "by any lawful means," their statement was taken by white supremacists as a call to arms.[49]

As soon as news of the manifesto was announced, Fulbright began receiving mail from all over the world. Students, teachers, ministers, rabbis, college presidents, Rhodes scholars, Fulbrighters, bankers, housewives, and a smattering of blue-collar workers expressed their opinions to the junior senator from Arkansas. Rather than the insulting, irrational attacks politicians usually receive in the heat of an emotional moment, they were thoughtful, eloquent, disbelieving, and anguished. Fulbright's correspondents professed not to understand how the author of a celebrated exchange program, a humanitarian, a man who had stood up against Joe McCarthy, could have cast his lot with the bigots and racists. "You might wonder that I am aggrieved by you in particular," one wrote. "The answer is that it is natural to single out certain leaders in any field, to follow their careers, to admire and be grateful for them. This was my attitude toward you. And, reasonable or not, I feel hurt."[50]

48 Quoted in Haynes Johnson and Bernard M. Gwertzman, *Fulbright: The Dissenter* (New York, 1968), 175.

49 Quoted in ibid., 170.

50 Quoted in ibid., 171.

A native of Selma, Alabama, spoke for many enlightened southerners:

> I do not think I can describe to you adequately the sickening shock I felt on the morning I heard the newscast of the Southern Manifesto, and learned that you were one of the signers. . . . When men of your caliber, education, intelligence – nationally and internationally known and respected – issue such statements in disregard of American principles and ideals, to whom can we of the South turn for responsible and morally sound leadership?[51]

The fact is that, although Fulbright felt the manifesto too extreme and did not want to sign it, and although he had done so for primarily political reasons, the junior senator still believed that integration was an idea whose time had not yet come. Sounding like a throwback to Booker T. Washington, he continued to insist that education in and of itself would over time eradicate prejudice and allow African Americans to take their rightful place in American society.[52] His reluctance to sign had stemmed from his respect for the law and his fear that defiance would spark racial violence in the South, not from a commitment to the principle of integration. As his activities in behalf of the desegregation of the University of Arkansas Law School indicated, the Arkansan believed that integration in public education would have to occur gradually and from the top down.

Surprisingly, Fulbright's signing of the Southern Manifesto did him little damage among the rapidly increasing ranks of Arkansas's African-American voters. By the mid-1950s black Arkansans had, despite their susceptibility to subornation and intimidation, become a political force with which to contend. Sixty-eight thousand African Americans paid their poll tax in 1954 and, according to the advice given Fulbright by Harry Ashmore and John Erickson, one hundred thousand would be eligible to vote in 1956. In 1955 Fulbright addressed the Arkansas Democratic Voters' Association headed by Isaac McClinton, a self-made African-American businessman from Little Rock. The junior senator, who was then doing his preemptive tour of the state in anticipation of the 1956 elections, went to great lengths to emphasize to McClinton and his colleagues that, had he not intervened, the Southern Manifesto would have been much more extreme than it actually was.[53] For the most part, Arkansas's black leadership generally accepted that gloss. Lawrence Davis, president of the all-black Arkansas AM&N, cabled Fulbright that he understood, and McClinton confided to Erickson that although he wished the senator "had not been put on the spot," he had had "no other choice but to go along with the manifesto."[54]

51 Quoted in ibid.
52 JWF to H. Alexander Smith, Aug. 3, 1956, BCN 84, F26, SPF.
53 Erickson to Redding Stevenson, Mar. 19, 1956, BCN 77, F19, SPF.
54 Redding Stevenson to Erickson and Yingling, Mar. 19, 1956, BCN 77, F17, SPF.

# 11

# *Massive retaliation, Suez, and the struggle for an alternative foreign policy*

Dwight Eisenhower had agreed to run for president because he was an intensely ambitious man who believed it his duty to save capitalism from creeping socialism and to protect America from the forces of international communism. Like Taft, Truman, Acheson, Fulbright, and the majority of the American people, Eisenhower believed in a monolithic communist conspiracy, directed from the Kremlin, whose aim was global domination through intimidation, subversion, and – unless the United States maintained its defenses – military aggression. Even so, Eisenhower did not share the Republican right wing's obsession with the menace of domestic communist subversion; the principal threat was from abroad and was best countered by American leadership in the formation of strong military alliances accompanied by programs of overseas military and economic aid. In short, Eisenhower and the internationalist wing of the GOP, despite their campaign promise to "roll back" the iron curtain in Eastern Europe and the Far East, essentially accepted the Truman administration's policy of containing communist power until, so the argument went, patience and firmness brought a loosening of the Kremlin's grip on the Russian and satellite peoples.

For various reasons, however, John Foster Dulles, Eisenhower's choice to be secretary of state, fought the cold war with unprecedented rhetorical vehemence. Indeed, in public Dulles adopted the stance of an uncompromising moralist, clothing the cold war in the language and imagery of a religious crusade. Epithets like "immoral," "enslavement," and "banditry" frequently spiced his public statements; his diplomatic approach to the Soviet Union and Communist China appeared to be consistently doctrinaire and uncompromising. Although he was a prominent Presbyterian layman and abhorred Marxism for its call to atheism, Dulles was far more flexible in his advice to Eisenhower and in negotiation than he was in public pronouncement. Indeed, his defenders argue that his public intransigence had more to do with the administration's desire to placate the GOP's right wing than anything else.

The Eisenhower administration accepted the premises and objectives of containment, but not the Truman administration's methods. Secretary of the

Treasury George Humphrey, the archconservative industrialist from Cleveland, and Secretary of Defense Charles Wilson, former president of General Motors, had little trouble convincing the conservative Eisenhower that the Keynesian assumptions underlying NSC-68 were erroneous and dangerous. Unrestrained spending, whether for military or nonmilitary purposes, could alter the very nature of American society, either through the debilitating effects of inflation or through regimentation in the form of economic controls.[1]

The principal task facing the Eisenhower administration in the area of defense and foreign policy, then, was how to reconcile a reduced budget with a militantly anticommunist posture. The administration's synthesis of the seemingly antithetical objectives of military economy and global defense was the doctrine of "strategic deterrence" or, in Dulles's terminology, massive retaliation. Relying mainly on the intercontinental striking power of the Strategic Air Command's hundreds of nuclear armed bombers, strategic deterrence was touted as a dramatic yet rational alternative to the Truman administration's practice of scattering funds among the three military branches. It was the essence of the Eisenhower administration's self-styled New Look in defense policy.

Even before the exigencies of the 1956 election compelled him to take up the cudgels and challenge Eisenhower's foreign policy, Fulbright denounced the concept of massive retaliation as a diplomatic strategy that would lead either to nuclear war or to a communist takeover of the developing world. During an SFRC grilling of Dulles in 1954, Fulbright asked the secretary of state incredulously whether the administration intended to rain atomic bombs on Moscow in response to "a local aggression in Burma, the Middle East or elsewhere." Such a policy was madness and would surely lead to World War III.[2]

Despite his growing contempt for the General and the Priest, as his staff referred to them, Fulbright rejected Walter Johnson's appeal to make a major political speech criticizing the New Look and the administration's failure to free the "enslaved" peoples of Eastern Europe as promised. The crisis over Dien Bien Phu was reaching its climax, Fulbright wrote, and he believed Eisenhower ready to declare war in French Indochina at any moment. The economy was sagging, and the GOP needed a little war to revive its popularity. Fulbright wanted to do nothing, he told the historian, to push the president or the Republican Party over the edge.[3] Moreover, as he confided to Chester Bowles, his duties as chairman of Banking and Currency made it impossible

1 John Lewis Gaddis, *Strategies of Containment: A Critical Appraisal of Postwar American National Security Policy* (New York, 1982), 139.

2 *Congressional Record,* Senate, Mar. 15, 1954, 3223.

3 Walter Johnson to JWF, May 13, 1954, and JWF to Johnson, May 20, 1954, BCN 84, F32, SPF.

for him to attend all but a few meetings of the SFRC.[4] There was another, more important, reason for Fulbright's reticence, however.

Following the Democrats' recapture of the Senate in the midterm elections of 1954, Lyndon Baines Johnson became the youngest Senate majority leader in the history of Congress. Intelligent, energetic, and intensely ambitious, Johnson was determined to use his new post to attract a national political following that would ultimately land him in the White House. Frontal assaults on the popular Eisenhower administration were not, he calculated, going to endear him to the masses. Indeed, Johnson perceived that his best bet was to act the role of cooperative partner with the executive branch. Eisenhower frequently found himself at odds with the right wing of his own party, particularly on internal security and foreign policy issues. By rounding up crucial support for the administration's economic development initiatives and internationalist foreign policies, Johnson could play the role of Washington power broker without offending the scruples of mainstream Democrats.[5]

Fulbright had first met Johnson when the Texan was elected to the Senate, by the barest of majorities, in 1948. The Arkansan was both attracted and repelled by him. Like Roberta, Johnson was a confirmed New Dealer and a dyed-in-the-wool Democratic loyalist. Like Roberta's son, Johnson had studied at the feet of Richard Russell and quickly mastered the mores and mechanics of the Senate. Fulbright admired Johnson's effectiveness and his nondoctrinaire pragmatism. "It is a politician's task to pass legislation, not to sit around saying principled things," Johnson once observed.[6] Like his liberal colleague from Illinois, Paul Douglas, however, Fulbright believed Johnson frequently went too far in his search for consensus and results. "Under Johnson," Douglas recalled in his memoirs, "the Senate functions like a Greek Tragedy: all the action takes place off stage, before the play begins. Nothing is left to open and spontaneous debate, nothing is left for the participants but the enactment of their prescribed roles."[7] For Fulbright and Douglas, the majority leader's approach was suspect because it denied the opportunity to examine alternatives, explore ideologies, and challenge perspectives. In addition, Fulbright was repelled by the "Johnson treatment." When the Texan wanted something from a colleague, he first resorted to shameless flattery, then arm twisting, backslapping, nose-to-nose persuasion, and finally coercion through withholding of a key dam or defense contract. As time passed, Fulbright began to perceive Lyndon Johnson as a man obsessed with process at the expense of substance: He did not care what was accomplished as long

4 JWF to Chester Bowles, Apr. 2, 1955, BCN 46, F31, SPF.

5 Kathleen J. Turner, *Lyndon Johnson's Dual War: Vietnam and the Press* (Chicago, 1985), 29, and Stephen E. Ambrose, *Eisenhower,* vol. II, *The President* (New York, 1984), 488–9.

6 Quoted in Turner, *Johnson's Dual War,* 30.

7 Quoted in ibid., 33.

as there was accomplishment. Moreover, he began to suspect that the Texan did not recognize the line between pragmatism and opportunism. "He once told me – this was after Johnson was majority leader – 'Lyndon doesn't know what's in a bill; he just wants it passed,'" an aide remembered.[8]

Both as minority and majority leader, Johnson developed a relationship with Fulbright that seemed on the surface to be not only businesslike, but warm and personal as well. "Over the years you have been an invaluable friend and a strong right arm in time of need," Johnson wrote in September 1955. "I will never forget how courageously and ably you stood up during the debate on the McCarthy Resolution and how you supplied the Senate with a calm, penetrating wisdom that was so badly needed." Indeed, in December, 1955 Fulbright and Betty spent a week at the Johnson ranch in Texas visiting Lyndon and Lady Bird while the majority leader was recuperating from his massive heart attack.[9] Nonetheless, neither man ever really understood or trusted the other. Jack Yingling recalled:

> It was a peculiar relationship. Johnson scared the pants off of him. They had desks side by side before Johnson became majority leader. Often, whenever Fulbright had something on the floor I would be sitting in a little chair drawn up between them. He called Fulbright professor about half the time and Fulbright would give it right back to him. On the other hand, I think Johnson could maneuver Fulbright as he could everybody else.[10]

Given Johnson's determination to pursue what he called "the politics of responsibility," Fulbright had to tread very carefully in criticizing the Eisenhower–Dulles foreign policies. Had he remained convinced that the New Look and the assumptions that underlay it were merely irrelevant, Fulbright might have kept the gloves on altogether, but he believed that dramatic developments in the Soviet Union were creating foreign policy opportunities that the president and his secretary of state must be made to seize, politics or no politics.

In March of 1953 Joseph Stalin died, and the communist world changed forever. "With Stalin ended the era when a decision by one man could change abruptly the whole course of foreign policy of the Soviet Union and world Communism," Adam Ulam has written. "His successors neither collectively nor singly would ever again have that power."[11] For two years a trio of

8 Interview with Jack Yingling, Oct. 12, 1988, Savannah, Ga.
9 LBJ to JWF, Sept. 21, 1955, BCN 105, F49, SPF.
10 Yingling interview.
11 Adam B. Ulam, *Expansion and Coexistence: Soviet Foreign Policy, 1917–1973,* 2d ed. (New York, 1974), 538.

would-be successors, comprising Lavrenti Beria, Nikolai Bulganin, and Nikita Khrushchev, struggled for control of the Kremlin. By the summer of 1955 Beria had been eliminated and Bulganin shunted aside to the largely ceremonial post of premier. It was Khrushchev who, as head of the Communist Party of the Soviet Union (CPSU), would thereafter wield the real power within the Kremlin. In July, Western leaders met with Bulganin and Khrushchev in Geneva to discuss disarmament and the reunification of Germany. Nothing concrete came out of the meeting, but observers reported that they sensed an intangible thaw in the cold war, a phenomenon American pundits dubbed "the spirit of Geneva." Smiling and amiable, Bulganin and Khrushchev stressed "peaceful coexistence" and "the relaxation of world tensions." Then in February 1956, at the Twentieth Congress of the Russian Communist Party, Nikita Khrushchev delivered a long recapitulation of the "crimes of the Stalin era." While insisting on the inevitable triumph of "socialism," he also reiterated the notion that different countries might choose "separate roads to socialism." Finally, Khrushchev suggested that further relaxation of the tight internal and external restrictions of the Stalin period was in the offing.[12]

To Fulbright the administration seemed completely insensitive to the possibilities opened up by the spirit of Geneva. From September 1954 through April 1955 Eisenhower and Dulles had repeatedly confronted Communist China over the fate of Formosa and the associated islands of Quemoy and Ma-tsu. Dulles's statements concerning Berlin and other cold-war hot spots were as moralistic and self-righteous as ever. While in Paris during the 1954 Geneva Conference, the secretary of state declared that the only way he would meet Chinese Premier Chou En-lai was if their automobiles collided. By 1956 Dulles had added the Southeast Asian Treaty Organization and the Middle East Treaty Organization to NATO in an effort to build a wall of alliances around the communist world. Fulbright thought this approach unsophisticated, and the administration's inability to distinguish between indigenous communist movements and Soviet imperialism potentially disastrous. The Arkansan chafed under the restraints imposed by Johnson's "politics of responsibility." "I do not believe as some Republican leaders seem to think," he wrote Walter Lippmann, "that people have to be treated like children – alternately to be soothed by paternalistic smiles and enraged by self-righteousness."[13] Larger questions of détente and world peace aside, if the Democrats were going to win in 1956, they would have to abandon the me-too line in foreign policy that Lyndon Johnson seemed to be advocating.

12 Charles C. Alexander, *Holding the Line: The Eisenhower Era, 1952–1961* (Bloomington, Ind., 1975), 178.

13 JWF to Lippmann, Jan. 10, 1956, BCN 103, F24, SNP.

By late 1955 Fulbright felt secure enough about his own position in Arkansas to turn his attention to national politics. Despite his reservations about Adlai Stevenson's toughness and effectiveness, Fulbright stumped dutifully for his Illinois friend.

In an effort to tie Fulbright down during the national campaign, the Republican National Committee persuaded Ben Henley, an Arkansas Republican of little consequence – a redundancy in the days before Winthrop Rockefeller – to challenge the junior senator in the general election. "On the whole, I think that the best strategy would be to ignore the fact the he is in the race," Erickson advised.[14] Fulbright agreed, and when Faubus officially invited him to attend the Democratic National Convention as a voting delegate, he accepted.[15]

During the ensuing presidential campaign Fulbright cast caution to the wind and launched an ongoing attack on the Eisenhower administration's foreign policy in general and Secretary of State John Foster Dulles in particular. In mid-February 1956 Dulles appeared before an executive session of the SFRC and told the assembled senators that the cold war was going very well: The administration's foreign aid program was winning the hearts and minds of Third World residents everywhere, and America was growing stronger daily. Faced with capitalist victories on every front and the crumbling of their own economy, the masters of the Kremlin were ready to cry uncle; what else could the so-called spirit of Geneva mean?[16]

"What we want and what we will support is a Secretary of State who will not treat us as children ready to clap in delight at every fairy story, however fanciful," Fulbright responded in a subsequent speech to the Senate. By emphasizing nuclear weapons and alliances, neglecting nonmilitary foreign aid, and aligning itself with dictatorial or colonial governments, the Eisenhower administration was opening the door to communism throughout the Third World. "Does the sight of tens of millions of people cheering Soviet leaders in India and Burma represent a dismal failure of Soviet policy?" he asked. "Does the dramatic and vigorous entry of Russia into the once forbidden zone of the Middle East represent a setback for the Kremlin?" They did not, he insisted.[17]

Despite Fulbright's impassioned sallies, the second Eisenhower–Stevenson campaign was a one-sided affair. The president was at the peak of his popularity and almost invulnerable to criticism. To make matters worse for the Democrats, Stevenson ran far less effectively than in 1952. He seemed unsure of himself and lacked much of the deft wit, courageous realism, and lofty elo-

14 Erickson to JWF, July 26, 1956, BCN 126, F42, and Erickson to Arnold M. Adams, June 29, 1956, BCN 77, F21, SPF.

15 Faubus to JWF, June 5, 1956, BCN 77, F38, SPF.

16 JWF to H. A. Wallace, May 9, 1956, BCN 101, F44, SPF.

17 *Congressional Record,* Senate, Feb. 27, 1956, 3369–75.

quence that had marked his first campaign. The sudden eruption of the Hungarian and Suez crises a few days before the election raised serious questions about the wisdom of recent American diplomacy, but most voters paradoxically assumed that the soldier-statesman's experienced leadership was more necessary than ever. November 6 brought an Eisenhower landslide of almost staggering proportions. Miraculously, the Democrats carried both houses, retaining their narrow majority in the Senate and slightly increasing their margin in the House. Lyndon Johnson, for one, was pleased; he promised the administration his and his party's continued cooperation. "I had a very gratifying talk with LBJ," Dulles wrote Eisenhower on November 13. "It was not only marked by great personal warmth but by a sincere desire to help to find a way to get bipartisan backing for our foreign policies." Johnson, it seems, "talked very frankly of some of his personal problems with fellow senators." According to Dulles, the Texan warned that "we might have some troubles with the Democratic side of the SFRC."[18] As usual Johnson was prescient.

Immediately after the election, Bill and Betty departed for Europe. The official purpose of the trip was a NATO parliamentarian's meeting in Paris – the alliance had spawned an auxiliary organization made up of representatives from member legislatures – but it was a vacation from first to last. At Helen Lippmann's suggestion, the Fulbrights decided to tour southern Italy. Following an obligatory appearance at the conference, they rented a red Fiat convertible, roved around Sicily for ten days, and then flew to West Germany.[19] After two rainy days in Bonn, Bill and Betty departed for home. Fulbright found the return depressing. "The truth is," he wrote Stevenson, "the prospect of Dulles for an indefinite period is so discouraging that it almost leads to defeatism – he really is a menace."[20]

Shortly after his return from Europe Fulbright appeared on network television and called for a full-scale congressional investigation of the administration's foreign policies, with special attention to the Middle East. "I confess that the Democrats did not function as an opposition party should during the past four years," he wrote Farnsworth Fowle of the *New York Times*. "There were many reasons for this, but the most obvious one was the ability of the administration to capture the leadership of the Democrats in Congress and make these men their own representatives."[21]

The Fulbrights got back to Washington in time to attend Walter and Helen Lippmann's traditional New Year's Eve party. Invitations to this annual ritual,

18 Dulles to DDE, Nov. 13, 1956, Dulles–Herter Series, Box 6, Folder Nov. 56 (1), Eisenhower Papers.
19 JWF to John W. Auchincloss, Oct. 29, 1956, BCN 105, F25, SPF.
20 JWF to Stevenson, Dec. 17, 1956, BCN 105, F65, SPF.
21 JWF to Farnsworth Fowle, Jan. 4, 1957, BCN 114, F6, SPF.

which brought together a carefully chosen collection of ambassadors, senators, government officials, art connoisseurs, and journalists, signaled one's arrival among the people who mattered. Among the regulars were *Washington Post* publisher Philip Graham, Oscar Cox, French ambassador Henri Bonnet, curator John Walker, and art collector Duncan Phillips. The guests customarily gathered at nine in the Lippmanns' elegant sunken living room, had drinks and supper, and at midnight, according to an iron rule, joined hands in a circle, sang "Auld Lang Syne," and kissed their neighbor.[22] Between cocktails and kisses, Fulbright expressed his misgivings about the collaborationist course Congress and the Democratic Party were taking. Lippmann, who criticized for a living, urged Fulbright to assume leadership of a movement that would indict not only Eisenhower's foreign policy, but the assumptions and values that underlay it. Given the Arkansan's education, his sponsorship of the exchange program, and his circle of friends, he was a natural.[23]

In fact, Fulbright was well positioned to develop an alternative foreign policy. Although his record on civil rights and his votes on the minimum wage separated him from the liberals of his own party – he was not a member of the ADA – he nevertheless had shared table and ideas over the years with many leaders of the liberal establishment, people like Arthur M. Schlesinger, Jr., John Kenneth Galbraith, Paul Douglas, Chester Bowles, and Averell Harriman. While Eisenhower dispensed his palliatives and Johnson collaborated, these individuals busied themselves developing a critique of Ike's America.

In a series of articles published in middecade, Arthur Schlesinger argued that the liberalism born during the Depression needed to be superseded by a liberalism adapted to the new age of abundance. Instead of a quantitative liberalism "dedicated to the struggle to secure the economic basis of life," Schlesinger called for a "qualitative liberalism dedicated to bettering the quality of people's lives and opportunities."[24] What the nation needed, John Kenneth Galbraith wrote in his best-selling *The Affluent Society,* was not more money for consumption, as the Eisenhower administration argued, but additional funds for the roads, schools, and public parks with which a truly cultured society could be created.[25] While not rejecting the cold war, these liberals hoped for an accommodation with the Soviets that would help end the arms race and allow the United States to focus on social and educational issues at home and economic development in the Third World.[26]

22 Ronald Steel, *Walter Lippmann and the American Century* (Boston, 1980), 465.

23 Executive Appointment Calendar, 1956, BCN 116, F44, SPF.

24 Quoted in Steven Gillon, *Politics and Vision: The ADA and American Liberalism, 1947–1985* (New York, 1987), 124–5.

25 Frederick F. Siegel, *Troubled Journey: From Pearl Harbor to Ronald Reagan* (New York, 1984), 115.

26 Gillon, *Politics and Vision,* 129.

Fulbright found many of Schlesinger and Galbraith's arguments stimulating. The materialism of the 1950s offended both his liberal and conservative sensibilities. Like other liberals, he believed that the wealth that America was amassing ought to be used for public and not private ends. At the same time, as a traditionalist he bemoaned the loss of purpose that seemed to be the inevitable result of the end of struggle. Welfare capitalism in service to the community might be a mixed good, Fulbright believed, but in service to the gratification of private, material appetites, it was an unmitigated evil. Like other conservatives Fulbright pined in the 1950s for a return to the lost world of frugality, private conscience, and individual responsibility. More pragmatically, the Arkansan believed that the politics of materialism would render the administration politically vulnerable. With his commitment to federal aid to education, intercultural understanding, and competitive coexistence with the Soviet Union he, no less than Schlesinger, Galbraith, and Chester Bowles, felt that it was not only possible but incumbent upon the Democrats to articulate an alternative to the stultifying Eisenhower–Dulles blend of morality and placebos.

The first week in January 1957 Fulbright met for lunch with John Sparkman and Chester Bowles to map out strategy for a Democratic offensive on foreign policy. All three agreed that the Republicans had ruthlessly exploited the Korean situation in 1952 to the tune of several million votes. Despite the fact that the Suez and Hungarian crises of late 1956 had exposed the administration's foreign policy for the amateurish effort it was, the president had emerged unscathed. The GOP's strategy was simple but effective: When the sailing had been smooth, the Republicans had claimed all the credit; when disaster loomed, Eisenhower and Dulles avoided blame by appealing for and receiving bipartisan support.

As the three Democrats saw it, two options were available to the party in its hour of need: It could declare a moratorium on partisan criticism of foreign affairs in return for the naming of Democrats to key administrative and foreign policymaking positions, including the National Security Council; or the Democratically controlled Congress could launch a series of subcommittee studies on a variety of topics, including foreign military assistance, overseas information, and specific issues such as the origins of the Middle East fiasco.[27] Fulbright supported the second option. The politics of cooperation may have benefited Lyndon Johnson, but it had kept the Democrats out of the White House. The party should take a harder line. The investigations would be launched in the most cooperative of spirits, he subsequently wrote Hubert Humphrey. "After such a study is underway, of course, it progresses as developments dictate."[28] Fulbright reminded Bowles and Sparkman of Robert

27 Chester Bowles to Lyndon Johnson, Jan. 2, 1957, BCN 112, F33, SPF.
28 JWF to HHH, Dec. 19, 1956, BCN 121, F25, SPF.

Taft's aphorism – "the business of the opposition is to oppose" – and cited the vigor of the British parliamentary system as evidence of the efficacy of that philosophy.

On January 5, 1957, President Dwight Eisenhower stood before a joint session of Congress and asked the assembled legislators to approve a joint resolution authorizing him to expend up to $200 million in economic and military assistance to preserve "the independence and integrity of the nations of the Middle East," and also to use American armed forces in support of any Middle Eastern state facing "overt armed aggression from any country controlled by international communism."[29] A week later Dulles appeared before a joint committee of the House and Senate for a detailed discussion of what the press was already calling the Eisenhower Doctrine. Following a tense grilling of the secretary by Democratic senators, Fulbright stunned the Republican members by introducing a motion requiring the administration to submit a "white paper" giving a chronology of the events that had led up to the Suez Crisis of the previous fall. The Eisenhower Doctrine was "a grandstand play . . . a gesture, not a policy," designed to cover up a record of incredible blundering, he charged.[30] With the Republicans bellowing and bleating all the way, the Democratic majority named Fulbright to head a special subcommittee to receive and examine relevant documents from the State Department. These proceedings, however, were not to hold up consideration of the president's resolution, the SFRC stipulated.

On January 29 Fulbright introduced a substitute for the resolution of approval for the Eisenhower Doctrine. It called for freedom of navigation through the Suez Canal; a comprehensive settlement of the Arab–Israeli conflict; and reaffirmation of America's right under Article 51 of the U.N. Charter to participate in systems of regional collective security, including those emerging in the Middle East.[31] It did not authorize U.S. military action to defend any and every nation in the region from communist aggression. The Arkansan declared that under no circumstance would he lend his name "to further the erosion of the power of this Senate." As Fulbright well knew, perceptions of who was a communist and what constituted aggression could differ dramatically.

Fulbright's "obstructionism" infuriated Eisenhower and Dulles. He was a pedant and a naysayer, they complained; the Arkansan's objections to the Eisenhower Doctrine were Stevensonian in their hair splitting. Indeed, it seemed to the administration that as a confirmed Atlanticist, Fulbright should have been one of the staunchest supporters of the Eisenhower Doctrine. Dulles be-

29 Quoted in Alexander, *Holding the Line,* 186.

30 "Eisenhower Middle East Doctrine 'Grandstand Play,' Solon Says," *Albuquerque Tribune,* Jan. 7, 1957.

31 *Congressional Record,* Senate, Jan. 29, 1957, 1066.

lieved that the Suez seizure was merely an opening gambit by Nasser to unify and dominate the entire Arab world. Having accomplished that, he would use his control of the region's oil and gas to bring Western Europe to its knees – the same Western Europe that the United States had fought two world wars and spent billions to save.[32]

Neither the joint committee members nor those of the Senate as a whole were willing to stand up to the administration and expose themselves to the charge that they had denied the president the money and weapons necessary to prevent Soviet domination of the Middle East. On March 5 Congress passed Joint Resolution 19 by a vote of 72 to 19.[33]

In disgust Fulbright turned to the task of dissecting the decision-making process that had led to the Suez Crisis. Maybe he could use the failed Aswan Dam deal to jar the Congress and public to their senses concerning the secretary of state. "I think Dulles was a fool," he later remarked. "Self-righteous, a religious fanatic; he thought he had a mission from the Lord. I don't think he was a smart man at all. You were either for or against us. You're either good people or you're bad people. You're good people if you support us and bad people if you don't."[34] "Their [Dulles and Fulbright] natures were so different," Douglas Dillon remembered. One was a moralist, that is, he saw the world in terms of a struggle between good and evil, and was committed to the triumph of good and to the notion of a harmonious and basically homogeneous world in which everyone would care for everyone else. The other was an idealist, one who believed in the efficacy of principles and institutions, who was convinced that the rule of law together with cultural exchange would make the world safe for diversity. As Dillon noted, however, Dulles had to deal with "practical" – that is, diplomatic and political – matters that made him appear "hypocritical" in Fulbright's eyes.[35]

As part of his modernization campaign, Egyptian prime minister Gamal Abdel Nasser had hoped to build a huge dam and hydroelectric power station on the Nile River at Aswan, some eight hundred miles south of Cairo. The proposed high dam would be one of the largest in the world and through irrigation would increase Egypt's arable lands by one-third. Because Egypt lacked resources to finance so vast a project, estimated to cost $1.3 billion, Nasser had sought outside assistance. In December 1955 the United States had offered an initial grant of $56 million to help finance the dam, and had Britain agreed to chip in $14 million. To Dulles's annoyance, Nasser had de-

32 Meeting with Bipartisan Congressional Group, Aug. 12, 1956, Box 3, Legislative Meeting Notes, WHOF–OSS, Eisenhower Papers.

33 United States, Congress, Joint Committee to Study the President's Middle East Proposal "To Promote Peace and Stability in the Middle East," 85th Cong., 1st sess., S. Rept. 70 (Washington, 1957), 4.

34 Interview with J. William Fulbright, Oct. 11–18, 1988, Washington, D.C.

35 Interview with Douglas Dillon, May 5, 1993, New York, N.Y.

layed acceptance and dickered with the Soviets for a larger package. Then in May 1956 he had added insult to injury by withdrawing recognition from Jiang Jie-shi's government and establishing diplomatic relations with Communist China. On July 19 Dulles peremptorily withdrew the offer of U.S. aid. A week later Nasser retaliated by nationalizing the Universal Suez Canal Co., an enterprise owned mainly by British and French stockholders, and announced that he would build the Aswan Dam from canal profits. Because he proposed to compensate the stockholders, the seizure did not violate international law. The British and French, in the last throes of imperial decline, viewed Egypt's takeover of the canal as an unbearable insult.

On October 29, 1956, Israel's army had knifed into Egypt with the twin goals of wiping out the fedayeen bases from which Palestinian guerrillas had been attacking the Jewish state and, if possible, of overthrowing Nasser. The week following, the British and French, who had secretly coordinated their plans with Tel Aviv, had dropped paratroopers into the Canal Zone and warned both sides to stay out of a ten-mile buffer zone on either side of the waterway. Egypt had then blocked both ends of the canal with sunken ships and prepared to wait out the crisis.

Frustrated and angry at what it considered the impetuous stupidity of its allies, the Eisenhower administration had gone to the Security Council and introduced a resolution calling on Israel and Egypt to stop fighting and demanding the immediate withdrawal of all foreign troops from Egypt. Faced by hostile world opinion, Soviet threats, and the opposition of their major ally, the British and French had swallowed their pride, stifled their resentment, and agreed to withdraw from Egypt. America's Middle East policy was in shambles.

Politics aside, Fulbright saw the Suez Crisis as a monumental foreign policy blunder. After having created the situation by withdrawing the offer to finance the Aswan Dam, Dulles had convinced the British and French not to use force until the 1956 presidential election was so far along that war in the Middle East would not affect it. That Eisenhower and Dulles be held politically accountable was in the interests of the country as well as of the Democratic Party, Arkansas's junior senator concluded.[36]

Over Fulbright's objections the Republicans on the Suez subcommittee – William Knowland (R–California), Levrett Saltonstall (R–Massachusetts), and Alexander Wiley (R–Wisconsin), insisted that the request to the State Department for pertinent documents go all the way back to 1946 rather than 1954. The volume of material that that requirement produced was breathtaking. By the end of July, James Jones – the author of *Fifteen Weeks,* whom Fulbright had hired to analyze the material – reported that he had only the

36 JWF to Irving Dillard, Feb. 19, 1957, BCN 113, F43, SPF.

documents for 1946 and 1947 and already his office was full. Declassification and delivery of more recent documents could take months if not years.

The delay, together with Dulles's sanctimonious statements in defense of his policy, raised Fulbright's blood pressure to the boiling point. After the secretary told the SFRC that, in the history of the world, no nation had been as free from the temptation to use its power for selfish purposes as the United States, the Arkansan momentarily lost control.[37] In press conferences, on *Face the Nation,* and in other forums he lambasted the secretary as "pompous, self-righteous, and inept." Indeed, he went so far as to spread rumors that the secretary of state had been involved in shady real estate dealings, and recalled that in 1939 Dulles had referred to Germany, Japan, and Italy as "dynamic, progressive" societies.[38] "Personal attacks so often backfire and hurt the attacker more than the one attacked," Anne Teasdale admonished from St. Louis. "When we get started taking someone to pieces we often go much too far and forget what we're talking about is a human being who has feelings and hence cannot be dissected as if he were not human but an object." Teasdale, who had frequently witnessed her brother's insensitivity to those whom he regarded as fools, had touched a sore point. "I agree with you completely about personal attacks," he wrote back, "although as a practical matter it is rather difficult to disassociate a Secretary of State . . . from foreign policy – especially when that foreign policy is so completely ineffective and disastrous."[39]

The last week in July Fulbright called the subcommittee together and told the members that it was pointless to delay any further. The Republicans insisted that there was not enough information even to draft a report. Frustrated, angry, but undeterred, Fulbright decided to deliver his own personal indictment. On August 14, he rose from his seat in the well of the Senate and began his litany of Suez sins. The administration had mistakenly equated Egyptian nationalism and neutralism with communism. Ironically, however, the State Department's actions had driven Nasser closer to the Kremlin. The department had, in addition, precipitated a war between Egypt on the one hand and Britain, France, and Israel on the other. America's principal allies were completely alienated, and the Arab–Israeli dispute much further from resolution than it had been before the crisis.[40]

Stevenson, Lippmann, Reston, Bowles, and a handful of other prominent liberals applauded Fulbright's attack. Indeed, as was so often the case, there

37 JWF to R. B. McCallum, Mar. 21, 1957, BCN 105, F54, SPF.

38 JWF to Raymond Brandt, Feb. 23, 1957, BCN 112, F44, and Some Notes on John Foster Dulles, BCN 114, F3, SPF.

39 Anne Teasdale to JWF, Apr. 1957, and JWF to Teasdale, Apr. 17, 1957, BCN 105, F68, SPF.

40 *Congressional Record,* Senate, Aug. 14, 1957, 14701–9.

was a degree of coordination between Fulbright and Lippmann, with the columnist advancing on a topic from the world of journalism and Fulbright discoursing simultaneously from the Congress, with each quoting the other. "I have been ill with persistent and rather high fever for some six days and was not able to get to the floor this morning where I would have loved to have inserted your column of August 6," Fulbright wrote Lippmann during the height of the attack on the Eisenhower–Dulles foreign policy. At the same time, the columnist was hailing Fulbright as the Senate's only true intellectual and as the spokesman for a rational, activist foreign policy.

Stevenson, fresh from a trip to Africa, wrote: "Bless you for that blast on Aswan. It is the first time anyone has documented the sequence of events which should be so well known and which I tried so hard to talk about in the last campaign."[41] That Stevenson read and praised the speech was symbolic; the average American paid little attention. Fulbright's attacks received almost no coverage in the papers. Republicans certainly paid it no mind. Even most liberals ignored it. The ADA, with its substantial Jewish membership, was busy attacking the administration for sponsoring a U.N. resolution calling for the pullout of foreign troops from Egypt.[42] The Democratic leadership was indifferent to hostile regarding Fulbright's investigation. If anything, Lyndon Johnson, who was intensely pro-Zionist, was angry with the administration for not being more supportive of the Anglo–French–Israeli bloc.[43]

In the end, Fulbright's main contribution was historical. His interpretation of the Suez Crisis, which foreshadowed Sir Robert Vansittart's "garden path" thesis, became standard among historians until release of classified documents in the mid-1980s. Any hope of keeping the Suez fiasco alive as a political issue ended in the fall of 1957 with the coming of the Little Rock integration crisis – an issue on which the administration was certainly vulnerable, but one that Fulbright found himself in no position to exploit.

41 Stevenson to JWF, Aug. 19, 1957, BCN 121, F28, SPF.
42 Gillon, *Politics and Vision,* 120.
43 LBJ to Dulles, Feb. 11, 1957, BCN 114, F2, SPF.

# 12

# *Little Rock and foreign aid*

The Little Rock crisis of 1957–8 was a landmark in the history of the civil rights movement and perhaps the most traumatic event in Arkansas's history. The city's name became a rallying cry for white supremacists and civil rights activists for a generation. At home and abroad it established an image of the state as a primitive, racist, irrational community dedicated to blocking change at any cost. For that reason alone it had profound implications for J. William Fulbright and his future.

On the day following announcement of the *Brown* decision, the Little Rock school board instructed Superintendent Virgil T. Blossom to draw up a plan for compliance. Neither Blossom nor the board was enthusiastic about integration, but they had no intention of defying the Supreme Court ruling. The Little Rock Phase Program that Blossom announced in May 1955 provided for token desegregation starting in September 1957 at one senior high school and ending in 1963 with small numbers of blacks attending class in the city's elementary schools. Under pressure from Little Rock's social and business elite, Blossom subsequently amended his proposal to delay desegregation until 1957, when construction on the new Hall High School would be completed. At that point the city would be served by three secondary schools: the predominantly black Horace Mann, Hall High situated near exclusive Pulaski Heights, and Central High in midtown. Central, located in an overwhelmingly working-class neighborhood, would be the only secondary school integrated. While the Little Rock school board was quietly preparing to integrate, Arkansas segregationists were preparing for the coming struggle.[1]

Governor Faubus seemed determined to remain above the fray, but then the "segs," as moderates referred to them, put forward a fire-breathing, implacable white supremacist named Jim Johnson to run against him in the 1956 gubernatorial primary. The previous year Johnson, who was an associate justice of the Arkansas Supreme Court, had urged a Pine Bluff audience to "do what needs to be done" to stop integration.[2] Johnson lost, but Faubus re-

[1] Tony A. Freyer, "Politics and Law in the Little Rock Crisis, 1954–1957," *Arkansas Historical Quarterly*, 40 (Autumn 1981), 206–7.

[2] "Bias on the Dais," Aug. 22, 1955, BCN 123, F27, SPF.

sponded to the segregationist challenge by throwing his support behind a campaign to get an interposition amendment on the November ballot. From that point on, the governor was tarnished in the eyes of the moderates, and he gravitated silently but relentlessly toward Arkansas's white supremacists. William Penix, Fulbright's friend who had represented the Hoxie school board, found Faubus to be a liberal throughout that controversy. He later argued that the governor's defiance over the integration of Central High was a deliberate strategy, a temporary move to gain short-term political advantage.[3]

With nine black children scheduled to enter Central High the following morning, the governor appeared on television on the evening of September 2 and reminded Arkansans that a majority of voters had approved an interposition amendment to the U.S. Constitution in 1956. As governor he was bound to enforce this legislation until it was declared unconstitutional. For this reason and to avoid violence, the state's National Guard would be stationed around Central High to prevent any black children from entering.[4] That same evening Blossom and the school board released a public statement asking the "Little Rock nine," as they came to be called, to remain at home until the legal issues involved had been settled. When, however, federal district judge Ronald Davies ordered the board to carry out its desegregation plan, the nine would-be pupils braved the mob surrounding Central High on September 4 only to be refused admittance by armed guardsmen.[5]

On September 21 Judge Davies ordered Faubus to cease his obstructionist tactics. The governor promptly removed the guard, departed for a southern governors' conference, and predicted violence if blacks again attempted to enter Central High.[6] On Monday morning, September 23, desegregation began under the protection of city police and a limited number of state troopers. The nine black children, carefully trained by Daisy Bates and other local civil rights leaders, braved a gauntlet of abuse. A shrieking crowd surrounded them shouting, "two, four, six, eight, we ain't going to integrate," and "niggers, keep away from our school. Go back to the jungle."[7] The students entered Central High, but by lunchtime the mob outside had become so large and belligerent that they were removed. "They might go in there," one Little Rock man who lived in the neighborhood remarked on national television, "but I bet they don't come out." That afternoon the mayor asked the Eisenhower administration for federal troops to restore order. The president imme-

3 Interview with William Penix, Apr. 17, 1991, Fayetteville, Ark.
4 Freyer, "Politics and Law," 213.
5 Numan V. Bartley, *The Rise of Massive Resistance: Race and Politics in the South during the 1950s* (Athens, Ga., 1959), 265.
6 Ibid., 267.
7 Quoted in William H. Chafe, *The Unfinished Journey: America since World War II,* 2d ed. (New York, 1991), 158.

diately federalized the National Guard, and that evening units of the 101st Airborne Division arrived in Little Rock. The following morning paratroopers escorted African-American students to Central High School and cleared the mobs from the school area.

By this point Little Rock had become the focus of southern resistance to court-ordered integration. "I must vigorously protest the highhanded and illegal methods being employed by the armed forces of the United States . . . who are carrying out your orders to mix the races in the public schools of Little Rock, Arkansas," Richard Russell cabled Eisenhower.[8] Segregationist speakers poured into the city from throughout the South. Race relations deteriorated, and the white supremacist Capital Citizens' Council suddenly became a major player in city politics. Central High School assumed the appearance of an armed camp, and the nine black students were subjected to a daily ordeal of spit, obscene gestures, and physical threats. The faces of their tormentors, contorted with hatred, shocked the nation. All the while, Governor Faubus displayed a growing talent for demagoguery, denouncing the federal presence as foreign occupation and accusing the soldiers of entering the girls' physical-education dressing rooms.[9]

As Little Rock writhed in the coils of racial animosity and political intrigue, Bill and Betty Fulbright were enjoying the charms of the Old World. With Orval Faubus preparing to bar the door of Central High, the happy couple arrived in London for the opening session of the Inter-Parliamentary Union. Following a round of meetings and social functions, Bill and Betty flew to Madrid, where they spent the next several days sightseeing, dining, and attending a bullfight with Ambassador John Lodge and his wife, Francesca. The Fulbrights then rented a car and toured southern Spain for a week.[10]

For Fulbright the drive through Valencia and environs was a troubling one. On September 13 John Erickson had sent him a sheaf of clippings on the integration crisis. "The Washington papers have given almost as full coverage as have the Little Rock papers," he moaned. David Lawrence and Dorothy Thompson had written columns denouncing Faubus, and rumor had it that a reporter from the *Times* of London was in town. The only silver lining, he wrote, was that the whole affair just might give Eisenhower a black eye.[11] For Fulbright there was no silver lining. On the issues, he had made it clear that, as he put it, "defiance of constituted authority should not be permitted" and that the key to peaceful integration of the South was the ability of local school boards to act under the liberal guidelines of *Brown II,* the Supreme Court's implementation order commanding segregated school districts to pro-

8 Russell to DDE, Tel., Sept. 26, 1957, Little Rock, Russell Papers.
9 Bartley, *Rise of Massive Resistance,* 268.
10 JWF to John Lodge, Aug. 26, 1957, BCN 105, F51, JWF Papers.
11 Erickson to JWF, Sept. 13, 1957, BCN 77, F13, SPF.

ceed with all deliberate speed.[12] Indeed, under the leadership of his brother-in-law Hal, the Fayetteville school district had peacefully integrated in 1955. In Fulbright's view, Faubus had interfered with that process in Little Rock and provoked a confrontation with the federal government that Eisenhower could not avoid. Walter Lippmann expressed his friend's sentiments when in "Today and Tomorrow" he accused the Arkansas governor of setting the cause of racial moderation in the South back a decade. With the advent of the Little Rock crisis, those southern Senators who refused to filibuster the 1957 Civil Rights Act had come under intense attack by segregationists, Lippmann pointed out. The moderates, "this country's only hope of domestic peace through an accommodation," would be driven underground by demagogues like Faubus.[13] The confrontation at Central High was "a great tragedy for the state," Fulbright wrote his brother-in-law Gilbert Swanson. "There was no excuse whatever for the action taken by the Governor, but we will all have to pay for it, nevertheless."[14]

Fulbright's immediate impulse upon his return was to deliver a public blast at Faubus and take a stand in behalf of law and order. "He was pissed off something awful when he came back," Jack Yingling remembered. Suddenly Fulbright claimed to see in Faubus foreshadowings of Hitler, Stalin, and McCarthy. As he wrote to James Reston during the Little Rock troubles:

> [A]side from the dangers that beset us from the outside, if we do not get leaders who bring out the best in us in a time of unspeakable danger, we shall get leaders eventually – and not too far off – who will appeal to the lowest instincts within us, and, utilizing our own baseness, make us slaves to their own base purposes.[15]

Faubus had not only set the cause of moderation back a decade, he had done something worse. He had embarrassed Fulbright by holding Arkansas up to national and international ridicule. "If I could rest anywhere it would be in Arkansaw," I. F. Stone quoted Davy Crockett in derision, "where the men are of the real half-horse, half-alligator breed such as grow nowhere else on the face of the universal earth."[16]

Harry Ashmore urged Fulbright to speak out, as did an old friend from Mountain Home, Harold Sherman;[17] Fulbright, however, held his tongue. Another longtime friend – Jim Neal, a college acquaintance from West Memphis – had come into the office shortly before Fulbright's return from Europe and insisted that Yingling have the senator call him before he did anything on

12 *Congressional Record,* Senate, July 9, 1957, 11081, and July 23, 1957, 12448.
13 Walter Lippmann, "Today and Tomorrow," *Washington Post,* Sept. 12, 1957.
14 JWF to Swanson, Oct. 21, 1957, BCN 105, F64, SPF.
15 JWF to Reston, Aug. 25, 1958, BCN 105, F61, SPF.
16 *I. F. Stone's Weekly,* Sept. 22, 1958.
17 Harold Sherman to JWF, Oct. 22, 1957, BCN 111, F43, SPF.

Little Rock. Neal, a delta lawyer, told Fulbright that it was too late. So did Fred Pickens, a wealthy businessman-planter from Newport and longtime Fulbright supporter. The tide had turned, they said; Arkansas was with Faubus. If Fulbright got in the way of the firestorm of racial hatred and xenophobia that was sweeping the state, his budding career would come to a sudden end.[18] Fulbright listened.

Weeks passed, and the crisis refused to abate. Egged on by Faubus, Arkansans and segregationists throughout the South raged against the "federal occupation" of Little Rock. The inflammatory rhetoric of the Arkansas governor and other firebrands like Russell, Talmadge, and Thurmond had made Faubus's prophecy of violence and bloodshed a concrete threat. Ironically, the Little Rock school board pleaded with Richard Russell to intervene with President Eisenhower to ensure that federal troops were not removed from Little Rock. "In my opinion if the troops are all removed we will have a riot that will make September 23rd look like a Sunday school picnic," R. A. Lisle wrote the Georgian.[19] In February of 1958 Faubus and the archsegregationist attorney general, Bruce Bennett, succeeded in having the Arkansas NAACP's nonprofit status revoked and then banned it for nonpayment of taxes.[20] Six months later, declaring the organization "riddled with Communists," Bennett launched an investigation into the NAACP's "subversive" activities.[21] L. D. Poynter, chairman of the Association of Citizens' Councils of Arkansas, started a statewide drive to have the legislature pass a law requiring the racial labeling of blood used in transfusions.[22] Following a television interview in which Fulbright observed that racial integration was a debatable question, he received a spate of angry letters. "Segregation is here to stay and there is no middle ground," a constituent wrote. "The people of Arkansas, in the future, are going to insist that all candidates openly declare themselves on this question and any man who is not wholeheartedly behind his people in this fight is certain of defeat."[23]

By May, Anne Teasdale – strong willed, civic minded, and the only one of the Fulbright sisters with the fortitude to challenge Bill and Jack – could stand the silence from her brother no longer.

> Ever since you've been in public life you have represented, to many people in this country, and others, too, I'm sure, the moderate, rational, thoughtful unprejudiced point-of-view. Your exchange

[18] Interview with Jack Yingling, Oct. 12, 1988, Savannah, Ga., and interview with John Erickson, Oct. 13, 1988, Atlanta, Ga.

[19] Lisle to Russell, Feb. 1, 1958, Little Rock, Russell Papers.

[20] "Franchise of NAACP Revoked," *Arkansas Democrat,* Feb. 13, 1958.

[21] Ernest Valachovic, "Bennett Tells Briton NAACP Is Led by Reds," *Arkansas Gazette,* Sept. 19, 1958.

[22] Poynter to JWF, Feb. 28, 1958, Series 5:8, Box 11:1, SPF.

[23] Jack Greathouse to JWF, Feb. 2, 1958, BCN 123, F17, SPF.

> program implies feelings about the importance of understanding and appreciation of other races and cultures and the necessity of learning to live together. . . . So I think it's been very hard to understand your not speaking out against the lawlessness, violence, and hatred shown in Arkansas. The old saying "Silence means consent" is accepted by people, I think.[24]

Fulbright's reply was defensive and disingenuous. Faubus was wrong in calling out the guard, he declared; clearly he did so only because he was planning to run for a third term. The violence and lawlessness in Little Rock were inexcusable although, in his opinion, they were "not quite as vicious as the gratuitous and rather aimless violences that occur every day in New York, Brooklyn, and recently in Philadelphia." He had not spoken out against these incidents because he did not conceive it his duty to do so. The same was true of Little Rock. "I have no doubt," he concluded, "that in the course of time, an occasion will arise at which I will have to make a statement about the Governor's action."[25] That moment would not come until two years later.

By the spring of 1958 concern over the deterioration of the educational process at Central High was such that the school board requested from the federal district court a two-and-a-half-year delay in the implementation of the integration order. Publicly, the school board argued that the hiatus would provide a cooling-off period, after which local opinion might be more amenable to the idea of black and white children attending classes together. Privately, the members admitted that they were motivated in part by the hope that Faubus would no longer be governor by 1960. In June 1958, federal district court judge Harold Lemley granted the delay, but the NAACP appealed at once. After a series of procedural maneuverings, the court of appeals overturned Lemley's decision. Meanwhile, Faubus won a landslide victory in the Democratic primary, ensuring him a third term in the governor's mansion. "Mr. Faubus won nomination . . . on the strength of his actions last fall in the Little Rock crisis," the *Gazette* observed, "and the unprecedented vote for him armed him with a mandate to continue his fight against the federal government." In August the school board appealed to the Supreme Court to uphold Judge Lemley's decision.[26]

At last, Fulbright believed, the time had come, if not to strike at Faubus, then to defuse the situation in Little Rock, revive the reputation of his native state, and create an opening for moderation. On August 23 the junior senator filed an amicus curiae brief with the Supreme Court in behalf of the Little Rock school board in *Aaron* v. *Cooper.*[27]

24 Teasdale to JWF, May 20, 1958, BCN 105, F67, SPF.
25 JWF to Teasdale, May 27, 1958, BCN 105, F67, SPF.
26 Freyer, "Politics and Law," 214.
27 "Fulbright Asks to File Brief Seeking Delay," *Arkansas Gazette,* Aug. 28, 1958.

The seeds of the legal and sociological argument he would make to the Court had been germinating in his mind since a conversation he had had with Sol Linowitz following an address to the City Club of New York in early February. In his speech Fulbright had made the point that the South would accept integration over time; Supreme Court mandates and federal intervention only played into the hands of the extremists. Faubus and the Little Rock crisis had derailed a most promising experiment. Linowitz suggested that his guest read Judge Learned Hand's Bill of Rights and review a series of lectures Hand had just delivered at Harvard.[28]

Fulbright briefly considered a challenge to the original *Brown* decision but then rejected the idea; that time had passed. The task, he and aide Lee Williams, decided, should be to prove that Lemley's decision was in conformity with the *Brown II* decision's ruling that integration should proceed "with all deliberate speed," with pace being determined primarily by local authorities. Another of Fulbright's advisers, David Cohn, convinced him, however, that if he were to carry the day with the court, he would have to persuade the justices that there was a separate "mind of the South," and that that mind was not antithetical to the interests of black Americans. Fulbright agreed and, following several conversations with Learned Hand, assigned the task of writing a first draft to Williams and Cohn.[29]

In fact, more than Ashmore, Williams, and Hand – certainly more than Lippmann – David Cohn helped shape and articulate J. William Fulbright's views on race and the South during the 1950s. Cohn was a remarkable man, a southerner and a Jew, one of several who was to make a lasting mark on Fulbright's life. He hailed from Greenville, Mississippi, a small delta community with a national reputation as a birthing ground and nurturer of intellectuals and liberals. At a time when the Southern Manifesto, the Montgomery Boycott, and Little Rock were bringing deep-seated racial hatreds to the fore throughout the South, Hodding Carter, Jr., the local newspaper editor, was calling upon the region to respond to the best features of its heritage: humility, compassion, and a deep appreciation of the crucial role of blacks in southern culture. Cohn was profoundly influenced by Greenville and by people like Carter and W. J. Cash, author of *The Mind of the South,* but it was not until later that he decided to lead a public life. After earning degrees from the University of Virginia and Yale, he established a chain of department stores that made him a millionaire.

In 1946 at age forty, Cohn forswore the business world for a life of literature. Like most accomplished writers, he wrote about what he knew best – in this case, the American South. His *Gods Shakes Creation* took its title from a sermon by a black preacher. In it he painted a sensitive and realistic portrait

28 Linowitz to JWF, Feb. 3 and 6, 1958, BCN 105, F51, SPF.
29 JWF to Hon. Learned Hand, May 6, 1958, BCN 105, F47, SPF.

of African-American culture in the Mississippi Delta. It was Cohn who used thirty-five years of the Sears, Roebuck catalogue to write a social history of the United States entitled *The Good Old Days.* There were other books, nine in all, and numerous articles for the *Saturday Review, Atlantic Monthly, Esquire,* and *Coronet.* In his innumerable letters to the editor, Cohn stumped for free trade, decency in politics, and defense preparedness. In Washington, where he spent his winters at the Hotel Jefferson, he maintained a "salon" at which he held forth to such friends as Sam Rayburn and Lyndon B. Johnson.[30] Fulbright first met him in 1952 in Springfield, where Cohn was writing speeches for Adlai Stevenson. The two men became immediate friends. Cohn was self-effacing, witty, and irreverent; and he was quintessentially, fervently southern.

Beneath the South's deceptively simple exterior, Cohn claimed, an infinitely complex culture lay. "Here each white is deeply affected by the Negro, just as each Negro is deeply affected by the white." Both were prisoners of history – slavery, the Civil War, and Reconstruction. The two races coexisted in a state of economic and psychological interdependency marked by "a labyrinthine code of manners, taboos, and conventions." Such a culture was a minefield for would-be reformers: "Upon such a society one must not lightly pass judgment; nor must one seek to apply patent remedies, for to do so is to play recklessly with explosives." Any "solution" to the racial problem, Cohn concluded, depended upon recognition of three things: that the "Negro question," like all social problems, was extremely complex; that in the minds of whites, "it is at bottom a blood or sexual question"; and that all differences between the races, "except that of social segregation," may be adjusted through the exercise of patience, wisdom, and good will.[31] It was these principles that underlay the amicus curiae brief.

In his presentation to the Supreme Court that sweltering day in August 1958, J. William Fulbright asked the justices to follow the guidelines they had laid down in *Brown II.* The Little Rock school board had presented a plan to integrate the public schools. Through actions beyond their control – Governor Faubus's ordering out the guard to block the plan and the Eisenhower administration's use of force to implement it – "bedlam and turmoil," to use the appellate court's phrase, had overwhelmed the school district. "The people of Arkansas are as law abiding," he pled, "as respectful of the traditions of our Anglo–Saxon heritage as are their fellow Americans; they abhor anarchy and disorder." Arkansans had no desire to be caught in "a conflict between two sovereignties," he declared, quoting a recent column of Walter Lippmann's. They must be given a chance to gain control of the situation, and Judge Lemley's two-and-a-half-year hiatus would provide them that opportunity. Exist-

30 *New York Times,* Sept. 13, 1960.
31 David L. Cohn, "How the South Feels," *Atlantic Monthly,* 173 (Jan. 1944), 47–51.

ing systems of education must be respected and "social experimentation in them made tolerable to their purposes."

It was dangerous, Fulbright warned, to ignore the existence of what might be called a "Southern mind." "History tells us that race memories long endure. They are perpetuated in myths, and monuments, and a mother's lullaby. They are sentimental and emotional and when stirred up, they become irrational." Certain problems – anti-Semitism, Irish nationalism, the Hindu–Muslim rivalry – had proved impervious to social engineering. So too might the "Negro question" in the South. At the very least, the Court could afford to grant Little Rock two and a half years to come to grips with integration. Did not Jesus of Nazareth come into the world to save the Jews from clericalism and legalism?

> Jesus's protest that the Sabbath was made for man, not man for the Sabbath, cuts to the foundation of all legalism and clericalism. It makes us see the profound foolishness of those who, like Cato, would adhere to the law even though the Republic be thereby destroyed.[32]

Quoting from R. Cohen's *Law and the Social Order,* he warned:

> Without a legal order and some ministry of religious insight, the path to anarchy and worldliness is indeed dangerously shortened. But without a realization of the essential limitations of legalism and clericalism, there is no way of defending the free human or spiritual life from fanaticism and superstition.[33]

The amicus curiae brief was an eloquent, poignant plea to preserve the South's caste system. The Court appreciated it but ignored it, unanimously rejecting Fulbright's plea for delay, and ordering immediate compliance with the integration order that had been rendered in 1956. To have done otherwise would have placed the Court's tacit seal of approval on Orval Faubus's obstructionist tactics. Lippmann was right: Little Rock had been caught between two clashing sovereignties, and there was no real doubt as to which would prevail. Fulbright did not bother to wait for the Court's decision; immediately after delivering his brief he departed for India on an SFRC fact-finding trip.[34]

According to Jack Yingling, Fulbright and his staff knew that the Court would not rule in their favor. The idea was to point Congress in a certain direction in the area of civil rights and to prepare the Court to approve when the House and Senate legislated in that direction. "Of course, the Supreme Court

32 Brief of J. W. Fulbright Amicus Curiae, in the Supreme Court of the United States, Aug. Special Term 1958, BCN 105, F1, SPF.

33 Ibid.

34 Norvill Jones to JWF, Sept. 30, 1958, BCN 105, F41, SPF.

didn't accept it, but we knew they wouldn't. David Cohn knew [Justice Felix] Frankfurter, and he thought it [the amicus curiae brief] would especially appeal to him. The main idea was to put the whole burden of desegregation on the school system."[35]

The governor and state legislature responded to the Supreme Court's ruling by closing all of Little Rock's high schools for the 1958–9 academic year. They then attempted to develop a plan whereby the state would fund, with taxpayer money, a system of segregated private schools. Continuing unfavorable national publicity, the paralysis of the city's educational system, and the decision of several out-of-state industries to locate branch plants elsewhere, crystallized opposition to Faubus and the segregationists, however. Moderates mobilized enough community support to win a special school board election in May 1959. This election, in turn, led to the return of the school to local public control on a limited, integrated basis. More important, it broke the governor's power over Little Rock's public school system. Despite segregationist bombings of the mayor and fire chief's homes and a tear-gas raid on the school board, all of Little Rock's high schools opened in the fall of 1959 with a handful of blacks attending classes.[36]

Liberals at the time and subsequently were convinced that the confrontation at Little Rock had set the cause of peaceful integration in the South back a decade. By predicting violence and provoking a direct confrontation between a state of the old Confederacy and the federal government, Faubus had enabled white-power extremists to play on the South's memories of the Civil War and Reconstruction, and barely submerged fears of black retribution for generations of exploitation and oppression. More recently scholars like Numan Bartley have argued that, in forcing the federal government to take a stand and in provoking intervention, Faubus had actually speeded up the integration process. What is certain, however, is that the Little Rock crisis gravely tarnished Arkansas's reputation and intimidated would-be moderates like Fulbright.

As the Little Rock crisis illustrated, Fulbright had a somewhat paradoxical relationship with his staff, virtually all of whom were skilled, educated, and dedicated. He was both aloof and intimate with them, solicitous of and then indifferent to their advice, dependent and independent of them. In some areas "the senator," as he was invariably called, expected them to tell him what to do. John Erickson recalls that shortly after Fulbright hired Yingling away from the navy, he almost fired him for not recommending a vote on a farm

35 Yingling interview.
36 Freyer, "Politics and Law," 215, and "Bombings Bring Irate Response at Little Rock," *Arkansas Gazette*, Sept. 9, 1959.

bill.[37] Yingling soon learned to assert himself, and he alone among the staff urged Fulbright to hold his tongue following his return from London.[38] In other situations, Fulbright repeatedly ignored his aides. He shunned Erickson and Lee Williams's advice to take a more advanced position on civil rights even during the late 1960s, when there was much less political risk involved.

Nonetheless, the staff uniformly recalled that an atmosphere of trust and respect prevailed in the office. "The senator" did not browbeat his subordinates or submit them to tongue-lashings; but neither did he praise directly. Yingling recalled:

> Now, if you expected him to pat you on the back, you had another think coming. I can't think of a case where he paid me a compliment directly. I know of a number of cases where people told me, like Mrs. Fulbright, how much Fulbright thought of me. I know one time I wrote a speech for him . . . it was the oleomargarine thing – and afterwards he said to me, "You know, Dick Russell said to me that that was the finest parliamentary argument he ever saw and Dick Russell knows what he's talking about."[39]

"He trusted us," remembered Erickson, "and I don't think we ever betrayed that trust."[40]

Yet Fulbright considered his staff socially inferior: Of his speechwriters and legislative and administrative assistants, only Seth Tillman, who came on board in 1960, was ever invited to dinner at Belmont Road. Moreover, he could be incredibly inconsiderate; to his mind the staff existed for his edification and convenience. Sara Lou Erickson recalled: "One time he called at four o'clock in the morning. 'Are you asleep?' he asked. 'Oh, no, Senator. We're just reading in bed.' He was leaving the country and something had gotten mixed up and he needed to talk to John."[41]

Neither Erickson nor Yingling had dinner with their families more than once a week, and they worked at least half a day on Saturdays. Ever since his father had died suddenly, Fulbright had been frightened of a premature death. His anxiety manifested itself in obsessive daily exercise routines. Erickson remembered it this way:

> The Senate would quit about 5:30 or 5:45 and Fulbright would go to the gym and work out. So we worked out a system. I and Jack had a lot of things we needed to talk about. So we would sit there waiting which is sort of selfish [on Fulbright's part]. He might have a dinner at eight o'clock. So he would get back to the office about 7:00. Our wives would be feeding our kids and putting them to

37 Erickson interview.
38 Yingling interview.
39 Ibid.; re oleo bill, see Chapter 7, n. 51.
40 Erickson interview.
41 Ibid.

> bed. We would have a drink. Jack, Lee, and I would not start home before 7:30. He would dress and go on to dinner. And here we were with a forty minute drive.[42]

Ironically, while J. William Fulbright was working to slow the pace of the civil rights movement during the mid-1950s, he was castigating the Eisenhower administration for adopting a rigidly counterrevolutionary position in regard to the anticolonial, nationalist revolutions that were simultaneously, and perhaps not coincidentally, sweeping the Third World. From late 1956 through 1960 the Arkansan repeatedly criticized Dulles and Eisenhower for presenting a foreign aid program that stressed military aid at the expense of economic support and cultural exchange. In so doing, he argued, the United States was converting tribal and regional rivalries from minor military confrontations fought with primitive weapons into modern, deadly wars capable of wiping out entire populations. In addition, in its obsession with the cold war the administration was giving aid to nations in ways that added fuel to the flames of regional disputes. Pakistan, which was pro-Western and received huge shipments of arms, and India, which was nonaligned and did not, were prime examples: The feud between those two nations had nothing to do with communism or capitalism but with the ancient Muslim–Hindu rivalry and the Kashmir territorial dispute, Fulbright pointed out. Aid to Pakistan in the name of anticommunism threatened to upset the balance of power in the subcontinent, and it alienated from the United States the world's second most populous nation. Finally, Fulbright argued, the administration's bipolar view of the world caused it to give aid to corrupt and reactionary regimes that merely declared themselves anticommunist. Such aid made a mockery of America's paeans to democracy, national self-determination, and human rights.

In criticizing the Eisenhower foreign aid program, Fulbright had to walk a very fine line, however. The United States had traditionally rejected the concept of aid to foreign nations as absurd. America's opposition to lending support to other nations was a corollary of the Republican, protectionist trade policies of various post–Civil War governments, of the American creed that preached self-reliance and rugged individualism, and of the gospel of work that viewed poverty as a badge of moral degradation and charity as a dangerous crutch for the improvident. Indeed, the United States had not inaugurated a peacetime foreign aid program until after World War II. With the conservative coalition growing stronger by the day, the Roosevelt and Truman administrations had rejected appeals from British officials and American liberals to continue Lend–Lease into the postwar period. It had taken the "lessons" of

42 Ibid.

World War II, the advent of the atomic age, and a putative global struggle between communism and the free world to persuade Congress and the American people to support the Marshall Plan, Point Four, and the various mutual security acts. Even then there had been a great deal of residual opposition, especially from the Taft wing of the Republican Party and some southern Democrats. Indeed, the principal opposition to the Eisenhower foreign aid program came from Republican congressional leaders such as Leverett Saltonstall, Everett Dirksen, and John Vorys. Moreover, of course, foreign aid continued to be the bête noire of the radical right.[43]

Fulbright had been a staunch supporter of foreign aid since its inception. He had voted and spoken in behalf of Lend–Lease, the British loan, the Marshall Plan, Point Four, and the various mutual security acts. He had done so because he believed that foreign aid drove the exchange program, but also because he had been convinced that it served the national interest. While he would come to argue vehemently that there was an imbalance in the resources devoted to military and nonmilitary aid – money to solve economic and social problems was more important than money for arms – Fulbright never argued against defense expenditures or military aid per se during the 1950s.[44] It was not that economic and technical aid should replace military aid, he believed, but rather that funding for nonmilitary support should be increased. Given the fact that Nikita Khrushchev had targeted developing, Third World nations as potential Soviet client states, aid to alleviate social and economic problems was and would continue to be more important than tanks and bullets. In taking this position, it should be noted, Fulbright found himself acting in unison with Democratic liberals including Robert Nathan of the ADA and Walter Reuther, head of the UAW, as well as with Republican internationalists such as Henry Cabot Lodge and Douglas Dillon.[45]

To Fulbright's delight the foreign aid bill for 1957–8 reported out to the Senate by the SFRC incorporated virtually all of the reforms he had been urging since his appointment to the committee. The measure provided for a $2 billion Development Loan Fund (DLF) with appropriations spread over three years. The International Cooperation Administration (ICA) would administer the fund, but all loans over $10 million would have to be approved by an Advisory Loan Committee headed by the assistant secretary of state for economic affairs – in this case, Fulbright's friend Douglas Dillon, whom Eisenhower brought back from Paris in February 1958. In a symbolic act the committee cut the military appropriation by $100 million and the defense support budget

43 *Manion Forum,* Jan. 27, 1957, BCN 112, F39, SPF.
44 JWF to A. M. Anderson, Jan. 7, 1958, BCN 109, F34, SPF.
45 Nathan to JWF, May 26, 1955, BCN 46, F29, and Reuther to JWF, Apr. 5, 1957, SPF.

by another $100 million. Perhaps most important, it separated military and nonmilitary aid, over Richard Russell's vehement protests, by placing appropriations for military support in the regular Department of Defense budget. As a consequence, Armed Services, which Russell headed, would no longer have any input into the nonmilitary foreign aid program.[46]

The first week in August House conferees utterly destroyed the product of nine months of laborious work. Led by John Rooney and Otto Passman (D–Louisiana) – who once told a State Department official: "Son, I don't smoke; I don't drink; my only pleasure in life is to kick the shit out of the foreign aid program of the United States"[47] – the House succeeded in cutting the total appropriation for the Development Loan Fund to $500 million and eliminating the multiple-year authorization from the foreign aid bill. It returned military aid to the mutual security program, ensuring that the two armed services committees would continue to have a say in the nonmilitary aid program.

While Fulbright did battle with hostile members of the conservative coalition over foreign aid in late 1957 and 1958, he was increasingly distracted by worries about the health of his twin sisters. Roberta, energetic, unfocused, frustrated, was drinking heavily and had separated from Gilbert Swanson. Helen, meanwhile, had suffered a nervous breakdown and would spend more than a year and a half at the Menninger Clinic in Topeka, Kansas. According to her son Doug, Helen was suicidal for much of the last five years of her life.[48] "I think you and Helen should devote your minds to getting completely well in every respect and that some well organized trips to Florida, Mexico, or some such place, would be beneficial," Fulbright wrote Hal.[49] At the same time, however, he attempted to dissuade Douglas from selling the house on Mount Nord and moving to the country. Hal thought a fresh start would be good for Helen; but Fulbright, despite his concern for his sister, was loath to part with a structure that held so many wonderful memories for him. Indeed, Fulbright, at fifty-two deeply mired in the miasmas of middle age, was frequently overcome with fits of nostalgia tinged with self-pity. To an acquaintance he wrote:

> Unfortunately, my family is scattered in all directions and I seldom see them, especially since Mother died. We used to gather every year at Christmas time with Mother and renew our bonds, but since she is gone we have not had such a gathering and I see so little of my sisters and their children that I scarcely know them. Politics al-

46 *Congressional Record,* Senate, June 13, 1957, 8984–90.

47 Quoted in Chester J. Pach, Jr., and Elmo Richardson, *The Presidency of Dwight D. Eisenhower* (Lawrence, Kans., 1991), 165.

48 Interview with Doug Douglas, Apr. 12, 1993, Fayetteville, Ark.

49 JWF to Douglas, Jan. 24, 1958, BCN 105, F37, SPF.

> most destroys private family life in any case, as it requires visiting over the entire state during recesses and while in Washington everyone is a visitor.[50]

Closely intertwined with his efforts to separate military from economic aid, to emphasize the latter at the expense of the former, and to increase State Department control over the program so that it would serve the long-range foreign policy goals of the United States, was Fulbright's continuing struggle to save and enhance the exchange program. Reports from ecstatic Fulbrighters moved the Arkansan deeply. "My experience as a Fulbright scholar was not only significant to me as a student of music," wrote Beatrice Brown, "it was the richest experience of 'living' I have ever been exposed to." Traveling about central Europe with noted performer and conductor Hermann Scherchen, Brown claimed to have learned not only the dynamics of German musical form and the nuances of French composition, but to have imbibed the essence of those cultures as well. Nor were those with whom she came in contact immune to the process. "Even with a man as great as Hermann Scherchen, the many small misconceptions he had concerning the American way of life, were instantly eradicated when I became a 'member of his household.' "[51] Unfortunately, John Rooney and his know-nothing cohorts considered such gallivantings at best a waste of money and at worst un-American.

In the spring of 1955 the House of Representatives, with Rooney and Thomas Curtis (R–Missouri) in the lead, slashed funding for the exchange program from $22 million to $12 million. Shunning more traditional methods of congressional politics, Fulbright immediately counterattacked in the press. At the same time, he urged the Teasdales to marshal the troops against Curtis, who represented suburban St. Louis, and to persuade the *Post-Dispatch* to run an editorial denouncing the congressman. The Arkansan became so intemperate in his public utterances that Anne once again had to warn him to tone it down. "I don't think sarcasm is an effective way to win people over," she advised.[52]

Meanwhile, Fulbright struggled to crack the adamantine Rooney. He contacted various influential New Yorkers and Little Rock friends like Sam and Dave Grundfest, who had New York connections, urging them to threaten to pull the plug on Rooney's campaign fund if he did not lay off the exchange program. As usual, the Arkansan's efforts came to naught. "Remember Rooney comes from Brooklyn," Alfred Knopf wrote. "In many ways he is a preposterous character – he wrote me once that only people driving Cadillacs got

50 JWF to Dr. James Jewell, Aug. 5, 1957, BCN 105, F49, SPF.
51 Brown to JWF, BCN 106, F21, SPF.
52 Teasdale to JWF, June 1955, BCN 105, F68, and JWF to Anne Teasdale, May 12, 1955, BCN 109, F37, SPF.

any attention in National Parks – but he has a good machine to keep him in the House."[53]

In no small part, the difficulties that the exchange program encountered in the 1950s stemmed from Fulbright's inability or unwillingness to cultivate his colleagues, particularly those for whom he had no respect. John Erickson once observed:

> Fulbright's kind of tough. He's not the most gregarious kind of person, constantly building relationships, maneuvering. He has an objective that he sees, and I don't think he does all the work that might be done to build coalitions and support. . . . If people don't have sense enough to know what he's talking about then he doesn't have much time for them. . . . He is sort of contemptuous of coalition-builders.[54]

The appropriation bill for the exchange program went to conference in late June 1955. The conferees restored $6 million to the House figure, but the total, $18 million, was $4 million lower than the Senate version called for and $577,000 below the 1955 appropriation. Eisenhower and Dulles had not lifted a finger to save their original proposal. If ever proof were needed that anti-intellectualism was abroad in the land, that America, in a fit of complacency, was turning inward, and that the nation was growing soft, Fulbright believed, it was Congress and the administration's attitude toward the exchange program.[55]

In the 1956 presidential campaign, the Democrats had feebly attempted to make education an issue. Stevenson had asked William Benton, then back at his post with *Encyclopaedia Britannica,* to develop a series of speeches taking Eisenhower and the Republicans to task for emphasizing conspicuous consumption and promising to maximize middle-class leisure time rather than putting money into the nation's schools and colleges and touting the virtues of excellence in education. Benton gave it a try and at the same time tried to draw in Fulbright. "You are in a dream position" to take the point in such an area, he wrote the Arkansan. Fulbright made several speeches on the subject but quickly sensed that the American people were not in the least interested. That apathy continued to prevail until a series of events in the fall of 1957 startled the country from its somnolence and provided the Democrats with an immensely profitable issue for the 1960 campaign.

53 Knopf to JWF, May 18, 1955, BCN 109, F37, SPF.

54 Erickson interview.

55 Telephone conversation between Russell Riley and JWF, May 15, 1956, BCN 84, F26, SPF.

On October 4, 1957, the Soviets rocketed into earth orbit the first artificial satellite. Named *Sputnik,* a Russian acronym meaning "fellow traveler of Earth," the satellite and its instrumentation package weighed 184 pounds. After Western observatories confirmed the existence of *Sputnik,* there could be no doubt that the Russians possessed a powerful rocket and had solved the essential problems of control and guidance necessary to deliver a thermonuclear warhead to its target. Even more startling and alarming to westerners was the Soviet launch on November 3 of *Sputnik II,* a space capsule weighing an astonishing 1,120 pounds.[56] According to Eisenhower's critics, the newly discovered "missile gap" stemmed from the Republican administration's antipathy toward spending for educational purposes, together with its condoning of "progressive education," with its emphasis on process rather than substance, on courses in "life adjustment" rather than a classical, liberal curriculum.[57] As Benton had noted, it was a battlefield for which J. William Fulbright was ideally suited; and after the shock of *Sputnik,* a frightened public was willing to listen.

Following an extended correspondence with John Kenneth Galbraith and Walt W. Rostow, an ambitious young MIT economist specializing in development theory, Fulbright took to the floor of the Senate in early 1958 to launch a scathing attack on the administration for presiding over an intellectual and educational slow rot that was giving the edge to the Soviet Union in the cold war.[58] He was, Fulbright said, aware of the fate of couriers bearing bad news, but "precisely because I feel that the stuff of greatness had not gone out of the bones of America," he was going to speak the truth. The fact was that the Soviet Union was eclipsing the United States in the field of education and basic research. The Russian hierarchy had attracted and developed its best minds through a steep and rigid system of incentives. That the launching of the *Sputnik*s was the result of totalitarian methods was irrelevant; results were what counted. Intimidated by the anti-intellectualism of the McCarthy era and then lulled into a false sense of security by the Eisenhower administration, America had become comfortable and complacent. "Fat, rich nations – like fat, rich old men – are prone to overestimate their powers," he declared. "They tend to believe that they are entitled to the admiration and respect of others because of their wealth." Shortly thereafter, Arkansas's junior senator cosponsored a bill "to strengthen the national defense, advance the cause of peace, and assure the intellectual preeminence of the United States . . . through programs designed to stimulate the development and to increase the

56 Charles C. Alexander, *Holding the Line: The Eisenhower Era, 1952–1961* (Bloomington, Ind., 1975), 214.

57 Quoted in Steven Gillon, *Politics and Vision: The ADA and American Liberalism, 1947–1985* (New York, 1987), 94.

58 JWF to J. K. Galbraith, Feb. 8, 1958, BCN 121, F27, and JWF to W. W. Rostow, Dec. 18, 1957, BCN 121, F28, SPF.

number of students in science, engineering, mathematics, modern foreign languages, and other disciplines."[59] His proposal was the forerunner of the National Defense Education Act. At the same time he suggested the creation of a legislative counterpart to the National Security Council.

In the wake of the Democratic triumphs in the off-year elections in 1958, however, Lyndon Johnson announced that as majority leader he would continue to take a bipartisan line in foreign policy. With the Russians pressing for "free" elections in West Berlin and threatening once again to cut off Western access to the beleaguered city, he did not want the Kremlin to get the idea that America was divided, he told reporters.[60] It would take an ambitious young senator named John Fitzgerald Kennedy to exploit the opening Fulbright had helped create.

59 *Congressional Record,* Senate, Jan. 23, 1958, 871–7.
60 James Reston, "Bipartisan Maneuvers," *New York Times,* Nov. 13, 1958.

# 13

# *A changing of the guard*

In early 1959, ten years after his appointment to the Senate Foreign Relations Committee, J. William Fulbright became its chairman. Although from the beginning he had been closely identified with foreign affairs, Fulbright's rise to a position of influence on the committee had been unusually swift. Through deaths, departures, and defeats, and through the seniority system he had initially deplored, he moved upward rapidly. By 1956 he was the number two man. Tom Connally, the chairman when Fulbright joined the committee, had left the Senate in 1952 at the age of seventy-five. Alexander Wiley of Wisconsin, who became the Republican chairman under Eisenhower, was sixty-nine and seventy during the two years he held the post. When the Democrats regained control of the Senate in 1954, Walter George assumed the reins at the age of seventy-seven. After Herman Talmadge took George's seat, the aged Theodore Francis Green became the chairman.

By 1959 Green was ninety years old and, understandably, found it difficult to keep up with what day it was, much less the complexities of foreign affairs. The de facto chairman of the SFRC was Chief of Staff Carl Marcy. During the debates over the mutual security bills, it was customary for the press to be admitted to the committee room where in executive session the members had "marked up," that is, made specific revisions in, the administration's proposed measures. "Senator Green loved to have the press come storming into the room so he could tell them what happened," Marcy remembered. The reporters would ask a question or two and then leave. As soon as Green departed, very pleased with himself, the press would return and get the real lowdown from Marcy.[1]

In an indiscreet moment Marcy remarked to Carroll Kilpatrick of the *Washington Post* that Green was getting so confused that in effect he, Marcy, was having to act in his place. Shortly thereafter a story appeared in the *Providence Journal* to the effect that Rhode Island's native son was senile and needed to step down. Deeply hurt, Green submitted his resignation as chairman of the SFRC to Lyndon Johnson in the middle of January 1959.

1 Interview with Carl Marcy, Oct. 10, 1988, Washington, D.C.

A week later Johnson ordered Marcy to gather the committee together. Although he was not a member of the SFRC, no one dared object when Johnson not only sat in but acted as chairman. He solemnly informed the assemblage that Senator Green had submitted his letter of resignation and, shedding copious crocodile tears, declared, "Theodore, you can't do this, it's the goddamn press that's picking on you, you know they're a bunch of so-and-sos; you're the greatest chairman that the Committee has ever had. I plead with you to reconsider." That theme was echoed around the table and it soon became apparent that LBJ had overdone it.

As Green wavered, Johnson whispered in desperation to Marcy: "Carl, I'm going to get him out of the room, you go out with him." Johnson put his arm around his aged colleague and said, "Theodore, you're feeling very strongly about this; I wish you'd go outside and think about it a little bit. It's a very important decision that you're making." As soon as the pair was out of the room, Johnson changed his tone. The old man was sick and tired, he told the members; if they did not get him out he would continue to embarrass the party and probably die on their hands to boot. Though he had not been told explicitly, Marcy knew what to do. He took Green into the back room where Eddy Higgins, the senator's longtime administrative assistant, was waiting. The two staffers argued that Green had submitted his resignation and ought to stick with it. Some very distinguished men had stepped down from the same post. It was up to Green to set an example, they said. The aged Rhode Islander made his way back to the committee and informed Johnson, with great solemnity, that he was standing by his decision.

A delighted Johnson slapped Green on the back, a gesture which sent the ninety-year-old into a fit of uncontrollable shaking, and proposed that he be made chairman emeritus. The committee voted unanimously to approve. The majority leader then turned to Fulbright and said: "Bill, you're the chairman." With that the meeting broke up.[2]

For Fulbright his ascension to the chairmanship marked the end of one journey and the beginning of another. He had decided early on to be a "national" senator and to make his mark in the field of foreign affairs. That particular ambition could have but one goal: chairman of the SFRC. From his new vantage point, Fulbright – like Henry Cabot Lodge, William Borah, and Arthur Vandenberg – could critique and at times influence American foreign policy. He would be sought out for his opinions, courted by various administrations dependent upon him to shepherd treaties and foreign assistance bills through Congress. What attracted Fulbright about his new post was that he could retain what he perhaps coveted most: independence of judgment and action, and, to a certain extent, control over his time.

2 Donald A. Ritchie, interviewer, *Oral History Interviews: Carl A. Marcy* (Senate Historical Office: Washington, D.C., 1983), 96–100.

Though it was not apparent at the time, Fulbright's assumption of the post of chairman of the Senate Foreign Relations Committee in 1959 was a significant development in contemporary American history. No one since Henry Cabot Lodge brought such intellect, such vision, such ambition, and, if his detractors are to be believed, such perversity to the position. It is true that the powerful progressive Republican, William E. Borah, had intimidated presidents and secretaries of state during 1924–32, but despite the claims of his defenders, the Idahoan had been an isolationist emotionally, intellectually, and ideologically. Borah was both ignorant and fearful of foreign powers and cultures. His role in twentieth-century foreign affairs was that of a stubborn and effective reactionary.[3]

Like Lodge, who had held a Ph.D. in history from Harvard, Fulbright revered the past and was determined to preserve American traditions and values from onslaughts by selfish special interests and materialistic know-nothings. Both saw themselves as national senators and the Senate Foreign Relations Committee as a full partner with the executive in the framing if not the conduct of American foreign policy. Like Lodge, Fulbright admired the British parliamentary system and believed that political parties in America ought to take clear-cut positions on vital issues. Moreover, when Congress and the executive were controlled by the same party, the legislative majority and the White House ought to work hand-in-hand to advance those positions; when they were not, the SFRC majority ought to hammer out an alternative foreign policy. The committee's two most formidable chairmen differed on substance, at least initially. Lodge had been a Rooseveltian imperialist and a nationalist of the first order; Fulbright was a Wilsonian internationalist who continued to believe that the hope of the world lay first in regional groupings and then in a world federation whose member states surrendered a portion of their national sovereignty for the common good. Like Lodge, Fulbright was proud, stubborn, and intellectually arrogant; likewise, he was a natural dissenter. At the outset of his career as the SFRC's longest-reigning chairman, Fulbright believed that he could look forward to the same relationship first with John F. Kennedy and then with Lyndon Johnson that Lodge had enjoyed with Theodore Roosevelt. He could not know that, although he and Johnson were of the same party, their relationship, once the Texan was president, would rather come to resemble that between Henry Cabot Lodge and Woodrow Wilson.[4]

3 See Robert J. Maddox, *William Borah and American Foreign Policy* (Baton Rouge, 1970).

4 William C. Widenor, *Henry Cabot Lodge and the Search for an American Foreign Policy* (Berkeley, 1980), 30–1, 48–50, 26–7, 37–9, 52–4, 266–300.

In his effort to convert the SFRC into an effective, long-term critic and framer of foreign policy, Fulbright was aided and abetted by the committee's formidable chief-of-staff, Carl Marcy. The son of a Methodist minister, Marcy had grown up in the Willamette Valley in Oregon and then earned a master's and doctoral degree in international law and relations and an LL.B. from the Columbia School of Law. Professor Lindsay Rogers – author of *The American Senate* as well as a great defender of the filibuster and of the prerogatives of the legislative branch of government – had directed Marcy's 1943 dissertation on presidential commissions. During 1942–50 Marcy had worked for Charles Bohlen, who was then State Department liaison with Congress. In 1950 at the invitation of Francis Wilcox, the SFRC's first chief of staff, Marcy joined the committee and served as one of its four permanent professional members. When Wilcox left in 1955 for an assignment in the State Department, Marcy became chief of staff, a position he would hold until 1974.[5]

Carl Marcy was the ultimate Capitol Hill éminence grise. The mustachioed, dapper Oregonian was a man of medium build but massive ego. He was educated, intelligent, organized, and ambitious to the point of obsession. He identified totally with the SFRC and, after Fulbright's accession to the chair, with its chairman. In the junior senator from Arkansas, Marcy had found a man he could serve – indeed, a man worth serving. This was no provincial hayseed or tottering octogenarian, but rather the architect of a massive educational exchange program and the author of the U.N. resolution – smart, sophisticated, and respected by the eastern establishment press. "I was already somewhat in awe of Fulbright by the time he became chairman," Marcy recalled.[6] Fulbright returned Marcy's loyalty with absolute trust. Each saw in the other a man who could help convert the SFRC into not only a forum for the discussion of contemporary foreign policy but a major contributor to the formulation of that policy.

From the time of his accession to the post of chief of staff in 1955, Marcy had envisioned the SFRC as an institution that would reflect the attitudes and interests of the populace as a whole and command the respect if not the admiration of the State Department. Marcy believed that the Congress ought to be a coequal partner with the executive in the framing of American foreign policy. "There is no constitutional reason," he wrote Lindsay Rogers, "why the Senate should not be asked for its advice and consent prior to the signing of a treaty, especially one of significance."[7] Green's age, conservatism, and lack of stature made that impossible, however, and it was not until Fulbright took over the top spot that Marcy was able to make any headway.

5 Ritchie, *Interviews: Marcy,* 1–18.
6 Marcy interview.
7 Marcy to Lindsay Rogers, Sept. 10, 1963, Box 4, Folder June–Sept., Marcy Papers, SFRC, RG 46, NA [hereinafter referred to as Marcy Papers].

From the outset Fulbright took the position that the SFRC ought to be above party politics, a stance that Carl Marcy enthusiastically endorsed. By that Fulbright did not mean that the Democrats should not dominate the positions and policies taken by the committee: Such domination would occur naturally by virtue of the fact that his party was in the majority. No matter how much the Democrats differed among themselves, they would not allow issues to be used against them for partisan advantage. Fulbright did not, however, intend to permit representatives of either party to manipulate international crises and foreign policy issues simply to embarrass the opposition. The committee should take rational, enlightened positions rooted in a realistic internationalism and then let the chips fall where they might. Courtesy and consultation were the keys, he believed, to preserving what he called "unpartisan" foreign policy.[8] As a result, Fulbright made a great effort to get along with the stodgy, pedestrian Bourke Hickenlooper of Iowa; indeed, the two became quite close. The Iowan was a conservative but not a reactionary, and he hated demagoguery. Each man believed himself to possess qualities that complemented those of the other. Hickenlooper valued Fulbright's knowledge of history and foreign cultures, while Fulbright saw Hickenlooper as a simple, down-to-earth fellow, a farmer from the Midwest who was close to the people.[9]

Marcy took great pride in the ability of himself and the staff to satisfy both Democrats and Republicans on all but a few occasions. "We tried to serve all the members of the Committee with equal attention," he would later insist. "After all, they were senators and we didn't think very much about whether they were Republicans or Democrats." The staff thought of itself as a law firm – "one day it would make the case for the plaintiff, the next for the defendant."[10] If Carl Marcy really believed this, he was deceiving himself. He and the rest of the staff were all foreign policy activists with a strong social conscience. They went out of their way to placate conservatives and isolationists on the committee but did nothing to advance their views. They did so because they were dependent on Fulbright for their jobs, but also because they shared his views. As the years passed, so completely did Marcy identify with his chairman that he plotted and schemed so that Fulbright's speeches, SFRC hearings that he chaired, and the timing of the positions that he took maximized his standing in the world, in the nation, and in Arkansas, if not in that order.

Carl Marcy had a passion for anonymity, and he absolutely forbade members of the staff to write about the committee's operations for publication or

8 Marcy to JWF, Feb. 24, 1959, Box 3, Folder Jan.–Dec., Marcy Papers.
9 Ritchie, *Interviews: Marcy,* 64–5.
10 Ibid., 45, 82–4.

to give interviews. Indeed, if interviews were to be given – not for attribution, of course – *he* would give them.[11] A past master at the strategic leak, Marcy spent hours each week cultivating and manipulating the press. Attracted by the chief of staff's forthcomingness and by Fulbright's ideals and charisma, a loyal band of congressional reporters attached themselves to the committee. The group included Ned Kenworthy and John Finney of the *New York Times* and Don Oberdorfer and Murray Marder of the *Washington Post.* They gathered outside the SFRC committee room before and after executive hearings to receive the official word from the chairman, and then assembled in the staff offices for an off-the-record briefing from Marcy.[12] Although Marcy's clandestine open door to the press enhanced Fulbright's image and gave the SFRC more clout, it occasionally got him and the chairman in hot water with Republicans on the committee and with the executive branch.[13]

The SFRC/Fulbright groupies were simply reporters, of course, and thus ranked a cut below columnists and news analysts like Walter Lippmann and James Reston, whom Fulbright and Marcy regarded as full-fledged partners in the business of framing an alternative foreign policy. Fulbright continued to consult Lippmann on virtually every issue. Although he saw a variety of other columnists on a regular basis, no other pundit ever attained the same degree of intimacy with the chairman except, occasionally, Reston.[14]

On September 15 Nikita Khrushchev, the first Soviet head of state ever to visit the United States, arrived at Andrews Air Force base outside Washington. In his response to Eisenhower's welcoming remarks, he pointedly referred to the Soviet *Lunik II* rocket, which had hit the moon on target less than two days earlier. The day following his arrival the Soviet leader journeyed to Capitol Hill to take tea with members of the SFRC and the leadership of both parties. Fulbright welcomed the man most Americans had come to regard with anxious ambivalence. "Ours are powerful countries with vast natural resources and energetic and talented people," the Arkansan intoned. "Even competitive coexistence, with significant mutual reduction of armaments, will give the world the opportunity to make vast strides in raising living standards of people everywhere." Khrushchev, clad in gray summer suit with dark red tie and the three customary medals, rose to reply.[15] At his most conciliatory, the Soviet leader insisted that his famous remark, "We will bury

11 Marcy to Roger Hilsman, Dec. 10, 1959, BCN 139, F2, SPF.
12 Ritchie, *Interviews: Marcy,* 122–3.
13 Hickenlooper to JWF, Oct. 11, 1963, Series 48:1, Box 5, F4, SPF.
14 Marcy, memorandum of conversation, June 24, 1959, Box 3, Folder Jan.–Dec., Marcy Papers.
15 Khrushchev Visit to SFRC, Tea, Sept. 16, 1959, BCN 135, F7, SPF.

you," referred to peaceful competition between two rival socioeconomic systems.

Fulbright was enormously impressed. "The heart of his statement," he later remembered, "was to the effect that future relations between the Soviet Union and the United States depended upon our recognizing that a new society had appeared among the community of nations – meaning, as I heard it, that we should recognize them as a socialist society that had a legitimate right to exist."[16] The Arkansan came away from the meeting more convinced than ever that the Soviet Union was well down the road toward becoming a peaceful, status quo power whose primary foreign policy goals were security and coexistence.

"The SFRC under your chairmanship now has an opportunity to serve as a rallying point for critical and constructive opinion in this country," Chester Bowles wrote, "and I am confident that you will use this new opportunity with maximum effectiveness."[17] Lyndon Johnson had his staff let the press know that Bill Fulbright was "his boy" on foreign policy and that all questions dealing with international affairs should be directed to the new chair of the SFRC. Unfortunately, there was nothing really for Fulbright to get his teeth into. Following the overwhelming Democratic victory in the 1958 midterm elections, Eisenhower had taken the political offensive and, as a result, had improved his ratings dramatically. During the fall of 1959 the Arkansan made a couple of listless speeches charging Ike with "using the full power of the Presidency to thwart Congress' attempt to give him the necessary means to strengthen the United States in a time of national peril"; criticizing the Republicans for allowing too much of the GNP to go to "luxuries" rather than having the courage to tax for education and national defense; and, of course, continuing to decry the missile gap.[18] With Eisenhower apparently committed to détente with the Soviet Union, however, the chairman's heart was simply not in the fight. The foreign policy opening for which Fulbright and the Democrats had been waiting came finally in the late spring of 1960 when one of the Eisenhower's greatest foreign policy disasters, the U-2 affair, emerged in the midst of what was to be one of its greatest triumphs, the Eisenhower–Khrushchev summit. That it threatened Fulbright's most cherished foreign policy goal – rapprochement between East and West – made for a welcoming conjoining of politics and principle.

16 J. William Fulbright with Seth Tillman, *The Price of Empire* (New York, 1989), 12–13.

17 Bowles to JWF, Feb. 7, 1959, BCN 135, F9, SPF.

18 "Fulbright Scores President's Aims," *New York Times,* Sept. 8, 1959; John Starr, "Soviet Threat Means Fewer U.S. Luxuries," *Arkansas Democrat,* Sept. 28, 1959; and "Fulbright Slaps Missile Program," *Arkansas Gazette,* Dec. 1, 1959.

In 1958 Khrushchev had threatened to sign a separate peace treaty with East Germany, thus turning over to that country the access route from West Germany to West Berlin. If Khrushchev made good on his threat, the Western allies would have to deal directly with the GDR in order to supply the ten thousand Western troops in Berlin across 110 miles of East German territory. In so doing, NATO would have to acknowledge the legitimacy of the East German regime and accept the permanent division of Germany, something the United States and its allies had steadfastly refused to do. East–West negotiations on a deadline dragged on through the remainder of 1958 and 1959. At the urging of British and French leaders, Eisenhower and Khrushchev agreed to a summit in the spring of 1960 on the German question.

Shortly before the president departed for Paris, the Soviets announced that they had shot down a U-2 reconnaissance plane over Sverdlovsk, and Khrushchev vehemently denounced the United States for violating Soviet air space. When, subsequently, the State Department announced that the aircraft was a weather plane that had strayed off course, Khrushchev sprang his trap: The pilot, Francis Gary Powers, was in custody and had confessed to being a CIA operative. On May 11 Eisenhower publicly took full responsibility for the whole U-2 intelligence program, which dated back to 1956. Espionage was a "distasteful but vital necessity" to protect the United States and the free world from "another Pearl Harbor," he told a press conference.[19] The Paris summit opened as scheduled but then ended abruptly when Khrushchev angrily denounced the United States for spying on his country, demanded that Eisenhower punish those responsible, and walked out.

The moment it became apparent that the summit was in danger, Eisenhower, Herter, and Dillon decided typically that bipartisanship was in order. On May 12 Fulbright had departed on a long-scheduled, ten-day speaking tour of the Middle East. On the sixteenth, the day of Khrushchev's diatribe, Herter called Fulbright in Cairo and asked if he would not join the American delegation in Paris. Fulbright hurriedly packed his bags and departed on the jet that had been provided him; by the time he arrived, however, the summit had effectively collapsed. He canceled the rest of his Middle East trip and flew home with Herter and his entourage.[20]

The day following his return from Paris Fulbright informed newsmen that he was going to ask the Senate to authorize the SFRC to investigate the U-2 affair. It would be "good for the soul of the country to get an understanding of what happened."[21] The Republicans, sensing an impending disaster, moved to seize the initiative. Everett Dirksen (R–Illinois), the GOP's wavy-haired, honey-voiced hatchet man in the Senate, greeted Fulbright's request with an

19 Chronology on U-2 Plane Incident, undated, BCN 147, F50, SPF.

20 *Washington Evening Star,* May 22, 1960.

21 Warren Duffee, "Fulbright Calls for U-2 Probe," *Washington Post,* May 22, 1960.

attempt to blame the summit debacle on Adlai Stevenson. Stevenson, who had repeatedly urged negotiations over Berlin, was "soft on communism," he proclaimed. After an unseemly partisan shouting match, the Senate authorized Fulbright to proceed with his investigation. For once on the defensive, Eisenhower pledged full cooperation with the Fulbright probe.[22]

The last week in June Fulbright delivered the SFRC's verdict on the U-2 matter. His speech was a surgical strike that brought delight to the hearts of Democrats everywhere. The U-2 incident and the Eisenhower administration's handling of it "were the immediate cause of the collapse" of the summit. He spoke with "a heavy heart and some regret," Fulbright told the Senate, but it was clear that "we forced Khrushchev to wreck the conference by our own ineptness." The first mistake was not to suspend flights in mid-April; the second was for the president, "who embodies the sovereignty and dignity of his country," to have publicly accepted responsibility; and the third was for the administration self-righteously to justify the flights and their continuance. Truth-telling was an admirable quality, as the president's defenders readily emphasized, but young George Washington, having admitted chopping down the cherry tree, did not go on to say: "Yes, I did it and I'm glad. The cherry tree was offensive to me, because it had grown so tall. I needed some cherries, and I shall chop down other cherry trees whenever I want more cherries."[23] There were many lessons to be learned from the U-2 incident, Fulbright declared solemnly, but he was not certain that the administration had learned any of them.

What the Democratic candidates for the 1960 presidential nomination believed they had learned from the U-2 incident was that, given the fact that they would have to face neither the person of Dwight Eisenhower nor his untarnished reputation, one of them had a realistic chance of winning in 1960. Encouraged by this prospect, a series of aspirants eyed the field. By primary season, however, the number had dwindled to four: Senators Hubert Humphrey of Minnesota, John F. Kennedy of Massachusetts, Lyndon B. Johnson of Texas, and Stuart Symington of Missouri. In addition, although Adlai Stevenson never became a formal candidate in 1960, he let his supporters know he was amenable to a draft.

The forty-two-year-old Kennedy, the first Roman Catholic seriously to contend for the presidency since Al Smith in 1928, quickly emerged as the Democratic front-runner. His triumph over Humphrey in the Wisconsin primary on April 5 was inconclusive given the fact that most Kennedy support

22 "GOP Charges Adlai Scuttled Summit," *Arkansas Gazette,* May 24, 1960, and "Ike Approves Congressional Probes of Summit Collapse, Promises Full Cooperation," *Arkansas Democrat,* May 26, 1960.

23 *Congressional Record,* Senate, June 28, 1960, 14734–7.

came from Wisconsin's strongly Catholic districts; but five weeks later, in heavily Protestant West Virginia, Kennedy's superbly run campaign ended with a sweeping triumph over the Minnesotan. Humphrey thereupon withdrew, and Kennedy went on to record impressive primary victories in Nebraska, Maryland, and Oregon. As he had hoped, these victories, together with earlier successes in New Hampshire and Indiana, caused Democratic leaders in the East and West to climb on his bandwagon. Kennedy and his managers came to the Democratic convention in Los Angeles on July 11 already confident of at least 600 of the 761 votes necessary for the nomination.

Fulbright was strangely pessimistic and passive during the 1960 campaign. It was difficult for him to whip up any real enthusiasm for the candidate. "I think Senator Johnson, the Majority Leader, is probably the best qualified man – by experience and temperament – to make a forceful President," he wrote McCallum, "but unfortunately, he comes from the wrong part of the country." Kennedy was able, he conceded, but young and inexperienced. It was unlikely, Fulbright predicted, that he would be able to hold his early lead. Humphrey, he told his tutor, was a talented orator but was anathema to the South because of his record on civil rights and his close ties to organized labor. Symington was the most likely compromise candidate, but his lack of speaking ability and charisma would render him easy pickings for Richard Nixon.[24] Stevenson was a two-time loser. In the end, Fulbright supported Johnson. The Texan was admittedly uncouth, ruthless, and relentlessly ambitious; but his intelligence, his moderation on civil rights, his progressive social views, his southernness, and his apparent willingness to defer to Fulbright on foreign policy matters quieted the Arkansan's misgivings. Although Fulbright did not attend the Los Angeles convention (he was then at odds with Orval Faubus, who headed the state's delegation), he wrote every delegate to laud Johnson's talents. "I believe," he declared, "he has the energy, experience and mature judgment which our candidate and our President must have to win the election and, more important, the world-wide contest with Communism."[25] Throughout the preconvention campaign Carl Marcy and the staff of the SFRC drafted speeches for Johnson on various foreign policy questions.[26] Fulbright had picked the wrong horse, however.

Delegates converged on Los Angeles in a sober mood, shaken by recent international events and tensed by the knowledge that the nomination was still up for grabs. Though Fulbright did not actively participate in its drafting, the party platform bore his mark. Adopted on July 12, it proclaimed that an enduring peace could be obtained only by restoring American "military, economic and moral" strength. It charged the Eisenhower administration with

24 JWF to McCallum, Jan. 14, 1960, BCN 105, F54, SPF.
25 JWF to Delegates, July 5, 1960, Box 3, Folder Jan.–Dec., Marcy Papers.
26 Marcy to LBJ, June 24, 1960, Box 3, Folder Jan.–July, Marcy Papers.

having lost America's "position of pre-eminence," and it promised to streamline and modernize the nation's military machine. Other Democratic pledges included more systematic planning for disarmament and the reshaping of foreign aid, with a new emphasis upon economic assistance and long-range international cooperation. One plank that did not bear Fulbright's stamp was civil rights, the strongest statement in the party's history.

After the most intricate and strenuous political maneuvering, the convention then proceeded to nominate John F. Kennedy on the first ballot. "The World is changing," Kennedy proclaimed in his acceptance speech on July 15. "The old era is ending . . . and we stand today on the edge of a New Frontier – the frontier of the 1960's. . . ." No comparable struggle for the presidential nomination took place within the Republican Party. It had been clear for months that Vice-President Richard M. Nixon enjoyed overwhelming support from party regulars in all parts of the country. He was nominated on the first ballot on July 28 in Chicago.

Arkansans were extremely displeased with the civil rights plank in the Democratic platform, and as of late August none of the Arkansas delegation had publicly committed to the Kennedy–Johnson ticket. Gradually, under heavy lobbying from Johnson, Arkansas, like most of the rest of the South, began to come around. Fortunately for Fulbright, John McClellan, who had hired Robert Kennedy to be chief counsel of his labor rackets investigating subcommittee and who was close to the Democratic candidate, was willing to take the lead. When Kennedy visited the state in early September, the entire congressional delegation turned out for him.[27]

Following his return from a trip to the Middle East in early October, Fulbright hit the campaign trail in earnest, delivering speeches up and down both coasts. Marcy wrote most of these partisan broadsides, carefully planning the time, delivery, and sequence for maximum effect. He advised Fulbright:

> Before trying to draft the four or five page essence of each release . . . I suggest trying to think of what kind of headlines you want – and then drafting to see if you can get them. For example: FULBRIGHT CHARGES U.S. PRESTIGE AT ALL TIME LOW; FULBRIGHT DEMANDS FOREIGN POLICY BASED ON RECOGNITION OF REALITIES; FULBRIGHT LISTS SPECIFIC STEPS TO BUILD U.S. STRENGTH AND PRESTIGE.[28]

Meanwhile, the campaign had begun to shift markedly in Kennedy's favor, primarily the result of the first of four nationally televised debates between him and Nixon broadcast during September 26–October 21. Democratic confidence and Republican gloom waxed steadily as election time neared; but ef-

27 Leslie Carpenter, "Possibility of 'Free Electors' Bolt Diminishing," *Arkansas Gazette,* Aug. 28, 1960, and *Hope Star,* Sept. 15, 1960.

28 Marcy to JWF, Oct. 11, 1960, BCN 146, F4, SPF.

fective stump speeches by President Eisenhower and a massive Republican television effort during the last week of the campaign produced a marked Nixon resurgence and reduced Kennedy's margin to the vanishing point. Kennedy won, but with one of the slimmest margins of victory in American political history: a hundred and twenty thousand votes, or one-fifth of 1 percent.

Although Fulbright had worked energetically in Jack Kennedy's behalf, he, like so many others, knew America's youngest president primarily by reputation. He remembered the Kennedy family's close ties to Joe McCarthy, but Fulbright was not one to begrudge a colleague his or her political expediency. Actually, during Kennedy's tenure in the Senate, Fulbright had regarded him as a lightweight.[29] "I'd never really had a conversation with Jack to be frank about it – never had occasion," Fulbright later recalled. "He traveled in a different world."[30] But Kennedy's elevation to the presidency and Fulbright's tenure as chairman of the SFRC meant that the two would have to speak and to tread the same path, even if they did not do it hand in hand.

In appearance, they were opposites: Kennedy with his flashy good looks, his aggressive, driving if suave style; Fulbright reserved, tweedy, sardonic. There was some common ground, however: Both were attracted by words and ideas, reveled in the pithy quote, read and appreciated learning and art, tolerated mistakes from talented subordinates, and inspired loyalty and affection from followers who saw them as men of principle attempting to chart a firm course in a sea of expediency. Kennedy and Fulbright also detested pretentiousness and delighted in deflating overblown egos. In the end each man viewed the other as someone with whom to reckon. Fulbright was an Arkansan and a senator, but he was a regional aristocrat with Oxford credentials – and he was chairman of the SFRC. Kennedy could and did play the role of a superficial young playboy, but he was smart and shrewd – as well as president of the United States.

In the aftermath of the 1960 election, rumors abounded in the national press that J. William Fulbright would be the next secretary of state. Neither President-elect Kennedy nor his acting chief of staff, Theodore Sorensen, did anything to discourage the speculation. In a lead article on the new administration, no less a publication than Henry Luce's *Time* magazine listed Fulbright as a sure thing.

29 Ritchie, *Interviews: Marcy*, 126.
30 Quoted in Haynes Johnson and Bernard M. Gwertzman, *Fulbright: The Dissenter* (New York, 1968), 195.

Shortly thereafter Fulbright, Vice-President–elect Johnson, and the rest of the American delegation to the 1960 NATO Parliamentarians' Conference departed for London. An expansive Johnson greeted crowds as if he were Woodrow Wilson on tour following World War I. After the meeting, the key delegates, including Fulbright and Johnson, dined with Prime Minister Harold Macmillan and then enplaned for home. In the midst of recitations of past battles won and his vision of the future, Johnson assured Fulbright that he would be the next secretary of state and pooh-poohed his misgivings. After a few days in Washington, Betty and Bill departed for Fayetteville for an extended Christmas holiday.

Before he left, Fulbright called Jack Yingling into the office. "This business about me getting appointed secretary of state is getting serious," he said. "You'd have to take it if they offered it to you," Yingling replied. "Damn it, that's not what I'm talking about," Fulbright exclaimed. "I'm talking about how in the hell do I stop it. You'd better figure out some way to stop it because if I go you're going to have to go with me. I don't want to spend ninety percent of my time greeting ambassadors and entertaining."

Yingling went back to his office and began reading the newspaper. An article on an impending trip to Palm Beach by Richard Russell sent him rushing back to Fulbright's office. "Why don't you talk to Russell and tell him that you think you'd be a lousy secretary and get him to tell Kennedy," the aide suggested. Fulbright replied that he thought that was a hell of a good idea and he picked up the phone and called his old friend.[31] As Pat Holt, the SFRC's Latin American expert remembered it, Fulbright told Russell:

> Dick, for God's sake, I don't want to be secretary of state! I don't want him to ask me to be! And I can be a whole lot more help to him in the Senate as chairman of the committee than I can as secretary. And furthermore, if I resign from the Senate my successor is most likely to be Orval Faubus, and Kennedy doesn't want him in the Senate.[32]

According to one version, Russell demurred, telling Fulbright that he would be a great secretary of state.[33] Yingling, convinced that Fulbright did not really want to be secretary, believed that Russell indeed told Kennedy that Fulbright would not accept. Russell later insisted to Fulbright that he had passed along the message.

Kennedy still refused to rule out Fulbright, however, and the rumors intensified. Later in the month the Arkansan received a telephone call in Fayetteville from an acquaintance, Gene Farmer of *Life* magazine. It was definite,

31 Interview with Jack Yingling, Oct. 12, 1988, Savannah, Ga.

32 Donald A. Ritchie, interviewer, *Oral History Interviews: Pat M. Holt* (Senate Historical Office: Washington, D.C., 1980), 149–50.

33 Johnson and Gwertzman, *Fulbright: The Dissenter*, 170.

Farmer said. He had heard directly from the Kennedy camp that Fulbright was going to be appointed secretary of state. He wanted to come down to Fayetteville immediately to begin work on a profile.

Although Fulbright put Farmer off – it was entirely too soon for an article, he said – the call touched off a family conference. Hal Douglas, the senator's brother-in-law, remembered sitting around the living room in Fayetteville weighing the possibilities. Douglas also recalled Fulbright saying emphatically that he did not want the job – but, of course, if the president offered it, he would have to accept.[34]

Rumors that Fulbright was under serious consideration were certainly true. As Bobby Kennedy later wrote, Jack "had worked with Fulbright, knew him better, was very impressed with the way he ran his committee." In fact, although Kennedy initially regarded him as somewhat pompous and opinionated, he quickly came to respect the man from Arkansas.[35] Later, Kennedy's close friend Charles Bartlett admitted that "Fulbright was the preferred candidate," and insisted that at one point the president-elect had actually decided on him. Kennedy considered and rejected a series of alternatives: Adlai Stevenson (whom Fulbright had recommended), Chester Bowles, and McGeorge Bundy. To his mind, none could compare.[36] Wrote Arthur M. Schlesinger, Jr.:

> When I talked to Kennedy on December 1, it was clear that his thoughts were turning more and more to Fulbright. He liked Fulbright, the play of his civilized mind, the bite of his language, and the direction of his thinking on foreign affairs. Moreover, as chairman of the Senate Foreign Relations Committee, Fulbright had considerable influence on the Hill. . . . [But] there were problems too.[37]

Among these "problems" was Fulbright's civil rights record, which had antagonized the NAACP. The same day that Schlesinger talked to Kennedy, John A. Morsell, assistant to the NAACP's executive secretary, issued a public statement declaring that naming Fulbright secretary of state "would be one of the most colossal blunders of any administration." He called upon the four-hundred-thousand-member organization to launch a nationwide campaign to keep Fulbright or any other signer of the Southern Manifesto out of the cabinet. L. C. Bates, Arkansas's field secretary, warned Kennedy that black Americans were unalterably opposed to Fulbright's selection. He reiterated his wife's statement, made at the time of the Little Rock crisis, to the effect that Faubus was more to be trusted than Fulbright because "at least we know

34 Ibid.

35 Herbert S. Parmet, *JFK: The Presidency of John F. Kennedy* (New York, 1983), 67.

36 Johnson and Gwertzman, *Fulbright: The Dissenter,* 201.

37 Arthur M. Schlesinger, Jr., *A Thousand Days* (Boston, 1965), 139.

where Faubus stands."[38] Scores of state chapters responded to Morsell's appeal.[39] Bobby Kennedy, for one, believed that the civil rights issue was compelling. He pointed out to his brother that the black vote had gone overwhelmingly Democratic in the presidential election and, it could be argued, had provided the margin of victory. Fulbright's appointment would alienate not only African Americans but nonwhites everywhere.[40] Much of the heat of Bobby's argument, of course, came from the fact that Fulbright had supported the despised Lyndon Johnson for the 1960 presidential nomination.

Adding to Fulbright's woes was the fact that UAW chief Walter Reuther had set up camp in Washington the last week in November and mounted a massive lobbying effort against one of organized labor's oldest and most consistent foes. Indeed, those close to Reuther were surprised by the vehemence of his attacks on Fulbright, whom he repeatedly criticized as a "segregationist who would hurt our international relations."[41]

Other voices were raised against Fulbright. Dean Acheson seconded Bobby Kennedy's arguments concerning the SFRC chairman's civil rights record and his ability to deal effectively with the nonwhite, developing nations. The acerbic Acheson had never forgiven Fulbright for his criticism of Harry Truman. The suggestion in 1946 that Truman resign in favor of a leading Republican legislator, in order that both the legislative and executive branches of government be controlled by the same party, had branded Fulbright as naïve, if not malicious, in Acheson's mind.[42] He told Kennedy he considered the senator somewhat of a dilettante and felt he was less solid and serious than the kind of man needed for the job. "He likes to criticize," Truman's former secretary of state told the president-elect, "he likes to call for brave, bold new ideas, and he doesn't have a great many brave, bold new ideas."[43]

Perhaps the most powerful voices raised against Fulbright's candidacy for the top diplomatic post, however, were those of Israeli officials and American Zionists. In the aftermath of World War II Fulbright had supported the creation of the State of Israel, but he had been critical from time to time of the lobbying tactics employed by American Jewish groups on behalf of Israel. When in 1960 American labor unions refused to unload the Egyptian ship *Cleopatra* in retaliation for Nasser's closing of the Suez Canal to Israel, Fulbright dared to denounce them on the floor of the Senate.[44] During the weeks that fol-

38 "NAACP Opposes Post for Senator," *Arkansas Democrat,* Dec. 1, 1960.
39 Gloria Newton to JFK, Dec. 8, 1960, Fulbright Name File, Papers of John F. Kennedy, Kennedy Library, Columbia Point, Boston, Mass.
40 Drew Pearson, "The Fulbright Dilemma," *Washington Post,* Dec. 7, 1960.
41 *Kansas City Star,* Dec. 1, 1960.
42 Interview with William Bundy, July 5, 1990, Princeton, N.J.
43 "Newsweek Reports Acheson Against Fulbright in Cabinet," *Arkansas Gazette,* Aug. 24, 1970.
44 *Fort Smith Southwest Times Record,* Nov. 14, 1960.

lowed, American Jews and officials of the Israeli embassy bombarded members of Kennedy's entourage with entreaties to pick anybody but Fulbright.[45]

Fulbright was in Little Rock when the call came from Kennedy, who was vacationing at West Palm Beach. Clara Buchanan, Lee Williams's secretary, was in the office and answered the phone. When she told Fulbright, he asked her to give him a few minutes to think. She recalled:

> We had two offices in the old federal building down town. The partition didn't go all the way up to the top. When he finally asked me to place the call I heard him say, "No, I know who he is but I don't know him very well." They were talking about Dean Rusk, of course. Kennedy was calling him to tell him that he was going to name Dean Rusk. He [Fulbright] was very quiet for a long time.[46]

At the same time Kennedy broke the news to Fulbright over the phone, he invited him to Palm Beach to discuss personnel matters and the shape and direction of the new administration's foreign policy. "The whole purpose was to try to soften the blow," Fulbright recalled of that meeting in Florida. "He thought it was a terrible blow, I guess. He more or less apologized for the publicity, which he regretted, he said, but he couldn't help it." Whatever reservations Fulbright had had earlier about Kennedy were removed by the manner in which Kennedy handled that Palm Beach visit. "I don't think I've ever seen a man of such importance, with more consideration, more sympathy for another politician, than this man was," he said later.

During his stay at the Kennedy compound, the "ambassador," Joseph P. Kennedy, took Fulbright aside and told him that the liberals, the NAACP, and the Zionists "just raised hell" when they heard about the possibility of his becoming secretary of state. When Fulbright returned to Washington, he found a case of Scotch at his house, compliments of "the ambassador."[47]

There is no doubt that J. William Fulbright was interested in being secretary of state – no one committed to public service with a focus on foreign affairs would not be – but his reservations about his suitability for the position were authentic. He would have made a terrible bureaucrat and ceremonial chief. There is little doubt that he would have resented surrendering his independence and privacy. Moreover, there was much to Fulbright's argument that he could have a greater impact on the course of American foreign policy as chairman of the SFRC than as secretary of state under a man who clearly was determined to control foreign affairs himself. The prospect of working in

45 Bill Gottlieb, American Council for Judaism, to JWF, Dec. 7, 1960; Lee Williams to Marschal D. Rothe, Jr., Dec. 9, 1960, Series 48:1, Box 1, F2, SPF; and "Dear Mr. President," Dec. 4, 1960, Fulbright Name File, Kennedy Papers.

46 Interview with Clara Buchanan, June 7, 1989, Little Rock, Ark.

47 Quoted in Johnson and Gwertzman, *Fulbright: The Dissenter,* 202.

an undivided government with a president whom he respected was most appealing. Fulbright sensed in the Kennedy administration the potential for a creative foreign policy, one that would break down barriers between the communist and noncommunist worlds and improve America's image in developing areas. Nevertheless, he would have taken the job if offered it and was deeply disappointed at not being asked.

# 14

# *Camelot and Cuba*

Fulbright was excited about the new administration, in part because he had had much to do with its composition. The chairman of the SFRC corresponded with, talked with, and played golf with Jack Kennedy throughout the last week in December and the first week in January.[1] He was responsible for the appointment of George Ball, Adlai Stevenson's former campaign adviser, as undersecretary of state. He was among those who successfully urged Kennedy to appoint East Asian expert Edwin O. Reischauer as ambassador to Japan.[2] He championed the cause of William Benton as ambassador to the Court of St. James, a post that went to another Fulbright friend, David Bruce. He recommended Philip Stern, a Stevensonian from the 1952 campaign, as assistant secretary for congressional relations. He did not know the new secretaries of state and defense, Dean Rusk and Robert McNamara, but they were reputed to be men of integrity and vision; nor was he acquainted with McGeorge Bundy, the dean of the faculty at Harvard, whom Kennedy selected to be his national security adviser, but the Arkansan had a weakness for academics from prestigious institutions. He did know Arthur Schlesinger and Kenneth Galbraith, both of whom received appointments in the new administration. During a golf game with Kennedy the two discussed the possibility of a summit with Khrushchev in 1961, the structure and function of a new organization to build bridges to young people in developing nations, and the possibility of troop reductions in Europe to halt the outflow of gold and dollars from the United States.[3] The Arkansan also found time to wring a commitment from Kennedy for the government to purchase the entire 1961 output of Reynolds Aluminum.[4]

Kennedy's election seemed to bring to an end the traditional animosity between the State Department and the SFRC. Even that archproponent of congressional prerogatives, Carl Marcy, seemed pleased. "I am delighted you are

1 "During Talks with President-Elect Kennedy Fulbright Hits on Arkansas Topics," *Northwest Arkansas Times*, Dec. 30, 1960.
2 JWF to JFK, Jan. 14, 1961, Series 1:1, Box 1, F4, SPF.
3 Marcy to JWF, Dec. 27, 1960, Series 48:7, Box 1:2, SPF.
4 "During Talks with President-Elect Kennedy. . . ."

to take over," he wrote Rusk shortly after the latter's appointment. "My only concern is that you may find the situation is just as a Republican friend in the Department remarked last week: 'We're getting out of there just in time; everything is ready to break loose.' "[5]

There was from the outset a basic contradiction in the foreign policies of John Fitzgerald Kennedy. He and his advisers insisted that they were out to make the world safe for diversity, that under their leadership the United States would abandon the status quo policies of the past and support change, especially in the developing world. The Kennedy people did not object to the Eisenhower administration's intervention into the internal affairs of other nations, but to the fact that it usually intervened ineptly and always to prop up the status quo. According to Arthur Schlesinger, Jr., Kennedy fully understood that in Latin America "the militantly anti-revolutionary line" of the past was the policy most likely to strengthen the communists and lose the hemisphere. He and his advisers planned openings to the left to facilitate "democratic development."[6]

At the same time, the administration saw any significant change in the world balance of power as a threat to American security. Kennedy, Bundy, Rusk, and McNamara took very seriously Khrushchev's January 1961 speech offering support for "wars of national liberation"; it was, they believed, evidence of a new communist campaign to seize control of anticolonial and other revolutionary movements in economically underdeveloped regions. If the Third World was not to succumb to the siren's song of Marxism–Leninism, with all the implications that that would pose for the international balance of power, then the United States and other "developed" countries would have to demonstrate that economic progress could take place within a democratic framework. However, the logic of this position, as John Gaddis has pointed out, was that the United States really would need a world resembling itself in order to be secure.[7]

Fulbright seemed to embrace the new administration's philosophy of foreign affairs enthusiastically. Consciously or unconsciously, Kennedy and his advisers were reacting to the criticisms of Eisenhower Fulbright had voiced during the preceding six years. Here was an educated, interested president surrounded by activist intellectuals rather than unimaginative businessmen. No longer would the foreign policy establishment surrender Third World

5 Marcy to Dean Rusk, Dec. 13, 1960, Box 3, Folder Aug.–Dec., Marcy Papers. In fact, Marcy had strongly recommended Rusk to the Kennedy transition team. Interview with Carl Marcy, Oct. 10, 1988, Washington, D.C.

6 Arthur M. Schlesinger, Jr., *A Thousand Days* (Boston, 1965), 201.

7 John Lewis Gaddis, *Strategies of Containment: A Critical Appraisal of Postwar American National Security Policy* (New York, 1982), 208–9.

areas to the communists in the name of a balanced budget. Galbraith, Schlesinger, and Rostow's advice appeared to reflect the Arkansan's notion that, given the balance of nuclear terror, the focus of competition between the communist and noncommunist worlds must shift to education, culture, and economic development. By all indications the White House and State Department recognized the crucial importance of the kind of people-to-people contact Fulbright had been advocating for a quarter century. The Peace Corps and the Alliance for Progress, a multi-billion-dollar, long-term aid program that the Kennedy administration hoped would do for Latin America what the Marshall Plan had done for Western Europe, seemed to the Arkansan to be steps in the right direction.[8] Indeed, Fulbright had been waiting for Kennedy's enlightened activism since 1945.

It was not surprising, then, that during the spring and summer of 1961 Fulbright more than any other figure associated with the Kennedy administration articulated the liberal activist philosophy that underlay Camelot's foreign policy. Effective resistance against the forces of international communism involved not only military strength, he told the Senate in June, but a willingness to help developing nations "toward the fulfillment of their own highest purposes." Noting that the focus of the cold war was now on the undeveloped and newly emerging nations, Fulbright insisted that the United States could never guarantee the borders of a neutral country against infiltration, or protect its villages from subversion; what it could do was instill in those people a willingness themselves to resist. What America had to offer was its values – "liberty and individual freedom . . . international peace, law and order, and constructive social purpose."[9]

Although one of the principal proponents of the liberal activism espoused by Schlesinger and Rostow, Fulbright perceived quite early the contradiction in the Kennedy foreign policy. He sensed, he told the Senate – in the same speech in which he declared that the United States must align itself with the forces of social progress – that there were powerful voices abroad in the land declaring that any change in the status quo around the world was the result of a communist conspiracy and must be met by force. "This is a dangerous doctrine," he warned; "nothing would please communist leaders more than to draw the United States into costly commitments of its resources to peripheral struggles in which the principal communist powers are not themselves directly involved." The event that first created doubts in Fulbright's mind about the Kennedy administration's willingness to allow social revolutions to run their course was the abortive Bay of Pigs invasion.

8 *Memphis Press-Scimitar,* Mar. 17, 1961.
9 *Congressional Record,* Senate, June 29, 1961, 11703–5.

Fulbright followed Fidel Castro's rise to power through the perceptive eyes of the SFRC's Latin American expert, Pat Holt. A journalist by training, Holt boasted degrees from the University of Texas and the Columbia School of Journalism. Drafted into the army in 1941, he had served as a Japanese-language translator and then elected to stay on in Washington after the war, where he worked for the *Reporter* and the precursor to the *Congressional Quarterly*. Holt's father was a friend and political supporter of Senator Tom Connally, and in 1950 the senior senator from Texas hired Holt as one of the four permanent staff members of the SFRC.[10]

Pat Holt was a tough, raw-boned Texan, his lean frame sheathed in skin that seemed perpetually sunburned and his angular face topped by a thatch of prematurely white hair. He was bluntly outspoken and almost as intolerant of fools as Fulbright. Intelligent without possessing a great deal of imagination, Holt was the stereotypical hard-bitten journalist. Although he had little empathy with ivory-tower academics such as Schlesinger and Rostow, the SFRC's Latin American specialist endorsed their stated determination to create openings to the Democratic left and to identify the United States with peaceful change in Latin America.[11]

According to Holt, he, Fulbright, and the SFRC were quickly disabused of the idea that Castro was an enlightened social democrat with whom the United States could deal. The issue was not whether or not Castro was a communist, or whether he was a "tool of the Kremlin," Holt recalled. The problem was that Castro was "a mercurial, very unreliable, and largely unknown quantity."[12] Nonetheless, Fulbright and Holt were deeply committed to the principle of nonintervention except in the most dire circumstances. Fulbright wrote a constituent:

> Of course I agree with you that our nationals are entitled to prompt, adequate, and effective compensation for their expropriated property in Cuba. What particularly troubles me is how we can effectively insist on this if the Cuban government proves obdurate. I think any kind of intervention in the manner of Teddy Roosevelt would only be self-defeating, not only in Cuba, but elsewhere in the hemisphere.[13]

By the fall of 1959 certain figures in the Eisenhower administration had come to the conclusion that Castro was a communist, a tool of the Kremlin,

10 Donald A. Ritchie, interviewer, *Oral History Interviews: Pat M. Holt* (Senate Historical Office: Washington, D.C., 1980), 1–15.
11 Ibid., 118–19.
12 Ibid., 116–17; also Erickson to Holt, Apr. 6, 1960, and Holt to Erickson, Apr. 11, 1960, BCN 147, F44, SPF. See also Eugene Carusi to JWF, Mar. 9, 1959, and Holt to JWF, Apr. 24, 1959, BCN 140, F57, SPF.
13 JWF to W. W. Jackson, July 30, 1959, BCN 139, F4, SPF.

and a nationalist hell-bent on driving American interests out of Cuba. Over the protests of Fulbright's friend Christian Herter, who argued that the unilateral use of force would "be inconsistent with our treaty obligations and would create widespread disillusionment, if not hostility, throughout Latin America and other areas of he world," Eisenhower had decided to facilitate Castro's overthrow.[14] In 1960 his administration had authorized the training and arming of a Cuban exile army of liberation under direction of the CIA.

On January 20, 1961, John F. Kennedy inherited both the plan and an armed force already highly trained in secret Guatemalan bases and ready to go. The CIA authors of the scheme naturally advocated it, asking the president whether he was as willing as the Republicans to permit and assist these exiles to free their own island from dictatorship, or whether he was willing to destroy well-laid preparations, leave Cuba to subvert the hemisphere, disband an impatient army in training for nearly a year under miserable conditions, and have it spread the word that Kennedy had betrayed its attempt to depose Castro.

During the winter of 1960–1 Pat Holt began to pick out straws in the wind that the CIA was training a brigade of Cuban exiles somewhere in Central America to overthrow Castro. He constructed a scenario that turned out to be close to the plan that was actually implemented. The problem was that he could not prove his suppositions and did not feel he should bother Fulbright with rumors: One did not persuade the chairman with gossip and innuendo. By chance, one day in early 1961 following a hearing, Fulbright, as was his custom, stayed in the SFRC room to chat with the staff. Apprehensively, Holt told him that he suspected the administration was going to support a Cuban exile invasion. "I don't think it will work," Holt ventured, "and I don't think we ought to try it if it would work." To Holt's surprise, Fulbright said, "I agree with you; I think that's what they've got in mind."[15]

Actually, the Cuban invasion was already an open secret. In Miami talkative exiles were boasting of the forthcoming action, and the "secret" training camps in Guatemala were secret in name only. American reporters had filed on-the-scene dispatches about the camps, and Fidel Castro had for weeks been ostentatiously preparing for the CIA-sponsored invasion.

Fulbright ordered Marcy to prepare a memorandum outlining the pitfalls of a U.S.-sponsored reinfiltration. Meanwhile, he would work on the problem of how to bring it to President Kennedy's attention, he told his Latin American specialist. As luck would have it, on March 23, 1961, President Kennedy hosted a reception at the White House for thirty-three members of Congress, Fulbright among them. Although Kennedy had called Fulbright frequently, it

14 Herter to DDE, June 30, 1960, Whitman File, Dulles–Herter File, Box 10, Eisenhower Papers.
15 Ritchie, *Interviews: Holt,* 151–3.

was the first time the senator had been with the new president since the inauguration. During the coffee hour, the two men chatted:

"Where are you going for Easter?" Kennedy asked.

"We're going to Delray Beach [just below Palm Beach] to stay with Betty's aunt," Fulbright said.

"Well, I'm going to Palm Beach. How'd you like a ride?" the president asked.

Fulbright accepted. Here was his chance to present his views on the Cuban invasion.[16]

When he got back to the office, Fulbright summoned Holt and told him to redouble his efforts to produce a memo. Easter was in March that year, and it was just a matter of days until Fulbright would board Air Force One for Florida. Holt recalled that he worked night and day, consulting periodically with both Fulbright and Marcy. The United States, Fulbright and his staffers believed, faced two practical options in its dealings with Castro: to seek his overthrow, or to tolerate his existence while working to isolate him and insulate the rest of the hemisphere from his revolution. Fulbright and Holt came down squarely in favor of the latter course. If the Cuban exiles succeeded, and the United States extended recognition, the operation would acquire a patina of legality, but this would do nothing to "lessen the universal popular impression that the whole operation was a brainchild and puppet of the United States." Most Latin American governments would be sufficiently intimidated to go along, but Washington's concern should not be with soldiers and politicians but with workers, peasants, and students. The Cuban revolution was already spreading, and a Yankee-led plot to overthrow Castro would give his revolution more credibility than it would otherwise have had.

On March 30, the day after the final memo was completed, Fulbright boarded the presidential plane to fly to Palm Beach. Several times during the course of Fulbright and Kennedy's wide-ranging talk, the president's aides broke in to discuss some aspect of the planned Cuban invasion. At last the Arkansan pulled the memo out of his pocket. "I have something to offer to the debate," he said. After Kennedy quickly scanned it, he and Fulbright mulled over the pros and cons of the enterprise. Fulbright emphasized his belief that the invasion would be a great mistake; Kennedy remained noncommittal. Minutes later, the plane landed and Bill and Betty Fulbright left for Delray Beach. The Arkansan departed convinced that his arguments had fallen on deaf ears.

The Fulbrights were planning to return by commercial flight when the phone rang Easter Sunday. It was President Kennedy and he wanted Fulbright to return with him on Air Force One on Tuesday, April 4. On the trip

16 Quoted in Haynes Johnson and Bernard M. Gwertzman, *Fulbright: The Dissenter* (New York, 1968), 204.

back nothing was said about Cuba until shortly before landing. Rather offhandedly Kennedy told Fulbright:

> I'm having a meeting to discuss the subject of your memorandum at five o'clock this afternoon on the seventh floor of the State Department, and I'd like you to come along. I'm going to the White House first, then over to the [State Department] Auditorium for a press conference and from there I'll go on upstairs to join you. You can go to the press conference if you like.[17]

From his conversation with Kennedy, Fulbright had expected a small, perhaps informal, meeting. Instead, he found confronting him as he walked into the State Department conference room as intimidating an array of American officials as had ever been assembled in one place. Three members of the Joint Chiefs of Staff, including Generals Lyman Lemnitzer and Thomas D. White, resplendent in their uniforms and campaign ribbons, were there. So was the pipe-smoking chief of the CIA, Allen Dulles. To his left was seated the secretary of defense, Robert McNamara, and his assistant, Paul Nitze. Adjacent to them were Secretary of State Dean Rusk and his assistant for Latin American affairs, Thomas Mann. Fulbright was momentarily cheered by the presence of his friend Douglas Dillon, now serving as Kennedy's secretary of the treasury. Old Latin American hand Adolph Berle was there. Completing the circle around a long table surrounded by maps and charts were two of Kennedy's special assistants, Richard Goodwin and Arthur M. Schlesinger.

"God, it was tense," Fulbright would remember. "I didn't know quite what I was getting into."[18] It was, in fact, the full-dress and final major policy review for the Bay of Pigs operation.

Kennedy waved Fulbright to a seat near him and directly in front of Dulles. Seated next to the CIA head was a heavy-set man in civilian clothes who had just returned from the secret training camp in Guatemala. Dulles introduced him and said he was there to give "the very latest" word on the operation. The man spoke in glowing terms of the combat readiness of the Cuban soldiers, Brigade 2506, of their zeal and determination, and of the American belief that everything was ready for the successful invasion.

"Then Dulles took it up and made his pitch," Fulbright recalled. "He told what would happen in Havana and all over Cuba after the landing. After the landing their source in Havana believed there would be a sympathy uprising."

The CIA representatives argued forcefully that the invasion could not be abandoned at that late date. What would the president do with all those emotional Cubans the United States had trained and implicitly promised to support? They would be disillusioned and embittered, and certainly would accuse

17 Quoted in Johnson and Gwertzman, *Fulbright: The Dissenter*, 207.
18 Quoted in ibid.

the United States of going back on its pledge, of being weak, and perhaps even of being soft on communism.

"I remember also their discussing at considerable length that if anything unexpected happened to thwart them from moving on toward Havana," Fulbright recalled, "they could easily escape to the Escambray Mountains. So it couldn't fail."[19]

Although it was the first time he had heard any details of the invasion plan, Fulbright was singularly unimpressed with the arguments advanced by the CIA. Dulles's contention that the United States would be placed on the horns of an unbearable dilemma if the invasion did not come off "didn't appeal to me a damn bit," he later recalled. Given his experiences in the 1950s with the Dulles brothers, he was highly dubious of their advice anyway.

The president went around the table calling on specific people for assessments – feasible or unfeasible. No one opposed the invasion until the president reached Fulbright. The chairman of the SFRC later admitted that he was somewhat intimidated, a bit flustered, and unprepared for the formal presentation that it seemed was expected of him. Typically, intimidation turned to irritation and then defiance. "Fulbright," Arthur Schlesinger later recalled, "speaking in an emphatic and incredulous way, denounced the whole idea."[20]

The Bay of Pigs operation would damage the national interest no matter how one looked at it, he said. If it succeeded, Cuba would inevitably become a dependency of the United States, and the world would brand the members of the Kennedy administration as a band of brutal imperialists. If it failed, America would be made to appear weak and ineffective. Despite what he had heard, Fulbright said, he was unconvinced the CIA's scheme was foolproof. More important, the projected invasion was a clear violation of America's principles and treaty obligations. No matter what the outcome, it would compromise the nation's moral position in the world. "He gave a brave, old-fashioned American speech, honorable, sensible and strong," Schlesinger later recounted; "and he left everyone in the room, except me and perhaps the President, wholly unmoved."[21]

In fact, neither Schlesinger nor Kennedy was all that moved. Early in the morning of Monday, April 17, 1961, the members of Cuban Exile Brigade 2506 – some 1,450 Cubans of every class, race, occupation, well trained and well led – landed at the Bay of Pigs, achieved tactical surprise, fought well, and – until they ran out of ammunition – inflicted heavy casualties upon Castro's forces, which soon numbered some twenty thousand. By nightfall of the following day all of Cuba's would-be liberators were either dead, imprisoned, or crawling through the swamps that ran inward from the Bay of Pigs.

19 Interview with J. William Fulbright, Oct. 11–18, 1988, Washington, D.C.
20 Schlesinger, *Thousand Days,* 252.
21 Ibid.

Fulbright learned of the invasion while he and Pat Holt were returning with Douglas Dillon from a meeting of the Inter-American Development Bank in Rio de Janeiro. They were shocked. While the party was in Rio, Kennedy had told a press conference that American forces would not participate in any attempt to liberate Cuba. Fulbright and Holt interpreted this to mean that the Bay of Pigs operation had been canceled. At their stopover at Ramsay Air Force Base in Puerto Rico, they learned that the exiles had in fact landed. The chairman of the SFRC and his Latin American adviser returned to Washington in a somber and apprehensive mood.[22]

As Castro's forces were mopping up, President Kennedy was hosting, in white tie and tails, a White House reception for his cabinet and the members of Congress and their wives. Shortly before midnight he slipped away to meet privately with his top advisers and congressional leaders. They were all there, including Dulles, Lemnitzer, Johnson, McNamara, Rusk, Russell, Rayburn, and Fulbright.

Solemnly Kennedy reported that the Bay of Pigs operation was an abject failure. There would be no American rescue and he, as president, would accept full responsibility. There were no excuses, no recriminations. As he passed Fulbright on his way out, he turned and said clearly enough for those present to hear: "Well, you're the only one who can say I told you so."[23]

Five days after that White House meeting, Fulbright appeared on *Meet the Press.* As he and Marcy anticipated, most of the questions were about Cuba. Citing executive privilege, he refused to say whether he had advised Kennedy not to proceed with the Bay of Pigs operation, and he defended the administration by insisting the Cuban refugees were an unruly lot, not susceptible to being controlled by anybody. He did deliver a long diatribe against U.S. intervention in Laos, where the pro-Western government was then under siege by the Pathet Lao.[24] The following week Walter Lippmann, unable to bear anonymity for his protégé, ran an "I told you so" column. "He [Fulbright] foresaw what would happen, he warned the President that the right policy was not to attempt to oust Castro but to contain him while we worked constructively in Latin America," Lippmann gloated in "Today and Tomorrow." "Senator Fulbright was the only wise man in the lot."[25]

The White House was furious. Ted Sorensen, Bobby Kennedy, and Arthur Schlesinger were convinced Fulbright was trying to show up the president. Kennedy suddenly recalled Fulbright's imperiousness when, as a member of that privileged clique of southern congressional chairmen, he used to send SFRC staffers to dragoon the very junior senator from Massachusetts into

22 Ritchie, *Interviews: Holt,* 153.
23 Quoted in Johnson and Gwertzman, *Fulbright: The Dissenter,* 210.
24 Holt to Marcy, Apr. 24, 1961, Series 48:1, Box 2:2, SPF.
25 Walter Lippmann, "Today and Tomorrow," *Washington Post,* May 2, 1961.

attending committee meetings. Shortly after Lippmann's column and a similar one by the *New York Times*'s Arthur Krock appeared, Rowland Evans ran a front-page story in the *New York Herald-Tribune* declaring that relations between the SFRC chairman and the White House had reached "a highly sensitive stage."[26] As was well known, Evans was a close personal friend of the president.

Worried that he would henceforth be shut out of administration councils, Fulbright hurriedly paid a courtesy call at the White House. After an hour in the Oval Office, he emerged to tell reporters that he and Kennedy were in perfect accord. The president did his bit the next day at his regular press conference. "I think his counsel is useful," he told reporters. "I think he should say what he thinks. If he had indicated disagreement on occasions, he has indicated general support on a good many other occasions."[27]

In late July 1962, shortly after a visit to Moscow by Raul Castro, Cuba's defense minister and brother to Fidel, the Soviet Union began sending weapons and personnel to Cuba. The Russians, citing the abortive Bay of Pigs invasion, explained that the arms they were shipping to the Caribbean would enable Fidel Castro to defend his regime against future American attacks. On the night of October 15 presidential advisers viewed new photographs from a U-2 flight showing a launching pad and other installations for medium-range nuclear missiles in a field near San Cristobal. After consulting with others, McGeorge Bundy decided that the matter could wait until the president awoke. Kennedy and his advisers interpreted the work of Soviet technicians, who were readying other sites, as a challenge to the Monroe Doctrine and an effort by the Soviet Union to shift the international balance of power in its favor. Ruling out an air strike to destroy the missile sites on the grounds that it would kill thousands of civilians and further undermine America's moral position in the world, the president decided, as a first step, to blockade Cuba. This would prevent entry of additional offensive weapons while the administration decided what to do about those already in place.

Eventually the rumors that swirled about Washington concerning the nature of the Soviet buildup in Cuba found their way to Arkansas, where Fulbright was campaigning for his fourth term in the Senate. When his opponent, Republican Kenneth Jones, asked where he stood on the communist threat that was being mounted against the United States, Fulbright assured the electorate that all weapons in Cuba were defensive in nature and that nothing

26 Rowland Evans, "Why Fulbright's Glaring at the White House," *New York Herald Tribune*, May 4, 1961.

27 Leslie Carpenter, "Fulbright Rates High in Councils At White House," *Arkansas Gazette*, May 21, 1961.

would be accomplished if the United States smashed that "poor, bedraggled country."[28] In fact, on September 14 Holt had cabled Fulbright that administration officials were assuring the Senate that the additional Soviet equipment recently arrived in Cuba "is of an essentially defensive nature – as, for example, anti-aircraft weapons." He and his contacts in the State Department were confident that the real menace posed to United States interests by Castro was his determination to subvert friendly governments in Central and South America. Even there, Holt had told Fulbright, the outlook was bright, because as the degree of Soviet intervention in Cuba became obvious, intensely nationalist Latinos were sure to sour on Castro. The only clouds on the immediate horizon were the "highly irresponsible" Cuban exiles whose main goal in life seemed to be "to involve the United States in military action to overthrow Castro."[29]

To deflect the Republican attacks on the administration's Cuban policy, the Democratic majority in Congress had passed on October 3 a joint resolution stating that the United States was "determined . . . by whatever means may be necessary, including the use of arms," to prevent Cuba from subverting the other governments of the hemisphere or "to prevent in Cuba the creation or use of an externally supported military capability endangering the security of the United States."[30] Fulbright did not have to vote on the resolution and was thankful for it. "I agree that all of Latin America appears to be unstable and dangerous," he wrote his old friend, Will Clayton, "but I have very little confidence in armed intervention . . . it won't work, just as it didn't work in Mississippi."[31]

Then, late on the day of October 21, while he was touring Arkansas, Fulbright received an emergency phone call from the White House. He should return at once to Little Rock, where an air force plane would pick him up and bring him back to Washington for a top-secret briefing on the Cuban situation. Congressional leaders gathered at the White House at five o'clock on the twenty-second, two hours before the president was scheduled to address a national television audience. Kennedy showed his guests the most recent U-2 photographs. According to Richard Russell's notes, the president confessed that there were in Cuba thirty medium-range missiles, forty MIG 21's, and twenty IL 28 bombers with a range of 2,200 miles. Clearly, Khrushchev

28 "Jones Asks – and Fulbright Answers with Views on Cuba," *Arkansas Gazette,* Sept. 11, 1962.

29 Holt to JWF, Sept. 14, 1962, Series 48:1, Box 4:3, SPF.

30 Marcy to Morse, Oct. 26, 1962, Box 4, Folder Jan.–May, Marcy Papers.

31 Federal marshals and National Guardsmen had earlier that year fought a pitched battle with segregationists in Oxford, Mississippi. The mob, egged on by the state's racist governor, had been attempting to prevent the integration of the University of Mississippi. JWF to Clayton, Oct. 5, 1962, Alpha File (1954–62), Folder FU, Papers of Will Clayton, Truman Library, Independence, Mo.

was threatening the international balance of power. The real issue, Kennedy declared, was whether or not the United States would continue to be a first-class power. He and his advisers were afraid that Khrushchev was not bluffing. Air Force General Curtis LeMay assured him, Kennedy said, that his planes could go in and knock out the bases, but there was every chance the Soviets would retaliate against West Berlin. He then outlined his plans for a blockade: A naval picket line would prevent additional Soviet ships from landing hardware and personnel in Cuba while the United States worked, through the United Nations and Organization of American States, to force Cuba to dismantle existing facilities.

To Kennedy's surprise, Russell and Fulbright urged him to go further. The blockade would not remove the danger; both Khrushchev and Castro had been repeatedly warned. The United States should either destroy the Russian missiles and planes through a surgical air strike or invade Cuba and through conventional ground action take out those weapons that posed a threat to the security of the United States. The fact that the principals had been warned negated the fears expressed by Robert McNamara that the United States would open itself to charges that it had staged a "sneak attack" à la Pearl Harbor. Kennedy listened courteously but reiterated his intention to follow the course he had outlined. All right, Russell responded, but why not use the word "quarantine" instead of "blockade"? Blockade is an act of war whereas there was no precedent or definition in international law for quarantine. It was the only bit of advice Kennedy accepted from the legislative leaders.[32]

The president was taken aback by Fulbright's bellicosity. Arthur Schlesinger later wrote that Kennedy reconciled the apparent discrepancy between the Arkansan's position on the Bay of Pigs and the missile crisis thus: "The trouble is that, when you get a group of senators together, they are always dominated by the man who takes the boldest and strongest line. That is what happened the other day. After Russell spoke, no one wanted to take issue with him. When you can talk to them individually, they are reasonable."[33]

The missile crisis moved to a denouement, the participants at times numb with anxiety. Through intermediaries, Khrushchev proposed a trade-off: the Soviet Union would remove the missiles from Cuba under inspection of the United Nations if the United States would lift the blockade and promise publicly not to invade Cuba. In this message and a subsequent letter, Khrushchev pressed Kennedy in addition to dismantle Jupiter missiles stationed in Turkey. Although he was prepared to consider a missile trade if the crisis dragged on into a third week, the president and his advisers offered a simple pledge not to invade Cuba in return for removal of the Soviet launchers and war-

32 Conference at White House, Oct. 23, 1962, General File, Box EE 3, Special Presidential File, Russell Papers.

33 Quoted in Schlesinger, *Thousand Days,* 812.

heads. Khrushchev accepted.[34] The world had survived its first and perhaps greatest thermonuclear crisis.

It is possible that Fulbright and Russell's advice, if taken, would have touched off World War III. In the spring of 1992 American, Soviet, and Cuban participants in the 1962 missile crisis came together in Havana for a commemorative conference. During those proceedings it was revealed for the first time that there had been tactical as well as strategic warheads in Cuba. Moreover, Soviet field commanders had had permission to use tactical nuclear weapons against an American invasion without permission from Moscow. Robert McNamara, then secretary of defense, admitted that had the Soviets used such weapons against an American force, the demand for a nuclear response against the Soviet Union would have been overwhelming.[35]

It soon became public knowledge that Fulbright had reversed his Bay of Pigs position and urged an armed invasion of Cuba as part of an effort to destroy the missile sites. In a cruder version of Kennedy's interpretation, some charged that Fulbright, in the midst of his reelection campaign, had caved in to the perceived need to appear tough in the eyes of the home folks. Indeed, strident anticommunists inside and outside the Republican Party had spread the word that Fulbright had been personally responsible for holding back an American air strike that would have saved the Cuban brigade during the Bay of Pigs operation.[36] Fulbright continued to insist that his course was the one most likely to avoid World War III. If the Soviets had attempted to run the American naval blockade, or if U.S. personnel had attempted to board Soviet freighters headed for Cuba, he told reporters, it would have brought the Soviet Union and the United States into direct, cataclysmic conflict.

Actually, Fulbright's position had been worked out by his new speechwriter, Seth Tillman. Though he had been with the staff barely a year, the young international affairs expert had already gained Fulbright's confidence and moved to fill the void created when David Cohn had died suddenly in 1960. A graduate of Syracuse University, Tillman during 1955–9 had studied at the Fletcher School of Law and Diplomacy under historian Ruhl Bartlett, a traditional Wilsonian.[37] While an assistant professor of international relations at MIT, Tillman had applied for and received an American Political Science Association congressional internship in 1961. He served for six

34 James N. Giglio, *The Presidency of John F. Kennedy* (Lawrence, Kans., 1991), 210–14.

35 On October 27, holed up in a bombproof bunker, Fidel Castro asked Khrushchev to authorize a preemptive nuclear strike against the United States to thwart an anticipated invasion. Arthur Schlesinger, Jr., "Four Days with Fidel: A Havana Diary," *New York Review of Books,* Mar. 26, 1992, 22–9.

36 Ned Curran, "Fulbright Switch? No Such Thing, Says the Senator," *Arkansas Gazette,* Oct. 28, 1962.

37 Interview with Seth Tillman, Oct. 6, 1988, Washington, D.C.

months in the office of a young Republican congressman named John V. Lindsay, whom Lee Williams knew. When Tillman's six months with Lindsay were up, Williams persuaded Carl Marcy to allow him to do his Senate stint with the SFRC.[38] Within the year, Fulbright had set up Tillman with his own office, given him direct and unrestricted access to his inner sanctum, and placed him on a level above the rest of the staff.

Congress had not been in session at the time of the missile crisis. Pat Holt was in Brasilia at an Interparliamentary Union meeting, shepherding a group of senators.[39] From Little Rock before he departed aboard Air Force One for Washington, Fulbright called Tillman and told him to draft a memo for his forthcoming meeting with the president. Tillman desperately tried to find out what was going on, but, as he later put it, "the White House wasn't taking calls that day." From the newspapers and the *Congressional Record,* he managed to piece together an approximation of the crisis. Tillman later recalled:

> I came up with the idea that it might be wise to actually mount a force to dismantle the missiles. But the premise upon which I was proceeding was not that we do this in the most drastic confrontational mode, but rather that this would be a safer way than confronting the Russians directly. . . . We land a force which allows the Soviets to stand aside.[40]

Fulbright later insisted that he bought the argument, flawed as it was, on its merits, and only secondarily because it might stand him in good stead with his constituents. As late as June 29, 1962, however, he had been warning against unilateral U.S. intervention in Cuba. "I suppose we would all be less comfortable if the Soviets did install missile bases in Cuba," he observed, "but I am not sure that our national existence would be in substantially greater danger than is the case today. Nor do I think that such bases would substantially alter the balance of power in the world."[41] It may have been that Fulbright had recommended intervention because he unquestioningly accepted the recommendations of a novice staff member, or that he had been overly influenced by Richard Russell. Another explanation is that the Arkansan believed, ironically, that a "surgical" invasion would serve to outflank the Republicans and those Americans who were clamoring for World War III.

As was true throughout his tenure as chairman of the SFRC, Fulbright wanted to avoid a great-power confrontation. He believed that the Bay of Pigs fiasco had so alarmed Castro and Khrushchev that they had staged the military buildup in Cuba to thwart future invasion attempts. Fulbright was also convinced that the Bay of Pigs humiliation had made John F. Kennedy

38 Williams to JWF, Apr. 14, 1961, Series 48:1, Box 2:2, SPF.
39 Ritchie, *Interviews: Holt,* 160.
40 Tillman interview.
41 Fulbright interview.

more bellicose than he would otherwise have been, prompting him to confront the Soviets over Berlin and to overcommit the United States in such Third World areas as Vietnam. Nevertheless, Fulbright steadfastly refused to criticize the young president either publicly or privately. He urged Kennedy's detractors to be patient, for he was convinced that the president was well intentioned and would mature in time. Perhaps most important, Fulbright believed that Kennedy needed all the help he could get in resisting pressure from a revived radical right. Indeed, the threat of a third Red Scare in America during the early 1960s ensured that the differences between the chairman of the SFRC and the White House remained minor.

# 15

## *"Freedom's Judas-goat"* [1]

Like Lippmann, Reston, and other observers of American foreign relations, Fulbright sensed that in the wake of the Berlin and U-2 crises, the Bay of Pigs fiasco, and the Cuban missile confrontation, the American people were once again growing frustrated with and weary of the burdens of world leadership. The great danger in all of this, he believed, was that the country was ripe for an isolationist resurgence. In 1959 Eugene Burdick and William Lederer published an immensely popular indictment of American involvement in developing nations, entitled *The Ugly American.* Fulbright believed the book to be simultaneously a reflection and a cause of America's weakening will to compete with international communism. Typically, he set about counteracting what he considered its baneful influence.

Much of *The Ugly American* was set in Sarkhan, an imaginary country situated in Southeast Asia that, despite massive American aid, was flirting with communism. The Soviet and American ambassadors, who arrived within a week of each other, were a study in contrast. The latter was a recently defeated politico with no knowledge of Sarkhanese, Southeast Asian culture, or American foreign policy. The Russian, a professional diplomat and veteran Comintern operative, was thoroughly familiar with his host country. Not surprisingly, the Soviet emissary proceeded to best his counterpart in a number of embarrassing encounters. When the United States shipped tons of rice to a famine-ridden section of Sarkhan, the ambassador and local communists convinced the populace that the food was a present from the Soviet Union. They even managed to stencil on the recently unloaded crates, "This is a gift from Russia." In their novel, which the authors insisted was "based on fact," U.S. aid workers were portrayed as incompetent and inefficient, living lives of luxury in Sarkhanese cities, totally isolated from the common people. They were mediocrities lured from well-deserved obscurity by the promise of fat pay-

1 "J. William Fulbright: Freedom's Judas-Goat" (Liberty Lobby: Washington, D.C., 1965). A "Judas goat" (or "Judas sheep") is "the animal that leads other animals to slaughter"; William and Mary Morris, eds., *Morris Dictionary of Words and Phrase Origins,* 2d ed. (New York, 1962), 328.

checks. When not co-opted by the communists, American aid went into the pockets of corrupt local officials.[2]

Despite his ongoing campaign against political appointees, Fulbright feared that *The Ugly American* might just be enough to turn public and congressional opinion against foreign aid once and for all. The Arkansan rose on the floor of the Senate in mid-May to deliver a withering attack on the book and its authors. *The Ugly American* was a libel on the Foreign Service, the Arkansan declared, and an attempt to destroy America's principal weapon in the cold war: foreign aid. There were, Fulbright pointed out, nothing but career personnel serving as ambassadors in Southeast Asia. The book was full of "oversimplifications" and "romantic nonsense" that were misleading a number of gullible Americans, including more than one senator.[3] Burdick and Lederer's diatribe, the chair of the SFRC subsequently told reporters, was a part of the new isolationism being purveyed by the radical right. The thrust of *The Ugly American* was that the United States was engaged in a political struggle that it had neither the talent nor the will to win. Its title character was actually "a panic-stricken American in hysterical retreat from a job he finds too tough to handle."[4]

Fearing for sales, Burdick and Lederer screamed libel and demanded a public apology. When none was forthcoming, they humbly requested an audience with Fulbright so that any "misunderstanding" could be worked out. They were told that the chairman would be tied up indefinitely.[5]

News that Hollywood was going to put *The Ugly American* on the silver screen and that it had requested technical assistance from the federal government produced a fresh outburst from Fulbright. Any movie that derived from that "false and shameful" book was sure to be equally false and shameful, he told reporters. He had heard from one of the producers, he said, that the story line revolved around a lush who lived with "a Eurasian dame to whom he spills American secrets." "Translating this from Hollywood language, this means that the U.S. Ambassador to a Southeast Asian country is a drunkard who has a Eurasian mistress to whom he betrays secrets of our foreign policy."[6]

The producers of the movie and its star, Marlon Brando, journeyed to Washington to appeal to their tormentor to cease and desist, but Fulbright would have none of it. "It is apparently enough for the producers," he told a

2 *Congressional Record,* Senate, May 19, 1959, 8445–7.

3 Ibid.

4 John R. Hoover, "Many Examples of Success Found in Foreign Aid Plan," *Memphis Commercial Appeal,* October 26, 1959.

5 Burdick and Lederer to JWF, Sept. 17, 1959, Series 48:6, Box 26:2, SPF, and Marcy to JWF, Mar. 7, 1960, Box 3, Folder Jan.–July, Marcy Papers.

6 Warren Duffee, "Fulbright Opposes Aid for 'Ugly American,'" *Washington Post,* Sept. 8, 1959.

press conference, "that they can make money out of it [the movie] even at the cost of their country."[7] Brando was highly incensed, accusing Fulbright of censorship and "a lack of good manners." It was the Arkansan who was the real ugly American, he proclaimed.[8]

Despite Fulbright's denunciations – and perhaps, in part, because of them – *The Ugly American* became a best-seller, and Marlon Brando was nominated for an Academy Award for his role in the movie version. The Arkansan's attacks on the book and movie were not, as some longtime Fulbright-watchers believed, a case of temporary obsessional behavior; rather, the senator had sensed correctly that *The Ugly American* was a sign that America was preparing for a third Red Scare.

In the spring of 1961 Fulbright began to receive reports from friends and admirers across the country that the United States military had embarked on a carefully orchestrated campaign to acquaint the American public with the dangers of communism. In the process they were providing a forum for right-wing Russophobes, who not only denigrated the Soviet Union but equated liberalism with "socialism" and "communism." Fulbright first became concerned about the military's self-appointed role as a propaganda agency for the right when James McCormick, an employee of *Stars and Stripes,* wrote him complaining that members of the U.S. command in Germany had forbidden the paper to publish stories on recent SFRC hearings in which Fulbright and others had criticized aid to Turkey.[9] Fulbright immediately complained to Secretary of Defense Thomas Gates and demanded that censorship of *Stars and Stripes* cease at once. Gates's reply was far from satisfactory, but Fulbright assumed that, with the election of John F. Kennedy, the military would stick to purely military matters.[10] He was mistaken.

On April 19, 1961, Marcy passed Fulbright a letter that one of his contacts in the DOD had given him. It was from a newly reenlisted Air Force Reserve officer who had attended a showing of the film strip "Communism on the Map." Portraying the United States as a bastion of freedom surrounded by a hostile world, the narrator of the film explained that countries like France, Sweden, and Norway were for all practical purposes already in the communist camp. USSR stood for Union of Soviet *Socialist* Republics, after all.[11] It was not so much the film that bothered him, the reservist wrote, but the harangues that followed:

> The "discussion" did not stop with criticizing past Presidents, but the speakers repeatedly called attention to and stated as a fact that

7 "Movie Producer Brands Fulbright Attack on Film 'Sinister, Irresponsible,'" *Arkansas Gazette,* Oct. 22, 1959.
8 "Marlon Speaking," *North Little Rock Times,* May 2, 1963.
9 James McCormick to JWF, Apr. 24, 1960, Series 4:19, Box 27:3, SPF.
10 JWF to Thomas Gates, May 4, 1960, Series 4:17, Box 27:3, SPF.
11 Philip Horton, "Revivalism on the Far Right," *Reporter,* July 20, 1961.

> welfarism leads to communism and that we were becoming more and more a welfare state . . . the whole tenor of the meeting was that the programs President Kennedy is for are programs which will lead us to communism.[12]

Then on April 21, Willard "Lefty" Hawkins, a friend of John Erickson and Jack Yingling's, reported on three simultaneous Strategy for Survival conferences that had just been held in Little Rock, Fort Smith, and Fayetteville, Arkansas. The conferences – which had drawn fourteen hundred in Little Rock, a thousand in Fort Smith, and around a hundred in Fayetteville – had seen members of the active-duty military and the Freedom Forum join hands to deliver a comprehensive "threat briefing" to the people of Arkansas. The crowd in Fort Smith, a mostly conservative community situated on the edge of the Fort Chaffee military reserve, had cheered as the beribboned officers warned against the Soviet military menace abroad while Dr. George Benson, president of Harding College, a small fundamentalist institution located in Searcy, and his assistant, Dr. Clifton Ganus, equated liberalism with socialism and attacked members of the Arkansas congressional delegation.[13] In a talk entitled "The Moral Foundations of Democracy," Ganus declared that Congressman J. W. Trimble, a soft-spoken, well-liked, and generally conservative politician representing Fulbright's old district, "has voted eighty-nine percent of the time to aid and abet the Communist Party." Not all in attendance were amused.[14] Fulbright and his staff sensed that the Strategy for Survival seminars were evidence not only of a resurgent radical right rooted in McCarthyism, but of the fact that the movement had penetrated the federal government.

Fulbright's fears were well founded. The 1960s had begun not only with the political triumph of a young, activist, progressive president but also – and perhaps not coincidentally – with the emergence of a new American radical right whose members *Time* magazine labeled "the ultras." In 1961 Americans worried about the problems of the cold war – Cuba, Berlin, Laos, and the H-bomb – but those problems seemed so distant and massive to individual citizens that they despaired of being able to do anything about them. Those frustrations provided the breeding ground for the ultra movement, whose leaders offered ready-made solutions to apparently insoluble problems. Like fundamentalists who promise to make a remote, transcendent God immanent, leaders of the radical right promised to make communism a tangible problem

12 Kenneth R. Loebel to Carlisle P. Runge, Asst. Sec. of Defense, Apr. 19, 1961, Series 4:19, Box 33:4, SPF.

13 Willard Hawkins to JWF, Apr. 21, 1961, Series 4:19, Box 26:1, SPF.

14 Pryor to Yingling, Aug. 9, 1961, Series 4:19, Box 26:1, JWF Papers. Trimble dismissed the incident with a joke, but Fulbright and his staff were infuriated and alarmed. J. W. Trimble to Leland F. Leatherman, May 8, 1961, Series 4:19, Box 26:1, SPF.

with which the average American could come to grips. As did the McCarthyites of the previous decade, the ultras argued vehemently that the real threat to the nation's security resided not so much in Sino–Soviet imperialism overseas but in communist subversion at home. Appealing to the American penchant for action, they urged citizens to fight this subversion by keeping a close eye on their fellow citizens, scrutinizing voting records, writing letters, and generally raising a hue and cry across the land. If they could not fight the communists in Cuba or Laos, at least they could smite the ones alleged to be at their elbows. "Don't worry about the atomic bombs or H-bombs," said former FBI counterspy Matthew Cvetic. "It's right here we'll lose the fight."

Above all, the ultras were extremists – "true believers," Fulbright called them. They brooked no compromise. "You're either for us or against us," insisted a California electronics company executive. "There's no room in the middle any more." Indeed, these fanatics of the right saw those who would compromise – liberals – as perhaps the greatest danger to American society. Declared TV commercial producer Marvin Bryan: "We don't want to coexist with these people. We don't want our children to play with their children."[15] Like other reform movements, the radical right of the 1960s produced and thrived upon a group of colorful and eccentric demagogues who, while attracting their own cult following, continued to emphasize themes common to the ultra movement as a whole.

Early in 1959 Robert H. W. Welch, Jr., a fudge-and-candy manufacturer from Massachusetts, had gathered eleven of his friends in an Indianapolis hotel where, in due course, they founded the John Birch Society. The organization, which spread like wildfire for two years, was a semisecret network of "Americanists" dedicated to fighting Communists by deliberately adopting some of communism's own clandestine and ruthless tactics – including the deliberate destruction of democracy, which Welch contemptuously described as government by "mobocracy." For Welch and the Birchites, Barry Goldwater was at least two shades too liberal. Most domestic programs, in the Welch view, were socialistic "welfarism" and a communist plot to destroy the republic. He railed against Earl Warren, telling his followers that their campaign to impeach the chief justice would deliver a crippling blow to international communism. In that same vein, the *Brown* decision was portrayed as a product of the "radicalism" that dominated the court and would lead to absorption by Russia without a struggle. To his devoted followers Welch – known as the "Stranger" – was a strongman who had sounded the tocsin just

15 "The Ultras: Ultraconservative Anti-Communism," *Time,* Dec. 8, 1961, 22–5.

in time and was bravely rallying the true believers for the decisive battle against communism.[16]

Meanwhile, from Tulsa, Oklahoma, the Reverend Billy James Hargis had launched the Christian Crusade ("America's largest anti-Communist organization"). The pink-faced, jowly evangelist specialized in coast-to-coast revivalist meetings, during which he delivered fundamentalist, anticommunist sermons, and in organizing Christian youth to combat the Red Menace. Joining Hargis on the stump was Dr. Fred C. Schwarz, a medical doctor from Australia, whose Christian Anti-Communism Crusade took in a million dollars in 1960. He promised Americans a lurid end if they were not ever vigilant: "When they come for you, as they have for many others, and on a dark night, in a dank cellar, they take a wide bore revolver with a soft nose bullet, and they place it at the nape of your neck."[17] Virtually every radical right movement of the postwar era was bankrolled by Texas oil money, and the ultras were no exception. The most colorful of the right's deep pockets was Haroldson Lafayette Hunt, an eccentric billionaire who lived in secluded splendor in a Dallas replica of Mount Vernon. His tax-exempt Life-Line Foundation, Inc. broadcast his right-wing views over three hundred radio and TV stations.[18]

Racism was a sometimes implicit, sometimes explicit feature of the radical right of the 1960s. The Arkansas Minute-Men Association denounced *The Diary of Anne Frank* as a Jewish conspiracy to whitewash Joseph Stalin.[19] Before the decade was out most members of the radical right claimed to see a link between the civil rights movement and international communism.[20] The degree to which the ultra movement and white supremacy had become intertwined was highlighted when the *Citizen,* the national publication of the white-supremacist Citizens' Councils of America, featured J. William Fulbright on the cover of its first issue. The publication did not laud Fulbright for his segregationist voting record but rather denounced him as one of the nation's most dangerous liberals.[21]

From the outset Fulbright was a favorite target of the new right. His sophistication and Oxford education made him anathema to a movement that featured fundamentalist religion and appealed strongly to members of the working and lower middle class. To these xenophobes, Fulbright's advocacy

16 George Barrett, "Close-Up of the Birchers' 'Founder,'" *New York Times Magazine,* May 14, 1961, 13, 89, 91–2.
17 Horton, "Revivalism on the Far Right."
18 Jack Anderson, "Oil-Rich Hunt Sees Self as Nation Saver," *Washington Post,* June 30, 1963.
19 Arkansas Minute-Men Association to Associated Press, May 27, 1959, BCN 147, F66, SPF.
20 *Congressional Record,* House, Feb. 17, 1959, 2317–20.
21 "Racist Magazine Scores Fulbright," *New York Times,* Nov. 11, 1961.

of cultural and educational interchange threatened to expose young Americans to dangerous foreign ideas, to open the nation's doors to aliens who would subvert its institutions and mores, and even to mongrelize the pure American race. He preached the ultimate heresies: peaceful coexistence and toleration of foreign ideologies. Right-wingers like Dan Smoot – a former FBI agent who harangued the nation on the dangers of communism on his weekly radio and television program – saw Fulbright as part of an internationalist conspiracy that began with Colonel Edward House, the headmaster of "the eager young socialist intellectuals around Wilson," and that blossomed during the regime of Franklin D. Roosevelt. The objective of "the great cabal" of which Fulbright was a part, Smoot told his listeners, was the same as the objective of international communism: "to socialize the economy of the United States and make this republic a dependent unit in a one-world socialist system." It was clear to Smoot and his followers that "Fulbright wants the President free from constitutional restraints so that he can surrender the sovereignty of the United States to a world government."[22]

For Michael Bernstein – minority counsel of the Senate Committee on Labor and Public Welfare, an ultra, and one of the driving intellectual forces behind Strom Thurmond and Barry Goldwater – Fulbright was a traitor, not in the sense of being a communist, but in the sense of being loyal to something other than the United States. The Arkansan had pledged his allegiance to internationalism rather than to American nationalism, Bernstein insisted. The former Rhodes scholar was a snob, an intellectual who despised the clods who comprised the mass of Americans. Clearly, he was one of Welch's "compromisers," a leading spokesmen for H. L. Hunt's "the Mistaken." "I don't say the phone rings in Fulbright's office," declared Colonel Fred A. Kibbe of the Florida Minutemen, "and a voice says, 'This is Khrushchev,' and tells him what to do, but I do say Fulbright helps the Communist cause."[23]

When in 1961 Fulbright set about exposing the military's involvement in the ultra movement, full-scale war erupted between him and the radical right. The Arkansan was convinced that it was not communists who had penetrated the federal government and were subverting American institutions, but rather fascists masquerading as conservatives. In fact, although many of the crusaders attacked the usefulness of the national defense program, some of their most ardent collaborators were high-ranking members of the officer corps.

In the wake of the Fort Smith Strategy for Survival conference, Fulbright asked Jack Yingling to investigate. Had members of the active military been involved in organizing the meeting? Had speakers equated liberalism with so-

22 *The Dan Smoot Report,* June 18, 1962.
23 Fletcher Knebel, "Who's on the Far Right?" *Look,* Mar. 13, 1962.

cialism and socialism with communism? Was the thrust of the program that America's greatest threat came from communist penetration of domestic institutions and the federal government? Had Trimble and other members of the Arkansas delegation been slandered? Yingling discovered that not only were all of these things true but that the Fort Smith, Little Rock, and Fayetteville meetings were part of a burgeoning national movement. He recalled:

> I was always kind of anti-military and Fulbright was too. I began to read more and more. The fellow that worked for [Democratic Senator] Joe Clark brought me some clippings about meetings in Pennsylvania. Come to find out this was an organized thing that derived from a directive that Eisenhower put out. It said that the military should educate people about the evils of communism.[24]

In fact, in 1958 the National Security Council had entrusted the military with the task of educating not only troops but the American people concerning the dangers posed to the nation by international communism and Soviet imperialism.

Following a month of study, Yingling prepared a lengthy memorandum that listed eleven instances in which Strategy for Survival programs sponsored by military personnel "made use of extremely radical right-wing speakers and/or materials, with the probable net result of condemning foreign and domestic policies of the administration in the public mind." The thrust of many of these conferences was that "much of the administration's domestic legislative program, including continuation of the graduated income tax, expansion of social security . . . federal aid to education . . . would be characterized as steps toward communism."

The memo confirmed Fulbright's worst fears: The radical right had penetrated the military and was using it to expound "the thesis of right-wing radicalism."[25] Noting that civilian control of the military was one of the most hallowed and jealously guarded principles of the republic, Fulbright recommended in a postscript to the document that the Department of Defense revise the 1958 directive to forbid political or ideological activities by military personnel acting in their official capacities.[26]

In mid-June President and Mrs. Kennedy asked the Fulbrights to join the official party that was to welcome President Mohammed Ayub Kahn of Pakistan. The evening of June 11 was relatively mild by summertime Washington standards, and the Kennedys, Fulbrights, Ayub Kahns, and other members of the official party were comfortable in their evening clothes as they boarded the presidential yacht for a cruise down the Potomac to Mount Vernon.

24 Interview with Jack Yingling, Oct. 12, 1988, Savannah, Ga.
25 JWF to JFK, June 28, 1961, Box 639, WHOF, Kennedy Papers.
26 "Memorandum Submitted to Department of Defense," Aug. 2, 1961, Series 4:19, Box 26:1, SPF.

Aboard ship Fulbright encountered Robert McNamara and decided to seize the moment. He told the former Ford executive:

> I've got a memo on my desk concerning something that happened in my state. In Fort Smith, Little Rock and Fayetteville, my home town, there have been so-called defense seminars, conducted by the Chambers of Commerce, but apparently sponsored by high-ranking military officers. I'd like to call it to your attention if you're interested.[27]

McNamara was indeed interested. The Bay of Pigs fiasco had reinforced the Kennedy administration's commitment to the principle of civilian control of the military. Shortly after they had taken over at DOD, McNamara and his deputy, Roswell Gilpatric, had let it be known that under their rule there would be no interservice squabbling, civilian authority would rule the military, and policy statements would be delivered by civilians rather than military officials. Unaware of the 1958 Eisenhower directive, McNamara in May had ordered all officials of the Department of Defense to limit themselves to defense matters in their public statements. His worry, however, had been about DOD encroachment on State Department turf, not that Defense would become a mouthpiece for the radical right.[28]

Both Kennedy and McNamara gave the Fulbright memo a careful and sympathetic reading, but before the DOD chief could prepare a directive incorporating Fulbright's recommendations, ultra officers in the Pentagon alerted Strom Thurmond, a major general in the Army Reserve and a leading spokesman for the new right, to what was happening. Thurmond immediately stormed down to Fulbright's Senate office. He encountered legislative assistant Lee Williams and demanded to see Fulbright at once. Upon being told that the senator was out of the office, he insisted on being given a copy of the infamous memo. He would have to check with his boss, Williams replied, and managed to persuade the indignant Thurmond to leave. When Fulbright returned to the office an hour later, Williams asked what he should tell Thurmond. "Tell him to go to hell," Fulbright answered.[29]

Unfortunately for Fulbright, the *Washington Post* and the *New York Times* obtained synopses of the memo and ran stories on it on the twenty-first. That afternoon Thurmond, unwilling to risk a second rebuff by one of Fulbright's staffers, sent the Arkansan a note demanding a copy of the memo within the hour. The memo on the military was part of his private correspondence, Fulbright replied. It did not have the sanction of the SFRC; indeed committee members were not aware of its existence. "Since it is a private communica-

27 Holmes Alexander, "Sen. Fulbright's Aide Wrote Controversial Memo," *Washington Star,* Aug. 14, 1961.

28 Department of Defense Directive, May 31, 1961, Series 4:19, Box 26:5, SPF.

29 Yingling interview.

tion to the Secretary of Defense, I have not felt that it is necessary to make it available to anyone else. Where it [the press] obtained the memorandum is a mystery to me."[30]

On July 29 Strom Thurmond decided that he could wait no longer. He took to the floor of the Senate to announce "that there is a concerted attack under way against the anti-Communist indoctrination of the American people and our troops in uniform and particularly against participation in this effort by our military officers." The attack, he said, had been begun by the Communist Party, USA, in its official organ, the *Worker,* and was now being carried forward by "innumerable sources." He then quoted an article in the *Worker* praising the Fulbright memorandum. Karl Mundt, Thomas Dodd (D–Connecticut), and other professional anticommunists leapt gleefully into the fray.[31]

On August 2 Fulbright inserted a copy of his memo and recommendations to McNamara in the *Congressional Record.* He was doing so, he said, not because he recognized the right of senators to demand access to the private correspondence of their colleagues, but because, apparently, some of his fellow senators believed that the principle of civilian control of the military was still debatable.[32]

Two days later Senator Styles Bridges of New Hampshire, the ranking Republican on the Armed Services Committee, declared that he found the contents of the Fulbright memo "shocking." He was going to ask Armed Services to launch a thorough investigation. In the House, Representative Robert Sikes (D–Florida) deplored any and all efforts to "muzzle the military." From that time forward Fulbright and Yingling's creation was known as the "muzzling the military" memo.[33]

As Thurmond and his contacts had hoped, Fulbright became the target for ultra attacks all across the nation. Among the milder denunciations was that of the Southern States Industrial Council, whose vice-president blasted Fulbright as a liberal who had no confidence in the people. The notion that the average American did not need to be educated concerning the communist menace was "the most incredible statement to be made by a prominent American in recent years."[34] Robert Welch urged Birchites everywhere to deluge their congresspeople and senators with letters and telegrams in an effort to head off "Operation FIB (The Fulbright Intimidation Binge)."[35] In his weekly

30 JWF to Thurmond and Thurmond to JWF, July 21, 1961, Series 4:19, Box 26:4, SPF.

31 *Congressional Record,* Senate, July 29, 1961, 13998–9.

32 "Memorandum Submitted to Department of Defense," Aug. 2, 1961, Series 4:19, Box 26:1, SPF.

33 "Investigation Urged on Fulbright Memo," *Arkansas Gazette,* Aug. 4, 1961.

34 Thurman Sensing, "Government by the People," Aug. 13, 1961, Series 4:19, Box 29:6, SPF.

35 John Birch Society, *Bulletin for October,* Oct. 2, 1961, Series 4:19, Box 26:6, SPF.

broadcasts the Christian Crusade's Rev. Hargis began referring to Fulbright as "the red-wing Senator from Arkansas,"[36] while Dan Smoot declared that the memo proved beyond a shadow of a doubt that Fulbright was "the darling of the one-world-welfare-state conspirators" who sought to make America just another province of bolshevik Russia.[37] "Piltdown Clique Stalks Fulbright," declared the *Pittsburgh Post-Gazette.*[38]

The whole affair proved quite exasperating to Lee Williams who, although he sympathized with Fulbright's position, was responsible above all for his senator's political well-being. Williams told his boss:

> As a result of your Senate speeches, press conferences, television appearances and other public utterances in the past two weeks, you have succeeded in arousing the ire of practically every organized segment of world public opinion. This is reflected in the mail you have received during this period. The following is a list of the groups from which you have had messages indicating their displeasure with your expressed opinions: John Birchers, McCarthyites, Goldwaterites, Thurmondites, Dixiecrats, militarists, isolationists, Zionists . . . Chinese Nationalists, Koreans, N.A.A.C.P.-ers, A.D.A.-ers, Communists, private powerists, veterans, farmers' cooperatives.[39]

Despite the ever-present risk of being labeled soft on communism, John F. Kennedy and Robert McNamara did not hesitate in defending Fulbright's warning and recommendations publicly. At his press conference the first week in August, Kennedy told reporters that Fulbright had performed a useful service in sending the Department of Defense a memorandum on political activities of the military. In fact, Kennedy said, McNamara had asked the junior senator from Arkansas for his observations and recommendations. It was manifestly in the interests of the military that its officers not be exploited for political purposes.[40] Indeed, on July 20 the DOD had issued a new set of directives laying down strict guidelines governing military participation in public programs.[41]

Meanwhile, the Senate on September 20 approved Thurmond's resolution authorizing the Armed Services Committee to investigate reports of censor-

36 Fred Michel to JWF, Sept. 26, 1961, Series 4:19, Box 31:3, SPF.

37 *The Dan Smoot Report,* June 18, 1962.

38 "Piltdown Clique Stalks Fulbright," *Pittsburgh Post-Gazette,* Oct. 22, 1961.

39 Quoted in E. W. Kenworthy, "Fulbright Becomes a National Issue," *New York Times Magazine,* Oct. 1, 1961, 21.

40 Statement on Fulbright Memorandum, undated, Box 29a, President's Office File, Kennedy Papers.

41 *Congressional Record,* Senate, Aug. 11, 1961, 15544–5, and McNamara to Sec. of Army et al., Oct. 5, 1961, Series 4:19, Box 26:5, SPF.

ship in the DOD. The Democratic majority on the committee, which included John Stennis and Richard Russell, were not enthusiastic about criticizing Fulbright and had no desire to take on the Kennedy administration, but a coalition of Russophobes and Republicans had forced its hand. To Thurmond's chagrin, however, the committee insisted on styling their exercise a "study and appraisal" rather than an investigation.[42] Richard Russell, chairman of Armed Services, then appointed a subcommittee headed by Stennis and including Thurmond and Stuart Symington, to hold hearings.

Styles Bridges and Strom Thurmond, for both political and ideological reasons, were content to let their ultra allies smear Fulbright. They believed that the muzzling the military memo and the Armed Services Committee inquiry presented an opportunity to indict the entire Kennedy administration, of which Fulbright was just a part.[43]

For two days during the first week in September, McNamara testified on the muzzling the military memo. The committee room was packed and the atmosphere tense. Several members of a women's ultra organization spat on the secretary of defense as he strode in. With John Stennis in the chair, the committee grilled McNamara for two days, demanding that he give them the names of the DOD review committee. With names, Thurmond and the ultras believed, they could utilize the intimidation tactics that had been employed so successfully by that heroic anticommunist of yesteryear, Joe McCarthy. McNamara, however, refused to comply with the committee's insistent requests. To do so would violate the principles of "sound management," he said.[44] At that point McNamara pulled out a letter from President Kennedy invoking executive privilege.

Stymied in their effort to link the Fulbright memo directly to the Communist Party, the Armed Services Committee turned to the case of General Edwin Walker, one of the Army's most decorated combat veterans. During World War II, Walker had led the elite First Special Service Force through Italy, France, and Germany. In Korea he had commanded the artillery at Heartbreak Hill.[45] On April 16, 1961, the *Overseas Weekly* reported that Walker, then in command of the 24th Infantry Division in Germany, had used materials of the John Birch Society and had described a number of prominent Americans as "pinkos" in discussion groups involving soldiers and dependents under his command.

The charges were true. Specifically, Walker had made "derogatory remarks on the leftist influence or affiliation of Harry Truman, Dean Acheson, and

42 "Muzzling Probe Set," *Arkansas Democrat,* Sept. 20, 1961.
43 Interview with Robert McNamara, Aug. 2, 1991, Washington, D.C.
44 "McNamara Backs Review of Military Leaders' Speeches," *Arkansas Democrat,* Sept. 7, 1961.
45 "Armed Forces: I Must Be Free. . . ," *Time*, Nov. 10, 1961, 27.

Eleanor Roosevelt." He had implied that journalists Edward R. Murrow (then head of the USIA), Eric Sevareid, and Walter Cronkite were fellow travelers. Walker, Pentagon investigators discovered, was a member of the John Birch Society and had distributed Birchite material to his troops. Most important and most damaging, the general had attempted to influence the outcome of the 1960 congressional elections. Through an editorial in the division's newspaper, he had urged his troops to base their choice on an index of congressional voting patterns prepared by the ultraconservative Americans for Constitutional Action and published by the right-wing magazine *Human Events.*[46]

Walker's reprimand, coupled with his relief as commander of the 24th Infantry, became an instant cause célèbre among the ultras. In the House of Representatives, Congressman Dale Alford was appointed chairman of a Congressional Committee for Justice for General Walker. Thurmond and Senator John Tower, a former political science instructor from Wichita Falls, Texas, called on the secretary of the army to demand an explanation. Given the fact that Walker's transgressions had been mentioned prominently in Fulbright's memo, it was natural for the Armed Services Committee to include the general in its muzzling the military investigation. Thurmond bore in on McNamara concerning Walker's rebuke. It was a national disgrace, the South Carolinian railed, for this decorated war hero, a man Hanson Baldwin had accurately labeled "a soldier's soldier," to be reprimanded for warning his troops against the dangers of communism.

At that point Harry Byrd interrupted. Was it not true, he asked, that General Walker had commanded federal troops at Little Rock? A hush fell over the room. When McNamara answered in the affirmative, Chairman Richard Russell exploded: "General Walker was in command at Little Rock! I thought at the time that he exercised high-handed, arbitrary, and intimidating methods." What could one expect from a man who had used "bayonets and rifle butts" to drive citizens off of private property?[47]

In fact, Russell's outburst had been carefully staged. Neither he, nor Stennis, nor Byrd, nor Symington had any desire to besmirch the Democratic administration. They were not isolationists who believed America's greatest threat came from within.[48] As Russell wrote a constituent, "I am frank to say that I think we are a long ways from the Communists putting anyone against the wall in this country."[49] Rather, these senators all represented southern states whose economies were benefiting immensely from massive defense contracts. They did not want to do anything to jeopardize this Pentagon-driven

46 John J. Lindsay, "The Case of Gen. Walker," *Nation,* Oct. 14, 1961, and DOD press release, June 12, 1961, Series 4:1, Box 1:1, SPF.

47 Drew Pearson, "Drive on Fulbright Boomerangs," *Washington Post,* Sept. 18, 1961.

48 Mike Manatos to Mike Feldman, June 12, 1962, Box 1, Papers of Mike Manatos, Kennedy Library.

49 Russell to R. A. Williams, Dec. 1, 1961, Walker Hearings, Russell Papers.

prosperity. Indeed, immediately after the Walker hearing, Russell left for Georgia to attend a dinner in his honor. The chief sponsor was Robert S. McNamara.[50]

Fulbright's tête-à-tête with the radical right sent the Arkansan's stock with American liberals soaring. The *Advance,* official publication of the Amalgamated Clothing Workers, praised Fulbright for saving the United States from takeover by a military junta. Southern liberal par excellence Ralph McGill praised him in his *Atlanta Constitution* column.[51] The Religious Freedom Committee, composed of Jewish, Catholic, and Protestant clerics of every denomination, denounced the political activities of certain military officers. "The United States government, in effect," the committee declared, "has been taking sides in a religious controversy – the attack by certain fundamentalist religious groups on liberal elements in the Protestant churches." It went on to praise Fulbright for the "courageous stand" he had taken.[52] To the right, however, he had become public enemy number one. "You are a stinking communist infiltrator," one superpatriot wrote in September 1961. "I call for your execution."[53]

By the midpoint of his first year in office, John F. Kennedy was under intense pressure from the radical right and the unscrupulous politicians who were waiting in the wings to reap the political whirlwind their more extremist brethren were sowing. "We need a man on horseback to lead this nation," E. M. Dealy, chairman of the board of the *Dallas Morning News,* told the president, "and many people in Texas and the southwest think that you are riding Caroline's bicycle."[54] Late in 1961 a man stepped forward to offer himself as America's Boulanger: Barry M. Goldwater, Arizona's Republican junior senator. Arthur Schlesinger, the White House's resident intellectual, attempted to damn Goldwater and the ultras with faint praise, but Kennedy and his advisers realized that this union of traditional conservatives and the radical right posed a genuine menace that had to be confronted.[55] The man who stepped forward to challenge Goldwater was J. William Fulbright. Indeed, the muzzling the military memo touched off a major debate over foreign policy, democratic ideology, and national purpose, a debate that established

50 Richard Russell to Rudy Simpson, Nov. 30, 1961, Walker Hearings, Russell Papers.

51 Max Awner to JWF, Oct. 17, 1961, Series 4:19, Box 31:2, SPF, and Ralph McGill, "The Incredible Generals," *Atlanta Constitution,* Oct. 13, 1961.

52 Rev. William Howard McLish to JWF, Oct. 12, 1961, Series 4:19, Box 31:3, SPF.

53 Hoover to SAC, Chicago, Sept. 25, 1961, "Hoover's Official and Confidential File," FBI Files.

54 Quoted in Arthur M. Schlesinger, Jr., *A Thousand Days* (Boston, 1965), 752.

55 Arthur Schlesinger, Jr., "The 'Threat' of the Radical Right," *New York Times Magazine,* June 17, 1962, 10, 55, 58.

the boundaries of political dialogue for the remainder of the Kennedy administration.

Fulbright's sweeping survey of American foreign policy, delivered in late June of 1961, infuriated Goldwater. In it, the Arkansan had urged the administration to continue to align itself with the forces of social progress in developing nations, to pursue a course of competitive coexistence with Communist China and the Soviet Union, to adopt a stance of toleration/isolation toward Castro's Cuba, and to avoid military intervention in peripheral areas of the world. Air Force Reserves General Goldwater already had his sights set on the 1964 presidential election, and he decided that Fulbright would make the perfect foil. Two weeks after Fulbright delivered his address, Goldwater rose in the well of the Senate and heaped ridicule on his colleague's remarks. He was "surprised, amazed, and alarmed" by Fulbright's views; they were an argument for "continued drifting in the wrong direction." Those who thought that America could wipe out communism by wiping out poverty were naïve – or worse. Fulbright, who he said was clearly speaking for the Kennedy administration, was foolishly preoccupied with a world opinion that seemed to prefer communism over democracy. The right course to follow, the only course to follow, Goldwater told the Senate, was for the president to declare "total victory as our fundamental purpose."[56]

Two days later Fulbright made his classic reply. In an age of ideological conflict and nuclear weapons, what exactly did Goldwater mean, he asked sarcastically, by "total victory"? Was he recommending that the United States stage a preemptive nuclear strike "which at the very least would cost the lives of tens of millions of people on both sides, devastate most or all of our great cities, and mutilate or utterly destroy a civilization which has been built over thousands of years?" What price victory! Or did he mean that he had developed some brilliant stroke of diplomacy or compelling argument of logic that would cause the communists to admit the error of their ways and voluntarily embrace capitalism? Should the United States invade Cuba, thus alienating all of Latin America and acquiring a new, ungovernable dependency? The arena of world politics was not like a college football game or medieval joust where there were clear winners and clear losers, the Arkansan declared.

In his contempt for global opinion, Fulbright continued, Goldwater did a great injustice to the peoples of the world. It was not communism that attracted them. The emergent peoples of Asia, Africa, and Latin America hoped for peace, a decent material life, and national self-determination. Only to the extent that communism was able to identify itself with these aspirations did it earn prestige, allegiance, and respect.

56 Robert S. Boyd, "Senate Argues Foreign Policy," *Memphis Commercial Appeal,* Aug. 29, 1961.

He was not, as Goldwater charged, a noninterventionist, but rather an advocate of "long-range intervention in depth" using all the instruments of foreign policy to identify the United States with social and political progress. "Our proper objective," Fulbright concluded, "is a continuing effort to limit the world struggle for power and to bring it under civilized rules." Total victory would consist of the triumph of "a world-wide regime of law and order and peaceful procedures for the redress of legitimate grievances."[57]

The Fulbright–Goldwater debate gained front-page headlines and spawned numerous editorials during late 1961 and 1962. "Fulbright Becomes a National Issue," was the title of a feature article by Ned Kenworthy in the *New York Times Magazine*.[58] "Clash of Irreconcilable Philosophies Involved" proclaimed Holmes Alexander in a column on the Fulbright–Goldwater encounter. "The forces of the left and right have joined battle on the deep-going principles expressed and implied in the Fulbright memo," producing "a clash that will be resounding throughout the sixties," he declared.[59] Conservative broadcaster Paul Harvey told his listeners that the debate could very well define the national purpose for an entire generation of Americans. Walter Lippmann, who had spent most of his life trying, futilely, to generate a national debate on one issue or another, defended Fulbright in his battle with the radical right, terming him a true conservative, "liberal in temper and progressive in policy."[60]

Lippmann, Kenworthy, Reston, and others' defense of Fulbright stemmed in part from the fact that the new right had targeted Fulbright for defeat in his 1962 bid for reelection. There was virtually no chance that a Republican could win in Arkansas, but Barry Goldwater and Styles Bridges believed that Orval Faubus would be a far less irritating thorn in their side than J. William Fulbright. Indeed, his election would provide a double benefit, removing an articulate critic of the GOP from the Senate and elevating to the national scene a living symbol of the racist traditions of the southern wing of the Democratic Party.

There is no doubt that Faubus could have beaten Fulbright in 1959, 1960, or 1961. The governor and his principal adviser, William J. "Bill" Smith, commissioned polls throughout this period. During the three-year span in

57 *Congressional Record,* Senate, July 24, 1961, 13246–7.

58 Kenworthy, "Fulbright Becomes a National Issue," 21, 89, 92, 96–7.

59 Holmes Alexander, "Clash of Irreconcilable Philosophies Involved," undated, Series 4:19, Box 27:2, SPF.

60 Walter Lippmann, "Fulbright Great Conservative," *Washington Post,* Oct. 13, 1961.

question, his surveys indicated that Faubus would take at least 60 percent of the vote in any head-to-head contest with Fulbright.[61]

Although many members of Arkansas's middle class, especially in the business community, were disgusted with Faubus over the black eye he had given to the state, his strength, as Harry Lee Williams noted, was still deep and wide in the towns and villages of rural Arkansas. While segregationists continued to idolize him, his control of patronage had raised up a small army of officeholders, both black and white, who were fervently loyal to him. Indeed, Louis Lomax, a black journalist who wrote an article on Arkansas for *Harper's* in 1960, noted with distress that a number of influential African Americans in Little Rock and Pine Bluff had supported Faubus for governor in 1958 and planned to do so again in 1960. He had won friends and influenced people within the state's black educational community by helping its members obtain administrative positions and posts in the state's Department of Education.[62]

In the spring of 1960 Betty and Bill Fulbright momentarily put aside their political anxieties to revel in the happiness of their eldest daughter. The last week in April Betsy Fulbright married a young medical student, John Winnacker.[63] Groom selection is the prerogative of the bride, but weddings often belong to mothers of the bride. Betty planned every aspect of the traditional ceremony held in Washington. Hal and Helen came from Fayetteville, and Anne and Kenneth Teasdale made the trip from St. Louis. Even Gilbert Swanson flew in from Omaha. Fulbright was unusually mellow and indulgent, even nostalgic. "As you know," he wrote a friend, "I have been in Washington since '43 and this is the first time we have been able to get the family together here, although it was only for two days."[64] Bosey, then a senior at Berkeley, divided her attention between her duties as bridesmaid and her new beau, Tad Foote, a tall, handsome Yale student. In June she and Foote announced their engagement.

As the campaign season approached, the Fulbright camp was uneasy and confused concerning the proper course to pursue in Arkansas. David Cohn, Fulbright's chief speechwriter and sometime adviser on southern strategy, had died suddenly in 1960 during a trip to Scandinavia. His demise was a per-

61 Interview with Orval Faubus, May 31, 1991, Conway, Ark., and interview with William J. Smith, May 23, 1990, Little Rock, Ark.

62 Louis Lomax, "Two Millionaires, Two Senators, and a Faubus," *Harper's,* Mar. 1960, 73–6, 82–6.

63 JWF to Lady Kathleen Wylie, Apr. 8, 1960, BCN 105, F72, SPF.

64 JWF to Clarence Byrns, Apr. 26, 1960, BCN 105, F32, SPF.

sonal as well as a professional blow. "Betty and I certainly miss David," Fulbright wrote a friend. "He was good company, and one of the most stimulating conversationalists I have ever known" – in Fulbright's eyes, perhaps the ultimate virtue.[65] Further complicating matters was John Erickson's decision to leave at the end of that year for a better-paying job with Ford Motors; his and Sara Lou's wise counsel and statewide network of friends would be sorely missed.[66] Lee Williams, the thirty-four-year-old lawyer from Fayetteville, agreed to move up from legislative to administrative assistant, and Norvill Jones was drafted to fill Williams's position.[67] Resilient, idealistic, and absolutely devoted to Fulbright, Williams would come to be an effective political counselor. He was more rough-edged than Erickson, and the second half of Fulbright's political career was correspondingly rockier than the first half; but that had to do as much with the controversial nature of the positions Fulbright took as with Williams's political management.

Fulbright and his staff believed that his high standing with the Kennedy administration and the national press would have little impact on his political fortunes in Arkansas. However quietly, Fulbright would have to continue to oppose the integration of schools and public facilities. Indeed, following his *Face the Nation* blast at Faubus, Fulbright went out of his way to pay tribute to the state's Democratic leadership and to call for party harmony. Behind the scenes, however, the junior senator worked diligently to erode his would-be rival's popularity and power.

Faubus was planning to run for an unprecedented fourth term in 1960, and the Fulbright camp decided that it would serve their candidate's interests to see that he had some respectable opposition. The governor was a segregationist (in fact, if not in philosophy) and, judging from his statements on foreign aid, an isolationist. In addition, the national leadership of the Democratic Party mistakenly viewed Faubus as an unlettered demagogue, a throwback to Theodore Bilbo and Pitchfork Ben Tillman. In late March Fulbright and Averell Harriman – wealthy industrialist, former adviser to presidents Roosevelt and Truman, and a leading figure in the Democratic Party – met and decided that, for the good of both the party and Fulbright, former governor Sid McMath should be persuaded to challenge Faubus. Harriman indicated that Truman believed Faubus to be a disgrace to the party and hence would be the perfect person to solicit McMath. Fulbright agreed to make the Truman–McMath connection.

By 1960 any sign of animosity between the former president and the junior senator from Arkansas had disappeared. "I never made any reflection on your personal character nor on your mother," Truman wrote Fulbright of their

65 JWF to George Carbone, Oct. 29, 1960, BCN 105, F37, SPF.
66 "A Good Man's New Work," *Arkansas Gazette,* May 21, 1960.
67 "Lee Williams Is Promoted by Fulbright," *Arkansas Gazette,* May 27, 1960.

1946 encounter over whether Truman should resign in favor of Vandenberg. All he had done in that heated moment before the Press Club dinner at the Statler was to suggest that if Fulbright had attended a land-grant college he would never have made the statement.[68] He was more than happy to accept the ex-president's explanation, Fulbright wrote back, although he felt he must point out that he *had* attended a land-grant institution – the University of Arkansas.[69] Truman readily agreed to contact McMath about challenging Arkansas's notorious governor. In the end, McMath – although he had been a public and vocal critic of Faubus and his handling of the integration crisis – rejected appeals by the party's national leadership to take on Arkansas's most famous segregationist.[70]

Frustrated and somewhat desperate, Fulbright, Erickson, and Williams decided that they would have to take the dangerous step of intervening directly in the 1960 gubernatorial campaign. Using Bob Lowe of the *Gazette* as an intermediary, Williams and Erickson tried to persuade various politicos to enter the fray.[71] Four eventually decided to take the plunge: former attorney general Bruce Bennett; H. E. Williams, president of Southern Baptist College at Walnut Ridge; Joe Hardin, a planter from Grady; and Hal Millsaps, a Siloam Springs businessman. Bennett, a protégé of Carl Bailey's, had always been on good terms with Fulbright. Millsaps entered with the express purpose of helping the junior senator "by knocking off Faubus."[72]

In deciding to take a hand in the 1960 gubernatorial campaign, Fulbright ran the risk of offending both the average Arkansan, who would resent senators interjecting themselves in campaigns other than their own, and the Darby–Pickens–Murphy–Stephens crowd, who supported both Faubus and Fulbright. In May, in fact, Bill Darby called to complain over the fact that Fred Livingston, who had left Fulbright's staff the previous fall, was working the state in behalf of Joe Hardin. Darby wanted assurances that Fulbright would stay out of the race. The senator would give such assurances, Erickson told the insurance magnate, if Faubus would promise not to challenge Fulbright in 1962.[73]

The Fulbright camp envisioned a scenario in which Faubus's opponents would force the governor into a runoff election against the top candidate, whereupon his opponents would combine forces to beat him. With weeks still to go before the preferential election scheduled for July 26, however, the

68 Truman to JWF, Mar. 14, 1960, BCN 105, F67, SPF.
69 JWF to Truman, Mar. 16, 1960, PPNF, Fulbright, J. William, Truman Papers.
70 JWF to HST, Mar. 31, 1960, PPNF, Fulbright, J. William, Truman Papers.
71 Williams to Erickson, Apr. 21, 1960, Williams Papers.
72 Erickson to JWF, May 4, 1960, Williams Papers.
73 Erickson to JWF, May 21, 1960, Williams Papers.

anti-Faubus coalition began running dangerously low on funds. In an effort to keep Bennett, Milsaps, and company afloat, Williams, who was well on his way to becoming one of Washington's most accomplished political money men, launched a major fund-raising campaign in their behalf. Using Sid McMath and Brooks Hays as intermediaries, Williams raised tens of thousands of dollars in New York alone for the anti-Faubus coalition.[74]

It was all for naught. Faubus overwhelmed his Democratic challengers in the primary, outpolling all of them combined. He went on to thrash his GOP opponent in the general election, and Arkansas was once again rife with rumors that the man from Greasy Creek would challenge the Rhodes scholar in 1962.

"The important thing is, don't under any circumstances, get in the position where Alford or Faubus can appear to be defending 'Americanism' under any sort of phony label," Willard "Lefty" Hawkins wrote a member of Fulbright's staff during the early stages of the senator's tête-à-tête with the ultras. "Never underestimate the number of idiots in this state who are suspicious of anything 'foreign' whether it involves foreign aid, or whatever."[75]

By that point, however, ultras in the Pentagon had alerted Thurmond and leaked word of Fulbright's memo to the press. The fat was in the fire, as Arkansans liked to say. Congressman Dale Alford, "the amiable popinjay" whom the national press generally regarded as a stalking horse for Faubus, accused Fulbright in early August of making "a clandestine assault on the very foundations of our system of government."[76] Later in the month Faubus told reporters, "It appears to me that a man in uniform should be able to speak against what he is expected to shoot against. I see no indication that the military has any desire to participate in partisan politics."[77] The Faubus-controlled statewide weekly, the *Arkansas Statesman,* lambasted Fulbright in back-to-back editorials for "wanting to ditch" the Constitution. It urged the forced retirement of the "chief senatorial foe of the anti-Communist alerters."[78]

Meanwhile, to Faubus, Alford, and Goldwater's delight, the ultras were mounting their own campaign to unseat Fulbright, one that these more traditional politicians exploited to the fullest. A letter to the editor in the *Arkansas Gazette* from the John Birch Society promised that millions of dollars of Tex-

74 Williams to JWF, June 20, 1960; Williams to Carl Marcy, June 20, 1960; and Williams to JWF, June 2, 1960, Williams Papers.

75 Hawkins to Bob Lowe, July 21, 1961, Series 4:19, Box 28:4, SPF.

76 E. W. Kenworthy, "Alford Scores Fulbright's Memo," *New York Times,* Aug. 8, 1961, and "They're Out to Get Fulbright," *New Republic,* Oct. 9, 1961.

77 *Arkansas Gazette,* Aug. 28, 1961.

78 Ernest Valachovic, "Faubus Weekly Steps Up Attack on Fulbright," *Arkansas Gazette,* Sept. 10, 1961.

as and Oklahoma oil money would go into the effort to defeat Fulbright in 1962.[79] In December Robert Snowden, a right-wing planter from Hughes, Arkansas, sponsored a "Survival U.S.A." meeting in Memphis. The subject was "Dangers of Muzzling the Military," and the guest speaker was Strom Thurmond, who proceeded to impugn Fulbright's patriotism and call for his ouster from the Senate. Ken Courtney of New Orleans, publisher of the *Independent American* and author of *The Case for General Walker,* flooded Arkansas with anti-Fulbright literature.[80]

Fulbright struck back as best he could. In some forty appearances across the state, he defended the principle of civilian control of the military and repeated his charges that the ultras were "soft" and unwilling to stand up to the communists over the long haul.[81] Red-baiting was hardly Fulbright's forte, however, and he chose instead to remind Arkansans what his seniority and persuasiveness had done for their pocketbooks. The strategy began to pay dividends. In Ozark, a western Arkansas community situated in an area where the Ozarks met the Arkansas River, Jeta Taylor and Harold Dodgen hosted an overflow crowd of four hundred to hear the senator. Taylor, vice-president of the Arkansas River Basin Association, heaped praise on the junior senator for his tireless efforts in behalf of river navigation, flood control, and power generation. No man had done more to break down foreign trade barriers against Arkansas poultry than Fulbright, declared Dodgen, a poultry raiser and processor whose plant at Ozark employed four hundred workers. Both described as "a lot of nonsense" the alarms over penetration of the American clergy and schools by communists.[82] To the chuckles of the crowd, Fulbright declared: "I don't have any doubt that there are some of those [communists] in New York. It may well be; you can find almost anything in New York, but how many Communists do you know in your hometown?"[83]

A week later, with raindrops beating gently on his felt hat and a dead buck at his feet, Fulbright chatted with reporters who had followed him on a deer hunt on Hugh Brinkley's huge eastern Arkansas plantation. He had to get back on the fried chicken circuit, he told them; it was a dangerous time for an incumbent to become complacent.[84] Gradually the muzzling the military issue and the third Red Scare seemed to retreat into the background. Whenever Walker did come up, Fulbright never failed to mention that he had command-

79 "They're Out To Get Fulbright," *New Republic,* Oct. 9, 1961.

80 "Let's Tell All the Facts On Communism, Thurmond Urges," *Memphis Press-Scimitar,* Dec. 4, 1901.

81 Ernie Deane, "Fulbright Tosses Political Straw," *Arkansas Gazette,* Nov. 19, 1961.

82 "Back in Arkansas," *Newsweek,* Nov. 13, 1961, 24–5, and "Fulbright Says Chaffee Slated for Reopening," *Arkansas Gazette,* Sept. 27, 1961.

83 "Back in Arkansas," *Newsweek,* Nov. 13, 1961, 24–5.

84 Ibid.

ed federal troops at Little Rock. It was hard for Arkansans to believe that their native son was a fellow-traveler. After all, asked one newsman rhetorically, "How can a onetime Razorback half-back be soft on Communism?"[85]

Suddenly, rumors began to circulate that Faubus would in fact not challenge Fulbright in 1962. His shy wife, Alta, did not want to leave Little Rock for Washington. Faubus himself, it was said, was afraid of being shunned by the administration if he should win Fulbright's seat. These were all rumors, however. Faubus continued to denounce foreign aid and DOD censorship of America's gallant officer corps. Despite the inroads Fulbright had made in the fall of 1961, it was clear to all concerned that had Faubus decided to run, "it'll be a helluva fight," as one Little Rock lawyer put it.[86]

Fulbright's 1961 anti-Faubus tour received major play in the national and international press. Lippmann, Reston, the *New Republic,* the *Nation,* and other moderate-to-liberal political publications declared that Fulbright must win in order to demonstrate to Goldwater, Bridges, Stennis, and Russell that alliance with the ultras would taint them as extremists and alienate mainstream voters. Indeed, if a cosmopolitan figure like Fulbright could win in a state as backward and susceptible to the appeals of the radical right as Arkansas, the "flatearthers," as John Erickson termed the ultras, would be permanently discouraged.[87] From the United Kingdom, the *Economist* portrayed the contest as one between racial moderation and enlightened internationalism on the one hand, and extremism and isolationism on the other.[88]

In February 1962 Fulbright was notified by several reliable sources that Faubus would seek another term as governor rather than run for the Senate in 1962.[89] Indeed, so comfortable did Fulbright feel that at the last minute he reversed a decision to miss the Inter-parliamentary Union meeting scheduled for Bermuda. He and Betty left on the fifteenth for a few days of golf and sun in the Caribbean.

The reasons behind Faubus's decision not to run have been the subject of much speculation. In the first place, all the deep pockets that Faubus and Fulbright shared – Darby, Stephens, Pickens – told the governor that if he challenged Fulbright, he would not have their support.[90] Faubus later observed that he had never really wanted to go to Washington; he enjoyed being gover-

85 Ibid.

86 Ibid.

87 See, for example, Walter Lippmann, "Nation's Eyes Swing to Fulbright," undated, Series 4:1, Box 1:2, SPF.

88 "Fulbright Given Boost by Leading Canadian Magazine," *Evening Times,* Sept. 9, 1961, and "Fulbright's Fight for Survival," *Economist,* Nov. 18, 1961.

89 Marcy to Holt, Feb. 13, 1962, Box 4, Folder Jan.–May, Marcy papers, SFRC, RG 46, NA.

90 Interview with Witt Stephens, May 24, 1990, Little Rock, Ark.

nor and he was good at it. The reason he had not deflated the rumors earlier was to punish Fulbright for "turning on him" in 1959;[91] in fact, Faubus and his principal adviser, Bill Smith, had simply wanted to show their spurs to the Fulbright people, to demonstrate who was boss. Even had he won, Faubus would have been dealt with much as Harry Truman was by the Roosevelt administration in the 1930s, if for different reasons, and he knew it.

During the fall of 1961 President Kennedy had stopped over in Fort Smith to deliver a ringing endorsement of Fulbright.[92] Shortly thereafter, Faubus had been invited to visit with the president at the luxurious Poteau, Oklahoma, ranch of Senator Robert S. Kerr, one of the Senate's richest and most powerful members. Present also were Attorney General Robert F. Kennedy and a few close aides of the three men. Shortly after the first drink, Bobby had moved in close to Faubus. Looking him square in the eye, the attorney general said, "Orval, we know that you can beat the hell out of Bill Fulbright if you run against him. But let me make you a promise: if you do you will not get one damn thing out of us for patronage. . . . We like you, Orval, but in Arkansas – not in the Senate." Kerr chimed in: "If you come to Washington, I promise you that you will not get anything for Arkansas out of the Senate. You will be as isolated as a Baptist in Miami Beach."[93]

Faubus's decision not to run meant that Fulbright was home free in the 1962 Democratic primary – almost. In April of that year one of Arkansas's most forgettable political figures, Winston G. Chandler, announced that he would challenge Fulbright because "he's too liberal." Chandler, president of a mobile-home convoy firm and a segregationist member of the Pulaski County school board, had decided to run partly at the behest of George S. Benson of Harding College. Touting his membership in the American Legion and Church of Christ, Chandler and his calico-beclad wife, Quida, hit the campaign trail to denounce the United Nations, federal aid to education, and other liberal errors. Questioned about Fulbright's muzzling the military memo, the Democratic challenger declared forthrightly: "He didn't think people should be woke up [*sic*] in this country about the threats of communism and I disagree with this."[94] Chandler's only break came when a BBC crew, mistaking him for Faubus, followed him around the state for a week.[95]

91 Faubus interview.

92 J. H. Yingling to Myer Feldman, Oct. 23, 1961, Series 1, Box 1:6, SPF.

93 Quoted in "J. William Fulbright: Freedom's Judas-Goat." See also "Kennedy Is Fearful of Fulbright's Defeat," *Pontiac Press,* Dec. 8, 1961.

94 "Chandler Says He'll Oppose Fulbright: 'He's Too Liberal,'" *Arkansas Gazette,* Apr. 29, 1962.

95 "Telstar to Relay Pictures of Chandler on Vote Hunt," *Arkansas Gazette,* Apr. 29, 1962.

With the tension of Fulbright–Faubus confrontation avoided, political pundits in Arkansas approached state politics in a better humor. A series of political doll jokes began making the rounds:

> The Winston Chandler doll – You wind it up and it makes an old Dale Alford speech.
>
> The Dale Alford doll – You wind it up and it makes an old Strom Thurmond speech.
>
> The J. William doll – You wind it up once every six years.
>
> The Orval Faubus doll – You don't wind it up; it runs on gas.[96]

In a campaign in which he almost completely ignored his primary opponent, Fulbright beat Chandler by a 2 to 1 margin. The incumbent, sensing that the ultras and the Republican Party had lost interest in the primary once Faubus had decided not to campaign, concentrated instead on the uncontested winner of Republican primary, Dr. Kenneth G. Jones. Jones, a Little Rock ophthalmologist and political reactionary, was of no consequence himself; but, as the Fulbright camp quickly learned, he had attracted some serious supporters.

Barry Goldwater, who headed the GOP Senatorial Campaign Committee in 1962, denied that his party was out to unseat Fulbright. "Why should we want to beat Fulbright?" Goldwater asked reporters. "We'd just get another Democrat. We don't have anything against Bill and we certainly haven't got any chance to elect a Republican to the Senate in Arkansas."[97] Perhaps not, but the ideologues behind the Arizona senator believed that if the ultras and the GOP joined forces, they could make their weight felt in the Arkansas election. The campaign could be used to link Fulbright to "Mrs. Roosevelt, Chester Bowles, and Adlai Stevenson," as Michael Bernstein put it. Fulbright's loyalty was to international institutions and ideals rather than to the United States, the radical right was convinced, and the nation must be alerted to the fact.[98] Letters from Tulsa, Dallas, Shreveport, and New Orleans signed by Rev. Billy James Hargis, Ken Courtney, and other ultras began flooding into Arkansas.

In the end Dr. Jones, even with the help of the radical right and the GOP Senatorial Campaign Committee, was no match for Fulbright. At the Hotel Milner-Noble in Jonesboro, Fulbright told an overflow crowd:

> I'm for the right "isms." My Republican opponent . . . has accused me of being guilty of socialism, statism and liberalism, and

96 *Pine Bluff Commercial,* June 10, 1962.
97 "Fulbright Hears GOP Is Planning Opposition for Him," *Arkansas Gazette,* Aug. 10, 1961.
98 Stewart McClure to Jack Yingling, Oct. 12, 1961, Series 4:19, Box 27:2, SPF.

> vaguely insinuates that these are the same as communism. I deny these charges. But since he likes to use the "isms," I am guilty of favoring cotton-ism, rice-ism, river-ism, poultry-ism, school-ism, road-ism, hospital-ism, tourism, forestry-ism, capitalism and above all, Arkansas-ism.[99]

Bill, Betty, and various staff members crisscrossed the state as if the election were in doubt. Members of his entourage were shocked to see the junior senator making small talk with total strangers.

Arkansans voted overwhelmingly to return Fulbright to the Senate; he received 214,867 to Jones's 98,013. "I appreciate your wire about the election," Fulbright cabled President Kennedy. "This was my first encounter with a Republican . . . while it was unpleasant at the time, the outcome was highly satisfactory."[100]

Somewhat surprisingly, race played almost no role in the shadow contest between Faubus and Fulbright or in the general election. It did not in part because J. William Fulbright was careful to stay to Orval Faubus's right on the major civil rights issues of the day. Members of Fulbright's staff, especially Norvill Jones, Lee Williams, and Seth Tillman, periodically screwed up their courage and pressed Fulbright to break with Russell and the hard-liners, issue a call for the South to comply with the law, and, at the head of the forces of moderation, lead Dixie into the twentieth century. Jones even went so far as to call for a new Southern Manifesto that would (1) express sympathy with black aspirations for justice and fair play, (2) recognize the validity of all Supreme Court decisions, and (3) stress the importance of local leadership in bringing about compliance lest the federal government be compelled to intervene again. "It is conceivable," he wrote Fulbright, "that the emotional climate will become so strong in favor of the Negro movement that the Southerner's position in Congress, i.e. the seniority system, will be threatened."[101] The national press, especially in the wake of the muzzling the military controversy, also looked to Fulbright to lead the South into a new age of enlightened race relations. "If a single Southern senator were to advocate the truly national interest . . . elimination of segregation in public schools and places of public accommodation," declared the *Washington Post*, "the present crisis which called into question America's commitment to democracy and equal justice under the law could be ended in the twinkling of an eye." Fulbright,

99 Roy Reed, "I'm for Right 'Isms,' Fulbright Declares," *Arkansas Gazette*, Sept. 22, 1962.

100 JWF to JFK, Dec. 4, 1962, Series 1:1, Box 1:1, SPF.

101 Jones to JWF, June 12, 1963, Series 39:2, Box 9:5, SPF.

proclaimed the *Post,* seemed to be the ideal Moses.[102] J. William Fulbright would have none of it.

On February 1, 1960, four students from the Negro Agricultural and Technical College in Greensboro, North Carolina, entered a variety store, made several purchases, and then sat down at the lunch counter and ordered coffee. In the wake of that first sit-in, young people, white and black, participated in similar peaceful forms of protest against segregation and discrimination. They sat in white libraries, waded in white beaches, and slept in lobbies of white hotels. Many were arrested for trespassing, disorderly conduct, and disobeying police officers. Indeed, the lunch counter demonstration in Greensboro set the stage for what John Hope Franklin has called "the most profound, revolutionary changes in the state of black Americans that had occurred since emancipation."[103]

The Dixie association, those eighteen senators who still gathered regularly in Richard Russell's office, remained unmoved in the face of these electrifying events. They continued to gather occasionally with their counterparts in the House to map out strategy and have a little fun. At a special meeting of the "Old Dixie Study Group," which convened in the Rules Committee hearing room, Howard Smith (D–Virginia) spoke on "The Lynching of Orderly Process," while Strom Thrumond held forth on "Bowel and Urinary Problems of Filibustering" and displayed the "leg-strap pitoc tube" members of the Dixie association used to survive ten hours on their feet. The White Citizens Council Quartet featuring L. Mendel Rivers (D–South Carolina), John Bell Williams (D–Mississippi), and Dale Alford treated the assembled to a rendition of "Nigra Stay Way from Them Polls."[104] After the happy group disbanded, Russell busied himself with gathering statistics showing that integration had produced an alarming rise in the number of "mixed-bloods" in the United States.[105]

Following passage of the 1957 Civil Rights Act, the Commission on Civil Rights had held hearings on black voting in several cities, North and South. It discovered, to few people's surprise, that blacks were being regularly denied the right to vote by certain white registrars in the South. As part of an effort to afford added protection, the Eisenhower administration had submitted to Congress the Voting Rights Act of 1960. The measure empowered federal courts to appoint referees to examine state voting-qualification laws and practices whenever a petitioner had been deprived of the right to register or vote

102 WTOP Editorial, June 12, 1963, Series 39:2, Box 9:5, SPF.

103 John Hope Franklin, *From Slavery to Freedom: A History of Negro Americans,* 5th ed. (New York, 1980), 439.

104 Old Dixie Study Group, Feb. 20, 1960, Civil Rights, Russell Papers.

105 Russell to R. Carter Pittman, Aug. 8, 1962, Dictation Series, Box I.F.9, Racial Folder, Russell Papers.

because of race or color. The referees could issue certificates entitling the aggrieved to vote in federal elections.[106]

On February 15 Richard Russell, having divided his colleagues into three teams of six senators each, launched what became known as the "filibuster of reason." The seven-week event lacked some of the "vaudeville" appeal of previous performances, Liz Carpenter noted in her column. In the old days, crowds would gather to listen to the reading of lengthy recipes for southern dishes or witness fiery defenses of Confederate womanhood by some of the worst old lechers who ever came to Washington. The new oratory featured philosophy, history, and constitutional law. Fulbright, not surprisingly, was the star.

Serving on the team of Senator Allen Ellender of Louisiana, with eight hours' duty every three days, the Arkansan delivered four major speeches during 125 hours of consecutive debate.[107] On March 1, he made a detailed review and analysis of federal and Arkansas law to demonstrate that there was more than enough legislation in place to protect the voting rights of all citizens. "The Negroes of my State vote freely and without coercion," he declared. He accused the North of attempting to force its cultural will on the South, a situation that "could well be taken advantage of by the Communists." Again, unconsciously echoing the radical right, he went on to ridicule the notion of universal suffrage. "I do not know what proof there is that the greater the vote the better the result," he observed.[108] On March 5 at 3:30 in the morning he delivered a scathing indictment of the Eisenhower administration's foreign policies, a speech that captured national headlines and led to the coining of the phrase "filibuster of reason."[109]

The junior senator from Arkansas may have been the picture of logic and reason when it came to foreign policy, but to all appearances he continued to buy into the southern myth of Reconstruction. On April 5 Fulbright told the Senate that many of the proposals in the so-called civil rights bill were virtually identical to the punitive measures offered during the original Reconstruction period following the Civil War, a decade that historians had labeled "one of the darkest and most unhappy eras since the founding of the nation." Federal intervention in and control of elections would not only violate the Constitution, but set off a backlash that eroded rather than promoted the rights of

106 Franklin, *From Slavery to Freedom,* 440, and Legislative Meeting Notes, Box 6, WHOF-OSS, Eisenhower Papers.

107 Elizabeth Carpenter, "Fulbright Symbol of 'New' Filibuster Technique of 1960," *Arkansas Gazette,* Apr. 17, 1960.

108 *Congressional Record,* Senate, Mar. 1, 1960, 3976–81.

109 Leslie Carpenter, "Filibuster's Wee Hours Drag for Weary Senators," *Arkansas Gazette,* Mar. 6, 1960.

black Americans. "The South lost the war in 1865," he observed with some bitterness. "Why are there so many in the North who wish to prolong it?"[110]

Despite Fulbright and the filibuster of reason, the Senate moved inexorably toward a vote. The eighteen irreconcilables found themselves increasingly isolated. With his sights set squarely on the Democratic nomination, Lyndon Johnson was relentless in pressuring for passage, so much so that Richard Russell began to waver. "LBJ personality overpowering," he scribbled in his journal. "Around the clock. Exhaustion . . . Do we really want a bad bill? this will fix our relations for years to come."[111]

The filibusterers barely beat back an amendment to the 1957 act that would have put Congress on record in support of the Supreme Court's 1954 school decision. The move was seen by many in the Senate as an attempt by northern liberals to rub the Dixie association's nose in the dirt. In the end, the Senate voted to approve the Civil Rights Act of 1960 by a vote of 82 to 18.[112]

Despite his eloquence, the liberal press blasted Fulbright during the course of the 1960 civil rights debate. "No Colossus of Rhodes," ran the title of a *Washington Post* editorial. Given proven and repeated voting irregularities in Louisiana and Georgia, could the chairman of the SFRC really believe that existing legal protections were adequate? Could he seriously contend that "apathy" was responsible for low voter turnout among African Americans? Because he was more intelligent, because more was expected of him, Fulbright deserved more opprobrium for "joining in this cabal of know-nothingism."[113] The criticism, indeed the controversy, bored and annoyed rather than distressed Fulbright. "I am sure you have noticed from the press that the Senate is tied up in a very wearisome controversy over civil rights again which seriously interferes with the ordinary conduct of the government," he wrote a friend in Puerto Rico.[114]

In February 1963 President Kennedy sent a special message to Congress recommending legislation to strengthen voting rights. The following June – largely in response to the use of dogs and high-pressure hoses against Martin Luther King, Jr., and his fellow marchers in Birmingham, Alabama – Kennedy submitted a new and broader civil rights program. The revised measure outlawed discrimination in public accommodations and interstate commerce. Segregationists, including Fulbright, denounced it as an unconstitutional and unwarranted interference with property rights.

110 *Congressional Record,* Senate, Apr. 5, 1960, 7321–6, and Apr. 8, 1960, 7728–30.

111 Personal Notes During 1960 Filibuster, Mar. 24, 1960, Personal History Series, Box 45, Folder JKL, Russell Papers.

112 "Senate Vote Rejects Congress' Support of '54 School Ruling," *Arkansas Gazette,* Apr. 5, 1960.

113 "No Colossus of Rhodes," *Washington Post,* Mar. 3, 1960.

114 JWF to Horace E. Thompson, Mar. 7, 1960, BCN 105, F67, SPF.

As Congress and the nation debated the proposed civil rights bill, the "March on Washington for Jobs and Freedom" occurred. From the outset the march received broad support from many sectors of American life. On August 28, 1963, more than two hundred thousand blacks and whites from all over the United States staged the largest demonstration in the history of the nation's capital. After the stately procession moved from the Washington Monument to the Lincoln Memorial, King delivered his incomparable "I Have a Dream" speech.

Congressional opponents of civil rights legislation had insisted that they would not be intimidated by the giant rally. Some members of Congress were "out of town" or "previously engaged" when constituents who were marching called to enlist their support. One who was "out of town" was J. William Fulbright. "I am sorry that I missed your call yesterday," he wrote John Stennis, "but not having a part in the 'March on Washington' I left early for the country."[115]

Nonetheless, when Fulbright came into the office the next day, members of the staff seemed to notice something of a change, a glimmer of an awakening. He had watched the march and King's speech on television and had been impressed both by the size and orderliness of the demonstration and King's inspiring rhetoric. The national press never believed that a man as intelligent as Fulbright actually thought that the only things holding back the black population of Arkansas and other southern states were poverty and ignorance, but he did. His ignorance was appalling, his apathy deplorable, but those were his faults – not a racism rooted in a Russell-like fear of "race-mixing." For such a person a moral awakening was still possible.

115 JWF to John Stennis, Aug. 29, 1963, Series 48:5, Box 20:3, SPF.

# 16

# *A creative tension*

Over the years Carl Marcy, other staffers, and various SFRC members had been contacted by persons who presented an apparently impartial point of view in behalf of a foreign interest or leader, usually in connection with the foreign aid bill.[1] Only later did the committee learn that they were being lobbied by paid agents. "Activities of the China Loby [*sic*], the Spanish Lobby, the Dominican lobby, the Vietnamese lobby, and others, are frequently referred to in the press," Marcy observed to Fulbright, "but there is no very precise information on what they do or how they do it." The Foreign Agents Registration Act, passed in 1938 mainly to counteract Nazi propaganda and subversion, required all nondiplomatic agents of foreign governments to register with the Justice Department and to report their earnings, expenses, and activities on a regular basis. With the coming of the cold war, the law was used mainly against suspected communists; for the most part it went unenforced.[2] The subject seemed a proper one for the SFRC to probe, Marcy suggested. He concluded with a word of warning: "An investigation along these lines could be explosive in the extreme." There was no telling, the chief of staff presciently observed, where the trail might lead.[3]

As was true of all congressional inquiries, the results of the probe would depend on the quality of those who conducted it. After several phone calls, Fulbright and Marcy decided to hire a young investigative reporter named Walter Pincus. In 1960 Pincus, a New Yorker who had graduated from Yale and done a stint with army counterintelligence, wrote a long piece with Don Oberdorfer for *Life* magazine on congresspeople who cheated on their expense accounts. He followed that with two articles for the *Reporter,* the first on lobbyists for foreign governments in general and the second on sugar lobbyists in particular. When Marcy called in mid-1961, Pincus agreed to go to work for the SFRC but not until the following year, when his current assign-

1 "Nondiplomatic Activities of Representatives of Foreign Governments," Report of the SFRC, July 9, 1962, Series 48:1, Box 4:2, SPF.

2 Ned Curran, "Fulbright's Look at Alien Lobbies Gains Momentum," *Arkansas Gazette,* Feb. 10, 1963.

3 Marcy to JWF, Mar. 17, 1961, Box 3, Folder Jan.–June, Marcy Papers.

ment was completed. "I was twenty-eight," Pincus later recalled, "and at that point willing to try anything."[4]

As soon as he was free, Pincus met with Fulbright. "He's a great person to work for," Pincus later recalled, "because if you proposed something that was unusual and could support it, he'd let you do almost anything. The theory was that if it didn't work, you'd have trouble with the next one."[5] At their first meeting it was Fulbright who did the proposing, however. Just you and a lawyer, Fulbright told Pincus, will work for six months investigating the activities of unregistered foreign agents. If, at the end of that period, there was enough material, the committee would hold hearings and disclose everything. Pincus readily agreed. So confident was Fulbright in his new investigator and in the importance of the project, that he persuaded the Senate in July 1962 to fund the SFRC's investigation of unregistered agents.[6]

After a short search, Pincus came up with a lawyer, Tony Sifton, and the two immediately set to work. Fulbright and Marcy accorded them almost total freedom. After some deliberation, Pincus and Sifton selected ten lobbyists for investigation, about most of whom Pincus had already written. During the probe one of the reporter's sources told him that before Rafael Trujillo's assassination in the summer of 1961, the dictator had bribed several congressmen and senators to secure a large slice of Cuba's suspended sugar quota. The few sugar quotas granted to foreign nations – the Philippines, Peru, the Dominican Republic, and Cuba before Castro – allowed those nations' growers access to the lucrative U.S. market and were worth hundreds of millions of dollars. In 1960 the Eisenhower administration had persuaded Congress to suspend the Dominican Republic's sugar quota in order to undercut support for the brutal Trujillo.[7] For a variety of reasons, the Kennedy administration continued the ban on Dominican sugar, although the policy was under active review when the committee on foreign lobbyists began its work. The information that Trujillo had suborned several U.S. legislators in an attempt to have his nation's quota restored was potentially sensational. The problem confronting the SFRC investigators was that they could not prove anything.

In the fall of 1962 Pincus flew to Santo Domingo and contacted an old friend of his who happened to be a member of the three-man junta that had succeeded Trujillo. The journalist had met him in New York when he was, as an anti-Trujillo politician, in voluntary exile. After the dictator's death, the Dominican had returned and managed to secure a spot on the governing council.[8]

4 Interview with Walter Pincus, Mar. 11, 1990, Washington, D.C.
5 Ibid.
6 "Nondiplomatic Activities of Representatives of Foreign Governments," Report of the SFRC, July 9, 1962, Series 48:1, Box 4:2, SPF.
7 *Congressional Record,* Senate, June 27, 1962, 11879.
8 Dean Rusk to JFK, July 2, 1962, Box 66, National Security Files [hereinafter referred to as NSF], Kennedy Papers.

When Pincus arrived, Trujillo supporters were still a force on the island – Trujillo's son was a member of the junta – and the opposition, including Pincus's friend, was searching for ways to discredit the former dictator. Indeed, despite the fillip given the left by the deteriorating economic situation, the anti-Trujillo forces were more afraid of the former dictator and his allies than of the Castroites. Elections were scheduled for the fall of 1962, and widespread intimidation by the right was expected. Thus it was that Pincus's request to see secret government files pertaining to the U.S. sugar quota fell on receptive ears. The American and his government contact worked out a system whereby Pincus would stay in the official's house twenty-four hours a day. In the evening, the Dominican, having been given a list of names, "a member of congress, a lobbyist, somebody who had been involved with Trujillo," would bring in an armload of documents. Pincus would stay up all night photographing the evidence with a special Kodak camera, and the official would return them to their government hiding place the next day. It was dangerous business, physically for Pincus's contact because the Trujillo people still occupied positions of power on the island, and politically for Pincus because the investigation involved some of Washington's most important figures.

Back in Washington Pincus described his adventure for Fulbright. Among the more interesting items he had photographed was a signed contract between Trujillo and Igor Cassini, brother of the world-famous fashion designer, Oleg Cassini. Igor wrote a gossip column and operated a successful public relations agency in Washington. Soon after the Kennedy administration came to power, Trujillo hired Igor Cassini, who promised to use his connections with Oleg to get to Jack Kennedy. Working through Jackie, for whom Oleg designed clothes, and through Joe Kennedy, who was a longtime friend, Igor assured the dictator that he could get the Dominican sugar quota restored. The Cassini connection worked. At the time Pincus was conducting his investigation, Loy Henderson of the State Department was in the Dominican Republic at Kennedy's direction; matters were clearly moving toward either a restoration of the Dominican quota or a massive aid program.[9]

Revelation of the Trujillo–Cassini–Kennedy connection would step on some large and sensitive toes, Fulbright realized. He met with George Aiken and Hickenlooper, neither of whom had any particular love for the Kennedys, and they decided to press on despite the possible political fallout. The object, the three agreed, however, should be to get the administration to clean up its act and to begin enforcing the Foreign Agents Registration Act. If it would do so, the committee could legitimately avoid publicity. Hickenlooper and Fulbright decided that because the situation involved violation of the law, the matter should be placed in Robert Kennedy's hands. At that time Pincus was dating the president's secretary and was thus known to the first family. Consequent-

[9] Pincus interview.

ly, it fell to his lot to act as messenger. Fulbright instructed him to go to Robert, describe the situation, and tell him the administration had six months to indict Igor Cassini. If it did not, the SFRC would hold public hearings and the Kennedys would be implicated. The time was October 1962 precisely, in the middle of the Cuban missile crisis.

Pincus later recalled his meeting with the attorney general: "So I had to go down and tell Bobby this. He hated Fulbright, did not trust him because he had been for Johnson. He also did not believe that we would do this. He was getting dressed to go to dinner. He said he would look into it." Two days later the Justice Department sent an agent to the Dominican Republic. He met with Pincus's contact and asked for the incriminating documents. The Dominican refused, and then called Pincus to tell him what was going on.

Six months later the assigned day arrived with no sign of Justice Department action. With time running out, Robert Kennedy called Marcy and asked for thirty minutes with Fulbright. For the first twenty-five minutes he made small talk and then asked, "I guess you are interested in what's going on and I just want to tell you that at three-thirty Igor was indicted." Within two months, Igor Cassini pleaded nolo contendere, lost his job, and seen his wife commit suicide.[10]

The second major focus of Pincus's investigation was the Philippines Claims Commission and its U.S. operatives. In 1946 Congress had passed the Philippine Rehabilitation Act authorizing $500 million for the reconstruction of the war-devastated Philippine economy, which was to be accomplished through the payment of private property claims for war damages. As the Arkansan fully realized, the new legislation opened the door to a massive campaign of graft.[11] Over the next ten years a Washington lobbyist named John P. O'Donnell and members of a Manila law firm that included Philippine President Diasdado Macpagal conspired to influence Congress to pass additional war-damage legislation and to collect fees from the recipients of American largesse. Their biggest clients were the Catholic Church and Philippine sugar growers. The church, through Bishop Fulton J. Sheen, and the sugar interests in turn funneled thousands of dollars into a special account from which some twenty U.S. congresspeople and senators were paid over the years. The bulk of the money went to Representative Clement Zablocki (D–Wisconsin), but the others, including Hubert Humphrey, received substantial sums as well. They in turn voted and argued for supplementary legislation that appropriated more than $150 million, two-thirds of which went to six claimants.

10 Ibid.

11 Hearing of the Special Subcommittee appointed to consider "A bill to amend further the Philippine Rehabilitation Act," Apr. 17, 1950, SFRC, Selected Documents, Box 8, Truman Papers.

By April 1963 the foreign agents registration hearings were in full swing and the fur was flying. With implicated congressmen pleading with and raging at their party's leadership, both Republicans and Democrats appealed to Fulbright to relent. So did the administration.[12] Fulbright refused. In the ensuing revelations, more than twenty legislators, including Hubert Humphrey and Clement Zablocki, were proven to have taken money from unregistered foreign agents. Humphrey and Zablocki were unrepentant to the end. Despite the fact that the Minnesotan was deluged with letters accusing him of taking "bribes" and demanding that he resign, he actively lobbied against Fulbright's bill to amend the Philippine claims bill.[13] Meanwhile, the infuriated Zablocki convinced his colleagues in the House that the SFRC investigation was an attack on the integrity of their chamber. "We do not like your arrogant attitude," Wayne Hays (D–Ohio) told Fulbright in arguing against direct payment of the Philippine claims money to the Philippine government, and suggested that he retire to Arkansas and become a chicken farmer.[14] All of this was a tempest in a teapot, however, compared to the firestorm that threatened to break upon Fulbright and the SFRC when it became known that their list of subjects to be investigated included the American–Israeli lobby.

In late May word leaked out that SFRC investigators were going to call representatives of the Jewish Agency–American Section to testify before the committee. The Jewish Agency was the American representative of the Jewish Agency for Israel, the successor organization of the World Zionist Executive.[15] It was composed of wealthy, influential Jewish Americans, and its sole purpose was to raise money for the state of Israel. Even in the early 1960s it was the most successful foreign lobby on Capitol Hill.

By 1962 J. William Fulbright had already acquired a reputation for being anti-Israeli and pro-Arab.[16] Foreign aid to the state of Israel exceeded aid to all the Arab states put together, a fact that continued to exasperate the Arkansan. He had outraged Zionists by attacking the annual congressional subsidy to Israel and by his stand during the *Cleopatra* affair. Fulbright was hardly anti-Semitic, but he did believe that the United States and Israel were sovereign nations each with their own national interests, and that at times those interests did not coincide. For most Zionists, however, that notion was ipso facto proof of anti-Semitism. In 1961, as he was preparing for the forthcom-

12 WF to CM, Jan. 25, 1963, Box 4, Folder Jan.–May, Marcy Papers, and Pincus interview.

13 Win Griffith to Rein Vander Zee, Apr. 25, 1963, and Humphrey to JWF, Apr. 20, 1963, Series 48:6, Box 26:2, SPF.

14 Marcy, memorandum of conversation, Apr. 23, 1963, Box 4, Folder Jan.–May, Marcy Papers, and "A House Divided," July 7, 1963, Series 48:1, Box 5:1, SPF.

15 Zvi Ganin, *Truman, American Jewry, and Israel, 1945–1948* (New York, 1979), 37.

16 See, for example, Dick Goodwin to McGeorge Bundy, June 8, 1961, NSF, Box 66, Kennedy Papers.

ing struggle with Orval Faubus, a group of supporters had asked Fulbright to New York to speak to a fund-raiser in his behalf. Most of those present were Jewish and ardent Zionists. To Fulbright's embarrassment and enragement, when he got up to talk, his hosts insisted on grilling him about his "anti-Israeli" views and repeatedly implied that he was anti-Semitic.[17] In the end, however, the decision to expose the Israeli lobby was not Fulbright's but Pincus's, who was himself Jewish. His investigation had revealed clearly that agents of the Jewish Agency and other American Zionists had violated the provisions of the Foreign Agents Registration Act.[18]

Almost immediately Fulbright and the SFRC came under pressure to suppress the information Pincus and Sifton had gathered concerning the activities of American Zionists. After several prominent American Jews had learned that they were mentioned in the materials the investigators had gathered, they asked to testify; but there were conditions. On the evening of June 18, 1963, Maurice Boukstein, the Jewish Agency's chief lawyer, called Marcy and threatened to cancel the appearances of those Zionists who had requested to be heard unless Marcy guaranteed they would not have to testify under oath, that no transcript would be kept of the meeting, and that nothing concerning the meeting would be made public. His clients, he said, were concerned with the impact adverse publicity might have upon fund-raising activities in the United States. Marcy indicated that that was really none of the committee's concern. Boukstein insisted that his clients were prominent individuals who could not "be ordered around" and implied that they might not be able to appear on the appointed day. Fine, said Marcy; the committee would simply release to the press the material Pincus had dug up on the lobbying activities of American Zionists.[19] His clients would be there, Boukstein said.

The first week in August Isadore Hamlin, executive director of the Jewish Agency–American Section and his deputy, Gottlieb Hammer, appeared and testified before the committee. Although Fulbright informed the press that the two were appearing as part of the committee's investigation of unregistered agents for foreign governments, a transcript of the closed-door hearings was never released.[20] When the Kennedy White House, already deeply immersed in planning for the 1964 election, learned that the SFRC was investigating the Jewish Agency, it appealed to Fulbright to pull back. When he refused, the Kennedys, working through Stuart Symington, mustered a majority on the SFRC that voted to allow Hamlin and Hammer to testify in executive ses-

17 Interview with Jack Yingling, Oct. 12, 1988, Savannah, Ga.

18 Pincus interview.

19 Marcy, memorandum of conversation, June 18, 1963, Box 4, Folder Jan.–Sept., Marcy Papers.

20 UPI 40, July 30, 1963, Series 48:6, Box 26, F5, SPF.

sion.[21] Undeterred, Fulbright and Pincus went ahead with plans to read portions of the two men's testimony on the floor of the Senate as part of the effort to garner support for modification of the Foreign Agents Registration Act. Only a last-minute appeal by Lyndon Johnson stopped them. In their testimony, the representatives of the Jewish Agency admitted that they had paid the expenses of Johnson and his entourage at the 1960 Democratic National Convention.[22] Despite the fact that the dubious activities of their representatives remained secret, the Israeli government and American Zionists would neither forget nor forgive Fulbright and Pincus's "humiliation" of Hamlin and Hammer.[23]

The upshot of the Pincus investigation was a major revamping of the Foreign Agents Registration Act. In September Fulbright and Hickenlooper successfully cosponsored a series of amendments to the 1938 measure that, among other things, outlawed political contributions by foreign governments or corporations through their agents, required registration by agents of foreign interests with the Justice Department and full disclosure of their financial dealings, and constrained these individuals to declare for whom they were working when they contacted legislators.[24]

If the principal goal of John F. Kennedy's liberal-activist foreign policy was peaceful change and socioeconomic progress in emerging and developing nations, the chief weapon in his diplomatic arsenal, of necessity, was foreign aid. During the 1960 campaign Kennedy had hammered away not only at the missile gap but also the "economic gap." Reflecting the views of his task force on foreign economic policy, which included George Ball, Walt Rostow, and Ken Galbraith, and the philosophy of both Douglas Dillon and J. W. Fulbright, the president had argued that the solution to the foreign aid problem was "a substantial, long-term program of productive loans to underdeveloped areas from a fully capitalized central fund."[25]

Fulbright was initially much encouraged by the new administration's emphasis on development and reform of the nonmilitary aid program. Indeed, he participated in foreign aid task force meetings throughout 1961.[26] Sometime

21 Alan Otter, "White House Increases Activities That Would Aid Democrats in 1964," *Wall Street Journal,* May 28, 1963, and Marcy memorandum, June 18, 1963, Box 4, Folder June–Sept., Marcy Papers.

22 The Jewish Agency also picked up the tab for Hubert Humphrey, Drew Pearson, and Jack Anderson; Yingling interview.

23 Pincus interview.

24 JWF to SFRC members, Aug. 13, 1963, Series 48:1, Box 5:3, and UPI 189, Sept. 10, 1963, Series 48:6, Box 26:5, SPF.

25 Quoted in Arthur M. Schlesinger, Jr., *A Thousand Days* (Boston, 1965), 591.

26 JWF to Peter Kilby, Feb. 2, 1961, and Carl Marcy to JWF, Feb. 6, 1961, Series 48:1, Box 2:2, SPF.

in 1962, however, he decided that isolationist-militarists in Congress, together with rabid anticommunists in the foreign policy establishment, were turning the aid program into an instrument of imperialism and oppression.

Opponents of foreign aid not only insisted that the 1962 and 1963 bills retain the annual appropriations provision, but also imposed unprecedented dollar cuts. At the same time, Wayne Morse, Ernest Gruening (D–Alaska), and other liberal Democrats in the Senate, alienated by the persistent emphasis on military aid, began to kick against the program. Indeed, when Morse moved to kill the 1962 foreign aid bill completely by recommitting it to the SFRC, twenty other like-minded Democrats voted with him.[27] The liberal–conservative alliance produced a cut in the 1962 request from $4.9 to $3.9 billion and reduced development loans by 20 percent. In 1963 the appropriation was $3.2 billion, the smallest amount in the history of the program.[28] There is little doubt that the cuts would not have been as deep as they were had J. William Fulbright fought for the program as enthusiastically as he had done in 1961.

Though not as disillusioned as Morse and Gruening, Fulbright concluded by 1962 that the foreign aid program was fatally flawed. In 1961 an Iranian American living in Teheran, an old acquaintance, had penned a scathing account of American aid. Because the shah oppressed and exploited his people, Fulbright's source reported, he did not enjoy popular support. Indeed, the only thing that kept the dynasty in place was American money and material, particularly military aid. Most of the nonmilitary equipment was siphoned off into the pockets of the minions of the Peacock throne; little of it reached the common people. The shah was not a benevolent ruler surrounded by corrupt underlings; indeed, he selected his lieutenants and worked through them. In addition, Washington's paeans to democracy in Iran were absurd. American officials and technicians in Iran were arrogant and incompetent. "You don't act like an American," had become the highest compliment one Iranian could pay to another. (Indeed, democracy was nonexistent. The shah and his secret police, funded with American money, tolerated no political dissent, organized or otherwise.)[29]

Fulbright was deeply repelled by this and other reports coming into his office. Foreign aid, it seemed, was being used to support repressive client governments rather than promote democracy and economic diversification. Brutal South American dictators continued to extract money from the United States to maintain "internal security" against alleged communist-led guerrillas. In reality, Fulbright and Pat Holt believed, the insurgents represented the interests of a peasantry oppressed and exploited by the military and the wealthy landowners and foreign interests for whom they fronted. In short, Fulbright was

27 Joseph Alsop, "Democrat Group Fights Foreign Aid," *Arkansas Democrat,* Nov. 16, 1963.

28 Schlesinger, *Thousand Days,* 596, 599.

29 FWM to JWF, May 2, 1961, Series 48:1, Box 2:2, SPF.

increasingly disturbed at the gap between Kennedy's rhetoric and his programs. "Openings to the left" had given way to blind anticommunism.[30] "I have the strong feeling," Marcy wrote Fulbright, "that the political officers in the DOS simply haven't considered the impact of aid programs on our political relations with the countries receiving aid."[31]

Wrote Fulbright to Kennedy in June 1961:

> Were I to vote now and express my judgment on the merits of the [foreign aid] bill before the Senate, I would vote to reduce the military program and to reorient the economic programs drastically. I would move rapidly away from support of such regimes as that in Korea, putting those funds instead into priority areas where we might expect some degree of self-sufficiency and reliable political maturity within the next five years.

But he went on to assure the young chief executive that he would support the 1962 aid bill in the knowledge that the administration was new and inexperienced, and in the hope that it would consider reforming the program along the lines he had suggested.[32]

Fulbright's disappointment and frustration over the administration's handling of foreign aid were partially offset by his enthusiasm for its European policies and what he regarded as its successes. Although somewhat discouraged by the failure of his efforts in the late 1940s and early 1950s to see established first an Atlantic Union and subsequently a federation of Europe, the Arkansan never abandoned the conviction – hardened by the vagaries of the cold war – that the Atlantic nations, given their common heritage and values, constituted one of the great potential sources for stability and prosperity in the world.

Fearful that competition between two rival economic blocs – the Inner Six led by France and the Outer Seven led by Great Britain – would threaten the unity of NATO, the United States intervened by bringing the two bodies together in 1960 in a special economic committee, and in the following year helped establish the Organization for Economic Cooperation and Development (OECD), comprising eighteen European nations plus the United States and Canada.[33]

Not surprisingly, Fulbright was an enthusiastic supporter of the OECD and made Senate approval a top personal and committee priority for 1961. With Will Clayton, William Batt, and other Atlanticists cheering them on, Fulbright and Undersecretary of State George Ball made a convincing case before the

30 Marcy to Art Kuhl, Apr. 11, 1963, Box 4, Folder Jan.–May, Marcy Papers.
31 Marcy to JWF, June 9, 1961, Box 3, Folder Jan.–June, Marcy Papers.
32 Marcy to JWF, June 26, 1961, Box 1, Folder Misc. 1961–62, Marcy Papers.
33 The United States and Europe, Feb. 9, 1963, NSF, Box 314, Kennedy Papers.

SFRC, the Senate, and the nation. Because the new organization's twin goals were to promote economic stability and growth among member nations, and to develop a strategy for assisting less-developed nations, it would be a key instrument in the West's ongoing socioeconomic and political struggle with the forces of international communism, they argued.[34]

As Fulbright had anticipated, the "troglodytes" came out in full force against OECD and attacked him personally for supporting it. "The most dangerous man in America may well be Sen. J. William Fulbright of Arkansas," declared ultra columnist George Todt. Fulbright was a member of the top-secret "Bilderburg Group," he charged, a "form of Atlantic Union type of fellowship dedicated to erosion or loss of U.S. sovereignty." As a former Rhodes Scholar, educated at Oxford, "that hotbed of Fabian socialists," Fulbright was dedicated to subsuming American sovereignty to that of Britain.[35]

Despite virulent attacks by the radical right, the agreement authorizing the OECD breezed through the Senate. Cynics insisted that the ease with which it was ratified had to do with the fact that membership bore no price tag.

Meanwhile, the cold war refused to wait on anyone. Soviet and American acquisition of nuclear weapons and intercontinental delivery systems had given a new meaning to the term "crisis management." Images of Hiroshima and Nagasaki continued to haunt Fulbright, and they became more vivid as the nuclear arms race intensified during the early stages of the Kennedy administration. While continuing to hope and work for European integration and an Atlantic Union, the chairman of the SFRC turned his attention to a more immediate and pressing problem – the avoidance of Armageddon.

In the spring of 1961 President Kennedy and his advisers decided to implement a policy of peace through strength; that is, to ensure by establishing overwhelming American superiority in number and quality of nuclear weapons that the communists would never launch a nuclear strike. In the wake of the Bay of Pigs fiasco, consequently, the president asked for and received from Congress a multi-billion-dollar addition to the defense budget. The result by mid-1964 was an increase of 150 percent in the number of nuclear weapons available, a 200 percent boost in deliverable megatonnage, the construction of ten additional Polaris submarines (for a total of twenty-nine) and 400 additional Minuteman missiles (for a total of 800) above what the previous administration had scheduled.[36]

34 Clayton to JWF, Feb. 23, 1961, Alpha File (1954–60), Folder FU, Clayton Papers, Truman Library and Organization for Economic Cooperation and Development, Report of the SFRC, Mar. 8, 1961, Series 48:1, Box 2:1, SPF.

35 George Todt, "'Give Me Liberty . . . or!'" *Los Angeles Times,* Aug. 2, 1961.

36 John Lewis Gaddis, *Strategies of Containment: A Critical Appraisal of Postwar American National Security Policy* (New York, 1982), 207–8.

At the most, Khrushchev and his advisers believed, the United States intended to wage a preemptive war and at the least to use its advantage to overturn governments friendly to international communism. Determined to demonstrate that he could not be intimidated, Khrushchev at his meeting with Kennedy in Vienna in June 1961 revived the Berlin crisis by repeating his demands of 1958 and setting a new deadline of six months for determining the permanent status of the city. It was upon his return from this meeting that the president, egged on by Dean Acheson, asked Congress for $3 billion for defense and mobilized the reserves.[37] The new Berlin crisis loosed a flood of East German immigrants into West Berlin. By late July 1961, two thousand refugees a day were streaming into the enclave.

The deterioration in Soviet–American relations during that first, hopeful year of the Kennedy administration was intensely disappointing to J. William Fulbright. As tensions mounted over Berlin, the chairman of the SFRC searched desperately for a solution that would break the logjam and nip the spiraling arms race in the bud. After consulting with Walter Lippmann, he proposed to Dean Rusk that the West counter Khrushchev's ultimatum with a proposal to convert West Berlin into a "free city" under U.N. supervision. In return for the "neutralization of Berlin" – that is, a promise by the West not to position nuclear weapons there – token forces from NATO and the United Nations could remain in the city, and the West would be guaranteed continued free access. Lippmann argued, and Fulbright agreed, that East and West Germany were political, diplomatic, and strategic realities. It was folly for Washington to expose the world to nuclear war out of a stubborn determination not to sign an agreement that recognized the sovereignty of the German Democratic Republic.[38]

When the State Department did not respond, Fulbright went public with his suggestion. "We should have conferences at the ministerial level to avoid a showdown leading to nuclear war," he told a group of reporters. "I believe in negotiation and discussion as opposed to ultimatums and showdowns." At the close of the news conference, in an offhand remark, Fulbright wondered out loud why East Germany had not staunched the outflow of refugees from East to West Berlin, and why Western authorities had not cooperated. The immigrants constituted a tremendous burden on the resources of West Berlin, were a continuing source of embarrassment to the communists, and could be stopped by the East Germans at anytime anyway.[39]

37 Memorandum of discussion in the National Security Council on July 13, 1961, NSF, Box 313–14, Kennedy Papers.

38 Walter Lippmann, memorandum on Berlin, June 7, 1961, and JWF to Dean Rusk, July 3, 1961, Series 48:16, Box 42:1, SPF.

39 "Fulbright Calls on U.S. to Take Lead in Dispute Over Berlin," *Arkansas Gazette*, July 30, 1961.

Fulbright's remarks, as he should have anticipated, placed him at once at the center of a storm of controversy. "Two of the best German correspondents, old friends of mine from Berlin, called me this morning," Pierre Salinger's assistant reported to him. "Their editors kept them up all night with bulletins and requests regarding Senator Fulbright's statement . . . he occupies a special position, and the West Germans, particularly Berliners, are very uneasy about the matter."[40] The status of Berlin was not negotiable, Rusk subsequently announced, and the United States would never sign a treaty recognizing the existence of a government – the DRG – imposed on the German people against their will. West Berlin mayor Willy Brandt declared that the chairman of the SFRC must have been misquoted.[41] On August 13 Soviet and East German troops began sealing off the border between East and West Berlin. They started with barbed wire and ended with a concrete block wall twenty-eight miles long.

The White House let its spokespeople in the press know of the president's displeasure at Fulbright's lack of "diplomacy," and reiterated Kennedy's determination not to negotiate in the face of "ultimata and threats." (To underscore his and America's commitment to Berlin, Kennedy in June 1963 would fly to the beleaguered city to proclaim dramatically, if ungrammatically, "Ich bin ein Berliner.") J. William Fulbright's statements in the summer of 1961 had had little or nothing to do with the East Germans and Russians erecting the Berlin Wall, but they would continue to be a source of ammunition for his enemies.

Actually, the president saw the wall as a sure sign that Khrushchev did not intend to take West Berlin by force. He agreed that a halt to the outflow of refugees was in everybody's interests, except, perhaps, prospective refugees. "It's not a very nice solution," he told his aides, "but a wall is a hell of a lot better than a war." But he dared not say such things in public: Cold warriors in America and Western Europe would accuse him of appeasing the Soviet Union.[42]

Indeed, despite the hard line he took in public over Berlin, Jack Kennedy and his advisers did not believe that the Soviet Union's being a communist state was, in itself, cause for overt conflict; rather, the United States should acknowledge the USSR's position as a great power and hold out to it the prospect of "constructive participation" in world affairs. "This will not change the basic policy of Soviet leaders now in power," Walt Rostow contended, "but it may have some moderating effects on their conduct, or that of their successors."[43] If the administration was not willing to negotiate a halt to the

40 Memorandum to Mr. Salinger, Feb. 20, 1963, Fulbright Name File, Kennedy Papers.
41 "Fulbright Quote Creates Storm," *Arkansas Gazette,* Aug. 3, 1961.
42 Michael R. Beschloss, *The Crisis Years: Kennedy and Khrushchev, 1960–1963* (New York, 1991), 278.
43 Gaddis, *Strategies of Containment,* 228.

arms race in which it enjoyed such a distinct advantage, it did prove willing to reach agreement on a test-ban treaty. On September 1, 1961, Russia broke the informal moratorium on nuclear tests that had been in place since 1958 with an explosion over central Asia. Before completing their tests in November, the Soviets detonated some fifty thermonuclear devices that increased radioactive contamination of the atmosphere by one-half. This two-month series, moreover, included detonation of a fifty-eight-megaton bomb three thousand times as powerful as the one that destroyed Hiroshima. Denouncing the Soviet action as "atomic blackmail," Kennedy resumed American testing by authorizing several underground explosions in Nevada.

In his desperate search for a gesture that would reverse the downward spiral of Soviet–American relations, Fulbright embraced the notion of a comprehensive test-ban treaty. He was convinced that such a pact was both technically and politically feasible. An easing of the arms race was manifestly in Khrushchev and the Soviet Union's interests.[44] Even assuming that Khrushchev and his fellows in the Kremlin were the paranoid, xenophobic creatures that many Kremlinologists portrayed them as, Fulbright reasoned, the best method for dealing with them was to build trust, not engage in confrontation. By 1960 one of the Arkansan's most frequent correspondents was Dr. Jerome D. Frank, a Johns Hopkins psychiatrist who was then advancing the notion that the principles he had gleaned from working with hostile, frightened psychiatric patients could be applied to international relations. Paranoid nations, like individuals, he argued, tried to protect themselves by maintaining "a suspicious, belligerent attitude, thereby engendering the very hostile feelings that he anticipates." They tended to withdraw and to seek immediate relief from their anxiety regardless of ultimate consequences. Russia fit this prototype, Frank insisted to Fulbright. The best method for dealing with sick nations, like sick people, was to listen to them patiently. The United States should negotiate in a nonjudgmental way with the Soviet Union and, more specifically, "sign a test ban agreement even with inspection provisions we regard as inadequate." "Just as mistrust begets mistrust, so trust begets trust," he advised the chairman of the SFRC.[45] Henry Wallace could not have said it better.

So compelling did the chairman find Frank's arguments that he appealed directly to the White House. "While I have no doubt of Khrushchev's desire to 'do us in,' preferably by peaceful means," Fulbright wrote Kennedy, "I do believe he understands that our mutually destructive capacities are so over-

44 Neither Fulbright nor Marcy, however, was naïve concerning Soviet motives, and they were not going to support an agreement that allowed the Soviet Union to gain a strategic edge over the West. Marcy to Kuchel, Apr. 18, 1958, Box 2, Folder Apr.–Dec., Marcy Papers.

45 Frank to JWF, Sept. 13, 1960, Series 48:7, Box 1:2, SPF.

whelming that a military confrontation must be avoided else we will both be destroyed."[46] The president proved receptive.

In the wake of the Cuban missile crisis, Kennedy and his advisers sensed a slight thaw in Soviet–American relations. The Russians had made good on their promise to allow the U.S. Navy to inspect ships carrying dismantled missiles out of the Ever Faithful Isle. In 1963, as a result of the Cuban confrontation, Kennedy and Khrushchev agreed to an emergency phone and teletype, or "hot line," connection between Washington and Moscow. It provided instant communication between the heads of the two superpowers when one or the other feared miscalculation in a crisis. Walt Rostow and Kennedy's science adviser, Jerome Wiesner – both of whom had been American delegates to the 1960 Pugwash Conference, a privately funded international meeting designed to reduce the chances of nuclear war – urged the president to make a test-ban treaty part of détente. The National Committee for a Sane Nuclear Policy (SANE), founded by Norman Cousins in 1957, had become a major lobbying force by 1963; its top priority was negotiation of a test-ban treaty. In March Kennedy authorized his arms control representatives in Geneva to begin discussions in earnest on a treaty, and in June announced that the United States would no longer test nuclear arms in the atmosphere "so long as other states do not do so."

In late July 1963 British, American, and Soviet representatives initialed a test-ban treaty. Signatories promised not to conduct nuclear tests in the atmosphere, in outer space, or underwater, and not to abet tests by others. The new accord permitted underground testing and stipulated that inspection was to be carried out through listening stations rather than on-site visits. Immediately upon his return from the meeting in Moscow, special negotiator Averell Harriman briefed Fulbright and the rest of the SFRC in a closed-door meeting. At its conclusion, the chairman emerged arm in arm with Harriman and announced to reporters that the pact had his full support.[47] A week later Fulbright departed Washington for Moscow as part of the American delegation to the official signing. For five intoxicating days Americans ate caviar, drank vodka, and envisioned global peace. The test-ban treaty, the Arkansan concluded, just might be the breakthrough to rapprochement for which the world had been waiting.

Fulbright anticipated a difficult ratification struggle. In negotiating the test-ban treaty, Kennedy, Rostow, McNamara, and Rusk had largely bypassed the Joint Chiefs of Staff.[48] Permanent senatorial representatives of the military, such as Richard Russell and John Stennis, might possibly ally with the

46 JWF to JFK, May 27, 1961, Box 3, Folder Jan.–June, Marcy Papers.

47 "Fulbright Endorses Pact After Briefing," *Arkansas Gazette,* July 30, 1963.

48 Memorandum of Conference with the President, July 18, 1963, NSF, Box 66, Kennedy Papers.

know-nothings and succeed in blocking two-thirds approval. For ten days a variety of administration officials, from Dean Rusk to the scientists who had advised Kennedy on the technical aspects of the treaty, paraded before the SFRC, assuring Fulbright and his colleagues that the ban was enforceable, would drastically reduce atmospheric fallout, and would not jeopardize the security of the United States. The principal naysayer was nuclear physicist Edward M. Teller, the "father of the H-bomb." A refugee from communist Hungary who had something of the mad scientist about him, Teller railed against the ban: It was full of technical holes; the perfidious Soviets could and would cheat; the treaty was an exercise in appeasement such as the world had not witnessed since the 1930s. Fulbright was not impressed. "Teller's an educated fool, you know," he would later recall. "I've never seen anybody quite as crazy as he is."[49] The committee voted 16 to 1 to recommend passage to the full Senate. It attached one reservation only: Nothing in the test-ban agreement should be construed as barring the United States from employing nuclear weapons in time of war.

The nation's attention was riveted on the Senate when Fulbright opened the debate on the test-ban treaty on September 9. National polls indicated only a bare majority in favor of the pact, and Fulbright's mail ran 4 to 1 against.[50] The Arkansan was at the height of his powers; a laudatory biography entitled *Fulbright of Arkansas* had reached number 3 on the *New York Times* bestseller list in March.[51] In reviewing the reasons why the test ban was manifestly in the interests of both the United States and the Soviet Union, Fulbright ranged from the technical to the historical to the philosophical. He sensed, he said, the same atmosphere in international relations that had existed prior to the Great War, when a mindless arms race had propelled unwilling nations into a global conflict. The public wanted an end to the constant threat of annihilation, of sending their children off to school not knowing whether mass destruction raining down from the skies would separate them forever. The test ban was a small first step to relieving that anxiety. "Extreme nationalism and dogmatic ideology are luxuries that the human race can no longer afford," he concluded. "It must turn its energies now to the politics of survival."[52]

When Russell proposed a number of "reservations" to the treaty, à la Henry Cabot Lodge and the Treaty of Versailles, and declared that the pact was a first step toward "unilateral disarmament," Fulbright lashed out on the NBC *Today* show. Any reservation would require renegotiation and kill the treaty, he told Dave Garroway. The Joint Chiefs had been privately lobbying against

49 Interview with J. William Fulbright, Oct. 11–18, 1988, Washington, D.C.

50 Williams to JWF, Aug. 10, 1963, Series 48:4, Box 20:2, SPF.

51 "What Washington Is Reading," *Washington Post,* Mar. 10, 1963.

52 *Congressional Record,* Senate, Sept. 9, 1963, 16525–40.

the treaty, he revealed. The chairman and all of the service heads had testified before his committee; each had signified their approval. If they felt otherwise, they should say so publicly or stop undercutting their commander-in-chief.[53]

Fulbright's management of the test-ban treaty, and particularly his eloquence in its behalf, helped pave the way for its ratification. Indeed, it was largely his skill and eloquence that contained the hawks and turned public opinion around.[54] In the wake of the Berlin and Cuban missile crises, the American people had built their fallout shelters and in the process assumed a bunker mentality. The test-ban treaty, as Fulbright repeatedly emphasized, offered a glimmer of hope, a ray of sunshine. Perhaps the holocaust was not inevitable. From mid-August to mid-September the percentage of Americans favoring the treaty rose from 52 percent to 81 percent.[55]

J. William Fulbright was in a buoyant mood as the fall of 1963 approached. The great desiderata of American foreign policy – avoidance of nuclear war and its corollary, détente with the Soviet Union – seemed at last within reach. After four years as chairman of the SFRC, the Arkansan was hitting his stride. Working through Carl Marcy, he had managed to put together what Richard Moose would later call the "Fulbright majority," a bipartisan coalition on the committee that trusted the chairman on all procedural and most substantive matters, and that could be counted on to follow his lead. His prestige at home and abroad was reaching an all-time high. True, the radical right and American Zionists had come to view him as the archenemy; but liberal intellectuals in academia and in the press chose for the most part to ignore his position on civil rights and focus on his "enlightened" stance on foreign affairs. Finally, though it had had its ups and downs, Fulbright's relationship with the White House was sound. The junior senator looked forward to 1964 and beyond, to four more years of competitive but peaceful coexistence with the communist bloc, and to cooperation with the executive branch.

53 UPI 41, Sept. 12, 1991, Series 48:1, Box 5:3, SPF.
54 Marcy to Hickenlooper, Sept. 12, 1963, Box 4, Folder June–Sept., Marcy Papers.
55 *Congressional Record,* Senate, Sept. 16, 1963, 17050.

# 17

# *Of myths and realities*

During the fall of 1963 President Kennedy and his advisers seemed to be devoting more attention than usual to politics. In September the president toured eleven western states and then made a series of major speaking engagements on the East Coast. Given the fallout from the administration's efforts in the field of civil rights, Ted Sorensen and Bobby Kennedy were particularly worried about Democratic prospects in the South. In the 1964 presidential election Texas would be crucial, and Lyndon Johnson's presence on the ticket was no guarantee that the Lone Star state would remain loyal. In 1963 the party machinery was paralyzed by a bitter feud between a liberal faction headed by Ralph Yarborough and the conservative wing dominated by Governor John Connally. Following a visit to Florida in mid-November, Kennedy flew to Texas for speaking engagements in several cities, an inspection of the space facilities in Houston, and mediatory talks with party leaders.

Exactly four weeks before, Adlai Stevenson had gone to Dallas to attend a meeting on United Nations Day. The radical right decided to counter this visit by holding a "United States Day" just prior to Stevenson's arrival, with General Edwin A. Walker as the main speaker. The day after Walker's appearance, handbills with photographs of the president of the United States – full-face and profile – appeared on the streets of Dallas. "Wanted for Treason," read the caption. That evening many of Walker's partisans appeared at the U.N. meeting to curse and spit on Stevenson. Talking with Arthur Schlesinger shortly thereafter, Stevenson remarked, "[T]here was something very ugly and frightening about the atmosphere. Later I talked with some of the leading people out there. They wondered whether the President should go to Dallas and so do I."[1]

J. William Fulbright shared that sense of foreboding. In early November Kennedy flew to Arkansas to dedicate the newly completed Greers Ferry dam near Heber Springs and to throw a few political bouquets in the direction of the junior senator. When Fulbright learned of the president's planned campaign swing through Texas, he begged him to avoid Dallas. "Dallas is a very dangerous place," he told Kennedy as the two drove from Little Rock to He-

[1] Quoted in Arthur M. Schlesinger, Jr., *A Thousand Days* (Boston, 1965), 1021.

ber Springs. "I wouldn't go there and don't you go."[2] (Indeed, Jim Garrison, the Louisiana attorney general who would undertake his own personal investigation of the Kennedy assassination, later reported that in 1962 the Kansas City chapter of the Minute Men had commissioned a Dallasite named John Moriss to shoot Fulbright.[3]) The president listened but told Fulbright he could not appear to be running scared.

The morning of November 22 Fulbright attended a routine executive session of the SFRC devoted to amending the Foreign Assistance Act of 1961. He met his close friend Eugene Black, head of the World Bank, at the F Street Club. There, during lunch, they learned of Kennedy's assassination. Later that afternoon, the White House notified Fulbright that the new president wanted him to be at the executive mansion at six o'clock. Johnson arrived at the White House at 6:45 to began conferring with the Capitol's movers and shakers. The first person he saw was his old acquaintance from Arkansas.[4]

News of John F. Kennedy's sudden and tragic death stunned and saddened Fulbright no less than the rest of the American people; and, as was the case with so many others, the president's demise and the circumstances surrounding it caused Fulbright to remember the best about Kennedy. During a radio interview that weekend, the head of the SFRC recalled the president as the most approachable chief executive he had ever known. There was never a trace of arrogance, he insisted. Kennedy was wonderfully sensitive with foreign guests. "Every time I went to a White House dinner, or any kind of ceremony, I was very proud of the way he represented me and my country."[5]

Struck down in his prime and at a time when his presidency seemed on the verge of realizing its promise, Kennedy was transformed almost overnight into a supernatural figure, his every action encased in an aura of romance. "What was killed in Dallas," journalist James Reston wrote, "was not only the President but the promise. The death of youth and the hope of youth, of the beauty and grace and the touch of magic."[6] Americans found it difficult to comprehend such tragedy; only the province of mythology seemed capable of lending meaning to an act so shocking and irrational, historian Dewey Grantham has written. Out of this need was born the naïve legend of Camelot, whose gallant young prince had given the nation a moment of glory before dying for its sins, but who also opened the way for change and reformation.

Fulbright reacted to Jack Kennedy's death not by romanticizing it but by seeking to identify the societal causes of the assassination and demanding that

2 Fred Livingston to Robert S. McCord, Mar. 31, 1969, Series 48:1, Box 9:3, SPF.

3 Correlation Summary, Mar. 13, 1969, 62-71126, FBI Files.

4 Interview with J. William Fulbright, Oct. 11–18, Washington, D.C.

5 Quoted in Haynes Johnson and Bernard M. Gwertzman, *Fulbright: The Dissenter* (New York, 1968), 217.

6 Quoted in Dewey W. Grantham, *Recent America: The United States since 1945* (Arlington Heights, Ill., 1987), 254.

they be rooted out. Americans were, for the most part, decent, civilized, and humane, he told the Rockefeller Public Service Awards luncheon at the Shoreham the first week in December; but there was a darker side, a strain of intolerance and violence. It manifested itself in savage urban crimes, in the malice and hatred exhibited by extremist political movements, and in "the cruel bigotry of race that leads to such tragedies as the killing of Negro children in a church in Alabama." He called for a long and painful self-examination, a rejection of "moral absolutism." Medieval Christians who burned heretics alive did so not because they were cruel and sadistic, he reminded the Senate; "they did it because they wished to exorcise evil and make men godly and pure." The frontier experience taught the values of self-reliance and individual initiative, but it also glorified violence. Kennedy's assassination was the product of "vigilante justice," a blending of Puritan intolerance and the frontier ethos. The United States stood at a crossroads, Fulbright declared. "Throughout the 20th century American foreign policy has been caught up in the inherent contradiction between our English heritage of tolerance and accommodation and our Puritan heritage of crusading righteousness." Those who took the president's life were intellectual and moral brothers of those who "in their fear and passion, seem ever ready to plunge the nation into conflict abroad and witch hunts at home." It was to be hoped, he concluded, that there would be some redemption for the death of the president. "That redemption could issue from a national revulsion against extremism and violence, and from a calling forth of the basic decency and humanity of America to heal the wounds of divisiveness and hate."[7] At the conclusion of Fulbright's declamation John J. McCloy, David Rockefeller, Henry Wriston, and others in attendance at the Shoreham rose to give the Arkansan a standing ovation.[8]

Most important, perhaps, the Kennedy assassination seemed to remind Fulbright that foreign and domestic policy were inextricably bound up, that mean-spiritedness and insensitivity at home were bound to translate into xenophobia and a foreign policy grounded in militarism and economic exploitation. As the New Frontier turned into the Great Society, the Arkansan decided that he must put his shoulder to the wheel of domestic reform. If his country were ever to pursue a policy of reason, restraint, and understanding abroad, it must do so at home as well.

Fulbright's newfound liberalism on domestic matters and his liberal-activist views on foreign policy seemed to foretell a unique and fruitful partnership with the man who had replaced John F. Kennedy in the White House.

Tall, powerfully built, simultaneously as ugly and handsome as the hounddogs he raised on his Texas ranch, Lyndon Baines Johnson stood in marked

7 *Congressional Record,* Senate, Dec. 6, 1963, 23726–8.
8 Wriston to JWF, Dec. 13, 1963, Series 48:1, Box 5:5, SPF.

contrast to John F. Kennedy. His rural, southwestern background, teachers' college education, drawling speech, and backslapping demeanor seemed the antithesis of Kennedy's northeastern, metropolitan youthfulness, his Harvard training, eloquence, and urbanity. The latter's tragic death seemed to erase in the public mind memories of Kennedy's working-class, Boston-Irish, ward-heeling ancestry. Johnson lacked his predecessor's graceful style on the speaker's platform, and his crude language and penchant for hyperbole dismayed many intellectuals. When warned by a staff member that, in bringing a certain political figure into his administration, the new president was hiring a chronic troublemaker, Johnson retorted (one of his favorites): "I'd rather have him inside the tent pissing out instead of outside the tent pissing in." But Johnson had a flair for the dramatic, and he was a man of enormous energy, drive, and determination.

Personally, Lyndon Johnson was a bundle of conflicting insecurities and ambitions. Like a number of other white southerners, he understood and empathized with the black revolution long before many northern politicians did. A man of self-made and conjugal wealth, Johnson had experienced financial difficulty and witnessed poverty firsthand in the Hill Country and Houston. A product of a rural political oligarchy, he preached the politics of populism minus its nativism. Though he would win the 1964 election by the largest margin of any presidential candidate in U.S. history, the Texan felt unloved and even ridiculed. He was candid and deceitful, considerate and cruel, coarse and subtle, intelligent but capable of stubbornness to the point of stupidity.

Despite his statement that he was but the trustee of the Kennedy legacy and his oft-repeated promises to enact the Kennedy program, the man from Johnson City was determined to be his own president. Shortly after returning to Washington from Dallas, Johnson summoned Princeton historian Eric Goldman, who, along with Walt Rostow, would become a resident White House intellectual in the new administration. Bill Moyers brought Goldman into the Oval Office and then sat somewhat apprehensively to one side. As their interview opened, Johnson was pleasant but quiet. He wanted to hear what the author of *Rendezvous with Destiny* had to say. Nervous, Goldman rambled a bit and then demurred: "I don't want to subject you to a history lecture." "Go on," Johnson remarked with a quick grin. "I can use a history lecture."

Confronted with death and division, Goldman declared, past presidents had drawn the country together by invoking the national interest. Avoiding partisanship and ideology they had thrown their weight behind a broad domestic and diplomatic program that represented what a variety of significant groups could agree upon or could be persuaded to agree upon. Theodore Roosevelt had brought the country out of the divisiveness of the 1890s by posing as the "steward" of the needs and aspirations of the general population. A too-sharply divided nation was an immobile and potentially self-destructive one. The task ahead was to move beyond the class warfare of the 1930s and the shibboleths of the cold war. A foreign policy for the 1960s would concentrate on moving Soviet–American relations from confrontation to competitive coexistence. At home, the president could clean up essential, unfinished business, such as action directed toward educational needs, the legitimate restiveness of the African American, and the dangerously mounting costs of medical care. Johnson, Goldman recalled, was entranced. "His long face was fixed on me and he would interject an occasional 'Yes.'" The historian had articulated Johnson's thinking precisely.[9]

Goldman later observed that most politicians seeking national office extol unity; it was the obvious political ploy. Johnson, however, meant it. The Texan had his own political reasons in declaring that he sought to be "the President who unified the nation";[10] but he also kept repeating this theme because it had deep emotional appeal for him. It was his dream to be remembered as the consensus president, a political reincarnation of Franklin D. Roosevelt. He was determined to persuade, cajole, coerce, or bludgeon everyone into hopping aboard his bandwagon.

Fulbright was more excited about the prospect of working with Johnson than with any of his predecessors. Past apprehensions were nowhere in evidence during the first days of the new administration. The goodwill the president enjoyed in Congress and his unparalleled achievements as legislative manager seemed to Fulbright to augur an end to the divided government he had so long lamented. The Texan could get the country moving in the direction in which Kennedy and Fulbright wanted it to go. Indeed, as 1964 began, Fulbright and Johnson shared a common vision. These two representatives of the New South would bring to the nation and the world a new era characterized by peace, social progress, and enlightened leadership. While Johnson concentrated on civil rights and poverty, Fulbright would devote his efforts to foreign affairs. On a personal level, the Fulbright–Johnson relationship had never been better. Johnson conferred with the chair of the SFRC throughout December. Just after Christmas the president sent Fulbright a picture of the two having breakfast aboard Air Force One. The inscription read: "To J. William Fulbright, than whom there is no better. Lyndon B. Johnson."

Jack Kennedy's assassination, the blight of the radical right, a wave of segregationist violence in the South, and Lyndon Johnson's accession to the presidency combined to convert Fulbright into an active supporter of many of the administration's domestic programs. To the Arkansan's delight and with his help, Johnson pushed through Congress the massive tax cut Kennedy had proposed but had been unable to effect, and that Fulbright had been urging since the late 1940s. Fulbright was similarly enthusiastic about Johnson's

9 Eric F. Goldman, *The Tragedy of Lyndon Johnson* (New York, 1969), 6–7.
10 Ibid., 201.

War on Poverty and its various components – the food stamp program, VISTA, Head Start, and the Office of Economic Opportunity (OEO). For too long had American domestic policy been robbed by the demands of the cold war, he told the national Association of Secondary School Principals:

> Far more pervasively than the United Nations or the "Atlantic community" could ever do, the cold war has encroached upon our sovereignty; it has given the Communists the major voice in determining what proportion of our federal budget must be allocated to the military and what . . . cannot be made available for domestic social and economic projects. . . . We can no longer afford to defer problems of slums and crime and poverty and inadequate education until some more tranquil time in the future.[11]

When the Economic Opportunity Act made its appearance in Congress, elements of the old conservative coalition railed against it. Some southern senators and representatives attacked the legislation because the planters and manufacturers they represented feared the loss of cheap, unskilled labor. Republicans denounced the measure creating the OEO as a partisan scheme to win votes in an election year, just a warmed-over version of the Works Progress Administration. Fulbright spearheaded the counterattack. "This bill," he told the Senate, "is designed to help those people – and particularly those children – who did not have the wisdom and foresight to be born of the right parents or in the right place." Its goal was to provide opportunity and not charity. The unemployed and unemployable did not pay taxes, the Arkansan pointed out; they ate them. The charge that the act was a scheme to buy votes was "hogwash." Responding to the rhetoric of Fulbright and other supporters, as well as to Johnson's behind-the-scenes whip cracking, the antipoverty bill passed the Senate by a margin of 52–33.[12]

On one level Fulbright's support of the antipoverty program made political sense. Despite the economic gains stemming from the modernization of agriculture in the Arkansas Delta and Ozark highlands, poverty was still pervasive in Arkansas. Indeed, as Fulbright pointed out in his defense of the OEO legislation, 60 percent of Arkansas families in 1960 made less than $4,000 a year, 47 percent less than $3,000, and 14 percent attempted to get by on less than $1,000. Margueritte Gilstrap, an Arkansan and an employee of the Farm Security Administration, recalled finding a white family living in a cave dugout near the north-central Arkansas community of Yellville. When she first encountered the family, the head of the household was lying on the floor wrapped in a blanket and dying of tuberculosis. The children played and bathed in an open trench. The year was 1962.[13]

11 "Fulbright Urges Priority Be Centered on Promoting Welfare of Americans," *Arkansas Gazette,* Jan. 17, 1965.
12 *Congressional Record,* Senate, July 23, 1964, 16764.
13 Interview with Margueritte Gilstrap, June 23, 1989, Washington, D.C.

Nonetheless, there was political risk in Fulbright's newfound liberalism as well; not all Arkansans confronted the prospect of social progress with equanimity. Gilstrap recalled going into the Delta town of Marianna and finding more than a thousand unemployed, able-bodied youths (90 percent of them black). She wrote a hundred-thousand-dollar grant for the town that would provide job training and minimal employment for virtually all of the young men. The city authorities rejected it: All they needed, they told Gilstrap, was a $7,000 grant to landscape the town center. The planters and small businessmen of Arkansas did not want the federal government coming in and "pricing the labor force out of sight." They sensed that education and prosperity for the poor, particularly the African-American poor, would eventually put an end to the region's hallowed caste system; but, more important, it would cost the planter-businessmen money.

Fulbright was well aware of the political pitfalls of supporting Johnson's antipoverty program. His voting record on civil rights attested to his sense of reality. He truly believed, however, that education and employment would solve the racial problem. The concrete gains to be realized from Johnson's antipoverty legislation were too great to ignore. Fulbright also suffered pangs of guilt over his opposition to civil rights legislation over the years. He would not have hired and retained the staff he did – liberal almost to a person on the race issue – had he not harbored some sympathy for the plight of African Americans. Moreover, the atrocities depicted on television and in the newspapers affected him no less than it did the average white, middle-class American. Fulbright and Lee Williams pressed Sargent Shriver, director of the OEO, to include raw cotton, cotton cloth, and cotton clothing in the food stamp program. They lobbied to have the Fort Chaffee reservation, then used only for military reserve training in the summer, converted into a huge Job Corps center.[14] When in January 1965 the administration introduced legislation launching an Appalachian development project, Fulbright labored to have the Ozarks included.[15] In 1965 he cosponsored the Public Works and Economic Development Act, which appropriated millions of dollars to finance water and sewer projects, roads, airports, and industrial parks in underdeveloped regions of the country.[16]

Nevertheless, pragmatist that he was, the chairman of the SFRC was willing to criticize portions of the administration's domestic program when he deemed them bombastic, irrelevant, or counterproductive. At the same time he went to the mat for the president's antipoverty measures, he blasted Johnson's proposals to increase the National Aeronautics and Space Administra-

14 Pat Fleming to JWF, July 20, 1964, F6, and JWF to Sargent Shriver, Sept. 2, 1964, Series 1:14, Box 11, F7, SPF.

15 "Fulbright Asks Economic Aid for the Ozarks," *Arkansas Gazette,* Jan. 26, 1965.

16 *Congressional Record,* Senate, June 1, 1965, 12152–3.

tion budget by 37 percent and ridiculed his promise (first made by Kennedy) to put a man on the moon by the end of the decade. The $35 billion price tag for that project could build ten TVAs, he pointed out. "At the risk of being considered something of a troglodyte, I cannot bring myself to believe that going to the moon is essential simply because it is new and creative and adventurous."[17] By 1965 Fulbright was ridiculing proponents of the space program as simpleminded jingoes whose nationalist fervor to beat the Russians in the lunar race was analogous to sports-crazed fans at a basketball game. Year after year the chair of the SFRC had struggled to fend off cuts to the exchange program, the Development Loan Fund, and other programs he considered farsighted and enlightened. Now, the know-nothings and flat-earthers were ready to vote $5.3 billion for the 1964 space program without blinking an eye. It was all so irrational, he declared.

Periodically during his career J. William Fulbright demonstrated the most striking ignorance of human nature and lack of insight into the simple rules of psychology. Nowhere was this more apparent than in his relations with Lyndon Johnson. He had spent years in the Senate with Johnson; no one had had a greater chance to experience firsthand the Texan's ego and insecurity. Johnson's demands for absolute loyalty from his staff were notorious, as was his unwillingness to abandon a bill or program once embraced. The space program was, like the president, larger than life. It would be a monument to his vision, to his leadership, as well as his economic legacy to the greater Houston area. Yet the moon race made no sense to Fulbright; therefore, it was nonsensical.

Fulbright's attacks on NASA were bound to anger the president. Marcy knew it, and tried to warn Fulbright. "I have thought for some time that you tend to go too far in beating the moon race over the head," he wrote Fulbright after his speech comparing the space race to an athletic contest.[18] Fulbright was not to be deterred, however, and his sarcasm-laden efforts to slow down the space program planted seeds of doubt in Johnson's mind concerning Fulbright's "reliability." There were to be others.

In the same address in which he urged lawmakers to enact a major tax cut, President Johnson also called for "the earliest possible passage" of Kennedy's civil rights bill. The new chief executive soon made it clear that he was totally committed to the enactment of this broad equal rights measure and that he was prepared to push on boldly to advance the cause with additional legislation and with executive action. "We have talked long enough in this country about equal rights," Johnson declared on November 27, 1963. "We have

17 Ibid., Nov. 19, 1963, 22361, and June 24, 1964, 14871–3.
18 Marcy to JWF, Mar. 29, 1965, Box 5, Folder Mar., Marcy Papers.

talked for one hundred years or more. It is time now to write the next chapter, and to write it in the books of law." To Johnson's mind, civil rights constituted the acid test of his credentials as a liberal, a reformer, and a national leader.

The measure that eventually became the Civil Rights Act of 1964 was the most far-reaching and comprehensive legislation in support of racial equality ever considered by any deliberative body in America. It empowered the attorney general to join civil suits filed by private citizens against discrimination and segregation in voting, education, and the use of public facilities. It forbade discrimination in most places of public accommodation, armed federal courts with broad injunctive powers, and empowered them to hold in contempt public officials blocking enforcement.

When the second session of the Eighty-eighth Congress began its work in January 1964, the Johnson administration mobilized all of its considerable forces behind the effort to pass the omnibus civil rights bill. Thousands of people poured into Washington to press for congressional approval, and scores of national organizations working through the Leadership Conference on Civil Rights labored to rally the nation. In late January, Emmanuel Celler (D–New York) steered the measure through the House. The final tally was 290 to 130. As always the great obstacle to be overcome was the Senate of the United States.

There was never any chance that the band of Confederate brothers under Richard Russell would actually support a civil rights measure, or that they would refrain from filibustering; but by 1964 they were growing weary. A few, like Fulbright, had become sensitized to the plight of African Americans. Indeed, following the bombing of a black church in Birmingham in the fall of 1963, a blast that had taken the lives of four young girls, the Arkansan had called the White House and offered to help pass a new, comprehensive civil rights bill.[19] Others like Ellender, Ervin, and Russell saw themselves as fighting a rearguard action designed to preserve as much regional autonomy for the South in the area of race relations as possible. Throughout the struggle over the 1964 and 1965 civil rights bills, Richard Russell's relationship with Lyndon Johnson remained close. The president and Lady Bird continued to have the Georgia bachelor to dinner at the White House on a regular basis. Perhaps most important, the Dixiecrats would become the president's chief supporters on Vietnam: Georgia, South Carolina, and Alabama would be the principal beneficiaries of bountiful defense contracts let by the ever-expanding Pentagon. Although they clung to their segregationist views, the deep South diehards had no intention of taking a position on the civil rights bill that would

[19] Mike Manatos to Larry O'Brien, Oct. 1, 1963, Box 18, Papers of Lawrence F. O'Brien, Kennedy Papers.

split the Democratic Party and make it impossible for Lyndon Johnson to govern.

The filibuster that began in March 1964 over the civil rights bill would last a grueling eighty-three days. J. William Fulbright dutifully attended the strategy sessions in Russell's office and took his turn on the floor. The points he made were familiar ones: The North was trying to impose its social ethic on the South, a code it was not even willing to abide by itself. The race problem was national and not regional. He and his brethren could not turn the clock back to 1619. He pled with his colleagues in the Senate to "recognize that the eternal problem posed by racial or religious minority yield[s] ultimately to the slow conversions of the human heart and mind."[20] Inspired by C. Vann Woodward's *The Burden of Southern History,* he brooded aloud on the plight of his native region:

> The people of the South are burdened with a historical legacy that the rest of the nation does not share. They are marked in some strange ways by a strange disproportion inherited from the age of Negro slavery. The whites and Negroes of Arkansas and the South are equally prisoners of their environment and no one knows what either of them might have been in a different environment or under other circumstances. Certainly no one of them has ever been free with respect to racial relationships to the degree that the Vermonter or the Minnesotan had been free. The society of each is conditioned by the presence of the other. Each carries a catalog of things not to be mentioned. Each moves through an intricate ritual of evasions, of make-believe, and suppressions. In the South one finds a relationship among men without counterpart on this continent.[21]

Despite the length and strength of the Dixiecrats' collective diatribe, Russell and his minions sensed from the very beginning that this time their efforts would be fruitless. The social consciousness that had been awakened in Fulbright by Kennedy's assassination and Johnson's accession to the presidency was a national phenomenon. On June 10, for the first time in its history, the United States Senate voted for cloture. The final tally showed 71 for and 29 against cutting off debate.[22] On June 19 the Senate passed the Civil Rights Act of 1964 virtually as it had been submitted by the White House by a vote of 73 to 27.

Throughout May the *Arkansas Gazette* and the national press were full of rumors that Fulbright would desert his brethren and vote for cloture. Some even whispered that Johnson had offered his old friend the position of secre-

20 *Congressional Record,* Senate, Mar. 18, 1964, 5639.
21 Ibid.
22 JWF to Don Weiner, June 10, 1964, Box 12, Series 39:2, F1, SPF.

tary of state in 1964 in return for his help in ending debate. The rumors proved ill founded: Fulbright voted against both cloture and the final bill.

Lee Williams later recalled that he and other staff members had argued long and hard to Fulbright that the times were such that he could finally afford to vote his convictions. Their boss seemed receptive. Indeed, according to Williams, as Fulbright was leaving for home the night before the vote, he indicated that he would vote yea. Williams and the others did not learn that he had voted nay until Fulbright returned from the floor the next day. The staff, of course, said nothing, but they were intensely disappointed and curious as to who had turned Fulbright around. More than likely, it had been Betty. The family had sacrificed too much for Bill's political career. Civil rights, she had probably convinced him, was just not an issue that warranted a political life-or-death stand. Most important, however, Fulbright's vote was not needed for cloture.

As had been the case in 1957 and 1960, Fulbright justified his votes on political grounds. The people had elected him in 1962 in no small part because of his record on civil rights; he would be betraying a sacred trust by changing horses in midstream. There is much evidence, however, that Lee Williams had been right: By 1964 a large number of Arkansans had come to feel that it was their Christian duty to acquiesce in federal laws outlawing discrimination against African Americans. Indeed, dozens of prominent clergymen representing virtually every denomination had written Fulbright urging him to vote for the omnibus civil rights bill.[23] The priests at Subiaco Academy had had their students write. The ministerial alliance of Pine Bluff, that ultraconservative, racially divided remnant of the old Confederacy, had wired their support for the bill.[24] The state's business community, grievously damaged by the publicity surrounding the Little Rock crisis, had come to the conclusion that Arkansas could no longer afford Jim Crow.[25] Even some of Fulbright's most important political advisers, individuals who had urged caution during the Little Rock crisis, told him that the time was now propitious.

Fulbright's role in the struggle over the 1964 Civil Rights Act was not entirely negative. He spoke the language of moderation. He pointed with pride to the fact that 123 black children attended mixed schools in Arkansas in 1964. Shortly after passage, Fulbright publicly urged calm and restraint on the part of those who had opposed the bill, and he expressed confidence that Johnson would administer the law with "fairness, compassion and an under-

23 Mann to JWF, Nov. 18, 1963, Series 39:2, Box 10:2, SPF, and Shoemaker to JWF, Nov. 26, 1963, Series 39:2, Box 9:1, SPF.

24 Theresa Seredynski to JWF, Feb. 16, 1964, and A. M. Roberts to JWF, Mar. 24, 1964, Series 39:2, Box 12:4, SPF.

25 "Business in Dixie: Southerners Say Racial Tension Slows Gains," *Wall Street Journal,* May 26, 1961.

standing of local sentiment which cannot be changed overnight."[26] Both Majority Leader Mike Mansfield and President Johnson wrote Fulbright thanking him for helping to prevent schisms in the Senate "which would have been years in closing" and for appealing for calm.[27] To his mind, he had fulfilled the pledge of help he had made to the Kennedy administration in the wake of the Birmingham church bombing. In fact, his position had changed little since the signing of the Southern Manifesto.

Above all, Fulbright continued to believe that the South had a right to decide its own destiny. If integration was to come to the region, its residents, white and black, would have to support it. He continued to be highly sensitive to the perceived issue of cultural imperialism. That summer William Edens, an old friend who worked in the American embassy in Pretoria, wrote complaining that the State Department had forced American officials in South Africa to include Negroes in their Fourth of July parties. When the South African government had complained, the U.S. ambassador had told it not to bother to send representatives. It was dangerous, Edens wrote, to offend the most powerful country in Africa. The Afrikaners thought like many Americans. "The attempt to force your way on another is why we are resisting the Russians," he warned.[28] Fulbright agreed and complained to his old friend George Ball: "It does seem to me that we should be guided in the main by the practices of foreign countries in which we have embassies," he wrote, "and that we should not try to impose upon them our particular ideas of morality."[29] Ball replied, somewhat indignantly, that it was imperative that foreign embassies of the United States reflect "our government's goals of equal treatment and opportunity for all."[30] Fulbright remained unconvinced. The object of American foreign policy should be to make the world safe for diversity, not remake it in the American image.

During the latter stages of the 1964 filibuster in early May, President Johnson dispatched Fulbright to Athens and Ankara to mediate the increasingly dangerous Greek–Turkish confrontation over Cyprus.[31] The senator decided to take Betty with him, and the two departed May 1 for a nine-day "whirlwind" tour of Europe and the Near East. "We traveled 13,632 miles, met the great, the near-great, and the would-be great, and ate every known kind of 'good-

26 "Fulbright Says Calmness Vital," *Arkansas Democrat,* July 10, 1964.

27 Mansfield to JWF, June 22, 1964, Series 39:2, Box 11:1, SPF, and LBJ to JWF, July 23, 1964, Box 3, WHCF, Papers of Lyndon B. Johnson, Johnson Library.

28 Edens to JWF, July 3, 1964, Series 2:1, Box 4:1, SPF.

29 JWF to Ball, July 23, 1964, Series 2:1, Box 4:1, SPF.

30 Ball to JWF, Aug. 3, 1964, Series 2:1, Box 4:1, SPF.

31 "Fulbright Delivers Johnson's Appeal to Greek Premier," *Arkansas Gazette,* May 7, 1964.

ie'," Betty wrote Judy Foote, Bosey's mother-in-law. While Bill "coped with various and sundry political prima donnas" at the International Court, Betty surveyed Holland's tulip fields from a helicopter and admired the works of Vermeer and other masters at The Hague. The Fulbrights dined at the foot of the Athenian Acropolis and took coffee on their balcony overlooking Ataturk's tomb. Their schedule was crowded to the point where they slept a maximum of five hours a night, every night in a different city, but Betty found the trip exhilarating. The time on planes and trains allowed her the first real access to her husband she had had since Christmas.[32]

Allen Matusow has written that Lyndon B. Johnson was a "complex man notorious for his ideological insincerity."[33] If by that Matusow meant that Johnson was nonideological or that he wielded ideological justifications for pragmatically based policies already decided upon, he was right. He also shared that trait with most other successful presidents, notably the two Roosevelts. Lyndon Johnson was in basic agreement with the foreign policies of the Kennedy administration: Military preparedness and realistic diplomacy would contain communism within its existing bounds. In order to keep up morale among America's allies and satisfy hard-line anticommunists at home, the United States must continue to hold fast to Berlin, oppose the admission of Communist China to the United Nations, and continue to confront and blockade Cuba. He was aware of the Sino–Soviet split and the possibilities inherent in it for dividing the communist world. He also took a flexible, even hopeful view of the Soviet Union and Nikita Khrushchev. It was just possible, he believed, that the USSR was becoming a status quo power and as such would be a force for stability rather than chaos in the world. The United States must continue its "flexible response" of military aid, economic assistance, and technical/political advice to the threat of communism in the developing world, but there was nothing wrong with negotiating with the Soviets at the same time in an effort to reduce tensions. Insofar as Latin America was concerned, Johnson was an enthusiastic supporter of the Alliance for Progress; as a progressive Democrat he was drawn to the Schlesinger–Goodwin philosophy of seeking openings to the democratic left. At the outset of his administration, it appeared that the new president did not buy into the myth of a monolithic communist threat. He was a staunch supporter of trade with Yugoslavia and Poland. Above all, he seemed a flexible, pragmatic cold warrior, a position very congenial to J. William Fulbright.[34]

32 Betty to Judy Foote, May 16, 1964, Letters in possession of Bosey Foote.
33 Allen J. Matusow, *The Unraveling of America: A History of Liberalism in the 1960s* (New York, 1984), 94.
34 See *Congressional Record,* Senate, Jan. 21, 1964, 893.

One evening in late March, in the midst of the civil rights filibuster, Lyndon Johnson had Fulbright to dinner at the White House.[35] The discussion ranged over many topics. The president urged Fulbright to rethink voting against cloture: He knew it was impossible for the Arkansan to support the final bill, the president said, but a vote for cloture would be of tremendous value. It would also help dispel the myth in foreign chanceries that Fulbright was a racist. The two talked of Vietnam, where some twenty thousand American military advisers were trying to shore up the struggling government of South Vietnamese general (and now prime minister) Nguyen Khanh against Vietcong attacks and North Vietnamese incursions; and where the Agency for International Development (AID), established under Kennedy, was working to build an economically self-sufficient society. In addition, Johnson informed Fulbright that secret negotiations were underway between Panama and the United States. In January riots had erupted in the Canal Zone over the display of Panamanian and American flags. Panamanian President Roberto Chiari had subsequently severed diplomatic relations with the United States and demanded a revision of the 1903 treaty under which the Americans had built and operated the canal. Both Fulbright and Johnson agreed that the canal issue had been blown all out of proportion by the radical right, but that its symbolic importance made it a political hot potato. The two analyzed the emerging controversy over East–West trade, about which they agreed, and policy toward Cuba, about which they did not. They also talked of politics. Johnson expressed his desire to win an overwhelming victory over the probable Republican candidate in 1964, Barry Goldwater. He wanted to unify the country behind his domestic programs, Johnson said, and discredit the radical right once and for all. Fulbright promised to do all in his power to help.

When Fulbright rose in the Senate chamber on the afternoon of March 25 to take his turn in the civil rights filibuster, the hall was virtually empty. Morse was there and so was Sam Ervin, but only a handful of others bothered to attend. In a low monotone Fulbright delivered one of the most important foreign policy speeches of his career. It would attract national and international attention.

In their dealings with the communist world, Fulbright declared, Americans must abandon old myths and adapt themselves to new realities. The character of Soviet–American relations had changed. Washington had demonstrated clearly to Moscow in the Cuban missile crisis that "aggression and adventure" involved unacceptable risks. Khrushchev had retreated from his dream of world conquest, and in signing the test-ban agreement the two nations had tacitly relinquished their quest for "total victory." In this new era of "peaceful

35 Rowland Evans and Robert Novak, "Fulbright's Opportunity," *Washington Post,* Apr. 14, 1964.

coexistence" it was imperative that Americans adopt a more flexible, sophisticated approach to their former adversaries. "We must dare to think about 'unthinkable things,' because when things become 'unthinkable,' thinking stops and action becomes mindless."

The tendency to view the communist world as a monolith bent on military destruction of the free world was an anachronistic if understandable holdover from the Stalinist era. The Sino–Soviet split and the growing independence of Poland, Yugoslavia, and Hungary were clear indications that the formerly homogeneous communist bloc was maturing into a diverse collection of nation-states with each of whom the United States must develop a separate, distinct relationship.

Too many Americans, Fulbright declared, returning to another favorite theme, confused means with ends. They tended to equate freedom and democracy with capitalism, federalism, and the two-party system. The latter were merely the mechanisms Americans preferred for achieving the former. It was quite possible for freedom and democracy to exist in a socialist or communist country, the Arkansan pointed out. What mattered was not the principles around which a society organized its economy, but that society's aggressive intent. "Insofar as a great nation mobilizes its power and resources for aggressive purposes," Fulbright declared, "that nation, regardless of ideology, makes itself our enemy. Insofar as a nation is content to practice its doctrines within its own frontiers, that nation, however repugnant its ideology, is one with which we have no proper quarrel." If the United States continued to view all communist regimes as equally hostile and equally threatening, it would be imposing on the communist bloc a degree of unity that the Soviet Union had proved quite incapable of enforcing. What then, should American policy be toward the communist nations and those vulnerable to Sino–Soviet penetration?

This country was going to have to come to grips with the fact that Castro and Castroism were not going to disappear in a season. Efforts to bring down the charismatic Cuban through a policy of political and economic boycott had failed. Cuba, Fulbright declared – repeating a point he had made during and after the abortive Bay of Pigs invasion – was a thorn in the side but not a dagger in the heart. Certainly Castro was attempting to export his revolution, but he was failing. Through a combination of military and economic aid, the United States had enabled states such as Venezuela to defeat communist-led domestic insurrections.

In the long run, Fulbright concluded, the United States was going to have to abandon the notion that meaningful social change could take place in Latin America without violence. Long-established ruling oligarchies were so deeply entrenched and so repressive that in some cases armed insurrection was the only path to democratization and socioeconomic reform. Such uprisings were not by definition communist inspired or communist led. He was not advocating violent revolutions, he said, but the United States must confront socioeconomic change in the developing world with an open mind.

In the "old myths and new realities" speech, Fulbright did not go so far as to call for the admission of Red China to the United Nations, but did reiterate his belief that there was only one China – mainland, communist China – and that the United States should deal with it and it alone. America could not tolerate Chinese expansion, but it should act with patience and flexibility in dealing with Beijing. If Mao and Chou should ever forswear their intention to reconquer Formosa, then Washington should consider normalizing relations.

Vietnam, Fulbright continued in his sweeping review of the nation's foreign policy, was perhaps the most complicated and pressing problem facing the Johnson administration. "Other than withdrawal, which I do not think can be realistically considered under present circumstances, three options are open to us," the Arkansan declared. The United States could continue the antiguerrilla campaign then underway, stepping up military and economic aid to the South Vietnamese; it could seek immediately a negotiated settlement looking toward the neutralization of all of South Vietnam; or, finally, it could widen the war through the introduction of American troops or sponsorship of a South Vietnamese attack on the North. Fulbright ruled out negotiations. "It is extremely difficult for a party to a negotiation to achieve by diplomacy objectives which it has conspicuously failed to win by warfare." The American–South Vietnamese position was then too weak to expose it at a peace conference. The only two realistic options were to step up American aid to Saigon to enable it to prosecute more effectively the counterinsurgency then underway, or to widen the war. Surprisingly, Fulbright did not indicate a preference. Whatever the Johnson administration's decision, he concluded, "it should be clear to all concerned that the United States will continue to meet its obligations and fulfill its commitments with respect to Vietnam."[36]

Although the Senate was virtually empty on March 25 as Fulbright spoke of old myths and new realities, the wire services reported it verbatim on the twenty-sixth, and the national press gave it extensive and immediate coverage. By the end of the week virtually every press pundit of note had written at least one column on the speech. "Fulbright Shows His Skill Again," proclaimed Drew Pearson in "The Washington Merry-go-Round." "The significant thing about the recent Fulbright full-dress speech . . . is that its author has an almost perfect score on foreign affairs," Pearson proclaimed. "It was one of the most important foreign policy statements made by any Senator in this decade."[37] The junior senator from Arkansas had launched a much-needed and long-delayed national debate, declared Arthur Krock in the *New*

36 *Congressional Record,* Senate, Mar. 25, 1964, 6227–31.

37 Drew Pearson, "Fulbright Shows His Skill Again," *Washington Post,* Apr. 1, 1964.

*York Times.* That postwar American foreign policy had been rigidly moralistic and punctuated by glaring failures was undeniable.[38]

To the delight of the radical right, *Pravda* called Fulbright's speech a "light which has lit up a new realistic tendency in Washington's political thinking." *Izvestia* devoted nearly three columns to a glowing appraisal.[39] Cuba's unofficial minister in charge of revolution, Che Guevara, thanked Fulbright for recognizing that "Cuba is here to stay."[40]

Convinced that Fulbright had led the Democratic Party into the "soft on communism" trap that had been set ever since the fall of China in 1949, Republican politicians and conservative columnists lined up to attack the "old myths and new realities" speech. Strom Thurmond, William E. Miller, chairman of the GOP national committee, and John Tower all charged Fulbright with "appeasement." Tower further accused the chairman of the SFRC of urging "an even softer line toward international communism than we now have."[41] Thurmond inserted in the *Congressional Record* an article on the Fulbright speech by labor leader George Meany entitled "A Return to Appeasement."[42] Declared Miller:

> This is a trial balloon which the Johnson administration is sending up to prepare public opinion for the acceptance of a foreign policy that could lead only to disaster for the Untied States and other free nations. The course Senator Fulbright advocates is the same road which Neville Chamberlain traveled in the 1930s.[43]

Response from the noncommunist world was sharp and mixed. The British were appreciative: The *Times* of London praised Fulbright's speech as "a landmark in the evolution of American policy," and Karl Meyer wrote in the *New Statesman* that Fulbright had created an atmosphere in which Rusk and Johnson would have much greater room for maneuver.[44] Although most of their governments were anti-Castro, Latin American diplomats generally approved Fulbright's analysis of the Cuban situation. They did not believe that current American policies would bring down the Cuban regime, and they were even more outspoken in praise of Fulbright's suggestion that the United

38 Arthur Krock, "Fulbright Has Started the Debate He Wanted," *New York Times,* Apr. 1, 1964.

39 "Fulbright Speech Praised in Pravda," *New York Times,* Mar. 29, 1964.

40 "Guevara Says Fulbright Talk Set Right Attitude," *Washington Evening Star,* Mar. 31, 1964.

41 "Tower Says Fulbright Urges 'Even Softer Line' on Reds," *New York Tribune,* Apr. 5, 1964.

42 *Congressional Record,* Senate, May 8, 1964, 10438–9.

43 Ned Curran, "Critics Claim Fulbright Hit at LBJ Policy," *Arkansas Gazette,* Mar. 26, 1964.

44 "U.S. Foreign Policy – The Feeling In Four Major Capitals," *New York Times,* Apr. 11, 1964.

States could afford to be more generous in its treatment of Panama.[45] Jiang Jie-shi, in a speech addressed to the youth of Taiwan on March 29, declared that his government would not tolerate the illusion of "international appeasement." The Fulbright speech, he subsequently told a reporter, would only encourage the communists "to hate and insult your country more."[46]

The Johnson administration's public reaction to "old myths and new realities" was guarded. Secretary of State Rusk told a news conference that he agreed with many of the points made by Fulbright, particularly about rapid changes in the communist and noncommunist worlds; but in regard to Cuba, Rusk insisted that Castro was "more than a nuisance" and that the economic boycott must continue. He denied that the speech was a trial balloon as Miller had charged, but welcomed Fulbright's efforts to stimulate a debate.[47] Some in the press and among the Democratic leadership – most notably the knee-jerk anticommunist speaker of the House, John McCormack – accused Fulbright of attacking not only American foreign policy but his old friend, Lyndon Johnson.[48]

In reality, while Johnson, Rusk, and McNamara were a bit apprehensive lest the public fall victim once again to the GOP's efforts to portray the Democratic party as weak on communism, they were generally pleased. Fulbright had in effect carved out the middle ground that the Democrats could occupy, it was to be hoped, during the forthcoming presidential election campaign. Liberals could rally around the call for flexibility, any yet the speech had really given away nothing. It rejected recognition of Red China, allowed room for a stepped-up commitment in Vietnam, and urged a diplomacy that had as its objective the breakup of the Soviet empire. Moreover, the administration was free to dissociate itself from various aspects of the speech, which Rusk did in regard to Cuba. Fulbright's speech would definitely aid the Johnson campaign in its efforts to portray Goldwater, almost certain to be the Republican candidate, as a go-for-broke cold warrior dedicated to total military victory over the forces of international communism.[49]

The "old myths and new realities" address launched what columnist Max Frankel referred to as the "Fulbright phenomenon." In early April more than seventeen hundred students, teachers, and townspeople turned out on a rainy Sunday night at the University of North Carolina to hear the Arkansan appeal for a more rational division of resources between military and human welfare

45 "U.N. Diplomats Praise Fulbright," *St. Louis Post-Dispatch,* Apr. 8, 1964.

46 Thomas Hughes to Acting Secretary, Apr. 10, 1964, NSF, Box 3, Johnson Papers.

47 "Fulbright's Stand on Cuban Policy Rejected by Rusk," *Arkansas Gazette,* Mar. 28, 1964.

48 See Marianne Means, "LBJ 'Friends' Helping GOP," *Washington Post,* Mar. 29, 1964.

49 See Evans and Novak, "Fulbright's Opportunity."

programs. The *Daily Tar Heel* praised him as a "man of political guts" and, referring to his position on civil rights, lamented the fact that he was one of a number of southern legislators "chained to a role they must act out."[50] John Fitzgerald Kennedy's death had left a vacuum, especially among the idealistic youth that the Kennedy family had politicized, and, despite his record on civil rights, Fulbright seemed to many liberals to be the man who could fill it. His appeal was not limited to college students, however. In his book *A Thousand Days,* the first comprehensive history of the Kennedy administration, Arthur Schlesinger, Jr., would write about the historical mind and the assassinated president. He would argue that Kennedy had been attuned to the complexity of human existence, its tensions, contradictions, shadings. He had not looked for morals, made sweeping judgments, and tried to come up with final solutions. These qualities, Schlesinger would insist, were the essence of the historical and liberal mind. In so doing, he could not have more aptly described J. William Fulbright, and these very attributes were in large part what made the Arkansan appealing to liberal intellectuals as well as to so many young people.

To all appearances the Fulbright–Johnson relationship continued to flourish as the new president settled into his duties. During the early weeks of the transition, the president was on the phone with Fulbright regularly. Indeed, Fulbright at times felt overconsulted. After Johnson called him at home at eleven o'clock in the evening, he complained to Pat Holt: "Geez, he just won't hang up, and you can't hang up on him!" The two families saw a good deal of each other. The Christmas following the assassination, Betty did the president's shopping for Lady Bird, Lynda, and Luci.[51] In mid-April Johnson sent Fulbright an advance copy of a major address he was scheduled to deliver, asking for his advice.[52]

50 Max Frankel, "Arkansas's Fulbright a New Hero to Youth," *New York Times,* Apr. 6, 1964.

51 Donald M. Ritchie, interviewer, *Pat M. Holt: Oral History Interviews* (Senate Historical Office: Washington, D.C., 1981), 165–6.

52 Bundy to LBJ, Apr. 18, 1964, NSF, Memos to President, Bundy, Box 1, Johnson Papers.

# 18

# *Avoiding Armageddon*

From 1882 until 1941 Laos, Cambodia, and Vietnam had comprised French Indochina, France's richest and most important colony. Following France's surrender to Germany in June 1940, the region had been occupied by Japan – either directly or indirectly – until 1945. In 1946 the French had returned to Southeast Asia determined to reestablish control in their former possessions.

The war in the Pacific had given a strong fillip to anticolonial movements throughout the area, and Indochina was no exception. Shortly after Japan's surrender in August 1945, Ho Chi Minh – leader of the Vietminh, a broad-based but communist-led resistance movement – had proclaimed from Hanoi the existence of a new nation, the Democratic Republic of Vietnam (DRV). Over the next year and a half, however, the French, with the help of the British in the south and the Chinese Nationalists in the north, had managed to reestablish themselves firmly in the south and tentatively in the north. In November 1946 a bitter colonial war had then erupted between the French and the Vietminh, culminating in 1954 with France's defeat at the battle of Dien Bien Phu. A subsequent peace conference at Geneva had provided for the temporary division of the country at the Seventeenth Parallel. The French had withdrawn from the peninsula but left an anticommunist regime in place in the south – the Republic of Vietnam (RVN) – under emperor Bao Dai and his prime minister, Ngo Dinh Diem. Within a year Diem had ousted Bao Dai and instituted a presidential system with himself as chief executive. Meanwhile, in the north Ho had established the one-party, socialist DRV.

There was no doubt that Ho, one of the original members of the French Communist Party, was a Marxist–Leninist or that the DRV was a totalitarian regime. After both Moscow and Beijing recognized Ho's government as the legitimate ruler of all of Vietnam in 1950, the United States had concluded that the DRV was a Sino–Soviet satellite and that Ho was a puppet of Stalin and Mao Zedong. Throughout the 1950s the Eisenhower administration had then poured economic and military aid into Vietnam. Diem, a principled, patriotic man, had briefly attempted land and constitutional reform, but proved unsuited to the task of building a social democracy. A devout Catholic and traditional mandarin by temperament and philosophy, he distrusted the masses and had contempt for the give-and-take of democratic politics. Increasingly, Diem had relied on his family and loyal Catholics in the military and civil service to rule a country in which 90 percent of the population was Buddhist. His brother Ngo Dinh Nhu used the Can Lao Party, the press, and the state police to persecute and suppress opponents of the regime. As corruption increased and democracy all but disappeared, a rebellion had broken out in the south against the Diem regime. In 1960 the DRV had decided to give formal aid to the newly formed National Liberation Front (NLF), as the anti-Diemist revolutionaries called themselves.

A variety of factors had combined to ensure that President Kennedy would attempt to hold the line in Southeast Asia. He viewed the conflict in South Vietnam as one of Khrushchev's wars of national liberation, a test of his administration's resolve just as much as Berlin or Cuba. Kennedy and his advisers had fully accepted the "domino theory," whereby it was assumed that the fall of one government in a particular region threatened by communism would lead to the fall of all noncommunist governments in the area. His agreement in 1961 to the neutralization of Laos, a landlocked nation wracked by communist insurgency, had further strengthened his resolve to ensure that South Vietnam remained a "free world bastion." The number of American uniformed personnel would grow from several hundred when Kennedy assumed office to sixteen thousand by 1963.

Despite American aid, the Diem regime became increasingly isolated from the masses. Bribes and intimidation by civil servants and military officials alienated peasant and urban dweller alike. Law 10/59, which the government had pushed through the rubber-stamp national assembly, had given Nhu's police and special forces the power to arrest and execute South Vietnamese citizens for a wide variety of crimes including black marketeering and the spreading of seditious rumors about the government. By 1963 the nation was teetering on the brink of chaos, with the Vietcong (the military branch of the NLF) in control of the countryside, students and intellectuals demonstrating in Saigon and Hué, Buddhist monks burning themselves in protest, and high-ranking military officers hatching a variety of coup plots.

Shortly before his own assassination in November 1963, Kennedy had tacitly approved a military coup in Saigon that led to the deaths of both Diem and Nhu. The president had sensed that the United States was on the verge of plunging into a morass from which it could not extricate itself; only the South Vietnamese themselves could establish a broad-based, noncommunist government and make the sacrifices necessary to sustain it. Without that commitment on their part, all the American aid in the world would be for naught. Still, he had been unwilling, for both political and strategic reasons, to stand by and see Vietnam fall to the communists.

Lyndon Johnson was no more ready than his predecessor to withdraw unilaterally from South Vietnam or seek a negotiated settlement that would lead to neutralization of the area south of the Seventeenth Parallel. First of all, he was, as McGeorge Bundy has noted, "a hawk."[1] Like so many other Americans of his generation, Johnson had learned the lessons of Munich. He would not reward "aggression" with "appeasement" in Southeast Asia or anywhere else. In a typically vulgar analogy, he declared: "If you let a bully come into your yard one day, the next day he'll be up on your porch, and the day after that he'll rape your wife in your own bed." He seemed smitten with Diem and with the determination of the "brave people of Vietnam" to resist a communist takeover.[2] As the nation and the world would learn, Johnson was that variety of southerner for whom compassion was an all-consuming obsession.

In addition, the Texan felt duty-bound to carry out the policies of his predecessor. He was acutely sensitive to the fact that he had not been elected in his own right.[3] Moreover, Johnson felt constrained to demonstrate to the world, friend and foe alike, that America's period of grief and self-searching would not diminish its strength or weaken its commitment to its allies. Thus it was that in his first message to Congress and the nation on November 27, 1963, Lyndon Johnson assured his audience that he would uphold American commitments "from South Vietnam to West Berlin."[4]

An even more potent factor in the Indochinese equation was the president's fear that right-wing adversaries would prevail over him should South Vietnam fall to communism, just as Harry Truman had been hounded and his policies circumscribed by Joe McCarthy after the fall of China. Even though, as he indicated in his conversations with Fulbright, he may have wanted to question the assumptions that underlay the original containment policy – including the monolithic communist threat and the domino theory – he dare not, lest the debate fracture the domestic consensus he so desperately desired. In a word, Lyndon Johnson had no intention of allowing the charge that he was soft on communism to be used to destroy the Great Society programs.

On November 24, 1963, President Johnson instructed Ambassador Henry Cabot Lodge, Jr., to assure the generals who had overthrown Ngo Dinh Diem that they had the full support of the U.S. government. Two days later the National Security Council incorporated his pledge into policy, affirming that it was "the central objective of the United States" to assist the "people and Government of South Vietnam to win their contest against the externally directed and supported communist conspiracy."

1 Interview with McGeorge Bundy, Aug. 1, 1991, New York.

2 Quoted in Kathleen J. Turner, *Lyndon Johnson's Dual War: Vietnam and the Press* (Chicago, 1985), 53.

3 Doris Kearns [Goodwin], *Lyndon Johnson and the American Dream* (New York, 1976), 177.

4 Quoted in Turner, *Lyndon Johnson's Dual War,* 54.

Lyndon Johnson was well aware of his inexperience in foreign affairs; as a consequence, he retained Kennedy's top advisers and relied heavily on them. Rusk in State, McNamara in Defense, and National Security Adviser McGeorge Bundy had all played prominent roles in shaping Kennedy's Vietnam policy and, as George Herring and others have pointed out, they had a deep personal stake in upholding that policy. The new president assumed that J. William Fulbright, as a longtime exponent of executive prerogatives in foreign affairs, was part of his team and, if the "old myths and new realities" speech was any guide, shared his assumptions concerning Vietnam.

Indeed, if there had been a constant in the Fulbright philosophy of diplomacy, it was that the chief executive should possess and wield the broadest possible authority in the conduct of foreign affairs. "The American people have a long tradition of looking at the world in terms of absolute good and absolute evil," he had told a college audience in 1963. "But in a world of power politics the statesmen must often think in terms of relative values, in terms of power and the struggle for power, in terms of what is possible as well as what is desirable." Echoing Dean Acheson and George Kennan, Fulbright declared that he favored open policies, but not open negotiations. Diplomats should be allowed to bargain in secret; they could then be held accountable for the results at election time. If negotiations were the subject of public scrutiny, failure was all but certain.[5]

At the outset Johnson and his civilian advisers were absolutely opposed to a massive commitment of land forces on the Asian mainland. Infusion of U.S. combat troops, they reasoned, would undercut South Vietnam's prospects for self-reliance, provoke hostile propaganda throughout the developing world, and generate domestic dissent that would threaten the Great Society programs and Johnson's chances for reelection. What course, then, should the United States follow?

He was strongly leaning, the president told Fulbright in a telephone conversation on March 2, 1964, toward doing what the United States had been doing – only better. When the Arkansan asked him if there were any hope of getting "that damn Vietnam straightened out," Johnson outlined the options available. American support for neutralization would lead to the same result as unilateral withdrawal, he declared. He could send marines and U.S. forces in "à la Goldwater," but that would involve American boys in a war "100,000 miles from home," possibly against masses of Chinese Communist troops. The current policy of providing technical and economic aid had not yet failed and he intended to keep it up until it did. Fulbright agreed: "I think that's

5 "Diplomats Backed by Fulbright," *Washington Post,* Mar. 10, 1963.

right . . . that's exactly what I'd arrive at under these circumstances at least for the foreseeable future." He was sending McNamara on a fact-finding trip to Vietnam, Johnson continued. If he found that the United States and its ally were losing, "we've got to decide whether to send them in or whether to come out and let the dominoes fall. That's where the tough one is going to be. And you do some heavy thinking and let's decide what we do."[6]

On March 15, the day following McNamara's return from Saigon, Fulbright went to lunch at the White House. He, Johnson, and Rusk heard from the secretary of defense that the situation had deteriorated since September. In twenty-two of the forty-four provinces the Vietcong controlled 50 percent or more of the land area. There were widespread signs of apathy and indifference. Desertion rates in the South Vietnamese army (ARVN) were on the rise, and draft dodging was pervasive. Morale among the hamlet militia and the Self Defense Corps was failing. General Khanh, head of the ruling Military Revolutionary Council, "though a very able man," lacked broad-based political support and was unsure of the military. After McNamara reiterated his belief that, unless the United States could maintain an independent, noncommunist South Vietnam, all of Southeast Asia would fall into enemy hands, the DOD chief reviewed the objectives with his typical machine-gun delivery. He came down where Johnson wanted him to: The administration should postpone a graduated program of pressure against North Vietnam, including bombing, until needed; the president ought to commit American troops only as a last resort. Through the utilization of military advisers, AID workers, and the latest techniques and equipment, both military and civilian, American personnel should continue to act on the "oil spot" theory, helping the South Vietnamese work outward from areas they already controlled to provide physical and economic security to contiguous territory.[7]

As the Vietnam section of the "old myths and new realities" speech indicated, Fulbright fully supported these recommendations. "I sincerely hope we can keep the situation from collapsing," the Arkansan wrote Will Clayton in early April. A communist takeover in Indochina "would have serious repercussions at home, as well as in Asia."[8]

The dire consequence Fulbright feared at home was the triumph of Barry Goldwater. By the time McNamara made his report, the preconvention campaign of 1964 was well underway. At the Republican convention in San Francisco in mid-July the conservatives completed their long-awaited conquest of

6 Quoted in Kearns, *Johnson and the American Dream,* 204–5.
7 McNamara to LBJ, Mar. 13, 1964, NSF, Memos to President, Box 1, Johnson Papers.
8 JWF to Clayton, Apr. 6, 1964, Alpha File, Folder FU, Papers of Will Clayton, Truman Library.

the GOP. With Goldwater partisans in the driver's seat, the convention derided Governor Nelson Rockefeller of New York, Governor William W. Scranton of Pennsylvania, and moderate, internationalist Republicanism in general. Goldwater was easily nominated on the first ballot, and William E. Miller, a conservative House member and political hatchet man from upstate New York, was chosen as his running mate. "Extremism in the defense of liberty is no vice!" Goldwater told the enraptured delegates in his acceptance speech, adding for good measure "moderation in the pursuit of justice is no virtue!"[9] Goldwater spoke for the "respectable anarchists who wrapped the flag about high-speed Cadillacs and called it American individualism," Harry McPherson has written.[10]

Johnson was just as firmly in control of the Democratic Party machinery as Goldwater was the Republican. There were disgruntled factions: The Kennedyites held the Texan in barely concealed contempt, but because they filled most of the important posts in the administration, they were not about to lead a rebellion. The South was furious with Johnson for his civil rights crusading, but unlike John F. Kennedy, he was one of them. His remarkable success with Congress and his impressive performance as executor of the Kennedy political legacy put him far ahead in the early public opinion polls.

Nonetheless, Goldwater alarmed J. William Fulbright. In Goldwater's person and candidacy, Fulbright believed, were concentrated all of the ignorance, chauvinism, and absolutism against which he had been struggling throughout his political life. Above all, he was worried that Goldwater was fully capable, under the proper circumstances, of touching off World War III. The Republican candidate had earlier urged that NATO commanders be given control of tactical nuclear weapons, and when asked about the situation in Southeast Asia had said, "I'd drop a low-yield atomic bomb on the Chinese supply lines in North Vietnam or maybe shell 'em with the Seventh Fleet."[11] Thus it was that when the Johnson administration came to Fulbright in early August 1964 and asked him to punch through the Senate a resolution authorizing the president to use military force to contain the spread of communism in Indochina, he readily agreed.

As part of his effort to do more of the same and do it more efficiently, Lyndon Johnson appointed General William Westmoreland to head the Military Assistance Command, Vietnam (MACV). Tall, erect, handsome, "Westy" was a fifty-year-old veteran of World War II and Korea with a chestful of

9 Quoted in Dewey W. Grantham, *Recent America: The United States since 1945* (Arlington Heights, Ill., 1987), 257.

10 Harry McPherson, *A Political Education* (New York, 1972), 73.

11 Quoted in Grantham, *Recent America,* 258.

medals. Westmoreland was a corporate executive in uniform, a diligent, disciplined organization man who would obey orders. Like his superior, Robert McNamara, the general saw the war as basically an exercise in management. At the same time he appointed Westmoreland, Johnson named General Maxwell Taylor to replace Lodge, who had allowed the U.S. country team in Vietnam to degenerate into warring factions. A former chairman of the Joint Chiefs of Staff under Kennedy, Taylor, a combat veteran who spoke several languages, was seen as a tough-minded, sophisticated individual who, together with his new deputy, career diplomat U. Alexis Johnson, would blend AID, CIA, MACV, and embassy personnel into an efficient nation-building machine. Within weeks, the new leadership had put together the most formidable American presence in a foreign country ever assembled. American experts in the provinces were teaching Vietnamese peasants to dig wells, breed pigs, build houses, and kill communists. The United States underwrote all of these activities as well as imports of milk, gasoline, fertilizer, and other products with a huge supplemental appropriation – $50 million for military aid and $76 million for nonmilitary – pushed through Congress in mid-1964.[12]

Still the situation in the South continued to deteriorate. As of mid-1964 the Vietcong controlled more than 40 percent of the territory and 50 percent of the population of South Vietnam. Where it could function freely, the government was hampered by a shortage of skilled officials and a lack of clear-cut goals. High desertion rates persisted, with the result that the ARVN remained well below authorized troop levels.[13] All the while, North Vietnam was becoming more deeply involved in the struggle in the south. In mid-1964 Hanoi launched a program to convert the Ho Chi Minh Trail, which ran southward from North Vietnam through Laos and Cambodia entering South Vietnam at various points, from a network of jungle trails to a modern transportation system. This, coupled with the decision taken earlier in the year to introduce regular North Vietnamese Army (NVA) units into the south, meant that by summer's end hundreds and then thousands of veteran North Vietnamese soldiers were taking up positions below the Seventeenth Parallel.

In response to this worsening picture, a number of Johnson's advisers urged him to authorize the use of "selected and carefully graduated military force against North Vietnam."[14] Precisely orchestrated attacks on the north would serve several purposes. "We should strike to hurt but not to destroy," McGeorge Bundy told Johnson, "and strike for the purpose of changing the

12 Bundy to LBJ, May 15, 1964, NSF, Memos to President, Bundy, Box 1, Johnson Papers.

13 NSF Meeting, May 15, 1964, NSC Meeting Notes, Box 1, Johnson Papers.

14 McGeorge Bundy to LBJ, May 25, 1964, NSF, Memos to President, Box 1, Johnson Papers.

North Vietnamese decision on intervention in the south."[15] Johnson's experts also portrayed an attack on the north as the one thing that could save the Khanh government and bring political stability to the south. Bundy and company somehow believed that one major military triumph would suddenly end Buddhist–Catholic infighting, alleviate corruption, raise up a pluralistic democracy, and transform Khanh into a South Vietnamese version of Franklin D. Roosevelt.

Virtually everyone in Johnson's inner circle agreed that it would be necessary to go to Congress for a resolution of approval prior to raining blows on North Vietnam.[16] From May through July Bundy and the NSC staff worked on the content of a congressional resolution and a strategy for passing it. All agreed that the administration should not go to Congress unless and until it was sure of overwhelming support. To this end, it was imperative to wait until the civil rights bill was passed. It would also be necessary to cultivate individual congresspeople and senators and to convince them that the United States had made every effort to solve the Vietnamese problem through the United Nations and other diplomatic channels. The resolution would permit "selective use of force" but would not be a blank check. Administration spokespersons would assure doubters that "hostilities on a larger scale are not envisaged."[17]

According to Robert McNamara, Johnson needed no convincing. Uppermost in the president's mind was the memory of the criticism Harry Truman had sustained for not securing congressional approval for the introduction of troops into Korea. "By God, I'm going to be damn sure those guys are with me when we begin this thing," McNamara remembered Johnson as saying. "They may try to desert me once we get in there!" He was not planning an escalation, McNamara insisted, but he was shrewd enough to realize that events might outrun his ability to control them.[18]

Sensing some unease on Capitol Hill, President Johnson ordered the State Department to schedule meetings with the most powerful members of Congress, especially the Senate, to answer their questions and to line up support for a congressional resolution. Throughout June and July, first the president, then Rusk, and finally Undersecretary of State George Ball met with Mansfield, Russell, Stennis, and Fulbright as well as Minority Leader Dirksen. At those meetings Johnson and his lieutenants assured the senators that the administration did not want nor were they even thinking about a wider war. The congressional resolution they had in mind was designed to demonstrate

15 Bundy to LBJ, May 22, 1964, NSF, Memos to President, Box 1, Johnson Papers.
16 Bundy to LBJ, May 25, 1964, NSF, Memos to President, Box 1, Johnson Papers.
17 Bundy Memo for Discussion, June 10, 1964, NSC File, Memos to President, Box 2, Johnson Papers.
18 Interview with Robert McNamara, Aug. 2, 1991, Washington, D.C.

American unity to Hanoi and to pressure the communists not to overrun South Vietnam and Laos.[19]

The man assigned to deal with Fulbright was George Ball. The two had first met when Ball had testified before Congress on Lend–Lease during World War II. As assistant general counsel to the Lend–Lease Administration, Ball had worked for Oscar Cox, a man for whom Fulbright had immense respect. At the time, Ball had been struck with the young senator's ability to grasp the complexities of the program, especially compared with his colleagues. Over the years Ball, Lippmann (who was Ball's next-door neighbor), Reston, and Fulbright had become personal friends. Like Fulbright, Ball was an Atlanticist – indeed, his assigned task during the Kennedy administration was to secure full British participation in the EEC – and he was skeptical concerning the overall strategic importance of Vietnam. In the summer of 1964, the undersecretary argued to Fulbright that Johnson could be counted on to resist the blandishments of the hawks, especially those on the JCS who wanted to launch a full-scale air and land assault on North Vietnam and communist enclaves in Laos and Cambodia. A Senate debate and resolution, he argued, would be one way to slow down or even prevent escalation.[20]

On the evening of July 26 Fulbright had dinner with the president at the White House. The Arkansan sensed that something was about to happen in Indochina. The Khanh regime was in serious trouble, and it might be necessary to employ additional American force to save it, Johnson confided. He would soon go to Congress and ask for the resolution Ball had been discussing with the Democratic leadership.[21] The president assured him that if for any reason the American mission changed character, he would seek fresh authority from Congress. Then there was the matter of Goldwater, a man who represented everything Fulbright detested: Johnson was determined, he said, to take the "soft on communism" issue away from the Republicans. Fulbright sympathized completely. "I didn't suspect that he [Johnson] was misleading us," he later recalled. "This was in the beginning of the contest between Johnson and Goldwater. I was just overpersuaded, I guess you'd say, in my feeling that I ought to support the president, that he was right and he was not going to escalate the war."[22]

When early in 1964 North Vietnam began to step up its infiltration into the south, the Johnson administration had issued a series of not-so-veiled threats of retaliation. To help counter any possible moves that the Americans and

19 William C. Berman, *William Fulbright and the Vietnam War: The Dissent of a Political Realist* (Kent, Ohio, 1988), 20.
20 Interview with George Ball, July 6, 1990, Princeton, N.J.
21 Berman, *Fulbright and the Vietnam War,* 22.
22 Charles Morrissey interview with J. William Fulbright, "Modern Congress in American History" (Library of Congress, Washington, D.C.), 22.

South Vietnamese might make, Hanoi persuaded the Russians to install modern antiaircraft missiles and radar stations around North Vietnam's main cities and along the broken coastline of bays and islands on the Tonkin Gulf. As contingency planning for possible bombardment, blockade, or invasion of North Vietnam got underway in Washington, military intelligence began gatherng information on this protective network. U-2 flights were able to photograph inland sites, but they were incapable of mapping the coastal installations. For this task, intelligence enlisted South Vietnamese commandos to harass the enemy radar transmitters, thereby activating them so that American electronic intelligence vessels cruising in the Tonkin Gulf could chart their locations. In addition to these operations, code-named DeSoto missions, a State Department–CIA task force under McGeorge Bundy was coordinating OPLAN-34, a top-secret program of infiltration and harassment of North Vietnam by South Vietnamese covert operatives. As 1964 progressed, then, North Vietnamese positions along the gulf coast were subjected to repeated attacks by the high-speed, heavily armed Norwegian speedboats used in the DeSoto program and to landings by OPLAN-34 operatives.

In July Admiral Ulysses Grant Sharp, Jr., commanding U.S. forces in the Pacific, ordered the aircraft carrier *Ticonderoga* to the entrance to the Tonkin Gulf and instructed the destroyer *Maddox* to engage in DeSoto-type patrols off the North Vietnamese coast.

On the night of July 30–31 South Vietnamese commandos in four patrol boats assaulted North Vietnamese positions on the islands of Hon Me and Hon Ngu, three and four miles from the North Vietnamese mainland, respectively. The crackle of North Vietnamese radar signals and radio traffic triggered by the attacks was monitored aboard the *Maddox* and transmitted to a special American intelligence center in the Philippines.

At eleven o'clock on the morning of August 2 the *Maddox* was situated some ten miles out to sea, adjacent to the Red River delta, the northernmost point of its circuit. Suddenly from behind the island of Hon Me, three North Vietnamese patrol boats attacked. As the trio fired their torpedoes, missing, the *Maddox* opened fire and signaled for air support from the *Ticonderoga*. The skirmish, which lasted a bare twenty minutes, ended in a clear-cut American victory. A single bullet struck the *Maddox* harmlessly, while U.S. fire sank one hostile craft and crippled the other two.[23]

Reports of the incident reached Lyndon Johnson on the morning of the same day, Sunday, August 2. Because no American had been hurt, he told his staff, further action was unnecessary; he specifically rejected suggestions

[23] CINCPAC Communiqué, Aug. 3, 1964, Meeting Notes File, Box 2, Johnson Papers.

from the military for reprisals against North Vietnamese targets. At the same time, however, Johnson directed the *Maddox* and another destroyer, the *C. Turner Joy,* as well as protective aircraft, to return to the gulf. The commanders bore with them orders to "attack any force that attacks them."[24] Meanwhile, the JCS and their commanders in the Pacific placed U.S. forces in South Vietnam and Thailand on alert. They pinpointed such targets as harbor installations and oil depots for retaliatory raids.[25] Finally, on August 3, Rusk, McNamara, and Earle Wheeler, chairman of the Joint Chiefs, briefed a combined meeting of the SFRC and Armed Services Committee in executive session. They described the attack on the *Maddox* and the generally deteriorating situation in South Vietnam. Wayne Morse, among others, came out of the meeting convinced that the administration was determined to go to war with North Vietnam. Speaking years later, Fulbright declared that Johnson had missed the significance of the August 2 attack and, realizing that this was just the situation he had been waiting for, maneuvered quickly to create a second one;[26] but if the Arkansan had any such suspicions at the time, he did not voice them.

The night of the fourth was a stormy, moonless one. Around eight o'clock Captain John J. Herrick of the *Maddox* intercepted radio messages seeming to indicate that communist patrol boats were bracing for an assault. Sonar began picking up bleeps on this night that one sailor later described as "darker than the hubs of hell."[27] An hour later the two destroyers started firing in all directions and taking evasive action to avoid North Vietnamese torpedoes. Their officers reported sinking two or perhaps three communist craft during the raid.

The battle report and traffic between the *Maddox* and Honolulu were monitored directly in the situation room in the basement of the White House. Duty officers summoned the president at once. Though his information was still sketchy, Johnson called the congressional leadership, including Fulbright, to the White House on the morning of the fourth and announced that there had been a second, unprovoked, deliberate attack on the *Maddox* and *Turner Joy.* This time, he said, the United States had no choice but to retaliate, and he intended to ask for a resolution of support. After huddling briefly with Fulbright, Aiken, and Hickenlooper, Mansfield "read a paper expressing general opposition." Richard Russell supported retaliation in principle but voiced concern about whether or not the United States had enough manpower and equipment in the area to do the job. Should the United States continue to allow the

24 Quoted in Stanley Karnow, *Vietnam: A History* (New York, 1984), 369.

25 Ibid., 370.

26 Berman, *Fulbright and the Vietnam War,* 23.

27 Quoted in George C. Herring, *America's Longest War: The United States and Vietnam, 1950–1975,* 2d ed. (New York, 1986), 120.

North Vietnamese "to murder us from bases of safety," McNamara asked incredulously. "I think I know what the reaction would be if we tucked our tails."[28] At this point, Johnson chimed in: "Some of our boys are floating around in the water," he said. The Republican leadership – Saltonstall, Halleck, and Dirksen – all expressed support and promised to vote for a congressional resolution. Fulbright came away from the meeting convinced that both attacks had occurred, that they were part of a communist test of American resolve, as Rusk put it, and that the assaults would continue unless the United States responded.[29]

Johnson strolled back to the Oval Office from the meeting with Kenneth O'Donnell, a former Kennedy aide who had stayed on at the White House. Speculating on the potential political effect of the crisis, they agreed that Johnson was "being tested" and would have to respond firmly to defend himself, not against the North Vietnamese but against Barry Goldwater and the Republican right wing. As O'Donnell later wrote, they felt that Johnson "must not allow them to accuse him of vacillating or being an indecisive leader."[30]

Still, Lyndon Johnson, despite his later claims that he did not really need a resolution from Congress to employ additional force in Vietnam or that retaliation against the north in that instance preordained escalation in the future, sensed that he was about to take a momentous step. He ordered McNamara to obtain verification of the second North Vietnamese strike. Unfortunately, Captain Herrick had begun to have second thoughts about whether or not an actual attack had occurred. On the afternoon of the fourth, he cabled CINCPAC, Sharp's headquarters. The entire action had left many doubts, he reported, and he was conducting an immediate investigation. Several hours later he cabled: "Review of action makes many reported contacts and torpedoes fired appear very doubtful. . . . Freak weather effects and overeager sonarmen may have accounted for many reports. No actual sightings by *Maddox*. Suggest complete evaluation before any further action."[31]

Meanwhile, however, the White House believed that it had obtained independent verification that the second attack had occurred. Naval intelligence provided McNamara with a batch of intercepts of North Vietnamese radio flashes that seemed to be ordering their patrol boats into action. Although he was in Martha's Vineyard at the time and was not summoned back to Washington until the afternoon of the fourth, Assistant Secretary of State William Bundy recalled that the intercepts – "get ready, go, we are attacking" – were

28 Summary of Leadership Meeting, Aug. 4, 1964, Meeting Notes File, Box 1, Johnson Papers.

29 Notes Taken at Leadership Meeting, Aug. 4, 1964, Meeting Notes File, Box 1, Johnson Papers.

30 Quoted in Karnow, *Vietnam: A History*, 371.

31 George McT. Kahin, *Intervention: How America Became Involved in Vietnam* (Garden City, N.Y., 1987), 221.

compelling. "These intercepts were certainly taken by all concerned to prove beyond a shadow of a doubt that there had been a second attack."[32] According to McNamara, he and others were not so certain:

> My first reaction was that the first attack might not have occurred, because we'd been wrong on so many damn things – the Cuban missile crisis. So many times we'd gotten erroneous information. . . . We made extensive efforts to insure that we found out what happened inclusive of obtaining fragments of the shells off the deck of the *Maddox*. And actually we had them flown to Washington to be sure that it was the goddamn case. Because the sonar and other evidence is very difficult to interpret. The second attack – to this day I doubt it ever occurred. I think the people who reported it were not trying to deceive. They were reporting their judgment about the sonar evidence. Then, finally we had intercepts of North Vietnamese transmissions indicating that they were saying that the attack had occurred.[33]

Although the Command and Control study of the Tonkin Gulf incident that the Pentagon completed in early 1965 assumed that it did, in all probability the second attack did not occur. In the minds of Johnson and his colleagues, however, the August 4 assault really did not matter.[34] The first had occurred, and to their thinking it had been an unprovoked North Vietnamese assault on American craft in international waters. McNamara later recalled:

> It never entered my mind that they might have been responding to what they considered to be our attack – the covert operations – because they were so unimportant. They were pinpricks; they were accomplishing nothing. I don't believe Bill Bundy or I ever believed they were worth a damn. It never occurred to me that we should check and see whether one of those things was underway at the time.[35]

Johnson accepted his brains trust's conclusions without question and in the late afternoon authorized retaliatory air strikes against North Vietnamese torpedo boat bases and nearby oil storage dumps. The strikes destroyed or

32 Interview with William Bundy, July 5, 1990, Princeton, N.J.

33 McNamara interview. Indeed, in my interview with him McNamara admitted that the intercepts probably were delayed broadcasts relating to the first attack. When confronted with McNamara's admission William Bundy responded: "Mr. McNamara, if I may say so, is an extraordinarily unreliable witness on this and all other matters relating to Vietnam." W. Bundy interview.

34 Office of the Director of Defense Research, Critical Incident Report No. 7, Command and Control of the Tonkin Gulf Incident, Feb. 26, 1965. Document provided to the author by Professor Edwin E. Moise, Clemson University.

35 His testimony is belied by other portions of the historical record. See Kahin, *Intervention,* 221.

damaged twenty-five patrol boats and 90 percent of the oil storage facilities at Vinh. As American jets lifted off the *Ticonderoga* and *Constellation,* Lyndon Johnson appeared on television to report to the nation that an unprovoked attack had taken place against American vessels on the high seas. "Repeated acts of violence against the armed forces of the United States must be met not only with alert defense, but with positive reply. That reply is being given as I speak to you tonight."[36]

On August 5 Fulbright went to the White House, where he agreed to manage the congressional resolution that Johnson would submit to Congress that day. It was clear that the Arkansan never knew about the DeSoto patrols. While Fulbright was closeted with Johnson and McGeorge Bundy on the fifth, the national security adviser assured him that there was no connection between the OPLAN-34-A missions and the presence of the American destroyers in the gulf. Bundy knew better. At the NSC meeting on August 4, when Johnson had asked if Hanoi wanted a war by attacking U.S. ships in the gulf, CIA Director McCone had replied "No. The North Vietnamese are reacting defensively to our attacks on their off-shore islands."[37] Most important, the chairman of the SFRC was not informed about the communiqué from Captain John Herrick of the *Maddox* suggesting the second North Vietnamese attack may not really have occurred. According to Fred Dutton, Fulbright alone among the members of the Democratic leadership had been kept in the dark regarding contingency planning for a military escalation in Vietnam during the spring and summer of 1964. McGeorge Bundy remembered that Johnson already considered Fulbright "a leaker," a man who could not be trusted with sensitive information.[38] Nevertheless, by his own admission Fulbright had known as a result of his July 26 dinner with the president that the administration had been planning some new move in Southeast Asia. He was not surprised by the retaliation against the North Vietnamese patrol boats. What he was ignorant of was the bombing campaign against the north then being considered and that the congressional resolution he was being asked to support would be used as justification for a wider war. In the end Fulbright, who had opposed the 1957 Middle East Resolution, agreed to support and manage a Vietnam resolution. In 1957 he had not trusted the man in the White House; in 1964 he did. Given that he believed Johnson when he said he would not escalate, and needed to demonstrate to the country that he could be tough with North Vietnam in order to fend off Goldwater, it would not have mattered if Fulbright had had the full picture, including Herrick's reservations. What subsequently infuriated him was that he had not been given all

36 Quoted in Karnow, *Vietnam: A History,* 372.
37 Summary Notes of 538 NSC Meeting, Aug. 4, 1964, NSC Meeting Notes File, Box 1, Johnson Papers.
38 McG. Bundy interview.

the pertinent information. J. William Fulbright did not like to be deceived, and he did not like to be used.

On the morning of August 6, George Ball met in Majority Leader Mansfield's offices with him, Fulbright, Russell, Saltonstall, and Aiken. Both Pat Holt, then acting director of the SFRC, and his counterpart for Armed Services, William Darden, were there as well. There was no discussion of substance. It was decided that Fulbright would introduce the resolution as soon as possible, with Russell, Hickenlooper, and Saltonstall cosponsoring. The SFRC and Armed Services committees would hold perfunctory hearings on the morning of the seventh; passage, they anticipated, would come easily that afternoon. Holt and Darden listened with growing incredulity. They remembered the endless debate and soul-searching that had taken place over similar resolutions pertaining to Formosa and the Middle East.[39]

That afternoon Fulbright introduced the Gulf of Tonkin Resolution, which authorized the president to take "all necessary measures to repel any armed attacks against the forces of the United States and to prevent further aggression."[40] Also on the sixth McNamara appeared before a joint session of the SFRC and Armed Services to testify on the resolution. It was plain from the beginning that he would face little opposition. Opinion polls showed that 85 percent of the American people stood behind the administration; most newspaper editorials reflected this support. Nothing was said about the covert raids. Official reports indicated that the *Maddox* was engaged in routine patrols in international waters. The incidents were portrayed as "deliberate attacks" and "open aggression on the high seas."[41] That morning, however, a Pentagon officer had telephoned Wayne Morse with a tip. The *Maddox* had been intimately involved with South Vietnamese raids north of the Seventeenth Parallel, he confided. When the lean, humorless Morse confronted McNamara, however, the Defense secretary flatly denied any relationship. By that point Morse was regarded by many as part of the lunatic fringe, and his insinuations were brushed aside.[42] Indeed, Fulbright and others congratulated the administration on its restraint in dealing with North Vietnam.

Congress responded to the administration's request with amazing alacrity. Senator Ernest Gruening of Alaska attacked the resolution as "a predated declaration of war," and Senator Gaylord Nelson (D–Wisconsin) pointed out that the resolution amounted to a sweeping grant of authority to the executive. Morse demanded to know why American war vessels were menacing the coast of North Vietnam. George McGovern of South Dakota asked incredul-

39 Donald A. Ritchie, interviewer, *Oral History Interviews: Pat M. Holt* (Senate Historical Office: Washington, D.C., 1980), 177–8.

40 Quoted in Herring, *America's Longest War,* 122.

41 Quoted in ibid.

42 Karnow, *Vietnam: A History,* 375.

ously why a tiny nation like North Vietnam would want to provoke a war with the greatest superpower in the history of the world. One by one Fulbright responded to the questions and criticisms. The *Maddox* had been attacked without provocation, and the American reaction was entirely justified as an act of self-defense under article 45 of the U.N. Charter. "It would be a great mistake," he declared, "to allow our optimism about promising developments in our relations with the Soviet Union and Eastern Europe to lead us to any illusions about the aggressive designs of North Vietnam and its Chinese Communist sponsor." He did not know what the limits on the president's power to take action in Vietnam were under the terms of the resolution, he told Nelson. "I personally feel it would be very unwise under any circumstances to put a large land army on the Asian Continent," he said, but that decision was one for the executive to make. It could be trusted. What was needed at that point was national unity and proof of resolve, and that is precisely what the resolution provided.[43] Behind the scenes Fulbright gave his personal assurances to McGovern and other doubters.[44]

The Senate debated the Gulf of Tonkin Resolution less than ten hours; for much of the time the chamber was less than one-third full. Fulbright carefully guided the resolution through, choking off debate and amendments. In the Senate only Morse and Gruening dissented; the final vote was 88 to 2. Consideration in the House was even more perfunctory, passage taking a mere forty minutes. With the Gulf of Tonkin Resolution out of the way, Fulbright could turn his attention to the final stages of the 1964 campaign.

When the Democratic delegates to the national convention met in Atlantic City in mid-August, Johnson's nomination was a foregone conclusion. The gathering divided its time between tributes to the Texan, who was nominated on his fifty-sixth birthday, and attacks on the bellicose conservative from Arizona. With Betty and Lady Bird watching together from the galleries, Fulbright stood before the assembled delegates to deliver the second nominating speech:

> I know him well. He has a genius for reconciling the irreconcilable, for resolving differences among many of deep conviction. The same understanding of human nature which enabled him to lead the Senate so effectively during a difficult period in our history will enable him to find a way to resolve differences which exist among nations. . . . I commend Lyndon Johnson to this convention and to all our people as a man of understanding with the wisdom to use the great power of our nation in the cause of peace.[45]

43 *Congressional Record,* Senate, Aug. 6, 1964, 18399–407.
44 Interview with George McGovern, June 27, 1991, Washington, D.C.
45 Ned Curran, "Fulbright Seconds Nomination of LBJ with High Praise," *Arkansas Gazette,* Aug. 27, 1964.

With Johnson's pro-forma nomination wrapped up, Fulbright hit the campaign trail with a vengeance:

> The foreign policy issue in this campaign is as profound as any that has ever arisen between the two great American political parties. The Goldwater Republicans propose a radical new policy of relentless ideological conflict aimed at the elimination of Communism and the imposition of American concepts of freedom on the entire world. The Democrats under President Johnson propose a conservative policy of opposing and preventing Communist expansion while working for limited agreements that will reduce the danger of nuclear war.[46]

In a speech dripping with sarcasm, Fulbright compared Goldwater's view of Soviet–American relations with a Gary Cooper movie: "Who ever heard of cowboys coexisting with Indians? Who ever heard of Wyatt Earp coexisting with Jesse James?"[47] In early October he delivered two speeches in Phoenix, Goldwater's hometown. "I'm just returning his visit," a grinning Fulbright told reporters.[48] As the campaign progressed, the Democrats hammered away at "Goldwater the Trigger Happy."[49] The Republicans thought that they might turn the campaign around when in October longtime Johnson aide Walter Jenkins was caught in a compromising position in a YMCA men's room in Washington; but alas for the GOP, the people were not interested.

The election returns on November 3 confirmed the opinion polls' forecast of a Democratic landslide. The Johnson–Humphrey ticket received a total of 43.1 million popular votes to 27.1 million for Goldwater and Miller. The Democrats carried forty-four states with a record 486 electoral votes. Only an unusual amount of ticket splitting saved the Republicans from being annihilated in the congressional races; still, the Democrats added to their existing majorities by gaining thirty-eight seats in the House and two in the Senate.

Of the southern senators, it was Fulbright who had worked the hardest for Lyndon Johnson. He was primarily responsible for keeping Arkansas in the Democratic column while five other southern states went Republican. Sensing Goldwater's strength, Faubus had remained on the sidelines.[50] Betty Fulbright wrote Judy Foote describing the campaign in Arkansas:

> We are down here until election, – trying to do what we can to help the ticket. It is quite frightening – the number of otherwise sane and sensible people who are just blindly for Goldwater. It is nearly all based on the race question and Bill is thinking of doing a speech

46 *Congressional Record,* Senate, Aug. 15, 1964, 19786.
47 Ibid.
48 Curran, "Fulbright Seconds Nomination."
49 Quoted in Allen J. Matusow, *The Unraveling of America: A History of Liberalism in the 1960s* (New York, 1984), 147.
50 Lee Williams to J. R. Johnson, Sept. 2, 1964, Series 2:6, Box 23:2, SPF.

> on television asking if they want to turn off the road of progress – down a blind alley of bitterness and frustration.[51]

It was indicative of how great a threat Fulbright considered Goldwater that he did in fact appeal to his fellow Arkansans to bury the civil rights issue and move on to more important business. When Rev. Billy James Hargis, chaplain to the radical right, began openly campaigning for Goldwater, Fulbright succeeded in persuading the IRS to revoke the tax-exempt status of his Christian Crusade.[52] By contrast, Richard Russell went to Europe, and Georgia went Republican for the first time in a hundred years. When, following the election, Johnson had Russell to the ranch for a three-day visit while ignoring Fulbright, the Arkansan was hurt. Nevertheless, he and Betty cabled the Johnsons: "What a team you are!! Heartfelt congratulations to both of you from both of us, and all best wishes for happy and fulfilling years ahead."[53]

Some have speculated that Fulbright's enthusiasm for Johnson – indeed, his support of the Gulf of Tonkin Resolution – stemmed from his desire to replace Dean Rusk as secretary of state. There is no doubt some truth in the argument. A number of people had been touting the Arkansan. "I have never talked with you about Bill Fulbright," John Kenneth Galbraith wrote Johnson. "It has always been my feeling that Kennedy's most serious mistake was in not following his first instincts and making Bill Secretary of State."[54] But there was never any chance that Johnson would have chosen Fulbright. The Texan demanded absolute loyalty from his team; once a decision was made there must be no dissent or hanging back, and certainly no public discussion. The Arkansan, Johnson and Bundy perceived, could not be counted on. If he felt the administration was headed in the wrong direction, he would "leak" – a term Johnson applied to those who voiced their misgivings in public.[55]

Fulbright would deny that he wanted to be Johnson's secretary of state just as he rejected the notion that he would have accepted the job from John F. Kennedy. Whatever his innermost ambitions, he would have supported Johnson and the Gulf of Tonkin Resolution anyway. The Texan's shortcomings, his tendency to equate process with substance, means with ends, his willfulness and impetuosity, his personal insecurity, his penchant for blurring ideological and policy lines for the sake of consensus – these paled in contrast to Goldwater. All things were possible with Johnson, Fulbright was convinced, whereas with Goldwater disaster was a certainty.

51 Betty Fulbright to Judy Foote, Oct. 15, 1964, letter in possession of Bosey Foote.
52 JWF to Douglas Dillon, Aug. 7, 1964, Series 3:4, Box 6:4, SPF.
53 Betty and Bill to Lyndon and Lady Bird, Nov. 6, 1964, letter in possession of Bosey Foote.
54 Galbraith to Johnson, Feb. 21, 1964, Conference File, Box 139, SPF.
55 McG. Bundy interview.

With Roberta dead and Helen in poor health, the prospect of traveling to Fayetteville for Christmas had grown less and less attractive for Bill and Betty. Both Betsey and Bosey were married, the latter in April 1964 to Thaddeus (Tad) Foote, the young lawyer and cousin of Adlai Stevenson with whom she'd attended her sister's wedding four years earlier. The Winnackers, who now had two small children, lived in Washington, whereas Bosey and Tad had put down roots in St. Louis. With Roberta gone, there was no one in Fayetteville to manage the logistics of family get-togethers, and the Fulbrights were never ones for pitching in and helping out. Consequently, Bill and Betty spent the Christmas of 1964 at home in Washington.

Despite his increasingly high profile, Fulbright remained one of the most private people in Washington. Unlike others whose names were household words, neither Cave Dwellers nor members of official Washington heard stories about Fulbright's personal life; his name seemed forever absent from the gossip-cocktail circuit. He remained personally self-effacing. His staff recalled that when he took the underground tunnel from the Senate Office Building to the Capitol, he inevitably walked instead of taking the trolley, and he always kept deferentially to the wall, like a novice in training for convent. This was quite in contrast to figures like Jacob Javits and Henry Jackson of Washington, who were followed virtually everywhere they went by an entourage of staffers and admirers.

If there were other women in Fulbright's life, there is no evidence of a meaningful relationship. He most certainly had opportunities. Fulbright was still a striking man. His obsession with health and exercise kept him fit. The ex-Razorback weighed only five pounds more than he had in college. His hair was thinning in front and was more gray than not, but his chiseled features, dimpled chin, and cool blue eyes still turned female heads. Fulbright liked women and could be as charming as anyone in Washington.

As a couple, the Fulbrights were much more eastern establishment than southern aristocrat. Their friends were the Lippmanns, the Cliffords, Douglas Dillon and his wife, and Eugene Black. It was not unusual for Bill and Betty during their intermittent trips to New York to lunch with John D. Rockefeller III and his wife, Blanchette.[56] In 1959, to the delight of R. B. McCallum, then the Master of Pembroke College, Fulbright was appointed a Regent of the Smithsonian. "You must be the first member of the College to hold that position," McCallum remarked, and noted that Smithson had once attended Oxford under the name of Macey.[57] Meanwhile, Betty became a prime mover in the International Student House. They both took an intense interest in developing the capital city's cultural life, which was retarded to say the least.

56 JWF to Rockefeller, Dec. 22, 1964, Series 1:2, Box 5:1, SPF.
57 McCallum to JWF, May 18, 1959, BCN 105, F54, SPF.

In the mid-1950s the Fulbrights had attended the Bolshoi Ballet with the Russian ambassador. The gala event was staged in the city's largest and finest theater: a tiny, drafty, outdated wooden structure located downtown. Fulbright remembered being acutely embarrassed. Here was the world's greatest power hosting one of the world's most celebrated cultural entities in surroundings befitting a Little Theater group. To him the event seemed to symbolize the materialism that had gripped America and to highlight the nation's cultural and educational backwardness, even in comparison to a "backward" and totalitarian society like the Soviet Union. He resolved to remedy this shortcoming.[58]

In 1958 Fulbright had shepherded through both houses of Congress legislation creating the National Cultural Center. Its focus was to be on the performing arts: theater, opera, and folk and classical music. The legislation donated federal land for the project – but provided for no appropriations. Fulbright and Lee Williams actually drove around the city and picked out the site. The preferred location was on the Mall just down from the Smithsonian, but that was preempted by the Air and Space Museum. The two Arkansans finally settled on an undeveloped tract of land on the banks of the Potomac near Georgetown. Fulbright persuaded the president of the Riggs National Bank to become treasurer of a private fund-raising drive, and over the next five years, Betty, Bill, and their helpers raised $14 million for the estimated $45 million project.[59] John F. Kennedy's death spawned a dozen or more memorial projects. Sensing an opportunity, Fulbright introduced legislation two weeks after the assassination renaming the National Cultural Center the John F. Kennedy Center for the Performing Arts. The new bill appropriated $15.4 million and authorized another $15.4 million in loans.[60] Work on what was to be the finest cultural facility of its day was completed in 1971. The architect for the Kennedy Center was none other than Edward Durell Stone, Fulbright's old Fayetteville chum.

58 Interview with J. William Fulbright, Oct. 11–18, 1988, Washington, D.C.

59 Ibid.

60 *Congressional Record,* Dec. 18, 1963, 25032–3.

# 19

# *Escalation*

John Newhouse, the SFRC's designated Southeast Asia expert, recalled that he had experienced considerable difficulty in persuading Fulbright to focus on Vietnam during the Kennedy administration and the first stages of the Johnson presidency. He seemed more interested in Europe, in foreign aid, and the exchange program. Several times when Newhouse brought up the Indochinese situation, Fulbright accused him of trying to make a mountain out of a molehill.[1] Then, in May of 1964, a horrifying picture in the *Washington Post* caught Pat Holt's attention. A prostrate Vietcong guerrilla, clad only in his undershorts, was being chained to an armored personnel carrier on a riverbank by South Vietnamese soldiers. They would drag him back and forth through the stream in an effort to get him to talk. Revolted and angered by the scene, Holt took the picture to Fulbright, who reacted similarly. "I want to know if this is the kind of advice the numerous American advisers are giving the Vietnamese," Fulbright subsequently wrote Robert McNamara. Aside from the fact that torture was morally repugnant, he declared, it was counterproductive as well. If the struggle in Vietnam was basically political, that is, one for the hearts and minds of the Vietnamese people, then such abuses would play into the hands of the communists, especially in view of the fact that they came hard on the heels of reports of "napalm bombing of innocent villagers simply because the presence of Viet Cong is suspected." Even without reports of torture and indiscriminate bombing, Fulbright told McNamara, he had become "gravely concerned" over the situation in Vietnam.[2]

In fact, Newhouse's warnings concerning the deteriorating situation in Vietnam had not, as he first thought, fallen on deaf ears. One of his best friends and most reliable contacts in East Asia, *Time–Life* correspondent Stanley Karnow, had been providing Newhouse with detailed reports on the situation in Indochina. "Militarily we may be dropping more napalm than ever," he wrote in one, "but this is a political situation, and the heart of the matter is that we're trying to help a regime that can't help itself."[3] Fulbright,

1 Interview with John Newhouse, June 27, 1991, Washington, D.C.
2 JWF to McNamara, Box 2, JWF Papers, SFRC, RG 46, NA.
3 Newhouse to JWF, Dec. 25, 1964, Series 48:1, Box 35:1, SPF.

and more important perhaps, Marcy and Holt, read those reports. In December Fulbright played golf with David Ness, a Foreign Service officer with extensive experience in Vietnam. "In selecting Vietnam to demonstrate that we can meet successfully the challenge of 'wars of liberation,'" he told the Arkansan, "we could not, in my opinion, have chosen more disastrously."[4]

By the end of November 1964 the movement within the Joint Chiefs of Staff, the Pentagon, and certain levels of the State Department in support of what Maxwell Taylor described as a "carefully orchestrated bombing attack" against North Vietnam was cresting. A variety of justifications in behalf of air warfare emerged: Bombing would force Ho and his colleagues to halt infiltration into the south, it would reassure Saigon of America's commitment, and it might even force an end to the fighting in South Vietnam. For many in the military, there merely seemed to be a job to do and they were eager to do it.[5]

Despite Lyndon Johnson's obsession with secrecy, reports that the administration was considering a bombing campaign against North Vietnam began appearing in the press in early December. Hints of an impending escalation, coupled with reports of a deteriorating political and military situation in Vietnam, prompted Carl Marcy to write a comprehensive analysis for his boss. In the first place, he insisted, the assumptions underlying escalation were erroneous. As proved to be the case in Europe during World War II and then in Korea, destruction of the enemy's industrial base by air had very little impact on their will or ability to fight. In the second, it was absurd and contrary to historical precedent to believe that, once Americans became directly involved in carrying out combat missions, the country would permit defeat. Escalation could very well lead to a protracted, bloody conflict. Moreover, Marcy inquired, was there a political and cultural entity south of the Seventeenth Parallel to defend? In its effort to build a nation, the Johnson administration was relying on a military dictatorship and in the process offending the democratic sensibilities of both Vietnamese and Americans. It was probably an ironic truth that only a totalitarian regime would be strong enough to fight a war against the communists and keep the peace in South Vietnam; but in the end, such a regime would prove incapable of winning the hearts and minds of the people and so incapable of ruling. In addition, without the quick knockout on which the administration was clearly counting, the American people would begin to question the ideological justification for the war and ultimately to ask whether their interests were really tied up with those of Southeast Asia. As it

4 Ness to JWF, Dec. 16, 1964, Series 48:11, Box 35:1, SPF.

5 Quoted in George C. Herring, *America's Longest War: The United States and Vietnam, 1950–1975,* 2d ed. (New York, 1986), 124.

became apparent that they were not, "the American public would object vigorously."

Echoing earlier administration papers on the subject, Marcy asserted that the United States had three options available to it in Vietnam. It could continue on its present course, expand its military role, or initiate "a planned, phased contraction of United States military assistance" ending with "neutralization and ultimate withdrawal." It was the third course that the chief of staff recommended. Withdrawal and neutralization would not have the dire consequences American hawks predicted. "The 'domino theory' has never been proven in history," he pointed out. "Faced by foreign domination of a great power, coalitions have always emerged to challenge that power." The specter of Chinese imperialism had only served to stimulate Japanese, Filipino, Indonesian, Indian, and Pakistani nationalism. The United States and the Soviet Union, Marcy concluded, had become the world's most important status quo powers. There was every possibility that the two could cooperate in fostering an independent, unified, and truly nonaligned Vietnam.[6] Thus in a single memo did the chief of staff explode the myths that underlay American involvement in Vietnam and foreshadow the disaster that was in store for the nation.

Fulbright conveyed his and Marcy's concerns over Vietnam to Johnson during various conversations, but the president and his advisers attributed the Arkansan's warnings to personal pique rather than to any true insight into the problem. The first week in December, McGeorge Bundy told Johnson:

> Carl Marcy called me this morning to say that Fulbright is in a rather difficult mood at the moment because he fears war in Vietnam and is at odds with us also on the organization of the AID program. Finally, his nose is out of joint over the Cultural Center, where he thinks Eisenhower has been given too much credit and he too little. I relate it not to add to your troubles, but simply to mark it down as an objective report in case you happen to want to give Fulbright a coat of butter.[7]

If Johnson subjected Fulbright to "the treatment," it apparently did not take, and the chairman began to air his concerns in public. Stepping up the war in Vietnam would be "senseless," Fulbright told students at Southern Methodist University in December 1964, and declared America's involvement to have been a mistake in the first place. He agreed with General Douglas MacArthur, he told a press conference that followed: The United States should never become bogged down in a land war in Asia.[8] Surprisingly, Fulbright's Dallas

6 Memorandum on Vietnam, Dec. 22, 1964, Box 4, Folder Oct.–Dec., Marcy Papers.

7 Bundy to LBJ, Dec. 9, 1964, NSF, Memos to President, Bundy, Box 2, Johnson Papers.

8 UPI 27, Dec. 9, 1964, Series 48:1, Box 6:3, SPF.

speech received almost no attention in the national press, and Marcy's efforts to peddle it to *Foreign Affairs* fell flat.[9]

Fulbright was not alone among Democratic congressional leaders in his misgivings and warnings. Mike Mansfield, a Pacific veteran and self-appointed expert on Asia, had never forgiven Kennedy's advisers for their complicity in the demise of the Ngo brothers. He told Johnson that escalation would involve the United States in a prolonged, costly conflict and saddle the country with a permanent dependency.[10] In mid-December Senator Frank Church (D–Idaho) called for a congressional debate on Southeast Asia. In a survey of eighty-three senators the AP reported that only seven favored the dispatching of troops or the bombing of North Vietnam, whereas a substantial number supported negotiations either then or whenever the military balance would permit.[11] Given the administration's commitment to maintain an independent, noncommunist South Vietnam, however, there was nothing to negotiate.

In vain did Johnson, Rusk, the Bundy brothers, and McNamara wait for a Vietnamese Winston Churchill to emerge from the political morass in Saigon. In late 1964 General Nguyen Khanh sacked his civilian cabinet and instituted military rule in South Vietnam. Buddhist-led demonstrations swept the country, and in late January five thousand students rampaged through the United States Information Service library in Hué, destroying everything in their path.

On the very day that Khanh ousted his civilian government, McGeorge Bundy and Robert McNamara met with Lyndon Johnson to have "a very private discussion of the basic situation in Vietnam." The policy of the United States, they observed, had been just to sit around and wait for a stable government to emerge in the south. That, it was obvious, was not going to happen by itself. The United States was going to have to take a more active role – not politically, or economically, but militarily.[12] Instead of attributing the instability in Vietnam to the absence of experienced political parties, a tradition of democracy, sectarian hatreds, or military domination of the political system, Bundy and McNamara told their chief that lack of physical security in the provinces and the United States' refusal to do anything about it was to blame.

9 Marcy to Hamilton Fish Armstrong, Dec. 18, 1964, Box 4, Folder Oct.–Dec., Marcy Papers.

10 Bundy to LBJ, Dec. 16, 1964, NSC File, Memos to President, Box 2, Johnson Papers.

11 William C. Berman, *William Fulbright and the Vietnam War: The Dissent of a Political Realist* (Kent, Ohio, 1988), 33.

12 Bundy to LBJ, Jan. 27, 1965, NSC File, Memos to President, Box 2, Johnson Papers.

Despite the fact that their recommendations made absolutely no sense, except in the context of the "good doctor" analogy, and that Dean Rusk, who was out of town at the time, disagreed with them, Johnson bit. Suddenly the patient who was too sick to fight seemed in danger of being murdered. No formal decision was taken, but by the close of 1964 most administration officials agreed that the United States should seize the first opportunity to launch air strikes and then build that initiative into a sustained bombing campaign against North Vietnam.

In early 1965 America was so deeply involved in every aspect of the war in Vietnam that an incident that could be used to justify a bombing campaign occurred virtually every week. On February 6, Vietcong units attacked a U.S. Army barracks in Pleiku and a nearby helicopter base, killing nine Americans and destroying five aircraft. Following a brief evening meeting with his advisers, Johnson ordered retaliatory strikes. In accordance with Flaming Dart, a plan of reprisal already drawn up by the JCS, American aircraft struck North Vietnamese military installations just across the Seventeenth Parallel.

On February 8 Johnson met with congressional leaders, including Fulbright, to brief them. He cited the Gulf of Tonkin Resolution and "the legal power of the Presidency" as justification for his action. His intent he said, was "to carry out at a manageable level an effort to deter, destroy and diminish the strength of the North Vietnamese aggressors and to try to convince them to leave South Vietnam alone." The views of a few senators would not be allowed to control his actions, he warned.[13] Fulbright's only response was to express misgivings about bombing the north while Alexsei Kosygin, who at the time was paying an official visit to Ho Chi Minh in Hanoi, was in the vicinity.[14] There was little danger of a break with the Soviets, administration spokesmen declared, because the bombing was a specific retaliation for the attack on the American barracks at Pleiku.

Sensing disaster, George McGovern, then a young, first-term senator from South Dakota, screwed up his courage and made an appointment with the president. The Oval Office with Johnson's persona inhabiting it was more than a little intimidating, McGovern recalled. Well aware that his guest was opposed to escalation, the president began. "Well, George," he said, "you know, we're dealing with a bunch of communist bastards here. John McCone [head of the CIA] was in here the other day. He reported that the communists are moving in Central America. The Chinese are moving into Africa. You know that they want to take over Asia." McGovern dared to point out that the Chinese and Vietnamese had been fighting each other for a thousand

13 Summary Notes of 547th NSC Meeting with Cong. Leaders, Feb. 8, 1965, NSC Meeting Notes, Box 1, Johnson Papers.

14 Berman, *Fulbright and the Vietnam War,* 34.

years. "It's hard for me to believe that Ho Chi Minh is a stooge of the Chinese." The Texan exploded: "Goddamn it, George, you and Fulbright and all you history teachers down there. I haven't got time to fuck around with history. I've got boys on the line out there. I can't be worried about history when there are boys out there who might die before morning."[15]

When the Vietcong on February 10 attacked an American enlisted men's quarters at Qui Nhon, the president ordered another, even heavier series of air strikes. In April American and South Vietnamese pilots flew a total of thirty-six hundred sorties against North Vietnamese targets. The White House approved the use of napalm, and pilots were given the authority to strike alternative targets without prior authorization if the original targets were inaccessible.

In explaining the bombing campaign to Congress and the American people, Johnson was, to use George Herring's phrase, "less than candid."[16] Clearly, Rolling Thunder was a turning point in the eyes of the administration. "We face the choice of going for war or running," the president had told his advisers on February 8. "We have chosen the first alternative."[17] But Johnson and his spokesmen justified the air strikes as a response to the attacks on Pleiku and Qui Nhon and emphatically denied implementing any basic change of policy.[18] "Those dirty rotten bastards sneaked up on them [the American soldiers at Pleiku] in the middle of the night and plugged them right in their beds," Johnson told George McGovern.[19]

In the days following the decision to bomb, pressure mounted on the administration from both the right and left to justify its actions publicly. National Security Adviser McGeorge Bundy urged his chief to resist that pressure and avoid mobilizing public opinion. The task ahead was to make it clear to the foreign affairs establishment and the military that a "major watershed decision" had been taken while concealing from the American public that the United States had assumed direct responsibility for the war.[20] The president acceded. Johnson, in fact, seemed not nearly as worried about congressional and public opinion – he could control those, he was sure – as he was about future investigations and his place in history. Throughout the decision-making process, Johnson insisted on a full and free debate – for the record at least. "At some time in the future a brutal prosecutor like Tom Dewey might be

15 Interview with George McGovern, June 27, 1991, Washington, D.C.

16 Herring, *America's Longest War,* 131.

17 Partial Record of Feb. 8, 1965, Meeting with President by group that met before NSC Meeting, Feb. 8, 1965, NSC Meeting Notes, Box 1, Johnson Papers.

18 "At an appropriate time we could publicly announce that we had turned a corner and changed our policy," Bundy had advised Johnson, "but . . . no mention should be made now of such a decision." Summary Record of NSC Meeting No. 548, Feb. 10, 1965, NSC Meeting Notes, Box 1, Johnson Papers.

19 McGovern interview.

20 Bundy to LBJ, Feb. 16, 1965, NSC File, Memos to President, Box 2, Johnson Papers.

asking how we got into these troubles," he confided to his advisers, "and he wanted to be sure that the answers would be good."[21]

Fulbright was present at the various briefings on Vietnam and spoke with Johnson personally on both February 8 and 14. The president convinced him that the bombing of the north was necessary to get the negotiating process started:

> We face several bad alternatives. The thing is to find one resulting in the least evil. The raids in North Vietnam are intended to create conditions that will make the Communists want to negotiate. As of now, there is no one to negotiate with and nothing to negotiate about, so we have to build up pressure for negotiation.[22]

Convinced that the bombing was only a tactical maneuver designed to avoid a much larger war, the Arkansan promised Johnson his continued public support. In mid-March on *Meet the Press* Fulbright again expressed his conviction that the air raids were necessary, and declared that the situation in Vietnam was then so critical that a public debate either by the SFRC or the Congress as a whole would be dangerous.[23] Like most other Americans, Fulbright did not realize that a most important corner had been turned, that the administration was assuming direct responsibility for winning the war.

Anticipating Vietcong attacks against U.S. air bases in retaliation for the bombing of the north, General Westmoreland in late February urgently requested two Marine landing teams to protect the air base at Danang. Although Maxwell Taylor objected and pointed out some of the long-term implications, Johnson and his advisers agreed almost routinely. On March 8 two battalions of Marines, clad in full battle dress and complete with tanks and eight-inch howitzers, splashed ashore near Danang, where they were welcomed by the mayor and a delegation of local beauties who adorned the soldiers with leis.

As Taylor had predicted, once troops were introduced, it proved very difficult to control the escalation process. At a summit conference in Honolulu in late April, McNamara, Taylor, and the Joint Chiefs put aside their differences and agreed upon a strategy whose object was to "break the will of the DRV/VC by depriving them of victory."[24] They decided to dispatch to Vietnam some forty thousand additional combat troops. Rather than being used without restriction to help the ARVN defeat the Communists as Westmoreland wanted, however, they stipulated that the additional soldiers were to be employed in an "enclave strategy." Positioned around major American military installations, the troops would restrict their operations to a fifty-mile radius of

21 Memorandum for the Record, NSC File, Memos to President, Box 2, Johnson Papers.
22 Quoted in Berman, *Fulbright and the Vietnam War,* 35.
23 *Meet the Press,* transcript, Mar. 14, 1965, Vol. 9, No. 9, Merkle Press.
24 Quoted in Herring, *America's Longest War,* 132.

their base. The administration hoped that this limited commitment of forces would be adequate to prevent the enemy from delivering a knockout blow, thus allowing time for the South Vietnamese to establish a viable government and to build an effective fighting force.

News that the administration had introduced ground combat troops into Vietnam and that Westmoreland was asking for a gradual buildup to three hundred thousand, coupled with the international outcry over the bombing of the north, caused Fulbright increasing anxiety. The second week in March Lee Williams attended a cocktail party at the Bulgarian Embassy and reported that "the Russians are terribly disturbed about our aggressive actions in Viet Nam." That report was confirmed when Fulbright subsequently spent two hours with Ambassador Anatoly Dobrynin at the Soviet embassy. The strikes on North Vietnam were "causing deep embarrassment and concern" to the Kremlin, Fulbright's Russian friend told him, and it would be necessary at the very least for the Soviet Union to step up arms aid. For Fulbright the central issue of the age continued to be peace and rapprochement with the Soviet Union. He was terrified that the conflict in Southeast Asia would lead to a great-power confrontation.

In Fulbright's view, it was the duty of the Democratic leadership to present the president with alternatives, and that is what the chairman of the SFRC, in consultation with Lippmann and Marcy, set out to do in the spring of 1965. Following his conversations with Dobrynin, the Arkansan proposed a halt in the bombing in return for Russian pressure on North Vietnam to staunch the flow of men and material into the south. According to the scenario that he developed, as hostilities ground to a halt in Indochina, the USSR and United Kingdom would reconvene the Geneva Conference, with all parties agreeing to abide by the results of free, nationwide elections in Vietnam. He was convinced, he said, that overtures toward negotiations would be "received with rejoicing" in Moscow.[25] The United States must be willing to accept the legitimacy of an independent, nationalist, and united Vietnam. By strengthening its ties to the Soviet Union, this Yugoslav-style entity could serve as a counterweight to China. At all costs the United States must avoid committing a large land army to the war in Vietnam because such a move would inevitably involve the country in a "bloody and interminable conflict in which the advantage would lie with the enemy." A major war in Asia, Fulbright predicted, "could be expected to poison the political life of the United States, undoing the beneficial results of the election of 1964 and reviving the influence of irresponsible and extremist political movements."[26]

25 JWF to Rusk, Mar. 12, 1965, Series 2:1, Box 4:2, SPF.

26 Quoted in Berman, *Fulbright and the Vietnam War,* 36.

Fulbright voiced his criticism of America's course in Vietnam privately, but others were not so discreet. Although the administration had attempted to conceal the direction of its policy, the obvious expansion of the war, particularly the bombing, had created widespread misgivings and provoked isolated outcries. White House mail ran heavily against the aerial assault. A few newspapers had joined with the *New York Times* in warning of the cost of "lives lost, blood spilt and treasure wasted, of fighting a war on a jungle front 7,000 miles from the coast of California."[27] Faculty members at Harvard, Michigan, and Syracuse conducted all-night "teach-ins"; students on various campuses held small protest meetings and distributed petitions against the bombing; and in April twenty thousand young people gathered in Washington to march in protest against the war. Congressional doubters, such as Frank Church, Wayne Morse, and George McGovern, echoed Charles de Gaulle's call for a negotiated settlement. The White House responded by organizing "Target: College Campuses." White House staffers and State Department personnel fanned out across the country to spread the gospel of a holy war against communism. Morse and company suddenly found their control over federal patronage threatened.

Johnson did not respond directly to Fulbright's proposal. Instead he delivered a major policy address on Vietnam at Johns Hopkins on the evening of April 7. The speech was carefully crafted to appeal to both hawks and doves – those terms had just come into current usage – and as a result it featured both carrot and stick. The Texan consulted frequently and extensively with Lippmann prior to the speech and closeted himself for ninety minutes with Mansfield and Fulbright going over the draft in detail. The president began by condemning communist aggression in Southeast Asia and reiterating America's determination to stand by its gallant allies in South Vietnam. Shifting to neutral ground, Johnson declared his administration ready for "unconditional discussions." He then moved on to the bait. If the people of North Vietnam would agree to act henceforward in a spirit of "peaceful cooperation," the United States would put up $1 billion to fund a massive regional development project that "would dwarf even our own TVA."[28] The afternoon of the seventh Johnson called Eugene Black, head of the World Bank, and asked him to administer the project. Black protested that he was too busy, but then succumbed to the Johnson treatment. The president knew that Black and the chairman of the SFRC were close friends; inclusion of the financier would, as Bundy put it, "neutralize Fulbright."[29]

Despite the Johns Hopkins speech, the United States had no real desire to begin negotiations when its political and battlefield positions were so weak.

27 Quoted in Herring, *America's Longest War,* 133.

28 Kathleen J. Turner, *Lyndon Johnson's Dual War: Vietnam and the Press* (Chicago, 1985), 128–9.

29 Ibid., 127.

The administration had not even developed goals and strategy for the "unconditional" talks it had proposed. Most important, the president had made it clear in his Johns Hopkins speech that the United States would not compromise on its fundamental objective: the preservation of an independent, noncommunist South Vietnam.

Fulbright was encouraged by the Johnson's April 7 address, particularly by the invitation to North Vietnam and the Soviet Union to participate in the Mekong River project; but at the same time he had come to the conclusion that North Vietnam had been "softened up" enough and that negotiations could never start without a bombing halt. He did not relish differing with the administration in public, Fulbright told reporters, but the bombing was only causing the North Vietnamese to "dig in" and the Russians to refuse to talk. What harm, he asked, would there be to stopping the aerial assault temporarily in an effort to get talks started?[30] When Dean Rusk publicly brushed off the chairman's proposal, Carl Marcy blew his top. "I think the time has come for Mr. Rusk to go," he told Fulbright. He had been all right under Kennedy, who was able to act as his own secretary of state, but Lyndon Johnson was "a babe in the woods in the field of foreign policy."[31]

Fulbright's pleas for a bombing halt struck a chord with the public. Although Joseph Alsop, America's most hawkish commentator, berated him, the Arkansan's mail ran strongly in favor of a bombing suspension. Marcy released the figures to reporters, which in turn led to direct pressure on the White House.[32] In early May, reluctantly, indeed resentfully, Johnson approved a five-day suspension of American air raids. In reality, he accepted the idea only because the administration could then tell "Mansfield, Fulbright and the *New York Times*" that the administration had held out the olive branch, and Hanoi had "spit in our face." Even then, the Texan thought it all a waste of time. Increasingly influenced by Dean Acheson, he declared, "I'm afraid if we play along with this group, we will wind up with no one on our side. My judgment is that the public has never wanted us to stop the bombing."[33] During the pause the State Department informed Hanoi that if and when NVA and VC military activity decreased, air attacks would be permanently scaled down. Ho Chi Minh denounced the bombing pause as a "worn-out trick of deceit and threat," and refused to curb military operations.

30 "Stopping Raids Might Pay Off, Fulbright Says," *Arkansas Gazette*, Apr. 19, 1965.

31 Marcy to JWF, Apr. 20, 1965, Box 5, Folder Apr., Marcy Papers.

32 Joseph Alsop, "Pompous Ignorance," *Washington Post*, Apr. 21, 1965, and Norvill Jones to JWF, Apr. 23, 1965, Series 48:11, Box 35:2, SPF.

33 Meeting with Foreign Policy Advisors on Vietnam, May 16, 1965, NSC Meeting Notes, Box 1, Johnson Papers.

In March the SFRC added an important new member to its staff, replacing John Newhouse, who had resigned the previous fall to take a position in business. As part of a round-the-world fact-finding trip in 1963, Marcy had stopped in Yugoslavia to survey the situation in the Balkans; there, Ambassador George Kennan had assigned his young political officer, James Lowenstein, to be Marcy's control officer. The two men had become fast friends. At the time of Newhouse's departure, Lowenstein was in Washington working in the State Department, bored to death. Though it meant leaving the Foreign Service with no guarantee of return, Lowenstein responded enthusiastically to Marcy's invitation to apply for the vacant staff position. Following an interview with Fulbright and the committee, he got the job. Fluent in French and a veteran of a dozen years in the Navy, the ivy-league-educated Lowenstein inherited Newhouse's job as Southeast Asia expert.[34]

As of the spring of 1965 Fulbright still believed that Lyndon Johnson was the main advocate of restraint in an administration of hard-liners. "I am doing all that I can to influence the President not to expand this war and to find a way to the Conference table," he wrote a constituent. "You must remember he inherited the involvement and it is not easy to overcome past mistakes."[35] Carl Marcy was not so sure; it seemed to him that Johnson had already sold out to hard-liners inside and outside his administration. Moreover, his anxiety over the diminution of the prerogatives of the SFRC and its chairman was becoming intense. The chief of staff was far less willing to give Johnson the benefit of the doubt, and he worked assiduously throughout the summer of 1965 to generate some skepticism in his boss. Marcy had come to suspect that Lyndon Johnson, in his obsession with "consensus," was bending over backward to appease the radical right.

Fulbright took Marcy's views seriously, but he continued to resist an open break with the Texan. He still believed that mild public opposition to the administration's policies, together with repeated statements of support for the president personally, would have the desired effect. He continued to treasure what he believed to be his close relationship with Johnson. When the president sent him a series of pictures showing the two in rapt conversation in the Oval Office – inscribed "To Bill, I can see I haven't been very persuasive" and "To Betty Fulbright, Delightful wife of an eloquent husband" – Fulbright hung them on his office wall.

In fact, Marcy's aphorism that all presidents and foreign policy establishments come to view Congress in general, and the Senate in particular, as either a nuisance to be circumvented or an asset to be manipulated was at no

34 Interview with James Lowenstein, Oct. 3, 1991, Washington, D.C.
35 JWF to Rev. Daniel H. Evans, July 29, 1965, Series 48:1, Box 7:3, SPF.

time truer than during the Johnson administration. Neither Rusk, Bundy, nor McNamara had never held elective office. Like George Kennan and Dean Acheson they believed that the executive should be free to make foreign policy decisions that would be judged by the general electorate every four years. Bundy in particular, the ivy league academic come to Washington, was contemptuous of Congress. Senators were a collection of uninformed yahoos, he insisted. Like everyone and everything else, they should be cajoled and coerced into supporting the policies that the executive in its wisdom had devised. The uncooperative should be cast out into the darkness. "They [Congressional opponents] are quite free to oppose you if they choose," Bundy wrote the president, "but they are not free to make statements that you regard as damaging and pretend that they are speaking as your friends and supporters."[36]

Indeed, instead of opening up the decision-making process, as Fulbright and Marcy wanted him to, Johnson was gradually circumscribing it. He came to distrust National Security Council meetings; they were too large and too often the source of the hated leak. Most important decisions were made at the famous Tuesday luncheon meetings at which only the president, Bundy, McNamara, Rusk, and one aide each were present. The conclusions reached there were carefully presented in a stage-managed fashion first to the NSC, then to the congressional leadership, and subsequently to the nation as a whole. Though Marcy and Fulbright did not yet realize it, they were going to be able to affect policy not by being part of the "team," not by forcing access through legislation, but through open and relentless opposition designed to erode the consensus that Lyndon Johnson so treasured.

In the middle of June 1965, Johnson called Fulbright to the White House and asked him to make a public statement in support of administration policies in Vietnam. He needed help, he told the Arkansan, in fighting off the hard-liners and getting negotiations on track. The following day Fulbright rose on the Senate floor to proclaim that President Johnson was showing "steadfastness and statesmanship" in his handling of the Southeast Asia situation. On the one hand military victory, though possible, was not worth the cost; on the other, withdrawal from South Vietnam would "betray our obligation to people we have promised to defend." The only answer was a compromise settlement based on major concessions by both sides:

> In the months ahead we must try to do two things in South Vietnam. First we must sustain the South Vietnamese Army so as to persuade the Communists that Saigon cannot be crushed and that the

[36] Bundy to LBJ, Mar. 15, 1965, NSC File, Memos to President, Box 3, SPF.

> United States will not be driven from South Vietnam by force; second, we must continue to offer the Communists a reasonable and attractive alternative to military victory.[37]

He was convinced, he said, that the Vietcong believed that the rainy conditions of the current monsoon season gave them a military advantage and therefore would not respond to invitations to talk. Consequently, he concluded, "I approve of the President's efforts to strengthen South Vietnam and to maintain its security through . . . November or December."[38] The chairman had delivered his message of support, but it was conditional and terminable.

Indeed, even at this early date Fulbright believed that any settlement in Indochina ought to include a political role for the communists. When, on the morning following his Senate speech, Fulbright was asked by Sander Vanocur on the *Today* show whether the Vietcong ought to be allowed to participate in negotiations, Fulbright responded with an unqualified yes. Legalities were irrelevant; the VC were major players in the game. Republicans immediately screamed sellout. If the administration sanctioned any negotiations that "would include Communist elements in a coalition government," it could forget bipartisan support, Dirksen and company warned.[39] Johnson quickly disassociated himself from Fulbright's TV remarks, but at the same time expressed satisfaction with his old colleague's Senate remarks and chose to interpret them as endorsement of a massive troop buildup.

Throughout May, June, and July, despite the bombing, continued increases in U.S. aid, and the small infusion of American ground forces, the military situation in South Vietnam continued to deteriorate. Following a whirlwind tour of South Vietnam the last week in June, McNamara returned to report that the situation was desperate. The United States must escalate before it was "too late to do any good." There were great risks involved in increasing the national commitment, but decisive and immediate action might "stave off defeat in the short run and offer a good chance of producing a favorable settlement in the longer run." Most important, General Westmoreland must be given the authority to use American troops and firepower whenever, however, and wherever he chose. JCS Chairman Earle Wheeler's advice – "You must take the fight to the enemy. . . . No one ever won a battle sitting on his ass" – seemed compelling.[40] Accordingly, Johnson delegated to Westmoreland, in consultation with Khanh's Military Revolutionary Council (MRC), the authority to move beyond the enclave strategy and do whatever was necessary to win the war. Johnson promised his field commander all the logistical and

37 *Congressional Record,* Senate, June 15, 1965, 13657.
38 Ibid.
39 Quoted in Berman, *Fulbright and the Vietnam War,* 43.
40 Quoted in Herring, *America's Longest War,* 138, 137.

troop support that he needed. At this point the war had cost America 420 combat dead, surpassing the total of the Spanish–American conflict (385).[41]

On June 28 Johnson once again asked the chairman of the SFRC to the White House. During a stroll through the Rose Garden, the president outlined the desperate situation in Vietnam and told Fulbright he was going to have to send more troops and equipment to hold the line until the United States and its ally could establish a firm negotiating position. The Republicans and their ultra allies were waiting in the wings like so many vultures, ready to pounce should the administration falter. Fulbright was sympathetic. He subsequently told *Newsweek*'s Samuel Shaffer:

> As the Republicans see it, the President is damned if he does and damned if he doesn't. If there are a lot of American casualties, they'll talk about the "Johnson War" the way they talked about "Truman's War" in Korea. If the war is settled by negotiation, they'll claim we "lost" Vietnam the way we "lost" China.[42]

Carl Marcy's contacts and sensors within the executive branch were extensive. Leaks from these sources and information provided by Ned Kenworthy of the *New York Times* convinced him that something more significant than just "holding the line" was taking place. Marcy tried to warn Fulbright. "We seem to be on the verge of another important decision regarding Vietnam," he told his superior, "one on which the views of the Senate will not be sought until after the decision. There is now a last chance to do something that may halt this constant progression toward war."[43]

Urged on by the SFRC chief of staff, Fulbright met with Walter Lippmann throughout early July. The journalist's estimation of the situation matched Marcy's. He convinced Fulbright to join him in putting forward an approach that they believed would lead to a negotiated settlement without a provocative escalation. As the president was telling Westmoreland to go ahead and use his troops in offensive operations throughout Vietnam, Fulbright and Lippmann suggested an enclave strategy whereby American troops would pull back to strong points with their backs to the sea. While avoiding a general or even "Korea-sized" war, this strategy, they insisted, would deny North Vietnam and the Vietcong control over all of Vietnam. Rather than exhaust themselves attacking impregnable strongholds, the communists would eventually sit down at the negotiating table.[44] This, of course, was the very tactic that Johnson had imposed on Westmoreland in April and that was in the process of being scrapped. That Marcy, Fulbright, and Lippmann regarded it as an imag-

41 "The Road Past North C Pier . . . " *Newsweek,* June 28, 1965.
42 Ibid.
43 Marcy to JWF, Box 5, Folder July, Marcy Papers.
44 "Two Alternatives in Vietnam War," *Arkansas Gazette,* July 14, 1965.

inative new initiative demonstrated just how isolated they were from the decision-making process and how out of touch they were with what was really transpiring in Vietnam.

Although he found lobbying his colleagues extremely distasteful, Fulbright on the afternoon of July 27 met with the Senate's foreign policy heavyweights in Mansfield's office.[45] Fulbright picked the Montanan's suite not only because he was majority leader but also because up to that point he had been the most consistent, thorough, and – so his colleagues believed – credible critic of U.S. involvement in Vietnam. As a professor of political science at the University of Montana he had specialized in East Asia. He had taken innumerable trips to Indochina and had been personal friends with the Diems before their demise, with Norodom Sihanouk of Cambodia, and with Ne Win of Burma. Throughout 1964 and early 1965 Mansfield had periodically dispatched to the White House long, turgid memos prepared by his chief aide, Frank Valeo, another China–Burma–India veteran, decrying American involvement in Vietnam. He pressed his dissent with what McGeorge Bundy called "mousy stubbornness," but his lack of personality and his unwillingness to confront the president publicly would make him a largely ineffective dissenter.[46]

Indeed, on the morning before Fulbright and the others gathered in his office, Mansfield had attended a legislative leadership meeting on Vietnam at the White House. "We owe this government nothing," he had declared, "no pledge of any kind. We are going deeper into war. Escalation begets escalation. The best hope for salvation is quick stalemate and negotiations." Having indicted the war in Vietnam and the assumptions that underlay it, he had then declared he would support the president "as a Senator and Majority Leader," whatever course he chose to follow.[47]

Fulbright found a surprising, gratifying degree of consensus in the group that gathered in Mansfield's office – Russell, Sparkman, Aiken, and John Sherman Cooper (R–Kentucky). There was full agreement that "insofar as Viet Nam is concerned we are deeply enmeshed in a place where we ought not to be; that the situation is rapidly going out of control; and that every effort should be made to extricate ourselves." Russell and Stennis, both southerners and members of the Armed Services Committee, had been arguing for all-out bombing of the north, but they readily agreed at the meeting that the bombing should never have been started in the first place – indeed, that Vietnam was of only marginal strategic importance to the United States. The five drafted a letter embodying their views and sent it to Johnson post haste. Most

45 Vietnam Chronology, July 24 and 27, 1965, Box 5, Folder July, Marcy Papers.

46 Bundy to LBJ, May 31, 1965, and Mansfield to LBJ, June 5, 9, and 14, 1965, NSC File, Memos to President, Box 3, Johnson Papers.

47 Cong. Leadership Meeting, July 27, 1965, Meeting Notes File, Box 1, Johnson Papers.

people backing the president on Vietnam did so primarily because he was president, the group told the Texan, and not out of any understanding or sympathy with administration policies.[48]

Fulbright was most hopeful that the meeting and resulting letter would halt what he considered to be a descent into full-scale war. The signatories did not include Morse, McCarthy, McGovern, Church, or Joseph Clark, the liberal Democratic senator from Pennsylvania, men whom he and Marcy knew the White House regarded as dangerous visionaries or political opportunists. No one could ever accuse Richard Russell or John Sparkman of being soft on communism or of being unwilling to take their country into war to defend its interests. In short, the chairman and his chief of staff were sure that they had assembled a group that Johnson could not afford to ignore. They were wrong.

The day following receipt of the Mansfield letter, Johnson called the dissidents to the White House. After outlining the deteriorating military and political situation in Vietnam, he told Fulbright and company that there was no turning back. America was in for the duration. The war could well last six or seven more years.[49]

Johnson's frank review of the situation stunned and then infuriated Fulbright. He had supported the president and his escalation of the war to that point out of a belief that limited bombing and introduction of troops were necessary to placate American hard-liners and get all sides to the negotiating table. Now it turned out that the administration was committed to winning a battlefield victory, to making all of South Vietnam physically secure and then bombing North Vietnam to the peace table. Could it be, he asked himself, that Carl Marcy was right? That in his desire to appease the hawks, Lyndon Johnson was selling out to them?

48 Mansfield to LBJ, July 27, 1965, NSF, Name File, Box 6, Johnson Papers.
49 Berman, *Fulbright and the Vietnam War,* 44.

# 20

# *Texas hyperbole*

At 4:40 on the afternoon of April 28, 1965, Lyndon Johnson sat down with Rusk, McNamara, Ball, Bundy, and presidential aide Bill Moyers to discuss the perilous situation in Vietnam. An hour into the meeting President Johnson was handed a cable marked "critic" (critical) from Ambassador W. Tapley Bennett in Santo Domingo. The Dominican military had split into at least two factions, and one was arming the populace in an effort to seize power. "Regret report situation deteriorating rapidly," it stated; "[C]ountry team unanimously of opinion that time has come to land the marines . . . American lives are in danger." After conferring with his advisers, all of whom approved intervention, President Johnson ordered four hundred marines to proceed to the Dominican capital at once. Rusk rushed off to inform all the Latin American embassies in Washington, and Moyers left to set up a briefing session in the Cabinet Room for congressional leaders later that evening.[1]

When Johnson and his advisers closeted themselves with the congressional leadership, Rusk stressed that the administration's decision to intervene had been based on the need to protect American lives. Newly named head of the CIA Admiral William "Red" Raborn declared that there had been "positive identification of three ring-leaders of the Rebels as Castro-trained agents." Everett Dirksen and John McCormack immediately warned of the danger of allowing another Castroite regime to emerge in the hemisphere and declared their support for armed intervention. Fulbright's only contribution to the council of war was to recommend that the Organization of American States (OAS) be involved. When asked whether American troops, soon to number some twenty-four thousand, would be pulled out immediately or allowed to remain there, Johnson answered that that bridge had not yet been crossed.[2]

On April 29 Richard Goodwin, coarchitect with Arthur Schlesinger of the Kennedy administration's Latin American policy, pleaded with Johnson to continue to justify the Dominican intervention on the grounds that American

1 Chronology of Pertinent Events in the Dominican Republic Situation, undated, NSF, Box 8, Johnson Papers.

2 Meeting with Congressional Leadership on Dominican Republic, Apr. 28, 1965, Meeting Notes File, Box 1, Johnson Papers.

lives were in danger. The administration was treading on dangerous ground, he warned; the event could be as costly "as the Bay of Pigs invasion itself." The marine landing, he reminded Johnson, would be the first military intervention in Latin America since U.S. troops left Nicaragua in the 1920s. It contravened the charter of the OAS and violated the spirit of the Good Neighbor Policy. Goodwin insisted that President Johnson not put himself in the position of suppressing a popular revolution against military rule. Still, he concluded, "I agree that anything, including military intervention, should be done if essential to prevent another Castro-type takeover in the Caribbean."[3]

The following day, as Dean Rusk advised reporters to play down "the ideological aspects of this thing," Johnson met with McNamara and General Wheeler.[4] He asked them, John Bartlow Martin later wrote, "what they would need to take the republic." One or two divisions, they replied. Martin, a former ambassador to the Dominican Republic whom Johnson had decided to send down on a fact-finding mission, recalled Johnson's motives as he stated them: "The President said he foresaw two dangers – very soon we would witness a Castro/Communist-dominated government in the Dominican Republic, or we would find ourselves in the Republic alone without any support in the hemisphere. He didn't want either to happen." Anticipating the criticism that was to come, the president declared that he had every intention of working through the OAS, but that he did not intend "to sit here with my hands tied and let Castro take that island. What can we do in Vietnam if we can't clean up the Dominican Republic?"[5]

The causes of the Dominican Republic's many troubles were varied, but most were rooted in the thirty-year dictatorship of Rafael Leónidas Trujillo Molina. That villain had brutally suppressed all opposition, turned the army into his personal palace guard, and ravaged his country's fragile economy. Then, in the summer of 1961, assassins had shot him through the head. His family had tried to perpetuate his tyranny, but failed and fled into exile. In December 1962 the Dominicans had elected the liberal intellectual Juan Bosch president. Ten months later a military coup had overthrown him, its leaders charging that he was too tolerant of communists and communism. Despite support from the Johnson administration for the new government of Donald Reid Cabral and the presence of some twenty-five hundred Americans on that island of some three-and-a-half million souls, stability eluded the Dominicans. Drought, widespread unemployment, strikes, sabotage, and continuing opposition from dissidents kept the country in constant turmoil. From exile in

3 Goodwin to LBJ, Apr. 29, 1965, NSF, Name File, Box 8, SPF.

4 Quoted in Haynes Johnson and Bernard M. Gwertzman, *Fulbright: The Dissenter* (New York, 1968), 247.

5 Quoted in John Bartlow Martin, *Overtaken by Events: The Dominican Crisis from the Fall of Trujillo to the Civil War* (New York, 1966), 661.

Puerto Rico, where he was employed as a college professor, Juan Bosch directed the disruptive activities of the Dominican Revolutionary Party (PRD).

The spring of 1965 found the Dominican military deeply divided. A minority were devoted to Bosch's return, but the majority regarded him as a dangerous revolutionary who would "open the door to the communists" and, not coincidentally, do away with the military's privileges.[6] When officers loyal to Reid Cabral had attempted to arrest some of their fellows for plotting against the government in behalf of Juan Bosch, the PRD, with the support of some military officers, had declared a general uprising and surrounded the presidential palace. At this point, the anti-Bosch military, led by the pious and thoroughly reactionary General Elias Wessin y Wessin, had issued an ultimatum to the PRD demanding that it turn over power to the army. Wessin had become convinced that Bosch and the PRD were encouraging the Castroite Fourteenth of June Movement.[7] When the rebels ignored his demand, air force planes had begun bombing and strafing the palace, as well as the slums of Santo Domingo, which were Bosch strongholds and, in the minds of the military, seedbeds of communist agitation. The brutal attacks inflamed the population, who had then flooded into the streets in response to calls from the PRD. At this point Santo Domingo was teetering on the edge of chaos. Under the auspices of U.S. Ambassador Bennett, who now decided that the embassy could no longer remain aloof, the anti-Bosch military had put together a junta headed by Colonel Pedro Bartolome Benoit. The sole purpose of this government was to request armed intervention by the United States.

On the afternoon of April 28, while President Johnson met with his advisers on Vietnam, Bennett exchanged a flurry of telegrams with Undersecretary Thomas Mann, the State Department's leading expert on Latin America. Bennett managed to convince the State Department that, given General Wessin and Colonel Benoit's inability to control the situation in Santo Domingo, there was a very real danger of a communist, Castro-controlled takeover in the Dominican Republic. All "responsible" elements agreed that the U.S. Marine Corps should be dispatched at once, and he agreed with them, Bennett declared. Mann then advised the ambassador that he must compel Benoit to base his request for American intervention on the need to protect American lives. "We did instruct our Ambassador to go back to Benoit . . . and in order to improve our juridical base asked him to specifically say that he could not

[6] There were as of that year three communist factions present in the Dominican Republic: the Dominican Popular Movement (MPD), illegal since 1963, which was Maoist and claimed some five hundred hard-core supporters; the Dominican Popular Socialist Party (PSPD), Moscow-oriented and between seven hundred and a thousand strong; and the Fourteenth of June movement (PACJ), which was financed by and loyal to Fidel Castro. U.S. Senate, Committee on Foreign Relations, *Executive Sessions of the SFRC,* Vol. 17, 1965 (Washington, 1990), 805.

[7] SFRC, *Executive Sessions,* Vol. 17, 1965, 491.

protect the lives of American citizens," Mann subsequently admitted to the SFRC.[8] In his later cables, as a result, Bennett insisted that the large number of Americans residing at the Hotel Embajador were in danger of being killed or wounded.

The first week in May reporters flooded into the Dominican Republic determined to check out the administration's version of events. They quickly discovered that no American civilian had been killed or even wounded at the Ambassador Hotel or anywhere else on the island. When pressed, anonymous sources in the American embassy declared that they had in their possession the names of fifty-eight card-carrying communists who had led the uprising against Reid Cabral. Editorials in the *New York Times,* the *New York Herald-Tribune,* and the *Washington Post* began to question the administration's reasoning and veracity. The notion that fifty-eight communists posed a massive threat in any Latin American country, even one as small as the Dominican Republic, seemed ludicrous.[9]

The ever-sensitive Johnson overreacted. He began exaggerating; he described scenes that had never taken place, misquoted cables for dramatic effect, and ridiculed his detractors. Throughout Sunday, May 2, the president briefed various congressional leaders and railed against his critics. More troops were going into Santo Domingo; the issue was now greater even than the loss of American lives, he proclaimed; now the Dominican Republic must be saved from "other evil forces."[10] On TV that night, solemn, intense, the president told his audience:

> The American nation cannot, and must not, and will not permit the establishment of another Communist government in the Western Hemisphere. . . . I want you to know and I want the world to know that as long as I am President of this country, we are going to defend ourselves. . . . We do not want to bury anyone as I have said so many times before. But we do not intend to be buried.[11]

The next afternoon at a union convention in Washington he told how he had received Bennett's urgent cable. "You must land troops immediately," he quoted it as saying, "or blood will run in the streets, American blood will run in the streets." Then, in a veiled reference to John F. Kennedy's handling of the Bay of Pigs he declared:

> What is important . . . in this hemisphere . . . [is] that we know, and that they know, and that everybody knows, that we don't propose

8 Ibid., 827.

9 See Tad Szulc, *Dominican Diary* (New York, 1965), for a critical contemporary account of the intervention.

10 Bundy to LBJ, May 2, 1965, NSC File, Memos to President, Box 3, Johnson Papers.

11 Quoted in Johnson and Gwertzman, *Fulbright: The Dissenter,* 248.

> to sit here in our rocking chair with our hands folded and let the Communists set up any government in the Western Hemisphere.[12]

At this point, Fulbright's attention was focused on Vietnam; it remained to others on the SFRC to look behind the president's rhetoric and challenge his justifications. Wayne Morse, the SFRC's Latin American expert, and Pennsylvania liberal Joe Clark were profoundly disturbed at the administration's bypassing of the OAS and convinced that the State Department had overreacted. Thomas Mann and Tapley Bennett, in their view, were throwbacks to the days of Big Stick diplomacy, men determined to work with and support only Latin leaders who were "good-suited" and pro–United States. Clark was convinced that Johnson had been captured by McNamara, Bundy, and other of his hard-nosed advisers, and was being misled by "McCarthyite–CIA" reports. Both Morse and Clark were as yet afraid to break with Johnson publicly, but they did persuade Fulbright and the rest of the committee to request Johnson to have Mann and others brief the committee in executive session.[13]

In May, Mann and Rusk painted fairly lurid pictures of alleged outrages committed against Americans at the Ambassador Hotel, and they emphasized that the possibility of a communist takeover in the days following Reid Cabral's resignation was very real. "A large rebel group . . . armed with tommyguns came in and emptied all Americans out of the hotel . . . got them outside the hotel, separated the men from the women, ordered the women back into the hotel, lined the Americans up against the wall as if they were going to shoot them." As for the communist threat, Mann declared, "really you can make a very good argument on the basis that the real intervention in the Dominican Republic took place when these 85 people were trained to overthrow the Government of the Dominican Republic, to institute in its place a Communist dictatorship."[14] Morse and Clark were skeptical, whereas Hickenlooper, Symington, and the sycophantic Frank Lausche (D–Ohio) were supportive. Fulbright seemed relatively indifferent.

Meanwhile, reports from the media steadily eroded the administration's credibility. Charles Kuralt and a CBS-TV crew transmitted live from the neutral zone that had been set up in the middle of Santo Domingo and was being guarded by American troops. He could not help but notice, Kuralt announced, that U.S. authorities were facilitating the movement of troops loyal to the Benoit junta while blocking rebel soldiers.

During the brouhaha over the Dominican crisis, a number of observers noted that for the first time the administration seemed to be encouraging Russo-

12 Quoted in ibid., 249.

13 Bundy to LBJ, May 5, 1965, NSC File, Memos to President, Johnson Papers, and JWF to Rusk, June 2, 1965, Box 5, Folder June, Marcy Papers.

14 SFRC, *Executive Sessions,* Vol. 17, 1965, 498, 514.

phobes and reactionaries in Congress and, because of this, the strength of the radical right in America had increased geometrically. They also noted a tendency by the administration to promote men like Thomas Mann and Douglas MacArthur III in the State Department, men who had matured during the era of unsophisticated, monolithic anticommunism. The president, one reporter noted, "had gone soft on Goldwaterism."[15]

By June 17 a shaky peace prevailed in the Dominican Republic, but public criticism had not abated. On that date Johnson gave an unforgettable performance at an untelevised press conference. Away from the glare of the television lights he shouted and snapped his fingers under the noses of reporters, thumped the desk, and brandished what he said were top-secret documents. He gave a new version of the scene that had allegedly prompted Tap Bennett to ask him to intervene. "In this particular instance, a fact that has been emphasized all too little [is that] some 1,500 innocent people were murdered and shot and their heads cut off." In that same press conference he also told reporters that Bennett "was talking to us from under a desk while bullets were going through his windows and he had a thousand American men, women, and children assembled in the hotel who were pleading with their President for help to preserve their lives."[16] To Johnson his statements concerning heads rolling in the streets of Santo Domingo and Tap Bennett hiding under his desk while bullets whizzed overhead were not fabrications but embellishments of a basic truth. "Those weren't lies," McGeorge Bundy would later insist. "He was building up, 'argufying'; he was certainly going beyond the truth, but that's not the same as lying. In his mind. He was 'trying to make the whole situation totally clear.'" He had a terrible time, Bundy recalled, trying to keep some sort of limit on the President's "unfettered exposition."[17]

J. William Fulbright did not appreciate Texas hyperbole. Johnson's description of events seemed at odds even with the version presented to the SFRC by the president's aides. He set about proving to himself whether or not the administration was lying. From mid-July through mid-August 1965, Mann, Bennett, Raborn, Assistant Secretary of Defense Cyrus Vance, and Assistant Secretary of State Jack Hood Vaughn testified at length before the SFRC. The committee was still split, but this time Fulbright took charge. He was every inch the trial lawyer, questioning, probing, careful not to antagonize the Republican members or proadministration Democrats. He asked for and received virtually all the cable traffic that had passed between Santo Domingo and the State Department. Pat Holt conducted his own investigation,

15 *Congressional Record,* Senate, Oct. 7, 1965, 26239.
16 Quoted in Johnson and Gwertzman, *Fulbright: The Dissenter,* 249.
17 Interview with McGeorge Bundy, Aug. 1, 1991, New York.

and Seth Tillman interviewed Tad Szulc, who was shortly to publish his first-hand and very critical version of the intervention, entitled *Dominican Diary*. From all of this evidence Fulbright was finally able to piece together an accurate picture.

Bennett and his staff had at first refused to act, allowing chaos to reign, and then overreacted to the threat of a communist takeover. Fulbright forced Mann to admit that Washington had instructed Benoit to alter his appeal to emphasize the need to preserve American lives. He then demonstrated that not only had there been no American civilian casualties, but that any threat to U.S. citizens had been greatly exaggerated.[18] Behind the scenes Pat Holt argued that Johnson and Tom Mann had set their faces against a return to power by Juan Bosch, in their eyes a weak and vacillating man who would open the door to the Castroites. It had been to prevent this eventuality, and not to save American lives, that the marines had been landed.[19]

During the course of the investigation, Holt learned that Johnson had not only lied to Congress and the American people but had attempted to compromise the CIA, whose operatives had delivered accurate intelligence reports on the crisis. When the Dominican affair erupted, CIA director Raborn had been in office for only a few days. Shortly after American troops landed, Johnson had asked Raborn to produce evidence of communist involvement in the unrest on the island. The admiral returned to Langley and appealed for help, but the Latin American experts in the agency told him that they could not come up with any communists for the president. Infuriated, Johnson had called in J. Edgar Hoover. "Find me some Communists in the Dominican Republic," he had commanded. The FBI director then secretly flooded the country with agents, who generated the list of fifty-three that Szulc and Kurzman subsequently discredited.[20] Johnson also attempted a mild subornation of Fulbright.

Monday morning, the first week in August, during a lull in the hearings, Carl Marcy received a call from Fulbright asking if he would be interested in flying down to Rio the next weekend. Marcy said he would and asked what was up. "Well, Betty and I were having dinner last night with Lyndon and Lady Bird," Fulbright replied, "and Lyndon said, 'Betty, how would you like to go to Rio next weekend? . . . It's a wonderful place for you to go because you can get jewels in Brazil at a very low price. It's a wonderful place to shop. . . . Take Air Force One.'"[21]

18 SFRC, *Executive Sessions,* Vol. 17, 1965, 737–95, 841–937, 1111–17.
19 Donald A. Ritchie, interviewer, *Oral History Interviews: Pat M. Holt* (Senate Historical Office: Washington, D.C., 1980), 185, and Memo of Conversation between Peter H. Freeman and Holt, July 26, 1965, Series 48:14, Box 38:5, SPF.
20 Ritchie, *Interviews: Holt,* 187.
21 Ibid., 162–3.

The ostensible purpose of the Fulbright trip was a commercial mission to the new anticommunist, conservative government of Humberto Castello Branco. Castello Branco had just succeeded in ousting Joao Goulart, a man seen by Washington as a dangerous social revolutionary and a "neutralist" in the cold war.[22] Johnson, Rusk, and Mann had set up the trip to reassure Castello Branco of Washington's willingness to provide trade and aid.

The plane was full of government officials when the Fulbrights boarded, but they and Marcy had been assigned the presidential suite. Shortly after takeoff Fulbright discovered the real purpose of the trip: Johnson had sent Tom Mann along "to try to convert Fulbright, to explain to him what we were doing," as Mann later put it. He was to "soften Fulbright's criticism, and even get him to come around" if possible.[23] To Mann's consternation, however, as soon as he learned what was afoot, Fulbright locked the forward compartment and would not come out.

The trip itself proceeded very smoothly. "Senator Fulbright performed flawlessly as the chief of the delegation and spokesman for the group," Johnson aide Jack Valenti reported to the president. "In several encounters with the press he made not one miss-step [*sic*]. The name Fulbright is universally and favorably known in Latin America."[24] In private discussions, the Arkansan lamented U.S. involvement in Vietnam but refused to criticize Johnson. On the Dominican Republic, Fulbright merely stated that the SFRC was investigating.

The Brazilian trip left the administration perplexed as to where Fulbright stood. "Tom Mann thinks the Committee is split down the middle," Valenti related to Johnson, "and while Fulbright would prefer an anti-intervention report, he can't get it through his fellow members."[25]

Mann was exactly right. Morse, Clark, Clifford Case (R–New Jersey), Minnesota's Eugene McCarthy, and Fulbright favored an SFRC report on the Dominican intervention, but Hickenlooper, Lausche, Symington, Gale McGee (D–Wyoming), and others were opposed. The matter might have ended there had the White House not unleashed Thomas Dodd of Connecticut on Fulbright. Dodd, a professional anticommunist and Johnson lackey, hated Fulbright for many things, but primarily for uncovering his ties to the government of Nicaragua, for which he had been an unregistered and highly paid lobbyist.[26] Although Dodd, an SFRC member, had attended less than 10

22 Valenti to LBJ, Aug. 10, 1965, WHCF, Box 7, Johnson Papers.
23 Interview with Thomas Mann, May 10, 1991, Austin, Tex.
24 Valenti to LBJ, Aug. 10, 1965, WHCF, Box 7, Johnson Papers.
25 Valenti to LBJ, Aug. 11, 1965, Box 7, Confidential File, CO 37, Brazil, Johnson Papers.
26 It was Dodd, moreover, who as a member of the Internal Security Subcommittee had helped ruin the career of William Wieland, the State Department desk officer in charge of Cuba at the time of Castro's rise to power.

percent of committee meetings and only part of one hearing on the Dominican Republic, he issued a press release on August 22 condemning Fulbright for slanting the hearings against the administration and deliberately excluding information supporting the case for intervention.[27]

On September 14 McGeorge Bundy was tipped off by "friendly newspapermen" that Fulbright was going to deliver a major address the next day indicting the administration for mishandling the Dominican situation and then intervening to no good purpose. He went to Johnson at once. Bundy did not have a copy, but he understood, he said, that the speech would be particularly hard on Bennett.[28]

The decision to give a speech on the Dominican Republic had been the subject of an intense, two-day debate among Fulbright's aides and the staff of the SFRC. Pat Holt, who had presided over the investigation and drafted the bill of particulars, and Seth Tillman, who had written the speech following close consultation with Fulbright, were in favor of going ahead. "Pat and I felt there was an obligation to speak out and address the country," Tillman remembers. "Our action was an outrageous violation of the OAS charter and a major mistake in policy."[29] Lee Williams, with an eye to the long-range interests of his boss, was adamantly opposed. He could read what Johnson's reaction would be, and the SFRC staff could not, he said: In a fit of rage the president would sever all ties with Fulbright; the senator would lose his channel to the White House, and his influence and that of the SFRC would be greatly diminished.[30] Even more important from Holt's point of view, Fulbright would never get another nickel for federal projects in Arkansas.[31] To his surprise, Marcy agreed: It was crucial for Fulbright and for the work of the SFRC that the chairman retain his close personal relationship with the president. Fulbright cut him short: "All I want to know, Carl, is whether you think this is a fair statement of what we found out during the hearings." He, Fulbright, would deal with the political fallout. When Marcy replied in the affirmative, Fulbright declared that he would deliver the speech the next day. "At least send Lyndon an advance copy," Williams pled. His boss finally agreed, but the White House received the speech only hours before it was delivered.[32] "I [had] thought I could influence him . . . [but] I decided there was no longer any hope," Fulbright later recalled.[33]

27 *Congressional Record,* Senate, Aug. 24, 1965, 21518–19.
28 Bundy to LBJ, Sept. 14, 1965, NSF, Memos to President, Bundy, Box 4, Johnson Papers.
29 Interview with Seth Tillman, Oct. 6, 1988, Washington, D.C.
30 Interview with Lee Williams, June 20, 1989, Washington, D.C.
31 Charles Morrissey interview with J. William Fulbright, "Modern Congress in American History" (Library of Congress, Washington, D.C.), 22.
32 Donald A. Ritchie, interviewer, *Oral History Interviews: Carl A. Marcy* (Senate Historical Office: Washington, D.C., 1983), 165–6.
33 Morrissey interview with Fulbright, "Modern Congress."

The Dominican address was indeed a devastating indictment. After laying out the chronology, Fulbright blasted Bennett for first underreacting and then overreacting. The embassy was paranoid concerning the threat that Castro and communism posed to the hemisphere, he said. Bennett had solicited armed intervention only after it appeared that the PRD and its allies might win, and the sole purpose of that intervention was to create and then maintain an anticommunist, pro-U.S. regime. The threat to American lives, greatly exaggerated, was a mere pretext, he declared. "In their apprehension lest the Dominican Republic become another Cuba, some of our officials seem to have forgotten that virtually all reform movements attract some Communist support."[34]

There is no doubt that Fulbright's speech on the Dominican Republic destroyed his relationship with Lyndon Johnson. The president was willing to listen to dissenting views – indeed, he at times demanded them of his subordinates – but once a decision was made, he expected his lieutenants to close ranks. "From Lyndon Johnson's point of view, anything less than 100% support was rank desertion," McGeorge Bundy remembered.[35] His was not an unreasonable expectation regarding members of the executive branch; the trouble was that Lyndon Johnson extended that criterion to virtually everyone in America, including Democratic members of Congress and Fulbright in particular. Like Woodrow Wilson, Franklin D. Roosevelt, and any number of lesser political figures, Johnson believed that he personified the country, was the receptacle of its hopes and the font of its wisdom. It was not surprising that the Texan was wont to convert differences over policy into personal feuds. Fulbright was part of his "team," and Johnson expected the Arkansan to manage the SFRC so as to facilitate and not obstruct administration policy. As he so often did when someone challenged him in public, Johnson felt "betrayed." He wanted to be loved, expected to be loved, and was bitterly disappointed when he believed he was not.

Even among those who differed with him, however, Johnson singled out Fulbright for special treatment. In late 1965 no fewer than three state dinners were held at the White House, one a gala affair for Chancellor Ludwig Erhard of West Germany; the chairman of the SFRC was excluded from all of them.[36] In November the White House denied Fulbright the use of a government jet to transport him and a senatorial delegation to Wellington, New Zealand, to attend a meeting of the British Commonwealth Parliamentarians' Association. To the chairman's chagrin, he and his party had to make the trip, which stretched half-way round the world, in a lumbering, prop-driven C-118. In addition, Fulbright would be banned from all official functions at the White House for more than a year. Johnson would curse and ridicule the Ar-

34 *Congressional Record,* Senate, Sept. 15, 1965, 23855–63.
35 McG. Bundy interview.
36 "Unbecoming a President," *Detroit News,* Dec. 22, 1965.

kansan to his staff and visiting dignitaries alike. All the while, the Texan continued to "consult" with Mansfield and Morse, both publicly and privately. "I spoke publicly the fifteenth of September . . . in '65," Fulbright later recalled, "and Johnson never after that had another private conversation with me" (which was not true).[37]

The break with Fulbright seemed to unleash resentments that had long been festering within Lyndon Johnson. Above all, there was the Texan's educational inferiority complex. "The Johnsons were as close to the Fulbrights as to any other couple in Washington," William Bundy recalled, "and at the same time there was that subtle difference deriving from what George Ball eloquently described as not LBJ's inferior education but his belief that he had had an inferior education."[38] Although he liked having Rhodes scholars like Rostow and Rusk on his team, Johnson was ambivalent toward people with gold-plated academic credentials and "intellectuals." He resented them and at the same time longed to please them. Johnson hated the Kennedys, and the Kennedys had gone to Harvard. He detested Arthur Schlesinger, the ultimate ivy league professor, because he was the most loyal of Kennedy loyalists. In the aftermath of the Dominican Republic speech, the president began to lump Fulbright and Schlesinger together. Although the Arkansan had no particular tie to the Kennedys, he was an intellectual and he shared their contempt for him, Johnson believed.

In the fall of 1965 many of those who had Johnson's ear curried favor by denigrating Fulbright. Dean Acheson and Averell Harriman had never forgiven the Arkansan for his "treachery" toward Harry Truman. "I often saw him through the eyes of Dean Acheson and William S. White," said William Bundy, Acheson's son-in-law. "They were often quite critical of him because they were pragmatists. When he suggested in that 1946 election . . . well, how can you take a guy seriously who made that suggestion?"[39] On a copy of Fulbright's Dominican address sent him by the White House, Harriman wrote: "This speech cheered in Moscow. Takes no regard of announced commie plans."[40] Thomas Mann – a lawyer from Laredo, Texas, who had graduated from Baylor University – whispered in Johnson's ear that, like Arthur Schlesinger, Fulbright had become a champion of violent social upheaval.[41]

37 Morrissey interview with Fulbright, "Modern Congress," 21.

38 Interview with William Bundy, July 5, 1990, Princeton, N.J.

39 Ibid.

40 Statement by JWF on D.R., Sept. 15, 1965, Box 462, Papers of W. Averell Harriman, Library of Congress, Washington, D.C.

41 In his April 27 speech to the School of Advanced International Studies, Fulbright had declared that "true" social revolution "is almost always violent and usually it is extremely violent; its essence is the destruction of the social fabric and institutions of a society and an attempt, not necessarily successful, to create a new social fabric and new institutions." Thomas Mann, *Be There Yesterday: The Adventures of a Career Foreign Service Officer, 1942–1966,* unpublished manuscript, 259–60.

Fulbright, Mann insisted, was calling for unqualified U.S. support for all social revolutions in Latin America whether they were "Marxist–Leninist" or not. Lyndon Johnson was more than ready to believe that his erstwhile friend was now a naïve intellectual whose recommendations would open the door to communist aggression in those areas of the globe still free of Sino–Soviet domination.

The image of Fulbright that formed in Johnson's mind, then, was that of a traitor and a coward. He was a traitor in the sense of putting his doubts above the interests of his country and his president. Unlike Morse, who would "whack him in the open," Fulbright would sneak around behind his back. He was not a "stand up kind of guy," McGeorge Bundy remembered Johnson as saying.[42]

Not content to freeze Fulbright out of official functions, Johnson counterattacked vigorously. He had Bundy draft a letter to Fulbright accusing him of cowardice and malice. "Your charges are ostensibly directed at Ambassador Bennett," the president wrote self-righteously, "but in reality they are directed at me. . . . You should not seek to avoid an attack on me by hitting at a man who cannot hit back." How, given American support for the enlightened governments of Venezuela, Chile, and Colombia, could Fulbright accuse the administration of always siding with military juntas and economic oligarchies?[43] Despite the warnings of John Bartlow Martin that official denials would only make matters worse, Johnson ordered the State Department to put everything else aside and draft a white paper on the Dominican Republic, a document that would completely exonerate everyone concerned.[44] When it became clear that most Latin American press opinion supported Fulbright's position, Johnson had Bill Moyers instruct the State Department to label all such comment as leftist- or Marxist-inspired.[45] Finally, the president unleashed his personality and his lieutenants on Congress with devastating effect. Dodd, Russell Long, George Smathers (D–Florida), and Richard Russell rose to blast Fulbright. How could anybody libel a good Georgia boy like Tap Bennett? Russell asked. Fulbright was opening the door to Castro, Dodd and Long declared. The House, by an overwhelming margin, passed a resolution endorsing direct military intervention in Latin America to prevent "subversive action or the threat of it."[46] Only Clark, Morse, and McCarthy had the nerve public-

42 McG. Bundy interview.
43 LBJ to JWF, Sept. 17, 1965, NSF, Memos to President, Box 4, Johnson Papers.
44 Bundy to LBJ, Sept. 23, 1965, NSF, Memos to President, Bundy, Box 5, Johnson Papers, and Martin to LBJ, Oct. 5, 1965, NSF, Memos to President, Box 5, Johnson Papers.
45 Luncheon Meeting with president, Ball, McNamara, Bundy, Raborn, Moyers, and Califano, Sept. 29, 1965, Meeting Notes File, Johnson Papers.
46 *Congressional Record,* Senate, Oct. 7, 1965, 26239.

ly to defend the Arkansan. The administration's reaction to Fulbright and his speech, wrote Joseph Kraft, "was not unlike the stoning reserved by the high priests of primitive communities for those who question the efficacy of blood sacrifice."[47]

So intense was the criticism and so isolated from his colleagues did Fulbright feel that he took the unusual step of rising on the floor of the Senate to defend himself. He was shocked at the virulity of the White House and his colleagues' reaction, the Arkansan declared. He did not like being told, he said, that "my statement was 'irresponsible' or that it has given aid and comfort to the enemies of the United States." His criticism had been of policies and not persons (which was not true). It was his duty as chair of the SFRC to offer the best advice he could on matters of foreign policy. "Insofar as it represents a genuine reconciliation of differences, a consensus is a fine thing," he scolded; "insofar as it represents the concealment of differences, it is a miscarriage of democratic procedure." Beware, he concluded dramatically, the "tyranny of the majority."[48]

At the height of the Dominican controversy, Betty suffered a serious heart attack. Her childhood bout with rheumatic fever had left her susceptible to heart disease, and that, coupled with the stress caused by the Dominican imbroglio, brought her low. Fulbright was temporarily embittered. "This country has gotten to where you are not supposed to speak out," he told a friend. If you do, "everyone jumps down your throat."[49] Betty Fulbright had always been an intensely social, outgoing person. Following her heart attack, the couple had to curtail their social engagements sharply. Fulbright did not miss the cocktail parties and receptions, but he pined for his wife's vivaciousness and energy. Her illness and the break with Johnson introduced a kind of grimness into Fubright's existence that had not hitherto existed.

What in fact lay behind the Arkansan's momentous decision to break with Lyndon Johnson? Some attributed Fulbright's broadside to "moodiness" and "oversensitivity." He was in many ways a typical youngest child (the twins had been an afterthought as far as Jay, Roberta, and the older siblings were concerned). The only one of the Fulbright children close to both of his parents, Bill had become adept at pleasing both. As he had shown throughout his life, he was driven to live beyond reproach, to be the perfect child and husband, if not father (reflecting, in part, his own father's aloofness), and the ideal citizen. Fulbright took life very seriously, and he had been taught to take responsibility for his social environment. He brooded over personal slights, aspersions cast on his native region, imperfections in the nation's for-

47 Ibid.

48 *Congressional Record,* Senate, Oct. 22, 1965, 28371–2.

49 Quoted in Johnson and Gwertzman, *Fulbright: The Dissenter,* 260.

eign policy, and flaws in those whom he had helped elevate to power. Wayne Morse, who gloried in public combat, shrewdly commented on the differences between himself and Fulbright. In the fall of 1965 Morse went to the White House for a ceremonial function. Johnson, who was then doing bitter battle with the burgeoning antiwar movement, of which Morse was a prominent member, greeted the Oregonian cordially: "Wayne, I've never seen you looking so fit. How do you do it?" Morse replied: "Well, Mr. President, I'll tell you. Every time I read in the papers what you're doing about Vietnam, it makes my blood boil. That purges me; it keeps me fit." But Fulbright was different, Morse later observed. "Bill's a bleeder. He keeps agonizing over it."[50]

In addition, Fulbright's natural, rather mild arrogance, had been sharpened by association with Seth Tillman. A Massachusetts native from a middle-class background, Tillman had attended Syracuse University and taught public school before earning his Ph.D. in international relations at Tufts. Tillman was a gifted speechwriter, "as good as Sorensen, better than Goodwin," according to James Lowenstein. He had published his dissertation, and he could not help but feel superior to the "Arkansas Mafia" and other staffers on the hill. Tillman believed that the combination of his prose and Fulbright's vision could change the world, that the Fulbright persona was an island of rationality and insight in a sea of know-nothingness.[51] In fact, the interaction between the two men produced a combination of voice and vision that made Fulbright far more formidable than he would have been alone; but Tillman's personality also fed an already deep-seated intellectual arrogance and self-righteousness in Fulbright. To the speechwriter and his boss, Lyndon Johnson was an unlettered Texan desperately in need of enlightened guidance in matters of foreign policy. That he would not take it from the best available source – Fulbright and Tillman – was infuriating. It was Tillman's advice Fulbright was taking when he asked Carl Marcy if the Dominican speech were correct and then told him that he would handle the political consequences.

Finally, there was Carl Marcy. By 1965 his determination to preserve congressional prerogatives in the area of foreign policy had become an obsession. Over the years the executive branch's unfailing habit of ignoring, circumventing, or manipulating the Senate in general and the SFRC in particular had created a smoldering resentment in the Oregonian. He believed that his committee under Fulbright was fully as competent to judge the national interest as the State or Defense departments. He had long ago identified his not-inconsiderable ego with the SFRC; indeed, his reservations about the Dominican speech concerned the probable loss of influence and status that would

50 Quoted in ibid.

51 Tillman interview, and interview with James Lowenstein, Oct. 3, 1991, Washington, D.C.

ensue for both Fulbright and the committee rather than any questions about the correctness of the chairman's position.

The White House's decision to deny a government jet to Fulbright and the senatorial delegation to New Zealand humiliated and infuriated Marcy. One of the most powerful men in Washington, the personification of the SFRC and the Senate's constitutional role in foreign policymaking, was going to have to spend two uncomfortable days in a lumbering, prop-driven C-118 sleeping in a bunk. Accommodations were Marcy's responsibility, and the White House's cattiness was more a slap at him than his boss.[52] Bundy and Johnson twisted the knife by arranging for Mike Mansfield to travel abroad on Air Force One at the same time Fulbright inched his way across the South Pacific. (Marcy retaliated by prompting Ned Kenworthy to write an article in the *New York Times* condemning the Johnson White House's pettiness. To his delight Bundy and Johnson both squealed. "We do not enjoy having these cases tried in the newspaper," Bundy sniffed to Marcy.)[53]

That Marcy's feathers were ruffled is not surprising. What is puzzling is Fulbright's surprise and dismay at the intensity of the Johnson counterattack. After all, what did he expect? His staff had warned him; he had known Lyndon Johnson for years. "If you took issue publicly with President Johnson," he later declared, "that's the end of you from his point of view. You're on his team or you're not."[54] Johnson's claims that heads were rolling in the streets of Santo Domingo were absurd, but he had been expostulating thus in public life for thirty years. What startled him, Bundy later declared, was that Fulbright was so distressed: "He must have known this about him. If I could get used to it in my cold-roast New England way, why couldn't Fulbright?"[55]

As was true of so many people with a minimum of imagination and a maximum of security, Fulbright frequently found it difficult to identify with others. The same inability to empathize with poor black sharecroppers in the Arkansas delta made him a very poor handler of presidents. Perceived ignorance or deceit rendered him caustic, sarcastic, condescending; having roasted Johnson, the object of his scorn, he subsequently expressed shock and hurt at the cutting response his scathing remarks elicited. Such a response was typical for Fulbright, however: Whether he was deriding a family member for his or her ignorance or dressing down public figures like John Foster Dulles or Lyndon Johnson for their errors, he always subsequently claimed to have been misinterpreted, not to have meant his remarks personally. What amazing ignorance of human nature, not to have realized that people invest their egos in their vocations!

52 Interview with Pat Holt, Oct. 7, 1988, Washington, D.C.
53 Bundy to LBJ, Dec. 21, 1965, WHCH, Box 42, Johnson Papers. See also Marcy to Dean Rusk, Nov. 2, 1965, Box 5, Folder Nov., Marcy Papers.
54 Morrissey interview with Fulbright, "Modern Congress," 21.
55 McG. Bundy interview.

Unwilling to speculate on sibling traits and oedipal complexes, William Bundy attributed Fulbright's "perverseness" to the Oxford environment, where, Dean Rusk once remarked, it was considered a sign of weakness or stupidity ever to agree with anyone.[56] In challenging Dulles and Johnson, Bundy speculated, he was at last gaining the respect of the brutally arrogant British schoolboys who had made him feel so inferior a generation earlier.

If J. William Fulbright misunderstood the implications of the Dominican speech and the break with the White House for his career, so too did Lyndon Johnson underestimate the impact of Fulbright's alienation on his presidency and the course of American foreign policy. One snowy afternoon in November, several weeks before the New Zealand trip, Fulbright, Holt, Marcy, and Lowenstein were sitting around the office discussing the war in Vietnam. Fulbright had just read *Street Without Joy* by Bernard Fall. Intrigued, he asked if anyone knew Fall, who was then teaching at Howard University in Washington. Lowenstein said that he did. When Fulbright asked him to set up a meeting, Lowenstein got in a cab, went immediately to Fall's Georgetown home, and persuaded the journalist-scholar to agree to come to lunch the following Monday.[57]

A French-born expert on Southeast Asia, Fall interspersed long trips to Vietnam during the 1950s and 1960s, where he absorbed the warp and woof of village life and flew on combat missions with both the French and Americans, with teaching stints in Europe and America. Until his death in 1967, killed by a Vietcong land mine, he would spend much of his time warning the United States of the complexities of the Vietnam conflict. He repeatedly urged Washington to treat the encounter as "a revolutionary war, that is, a military operation with heavy political overtones. To win the military battle but lose the political war could well become the U.S. fate in Vietnam."[58] Marcy's opinion carried great weight with Fulbright, but Fall was a scholar and combat journalist. The break with Johnson over the Dominican intervention had created in the Arkansan alienation sufficient to prepare him emotionally for open conflict with the administration over Vietnam. The lunch with Fall marked the beginning of Fulbright's effort to educate himself on every aspect of the war in Southeast Asia.

As part of his effort to inform himself concerning the complexities of East Asia, Fulbright brought along *The Crippled Tree* by Chinese-Belgian author Han Suyin on the long trip to New Zealand.[59] The book was a personal and vivid account of China's ill-treatment at the hands of the West. More impor-

56 W. Bundy interview.

57 Holt interview and Lowenstein interview.

58 Quoted in Charles DeBenedetti with Charles Chatfield, *An American Ordeal: The Antiwar Movement of the Vietnam Era* (Syracuse, 1990), 84.

59 Johnson and Gwertzman, *Fulbright: The Dissenter*, 265.

tant, among the senators on the trip was Republican Hiram Fong of Hawaii. As the two engaged in long conversations on the culture and politics of the East, Fulbright began to realize for the first time that his country had undertaken a task that it could not accomplish, that it was attempting to "save" a culture that it did not understand, and that, in fact, in its obsession with the cold war, America had interjected itself into a conflict whose roots were largely indigenous.

# 21

# *The hearings*

"The war is not only not going well," Clyde Pettit wrote Lee Williams from Bangkok in January 1966; "the situation is worse than is reported in the press and worse, I believe, than is indicated in intelligence reports." Pettit, a lawyer-turned-journalist who had just finished interviewing some two hundred military personnel for the Arkansas radio network, instructed his friend to show the letter to Fulbright but otherwise to keep it confidential. That communication, a devastating account of the political and military situation in Southeast Asia, would become the existential basis for Fulbright, Marcy, and Williams's already deeply rooted philosophical and historical dissent from the war.

For the most part, the American military buildup was having little effect on the war because most U.S. troops "are literally confined in closely-guarded compounds, protected by moat-like defenses of concertina-wire and incessant barrages of U.S. artillery," Pettit wrote. Among American enlisted personnel and lower- and middle-ranking officers, particularly in combat areas, morale was unbelievably high. This gung-ho attitude made U.S. soldiers vigorous and effective fighters, but, ironically, rendered them useless in the battle for the hearts and minds of the South Vietnamese. Their "messianic attitude of anger" made pacification most difficult.

> It is strange to talk to these men in the field who are against any compromise, any cease-fire, any even temporary cessation of hostilities, and who talk blithely of remaining ten years and wanting to die there if necessary, and then to talk to the colonels in Saigon who . . . are infinitely more pessimistic, more cynical, and more realistic.[1]

One erudite officer had told him that "If there is a God, and he is very kind to us, and given a million men and five years and a miracle in making the South Vietnamese people like us, we stand an outside chance of a stalemate."[2]

As Fulbright and Williams sensed immediately, Pettit and his cynical officer were not exaggerating. Americans had repeatedly identified themselves with a French colonial regime that had denied the Vietnamese an education, a

[1] Pettit to Williams, Jan. 13, 1966, Series 48:17, Box 43:1, SPF. [2] Ibid.

decent living, a sense of independence, and that had "insulted a national dignity in countless ways." American officers, Pettit reported, insisted on inhabiting the old French colonial mansions that served as constant reminders to the Vietnamese of their past exploitation. "We are Westerners, the outsider, the alien," Williams's friend observed. "To the leftists, we are villains; to the rightists we are fools."[3] Pettit's reports were confirmed by Bernard Fall, Stanley Karnow, and a host of other sources.

In brief, in early 1966 the books that Fulbright was reading and the people to whom he was talking convinced him that the war in Vietnam was a civil conflict in two senses. On one level the struggle was between the people of North Vietnam and the inhabitants of South Vietnam. On another it was a battle within South Vietnam between the forces of democracy and pluralism on the one hand and the "Saigonese," to use historian George Kahin's term – the corrupt and dictatorial MRC and their hangers-on – on the other. The opponents of the regime in Saigon, both communist and noncommunist, had seized the banner of nationalism, whereas the generals in charge of the South Vietnamese government and their American sponsors were identified in the popular mind with colonialism. "It is fundamental in the affairs of men," Pettit concluded in his report, "that when you see the imminent and inevitable death of an ancient regime, that you go to the funeral, but you are amiable to the heirs and do not sit forever holding hands with the corpse in necrophilial devotion."[4]

Fulbright was not alone in his growing alienation. If they were not as privy to the deteriorating situation in Vietnam as were Fulbright, Morse, and Mansfield, a number of Americans by 1966 had, nonetheless, come out into open opposition to the war. Traditional pacifists, such as A. J. Muste, and the organizations they headed, such as the Fellowship of Reconciliation and the War Resisters League, spoke out against the carnage in South Vietnam because they were against all wars; the taking of human life, no matter what the reason, was immoral. Antinuclear activists who had organized the Committee for a Sane Nuclear Policy (SANE) in the mid-1950s opposed the war in Vietnam because they feared it would lead to a nuclear confrontation between the United States and the communist superpowers. Student activists who, energized by the civil rights movement, formed the Students for a Democratic Society (SDS) in 1962, enlisted in the antiwar movement as part of a larger campaign to alter American society fundamentally. SDS members and their academic mentors formed what came to be known in intellectual circles as the New Left. They espoused the radical critique of American foreign policy that William Appleman Williams had put forward in his famous 1959 book, *The Tragedy of American Diplomacy.* Building on the economic determinist interpretations of Charles Beard and Fred Harrington, Williams and the New Left-

[3] Ibid. [4] Ibid.

ists insisted that America, because it was a capitalist society, was dominated by financiers and manufacturers who, having subdued the American proletariat and exploited the nation's resources in the nineteenth century, set out to establish their economic hegemony throughout the rest of the world in the twentieth; and since politics always follows economics, the government and military were permanently and primarily committed to Wall Street's cause. Liberals of a more moderate stripe, concentrated in one wing of the ADA, had become convinced by the end of 1965 that the war in Southeast Asia was a perversion of the liberal internationalism they had espoused since the end of World War II: In its quest to protect democracy and liberty from communist totalitarianism, the United States was allying itself with brutal military dictatorships and facilitating the murder of thousands of innocent people. Finally, the Quakers and elements within the other major religious denominations began denouncing the war in Vietnam, some because they thought the whole enterprise unjust, others because they deplored the indiscriminate and brutal taking of civilian life, and still others because they were appalled at the spectacle of the richest, most powerful nation in the world attempting to bomb into submission a tiny, fifth-rate power situated halfway around the world. In October 1965 the Reverend Richard Neuhaus, Rabbi Abraham Heschel, and Father Daniel Berrigan formed Clergy Concerned About Vietnam.[5]

During a marine search-and-destroy mission in Cam Ne in August 1965, American troops rousted the villagers, suspected of collaborating with the Vietcong, from their huts, which they then set on fire with cigarette lighters. CBS newsman Morley Safer and his camera crew taped the scene, which included anguished, pleading villagers. Despite the outraged protests of the White House, the tapes were shown during the six o'clock news in homes all across America.[6] In October antiwar activists sponsored the International Days of Protest. Nearly a hundred thousand people in eighty cities and several nations participated.[7]

Far more troubling to the president than these public displays, however, was the discomfiture of those "liberals" in Congress who were increasingly uneasy about the bombing and escalation. Following testimony on the Hill, McNamara reported that support in the House and Senate was "broad" but "thin." "There is a feeling of uneasiness and frustration. There is criticism of our allies for not helping more in Vietnam," he reported.[8]

In December Bundy, Ball, Rusk, and others began to urge Johnson to consider a Christmas bombing halt. What was needed, as presidential aide Jack

5 Charles DeBenedetti with Charles Chatfield, *An American Ordeal: The Antiwar Movement of the Vietnam Era* (Syracuse, 1990), 144.
6 Harriman to Rusk, Aug. 28, 1965, Box 499, Harriman Papers.
7 DeBenedetti and Chatfield, *American Ordeal,* 125.
8 Notes of 554th NSC Meeting, Aug. 5, 1965, NSC Meeting Notes File, Johnson Papers.

Valenti put it, was something that would "de-fang the leftists, and comfort the moderates."[9] On Christmas Eve 1965, the constant pounding of NVA positions between the Seventeenth and Twentieth Parallels that had been going on continuously since May suddenly stopped. Immediately a small army of diplomats headed by ambassador-at-large Averell Harriman departed for various European and Asian capitals with much-publicized instructions to leave no stone unturned in their search for a negotiated settlement. Before Harriman left, Johnson told him that the object of the trip was to enable the envoy "to testify [before Congress] . . . that he had sent me to go the last mile in trying to come to a settlement."[10]

From the beginning Carl Marcy sensed that the bombing halt was a ploy by the administration to undercut and divide congressional opposition to the war. He felt the country moving inexorably toward massive intervention into Vietnam, and he was desperate to stop the drift. "The present bombing pause and negotiation initiative offer the last clear chance to stop short of unlimited escalation," he warned Fulbright. "If the United States moves ahead now it must be prepared to go the whole way – even to the use of nuclear weapons." Though he admitted that "the Birch society will get a new lease on life," he reiterated his view that it was time to withdraw from Southeast Asia – conditionally or unconditionally. Quite aside from the national interest, the president's political fortunes as well as the future of the Democratic Party demanded it. Johnson and the Democrats could win in 1968 only if they ran on a peace program. "The fundamental issue between Johnson and Goldwater was whether the United States was to become more deeply involved in land war in Asia, and the American people voted against that, not for Johnson."[11]

Shortly after Christmas, Bill and Betty departed for Puerto Rico and a week in the sun. Hal Douglas joined them en route. It had been a difficult year for everyone. Following a year and a half in the Menninger Clinic in Topeka, Helen had died in the summer of 1965. She had been sitting on the couch in the living room at 5 Mount Nord talking to Hal before he returned to work after his lunch break. Her heart had given out in midsentence. Though Betty was still recovering from her own heart problems, she and Bill had made the trip to Fayetteville for the funeral. Then there had been Fulbright's break with Johnson and the accompanying tension. For a week Betty lay in the sun and wrote letters while Bill and Hal golfed. For Fulbright Puerto Rico was just a brief calm before another stormy encounter with the administration.

9 Valenti to LBJ, Dec. 6, 1965, WHCF, Nat'l. Sec./Def., Box 218, Johnson Papers.
10 Harriman to Rusk, Dec. 28, 1965, Box 499, Harriman Papers.
11 Vietnam, Jan. 10, 1966, Box 6, Folder Jan., Marcy Papers.

The third week in January the SFRC, with some difficulty, persuaded the secretary of state to testify on a supplemental appropriations bill for Vietnam. The bombing pause had been accompanied by the most intense congressional debate on Vietnam to date. When Rusk entered the Foreign Relations hearing room he found it unusually full. In addition to the regulars – Fulbright, Mansfield, Symington, Hickenlooper, and Aiken – Clifford Case (R–New Jersey), Eugene McCarthy (D–Minnesota), Lausche, Mundt, Williams, Clark, and Claiborne Pell (D–Rhode Island) were on hand as well. He would be frank with the committee, Rusk said. The Soviet Union was willing to accept a Korea-like settlement in Vietnam, to interpret the Geneva conventions in such a way as to allow separate elections below and above the Seventeenth Parallel. However, because of "their contest with Peiping" they had "given their proxy to Hanoi"; thus, the road to a negotiated settlement had reached a dead end. Meanwhile, the North Vietnamese were using the bombing pause to pour men and equipment into the south. The administration's goal was to convince the other side it could not win. That was what had happened during the Berlin blockade and the Korean War:

> [T]here was no objective reason in terms of necessity as to why the other side lifted the Berlin blockade when it did, but, for reasons better known to them than to us, there came a point when they seemed to find that it was desirable to do so. . . . There was no major objective reason why the other side had to end the Korean War when it did.[12]

The implication was clear: If the United States and its allies remained firm, the communists would eventually give up in Vietnam.

Had the administration offered to negotiate with the NLF or the Vietcong, Fulbright asked? No, Rusk replied. Both were creatures of the government of North Vietnam. "Hanoi organized the VC, the NLF, in Hanoi in 1960," he declared, "and immediately started the infiltration of men and arms into South Vietnam." Had not the VC, NLF, and Vietminh originally been part of the same movement, a nationalist movement that, following World War II, had been spurned by the United States and only then had turned to Moscow and Peiping for help, the chairman queried?

Rusk squirmed; his eyes flashed. Frank Lausche tried to run interference. What gallant composure under fire Rusk was showing, the Ohio Democrat interjected. Upon seeing the secretary's strained, beleaguered face on television the night before (Rusk had appeared on a network news program to discuss Vietnam), Lausche declared, "I pretty nearly wept." Rusk and Fulbright ignored him.

12 Briefing by Secretary Rusk on His Recent Visits Abroad, Jan. 24, 1966, Executive Sessions, SFRC, RG 46, NA.

Fulbright then proceeded to read from testimony given by then-CIA Chief John McCone in October 1963 to the effect that the Diem regime was a dictatorship operating under the facade of a democracy, and then from Rusk's statement given a month later assuring the committee that Diem's regime was a constitutional government chosen by the people. The secretary of state, Fulbright seemed to be saying, did not know what he was talking about. "Never criticize a man out of his own mouth," Lyndon Johnson once advised McGeorge Bundy; it was a sure way to make a lifelong enemy. Rusk was furious. His eyes narrowed and his austere face drawn into a hard mask, he murmured to Fulbright that he was sure South Vietnam would choose "something that is not communism" over communism if there were free elections.

"I do want to say that there is one subject on which I am extremely sensitive, and that is the question of credibility and integrity," Rusk declared with all the gravity he could muster. "When I came into this job I made a firm resolution . . . that I would never lie to the press." Silently, Rusk promised himself that he would never again be forthcoming with Fulbright or Marcy.[13] One way to keep from being caught in a lie was to not provide any information.[14]

The clash between Fulbright and Rusk, between the State Department and the SFRC, had been building a long time. In August of 1965 Marcy had written an impassioned assessment of American foreign policy for Fulbright. What had happened to "turn the liberal supporters of President Kennedy into opponents of the policies of President Johnson?" The answer was obvious, Marcy declaimed. "We have tried to force upon the rest of the world a righteous American point of view which we maintain is the consensus that others must accept. Most of the tragedies of the world have come from such righteousness."[15] The chief purveyor of the American worldview, Marcy believed, was Dean Rusk. No longer the impotent bureaucrat of his earlier imaginings, Rusk had assumed the role of lead villain in the escalation drama. At the close of World War II the United States had been thrust into a position of international leadership; very quickly it had defined its mission as saving the world from the scourge of communism. Rusk had grown up in and been part of that national conversion to a secular religion.[16] Neither Mar-

13 Interview with Dean Rusk, Oct. 14, 1988, Athens, Ga.

14 Fulbright began by notifying Rusk that the committee had voted not to allow transcripts of closed hearings to leave its offices under any circumstances. The previous fall, following George Ball's testimony on Vietnam in executive session, Rusk had asked for a copy of the transcript. Fulbright had agreed but with an "eyes only" stipulation. In an effort to prove that the committee was deeply divided over Vietnam, State had leaked various senatorial statements to the press.

15 Briefing by Secretary Rusk on His Recent Visits Abroad, Jan. 24, 1966, Executive Sessions, SFRC, RG 46, NA.

16 Marcy to JWF, Aug. 17, 1965, Series 48:1, Box 16:2, SPF.

cy nor Fulbright could ever forget that Rusk's chief backer for the position of secretary of state had been Henry Luce.[17]

In fact, Dean Rusk was both an impotent bureaucrat and a naïve missionary. Born on a farm in Cherokee County, Georgia, Rusk had moved with his family to Atlanta, where his father had secured a job as a mail carrier. An excellent student, he had earned a scholarship to Davidson and subsequently a Rhodes to Oxford. During World War II Rusk had served in the China–Burma–India theater and subsequently secured a position in the State Department working under George C. Marshall, whom he had worshiped. During the Eisenhower years, Rusk had taught briefly and then become head of the Rockefeller Foundation, the position he had abandoned for the secretary of state's job in 1961.[18]

The Georgian was a gracious, self-effacing, driven man: driven to serve his country, to prove himself in battle, whether for Marshall in Southeast Asia during World War II or for Lyndon Johnson before the Klieglights in the SFRC hearing room. Rusk's intellect was undiscriminating, and much of his intelligence derivative. He absorbed the ideas and assumptions of the authority figures he found himself serving. His views on foreign policy had become fixated during the late 1940s and early 1950s, when international communism really had been directed from the Kremlin and the domino theory had gained currency. His justifications for the Vietnam War sounded anachronistic even to his colleagues in the State Department in the 1960s. Rusk was no hypocrite, however – he believed them.

Dean Rusk came to have questions about the war, to doubt the efficacy of bombing, to wonder if there was any chance of winning with the nation only half mobilized; but, incredibly, he did not believe that it was his duty to express those doubts. Kennedy, wanting to control foreign affairs personally, had selected Rusk; soon discovering that he had time to focus on only the most pressing issues and most important crises, the president had become frustrated with the Georgian. "I can't get Rusk to take any responsibility," Kennedy had once complained to Douglas Dillon. "He sends cables – every paragraph – over here and wants me to sign." Dillon recalled that, during the Cuban missile crisis, the secretary of state sometimes had not attended the meetings of the Executive Committee of the National Security Council, and when he had, he'd rarely spoken.[19] Matters did not change under Johnson. Rusk insisted that it was not his job to give advice to the president in a cabinet meeting or in front of the NSC; that must be left to one-on-one conversations

17 Donald A. Ritchie, interviewer, *Oral History Interviews: Carl A. Marcy* (Senate Historical Office: Washington, D.C., 1983), 187–8.

18 Dean Rusk as told to Richard Rusk, *As I Saw It* (New York, 1990), 27–32, 93–8, 193–200.

19 Interview with Douglas Dillon, May 5, 1993, New York, N.Y.

with his boss. McNamara, for one, doubted that Dean Rusk ever gave Lyndon Johnson any advice, even when they were alone.[20]

Rusk's January 24 testimony before the SFRC seemed to Fulbright to demonstrate beyond a shadow of a doubt that the administration was locked into its blind anticommunist assumptions and that it would not meet the minimum conditions for beginning negotiations, namely, recognition of the NLF.[21] Fulbright hoped against hope that Johnson would continue the pause, but in his heart he knew that Carl Marcy was right: The president and his men had already set their course. Before Rusk left the Hill, Fulbright asked that at the very least the committee be consulted before a decision on resumption was taken.

Lyndon Johnson was eager to resume bombing North Vietnam as soon as the New Year began, and he only became more anxious and determined as time wore on. When the Joint Chiefs were able to produce statistics showing a dramatic increase in infiltration, McNamara pointed out that it was the dry season and this was to be expected. The CIA continued to insist that bombing had had no impact on the north's willingness or ability to infiltrate, and that the assault from the air would continue to be ineffective.[22] They argued in vain. From Saigon, Cabot Lodge, under intense pressure from Westmoreland, railed against the pause. On Christmas Day alone, he reported to Johnson, "1,000 North Vietnamese soldiers were reliably observed entering South Vietnam."[23] "Every day increases their capability in the South," Earle Wheeler insisted to Johnson, and he called for a full-scale air assault on Hanoi.[24]

By January 20 Johnson had made the decision to resume bombing. He could not bear the thought that he was letting America's fighting men down. The president's friend, Jack Valenti – the Houston public relations expert and campaign aide whom Johnson had brought with him to the White House – advised the president to resist Fulbright, Lippmann, and the other "Lyndliners."[25] Former governor John Connally bombarded Johnson with hawkish advice throughout the pause. He told the president to remember that there were only two hundred thousand boys in Vietnam and they had only four

20 Rusk, *As I Saw It,* 16, and interview with Robert McNamara, Aug. 2, 1991, Washington, D.C.

21 "Continue Bombing Lull, Fulbright Urges U.S.," *Washington Star,* Jan. 24, 1966.

22 Meeting between President, Rusk, Bundy, McNamara, Ball, Moyers, Valenti, Jan. 3, 1966, and Meeting between President, Rusk, Helms, McNamara, Harriman, Taylor, Ball, Raborn, Thompson, Goldberg, Bundy and Valenti, Jan. 22, 1966, NSF, Meeting Notes File, Box 1, Johnson Papers.

23 Lodge to LBJ, Jan. 5, 1966, NSF, Memos to President, Box 6, Johnson Papers.

24 Cabinet Meeting, Jan. 10, 1966, Meeting Notes File, Box 2, Johnson Papers.

25 Historian and peace activist Staughton Lynd had gone to Hanoi in early January to try to start negotiations himself. As the administration well knew, he was in touch with Fulbright during and after his trip. Marcy to JWF, Jan. 17, 1966, Box 6, Folder Jan., Marcy Papers.

hundred thousand parents; their one advocate was Lyndon Johnson. The real question was whether the president was going to provide America's fighting men with the equipment and support they needed to win the war.[26]

Although he had been wounded by his confrontation with Fulbright on the twenty-fourth, Dean Rusk persuaded Johnson to meet with the chairman. "The committee would have no serious problem if you see Fulbright," he advised.[27] The president agreed, but only on condition that the Arkansan be bracketed by hawks. On the evening of the twenty-fifth Johnson met with the entire congressional leadership. Dirksen, Russell, McCormack, Hickenlooper, Carl Albert, and others urged the president to resume and even expand the bombing; only Mansfield and Fulbright spoke out for a continuation of the pause.[28]

On January 31, 1966, American fighters and fighter-bombers took off once again and struck bridges and staging areas north of the Seventeenth Parallel. Resumption would, Johnson hoped, compel the North Vietnamese to "show their ass before we showed ours."[29]

With Lyndon Johnson's decision to resume the bombing of North Vietnam, J. William Fulbright's pent-up anger and frustration burst forth. On the evening the bombing resumed he appeared on a CBS national television hookup to declare the war morally wrong and counterproductive to the interests of his country. The world's largest, richest, most powerful nation had no business, he told Martin Agronsky and Eric Sevareid, laying waste to a small, desperately impoverished, weak, and divided state like Vietnam. No matter how the conflict ended, the United States had lost stature by participating in a struggle beneath its dignity and even its notice. The administration, the Arkansan declared, was still a prisoner of the Munich analogy, a comparison totally inapplicable to Southeast Asia. As visualized by its architects, containment was designed to prevent the spread of Soviet aggression; as it had evolved under Johnson, it was an attempt to contain a worldwide movement toward self-government and self-expression by peoples formerly yoked to European empires. This misreading of reality and a failure to distinguish between "big C" and "little c" communist revolutions lay at the very heart of the

26 Marvin Watson to LBJ, Feb. 21, 1966, SHCV, Box 342, Johnson Papers.

27 Meeting of Foreign Policy Advisors, Jan. 24, 1966, Meeting Notes File, Box 1, Johnson Papers. A number of senators had spoken to him privately, Rusk said, complaining about the fact that the chairman of the SFRC was not included in White House meetings with the congressional leadership. Rusk to Johnson, Jan. 24, 1966, NSF–NSC History, Box 44, Johnson Papers.

28 Bipartisan Congressional Meeting, Jan. 25, 1966, Meeting Notes File, Box 1, Johnson Papers.

29 Meeting with Foreign Policy Advisors on Vietnam, Jan. 20, 1966, Meeting Notes File, Box 1, Johnson Papers.

Vietnam misadventure. He ended by expressing deep regret at the role he had played in ushering the Gulf of Tonkin Resolution through the Senate.[30]

With the end of the Christmas bombing halt, Fulbright and Marcy proceeded with plans to hold public hearings on the war in Southeast Asia. It was now more than ever necessary to generate a congressional and public debate over Vietnam, to start a controversy over a very controversial subject, they believed. Fulbright had learned to his deep dismay during the Dominican crisis that an articulate, thoughtful, and provocative speech was not sufficient to arouse the nation. That tactic had left him isolated, "dangling in the wind," to anticipate a phrase. Public hearings with establishment figures in which he and other doubters questioned both the assumptions underlying the war in Vietnam and the tactics being employed to fight it might just do the trick – especially if they were televised. On February 3 the SFRC met in executive session; Fulbright, Gore, Morse, and Aiken persuaded the others to authorize hearings not just on the pending $415 million supplemental aid bill for Vietnam but on the war in its broadest sense. The hearings were to be public, and Carl Marcy was directed to obtain the widest possible exposure.

By early 1966 a majority of the SFRC were either deeply disturbed by U.S. involvement in Southeast Asia or overtly opposed. Those who had previously been willing to give the administration the benefit of the doubt had run out of patience. A number, including John Sparkman (D–Alabama), had lost confidence in the administration because of its overly optimistic and consistently wrong predictions in the past – we are winning in Vietnam, light at the end of the tunnel–type statements. Moreover, several members feared that Vietnam had brought the United States and China to the brink of a major war. A consensus existed on the SFRC that John Stennis, second-ranking member of Armed Services, was plugged into the decision-making process in the White House: The Mississippi hawk had correctly and accurately predicted the troop buildup that had taken place in the fall of 1965. On January 27, 1966, he had stated in a speech to the Mississippi legislature that by the end of the year there would be six hundred thousand men in Vietnam, and that if the United States were to go to war with China, he favored the use of tactical nuclear weapons. Fulbright and the majority of SFRC members believed that Stennis was accurately foretelling the future, and they were frightened. The only dissenters from what one staffer referred to as "the Fulbright majority" were Lausche, Dodd, Symington, and Hickenlooper.[31]

30 William C. Berman, *William Fulbright and the Vietnam War: The Dissent of a Political Realist* (Kent, Ohio, 1988), 55.

31 Hearings on S. Res. 217, Authorizing and Directing the Committee on Foreign Relations to Conduct a Full and Complete Investigation of All Aspects of United States Policies in Vietnam, Executive Sessions, Feb. 3, 1965, SFRC, RG 46, NA, and Henry H. Wilson to LBJ, Feb. 18, 1966, WHCF, Subject File, Box 342, Johnson Papers.

Fulbright and Marcy were realistic about what precisely the televised hearings could accomplish. To listen to the "armed services boys," the chairman wrote Marriner Eccles, it would seem that "although we ought to get out, it is actually impossible, and it even discredits one to suggest that we do so." Given this mind-set, "the most favorable thing the hearings can possibly accomplish is to prevent the enormous escalation of this war."[32]

As soon as the SFRC decided on public hearings and the meeting broke up, Marcy got on the phone with executives from the major television networks. He described the scope of the hearings, and ticked off the impressive list of witnesses scheduled to appear.[33] On January 28 Dean Rusk had testified in public session on the supplemental appropriations bill; he and Fulbright had taken up where they had left off on the twenty-fourth. Both the CBS and NBC nightly news had carried clips of the clashes between the two Rhodes scholars: The networks realized that this was the stuff of real-life television drama.[34] Thus, when Marcy called with news of the wider hearings and list of witnesses, CBS and NBC ordered their crews to be prepared to occupy the Hill.

Mike Mansfield, as he would do throughout the remainder of the Johnson administration, immediately briefed the White House as to what was afoot. In turn, Johnson ordered his aides to spare no effort to sabotage the "Fulbright hearings." When Fulbright requested permission from the Senate as a whole to hold hearings during the regular session of the Senate, Senate Minority Leader Everett Dirksen, at Johnson's behest, blocked him.[35] Fulbright and Marcy forced Dirksen to back down by threatening to hold the Vietnam inquiry in the evenings, during prime time.[36] Then, on the night of February 3, without telling any of his aides, Johnson decided to hold an impromptu summit meeting with South Vietnamese Prime Minster Nguyen Cao Ky in Honolulu. The meeting would take place during Fulbright's show.

The Honolulu conference was, to use McGeorge Bundy's description, "a big farrago, meant to take the spotlight off the hearings."[37] After talking with Valenti, Johnson ordered the American Embassy in Saigon to roust Ky out of bed on Thursday night, the third, and have him invite Johnson to a summit meeting to be held on Saturday and Sunday. The first Bundy or any of Johnson's other aides heard of the trip was when the president announced it at a press conference on Friday the fourth.[38] The meeting opened with neither

32 JWF to Marriner Eccles, Mar. 1, 1966, Series 48:18, Box 47:7, SPF.

33 Donald A. Ritchie, interviewer, *Oral History Interviews: Pat M. Holt* (Senate Historical Office: Washington, D.C., 1980), 204.

34 Melvin Small, *Johnson, Nixon, and the Doves* (New Brunswick, N.J., 1988), 78.

35 "Senate Nears Vietnam Inquiry," *Los Angeles Times*, Feb. 3, 1966.

36 Godfrey Sperling, Jr., "Backstage at Senate's Great Debate," *Christian Science Monitor*, Feb. 14, 1966.

37 Interview with McGeorge Bundy, Aug. 1, 1991, New York.

38 Note (anonymous), 1966, NSFA, NSC History, Box 44, Johnson Papers.

adequate preparation nor even a precise agenda. Johnson used the occasion to give a pep talk and to exhort the American and Vietnamese military to renew their efforts. He wanted "coonskins on the wall," he told them. When Ky finished his speech, an optimistic set piece that promised not only victory but a new era of political stability, Johnson leaned over and whispered to him, "Boy, you talk just like an American." Small wonder: Ky's speech had been prepared by the American Embassy. Johnson could not leave Honolulu without a blast at Fulbright, Morse, and his congressional detractors. He warned America that the war effort was being hampered by "special pleaders who counsel retreat in Vietnam."[39]

Fulbright and Marcy had intended to mix administration figures with prominent dissidents during the open hearings, but the administration had no intention of cooperating. To Fulbright's chagrin, Johnson took both Maxwell Taylor and Alexis Johnson, then deputy undersecretary of state, with him to Hawaii.[40] Both McNamara and Rusk refused to appear in open hearing. Not all were able to escape, however. On the morning of the fourth, with Lyndon Johnson watching on television, David Bell testified before the SFRC on the aid program in Vietnam and was subjected to withering cross-examination.

At stake in the 1966 SFRC hearings was control of the television airways and, through them, American public opinion. Fulbright and Marcy had become acutely aware of the executive's ability to dominate the media and especially television. Since the time of Franklin D. Roosevelt, powerful presidential personalities had co-opted and manipulated print and broadcast newspeople. The White House was easier and simpler to cover than Congress, and the president's press secretaries ensured that reporters were furnished with an abundance of interesting stories and photo opportunities. Most shared the presidents' contempt for Congress, a complex, perverse place very difficult to squeeze into a brief time slot. One who was different was Fred W. Friendly, head of CBS news and protégé of Edward R. Murrow. Throughout his career, Friendly had been pressing television to devote more space and money to news, particularly to live coverage. The Fulbright hearings offered him his opportunity. After persuading his superiors to agree to thirty-minute coverage for the Fulbright hearings, Friendly took personal charge and kept the hearings on throughout the morning and into the afternoon. *Captain Kangaroo* and various soap operas were preempted, and Friendly's superiors were furious.[41]

When the committee met again in public session and on television, it heard testimony from General James Gavin, who presented the case for the enclave strategy that Fulbright and Lippmann had earlier advocated, and that the John-

39 Bryce Nelson, "Fulbright Sees Active Congress Role In Vietnam," *Washington Post*, Feb. 8, 1966.
40 JWF to John B. Oakes, Feb. 5, 1966, Series 438:18, Box 49:4, SPF.
41 David Halberstam, *The Powers That Be* (New York, 1979), 504.

son administration had already discarded. Fulbright was able to persuade Korean War hero Matthew Ridgway to submit a letter to the committee endorsing this approach. On February 11, Fulbright and Marcy pulled out their big gun: George Kennan. No individual in or out of government had more prestige as a foreign policy analyst. As the father of containment policy, Kennan was hardly subject to the criticism that he was soft on communism; at the same time he had endeared himself to cold-war liberals by his calls for a defense policy that matched means with ends, his attacks on massive retaliation and brinkmanship, and his advocacy of patience in dealing with the Soviets. A distinguished scholar, the former ambassador to Yugoslavia and the Soviet Union was a model of decorum, precisely the establishment figure Fulbright needed to question Johnson's policy. Kennan agreed with Gavin that it was essential to avoid further escalation, and he urged also that the war be liquidated "as soon as this could be done without inordinate damage to our prestige or stability in the area." If the United States sought to resolve the problem of Vietnam by winning a clear-cut military victory over Ho and DRV cofounder General Vo Nguyen Giap, there was every chance that full-scale war with China would ensue.[42]

Like the Kefauver crime investigations of 1951 and the Army–McCarthy encounters of 1954, the Vietnam hearings impinged on the lives of virtually all Americans. Those that did not watch directly caught excerpts on the six and ten o'clock news. Fulbright, the questioner, and Gavin, Kennan, and the other witnesses were not irresponsible students or wild-eyed radicals but conservative, establishment figures. Maybe, some Americans began to think, Vietnam was not analogous to World War II or Korea. Even more began to suspect that the country had become involved in a situation that it did not truly understand.

Worried by the attention the hearings were receiving, Lyndon Johnson called Frank Stanton of CBS and demanded that he cease coverage. On February 10, the network abandoned the hearings and ran its normal daytime fare, including reruns of the *I Love Lucy* show; only after respected news director Fred W. Friendly resigned over the incident did CBS resume coverage. NBC carried the entire proceeding, however, including Kennan's telling testimony.[43]

With each day that the hearings continued, Johnson became more and more distraught. His public relations people were maddeningly candid: Do not worry about the effect that the hearings were having on Beijing and Hanoi, presidential adviser George Reedy told him, worry about their impact on the

42 "Fulbright Fears U.S. Eliminating Chance for Peace," *Arkansas Gazette,* Feb. 11, 1966.

43 "Hearings Coverage Draw Heavy Fire," *Washington Star,* Apr. 4, 1966, and Small, *Johnson, Nixon, and the Doves,* 78.

American people. Fulbright's show, he said, was deeply divisive; it was doing nothing less than polarizing the electorate. "At the present time, the debate is being conducted in the tone of a 'hawks' and 'doves' clash with the 'hawks' convinced that anyone outside of their ranks is a 'chicken' and the 'doves' convinced that anyone outside of their ranks is a 'vulture.'" Moreover, whenever the doves held centerstage, the administration came off as hawkish, and when the hawks grabbed the microphone, it was made to appear dovish. The end result was a divided country and the appearance of a vacillating government.[44] "Dick Goodwin called yesterday to say that everywhere he speaks, he runs into deep concern about the situation in Vietnam," Joseph Califano told the president on February 19. "He said he is personally and firmly convinced that you are pursuing the correct course, but that the Fulbright hearings particularly are doing a tremendous amount to confuse the American people."[45]

At this point Dirksen, Symington, Russell Long (D–Louisiana), and Hickenlooper intervened with Johnson and persuaded him to allow Maxwell Taylor and Dean Rusk to appear.[46] With "hostile" witnesses on the stand, Fulbright abandoned the sympathetic, solicitous manner he had used with Gavin and Kennan, and adopted the prosecutorial style for which he was becoming famous. The public was treated for the first time to images of the chairman – leaning forward intently toward the witnesses, eyes shielded by dark glasses from the glare of the powerful television lights, questioning, probing, confronting witnesses with history and logic. It was standing room only in the Klieg-lit hearing room as Taylor, bespectacled and civilian-suited, took his seat. Conspicuously occupying a front-row chair was Senator Robert F. Kennedy's wife Ethel; the senator himself stood in the back of the room. (So fond of Taylor were the Kennedys that they had named their one-year-old son after the general.) Was not the American Revolution a "war of national liberation?" Fulbright asked Maxwell Taylor. Wasn't it true that politically there was no such thing as South Vietnam? Taylor, who had been carefully coached by Stuart Symington, could only defend administration policy as "the best that has been suggested."[47] Fulbright then read a letter from an "anonymous but articulate" observer in Southeast Asia who declared that the United

44 Reedy to LBJ, Feb. 17, 1966, WHCF, Nat'l. Sec./Def., Box 219, Johnson Papers.

45 Califano to LBJ, Feb. 19, 1966, Box 219, WHCF, Nat'l. Sec./Def., Johnson Papers.

46 Mike Manatos to LBJ, Feb. 16, 1966, WHCF, Subject File, Box 342, Johnson Papers. During the hearings presidential aides were in constant contact with their friends on the committee, especially Dodd and Lausche, supplying them with questions and giving them encouragement. Manatos to LBJ, Feb. 17, 1966, Box 342, WHCF, Subject File, Johnson Papers.

47 "New Kind of War for Gen. Taylor," *New York Herald Tribune,* Feb. 18, 1966, and Mike Manatos to LBJ, Feb. 16, 1966, WHCF, Subject File, Box 342, Johnson Papers.

States was losing the war. The countryside was insecure, the Army of the Republic of Vietnam was well-meaning but ineffectual, and the threat of terrorism ever-present. The author, of course, was Clyde Pettit.[48] The hearings climaxed when Rusk appeared on February 18. In what constituted a summation of the proceedings, the secretary of state articulated the case for continuation of the war in Vietnam and Fulbright the case against:

> FULBRIGHT: I think there is something wrong with our approach. There must be something wrong with our diplomacy.
>
> RUSK: Senator, is it just possible that there is something wrong with them [the North Vietnamese and NLF]?
>
> FULBRIGHT: Yes. There is a lot wrong with them. They are very primitive, difficult, poor people who have been fighting for twenty years and I don't understand myself why they can continue to fight, but they can.
>
> RUSK: And they want to take over South Vietnam by force.
>
> FULBRIGHT: It is said the liberation front would like to take it over by election.[49]

So threatened did the president feel by the hearings that on February 19 he called J. Edgar Hoover and ordered him to have the FBI "cover Senate Foreign Relations Committee television presentation with a view toward determining whether Senator Fulbright and the other Senators were receiving information from Communists." The bureau obliged by drawing "parallels" between presentations made at the hearings and "documented Communist Party publications or statements of Communist leaders."[50] Shortly after the hearings ended, Johnson had Fulbright and several other Senate doves placed under strict FBI surveillance.[51] Perhaps the president hoped Hoover would expose some link between his critics and the international communist conspiracy; more likely, he anticipated that the director would be able to uncover an illicit love affair, a financial wrongdoing, or some other personal peccadillo that could be used to silence his tormentors. At the same time, the White House ordered the research division in State to ferret out Fulbright's public statements during the period when mainland China was being overrun by Mao. Johnson may have feared a revival of McCarthyism, but he was not above appropriating Tail Gunner Joe's techniques.[52] "The criticism from the

48 Ned Curran, "Fulbright Reveals Note from Vietnam Saying U.S. Losing," *Arkansas Gazette,* Feb. 19, 1966.

49 Quoted in Haynes Johnson and Bernard M. Gwertzman, *Fulbright: The Dissenter* (New York, 1968), 281.

50 Athan G. Theoharris, *From the Secret Files of J. Edgar Hoover* (Chicago, 1991), 237.

51 Berman, *Fulbright and the Vietnam War,* 68.

52 Marcy to JWF, Feb. 22, 1966, Box 6, Folder Feb. 66, JWF Papers, SFRC, RG 46, NA.

Executive is becoming bitter and mean," Fulbright complained to a constituent.[53]

Unbeknownst to Fulbright, Johnson ordered J. Edgar Hoover to provide Everett Dirksen and Bourke Hickenlooper with "evidence" that the chairman of the SFRC was either a communist agent or a dupe of the communists. Given the frequent contacts between Fulbright and his staff and personnel from the Soviet and East European embassies, this was not difficult. The first week in March the director's assistant, C. D. DeLoach, visited the two Republicans. He indicated that he was coming at the president's specific request and asked that their conversations be held in the strictest confidence. Both were more than ready to believe that the Arkansan was "deeply involved and very much obligated to communist interests," as DeLoach subsequently reported. According to the bureau, Hickenlooper observed that Fulbright's willingness to betray the interests of his country stemmed from his resentment at not being named secretary of state. Both promised to do everything in their power to counteract his baleful influence.[54]

It should be pointed out that Fulbright was not calling for unconditional withdrawal from Vietnam. What he advocated in early 1966 was an end to the bombing of the north, the withdrawal of American troops to enclaves around South Vietnam's major cities, the reconvening of the 1954 Geneva Conference looking toward national elections in Vietnam, and, following a negotiated political settlement, the removal from Vietnam of all foreign troops. The Johnson administration was adamantly opposed to this strategy because it was certain that it would lead to the electoral triumph of Ho Chi Minh and the communization of all of Vietnam. That development, in turn, would represent a clear victory for the forces of international communism and tip the scales in favor of Moscow and Beijing. "I regard the analogy between the Cuban missile crisis and the Viet Nam war as legitimate," Walt Rostow, then head of the policy planning staff in the State Department, wrote Averell Harriman. "Both are conscious and purposeful Communist efforts to shift the balance of power against us at a decisive point."[55]

Fulbright was still unsure of Johnson's motives, of the sources of his erroneous policy in Southeast Asia. It was probably a combination of things, he guessed. In his obsession with consensus, the president was too ready to collaborate with the Goldwaterites. In his ignorance, he was too willing to rely on advisers who had a vested intellectual and bureaucratic stake in victory

53 JWF to M. S. Craig, Feb. 11, 1966, Series 48:18, Box 47:5, SPF.

54 DeLoach interview with Everett Dirksen, Mar. 7, 1966, and DeLoach interview with Bourke Hickenlooper, Mar. 8, 1966, "Hoover's Official and Confidential File," FBI Files.

55 W. Rostow to Harriman, Jan. 28, 1966, Box 499, Harriman Papers.

in Vietnam. In his altruism, he overestimated America's ability to save the world. Indeed, it was this latter tendency to see himself as "a combination of Santa Claus and God whose personal destiny it is to insure life, liberty, happiness, wealth, health, education, etc., not only for every person in the U.S. but to all the world," that was at the root of the problem[56] – which made it hard for Fulbright to harden his heart completely against his old Senate colleague. Young men were dying, however, and a foreign culture teetered on the brink of destruction because of Lyndon Johnson's tragic flaws.

Public and press reactions to the 1966 hearings were mixed. The national print media split, with critics headed by the *Washington Post* – intensely pro-Johnson since Ben Bradlee's transfer from *Newsweek* – and supporters spearheaded by the *New York Times*. For the most part, television news just reported; what editorial comment there was tended to be pro-Fulbright. Roger Mudd, for example, praised the Arkansan for being able "to shed his American clothes and look at a situation objectively." His "disinterest" was good for the country, and it was in the national interest that "he continues to be elected."[57] Of 1,207 letters sent to the State Department, 1,028 were counted as approving Rusk's presentation; but the White House was soon chastising the State and Defense departments for exaggerating or distorting the contents of opinion mail. Of the 924 "pro" letters the DOD claimed it received during January 1–February 14, 1966, only 30 were deemed reliable enough in the end to turn over to newspeople.[58] Marcy and the SFRC staff claimed that the committee's mail ran 30 to 1 against escalation in the wake of the hearings. They took great pains to circulate a congratulatory letter from General Matthew Ridgway, the hero of Korea: "Having sat before the TV screen throughout all of the hearings," he wrote Fulbright, "may I state, sir, my respectful opinion that you conducted them in the finest traditions of the Senate, and that you and your colleagues performed a signal service to our people."[59] The Vietnam inquiry was not a complete public relations success, however. One Cleveland woman demanded that the committee hold its hearings in private or move them from 4:30 to 7:30: "Interference of [*sic*] regular daytime television programs is losing you the support and the votes of housewives."[60]

The hearings created almost as much attention abroad as they did at home. On February 14 the BBC ran Kennan's testimony and Fulbright's cross-examination almost verbatim. Various members of the ruling Labour Party went on talk shows to voice their agreement with the doubts that had been expressed.[61]

56 JWF to Jim Ballard, Series 48:18, Box 47:2, SPF.
57 PW to JWF, 1966, Series 48:17, Box 43:3, SPF.
58 Larry Levinson to Joe Califano, Feb. 12, 1966, WHCF, Box 134, Johnson Papers.
59 Ridgway to JWF, Feb. 19, 1966, Series 48:17, Box 43:1, JWF Papers.
60 "Fulbright Mail Runs 30 to 1 For War Stand," *Arkansas Gazette*, Feb. 12, 1966.
61 Hilary A. Marquand to JWF, Feb. 15, 1966, Series 48:18, Box 49:3, SPF.

At first glance, Fulbright and Marcy's media event seemed not to have had a significant impact on public opinion.[62] A Louis Harris poll taken a few days afterward revealed that only 37 percent of those queried had heard about the committee's hearings, and a majority of those were college educated. Of people with opinions, 55 percent believed that the hearings had been helpful, whereas 45 percent thought otherwise.[63] The vast majority of congresspeople and senators continued publicly to support the war in Vietnam – although, to Johnson and Russell's enragement, a $4.8 billion Vietnam appropriations bill stalled in the Senate for two weeks while thirty-five senators made speeches attacking the war or the tactics being used to fight it.[64] Antiwar activists had certainly expected more; most agreed with George Ball, who found the hearings "disappointingly docile."[65] Jack Valenti assured his boss that the administration had sustained only minor damage; John Connally told the president that the hearings had not changed anyone's mind, and that the "concerned people" with whom he had talked "are not questioning U.S. foreign policy."[66]

Valenti and Connally, two of Johnson's most hawkish advisers, were just telling him what they wanted him to hear. The fact that many people reacted negatively to the hearings did not mean that their attitude toward the president and his handling of the war had not been adversely affected. George Reedy was right, the administration was getting hit from both sides; and Lyndon Johnson knew it. In late February, Bill Moyers reported to the president that the approval rating for his handling of the war had in one month – from January 26 to February 26 – dropped from 63 percent to 49 percent.[67] "Never have I known Washington to be so full of dissonant voices as it is today," Moyers wrote to Theodore H. White.[68]

More important, perhaps, Kennan and Gavin's testimony and Fulbright's cross-examination made it respectable to question, if not oppose, the war. On February 26 Robert Komer, McGeorge Bundy's top aide, reported to Johnson that the New York business community was getting cold feet. If, as they suspected, the administration was going to spend $10 billion and then get out of Vietnam following the 1966 congressional elections, then it ought to get out at once.[69]

62 Small, *Johnson, Nixon, and the Doves,* 79.
63 Berman, *Fulbright and the Vietnam War,* 60–1.
64 "Fulbright Wants to Zero In on Humphrey," *New York Herald Tribune,* Feb. 17, 1966.
65 Marvin Watson to LBJ, Feb. 21, 1966, WHCF, Box 342, Johnson Papers.
66 Ibid.
67 Meeting in Cabinet Room, Feb. 26, 1966, Meeting Notes File, Box 2, Johnson Papers.
68 Moyers to White, Mar. 7, 1966, Box 219, WHCF, Nat'l Sec./Def., Johnson Papers.
69 Meeting in Cabinet Room, Feb. 26, 1966, Meeting Notes File, Box 2, Johnson Papers.

The February hearings, in short, opened a psychological door for the great American middle class. It was Fulbright's ability to relate to this group, as well as his capacity for building bridges to such conservative opponents of the war as Russell, Sparkman, and Symington – rather than his being a symbol of and a catalyst for the political left – that would make him important to the antiwar movement. As Johnson correctly noted, the hawks were and would continue to be a majority in the country. It would be Fulbright rather than A. J. Muste, Staughton Lynd, or Tom Hayden who could speak to them. If the administration intended to wage the war in Vietnam from the political center in America, the 1966 hearings were indeed a blow to that effort.

Johnson could not help but note that Robert Kennedy took pains to associate himself with the SFRC and the hearings. Appealing as he always did to the president's worst instincts, John Connally told him that Bobby was "the motivating force behind the Senate hearings."[70] Fresh from a visit to the University of Chicago, George Reedy reported: "The students, though polite, are quite frank in their preference for President Kennedy [in comparison]. They state that somehow you do not 'come across' to them and that even though they like your domestic programs, they have some deep reservations."[71] As Tom Mann observed, if one did not understand the mutual hatred between the Kennedys and Johnson, one could not understand anything about the 1960s. By sticking in and saving Vietnam, Lyndon Johnson believed he could win a victory over the ghost of his assassinated predecessor. During the Bay of Pigs invasion, Kennedy's enemies charged, the president had lost his nerve, leaving Castroism free to infect the hemisphere. Just as Truman had in Korea, Johnson would hold the line in Vietnam. History would view the Texan as the man who had not only passed Kennedy's legislative program, but fulfilled the nation's commitment to contain Sino–Soviet imperialism. Now here were the ex-president's brother and Fulbright joining forces to attack him for pursuing a policy that they had once fully supported. In May, Johnson joked bitterly at a public meeting, "You can say one thing about those hearings, but I don't think this is the place to say it."[72] Johnson had J. Edgar Hoover and the national commander of the American Legion to the White House, where he asked them to coordinate a letter-writing campaign to demonstrate to Fulbright that the nation was solidly behind the war in Vietnam.[73] "Those hearings were a declaration of war," McGeorge Bundy recalled, "and were so taken by the White House."[74]

70 Marvin Watson to LBJ, Feb. 21, 1966, WHCF, Box 342, Johnson Papers.
71 Reedy to LBJ, Jan. 27, 1966, WHCF, Nat'l. Sec./Def., Box 219, Johnson Papers.
72 Quoted in Small, *Johnson, Nixon, and the Doves,* 80.
73 Hoover to Tolson, Mar. 3, 1966, "Hoover's Official and Confidential File," FBI Files.
74 McG. Bundy interview.

In the wake of the Vietnam hearings, Fulbright came to the conclusion that the key to peace in Southeast Asia was Communist China. He did so not because he mistakenly assumed that Ho and the NLF were puppets of Beijing; rather, he recognized that the Soviet Union wanted peace in the region and favored a negotiated settlement, but that its rivalry with China paralyzed it and allowed Hanoi to play one communist superpower off against the other. Beijing's aggressiveness, Fulbright believed, was due to revolutionary fervor but also to fear of being squeezed between the Soviet Union and the United States.[75] If, Fulbright reasoned, the United States could build the same trust with China as it had with the Soviet Union after the missile crisis, and convince it that the United States was a satiated, status quo power, perhaps it would agree to a "neutral" Southeast Asia. In March of 1966 the junior senator from Arkansas called for a "general accommodation" with the world's most populous Marxist republic.[76]

The chairman labored under no illusions about the political difficulty of achieving such an accommodation with the communist regime in Beijing. Since the "fall" of China in 1949, Congress had been unable to conduct a rational and dispassionate debate on the subject. Henry Luce and the China Lobby continued to promote Jiang Jie-shi as democracy's last, best hope in Asia. Professional anticommunists in the Republican Party, like Richard Nixon, had made a career of rolling back the Bamboo Curtain. Those in Congress who dared to suggest that the question of Communist China's admission to the United Nations was a proper subject of debate had been labeled soft on communism. If there was going to be a reassessment of American relations with Beijing, and if the true China experts in the State Department were to be empowered, Fulbright decided, the prevailing myths would have to be exploded and the American people reeducated.[77]

On the day following his Senate call for a review of China's relationship with the West, Fulbright presided over the first of a series of public hearings on the history and culture of the world's most populous nation. For three weeks prominent sinologists and experts in international affairs paraded in and out of the SFRC. Among the most noteworthy were Doak Barnett, John K. Fairbank, and Donald Zagoria. Not all were doves on Vietnam – Fairbank, for example, approved of America's nation-building efforts in South Vietnam – and none of them was enamored of Mao's totalitarian regime; but,

[75] In fact, Zhou En-lai, acutely aware that his country had suffered a million casualties in the Korean War, was frightened of America's growing military presence in South Vietnam. However, the Chinese leadership did not really believe that the United States would withdraw from the Indochinese peninsula if Hanoi and Saigon worked out a negotiated settlement. Better that the Vietnamese harry the Americans into leaving, and then China could move in and once again dominate Vietnam.

[76] *Congressional Record*, Senate, Mar. 1, 1966, 4377–85.

[77] JWF to Charles Taylor, Feb. 24, 1966, Series 48:11, Box 35:3, SPF.

to Fulbright's delight, the participants in the China hearings put that nation's post–World War II domestic and foreign policy in historical context. All of them urged more contact between Americans and Chinese on every front. The testimony demonstrated to the American people, Fulbright believed, that China was not the monolithic, expansionist international outlaw that McCarthy, Nixon, and Luce had portrayed it to be.

Intrigued by U.N. Secretary General U Thant's comment that Communist China was analogous to a person who had suffered a nervous breakdown, Fulbright invited psychiatrist Jerome D. Frank of the Johns Hopkins Hospital in Baltimore to testify. Perhaps the task facing the United States, the Arkansan wrote Frank, was to decide whether to treat the patient in the old-fashioned way, by "throwing her into the international snake-pit" and treating "her as a pariah," or whether "to seek to rehabilitate her and make her a useful member of the community of nations."[78]

According to FBI confidential files, both Everett Dirksen and Bourke Hickenlooper believed that, in launching the China hearings and pressing for normalization of relations, Fulbright was acting at the direction of communist agents.[79] Hickenlooper subsequently huddled with Senator Henry Jackson (D–Washington) and lined up witnesses to counter Fulbright's slate, which they regarded as "leftist." The Iowa Republican also culled the files of the Senate Internal Security Subcommittee for information that could be used to discredit Fairbank and company.[80]

Fulbright was delighted with the response that the hearings provoked. Teach-ins on China swept the nation's college campuses, including Michigan, Wisconsin, and Berkeley. The League of Women Voters sponsored public discussions on China, as did the Foreign Policy Association. CBS even produced a television seminar on China and Vietnam, with Fulbright and Fairbank serving as discussants. Valuable as the chairman felt the hearings had been, however, he was soon made to realize that they were not going to produce any significant change in America's Vietnam policies. Nor were they going to cause Beijing to abandon the DRV or the NLF. "I do not believe that the Communist Chinese at this point will encourage Hanoi to talk and to settle the matter," Senator Joseph Clark (D–Pennsylvania) told the Senate, "for, after all, they are fighting to the last American and to the last North Vietnamese. I think they are quite happy with the situation."[81]

Much later Clark Clifford would describe the evolution of his own position on Vietnam as moving from a doubt to an opinion to a conviction to an ob-

78 JWF to Dr. Jerome D. Frank, Mar. 30, 1966, Series 48:18, Box 48:1, SPF.

79 DeLoach interview with Dirksen, Mar. 7, 1966, "Hoover's Official and Confidential File," FBI Files.

80 DeLoach interview with Hickenlooper, Mar. 8, 1966, "Hoover's Official and Confidential File," FBI Files.

81 *Congressional Record,* Senate, Mar. 21, 1966, 6416.

session. The same could be said about Fulbright. As casualties mounted and the war threatened to spill over into Thailand, Cambodia, and Laos, the chairman began to see Vietnam as more than a symptom of the nation's anticommunist phobia; it had become a destructive force in and of itself. Effect had become cause. "The longer the Vietnamese war goes on without prospect of victory or negotiated peace, the war fever will rise; hopes will give way to fears and tolerance and freedom of discussion will give way to a false and strident patriotism," he told students at Johns Hopkins.[82]

[82] Ibid., Apr. 25, 1966, 8871.

# 22

# *The politics of dissent*

Frustrated by his inability to convince the Johnson administration and the American people that the domino theory and the notion of a monolithic communist threat were fallacious, Fulbright decided to turn his searchlight once again on the national character. Jim Lowenstein later remarked that Fulbright's genius was not his knowledge of foreign cultures and political systems – he was frequently naïve about the Soviet Union and Communist China – but his knowledge of the American people.

> He really understood their reaction to overblown rhetoric, prejudice, what would happen to them in Vietnam. . . . His great genius is the exact opposite of what people thought it was – that he was an expert in foreign policy but was distant from his own people. I think he understood the American people far better than anyone else.[1]

The third week in March 1966, Fulbright traveled to Storrs, Connecticut, to deliver the Brien McMahon Lecture at the land-grant university there. He was glad for the opportunity to honor his late friend and Senate colleague. It was an appropriate occasion, Fulbright decided, to attempt to start a searching national self-examination. He told his audience:

> There are two Americas. One is the America of Lincoln and Adlai Stevenson; the other is the America of Teddy Roosevelt and General MacArthur. One is generous and humane, the other narrowly egotistical; one is modest and self-critical, the other arrogant and self-righteous; one is sensible, the other romantic; one is good-humored, the other solemn; one is inquiring, the other pontificating; one is moderate and restrained, the other filled with passionate intensity.[2]

After thirty years as a superpower, America stood at a crossroads, he told the students and faculty. The United States would have to decide which of the two sides of its character would prevail – "the humanism of Lincoln or

[1] Interview with James Lowenstein, Oct. 3, 1991, Washington, D.C.
[2] *Congressional Record,* Senate, Mar. 25, 1966, 6749.

the aggressive moralism of Theodore Roosevelt." He was, he said, afraid that America's better half was in eclipse. The nation's aggressive, militaristic spirit had in part been responsible for the Vietnam War, and that conflict was in turn reinforcing the dark side of the American character. The war would destroy Lyndon Johnson's vision of a better America just as surely as it would destroy Vietnam. "The President simply cannot think about implementing the Great Society at home while he is supervising bombing missions over North Vietnam," Fulbright insisted. Not only was the war consuming the nation's generous, humanitarian, instincts, it was eating up the resources necessary to give substance to those instincts.

The fundamental dualism in the American character was reflected in the two dominant strains in postwar American foreign policy: opposition to communism and support for nationalism, Fulbright continued. "The tragedy of Vietnam is that a revolution against social injustice and foreign rule has become a contest between Asian communism and the United States," he said. Had it not been for Western colonialism and the unwillingness of the Great Powers to decolonize wisely, the oppressed of Asia would never have turned to communism. He then uttered the ultimate heresy: "American interests are better served by supporting nationalism than by opposing communism, and . . . when the two are encountered in the same country, it is in our interest to accept a Communist government rather than undertake the cruel and all but impossible task of suppressing a genuinely national movement."[3]

While the televised hearings and Fulbright's call for America to accept and even support communism under some circumstances unsettled some Americans, it infuriated others. In March 1966 a Missouri chapter of the Minutemen, a right-wing terrorist organization, developed plans to assassinate the chairman of the SFRC. After his arrest by the FBI, Jerry Milton Brooks testified in Kansas City that his orders to shoot Fulbright were called off at the very last minute. The assassination, he said, was part of a plan to intimidate certain members of Congress into "voting American."[4]

The McMahon Lecture was to be the first installment of a national speaking tour that Fulbright and Marcy planned for the spring of 1966. The SFRC had entered the fray, Marcy observed to Fulbright, and was actively competing with the president for the attention of the nation. They were under no illusion as to how easy their task would be; the White House would counterattack with an unprecedented propaganda blitz, a campaign as ferocious in its way as the aerial bombardment being visited on the Vietnamese. There was no way the SFRC could co-opt the mass media and reach the number of people that the executive could on a day-to-day basis, Marcy warned. "He can command radio, TV, the press, and he has his own publications." Speeches by the

3 Ibid., 6749–53.
4 "Talk of Killing Fulbright Laid to Minutemen," *Arkansas Gazette*, Apr. 8, 1966.

chairman and individual members would not suffice. Though such a course would be "politically dangerous," the chief of staff favored holding additional hearings on Vietnam in order, he said, to control the public spotlight and to "keep the Committee in the midst of the crucial decisions relating to war and peace."[5] But Fulbright said no: It was too soon; people would tire of the subject and tune out him and the committee. It would be better to concentrate his efforts during the next few months on persuading and galvanizing the opinion-making elite.

During the last part of April and the first part of May Fulbright delivered the Christian A. Herter Lectures at Johns Hopkins University. In late April he traveled to New York to address the Associated Press and the American Newspaper Publishers Association. In his speeches, he repeated earlier themes: that erroneous assumptions underlay America's Vietnam policy, that the United States must adopt a realistic policy toward China, and that the war in Vietnam must be ended through negotiation. Throughout the tour Fulbright worked under intense pressure – externally and internally. There were the smear campaign directed by the White House and snubs by the president. While addressing a congressional dinner in Washington in mid-May, Johnson looked directly at Fulbright and said, "I am delighted to be here tonight with so many of my very old friends as well as some members of the Foreign Relations Committee."[6] Not even Wayne Morse had been so singled out by Johnson. A visible shudder went through the crowd. The president, whose control over federal largesse could make or break senators and congresspeople, was labeling the Arkansan a pariah. Fulbright quickly came to realize that not only Johnson but the American people were also angry with him – angry because he was telling them the truth and, in fact, foretelling their future.

James Lowenstein, a longtime student of French politics, frequently compared Fulbright to Charles de Gaulle – behind his back, of course. Not only did he know his own people intimately, instinctively, like *le grand Charles,* but the Arkansan was always a bit too early with his political judgments. "He was too far ahead of the popular view," Lowenstein observed. "He would say things to the American public they weren't prepared to accept, and they didn't like it."[7] During the hearings a Tennesseean wrote that he had "stomached about as much as I can of the pious and profound statements coming out of the Senate Foreign Relations Committee and from numerous senators in the Majority party," who had so obviously joined with "the beatniks, the professional marchers, the civil rights workers, the Communists and the draft dodgers."[8]

5 Marcy to JWF, Mar. 23, 1966, Series 48:3, Box 16:3, JWF Papers.
6 Quoted in William C. Berman, *William Fulbright and the Vietnam War: The Dissent of a Political Realist* (Kent, Ohio, 1988), 67.
7 Lowenstein interview.
8 UPI 160, Apr. 21, 1966, Series 48:1, Box 7:4, SPF.

In response to the pressure, Fulbright's speeches and public statements in March and April became more strident. His country was succumbing to "that arrogance of power which has afflicted, weakened and in some cases destroyed great nations in the past" and it must be saved from the error of its ways.[9] Three weeks later he told a group of reporters that America was killing what it wanted to save in South Vietnam. If the United States did not stop, its AID programs, its money, and its massive military presence would destroy traditional Vietnamese society. Saigon, in fact, was well on its way to becoming "an American brothel," with thousands of Vietnamese, seduced by the almighty dollar, putting their wives and daughters to work as bargirls.[10] During one of his talks in New York he likened the United States in its "current imperial mode" to Nazi Germany.[11] Those who were openly protesting the war deserved the country's sympathy and respect, the Arkansan proclaimed, although he urged youthful demonstrators to abjure "direct dissent" like draft-card burning. He quoted Albert Camus's "Letters to a German Friend": "This is what separated us from you: we made demands. You were satisfied to serve the power of your nation and we dreamed of giving ours her truth."[12]

More significant, in the wake of the 1966 hearings Fulbright abandoned his longtime advocacy of executive predominance in foreign policy. Since he had first been elected to Congress, the Arkansan had urged the nation to accept the need for an active presidency with maximum freedom to conduct diplomacy and contain communism through armed strength and foreign aid. His principal criticism of the Eisenhower administration had been that it was too passive. However, over the years, in response to crisis after crisis, the balance had shifted too far. He decried the transformation in his first Herter Lecture:

> Congress, inspired by patriotism, importuned by Presidents, and deterred by lack of information, has tended to fall in line behind the Executive. The result has been the unhinging of traditional constitutional relationships; the Senate's constitutional powers of advice and consent have atrophied into what is widely regarded . . . to be a duty to give prompt consent with a minimum of advice.[13]

Fulbright's primary concern was not to a particular interpretation of the Constitution in regard to foreign affairs, but to his country's interests economically, strategically, and culturally defined. He was a true internationalist, committed to the notion of cultural pluralism and convinced that economic interdependence advanced the interests of all peoples. In the aftermath of World

9 "Fulbright Mail Runs 30 to 1 for War Stand," *Arkansas Gazette,* Feb. 12, 1966.
10 "Fulbright Calls Saigon 'An American Brothel,'" *Saigon Post,* May 9, 1966.
11 "Views on Viet Nam Policy," *Rochester Times-Union,* Apr. 30, 1966.
12 "Fulbright Calls Saigon 'An American Brothel,'" *Saigon Post,* May 9, 1966.
13 Quoted in Berman, *Fulbright and the Vietnam War,* 64.

War II, with the tide of isolationism still running strong and deep in the United States, an assertive, active executive was needed to advance the cause of internationalism and keep the peace. Over the years, however, the stresses and strains of fighting the cold war under the shadow of a nuclear holocaust had taken their toll. The executive, its actions at times circumscribed and at times dictated by fanatical anticommunist elements at home, had adopted a missionary attitude that assumed America had the duty and the power to make the world over in its own image. "America is showing some signs of that fatal presumption, that overextension of power and mission, which brought ruin to ancient Athens, to Napoleonic France and to Nazi Germany." The war in Vietnam was both a sign of that trend and an accelerator of it. If the war continued and America became "what it never has been, a seeker after unlimited power and empire, then Vietnam will have had a mighty and tragic fallout indeed." One of the answers to the problem of creeping imperialism, he declared, was "to find a way to restore the Constitutional balance, to find ways by which the Senate can discharge its duty of advice and consent in an era of permanent crisis."[14]

Fulbright's indictment of imperial America and the grasping, insensitive executive that served it was a reflection of not only his own views but also those of Carl Marcy. The trend toward executive usurpation that had begun in the early stages of the cold war had culminated in the Johnson presidency, the chief of staff believed. Not only had the White House alternately ignored and manipulated the Senate; it was deliberately deceiving the American people. In mid-May, for example, Marcy learned that a Rand survey of Vietcong defectors commissioned by the Pentagon had been rejected and then doctored. The original report did not depict the Vietcong cadre as demoralized and out of touch with the people of South Vietnam, as Westmoreland, Walt Rostow, and Cabot Lodge were arguing – far from it; hence the survey, from which McNamara quoted extensively at an NSC meeting, was made over to show that the people of Vietnam viewed the VC as alien oppressors and that American military operations, particularly air operations, had the guerrillas on the ropes.[15]

In response to this and other evidences of administration fraud, Marcy began to develop plans for what could only be called an alternative State Department. What he proposed was a system whereby professional staff people would either assume permanent stations in Europe, Latin America, Southeast Asia, Africa, and other locations or be sent there on special assignment to report independently to the SFRC. He had considered the approach before,

14 Quoted in ibid., 66, 64.

15 Report to Larry Henderson from Leon Goure, Rand Corp., May 9, 1966, NSF, Memos to President, Box 8, Johnson Papers; Summary Notes of 557th NSC Meeting, May 10, 1966, NSC Meeting Notes File, Box 2, Johnson Papers; and Marcy to JWF, May 12, 1966, Box 6, Folder May, Marcy Papers.

he told Fulbright, but had rejected it because it smacked of McCarthyism and would create doubt in the minds of foreign nations as to who was in charge of American foreign policy. However, the administration could not be trusted; the information given the SFRC and the public was either slanted or false. In addition it put the committee at a disadvantage to have to quote an unnamed source in AID, for example, or an article in the *New York Times*.[16] Fulbright pointed out, and Marcy agreed, that the committee members would have to be won over to this concept – aside from their fear of Johnson, many viewed staffers as peons – but the chairman agreed to take the matter under advisement.

It should be noted that, despite Johnson and Rusk's efforts to convince the American people otherwise, Fulbright had not become an irresponsible radical. He still believed that the United States had a role to play as the major stabilizing force in world politics, and he continued to advocate the use of air and sea power to contain China. As Omar Bradley had said of MacArthur's proposal to invade North Korea, Vietnam to Fulbright was "the wrong war in the wrong place at the wrong time." It was one thing, the Arkansan believed, for his country to play the role of balancer of power, and quite another for America to attempt to remake the world in its own image and to try to solve every problem that plagued the "global village," to use Marshall McLuhan's term, then in vogue.

Though certainly not an isolationist in the strictest sense, Fulbright at times sounded like Charles Beard or Robert Taft. He declared:

> If America has a service to perform in the world – and I believe it has – it is in large part the service of its own example. In our excessive involvement in the affairs of other countries, we are not only living off our assets and denying our own people the proper enjoyment of their resources: we are also denying the world the example of a free society enjoying its freedom to the fullest.[17]

In September he joined with Mike Mansfield in cosponsoring a resolution calling for the withdrawal of a substantial number of American troops from Europe.

Within the imperatives Fulbright had outlined, the Johnson administration could not "win" in Vietnam. During 1965 and 1966 the United States struggled desperately to create south of the Seventeenth Parallel a nation it could defend. To a degree, the American war effort hinged upon the ability of the U.S. country team to help establish a broad-based government capable of holding the allegiance of Buddhist and Catholic, student and worker, peasant and entrepreneur, and residents of both Saigon and the Mekong Delta. It had

16 Carl Marcy to JWF, May 16, 1966, Series 48:4, Box 19:1, SPF.
17 *Congressional Record*, Senate, May 17, 1966, 10808.

to reach out into the complex of villages, secure them, and create a life for which the average Vietnamese was willing to fight and die. To win, America would have to intervene in Vietnam on a massive scale, and the transposition of its values, institutions, and culture to that far-away land was inevitable; but what the Vietnamese wanted, Fulbright insisted, was simply the freedom to work out their own destiny. He refused to acknowledge that the Marxist–Leninist theories and the totalitarian techniques employed by Ho and Giap were as alien to Vietnam as the institutions and processes of the Great Society. Years later, when McGeorge Bundy was asked whether South Vietnam had died of too much democracy, of the American insistence on elections and representative government, he agreed. What South Vietnam had needed was "leadership": someone who would use noncommunist institutions and theories to dominate, galvanize, and mobilize the south as Ho had in the north. Diem was dead, however, Washington could not resurrect him, and Fulbright would not have tolerated such a figure anyway. The only alternative, in the Arkansan's view, was a negotiated withdrawal.[18]

Insofar as a diplomatic settlement in Vietnam was concerned, the key difference between Fulbright and the Johnson administration in 1966 was the inclusion of the NLF in a coalition government in South Vietnam. From June 1964 through August 1965, J. Blair Seaborn, the chief Canadian delegate to the International Control Commission on Indochina, had made five trips to Hanoi with Washington's approval. His proposal to Ho had been simple and straightforward: If Hanoi would stop its assistance to the Vietcong and withdraw its forces from South Vietnam, the United States would remove its troops from South Vietnam and extend economic assistance and diplomatic recognition to North Vietnam. Through the Canadian diplomat Rusk had warned the North Vietnamese that if they did not respond favorably, air and sea operations would commence north of the Seventeenth Parallel. Ho had responded by demanding that American forces withdraw from Vietnam and that the NLF be included in a coalition government in Saigon.[19]

Although unaware of Seaborn's mission, Fulbright, joined by Robert and Edward Kennedy, George McGovern, and others, tacitly supported Hanoi's position, insisting that South Vietnamese communists would have to be admitted to any provisional government if there was to be a compromise settlement. The administration's position was and would remain that the NLF was simply an instrument of Hanoi, and that it would use its position in a coalition government to subvert that regime, control elections, and facilitate communization of the entire country. There was thus no difference between Hungary in 1946, Czechoslovakia in 1948, and South Vietnam in 1966. When the administration declared during the peace initiative of 1965 that "We have

18 Interview with McGeorge Bundy, Aug. 1, 1991, New York.
19 Dean Rusk as told to Richard Rusk, *As I Saw It* (New York, 1990), 461.

put everything into the basket of peace except the surrender of South Vietnam," it had included in its use of the word "surrender" NLF participation in a coalition government.[20] In vain did Fulbright, Albert Gore (D–Tennessee), McCarthy, and Mansfield point out to the administration that to refuse to negotiate with the Vietcong – which, as of the spring of 1966, controlled three-fourths of the territory of South Vietnam and comprised 80 percent of the military force with which the United States was contending – was to refuse to negotiate at all.[21]

In his speech Fulbright had appealed to his countrymen to respond to a "higher patriotism," one that conceived of America as a nation of principles and ideals rather than one that was rooted in blood-and-soil nationalism. In so doing he had clearly and unequivocally embraced the role of dissenter, and in the process had put himself at emotional and psychological odds with his president and a substantial majority of his countrymen. Lyndon Johnson was committed to consensus; Fulbright was not. The president had a visceral dislike of conflict and discord; he was a reconciler. Like so many academics, Fulbright was uneasy with consensus, and he thought his country's obsession with it a great flaw. In his higher-patriotism speech, he observed with distaste that intolerance of dissent was a typically American characteristic. He insisted that what de Tocqueville had said of the United States 150 years earlier was still true: "I know of no country in which there is so little independence of mind and real freedom of discussion." Fulbright realized that his was a society that was unnerved by dissent because it had experienced so little of it, but he insisted nonetheless that unanimity was tantamount to complacency. In the absence of debate and dissension, errors were likely to be made. "Freedom of thought and discussion gives a democracy two concrete advantages over a dictatorship in the making of foreign policy," he declared; "it diminishes the danger of an irretrievable mistake and it introduces ideas and opportunities that otherwise would not come to light."[22]

Much has been made of Fulbright's aversion to the protest movement, to the fact that his establishment credentials prevented him from being embraced by the SDS or the New Left, much less the Yippies. It was true that he was much too conventional in his personal life to march or demonstrate, and he rejected draft-card burnings, sit-ins, and other "symbolic" and frequently illegal forms of dissent. "We are, for better or worse, essentially a conservative society," he told the protesters. Symbolic acts inflamed passions, closed ears, blocked channels. Ignoring the fact that extremists have constituted the van-

20 Ibid., 465.

21 Discussion with Vice-President Humphrey, Mar. 2, 1966, Executive Sessions, SFRC, RG 46, NA.

22 *Congressional Record,* Senate, Apr. 25, 1966, 8869–72.

guard of every effective reform movement, Fulbright insisted that the object of dissent was to change society. Forms that were counterproductive to that goal, that is, that alienated moderates, should be rejected. Nevertheless, Fulbright not only endorsed the antiwar movement, but over time gradually came to embrace it – intellectually if not philosophically and culturally. Indeed, during his spring 1966 speaking tour he went out of his way to identify himself with those who were demonstrating. "The wisdom and productivity of the protest movement of students, professors, clergy and others may well be questioned, but their courage, decency, and patriotism cannot be doubted," he declared. The mass uprising against the war that developed in the mid-1960s was "a moral and intellectual improvement on the panty raids of the 1950s," he told the students at Johns Hopkins. The new radicalism was not shallow and sophomoric, and opposition to the war was not "hypocritical" as the superpatriots were charging. Critics of the war were rebelling against a "corrupt vision of society," he insisted, and only a fool would refuse to make moral distinctions between wars for fear of being called inconsistent or unpatriotic.[23]

Nevertheless, as his family and his staff frequently observed, Fulbright was a pragmatist, not an ideologue or a zealot. To him, his critique of the war was logical, sensible, and correct, but he had no desire to go down in history as a Cassandra or an Old Testament prophet who gloried in the approval of the Almighty as his people trod the path of destruction. Moreover, despite his public outbursts of early May, Fulbright and his staff, Lee Williams recalled, were afraid of appearing to be extremists. If the public began to lump the chairman with people like Wayne Morse, notorious for his negativism, he would lose his credibility and effectiveness.

Further tempering Fulbright's public statements if not his views was the fact that it was very difficult for him to give up on Lyndon Johnson – personally and politically. He wanted to believe that Johnson would do nothing to endanger Democratic prospects either in the midterm elections or the 1968 presidential campaign.[24] His breach with the White House left him feeling "isolated and discouraged," as a *Washington Post* headline put it. He complained to Helen Gahagan Douglas that, although opposition to escalation was widespread, the president "tends to think I am the only one not supporting him."[25] She and other friends tried to comfort him: "I am so grateful to you and deeply appreciative of your willingness to confront the administration publicly," she wrote.[26] George McGovern quoted to him from *The Memorials of Alfred Marshall:* "It is almost impossible for a student to be a true

23 Ibid., 8871.
24 JWF to Arthur Schlesinger, Mar. 15, 1966, Series 48:8, Box 50:1, SPF.
25 JWF to Douglas, May 18, 1966, Series 48:1, Box 47:6, SPF.
26 Douglas to JWF, May 16, 1966, Series 48:1, Box 47:6, SPF.

patriot and have the reputation of being one at the same time."[27] Numerous members of the federal bureaucracy reached out to him: "As you know," wrote one top-level government employee, "I work for Interior, so I cannot support you actively by word or work or writing, but I do want you to know that I admire your bravery very much."[28]

During a speech before the National Press Club on May 17, Fulbright expressed regret for calling Saigon a whorehouse and comparing the United States to the Third Reich. At the same time he wrote Johnson complaining that his statements had been misconstrued. The president's reply was surprisingly conciliatory. He agreed that "statements can be taken out of context and interpretations can draw a different meaning than you mean from your words. It's happened to me!" While defending his policies, Johnson seemed to invite reconciliation: "I cannot believe our differences over policy have erased the friendship we have shared for so long. I have a fondness for you and Betty that is real. . . . I am sorry that careless people have appeared to paint another picture."[29] When Fulbright failed to show up at the White House signing of a bill creating an Asian Development Bank to which he had been invited, Johnson had one of his aides call to tell him he had been missed.[30] Indeed, in late April Johnson had invited Bill and Betty to fly to Houston with him and Lady Bird.[31] Fulbright's New York speech forced him to turn down the invitation, but he thanked Johnson profusely. When, a couple of weeks later, Johnson complained about Fulbright's use of the term "arrogance of power" in relation to the administration, the Arkansan wrote him: "Never at any time have I spoken, or even thought, of you in connection with arrogance."[32]

27 McGovern to JWF, May 16, 1966, Series 48:18, Box 49:1, SPF.
28 Franks to JWF, May 23, 1966, Series 48:18, Box 48:1, SPF.
29 LBJ to JWF, May 27, 1966, NSF, Memos to President, Box 7, Johnson Papers.
30 Mike Manatos to LBJ, Mar. 17, 1966, WHCF, Subject File, Box 18, Johnson Papers.
31 Lee Williams to JWF, Apr. 25, 196, Series 1:1, Box 3:5, Johnson Papers.
32 JWF to LBJ, May 9, 1966, Series 1:1, Box 3:5, SPF.

# 23

# *Widening the credibility gap*

The temporary thaw in the Johnson–Fulbright relationship led to several face-to-face meetings between the two during the first half of June; but Fulbright soon learned that Johnson's apparently softening attitude toward him did not indicate a change of heart concerning the war. By the time Nguyen Cao Ky had returned to Vietnam from the Honolulu conference in February, Vietnamese Buddhists had been demonstrating in behalf of a return to democratic rule and the end of foreign, that is, American, domination of their country. In March, an angry mob had set fire to the U.S. consulate in Hué, and firemen had refused to put out the blaze. The American country team had labored mightily but unsuccessfully to reconcile the dissenters to the Saigon regime. As the crisis worsened, some administration officials had proposed abandoning Ky, whereas others had began to develop plans for yet another escalation of the war.[1]

In light of the deteriorating situation in Vietnam, Robert McNamara had come to the conclusion by the summer of 1966 that the United States should abandon its crusade in South Vietnam. According to Averell Harriman, McNamara told him on May 14 that Washington should "get in touch direct with the NLF, also the North Vietnamese, but particularly the NLF, and begin to try to work up a deal for a coalition government."[2]

Counteracting naysayers inside the administration and outside, however, was the U.S. embassy in Saigon, which explained that Vietnamese were not like Americans and that South Vietnam could achieve military security and realize the fruits of pacification without a stable, broad-based government. In a remarkable cable sent to Johnson in late April, Henry Cabot Lodge observed that Vietnam "was not going to be stable in our meaning of the word for a long, long time." But it did not matter, Lodge insisted. The United States could still succeed, Vietnam could "evolve":

1 Meeting of Foreign Policy Advisors on Vietnam, Apr. 4, 1966, Meeting Notes File, Box 1, Johnson Papers.

2 Memorandum of conversation with Secretary McNamara, May 14, 1966, Box 486, Harriman Papers.

> Silence and action; first-rate policies on land reform and universal education; talented and persuasive liaison men – these things will enable us to be largely indifferent to the lack of "stability" and to the general uproar going on while this country carries on its evolution and finds its way.[3]

Walt Whitman Rostow, who had succeeded Bundy as national security adviser on April Fool's Day 1966, was even more unrealistic than Lodge. In a conversation with Averell Harriman in early 1966, Rostow outlined the course America must follow. The head of the policy planning staff wanted to fight a war of attrition against the enemy in the south and blast the north. He wanted to bomb not only oil storage facilities but electric power plants, and to mine Haiphong harbor. "I would use our air power as our equivalent to guerrilla warfare."[4] He supported pacification, he told President Johnson, but it would not win the war; only punishment of North Vietnam and defeat of its main force units would do that.[5]

In spite of clear evidence of political and military paralysis in South Vietnam, Lyndon Johnson decided to press ahead. To their credit, Dean Rusk and Averell Harriman argued that it would be unwise to escalate bombing of the north with political chaos threatening the south; but Johnson swept their objections aside.[6] They had spent too much time considering new proposals and changes in policy, he told his more hesitant advisers in mid-May:

> Our strategy has been the same for three years. There are island hoppers who jump from issue to issue and there are those who would put a bag of cement on the back of the man running the race. We are committed, and we will not be deterred. We must accept the fact that some will always oppose, dissent and criticize.[7]

In mid-June when the Joint Chiefs of Staff reported that the number of NVA trucks on the Ho Chi Minh Trail had jumped from sixty-nine hundred to ten thousand per month, and that the North Vietnamese were preparing for a major push into northern South Vietnam, Johnson authorized the bombing of petroleum storage facilities in Hanoi and Haiphong.[8]

Shortly before this onslaught, Johnson summoned Fulbright to the White House. He must strike at the north, he told the Arkansan, in order to stop the

3 Lodge to LBJ, Apr. 29, 1966, NSF, Memos to President, Box 7, Johnson Papers.
4 Rostow to Harriman, Jan. 28, 1966, Box 499, Harriman Papers.
5 Rostow to LBJ, Apr. 5, 1966, NSF, Memos to President, Box 7, Johnson Papers.
6 Harriman to Rusk, May 10, 1966, Box 499, Harriman Papers.
7 Summary Notes of 557th NSC Meeting, May 10, 1966, NSC Meeting Notes, Box 2, Johnson Papers.
8 Summary Notes of 559th NSC Meeting, June 17, 1966, NSC Meeting Notes File, Box 2, Johnson Papers.

NVA buildup in the south. With communist staging areas and supply lines destroyed or disrupted, Westmoreland would be able to smash the main units of the North Vietnamese Army in pitched battles along the demilitarized zone (DMZ) during the monsoon season. Hanoi would then be receptive to another peace offensive he was planning for the winter.[9] Fulbright listened, and then repeated his arguments in behalf of disengagement. They fell on deaf ears. On June 29 and 30, at Johnson's direction, American planes struck oil refineries and tanks in and around Hanoi.

On July 1 Fulbright rose in the Senate to denounce the attacks on Hanoi and Haiphong. He described the escalation as a long step toward "ultimate war" and proof that once more the administration had been mesmerized by the vision of total military victory in Vietnam.[10] What gave a particular sharpness and urgency to his comments, however, was his belief that the renewed aerial assaults were not meant to be a prelude to negotiations and ultimate American withdrawal, but were rather an indication of the administration's determination to play a larger, permanent role in Asia.

Many within the Johnson administration believed that Fulbright's opposition to the war stemmed from his racism. Wrote White House staffer Fred Panzer to a coworker:

> It appears that Fulbright, identifying with the anti-bellum [*sic*] Southern gentry, is still wrangling from the seething hatreds of the Civil War. Vietnam is his ancestral plantation, the Vietnamese – especially the Viet Cong – are an amalgam of his tattered gallant Rebels and his devoted and dedicated darkies, and the American presence is those hated carpet baggers and damn yankees.[11]

Certainly Lyndon Johnson and Dean Rusk believed that Fulbright's opposition to the war in Vietnam stemmed from his racism – the yellows, blacks, and browns of the world were just not worth bothering about.

Whenever Fulbright bloodied his nose, Johnson frequently responded by ostentatiously assuming more responsibility for the care and feeding of the poor, illiterate, and undernourished of Southeast Asia. At the same White House meeting where he learned that the hearings had knocked his approval rating down thirteen points, he blurted out: "Why don't we do a real study on brown men – and Asia – Task Force on Asia – heavy thinking on Asia –

9 James Reston, "Prognosis in Vietnam Is More of the Same," *Arkansas Gazette,* June 20, 1966.

10 "Fulbright Fears New Raids Step to 'Ultimate War,'" *Arkansas Gazette,* July 1, 1966.

11 Fred Panzer to Hayes Redmon, May 10, 1966, Office Files of Fred Panzer, Box 361, Johnson Papers.

potentialities and solutions – liven it up – Asian Task Force."[12] Following the Buddhist crisis of 1966 the United States made pacification a top priority in South Vietnam. "Dammit," Johnson exploded on one occasion, "we've got to see that the South Vietnamese government wins the battle . . . of crops and hearts and caring." In the aftermath of Fulbright's broadside, the Texan declared on July 12 at White Sulphur Springs, West Virginia, that the United States was a Pacific power and would seek to use its resources to promote prosperity and cooperation throughout the entire region. The future was secure for the people of the Pacific rim as long as "we stand firm in Vietnam against military conquest."[13] The press subsequently dubbed the president's pledge the "Asian Doctrine" or "Johnson Doctrine."

On the last day of July, Fulbright rose from his desk once again to sound the alarm. The Senate, which used to be asked for its advice and consent, ought to consider the sweeping implications of Johnson's unilateral pledge to an entire region before it became an "irrevocable national commitment." The president had escalated not only the war but American war aims. The United States, warned the Arkansan, was "taking on the role of policeman and provider for all of non-Communist Asia."[14]

Bill Moyers, Harry McPherson, and other Johnson aides who were on good terms with Fulbright tried to soft-pedal the confrontation and cool off the chairman. At a White House press conference on July 22, Moyers declared that the president found Fulbright's reasoning "difficult to follow" and "disappointing."[15] At the same time he and McPherson, with Johnson's encouragement, tried to draw Fulbright into a private, discreet dialogue, but they were rebuffed. Hints that the president would like to spend a quiet evening discussing the future of American policy in Asia were met with stony silence.[16]

After giving the administration a rhetorical bludgeoning over the Asian Doctrine, Fulbright joined in tacit alliance with Everett Dirksen and the Republicans to hack away at administration programs. First up was foreign aid. Reversing the position he had taken on previous aid bills, Fulbright, the measure's floor manager, led the fight to cut the authorization from five years to one. "I would be much more inclined to support multiyear authorizations if there were not this tendency to escalate our commitments," he said. Indeed, over the vehement objections of the White House, he did away with the multi-

12 Meeting in Cabinet Room, Feb. 26, 1966, Meeting Notes File, Box 2, Johnson Papers.

13 Quoted in William C. Berman, *William Fulbright and the Vietnam War: The Dissent of a Political Realist* (Kent, Ohio, 1988), 70.

14 "From Fulbright: A Sweeping Attack on LBJ's 'Asian Doctrine,'" *U.S. News and World Report,* Aug. 1, 1966, 12.

15 Ibid.

16 Rowland Evans and Robert Novak, "Fulbright Stands Pat," *Washington Post,* July 31, 1966.

year authorizations for the Development Loan Fund and the Alliance for Progress, provisions he had been instrumental in getting through the Senate in 1961 and 1962.[17] He then stood idly by as Dirksen and the Senate struck $142 million from the $3.2 billion aid bill and another $250 million from the DLF.[18] In August he introduced an amendment to cut Johnson's $5 billion, two-year Food for Peace proposal to one year and $1 billion.When Allen Ellender pointed out that his "friend" from Arkansas was doing an about-face on foreign aid, Fulbright replied, "it seems to me that anyone at all perceptive should change his opinion about the interference of our country in the internal affairs of other countries, and what it leads to."[19] Given the heavy Arkansas agricultural participation in the project, it was rather a daring position for Fulbright to take.

In truth, the pacification program in Vietnam had convinced Fulbright that much of the foreign aid program was futile if not counterproductive. No matter how well intentioned, American aid was ripping the fabric of Vietnamese life, distorting that nation's economy, undermining its religious beliefs, disparaging its material culture, and threatening its very identity. He was not surprised, he declared, at the anti-American tone of the antigovernment demonstrations in Danang and Hué. The Vietnamese were suffering from the "'fatal impact' of the rich and strong on the poor and weak." Dependent on it though the Vietnamese were, "our very strength is a reproach to their weakness, our wealth a mockery of their poverty, our success a reminder of their failures." Consciously or unconsciously, the Vietnamese feared for the very survival of their society.[20]

At the same time Fulbright was harassing the foreign aid program, he embarked on a crusade to expose and discredit the administration's vast propaganda campaign in behalf of the war in Vietnam. In April 1966, Carl Marcy informed his boss that the lead article in the spring issue of the prestigious journal *Foreign Affairs* had been written by George A. Carver, who was then a full-time CIA analyst. His piece, "The Faceless Vietcong," was a compilation of the evidence supporting the administration's contention that the NLF was a "contrived political mechanism" of North Vietnam. The article itself seemed contrived, but that was not what angered Fulbright. Carver was not even identified as an employee of the federal government, much less the CIA.[21] Fulbright complained to Admiral William F. "Red" Raborn, Jr., who

17 David Bell to LBJ, May 27, 1966, WHCF, Box 4, Johnson Papers.
18 UPI 139, July 7, 1966, and "From Fulbright: A Sweeping Attack on LBJ's 'Asian Doctrine,'" *U.S. News and World Report,* Aug. 1, 1966, 12.
19 UPI 13, Aug. 30, 1966, Series 78:3, Box 33:2, SPF.
20 *Congressional Record,* Senate, May 17, 1966, 10807.
21 UPI 61, Mar. 7, 1962, Box 1, Miscellaneous 1961–62 Folder, Marcy Papers.

headed the agency, but Raborn refused to do anything about the article or to promise that his employees would not again engage in such activities. To Raborn and Johnson's enragement, Marcy leaked the contents of their letters to Martin Agronsky, who went into the issue on his CBS morning news broadcast.[22]

Over the years Fulbright had become increasingly alarmed at the growth of the CIA and the fog of secrecy in which it insisted on operating. Like many others, he believed it had been primarily responsible for the Bay of Pigs fiasco, and he suspected that the agency had had a hand in sabotaging the 1960 summit meeting between Eisenhower and Khrushchev. He was also irritated by the CIA's habit of using American embassies abroad as "cover" for its activities.[23] Most important, Fulbright recognized that the CIA was intimately involved in the making and implementation of American foreign policy, and as such should be made responsible to the SFRC as well as to Armed Services.

The agency reported to a special subcommittee of the Senate Armed Services Committee – the "secret seven" as it was dubbed by the *New York Times* – chaired by Richard Russell.[24] In 1954 Mike Mansfield, seconded by Fulbright, had attempted to expand the membership of the committee, making it a joint committee of the House and Senate. Russell, ever-jealous of his prerogatives, beat back the attempt.[25] Although Fulbright and the SFRC's attitude toward the CIA improved somewhat under Kennedy's appointee, John McCone, Russell continued to insist that the SFRC and its chief be kept in the dark concerning America's intelligence operations. In 1962 when Francis Gary Powers and John McCone testified on the U-2 incident, the SFRC was the last committee to hear their comments although it had been the first to request them.[26] The 1966 Carver article convinced Fulbright that not only was the CIA making and implementing foreign policy, it was also propagandizing the American people in behalf of those policies.

Throughout April Fulbright attempted to persuade Richard Russell to add three members of the SFRC to the secret seven voluntarily, but he consistently refused. Armed Services had originated the legislation in 1946 creating the CIA as well as the NSC, and it would retain oversight, the Georgian declared.[27] Frustrated, Fulbright, Mansfield, and McCarthy in mid-May 1966 persuaded the SFRC to report out a measure that would transform the secret

22 Russell to JWF, Apr. 30, 1966, Series 48:3, Box 16:3, SPF.
23 Moose to JWF, May 19, 1966, Series 48:3, Box 16:3, SPF.
24 Gilbert C. Fite, *Richard B. Russell, Jr., Senator from Georgia* (Chapel Hill, 1991), 391.
25 *Congressional Record,* Senate, Mar. 10, 1954, 2986–7.
26 UPI 61, Mar. 7, 1962, Box 1, Miscellaneous 1961–62 Folder, Marcy Papers.
27 Russell to JWF, Apr. 30, 1966, Series 48:3, Box 16:3, SPF.

seven subcommittee into the Full Committee on Intelligence Operations.[28] The proposed new body, consisting of three members each from Foreign Relations, Armed Services, and Appropriations, would oversee the intelligence activities of all government agencies, including the CIA.

In the midst of his tête-à-tête with Russell, Fulbright received disturbing reports that the CIA had penetrated the exchange program and was using Fulbrighters abroad to gather information. Although spokesmen for the agency promised that their operatives were not exploiting the exchange program, or that if it had, they would stop, Fulbright ordered Marcy to investigate.[29] When, shortly thereafter, the chief of staff reported that not only had the CIA penetrated Fulbright's creation, but it was subsidizing such diverse organizations as the National Student Association, the American Newspaper Guild, and the Retail Clerks International Association, the chairman called for a special investigation. The extent of the CIA's activities "was much greater than I had ever imagined," he declared on ABC's *Issues and Answers*.[30]

Richard Russell was still one of Lyndon Johnson's closest friends – he could be depended upon not to "leak" – and he had no intention of allowing Fulbright to "muscle in" on his territory.[31] He, Johnson, and Raborn were convinced that if Fulbright penetrated the oversight committee, he would deliberately sabotage the agency's operations by revealing its sources and methods. Indeed, the CIA director pleaded with both Johnson and Russell to go to any lengths to block the measure.[32] At a going-away party for Thomas Mann, Raborn, Johnson, and J. Edgar Hoover agreed that Fulbright was engaged in a conspiracy to "disrupt intelligence operations" throughout the executive branch.[33] Prior to Senate consideration of the CIA bill, Russell and various White House staffers did their best to convince other senators and the press that the SFRC under Fulbright and Marcy had consistently leaked information affecting the national security during both the Dominican crisis and the Vietnam escalation.[34] After hours of debate, the full Senate in mid-July turned back Fulbright and the SFRC by a vote of 61 to 28.[35] The new director of the CIA, Richard Helms, who had been appointed but a month before to re-

28 Although Eugene McCarthy was the official sponsor of the resolution, Marcy had drafted it. Marcy to McCarthy, Oct. 8, 1965, Box 5, Folder Oct., Marcy Papers.

29 Richard Helms to Marcy, Dec. 7, 1966, and Marcy, memorandum of conversation, Dec. 15, 1966, Box 2, JWF Papers, RG 46, NA.

30 "Fulbright Urges Special Probe of CIA's Funding Operations," *Washington Post*, Feb. 20, 1967.

31 Interview with McGeorge Bundy, Aug. 1, 1991, and Fite, *Russell*, 391.

32 Rostow to LBJ, June 1, 1966, NSF, Memos to President, Box 8, Johnson Papers.

33 Hoover to Tolson, July 1, 1966, "Hoover's Official and Confidential File," FBI Files.

34 The chairman and his chief of staff did not deny they had leaked, but insisted that none of the information released affected the national security. Memorandum for Possible Use During Debate on CIA Resolution, June 29, 1966, Series 48:3, Box 16:3, SPF.

35 Fite, *Russell*, 390–1.

place the never-effective Raborn, could not refrain from gloating. When the conservative *St. Louis Globe-Democrat* boasted editorially that Fulbright had at last got his "come-uppance," Helms wrote a letter to the editor congratulating him on the impartiality and insightfulness of his observations. Although Helms's letter infuriated the Senate, and Fulbright succeeded in forcing him to apologize to the SFRC in person, the secret seven remained in control, and the CIA continued to play an active role in the administration's propaganda campaign.[36]

Marcy and Fulbright had long recognized that their struggle with the administration was essentially a competition for the attention of the press – that to change American foreign policy, they would have to have massive exposure and gain the support of a significant number of public opinion makers. During the Vietnam War a fundamental change took place in the relationship between the press and the political power structure in America. Throughout World War II and the Korean conflict, American news reporters had become an extension of the war effort. With some grumbling the press had accepted the dichotomy that Franklin Roosevelt posed during World War II between the civilian realm and the military, between war and peace, as well as his insistence, in effect, that they join the military and help fight the war. Ernie Pyle had been the embodiment of the patriotic "combat correspondent." This marriage was shattered by the Vietnam War. Reporters such as Malcolm Browne, Stanley Karnow, Neil Sheehan, Morley Safer, and David Halberstam were alienated by the discrepancy that existed between the view of the war presented by embassy personnel in Saigon and what they saw with their own eyes and heard with their own ears. They rebelled, and by 1966 their reports in many instances were contradicting the official version of the war. This new breed, moreover, came to think of themselves as actors in the drama, players in the game. Safer's August 1965 telecast of the marine burning of Cam Ne was quite calculated. Harrison Salisbury went so far as to report from North Vietnam on the effects of U.S. bombing on the civilian population. In 1966 two of Fulbright's closest friends in the press, Harry Ashmore and William Baggs of the *Miami News,* undertook their own private peace mission to Hanoi.[37] The independence of the press was accelerated by the activities in the mid-1950s of a group of self-styled foreign policy pundits like Walter Lippmann and Joseph Alsop (who criticized from the right), who believed that only they could provide long-term perspective, and hence proper guidance, to U.S. diplomacy.

36 "CIA Chief Rebuked for Letter Praising Attack on Fulbright," *Arkansas Gazette,* July 29, 1966.

37 William C. Baggs to JWF, Dec. 27, 1965, Series 48:1, Box 8:1, SPF.

As Kathleen Turner and others have pointed out, Vietnam-era presidents in general, and Lyndon Johnson in particular, mishandled the press and contributed to the alienation of the media. Johnson viewed the Washington press corps as "one hundred enemies and one good reporter named Bill [William S.] White," as McGeorge Bundy put it.[38] The president might leak stories to favored reporters, but he was determined that no one else would. More important, Johnson's refusal to publicize his escalation in Vietnam, his hyperbole, and the efforts of U.S. military and embassy spokespersons to put the best face on the war in Vietnam had by 1966 created a huge "credibility gap."

The American youth who populated the nation's college campuses felt that "without exception" they had not been told "'the full truth'" about Vietnam, George Reedy confided to the president. It was not only the "light at the end of the tunnel" statements, he said. Young people seemed to be acutely aware that McNamara had once promised that all troops would be out of Vietnam by the end of 1965. It had been "'proven'" that American nationals in the Dominican Republic had not been in danger, the students had told him. "They have a surprising fund of information and misinformation on the Dominican Republic and apparently the action impressed them deeply," Reedy reported.[39]

Fulbright and Marcy cultivated their ties with independent reporters and did their best to widen the credibility gap. In early August Fulbright notified Leonard Marks, head of USIA, that he was going to hold hearings on the information agency's activities in Vietnam, specifically its practice of providing free trips to Southeast Asia to selected journalists. The USIA chief knew perfectly well what Fulbright intended to do. He frantically tried to arrange for a private meeting with the chairman to plead with him not to question too closely or to demand to know the names of the junketeers, lest he give the communists "propaganda leverage." Unfortunately for the administration, Fulbright's schedule was "too full" to permit a conference with Marks.[40] No sooner had the hearings opened than Fulbright gained the floor. Why, he asked Marks, was the USIA using taxpayers' money to fund media trips to Vietnam when he knew that it would bias reporting on the war. Marks insisted that his agency's motives were pure, and he refused to reveal the names of his press guests.[41] Nevertheless, the blow had been struck. The national press carried

38 McG. Bundy interview.

39 Reedy to LBJ, Jan. 27, 1966, WHCF, Nat'l. Sec./Def., Box 219, Johnson Papers.

40 Kinter to Johnson, Aug. 15, 1966, Box 13, Confidential File, CO 312, Johnson Papers.

41 Frank Starzel, retired president of AP; Frank Stanton of CBS; and Palmer Hoyt of the *Denver Post.*

the story on its front pages; "Fulbright Hints Junkets Used to Manage News" ran a typical headline.[42]

The White House and State Department continued with their propaganda campaign in behalf of the war and offered speakers to any and every forum, although college campuses were already becoming hostile environments by 1966 and the demonstrations that frequently accompanied official visits sometimes rendered them counterproductive. The president sought to highlight his domestic record. Indeed, Walt Rostow suggested that the administration "fight a major political battle before the public on an issue other than Vietnam in the weeks and months ahead." What he had in mind was civil rights. "We ought to be able to mobilize a considerable part of the liberal community and isolate Fulbright, Morse and Lippmann," he advised Johnson.[43] White House staffers lobbied congresspeople and senators, and wrote speeches for the Dodds and Lausches to deliver in response to the Fulbrights and Morses.

From mid-1966 on, the administration attempted to portray its congressional opponents, and especially Fulbright, as men who were cowards and who would not only welch on their promises but have their country betray its commitments as well. For Dean Rusk the ultimate rationale for the war in Vietnam was the American "commitment" under the SEATO treaty. Although the signatories to that document pledged only to "counter armed attack" against the nations of Southeast Asia, and to do so in accordance with their "constitutional processes," the secretary regarded it as "the law of the land" that "linked South Vietnam to the general structure of collective security."[44] Because Congress had ratified the SEATO treaty and passed the Gulf of Tonkin Resolution, all "constitutional processes" had been satisfied to his way of thinking.[45] Some like Rusk and Rostow actually believed that. (Whether or not they knew that the government of South Vietnam had never officially requested troops from the United States is unclear.) "Taking it all in all, the conclusion is quite simple from the full range of his [Fulbright's] speechmaking," Rostow told Johnson. "He is unwilling to acknowledge that the role of force is a legitimate element in U.S. foreign policy."[46] Fulbright had signed on,

42 "Fulbright Hints Junkets Used to Manage News," *Arkansas Gazette,* Aug. 17, 1966. After checking with LBJ, Marks scheduled a new round of trips. Kinter to President, Aug. 15, 1966, Box 13, Confidential File, CO 312, Johnson Papers.

43 Rostow to LBJ, May 25, 1966, NSF, Memos to President, Box 7, Johnson Papers.

44 George McT. Kahin, *Intervention: How America Became Involved in Vietnam* (Garden City, N.Y., 1987), 74, and Dean Rusk as told to Richard Rusk, *As I Saw It* (New York, 1990), 427.

45 Rusk, *As I Saw It,* 445, and Summary Notes of 557th NSC Meeting, May 10, 1966, NSC Meeting Notes, Box 2, Johnson Papers.

46 Rostow to LBJ, May 24, 1966, NSF, Memos to President, Box 7, Johnson Papers.

Rusk later wrote, and then gotten cold feet. In the spring of 1966 White House staffers dredged up Fulbright's speeches and votes on the treaty and resolution and gave them to friendly senators and journalists.[47] The president's intent was to condemn the Arkansan out of his own mouth.

The White House's counteroffensive did nothing, however, to close the credibility gap. By the summer of 1966 Johnson's "peace offensive" had come to be widely viewed as the staged affair that it was. The administration frequently declared that it would "negotiate anywhere at any time without reservations," but in fact it continued to refuse to negotiate with the Vietcong. Even Walt Rostow noted that although there were good reasons for the latter, it was "not consistent with the former." The administration's unwavering habit of hailing every change of government in Saigon as a "good" change had made it seem either stupid or devious.[48] Moreover, it lied about casualties. Not only did the Pentagon exaggerate VC and NVA dead and wounded, it misled Congress and the public concerning the number of North Vietnamese civilians killed by the bombing. At the same time the military was telling Fulbright and the SFRC that only six civilians had been killed in Vietnam as a result of all American military action during the first two months of the bombing war, the First Cavalry Division alone was reporting 131 deaths; and this was in South Vietnam only.[49] In June Rostow admitted to Johnson that "we may have killed in the first year of bombing the North three to four thousand civilians."[50]

Then, too, there was the justification for the war. Eric Sevareid told his television audience:

> The immediate difficulty for the administration is that it is trying to fight a limited war under an unlimited rationale. It is foolish to talk about fighting for democracy in a country that has never known it; it is dangerous to talk about China as the real source of the trouble when the last thing you want is a war with China; it is unconvincing to talk as if this aggression is an integral part of a generally advancing Communist tide in Asia when so many hard facts suggest it may be neither general nor advancing.[51]

Further contributing to the credibility gap among college students, the press, and certain members of Congress was the growing rift within the administration itself. McNamara continued to argue that the bombing of the north was counterproductive. Despite Henry Cabot Lodge's laboriously opti-

47 Alexis Johnson to White House, Feb. 11, 1966, NSF, Memos to President, Box 6, Johnson Papers.
48 Rostow to LBJ, June 10, 1966, NSF, Memos to President, Box 8, Johnson Papers.
49 JWF to McNamara, Mar. 21, 1966, Box 2, Fulbright Papers, SFRC, RG 46, NA.
50 Rostow to LBJ, June 16, 1966, NSF, Memos to President, Box 8, Johnson Papers.
51 Eric Sevareid, "Viet Inquiry Essential," *Arkansas Gazette*, Feb. 13, 1966.

mistic reports from Saigon, it was plain for all to see that "South Vietnam" as a viable political entity did not exist. There was increasing doubt as to the willingness of the citizens of that contrived republic to fight in their own behalf. As Richard Russell privately admitted, "the South Vietnamese just can't hack it."[52] Nicholas deB. Katzenbach, who would become undersecretary of state in December 1966, recalled that he never had any problem with the rationale for America's presence in Vietnam. "The notion of trying to keep the North Vietnamese from taking over South Vietnam seemed to me to be a perfectly reasonable thing to do," he later observed. "The problem was that there was no government there to do it."[53] In the absence of one, the United States would have to do the job itself. If that was the case, then what, in fact, was the country fighting for in Southeast Asia? Katzenbach was forced to ask himself. Johnson, Rostow, and the White House public relations experts liked to think that dissent was limited to the spoiled and irresponsible children of America's upper middle class and to a liberal–intellectual coalition spearheaded by Fulbright, Reston, and Lippmann and made up of college professors, professional liberals, pretentious senators, and the *New York Times*.[54] The cancer had spread to the president's inner circle, however, and McNamara, Moyers, presidential speechwriter Harry McPherson, and East Asian specialist Roger Hilsman's loss of faith in America's mission in Vietnam both reflected and accelerated a similar loss of faith among the general citizenry.

To the consternation of the White House, Fulbright managed to make war on the conflict in Vietnam and at the same time avoid being labeled part of the lunatic fringe by the national press and the great American middle class. "There still is no doubt that once his name is attached to a particular position," Brock Brower wrote in *Life,* "even his boldest detractors are forced into a grudging respect for it. . . . Senator Fulbright belongs at this critical moment not to Arkansas but to world opinion."[55] He managed to convey the impression that he was genuinely interested in the welfare of all parties concerned, that he was a disinterested observer, a man of goodwill who did not have all the answers but who wanted nothing so much as to see the peoples of the world enjoy peace and self-determination; this, despite his civil rights record. His staff, all of whom deplored his public posture toward the rights of African Americans, never doubted his sincerity. When Jim Cash suggested that his boss throw in the towel over Vietnam in order to save his political

52 Interview with William Bundy, July 5, 1990, Princeton, N.J.

53 Interview with Nicholas deB. Katzenbach, July 5, 1990, Princeton, N.J.

54 See Robert Kintner to LBJ, July 1 and 5, 1966, WHCF, Confidential File, Box 83, Johnson Papers.

55 Brock Brower, "The Roots of the Arkansas Questioner," *Life,* May 13, 1966, 92–115.

neck, Lee Williams rebuked him. In addition to the fact that Fulbright was right and Johnson wrong, he declared,

> a capitulation by the Senator would have incalculable effect upon our adversaries, primarily the Russians, but also the bloc nations who look to Fulbright and those of his persuasion as the voice of reason in the U.S. Government. If Fulbright gives up, I think their tendency would be to abandon all hope for a rational settlement of the conflict.[56]

The third week in August, Captain Murphy Neal Jones, who had been shot down during the first American raid on the Hanoi oil depots, admitted to reporters that he had taken off from Takhli Airbase in Thailand. Immediately, members of the American press corps began pouring into this supposedly neutral country. What they found was the largest B-52 base in the world. By late in the summer of 1966 the United States had thirty thousand uniformed personnel there. "Thailand is already so crowded with American air power," Clayton Fritchey wrote, "that it is beginning to look more like an air base than a country."[57] Fulbright inserted Fritchey's article into the *Congressional Record* and announced that SFRC hearings on U.S. commitments to Thailand would begin in a month. America was then at the same point with Thailand as it had been with Vietnam at the time of the Gulf of Tonkin, the chairman of the SFRC declared.[58] "Fulbright Fears U.S. May Fight War In Thailand," proclaimed the headlines.[59]

Rusk and McNamara managed to dodge the public spotlight over Thailand, but Nicholas deB. Katzenbach, the former assistant attorney general who had replaced George Ball in the State Department, was not so lucky. As public criticism of the administration mounted for its refusal to face the SFRC in public, Johnson ordered Katzenbach to sacrifice himself.

Referring to the military buildup then underway in Thailand, Fulbright questioned the lawyer-turned-diplomat closely on his constitutional views. Could the United States make a commitment to defend another country without the advice and consent of Congress? Had not the president already made irrevocable commitments without consulting Congress? Katzenbach insisted that President Johnson had not nor would he ever exceed his constitutional powers. Outside the hearing room Fulbright held court once again with the Capitol press corps. With his hand occasionally resting on a copy of *The*

56 Williams to Cash, July 1, 1966, Williams Papers.
57 *Congressional Record,* Senate, Aug. 22, 1966, 20191.
58 Marcy to JWF, Aug. 26, 1966, Box 6, Folder July-Sept., Marcy Papers.
59 UPI 128, Oct. 3, 1966, Series 78, Box 33:2, SPF, and "Fulbright Fears U.S. May Fight War in Thailand," *Arkansas Gazette,* Sept. 1, 1966.

*Heart of Man* by psychoanalyst Erich Fromm, Fulbright announced that although the Pentagon continued to deny it, the United States was building another B-52 base and a deep-water port in Thailand. Americans had better gear up for yet another war under the Asia Doctrine.[60]

60 "Fulbright Swings at State and Marcos," *Washington Post,* Dec. 5, 1966.

# 24

# *The war in Washington*

Throughout the early weeks of 1967 American newspapers were filled with pictures of wounded GIs and screaming Vietnamese children, their clothes burned off by napalm. Stories of American atrocities began to mount. Letters from GIs sickened by the war poured into Fulbright's office. He read many of them.[1] One of the most poignant was written by a battle-hardened second lieutenant serving near Tuy Hoa:

> I have been meaning to write this letter to you for a long while. This evening the pressures are too great to be ignored, even though they are the result of several small occurrences rather than one large disaster. Although, in one sense, the large disaster surrounds me. Adding fresh dimensions of madness daily.
>
> It is just that, in the past few months as an advisor to the VN Coastal Force, I have seen too often the real casualties of this conflict – the farmers and their families in the Delta mangled by air strikes, and the villagers here killed and burned out by our friendly Korean mercenaries.
>
> Of course, I do my share in the lunatic ward. I have even been reprimanded for over-enthusiastic pursuit of VC. Part of it is just compensation – it is refreshing, after seeing so many innocent people suffer, to meet real, live hostile forces capable of striking back.
>
> This evening they showed the JFK documentary film here in the MACV compound. I could not help but feel a great sense of loss as I listened to the richly rolling phrases – what ever has become of our dream? Where is that America that opposed tyrannies at every turn, without inquiring first whether some particular forms of tyranny might be of use to us? Of the three rights which men have, the first, as I recall, was the right to life. How then have we come to be killing so many in such a dubious cause?
>
> As you are probably aware, I am possibly violating seventeen thousand directives in writing to you. But it is not possible to keep silent, as you so amply demonstrate. You remind me of Kent, in *Lear,* who in the face of dire threats from his king replied: "Whilst

1 See, e.g., Capt. James E. Terrell to JWF, July 21, 1967, Series 48:18, Box 53:4, SPF.

> my tongue can yet give vent to clamor, I'll tell thee thou doest evil!" I pray that you fare better than Kent. . . . Good night sir. God keep you well and safe.[2]

Fulbright was overwhelmed. "I agree with everything you have written," he replied to the author, Lieutenant Karl Phaler, "and am ashamed of the fact that I have been unable to persuade this Administration to make a reasonable and timely offer of negotiations so that we might bring this tragic conflict to an end."[3]

No one would ever characterize J. William Fulbright as a brooder or a dreamer. He was not cursed with an overactive imagination; indeed, Paul Greenberg, one of the senator's most relentless critics, once observed that Fulbright feared prophets who claimed to hear the voice of God whispering in their ear. Fulbright was a man much closer to Henry V than Hamlet;[4] yet, by 1967 Vietnam had begun to haunt him.

Indeed, had the war not changed Fulbright, he would never have been able to change it. By 1967 for him the issue was not just strategic, or constitutional, or political, but moral as well. He was not really sure what that meant, as his halting approaches to theologian Reinhold Niebuhr indicated. Throughout his life he had had little time for moral philosophy, much less theology; but the more the Vietnam War impinged on his consciousness, the more time he had for both. Indeed, in the summer of 1967 he wrote an introduction and commentary to a life of Mahatma Gandhi. In the master's spiritualism, if not in his tactic of nonviolent disobedience, were to be found the tocsins that would call the American people back to their fundamental humanity and decency, he declared.[5] However, as Fulbright realized better than anyone, combat with Lyndon Baines Johnson required more than morality and spiritualism.

The administration gave General William Westmoreland broad discretion in developing a strategy to defeat the enemy on the ground in South Vietnam (in contrast to the air war, over which it retained tight control). Westmoreland's "search and destroy" strategy demanded more and more men. In June 1966 the president had approved a force level of four hundred thirty-one thousand to be reached by mid-1967. As this buildup was taking place, Westmoreland put in a new request for an increase to five hundred forty-two thousand troops by the end of 1967.

2 LTJG Karl J. Phaler, May 17, 1967, Series 48:18, Box 53:1, SPF.
3 JWF to Phaler, May 17, 1967, Series 48:18, Box 53:1, SPF.
4 Interview with Paul Greenberg, June 9, 1989, Pine Bluff, Ark.
5 Thomas C. Mulholland to JWF, Aug. 1, 1967, and JWF to Mulholland, Aug. 4, 1967, Series 48:1, Box 8:5, SPF.

The massive infusion of American uniformed personnel between 1965 and 1967 may have forestalled a military collapse in South Vietnam, but Westmoreland's approach was based on a number of erroneous assumptions. Inherent in any attrition strategy was the notion that one could inflict intolerable losses on the enemy while keeping one's own losses within acceptable bounds. In Vietnam that proved not to be the case. Because an estimated two hundred thousand North Vietnamese reached draft age each year, Hanoi was able to replace its losses, counter each American escalation, and frustrate Johnson's hopes for a quick victory. General Vo Nguyen Giap, commander of North Vietnamese forces, understood quite precisely what it would take to win the Second Indochina War, and he took full advantage of the special opportunities available to military men in a totalitarian society. Not having to worry about public opinion and elections, he and Ho could mobilize North Vietnam down to the last person and sacrifice life on the battlefield on a scale unheard of in a democracy. To North Vietnam's strategic benefit, Giap proved absolutely ruthless. Consequently, the United States was able to achieve only temporary military advantage. The North Vietnamese and Vietcong had been hurt, in some cases badly, but their main forces survived; able to choose the time and conditions of battle, and free of time constraints, they retained the strategic initiative. In an effort to force the South Vietnamese to assume responsibility for defending their country, and in response to perceived political opposition to calling up the reserves, Johnson and McNamara deliberately held U.S. troop levels to one-half million; but as a result, Westmoreland did not have sufficient forces to wage war against the enemy's regular units and to control the countryside.

Throughout late 1966 Fulbright's detractors had demanded that he either stop criticizing the administration or offer a concrete alternative for ending the war, one that was politically and strategically viable. In December Random House published *The Arrogance of Power,* a compilation of Fulbright's Johns Hopkins speeches topped off with his eight-point plan for negotiation, American withdrawal, and eventual neutralization of all of Southeast Asia. As with all of Fulbright's books, *The Arrogance of Power* was an amalgam of ideas worked out by Fulbright and his staff and then skillfully edited by Seth Tillman. Combining the Gavin enclave strategy with his own call for the neutralization of Southeast Asia, his eight-point program prescribed an end to the bombing of the north, recognition of the NLF as a party to negotiations, and concentration of American troops in defensible enclaves as a prelude to withdrawal. Hanoi's continuing unwillingness to give assurances that it would halt infiltration and cease hostilities in return for a suspension of the American bombing campaign, coupled with Johnson and Rostow's hostility to a negotiating role for the NLF, made Fulbright's plan unworkable.

Nonetheless, Fulbright's reputation as America's most articulate and influential dove continued to grow. The book made the *New York Times* best-seller list, and by June 1967 Random House had sold a hundred thousand copies. Italian, Spanish, German, Japanese, and Swedish editions followed. One Japanese journalist recalled that the book became virtually required reading for graduate students in his country. "Since leaving the United States I have visited other countries," an English M.P. wrote Fulbright, "and . . . when the word 'Vietnam' is mentioned, invariably your name comes into the conversation. . . . The fact that you are risking your political neck in differing from the views of your Administration is one of the things that will serve the United States in good stead in the future."[6] Ultimately, *The Arrogance of Power* sold over four hundred thousand copies, making it one of the most widely known works of its time.

The notoriety of *The Arrogance of Power* hinged far more on Fulbright's analysis of the role of the nation-state in international affairs and his critique of American foreign policy than it did on his eight-point program to end the war. Max Frankel noted in the *New York Times Book Review* that while Fulbright's book was "an invaluable antidote to the official rhetoric of the government," it was "not a satisfying prescription for alternatives to the policies it condemns." Writing in the *Washington Post,* Ronald Steel grasped the larger point when he observed that "*The Arrogance of Power* marks the passage of Senator Fulbright from a relatively orthodox supporter of the liberal line on foreign policy to a spokesman for the post-cold-war generation."[7] Steel, who had worked briefly for the SFRC, was in an excellent position to make that judgment. Later that year his book *Pax Americana: The Cold War Empire and the Politics of Counterrevolution,* one of the basic texts of the New Left, would be published.

Fulbright and Marcy understood more clearly than ever in early 1967 that the key to eroding congressional and public support for the war was alienation of the hawks. At the same time he was participating in the burgeoning New Left critique of American society, the Arkansan searched for arguments that would appeal to Russell, Sparkman, Symington, and conservative Republicans. He could not very well take overt advantage of their frustration over Johnson's determination to fight a limited war, but he could exploit their traditional commitment to a strict construction of the Constitution and their opposition to a powerful, activist executive. Many of the congressional hawks were, after all, either founders or political heirs of the old conservative coalition that had bat-

6 A. J. Levin to JWF, Apr. 12, 1967, Series 48:18, Box 52:4, SPF.

7 Quoted in William C. Berman, *William Fulbright and the Vietnam War: The Dissent of a Political Realist* (Kent, Ohio, 1988), 78.

tled Harry Truman over the Fair Deal and that had managed to stymie John F. Kennedy's New Frontier. In late February Senator Joseph Clark offered an amendment to a $4.5 billion supplementary appropriations bill for Vietnam. Fulbright used the debate over the Clark amendment – which would require a declaration of war for the further expenditure of funds for military operations in or over North Vietnam and for an increase in U.S. military personnel above five hundred thousand – to provoke Richard Russell into breaking with the administration.[8] Did he not recall that the framers of the Constitution initially reserved to Congress the right not only to declare but to conduct war, he asked the Georgian? Only with great reluctance did they allocate to the executive the power to oversee military operations. Was not the Johnson administration conducting military operations without a declaration of war? How many troops would Russell countenance in Vietnam without a declaration? One million? Two million? They had been allies in disciplining the executive over "domestic" (civil rights) matters, Fulbright reminded his colleague; why could they not act in harness over foreign policy as well?[9]

Russell refused to be entrapped, at least for the moment. He readily admitted that he was a longtime defender of congressional prerogatives, but in the case of Vietnam the legislative branch had been consulted, he argued. All it had to do if it did not like the war in Vietnam was to pass a concurrent resolution, which was not subject to presidential veto, terminating the Gulf of Tonkin Resolution.[10]

As Russell well knew, Fulbright was walking a tightrope. The Arkansan did not, in fact, want a formal declaration of war; nor did he wish for a congressional vote on the Gulf of Tonkin Resolution. Historically, no congressperson or senator had ever voted to withhold support from American troops once they were in the field without suffering politically as a result. In 1967 Lyndon Johnson was sure to win any vote on the war decisively.

Yet, as Fulbright sensed, the hawks were becoming restive. Russell had not supported intervention in 1954, and he had opposed the introduction of American troops under Kennedy; now he chafed under the restrictions Johnson had imposed on the JCS. "Our great difficulty is that we are fighting the kind of war our enemy wants and not using all of the resources that are available to us," he complained to a constituent.[11] The influential Stuart Symington, a former secretary of the air force who sat on both Armed Services and Foreign Relations, was intensely angry with the DOD for what he considered its "arrogance" in not heeding his demands for an all-out air war. Privately he

8 John Herbers, "Fulbright Backs Vietnam Limit of 500,000 G.I.'s," *New York Times*, Mar. 1, 1967.

9 *Congressional Record*, Senate, Mar. 13, 1967, 6427–9.

10 Ibid., Feb. 28, 1967, 4714–17.

11 Russell to General L. O. Grice, Mar. 21, 1967, Dictation Series, Box I.J. 34e., Vietnam Folder, Russell Papers.

admitted to Carl Marcy that his conviction that the United States ought to be in Vietnam was crumbling under Fulbright's onslaughts.[12] Both men were alienated by Johnson's unabashed use of such mindless flag-wavers as Frank Lausche and Thomas Dodd.

Fulbright also sensed mounting support for his position from the liberal, internationalist wing of the Republican Party. In the spring of 1967 Clifford Case (R–New Jersey) and John Sherman Cooper (R–Kentucky) toured Vietnam and returned filled with apprehension over the political situation and the pace of pacification.[13] The ambitious young mayor of New York, John V. Lindsay, denounced the war for diverting funds that were desperately needed to rebuild the inner cities' rotting ghettos and crumbling infrastructures.[14]

Finally, traditional Republican isolationists began to find Fulbright's critique congenial to their views. After all, the notion that the United States ought not to fight a land war in Asia but should defend its interests in the Pacific by means of a ring of naval and air bases was the essence of the "unilateralist" approach propounded by Robert Taft and Herbert Hoover in 1950. In fact, in early 1967 Fulbright had struck up an admiring correspondence with FDR's old isolationist bête noire, Burton K. Wheeler.[15] Vermont's venerable George Aiken had never been enthusiastic about Vietnam, and in the late spring of 1967 he took to the floor of the Senate, armed with a speech prepared by Carl Marcy, calling for an "Asian" settlement to the war. If the countries of the region, who had the most to lose by a communist triumph, did not agree to shoulder their fair share of the burden in Vietnam, the United States should gradually withdraw.[16]

In April 1966 Argentine President Arturo Illia had suggested a summit meeting of the presidents of the American republics to discuss ways to strengthen the Alliance for Progress. Johnson had immediately been attracted by the proposal; it offered an opportunity to reverse an anti-U.S. trend that had been building south of the border in the wake of the Dominican intervention.[17] With the meeting tentatively scheduled for April 1967, Johnson and his advisers developed a plan for the creation of a hemispheric common market. The United States would offer to fund inter-American highways and telecommunications as an incentive to the republics to give up their trade barriers. Following publication of an article entitled "The Alliance That Lost Its Way,"

12 Marcy to Bader, Mar. 4, 1967, Box 7, Folder Jan.–Mar., Marcy Papers.
13 Clifford P. Case to JWF, Feb. 27, 1967, Series 48:1, Box 8:4, SPF.
14 Jack Files to JWF, Mar. 13, 1967, Series 48:17, Box 4:1, SPF.
15 JWF to Burton K. Wheeler, Oct. 30, 1967, Series 48:18, Box 53:5, SPF.
16 Marcy to Aiken, May 8, 1967, Box 7, Folder Jan.–Mar., Marcy Papers.
17 Lyndon Baines Johnson, *The Vantage Point: Perspectives of the Presidency, 1963–1969* (New York, 1971), 348.

by Chilean President Eduardo Frei Montalva, the president decided to add health, education, and agriculture to the categories of projects the United States would help fund. Following a meeting between Rusk and his Latin counterparts in February, the administration decided to ask the House and Senate for a $1.5 billion supplement to the Alliance for Progress.

Despite its elephantine insensitivity, the State Department by 1967 had begun to perceive that Congress was in a somewhat restive mood and no longer ready to rubber-stamp any foreign policy initiative that the administration might propose. Rusk and Katzenbach persuaded the president, somewhat against his better judgment, to ask Congress not only to approve the administration's objectives for the forthcoming meeting to be held in Punta del Este, Uruguay, but to endorse the aid amount as well. A resolution drafted by the State Department and submitted on March 13 sailed through the ever-compliant House Committee on Foreign Affairs. Immediately, President Johnson announced that he and Lady Bird would entertain thirty-five Latin American ambassadors and their wives at the LBJ Ranch as a prelude to the summit gathering.[18] Being a Texan, he knew Mexico well, Johnson told reporters. He had always had a soft spot in his heart for Latin America, a land of "sunshine and flowers and pretty girls."[19]

Just prior to submission of the Punta del Este Resolution, Sol Linowitz, U.S. ambassador to the OAS, approached Fulbright about acting as Senate sponsor. The chairman bristled, refused, and then mischievously suggested that Linowitz approach Wayne Morse, chairman of the SFRC subcommittee on Latin America, and ask him to sponsor it. Fulbright reasoned that Morse, whose anti-Vietnam rhetoric had been far more extreme than his, would indignantly decline; but to his surprise, the enigmatic Morse readily agreed and became not only the Punta del Este Resolution's sponsor but its most ardent advocate. Linowitz mistakenly assumed that although Fulbright would not support the administration's new Latin American initiative, neither would he actively oppose it. Thus, after congressional leaders, including Mansfield, Hickenlooper, and Morse, assured Johnson of their support at a White House meeting on March 10, the administration moved confidently into the breach.[20]

Referring repeatedly to the Gulf of Tonkin Resolution, to the Formosa Resolution (for which he had voted), and to the Middle East Resolution (which he had opposed), Fulbright rose on the floor of the Senate to blast the president. The Punta del Este Resolution, he declared, constituted the most gratuitous and egregious effort to usurp congressional prerogatives in the post–

18 J. Y. Smith, "Latin Aid Resolution Is Approved," *Washington Post,* Mar. 18, 1967.

19 "Rocky Road to the Summit," *Washington Star,* Mar. 23, 1967.

20 Hugh Sidey, "L.B.J.'s Diplomatic Foray into South America," *Life,* Apr. 14, 1967, 38b.

World War II period. The administration was once again trying to impale the House and Senate on the horns of a dilemma:

> If the resolution is rejected, it will be argued that the Congress has weakened the position of the President at Punta del Este. If the resolution is approved, Congress will be committing itself in advance to support courses of action which will lead, it knows not where, and which will cost, it knows not what, or as they say in Arkansas, we will have bought a pig in a poke.[21]

He would approve nothing in advance, he said, and proceeded to offer a "compromise." Under Fulbright's substitute, funds would be made available for the project "only in keeping with Constitutional processes and as specifically authorized and appropriated from time to time by the Congress." To the consternation of the White House, the SFRC immediately voted out the Fulbright version of the Punta del Este Resolution.[22]

Johnson was beside himself with rage. The Texan had once told Joseph Califano, following a multiple bill-signing ceremony, that Congress had to be "mounted like a woman." Not only was Fulbright refusing to succumb to the Texan's unique charms, he was yelling rape. What the hell was he going to tell all those Latinos he was having to the ranch? On April 4 the president called a press conference and condemned both the committee and its chairman. That night Betty and Bill, ignorant of the White House's latest blast, arrived at the executive mansion to attend a state dinner in honor of the president of Turkey. As soon as he learned that Johnson had publicly denounced him, Fulbright got up in the middle of dinner and told Betty, "Let's go." When she lingered, talking to another guest, he angrily grabbed her elbow and said "I said 'come on.'"[23]

His abrupt departure from the Turkey dinner at the White House was one of the few public demonstrations of anger at Lyndon Johnson that Fulbright allowed himself. He knew well that if the Democratic leadership decided that he was allowing personalities to affect the national, and more important the party's, interest, it could and would remove him as chair of the SFRC. In 1871 Senator Charles Sumner, a powerful and senior member of the Republican Party and a sharp critic of President Ulysses S. Grant, had become outraged when his close friend, John Motley, was replaced as minister to London. When he had refused to meet or talk socially with either the president or Hamilton Fish, the secretary of state, Sumner's Senate colleagues had voted to oust him as chairman of the SFRC.[24]

21 *Congressional Record,* Senate, Mar. 16, 1967, 7057.
22 "Rocky Road to the Summit," *Washington Star,* Mar. 23, 1967.
23 *Chicago Sun-Times,* Apr. 13, 1967.
24 Charles Bartlett, "Is Feud Hurting U.S. Interests?," *Chicago Sun-Times,* Apr. 12, 1967.

To the Washington press corps' surprise, Johnson decided not to make a fight of it. He withdrew the Alliance for Progress resolution and went to Punta del Este with nothing but promises. Puzzled observers insisted that he had the votes and that the State Department was adamantly opposed to giving in to Fulbright; but Johnson, a consummate and peripatetic vote counter, was not so sure. Frank Church and Stuart Symington as well as Albert Gore had supported Fulbright. If the administration lost over Punta del Este, it could well signal an open revolt in Congress against executive control of foreign policy, one that could end in a forced, unilateral withdrawal from Vietnam. In the midst of the Punta del Este controversy, Fulbright had spoken to a packed house at Bennett College, where he declaimed against "welfare imperialism." Here, the Arkansan realized, was a rallying cry that had the potential to bring together liberals and conservatives, Democrats and Republicans.[25]

In late April 1967 General William Westmoreland returned to Washington for "consultations." He coupled private warnings to Johnson that the war could go on indefinitely unless the administration acceded to his requests for more troops with public pronouncements that victory was just around the corner. Though he made numerous public appearances in New York and Washington and granted a private audience to the Council on Foreign Relations, he refused Fulbright's request to appear before the SFRC.[26] He further antagonized the chairman by libeling the antiwar movement. "The magnificent men and women I command in Vietnam," Westmoreland told executives of the Associated Press, "have earned the unified support of the American people"; but a "noisy minority" was denying them that support. He and his troops were "dismayed" by "recent unpatriotic acts" in the United States, he said, acts that were clearly costing American as well as Vietnamese lives.[27]

On Friday April 28 Westmoreland delivered a rousing, flag-waving address to a joint session of Congress. To Fulbright's disgust, his colleagues gave the Vietnam warrior a prolonged standing ovation. Shortly thereafter, representatives of the Liberty Lobby and the John Birch Society circulated recall petitions in Idaho, accusing Frank Church of killing American soldiers in Vietnam by his opposition to the war. Bill Fulbright and Wayne Morse were next on the hit list, petition organizers declared.[28] The Westmoreland sally and the wave of patriotism that it provoked put Fulbright on the defensive. Participating in a CBS televised postmortem on the general's speech, the chairman took pains to point out that his quarrel was not with Westmoreland

25 *Congressional Record,* Senate, Apr. 25, 1967, 10621.
26 Marcy to JWF, Apr. 25, 1967, Box 7, Folder Apr.–June, Marcy Papers.
27 *Congressional Record,* Senate, Apr. 25, 1967, 10621.
28 "Senate War Foe Faces Recall Petitions," *Arkansas Gazette,* May 26, 1967.

or his troops but with the policy that had placed them in harm's way.[29] Indeed, so intimidated were Senate doves that some fifteen, including Fulbright, signed an open letter to Ho Chi Minh drafted by Frank Church stating their opposition to a unilateral American withdrawal and urging negotiations.[30]

Privately Fulbright was angry and depressed. "The Administration's drive at total consensus, climaxed last Friday by General Westmoreland's appearance at the Joint Session, is leading us into a frenzy of chauvinism," he wrote actor Carl Reiner, a longtime Fulbright admirer.[31] Government propaganda and the war had turned Americans into a bunch of flag-waving sheep, he complained to Sey Chassler, editor of *Redbook.* The mood in the country was not unlike that in Germany in the 1930s. He feared the worst, he confided.[32]

The Arkansan was not alone in his apprehension. Antiwar columnists, most of whom were in intermittent contact with Fulbright, warned that the war and Johnson's drive for consensus were laying the groundwork for a new wave of McCarthyism. "No precedent exists for an American President bringing home the field commander of American forces at war to plead in public for support of that war and an end to protest and dissent against it," Doris Fleeson declared.[33]

Fulbright's drive to alienate congressional hawks from the administration was momentarily sidetracked by an indiscreet interview he granted to *Newsday,* the Long Island paper then being published by former White House staffer Bill Moyers. He bitterly denounced hawks within the administration and repeated the New Left charge that as errand boys for American capitalists, State Department, Pentagon, and White House officials supported the war in Vietnam because it benefited manufacturers and financiers in the United States. According to Fulbright, they viewed Vietnam as "a nice little war, not too much killing, but still a big help to the economy."[34] More important, he singled out Congressman L. Mendel Rivers (D–South Carolina), Senator Henry Jackson (D–Washington), and Richard Russell as legislators whose home districts abounded with defense industries and who supported the war because their constituents benefited from war-generated Pentagon contracts.

29 Berman, *Fulbright and the Vietnam War,* 82.
30 *Congressional Record,* May 17, 1967, 13011.
31 JWF to Carl Reiner, May 1, 1967, Series 48:18, Box 53:2, SPF.
32 JWF to Sey Chassler, Apr. 29, 1967, Series 48:18, Box 51:3, SPF.
33 *Congressional Record,* Senate, Apr. 27, 1967, 11042–3.
34 "Fulbright Charges News Story Aimed to Discredit Him," *Arkansas Democrat,* May 5, 1967.

Rivers and Jackson immediately cried foul. It was an unwritten rule of Congress that members did not accuse each other of crass political opportunism when they pork-barreled in behalf of their constituents. Fulbright had crossed the line, and he publicly apologized to his colleagues, claiming that *Newsday* was seeking to discredit him by quoting out of context an off-the-record interview.[35] Jackson, prowar, prolabor, and pro-Zionist, would never forgive the Arkansan; indeed, the two would remain bitter enemies until Fulbright's departure from the Senate.

Fulbright, as one family member put it, had the constitution of a horse. Throughout his life he had proved amazingly resistant to stress. His health problems had been largely limited to the aftereffects of his lacrosse injuries. In May, however, he came down with a cold that soon turned into bronchitis. His fever skyrocketed, and he was forced to check himself into Walter Reed Hospital for a week.[36]

Fully recovered, Fulbright, together with Joe Clark, Claiborne Pell, and several other legislators, traveled to Geneva the last week in May to attend the Pacem in Terris conference, an international gathering of parliamentarians, businesspeople, and scientists who had been meeting intermittently since the 1950s to try and figure out a foolproof way to avert nuclear war. Fulbright was one of the keynote speakers.

By the time he addressed the Pacem in Terris gathering Fulbright was being labeled by many in the United States as a neoisolationist. The application of that term to the Arkansan was an indication of how deeply the globalist assumptions in NSC-68 had become embedded in the popular mind. Shortly before the Geneva meeting Carl Marcy reread Admiral Alfred Thayer Mahan and prepared a new American foreign policy statement for Southeast Asia, a statement that summarized Fulbright's views. The goal of the United States should not be to defend and promote "freedom" and "democracy" – those were culturally relative values – but "to maintain such base facilities there [in the Pacific] as will protect the sea and air routes of the area from domination by hostile forces, and to do so without involving American manpower in combat with the manpower of Asia."[37] Surely, that position smacked of Theodore Roosevelt, and more recently, of Robert Taft and Herbert Hoover, men whom Democratic globalists like Dean Acheson (and J. William Fulbright) had labeled as neoisolationists. It should be pointed out, however, that neither they nor Fulbright favored an American withdrawal from world

35 Ibid.

36 Lee Williams to Theodore Matoff, May 13, 1967, Series 39:2, Box 14, SPF.

37 Summary Proposal for Disengagement in Vietnam, May 18, 1967, Box 7, Folder Apr.–June, Marcy Papers.

affairs; what the Arkansan advocated was a narrower definition of the national mission than that espoused by those who had been "present at the creation."

Fulbright coupled this scaled-down definition of America's strategic goals and responsibilities – dubbed the "new realism" by University of Chicago political scientist Hans Morgenthau – with a return to the internationalism of his first years in Congress. Since the birth of the nation-state system, Fulbright told the gathering in Geneva, extended periods of peace had been the result of a balance of power. When, as had been the case during the Napoleonic era, one nation, through overweening ambition and the acquisition of unlimited power, had destroyed the balance, the victims of that imperial impulse had attempted to form a permanent community to regulate competition and mediate conflicts. The Concert of Europe, formed in the wake of Waterloo, had collapsed in 1914, and the United Nations had fallen victim to the exigencies of the cold war. Initially it had been Stalinist Russia that threatened the balance of power, but now a different hegemonic power sought to force its will on the rest of the world, albeit for seemingly noble purposes. That nation was the United States. For his country's sake as well as for the good of the rest of the world, the United Nations was going to have to mediate international disputes, and multinational organizations such as the World Bank were going to have to attend to the socioeconomic problems of developing areas. America needed to be saved from itself.[38]

Reflecting his new interest in education, mass psychology, anthropology, and moral philosophy, Fulbright insisted that international community was the only alternative to nationalism, aggression, empire, and ultimately holocaust. It was the nature of humankind to deny its base origins:

> We pay lip service to Darwin, but, in our heart of hearts, how many of us really believe that we are not fallen gods but unusually precocious apes? Not many, I dare say. And why should we? Who wants to associate with chimpanzees when he has the words and the ideas which enable him to believe that he is only slightly lower than the angels?[39]

But humanity erred in denying its baser nature. The need for an international community that would restrain unbridled nationalism and thereby ensure the survival of the species was greater than ever.

The mainstays of Fulbright's political thought in 1967 were limited national commitment, international cooperation, and educational exchange. As the

[38] Throughout the remainder of 1967 Fulbright would suggest that the Security Council be asked to assume responsibility for mediating the Vietnam War. Specifically, the Council should pass a resolution calling for a cease-fire and then reconvene the Geneva Conference. "Fulbright Wants UN to Rule on Vietnam," *Christian Science Monitor,* Sept. 25, 1967.

[39] *Congressional Record,* Senate, June 7, 1967, 15018.

communist world diversified and Stalinism receded into history, there was no longer any need for an American crusade or symmetrical containment – if there ever had been. In seeking to fulfill its cold war mission, in acting as if the bipolar political system that had emerged from World War II continued to exist, the United States was threatening to become the hegemonic power it had frequently decried and occasionally combated. Vietnam was the mirror that would reflect the perversion of America's values and traditional policies, and Fulbright was determined to hold it before the nation's face.

What gave Fulbright's critique of American foreign policy special sharpness and poignancy was that he had been one of the principal architects of the very cold war liberalism he was now decrying. Indeed, his disillusionment both paralleled and accelerated disillusionment within the nation's preeminent liberal organization, the Americans for Democratic Action.

Because of Fulbright's record on civil rights, his numerous antiunion votes, and his intermittent attacks on American Zionists, the ADA did not, indeed could not, explicitly embrace him. Nonetheless, the moderate and reform wings of the organization were vastly influenced by the SFRC hearings and by the chairman's humane and intelligent criticism of the war. Fulbright bridged the gap between disillusioned cold warriors like Arthur Schlesinger and Chester Bowles on the one hand, and more radical antiwar figures like Curtis Gans and Allard Lowenstein on the other. In so doing he dealt the Vietnam consensus a serious blow; he also further damned himself in Lyndon Johnson's eyes.

Beginning in 1966 Lowenstein – a former student activist at the University of North Carolina at Chapel Hill, a past head of the National Student Association, and a leader of the reform wing of the ADA – launched a campaign to persuade the organization to support someone other than Lyndon Johnson for president in 1968. Though Lowenstein did not succeed, the National Board at its annual meeting in Washington in the spring of 1967 did denounce the war in Vietnam. At the same time, a group of antiwar enthusiasts in New York opened the "Citizens for Kennedy–Fulbright" headquarters in preparation for the 1968 presidential election.[40] In July the group organized some fifty former delegates to the Democratic National Convention and had them send a public letter to the president urging him not to run in 1968. Because of deep divisions over foreign affairs, they declared, "millions of Democrats will be unable to support Democratic candidates in local, state or national elections."[41]

From that time on, Lyndon Johnson viewed the ADA as nothing less than a "Kennedy-in-exile" government. The dump-Johnson organization also served

40 "RFK–Fulbright Group to Ignore Objections, Run in New Hampshire," *Arkansas Gazette,* May 5, 1967.

41 "'Help Party, Don't Run,' Dissenters Tell Johnson," *Washington Evening Star,* July 31, 1967.

further to identify Fulbright in Johnson's mind with the hated Bobby. Although he publicly repudiated the movement to draft him for the 1968 Democratic vice-presidential nomination, Fulbright continued to cultivate members of both the moderate and reform groups within the ADA. If the Texan heeded the antiwar consensus emerging among American liberals, he could save his presidency; if he did not, he would have to go down with his ship of war. Like Lowenstein, Fulbright believed that ending the war in Vietnam was far more important than saving Lyndon Johnson's presidency.

# 25

# *"The price of empire"*

In early February David Ness, deputy chief of the American mission in Cairo and an old acquaintance of Fulbright's, wrote the chairman warning him that the Middle East was teetering on the edge of an abyss, ready to plunge into war at a moment's notice. Arab nationalism, inflamed by the suffering of exiled Palestinians and fueled by Nasser's ambition, was reaching a fever pitch. Ambassador Lucius Battle (former head of cultural affairs in State and another acquaintance of Fulbright's) was scheduled to leave in March, and Washington had not even thought of a replacement. The region was ready to explode, and the Johnson administration did not have a clue as to what was going on. Ness pled with Fulbright to help. "I will try to get the word through [to the White House and State Department] in the best way I can," the chairman replied. "I need not tell you that things are testy here in Washington these days, and one has to watch his step."[1]

Throughout the late 1950s and early 1960s, Egypt, Syria, and Jordan offered their territory as staging grounds for Palestinian guerrilla attacks into Israel. In 1964 Gamal Abdel Nasser, who still aspired to head a pan-Arab union, persuaded other Arab leaders to join him in creating the Palestine Liberation Organization and financing a guerrilla army whose purpose it would be to wrest Palestine from Israel. This army, Al Fatah ("conquest"), began raiding Israel from Syria and Jordan. When Israel responded with devastating reprisal attacks against its two Arab neighbors, the Soviet Union declared its support for the Palestinian movement and began shipping large quantities of tanks and planes to Syria.

On May 22, 1967, Nasser, in an effort to exert pressure on Israel, closed the Straits of Tiran, the entrance to the Gulf of 'Aqaba, which separated the Sinai Peninsula from Arabia. The gulf was Israel's only opening to the south, and that nation operated a major oil terminal at its head. President Johnson denounced the closing on May 23. He then simultaneously appealed to Egypt to reopen the waterway and asked Israel to refrain from retaliation. He promised, moreover, to work out an international guarantee of free passage.

1 JWF to David G. Ness, Feb. 3, 1967, Series 48:11, Box 35:5, SPF, and "U.S. Ignored Crisis Signs in Mideast," *Baltimore Sun,* June 11, 1967.

Days passed and the Strait of Tiran remained closed. Meanwhile, Egypt, Syria, and Jordan massed troops along Israel's borders. On June 5 the Israeli military attacked. An air strike caught most of Egypt's planes on the ground, where they were obliterated, while the army raced across the Sinai Peninsula. Within a week the Israelis had driven the Egyptians back to the west side of the Suez; the Star of David flew over the entire Sinai. After Jordan entered the fray, the Israelis were able in addition to conquer the West Bank of the Jordan – including all of Jerusalem, the putative capital of *eretz* (greater) Israel – and to occupy the Golan Heights, strategic high ground just inside Syria. In the process, the Israelis became reluctant caretakers of some eight hundred thousand Palestinian refugees.[2] On June 10 the fighting stopped when all belligerents accepted the U.N. cease-fire proposal.

Once Fulbright and Marcy became convinced that the Johnson administration was not going to intervene unilaterally in the Six-Day War, they began to view the Middle East crisis through the prism of the conflict in Vietnam. Incredibly, they saw in the week-long conflagration an opportunity to hammer out a great-power rapprochement that would in turn make possible an end to the fighting in Indochina.

As soon as he received word of the closing of the Straits of Tiran, Rusk called Fulbright and other congressional leaders to the State Department for an extended meeting. He assured them that Johnson was determined to avoid a Soviet–American conflict and to see the crisis resolved peacefully.[3] Two days later Fulbright told reporters that it was "hypocritical" for the president to appeal to the Israelis to show restraint when he was attempting to bomb North Vietnam back to the Stone Age. Well aware that the vast majority of the American people were pro-Israeli, Fulbright and Stuart Symington declared that the United States was unprepared to mediate in the Middle East and to protect its "vital interests" – a euphemism for Israeli security – because it was bogged down in Vietnam. Johnson, Rusk, and McNamara were furious. What an irony, Rusk remarked bitterly; the dove was sprouting talons.[4]

In the aftermath of the 1967 war, which left Israel in control of the Golan Heights, Gaza, and the West Bank, Fulbright and Marcy claimed to see a certain symmetry in the Soviet and American positions in world affairs. Both had underestimated the power of nationalism in developing regions of the world; both had found their modern weaponry incapable of determining the outcome of regional conflicts; and both as a result had suffered a significant loss of prestige and influence. The opportunity was ripe, Fulbright asserted repeat-

2 Johnson to Truman, Augues 3, 1967, Box 15, Post-Presidential Files, Truman Papers.

3 JWF to Irma Jennings, May 22, 1967, Series 48:18, Box 52:2, SPF, and *Congressional Record,* Senate, May 24, 1967, 13788.

4 Memorandum for the Record, May 24, 1967, NSC Meeting Notes, Box 2, Johnson Papers.

edly, for Soviet–American cooperation in the context of the United Nations. In the Middle East, the two superpowers could defuse the situation by guaranteeing free international access to the Gulf of 'Aqaba in return for an Israeli withdrawal from the occupied territories. In Southeast Asia, the Soviet Union could use its good offices to bring Hanoi to the negotiating table.[5] What the chairman and his chief of staff hoped was that the Soviet Union's humiliation in the Middle East would blunt Russophobia in the United States and create enough political room for the president to accept a mediated settlement in Vietnam. They were, of course, wrong.

Deciding that two could play the Zionist card in regard to Vietnam, Johnson told Israeli foreign minister Abba Eban that traditional isolationism was on the loose in Congress. "We are almost back to the Gerald Nye days when the monstrous munitions maker was on every school child's tongue." Everyone with any sense knew that Israel was the free world's front line against communism in the Middle East and that the struggle there was part and parcel of the war in Vietnam. The growing sentiment against foreign commitments boded ill for Israel as well as South Vietnam, the president warned Eban. The same senators who opposed the war in Vietnam would abandon Israel in a twinkling of an eye. Putting words in Fulbright's mouth, Johnson told Eban that "one Senator" had told him that "we should abandon Southeast Asia because they are not our kind of people." If that was to be the basis of American foreign policy, he told Eban, "you've done had it." The message was clear: If Israel wanted continued help from the United States, it had better mobilize American Zionists in behalf of the war in Vietnam.[6]

The Six-Day War had only momentarily diverted Fulbright from his campaign to unify hawks and doves around the issue of executive usurpation of the congressional prerogatives in the field of foreign policy. Fulbright and Marcy focused increasingly on the idea of a national commitments resolution. Throughout June and the first part of July, Marcy, Don Newhouse, and the SFRC staff labored over a document that would, in Marcy's words, "unite the hawks and the doves, the North and the South, and the liberals and conservatives – all acting in glorious defense of the Constitution."[7]

Meanwhile, a series of events in the Congo had persuaded Richard Russell, the powerful chairman of Armed Services, that the administration had to be confronted lest America become involved in one Vietnam after another. Throughout the Congo's bloody struggle for independence from Belgium and

5 *Congressional Record,* Senate, May 24, 1967, 13788, and Possible Security Council Resolution, June 9, 1967, Box 7, Folder Apr.–June, Marcy Papers.

6 Notes on the President's meeting with Abba Eban et al., Oct. 24, 1967, Meeting Notes File, Box 2, Johnson Papers.

7 Marcy to Morse, July 24, 2967, Box 7, Folder July-Sept., Marcy Papers.

the civil strife that followed, the United States had acted to shore up the pro-Western, anticommunist government of President Joseph Mobutu. In June President Johnson had authorized the dispatch of three C-130 cargo planes and 150 military personnel to the central African republic. The American presence was necessary, Mobutu claimed, to help him suppress a major rebellion against his government. On July 8, shortly before the planes left, Rusk called Russell and Fulbright to inform them of the enterprise. He gave the impression in his telephone conversation that the purpose of the expedition was to rescue Americans about to be butchered in the jungle. The following day, however, Rusk called again and said that the planes would be used to move Mobutu's troops "around the Congo to deal with revolutionary elements."[8]

On July 10 Russell seized the floor in the Senate to criticize the administration sharply. The situation in the Congo, he said, was purely an internal conflict and one in which the United States should not become involved. Americans must not become bogged down in "local rebellions and local wars" in which the nation had "no stake and where we have no legal or moral commitment to intervene."[9] He had protested privately to the administration, he said, but his objections had gone unheeded.

Fulbright moved quickly to take advantage of the opening. During a long lunch in the Senate dining room, the Arkansan broached the subject of a national commitments resolution to his old friend from Georgia and urged him to introduce a bill embodying it. The document that Marcy and his staff had produced was a masterpiece, the chairman observed, one that "seems to me to come pretty close to expressing what I would guess is a nearly universal Senate view." It provided that a national commitment by the United States to a foreign power "necessarily and exclusively results from affirmative action taken by the executive and legislative branches of the United States Government through means of a treaty, convention, or other legislative instrumentality specifically intended to give effect to such a commitment."[10] Thus was planted the seed that would flower into the Hatfield–McGovern and Cooper–Church resolutions as well as the War Powers Act. The long, bitter struggle against the imperial presidency had begun.

After testifying before the newly formed Subcommittee on the Separation of Powers headed by Senator Sam Ervin (D–North Carolina), Fulbright met with the Capitol Hill press corps. He detected, he told them, a growing desire by the Senate to reclaim its prerogatives. He then departed for Idaho and a float trip down the middle fork of the Salmon River with James H. Doolittle of Tokyo air raid fame and executives of the Potlatch Forests Co. It was a fruitless attempt at diversion. In the middle of the trip Fulbright had the ca-

8 Quoted in Gilbert C. Fite, *Richard B. Russell, Jr., Senator from Georgia* (Chapel Hill, 1991), 451.

9 Quoted in ibid.

10 JWF to Richard Russell, July 14, 1967, Series 48:3, Box 16:4, SPF.

noes put ashore and ordered the guide to radio for a helicopter. Young men were dying, a congressional revolt was brewing, and he needed to get back to the scene of action. By the twenty-second Fulbright was once again in the capital ready to do battle.[11]

On July 25 Lyndon Johnson convened what he expected to be a routine gathering of Senate committee chairs. The group included Scoop Jackson, Allen Ellender, James Eastland, Mike Monroney (D–Oklahoma), Warren Magnuson (D–Washington) – all committed party-liners on the war – as well as Mansfield and Fulbright. The president thanked the group for their "experience, friendship and judgment," and invited comments. "Mr. President," Fulbright exclaimed, "what you really need to do is to stop the war. That will solve all your problems." Johnson's face reddened. He sensed a change in the attitude of his colleagues toward the conflict in Vietnam, Fulbright declared. Even Frank Lausche had called for an end to the bombing of the north. Senator Russell was very upset about having been lied to on the Congo, he continued. "Vietnam is ruining our domestic and our foreign policy. I will not support it any longer." By now Johnson's steely gaze was fixed on the Arkansan. The group was absolutely still. "I expect that for the first time in twenty years I may vote against foreign assistance and may try to bottle the whole bill up in the Committee," Fulbright warned.

Johnson exploded. If Congress wanted to tell the rest of the world to go to hell, that was its prerogative. "Maybe you don't want to help the children of India, but I can't hold back." He understood that, "according to Bill Fulbright at least," all of them felt under the gun when they came to the White House. He then dared the leaders to defeat foreign aid.

Fulbright refused to be intimidated. "Vietnam is central to the whole problem," he declared. It was unbalancing the budget and undermining the nation's foreign policy.

"Bill," Johnson responded, "everybody doesn't have a blind spot like you do. You say don't bomb North Vietnam on just about everything. I don't have the simple solution you have."

Turning to the group, the president said bitterly, "If you want me to get out of Vietnam, then you have the prerogative of taking out the resolution under which we are out there now. You can repeal it tomorrow. You can tell the troops to come home. You can tell General Westmoreland that he doesn't know what he is doing."[12] Mansfield interrupted to say that perhaps the group ought to move on to a discussion of governmental operations.

Six days after his explosive encounter with the president, Fulbright was ready to move on the national commitments resolution. "This could be a pretty

11 "Fulbright Cuts Float Trip Short," *Arkansas Democrat,* July 22, 1967.

12 Meeting of the President with the Senate Committee Chairmen, July 25, 1967, Tom Johnson Notes, Box 1, Johnson Papers.

important statement," Marcy told another staff member with vast understatement; "the break between JWF and LBJ openeth again."[13] On the thiry-first Fulbright introduced his nonbinding "sense of Congress" proposal. It was, he told his colleagues, a simple reaffirmation of the constitutional truth that a national commitment could be made only through formal executive and legislative action. Immediately Richard Russell rose to his feet. "I know of nothing that is more in need of clarification than the present state of the alleged commitment of the United States all over the world." Conservative North Carolinian Sam Ervin followed. "The Senator from Arkansas has rendered a real, a lasting, and a most significant service to the country in proposing the resolution which he has offered today," proclaimed the self-styled "country lawyer." A host of others followed – doves, hawks, northerners, southerners, liberals, conservatives.[14] At last Fulbright had in his fingers the thread that would unwind the congressional consensus in behalf of the Vietnam War. He had no intention of forcing an early vote, however. With the resolution pending, there would be a continual focal point for anti-Vietnam debate.

In addition, however, the national commitments resolution was a frontal assault on NSC-68 and the globalist assumptions that underlay it. Fulbright let newsmen know that he was drawing up a "diplomatic catechism" for Rusk to answer during his next appearance before the SFRC. These questions would force the secretary to define precisely American responsibilities under the forty-two bilateral and multilateral aid agreements the United States had concluded around the world. No one noted the irony of the fact that the sponsor of the national commitments resolution was the same person who had proved instrumental in defeating the Bricker amendment more than a decade earlier.

As if the imp of the perverse were pursuing him, Lyndon Johnson in 1967 seemed to lose the support of the group that had more than any other benefited from the policies of his administration: African Americans. Inevitably, the legal and political progress of the early 1960s had served to heighten black expectations that all too often were then not realized, leading in turn to greater frustration, bitterness, and anger. This was especially true of urban dwellers. On July 23, 1967, the bloodiest and most destructive American riot in a century erupted in Detroit. Beginning the usual way, with an incident of alleged police brutality, it spread like wildfire through fourteen square miles of black slums. Governor George Romney had no choice but to call out the National Guard, but police and Guardsmen were helpless in the face of this massive breakdown of public order. The carnage of the riot when it ended was stun-

13 Marcy to Newhouse, July 27, 1967, Box 7, Folder July–Sept., Marcy Papers.
14 "Bid to Curb Executive's Role Gains," *Baltimore Sun,* Aug. 1, 1967.

ning – 43 dead, 7,000 arrested, 1,300 buildings destroyed, and 2,700 businesses looted. Surveying his city, Mayor Jerome Cavanaugh grimly remarked, "it looks like Berlin in 1945."[15] The problem was only going to get worse, Hubert Humphrey told Johnson. According to the vice-president, there were fifty-two cities ready to explode. As of August 2, law enforcement agencies reported ten with "high tension" and eight undergoing "intense psychological warfare," including Washington.[16]

J. William Fulbright saw a connection between racial unrest in the United States and foreign affairs. Ten days after the Detroit riot the chairman of the SFRC flew to Honolulu to address the Hawaiian Bar Association. He opened by quoting a black veteran who had declared, standing in the smoke and rubble of Detroit, "I just got back from Vietnam a few months ago, but, you know, I think the war is here." Pointing out that during a single week in July 164 Americans had been killed and 1,442 wounded in Vietnam, while 65 Americans had perished and 2,100 were injured in city riots, Fulbright told the lawyers that "we are truly fighting a two-front war and doing badly in both." There was a subtle, moral connection between the conflict in Vietnam and the urban riots that were sweeping America, he said. It was impossible for the United States to pursue an imperial policy abroad, to carpet-bomb North and South Vietnam, and simultaneously attend to the demands of freedom and social justice at home. It was obscene that the administration had allocated $76 billion to the Pentagon for fiscal 1968 and only $15 billion to social programs.[17]

Fulbright's Hawaiian speech, entitled "The Price of Empire," was a powerful indictment of the Johnson administration and America, a philosophical and moral extension of the positions taken in the Herter Lectures and *The Arrogance of Power.* Critics of the war, which he once again went out of his way to hail, knew what policymakers did not, Fulbright said: "that it is ultimately self-defeating to fight fire with fire and that you cannot defend your values in a manner that does violence to those values without destroying the very thing that you are trying to defend."[18]

By the late summer of 1967, the antiwar movement had become a major force in American politics and culture. On April 4 Martin Luther King, Jr., had told the ritzy congregation at New York's Riverside Church: "I could never again raise my voice against the violence of the oppressed in the ghet-

15 Quoted in Allen J. Matusow, *The Unraveling of America: A History of Liberalism in the 1960s* (New York, 1984), 363.

16 Memorandum for the President, Aug. 2, 1967, Tom Johnson Notes, Box 1, Johnson Papers.

17 *Congressional Record,* Senate, Aug. 9, 1967, 22126–7.

18 Quoted in William C. Berman, *William Fulbright and the Vietnam War: The Dissent of a Political Realist* (Kent, Ohio, 1988), 86.

tos without having first spoken clearly to the greatest purveyor of violence in the world today – my own government."[19] Eleven days later, King led the biggest antiwar demonstration to date. The decision by the 1964 Nobel Prize winner to join the antiwar movement gave it a sudden infusion of much-needed prestige. King endorsed Fulbright's eight-point program for ending the war but, like Fulbright, explicitly rejected civil disobedience and draft evasion. In July King joined Benjamin Spock, whom Fulbright had publicly praised, and others in cofounding Vietnam Summer, an ambitious effort to organize liberals and radicals into local antiwar chapters. Following a December 1966 "We Won't Go" conference in Chicago, students at Chicago, Wisconsin, and Queens College independently announced in 1967 that they would not fight in Vietnam. In March Fulbright inserted into the *Congressional Record* a letter protesting the war signed by eight hundred former Peace Corps volunteers.[20] Only a February snowstorm prevented two thousand members of Women's Strike for Peace from demonstrating in Washington.[21] By July popular approval of the president's handling of the war had dropped to 33 percent.[22]

The White House had reason to fear the antiwar movement, not because it was a threat by alien and radical factions to destabilize the nation, but because it was an increasingly mainstream movement whose objective was to conserve American institutions and living standards. Support for the war among middle- and working-class Americans dropped sharply during 1967. By the summer of that year, draft calls exceeded thirty thousand per month, and more than thirteen thousand Americans had died in Vietnam. In early August, the president recommended a 10 percent surtax to cover the steadily increasing costs of the war.[23] Polls taken shortly after the tax increase was announced indicated that although they continued to oppose withdrawal, a majority of Americans for the first time indicated their belief that the United States had been mistaken in intervening in Vietnam. Public approval of Johnson's handling of the war plummeted to 28 percent by October.[24] A number of major metropolitan dailies shifted from support of the war to opposition in 1967, and the influential *Time–Life* publications, fervently hawkish at the outset, began to raise serious questions about the administration's policies.

19 Quoted in Charles DeBenedetti with Charles Chatfield, *An American Ordeal: The Antiwar Movement of the Vietnam Era* (Syracuse, 1990), 172.

20 *Congressional Record,* Mar. 7, 1967, 5635.

21 WSP to JWF, Feb. 9, 1967, Series 48:17, Box 44:1, SPF.

22 DeBenedetti and Chatfield, *American Ordeal,* 179.

23 George C. Herring, *America's Longest War: The United States and Vietnam, 1950–1975,* 2d ed. (New York, 1986), 174.

24 Sherwin Markman to Barefoot Sanders, July 11–14 and 20, 1967; and DeVier Pierson to Barefoot Sanders, Aug. 3, 1967, WHCF, Box 324, Johnson Papers.

Lyndon Johnson was a stubborn, controlling man, however. Had he accepted defeat easily he would have been neither the Senate's youngest majority leader nor president of the United States. Johnson's definition of victory in Vietnam, despite what Fulbright thought or said, did not include the conquest, or even military defeat, of North Vietnam. It did call for the protection and sustenance of a noncommunist South Vietnam; but that was the problem. Called upon to describe the political and cultural entity it was fighting to protect, the administration was hard pressed to come up with a convincing answer. Since the formation of nation-states, the willingness of citizens to bear arms in behalf of their country had been both a badge of their citizenship and a sign of the viability of their country. By that standard, as well as other political and cultural guidelines, South Vietnam did not exist: In July, while calling for additional American troops, military chief of state Nguyen Van Thieu rejected the notion of a general mobilization of his countrymen.[25]

Through sheer willpower, the Johnson administration had brought into being a South Vietnamese constitution in the spring of 1967 and persuaded Thieu and sitting Prime Minister Nguyen Cao Ky to schedule elections for September of that year. The process was flawed from beginning to end, however. The American embassy carefully "monitored" elections to a constituent assembly to ensure that "anti-Americanism" did not crop up and that NLF members and fellow-travelers were excluded.[26] The problem was that in seeking to keep anti-Americanism out of the election, the embassy virtually guaranteed that the Buddhists would not participate.

With members of the NLF excluded and the Buddhists boycotting, participants in the constituent elections were limited largely to members of the government and their clients. Fulbright, who had been following events closely, was disgusted. "If they had an honest election in South Vietnam they would tell us to go home," he wrote a constituent, "but there is not a chance to have an honest election when we control all modes of transportation . . . and for all practical purposes dominate the country."[27]

Assisted by John Roche, the same White House staffer who wanted to jail draft-card burners and other dissenters, the constituent assembly drafted a constitution that called for a two-house legislature and a powerful president. Fulbright was not impressed. Noting that the president could suspend the constitution for reasons of "security, national defense . . . national interest . . . public safety," he warned the Senate that the ballyhooed document was an invitation to tyranny.[28] When, subsequently, one of the 117 members of

25 Baggs to JWF, July 14, 1967, Series 48:18, Box 51:2, SPF.

26 Principles Governing U.S. Operations Concerning Elections and Constitutional Assembly in South Viet-Nam, May 12, 1966, NSF, Memos to President, Box 7, Johnson Papers.

27 JWF to Oscar Fendler, May 14, 1966, Series 48:18, Box 48:1, SPF.

28 *Congressional Record,* Senate, June 6, 1967, 14758.

the assembly who dared support negotiations with the NLF was murdered, Fulbright, appearing on *Meet the Press,* accused the Ky government of being responsible.[29] The charge infuriated Ky. The South Vietnamese ambassador delivered an official protest, and militant Roman Catholic youths burned effigies of Fulbright in Saigon.[30]

Though not flagrantly fraudulent by Ngo Dinh Nhu standards, the September elections were hardly fair and impartial. Only NLF members or sympathizers were excluded: The vast majority of Buddhists wound up voting – indeed, they had little choice. The Vietcong had called for a boycott of the elections, and the government warned that all Vietnamese who did not participate would be prosecuted. The ambitious Thieu forced Ky to take second billing on the ticket, and prepared for a landslide victory. He was sadly disappointed. The Thieu–Ky ticket polled barely 35 percent of the vote. Of further embarrassment to the government was the strong showing of Truong Dinh Dzu, an unsavory lawyer who had once put his wife up as collateral for a loan. Concealing his neutralist tendencies, Dzu slipped through the screening process and then campaigned as a dove. Immediately following the election, President Thieu, whose 35 percent still represented a plurality, had Dzu arrested and jailed.[31]

"These are our elections," Fulbright told reporters, "not the kind anticipated under the Geneva accords."[32] It was all one big farce, he said; the American-financed pacification program in Vietnam stemmed not from any commitment to the welfare of the people but to a determination to bribe them into voting for a pro-American government. In view of the "unsatisfactory political situation" in South Vietnam, Fulbright called on Johnson for "a major reassessment of our position."[33]

The administration, including Johnson and Lodge, were not so naïve as to believe that Western-style democracy could be exported to Vietnam, a land that had stubbornly resisted westernization for four hundred years. Many within the administration feared that a completely open government would lead to chaos. Indeed, by 1967 the Johnson administration had recast its definition of "victory" in Vietnam. Perhaps the best that could be hoped for, Lodge told Johnson, was a reduction in the level of terrorism, an open stretch of road

29 Notes on Senator Fulbright *Meet the Press* Interview, Jan. 24, 1967, Box 462, Harriman Papers.

30 JWF to Tran Van Do, Mar. 3, 1967, Series 48:18, Box 53:4, SPF, and "Fulbright, Others Burned in Effigy at Rally in Saigon," *Arkansas Gazette,* Feb. 26, 1967.

31 Stanley Karnow, *Vietnam: A History* (New York, 1984), 449–50.

32 Carolyn Lewis, "Fulbright Calls Vietnam Pacification 'Political,'" *Washington Post,* May 19, 1967.

33 JWF to LBJ, June 30, 1967, Box 2, RG 46, SPF.

from Camau (Quan Long) in the south to Quang Tri in the north along which civilians could travel safely. Victory, in the final analysis, could be defined as the absence of defeat.[34]

Unable either to establish a government that would satisfy its own publicly stated standards for democracy and viability, or to compel the Vietnamese to fight for a political edifice that was acceptable to Washington and the Vietnamese military, Johnson, Rostow, Lodge, and the Joint Chiefs turned once again – inevitably, it seemed – to the issue of physical security. If the North Vietnamese could be bombed into halting their infiltration of the south, and if the South Vietnamese countryside could be pacified, then perhaps, they hoped, there would emerge a South Vietnam for which its citizens would be willing to fight.

By the late summer of 1967 Robert McNamara's opposition to the bombing of the north had become so stubborn that Lyndon Johnson either had to order a stand-down or part company with his secretary of defense. The DOD chief was sick of the war, sick of being ignored by the president, and sick of war protesters, several of whom had burned down his condominium in Aspen. In December at McNamara's request Johnson recommended him to head the World Bank. He officially departed in February 1968.

Though he pared Westmoreland's troop request from two hundred thousand to fifty-five thousand, Johnson, upon the recommendation of McNamara's successor, Clark Clifford, significantly expanded the list of aerial targets in North Vietnam. In the fall of 1967 troop staging areas, rail yards, and munitions depots within the greater Hanoi–Haiphong area, as well as previously restricted supply routes along the Chinese border, came under attack.[35] The Johnson administration's decision to bomb so close to Chinese territory frightened and angered Fulbright. "I think it's very dangerous and extremely stupid," he told reporters.[36] Observers noted ominously that the decision to widen the bombing war came just as the Senate was preparing to debate the 1967 foreign aid bill.

No sooner had Johnson submitted his $3.2 billion aid measure than Fulbright and the SFRC immediately began hacking away at it. After some $200 million had been cut, both Rusk and McNamara suddenly found time to testify before the committee. For over a year Fulbright had been waiting to get the two in open session. The United States was running a negative balance of payments, the national debt was growing at a rate of $30 billion a year, the inner cities were suffering from neglect, and the president was thinking of imposing new taxes. How could it justify a multi-billion-dollar aid program,

34 Lodge to LBJ, Aug. 10, 1966, NSF, Memos to President, Box 9, Johnson Papers.

35 Notes of President's Meeting with Clifford and Taylor, Aug. 5, 1967, Box 3, T. Johnson Meeting Notes, Johnson Papers.

36 "Fulbright Calls Raid Widening a Great Risk," *Washington Star,* Sept. 10, 1967.

Fulbright asked? The United States must seek "to build a peace," Rusk replied. "When you talk about building a peace, do you consider the 12,000 deaths in Vietnam and the 70,000 wounded?" Fulbright asked. "That doesn't seem to be a typical figure of building a peace."[37]

By the time Fulbright "reluctantly" presented the foreign aid bill to the Senate as a whole, the SFRC had cut nearly three-quarters of a billion dollars from it. An amendment by Frank Church prohibited arms aid to countries whose economic development would suffer as a result of excessive military spending. The administration had been warned time and time again, Fulbright declared, and ignored the signals. Now it was time to pay the price.[38] In the end, the Senate cut another $100 million from the aid measure, approved the Church amendment, and passed the revised bill by a vote of 60 to 26.[39] While the national press trumpeted Fulbright's victory, Johnson fumed.

As the pressure on him mounted, the president increasingly indulged his fantasies. "I'm not going to let the communists take this government and they're doing it right now," he told a Tuesday luncheon meeting in early November. "I've got my belly full of seeing these people put on a Communist plane and shipped all over this country."[40] His restraint toward the antiwar movement disappeared. Johnson instructed the CIA to place leaders of the SDS, SANE, the Yippies (Youth International Party), Mothers Against the War, and other antiwar groups under surveillance and prove that they were communists operating on orders from foreign governments. This program, later institutionalized as Operation CHAOS, violated the CIA's charter, which prohibited domestic operations. As many as seven thousand Americans came under scrutiny by the agency. The war against the peace movement soon shifted from surveillance to harassment and disruption. Dr. Spock was indicted for counseling draft resistance. Not surprisingly, the FBI got into the act. Shortly after the Vietnam Veterans Against the War was formed, Hoover's men infiltrated the organization with a view to gathering information and, through agents provocateurs, staging violent confrontations with authorities that they hoped would discredit the movement.

The first week in October Everett Dirksen delivered a speech written by Rostow and approved by "the Boss," as Dirksen referred to the president, that accused Fulbright and his fellow doves of endangering the lives of American troops by eroding support in America for a just war in Southeast Asia and by encouraging Hanoi to fight on. The sage of Illinois, whose reputation as an

37 "Senate's Cuts in Aid Irk Rusk," *Chicago Tribune,* July 15, 1967.

38 *Congressional Record,* Senate, Aug. 14, 1967, 22549–51.

39 Manatos to LBJ, Aug. 16, 1967, WHCF–Leg., Box 57, Johnson Papers, and "Senate Supports Fulbright, Passes a Reduced Aid Bill," *Arkansas Gazette,* Aug. 18, 1967.

40 Luncheon Meeting with Rusk and McNamara, Rostow, Helms, et al., Nov. 4, 1967, Box 2, Meeting Notes File, Johnson Papers.

orator was so great that he would later record an album, quoted a bit of doggerel:

> No man escapes when freedom fails.
> The best men rot in filthy jails
> And those who cry "appease, appease"
> Are hanged by those they sought to please.[41]

"You've been quarreling for the last year with the conduct of the war," he shouted at Fulbright, waving his arms. "Tell us what you want to do – quit now and get out?"[42]

In the House, Speaker John McCormack received a standing ovation when he struck out at those who "dissent without responsibility" on Vietnam. "If I was one of them my conscience would be such that it would disturb me the rest of my life. . . . If I had an opinion I thought would be adverse to the interests of my country, I would withhold it," he declared, impugning not only the intelligence but the patriotism of antiwar activists.[43] Throughout the summer and fall of 1967 Fulbright's office was deluged with black umbrellas, the symbols of Chamberlain's appeasement of Hitler at Munich.

These attacks on his motives and patriotism left Fulbright momentarily embittered. He rose on the floor to answer Dirksen, but he could only speak in abstractions and generalities for fear of alienating the hawks he was trying to attract. "Ho Chi Minh couldn't care less about what I say or what any other senator says," Fulbright told a Little Rock crowd. "What I say wouldn't give him one additional gun or plane or anything else."[44] Later, in Hot Springs, he told the Arkansas Home Builders Association that Dean Rusk was carrying on a "McCarthy-type crusade" against opponents of the war. In Camden, when a reporter asked him whether he would support President Johnson for reelection in 1968, he lost his temper. The election was a year-and-a-half away; why was he asking him a stupid question like that "when I am trying to meet my people." He pushed the microphone away and stalked out of the meeting.[45]

White House charges that Fulbright was betraying his country sent him scurrying back to Arkansas to mend fences. Republican surveys taken during the 1966 elections gave Fulbright a favorable rating of only 57 percent whereas John McClellan had polled 74 percent. The GOP attributed the difference to

41 *Congressional Record,* Senate, Oct. 3, 1967, 27578–9.
42 "Fulbright Hits Dirksen Stand," *Arkansas Gazette,* Oct. 4, 1967.
43 Albert C. Albright, "Fulbright Hits Back at Dirksen," *Washington Post,* Oct. 12, 1967.
44 Jerol Garrison, "Fulbright Declares 'Ho Chi Minh Couldn't Care Less What I Say,'" *Arkansas Gazette,* Oct. 26, 1967.
45 "TV Man Gets Dressing Down by Fulbright," *Arkansas Gazette,* Oct. 21, 1967.

Vietnam. A year later a Little Rock television survey indicated that 54 percent of the viewers questioned indicated they opposed Fulbright's stand on the war whereas 46 percent approved.[46] As Williams and Arkansas staffer Parker Westbrook well knew, pro-Fulbright sentiment was likely to be highest in Little Rock – the state's only urban area – for socioeconomic and educational reasons.

The two personalities deemed most likely to unseat Fulbright in 1968 were former governors Sid McMath and Orval Faubus. McMath, a ruggedly handsome ex-marine, was a perfect foil to Fulbright's antiwar views. Beginning in the spring of 1967, he toured the state giving anti-Fulbright, prowar speeches. Lumping the junior senator with the cold-war liberals who had been instrumental in persuading the country to embrace globalism, McMath declared that the United States' "commitments and trials and tribulations in Vietnam are a direct result of policies which Senator J. W. Fulbright himself advanced and championed."[47] Meanwhile, in April Faubus told reporters that it was "very possible" and "mostly likely" that he would challenge Fulbright in 1968. "I agree with Gov. George Romney of Michigan when he said that Fulbright is aiding the enemy by his comments," the former governor declared.[48]

At this point the state Democratic Party was still in disarray. Faubus's abdication in 1966 had left the field open for "Justice Jim" Johnson. The avowed segregationist had won the Democratic primary but then been soundly trounced by Republican Winthrop Rockefeller. Throughout the fall of 1967, forces loyal to Fulbright, Wilbur Mills, and the moderate wing of the party struggled to gain control of the state party machinery. Fulbright promoted Little Rock attorney Jack Files, previously head of the Young Democrats and a Faubus opponent, to his Washington staff, and the moderates blocked selection of a former Faubus aide to the newly created post of executive director of the state Democratic Party.

Throughout October Fulbright hit the service club circuit, playing up his putative role as a conscientious country boy standing up to an arrogant bully. Rockefeller sensed that Fulbright had struck a responsive chord. Although a Republican, he put in a good word for the incumbent. "The folks here in Arkansas are proud of our boy who stands up and takes a position," he told Peter Jennings on ABC News.[49] Most important, however, was the public announcement of political kingmakers Jack Pickens and Bill Darby that they

46 "Fulbright Facing '68 Fight," *Washington Evening Star,* May 15, 1967, and "Fulbright's Stand Tested by TV Poll," *Arkansas Democrat,* Nov. 2, 1967.
47 "McMath Criticizes Fulbright, but Disavows Senate Race," *Arkansas Gazette,* Nov. 9, 1967.
48 "Faubus Says Fulbright Vulnerable," *Arkansas Democrat,* Apr. 27, 1967.
49 "Fulbright Facing '68 Fight," *Washington Evening Star,* May 15, 1967.

would support Fulbright in 1968. "I am going with Bill and I have told the governor so," Pickens declared.[50] Reporters were unsure as to which governor the construction millionaire meant: Like Darby, Witt Stephens, and other power brokers, Pickens played both sides of the street and then declared his undying support for whoever won. He had supported Faubus in 1964 and Rockefeller in 1966; but that made his declaration in behalf of Fulbright all the more impressive. It greatly reduced the senator's anxiety over his political future at a time when the war in Vietnam and, indeed, the fate of American foreign policy hung in the balance.

50 George Douthit, "Pickens Throws His Support to Fulbright," *Arkansas Democrat,* Oct. 1, 1967.

# 26

# *Denouement*

As the series of cease-fires in honor of Christmas and Tet, the Vietnamese lunar New Year, got underway in the last days of 1967, Ambassador Ellsworth Bunker threw a New Year's Eve party, inviting everyone to come "see the light at the end of the tunnel."[1] That light turned out to be fire in the hole. On the evening of January 31, 1968, Americans turned on their television sets to view the nightly news. They had become somewhat inured to film clips depicting American combat teams combing the countryside for the ever-elusive enemy and Vietcong rockets exploding among supposedly secure villages and troop compounds; but the war had seemed to be going better during the winter of 1967–8, and amid optimistic prognostications by Westmoreland and others, hope that the long nightmare might soon be over began to rise in the collective bosom. What the nation saw that January evening withered that hope and blasted any chance Lyndon Johnson had of maintaining his much-coveted consensus.

The previous night, nearly seventy thousand communist soldiers had launched a surprise offensive of extraordinary intensity and astonishing scope. Violating a truce that they themselves had pledged to observe during the Tet season, they surged into more than a hundred cities and towns, including Saigon, audaciously shifting the war for the first time from its rural setting to a new arena: South Vietnam's supposedly impregnable urban areas. "War Hits Saigon" screamed the front-page headline of Washington's afternoon tabloid *The News.* Print accounts paled beside the television images, however. Fifty million Americans saw the dead bodies lying amid the rubble, heard the rattle of automatic gunfire as dazed American soldiers and civilians ran back and forth trying to flush out the guerrillas.[2]

Once they recovered from their initial surprise, U.S. and South Vietnamese troops struck back quickly and effectively. Within days, they had cleared Saigon and the other provincial capitals of enemy troops. In the process they killed and captured tens of thousands of Vietcong cadre and seized valuable

1 Quoted in Marilyn B. Young, *The Vietnam Wars, 1945–1990* (New York, 1991), 216.
2 Stanley Karnow, *Vietnam: A History* (New York, 1984), 526.

caches of arms. The ARVN, perhaps because in many cases it was literally defending its homes and families, fought with vigor and tenacity. Only in Hué were the communists able to hold out for an appreciable time. The liberation of that city took nearly three weeks and required heavy bombing and intensive artillery fire, which in the end left the beautiful old city, in the words of one observer, "a shattered, stinking hulk, its streets choked with rubble and rotting bodies." As allied troops moved into the city they discovered the mass graves of twenty-eight hundred South Vietnamese murdered by VC and NVA troops.[3]

Tactically Tet was a devastating defeat for the North Vietnamese and Vietcong. The Thieu government did not collapse; the South Vietnamese people did not rise to welcome the attackers as liberators. Estimates of combined Vietcong and North Vietnamese losses ran as high as forty thousand. Indeed, Tet broke the back of the Vietcong, which had theretofore borne the brunt of the fighting in the Second Indochinese War. Superior American and ARVN firepower destroyed many of its main units, and the fighting killed or wounded an irreplaceable political cadre.

Strategically, however, the lunar New Year offensive was a grand success for the communists. American and South Vietnamese losses amounted to eleven hundred and twenty-three hundred killed, respectively. An estimated twelve and a half thousand civilians died in the fighting, and the communist offensive created as many as one million new refugees. Most important, Tet was interpreted by American journalists and their followers not only as proof that the United States was not winning the war but as evidence that the Johnson administration was out of touch with reality. "What, indeed, is the U.S. trying to save" in Vietnam? asked the *Wall Street Journal.* "If the Saigon government . . . doesn't really have the support of most of the people or the ability to save them from nation-wide terror and murder, how good is it?"[4]

Westmoreland and Johnson's hawkish advisers pointed out to him that Tet presented the greatest military opportunity of the war. The enemy was on the run; if the United States was willing to apply the necessary force, the Vietcong could be destroyed once and for all. With the indigenous guerrilla war over, the U.S. military and ARVN could seal South Vietnam's borders, à la South Korea, and put an end to North Vietnamese infiltration. The United States did not follow up, however, because it could not. Tet constituted a devastating blow to Johnson's prowar consensus. Fulbright and others had so weakened it, so highlighted the Texan's lack of credibility, that it could not survive. In the days and weeks following Tet, it was J. William Fulbright, rather than William Westmoreland, who was able to press his advantage.

3 George C. Herring, *America's Longest War: The United States and Vietnam, 1950–1975,* 2d ed. (New York, 1986), 190.

4 "Vietnam; The American Dilemma," *Wall Street Journal,* Feb. 6, 1968.

To Fulbright's great irritation, Dean Rusk frequented *Meet the Press* and other national television talk shows to discuss Tet while steadfastly refusing to testify in open session before the committee.[5] "These are more or less controlled exhibitions," Fulbright complained to reporters. The administration "can do everything except say to [*Meet the Press* moderator Lawrence] Spivak what the questions will be." Were he to object, Spivak "knows that he will be dropped from the list."[6] Should Rusk be replaced? David Brinkley asked Fulbright shortly thereafter. He did not want to make a "personal judgment," Fulbright said, but he had always believed that Secretary Rusk had never wanted any peace terms except the unconditional surrender of North Vietnam.[7] "We have gotten our Committee in a perfectly untenable position," he told the SFRC, "where it is assumed by the public . . . that we as Senators and members of the Foreign Relations Committee have less self-restraint and less responsibility than a bunch of newspaper people."[8]

The prospect of attacking the secretary of state in public, however, while the battle for Hué was raging continued to be an intimidating one for the SFRC. "I am not going to contribute to the continued disruption of our military operations and our military effort," Hickenlooper told Fulbright and his colleagues. Even the aggressively dovish Joseph Clark was dubious. He doubted, he said, whether "it is wise to put on a public show even if we could get him to come, until this present offensive is blunted." The administration was "at bay" and dangerous, he said. Fulbright, supported by Albert Gore, still held his ground. The most effective time to act was during a crisis, the chairman argued, when the country's attention was focused on the problem. When several suggested that Fulbright request a face-to-face meeting between the president and the SFRC, similar to the one Henry Cabot Lodge had arranged with Woodrow Wilson in 1919, Fulbright resisted. "The more traditional and time-proven way is public hearings," he insisted. The public was entitled to know what was going on. After all, "it is their boys who are being killed, it is their money that is being spent, it is their country that is being ruined and they ought to be given an opportunity to judge about the course of it." Following an 8 to 4 vote, Fulbright drafted a formal letter to the president asking him to direct Rusk to appear in public session.[9]

In the days that followed, Mike Mansfield worked frantically to hammer out a compromise. Perhaps Rusk would agree to appear in public session to

5 Marcy to Gore, Feb. 5, 1968, Box 8, Folder Jan.–Mar., Marcy Papers.

6 "Fulbright Hits 'Show,'" *Washington Post*, Feb. 7, 1968.

7 In a follow-up to the interview, Brinkley told his audience that Fulbright was particularly incensed that though he had just recently appeared on *Meet the Press*, Rusk still refused to testify before the SFRC in open session. Bob Fleming to LBJ, Feb. 16, 1968, WHCF, Box 287, Johnson Papers.

8 Discussion on Secretary Rusk's Appearance Before the Committee, Feb. 7, 1968, Executive Sessions, SFRC, RG 46, NA.

9 Ibid.

discuss the foreign aid bill, he told Fulbright. You tell the president, Fulbright retorted, that if Rusk did not get his butt up to the Hill there would not be a foreign aid bill to discuss.[10]

Reluctantly, Johnson called Rusk in and told him he would have to go before the SFRC and the television cameras again and take his punishment. Everyone must do his duty to help maintain public support for the war. The Georgian agreed, but he was bitter at Fulbright, at Marcy, and at Johnson.[11] During a backgrounder with the press on February 26, he lashed out. "There gets to be a point when the question is, whose side are you on?" he responded to a hostile questioner. "Now I'm Secretary of State of the United States and I'm on our side . . . none of your papers or your broadcasting apparatuses are worth a damn unless the United States succeeds."[12]

After extensive wrangling, Carl Marcy and Rusk's assistant for legislative affairs, William "Butts" Macomber, agreed on March 11 as the date for the secretary's appearance. The hearings would be covered live by CBS.[13]

While Fulbright, Marcy, and the rest of the SFRC prepared for Rusk, the Johnson administration was facing a turning point in the war. Since 1967 Westmoreland and the JCS had fought against suggestions by Fulbright and others that the United States revive the enclave strategy. To do so, argued Westmoreland and Wheeler, would be "to abandon a large portion of Vietnam to the control of the enemy and would preclude further significant broadening of the GVN's [government of Vietnam's] influence throughout the countryside."[14] The enemy's strategy depended on the establishment of prestocked bases in secure areas. These bases in turn were necessary to support the activities of regular NVA and main-force VC units, Westy insisted. Only by striking at these bases through search-and-destroy missions could "Free World Forces" divorce the enemy's various echelons from each other and defeat them. An enclave strategy would allow the NVA and VC to grow stronger and stronger.[15]

Confident that he could exploit the enemy's "defeat" at Tet, and buoyed by the president's dispatch of ten-and-a-half thousand additional men to Khe

10 Even though the State Department's legal adviser told him that Congress could not require an officer of the executive branch to appear, and if he did, that officer could impose whatever limitations he chose, LBJ gave in. Larry Temple to LBJ, Feb. 8, 1968, WHCF, Box 342; Manatos to LBJ, Feb. 15, 1968, WHCF, Box 287; and Mansfield to LBJ, Feb. 19, 1968, Box 102, NSF, Country File–Vietnam, Johnson Papers.

11 Harry McPherson to LBJ, Feb. 26, 1968, WHCF, Confidential File, Box 34, Johnson Papers.

12 "Rusk Is Identified as Critics' Critic," *New York Times,* Feb. 24, 1968.

13 JWF to Carl Marcy, Mar. 4, 1968, Series 48:3, Box 16:5, SPF.

14 Wheeler to LBJ, Feb. 3, 1968, Box 102, NSF, Country File–Vietnam, Johnson Papers.

15 Harold K. Johnson to LBJ, Feb. 1, 1968, NSF, Country File–Vietnam, Box 102, Johnson Papers.

Sanh, Westmoreland devised a "two-fisted" strategy designed to take advantage of the enemy's weakened condition. During a late-February visit to Saigon by JCS Chairman Wheeler, he and Westmoreland decided to propose an "amphibious hook" designed to take out North Vietnamese bases and staging areas across the demilitarized zone, attacks on the communist sanctuaries in Laos and Cambodia, and an intensified bombing campaign directed against North Vietnam. Wheeler was to return to Washington and ask for two hundred and six thousand additional men, a number sufficient to meet any contingency in Vietnam and an increase that would force the president to call up the reserves.[16]

Fulbright learned of the request for over two hundred thousand additional troops and permission to expand the war almost as soon as Wheeler returned to Washington. His source could have been any one of a number of people. Clark Clifford, the new secretary of defense, had deep reservations about lifting the administration's self-imposed limit of five hundred and twenty-five thousand men, and thus some reason for telling the chairman; some of the president's defenders would later claim that Johnson himself had leaked the information in order to contain the hawkish Wheeler and Westmoreland. Whatever the case, Fulbright rose on the floor of the Senate on March 7 and called for a full-fledged congressional debate on the rumored troop buildup. The administration was responding to "our recent defeats and difficulties" not by pulling back, but by putting in two hundred thousand more soldiers and expanding the war beyond the south, a reference to Westmoreland's "two-fisted" strategy. He had not, he told his colleagues, urged the Senate to adopt the Gulf of Tonkin Resolution out of the belief that it gave the president the authority to wage all-out war in Southeast Asia; indeed, the administration had presented the resolution as congressional authorization to respond to the torpedo boat attacks and nothing more. Reminding the Senate that Johnson had promised the American people during the 1964 campaign not to send American boys to fight an Asian war, Fulbright declared that the resolution "like any contract based on misrepresentation . . . is null and void."[17]

Fulbright's speech fell like a spark on dry tinder. A dozen senators vied for the floor; Robert Kennedy, Jacob Javits, Frank Church, and Gaylord Nelson rose to applaud Fulbright's speech and to call for a full-scale debate on the rumored expansion of the war. "If the Senator from Arkansas had stood on the floor of the Senate, in the middle of that debate in 1964," Nelson declared, "and had said that the resolution authorizes a ground commitment of an unlimited number of troops . . . he would have been soundly defeated."[18]

16 Herring, *America's Longest War,* 193–4.
17 *Congressional Record,* Senate, Mar. 7, 1968, 5644–54.
18 Ibid.

Only diehard hawks such as John Tower of Texas dared argue that the issue was none of Congress's business.

What the administration ought to do, Walt Rostow told his boss, was introduce legislation repealing the Gulf of Tonkin Resolution. Senators could then stand up and be counted for or against the country for all to see. It would be quite proper to make those who were then "wringing their hands, shedding crocodile tears, caterwauling," and expressing their "concern" to be forced to "stand up like men and vote one way or the other." Johnson was tempted. He knew that such a motion would pass overwhelmingly; but he also knew that senators would be so alienated by his rubbing their noses in the war that he could not count on their support on other issues.[19]

Meanwhile, the long-awaited day of the second televised confrontation between Dean Rusk and the SFRC had arrived. When the Klieglights lit up on Monday morning the cameras revealed a packed committee room and a tight-lipped witness peering apprehensively over his half-glasses at the members. They were, Rusk had to admit, more imposing than he remembered. There was George Aiken, his ancient head crowned with wisps of white hair; the square-jawed Sparkman; the mustachioed Wayne Morse, his brows perpetually arched; the dour-faced Mike Mansfield; and, at the center of the inquisitory board, Fulbright. Without makeup, tortoise-shelled dark glasses perched atop his nose, the chairman looked like a gargoyle in a three-piece suit.

"I am more than ever convinced that [U.S. strategy] is wrong and that our present policies in Vietnam have had and will have effects both abroad and at home that are nothing short of disastrous," Fulbright declared in his opening statement. When asked whether reports that the president was going to send two hundred thousand additional troops to Vietnam were true, Rusk declared that the president was considering all options and "it was not right to speculate on new numbers." Would Congress be consulted before any decision on escalation was taken, Fulbright inquired? The secretary replied that Lyndon Johnson had consulted Congress more than any president in the twentieth century.[20] And so it went.

The 1968 Rusk hearings were not the public relations event that the 1966 hearings had been. Polls showed opinion about evenly divided between Rusk and the committee's position. Still, the secretary of state's obfuscation, vagueness, and self-righteousness, coming as they did hard on the heels of Tet, did not sit well with the public. Moreover, the hearings revealed that the antiwar majority on the SFRC had expanded to include former hawks like Mundt and Sparkman.[21]

19 Rostow to LBJ, Mar. 8, 1968, Box 102, NSF, Country File–Vietnam, Johnson Papers.

20 "Troop Issue Still Open, Rusk Says," *Washington Evening Star,* Mar. 11, 1968.

21 Bob Fleming to LBJ, Mar. 11, 1968, and Ernest K. Lindley to Rostow, Mar. 29, 1968, WHCF, Subject File, Box 342, Johnson Papers.

Much more important in undermining the administration's position than the televised confrontation with Rusk was Fulbright's decision, made during the height of the Tet offensive, to reopen the whole Gulf of Tonkin debate. This time the chairman was prepared to go beyond his argument that the administration had misrepresented its intentions and exceeded its authority. This time he would insist that Johnson, McNamara, and Rusk had lied to Congress about the circumstances surrounding the attacks on the *Turner Joy* and the *Maddox* – and, in fact, that the second foray had never taken place.

Momentum toward a confrontation with the administration over the Gulf of Tonkin Resolution had been building for almost two years. The first hint that things had not been not as they had seemed on the nights of August 2 and 4, 1964, had come during the Senate's original consideration of the resolution. One of Wayne Morse's contacts in the Pentagon had called him and told him to ask McNamara for the *Turner Joy* and *Maddox*'s logbooks. McNamara at the time had told Morse that they were unavailable – still aboard ship. (In fact, they had been flown back to Washington.) Whether the Department of Defense had wanted to suppress the books because they indicated that the ships had been running cover for South Vietnamese DeSoto patrols, or because they showed that the second attack had not occurred, is unclear – probably both. Whatever the case, in August 1964 Fulbright had been a strong administration partisan and had viewed Wayne Morse as a humorless Don Quixote who was obstructing his efforts to help the president defeat Barry Goldwater.

As Fulbright's doubts about the administration's veracity grew – particularly in the aftermath of the Dominican crisis – and as the administration continually beat him about the head and shoulders with his sponsorship of the Tonkin resolution, the chairman began to recall the missing logbooks. Then in March 1966 he received a letter from retired Admiral Arnold True, a distinguished veteran of World War II, who wrote that the administration's account of the August 4 attack "sounds unrealistic."[22] Knowing that George Ball had been present throughout the 1964 crisis, Fulbright asked him whether the second attack had really occurred. "I'll tell you what the President told me," Ball said. "He said, 'Those goddamn admirals; they see a bunch of flying fish and they think they're ships. They don't know how to run the goddamn navy.'"[23] Ball did not, however, tell Fulbright that the CIA and the South Vietnamese had been running a covert operation in conjunction with the destroyer patrols; he did not because he had not been informed. Then, in mid-December 1967 Lt. (j.g.) John White told the Associated Press that no North

22 Quoted in William C. Berman, *William Fulbright and the Vietnam War: The Dissent of a Political Realist* (Kent, Ohio, 1988), 69.
23 Interview with George Ball, July 6, 1990, Princeton, N.J.

Vietnamese torpedoes had been fired during the second attack. He had been on duty aboard the *Pine Island,* the first ship into the war zone on August 4 after suspected enemy action had been reported. The sonarman aboard the *Maddox* had reported throughout the incident that no torpedoes had been fired into the water.[24]

Still, Fulbright was loath to charge the administration publicly with fabricating the whole incident. It would be difficult to prove, and although an investigation had the potential of destroying the president, it could also backfire and deflate the antiwar movement in Congress. What apparently changed Fulbright's mind was Nicholas Katzenbach's testimony in August 1967. When Fulbright castigated the administration for going to war without a declaration, and insisted that the Tonkin resolution had been limited to the incident in question, Katzenbach bristled. Why would the administration need a declaration of war? he asked rhetorically. "[D]idn't that Resolution authorize the President to use the armed forces of the United States in whatever way was necessary? Didn't it? . . . You explained it, Mr. Chairman."[25]

Several days later Fulbright asked William Bader, an SFRC staffer with a background in naval intelligence, quietly to begin an investigation. In mid-December the chairman planted the first seeds of doubt in the public's mind when he released portions of Assistant Secretary William Bundy's testimony given in executive session over a year earlier. Bundy had let slip that the State Department had prepared the Gulf of Tonkin Resolution months before the actual incident occurred.[26] Clearly, the administration had planned to escalate the war; it had either seized on or fabricated the Gulf of Tonkin incident to justify a policy that had been predetermined. Journalists and academics remembered FDR's duplicity over the USS *Greer* prior to America's entry into World War II. Finally, in early January 1968, with the national commitments resolution pending and the tide turning in Congress against both the war and Lyndon Johnson, Fulbright announced that the SFRC staff would conduct an official inquiry into the Gulf of Tonkin incident. Secretary McNamara and other relevant officials would be asked to testify in open hearings at the appropriate time.

On January 23, with Khe Sanh under siege and the Tet offensive just a week away, President Johnson was awakened at 2:24 in the morning. The duty officer informed him that the USS *Pueblo,* a highly sophisticated intelligence ship, had been surrounded and then seized by a North Korean flotilla of warships. The communists had captured the vessel fifteen and a half miles from the nearest land, outside the territorial limit, and had wounded four of

24 "Red Boats Fired No Shots in Tonkin, Ex-officer Says," *Arkansas Gazette,* Dec. 10, 1967.

25 Quoted in Berman, *Fulbright and the Vietnam War,* 88.

26 "War Resolution Drawn Up Early," *Arkansas Gazette,* Dec. 22, 1967.

the eighty-three-man crew, one mortally.[27] The consensus among Johnson's advisers was that the seizure was a diversionary tactic by the North Koreans designed to help Hanoi.[28] Fearful that the North Koreans might be willing to go so far as to "open a second front," the president rushed the nuclear carrier *Enterprise* to the scene. The huge ship cruised twelve miles offshore, broadcasting demands for release of the *Pueblo*'s crew.[29] As the nation held its breath over the incident, the forthcoming hearings on the Gulf of Tonkin took on special meaning.

"An intelligence ship off your coast is very irritating," Fulbright told a Pine Bluff audience. "People for some reason just don't like eavesdropping. . . . I can tell you now that I don't think there will be any 24-hour resolution on this incident."[30] A number of observers, including Arthur Schlesinger, credited the pending investigation of the Gulf of Tonkin Resolution with preventing the administration from launching an immediate attack on North Korea and then coming to Congress for approval.[31] In turn, the *Pueblo* incident whetted the public's appetite for the true story behind the Gulf of Tonkin incident. "We feel that the country should have all the facts on what happened in the Tonkin Gulf in August, 1964," editorialized the hitherto staunchly pro-administration *Washington Post.*[32]

Fulbright's announcement that the SFRC was resuming its Gulf of Tonkin investigation was made on the day the Tet offensive began. He went to great lengths not to appear to accuse the administration of a conspiracy. All the committee wanted to know, he told reporters, was why CINCPAC had dispatched two American destroyers on a sensitive mission off the coast of North Vietnam at the time that it had.[33]

Although he was determined to press ahead, Fulbright took no joy in his task. His country was in a terrible predicament, writhing in the coils of its own misguided altruism, reaching once again for the sword in its frustration. "There is literally a miasma of madness in the city, enveloping everyone in the administration and most of those in Congress," he wrote Erich Fromm. "I am at a loss for words to describe the idiocy of what we are doing."[34]

Robert McNamara, although he detested Fulbright and felt deep contempt for most of the rest of the members of the SFRC, agreed to run the gauntlet

27 Lyndon Baines Johnson, *The Vantage Point: Perspectives of the Presidency, 1963–1969* (New York, 1971), 533.
28 Notes of the President's Meeting with the NSC, Jan. 24, 1968, T. Johnson Meeting Notes, Box 2, Johnson Papers.
29 "U.S. Stations Nuclear Carrier Near N. Korea," *Arkansas Gazette,* Jan. 25, 1968.
30 "U.S. Ambitions Assailed," *Pine Bluff Commercial,* Jan. 26, 1968.
31 Schlesinger to JWF, Jan. 25, 1968, Series 48:16, Box 42:1, SPF.
32 J. R. Wiggins, ed., "Midwife to History," *Washington Post,* Jan. 27, 1968.
33 "Senate Panel to Re-examine Tonkin Case," *Arkansas Gazette,* Jan. 31, 1968.
34 JWF to Fromm, Feb. 1, 1968, Series 48:18, Box 54:5, SPF.

in order to try to cleanse his reputation before he left for the World Bank. From the beginning, it was clear that his intention was to manipulate the information at his command so as to prove decisively that the North Vietnamese had staged armed attacks on both August 2 and 4, even though he knew full well that there had been no second assault.[35]

When McNamara met with the SFRC in executive session on February 20, the atmosphere was predictably tense. The secretary as always was immaculately dressed, his straight hair slicked back, his lower lip protruding aggressively beneath his famous rimless glasses. Although he had brought a large entourage with him, he refused to read from his prepared statement until the SFRC staff left the room. During the grueling seven-and-a-half-hour cross-examination, the secretary read testimony from an "unimpeachable" North Vietnamese source stating that an assault had in fact taken place on the fourth. When Fulbright asked for copies, McNamara quickly reclassified the document.[36] When the secretary of defense denied that there had been any connection between the destroyer patrols and the OPLAN-34 raids being conducted on two North Vietnamese islands in the gulf by the South Vietnamese, Fulbright produced a message sent on August 3 by Capt. John J. Herrick, commander of the destroyer task force, to his superiors stating that the DRV considered the two connected and were determined to treat the *Turner Joy* and *Maddox* as aggressor ships. He also presented a copy of the cable Herrick had sent to the Pentagon in the early afternoon of August 4: "Review of action makes many recorded contacts and torpedoes fired appear doubtful. Freak weather effects and over-eager sonarman may have accounted for many reports. No actual visual sightings by *Maddox*." McNamara could only reiterate that he had copies of intercepted NVA cable traffic indicating that the attack had occurred.[37]

Before the Tonkin Gulf hearing closed both McNamara and Fulbright agreed that neither would say anything substantive to the phalanx of reporters who waited outside the committee room doors; but no sooner had the DOD chief made that commitment and exited his chamber of tribulation than he presented to the press a twenty-one-page document "proving" conclusively that both the *Maddox* and *Turner Joy* had been attacked by North Vietnamese torpedo boats in international waters on August 4, 1964. He blasted Fulbright and the SFRC for impugning his and the president's integrity. Any sugges-

35 Indeed, the Pentagon refused to provide any cable traffic or other information connected with the incident until Fulbright persuaded Richard Russell to intervene. The Armed Services chairman summoned Paul Nitze to his office and advised him to cooperate, but even then, the documentation was incomplete.

36 Gulf of Tonkin Hearing, Feb. 21, 1968, Executive Sessions, SFRC, RG 46, NA.

37 John W. Finney, "McNamara Says Destroyers in Gulf of Tonkin Warned of Enemy," *New York Times*, Feb. 25, 1968.

tion that the United States had induced the attack as part of an effort to find an excuse for its subsequent retaliation was "monstrous," he said.[38]

Infuriated at McNamara's duplicity, Fulbright tried to strike back. He called the committee into executive session on the twenty-first. Before he went in, he told reporters that it was "monstrous" to insinuate that members of the committee had accused the administration of a conspiracy. He then denounced the DOD chief for engaging in selective declassification designed to safeguard his reputation. "Security classification is intended to protect the nation from an enemy . . . not to protect the American people from knowledge of mistakes."[39]

The next day Fulbright showed his ace in the hole. Not only was the Johnson administration misleading the American people about the 1964 Gulf of Tonkin incident, an ambiguous event that had been used to justify a major escalation of the war, but it had locked up in a mental ward a navy commander who had volunteered to tell Congress what he knew of the affair.[40] The officer, a Commander Cowles who had worked in flag plot in the Pentagon at the time of the Tonkin incident, had indeed gone to see Fulbright in mid-November to express his reservations concerning the second attack. When, shortly thereafter, Cowles's commander had discovered the liaison, he had had the officer committed to the Walter Reed psychiatric ward for four weeks. In a public exchange of letters with Fulbright, McNamara insisted that Cowles had had a history of "neuroses" but had since been returned to active duty.[41]

On Sunday, February 25, Ned Kenworthy of the *New York Times* printed an accurate summary of the McNamara hearing transcripts. "McNamara Says Destroyers in Gulf of Tonkin Warned of Foe" and "9 on Fulbright Panel Feel U.S. Over Reacted to Tonkin Attack" ran the headlines.[42] "McCarthyism" screamed pro-Johnson columnist William S. White. "The violently dovish chairman of the Senate Foreign Relations Committee, J. William Fulbright, is employing its apparatus for a masked attack upon American policy in Vietnam."[43] During the weeks that followed enterprising reporters interviewed dozens of sailors who had served aboard the two American destroyers and published the results. The overwhelming consensus was that the *Turner Joy*

38 "Fulbright Hints McNamara Version of Tonkin Attack Misleading," *Northwest Arkansas Times,* Feb. 21, 1968.

39 Fulbright press release, Feb. 21, 1968, Series 48:6, Box 28:3, SPF.

40 "Fulbright Says Public Misled About Vietnam," *Malvern Daily Record,* Feb. 22, 1968.

41 "Uneasy Truce Descends on Tonkin Gulf Dispute," *Washington Post,* Feb. 2, 1968; Naval Inspector General to Secretary of the Navy, Feb. 24, 1968, Series 48:1, Box 9:1, SPF; and Marcy to Jones, Feb. 28, 1968, Box 8, Jan.–Mar. '68, RG 46, NA.

42 Finney, "McNamara Says Destroyers in Gulf of Tonkin Warned of Enemy."

43 *Congressional Record,* Senate, Feb. 26, 1968, 4009.

and *Maddox* had been on a secret mission in support of the South Vietnamese and that the second attack had never happened.[44]

The 1968 brouhaha struck a major and perhaps decisive blow at the president's credibility, and it did so at a crucial time. If Johnson had misled Congress and the American people concerning the North Vietnamese attack on the two American destroyers in 1964, then the Gulf of Tonkin Resolution, which the administration had so often invoked as justification for the presence of American troops in Vietnam, was invalid. In the context of the Tet offensive, this meant not only that Johnson lacked the authority to expand the war and give Westmoreland the troops he wanted, but also that he would have to withdraw the forces already in Vietnam.

The 1968 confrontations with Rusk and McNamara accelerated the erosion of the president's Vietnam consensus and enhanced the prestige of the SFRC. Somewhat surprisingly, Fulbright received little credit. Indeed, the media appeared more interested in other committee members. Liberals within the press and academia could not help but note that, during a committee recess in the midst of the Rusk hearings, J. William Fulbright had walked over to the Senate chamber and voted against the 1968 Civil Rights Bill.[45]

Some ten days later Martin Luther King, Jr., journeyed to Memphis to lead a demonstration in support of striking garbage workers. The protest degenerated into a minor riot. Back in the city on April 4, he was determined to lead a second march, in part to help the garbage workers, and in part to vindicate his nonviolent tactics, which were then under attack by black radicals. He was relaxing in the early evening on the balcony of the Lorraine Motel when a white drifter and escaped convict named James Earl Ray shot and killed him from ambush. Hours later, African Americans expressed their rage by rampaging through their ghettos in Washington and other cities. The next day federal troops ringed the White House and manned a machine-gun post on the steps of the Capitol. Before the week was over, 125 more riots broke out in ghettos across America, the U.S. Army patrolled streets in Chicago and Baltimore, and twenty-one thousand black Americans were charged with riot-related crimes. Resentment was not limited to urban areas. "This eastern Arkansas town is an armed camp," a Marianna resident wrote attorney general Ramsey Clark. "Each white man in this city owns a gun and is well supplied with ammunition."[46]

King's assassination pricked the consciences of white liberals and caused some of them to focus once again on their Vietnam champion's civil rights

44 Ibid., Mar. 14, 1968.

45 Lee Williams to JWF, Jan. 15, 1968, Series 39:2, Box 14:6, SPF, and interview with Lee Williams, June 20, 1989.

46 Lewis E. Clarke to Ramsey Clark, Apr. 17, 1968, Series 39:1, Box 4:5, SPF.

record. "Fulbright's Credibility Widens on Moral Issues," Ralph McGill proclaimed in his April 26 column in the *Atlanta Constitution.* The Arkansan had the gall, the famed southern liberal declared, to demand of Rusk why he did not seek peace so that America could have more money to spend on the problems of the nation's cities, the ghettos, and the poor, and on the very same day to vote against the open housing bill.[47] Hawks at home and abroad were not slow to take advantage of the chairman's apparent hypocrisy. In Bangkok the Thai foreign minister blasted "pseudodemocratic politicians" in America who preached "Little Rock democracy."[48]

The second week in March the senator's brother, Jack Fulbright, died; he was sixty-eight years old. Although he had been suffering from heart trouble for several years, his demise was quite unexpected. By the time he died, the elder Fulbright had at long last come to terms with life: He was happily married to his third wife and was living as a "born again" Baptist; he had retired from his last job with the Arkansas Oak Flooring Co. in Pine Bluff when he was sixty, and spent most of his time playing golf and visiting friends.[49] Despite Jack's mellowing, the passing years had not seen him and Bill draw any closer. "I have a very bad cold and bronchitis and the Dr. forbids my traveling in an air plane so I won't be able to get to Jack's funeral," he wrote Ted Wylie. "It is such a dreary time."[50]

Six weeks following the beginning of the Tet offensive, the gains made by the NVA and VC had been wiped out. Pressure on Khe Sanh eased as Giap transferred two of his three besieging divisions to other areas.[51] From various outlying districts American intelligence reported that VC activity was ebbing sharply. The communists had suffered unprecedented losses, an estimated fifty-eight thousand killed.[52] Yet public opinion polls in the United States showed that both disillusionment with the war and disapproval of the president's handling of the conflict were on the rise. Moreover, the man with whom Lyndon Johnson had replaced Robert McNamara as secretary of defense was beginning to see the war in Vietnam as strategically hopeless and politically counterproductive.

47 "Fulbright's Credibility Widens on Moral Issues," *Atlanta Constitution,* Apr. 26, 1968.
48 "Thai Assails Fulbright as Fake Liberal," *Washington Sun,* Dec. 5, 1967.
49 "Jack Fulbright, Brother of Senator, Dies in Memphis," *Commercial Appeal,* Mar. 14, 1968.
50 JWF to Ted Wylie, Mar. 15, 1968, Series 48:18, Box 55:5, SPF.
51 Memorandum for Record, Apr. 4, 1968, NSC Meeting Notes File, Box 2, Johnson Papers.
52 Clark Clifford, *Counsel to the President: A Memoir* (New York, 1991), 473.

Clark Clifford recalled in his memoirs that Lyndon Johnson had selected him because he had wanted a man who would support his position in Vietnam, end the struggle between the secretary of defense and the JCS, and improve relations with Congress.[53] Those three objectives were mutually incompatible. It was perhaps crucial to the history of the war that Johnson appointed Clifford to succeed McNamara in 1968. While his longtime friend Bill Fulbright was busily widening the credibility gap and eroding the domestic consensus in behalf of the war, Clifford, the man who had acted as political adviser to Democratic presidents since Harry Truman, was placed in a position to advise Johnson on strategic matters. This convergence of the political and strategic in the person of Clifford forced Johnson to realize that he could not win the war in Vietnam, and that having plunged the nation more deeply into the quagmire than any of his predecessors, he could not retain the presidency.

Fulbright applauded Clifford's appointment as secretary of defense. He was not publicly committed to a continuation of the war, the chairman told reporters, and would thus be able to persuade the president to stop the bombing of the north "without embarrassment." Terming Clifford a personal friend, Fulbright told reporters, "I feel that I could speak with him and have an opportunity to try to persuade him. In any case, I think he would listen."[54]

As he surveyed the scene from his office in the Pentagon, Clifford decided that the JCS, Westmoreland, and the American military did not know what it was doing in Vietnam and that the war was a millstone that would drag Lyndon Johnson and the Democratic Party down to defeat in 1968.[55] At a meeting of the Tuesday luncheon group on March 4, Clifford laid his cards on the table. Westmoreland and the Joint Chiefs had been overly optimistic, Tet had been both a military and public relations defeat for the United States and South Vietnam, and Westmoreland's troop request was just an invitation to pour more money and troops down a rathole, he declared. North Vietnam was showing an ongoing capacity to meet the United States man for man and gun for gun. Where would it stop? the new DOD chief asked. More than likely, two hundred and six thousand more men would not suffice. If the president continued to heed Westmoreland and the JCS, there would be one million American soldiers in Vietnam by the end of the year with still no end in sight. Johnson did not protest.[56]

Clifford's realistic appraisal broke the dike. Although Rusk and Rostow initially supported Wheeler and Westmoreland and insisted that the Thieu re-

53 Ibid., 465.

54 "Hanoi Desires End to War, Fulbright Feels 'Quite Sure,'" *Arkansas Gazette,* Jan. 22, 1968.

55 Clifford, *Counsel to the President,* 473–5.

56 Notes of Press Meeting with Senior Foreign Policy Advisors, Mar. 4, 1968, T. Johnson Meeting Notes, Box 3, Johnson Papers.

gime represented a viable state that deserved U.S. support, they quickly began to soften. During a mid-March meeting of the president and his top advisers, Rusk observed that the element of hope had been taken away from the American people by Tet, while Rostow acknowledged that Thieu would soon have to accept the NLF as part of the political system.[57]

By the time Johnson had to make his crucial decisions concerning an expansion of the war in Vietnam, he was already faced with a formal challenge to his presidency within the Democratic Party. In August 1967, during Nicholas Katzenbach's claim before the SFRC that Johnson had virtually unlimited constitutional authority to carry on the war in Vietnam, Senator Eugene McCarthy had gotten up and stalked out of the committee room. Marcy and Ned Kenworthy had followed him. "The Catholic Church has now abandoned the doctrine of Papal infallibility, but the Johnson administration has taken it up," McCarthy remarked when he reached the staff office. "Somebody's got to take these guys on and I'm going to do it even if I have to run for President."[58] By early 1968 McCarthy supporters had established campaign organizations in a dozen states and were preparing for the New Hampshire primary.

Although Eugene McCarthy had won the endorsement of the ADA, it was hard for Democratic Party leaders to take the Minnesota senator – a nonpartisan, soft-spoken, cerebral man – seriously; but then on March 12 McCarthy stunned the White House by making a strong showing in the New Hampshire primary. Johnson's name had not been on the ballot, but the party organization had mounted a vigorous write-in campaign for him. Thus, when "Clean Gene" won 42.2 percent of the vote and twenty of twenty-four convention delegates, the media declared New Hampshire to be a major defeat for the president and his policies – despite the fact that most of those voting for McCarthy were disgruntled hawks. To make matters worse, on March 14 William Randolph Hearst, Jr., a longtime Johnson supporter, announced in his huge chain of papers that the Hearst Corporation was changing its stance on the war.[59] Two days later Robert Kennedy entered the race for the Democratic nomination. With his name, glamour, party connections, and money, Kennedy appeared to be a serious threat to the Texan's renomination. Indeed, though the ADA had officially endorsed McCarthy, it was clear that the rank and file, particularly the moderates like Schlesinger, would work for Bobby.

57 Meeting with Foreign Policy Advisors, Mar. 19, 1968, Meeting Notes File, Box 2, Johnson Papers.

58 Donald A. Ritchie, interviewer, *Oral History Interviews: Carl A. Marcy* (Senate Historical Office: Washington, D.C., 1983), 201–2.

59 Williams to JWF, Mar. 14, 1968, Series 48:18, Box 55:1, SPF.

Johnson's longtime friend and adviser Jim Rowe urged him to do "something exciting and dramatic to recapture the peace issue."[60]

In these circumstances, the president rejected Westmoreland's request for two hundred and six thousand additional men and agreed merely to deploy thirteen and a half thousand support troops to augment the emergency reinforcements sent in February. At the same time, he recalled his field commander to Washington to become army chief of staff; but Lyndon Johnson had more demotions in mind.

Fulbright was scheduled to deliver a speech on Vietnam in Cleveland the night of March 31. Shortly before he left Washington, Clark Clifford told him that the president was going to announce a bombing halt the same night he was scheduled to speak. Fulbright decided to keep his engagement, but he interrupted his talk so that he and his audience could watch the president.[61]

Johnson's image on television, even with makeup, was shocking. His eyes betraying the immense strain he was under, his face deeply lined, the president seemed at a crossroads. He announced that the bombing of North Vietnam would henceforth be limited to the area just north of the DMZ, and that this would cease if there were evidence the enemy was scaling back its military activity. He named Averell Harriman his special representative should peace talks materialize. He then dropped his bombshell: "I shall not seek, and I will not accept, the nomination of my party for another term as your President."[62]

The country was much impressed. For Johnson, the ultimate political animal, voluntarily to relinquish the reins of the most powerful office in the world was clearly a sacrifice of the first order. There were, of course, thousands of individual reactions to that abdication speech, but none more dramatic than that of Wayne Morse. The Oregon maverick had jousted with Johnson over Vietnam, but avidly supported his civil rights stand. That Wednesday evening, Morse was part of a crowd gathered around a radio in the U.S. embassy in Mexico City. As Johnson announced that he would not seek reelection, the group sat in stunned silence. Roy Reed, then a reporter for the *New York Times,* looked up at Morse. Tears were streaming down his face.[63]

Fulbright and Marcy's initial reactions to Johnson's abdication speech were ones of relief and gratitude. At Lee Williams's urging, the chairman called the president to congratulate him and offered to do whatever he could to get the peace process started in earnest. Johnson thanked the Arkansan and accepted his offer of help.[64] The next day Marcy met with his contact in the Soviet

60 Quoted in Herring, *America's Longest War,* 202.
61 Berman, *Fulbright and the Vietnam War,* 97.
62 Quoted in Herring, *America's Longest War,* 206.
63 Interview with Roy Reed, Sept. 17, 1993, Fayetteville, Ark.
64 Memo for the Files, Apr. 1, 1968, Williams Papers.

embassy, Igor Bubnov, and told him that he was "absolutely certain" that the president was sincere in his stated desire for peace.[65] "I think this is a very useful move by the President," Fulbright told reporters. "I think the President's statement shows he is really determined to bring about peace, a liquidation of the war." The North Vietnamese would be "extremely foolish" if they did not respond immediately.[66]

Despite his initial optimism and the opening of preliminary peace talks in Paris on May 13, however, Fulbright soon began to have doubts about Johnson's willingness to change the substance of his position. Harry Ashmore, who had been in Hanoi the night of Johnson's speech, reported to the chairman that upon his return to Washington he had found the door just as firmly closed to compromise as it had been a year earlier. Rusk refused to budge from his position that Hanoi would have to deescalate in return for a complete American bombing halt.[67] Fulbright began to suspect that Johnson was hoping somehow to produce a military victory or, at the very least, preserve a stalemate that the next president might resolve in America's favor. Yet, as Johnson's skyrocketing public approval ratings indicated, he and the doves were going to have to show restraint and give the peace process a chance. Silence seemed all the more important given the fact that Fulbright was seeking election to his fifth term in the Senate in 1968.

65 Marcy, memorandum of conversation, Apr. 2, 1968, Box 8, Folder Apr.–June, Marcy Papers.

66 "Fulbright Hails President Johnson's Vietnam Peace Proposal," *Fort Smith Southwest Times Record,* Apr. 2, 1968.

67 Ashmore to JWF, Apr. 17, 1968, Series 48:18, Box 54:1, SPF.

# 27

# *The politics of a Dixie dove*

The last week in March, the junior senator had flown to Little Rock to file for office formally. As reporters trailed after him asking if he would support Lyndon Johnson in 1968, whether Arkansans would penalize him for his dissent on the war, and if the black vote that had proved so important to electing Governor Rockefeller would figure in his campaign, Fulbright had walked from his hotel first to the Democratic State Headquarters and then to the courthouse. Conspicuous by his presence in the senator's entourage was wealthy and powerful insurance tycoon Bill Darby. Fulbright wanted to show that once again the power was in his corner; and, indeed, to that point the only other person to file was Bobby K. Hayes of Calico Rock, a rural businessman who would have made Warren Harding look like an intellectual. War hero Sid McMath was still touring the state telling all who would listen that Fulbright's opposition to the conflict in Vietnam was helping the enemy, but he had not declared. McMath sensed that Fulbright was vulnerable, but Witt Stephens, Jack Pickens, Darby, and others had told him that he would be on his own if he challenged the incumbent.

The Arkansas power brokers had given the same message to Orval Faubus. At the time Fulbright filed, Faubus was crisscrossing several western states, ostensibly on vacation, but in fact seeing if conservative oilmen like H. L. Hunt would finance a campaign against the junior senator.[1]

As Fulbright toured Arkansas, the usual grumblings concerning his preoccupation with national and international affairs to the detriment of the state began to be heard. When Fulbright shed his three-piece suit for his checked shirt to attend a fish fry, reporters dusted off their "just plain Bill" jokes; but Fulbright knew that within months the $1.2 billion Arkansas River Navigation Project, the most extensive undertaking of its kind in American history, would be completed. The grateful benefactors of his efforts up and down the Arkansas River Valley had already notified him that they would hold a series of ceremonies in the summer to pay tribute to him.[2]

[1] Ernest Dumas, "Is Orval Prospecting for Campaign Gold?" *Arkansas Gazette,* Mar. 31, 1968.

[2] Charles D. Maynard to JWF, Apr. 29, 1968, Series 1:1, Box 4:1, SPF.

Indeed, as the closing date for filing drew near, Lee Williams, Norvill Jones, Parker Westbrook, and other Fulbright aides relaxed in anticipation of a clear sail through to the general election. Then, on May 1, the last day to file, former State Supreme Court Justice Jim Johnson, Arkansas's most outspoken racist, paid his entry fee. "He is a man of no character, but with a considerable ability for inflammatory demagoguery," Fulbright wrote his wealthy benefactor, Cyrus Eaton. "If there are riots this summer, as expected, he can be a dangerous opponent."[3]

In fact, the violence that followed in the wake of Martin Luther King's assassination produced a white backlash of major proportions. In spite of the fact that there was not one case of looting or arson reported in Arkansas, the state's residents were as much agitated by the specter of urban violence as any New Yorker or Washingtonian. Footage showing entire city blocks in flames and rioters hindering firemen, which flickered nightly upon the state's television screens, seemed to confirm Arkansas's worst fears about black retaliation for years of oppression – today Newark, tomorrow Forrest City. The Reverend Lewis Clark of Marianna told his Baptist flock:

> Watching the holocaust of recent days reduce our cities to a charred sodden mass has left us to stand staring, stirring in the dark gray ashes that were once a home, an office, or corner shop that provided a meager way of existence. The crack of a rifle, the backfire of a jeep, the thunder of marching feet of loyal American troops, the rumble of a tank, and the crashing of plate glass [together] with the sickening sound of police issuing the command to halt with upraised hands is enough to make Karl Marx, the father of riots, civil disorder, and rebellion shout, "I have overcome."[4]

Fulbright and his supporters considered Jim Johnson a threat not only because he was racist and anti-intellectual in his own right but because they viewed him as a stalking-horse for George Wallace. The Alabama governor – famous among white supremacists for his theatrical stand in the schoolhouse door during efforts to integrate the state university – had formed a third party, the American Independent Party, and was planning to run in 1968 as its presidential nominee. He was still a nominal Democrat, however, and hoped that a number of southern delegations, including Arkansas's, would support him at the Democratic National Convention in August. When in March "Justice Jim" blocked a move within the state committee to bind convention delegates to support the national ticket, and when subsequently he began circulating petitions to qualify Wallace for the Arkansas ballot, Fulbright decided he would have to act. Though he had never before attended a meeting of the

3 JWF to Cyrus Eaton, May 1, 1968, Series 2:1, Box 5:5, SPF.
4 Rev. Lewis Clark, "A Discourse on Civil Disobedience and the Death of Democracy," May 21, 1968, Series 39:1, Box 5:1, SPF.

Democratic State Committee, the junior senator showed up in Little Rock in person on June 27 with enough proxies to carry the day. Fulbright ran roughshod over Jim Johnson's people and got what he wanted: an uncommitted delegation that was bound in the end to support the party's regular nominees. Fulbright wanted not only to keep the state's representatives from bolting for Wallace, but to prevent them from prematurely casting their lot with Hubert Humphrey, who had entered the lists following Lyndon Johnson's abdication speech. Fulbright, who saw the two men as Tweedledee and Tweedledum on Vietnam, wanted to keep whatever pressure on the administration he could to press ahead with the Paris peace talks.[5]

As Fulbright moved back and forth between Washington and Arkansas during the tumultuous days of 1968, he kept one eye on state politics and the other on the peace negotiations. His initial pessimism only grew with each passing day. Days turned into weeks following the president's announcement that Hanoi and Washington had agreed to face-to-face negotiations. The two sides haggled initially over a meeting place. Although Johnson had vowed to send representatives "to any forum, at any time," he rejected Hanoi's proposed sites of Phnom Penh and Warsaw, where, he said, the "deck would be stacked against us."[6]

Soon after the Paris talks opened, the American delegation introduced a variant of the old San Antonio formula: The United States would stop the bombing "on the assumption that" North Vietnam would respect the demilitarized zone and refrain from further rocket attacks in the south, and that "prompt and serious" talks would follow.[7] It seemed, however, that the closer peace approached, the more fearful of it Lyndon Johnson became. "Some of you think we want resolution of this in an election year," he told his foreign policy advisers. "I want it resolved, but not because of the election. Don't yield anything on that impression."[8] Indeed, his instructions to the American negotiating team were to "let the enemy do his own negotiating and hold to our basic positions."[9] Averell Harriman ignored the president and worked for a quick peace in hopes of derailing Richard Nixon's candidacy.

The opening of the Paris peace talks placed tremendous pressure on the government of South Vietnam. The rivalry between Ky and Thieu intensified, fragmenting and paralyzing the government. The Buddhists remained more

5 "Fulbright Moves to Insure Loyalists Go to Convention," *Jonesboro Sun,* June 19, 1968, and Ernest Dumas, "Democrats Select Loyal Delegates; Slate Uncommitted," *Arkansas Gazette,* June 28, 1968.

6 Quoted in George C. Herring, *America's Longest War: The United States and Vietnam, 1950–1975,* 2d ed. (New York, 1986), 209.

7 Quoted in ibid., 210.

8 Notes of the President's Meeting with Foreign Policy Advisers, May 6, 1968, Meeting Notes File, Box 3, Johnson Papers.

9 Rostow to LBJ, May 21, 1968, NSF, Country File–Vietnam, Box 101, Johnson Papers.

alienated than ever, openly demanding formation of a peace cabinet and urging ARVN troops to lay down their arms. Both the Buddhists and newly active sects appeared to look forward to the collapse of the government. New political groups sprouted after the peace talks began, but they were riddled with dissension and incapable of forming a meaningful opposition.

During the early stages of the administration's peace offensive, both Johnson and Fulbright decided that a public show of reconciliation would serve their purposes. In early May, the president attended the opening of the National Collection of Fine Arts in Washington's historic Old Patent Office Building. Sharing the dais were the members of the Smithsonian Institution's board of directors. Johnson went out of his way to shake hands with Fulbright, a gesture greeted with thunderous applause by the audience.[10] Several days later, after Fulbright had departed for a speaking engagement in Arkansas, Johnson pointedly called to give the "stud-duck of the opposition," as the president referred to him, "a full and complete briefing" on the Paris talks.[11]

The intersection of the war, the 1968 presidential election, the Paris peace talks, the antiwar movement, the white backlash, and the increasingly embittered civil rights movement produced a confusion, fragmentation, and anguish that the country had experienced only once or twice before in its history. All the while, there seemed to be no figure on the horizon willing or able to appeal to people's better instincts, to pull America together. Harry Ashmore painted a vivid picture of wartime Washington in 1968:

> Dilettante diplomats motivated by self-aggrandizement and promotional self-interest; hysterical Jack Kennedy lovers mad with hatred of LBJ; soft-headed intellectuals of doubtful patriotism; political subversives trying to do a hatchet-job on behalf of Bobby Kennedy and Gene McCarthy; overweening egos frustrated because we can't dictate the foreign policy of the country.[12]

Lyndon Johnson's inability or unwillingness to get the peace talks off dead center loomed as a potentially mortal handicap to his heir-apparent, Hubert Humphrey. The Happy Warrior's candidacy, announced on April 27, three weeks after Johnson's abdication, had initially been buoyed by the Paris talks. Johnson's decision, and the simultaneous announcement of a partial bombing halt and new peace negotiations, had denied McCarthy and Kennedy their most compelling issue and forced them to resort to personalities. After the ADA endorsed McCarthy, the Democrats turned their attention to the important California primary scheduled for June 4. A poor showing in a televised debate convinced McCarthy and his aides that defeat was inevitable. As

10 "LBJ Tells Art Audience Peace Is Endless Effort," *Washington Post,* May 4, 1968.
11 Parker Westbrook to JWF, May 10, 1968, Series 1:1, Box 4:1, SPF.
12 Ashmore to JWF, Apr. 17, 1968, Series 48:18, Box 54:1, SPF.

he watched Robert Kennedy make his victory speech, McCarthy reached to turn his hotel TV off. He was frozen by the announcement that his rival had been shot by a deranged Jordanian, Sirhan Sirhan. Twenty-five hours later, without ever regaining consciousness, Bobby Kennedy died.

On June 7, shortly after Robert Kennedy's assassination, McCarthy called Carl Marcy and told him that, despite losing the California primary, he had decided not to withdraw. Now that Kennedy was dead, he was the only alternative to the policies of either Humphrey or Richard Nixon, who, it seemed, was sure to be the Republican candidate. What he needed, he said, was for one or two Democratic senators publicly to announce support.[13] The chief of staff was certainly supportive. Despite a directive he had written to his subordinates warning them to avoid political activity, Marcy had been writing campaign speeches for McCarthy and quietly plumping for him since December.[14] In fact, for Carl Marcy, Eugene McCarthy's candidacy marked the culmination of his crusade to bring the executive to heel and reestablish congressional influence on foreign policy.[15]

Fulbright certainly leaned toward McCarthy. He thought the Minnesotan somewhat ineffectual, but Humphrey too was frequently all sail and no anchor. Moreover, he and the vice-president had repeatedly clashed over Vietnam.[16] Finally, the Arkansan suspected that Humphrey might be a stalking-horse for Johnson. Writing Martha Gelhorn, an old family acquaintance then living in Kenya (and once married to Ernest Hemingway), he observed of Johnson's abdication speech, "no one can say at this time whether it was a ploy or trick or whether he means it." There was a good chance that "Hubert will withdraw at the last moment in favor of Johnson, who will be nominated by acclamation."[17] Nevertheless, Fulbright felt that he could not publicly endorse McCarthy. It was unwise for any incumbent senator running for reelection to tout a particular national candidate when that candidate was an uncertain quantity with his constituents.

By mid-June it began to dawn on Marcy and the staff of the SFRC that neither side in the Vietnam talks was committed to negotiating on matters of substance. The president had, they decided, agreed to talks merely to relieve pressure from congressional doves and antiwar activists in the United States, whereas Hanoi appeared to be willing to await the outcome of the fall elections before getting down to business. With both sides working feverishly to improve their military positions in Vietnam, and Americans killed averaging

13 Marcy to JWF, June 7, 1968, Box 8, Apr.–June, Marcy Papers.

14 Marcy to Staff, Mar. 22, 1968, Series 48:3, Box 16:5, SPF, and Marcy to McCarthy, Dec. 14, 1967, Box 7, Folder Oct.–Dec., Marcy Papers.

15 Marcy to Jean D. Andres, June 10, 1968, Box 8, Apr.–June, Marcy Papers.

16 See, for example, Summary Notes of 578th NSC Meeting, Nov. 8, 1967, NSC Meeting Notes, Box 2, Johnson Papers.

17 JWF to Gellhorn, Apr. 25, 1968, Series 48:18, Box 54:5, SPF.

five hundred per week, McCarthy broke the silence doves had imposed on themselves after Johnson's March 31 speech. Using memos prepared by Marcy and Jim Lowenstein, "Clean Gene" began publicly to question the administration's sincerity.[18]

In the midst of the presidential campaign and his own race for the Senate, Fulbright attempted once again to coerce the administration on Vietnam. Led by Fulbright and Frank Church, the SFRC rejected the administration's foreign aid bill and substituted a simple continuing resolution that would extend aid through fiscal 1969 at 80 percent of the previous year's level. In six months a new administration would be in place, and it deserved the opportunity to present an aid program of its own, Fulbright insisted.[19] Under the continuing-resolution arrangement, foreign aid reached an all-time postwar low.

Furious but helpless, the administration revenged itself on Fulbright's pet. The Arkansan's heart sank as he read the State Department's proposed budget for the exchange program in fiscal year 1969. Funds available for the academic year beginning in September were to be cut by 72 percent; as a result, Fulbright programs would have to be terminated in eighteen European countries. The department's funding reduction in the exchange of persons program was twice that suggested for other areas. Congress had been pushing federal agencies to eliminate threats to the balance of payments, and this was a good way to do it, declared a State Department spokesman.[20] Although Fulbright managed to retrieve some of the money, and the binational commissions in Germany, Britain, and other countries took up part of the slack, it would be twenty-five years before the Fulbright Exchange Program regained the funding level it had enjoyed before the great Johnson cut.[21] Upon receiving a doctor of laws degree from Texas Christian University, Johnson told the assembled crowd of students and faculty: "Having spent most of my life doctoring laws, it is nice now to have a license. I might even apply for a Fulbright scholarship, but I am not very hopeful."[22]

18 Lowenstein to Marcy, June 11, 1968, Series 48:3, Box 16:5, and Marcy to Lee Williams, July 10, 1968, Series 48:1, Box 9:2, SPF; and Marcy to McCarthy, June 12, 1968, Box 8, Apr.–June, Marcy Papers.

19 Jones to JWF, Feb. 9, 1968, Series 48:8, Box 30:4, SPF; Marcy to Boyd [House Committee on Foreign Affairs], May 21, 1968, and Marcy to Holt and Henderson, June 6, 1968, Box 8, Folder Apr.–June, Marcy Papers; and Gaud to LBJ, May 24, 1968, Box 57, WHCF, Legislation, Johnson Papers.

20 "Budget Cuts Imperil Fulbright's Program on Scholar Exchange," *Arkansas Gazette*, Sept. 27, 1968.

21 Interview with Ulrich Littmann, July 18–19, 1988, Bonn, FRG.

22 "Fulbright Scholarship On for LBJ?" *Hot Springs New Era*, May 30, 1968.

Meanwhile, in Arkansas, Fulbright was moving to shore up two of his shakiest constituencies: blacks and organized labor. At the state AFL–CIO convention president J. Bill Becker, a longtime Fulbright family friend and Democratic Party activist, urged his fellows to hold their noses and endorse the junior senator. There was a spontaneous floor revolt and a three-hour debate. In all his twenty-six years in Congress, declared former president Wayne Glenn, Fulbright had never given labor a vote on a "bread and butter" issue. How could the organization, consistently hawkish on Vietnam, endorse the man whom American soldiers in Southeast Asia had termed a "Judas-goat"? In the end, however, the AFL–CIO decided that support for Justice Jim was unthinkable; deeply divided, the convention gave Fulbright its stamp of approval.[23]

With an eye to his other potential weak spot, Fulbright in mid-June named a Pine Bluff minister and black civil rights activist, Ben Grinage, to his campaign staff. Fulbright's record on civil rights was "indefensible," Grinage told reporters, but it was no worse than other members of the Arkansas delegation.[24] As Williams and Fulbright well knew, the Pine Bluff cleric's appointment was a gamble. Williams and Jim McDougal, Fulbright's staff person in Arkansas, urged the African-American leader to do his utmost to organize and win the support of blacks, but to keep his activities as secret as possible from white political leaders around the state, lest there be a backlash. Indeed, McDougal wanted Grinage to operate via mail and telephone and not leave the Little Rock office.[25] (So sensitive were Grinage's reports of his activities among black voters that Williams kept them in a locked safe in his office.)

Johnson, as well as Fulbright's other rival, Bobby K. Hayes of Calico Rock, alienated most thinking Arkansans by the viciousness of their attacks. Terming Fulbright the "pin-up boy of Hanoi," Justice Jim toured the state telling all who would listen that the incumbent was giving aid and comfort to the enemy and was directly responsible for American casualties.[26] Hayes announced that the reason Fulbright had opposed the bombing of Haiphong harbor was that he was on a $150,000 retainer from Lloyd's of London, a company that insured many ships that moved in and out of the port.[27] In Little Rock a gun-toting Johnson–Wallace supporter accosted Lee Williams and

23 Bill Lewis, "COPE Endorses Boswell, Fulbright After Hot Debate," *Arkansas Gazette,* June 16, 1968.

24 "Grinage to Be Aide to Senator Fulbright," *Arkansas Gazette,* June 12, 1968.

25 Williams to JWF, Feb. 28, 1969, and Grinage to JWF, Feb. 28, 1969, Williams Papers.

26 "Fulbright Calls 'Hanoi Pin-Up Boy' Label 'Utter Trash and Hogwash,'" *Pine Bluff Commercial,* July 26, 1968.

27 "Hayes Ties Fulbright to Lloyds," *Arkansas Democrat,* June 23, 1968.

told him that true Americans would "get even" with him and Fulbright one way or another.[28]

Stung by these slanders and threats, and ever-mindful of the perennial appeal of demagoguery, Fulbright held his nose and cozied up to the farmers and "wool-hat boys" of rural Arkansas. When famed country-folk singer Jimmy Driftwood of Timbo announced that he was embarking on a seven-week international tour to promote world peace, Fulbright, along with Miss Arkansas, was on hand at the airport to see him off.[29]

Throughout July, Bill – clad in short-sleeved, blue-checked sportshirt in deference to the heat and his urbane image – Betty, Lee Williams, and various members of the campaign staff toured the state. The highlands were notoriously independent, but Fulbright could always appeal to local chauvinism in northwest Arkansas. Eastern Arkansas seemed well in hand under the expert management of Bill Penix. He always enjoyed campaigning in the delta, a grinning Fulbright told a Jonesboro businessman. One could gain a maximum number of votes by talking to a minimum number of people, he said, alluding to the large number of machine-controlled counties and to vote buying among poor sharecroppers. The south and west were more unpredictable and thus problematical.

One hot, dusty July day Fulbright and Lee Williams were campaigning in Texarkana. They decided to seek out the nearest watering hole for a little refreshment. As Texarkana seemed to be made up chiefly of Baptist churches, gas stations, and beer joints, one was not hard to find. Williams introduced the always-diffident Fulbright to one of the locals, a huge, semiliterate truck driver replete with long underwear and a Mack Truck cap. The local pumped Fulbright's hand and told him he had long been an admirer. After an extended, low-level discussion of national and local affairs, the two politicians made their exit. As Williams was walking out the door, the truck driver caught his arm. "You tell Senator McClellan, I hope he wins," he said.[30]

As election day approached, the campaign staff was guardedly optimistic. The senator predicted a first-primary victory with 65 percent of the vote. Arkansas political pundits were not so sure; Johnson was indeed an accomplished demagogue and the state, like the nation, was in a very unsettled condition. "Fulbright Faces Most Serious Challenge of His Career," ran a *Gazette* headline.[31]

[28] Williams appealed to the FBI, but the bureau decided not to take any action "in view of past unfavorable relations with Senator Fulbright." FBI, Little Rock to Director, July 29, 1968, 62-71126, FBI Files.

[29] "Driftwood Heads Abroad in Interest of Peace," *Arkansas Democrat,* July 1, 1968.

[30] Interview with Lee Williams, June 20, 1989, Washington, D.C.

[31] Bill Lewis, "Fulbright Faces Most Serious Challenge of His (24-Year) Career Tuesday," *Arkansas Gazette,* July 28, 1968.

The pundits were right. Although he led in sixty-eight of Arkansas's seventy-five counties, Fulbright garnered only 53 percent of the popular vote against candidates who consistently accused him of giving aid and comfort to the enemy. His victory was made possible by help from some unexpected quarters. Faubus not only shunned Johnson but organized Madison County for Fulbright – or so he claimed.[32] According to Ben Grinage, the incumbent received nearly forty thousand votes, 18 percent of his total, from Arkansas blacks.[33] Had the Man from Greasy Creek not remained neutral and had African Americans stayed home, Fulbright might have had to face a runoff.

All told, Charles Bernard, Fulbright's Republican opponent for the general election, was encouraged. A self-made millionaire, Bernard farmed seventy-seven hundred acres of rich delta land near his eastern Arkansas birthplace of Earle. He was convinced that if he followed in Winthrop Rockefeller's political footsteps and let Fulbright's record on Vietnam speak for itself, he could win.[34]

The approaching Democratic National Convention forced Fulbright to take time out from his reelection campaign and address national politics. Indeed, the two had, to his chagrin, become momentarily intertwined. By the time the Democratic State Committee met on August 10 to instruct its delegation to the Chicago convention, Chairman Leon Catlett had promised all of the state's thirty-three votes to Hubert Humphrey. McCarthy partisans were furious. The split reflected the growing division within the state party between younger, more liberal members and the old guard, many of whom had supported Orval Faubus. The Young Turks responded to Catlett's perceived perfidy by trying to ram through a resolution committing the delegation to vote for J. William Fulbright as Arkansas's favorite-son candidate.

The move presented Fulbright with a dilemma. His views on the war were much more in tune with McCarthy and the Young Turks, but he needed the old guard – Stephens, Darby, Pickens, and the others – to win. He hesitated only briefly. With the committee in turmoil, he officially notified it that he would not consent to be a favorite-son candidate and that, in fact, he was withdrawing his name from the list of delegates. Fulbright's decision left Arkansas liberals and Eugene McCarthy high and dry, and paved the way for an early Arkansas commitment to Hubert Humphrey.[35]

32 Faubus to Darby, Aug. 1, 1968, Williams Papers.

33 Grinage to Williams, Aug. 12, 1968, Williams Papers.

34 "Fulbright Still Has Challenge: WR-Backed Foe," *Hot Springs Sentinel Record,* Aug. 1, 1968.

35 "Fulbright Against Favorite-Son Movement in Party," *Pine Bluff Commercial,* Aug. 11, 1968, and "Fulbright Won't Be Delegate," *Mena Evening Star,* Aug. 16, 1968.

To compensate for his abandonment of McCarthy and the antiwar faction within the Arkansas delegation, Fulbright flew to Washington on August 20 to testify before the platform committee of the Democratic National Committee. American involvement in Vietnam was a national tragedy, he told the committee in remarks that were given wide coverage by the national press. Intervention was the product of a rigid cold-war mind-set that turned Ho Chi Minh "into another lunatic Hitler" and that posited the existence of a monolithic communist threat. As a result of that ill-advised crusade, old allies, like Britain and France, had abandoned the United States, the Great Society lay in shambles, and power had become centralized in the executive to the point where an "elective dictatorship" was ruling America. He then offered his model plank: With the ultimate goal of self-determination and neutralization of Southeast Asia, the United States should commit itself to an immediate bombing halt and cease-fire. He also asked the party to endorse his national commitments resolution.[36]

Hubert Humphrey did not want to repudiate the war in Vietnam, but he favored a plank that would promise to get the negotiating process in Paris off dead center. Lyndon Johnson would have none of it; he and Earle Wheeler agreed that there should be no "unilateral" concessions. He was determined, the president said, that the Democratic Party not be surrendered to the new isolationists.[37] Dean Rusk testified before the platform committee that it would be "neither wise or practicable" to spell out in detail the contents of an agreement with Hanoi. At the same time, the Texan summoned to the White House two of Humphrey's aides charged with drafting the Vietnam plank and told them he would not put up with any statement calling for an unconditional bombing halt. He also sent Charles Murphy, one of his chief troubleshooters, to Chicago to make sure that there was no slippage when the convention actually drafted the plank. There was none. Over the outraged protests of its dovish minority, the Democratic National Convention praised the administration for its efforts to halt aggression in South Vietnam and left the details of negotiation completely up to the executive.[38]

It was fortunate for Fulbright that he decided not to attend the Chicago convention. Following the angry floor debate over the party's position on Vietnam, Humphrey was easily nominated on the first ballot. McCarthy's quest for delegates had been undermined by his own introspective and enigmatic personality, the image of his campaign as a "children's crusade," and the fact

36 William C. Berman, *William Fulbright and the Vietnam War: The Dissent of a Political Realist* (Kent, Ohio, 1988), 101–2.

37 Bromley Smith to LBJ, Aug. 28, 1968, NSF, Country File–Vietnam, Box 102, Johnson Papers.

38 "Rusk Says Not to Dictate Terms of Vietnam Conflict," *El Dorado News,* Aug. 21, 1968, and John W. Finney, "How Johnson Got the Vietnam Plank He Wanted," *New York Times,* Aug. 27, 1968.

that most professional politicians distrusted him. Their candidate and their peace plank unceremoniously rejected, antiwar delegates decided to be as disruptive as possible and demonstrate to the national television audience watching the convention that they had been steamrolled.

While inside the convention McCarthy partisans grew increasingly irate at the high-handed tactics of convention managers, outside a drama of street violence was unfolding in central Chicago. Some ten thousand antiwar youths had descended upon the city, including radical elements of the New Left, such as Abbie Hoffman's Youth International Party (Yippies), to demonstrate against Johnson's Vietnam policy. City police were ordered by Mayor Richard J. Daley, the quintessential big-city political boss and an intense Humphrey partisan, to break up organized protests. When the Yippie-led demonstrators pelted police lines with obscenities, stones, and urine, the men in blue rioted. While a nationwide television audience watched in fascinated horror, Chicago's finest assaulted the youthful antiwar protesters with clubs, tear gas, and mace. America had seen nothing like it since Bull Connor's men and dogs had attacked civil rights marchers in Birmingham. Thankful that he had not been filmed in the midst of this mayhem and could not be tainted by association with the discredited Johnson administration, Fulbright turned his attention to the general election in Arkansas.

Shortly after he began crisscrossing the state in his Cessna-180 in August, Charles Bernard was joined by an up-and-coming right-wing fund-raiser named Richard A. Viguerie. Quickly Viguerie, who claimed to be able to defeat liberal candidates nine times out of ten, convinced Bernard to make the campaign more ideological. "Fulbright has pleaded for recognition of Red China," declared a Bernard For Senate circular. "He has worked for a 'hands off' policy toward Castro and Communist Cuba." "Do you think there should be a single, centralized system for setting of prices and allocation of resources in the United States?" another Bernard campaign letter asked. "J. William Fulbright does."[39] Viguerie began mining the Tulsa–Dallas–Shreveport crescent for campaign funds. Asked by reporters in that latter metropolis if he was supporting Bernard, H. L. Hunt declared that he was doing everything he could to bring about Fulbright's defeat in the November 5 election.[40]

Some members of the radical right wanted to use more than money to defeat Fulbright. On August 26 the FBI informed Lee Williams that its agents had uncovered a plot by the Longview, Texas, chapter of the Minutemen to

39 Robert Webb to "Fellow American," Oct. 8, 1968, and Robert Webb to Arthur Frankel, Oct. 14, 1968, Series 78, Box 26:5, SPF.

40 "Fulbright Tags Dallas Tycoon 'Eccentric' Foe," *Memphis Commercial Appeal,* Oct. 31, 1968.

assassinate the junior senator from Arkansas. One Marshall Ray Grissom had been assigned the task, but Hoover's men, Williams was assured, had infiltrated the organization and had the matter well in hand.[41]

Although Fulbright's new press secretary, Hoyt Purvis, denied it, the incumbent's campaign received more than a hundred thousand dollars from out-of-state liberals who were determined that their champion, tarnished by civil rights though he was, would not be done in by the know-nothings. Archibald MacLeish, America's poet laureate, sent a form letter to liberals all over the nation urging contributions to Fulbright's campaign.[42] Hundreds of Fulbright supporters around the country wrote Arkansas newspapers urging his election. "It is important to consider that certain Americans from the Boondocks are playing major roles in our destiny," C. W. Greene of Whitman, Massachusetts, indelicately wrote the *Pine Bluff News.* "I plead fervently to the citizens of Arkansas to keep Senator Fulbright on the national scene."[43] Meanwhile, Purvis busied himself distributing pictures of his boss holding a stringer of fish or kicking his famous field goal against SMU when he had been a Razorback.

As was true of the primaries, the two great unknowns in the general election were Vietnam and civil rights. An estimated hundred thousand blacks would vote in the general election, and it was this constituency that had carried the day for Winthrop Rockefeller in 1966. If the Republicans transferred Rockefeller's popularity to Bernard, Fulbright might be in trouble. Bill Penix decided to take no chances. He had several thousand posters printed up depicting Charles Bernard's campaign promises to help the poor and downtrodden on one side and a picture of his palatial home, complete with swimming pool, on the other. Penix then hired a small plane and rained the leaflets on the tar-paper shacks of eastern Arkansas.[44]

Ironically, Fulbright's stand on the war ended up helping him with conservatives as well as liberals. Arkansans who opposed the war were more than ever ready to support their hero, while conservatives, though disapproving of Fulbright's outspoken criticism of U.S. involvement in Vietnam, admired his courage in standing up to Lyndon Johnson, whom they blamed for miring the country in a war he was unwilling to win. "I didn't vote for Fulbright in the primary," one poll respondent declared, "because he was always going on TV complaining about the war. . . . But now no one knows what's going on. Maybe Fulbright is right. Anyway, he has courage going against Lyndon

41 Lee Williams, Memo for the Files, Aug. 26, 1968, Series 5:2, Box 3:8, SPF.

42 "Fulbright, Bernard Forces Go Outside of State Borders," *Jonesboro Evening Sun,* Oct. 13, 1968.

43 "Fulbright, A Political Immortal," *Pine Bluff News,* Aug. 15, 1968.

44 Interview with William Penix, Apr. 17, 1991, Fayetteville, Ark., and James T. Wooten, "Fulbright Caught Up in Complex Reelection Fight," *New York Times,* Oct. 9, 1968.

Johnson." The more undecided the situation in Vietnam appeared, the more attractive Fulbright became.[45]

In the end only one of the state's newspapers came out in support of Bernard, and Fulbright wound up winning 64 percent of the vote. Williams and company breathed a sigh of relief. They had been confident, but in a year when Arkansas voted for George Wallace for president, Winthrop Rockefeller for governor, and J. William Fulbright for senator, anything could happen.[46]

The rest of the national Democratic ticket did not fare as well as the junior senator from Arkansas. Although the early front-runner for the 1968 Republican nomination was liberal Governor George Romney of Michigan, the GOP convention meeting in Miami chose Richard M. Nixon on the first ballot. The putative "new Nixon" that won the New Hampshire primary was not the strident ideologue of old; the new Nixon was gracious, cool under fire, and eminently reasonable. Following his nomination in Miami, Nixon surprised most observers by selecting Governor Spiro T. Agnew of Maryland for second place on the ticket. The combative Agnew, although a national unknown, was the choice of such party ultraconservatives as turncoat Democrat Strom Thurmond. Anticipating the politics of division advocated by Pat Buchanan and Kevin Phillips, the GOP platform promised an "all-out" campaign against crime, reform of the welfare laws, an end to inflation, and a stronger national defense. On Vietnam, the platform pledged to "de-Americanize" the war, to engage in "clear and purposeful negotiations," and not to accept "a camouflaged surrender."[47]

By early September the national campaign was well under way. The Republicans, confident that they would be able to smash the divided Democrats, unleashed the most elaborate and expensive presidential campaign in United States history. Nixon campaigned at a deliberate, dignified pace, seeking to dramatize the nation's decline at home and abroad under two Democratic administrations. The Democratic effort, by contrast, started very badly: First, the disastrous Chicago convention still hung like a pall over the party; second, Humphrey and his running mate, Senator Edmund Muskie of Maine, faced a serious challenge for control of the South and Midwest from the third-party candidacy of former Democrat George Wallace.

Nevertheless, from a rock-bottom beginning Humphrey's campaign made steady progress. As was true in July, he needed to create some distance between himself and Johnson on Vietnam without seeming to repudiate the president. What he needed was some movement in the Paris peace talks them-

45 John Averill, "War Stand Helping Fulbright Survive," *Arkansas Democrat,* Oct. 11, 1968.

46 "Arkansas Embraces Wallace but Gives Fulbright Big Edge," *Arkansas Gazette,* Nov. 7, 1968.

47 Quoted in Dewey W. Grantham, *Recent America: The United States since 1945* (Arlington Heights, Ill., 1987), 307.

selves. In that way and that way alone would it be possible for Humphrey to have Johnson and the peace issue both.

Then on October 11 Le Duc Tho indicated that if the United States agreed to stop the bombing of the north, his country would drop their objections to participation by the Thieu government in the Paris talks. At the same time, a major NVA–VC offensive launched in September collapsed. Rusk and Wheeler – after checking with Ellsworth Bunker and General Creighton Abrams, Westmoreland's successor as field commander – decided that the communists, having been defeated on the battlefield, were ready to negotiate. At long last they assented to a bombing halt. Reluctantly, on November 1, just before the election, President Johnson called off aerial attacks over the north.[48] Unfortunately for the Democratic ticket, Nguyen Van Thieu denounced the bombing halt and refused to go to Paris.

Whether Thieu's refusal to negotiate led to Hubert Humphrey's defeat is unknowable. What is certain was that he fell short – by an agonizingly small margin. Nixon won 31,770,000 votes, or 43.4 percent of the total, compared to Humphrey's 31,270,000, or 42.7 percent. George Wallace finished a distant third with 13.5 percent.

More important, Richard Nixon's election in 1968 marked the end of eight years of Democratic rule and symbolized America's disillusionment with liberal reform both at home and overseas. Indeed, as the tumultuous decade approached its close, cold-war liberals found themselves under attack from all sides. From the left, intellectuals, students, and minorities complained about liberal complicity in waging an immoral war in Vietnam and creating an indifferent bureaucracy that resisted change. Disillusioned black radicals rejected the concept of nonviolent civil disobedience and denounced civil rights evolutionists as Uncle Toms. From the right came slings and arrows loosed by an emerging "silent majority" – working- and middle-class Americans who insisted that the nation reassert its commitment to patriotism, the work ethic, and "law and order."

Perhaps liberalism's bitterest critics were its disillusioned own. In his critique of postwar American foreign policy J. William Fulbright revealed that in their efforts to reconcile the ideal with the real, American liberals had allowed their obsession with social justice to be welded to the anticommunist crusade that pervaded the nation during the 1950s and 1960s. As a result, American foreign policy had become a missionary crusade that blinded Americans to the political and cultural realities of Southeast Asia as well as other developing regions. Had liberals not permitted themselves to be intimidated by McCarthyism and its radical-right offspring, then Vietnam could never have happened. The extension of the liberal impulse from the domestic to the international sphere made possible an unholy alliance between realpolitikers

48 Marcy to John Rielly, Sept. 6, 1968, Box 8, Folder July–Sept., Marcy Papers.

preoccupied with markets and bases and emotionally committed to the domino theory, and idealists who wanted to spread the blessings of freedom, democracy, and a mixed economy to the less fortunate of the world. The foreign aid program, with its dual emphasis on armaments and infrastructure, symbolized the marriage between the two. Conservatives were willing to accept nonmilitary aid because they were convinced that it was essential to halting the rise of communism, whereas liberals could reconcile themselves to massive military assistance on the grounds that America was simply protecting the recipients of its global social experiment.

In Vietnam Fulbright saw the ultimate product of liberal internationalism, and he spoke. The United States was battling an enemy that had long since changed in form and substance. America, acting in part out of altruism, was trying to impose its culture and institutions on nations whose folkways and political processes far antedated its own. In their anxiety to be politically relevant, to play the anticommunist card, American liberals had embraced the military–industrial complex and had thereby placed the very things they worshiped – freedom, democracy, diversity – at risk. John F. Kennedy and Lyndon Johnson's agenda had not triumphed over that of Barry Goldwater; the two had become joined. What gave Fulbright's insights – stated so eloquently in *The Arrogance of Power* and "The Price of Empire" – such sharpness and poignance was that he more than any other figure had been responsible for convincing his fellow Americans to embrace liberal internationalism.

# 28

# *Nixon and Kissinger*

Cheered by the thought of not having to campaign again for another six years, Arkansas's most famous son returned to Washington in January 1969 in a buoyant mood. Fulbright's reelection had elevated him to the top echelon of the Senate seniority system and earned him a spot on the Democratic Steering Committee. Despite the fact that Congress was in the hands of one party and the executive the other, Fulbright was cautiously optimistic concerning the prospects for a bipartisan foreign policy. The day following the election Nixon had called Fulbright to exchange congratulations and to emphasize his intent to consult the SFRC every step of the way. Fulbright was delighted with Nixon's choice of his old friend William Rogers to be secretary of state. Rogers, an urbane New York lawyer, had handled his duties as point man for the Eisenhower administration's civil rights program with tact and skill. He had repeatedly demonstrated that he was neither a right-wing ideologue nor an inflexible cold warrior. Fulbright, somewhat naïvely, anticipated that whereas manipulation had characterized bipartisanship under Dulles and Eisenhower, authentic cooperation would be the watchword under Rogers and Nixon. Nixon's consultation with him before naming a secretary of state pleased the chairman immensely. "A Sweet J. W. Fulbright," proclaimed Rowland Evans and Robert Novak in their biweekly column.[1]

Four days before Richard Nixon was inaugurated, the Senate bade farewell to Lyndon Johnson. Room S-207 was packed with senators and their staffs when the president, Lady Bird, Lucy, and Linda arrived. Johnson charged into the crowd with his accustomed enthusiasm. Encountering Frank Valeo, longtime secretary of the Senate and companion to Johnson on his 1961 trip to Vietnam, the president grabbed the much smaller man by the lapels, pulled him up to face level and said with vehement sincerity, "I want to take another trip with you!"[2] Fulbright came to the Johnson send-off, but he and his for-

1 Rowland Evans and Robert Novak, "A Sweet J. W. Fulbright," *New York Times*, Jan. 28, 1969.

2 Interview with Frank Valeo, Oct. 2, 1991, Washington, D.C.

mer adversary never spoke. Although Johnson had kept Fulbright posted on developments in Paris throughout January, the two men were too angry and too wary of each other for a true reconciliation.[3]

Inauguration Day dawned gray and ugly. The mood in Washington was as nasty as the weather. The only happy person in the entire city, columnist Russell Baker wrote, was Lady Bird Johnson. Baker overheard a black man and a white man exchange racial epithets as the crowd pressed them together. Even worse were the antiwar demonstrators. All along Pennsylvania Avenue they burned the small American flags distributed by the Boy Scouts and shouted "Ho, Ho, Ho Chi Minh, the NLF is going to win."[4] This was the first disruption of an inaugural parade or ceremony in the 180 years of the American presidency; not even at Lincoln's first, in 1861, had anything like it occurred. When the Nixons' limousine reached 13th Street, demonstrators cursed the couple and deluged their car with sticks, stones, beer cans, and bottles. By 15th Street, the motorcade had left the demonstrators behind, and the inauguration proceeded peacefully.

Bill and Betty attended the swearing-in ceremonies, sitting in Governor Winthrop Rockefeller's box. When they got to their seats whom should they see sitting in the Arkansas section but anti-Fulbrighter H. L. Hunt. Rockefeller, who was also just arriving, spotted Hunt at the same time. With Fulbright in tow, grinning and clapping, Rockefeller escorted the oilman from the box. The governor was not just being courteous to his junior senator; Hunt had on several occasions called Rockefeller a fellow-traveler.[5] It was the high point of an otherwise somber day for the Fulbrights.

Carl Marcy, Pat Holt, and the rest of the SFRC staff believed that the election and popular disenchantment with the war in Vietnam offered a rare opportunity for the Senate to reassert its prerogatives in the area of foreign policy. Indeed, Holt took great pains to point out to his superiors that one of the reasons Nixon was president was that the committee had insisted on playing its constitutional role in the creation of foreign policy.[6] The new administration would be staffed by novices, Marcy insisted, and he urged Fulbright to join with Mansfield and Aiken to form a Senate foreign policy council. This troika would "endorse, reshape, substitute, or reject Administration proposals," and

3 Mansfield and Dirksen to JWF, Jan. 16, 1969, Series 48:18, Box 56:7, SPF.

4 Quoted in Stephen E. Ambrose, *Nixon,* vol. II, *The Triumph of a Politician, 1962–1972* (New York, 1989), 245.

5 "H. L. Hunt Unseated, WR Recalls," *Arkansas Gazette,* Apr. 8, 1969.

6 Marcy to JWF, Jan. 8, 1969, Box 8, Folder Jan.–Mar., Marcy Papers.

its meetings would be far more important than pro-forma consultations with the secretary of state or the president.[7] The staff looked forward to a good grilling of Rogers and even urged Fulbright to demand the right in behalf of the SFRC to approve Secretary of Defense–designate Melvin Laird's nomination.[8] To Marcy's intense disappointment, however, Fulbright indicated that he intended to give the new administration every benefit of the doubt. Indeed, for the first time in history, the SFRC did not hold open confirmation hearings for an incoming secretary of state. "Rogers will never be impeached," he implored Fulbright. "The only chance the Senate has to examine him from a position of power is now";[9] but Fulbright was unmoved. Emerging from the closed hearing, the chairman pronounced Rogers "a broad-gauged man, not doctrinaire and capable of adjusting to change."[10] As it turned out, Rogers' confirmation hearing – indeed, his appointment – was largely irrelevant.

Richard Nixon nominated William Rogers to be secretary of state because he was convinced the New York lawyer would "make the little boys in the State Department" behave and because he knew next to nothing about foreign policy.[11] He was the perfect choice for a president who intended to run foreign affairs out of the White House. Typically, Henry Kissinger, Nixon's national security adviser, was both jealous and contemptuous of Rogers. He went out of his way to see that the State Department was kept in the dark during major negotiations. During both the Vietnam peace talks in Paris and the strategic arms limitations discussions in Vienna, Kissinger ordered negotiators to communicate directly with him through top-secret, "backchannel" networks. Rogers complained to Nixon, and the president promised to correct the problem, but he never did. Nixon knew about the rivalry and rather enjoyed it.[12]

Although a novice at bureaucratic infighting and power consolidation, Henry Kissinger proved superb at it. The offices of national security adviser to the president and executive director of the National Security Council remained separate in name but not in fact. As national security adviser, Kissinger enjoyed direct, primary access to the president, but he also chaired every NSC committee meeting, approving or disapproving its recommendations. In short, under Nixon the foreign-policymaking process was centered in the NSC rather than in the State Department, and Kissinger completely dominated the

7 Marcy to JWF, Nov. 26, 1968, Box 8, Oct.–Dec., Marcy Papers.

8 Marcy to JWF, Dec. 30, 1968, Box 8, Folder Oct.–Dec., Marcy Papers.

9 Marcy to JWF, Jan. 8, 1969, Box 8, Folder Jan.–Mar., Marcy Papers.

10 Chalmers M. Roberts, "Fulbright Closed Hearings So Rogers Could Talk Policy," *Washington Post,* Jan. 13, 1969.

11 Quoted in Ambrose, *Nixon,* vol. II, 234.

12 Quoted in Seymour M. Hersh, *The Price of Power: Kissinger in the Nixon White House* (New York, 1983), 103.

council.[13] The professor and the politician were well pleased with the setup. It would allow them, they believed, to bypass not only Foggy Bottom, but Congress as well.

Richard Nixon wanted to end the war in Vietnam, but prompted by the Joint Chiefs of Staff and his new military adviser, General Andrew Goodpaster, the president came to believe that he could do so by winning rather than losing. A week following his election Nixon met with General Creighton Abrams, Goodpaster, and the JCS. Despite Thieu's resentment over the Paris peace talks, there had been no "breach between the United States and South Vietnam militarily," the men in uniform reported. Moreover, the North Vietnamese were on the run. In 1967, having fought an unsuccessful guerrilla war, the communists had decided to change tactics; the result had been Tet, a disaster for the VC. This had been followed by NVA offensives in May and August 1968; both had been turned back, and in the process B-52s had pulverized enemy troop concentrations. The North Vietnamese had withdrawn forty thousand troops from the south and were in Paris because they had reached a dead end militarily.[14] If Goodpaster and the JCS were correct, the war was virtually won on the battlefield. America could afford to be tough and drive a hard bargain at the negotiating table.

Kissinger was much less sanguine about the military and particularly the political situation in Vietnam. The president was going to move toward a negotiated settlement and withdrawal, he told Averell Harriman nine days after the inauguration. Goodpaster was pushing Nixon to win the war in the next few months, but the president, he was sure, would act realistically.[15] As events would demonstrate, Kissinger was overestimating either Nixon's realism or his own influence with the new president.

There was no more willing congressional bride in the Nixon administration's honeymoon than J. William Fulbright. Calls for an immediate withdrawal of troops were premature, he told reporters: "I think we ought to give the people in Paris an opportunity to negotiate without making a serious change in the status quo," he informed *U.S. News and World Report.*[16] Indeed, later that month Fulbright got up at 5 A.M. to go to the airport to see Nixon off on his first overseas trip as president. At the same time he let it be known that his

13 William Shawcross, *Sideshow: Kissinger, Nixon and the Destruction of Cambodia* (New York, 1979), 80–1.

14 Notes of Presidential Meeting with President-elect Nixon, Nov. 11, 1968, Tom Johnson Meeting Notes, Box 3, Johnson Papers.

15 Memorandum of conversation with Henry Kissinger, Jan. 29, 1969, Box 481, Harriman Papers, LC. See also Haldeman Notes, Box 40, Papers of H. R. Haldeman, WHSpF, Richard M. Nixon Presidential Papers Project, National Archives, Arlington, Va.

16 "What U.S. Should Do about Vietnam: Survey of Key Senators," *U.S. News and World Report,* Feb. 10, 1969, 29–32.

tacit support stemmed from his belief that Nixon and Kissinger were committed to ending the war.

The same day he publicly bade farewell to the president, the chairman dropped by the George Washington University gymnasium to have his picture taken with an intramural basketball team named the "Fulbrights." They were all doves, captain Mark Plotkin told Bill and Betty. Indeed, the reason the team only had six members was that they had been carefully selected for ideological purity. "The Arrogance of Power" was printed on the backs of the team's jerseys.[17] Fulbright assured the college students that while he was willing to give the new administration time to end the war, neither his nor the nation's patience was infinite.

Some three weeks later, the chairman drove to the opposite end of Pennsylvania Avenue for a meeting with the president, Rogers, and Kissinger. In an effort to calm Fulbright and forestall a congressional uprising over Vietnam, Nixon had asked the chairman to come by and state his views. As usual, Fulbright was brutally frank. If the president did not liquidate the war by the midpoint of his first term, he warned, the administration "will be on an irreversible path toward repudiation."[18] Above all, he pleaded, do not escalate the conflict in Vietnam. There was no need to take any military action beyond that necessary to defend American troops already in country.[19] The president received Fulbright cordially, and Kissinger poured on the charm. For an hour and a half the two assured their guest that they would move quickly to end the war and would not repeat Lyndon Johnson's mistakes. "Just give us a year," Fulbright remembered them saying. The chairman wished them well, but he reminded Nixon that public confidence in the presidency, in the military, and in the complex of rationales for Vietnam was rapidly disintegrating.[20]

After Fulbright returned to his office. Lee Williams came in with a message from Dan Blackburn of Metromedia News. Instead of winding down the war, Blackburn confided, the Nixon administration had taken the offensive in Vietnam. Following his inauguration, the president had ordered General Abrams to intensify bombing activity above and below the Seventeenth Parallel and to apply full military pressure on the ground as well. In addition, Blackburn reported, rumor had it that the U.S. command in Saigon, in secret agreement with Prince Norodom Sihanouk, was planning to attack six North Vietnamese bases in Cambodia.[21] In fact, the bombing attacks on Cambodia

17 Phil Casey and Mary Wiegers, "Sen. Fulbright's Basketball Team," *Washington Post,* Feb. 24, 1969.

18 Marcy to JWF, Mar. 20, 1969, Box 8, Jan.–Mar., Marcy Papers.

19 William C. Berman, *William Fulbright and the Vietnam War: The Dissent of a Political Realist* (Kent, Ohio, 1988), 108.

20 Interview with J. William Fulbright, Oct. 11–18, 1988, Washington, D.C., and Berman, *Fulbright and the Vietnam War,* 107.

21 Lee Williams to JWF, Mar. 21, 1969, Series 48:17, Box 46:1, SPF.

had begun on March 18, 1969, three days before Fulbright's meeting in the Oval Office.

Nixon and Kissinger's strategy was to couple great-power diplomacy with force in an effort to win an "honorable" peace at the Paris negotiations. The president believed that military pressure had thus far failed because it had been applied in a limited and indecisive way. Encouraged by Goodpaster and the JCS, the president was prepared to threaten the very survival of North Vietnam in order to break the enemy's will. Analogizing between his situation and that faced by Eisenhower in Korea in 1953, Nixon believed that the threat of annihilation could be used just as effectively against Hanoi as it had against Pyongyang. His image as a hard-line anticommunist would make his warnings credible. "They'll believe any threat of force Nixon makes because it's Nixon," he told White House Chief of Staff H. R. Haldeman. "We'll just slip the word to them that, 'for God's sake, you know Nixon's obsessed about Communism . . . and he has his hand on the nuclear button.'"[22]

In March the president sent a personal message to Ho Chi Minh expressing his firm desire for peace and proposing as a first step the mutual withdrawal of American and North Vietnamese troops from South Vietnam and the restoration of the demilitarized zone as a temporary political boundary. He did not even wait for an answer. For years the JCS had urged Johnson to bomb communist supply routes and staging areas in Cambodia, but to no avail. Nixon gave the go-ahead, but insisted that the bombing be kept secret from Congress, the American people, and even his own administration. Under operation MENU, 3,360 B-52 raids were flown over Cambodia, dropping more than a hundred thousand tons of bombs. The stated military objective of the aerial assault was to limit North Vietnam's capacity to launch an offensive against the south, but Nixon's primary motive was to indicate that he was prepared to take measures that Johnson had avoided, thus frightening Hanoi into negotiating on his terms. The raids killed an untold number of civilians and accelerated the tragic destabilization of Cambodia. The North Vietnamese simply moved deeper into the Cambodian jungles.[23]

At a symposium on the military budget and national priorities, held on Capitol Hill the morning after his meeting with the president, Fulbright appeared depressed. He was pessimistic about the war, he remarked to several of those present. Because the administration was bent on achieving an "honorable" peace, the present lull in Vietnam was probably "the calm before the storm."[24] He said nothing about the impending assault on Cambodia of which Dan Blackburn had warned. He knew that the administration was full of unscrupulous demagogues who would not hesitate to charge him with treason

22 Quoted in George C. Herring, *America's Longest War: The United States and Vietnam, 1950–1975,* 2d ed. (New York, 1986), 225.

23 Shawcross, *Sideshow,* 25–36, 90–3.

24 Quoted in Berman, *Fulbright and the Vietnam War,* 108.

for discussing military operations then underway. Moreover, he had no hard evidence to prove that the bombing had taken place, and would not until the famous Moose–Lowenstein mission to Phnom Penh.

Fulbright well understood that it would be difficult for Nixon and Kissinger to withdraw from Southeast Asia – more difficult, perhaps than it would have been for Lyndon Johnson. It was true that the long, protracted struggle and the antiwar movement had eroded support for the war even among hawks, but there were powerful forces at work with a vested interest in continuing the conflict indefinitely. The military–industrial complex of which Dwight Eisenhower had warned was larger and more formidable than ever. Indeed, in the chairman's view, Robert McNamara had created an $80-billion-a-year monster that would be difficult for Nixon and Kissinger to control even if they were so inclined. Finally, of course, there were the increasingly frustrated and alienated blue-collar workers to whom George Wallace had appealed and for whom Nixon had had to compete. It was upon militarism, however, and specifically the military's growing influence on diplomacy, that Fulbright chose to focus.

The Arkansan's perception of the American officer corps was of an undereducated, isolated, overly professionalized body of men dedicated to creating a mission for themselves. Regular military officers "are a strong breed," his longtime friend John Bell, then chief political officer at McDill Air Force Base, advised him. They divided civilians into two groups: those "'for us'" and those "'against us.'" They were generally ignorant of foreign cultures and, for that matter, of American society. The country and the world consisted not of cities but of bases and PXs that the officers and their families rarely left. The key word to the modern military was "requirement": Once a requirement was established, it was seldom if ever reviewed; the test then became whether there was a "shortfall" in meeting the requirement. The concept included everything from chapels to wars.[25]

In February 1969 Fulbright learned that members of the officer corps were once again taking part in "national security seminars" conducted under the auspices of the Industrial College of the Armed Forces, an interservice institution responsible directly to the JCS. The 1969 edition of the seminars emphasized not the threat of communist infiltration of American institutions, but the need for the United States to continue to police the international community. "We must take over the guard all around the world, in order to fill the power vacuum left by the withdrawal of the British and other Western powers who no longer have the capacity," declared one beribboned conference

25 Memorandum for the File, Military and Foreign Policy, Jan. 9, 1969, Box 8, Jan.–Mar., Marcy Papers.

leader. "Our policy . . . is to contain Chinese imperialism – or communism – or whatever," proclaimed another. "To do this, we have to stay put as long as necessary to provide a balance of power in Asia."[26]

Predictably, Fulbright mounted the stump to warn his countrymen of the menace posed by the new militarism. Violence had become the country's leading industry, he declared repeatedly during the spring of 1969. "We are now spending about $80 billion a year on the military, which is more than the profits of all American business,"[27] he told an audience at Denison University. Militarism permeated every aspect of the national life:

> Millions of Americans have acquired a vested interest in the expensive weapons systems, which provide their livelihood and indirectly, therefore, a foreign policy that has plunged the United States into a spiraling arms race with the Soviet Union, made us the world's major salesman of armaments, and committed us to the defense of freedom – very loosely defined – in almost 50 countries.[28]

But more than rhetoric was necessary. If the public was not educated and the Pentagon cut down to size, the chairman had become convinced, America would be plunged into one Vietnam after another and be bankrupted in the process.

On February 3 Fulbright announced that the SFRC was creating an Ad Hoc Subcommittee on United States Security Agreements and Commitments Abroad. Stuart Symington would chair the panel, which would include Fulbright, Sparkman, Aiken, Cooper, Mansfield, and Jacob Javits. Fulbright noted that under existing treaties the United States could possibly be committed to using its armed forces in forty-two countries. The United States provided military aid to forty-eight countries, and 32 percent of all Americans under arms were stationed outside the continental United States, most of them in an elaborate network of overseas bases. The tendency of the military to fill a void and create a mission for itself, coupled with congressional delegation of authority to the executive, had created a system in which the United States was pledged to defend other nations without the public's knowledge or permission. Following lengthy and thorough investigations, Fulbright told reporters, the Symington subcommittee would identify these commitments. The unspoken goal of the panel was to get the military out of the foreign-policymaking business and to compel the executive once again to seek congressional approval for the diplomatic commitments that it made. Because Vietnam raised a number of "complicated and unique questions," it would be excluded from subcommittee scrutiny, Fulbright declared.[29]

26 "Fulbright Chokes on the Military's Rhetoric," *Baltimore Sun,* Feb. 22, 1969.
27 "Fulbright: Top Industry Is 'Violence,'" *Arkansas Gazette,* Apr. 20, 1969.
28 Ibid.
29 Fulbright press release, Feb. 3, 1969, Series 48:3, Box 17:1, SPF.

Symington's appointment was a stroke of genius. A former secretary of the air force, he had been one of the Senate's leading hawks on Vietnam until Fulbright had turned him. As a member of both the Armed Services and CIA oversight committees, the Missourian retained close ties with Senate conservatives and the Pentagon. No soft-headed peacenik, Symington could investigate the military with some credibility.

The day following the creation of the Symington subcommittee, Fulbright reintroduced the national commitments resolution. Promising his colleagues that the congressional statement of purpose he proposed would not affect current military involvement in Vietnam, the chairman insisted that the resolution would redress a constitutional imbalance that was the product more of natural forces than a conspiracy by would-be dictators. Napoleon long ago observed that "the tools belong to the man that can use them," he told the Senate. No executive could be expected to limit its freedom of action voluntarily; Congress would have to assert itself.[30]

The formation of the Symington subcommittee and the reintroduction of the national commitments resolution frightened and angered Richard Nixon. He, Haldeman, John Ehrlichman, Patrick Buchanan, and the other ad-agency types and ultraconservatives that comprised the bulk of the White House staff detested Fulbright. Despite his segregationist record and conservative stance on many socioeconomic issues, they regarded him as a would-be intellectual and a tool of the "eastern establishment press." His relentless advocacy of the United Nations, his opposition to the war in Vietnam, and his sharp criticism of aspects of American culture marked him out in their minds as a "liberal." Nixon recalled the Arkansan's opposition to McCarthyism and his partisan attacks on the missile gap in 1959 and 1960. Philosophically and politically he qualified for a top spot on the president's rapidly expanding list of personae non grata. Typically, Nixon saw the effort to rein in the military and limit the executive's ability to commit the United States to support other countries as a personal attack. Kissinger, who was infuriated at any effort to interfere with his freedom of action, raged against the Symington subcommittee and the national commitments resolution.[31] He was barely willing to brook opposition from the president of the United States, much less from a committee of Congress and its Arkansas chairman. Remembering that Fulbright had led the fight against the Bricker amendment, Nixon put out the word to his underlings to label the national commitments resolution as nothing more or less than a reincarnation of that anachronistic and isolationist document.[32]

30 *Congressional Record,* Senate, Feb. 4, 1969.
31 Interviews with James Lowenstein, Oct. 3, 1991, and Richard Moose, June 29, 1989, Washington, D.C.
32 Nixon notation, Apr. 1969, WHSpF, President's Office File, Pres. Handwriting, Box 1, Nixon Project.

With the globalization of the Truman and Eisenhower doctrines, the Pentagon had in fact blanketed the world with a maze of bases and promises. In the feverish days of the early cold war, the air force had scrambled to acquire facilities for the medium-range B-47 bomber, which had insufficient range to reach potential targets in the Soviet Union from airfields on American territory; but as Fulbright rightly suspected, over time the 429 bases that had been built overseas existed as much to ensure political stability in the host country as to deter the Soviet Union.[33] Fulbright and the SFRC staff were vaguely aware of the presence of American troops in Laos, Thailand, and perhaps Cambodia in connection with the Vietnam War. They also knew that the military had signed hundreds of agreements with governments in Latin America, Europe, Asia, and the Near East to cooperate in resisting communism; but the exact number and scope of those agreements were carefully guarded state secrets.

The task of the Symington subcommittee was to pull away that shroud of secrecy and define precisely the extent of existing commitments, while the goal of the national commitments resolution was to ensure that in the future Congress and the American people would be "in on the takeoff," to use Arthur Vandenberg's phrase, as well as the landing. Given Nixon and Kissinger's determination to control policy and the ongoing hysteria generated by the Vietnam War, Fulbright and Symington had set formidable tasks for themselves.

In late February, Marcy named Walter Pincus and Roland Paul to be the chief investigators for the Symington subcommittee. Pincus was the tough-minded, resourceful reporter who had uncovered the Trujillo–Kennedy–sugar quota scandal. Paul was a Washington lawyer with a reputation for thoroughness and combativeness. It was obvious that two men could not cover the waterfront; as a result, Fulbright, Symington, and Marcy decided that the investigators would concentrate on Europe and Asia, exclusive of Vietnam, and look for "targets of opportunity."[34] The first target that presented itself was Spain, and it was a juicy one.

In late February stories began to appear in the national press that the Pentagon was about to conclude a multi-million-dollar bases deal with the government of aged dictator General Francisco Franco. The SFRC staff had learned not only that the administration was keeping the bases agreement secret from Congress, but also that the Pentagon – specifically, Earle Wheeler

[33] "Rival to the State Department?" *Chicago Daily News,* May 9, 1969.

[34] Background and Suggestions for Organization of Ad Hoc Subcommittee on U.S. Security Agreements and Commitments Abroad, Feb. 24, 1969, Box 8, Jan.–Mar., Marcy Papers.

and a two-star general named David A. Burchinal, deputy to the Supreme Commander of NATO – rather than the State Department was negotiating terms. Fulbright called the Capitol Hill press corps together and told them he had serious questions as to whether or not the bases were strategically necessary and, if they were, why the United States should have to pay for the privilege of building and operating them.[35] What he suspected but did not say was that in "cooperating" with the Franco government, the American military had made a de facto commitment to defend that autocratic regime against enemies both external and internal.

The decision to send Pincus and Paul abroad by themselves was a break with precedent. Aside from Pincus's foray into the Dominican Republic, SFRC staffers had never before ventured overseas without a member. Free-lancing by the staff offended prima donnas on the committee, and both Marcy and Fulbright knew that such forays would revive memories of the notorious Cohn–Schine trips of intimidation during the McCarthy period. Nevertheless, a majority of the SFRC was convinced that if Congress and the public were not to be involved in an endless series of Vietnams by the national security state, it would have to initiate its own intelligence-gathering effort.

Before they left, Pincus and Paul sent a list of questions that the SFRC wanted answered to the U.S. embassy in Madrid and the military command at Torrejon, the huge military base outside Madrid. What was the American military's mission in Spain? What, in addition to money, had the officers who were negotiating the bases deal promised Franco? Were there joint military exercises and, if so, what were the objectives of those exercises?

Over coffee at the elegant officers' club at Torrejon, Pincus and Paul were told their schedule. That morning they would go with the base commander and watch him exercise his hunting falcons. After lunch they would get a sight-seeing tour. The two were free for dinner, but the base had secured theater tickets for the whole party later in the evening.

"Let me see the base phone book," Pincus said.

"What?" his handlers asked.

"The base phone book," he repeated.

As Pincus already knew, although the military command in Spain had gone to great lengths to conceal its mission and to shield certain operational facilities from the public, all units, classified and unclassified, were listed in the base phone book. He had no intention of spending the morning with Torrejon's commander – "an arrogant son-of-a-bitch" – and his falcons. Pincus tore up the schedule he had received. He and his partner would visit every classified unit on the base, alone, from eight in the morning to nine at night

35 "Rival to the State Department?" *Chicago Daily News,* May 9, 1969, and "Fulbright Panel Opens Probe on Spanish Bases," *Arkansas Gazette,* Apr. 3, 1969.

for as many days as it took, he declared. The receiving party immediately caved in. Assuming that Pincus and Paul would never have been admitted to a top-secret facility if they did not have top-secret clearance, the airmen and specialists at the various communications and missile sites were completely candid.[36]

The two SFRC investigators learned first that the mission of the Torrejon base was to provide forward support for a fighter-bomber squadron stationed in Turkey, whose mission was to rain atomic missiles on the Georgian and Ukrainian Soviet Socialist Republics in case of war with the Soviet Union. Were there atomic warheads stored in Spain, they asked? Sure, the airmen replied.

The precise locations of U.S. nuclear weapons were among America's most closely guarded state secrets. Although Torrejon had frequently been the target of Spanish antinuclear activists, the Nixon administration had staunchly denied that any warheads were stationed on the Iberian peninsula. The American ambassador did not even know of their existence.

The congressional snoops also discovered why the Spanish authorities, if not the Spanish public, were so supportive of the huge American presence. There were the loans and direct payments Madrid received from the United States; but, in addition, Torrejon boasted one of the largest PXs in the world. It was open not only to base personnel and embassy staff, but to high-ranking Spanish officers as well.

After they had finished with Torrejon, the SFRC investigators visited Meron, a limited-manned base outside Seville. Meron was run by a skeleton crew and, as Pincus soon discovered, was used primarily for joint Spanish–American military exercises once a year. He also learned that the scenario for these exercises was a domestic insurrection in which the American military intervened to save the Spanish government – the regime headed by Francisco Franco, onetime intimate of Adolf Hitler, brutal autocrat, cofounder of the fascist and anti-Semitic Falangist party! It was the Spanish Civil War with the United States intervening on the side of the fascists, and Washington was willing to pay $175 million for the privilege.[37]

Upon their return to the United States Pincus and Paul immediately huddled with Fulbright and Marcy. They would have to be careful; release of classified information could lead to charges of treason. It was decided that Marcy would use his excellent contacts with the press to leak word of the Spanish bases' nuclear mission. Meanwhile, the Symington subcommittee would hold hearings in which it would be revealed that the Pentagon had made a commitment to defend the Franco government from external aggression and internal subversion not only without congressional approval, but without public knowledge.

36 Interview with Walter Pincus, Mar. 11, 1990, Washington, D.C.

37 Ibid.

In early April Symington and his colleagues issued their report, citing the Spanish bases arrangement as a classic example of executive usurpation of congressional authority in foreign affairs. During the current negotiations, Symington told the press while handing out copies of the report, JCS Chief Wheeler had assured the Spanish in writing that the presence of American armed forces in Spain "constitutes a more significant security guarantee to Spain" than would a written agreement.[38]

Nixon, Kissinger, the Pentagon, and the Spanish were infuriated. The Spanish ambassador, the Marquis de Merry bel Val, flatly denied that his government would ever ask American troops to fight against Spaniards and demanded that the chairman apologize.[39] In late April Fulbright officially asked the administration to suspend negotiations on the Spanish bases agreement unless and until Congress was fully consulted.[40] Although neither Nixon, Rogers, nor Laird even bothered to reply, the Symington subcommittee had made an impact.

In June Washington and Madrid announced that an agreement had been signed. The United States agreed to pay Spain $50 million in military assistance with another $35 million in Export–Import Bank credits to follow. Instead of a ten-year renewal, however, the pact was limited to fifteen months. Both governments, their representatives told the press, had "serious reservations about any long-range extension."[41]

The second week in June Betty and Bill flew to Little Rock to attend the premiere of *True Grit,* a movie based on the novel by Arkansas native Charles "Buddy" Portis and starring John Wayne and Glen Campbell. Fulbright had helped bring the grand opening to Little Rock to raise money for the state Democratic Party, financially exhausted after years of trying to match Winthrop Rockefeller's deep pockets. The event combined the Old South sophistication of the Little Rock Club with the folksiness of the Grand Ole Opry. Campbell, from Delight, Arkansas, attended, and following the showing ticket holders retired to the Olde West Dinner Theater for a banquet.[42]

Back in Washington, Fulbright continued to pressure his colleagues to pass the national commitments resolution while the Symington subcommittee re-

38 The 1953 executive agreement, kept secret until this time, and under which the 1969 pact had been negotiated, provided that an attack on joint Spanish–American facilities would be viewed as a matter of "common concern" and that the Spanish had the right to use the American-built bases with or without Washington's permission. "Rival to the State Department?" *Chicago Daily News,* May 9, 1969.

39 "Fulbright Assures Spain on Row," *Baltimore Sun,* Apr. 12, 1969.

40 JWF to Rogers, Apr. 22, 1969, Box 8, Apr.–June, Marcy Papers.

41 "U.S.–Spain Renew Military Agreement," *Iowa Daily Tribune,* June 21, 1969.

42 "Showing of 'True Grit' to Bring in $30,000, Matthews Calculates," *Arkansas Gazette,* June 12, 1969.

vealed that there were fifty thousand American troops in Thailand. The presence of these soldiers, Fulbright told the Senate, "combined with Thailand's involvement in the Vietnam war, have created a de facto commitment going far beyond the SEATO treaty."[43] If Congress refused to rein in the executive and especially the Pentagon, the country would continue down the path toward "elective dictatorship," the chairman warned.

On June 26, 1969, with strong support from both liberals and conservatives, the U.S. Senate passed the national commitments resolution by a vote of 70 to 16. As amended by John Sherman Cooper, the measure defined national commitment to mean "use of the armed forces on foreign territory or a promise to assist a foreign country, government or people by the use of the armed forces or financial resources of the United States, either immediately or upon the happening of certain events." Although Vietnam was specifically excluded, the *Washington Post* declared that "throughout the debate, it was apparent it [the resolution] was the Senate's answer to the U.S. involvement in Vietnam."[44]

Fulbright did not need Lee Williams, Scotty Reston, or Walter Lippmann to tell him that a sure-fire way to discredit oneself with the American people, especially during wartime, was to appear to be antimilitary. Consequently, he scheduled a major address at the National War College – not, as one pundit put it "to go into the lion's den to beard the lion," but to try and convince the nation's officer corps and the nation that he was opposed to militarism and not to the military.

The atmosphere was electric as the nation's leading dove strode onto the stage of the huge auditorium at the National War College. His audience, composed of several hundred men who were committed to learning the art of war and sacrificing their lives for their country, greeted him with polite applause. Fulbright was a man of considerable personal courage; his voice did not quaver. "In the old Western movies," he began, "there was a standard climax in which the villain emerged from his hideout shielded behind the captive heroine and snarling: 'Shoot me and the girl dies!'" It reminded him, he said, of those officials responsible for the war in Vietnam. Everytime they were criticized, they wrapped themselves in the flag, hid behind the military, and declared, "Criticize me and the soldier dies."

The problem with contemporary American life was not the military but militarism, Fulbright declared. Every nation, he told the assembled officers, has a double identity; "it is both a power engaged in foreign relations and a society serving the interests of its citizens." In its role as arbiter of interna-

43 *Congressional Record,* Senate, June 19, 1969, 16617.
44 Warren Unna, "Senate Votes to Reassert Policy Role," *Washington Post,* June 26, 1969.

tional affairs the nation drew upon but did not replenish the people's economic, political, and moral resources. For three decades the United States had been preoccupied with its role as the world's greatest power "to the neglect of its societal responsibilities, and at incalculable cost to our national security." The 10-to-1 imbalance in military versus nonmilitary expenditures had undermined the nation's systems of education, welfare, health, and housing. The emergence of the national security state and the placing of the nation on what amounted to a permanent war footing had tipped the balance within the federal government dangerously in favor of the executive. The moral cost was reflected in the angry alienation of the nation's youth. "The 'dog of war,' which Jefferson thought had been tightly leashed to the legislature, has now passed under the virtually exclusive control of the executive," he warned.

When it came to the role that the military had played in this mounting tragedy, Fulbright did not mince words.

> Bringing to bear a degree of discipline, unanimity and strength of conviction seldom found among civilian officials, the able and energetic men who fill the top ranks of the armed services have acquired an influence disproportionate to their numbers on the nation's security policy. The Department of Defense itself has become a vigorous partisan in our politics, exerting great influence on the President, on the military committees of Congress, on the "think tanks" and universities to which it parcels out lucrative research contracts, and on public opinion.[45]

But there was a historic mistrust of power among the American people and "like a human body reacting against a transplanted organ, our body politic is reacting against the alien values which, in the name of security, have been grafted upon it."[46]

Perhaps stunned by Fulbright's audacity, the student body of the National War College responded with the same polite applause with which they had greeted him. Others were not so civil. His face working with emotion, Howard K. Smith, coanchor with Frank Reynolds on the *ABC Evening News,* accused Fulbright of inexcusable inconsistency. He had first promoted then denounced the Gulf of Tonkin Resolution. Having rejected his own offspring, the Arkansan had then proved incapable of summoning up the courage to work for its repeal. This southern conservative who had repeatedly voted against raises in the minimum wage dared fault the executive for neglecting social welfare programs. How could he talk about the well-being of underdeveloped peoples when he had consistently fought civil rights legislation? Most viewers were not surprised at the hawkishness of Smith's edito-

45 *Congressional Record,* Senate, May 20, 1969, 13056.
46 Ibid.

rial, only its bitterness. Few knew that his son had been grievously maimed in Vietnam.[47]

Generally, however, Fulbright's attack on the military–industrial complex struck a responsive chord in academia and the national media. Richard Harwood and Laurence Stern devoted two pages in the *Washington Post* to a description and analysis of the Pentagon and the defense industries that were dependent upon it. Former members of the Kennedy administration Richard Goodwin and John Kenneth Galbraith stepped forward to accuse Robert McNamara of having created a military–industrial complex that was threatening the nation's economic health, subverting its political institutions, and perverting its values.[48]

The first week in June, Nixon delivered a hard-hitting speech defending the military in all its various roles and blasting Fulbright and his supporters as neoisolationists. Speaking at the Air Force Academy, he declared that the current debate, centering as it did on America's proper place in the world, was of immense importance. One school of thought favored "a downgrading of our alliances and what amounts to a unilateral reduction of our arms." According to Nixon, this "isolationist" worldview was based on the absurd belief that "the United States is as much responsible for the tensions as the adversaries we face." He would, he said, no more sanction a global American retreat than he would countenance a recommendation for "unilateral disarmament."[49]

The Nixon speech hit a Fulbright nerve. The president was, the Arkansan declared, engaging in "a form of demagoguery that was very fashionable in the time of his old colleague, Joe McCarthy."[50] He saw in the smoke of the president's fusillade the apparition of the old "America right-or-wrong attitude" that had been used to justify a generation of overinvolvement and to discredit those who dared criticize Pax Americana. It was the term "neoisolationist" that rankled Fulbright, Marcy, Seth Tillman, and Lee Williams; but despite their denials and the fact that Nixon's motives were less than pure, by mid-1969 in many respects the label was apropos.

At times Fulbright's critique of American foreign policy seemed to parallel that of the New Left, but there were many more differences than similarities. Although radical historians like Gabriel Kolko and Eugene Genovese, as well as I. F. Stone and other left-wing columnists, admired the Arkansan's stand on the war and frequently quoted him, they never considered him one of their own. Given his segregationist voting record, his republicanism and elitism,

47 Reuben Thomas, "Howard K. Smith on Fulbright," *Arkansas Gazette,* May 28, 1969.

48 Tom Huston, "The McNamara Legacy," June 16, 1969, WHSpF, Box 2, Nixon Project.

49 Quoted in Berman, *Fulbright and the Vietnam War,* 111.

50 William F. Buckley, "On Tormenting Senator Fulbright," *Pine Bluff Commercial,* June 10, 1969.

and his personal revulsion at the burgeoning counterculture, how could they? He was a southerner, a conservative, and a champion of the Senate's undemocratic seniority system. Stone, who frequently hailed Fulbright in his weekly *Newsletter,* had no illusions. "He is not a liberal at all," he once remarked. "This is the landed civilized gentleman type . . . foreign to the American egalitarian tradition."[51] Yet, at the same time they regarded Fulbright as perhaps the most important critic of the system they were themselves indicting.

By 1969 Fulbright was referring to America as "sick," not because of its materialism, which had been his focus in the 1950s, but because of the alienation of its youth and neglect of compelling social problems. Fulbright did not believe in "participatory democracy"; he remained committed to the vision of America as a meritocracy based on education and equality of opportunity. During the 1960s he had been persuaded of the notion that inequality was the product of socioeconomic disadvantages and that the government had a responsibility to create conditions in which learning and achievement could take place. Thus did he throw his support behind the War on Poverty. He never endorsed the principle of equality of condition, however, and he remained wedded to the free-enterprise system. Fulbright had come to share the New Left's distrust and fear of the military–industrial complex, but he did not buy the idea of a pervasive corporate elite that was inherently immoral and exploitative. There were vast differences in interest, intent, and public-spiritedness in the American corporate structure. It was absurd to link the personalities and policies of General Dynamics and DuPont on the one hand and General Mills and Upjohn on the other. Fulbright's indictment was of the defense industry and the degree to which it was dominating the foreign policy and politics of the country.

Fulbright was more than ready publicly to repudiate liberal internationalism and the globalist foreign policy to which it had led; but like Gerald P. Nye, the famous isolationist of the Roosevelt era with whom he struck up a brief correspondence in 1969, Fulbright preferred the term "noninterventionist" to "isolationist."[52] Fulbright read and placed in the *Congressional Record* a defense of isolationism by a young revisionist historian named Thomas G. Paterson. In his article Paterson noted that throughout most of American history the term "isolationism" had hardly been one of reproach. The two-spheres idea was rooted in Washington's Farewell Address, Jefferson's first inaugural address, the Monroe Doctrine, and dozens of other hallowed documents in American history.[53]

51 I. F. Stone, "An American Anthony Eden," *New York Review,* Dec. 29, 1966; reprinted in idem, *In a Time of Torment, 1961–1967* (New York, 1967), quote on p. 328.

52 Nye to Robert E. Jakoubek, Aug. 22, 1969, and JWF to Gerald P. Nye, Sept. 11, 1969, Series 48:1, Box 9:4, SPF.

53 *Congressional Record,* Senate, Sept. 12, 1969.

Echoing anti-imperialists from George Washington to Abraham Lincoln to Charles Beard, Fulbright called upon America to retreat within itself and work to perfect its own institutions and social system, and thus to become a beacon to the rest of the world. In early June 1969, in the midst of his indictment of the military–industrial complex, Fulbright exhorted the foreign policy establishment to abandon its effort to create a "Pax Americana – the imposition of peace by a force of arms paid for by the American taxpayer," and instead make the United States a "humanistic example" to the rest of the world.[54]

Fulbright was uncomfortable with the notion that the war was immoral, although he did not hesitate to so label it, and instead periodically concentrated on the notion that Vietnam and American foreign policy in general were the products of flaws in the human psyche, flaws that were subject to being identified and controlled by modern social science. In mid-March Fulbright convened a group of sociologists, anthropologists, and psychiatrists in the SFRC conference room. He listened to Lionel Tiger of Rutgers declare that war was not a human problem, but a male problem: Unable to bond, modern males turned to more adolescent pursuits, of which war was one. He and Edward O. Wilson, a Harvard zoologist, described fantasies of aggression that people develop when their leaders insist they should adhere to policies over which they had no control.[55] Then in June, the Arkansan had the renowned psychiatrist Karl Menninger testify before the SFRC in open session. Vietnam was, he proclaimed, "a destructive, futile, pointless military bonfire which has created haunting anxiety and depression that is near to despair."[56] "I think a psychological interpretation of many of our historical experiences . . . can be more persuasive with my colleagues in the Congress and the people than a poorly informed politician," he wrote Louis Halle who had warned him that social scientists and academics possessed no magic formula to avoid war.[57]

Betty Fulbright never fully recovered from the heart attack she had suffered in 1967, and her diabetes continued its corrosive work, but by 1969 she was able to resume many of the old routines and friendships. She began having her hair done again once a week at Elizabeth Arden's, and she nearly always felt well enough to dress for dinner. The Fulbrights dined simply, their housekeeper Emmy Eichler recalled: cereal for breakfast and steak and eggs for Sunday brunch. Bill still got home around seven-thirty from the Senate.

54 "Fulbright: Halt 'Absurd' Arms Race," *Chicago Daily News,* June 4, 1969.
55 "Fulbright and the Scholars," *Washington Evening Star,* May 16, 1969.
56 Ed Johnson, "Fulbright Panel 'Psychoanalyzes' Foreign Policy," *Arkansas Gazette,* June 20, 1969.
57 JWF to Louis J. Halle, July 22, 1969, Series 48:18, Box 56:6, SPF.

The two would have a drink in the living room and talk over the day's events. They dined on chicken or fish, potato, and a vegetable – by candlelight in the dining room, of course. "After dinner they went up to the library," Eichler recalled. "They watched t.v. and read. He liked westerns like *Bonanza.*"[58]

Betty spent her days visiting the International House, meeting friends for lunch, and watching soap operas like *General Hospital* and *One Life to Live.* Unlike Bill, Betty was a night person. Eichler recalled that when they got home around twelve from a reception at the Egyptian or Japanese embassy, the senator would go to bed, but Betty would stay up until two or three in the morning writing letters. When Eichler was in Europe for two weeks visiting relatives, she received four eight-page letters from her employer. Most of Betty's correspondence comprised gushy, June Cleaver–type missives. "What mind-readers you are to know how much I love yellow tulips," she wrote Judy Baumgartner, Bosey's mother-in-law.[59] Her letters inevitably focused on problems involving domestic servants, arrangements for the next vacation, or descriptions of social events. What is striking about the many she wrote to her daughter's in-laws was her effusiveness concerning Tad: How happy he made Bosey, how attentive he was, how he concerned himself with the home and family, how involved he was with Julia, his and Bosey's first child. How different from her own husband.

Betty enjoyed visits from the grandchildren, who sometimes came and stayed for two weeks; Bill did not. "When the grandchildren didn't behave at the dinner table, that irritated him," Eichler recalled. She remembered her employers' marriage as being very solid.[60] Indeed, the only subject about which they really argued was the grandchildren. With the departure of Lyndon Johnson and the advent of an administration apparently committed to détente, however, Bill became almost affable with Bosey and Betsy's offspring.

The Arkansan's peace of mind was to be short-lived. The rationalist in Fulbright told him that whatever its motives or the character of its participants, the Nixon administration could not fail to recognize that Vietnam had defeated Lyndon Johnson and that the path to a second term was a negotiated peace and quick withdrawal. He understood the restraints imposed on the Nixon administration by militarism, anticommunism, and the military–industrial complex, and he was determined to help by continuing to expose the motives and methods of those who favored an imperial foreign policy. What he apparently failed to understand was how integral those forces and interests were to the political coalition that Richard Nixon had put together, and how determined the president and his advisers were to avoid the "humiliation" of defeat.

58 Interview with Emmy Eichler, July 21, 1991, Washington, D.C.
59 Betty to Judy and Walter, undated, letter in possession of Bosey Foote.
60 Eichler interview.

# 29

# *Of arms and men*

Fulbright's attitude toward the military–industrial complex was analogous to Theodore Roosevelt's stance toward big business during the early years of the Progressive Era: It should not be destroyed, but brought under control, made responsive to the democratic process and to the public interest. Like T. R., Fulbright was determined to get the mule's attention, and the bludgeon with which he intended to do it was the multi-billion-dollar antiballistic missile (ABM) system pending in Congress in the fall of 1969.

Nixon and Kissinger's new world order called for a stable relationship with the Soviet Union. The two were committed to containment but were not averse to the idea of dialogue, a position that had in part been responsible for the honeymoon with Fulbright; but the national security adviser believed that America's strategic position vis-à-vis the Soviet Union had steadily deteriorated under Jack Kennedy and Lyndon Johnson.[1] Implicit in Kissinger's version of détente was "linkage," an updated version of the old balance of power approach to international affairs. Instead of negotiating military, economic, and political issues piecemeal with the Soviets, Nixon and Kissinger would demand general settlements, linking problems such as Vietnam and the Middle East with concessions on trade and disarmament. In the area of arms control Kissinger and his boss saw negotiations with the Soviets as a means to extract concessions across a broad range of issues, including Vietnam. As far as the "balance of terror" was concerned, Kissinger, Nixon, and Secretary of Defense Melvin Laird were committed to establishing American supremacy, which, of course, they saw as the key to maintaining international stability.[2]

In 1966 United States intelligence had discovered that the Soviet Union was in the research and development stage of a rudimentary ABM system. The ultimate goal of that program was to ring Moscow and other cities with missiles that could destroy incoming enemy missiles and bombers in case of a nuclear attack. Possession of such a system by one of the superpowers and not the other would open up the possibility of a first strike (the possessor

1 Kissinger to Nixon, Oct. 13, 1969, WHSpF, Box 3, Nixon Project.
2 See Seymour M. Hersh, *The Price of Power: Kissinger in the Nixon White House* (New York, 1983), 147–9.

being invulnerable to retaliation) and thus upset the nuclear balance of power; but an ABM race would constitute a dangerous escalation of the arms race, one that could very possibly bankrupt the participants. Several times Johnson and Soviet Premier Aleksei Kosygin had discussed conducting negotiations on limiting both offensive and defensive weapons, but nothing had ever come of their conversations. Consequently, in 1968 Johnson had persuaded a reluctant Congress to pass legislation appropriating $1.195 billion for the construction of an American ABM system. When the Nixon administration took over the project, renamed it Safeguard, and announced that it was going to approach Congress for several billion dollars more, Fulbright and his colleagues decided that the time was propitious to make a stand against this particular weapons system and the military–industrial complex in general.[3]

Throughout March and April, Secretary of Defense Laird and his soft-spoken assistant, David Packard, attempted to convince the Senate, and specifically the SFRC, that the Soviets had achieved superiority in "individual payload" for their missiles and, as a result, in total megatonnage; hence, their construction of an ABM system would give the communists "a first strike capability." That is, the Kremlin, sure that it could protect its cities and missile sites from retaliatory annihilation, would feel free to attack the West at any time. Even if they did not do so, the Pentagon argued, they could threaten and intimidate the free world into innumerable and damaging concessions.

Packard, the ultimate chart turner, appeared before the SFRC in early March. A "testy" Fulbright wanted to know, in light of its recently announced support for the nuclear nonproliferation treaty, why the administration was not negotiating with the Soviets rather than trying to build a new missile system. Article 6 of the nonproliferation agreement required the nuclear powers to begin negotiations at an early date as part of an effort to halt the nuclear arms race. With NBC and CBS taping the proceedings, Packard moved ponderously through his charts as a bevy of beribboned aides stood at stiff attention. In the middle of his presentation Albert Gore moved in with his own charts, asked to borrow Packard's "wand," and proceeded to demonstrate that the United States had clear nuclear superiority over the Soviets. To move ahead with another system was "madness," he said. The White House was furious. "All in all, [the networks] had a great time turning the entire proceeding into one giant joke," Pat Buchanan reported to Nixon. The president characteristically ordered Herb Klein to "raise hell with N.B.C. on this."[4]

As the battle lines formed, the national press predicted a major political confrontation, a "dramatic struggle" between "those who support the military budget and those who want to redirect resources toward solving hard social

3 Laurence Stern, "Political Winds Stir Change in Military, Defense Climate," *Washington Post,* Feb. 5, 1969.

4 Television Analysis, Mar. 1969, WHSpF, Box 30, Nixon Project.

problems."[5] Cost estimates for the completed ABM system ran as high as $40 billion.[6] From the outset the opposition to Nixon's ABM system was deep and wide. Leading the revolt were Democrats Fulbright, McGovern, Symington, and Mansfield and Republicans Cooper, Javits, and Pearson. Even Everett Dirksen, responding to the cries of Chicagoans outraged at the scheduled construction of an ABM facility only thirty miles away, expressed reservations. However, the insurgents, as Laurence Stern pointed out, would be fighting an uphill battle. "The Defense Department has the biggest larder of benefits – money, real estate and plants – with which to foster friendliness and fealty. It maintains a congressional liaison establishment on Capitol Hill that is courteous, ever-willing and second to none among the executive agencies."[7] Taking point for the Pentagon were such proven cold warriors as John Stennis, John Tower, Robert Dole (R–Kansas), Robert Byrd, and Strom Thurmond; but the heart and soul of the ABM team was Senator Henry M. "Scoop" Jackson, who, though a liberal Democrat on most domestic matters, was a tiger on defense issues. Jackson was a committed cold warrior both philosophically and politically. Without the aerospace industry, he believed, Washington State's economy would collapse. The debate over ABM constituted the second chapter in the developing feud between him and Fulbright.

The third week in March Melvin Laird appeared before the SFRC Disarmament Subcommittee. The proceedings were televised live by two of the three networks. His bald dome glistening in the Klieglights, his brows arched, and his lips pursed, the DOD chief solemnly told the subcommittee that he wanted to be known as the "secretary of peace," and that Safeguard meant "people protection." Albert Gore asked a hypothetical question: Imagine the plight of a lonely lieutenant at a Safeguard site in Wyoming. The Soviet missiles are coming over the horizon, and the young officer calls the White House for instructions. Should he press the offensive (Minuteman) button or the defensive (Safeguard) button? "Tell him to press the panic button," Fulbright muttered, provoking a roar of laughter from the mostly young and antiwar audience. "This is a deadly serious matter," Laird thundered.[8] Provoked, the DOD chief made a portentous claim: The Soviet Union was working toward a first-strike capability; "there is no question about that," he said.[9]

Throughout March Fulbright and the staff of the SFRC received a flood of information that the administration's projected ABM system was technically

5 National Committee for an Effective Congress, Mar. 10, 1969, Series 48:6, Box 24:3, SPF.

6 Tom Wicker, "The Overwhelming Case Against ABM System," *Arkansas Gazette,* Mar. 13, 1969.

7 Stern, "Political Winds."

8 Mary McGrory, "Laird Like Adman on ABM," *Washington Evening Star,* Mar. 21, 1969.

9 "Russia Works on 1st Strike, Laird Insists," *Washington Evening Star,* Mar. 21, 1969.

deficient, that as soon as the installations were complete, they would be obsolete, and that the administration and defense contractors who would benefit from ABM were turning a deaf ear to criticism both from within the Pentagon and the scientific community at large. On March 27 David Packard appeared once again before the SFRC Disarmament Subcommittee. The Public Broadcast System was carrying the proceedings over the radio. Packard was reciting the usual litany when Fulbright interrupted him:

> FULBRIGHT: Have you consulted outside experts on this system?
>
> PACKARD: Yes, yes. Of course.
>
> FULBRIGHT: Who have you consulted?
>
> PACKARD: Well, we've consulted a lot of experts.
>
> FULBRIGHT: Yeah, but who?
>
> PACKARD: All the authorities.
>
> FULBRIGHT: Yeah, but who?
>
> PACKARD: I'm not sure I remember.
>
> FULBRIGHT: Now, Mr. Secretary, you've consulted all these experts. Surely you can remember just one name, just one name.
>
> PACKARD: [*after a long, pregnant pause*] I'll give you one name. Dr. Wolfgang Panofsky at the Stanford Linear Accelerator.

Fulbright thanked him and the questioning continued.

A half hour later, the phone rang in the back of the hearing room. Jim Lowenstein answered. "This is Wolfgang Panofsky," the voice said. "He's not telling the truth. He ran into me in the airport and said, 'What do you think of the ABM system?' I said, 'I think it's for the birds. It won't work.'"[10]

The next day Fulbright called a press conference. The Nixon administration, he charged, had made "no serious scientific review" of the ABM program; the whole thing was a "political gimmick." "The Defense Department doesn't take this committee of the Congress seriously. . . . They think they can pull the wool over our eyes." He then told the Panofsky story.[11] In late April a group of anti-ABM physicists picketed the White House carrying signs reading "Caution. The military–industrial complex is armed and dangerous" and "ABM is an Edsel."[12]

Nixon had staked his fragile ego on the ABM issue and, egged on by his top aides, he was determined to win. "A victory on this controversial issue is more than important; it is absolutely essential," Alexander Butterfield told him.[13] At Nixon's direction White House assistant Tom Huston lashed the

10 Interview with James Lowenstein, Oct. 3, 1991, Washington, D.C.

11 "Fulbright Charges No Serious Review Made of Safeguard," *Arkansas Gazette,* Mar. 29, 1969.

12 *Congressional Record,* Senate, Aug. 12, 1969, 23469.

13 Butterfield to Nixon, June 11, 1969, WHSpF, Box 2, Nixon Project.

troops to greater effort. "The attack on ABM and on defense spending has centered on the President because DOD, Congressional and Party officials are not doing their appropriate thing – sticking their necks out," he berated the cabinet and bureaucracy.[14] When National Educational Television ran a series critical of the ABM specifically and military spending in general, Nixon exploded. "I want to use every possible discreet means to see that public funds for this left wing outfit are dried up," he ordered Herb Klein.[15] The White House persuaded Wall Street lawyer and well-known superhawk William Casey to establish the "Citizens Committee for Peace with Security" to lobby for passage of ABM. Amply funded by the major defense contractors who would profit from the Safeguard system, the Casey committee was tremendously effective in controlling the airways and pressuring key legislators.[16]

While Nixon and his aides mounted their television and print campaign in behalf of ABM, Fulbright and the opposition pursued two stratagems. They focused first on Laird's claim that the Soviets were mounting a first-strike capability and that, once achieved, the Kremlin intended to annihilate the West at the first opportunity. They then labored to bring to the public eye the deep divisions within the administration over whether or not to go ahead with the system. Fulbright, Philip Hart (D–Michigan), and several other members of the opposition convened a scientific briefing at which anti-ABM scientists (which included virtually everyone except Edward Teller) briefed nineteen senators on the actual status of the Soviet arsenal.

The first test vote on Safeguard was scheduled for early June. As the date approached, most observers, including Fulbright, were predicting that the Pentagon would suffer one of its few setbacks since the beginning of the cold war. "If we can succeed in defeating the military forces in the Congress in one instance, it will greatly encourage the Congress to proceed in others," he wrote a supporter in Los Angeles.[17] "The ABM itself is not all that significant," he declared on *Face the Nation,* but "it is a symbol of our lack of concern and interest in disarmament."[18]

Predictions of defeat only seemed to whet Nixon's appetite for battle. "There must be no talk of compromise," he instructed the White House staff.

14 Tom Huston, "The McNamara Legacy," June 16, 1969, WHSpF, Box 2, Nixon Project.

15 Klein to Butterfield, July 10, 1969, WHSpF, Box 2, Nixon Project. In November White House staffer Peter Flanigan offered the Corporation for Public Broadcasting a $5 million increase to enable it to supplant NET. Flanigan to Nixon, Nov. 4, 1969, WHSpF, Box 3, Nixon Project.

16 Peter Flanigan to John Ehrlichman, June 25, 1969, June 25, 1969, WHSpF, Box 42, Nixon Project.

17 JWF to Harold Willens, May 17, 1969, Series 48:18, Box 57:7, SPF.

18 "Nixon Rules Out ABM Compromise," *Washington Post,* Apr. 28, 1969.

Indeed, Nixon had his own polls, and the White House headcount showed 50 for, 45 against, and five uncommitted.[19] As the tension mounted, the administration executed a shrewd diversionary move. The Pentagon "leaked" news that the Soviet Union was testing MIRVs (multiple, independently targeted reentry vehicles): clusters of nuclear-tipped rockets that would eventually sit atop the huge Soviet SS9.[20] With little additional effort, MIRVs would enable their developer to quadruple the number of enemy targets destroyed.

As the White House had hoped, the debate in the Senate shifted from ABM to MIRVs. It seemed to many fence sitters that the multiple-warhead threat made ABM necessary. Administration spokesmen let it be known that the ABM would be a crucial bargaining chip in the SALT talks as the United States attempted to keep the Soviets from deploying their multiple warheads. To vote down the Safeguard system would be to engage in "unilateral disarmament."[21] Fulbright worked frantically to keep the ABM insurgents from falling for the MIRV trap, but a number did.[22]

On June 28 the Senate Armed Services Committee approved the ABM bill by a vote of 10 to 7. Fulbright was encouraged. It was the closest vote on a major weapons system in twenty years. When George Aiken subsequently announced his opposition, John Chancellor and Roger Mudd declared on the six o'clock news that the Safeguard system was dead.[23] By this point Fulbright, Ted Kennedy, Albert Gore, and other ABM insurgents were receiving on a daily basis tips and documents from ABM opponents within the Pentagon. Using elaborate means to defeat wiretaps and microphones they assumed were hidden in their offices, anti-ABM officials provided the Senate with proofs that Safeguard computers were not fail-safe, that Safeguard sites were vulnerable to a first strike, and that it was the Nixon administration rather than the Kremlin that was pressing ahead with MIRV testing.[24]

The tension generated by the ABM fight sometimes reached excruciating levels. Though not an outdoorsman per se, Fulbright chafed under the constant confinement of office and committee room. When weather permitted he would abandon the Senate tunnel and walk the short distance from the Senate Office Building to the SFRC committee room across the picturesque Capitol grounds. Sometimes the staff would prevail upon him to stop by one of the

19 Butterfield to Nixon, June 11, 1969, WHSpF, Box 2, and Ken BeLieu to Nixon, June 10, 1969, WHSpF, Box 2, Nixon Project.

20 Ibid.

21 Marcy to JWF, June 9, 1969, Box 8, Apr.–June, Marcy Papers.

22 Discussion of Vietnam Resolutions, Dec. 1, 1969, Executive Sessions, SFRC, RG 46, NA.

23 "Senate Committee Approves ABM System," *Fort Smith Southwest Times Record,* June 28, 1969, and News Summary, July 1, 1969, WHSpF, Box 30, Nixon Project.

24 Bernard D. Nossiter, "ABM Foes Flooded with Tips," *Washington Post,* July 11, 1969.

Senate staff league softball games. In late June, clad in vest and shirtsleeves, he led his team to victory over Senator Alan Cranston's contingent. Fulbright knocked in two runs while the Californian, dressed in gym shorts and red striped socks, went hitless.[25]

The climactic debate over ABM began the first week in July. Leading the way for the defense establishment was Henry Jackson, the personification of liberal internationalism. The real issue, he told the Senate, was the nature of the threat facing the United States. Make no mistake about it, the Washingtonian proclaimed, "we face a very rough adversary, a very dangerous adversary, and an unpredictable one." That was not the issue at all, Fulbright responded. The issue was whether or not the Senate would be able "to reassert some control over the military department." If it did not, the United States would indeed become a national security state in which democracy, individual liberty, economic viability, everything, would be subsumed to the well-being of the military–industrial complex.[26]

After four weeks of debate, polls showed the Senate evenly divided with only Clinton P. Anderson (D–New Mexico) and John J. Williams (R–Delaware) uncommitted. The first and key vote would be on an insurgent amendment to continue research and development but to postpone actual construction of the first two Safeguard sites for a year; it was defeated on August 6 by a vote of 51 to 49.[27] The closeness of the vote was a triumph, Charles Percy (R–Illinois) told Fulbright in an effort to cheer him up. "In winning the support of half of all Senators, we established the principle that the Senate is no longer willing to accept without question the judgment of the military that a particular weapons system is vital to national survival."[28]

While Fulbright was publicly inveighing against the threat posed by the military–industrial complex, the investigative team of Pincus and Paul had shifted their attention from Spain to Laos. In 1967 and 1968 as the fighting in Vietnam had escalated, so too had the level of violence in Laos. While American personnel, including Ambassador William Sullivan, had insisted that the United States was respecting Laotian neutrality as provided for under the 1962 Geneva Accords, hundreds of military advisers, CIA operatives, and Air America personnel had flooded into that unfortunate country and directed the Royal Laotian armed forces in operations against NVA enclaves and parts of the Ho Chi Minh Trail. By 1968 American fighter-bombers stationed in

25 "Senatorial Softball," *Washington Post,* June 26, 1969.

26 *Congressional Record,* Senate, July 9, 1969, 18914.

27 David R. Boldt, "ABM Wins Crucial Senate Test," *Washington Post,* Aug. 7, 1969.

28 Percy to JWF, Aug. 12, 1969, Series 48:6, Box 24:5, SPF.

Thailand were pounding the Plain of Jars, a fertile region in northeastern Laos that had been under Pathet Lao control since 1964.[29]

With Nixon's election, Sullivan became deputy assistant secretary of state. Replacing him as ambassador in Vientiane was George McMurtrie Godley, whose experience in the Congo in 1964–5 had given him a taste for action. Washington ordered all restrictions on bombing, including the use of B-52s, removed. Godley, who personally directed air operations from a command post in the U.S. embassy, quickly acquired the nickname "air marshal." In the summer of 1969 Pincus and Paul arrived in the middle of this secret war. To their delight, it proved to be a simple task to uncover the Pentagon's covert operation. Pincus recalled their adventure:

> The thing that we were doing – we were bombing the trail, of course – but based in Laos were forward air controllers who went up in unmarked airplanes – Americans with no identification. The air attaché, most of the attachés, were really very honest. The first day I heard about it I asked him if I could go up in one of these planes. He said he would take it under consideration. The second day we were there, they took us out to one of these luscious French lunches. Suddenly, a colonel appears and says we are going up. So we go out to this air base. I sat in the back of one of these two seaters. He supposedly was marking the site of an NVA or a Pathet Lao base near the border. He gave me a hell of a ride. He would say "there they are" and plunge the plane straight down to the tree tops. I threw up. The third time my glasses flew up against the canopy. The Royal Laotian Air Force came roaring in and blew up [what was marked]. By this time we were short of gas. We landed in the middle of nowhere. Men appeared from the jungle, refueled the plane, and told us we were too close to the NVA. We had two minutes to leave. I was a hell of a mess. But it didn't matter. I had proved that there were Americans in Laos and that they were flying. It later proved terribly important because Nixon had denied that there was anybody there.[30]

The American embassy seemed not to have gotten the word that Nixon and Kissinger wanted the secret war in Laos kept secret, especially from Congress. Godley, whom Pincus referred to as the American "proconsul" in Laos, thoroughly enjoyed his military responsibilities and could not stop talking about them. The SFRC investigator was delighted:

> We proved that we had to go in and support one of the two groups in Laos in order to get them to allow us to go into Laos to support the war. It meant that the commitment was to perpetuate a group in

29 Marilyn B. Young, *The Vietnam Wars, 1945–1990* (New York, 1991), 235.
30 Interview with Walter Pincus, Mar. 11, 1990, Washington, D.C.

> Laos in order to help the war. What we were doing was we were showing that we were creating commitments way beyond what people knew.[31]

Throughout the summer of 1969 the Symington subcommittee deliberately maintained a low profile;[32] then, on September 30, the long-awaited public hearings on unauthorized national commitments began. As the magnitude of the work done by Pincus and Paul became apparent, the White House momentarily panicked. "Symington Committee staffers have obtained from DOD, State and field missions a vast amount of highly sensitive information," Kissinger wrote Nixon. "Much of this is the type that has never been given to the Legislative Branch in previous administrations. Their information includes such things as type and locations of nuclear weapons and data on covert operations in Laos."[33] After meeting with Symington and futilely attempting to persuade him to desist, Nixon ordered all executive branch personnel to stonewall on the location of nuclear weapons and on all military "contingency" plans. It was a proverbial barn-door directive.

The last week in October the Symington subcommittee turned its attention to Laos and Cambodia. "It's time people knew the facts," Fulbright told the Capitol Hill press corps. With copies of the Pincus–Paul report in their hands, Fulbright, Symington, and Mansfield grilled CIA Director Richard Helms, Secretary of Defense Laird, and military personnel brought back from Laos and Thailand specifically at the subcommittee's request. To the administration's enragement, Fulbright would regale reporters with tidbits of information gleaned by committee investigators after the closed-door hearings had ended. After Helms testified on October 29, Fulbright emerged from the committee room and announced to a phalanx of reporters that the United States had been fighting a secret war in Laos in direct violation of the 1962 Geneva Accords, which prohibited the introduction of foreign troops into that country. The CIA was illegally arming and training a clandestine Laotian army, he insisted, and the United States Air Force was operating inside Laos.[34]

The chairman and his supporters intended the hearings to be a prelude to concrete congressional action to prohibit U.S. involvement in overseas conflicts made under secret agreements. The White House knew what the anti-imperialists had in mind, but they did not know when or how they would act. On December 15 Fulbright and his cohorts struck. During a debate on the military appropriations bill, the chairman asked the measure's floor manager

31 Ibid.

32 Marcy to Lindsay Rogers, July 18, 1969, Box 8, Folder July–Sept., Marcy Papers.

33 Kissinger to Nixon, Oct. 1, 1969, WHCF, Box 20, Nixon Project.

34 "U.S. Waging War in Laos on the Sly, Fulbright Asserts," *Arkansas Gazette,* Oct. 29, 1969.

why it included $90 million for U.S. military assistance to neutral Laos. Before he could respond, Frank Church rose to propose that the Senate amend the Pentagon budget bill to bar the use of new defense funds "to finance the introduction of American ground combat troops in Laos and Thailand." In a massive show of force, hawks and doves banded together to approve the Church amendment by a vote of 73 to 17. When the dust had settled Congress had slashed $5.3 billion from the administration's military spending bill.[35]

Fulbright recognized an essential truth about the nature of North Vietnamese resistance that seemed to escape Nixon, Goodpaster, and the JCS. Ho Chi Minh and the soldier-citizens around him were willing to sacrifice everything to reunify the country under their leadership. They were not subject to threats. There was no significant evidence of a division within Ho's ranks. The United States had moved more tonnage of equipment and weaponry into Vietnam than it had into the European Theater of Operations during World War II. American body count put enemy deaths as of 1969 at 520,219. Nevertheless, the communists persisted. "There are some kinds of wars that can't be won by force, and some kinds of people that will die before they will surrender," Fulbright wrote Mrs. Albert Gore. The nature and origin of their motivation were irrelevant. Even if the NVA and VC soldiers were hopeless automatons, turned into suicide machines by a totalitarian government (which he did not believe), "the United States has taken on a hopeless task."[36]

Despite congressional and public impatience with the Nixon administration's policies in Vietnam, the president was no more willing to make the hard choices than Kennedy or Johnson had been. He was aware at the intellectual level of how strategically and politically counterproductive the war was; but he was convinced that an immediate, unnegotiated withdrawal would be interpreted by the Russians as a sign of weakness and lack of control. In addition, there continued to be powerful psychological forces at work that kept the president from withdrawing. Once Nixon became president and inherited responsibility for the war, he acquired ownership in it. He was enthralled with the notion of being commander-in-chief and terrified of being viewed by the military as weak. Like Johnson he came to believe that those who criticized the conflict were criticizing him. Indeed, the war and the debate over it activated Nixon's near-obsessive fear of defeat and humiliation. Those who opposed what he wanted to do in Southeast Asia, whatever that happened to be at the time, became in his mind "doctrinaire leftists."[37] What differentiated

35 Warren Unna and Richard Homan, "Hill Acts to Curb Asia Role," *Washington Post,* Dec. 16, 1969.

36 JWF to Mrs. Albert Gore, July 22, 1969, Box 8, July–Sept., Marcy Papers.

37 News Summary, May 20, 1969, WHSpF, Box 30, Nixon Project.

Nixon from his predecessors and made possible the prolongation of the war was that he was more successful in convincing both hawks and doves that he was heeding their advice, and in diverting popular impatience to his critics.

On May 14, 1969, the president had addressed a national television audience on Vietnam. "I know that some believe I should have ended the war immediately after my inauguration by simply withdrawing our forces from Vietnam," he said. "That would have been the easy thing to do and it might have been a popular move"; but he could not do it, the president declared somberly. Simply to withdraw would have been to have "betrayed my solemn responsibility as President." He intended to end the war permanently, Nixon declared, "so that the younger brothers of our soldiers in Vietnam will not have to fight in the future in another Vietnam some place in the world." The United States had given up on winning a purely military victory, Nixon told the American people, but neither would his government accept a settlement in Paris that amounted to a "disguised defeat." The United States would agree to withdraw its troops from Vietnam according to a specified timetable if North Vietnam would agree to withdraw its forces from South Vietnam, Cambodia, and Laos according to a specified timetable.[38]

Shortly thereafter William Rogers testified before the SFRC in executive session on his recent tour of Vietnam. As the secretary of state launched into his optimistic review, the chairman interrupted him:

> You sound exactly like Mr. McNamara and Mr. Taylor when they used to report to us year after year, and always the generals were always first-rate, the morale was fine, Bunker was fine, everything was just fine, which again leads me to believe that there is not the slightest idea of changing anything that the previous administration has been doing.[39]

Two weeks after Rogers's appearance Fulbright announced on ABC's *Issues and Answers* that the SFRC would hold a new series of hearings on Vietnam. The president's "new isolationist" speech at the Air Force Academy, he said, indicated that his policy was as bankrupt as Johnson's.[40] The first witness would be Clark Clifford, who had just recommended in *Foreign Affairs* that a hundred thousand troops be brought home by the end of 1969 and that all combat troops be removed by the end of 1970.[41]

Mcanwhile, Nixon's secret diplomacy and implied military threats were having no impact on Hanoi. Ho Chi Minh agreed with Fulbright: There was

38 Text of Televised Speech by the President on Vietnam, May 14, 1969, Series 1:1, Box 4:3, SPF.

39 Briefing on Secretary Rogers's Trip, June 6, 1969, Executive Sessions, SFRC, RG 46, NA.

40 Robert C. Jensen, "Fulbright Will Reopen Probe of Vietnam Policy," *Washington Post,* June 23, 1969.

41 JWF to Clark Clifford, June 21, 1969, Series 48:3, Box 17:1, SPF.

no significant difference between Nixon's negotiating position and Johnson's. To have accepted the notion of mutual, calibrated withdrawal that left the Thieu government in place and the NLF outside the power structure would have been to have relinquished goals for which Ho and his colleagues had been fighting for a quarter century. The North Vietnamese delegation publicly dismissed the proposal made in Nixon's May television address. They would, if necessary, sit in Paris "until the chairs rot," they said.[42] Certain that American public opinion would eventually force Nixon to withdraw from Vietnam, the North Vietnamese were prepared to wait him out, no matter how many soldiers and civilians had to die and how long it took.

Fulbright's and the SFRC's mounting frustration with the Nixon administration was accompanied by a revival of the antiwar movement, disorganized, demoralized, and largely dormant since the disastrous Chicago convention. A wave of protest and demonstrations disturbed nearly four hundred of the nation's twenty-five hundred college campuses. The 1969 disorders were more confrontational and violent than previous eruptions. Nerves on both sides of the picket line were raw. Patience was at a premium. Occupation of administration buildings seemed almost always to end with beatings and arrests. Authorities hauled away over four thousand students on campuses from San Francisco State to Swarthmore, while 7 percent of the country's schools reported violent protests involving property damage or personal injury.[43]

Despite this violence, or perhaps because of it, the main burden of regenerating the antiwar movement fell in 1969 upon its more conservative elements, primarily liberals who wanted to work within the system. The activities and makeup of the participants reflected this shift. The resurgence of springtime activism culminated in the organization of the moratorium and the New Mobilization, which, according to Charles DeBenedetti and Charles Chatfield, "combined. . . to rally the most potent and widespread antiwar protests ever mounted in a western democracy." On June 30, the Vietnam Moratorium Committee issued its call for a nationwide work stoppage to demonstrate opposition to the war in Southeast Asia. The New Mobilization Committee to End the War in Vietnam was determined to organize the broadest possible spectrum of antiwar citizens in "a legal and traditional protest action";[44] in pursuance of that goal, it called for a national demonstration in Washington to begin on November 13. Participants would demand America's immediate withdrawal from Vietnam.

42 Quoted in George C. Herring, *America's Longest War: The United States and Vietnam, 1950–1975,* 2d ed. (New York, 1986), 226.

43 Charles DeBenedetti with Charles Chatfield, *An American Ordeal: The Antiwar Movement of the Vietnam Era* (Syracuse, 1990), 242–3.

44 Ibid., 248, quote on 250.

On September 2, 1969, exactly twenty-four years after he had proclaimed the independence of Vietnam in the words of the American Declaration of Independence, Ho Chi Minh died. The previous May, his health already failing, Ho had written a testament that was now released. "We, a small nation, will have earned the unique honor of defeating, through a heroic struggle, two big imperialisms – the French and the American – and making a worthy contribution to the national liberation movement."[45]

On the morning of the sixth, Fulbright was sitting in his office reading his mail when the phone rang. It was the Reverend Mouzon Mann, an Arkansas clergyman and an ardent opponent of the war. Why not test the seriousness of the administration's intent to negotiate an end to the Vietnam conflict by proposing that it send a delegation to Ho Chi Minh's funeral?[46] An excellent idea, the chairman replied. To the administration's delight and to his personal staff's horror, Fulbright first put the suggestion in a letter to Nixon and then made it public. It would be "inadvisable," the White House replied, for Americans to pay tribute to the fallen North Vietnamese leader while his troops were still killing American boys.[47] With hawks blasting him as a traitor and doves wincing at his lack of judgment, Fulbright continued lamely to insist that an American presence at the funeral would facilitate negotiations.[48]

During the first months of 1969, while Fulbright had observed a self-imposed ban on criticism of the war, his visibility had diminished and his hate mail declined; but the Arkansan's blasts at the administration's Vietnam policy and his assaults on the military–industrial complex made him once again an object of intense public controversy. The editor of the *Newport* (Arkansas) *Daily Independent* advised its readers to write Fulbright and tell him "what a damned fool he is making of himself." America could win the war if "he will shut his mealy mouth and stop advocating tucking tail and running from a bunch of chinks."[49] Vice-President Spiro Agnew, addressing the Midwestern Governors Conference, lashed out at "self-professed experts" on Vietnam whose opposition was "undermining our negotiations and prolonging the war." The ever-combative superhawk denounced "the Fulbright-crats, the McGovern-crats and other kind of 'crats.'" "It is their stock in trade to downgrade patriotism and to downgrade the American fighting man."[50] Two weeks before Christmas an anonymous call came into the FBI office in Miami. "I have just returned from Vietnam," the calm, male voice declared. "I am going to kill Fulbright . . . I am leaving right now . . . I don't like Com-

45 Quoted in Young, *Vietnam Wars,* 238.
46 JWF to Bryan Langley, Dec. 4, 1969, Series 1:1, Box 4:4, SPF.
47 "Fulbright Urged Nixon to Send Representatives to Ho's Funeral," *Washington Daily News,* Sept. 10, 1969.
48 JWF to General W. Peyton Campbell, Sept. 8, 1969, Series 1:1, Box 4:3, SPF.
49 "Editorial," *Newport Daily Independent,* June 26, 1969.
50 "U.S. 'Fighting Without Hope,'" *St. Petersburg Independent,* July 5, 1969.

munists."[51] As the ardency of Fulbright's detractors increased, so did that of his admirers, however. "Each night before I lay me down I say a little prayer," Irene LeBreton of Chicago wrote. "'Thank you, dear God, for Senator Fulbright. Keep him well, make him strong, and let his wisdom prevail.'"[52]

51 FBI, Miami to Director, Dec. 8, 1969, 62-71126, FBI Files.
52 Irene LeBreton, to JWF, Oct. 2, 1969, Series 48:18, Box 56:7, SPF.

# 30

# *Struggle for the vital center*

On September 25, 1969, Senator Charles Goodell (R–New York) introduced an amendment to the foreign assistance bill requiring a complete suspension of funding for military activity in Vietnam after December 1, 1970. Applauding Goodell's courage, Fulbright declared his an original and workable approach, and announced he would soon hold hearings on the proposal. "Fulbright, more than any other person, probably holds the key to when the debate is resumed and to the line of attack against the Administration," observed the *New York Times.*[1] Not since the Whig rebellion during the Mexican War had Congress seriously considered cutting off funds for an army in the field.

Predictably, the White House "knocked down" Goodell's proposal, to use Nixon's favorite phrase, terming it "defeatist in attitude." Such initiatives inevitably "undercut and destroy the negotiating position we have taken in Paris," administration spokesmen declared.[2] The first week in October Nixon told nine Republican senators that he did not intend to be "the first President to preside over an American defeat" and let it be known that he was considering blockading Haiphong and invading the north.[3]

On the floor of the Senate, Fulbright declared that President Nixon had been in office nine months, "the normal period of gestation for humans." During the fall campaign the president had told the American people that he had a "secret plan" to end the war. What had happened to that alluring scheme? Noting that nearly ten thousand American soldiers had died in Vietnam since the new administration had come to power, he proclaimed that it was time for the United States to leave Vietnam; it was time for the Vietnamese to fight their own war. Fulbright also announced his support for the national moratorium scheduled for October 15, declaring it to be "in the best American tradition of peaceful protest for the redress of grievances."[4]

1 John W. Finney, "Goodell Calls for Pullout; Rockefeller Rebukes Him," *New York Times,* Sept. 26, 1969.

2 Quoted in William C. Berman, *William Fulbright and the Vietnam War: The Dissent of a Political Realist* (Kent, Ohio, 1988), 115.

3 "Nixon Quoted as Barring U.S. Defeat," *New York Times,* Oct. 2, 1969, and Bryce Harlow to LBJ, Oct. 6, 1969, Box 3, WHSpF, Nixon Project.

4 *Congressional Record,* Senate, Oct. 1, 1969, 2781–3.

As the antiwar movement veered sharply toward the political and cultural center in 1969, Fulbright became more closely identified with and important to it. Partial proof of this was the fact that he became anathema to the movement's more radical elements. In March, Fulbright had addressed the National Convocation on the Challenge of Building Peace. In the middle of his talk in the Grand Ballroom of the New York Hilton, several demonstrators disguised as hotel waiters appeared on the dais carrying platters bearing the heads of pigs. Donning masks of pig heads themselves, they began chanting "Ho Ho, Ho Chi Minh, NLF is gonna win." They then unfurled VC battle flags and ran out. When Fulbright attempted to resume speaking, several protesters in the audience interrupted him. "You're a racist, Mr. Fulbright," they shouted. "You're helping the U.S. kill Vietnamese."[5]

Far from disturbing Fulbright, these and other attacks from the fringes of the movement reassured him. No less than Richard Nixon or Lyndon Johnson, the Arkansan perceived that the battle on the home front was a struggle for the political center. It was to patriotic, law-abiding, churchgoing, property-owning Americans that the movement would have to appeal. To this end Fulbright repeatedly and publicly repudiated the tactic of draft resistance. Throughout 1967–9 young men planning to burn their draft cards or flee to Canada wrote the chairman of the SFRC, asking for his advice. His response was always the same. Your decision "is a profoundly personal one," he would write, and consequently, his advice had "no more than limited relevance." Although the war in Vietnam was unjustified, "I believe that if I were drafted I would serve," he wrote. "I would do so because I believe that our country, despite grave defects and mistakes, is basically a decent society and one, therefore, whose laws and requirements I would wish to comply with." The individual citizen could do more to correct the nation's "transgressions" by "staying within the system and laws than by going outside them."[6]

At the same time Fulbright sympathized with those who sacrificed their citizenship for their principles. Appearing on *Face the Nation,* he noted that some fifty thousand young people had emigrated because of their disillusionment with the war. For the most part, he told newscaster George Herman, "the best people, the most sensitive and most intelligent, are the ones who are the most alienated." Youths who were staying and backing the war to the hilt were "the raw material for the brown shirts."[7]

In an effort to deflate the antiwar moratoriums scheduled for the fall of 1969, the administration canceled the November and December draft calls. The action was the result of "progress in Vietnamization," the president an-

5 "Demonstrators Disrupt Talk by Sen. Fulbright," *Washington Post,* Mar. 6, 1969.
6 JWF to Richard H. Cook, Nov. 29, 1967, Series 48:18, Box 50:3, SPF.
7 "All but the 'Brown Shirts' Are Alienated," *Arkansas Democrat,* Apr. 30, 1969.

nounced;[8] but prospective antiwar protesters were not appeased. As reports from Attorney General John Mitchell's hundreds of spies in the movement began to roll in, it was clear that the forthcoming demonstrations would be well organized and large.

On October 15 the first phase of the Vietnam Moratorium Committee's operation began. The day started with a memorial service for American war dead held on Massachusetts's sea coast, and it spread westward as the day unfolded, attaining, in the words of DeBenedetti and Chatfield, "a diversity, pervasiveness and dignity unprecedented in the history of popular protest."[9] Moratorium activities ranged from lonely picketing to mass rallies, from public demonstrations to private conversations. Managers of businesses such as the Itek Corporation and Midas Muffler encouraged workers to take time off to support the moratorium. In New Haven, no less an establishment figure than Malcolm Baldridge, 1968 Connecticut Chairman for Citizens for Nixon–Agnew, denounced the war to a group of Yale students.[10] Fulbright was delighted. "They seemed to me to be extremely well-behaved and a very serious demonstration of disapproval of the tragic mistake . . . in Vietnam," he wrote a disgruntled constituent.[11]

His advisers might have been split over the sincerity and integrity of the antiwar movement, but Richard Nixon remained convinced that it continued to be led and organized by the Students for a Democratic Society, which he perceived to be a collection of Marxists, radicals, and anarchists, and that the goal of the student movement was destruction of the established political order.[12] Indeed, the president's true feelings were articulated by Spiro Agnew, who addressed a Republican gathering a few days after the October demonstrations. The Vietnam Moratorium Day activities were wrongheaded and dangerous demonstrations "encouraged by an effete corps of impudent snobs who characterize themselves as intellectuals," he proclaimed.[13] Most important, the president refused to believe that the antiwar movement included significant portions of the American center: The law-abiding, property-owning, churchgoing public would not tolerate defeat in Vietnam.

Nixon had justified the fall draft cancellations as part of his "new" policy of Vietnamization. Actually, it was an approach he had inherited from Lyndon

8 News Summary, Sept. 8, 1969, Box 30, WHSpF, Nixon Project, and News Release, Sept. 19, 1969, Series 4:1, Box 4:5, SPF.

9 Charles DeBenedetti with Charles Chatfield, *An American Ordeal: The Antiwar Movement of the Vietnam Era* (Syracuse, 1990), 255.

10 Butterfield to Haldeman, Oct. 21, 1969, Box 138, WHSpF, Nixon Project.

11 Quoted in Berman, *Fulbright and the Vietnam War,* 116.

12 Arthur Burns to Nixon, May 26, 1969, Box 2, WHSpF, Nixon Project.

13 "Agnew Says 'Effete Snobs' Incited War Moratorium," *New York Times,* Oct. 19, 1969.

Johnson. This approach, Melvin Laird explained, involved reliance "on indigenous manpower organized into properly equipped and well-trained armed forces with the help of materiel, training, technology and specialized military skills furnished by the United States."[14] Sir Robert Thompson, the British counterinsurgency expert who had advised the Eisenhower administration on Vietnam, reemerged to convince Nixon that South Vietnam was daily growing stronger and that if the United States continued to furnish large-scale military and economic assistance, the Saigon government might be strong enough within two years to resist a communist takeover without external help. Heartened by this evaluation, Nixon delivered an ultimatum to North Vietnam: If there were no diplomatic breakthrough by November 1, he would resort "to measures of great consequence and force."[15]

In a major television address on November 3, the president spelled out his Vietnamization policy in some detail. It seemed to offer the alluring prospect of reducing U.S. casualties and of terminating American involvement in an honorable fashion regardless of what North Vietnam did. He also announced a schedule for further troop withdrawals. Having apparently placated critics of the war, Nixon then went out of his way to antagonize them. He dismissed the protesters as an irrational and irresponsible rabble, and accused them of sabotaging his diplomacy. He openly appealed for the support of those he labeled the "great silent majority," and he finished his speech with a dramatic flourish: "North Vietnam cannot humiliate the United States. Only Americans can do that."[16]

In fact, Vietnamization was designed to appeal not to doves but to hawks and former supporters of the war who had become alienated. In the spring of 1969 Pat Buchanan and his conservative coworkers had identified the core of Nixon's political support and advised him on how best to enlarge it. Aside from the well-to-do industrialists, financiers, and professional people who traditionally voted Republican, Nixon's broadest potential appeal was to the lower middle class who, ironically, had been converted into haves from have-nots by the New Deal. Above all they were preoccupied with preserving their newly won wealth (modest though it was) and social status.

The new "forgotten American," to use *Time* and *Harper's* label (the term was first used in American politics by Raymond Moley), had little or no college education but possessed a steady job, a home mortgage, and two vehicles. He or she watched Ed Sullivan on Sunday night, read *Reader's Digest,* and frequented the horse races or the betting parlor. A number of common views bound these Americans together. This was, as *Harper's* put it:

14 Quoted in Marilyn B. Young, *The Vietnam Wars, 1945–1990* (New York, 1991), 240.

15 Stanley Karnow, *Vietnam: A History* (New York, 1984), 597.

16 Quoted in George C. Herring, *America's Longest War: The United States and Vietnam, 1950–1975,* 2d ed. (New York, 1986), 229.

> the man under whose hat lies the great American desert, who watches the tube, plays the horses, and keeps the niggers out of his union and his neighborhood, who might vote for Wallace (but didn't), who cheers when the cops beat up on demonstrators, who is free, white, and twenty-one. . . .[17]

These "forgotten Americans" still admired the military and respected the police. They were shocked to see respected clergymen, sometimes *their* clergymen, leading open housing demonstrations. They were appalled when they read of millionaires getting away with paying no taxes. They had saved to send their kids to a college they could never have attended and had then become enraged when their institution or one like it had disintegrated into protest and disorder. They were appalled at the drug use, bizarre dress, and impudence of young people. Most blamed "Marxism" specifically and college professors in general for alienating their children from them. They felt they were being forced to pay the real price of integration while assorted social planners and liberal moralists sent their children to private schools. There existed among the forgotten Americans a vague but deep-seated contempt and hostility toward the so-called establishment, centered in the Northeast and perceived to be predominantly liberal.

Tactically, the "silent majority" speech was a brilliant stroke. As the Democratic National Committee put it, "the national mood on Viet Nam is at the same time glum and tired, but unwilling to accept outright defeat."[18] Having announced a plan for ending the war, Nixon denounced those who had been demanding its end. In so doing he made it possible for the Americans who had at one time or another supported the war in Vietnam, but who had turned against it, to support a scheme for American withdrawal without seeming to oppose the war. A Gallup poll indicated that 77 percent of Americans backed the president's plan, with only 6 percent in opposition, and that by a 6-to-1 margin people agreed with him that antiwar protests actually harmed the prospects for peace.[19] Nixon was so thrilled with these opinion surveys that he twice called newsmen and cameramen into the Oval Office to see them;[20] and he had Bryce Harlow send Fulbright "personal" copies of the Gallup poll "in the event you had not noted it in the papers."[21]

Not surprisingly, the "silent majority" speech angered and depressed Fulbright. It was all he could do to contain himself when Bob Hope wrote pro-

17 The Forgotten Americans, News Summary, July 1969, Box 30, WHSpF, Nixon Project.
18 "Richard Nixon – One Year Later," Democratic National Committee, Dec. 19, 1969, Series 1:1, Box 4:4, SPF.
19 DeBenedetti and Chatfield, *American Ordeal,* 259.
20 "Nixon Thinks He Has Won a Referendum on the War," *Baltimore Sun,* Nov. 5, 1969.
21 Harlow to JWF, Nov. 5, 1969, Series 1:1, Box 4:4, SPF.

posing that the Arkansan join him in cochairing a "week of national unity."[22] President Nixon, Fulbright told reporters, "now has fully and truthfully taken on himself the Johnson war, and I think it is a fundamental error."[23]

A major assumption of the political strategy espoused by Buchanan, Kevin Phillips, and other conservative intellectuals, and one embraced by Nixon, was that their opponents were totally out of touch with the forgotten American. In the case of the chairman of the SFRC, they were quite right: No public figure was more remote from or less sympathetic with the silent majority than the junior senator from Arkansas. Despite Jim Lowenstein's claim that he possessed unique insight into his country and its national characteristics, the Arkansan lived in a world that took no notice of pickup trucks, country music, celebrity sports, or religious fundamentalism. His and Betty's only concessions to popular culture were addictions to *Bonanza* and the soap operas. Socially and materially secure himself, Fulbright did not understand the fears and anxieties of those who were not. He had never experienced personal debt; he once expressed amazement that his secretary and her husband had assumed a mortgage to pay for their house. Fulbright did not worry about blacks moving into his neighborhood; blacks already lived there – Ghanaian, Zambian, and Moroccan diplomats. His opposition to forced integration stemmed from his constitutional views and his old-fashioned progressive conviction that the government owed to the people equality of opportunity and not equality of condition. For the forgotten American the war in Vietnam was a test the nation could not afford to fail, a contest it dare not lose. Defeat meant loss of face, personal as well as national humiliation. Fulbright related primarily to the "international community," which was in fact a fairly close-knit network of well-educated political and cultural elites, rather than to the parochial, sports-minded, undereducated Americans who constituted the silent majority. From his perspective, it was the war itself that threatened the nation with humiliation: The worst thing that could have happened in Vietnam was for America to have won a military victory.

J. William Fulbright might have been out of touch with the silent majority and unmindful of the forgotten American, but he came at the war in Southeast Asia not as a liberal, as Nixon and his entourage asserted, but as a conservative. For him the war posed a threat to democracy, individual liberty, and the constitutional system of checks and balances. Moreover, it was threatening to displace those who had traditionally held power in America: independent businesspeople, professionals, well-to-do farmers, liberally educated journalists and clergy, and activist intellectuals. In his opinion, the void in American foreign policy was being filled by the true believers, vested interests, and politi-

22 Bob Hope to JWF, Nov. 6, 1969, Series 48:1, Box 9:4, SPF.

23 "Fulbright Critical of Nixon's Address," *Fort Smith Southwest Times Record,* Nov. 4, 1969.

cal opportunists who had a stake in the continuation of the war in Vietnam, the perpetuation of the cold war, and the maintenance and expansion of the network of bases and commitments that it had spawned. If Congress did not act, the nation would be dragged into one foreign adventure after another until, morally and financially bankrupt, it disappeared from the face of the earth like other empires before it.

Nixon's silent majority address was interpreted by many as an invitation to wage open warfare on opponents of the conflict in Southeast Asia. He was starting to receive "the most venomous and threatening letters since the days of Joseph McCarthy," Fulbright told a UPI reporter. In mid-November the Pentagon sponsored a tour of the United States by Major James Rowe, recently returned from five years in a North Vietnamese prison camp. Appearing before civic groups and specially selected congressmen and senators, the former POW denounced Fulbright as unpatriotic. The Arkansan was giving aid and comfort to the enemy, he declared. As part of their program of psychological torture, the North Vietnamese played excerpts of Fulbright's speeches to American POWs at the Hanoi Hilton and other camps.[24] Nixon and Agnew had aroused the "old tribal instinct to gather around and support the leader," the Arkansan complained to reporters.[25]

Fulbright, Aiken, Mansfield, and other members of the SFRC briefly considered a new round of hearings on Vietnam, but decided against them. Given the deep and widespread support for Nixon, the chairman confided to several journalist friends, the committee must take pains to appear "responsible and careful" and not do anything that might appear to be "antagonistic."[26]

Richard Nixon realized instinctively in 1968 and explicitly in 1969 that one of the principal strongholds of the forgotten American was the South, and that if he were going to sustain his presidency and preserve his Vietnam consensus, he would have to control that region. Although Nixon had a long-established record as a supporter of the civil rights movement, he had made significant inroads in the 1968 election into the old Confederacy, historically a Democratic stronghold.

Nixon was a master of taking away with one hand what he seemingly was offering with the other. This was as true in the area of civil rights as it was in Vietnam. "We are opposed to segregation in any form, legal and moral and we will take action where we find it, and where it amounts to a violation of

24 Charles H. Wilson to JWF, Nov. 25, 1969, Series 48:18, Box 61:6, SPF.
25 UPI, Nov. 1, 1969, Series 78:9, Box 65:3, SPF.
26 "Nixon and the War," *New York Times*, Nov. 11, 1969.

an individual's rights," Spiro Agnew had told an audience at Williamsburg, Virginia. "But our opposition to segregation does not mean we favor compulsory or forced integration; and we remain opposed to the use of federal funds to bring about some arbitrary racial balance in the public schools."[27] In short, the administration declared war on segregation and discrimination and then proclaimed itself powerless to do anything about it: local option instead of forced busing, states' rights instead of federal intervention.[28]

On the surface, the Nixon civil rights philosophy seemed to parallel Fulbright's quite closely. The Arkansan had long railed against judicial activism and federal intervention to coerce local communities into integrating their schools and public facilities. He had beaten Jim Johnson in 1968 by appealing to Arkansas's moderately conservative voters, estimated by some to constitute as much as 40 percent of the electorate. These businessmen, artisans, independent farmers, housewives, and professional women had rejected the white supremacist movement as it became identified with violence, lawlessness, and ignorance. They had proved willing to accord blacks equality under the law, and even over time to countenance racial integration; but they did not want to be coerced, particularly in the latter area.[29]

Nonetheless, by mid-1969 Fulbright began to sense that Nixon and Agnew were determined to appeal to America's fears rather than its hopes, to stimulate its prejudices rather than tap its reservoir of tolerance. By attacking welfare cheats in a period during which poverty was growing at a disproportionate rate among black families, by calling for law and order when many of the nation's cities had recently been wracked by racial rioting, and then invoking states' rights and local option, the administration was sewing the seeds of racial hatred and laying the groundwork for a return to Jim Crow. Fulbright catered to his constituents' prejudices; Nixon deliberately inflamed them.

In the fall of 1968 Fulbright (and John McClellan) had infuriated Lyndon Johnson and Democratic liberals by voting to block Abe Fortas's nomination to be chief justice of the Supreme Court; but Fulbright had opposed Fortas not because he was a liberal and a judicial activist, but because he was a close friend of Johnson's and because, in his opinion, the president had tried to ram the nomination down the Senate's throat. The man whom Fulbright had hoped would replace the retiring Earl Warren was U.N. Ambassador and former Supreme Court justice Arthur Goldberg, a prominent liberal on civil rights matters.[30] There were other signs that, like Booker T. Washington, Fulbright was willing during this period in his life to work behind the scenes

27 Desegregation, Sept. 1969, Box 30, WHSpF, Nixon Project.

28 Ehrlichman to Nixon, Feb. 5, 1969, WHSpF, Box 1, Nixon Project.

29 John L. Ward, *The Arkansas Rockefeller* (Baton Rouge, 1977), 162, 176.

30 "Bill Fulbright: Fortas Involves Independence," *Fort Smith Southwest Times Record,* Oct. 1, 1968, and "Fulbright Warns: Keep Police Powers Locally," *Arkansas Democrat,* Oct. 20, 1968.

to facilitate the civil rights effort while keeping silent in public. At the start of the 1969 congressional session, Fulbright had quietly switched his support from Russell Long as Senate majority whip to the liberal Edward Kennedy.[31] When late in 1969 congressional conservatives attached an amendment to the tax reform bill denying tax exempt status to the Southern Regional Council's Voter Registration Project – and thus destroying it – Fulbright voted against it. (Gene McCarthy, enigmatic to the end, voted for it.)[32] There were limits beyond which Fulbright felt he could not go, however.

In May 1969, under intense fire for having taken expensive gifts from financier Louis Wolfson, Abe Fortas resigned from the Supreme Court. Nixon had scored points with the legal community and pleased both liberals and conservatives by appointing the able and moderate Warren Burger as chief justice; the replacement for Fortas was another matter. "With this one," Ehrlichman remembered Nixon telling him, "we'd stick it to the liberal, Ivy League clique who thought the Court was their own private playground."[33] The president ordered Attorney General John Mitchell to come up with a strict constructionist from the South. The attorney general's choice, Judge Clement F. Haynsworth of South Carolina, chief judge of the Fourth Circuit Court of Appeals, was less than eminent. He was a wealthy segregationist with an undistinguished legal record who belonged to several exclusive clubs. Southerners of all political inclinations were initially gratified that Nixon had named one of their own, and northerners assumed that the new nominee would be as qualified as Burger; but as details of Haynsworth's background came to light, liberals took up sword and buckler to fight the nomination.

Feelings over the Haynsworth nomination in Arkansas ran strangely deep. Most believed that opposition to the South Carolinian stemmed from the traditional antisouthern bias of the "eastern establishment" or to liberal outrage over his opposition to busing. As the controversy mounted, Lee Williams, his feet suddenly turning cold, advised Fulbright that "you are hurting yourself badly by your continued adamant stand on the war," and told him that a vote against Haynsworth might finish him off at home.[34]

Fulbright consulted his longtime friends and political supporters Robert Leflar and Bill Penix. Leflar, who was then amassing a national reputation as a legal scholar, insisted that Haynsworth was a conservative, but reasonably fair and impartial. The South Carolinian, whom Leflar had taught in a seminar for judges, would honor Supreme Court reversals of his earlier opinions.

31 "Victory of Kennedy Draws Some Criticism in South," *Washington Evening Star,* Jan. 4, 1969.

32 Rowland Evans and Robert Novak, "Republican Lindsay," *Washington Post,* Nov. 22, 1969.

33 Quoted in Stephen E. Ambrose, *Nixon,* vol. II, *The Triumph of a Politician, 1962–1972* (New York, 1989), 296.

34 Williams to JWF, Nov. 17, 1969, Williams Papers.

Penix, more worried about Fulbright's political position than the conservative–liberal balance on the Court, agreed.[35] Gradually, Fulbright convinced himself that Haynsworth had not actually rejected Supreme Court decisions on civil rights but had merely been "timid" in applying them.[36] He suspected that the chorus of Democratic cries against Haynsworth was part of a campaign to pay Republicans back for having hounded Fortas from the Court for political and ideological reasons.

Fulbright's defense of Haynsworth was contrived, however. In addition to being subject to conflict-of-interest charges stemming from his hearing of cases affecting corporations in which he held stock, the South Carolinian had done his best to obstruct the Supreme Court's civil rights decisions. In *School Board of the City of Charlottesville* v. *Dillard,* Haynsworth had insisted that children in schools under desegregation orders be allowed to transfer. Contrary to the contentions of the Supreme Court in the *Brown* decision, he argued that integration increased rather than decreased the sense of inferiority among black students.[37]

Clement Haynsworth was a racist, and J. William Fulbright knew it. In the end he voted to confirm, but only after he was sure that the nomination would be defeated. Despite the fact that he received three hundred telegrams from Arkansas the morning of the confirmation vote urging him to support Nixon's choice, he was prepared to dissent if his vote was needed. Haynsworth went down by a vote of 55 to 45. "We lost by a big margin, thank God," one of Fulbright's staff was overheard to say.[38]

Throughout the fall and winter of 1969 Fulbright continued to receive letters from draft-age men who were opposed to the war asking his advice as to what they should do if they were called. Some were more difficult to answer than others. In December, Bill Penix of Jonesboro wrote and asked him to drop a line to his son, Bill Jr., who had been drafted and was serving in the Army Medical Training Center in Fort Sam Houston, Texas. Father and son were particularly close, but they had argued bitterly over the war. The senior Penix was not enthusiastic about the conflict in Vietnam, but he was a veteran and believed that young men had a duty to serve when called. His son had resisted fiercely, at one point even considering moving to Canada, but finally agreed to be inducted. Nevertheless, his doubts about the war and about his decision to submit to the system persisted. After the younger Penix received

35 William Penix to Author, Oct. 23, 1989; Leflar to JWF, Oct. 9, 1969, and Penix to Lee Williams, Apr. 10, 1970, SPF.

36 JWF to Guy Berry, Nov. 28, 1969, SPF.

37 *School Board of the City of Charlottesville* v. *Dillard,* 374 U.S. 827 (1963).

38 E. W. Kenworthy, "Williams and Griffin Held Most Persuasive," *New York Times,* Nov. 22, 1969.

his orders for Vietnam, his father wrote Fulbright and asked if he could not provide some words of consolation to his son. Fulbright agreed. His letter was an individualized version of a standard response. He began as usual by saying that his advice was purely personal, that the war was wrong, but that America was "basically a decent society" and that "the mistake in this case, though extreme, is reversible." Therefore, he advised young Penix, if drafted and ordered to Vietnam, he, Fulbright, would go. "I would think it more likely I could help to reverse our errors by staying within the system and its laws than by defying and going outside them."[39]

Fulbright was no doubt writing from conviction, but his oft-publicized advice to draft resisters was crucial to maintaining his credibility as a "patriotic" critic of the war. Apparently unbeknownst to Fulbright, his legislative aide, Lee Williams, was putting that reputation at grave risk at the same time Fulbright was advising Penix and others to serve.

In 1966 a bright, intensely ambitious young Arkansan named William Jefferson Clinton had obtained a job in Fulbright's office as a mail clerk. For the next two years Clinton had used that position to support himself while he attended Georgetown University. Williams, a kindhearted individual who prided himself on spotting and supporting political talent, took the young man from Hot Springs under his wing. As Clinton prepared to graduate from Georgetown in the spring of 1968, he was reclassified 1-A by his draft board. For one reason or another, Clinton's Hot Springs draft board then delayed his preinduction physical for ten and a half months. The delay allowed him to accept the Rhodes scholarship he had won and enroll at Oxford for a course of study that generally took two to three years. Finally, on February 3, 1969, the future president had taken his physical and been certified for induction into the armed services.[40]

At Oxford, Clinton had become deeply involved in the antiwar movement; he had desperately wanted to avoid having to go to Vietnam. Throughout the spring, Arkansas's latest Rhodes scholar had felt the heat of the draft blowing on his neck; his February induction notice, though not a surprise, was still a shock. Short of death or disability there was only one way of having one's induction notice canceled, and that was through enlistment. Again the draft board stayed its hand while Clinton considered his options. He had plans to return to the United States and attend the University of Arkansas Law School when he finished his Rhodes. Through his contacts in Arkansas he learned that he could participate in the Reserve Officers Training Program while attending law school. That summer, he simultaneously wrote the head of the ROTC program at the university asking to be admitted, even though he had at

39 JWF to Penix, Jan. 26, 1970, Series 48:18, Box 61:2, SPF.

40 William C. Rempel, "Draft Inquiry Hints Lobbying Helped Clinton," *Arkansas Democrat Gazette,* Sept. 2, 1992.

least another year at Oxford, and contacted Lee Williams asking him to help. Williams called Colonel Eugene Holmes, head of ROTC, and recommended that Clinton be accepted.[41] Holmes agreed, Clinton signed a letter of intent, and on August 7 Clinton's status was changed to 1-D, for "member of a reserve component or student taking military training."[42]

Clinton's ROTC deferment lasted only three months. The first week in December he wrote Colonel Holmes saying that he was not going to enlist in the ROTC but instead was going to submit himself to the draft. Although he was opposed to the war, he wrote Holmes, he had to relinquish his deferment in order "to maintain my political viability within the system."[43] The ROTC–Law School route, he had concluded, did not meet that requirement.

In 1969 Bill Clinton was politically inconsequential. What was significant was that an aide to J. William Fulbright had attempted to use the prestige of the senator's office to help the young man avoid going to Vietnam. Had that fact become known in 1969, Richard Nixon, Spiro Agnew, Henry Jackson, and Strom Thurmond would have used it to devastating effect.

Bill Penix, Jr., subsequently served a year's tour of duty in Vietnam.[44] He returned to Arkansas to become a social worker; years later a deranged welfare recipient stabbed him to death with a butcher's knife.

In mid-November Joseph Starobin, former editor of the *Communist Daily Worker,* then working in self-imposed exile as an assistant professor at York University in Canada, contacted Fulbright and told him that he had twice acted as a go-between for Henry Kissinger and North Vietnamese delegate Xuan Thuy in Paris. Charges made by Nixon in the silent majority speech that North Vietnam had rejected all overtures for a peace settlement, public and private, were untrue. Prior to the speech, the DRV had made several attempts to break the diplomatic logjam but had been rebuffed. Although Starobin had for much of his adult life been a communist, and there were questions concerning his reliability, Fulbright decided to break the story. He suspected, correctly, that Nixon had chosen to substitute "Vietnamization" for negotiation. In fact, on November 21 two top members of the U.S. delegation in Paris, Henry Cabot Lodge and Lawrence Walsh, would resign in apparent disgust at the administration's intransigence; but the Starobin revelation was a

41 Interview with Lee Williams, June 20, 1989, Washington, D.C. According to Robert Corrado, the only surviving member of the Hot Springs draft board, Williams had earlier called him and other members of the board asking that Clinton be given time to finish his course of study at Oxford. Rempel, "Draft Inquiry."

42 Mark Oswald and Joe Nabbefeld, "Bill Clinton & Vietnam," *Little Rock Spectrum Weekly,* Dec. 4–10, 1991.

43 Randy Lilleston, "Text of 1969 Letter to UA ROTC," *Arkansas Democrat Gazette,* Feb. 13, 1992.

44 Penix to JWF, Oct. 10, 1973, Series 39:1, Box 8:3, SPF.

public relations bust. Agnew and company simply cited the incident as further proof that the Arkansan was a willing or unwilling dupe of the communists.[45]

Late in 1969 Fulbright initiated a Senate debate on Laos. Six weeks earlier, in late October, with Roland Paul at their side, Fulbright and Symington had questioned former ambassador William Sullivan and CIA Chief Richard Helms on America's secret war in that unfortunate land. Under tough cross-examination, they had admitted that during 1964–9 B-52's operating out of Korat air base in Thailand had flown between seven hundred and fifteen hundred sorties against the Ho Chi Minh Trail and Pathet Lao positions in the Plain of Jars. There were 125 USAF officers assigned to the Air Attaché's Office in Vientiane. In addition, they conceded that the U.S. ambassador had complete authority to "validate" targets in Laos.[46]

When subsequently Fulbright began to describe American activities to the Senate, members of the Armed Services Committee jumped to their feet. The senator from Arkansas was leaking classified information of military use to the enemy, they charged. The executive branch had involved the United States in an undeclared war in Laos without the knowledge or consent of Congress or the American people, Fulbright replied. He was going to say what he was going to say. Mansfield quickly seized the floor and guided the Senate into executive session. As the chairman detailed American secret activities in Laos, his colleagues became visibly outraged. Some, like Mansfield, insisted that air strikes in Laos were necessary to the prosecution of the war in Vietnam, but all agreed that Congress had a right to know. Several days after the executive session, the House and Senate passed an amendment to a military appropriations bill sponsored by John Sherman Cooper and Frank Church forbidding the use of American ground troops in Laos without Congress's approval.[47]

To say that J. William Fulbright had welcomed the Nixon administration with high hopes when it assumed office in January 1969 would be an overstatement. He harbored no illusions concerning Richard Nixon's altruism; but he believed that the president's political opportunism boded well for the future. The election, Fulbright was convinced, had been a repudiation of Lyndon Johnson and his policies in Southeast Asia. During his conversations with

45 "Fulbright Quotes Intermediary," *Pine Bluff Commercial,* Nov. 12, 1969; Marcy, memo of conversation, Nov. 20, 1969, Box 8, Folder Oct.–Dec., Marcy Papers; and "Nixon Seen as Downgrading Talks, Stressing Vietnamization," *Arkansas Democrat,* Nov. 21, 1969.

46 Hearings on Laos, Executive Sessions, SFRC, RG 46, NA.

47 Berman, *Fulbright and the Vietnam War,* 119.

the president and Henry Kissinger in the spring, both had assured him that they realized their political future as well as the interests of the nation would be served by the earliest possible exit from Vietnam. Instead of scaling down the war and making meaningful concessions in negotiations with the North Vietnamese, however, Nixon had actually escalated the level of violence, continued a clandestine war in Laos, and engaged in the secret bombing of Cambodia.

By the summer of 1969 Fulbright had decided that, like Lyndon Johnson, Richard Nixon had become a prisoner of forces – the radical right, the military–industrial complex, his own psyche – of which he was only dimly aware and that he could not control even if he had so desired. The country was frightened and exhausted, afraid to lose in Vietnam, but increasingly convinced that it could not win. The junior senator from Arkansas was not optimistic about his or the Senate's ability to lead the country out of the wilderness – he did not think in such terms anyway – but someone had to sound the tocsin, and Congress was the only power center available around which to build support for an end to the war and a new foreign policy based on reason and restraint.

# 31

# *Sparta or Athens?*

"The true patriot," J. William Fulbright told the Senate in 1971, "is one who gives his highest loyalty not to his country as it is, but to his own best conception of what it can and ought to be." Those among his colleagues with an eye to history recalled William Lloyd Garrison and his invocation of a higher law. That speech, delivered during the height of the slavery controversy, had presaged a denunciation of the Constitution and the Fugitive Slave Act, and an appeal by Garrison to his abolitionist followers to ignore the law when it violated their moral scruples; but Fulbright's invocation of a higher loyalty foreshadowed instead a campaign to restore constitutional democracy to America. It was a call to arms to combat what he referred to as an "elective dictatorship" – what Arthur Schlesinger would subsequently dub "the imperial presidency."

As Congress began its deliberations in early 1971 Fulbright delivered an updated version of "The Legislator," the speech he had given at the University of Chicago twenty-seven years earlier. From time immemorial, presidents, prime ministers, premiers, generalissimos, and tribal chieftains, elected or otherwise, had grasped for greater power; it was their nature. It was the duty of legislatures to remain forever vigilant against this threat; but America's had failed. "Out of a well-intentioned but misconceived notion of what patriotism and responsibility require in a time of world crisis, Congress has permitted the President to take over the two vital foreign policy powers which the Constitution vested in Congress," Fulbright proclaimed: the power to declare war and the power to approve foreign commitments.[1] Theoretically, Congress had the authority to end the war in Vietnam; whether or not it had the will was the issue. One did not have to be a student of Plato, Thucydides, or Montesquieu to understand that the Vietnam War was not only polarizing the country but also eroding the political liberties of its citizens. In the heat of war and frustrated by the nation's inability to win a clear-cut victory, Congress and the American people during the Johnson years had deferred to an avaricious executive in thrall to a burgeoning military–industrial complex whose existence was justified on the grounds that it was bringing social justice, a higher stan-

1 *Congressional Record,* Senate, Feb. 5, 1971, 1867–8.

dard of living, and at least the possibility of democracy to those peoples of the world threatened by international communism. Although that crusade had proved to be an illusion, private interests and ideological fanatics had joined hands to perpetuate it. If Congress did not act, the nation would be dragged into one foreign adventure after another until, morally and financially bankrupt, it disappeared from the face of the earth like other empires before it.[2]

Not only had the trend toward executive domination of American foreign policy accelerated dramatically under Richard Nixon and Henry Kissinger, but there was no idealism in their notion of American exceptionalism. As a nationalist and card-carrying superpatriot, Richard Nixon continually paid lip service to the notion of American cultural superiority; but as an outsider and an episodic paranoid, he attached himself to those aspects of American culture that he felt would make him popular – sports, for example. He had no genuine passions or even hobbies beyond politics, much less a utopian vision or even a commitment to a moral code. Indeed, like the public relations men with whom he surrounded himself, Nixon was amoral, a humorless man seeking in the exercise of power the comfort and security that he was unable to find elsewhere.[3] Repeatedly referring to himself in the third person as "RN" in memos to his aides, Nixon hammered away at the person he wanted them to create in the public mind: "strong convictions . . . came up through adversity . . . cool . . . unflappable . . . a man . . . who is steely but who is subtle and appears almost gentle."[4]

The Nixon regime, because it was less idealistic than the Johnson administration, was both more and less formidable an adversary for Fulbright and those who wanted to end the war in Vietnam, reduce American commitments abroad, and restrict the power of the executive. Unlike Johnson, Nixon had no agenda for uplifting the downtrodden at home or abroad and was thus unable to tap the deep well of American idealism. He tried the New Republicanism in the form of the Family Assistance Plan, but abandoned it. Indeed, Richard Nixon cared nothing for domestic reform because he could not win with it. "International affairs is our issue," he told White House staffers John Haldeman and John Ehrlichman, and the Democrats must not be allowed to usurp it. Leave domestic affairs to them "because Libs can always promise more."[5] However, he thought of international relations in terms of power and control, not understanding and interdependence. His approach to the Ful-

2 Ibid.

3 Late in 1970 the president directed H. R. Haldeman to assign a designated "anecdotalist" to any public meeting or interview involving the president. That person was to be sure that out of every such encounter the press received a "warm human interest story" that portrayed Nixon as a sensitive, caring human being. Haldeman to Chapin, Dec. 9, 1970, WHSpF, Box 70, Nixon Project.

4 Nixon to Kissinger, July 19, 1971, WHSpF, Box 151, Nixon Project.

5 Notes on News Summary, Nov. 13, 1971, WHSpF, Box 35, Nixon Project.

bright exchange program was to view its participants as agents of cultural imperialism. He repeatedly told Kissinger that the United States should send more of its students abroad and accept fewer from foreign countries. Indeed, at times he blamed campus unrest on "radical" exchange students from other parts of the world.[6]

No one ever accused Henry Kissinger of being a bleeding heart either. The notion of replicating America around the globe seemed absurd to him, both because he had contempt for so much of what was American and because he recognized the pitfalls of "welfare imperialism," to use Fulbright's phrase. Like Nixon, Kissinger was interested in power for power's sake. As numerous historians have noted, the national security adviser aspired to be nothing less than arbiter of the international political system. For Kissinger as well as for Nixon to satisfy their needs, America had to be respected, and respect, they were convinced, was built primarily on fear. The vision of America as a moral exemplar and benefactor to the rest of the world – champion of human rights, elevator of living standards – held no attraction for them. Bases, bombs, missiles, and ships gave the United States credibility. In *A World Restored,* Kissinger acknowledged that diplomacy was "the art of restraining power," but he also observed that "in any negotiation it is understood that force is the ultimate recourse."[7] Those assumptions and goals placed the administration on a collision course with J. William Fulbright and the growing anti-imperialist clique within the United States Congress.

Throughout 1970 and 1971 Fulbright, together with George McGovern, John Sherman Cooper, and Mark Hatfield (R–Oregon), hammered away at the system of bases and overseas commitments and at the military–industrial complex that underlay them. Using the issue of executive usurpation of congressional prerogatives to attract conservatives, and capitalizing at every opportunity on the widespread discontent created by American involvement in Cambodia, Laos, and Vietnam, they sought to persuade the nation to redefine its foreign policy objectives in a rational, restrained way, one that would take into account cultural diversity and match America's ends to its diminishing means.

In 1969 Carl Marcy had persuaded Richard Moose to join the staff of the SFRC. Moose, an Arkansan and career Foreign Service officer, had worked first for Walt Rostow on the staff of the NSC and subsequently for Henry Kissinger in the same capacity. He had left the White House for a variety of reasons: He was tired of looking out his office window and watching his wife marching to protest the very war that he was planning; he was increasingly influenced by his radical friend I. F. Stone; and it soon became clear

6 News Summaries, Jan. 3, 1971, WHSpF, Box 32, Nixon Project.

7 Chalmers Roberts, "Kissinger vs. Fulbright," *Washington Post,* Apr. 26, 1970.

that "Henry" had his knife sharpened for him. A bright, personable man with a fine sense of irony, Moose found a kindred spirit in Jim Lowenstein.

Both Moose and Lowenstein had had a conversion experience over Vietnam, and they attacked American involvement there with all the ferocity guilty consciences could muster. In the fall of 1969 the pair had approached Carl Marcy and asked him about the feasibility of a fact-finding mission to Southeast Asia. Led by Spiro Agnew, supporters of the war were insisting almost daily that Fulbright himself go to Vietnam and find out the truth, a suggestion that the chairman had steadfastly resisted on a number of grounds. An SFRC staff mission, the two had argued, would hopefully spike the vice-president's guns. Moreover, Vietnamization had temporarily mesmerized the country and many members of Congress; with George Aiken and John Sherman Cooper openly supporting the policy, all momentum toward withdrawal had been lost.[8] Moose and Lowenstein suspected that the military/political situation was not as promising as the administration portrayed it, and that the GVN and ARVN were no more prepared to assume responsibility for the future of their country than they had been during the Johnson era.

Marcy hesitated. He had had a hard time selling committee members on the Pincus–Paul expedition, and there had been no partisan split on the committee then. After consulting Fulbright, however, he gave the go-ahead.

Fulbright found seductive the lull in the war on the home front that followed Nixon's Vietnamization speech. "The hate-mail has been very bad during the past year," he wrote Tony Austin of the *New York Times*. "Whatever may be the eventual limits of the President's Vietnamization program, it does have the immediate, beneficial effect of cooling down the temperature of the country."[9] But he and other critics of the war could not blind themselves to the knowledge that Vietnamization was not a viable plan for American withdrawal but a scheme to achieve military and political victory. "So far as I can see," Arthur Schlesinger wrote Fulbright in late January 1970, "the administration has been trying to ride two horses on Vietnam," and the two horses were going in different directions. "The negotiation idea is designed to bring the war to an end; the Vietnamization plan is designed to keep the war going . . . and even apparently in some sense to 'win' the war."[10] Fulbright had already come to that conclusion. "Vietnamization can only be taken as 'heads I win, tails you lose,' a strategy aimed at victory for the Thieu–Ky government," Fulbright wrote in the *Progressive*. This was an outcome the North Vietnamese and Vietcong "will never accept, unless it is forced upon them by military defeat."[11]

8 Interview with James Lowenstein, Oct. 3, 1991, Washington, D.C.
9 JWF to Anthony Austin, Jan. 21, 1970, Series 48:18, Box 59:1, SPF.
10 Schlesinger to JWF, Jan. 26, 1970, Series 48:48, Box 61:4, SPF.
11 J. William Fulbright, "Vietnam: The Crucial Issue," *Progressive*, Feb. 1970, 16–18.

Both Schlesinger and Fulbright believed that the key to reaching a negotiated settlement in Vietnam was the Thieu government. If the United States would abandon its client regime in Saigon and throw its support behind a new ruling coalition, the North Vietnamese would be willing "to accept a neutralist, independent South Vietnam which they would not seek forcibly to reunite with North Vietnam."[12] Privately, the chairman observed to Schlesinger that "the North Vietnamese are probably deeply interested in a negotiated settlement. The question is how to persuade the president to be interested in it and make a move in that direction before the Vietnamese change their minds. . . . The President has mesmerized the country for the present."[13]

Fulbright was wrong about Hanoi, if correct about Nixon and the American people. The North Vietnamese were in fact publicly taking the line that they would countenance a neutral, independent south, but in private conversations with Kissinger, negotiator Le Duc Tho refused to give any such assurances. Kissinger repeatedly warned Fulbright that the North Vietnamese were telling the doves one thing but him quite another; his arguments fell on deaf ears. Vietnamization would have to be exposed for the sham it was, Fulbright decided, and it was this conviction that led him to approve the Lowenstein–Moose probe.[14]

Lowenstein had been to Vietnam previously in 1967 with Senator Philip Hart and knew that if he and Moose were not careful, they would be swallowed up in the official public relations apparatus:

> They meet you and say that they are going to show you everything. Tomorrow they will take you to a specific place – it's two hours in the helicopter, two hours in a car, twenty minutes in the place, two hours in the car, two hours in the helicopter and the day's gone. They keep you moving all the time in a captive environment so you're always talking to the pilot, driver, plus an escort officer. As long as they keep you moving, they can keep you from talking to people. It's very subtle.[15]

As soon as Moose and Lowenstein arrived in Saigon on December 4, the two broke away from their uneasy hosts and struck out for the delta. Traveling at times by bicycle and at times by rickety automobile, they were passed from source to source, interviewing peasants, village chiefs, and field-grade American officers. In the company of a journalist friend of Lowenstein's the two spent the night in a supposedly secure hamlet, only to wake up the next morning to find that the headman's throat had been cut. In Saigon Moose and Lowenstein were met with hostile contempt by Ellsworth Bunker and the

12 Ibid.
13 JWF to Schlesinger, Jan. 30, 1970, Series 48:18, Box 61:4, SPF.
14 Press Release, Dec. 1, 1969, Series 48:3, Box 17:1, SPF.
15 Lowenstein interview.

military command, but the two SFRC staffers quickly learned that the upper echelon's control did not reach very far down into the ranks. Lowenstein recalled:

> The situation in the military was very bad by then. A lot of officers would talk to us about it . . . a lot of junior officers – lieutenants, captains, majors – who were very well educated. Out of the military academies. They were very upset. All the lies that went into the business about body counts were so flagrant and so obvious.[16]

The Moose–Lowenstein team returned to Washington just before Christmas to deliver its report. After describing the situation as they had found it – a much less optimistic image than that being projected by the administration – the SFRC investigators argued that Vietnamization would work only if there emerged a broad-based government capable of commanding the allegiance of all major groups, if ARVN became a highly motivated, efficient fighting machine, and if Hanoi continued its low level of military activity in the south. "Dilemmas thus seem to lie ahead in Vietnam, as they have throughout our involvement in this war that appears to be not only far from won but far from over," they concluded.[17]

No sooner had the two investigators filed their analysis with the SFRC than Carl Marcy leaked it to the press. Lowenstein recalled that the result was astonishing. All the major dailies carried front-page excerpts, and the nightly news anchors read portions of the text on the air.[18] At once the sense of tranquillity over Vietnam that Nixon and his minions had labored so hard to establish was shattered. All the old anxieties came flooding back. "This shows there is an establishment for peace at any price," the president wrote Kissinger. "Have your letters team give them hell – we must keep our silent majority group involved."[19]

Throughout February and March 1970, Fulbright and the SFRC staff received word from various sources that the secret war in Laos was escalating. Those rumors turned out to be true. Nixon had come under intense pressure from the air force to resume bombing North Vietnam. Kissinger pleaded with him not to take that dangerous step, one that was sure to derail his private negotiations with Le Duc Tho and to breathe new life into the antiwar movement. Nixon compromised by authorizing massive new bombing of North Vietnamese positions in Laos and the portions of the Ho Chi Minh Trail that

16 Ibid.

17 Quoted in William C. Berman, *William Fulbright and the Vietnam War: The Dissent of a Political Realist* (Kent, Ohio, 1988), 120.

18 See John W. Finney, "War-Policy Basis Is Called Dubious," *New York Times,* Feb. 2, 1970.

19 Notes on News Summary, Feb. 2, 1970, WHSpF, Box 31, Nixon Project.

ran through that country.[20] From the secret hearings held by the Symington subcommittee in October 1969, Fulbright and the other members knew that there were hundreds of American military advisers in Laos, and that American planes based in Thailand were flying numerous missions each week in support of the Royal Laotian Army's effort to clear the Pathet Lao out of the Plain of Jars. They had also learned that the U.S. military and CIA had for years supplied and trained a secret army under Major General Van Pao. Van Pao's troops – comprising Laotians but separate from the Royal Laotian Army – felt free to cross into Vietnam and Cambodia in pursuit of the communists.[21]

Despite the fact that Fulbright had detailed some of this activity to his Senate colleagues in executive session, the Nixon administration continued to argue privately that its operations in Laos were classified and to deny publicly that they existed at all. Indeed, so determined was Washington to hide its involvement, particularly on the ground, that CIA operatives killed in northeast Laos were routinely maimed by their fellows to prevent identification. "The Americans have orders they must not be captured," a Laotian official working with the CIA confided to a foreign correspondent. "If they are killed, other members of their patrol put a grenade on their face or shoot them up with their machine guns till they can't be recognized."[22]

Though he would not release verbatim portions of the transcript or cite precise numbers of advisers and sorties, Fulbright began giving Kissinger-style "backgrounders" to the press. The conflict in Laos had already turned into a Vietnam, he told an Arkansas reporter. The only difference was that because there were only three million Laotians, the number killed could never equal the number of Vietnamese killed.[23] The first week in March Fulbright backed a move by George McGovern to have the Senate once again go into executive session to consider the Laotian situation.[24] Still the Nixon administration refused to allow the SFRC to release its information.

Then on March 9, in an effort to head off the gathering storm, Nixon went on a national television hookup to inform the nation that there were four hundred American advisers in Laos and that American warplanes were bombing the trail and flying support missions for Prince Souvanna Phouma's Royal Laotian Army. However, he stated, no Americans had died in combat in Laos; moreover, he would abide by the 1969 congressional directive not to introduce American ground troops into that country. Three days later newspapers

20 Notes on News Summaries, Feb. 9 and Mar. 13, 1970, WHSpF, Box 31, Nixon Project.

21 "Rogers Explains His Stand on Laos," *New York Times,* Mar. 18, 1970.

22 "CIA Reportedly Maims Its Dead on Lao Patrols," *Washington Evening Star,* June 10, 1970.

23 "Concern Grows Over Laos," *Fort Smith Southwest Times Record,* Feb. 22, 1970.

24 George C. Wilson, "Secret Session on Laos Sought by McGovern," *Washington Post,* Mar. 4, 1970.

across the country reported that Capt. Joseph K. Bush, Jr., had been cut down by North Vietnamese machine-gun fire in northeastern Laos. Assistant Press Secretary Gerald Warren admitted to reporters at Key Biscayne that Bush was the twenty-seventh American combat death in Laos, but that the president had been unaware of the statistic when he had delivered his speech.[25] Fulbright suspected that Warren was lying, and he was not satisfied with the president's pledge. Three days after the White House statement he introduced a resolution prohibiting the use of U.S. forces "in combat in or over Laos" without prior congressional approval. "If the Senate is to remain silent while the President uses air forces in an Asian country without authority from Congress," he declared, "we should remain silent about his use of ground combat forces."[26]

Foreign policy was not the only area in which Richard Nixon displayed his contempt for the U.S. Senate. The upper house's rejection of Clement Haynsworth had humiliated and therefore incensed Nixon. In the aftermath of that debacle, he ordered Attorney General Mitchell to come up with another name for the Supreme Court. He wanted a southerner, a strict constructionist, and a man free of any possible conflict-of-interest charge, he said. Mitchell's choice was Judge G. Harold Carswell, a Floridian who had recently been appointed to the U.S. Court of Appeals for the Fifth Circuit. Carswell met Nixon's requirements, but he was also an ignoramus and a racist. As a candidate for the Georgia legislature in 1948, he had declared that "segregation of the races is proper and the only practical and correct way of life."[27] Furthermore, his qualifications for the high court were simply nonexistent. As a district and later circuit judge, Carswell was reversed on appeal 40 percent of the time. He had, moreover, been abusive to civil rights lawyers in his court and often dismissed their suits without a hearing.[28] Bryce Harlow, the Eisenhower assistant whom Nixon had brought in to handle congressional liaison, informed the president that the senators "think Carswell's a boob, a dummy. And what counter is there to that? He is."[29]

Why Richard Nixon picked such a grossly unqualified and politically vulnerable person was a subject of much debate at the time. Some speculated that he wanted to insult the Senate, others that he selected Carswell as a rebuke to

25 UPI 6, Mar. 9, 1970.

26 "Use of Planes for Laos War Called Illegal," *Arkansas Gazette*, Mar. 12, 1970.

27 Quoted in Stephen E. Ambrose, *Nixon*, vol. II, *The Triumph of a Politician, 1962–1972* (New York, 1989), 330.

28 William Safire, *Before the Fall: An Inside View of the Pre-Watergate White House* (New York, 1977), 342–4.

29 Quoted in Ambrose, *Nixon*, II:330.

the Supreme Court. Nixon was angry at the court for forcing busing on the South and in the process enabling George Wallace to attack the administration from the right. Moreover, the president was genuinely convinced that the high court was indeed forcing integration on Dixie while turning a blind eye to segregation in the North.[30] Nixon had not, however, deliberately selected a blatant racist and intellectual lightweight: He had assigned the task to John Mitchell, and Mitchell had botched it.[31] Nevertheless, once Carswell's name had been sent forward, the president became determined to fight to the bitter end to secure his nomination. Admitting to mistakes was not part of Nixon's repertoire.

The Haynsworth nomination had caused J. William Fulbright numerous political problems in Arkansas; his obvious lack of enthusiasm for the South Carolinian had alienated conservatives, and his vote for the nomination had eroded his standing with liberal opponents of the Vietnam War. It was therefore with a sinking heart that he heard Lee Williams brief him on Carswell's background. There would be no lesser-of-two-evils argument in this situation.

Many Arkansans continued to be up in arms about integration. In the fall of 1969 the Supreme Court had issued orders speeding up the process and authorizing extensive busing to implement its instructions. Although busing was hardly necessary in most parts of Arkansas, integration was well under way in a number of rural communities as well as Little Rock, Pine Bluff, Jonesboro, and Fort Smith. Just as Arkansans identified with the white "victims" of ghetto violence in 1968, they identified with the "victims" of forced busing then and in the years that followed. George Wallace had carried the state in 1968. Arkansans continued to feel oppressed and discriminated against, and they vented their spleen to their junior senator. He seemed to be intimidated. "I have always been sympathetic to the problems faced by local schools in administering their policies," Fulbright wrote a Rogers constituent, "and I believe that busing students against the will of either the student or his parent, for the sole purpose of achieving a racial balance, is not in the best interest of any of the parties concerned."[32] In February Fulbright supported an amendment to the HEW appropriations bill requiring that the entire country desegregate its schools at the same speed;[33] but then, on March 13, Fulbright voted for a five-year extension of the Voting Rights Act. It marked the

30 News Summaries, Jan. 13, 1970, WHSpF, Box 31, Nixon Project.

31 See News Summary, Feb. 1970, WHSpF, Box 31, Nixon Project.

32 JWF to William P. Snyder, Feb. 26, 1970, Series 39:3, Box 17:6, SPF.

33 Northern liberals were caught off guard and the amendment passed by a vote of 63 to 24. "South Wins Large Senate Vote to Equalize Integration Pace," *Arkansas Democrat*, Feb. 18, 1970.

first time since Reconstruction that an Arkansas senator had voted for a civil rights bill.[34]

A number of Fulbright's liberal supporters in Arkansas had urged him to vote for Haynsworth on the grounds that Nixon would only nominate someone worse. Carswell was indeed someone worse, they agreed. From Fayetteville Bob Leflar urged the junior senator to vote "no." Carswell just "didn't measure up," he advised.[35]

By the time the Senate began formal debate on the Carswell nomination in late March, the Floridian was taking hits from all directions. The ABA repudiated its earlier endorsement as evidence came to light that Nixon's choice for associate justice had belonged to an all-white Florida State booster club in the early 1950s and was cofounder of a segregated private golf club.[36] Even his supporters damned him with faint praise. Senator Roman Hruska (R–Nebraska) took to the floor of the Senate to defend the administration's nominee. "The President appoints these people," he declared, "and even if he were mediocre, there are a lot of mediocre judges and people and lawyers. Aren't they entitled to a little representation?" Russell Long agreed: "Brilliant . . . upside down thinkers" on the Supreme Court were destroying the United States. What the country needed, he declared, was a "B student or C student."[37]

In March Fulbright privately informed Senator Birch Bayh (D–Indiana) that he was seriously considering voting against the Carswell nomination. Bayh, who was leading the northern liberal opposition to the Floridian, was delighted. The best tactic for derailing the nomination would be a motion to recommit it to the Judiciary Committee for further study. Would Fulbright lead the way? Bayh asked. His prestige, coupled with the fact that he had voted for Haynsworth, would persuade a lot of fence sitters.[38]

On March 26, with the Senate deeply divided, Fulbright stood before his colleagues and moved that the Carswell nomination be recommitted. "A number of additional questions have been raised concerning Judge Carswell's qualifications," he declared, and the Judiciary Committee needed time to consider them.[39] To that point polls had shown a 2-to-1 majority in the Senate in favor of Carswell. Fulbright was the first southerner to express reservations, and his announcement started major bleeding. Within hours two Republicans, Mark Hatfield and Robert Packwood, both of Oregon, announced their oppo-

34 John W. Finney, "5-Year Extension of Voting Rights Passed by Senate," *New York Times,* Mar. 14, 1970.

35 "Back to the Licklog," *Arkansas Gazette,* Mar. 26, 1970.

36 *Congressional Record,* Senate, Mar. 26, 1970, 9611.

37 "Long Tells Senate Supreme Court Needs 'C Student,'" *Arkansas Gazette,* Mar. 17, 1970.

38 Birch Bayh to JWF, Mar. 24, 1970, and David Lambert, memorandum to JWF, Mar. 24, 1970, SPF.

39 *Congressional Record,* Senate, Mar. 26, 1970, 9610.

sition.[40] The Oregonians and other Republicans were furious because they believed the White House had withheld vital information from them concerning Carswell's racist record.

During the first week in April, Fulbright was deluged with mail by constituents who saw the opposition to Carswell as simply a northern liberal vendetta to block the appointment of a "strict constructionist . . . Southern judge" who opposed the Warren court's activism on civil rights. In vain did he argue that he was the strict constructionist whereas Carswell was a radical reactionary activist.[41] There were those, however, who saw Carswell as an anachronism, a crude racist whose nomination was a backhanded slap at the South. Orval Faubus's unwillingness to condemn Fulbright over his move to recommit was a sure sign that a large number of Arkansans shared the junior senator's reservations.[42]

In the face of mounting opposition, Nixon declared that Carswell had his "total support" and denied that the judge was a racist. "What is centrally at issue," he declared, "is the constitutional responsibility of the President to appoint members of the Court – and whether this responsibility can be frustrated by those who wish to substitute their own philosophy . . . for that of the one person entrusted by the Constitution with the power of appointment."[43]

For the previous six months Fulbright had been working assiduously to convince the Senate that the Nixon administration was destroying the system of checks and balances and creating an imperial presidency. As the votes on Laos and foreign aid indicated, he had made some headway. Many senators, however, had a hard time getting worked up about foreign policy matters and abstract questions of legislative–executive prerogatives; but the right of the Senate to pass on the executive's judicial nominees was another matter. Federal judges and other judicial officers were an important part of senatorial patronage; these individuals had the power to influence the lives of constituents in a dramatic fashion. Senators on both sides of the aisle rose to remind Nixon that as president his prerogative was to nominate; the consent of the Senate was necessary to appoint.

On April 5 a coalition of southern diehards and Republicans led by John Stennis beat back the motion to recommit Carswell's nomination to the Judiciary Committee by a vote of 52 to 44. White House jubilation quickly died down, however, when several Republicans announced that they had voted against recommittal because they wanted the chance to reject Carswell outright. A poll of the Senate on the eve of the confirmation vote showed a dead heat. The fate of the nomination, Clifford Case declared, would hinge on the

40 "Send Nomination Back to Panel, Fulbright Says," *Arkansas Gazette,* Mar. 27, 1970.
41 JWF to Randall Mathis, May 12, 1970, SPF.
42 "Send Nomination Back to Panel, Fulbright Says," *Arkansas Gazette,* Mar. 27, 1970.
43 Quoted in Ambrose, *Nixon,* II:337.

vote of J. William Fulbright. The Arkansan had informed reporters following the recommittal ballot that he would study the situation closely before deciding.[44] In the last hours before the vote, White House aides tried to repair the damage. A dozen western Democrats received calls promising no significant Republican opposition in their next elections if they supported Carswell.[45]

As the Senate prepared to take up the controversial nomination, a large crowd gathered on the steps of the Capitol. Inside, Senators and staff aides filled the well of the chamber. A number of distinguished guests, including 83-year-old Ernest Gruening, a veteran of liberal causes, filled rows of chairs five deep behind the senators' desks. The galleries were packed. Tension permeated the chamber as the clerk began to call the roll. There was scarcely a sound as the names were read. By the time the clerk reached Fulbright, the vote stood 19 to 9 for confirmation.

"Mr. Fulbright," the clerk intoned. There was a brief pause, then a quietly drawled "No." A huge collective sigh went up from the crowd. As the call continued the tension mounted again. It soon became apparent that Fulbright and a small band of southerners, together with a dozen liberal Republicans, were voting with northern Democrats. When the final vote tally was read, Carswell and Nixon had lost. The vote was 51 to 45. The packed gallery cheered and applauded. At the door to the corridor outside the chamber an African-American woman raced up to Clarence Mitchell, the veteran NAACP Washington director, and hugged him; others crowded around and patted him on the shoulder. On the Senate floor, Vice-President Agnew pounded the gavel, but the senators themselves paid him no heed. Richard B. Russell of Georgia, coleader of the southern Democrats, stood white-faced with emotion and said, "Order, we must have order." There was none on the floor or off.[46]

In the days following the Carswell vote Fulbright's offices received a flurry of hate mail. Martha Mitchell, the beehive-bouffanted Pine Bluff native who was married to the attorney general, called the *Arkansas Gazette* and urged the paper to "crucify" Fulbright for his opposition to Carswell. It would be one of many late-night telephone calls Mrs. Mitchell would make to the *Gazette* and other newspapers.[47] The furor, however, quickly died down. The national and international press heaped accolades on Fulbright. From London, Anthony Lewis declared that the SFRC chairman had done much by his vote against Carswell to free himself and his state of the taint of Little Rock.[48]

44 "Foes of Carswell Gather for Fight," *Pine Bluff Commercial,* Apr. 7, 1970.

45 "GOP Bid for Carswell Deal Reported," *Washington Evening Star,* Apr. 9, 1970.

46 "In Senate: A Gasp . . . Then Cheers," *Washington Post,* Apr. 7, 1970.

47 "Mrs. Mitchell Sounds Off," *Washington Evening Star,* Apr. 9, 1970.

48 Anthony Lewis, "The Significance of Senator Fulbright," *New York Times,* Mar. 28, 1970.

The Carswell vote embittered Richard Nixon. He called reporters into the Oval Office and told them that the Floridian's rejection was a slap in the face of the South. It was clear, he said, that no southern judge who was a strict constitutional constructionist would be named by the present Senate.[49] Privately, he told his staff that he was determined to show "those Senators . . . who's really tough."[50] Coming in the midst of a campaign by the JCS to persuade him to expand the war in Southeast Asia, Nixon's threat had ominous overtones for American foreign policy.

The first week in April Fulbright delivered a speech entitled "New Myths and Old Realities," an ironic play on the title of his famous 1964 address. He called for nothing less than American acquiescence in the communization of Vietnam:

> The master myth of Vietnam . . . is the greatly inflated importance which has been attached to it. From the standpoint of American security and interests, the central fact about Indochina, including Vietnam, is that it does not matter very much who rules in those small and backward lands. At the risk of being accused of every sin from racism to communism, I stress the irrelevance of ideology to poor and backward populations.[51]

The notion of a monolithic communist threat bent on conquering the world was an illusion. The Soviet Union was a "traditional, cautious, and rather unimaginative great power" incapable of co-opting nationalism in Southeast Asia. If the United States had not interfered in Vietnam, "we might now be dealing with a stable, independent, unified Communist country – no more hostile to the United States than Yugoslavia itself is today." North Vietnam was the paramount power in Indochina, and the sooner the United States recognized that fact the better. "We are fighting a double shadow in Indochina," he proclaimed: "the shadow of the international Communist conspiracy and the shadow of the old, obsolete, mindless game of power politics."[52]

Although Nixon and Kissinger would never have admitted it, there was much in this speech with which they agreed. "What happens in those [developing] parts of the world is not, in the final analysis, going to have any significant effect on the success of our foreign policy in the foreseeable future," Nixon wrote Kissinger in March.[53] They did not, however, regard power

49 Speech Insert, Apr. 10, 1970, WHSpF, Box 63, Nixon Project.

50 Quoted in George C. Herring, *America's Longest War: The United States and Vietnam, 1950–1975,* 2d ed. (New York, 1986), 235.

51 *Congressional Record,* Senate, Apr. 2, 1970, 10150–6.

52 Ibid., 10150–6.

53 Nixon to Haldeman, Ehrlichman, and Kissinger, Mar. 2, 1970, WHSpF, Box 138, Nixon Project.

politics as old, obsolete, or mindless; nor did they perceive the Soviet Union and especially Communist China to be satiated, unimaginative powers – rather, these countries would seize markets, bases, and political influence wherever and whenever they could, and it was up to the United States to contain and even dominate its adversaries. Nixon and Kissinger wanted to extricate the United States from Vietnam because the war weakened the nation's ability to combat Moscow and Peking and to influence events in other, more important regions of the globe. America could not simply pull out, however: To do so would lessen its credibility with friend and foe alike, and cause division at home that would impair the administration's ability to arbitrate abroad in those areas that were of vital interest.

"New Myths and Old Realities" was accorded a very different reception than the earlier speech to which it alluded. In 1964 Fulbright had conjured up visions of a better world based on peaceful coexistence. In 1970 he urged Americans to recognize that they had for the past seven years been involved in a long, bloody, and pointless failure in Vietnam. In the end, he said, it did not matter whether communism prevailed in Southeast Asia, and it had never mattered. The United States should negotiate the best deal it could and get out. "This is strong stuff," editorialized the *Washington Post*[54] – indeed, still too strong for most Americans. "Fulbright Would Surrender" proclaimed the *Richmond Times-Dispatch.*[55]

54 Benjamin C. Bradlee, ed., "Vietnam: The Missing Ingredient," *Washington Post,* Apr. 5, 1970.

55 "Fulbright Would Surrender," *Richmond Times-Dispatch,* Apr. 5, 1970.

# 32

# *Cambodia*

In April 1970 Fulbright became the longest-reigning chairman of the SFRC in American history. One after another, members of the club rose on the floor of the Senate to pay tribute. John Sparkman, Gale McGee, and Russell Long, all of whom he had differed sharply with him over Vietnam, praised Fulbright as a conscientious, independent, thoughtful statesman. Jacob Javits, whose unflinching support of Israel had repeatedly pitted him against the Arkansan, lauded him as "a man of very deep insight . . . a fine intellect." Virtually every member of the SFRC, Republican as well as Democrat, paid him homage.[1]

By the spring of 1970 the flaws in Nixon's policy of Vietnamization were becoming apparent. In an effort to build on the tranquillity that followed in the wake of the silent majority speech, the president announced in March 1970 the intended withdrawal of a hundred and fifty thousand additional troops during the coming year. No matter how useful Vietnamization was in terms of quelling domestic dissent in the United States, however, it was counterproductive to the goal of forcing North Vietnam to negotiate a settlement that would leave the Thieu government intact. The logic of the situation was that Hanoi had only to wait and refuse to make concessions; eventually the Americans would be gone and the pitifully weak Thieu regime could be summarily dispatched. Indeed, Creighton Abrams had bitterly protested the new troop withdrawals, warning that they would leave South Vietnam dangerously vulnerable to enemy military pressure. Increasingly impatient with the stalemate in Southeast Asia, Nixon began once again looking around for an opportunity to demonstrate to the North Vietnamese that "we were still serious about our commitment in Vietnam."[2] One was not long in coming.

Throughout the Vietnam War, Prince Norodom Sihanouk had worked desperately to perserve Cambodian neutrality. As part of an early understanding

1 "Fulbright Praised by Fellow Senators," *Arkansas Gazette,* Apr. 24, 1970.
2 Quoted in George C. Herring, *America's Longest War: The United States and Vietnam, 1950–1975,* 2d ed. (New York, 1986), 234.

with Hanoi, Sihanouk had agreed to ignore sanctuaries established by the Vietcong on the Vietnamese–Cambodian border. In exchange, Hanoi had promised not to aid the small Cambodian communist movement, the Khmer Rouge. The decision by the Nixon administration in 1969 to embark on its top-secret bombing campaign inside Cambodia helped upset the delicate balance Sihanouk had established. In March 1970 the prince, while in Europe, was overthrown by Prime Minister Lon Nol, who had the support of Cambodia's intensely anticommunist military commanders. Although the United States had played no direct role in the coup, according to George Herring and William Shawcross,[3] Lon Nol was well aware of Washington's disapproval of Sihanouk's neutralism and therefore believed that the United States would not only tolerate but reward a pro-Western coup. Following Sihanouk's overthrow, the United States quickly recognized the new government and began providing it with covert military aid.

For years the American military had wanted to do more than just bomb North Vietnamese and Vietcong sanctuaries in Cambodia. The JCS longed to invade and destroy the communist enclaves on the ground. With a friendly government now in power, they could act. Melvin Laird and William Rogers both opposed an incursion, whereas Kissinger managed to play both sides of the street. Nixon was determined to strike. Attacks on the sanctuaries could now be justified in terms of sustaining a friendly Cambodian government as well as easing the military threat to South Vietnam. The president knew the move would touch off a firestorm of controversy at home, but he was in one of his black moods. Angry with the Senate for rejecting his nominees to the Supreme Court and criticizing his handling of the war, he was determined to "show them who's tough." Nixon perceived himself as an individual who thrived on crises, even if he had to manufacture one. "When you bite the bullet, bite it hard – go for the big play," he subsequently told Nelson Rockefeller in describing his decision to invade Cambodia.[4] The mixed Western/football metaphor was vintage Nixon.

On April 29 South Vietnamese units with American air support attacked an enemy sanctuary on the Parrot's Beak, a strip of Cambodian territory thirty-three miles from Saigon. On the thirtieth, American forces assaulted Fishhook, a North Vietnamese base area fifty-five miles northwest of Saigon. That night Nixon went on national television and justified the invasion as a response to North Vietnamese "aggression." The real target of the operation, he explained, was the Central Office for South Vietnam (COSVN), the "nerve center" of North Vietnamese operations, although DOD had made clear to him that it was uncertain as to where COSVN was located or whether it even ex-

3 Ibid., 234; William Shawcross, *Sideshow: Kissinger, Nixon and the Destruction of Cambodia* (New York, 1979), 122.

4 Quoted in Marilyn B. Young, *The Vietnam Wars, 1945–1990* (New York, 1991), 247.

isted.[5] At a subsequent press conference on May 8, Nixon promised that all American units would be out of Cambodia by the second week of June and that all Americans, including advisers, would be out by the end of the month.

During the weeks preceding the invasion, the administration had worked assiduously to conceal its plans from Fulbright and the SFRC. On April 3, Secretary Rogers had assured a closed-door session of the committee that the administration was committed to maintaining the neutrality of Cambodia, and under no circumstances would American forces cross the border. A beaming Fulbright had emerged to tell reporters, "It is quite clear their policy is not to become involved in a general way." On the evening of the twenty-third Kissinger had met at Fulbright's house with the chairman and selected committee members to discuss foreign policy questions and mend political fences generally. Three times Nixon phoned and interrupted the meeting to discuss the forthcoming Cambodian operation; the national security adviser said nothing to his hosts.[6] On the twenty-seventh Rogers again appeared in executive session before the SFRC and assured Fulbright and the others that the president would do nothing in Cambodia without consulting Congress.[7]

Actually, Fulbright and the staff of the SFRC had almost been able to anticipate the invasion. By late April, Washington was full of rumors that the Nixon administration was secretly funneling unauthorized military aid to the Lon Nol government. Dick Moose and Jim Lowenstein were certain something more was afoot, and they subsequently convinced Marcy and Fulbright to send them out to investigate. "Maybe by going out there . . . if you can send us some information . . . maybe this won't happen," Moose remembered Fulbright as saying. The two investigators did not arrive in time. "We were in Hong Kong when the invasion of Cambodia occurred and we landed in Saigon the first day after it had happened," Moose recalled. "We were too late but we were able to dig right in to the rationale of the administration for doing what they had done."[8]

After taking in the standard round of briefings in Saigon, Moose and Lowenstein drove directly to Fishhook and the Parrot's Beak. They were shown mounds of captured equipment and heard how COSVN had been surrounded. "We've got them in the bottle; all we've got to do is put the stopper in," the U.S. commander told them. "It was all pure bullshit," Moose recalled. "If Lowenstein and I knew the attack was coming, you can be goddamn sure the NVA knew they were coming."[9]

5 Herring, *America's Longest War,* 236.
6 William C. Berman, *William Fulbright and the Vietnam War: The Dissent of a Political Realist* (Kent, Ohio, 1988), 124.
7 UPI 7, Apr. 27, 1970.
8 Interview with Richard Moose, June 29, 1989, Washington, D.C.
9 Ibid.

Nixon's Cambodian incursion had in fact produced only limited tactical results. According to the U.S. command, American troops killed some two thousand enemy troops, cleared over sixteen hundred acres of jungle, destroyed eight thousand bunkers, and captured large stocks of weapons. The invasion no doubt helped relieve pressure on ARVN and the Thieu government, thereby buying some time for Vietnamization; but COSVN turned out to be little more than a handful of thatched huts sitting atop a network of tunnels, and the NVA moved back into the area as soon as the Americans and South Vietnamese left.[10] Coming as it did in the wake of Sihanouk's overthrow, the invasion shattered Cambodian neutrality. "I think the effect is going to be – and already is – a terrible destruction to a rather fine little country that was not bothering anybody," Fulbright remarked prophetically to a group of reporters.[11]

Immediately Fulbright and other senators questioned the legal and constitutional power of the president, even as commander-in-chief, to send troops into a neutral nation. In a bitter Senate speech Mike Mansfield, a longtime friend of Sihanouk's, condemned the invasion and criticized Nixon personally. The time had come, he said, for the nation's leaders to show "a fitting sense of humility."[12] Senator Stephen Young (R–Ohio), attacking the "hallucination of victory in Vietnam," introduced a resolution to censure the president. In behalf of the SFRC Fulbright requested a face-to-face meeting with Nixon, the first such conference since Woodrow Wilson met with Henry Cabot Lodge's committee in 1919.[13]

Within minutes of the president's April 30 televised address, antiwar activists had taken to the streets in New York and Philadelphia, and protests erupted across the country in the days that followed. The scores of marches and rallies that engulfed campuses from Maryland to Oregon were characterized by a sense of betrayal; the war was being expanded under the pretense of ending it. On the evening of May 2 Fulbright addressed thirty-five hundred people at Indiana Central College under the sponsorship of the Hoosiers for Peace. Nixon's Cambodian intervention was "a clear, calculated, and utterly ill-advised decision to widen the war," he told the sympathetic audience. Nixon had taken this step, Fulbright explained, out of a personal fear of "humiliation and defeat," and because he still hoped to achieve victory by keeping Thieu and Ky as the undisputed rulers of South Vietnam.[14]

10 Herring, *America's Longest War,* 236.

11 Mike Trimble, "Allied Troops' Invasion to Destroy Cambodia, Fulbright Forecasts," *Arkansas Gazette,* June 17, 1970.

12 "Fulbright Panel Wants Session on Troop Move," *Washington Evening Star,* May 1, 1970.

13 "Lawmakers Demand President Explain Cambodia Decision," *Arkansas Gazette,* May 2, 1970.

14 "Fulbright Sees Fumble in Expansion of War," *Washington Evening Star,* May 2, 1970.

As criticism mounted and the first murmurings of impeachment began to be heard in Capitol Hill cloakrooms, Nixon reacted like a cornered animal. During a meeting on May 3 he urged aides to stand tough and instructed them in how to coach congressional supporters. They should accuse his detractors of "giving aid and comfort to the enemy" – he emphasized that phrase. "Don't worry about divisiveness. Having drawn the sword, don't take it out – stick it in hard. . . . Hit 'em in the gut. No defensiveness."[15] Kissinger later recalled that the president was "exhausted" and "deeply wounded by the hatred of the protesters."[16]

Meanwhile, the previously dormant antiwar movement continued to gain momentum. In Cambridge, Massachusetts, students occupied Harvard buildings to protest the university's refusal to take a stand against the Vietnam War or to withdraw its investments in racist South Africa. The first week in May, Kent State students protested the Cambodian invasion by rioting downtown and firebombing the ROTC building. Upon hearing the news, Nixon, at an informal briefing session at the Pentagon, called the student demonstrators a bunch of "bums." Meanwhile, Ohio Governor James Rhodes called out the National Guard and declared martial law. When he ordered guardsmen onto the campus of Kent State, students held a peaceful demonstration to protest. Suddenly the troops turned and opened fire. Their fusillade left four students dead and eleven wounded. Two of the young women killed were simply walking to class. Within days a million and a half students were participating in a boycott of classes, shutting down about a fifth of the nation's campuses for periods ranging from one day to the rest of the school year. Even the University of Arkansas, attended for the most part by conservative southern students, held a memorial service, and students and faculty circulated petitions calling for Nixon's impeachment.[17] Aroused by both the invasion and the Kent State shootings, more than a hundred thousand people gathered in Washington to show their disapproval.

"A whole new breed of student protesters are swarming into Washington," observed the UPI. "For these are the one-time 'silent majority' of university students – scrubbed, neat, well-dressed and determined instead of desperate."[18] Most had not participated in the demonstrations of the past; missing were the symbols of counterculture, even the peace symbol. Prominent among those who denounced the incursion as unconstitutional were the heads of the National Council of Churches, the United Presbyterian Church, the United Church of Christ, and the Council of Bishops of the United Methodist

15 Quoted in Charles DeBenedetti with Charles Chatfield, *An American Ordeal: The Antiwar Movement of the Vietnam Era* (Syracuse, 1990), 279.

16 Henry Kissinger, *White House Years* (Boston, 1979), 513, 514.

17 Brenda Blagg, "Mulins Declines Class Dismissal, Backs Memorial," *Arkansas Gazette,* May 7, 1970.

18 UPI 25, May 8, 1970.

Church. Even Billy Graham expressed "shock" at Cambodia and Kent State.[19]

In the summer of 1970, in the wake of the Cambodian demonstrations, an embittered president declared virtual warfare on those he considered his enemies: the "madmen" on the Hill, the "liberal" press, those who marched in protest. "Within the iron gates of the White House," Charles Colson later wrote, "a siege mentality was setting in. It was 'us' against 'them.' Gradually, as we drew the circle closer around us, the ranks of 'them' began to swell."[20] The day following the massive demonstration in Washington, Spiro Agnew, with a hundred National Guardsmen on duty for his protection, defended U.S. entry into Cambodia and accused J. William Fulbright of trying to "rekindle the debilitating fires of riot and unrest." In his address to a Republican campaign dinner at Boise, he classified Fulbright as one of America's Jeremiahs – "a gloomy coalition of choleric young intellectuals and tired, embittered elders."[21]

The Nixon administration's panicked reaction to criticism following Cambodia and Kent State sewed the seeds of its downfall. Shortly before the invasion of Cambodia, the Weathermen faction of the SDS had bombed the New York headquarters of three major U.S. corporations, including the Bank of America. Tom Huston subsequently told H. R. Haldeman that not only was the SDS determined to overthrow the government by force, it was fully capable of doing so.[22] In response to his aide's hysteria, the president authorized Huston to assemble a team of "countersubversives" who would ferret out and neutralize enemies of the Republic (and of Nixon – to him the two were interchangeable). In addition, under the Huston plan, intelligence agencies were directed to install wiretaps, open mail, and even break and enter to gather information that could be used to thwart opponents of the administration.

The May demonstrations in Washington heartened Fulbright because he saw in them the beginnings of a return by American liberals to the values of the 1930s and 1940s. The students who had come to the nation's capital, he noted in the *Progressive,* "seem to be in the process of becoming lobbyists for peace, making their views known, in a concerted, persistent, but peaceful and orderly way, to the elected representatives." They were following the path trod by American farmers, businesspeople, and labor unionists over the decades and in the process were reaffirming democracy. Although he was only dimly aware of the gathering storm of paranoia in the White House, Fulbright

19 "Four Church Leaders Say U.S. Incursion Unconstitutional," *Arkansas Gazette,* May 7, 1970.

20 Quoted in Herring, *America's Longest War,* 239.

21 "Spiro Defends U.S., Blasts Fulbright," *Paragould Daily Press,* May 9, 1970.

22 Huston to Haldeman, Mar. 12, 1970, WHSpF, Box 152, Nixon Project.

could not have disagreed more with Huston, Buchanan, and Nixon's views on the sources of instability in American society. Fulbright insisted that:

> [i]f there is any bias in our history . . . , it is not toward the Left but toward the Right. The "Red scares" of our past, from Sacco–Vanzetti to Alger Hiss to the "effete snobs" . . . of more recent vintage, have never amounted to much as far as threatening our society is concerned, but the anti-Red reactions have amounted to a great deal. [It is] the right wing bias of our past, the intense, obsessive fear of Communism, the disruption wrought by thirty years of chronic war, the power of the military–industrial–labor–academic complex which war has spawned [that threatens America].[23]

Fulbright continued to believe that with liberal internationalism discredited, the best bet for checking the right-wing radicalism spawned by the cold war was traditional conservatism. He remained convinced that the principal rallying point in his campaign to end the war and contain the burgeoning American empire was the Constitution. Only that hallowed document would offer sufficient political protection for those who would be accused of endangering America's national security. In addition, while Fulbright was convinced that the war in Vietnam was immoral, he had come to the conclusion that it was unwise and perhaps impossible to build a politically effective anti-imperialist campaign on abstract notions of right and wrong. He wrote in the *Progressive:*

> I am unattracted by that excess of conscience which leads individuals to invoke "a higher moral law." I mistrust too much conscience because it places too heavy a burden on human judgment. . . . I would rather be ruled by law than by conscience, because law, imperfect though it is, is the only means we have of protecting ourselves from the arbitrariness, capriciousness, and susceptibility of our own human nature.[24]

Carefully, meticulously, Fulbright and Marcy had been building support for the notion that the administration – first Johnson's, now Nixon's – was making international commitments and involving the country in future wars without its permission or even its knowledge, and in so doing was violating the basic law of the land. Not coincidentally, in the summer of 1970 the antiwar movement began to focus for the first time on the constitutional issue, both because the new leaders saw its potential for ending the war and because the new, more conventional majority tended to think in traditional political and legal terms. After the Cambodian invasion, Congress was inundated with the heaviest volume of mail on record. Fulbright alone received a hundred

23 J. W. Fulbright, "What Students Can Do for Peace," *Progressive* (June 1970).
24 Ibid.

thousand telegrams and letters in the first week. By mid-July the count was three hundred and fifty thousand. Clara Buchanan and the rest of the secretarial staff found their desks surrounded by mountains of mailbags each day. The chairman's letters and telegrams ran 60 to 1 against the decision to invade.[25]

Five days after Nixon announced the incursion, members of the SFRC accused him of usurping the legislature's warmaking power and denounced the "constitutionally unauthorized, Presidential war in Indochina."[26] The charge quickly became a rallying cry inside and outside of Congress. The president of the Amalgamated Clothing Workers Union demanded that congressional constraints be imposed on the president. The American Civil Liberties Union campaigned for an immediate end to the war on the grounds that it was not constitutionally declared and therefore deprived Americans of their civil liberties. Even the hawkish House was up in arms. Representative George E. Brown (D–California) introduced a resolution of impeachment, and Richard D. McCarthy (D–New York) proposed a declaration of war on North Vietnam in the expectation that it would be overwhelmingly defeated.[27]

On April 10, 1970, the SFRC voted unanimously to repeal the Gulf of Tonkin Resolution, which had remained in effect even after the 1968 SFRC hearings. A month later the committee added the Cooper–Church amendment to the 1971 Military Sales Bill. Authored by John Sherman Cooper and Frank Church, the amendment would cut off funds for U.S. military operations in Cambodia after June 30, 1970, the date Nixon had set for withdrawal in the midst of the postinvasion brouhaha. Fulbright was wildly enthusiastic about the latter proposal. The president ought to be completely supportive of Cooper–Church, he told the Senate. Had he not promised to pull all American troops out anyway? Congress was just helping him keep his word. The administration did intend to keep its word, did it not? he asked.[28]

The Nixon White House, being a collection of public relations experts, was uniquely equipped to deal with the daunting public relations problems posed by Cambodia and Kent State. Typically, Nixon and his men decided to take the offensive. "As in all battles the tide in this one ebbs and flows," H. R. Haldeman observed. "At this particular point the opposition has shot their wad. . . . We now have a chance to frighten off the enemy [anti-war critics]

25 The count was a much closer, 3 to 2, among the three thousand letters from Arkansas. JWF to David C. Rains, July 10, 1970, Series 48:18, Box 61:3, SPF.

26 Quoted in DeBenedetti and Chatfield, *American Ordeal,* 284.

27 "Fulbright Sees Constitutional Crisis," *Washington Evening Star,* May 6, 1970.

28 JWF to Lewis W. Douglas, May 12, 1970, Box 9, Apr.–June, Marcy Papers, and *Congressional Record,* Senate, May 15, 1970, 15726.

but we've got to do it in a strong, positive fashion and without any delay – without any letup."[29] Indeed, Pat Buchanan saw an opportunity in the situation: The administration should take the offensive and make Congress the whipping boy. "We are the beneficiaries of the visceral patriotism of the lower middle class," he told his boss, and now was the time to call on it. Haldeman and the president were enthusiastic. "Run a roll of shame," Haldeman suggested; administration spokesmen should imply that supporters of Cooper–Church were nothing less than traitors, willing to deny ammunition to American GIs and to see them die as a result. That was the ticket, Buchanan declared, but the president should appear to remain above it all: "[F]or the President . . . no epithets . . . for the Vice President, let's cut loose and see how much blood we can spill."[30]

What followed in the spring and summer was a campaign of calculated divisiveness waged by the administration. Nixon and his henchmen attempted to make Vietnam a symbol of the integrity of the presidency and of the nation's core values. Administration figures brandished the symbols of American nationalism at every opportunity. The White House sponsored a lavish "Honor America Day" in the capital on the Fourth of July. The president and his supporters began wearing flag jewelry. Throughout the summer, the American Legion, the John Birch Society, the Christian Crusade, and other right-wing organizations charged that the peace symbol was a Marxist emblem, an anti-Christian insignia, or a sorcerer's signature.[31]

Fulbright was one of the first to feel the lash. In mid-May White House loyalist Hugh Scott escorted the national commanders of the American Legion and the Veterans of Foreign Wars to the Senate Press Gallery for a press conference. Denouncing Fulbright and other doves by name, the commanders declared that the Cooper–Church amendment amounted "to a declaration of surrender to Communist forces and constitutes a stab in the back for our boys in combat."[32] Fulbright's hate mail became frighteningly explicit. "Inevitably you will be caught off guard, sometime, somewhere, somehow, and then bingo! a bullet right between the eyes," warned Edward Pretarski of Santa Ana, California. "Yes, Billy boy, the Vigilantes are coming."[33]

Though a man of personal courage and one not given to brooding about his image, the crush of criticism and threats was for Fulbright at times overwhelming. In the midst of this new onslaught by the administration and the radical right, he received a letter from a constituent that affected him as no

29 Talking Papers, May 20, 1970, Haldeman Papers, WHSpF, Box 152, Nixon Project.
30 Buchanan to Nixon, June 17, 1970, WHSpF, Box 139, Nixon Papers.
31 DeBenedetti and Chatfield, *American Ordeal,* 288–9.
32 "Scott Apologizes for Attack on Stand of 4 Colleagues," *Arkansas Gazette,* May 17, 1970.
33 Petrarski to JWF, June 7, 1970, Series 52, Box 310, SPF.

other he had ever received. The letter was from Russell Harper, a retired navy man farming near Gillham, Arkansas:

> I have never voted for you; I have never missed a chance to belittle you. But, deep inside me is a nagging suspicion that I have been wrong. As this world plunges headlong toward what may well be its own destruction, it gets increasingly harder to hear lonely voices such as yours calling for common sense, human reason and a respect for the brotherhood of mankind. But, be of good cheer, my friend. Keep nipping at their heels. This world has always nailed its prophets to trees, so don't be surprised at those who come at you with hammers and spikes. Know that those multitudes yet unborn will stand on your shoulders.[34]

Fulbright shut himself up with the letter for hours and then wrote Gillam a personal reply.

One of the Pharisees who came at the junior senator with hammer and nails was the Reverend Carl McIntire, a fundamentalist radio evangelist and professional red-baiter. In mid-May he gathered an audience at the Little Rock Convention Center and told them: "Senator Fulbright is the number one voice in the country asking us to do what Hanoi wants us to."[35] As McIntire toured the state whipping up support for a "March for Victory" rally in Little Rock on June 6, "Justice Jim" Johnson launched a recall movement designed to oust Fulbright from his Senate seat.

Although Arkansas was still an overwhelmingly Democratic state – with those on the political far right identifying with George Wallace rather than Richard Nixon – the White House gave what support it could to McIntire, Johnson, and the recall movement.[36] The principal problem facing Johnson and the anti-Fulbright forces was that Arkansas had no provision for recall of state officials. Consequently, the first priority for the movement was a constitutional amendment.[37] Johnson did his best, running solicitation ads in the *Los Angeles Times* and other national publications and enlisting the aid of the American Party machinery and the VFW. He aired numerous radio spots that faded in with strains from "America the Beautiful." There was, he said, an international communist conspiracy to enslave the world, and Senator Fulbright was aiding that conspiracy.[38]

Fulbright was sufficiently worried about the recall campaign to abandon momentarily the struggle over Cooper–Church and fly home for a quick

34 Harper to JWF, Mar. 15, 1970, Series 48:18, Box 60:2, SPF.
35 "McIntire Raps Fulbright at Resort Victory Rally," *Sentinel Record,* May 12, 1970.
36 Harry Dent to Nixon, May 22, 1970, WHSpF, Box 6, Nixon Project.
37 "Wording for Amendment on Recall of Fulbright Inadequate, Purcell Says," *Arkansas Gazette,* May 10, 1970.
38 Pat Walsh to JWF, July 2, 1970, Series 78:1, Box 26:5, SPF.

speaking tour. He defended his opposition to the war, explained Cooper–Church, and denounced the recall movement as an "exercise in futility."[39] In between speaking engagements, Bill and Betty, together with Hal and Jacquie Douglas (Hal had married Jacqueline Sterner, dean of women at the university, in 1966), hosted the annual family reunion. The Winnackers and Footes made the trek to Fayetteville as did virtually every nephew, niece, cousin, and step-child. After a business meeting on Saturday morning, the men departed for golf at the country club. Their round completed, everyone gathered for dinner and reminiscence. By Monday only Hal and Jacquie and Bill and Betty were left. That afternoon the Fulbrights hit the service-club circuit to do battle with Johnson and the recall forces.[40]

Before returning to Washington, Fulbright put together a committee of Arkansas lawyers to challenge the constitutionality of the recall amendment. Chaired by James B. Blair of Springdale, chief attorney for Tyson Foods, the committee included Fred Pickens of Newport, Richard Arnold of Texarkana, and a who's who of Arkansas establishment politics.[41] In June, former governor and ex-marine Sid McMath, who had at times been sharply critical of Fulbright's opposition to the war, announced that he favored withdrawal of all U.S. combat troops from Vietnam.[42] In July, the anti-Fulbright movement collapsed when Johnson failed to obtain the requisite number of signatures to get the recall amendment on the ballot.[43]

Despite the activities of the revived antiwar movement, public opinion polls taken in early June were still showing majority support for the incursion into Cambodia. Moreover, the politics of polarization began to take its toll on the tenuous anti-imperialist coalition as Robert Dole, Hugh Scott (R–Pennsylvania), and other administration supporters prolonged the congressional debate over Cooper–Church and pointed out the political consequences for those who voted to cut off funds for troops in the field.

As a result, the White House decided it was time for a test of strength. Nixon and Laird persuaded the flamboyant, conservative Robert Byrd of West Virginia, a man not known for political courage in the mildest of circumstances, to propose an amendment to Cooper–Church. It would authorize the president to send U.S. troops back into Cambodia after July 1 if he thought

39 "Fulbright Acts Nervous Over Recall Move," *Daily News,* June 6, 1970.

40 "Fulbright Family Reunion Held Here Over Weekend," *Northwest Arkansas Times,* June 16, 1970.

41 "Committee Formed to Stop Amendment on Fulbright Recall," *Arkansas Democrat,* June 18, 1970.

42 "Shift on War by McMath: 'Get Out Now,'" *Arkansas Democrat,* June 16, 1970.

43 Bill Rutherford, "Campaign for Recalling Sen. Fulbright Collapses," *Washington Post,* July 4, 1970.

redeployment was necessary to protect American forces in South Vietnam. Predictably, Fulbright, Javits, and McGovern denounced the Byrd proposal as nothing less than a scheme to "gut" Cooper–Church.[44]

In a major miscalculation, the Nixon administration forced a vote on the Byrd amendment on June 12. In what the *Washington Post* termed a "key rebuff" and "one of the most important foreign policy votes in years," the Senate rejected the Byrd amendment by a vote of 52 to 47. The coalition of thirty-nine Democrats and thirteen liberal Republicans had held firm.[45] Acting on orders from the White House, Scott, Dole, and company hurriedly put together a filibuster in order to prevent a vote on Cooper–Church itself.

Meanwhile, the administration intensified its media blitz with Spiro Agnew taking point. On June 20 the vice-president, speaking to a gathering of the party faithful in Cleveland, unleashed a furious attack on leading Democratic doves, including Fulbright, Edward Kennedy, Clark Clifford, and Averell Harriman, the latter two having appealed in various public forums in the aftermath of Cambodia for an immediate and unconditional end to the war. The whole lot were "sunshine patriots," Agnew declared, but Fulbright and Kennedy were particularly odious. They were, he proclaimed, nothing less than "apologists" for Hanoi.[46]

Fulbright managed to keep a sense of humor. "His [Agnew's] principal objective these days is raising money at Republican dinners," he wrote a friend, "and, as he says once in a while, he has to feed them some raw meat in order to inspire larger contributions."[47]

By late June, Griffin, Dole, Henry Bellmon (R–Oklahoma), John Williams (R–Delaware), and Hugh Scott were exhausted. They pleaded with Nixon to allow them to bring the brutal debate over Cooper–Church to a climax. Nixon wanted to press on – the public relations campaign in behalf of Cambodia specifically and presidential prerogatives in general had picked up a full head of steam – but he relented when Dole and Scott proposed a scheme in which passage of the amendment would actually increase rather than decrease the president's authority. Dole would first disarm supporters of a fund cutoff for Cambodia by proposing repeal of the Gulf of Tonkin Resolution, and then Robert Byrd would attach another amendment to Cooper–Church providing that nothing in the proposal would "impugn the exercise of a President's power as commander-in-chief to protect U.S. forces wherever deployed." The net effect, of course, would be to give a priori congressional approval for the executive to use force abroad wherever and whenever it wanted.[48]

44 *Congressional Record,* Senate, June 10, 1970, 19181.
45 Spencer Rich, "52–47 Vote Deals Nixon Key Rebuff," *Washington Post,* June 12, 1970.
46 Berman, *Fulbright and the Vietnam War,* 130.
47 JWF to Frederic Irish, Aug. 19, 1970, Series 48:18, Box 60:3, SPF.
48 Bryce Harlow to Nixon, June 22, 1970, WHSpF, Box 139, Nixon Project.

On June 22, during the fifth week of debate on Cooper–Church, Robert Byrd proposed his second amendment. Although Fulbright pointed out that American armed forces were "deployed" in practically every country in the world and that the West Virginian's addition would contravene the meaning of the original amendment, a majority of senators refused to expose themselves to the charge that they were denying the commander-in-chief the power to defend American soldiers overseas. The Byrd amendment passed overwhelmingly. Among the majority were Cooper and Church. "It's getting so you can't tell the players – even with a scorecard," observed the *Washington Post*.[49]

No sooner had the clamor over the Byrd amendment died than Dole, a gravel-voiced veteran who had been maimed during World War II, interrupted the proceedings to propose repeal of the Gulf of Tonkin Resolution. Administration supporters, he explained, were tired of being called warmongers. Fulbright leapt to his feet to object. A repealer had already been approved by the SFRC and had been placed on the calendar for debate after the Senate finished with Cooper–Church. He accused the Kansan of departing from established Senate procedure, which called for all measures to go through committee before being voted on by the Senate as a whole. Hugh Scott interrupted. The senator from Arkansas had often spoken of the need to repeal the resolution he had once so ardently supported. Now he had the chance. What was the problem? he asked mischievously.

Fulbright was trapped. If the Senate went ahead and passed the Cooper–Church amendment as altered by Robert Byrd and then repealed the Gulf of Tonkin Resolution, the net effect would be "to give the president a clear legislative history that Tonkin meant nothing when it was passed and means nothing by its repeal – thus confirming the president's claim to the power to do what he pleases as Commander-in-Chief."[50]

Confused, exhausted, angry, the U.S. Senate on June 24, 1970, voted to repeal the Gulf of Tonkin Resolution by a vote of 81 to 10. On the surface it appeared to be a groundbreaking victory for opponents of the war and the imperial presidency. Fulbright, who voted "no," knew better and said so. "We are in the process of making legislative history of the kind which I predict, we will regret as much as many of us have regretted our precipitant approval of the Tonkin resolution in 1964," he declared bitterly.[51]

Two days after his ironic vote on the Tonkin repealer, Fulbright rose on the floor of the Senate to vent his usually well-controlled spleen. The *Washington Post*, which had recently compared Vice-President Agnew to Joe McCarthy, had it wrong, he declared. Agnew was reminiscent of Joseph Goebbels, chief

49 "Fulbright's Complaint," *Washington Post*, June 24, 1970.
50 *Congressional Record*, Senate, June 23, 1970, 20988.
51 Philip D. Carter, "Senate Voids Resolution on Tonkin, 81–10," *Washington Post*, June 25, 1970.

propagandist and hatemonger of Hitlerian Germany. Goebbels and Agnew spoke with the power of the state behind them, whereas McCarthy had not.[52]

During his long career in the Senate J. William Fulbright had been alternately frustrated and gratified that the Congress of the United States was a deliberative body in the most complex, slow-moving, and inefficient sense of the word. At no time was he more grateful for that ponderousness than in the summer of 1970. With Dole and the White House in apparent command of the constitutional and political field, the doves regrouped and counterattacked. Three days before the scheduled showdown vote on Cooper–Church, the Senate by a vote of 73 to 0 approved a proposal by Jacob Javits that stated: "Nothing contained in this section shall be deemed to impugn the congressional powers of the Congress including the power to declare war and to make rules for the government and regulation of the armed forces of the United States."[53] The Javits proviso seemingly canceled out the Byrd amendment; or, put another way, the Senate had reasserted the respective powers of the executive and legislative branches in the area of foreign affairs. What was left was a warning that all funds for U.S. military action in Cambodia would be cut off in three days.

The last week in June, after six weeks of tumultuous debate, the U.S. Senate approved the Cooper–Church amendment to the military sales bill by a vote of 58 to 37. It was a momentous occasion, the first time the upper house had passed a clearcut anti–Vietnam War resolution. Fulbright, McGovern, Church, Javits, and Marcy sensed the possibility of victory in their grueling struggle to end the war in Indochina, place restraints on the burgeoning American empire, and reassert congressional prerogatives in the area of foreign policy.

On the eleventh Fulbright in behalf of the SFRC introduced the original repealer of the Gulf of Tonkin Resolution. Dole's bill had been an amendment to another, broader piece of legislation and, as such, subject to presidential veto. The Fulbright repealer was in the form of a concurrent resolution and consequently was not vulnerable to a veto. Fulbright alerted his colleagues to the difference:

> The two forms of repeal of the Tonkin resolution . . . , though nominally leading to the same result, in fact have radically different connotations. The one, coupled as it is with a legislative enactment which can be read as acquiescence in the Executive's claim to plenary war powers, represents an act of resignation, an attempt by Congress to give away its own constitutional war powers. The other, favored by the committee, would eliminate an illegitimate authorization and, in so doing, reassert the constitutional authority of Con-

52 Berman, *Fulbright and the Vietnam War,* 131.

53 "Senate Approves Javits Plan Citing War Policy Roles," *Washington Evening Star,* June 27, 1970.

> gress to "declare war," "raise and support armies," and "make rules for the Government and regulation of the land and naval forces."[54]

Even if Nixon did not veto the repealer, the Dole resolution would enhance the power of the executive by making it possible for the president to do so. The SFRC resolution passed by a vote of 57 to 5.

Shortly before enactment of the second Tonkin repealer, the House, still much more conservative and hawkish than the Senate, rejected Cooper–Church by almost 2 to 1. Mike Mansfield warned that unless the House reconsidered, the Senate would simply refuse to pass the huge arms-sales bill to which the Cambodian amendment was attached;[55] but Thomas E. ("Doc") Morgan (D–Pennsylvania) – chairman of the House Committee on Foreign Affairs and just as much a champion of the war and of executive prerogatives under Richard Nixon as he had been under Lyndon Johnson – refused to be intimidated. The measure remained locked up in conference committee for the next six months.

Cooper–Church was really a flank attack on the war in Southeast Asia. Emboldened by their success in the Senate, the doves decided to stage a frontal assault. George McGovern and Senator Mark Hatfield proposed attaching an amendment to a pending arm-sales bill cutting off funds for all U.S. military operations in Southeast Asia after December 31, 1970. It was the ultimate end-the-war measure.

To McGovern's surprise and dismay, Fulbright and Marcy were initially opposed to the proposal. Indeed, Fulbright went to McGovern and urged him to support a different, weaker resolution, one that stated that Congress would not fund a troop level beyond two hundred and eighty thousand after April 1, 1971. Nixon had already announced that he would pull a hundred and fifty thousand soldiers out of Vietnam by that date, thereby leaving two hundred and eighty thousand. Thus, as had been the case with Cooper–Church, the Senate could argue that it was merely helping the president keep his word.[56]

Apparently Fulbright's sudden reticence about an end-the-war resolution was the product of Henry Kissinger's influence. In spite of the bitterness of the fight over Cooper–Church and the chairman's anger over Cambodia, the two men had managed to maintain a working relationship. They continued to see each other at Washington social functions, and during crucial periods Kissinger would come to Fulbright's house on Belmont Road. In their talks Kis-

54 *Congressional Record,* Senate, 23711, July 10, 1970.

55 Philip D. Carter, "Senate Again Votes to Repeal Tonkin," *Washington Post,* July 11, 1970.

56 Draft Amendment to the Military Procurement Bill, Aug. 21, 1970, Box 9, July–Sept., Marcy Papers.

singer continually emphasized his long-range goals: détente with the Soviet Union and China, and a new pragmatic foreign policy free of the hysterical anticommunism and missionary zeal that had been responsible for missteps like Vietnam. "It was deeply satisfying to Fulbright to sit and exchange ideas [with Kissinger]," recalled Richard Moose who had worked for them both. "He was aware that Kissinger was a remarkable man. To be able to sit and talk about a great purpose in which they were both opposed by people who didn't understand" was heady stuff.[57] Fulbright could not know, of course, that at the same time the national security adviser was appealing to him to help restrain the unstable Nixon, he was denouncing the Arkansan to the president as a weak-kneed liberal and establishment opportunist.

Shortly after McGovern–Hatfield was conceived, Kissinger once again pleaded with Fulbright not to do things that would anger Nixon, that would tempt him to lash out at his domestic critics and the North Vietnamese. Fulbright was sympathetic. McGovern later recalled that the Arkansan told him that he did not want to coerce Nixon; there must be a more "civilized" way. McGovern refused to go along with the chairman's troop-level compromise, and Fulbright's name was not among the twenty-three cosponsors of the McGovern–Hatfield amendment.[58]

Fulbright had reservations about McGovern–Hatfield that had nothing to do with his relationship with Kissinger. The chairman's experience with the Gulf of Tonkin Resolution and the legalistic maneuverings of Nicholas Katzenbach had made him very wary of inadvertent actions by the Senate that could be used by the executive to further usurp Congress's prerogatives. Repeal of the Gulf of Tonkin Resolution had had the support of strict constructionists who believed President Johnson had exceeded his authority, as well as of blind supporters of executive power who, like Katzenbach, were convinced that "the President has full authority to make war under his powers as Commander-in-Chief, with or without Congressional approval." McGovern–Hatfield imposed restrictions on the use of the armed forces; given the fact that Congress had not in the first place authorized the use of such forces, the resolution could be interpreted to mean that, in the absence of restrictions, "the President can do whatever he pleases – anything goes, that is, unless it is explicitly prohibited."[59]

Although Cooper–Church and McGovern–Hatfield were the foci of Senate antiwar attention during the spring and summer of 1970, Fulbright and his allies were assaulting the military–industrial complex and the imperial presidency on a number of other fronts. At the close of the 1970 session the Ar-

57 Moose interview.
58 Berman, *Fulbright and the Vietnam War,* 133.
59 *Congressional Record,* Senate, Feb. 5, 1971, 1868–9.

kansan quietly attached an amendment to the Military Assistance Program limiting the number of foreign military officers trained in the United States to the number of Fulbright exchange scholars studying in the United States at any given time.[60] He proposed an amendment to the national draft law that would limit service by draftees abroad only to actions that "have been approved in accordance with the Constitution." Beginning in May Fulbright held up all presidential appointments that came before the SFRC because of what he called the State Department's "contempt" of Congress.[61] "Fulbright is conducting a form of the Chinese water torture on the administration," quipped Chalmers Roberts.[62]

The SFRC continued to hold intermittent hearings on the day-to-day conduct of the war and its impact on the United States. To Fulbright's delight, members of the business community began to take public stands against the conflict in Southeast Asia. Thomas Watson, head of IBM, testified that the war was not only stimulating inflation but undermining confidence abroad in the American economy and its products. Gordon Sherman, president of Midas Muffler, termed the war a "distraction" and urged Nixon to "get the deal" in Paris.[63] Three prominent American clerics – Dr. John C. Bennett, president of Union Theological Seminary, Bishop John J. Dougherty of the U.S. Catholic Conference, and Dr. Irving Greenberg of Yeshiva University – described the Vietnam war as a "moral disaster."[64]

In his battle with Fulbright and the SFRC, Nixon enjoyed the ongoing support of such illustrious personages as Frank Sinatra, Bob Hope, and John Wayne. Glen Campbell was "the only thing from Arkansas that I like," the Duke told the *Chicago Tribune.* "Senator Fulbright is the most miserable S.O.B. I've met in my whole life. He's a fraternity brother of mine [Sigma Chi], but he's an educated idiot."[65] In addition to right-wing celebrities, the White House also benefited from criticism of the Arkansan and his supporters by policy experts who feared that the anti-imperialists were going too far. Although he admired Fulbright's intelligence and courage, Hans Morgenthau thought him dangerously naïve concerning the threat posed by the Soviet Union and Communist China, and said so in an article published in 1970.[66]

60 Richard Homan, "Aid Act Snags Training of Foreign GIs," *Washington Post,* Feb. 7, 1970.

61 UPI 103, May 18, 1970.

62 Chalmers Roberts, "The Senate's Role," *Washington Post,* Apr. 12, 1970.

63 "'Get the Deal' in Paris, Nixon Advised," *Washington Evening Star,* Apr. 17, 1970.

64 UPI 171, May 7, 1970.

65 "In the News," *Arkansas Gazette,* July 8, 1970.

66 Like George Kennan, Morgenthau found fault with the way containment had been implemented, but not with the policy itself, or the assumptions that underlay it. See "J. William Fulbright" in Hans J. Morgenthau, *Truth and Power: Essays of a Decade, 1960–70* (New York, 1970), 174–83.

Morton Kaplan, another University of Chicago academic, saw Fulbright as just a sophisticated version of John Bricker. His suggested "reforms" would hobble policy, Kaplan wrote Gordon Allott (R–Colorado). "They would delay interventions until the situation had deteriorated and until enemy states had so overcommitted themselves that direct confrontations would be difficult to avoid."[67]

Even as late as 1970 the principal obstacle to be overcome by Fulbright and the doves were World War II and its lingering memories. The journalists, politicians, and academics that still shaped American foreign policy could not forget Munich, Lend–Lease, Cash–Carry, and the other landmarks in America's perilous but glorious victory over the Axis. The arguments used by William Allen White's Committee to Defend America by Aiding the Allies were invoked to justify Vietnamization and foreign military assistance in general. In an editorial attack on Fulbright, William Randolph Hearst lamented in the *San Francisco Examiner:* "Why can't he see that financial aid to help our allies resist communism is far more desirable than fighting their battles for them?"[68]

During the debate over the Cooper–Church and McGovern–Hatfield amendments, Fulbright became increasingly uneasy about the Nixon White House's efforts to intimidate the major networks. In May presidential adviser Clark Mollenhoff told his bosses that CBS had knowingly faked two films purporting to show American personnel aiding and abetting atrocities in Vietnam. One showed a Special Forces trooper with a knife and two VC ears and another a South Vietnamese soldier stabbing a prisoner while American advisers stood compliantly nearby. CBS should not be allowed to use "freedom of the press" to get away with "fraud by the press," Mollenhoff declared, and recommended an FCC investigation. Richard Salant, president of CBS, subsequently refused Pentagon and White House "requests" for information on how the film clips had been put together and who was responsible. In May, Jack Anderson published excerpts from the Mollenhoff memo and described White House efforts to pressure Salant.[69]

Leaping to the defense of the press, Fulbright cosponsored a bill designed to strengthen the first amendment and protect the confidential nature of newspeople's sources of information. "Any infringement of press freedom, any intimidation of journalists, particularly by the government, undermines the strength of our society and the role of the press as the public watchdog," he told the Senate.[70] The chairman of the SFRC revived old charges that the Pentagon regularly faked its own combat films for propaganda purposes, and

67 *Congressional Record,* Senate, June 5, 1970.
68 News Summaries, Nov. 22, 1970, WHSpF, Box 32, Nixon Project.
69 "White House Memo Cites CBS Faking," *Washington Post,* May 22, 1970.
70 "Fulbright Supports Newsmen," *Magnolia Daily Banner News,* Mar. 25, 1970.

he reminded the nation that the DOD maintained a multi-million-dollar propaganda agency at taxpayer expense.[71]

Despite Salant's brave showing against the White House and the press's traditional dislike of Richard Nixon, Fulbright and the SFRC staff noted with dismay that by midsummer broadcast journalists seemed, in fact, to have been intimidated. When Howard K. Smith of ABC, John Chancellor of NBC, and Eric Sevareid of CBS interviewed the president live the first week in July, they behaved, in the words of the *Washington Post,* "like three small town mill owners gathered in the living room of the local banker who held all their mortgages."[72]

Like a basketball coach whose rival is successfully baiting the game officials, Fulbright decided that he would have to do a bit of intimidating himself. Throughout the late summer of 1970 he denounced the major networks for allowing the executive to manipulate them and dominate the airwaves. "There is nothing in the Constitution which says that, of all elected officials, the President alone shall have the right to communicate with the American people," he told the Senate.[73] When the networks subsequently refused congressional requests for equal time, or even to allow antiwar advocates in Congress to purchase time, Fulbright and fourteen of those who had sponsored the McGovern–Hatfield amendment asked the Federal Communications Commission to intervene and coerce the networks. After the FCC declined, Fulbright introduced legislation that would have provided television time to Congress as an institution.[74]

Fulbright's bill never got off the ground, but the last week in August NBC announced that it was giving senatorial opponents of the war thirty minutes of prime time on the evening of August 31, the night before the decisive vote on McGovern–Hatfield. The doves chose as their spokesmen J. William Fulbright and George McGovern.[75] From 7:30 to 8:00 America's two most visible congressional doves harangued the nation on the erroneous assumptions that underlay its Vietnam policies and the evils that that conflict had wrought on both Vietnam and the United States. The Paris peace talks were deadlocked, Fulbright declared, because the administration was unwilling to make the "key concessions" necessary to break the stalemate, namely, "a willingness to take away from President Thieu the veto he presently exercises over American policy" and a "willingness to commit ourselves to a phased but total American military withdrawal from Vietnam to be completed by a speci-

71 "Fulbright Says War Film Fake," *Arkansas Gazette,* May 23, 1970.

72 Frank Mankiewicz and Tom Braden, "Three TV Interviewers Failed to Ask President a Single Hard Question," *Washington Post,* July 7, 1970.

73 *Congressional Record,* Senate, June 2, 1970, 17838.

74 John W. Finney, "14 Senate Doves Ask That F.C.C. Force the Networks to Provide TV Time," *New York Times,* July 9, 1970.

75 "Antiwar Senators Get Free Time from NBC," *Washington Post,* Aug. 22, 1970.

fied date." "A war is not a football game which you play to win for the sake of winning," he lectured. "A war is fought for political objectives, and when it is recognized that those objectives are unattainable at a reasonable cost, the appropriate course of action is to end that war in an orderly and expeditious way."[76] It was all for naught. The next day the United States Senate defeated the "Amendment to End the War," the official title of the McGovern–Hatfield proposal, by a vote of 55 to 39.[77]

News that the "Fulbright claque" had been turned back at the gate created euphoria within the White House staff. Charles Colson declared that the country had turned an important corner. He told the president:

> I can't recall any period in the past 15 years when there had been such a dramatic shift of political attitudes in so short a period of time. I believe that most Senators have decided that the President is in political control, will remain that way and that their own political future is better served by being with us rather than against us.[78]

He was, of course, being overly optimistic.

Richard Nixon was locked in a fierce struggle with congressional doves for control of the political middle ground on Vietnam. J. William Fulbright's dream was at long last coming true. No longer was the antiwar movement a protest of the liberal left. A majority of Democratic members of Congress and a sizable minority of Republicans were now actively opposed. Not for a hundred years had Congress mounted such a challenge to a commander-in-chief with troops fighting in the field as that mounted against Richard Nixon in the summer of 1970. In fact polls showed that, by late June, nearly half of all Americans advocated getting out of Vietnam immediately and only 15 percent favored staying in.[79]

76 "U.S. Concessions Will End Deadlock, Fulbright Asserts," *Arkansas Gazette*, Sept. 1, 1970.
77 "Senate Refuses to Set a Deadline to Get Troops Out," *Arkansas Democrat*, Sept. 1, 1970.
78 Colson to Haldeman, Sept. 9, 1970.
79 DeBenedetti and Chatfield, *American Ordeal*, 290.

# 33

# *A foreign affairs alternative*

One of the few things that J. William Fulbright and Richard Nixon had in common was a belief that American Zionists exerted too much influence on U.S. foreign policy.[1] Though Nixon's national security adviser was himself a Jew, he too favored a "balanced" approach toward the Middle East. During their musings on a new world order, Kissinger and Fulbright did not fail to outline a lasting settlement of the Arab–Israeli conflict, one that included an Israeli willingness to trade peace for land and an Arab willingness to recognize the legitimacy of the Jewish state and to sign peace treaties with it. Indeed, in 1970 Fulbright decided to jeopardize his carefully constructed anti-Vietnam coalition and to propose an extension rather than reduction of American commitment overseas as part of an effort to bring a lasting peace to the Middle East.[2]

Most of the Arab world had severed formal ties with the United States in the aftermath of the Six-Day War in 1967, in which the Israelis, utilizing American arms and supplies, had crushed the Soviet-supplied Egyptian and Syrian forces. During the fighting, the Israelis had seized and occupied portions of Egypt, Syria, and Jordan. Despite U.N. Security Council Resolution 242, which called upon Israel to return conquered lands to the Arabs in return for secure, recognized boundaries, peace continued to elude the Middle East. As of 1969 Israel had controlled all of the Sinai Desert up to the western bank of the Suez Canal; the Gaza Strip, a narrow coastal area jutting toward Tel Aviv from the Sinai; the Golan Heights, a strategic hill area from which, before the war, Syrian and Palestinian gunners had lobbed artillery shells into Jewish settlements; and East Jerusalem and the West Bank, both of which had been seized from Jordan.

The dilemma facing the Nixon administration in 1969 had been stark. The Arabs had insisted that Israel give up its conquered lands before serious ne-

1 Nixon, note to Haldeman, News Summary, Feb. 1970, WHSpF, Box 31, Nixon Project.

2 Complicating Fulbright's efforts to assemble and maintain an antiwar consensus in the Senate was the fact that a number of prominent doves – Javits, Goddell, and McGovern, for example – were ardent advocates of aid to Israel. See Goodell to JWF, Mar. 23, 1970, Box 3, Fulbright Papers, SFRC, RG46, NA.

gotiations leading to normalization of relations could start, whereas the Israelis had demanded recognition of Israel's right to exist as a state as the price for talks on disengagement. Yasir Arafat, head of the Palestine Liberation Organization, had insisted that much of Israel belonged to his people by right of two thousand years of continued occupancy. The goal of the radical fedayeen movement he led was the creation of a "democratic secular state" in which "Jews, Arabs, and Christians would live together with equal rights."[3]

As 1970 came to a close the level of conflict between the Palestinians and Egypt on the one and Israel on the other increased to the point where the Nixon administration decided it would have to take a gamble in an effort to break the diplomatic impasse and avert a general war. During an address to an audience of Foreign Service officers, Secretary of State Rogers suggested that Israel withdraw to its pre-1967 boundaries in return for recognition from Egypt. He also called for a broadly based settlement in the Middle East, involving negotiations between Israel and Jordan over the West Bank, the future of United Jerusalem, and the Palestinian refugee problem.[4] Israel and American Zionists immediately denounced the "Rogers Plan," as it was called, as a sell-out of Israeli interests.

As Israel continued its aerial assault on Egypt, Nasser flew to Moscow and persuaded the Soviets to provide him with advanced SAM-3 surface-to-air missiles capable of shooting down the American-made Israeli Air Force F-4 Phantoms. By April the first of what would be fifteen thousand Soviet soldiers and advisers began pouring into Egypt to assemble and man the SAM-3's. To counter this threat, Israel asked for 125 additional F-4's from the United States, a request the Nixon administration rejected. The president and his national security adviser, who had now fully interjected himself into the Middle East picture, hoped that by temporarily withholding jets from Israel, they could persuade both Moscow and Tel Aviv to show restraint and eventually preside over a settlement of the entire Arab–Israeli conflict.

Fulbright was only dimly aware of the bureaucratic infighting that accompanied American Middle East policy under Nixon, but he fully supported the Rogers peace plan and the administration's subsequent decision not to sell jets to Israel in the spring of 1970. When Charles Goodell requested an SFRC investigation of what he declared to be abandonment of a gallant ally, Fulbright, with George Aiken's full support, said no. The decision to defer sales "represents a sound and responsible policy" he wrote Goodell. "I believe it desirable at this juncture to allow the State Department to pursue new peace initiatives without the interjection of . . . the Committee."[5]

By late May, American Zionists were bringing intense pressure to bear on

3 Quoted in Seymour M. Hersh, *The Price of Power: Kissinger in the Nixon White House* (New York, 1983), 215.
4 Ibid., 217, 219–20.
5 JWF to Goodell, May 31, 1970, Box 3, Fulbright Papers, SFRC, RG 46, NA.

Congress and the administration over the jet sale issue. Some American Jews, suffering pangs of guilt that they were not in the front lines defending the homeland, were susceptible to manipulation by various Israeli governments. They were, in the words of Morris Rubin, editor of the *Progressive,* "more royalist-than-the-crown" and capable of expressing positions that "many Israelis would find rather naïve and unrealistic."[6] Naïve they might have been; powerless they were not. Seventy-three Senators, including Goodell, McGovern, Strom Thurmond, and Barry Goldwater, signed an open letter to Rogers demanding immediate sale of twenty-five F-4 Phantoms and a hundred A-4 Skyhawks to Israel.[7] On June 24 the Senate amended the Defense Procurement Act, authorizing the president to transfer to Israel all aircraft and other equipment necessary to maintain the military balance of power in the Middle East. The Democratic leadership bypassed the SFRC, referring the measure to the more sympathetic Armed Services Committee under John Stennis and Henry Jackson, cold warriors and Israeli supporters par excellence.[8]

During various Arab–Israeli crises Fulbright had come under intense pressure from the small but influential Jewish community in Arkansas to resist "hardline Soviet–Arab demands" and to "provide Israel the arms and economic aid needed to defend herself against hostile Arab forces continuously supplied with mountains of arms by the Soviet Union," as one rabbi put it.[9] The 1970 conflict was no exception. For Paul Greenberg, the *Pine Bluff Commercial* editorial page editor who had won a Pulitzer Prize for his civil rights commentaries, Fulbright was something of an obsession. A committed cold warrior and crusading Zionist, Greenberg never missed a chance to pillory the junior senator.[10]

For the most part, Fulbright chose to ignore Greenberg and the Zionist extremists. To him they were just a different version of the "true believers" he had been battling since the days of Joe McCarthy. Instead, the chairman continued to listen to a handful of Jewish intellectuals, like psychologist Eric Fromm and Israeli peace activist Nahum Goldman, who in 1970 served as president of the World Jewish Congress. These individuals were Jews and Zionists, but they were sympathetic to the plight of the Palestinians and committed to the idea of trading land for peace. A safe and secure homeland without the West Bank was preferable to a besieged police state with it, Fromm repeatedly told Fulbright.[11]

6 Morris Rubin to JWF, Sept. 1, 1970, Series 48:5, Box 40:3, SPF.

7 "58 Senators Sign Letter Backing Jets for Israel," *Arkansas Gazette,* June 1, 1970.

8 JWF to Stennis, June 26, 1970, Series 48:3, Box 17:4, SPF.

9 Rabbi Seymour Atlas et al., to JWF, Jan. 19, 1970, Series 48:15, Box 40:2, SPF.

10 See Paul Greenberg, "Tone-Deaf in Gaza," *Pine Bluff Commercial,* Sept. 3, 1970, and idem, "A Contemptible Performance," *Pine Bluff Commercial,* Nov. 4, 1970.

11 Eric Fromm to JWF, July 18, 1970, Series 48:15, Box 40:3, SPF.

The Arkansan was not unmindful of the historical burden borne by world Jewry; he understood the fears created in Jewish minds by the Holocaust. "As survivors of genocide, they [Jews] can hardly be expected to distinguish with perfect clarity between Nazi crimes and Arab rhetoric," he once remarked.[12] He understood that Jerusalem, with its Wall of the Temple, was sacred to the Jews. Fulbright never questioned the legitimacy of a Jewish state in the Middle East, and he recognized the precarious strategic situation faced by a tiny nation of three million surrounded by millions of hostile Arabs.

However, the Arab–Israeli conflict was not, Fulbright insisted, a case of right against wrong, good versus evil. It was, as I. F. Stone, another Jewish intellectual, put it, a classic tragedy, a case of "right against right," in which good men do evil to each other.[13] More than a million Palestinians had been dispossessed by the 1948 war, and their demand for a return to their lands was legitimate, Fulbright believed. The areas taken in the 1967 conflict were conquered territories; Egypt, Syria, and Jordan would never let Israel live in peace until their return. Israel would have to trade land for peace unless it was willing to conquer and hold the entire Arab world – a clear impossibility, a proposition, Fulbright was convinced, even more absurd than an American effort to conquer and hold Vietnam. Given unconditional American backing of Israel and the general sympathy in the West for the Jewish state, it was natural for the Arabs to view Zionism as another form of Western imperialism. The tighter the Israeli–American embrace, the more intense became Arab nationalism.

The Arab–Israeli conflict was to Fulbright's mind no less an indigenous phenomenon than the civil war in Vietnam; but the cold war had come to the Middle East just as it had to Southeast Asia, infusing into a regional struggle the potential for a worldwide nuclear war. For this reason if for no other, he was convinced, the Middle East crisis had to be settled. As it was, every fedayeen raid, every Israeli retaliation, brought the Soviet Union and the United States to the brink of war.

The last week in August 1970 Fulbright made a startling proposal. As part of an effort to establish a lasting peace in the Middle East, the United States should enter into a formal "treaty of guarantee" with Israel, under which the United States would promise to protect, through use of armed force if necessary, "the territory and independence of Israel within the borders of 1967." The treaty would also obligate Israel itself never to violate those borders. Under Fulbright's plan the American commitment would become effective only after the Security Council itself guaranteed such a settlement. In that way the great powers, including the Soviet Union, would be bound to recognize the pre-1967 boundaries of Israel. According to Fulbright's scheme, as

12 *Congressional Record,* Senate, Aug. 24, 1970, 29804.

13 Ibid., 29796.

Israeli troops withdrew from the Golan Heights, the Gaza Strip, and the West Bank they would be replaced by U.N. peacekeeping troops. Israel would agree to accept a certain number of Palestinians as Israeli citizens and help resettle the rest in a Palestinian state outside Israel. Fulbright made it clear that U.S. military action to defend Israel, once the guarantee went into effect, would not depend on prior Security Council action and that the Israelis would be free to defend themselves against fedayeen attacks.[14]

The Fulbright peace plan created an instant international furor. "Fulbright urges US–Israel treaty" ran the front-page headline of the London *Sunday Times.*[15] American observers of foreign affairs were enthusiastic. There was no hobgoblin in this Arkansan's large mind, declared Joseph Kraft. No matter that Fulbright had been straining every nerve and sinew since 1967 to reduce American commitments abroad. Never mind that he had been warning since 1960 of the insidious machinations of the American Zionist lobby to make America an Israeli cat's-paw in the Middle East. "A deep inner logic" governed Fulbright's ideas, Kraft declared. "He is one of the few actors on the world stage who knows how to take the cue of history."[16] James Reston, writing in the *New York Times,* agreed and predicted that Fulbright's proposal would carry great weight because of his reputation as an opponent of foreign entanglements and as a friend of the Arabs. Fulbright's "switch," Reston declared, was not unlike that made by another chairman of the SFRC. In January 1945, Arthur Vandenberg, a senator famed for his staunch isolationism, had shocked the Senate and the nation by calling for a system of treaties with other democracies to defend Western Europe against the scourge of communism; that speech had transformed American policy in the postwar world. Hopefully, Fulbright's would do the same for the nation's contemporary Middle Eastern policy.[17] No doubt the Arkansan shuddered at the comparison. Somewhat surprisingly, so did the Israeli government.

In 1970 Israel was still clearly in control of its own destiny, and the government of Golda Meir was not about to give up the territories won in the 1967 war. Fulbright's proposal came in the midst of a ninety-day cease-fire with Egypt and U.N.-sponsored peace talks in New York. Israeli militants in the Knesset were furious that the Nixon administration was withholding the 125 jets and angry with the government for agreeing to a cease-fire. On August 25, Foreign Minister Abba Eban, speaking to the Israeli legislature, flatly rejected the Fulbright peace plan. A U.N. or U.S. guarantee, he said, was

14 Ibid., 29796–809.

15 "Fulbright Urges US–Israel Treaty," *Sunday Times* (London), Aug. 23, 1970.

16 Joseph Kraft, "Fulbright Cuts Through the Middle East Miasma," *Arkansas Gazette,* Aug. 25, 1970.

17 James Reston, "Washington: Fulbright's Startling Proposal," *New York Times,* Aug. 23, 1970.

no substitute for an iron-clad treaty signed by all the Arab states recognizing Israel, including the territories taken in the 1967 war.[18]

With Tel Aviv up in arms, and Henry Jackson and American Zionists on the warpath, the administration immediately distanced itself from the Fulbright proposal. Most people applauded Nixon's efforts to arrange a cease-fire, but opinion polls showed that 46 percent of the public sympathized with Israel whereas only 6 percent supported the Arabs. The country was evenly divided over whether or not U.S. troops should intervene, even if Israel was about to be overrun by Soviet-backed Arab armies.[19]

The whole affair disgusted Fulbright. The Israelis were not even willing to act in their own self-interest, he lamented. At one point he suggested that the United Nations, backed by the force of a unilateral American guarantee, impose a peace on the Middle East. There was little chance of that, however, he admitted to a California supporter. The United States was in thrall to the Zionist maximalists who were in turn "extremely powerful . . . especially in the field of communications. The most prestigious newspapers in this country are devoted to this cause, and most of the TV networks are owned by people sympathetic to the same cause."[20]

One of the primary reasons a majority of Americans supported Israel was its demonstrated ability to fight its own battles – unlike the people of Southeast Asia. The Cambodian incursion may have bought some time for Vietnamization, but it also imposed clear-cut if implicit limits on the future use of American combat forces, and it increased pressure on the Nixon administration to speed up the pace of withdrawal. Nixon's efforts to intimidate his enemies at home and abroad produced just the opposite effect. Domestic divisiveness increased dramatically in the summer and fall of 1970. North Vietnamese and Vietcong delegates boycotted the formal Paris talks and promised they would not return until American troops had been withdrawn from Cambodia. The secret talks lapsed as well. Hanoi was content to bide its time, secure in the belief that the antiwar movement, with Fulbright among the vanguard, would destroy America's will to fight.

In an effort to keep Hanoi and the antiwar movement off balance, Nixon in October 1970 launched what he described as a "major new peace initiative."[21] On a nationally televised broadcast he proposed a cease-fire in Indochina, the immediate release of all POWs, the convening of a great-power conference on Southeast Asia, and the creation of a political process that would express

18 "Israel Rejects Fulbright Plan," *Baltimore Sun,* Aug. 26, 1970.

19 News Summary, Sept. 14, 1970, WHSpF, Box 32, Nixon Project.

20 JWF to Ronald Harris, Sept. 24, 1970, Series 48:15, Box 40:3, SPF.

21 Quoted in George C. Herring, *America's Longest War: The United States and Vietnam, 1950–1975,* 2d ed. (New York, 1986), 239.

the will of the people of South Vietnam. "I thought the President's speech represented a considerable improvement . . . in tone," Fulbright wrote David Bruce, the new American negotiator in Paris, "but I regret to say that I do not think that it is an offer the other side will accept."[22] He was right. Hanoi promptly rejected the president's suggestion for a cease-fire, which, it perceived, would restrict the Vietcong to areas they then controlled without assuring them of any role in a political settlement.

In fact, the October speech was intended primarily for domestic consumption. The midterm congressional elections were coming up, and the White House dreamed of a Republican landslide. Nixon followed up his address by touring ten states, angrily denouncing the antiwar protesters and urging the voters to elect men who would "stand with the President."[23] The White House hoped for a majority in the Senate because it would mean, among other things, the end of J. William Fulbright's tenure as chairman of the SFRC.[24] Agnew conducted his own tour in behalf of Republican candidates. He was particularly obnoxious, even for Agnew, and frequently singled out Fulbright for abuse. The conservatives managed to defeat three leading Senate doves – Albert Gore (D–Tennessee), Charles Goodell (R–New York), and Joseph Tydings (D–Maryland) – but about that number of hawks were also defeated. The bellicose Thomas Dodd lost in the Democratic primary in Connecticut. The Republicans gained only two seats in the Senate and lost nine in the House. The 1970 midterm elections were hardly the conservative, forgotten-American landslide that Pat Buchanan and Charles Colson had predicted.

By 1970 the number of American POWs held by the communists or listed as missing in Southeast Asia ran into the thousands, and the issue of their treatment and return had become one of the most sensitive of the war.[25] Both hawks and doves labored to take maximum propaganda advantage of the situation. To Fulbright's intense annoyance, the administration arranged through House Speaker John McCormack to allow Texas billionaire H. Ross Perot to hang a life-sized "tiger cage" in the rotunda of the Capitol. The bamboo cages, suspended several feet off the ground and exposed to the elements, were allegedly used by the North Vietnamese to house American POWs.[26] The rotunda display, the Arkansan asserted, was a public relations stunt that would only further inflame public opinion and prolong the war. In 1969 Fulbright had appealed directly to Ho Chi Minh – and, after his death in September, to

22 Quoted in William C. Berman, *William Fulbright and the Vietnam War: The Dissent of a Political Realist* (Kent, Ohio, 1988), 134.

23 Quoted in Herring, *America's Longest War,* 240.

24 News Summaries, Oct. 13, 1970, WHSpF, Box 32, Nixon Project.

25 Neil Sheehan, "U.S. Information on P.O.W.'s Appears Limited," *New York Times,* Nov. 24, 1970.

26 "Fulbright on the Prowl," *Washington Post,* Aug. 6, 1970.

Pham Van Dong, who succeeded Ho as premier – to publish an official list of those held and to repatriate the sick and wounded. The North Vietnamese, who had succeeded in coercing some of their American prisoners to tape "confessions" and appeals for peace, refused and used the occasion to tell POW families that their loved ones would return to them if only President Nixon would halt his war of aggression.[27]

Throughout the fall of 1970 Fulbright met repeatedly with the wives of POWs and MIAs, most of whom were then pressing for a quick end to the war as a means for getting their husbands home. It was significant that the innately hawkish families of missing and imprisoned servicemen were by the close of Nixon's second year in office willing to turn for help to a man they had once reviled as "Hanoi's little helper." During October, the national networks ran footage of POW–MIA wives going into and out of Fulbright's office.[28] The Arkansan assured the families that he was continuing to work to persuade the North Vietnamese to treat the POWs as a humanitarian issue unconnected to military and political considerations.[29]

Two weeks after the midterm elections in November, Nixon made a bold move to take the POW issue away from Fulbright and the doves. Early one Saturday, 250 American fighter-bombers struck targets across the DMZ and within the Hanoi–Haiphong "doughnut," the first resumption of bombing since the Johnson-initiated pause in the fall of 1968. The attacks, however, were a diversionary tactic to cover a daring raid by U.S. Air Force and Army Special Forces units on the Son Tay prison camp twenty-three miles west of Hanoi. The fighters swooped in and blasted guard towers and concertina-wire fences; but when the U.S. helicopters nestled in and disgorged their commandos, there was no sign of life. The communists had cleared out days before and taken their prisoners with them.[30]

Fulbright suspected from the first that the Son Tay prison raid was a public relations ploy. Indeed, when a somber but self-satisfied Melvin Laird – with Colonel Arthur Simonds, who had led the Son Tay raid, in tow – told newspeople that the "daring mission" highlighted the administration's "dedication" to the POWs and its determination to "do everything that we can in our power to accomplish their early release," Fulbright was sure of it.[31] The Arkansan dared not voice his suspicions without clear-cut proof, however, and he had none. Moreover, such raids were for the most part popular with the public, providing a temporary respite from the ever-present feeling of powerlessness

27 JWF to Pham Van Dong, June 24, 1970, and Ho Chi Minh to JWF, July 25, 1969, Series 48:6, Box 27:6, SPF.

28 News Summaries, Oct. 6, 1970, Box 32, WHSpF, Nixon Project.

29 See JWF to Olaf Palme, July 11, 1970, Series 48:3, Box 17:4, SPF.

30 William Beecher, "U.S. Rescue Force Landed Within 23 Miles of Hanoi, but It Found P.O.W.'s Gone," *New York Times,* Nov. 24, 1970.

31 JWF to Harry Ashmore, Dec. 3, 1970, Series 48:18, Box 59:1, SPF.

that had set in in the wake of the Tet offensive. In fact, so positive was public comment that Laird called Fulbright and volunteered to testify on Son Tay before the SFRC.[32] Fulbright could not deny the request, and the DOD took full advantage of the opportunity. Laird acknowledged that operations like Son Tay were risky, but with a view to defusing criticism from the POW–MIA families, he refused to rule out future raids. "If this country is willing to abandon its military men to death and captivity, we will have truly lost our national morality and our humanity," he declared sanctimoniously.[33]

Within days of Laird's appearance before the SFRC, however, the administration's story had begun to unravel. Laird claimed during his testimony that he and the president had authorized the raid upon hearing that several American POWs had died at Son Tay; but the two Americans from whom the administration claimed to have gotten that information – private citizens who had traveled to Hanoi and brought back the names of seventeen Americans killed over North Vietnam – denied that any of those had died at Son Tay or any other prison camp. "It [the list] could mean they were dead on hitting the ground, or found dead after wandering around in the mountains for weeks after they crashed, or died from wounds suffered while they were being shot down," Peter Weiss, a lawyer representing the POW families told reporters.[34] Writing in the *Washington Star,* Clayton Fritchey observed that even if the Son Tay raid had been successful, it would have subjected other Americans in captivity to torture and death. "There is a smell of desperation about this adventure," he mused. "It is not the considered action of a great power."[35]

On Sunday, November 9, Fulbright appeared on *Face the Nation* – as it happened, at the same time as South Vietnamese Vice-Premier Nguyen Cao Ky appeared on NBC's *Meet the Press.* (Ky was in the country as a guest of the Rev. Carl McIntire, the fundamentalist preacher who had fueled the recall Fulbright movement in Arkansas.) Fulbright astounded Marvin Kalb and his other questioners by accusing Laird of "misrepresenting the facts" about the Son Tay raid and the bombing of North Vietnam. "Now I wouldn't ever call anybody a liar in public except by inadvertence," he declared, but he made it clear that that was what he was doing. He then launched into an unprecedented indictment of the DOD and its representatives in Congress. Son Tay and the resumed bombing of the North were just symptoms of a general malady, the Arkansan declared. The Defense Department had completely eclipsed State

32 "Critics Stymied as Laird Invokes Honor, Morality," *Washington Post,* Nov. 25, 1970.

33 "1st Foray Justified, Hill Told," *Washington Post,* Nov. 25, 1970.

34 "Laird Accused of Distorting POW Deaths," *Arkansas Gazette,* Nov. 26, 1970.

35 Clayton Fritchey, "That Dubious Raid to Free the Hanoi Prisoners," *Washington Star,* Nov. 30, 1970.

and was not only making American foreign policy but also, with $80 billion a year to spend, selling and implementing that policy. "This is muscle, this is influence, this is power," the chairman observed. "It [the Pentagon] controls and influences everything that goes on in our government." Representing the interests of the military establishment in the Senate, he told Kalb and the others, were Richard Russell, John Stennis, Henry Jackson, and other members whose home states brimmed with defense plants. These men were the real power in the Senate. Compared with them, his position as chairman of the SFRC was "very secondary," comparable, he said, to the subsidiary position State was then occupying in relation to Defense. His journalist-hosts should not have been surprised. The Arkansan's new book, *The Pentagon Propaganda Machine,* had been published earlier in the month; it was a devastating attack on the military–industrial complex.[36]

By 1971 J. William Fulbright's international reputation was cresting. Years of advocating détente with the Soviet Union and arms control, coupled with his opposition to a war that even America's staunchest allies viewed as brutal and counterproductive, had won the Arkansan a following in Japan, Brazil, France, Indonesia, Australia, and dozens of other countries. Despite his well-known record on civil rights, Fulbright's admirers tended to be concentrated among the young, the educated, and those whose political views were moderate to leftist. Particularly important to his popularity was Fulbright's opposition to militarism and military regimes. In 1971, at the urging of British historian-philosopher Arnold Toynbee and several other international celebrities, he led a fight to cut off aid to Pakistan until it ceased slaughtering the inhabitants of the breakaway republic of Bangladesh.[37] Even more significant, however, was his decision in 1970 and 1971 to take on the brutal military dictatorship in Greece, a decision that placed him at the forefront of a "new" international reform movement: human rights.

In April 1967 a military junta headed by Colonel George Papadopoulos had overthrown the civilian government in Greece, suspended the legislature, and imposed martial law. The Johnson administration had responded by announcing that it would indefinitely withhold shipments of tanks, airplanes, and aircraft to its NATO partner. Over the next year and a half the junta had brutally stifled dissent. Eyewitness accounts of prolonged imprisonment, torture, and killings by right-wing death squads appeared in newspapers and magazines all over the world. Some of the beatings and mutilations had oc-

36 "Bombing Facts Misstated, Fulbright Says," *Los Angeles Times,* Nov. 30, 1970, and "Fulbright Says U.S. Action in Vietnam Has Intensified," *Baltimore Sun,* Nov. 30, 1970.

37 Toynbee to JWF, July 28, 1971, and JWF to Toynbee, Aug. 5, 1971, Series 48:11, Box 36:5, SPF.

curred in the headquarters of the Greek military police, only a block from the American embassy. That proximity would become symbolic under the Nixon administration.

Neither during the 1968 campaign nor during his first hundred days had Richard Nixon publicly mentioned the situation in Greece, but several factors had disposed the president and his NSC adviser to adopt a lenient position toward the junta. Greece served as an important strategic base for the U.S. Navy's Sixth Fleet, and it permitted U.S. Air Force planes full overflight and landing rights. Moreover, as the subsequent Watergate investigation revealed, a prominent Greek-American businessman, Thomas A. Pappas, had funneled contributions from the junta to the Nixon campaign during the 1968 election.[38] In 1969 Nixon had appointed career Foreign Service officer Henry J. Tasca ambassador and urged him to develop a close relationship with the colonels. He had been instructed to inform Papadopoulos that Washington would soon resume heavy weapons shipments; the United States would appreciate steps toward democracy, but it would not make restoration of the full aid program dependent upon them.[39] No sooner had Tasca arrived in Athens than the flow of heavy arms to Greece had begun, and on September 22, 1970, the Nixon administration had formally lifted the embargo.

In the summer of 1970 rumors had begun to circulate that the Pentagon had exceeded the congressionally mandated ceiling on aid to Greece by almost twenty million dollars. Fulbright had immediately convened the SFRC and launched an investigation. In the executive hearings that followed, he had compelled Defense and State Department officials to admit that the administration had resumed heavy-arms shipments and that there had in fact been no progress toward democracy under the colonels. Marcy had then promptly leaked the transcript to the press.[40] The chairman had subsequently cosponsored legislation with Senator Vance Hartke that would cut off all aid, military and nonmilitary, to Greece.[41] At that point Fulbright had become a hero to the Greek resistance movement and anathema to the colonels.

Early in 1971 Fulbright decided to send Dick Moose and Jim Lowenstein to Greece to gather evidence proving that the colonels had no intention whatsoever of moving toward a constitutional democracy, and that they were instead continuing to burn, electrocute, and shoot their countrymen into submission. The trip turned out to be something out of an Ian Fleming thriller. Tasca, "a real son-of-a-bitch," according to Lowenstein, was hostile and obstructive. The Greek KYP (secret police), heavily subsidized by the

38 Hersh, *Price of Power,* 136–9.

39 Ibid.

40 Tad Szulc, "Pentagon Doubles Arms Aid to Athens Despite Restriction," *New York Times,* Apr. 17, 1970, and "Athens Given U.S. Arms Despite Ban," *Washington Post,* June 3, 1970.

41 JWF to Jessie O'Kelly, June 9, 1970, Series 48:8, Box 31:1, SPF.

CIA,[42] shadowed the two SFRC investigators every step of the way. "Dick and I had two rooms in this hotel [in Athens]," Lowenstein recalled. "There was a room in between us. We could hear people in this room but we noticed that there were never any shoes outside the door. The key was never downstairs." Lowenstein would go to Geneva and call his contacts in Greece from a telephone booth. Led by an American who headed the American Farm School in Salonika and a Foreign Service officer who was disgusted with the embassy's constant kowtowing to the colonels, dozens of Americans and Greeks related tales of torture and provided documents proving that the colonels had no intention of restoring democracy to Greece.[43]

By late February Moose and Lowenstein had all the information they needed. Fulbright released their report within days of their return to Washington. It portrayed Ambassador Tasca as an "apologist" for the junta rather than the tough-minded spur to democracy the administration claimed him to be. American aid, together with the approval of the Nixon administration, constituted the most important assets Papadopoulos and his cronies enjoyed.[44] In October, following a trip to Athens by Spiro Agnew during which he heaped unreserved praise on the colonels, Fulbright led a Senate charge to cut off aid to the junta.[45] Though he was unsuccessful, the Arkansan had helped focus national and world attention on the plight of prodemocracy activists in Greece. Years later when Fulbright was in Athens to commemorate the signing of the exchange agreement, victims of the colonels' terror held a massive celebration in his honor. More than a score took the stage to pay tearful tribute to his concern and courage.[46]

As Congress prepared to reconvene in January 1971, Carl Marcy, as was his wont, surveyed the events of the previous year. He did not like what he saw. The administration had systematically continued the erosion of congressional prerogatives in the areas of warmaking and treaty ratification, he concluded. As the Cambodian invasion, the clandestine war in Laos, and the secret commitments to Thailand, Spain, and other countries indicated, the Nixon administration was not only proceeding unilaterally but deceiving Congress and the American people. In addition, Nixon and Kissinger were manipulating the bureaucracy in ways that allowed them to conceal their intentions and actions from the SFRC.[47]

42 Hersh, *Price of Power,* 138.
43 Interview with James Lowenstein, Oct. 3, 1991, Washington, D.C.
44 Bernard D. Nossiter, "Hill Report Cites Greek Repression," *Washington Post,* Mar. 5, 1971.
45 "Agnew, Heading Home, Praises Greek Regime," *New York Times,* Oct. 28, 1971, and UPI 90, Oct. 29, 1971.
46 Interview with Monroe and Mary Donsker, Oct. 19, 1990, New York, N.Y.
47 Marcy to JWF, Jan. 22, 1971, Box 10, Folder Jan.–Mar., Marcy Papers.

Marcy's analysis noted also that the executive had systematically withheld vital information from the Committee – the Thai contingency plan, the Tonkin Gulf command-and-control study, and the Spanish bases agreement. Diplomatic correspondents, foreign diplomats, and selected members of certain proadministration committees had greater access to foreign policy information than had the SFRC.[48] Although Rogers, Kissinger, and Laird gave frequent "backgrounders" to friendly congresspeople and members of the press corps, they had been unavailable for testimony in public session. When they or other executive branch officers did agree to appear, State Department officials would come to the Hill and brief individual SFRC members so that they would not show up for the scheduled meeting, thus embarrassing Fulbright and preventing a confrontation en masse.[49] "The Committee has had more significant meetings this year with Abba Eban, Willy Brandt, Suharto, and others than it has had with high level officers of the U.S. Government," Marcy lamented to Fulbright.[50] When executive branch officers did testify with any candor, the administration declared their remarks classified, thus preventing their release to the public.

On the positive side, the committee would remain Democratic and under the chairmanship of J. William Fulbright until at least 1974. Gore was gone, but there was still a "Fulbright majority" on the committee, to use Richard Moose's term. Stuart Symington and his subcommittee would continue to uncover clandestine commitments. The relentlessly dovish George McGovern would be back. In response to the bombing and invasion of Cambodia, Mike Mansfield had abandoned his long-held view that the Senate majority leader should be the handmaiden of the president no matter what his party, and was apparently prepared to work openly for the defeat of administration measures. Although Fulbright did not completely trust him, Frank Church, the boy orator from Idaho with the slicked-back hair and burning ambition, still perceived opposition to the war as good politics. The gaggle of Republican liberals – the chain-smoking and inarticulate John Sherman Cooper, the brilliant Jacob Javits, and the morally driven Clifford Case – would also return to strengthen the anti-imperialist coalition. "Between the conservatives of 15 years ago and the liberal internationalists of today," one journalist noted after surveying the new Congress, "there is a common concern over the President's ability to enter into foreign agreements without the consent or knowledge of Congress."[51]

48 Marcy to JWF, Sept. 30, 1970, Box 9, July-Sept., Marcy Papers.
49 Marcy to JWF, Jan. 22, 1971, Box 10, Jan.–Mar., Marcy Papers.
50 Marcy, memorandum, Nov. 5, 1970, Box 9, Oct.–Dec., Marcy Papers.
51 "Case Offers Bill to Disclose Pacts," *New York Times*, Dec. 3, 1970.

On February 1, 1971, the *New York Times* reported that B-52's were bombing enemy supply bases in southern Laos around the clock. Rumor had it that a massive South Vietnamese invasion, backed by American aircraft, was afoot. Because Military Assistance Command in Saigon had clamped an embargo on news coming out of both Laos and South Vietnam, stories about a possible incursion could not be immediately confirmed.[52] An alarmed Fulbright, believing that the administration had decided to cast caution to the wind and go for broke, immediately summoned the Capitol Hill press corps. If the raids in Laos failed to hamper the enemy, he told them, "it would be logical to go on further north" and overrun North Vietnam itself. He pointed out that there was no congressional restriction on the use of American troops for an invasion of North Vietnam; indeed, the Cooper–Church amendment was being interpreted as authorization for all actions not specifically forbidden.[53]

The Laotian incursion fueled the movement in the Senate to impose both specific and general limitations on the president's warmaking powers. Hatfield and McGovern asked Fulbright to join them in cosponsoring a reworked version of their 1970 "Amendment to End the War." It would "propose" that the president set a timetable for the withdrawal of all American armed forces from Vietnam by December 31, 1971. After that date, funds would remain available only for release of prisoners of war, protection of South Vietnamese "who might be endangered," and continued assistance to the government of South Vietnam.[54] Fulbright refused, primarily because the new amendment included continued aid for the Thieu regime. "Even our concept of 'peace' has been drastically modified," he told an assemblage of students and teachers at Florida State. "Where once it referred to a condition in which nobody is killing anybody, it now refers to a future state of affairs in which Asians will be killing Asians with American guns, bombs and air support." Quoting another critic of the war, he declared that "American policy in Indochina was being shaped 'as though America had no concern for the sanctity of human life, as such – as though, somehow, Americans cared only about American lives.'"[55]

Nor did Fulbright join other legislative efforts designed to limit the warmaking powers of the president. In mid-February Javits introduced the measure that would eventually become the War Powers Act. It required the president to end any future military action overseas after thirty days unless it was authorized by Congress. Javits's bill compelled the president to "report fully and promptly" to Congress, explaining the reason and authority for military

52 Terence Smith, "U.S. B-52's Strike Foe's Laos Bases Around the Clock," *New York Times*, Feb., 1, 1971, and Marcy to JWF and Williams, Feb. 1, 1971, Box 10, Jan.–Mar. 71, Marcy Papers.

53 UPI 27, Feb. 8, 1971, Series 48:3, Box 18:1, SPF.

54 Hatfield to JWF, Jan. 21, 1971, Series 48:17, Box 46:2, SPF.

55 *Congressional Record*, Senate, Mar. 12, 1971, 6395.

actions taken in the absence of a declaration of war. Unless authorizing legislation was forthcoming, the chief executive would have to terminate the action.[56]

Fulbright's apparent apathy puzzled the press. The *New York Times* reported that the Arkansan was "in a mood of despairing resignation, bored with criticizing the Administration and uninterested in pushing legislation." Fulbright admitted to being frustrated and pessimistic, but his intermittent despondency stemmed not from his belief that Congress would never pass an end-the-war resolution, but from his suspicion that such specific prohibitions were too little, too late.[57] That he was willing to let others take the lead on various end-the-war measures was merely indicative of the fact that he had decided to challenge the imperial presidency on other fronts.

56 "Javits Offers War Curb Bill," *Washington Evening Star,* Feb. 10, 1971.
57 JWF to Mrs. William Maloney, Mar. 2, 1971, Series 48:18, Box 63:1, SPF.

# 34

# *Privileges and immunities*

Since 1967 J. William Fulbright had decried and described the corrosive effect the war was having on both Vietnamese and American society. By 1971 his focus was almost entirely on the havoc being wrought on the U.S. economy, its Constitution, and its common ideals. "When a war is of long duration, when its objectives are unascertainable, when the people are bitterly divided and their leaders lacking in both vision and candor, then the process of democratic erosion is greatly accelerated," he declared in his Florida State speech. "Beset by criticism and doubt, the nation's leaders resort increasingly to secrecy and deception." That was what was happening in America in 1971 and, as a result, the very institutional foundations of the republic were at risk. "When truth becomes the first casualty," he warned the Senate, quoting a familiar aphorism, "belief in truth, and in the very possibility of honest dealings, cannot fail to become the second."[1]

In mid-March Fulbright decided to attack the whole concept of executive privilege. It lay, he was convinced, at the very heart of the imperial presidency, and it was being used to conceal American involvement in Southeast Asia and other real and imagined trouble spots around the world. By 1971 Nixon and Kissinger had succeeded in shifting most diplomatic policy and decision making from the cabinet departments to the NSC, which was part of the office of the president and as such exempt from congressional accountability. Unwilling to see anything slip through the veil of secrecy, however, the president extended executive privilege beyond the confines of the White House to cover even communications between himself and regular cabinet officers. Perhaps most important, the Nixon administration refused not only to provide information, but even to debate the rationale for the war or to discuss its plan for ending it. During an SFRC hearing earlier in the year, a high-ranking administration official had been asked if the government intended to withdraw from Southeast Asia unconditionally or whether it was determined to leave only after it had firmly established anticommunist governments. The official

1 *Congressional Record,* Senate, Mar. 12, 1971, 6395.

had declined to answer on the grounds that such information would aid the enemy.[2]

The Nixon administration based its virtually unlimited interpretation of executive privilege on a 1958 Justice Department memo. "Congress cannot, under the Constitution, compel heads of departments by law to give up papers and information; regardless of the public interest involved," it read; and anyway, "the President is the judge of that interest." That definition had had the same effect on the legislative and executive branches as a severance of relations would on two sovereign nations, Fulbright declared. The notion that the president and the president alone was the sole judge of the public interest was absurd, a mortal threat to the system of checks and balances. "As James Madison said in *The Federalist,*" Fulbright argued to the Senate, "neither the Executive nor the legislature can pretend to an exclusive or superior right of setting the boundaries between their respective powers."[3]

In an effort to create momentum in behalf of a congressional show of force against executive privilege, Fulbright submitted a bill requiring employees of the executive branch to appear in person before Congress or the appropriate committee when duly summoned. The chairman reasoned that even if, upon their arrival, the president's men did nothing more than invoke executive privilege, they would have put Congress and the public on notice that the administration was operating in secret.[4] He hoped the claim would have the same damning effect that witnesses' invocation of the Fifth Amendment had had during the McCarthy, McClellan, and Kefauver committee hearings. At the same time, he put Marcy to work on a draft amendment to the Constitution providing for censure or removal of a president without subjecting the country to the trauma of impeachment. Among those actions warranting censure or removal under the Fulbright–Marcy plan were "ignoring provisions of law such as the Cooper–Church amendment" and "the refusal of lawful requests for information."[5]

Amid Fulbright's ruminations on executive privilege and impeachment, one of the decisive events of the entire Vietnam era transpired. Following five months of testimony and investigation, a military court at Fort Benning, Georgia, convicted Lieutenant William Calley of murdering twenty-two innocent men, women, and children in the village of My Lai and sentenced him to twenty years in prison. The trial was conducted with scrupulous regard for

2 Ibid., Mar. 5, 1971, 5232. 3 Ibid. 4 Ibid., Mar. 12, 1971, 6396.

5 Referring to the 1867 impeachment trial of Andrew Johnson, Marcy observed that Congress and the courts had traditionally held that impeachment ought to be for "treason, bribery, and other high crimes and misdemeanors," and that referred only to criminal acts, not resistance to the will of one or both of the other branches of the federal government. Marcy to JWF, Apr. 27, 1971, Box 10, Apr.–June, Marcy Papers.

the rights of the defendant. The six judges were all combat veterans and five had served in Vietnam. After the evidence was presented, there was no doubt in their minds or in the minds of the vast majority of professional soldiers everywhere that Calley was guilty and that his conduct was inexcusable. "This is the guy," William Greider reminded his readers in the *Washington Post,* "who picked up a baby, threw him into a ditch and shot him. He is the soldier who butt-stroked an old man in the face, then shot him at point-blank range and blew away the side of his head."[6] As Aubrey Daniel, the army's chief trial counsel put it, "it is unlawful for an American soldier to summarily execute unarmed and unresisting men, women, children, and babies."[7]

Nonetheless, Calley's conviction seemed to outrage Americans as had no other incident in the war. The White House and various congressional offices were deluged with tens of thousands of letters of protest from both hawks and doves. Hawks felt the trial, not to mention the sentence, was grossly unfair, and final proof that the nation did not have the will to win. War was a collective decision to murder, they pointed out; once that line was crossed, conventional moral standards went out the window. Everyone knew that it was impossible to distinguish friend from enemy in Vietnam. "The most innocent looking child or old person can kill a person with a gun or grenade," a Little Rock woman declared. "Men are trained in the Army to kill the enemy and this is what happened at My Lai."[8]

Those who had served in Vietnam, who had lost relatives in the war, or who had relatives serving in Southeast Asia felt betrayed. "We have never been in sympathy with the Vietnam war, but our son went when his draft call came," Mrs. Ralph Barnett wrote Fulbright. "Our boys should not be tried and sentenced for killing the enemy when they are sent over to do just that." Mrs. Barnett's son had been killed in action three months earlier.[9]

Opponents of the war did not deny that Calley was guilty – indeed, since 1969 they had been insisting that My Lai was a disgraceful emblem of American imperialism and the ultimate example of the brutality of the war in Vietnam – but in the wake of Calley's conviction, doves insisted that the commander of Charlie Company had been made a scapegoat and called for an immediate end to the war followed by Nuremberg-type war-crime trials for those officials who had originally been responsible for committing America to war.[10] Fulbright's views on the trial were typical. It was "a rather questionable principle" to single out Calley for prosecution, he told reporters. He had been "put in a situation created by policy supported by the principal polit-

6 William Greider, "Calley's Trial: The Moral Question and Battlefield Laws," *Washington Post,* Apr. 5, 1971.
7 Daniels to Nixon, Apr. 3, 1971, WHSpF, Box 16, Nixon Project.
8 Debbie Tyler to JWF, Apr. 1, 1971, Series 4:10, Box 18:1, SPF.
9 Barnett to JWF, Mar. 30, 1971, Series 4:10, Box 18:3, SPF.
10 See Jack Baker to JWF, Mar. 31, 1971, Series 4:10, Box 18:5, SPF.

ical authorities in this country." It was Johnson, Westmoreland, and Abrams who should be held accountable, he said. "The principle that we applied to Yamashita [Japanese General Tomoyuki, commander of Japanese forces in Southeast Asia, executed as a war criminal in 1946] should be applied here."[11]

"Tide of Public Opinion Turns Decisively Against the War," ran the headline of an article on a Louis Harris poll taken in the wake of the Calley trial. By 60 to 26 percent Americans indicated they would favor continued withdrawal of American troops from Vietnam, "even if the government of South Vietnam collapses." For the first time, by 58 to 29 percent, a majority of the public agreed that it was "morally wrong" for the United States to be fighting in Vietnam.[12]

Buoyed by signs of pervasive disillusionment with the war, Fulbright and the SFRC the last week in April opened hearings on the end-the-war resolutions pending before Congress. Among the witnesses were former Johnson administration officials McGeorge Bundy, Arthur Goldberg, and George Reedy, all of whom endorsed the notion of setting a deadline and enacting legislation placing limits on the executive's ability to wage war.[13] One of the star witnesses at the 1971 hearings was John Kerry, a leading light in the newly formed Vietnam Veterans Against the War. Kerry and his compatriots, clothed symbolically in faded fatigues adorned with battle ribbons and peace symbols, had come to Washington from Detroit where, in a Howard Johnson's motel room, they had conducted their "Winter Soldier" investigation of U.S. war crimes in Indochina. Kerry's band gathered on the Capitol steps, bore witness to their own misdeeds in Vietnam, and ceremoniously tossed away their medals. Several days later, Fulbright met Kerry at a Georgetown party and invited him to appear before the SFRC.[14]

As the hearings opened, the committee room was filled with Vietnam veterans. Kerry, thrice-wounded as a riverboat commander, was eloquent in his appeal for an immediate end to the war. "How do you ask a man to be the last to die in Vietnam?" he asked the senators. "How do you ask a man to be the last to die for a mistake?"[15] Newspaper reporters and television commenta-

11 "Nixon Orders Calley Freed from Stockade," *Arkansas Gazette,* Apr. 2, 1971.
12 Louis Harris, "Tide of Public Opinion Turns Decisively Against the War," *Washington Post,* May 3, 1971.
13 Marcy to JWF, May 6, 1971, Series 48:3, Box 18:1, SPF, and "Harriman Assails Thieu on '68 Talks," *Washington Evening Star,* May 25, 1971.
14 Interview with Carl Marcy, Oct. 10, 1988, Washington, D.C.
15 Herbert Rainwater to JWF, June 3, 1971, Series 48:18, Box 63:3, SPF.

tors declared Kerry's testimony to be among the most dramatic of the war, and everyone complimented the veterans on their comportment.[16]

Later, however, as Fulbright and the SFRC were listening to establishment figures testify on the need to get out of Vietnam as soon as possible, the committee room was invaded by members of the Mayday Tribe, a new counterculture, antiwar organization that had come to Washington with the stated intention of "shutting the government down." While their comrades were outside conducting "lie-ins" on bridges and major thoroughfares and at the entrances of government buildings, three "tribesmen" interrupted Fulbright to accuse him and everyone involved in the proceedings of being imperialists and war criminals. The committee was "doing the dirtywork of the administration" by acting as a safety valve and diverting the attention of the antiwar movement. Both Aiken and Fulbright lost their tempers.

"Why the hell do you stay here if other countries are so much better?" the white-haired Republican asked. "If you were in an authoritarian country," Fulbright told the demonstrators, "you'd all be in jail."[17]

Positive public and press response to the end-the-war hearings seemed to stiffen the Senate's resolve. In mid-May the upper house began debate on a new Hatfield–McGovern amendment, which proposed to cut off funds for further military operations by the end of the year. Mike Mansfield revived his bill calling for a 50 percent reduction of American troops in Europe.[18] Stuart Symington asked for and got a secret session of the Senate, during which he briefed his colleagues on the extent of American bombing in Laos. He flatly accused the Nixon administration of deceiving Congress and the American people, and of violating the law.[19]

When the debate had ended, the doves seemed to have little to show for their efforts, however. The second Hatfield–McGovern amendment was defeated by a vote of 55 to 39 on June 16.[20] Shortly before, supporters of the administration had managed to down the Mansfield proposal to cut U.S. troops in Europe by a 63 to 36 tally.[21] These seemingly hawkish votes were

16 Actually Kerry was something of an establishment figure. While in Washington he stayed in the Georgetown townhouse of a friend of the Kennedy family's. Adam Yarmolinsky, a former Kennedy administration official, had helped script his SFRC testimony. In early June the VVAW leadership denounced him for using their organization to further a prospective political career.

17 UPI 28, Apr. 28, 1971.

18 *Congressional Record,* Senate, May 18, 1971, 15550–1.

19 Spencer Rich, "Senate Told Nixon Aid to Laos Illegal," *Washington Post,* June 8, 1971.

20 William C. Berman, *William Fulbright and the Vietnam War: The Dissent of a Political Realist* (Kent, Ohio, 1988), 145.

21 Spencer Rich, "Senate Defeats Compromises on NATO Cutback," *Washington Post,* May 20, 1971.

somewhat deceiving, however. The Nixon administration was then justifying its opposition to end-the-war resolutions almost solely on the grounds that it needed maximum leeway to protect American troops as they withdrew from Vietnam. The decisive defeat of the Mansfield bill stemmed from the fact that in May, Soviet leader Leonid Brezhnev had called for a mutual reduction of forces in Europe, and the administration had begged the Congress not to give away a bargaining chip in advance.[22] Moreover, while the House simultaneously voted down its own end-the-war resolution, the antiwar tally of 158 was the largest in the history of the Vietnam conflict.[23] Perhaps most important, the Senate's most effective and consistent hawk, John Stennis, announced to his startled colleagues that he was introducing his own legislation to curb the power of presidents to commit the nation to war without the consent of Congress. Fulbright, Symington, and McGovern joined with Sam Ervin, John Sparkman, and the *New York Times* to hail Stennis's speech as a potential turning point in contemporary American history, a key action that could lead to the redressing of the balance of power between Congress and the executive.[24]

Fulbright had not been on hand for the second vote on Hatfield–McGovern. Cambridge University had invited him to address its commencement exercises, and because he was able to arrange a pair (i.e., agree not to vote) with an opponent of the end-the-war proposal, he went. Fulbright's speech, delivered amid the medieval towers and rolling meadows of one of the world's most picturesque and prestigious universities, the site of his lacrosse triumph when he had been at Oxford, was a study in irony. Twenty-five years earlier he had created an academic exchange program that had had as one of its primary objectives the training of the best and the brightest for government service; but the ensuing participation by intellectuals in government, he told the graduates, had been a mixed blessing to say the least:

> I very much doubt that America's brilliant strategy in Vietnam could have been shaped without the scholarship and erudition of two Rhodes scholars and one former Harvard dean. More recently, we have been served at the highest policy level by an illustrious historian and strategic thinker whose special gift is an ability to shape American strategy in Southeast Asia in the light of the experience of Weimar Germany and Metternich's stewardship of the Hapsburg empire. . . . Eschewing false modesty, I am bound to confess that

22 Ibid.

23 "Senate End-the-War Faction Is Close to Majority, But . . . ," *Washington Evening Star,* June 20, 1971.

24 John W. Finney, "Stennis Seeks War Curb on President," *New York Times,* May 12, 1971.

> my country has solved the problem of drawing intellectuals into government. The problem is . . . how do we get them out?[25]

While he was in London, the *New York Times* began publishing the first portions of the *Pentagon Papers,* the top-secret Defense Department study of the war commissioned by Robert McNamara in 1967. The person who had furnished them to the *Times* was Daniel Ellsberg, a former DOD and Rand Corporation employee, an intellectual who had become intensely disillusioned with the war, and a newly converted activist who wanted to spread that disillusionment as widely as possible.[26] As a DOD employee with a top-secret clearance, he had been granted access to the forty-seven-volume study commissioned by McNamara. That compilation, he concluded, was a record of deceit and misjudgment without parallel in American diplomatic history. Its publication would be the final blow that would collapse the Vietnam consensus. In the late spring of 1970 Ellsberg summoned an old friend of his named Neil Sheehan to MIT, where Ellsberg was then working as a research fellow. Sheehan received the papers and subsequently succeeded in persuading his employer, *Times* publisher Arthur Sulzberger, to print them.[27]

From London where, having received his honorary degree from Cambridge, he was attending the British–American Parliamentary Conference, Fulbright hailed the decision to publish the *Pentagon Papers.* "I think it's very healthy for a democratic country like America to know the facts surrounding their involvement in such a great tragedy as the war in Vietnam," he told reporters. The chairman revealed for the first time that he and the SFRC had known of the study's existence and had unsuccessfully attempted to secure a copy from the administration. He himself had never seen the Pentagon documents, Fulbright insisted.[28]

Upon his return Fulbright asked the *Times* to turn over its copy of the *Pentagon Papers* to Congress so that the study could be published in its entirety. When Sulzberger refused, Fulbright officially requested a copy from Melvin Laird.[29] As he had in the past, Laird, after consulting with Nixon, said no. The study was a "compilation of raw materials to be used at some unspecified, but distant, future date." Giving the history to the SFRC "would clearly be contrary to the national interest," Laird concluded.[30] Meanwhile, the *Times* continued to run choice excerpts on its front page.

25 Quoted in Berman, *Fulbright and the Vietnam War,* 144.

26 Stanley Karnow, *Vietnam: A History* (New York, 1984), 633.

27 Sanford J. Ungar, "Daniel Ellsberg: The Difficulties of Disclosure," *Washington Post,* Apr. 30, 1972.

28 UPI 22, June 7, 1971.

29 JWF to Sulzberger, *New York Times,* June 16, 1971, Series 48:18, Box 63:3, JWF Papers, and Sulzberger to JWF, June 19, 1971, Box 10, Apr.–June, Marcy Papers.

30 James M. Naughton, "Laird Refused '69 Fulbright Request for the Pentagon Study on Vietnam," *New York Times,* June 17, 1971.

Publication of the *Pentagon Papers* shocked and angered both Nixon and Kissinger. At Nixon's direction the Justice Department filed suit to block further publication. Both men were worried that this "hemorrhage of state secrets," as Kissinger described the release, would undermine American credibility abroad and affect negotiations with both North Vietnam and China that were then underway.

Nixon was also angry that such a monumental leak had taken place during his term in office. Shortly after the Supreme Court turned down his request to block further publication by the *Times,* he threw a tantrum: "I want to know who is behind this and I want the most complete investigation that can be conducted. . . . I don't want excuses. I want results. I want it done, whatever the costs."[31] In early July the White House formed a secret internal police unit and began domestic operations aimed at destroying the credibility of Ellsberg and others in the antiwar movement.

On June 22 Fulbright announced that the SFRC would soon launch a full-scale investigation into the history of U.S. involvement in Vietnam, and he once again asked the administration to furnish the Senate with a complete copy of the *Pentagon Papers.* The following day Nixon agreed, although he told reporters that the report was still classified and it would be available only for senators to see and take notes. The papers would be guarded and they would not be made public.[32] What persuaded the president to make this "concession" was the knowledge that Fulbright and the SFRC staff had had a copy of the *Pentagon Papers* in their possession for sixteen months.

The first week in November 1969 Ellsberg, convinced that the Nixon administration was deliberately escalating the war in Vietnam in hopes of winning a military victory while deceiving Congress and the American people as to its true intentions, had gone to Washington and called on Jim Lowenstein. He and Lowenstein had first met during the latter's trip to Vietnam with Philip Hart. Ellsberg had also met Dick Moose while Moose was working for Henry Kissinger. Ellsberg had told Lowenstein that he had in his possession "a classified Executive Branch document regarding Vietnam" that would be useful to the committee.[33] After talking to Carl Marcy, Lowenstein had set up a meeting that afternoon between Fulbright and Ellsberg.

Ellsberg had been very familiar with Fulbright's views on the war, and particularly with his belief that Lyndon Johnson and Robert McNamara had

31 Quoted in Karnow, *Vietnam: A History,* 633.

32 John Herbers, "Nixon Will Give Secret Study to Congress," *New York Times,* June 24, 1971, and Elsie Carper, "Part of Study in Hand, Fulbright Seeks Rest," *Washington Post,* June 23, 1971.

33 Lowenstein to Jones, Mar. 23, 1973, Ellsberg File, Papers of Norvill Jones (in his possession).

lied to him and the Senate during the Gulf of Tonkin incident. The Arkansan, Ellsberg had believed, was the perfect person to receive and publish the papers. As a leader of the antiwar movement, Fulbright would draw attention to the secret history and maximize its impact on Congress and the public. His imprimatur would, moreover, help legitimize what some would characterize as an act of espionage. Most important, perhaps, Ellsberg had realized that if the *Pentagon Papers* were published under the auspices of Fulbright and the SFRC, he could avoid prosecution: Senators acting as senators were immune to prosecutorial action by the courts and Justice Department; logic seemed to dictate that that protection would extend to their sources.[34]

During the forty-five-minute meeting Ellsberg had briefly described what he had in his possession. To whet Fulbright and Marcy's appetite, he had given them a copy of the Gulf of Tonkin command and control study prepared by the DOD's Institute of Defense Analysis. The secret history of the war McNamara had ordered was a sordid tale of deception and ineptitude whose publication was sure to accelerate disillusionment with the war, he had insisted. Fulbright had expressed interest and suggested that the best approach might be to have Ellsberg testify before an executive session of the SFRC. He then instructed Lowenstein and Jones to follow up. The next day Ellsberg had brought a single-volume summary of the *Pentagon Papers* to Jones. The two agreed to lock the summary in the committee safe.[35]

The next day Fulbright had huddled with his staff to decide how to proceed. Marcy and Jones had urged the chairman to use caution. Ellsberg was a volatile personality, and he had obviously broken the law. "If the Committee had decided to hold hearings on the papers," Jones later observed, "the focus would have been on how the Committee came into possession of the documents and not their contents. It would have side-tracked the Committee's efforts to mobilize opinion against the war, thus playing into the Administration's hands." In addition, the climate in Congress was "already bitter," Fulbright's aides had told him, and release of the purloined documents would impair his efforts to weld hawks and doves into an anti-imperial coalition. Finally, there was little in the excerpts that Ellsberg had given them that they did not already know, namely, that the Johnson administration had engaged in deception "which amounted to fraud."[36]

Fulbright, Marcy, and Jones had perceived correctly that, Ellsberg being who he was, the *Pentagon Papers* would find their way into the public domain through another sphere. Why not use the situation to embarrass the ad-

34 See Donald A. Ritchie, interviewer, *Oral History Interviews: Carl A. Marcy* (Senate Historical Office: Washington, D.C., 1983), and Ungar, "Daniel Ellsberg."

35 "Ellsberg Matter," undated, Ellsberg File, Jones Papers, and Ungar, "Daniel Ellsberg."

36 "Why the Committee Did Not Act on the Pentagon History of the War," undated, Ellsberg File, Jones Papers.

ministration and discredit the use of "executive privilege"?[37] If the SFRC could get Laird to deny Congress access to the papers, citing executive privilege, and then the papers became public, it would be clear for all to see that the Nixon administration was abusing the classification power and the claim of executive privilege merely to cover up a trail of executive-branch misdeeds.

In late February 1970 Norvill Jones had begun receiving in the mail copies of twenty-five of the forty-seven volumes of the secret study. Some of them Ellsberg had simply mailed at the post office in the Brentwood section of Los Angeles. After looking them over, Jones and Marcy had conferred with Fulbright. The purloined volumes were later locked away in the safe in the committee's offices on the fourth floor of the New Senate Office Building.

Ellsberg's two children from his first marriage had helped photocopy the documents, and they had kept their mother apprised of what was transpiring, including their father's decision to mail copies of certain volumes to Fulbright. Shortly thereafter, FBI agents, casting their net widely for incriminating information on former administration officials who had turned against the war, had interviewed the first Mrs. Ellsberg. She had told all, including her ex-husband's liaison with the chairman of the SFRC. When Ellsberg had learned that Hoover's men were on his trail, he had resigned from Rand and taken the position with MIT. Meanwhile, FBI agents had made inquiries at Rand and been told that the documents in Ellsberg and Fulbright's possession did not involve national security. Despite its doubts, the bureau had immediately dropped its investigation – primarily out of fear of the link to Fulbright. The chairman was too powerful; officials decided that further inquiry could "embarrass the bureau."[38]

In the weeks that followed Ellsberg had pressed Fulbright to hold hearings for the specific purpose of revealing the contents of the *Pentagon Papers*. Fulbright had refused. Norvill Jones later told Fulbright:

> I am very leery about Dan Ellsberg and believe that we should keep him at arm's length. I have repeatedly warned him about not getting the Committee's name involved in any way in his efforts to do something with the material he wants to get out, but I fear that for his own purposes sometime he may let it be known that he has supplied the Committee with a copy.[39]

Indeed, during his various contacts with Ellsberg in the spring of 1970 he had found the former DOD official increasingly frantic. He knew that the FBI was tailing him, Ellsberg told Jones, and he was certain that he was going to jail.

37 Ibid.

38 Seymour M. Hersh, *The Price of Power: Kissinger in the Nixon White House* (New York, 1983), 327. See also SAC, Los Angeles to Director, July 7, 1970, 62-71126, FBI Files.

39 Jones to JWF, Apr. 1, 1971, Ellsberg File, SPF.

Ellsberg was a loose cannon, Jones had told Marcy, and it would be best to keep Fulbright and the SFRC out of his way.[40]

On July 10, 1970, Fulbright had written Secretary of Defense Laird again asking that the papers be made available to the committee. Three days later Laird had written back to say no. Fulbright had then denounced the decision on the floor of the Senate. "Nothing is secret for long in Washington," he had noted. "I hope that the first enterprising reporter who obtains a copy of this history will share it with the committee."[41]

Ellsberg had seen Fulbright one final time before publication in June 1971. On March 31, after his meeting with Sheehan, he had met with the chairman in Washington. Ellsberg had stressed that he was ready to go to jail if necessary to help bring the war to a close. At the same time he had pleaded with Fulbright to read a portion of the papers into the *Record* or to help him find a senator or congressman who would. Fulbright had told him that, in his opinion, publication of the papers would have minimal impact on the course of the war and would do little to help the various end-the-war resolutions. Ellsberg had called several times after that but, upon the advice of his staff, the chairman had not responded.[42]

Ellsberg did manage to secure congressional protection, but only after the *Times* had begun publication. Two days after the initial installment appeared, Senator Mike Gravel (R–Alaska) convened a meeting of his Buildings and Grounds Subcommittee and began reading portions of the *Pentagon Papers.* After bursting into tears several times, Gravel finally stopped at 1:12 A.M.[43]

The revelation that Fulbright and the staff of the SFRC had had a copy of the *Pentagon Papers* for months before their publication in the *Times* caused little outcry among either hawks or doves. Fulbright and the committee were far too valuable to the antiwar movement to have jeopardized their credibility by releasing the documents, opponents of the war concluded. Administration supporters muttered that the Arkansan should have turned Ellsberg over to the proper authorities, but by being circumspect Fulbright and company had avoided giving their enemies any real opening.

Although Fulbright never succeeded in forcing the Nixon administration to invoke executive privilege over the *Pentagon Papers,* the president's efforts to have the Supreme Court block publication had the effect of casting him in the role of an enemy of the First Amendment and as a tacit partner of Lyndon Johnson in an ongoing conspiracy to deceive the public. The whole affair, as

40 Interview with Norvill Jones, June 29, 1989, Washington, D.C.

41 Ungar, "Daniel Ellsberg."

42 "Background of Contacts with Daniel Ellsberg," undated, Ellsberg File, Jones Papers.

43 Spencer Rich, "Gravel Appears Unlikely to Be Disciplined by Senate," *Washington Post,* July 1, 1971.

Fulbright had hoped, further aroused strict constructionists, mostly southern conservatives, in Congress. For months Fulbright had been wooing the epitome of that breed, Senator Sam Ervin (D–North Carolina). During 1970 and 1971 he had written Ervin several times arguing that, whatever he thought of the war in Vietnam, he must admit that it was extraconstitutional. Its continuation and expansion without congressional approval or input was destroying the system of checks and balances.[44] Fulbright had ostentatiously supported Ervin's fight to eliminate the "no-knock" provisions from John Mitchell's notorious Omnibus Crime Bill. Although Ervin had been grateful, he had resisted suggestions that he extend his fight against the imperial presidency into the field of foreign affairs.

Fulbright's persistence, however, coupled with the brouhaha over the *Pentagon Papers* and John Stennis's declared intention to seek a congressional limit on the warmaking powers of the president, finally turned Ervin. In August the self-styled "country lawyer," his jowls shimmying and eyes flashing, opened hearings before his Judiciary Subcommittee on various pending measures designed to keep the executive branch from withholding information from Congress. The first item on the agenda was the Fulbright bill, and it was immediately clear that the measure had the North Carolinian's full support.[45]

Despite his defiant posture, Richard Nixon could feel the foundations of the Republic shaking beneath his feet during the summer and fall of 1971; or, more important from his perspective, he could see his prospects for reelection in 1972 diminishing by the day. The *Chicago Sun-Times* warned the president that it was "3rd and 20" for him on the war.[46] A team of Library of Congress researchers declared the Vietnam conflict to be "the second most expensive war in American history," and the once proud American military team in Vietnam continued to disintegrate slowly on the nightly news before the eyes of an anguished public.[47] As the purpose of the war became increasingly obscure to American GIs, incidents of individual and mass disobedience mounted. More than two thousand incidents of "fragging" – attempted murder of officers, often by grenade – were reported in 1970. The U.S. command estimated that as of that year as many as sixty-five thousand American servicemen were using drugs. At the same time racial tensions were becoming palpable; in some encampments black and white soldiers segregated themselves. "A sense of uselessness and lack of accomplishment dwells within our ranks," SP5 Donald Young wrote Fulbright from his fire base camp. "We

44 JWF to John Stennis, July 7, 1971, Series 48:1, Box 10:2, SPF.

45 "Senate G.O.P. Chief Backs Restrictions on President's Warmaking Powers," *New York Times,* July 27, 1971.

46 News Summaries, June 7, 1971, WHSpF, Box 33, Nixon Project.

47 "Impact of War Totaled," *Arkansas Democrat,* July 11, 1971.

do not believe our President when he says it must take time to bring our men home. Why does it take one day to become involved in a situation, but eleven years to admit our possible wrong and then gradually withdraw?"[48]

Although determined not to be stampeded, Nixon and Kissinger were sufficiently concerned about the course of the war and the state of the home front to try once again to break the stalemate in Paris. Kissinger repeatedly expressed fear that the administration might be hamstrung at any moment by Congress "giving the farm away."[49] Most important, Nixon suspected that he would need a peace settlement in order to win reelection. As a result, in May, Kissinger secretly presented to the North Vietnamese the most comprehensive peace offer yet advanced by the United States. In exchange for release of the American prisoners of war, Washington would withdraw all troops within seven months after an agreement had been signed. The United States also abandoned the concept of mutual withdrawal, insisting only that North Vietnam stop further infiltration in return for the removal of American forces.

In the midst of his Paris shuttle, the NSC adviser made a trip to Pakistan, ostensibly to consult American officials there. His agenda included a secret detour to China to make last-minute arrangements for an official visit by Nixon in 1972. Mao proved receptive, and on the evening of July 15 Nixon told a national television audience that he was going to Beijing to negotiate a normalization of relations with Communist China.[50]

Nixon's announcement stunned the nation and the world. No hatred was more sacred to anticommunists than that they harbored toward Mao's China. No bilateral relationship was more shrouded in mythology. Republicans had been pummeling the Democratic Party for the "loss" of China with great profit for a generation. During the early years of that drama, its star had been Richard Nixon. Jiang Jie-shi's government was appalled at Nixon's opening to mainland China, but outside of radical-right circles, the forthcoming trip was hailed as a coup by foreign policy observers and politicians at home and abroad.[51]

Long before Nixon or Kissinger sought to open the door to China, Fulbright had advocated a fresh approach to Mao's regime. His China hearings in 1966 had gone far to demythologize the entire subject. Ironically, as Kissinger shuttled back and forth between Beijing, Paris, and Washington, Fulbright's committee was holding new hearings on China, this time focusing

48 Young to JWF, Aug. 30, 1971, Series 48:19, Box 53:4, SPF.
49 Quoted in George C. Herring, *America's Longest War: The United States and Vietnam, 1950–1975,* 2d ed. (New York, 1986), 244.
50 Stephen E. Ambrose, *Nixon,* vol. II, *The Triumph of a Politician, 1962–1972* (New York, 1989), 450–3.
51 Weekend News Review, July 19, 1971, WHSpF, Box 33, Nixon Project.

on the issues of representation in the United Nations and the status of the Formosa Resolution of 1955, which authorized the president to use force to defend the Nationalist government.

Fulbright was generally positive about Nixon and Kissinger's gambit. "I would like to go to Peking. . . . I used to play Ping-Pong twenty years ago," he joked with reporters.[52] Indeed, he had been urging such openings to the communist world ever since Nikita Khrushchev had made his impassioned appeal for peaceful coexistence before the SFRC in 1959. At the same time, Fulbright used the 1971 hearings to launch a major attack on the policy of containment and to make sure that the right would not force the administration to retreat. To the enragement of Dean Acheson and other architects of the cold war, Fulbright's new China hearings depicted a Truman administration that had deliberately misled Congress and the American people as to the threat posed to their interests by Communist China and as to the true nature of Jiang Jie-shi's corrupt, repressive regime. John Stewart Service and John Paton Davies, the two Foreign Service officers savaged by Joe McCarthy twenty-five years earlier for allegedly betraying China to the Communists, came out of seclusion to reveal that their reports criticizing Jiang had been suppressed.[53] "We've been deceived for a long time," Fulbright told the Capitol Hill press corps, "much longer than we thought and much more profoundly."[54] Over the objections of the State Department, which declared that such action would "send the wrong signal" prior to Nixon's forthcoming visit to China, the SFRC voted to repeal the 1955 Formosa Resolution.[55]

As in the past, the whipping boy for senators frustrated by their exclusion from the foreign policy process was foreign aid. That was so not only because it was one of the few areas in which the executive was vulnerable to legislative pressure, but also because it was an expression of the liberal internationalism that Fulbright, Mansfield, and Symington were convinced had been responsible for American overcommitments around the world, including Vietnam. Throughout late 1970 and early 1971 a coalition consisting of traditional conservative opponents of foreign aid and antiwar activists waged a guerrilla war against various foreign aid "supplementals" for Cambodia and Laos.[56] As the date for the final vote on the administration's 1972 request approached, the White House applied maximum pressure. Dozens of lobbyists

52 "Fulbright Begins to Like Ping-Pong," *Washington Post,* Apr. 15, 1971.

53 UPI 11, July 21, 1971.

54 "Fulbright Panel Told Data on China Was [*sic*] Suppressed," *Baltimore Sun,* June 29, 1971.

55 Marcy to JWF, July 21, 1971, Box 10, July–Sept., Marcy Papers, and Henry Tanner, "Senate Unit Acts to Repeal Taiwan Defense Measure," *New York Times,* July 22, 1971.

56 *Congressional Record,* Senate, Feb. 18, 1971, 3009–11.

from the White House, State Department, Defense, and AID swarmed through Senate corridors and twisted arms in the off-floor office of Vice-President Spiro Agnew.[57]

No foreign aid bill had ever gone down to defeat in the history of the program; both the White House and the Republican leadership were confident – too confident. As the vote proceeded, however, the gallery began to buzz. One by one former supporters of the program answered "no": Bayh, Cranston, Magnuson, Saxbe, Smith, Spong. Defeat of a major bill on the floor of either house was very rare; usually the dirty work was done in committee.[58] When the final ballot was cast, the United States Senate had voted 41 to 27 on October 29, 1971, to kill the entire foreign aid program.

The Sunday after his victory Fulbright appeared on *Face the Nation.* He praised the Senate for defeating the foreign aid bill, which he denounced as a mechanism to ensure continued U.S. dominance over small nations. The way was now open to write a new bill emphasizing nonmilitary aid funneled through multilateral channels and featuring a multiyear authorization. At the same time, Senate Minority Leader Hugh Scott, white-faced with anger, appeared on *Meet the Press.* He charged "left wing Senators" with leading the bill to "slaughter." These people, he declared, were guiding the nation down the dangerous path of neoisolationism.[59] Nixon's reaction was reflected in a bitter commentary by his friend Joe Alsop: "The proof is now clear," he wrote the day following the vote, "that Senate majority leader Mike Mansfield and the chairman of the Foreign Relations Committee, Sen. J. William Fulbright, are actively, unashamedly eager to see the United States defeated in war."[60] In the end, the Senate voted to approve $1.14 billion for economic and humanitarian aid and $1.5 billion for foreign military support. The total was nearly a billion dollars less than the amount the administration had originally requested.[61]

57 Marcy, memorandum, Nov. 12, 1971, Box 10, Oct.–Dec., Marcy Papers.
58 Neil MacNeil, "Foreign Aid: Scrambling to the Rescue; How the Senate Foreign Aid Bill Died," *Time,* Nov. 15, 1971, 13–15.
59 News Summaries, Nov. 1, 1971, WHSpF, Box 35, Nixon Project.
60 Joseph Alsop, "Undercutting the War," *Washington Post,* Nov. 5, 1971.
61 Spencer Rich, "Military Aid Voted in Senate; $1.5 Billion Provided for Revived Bill," *Washington Post,* Nov. 12, 1971.

# 35

# *Divided minds*

In the spring of 1972 the SFRC, using the *Pentagon Papers* as a basis, held a series of hearings on the origins of American involvement in Southeast Asia. Among those testifying were Noam Chomsky and Arthur Schlesinger, Jr., two academics whose views on the Vietnam War reflected two principal strains in revisionist historiography. In his testimony, Schlesinger attributed the disaster to policies made out of "ignorance, improvisation and mindlessness."[1] He stressed the importance of the ideology of anticommunism, a belief system that equated capitalism with freedom and democracy, and state socialism with oppression and totalitarianism. Chomsky presented the structuralist or classic New Left interpretation. He contended that the war was an outgrowth of American opposition to a peasant-based revolutionary movement and as such was the product of "rational imperialism" rather than blind anticommunism. The overriding objective of American foreign policy and the raison d'être for the war in Vietnam, he said, was to prevent "any nibbling away at areas that provide Western industrial powers with free access to markets, raw materials, a cheap labor force and the possibilities for the export of pollution and opportunities for investment."[2]

Fulbright believed that both interpretations were equally credible. He had always fancied himself a pragmatist in both thought and action. Taken to task by a constituent for reversing himself on the issue of presidential power over foreign policy formulation, he replied:

> As a political officeholder, I do not make speeches designed to formulate abstract principles for all time, but I respond to the circumstances as I see them . . . for the purpose of trying to direct the policies of the country in a useful and orderly direction, preserving, if possible, our security and our prosperity.[3]

1 William C. Berman, *William Fulbright and the Vietnam War: The Dissent of a Political Realist* (Kent, Ohio, 1988), 155. On the whole, Chomsky's views tended to be more extreme and conspiratorial than other New Leftists, particularly historians such as William Appleman Williams, Lloyd Gardner, Barton Bernstein, Thomas Paterson, and Walter LaFeber.

2 Quoted in Berman, *Fulbright and the Vietnam War,* 155.

3 JWF to Kenneth Jones, Apr. 3, 1973, Series 48:18, Box 65:3, SPF.

As a pragmatist he could accept both Chomsky's and Schlesinger's interpretations of the origins of the war in Vietnam. In analyzing any diplomatic problem, Fulbright believed, an informed person had to take into consideration such historical constants as ideology, economics, geopolitics, domestic politics, and, after 1945, bureaucratic momentum; but each episode and movement was unique and had to be evaluated as such.

In January Fulbright and Tillman had published in the *New Yorker* a scathing indictment of the containment policy. "The anticommunism of the Truman Doctrine has been the guiding spirit of American foreign policy since the Second World War," they wrote. "Stalin and Mao Tse-tung and even Ho Chi Minh replaced Hitler in our minds as the sources of all evil in the world. We came to see the hand of 'Moscow communism' in every disruption that occurred anywhere." In this piece, entitled "In Thrall to Fear," and in subsequent articles and speeches, the Arkansan explained that in an effort to sell Congress and the American people on a massive foreign aid program and military buildup to combat a threat that they believed to be authentic, Harry Truman and his cohorts had oversold the evil of communism and the danger posed by Soviet imperialism. "The Truman Doctrine, which made limited sense for a limited time in a particular place, has led us in its universalized form to disaster in Southeast Asia and demoralization at home," he wrote. As 1972 opened, the Arkansan called upon America "to return to the practical idealism of the United Nations Charter," which he conceived to be peaceful coexistence and tolerance for cultural diversity;[4] but Vietnam, the ultimate manifestation of America's cold-war paranoia and its counterrevolutionary policies, would not go away.

Fulbright interrupted his musings on the origins of the cold war long enough to take Betty on a winter vacation to the West Indian island of St. Croix. They left Dulles on January 2 amid snow flurries and touched down in 80° weather and clear blue skies. For a week Bill played golf and snorkeled while Betty lounged on the beach and wrote Bosey and Betsy.[5] They were scheduled to return on the eighth, but they found St. Croix so luxuriously relaxing that they extended another week.

In mid-February Richard Nixon paused in his ongoing battle with Hanoi and American doves to embark on the greatest adventure of his presidency: the much anticipated journey to mainland China. The trip was more of a public-

4 "Fulbright Traces Foreign Failures to Truman Policy," *Arkansas Gazette*, Jan. 5, 1972.

5 Appointments calendar, Jan. 2–14, Papers of Lee Williams.

relations triumph than the buildup, if that was possible. The American people watched in disbelief as the man who had based his early career on professional anticommunism, who had for two decades derided the Democrats for "selling out" China to the communists, was escorted around the Forbidden City and shown the Great Wall by his Red Chinese hosts. He and Mao traded smiles and toasts, and much of the world hailed him and his German-accented adviser as pragmatic geniuses.

Richard Nixon and Mao Zedong discussed Southeast Asia during their summit, and the Chinese leader promised to help bring the war to an end. Whether or not he was sincere is unclear; what is certain is that he was unsuccessful. In March 1972, a hundred and twenty thousand North Vietnamese troops, led by phalanxes of Soviet tanks, smashed their way across the DMZ and drove into northern South Vietnam. At that point there were only six thousand American combat troops, out of a total of ninety-five thousand personnel, in Vietnam. Hanoi reasoned that, with a presidential election imminent, Nixon would not dare reverse the course of Vietnamization and put additional troops in Vietnam. It was also logical to assume that a major escalation in the fighting during an election year would generate irresistible pressure for peace in the United States.

Initially, the NVA offensive was an unqualified success. Communist troops advanced across the DMZ, in the Central Highlands, and across the Cambodian border northwest of Saigon. Thieu dispatched thousands of troops to defend the besieged towns of Quang Tri in the north, Kontum in the highlands, and An Loc just sixty miles north of Saigon. In the process, he opened the door for increased Vietcong activity in the Mekong Delta and the heavily populated areas around Saigon.

Richard Nixon would not be reconciled to the fall of South Vietnam. Typically, he convinced himself that the offensive was a tactic designed to force him out of the 1972 election as Lyndon Johnson had been driven from the field in 1968.[6] The president quickly approved B-52 strikes across the demilitarized zone and followed up with massive air attacks on fuel depots in the Hanoi–Haiphong area.

Shortly after the new wave of aerial assaults began, Bill and Betty went to dinner at the James Restons'.[7] As it always did when Fulbright was present, the conversation turned to international affairs. The Arkansan's discourse on the shortcomings of Richard Nixon's foreign policies began calmly enough, but after five minutes he was ranting and raving. After another five minutes, with the other guests stirring uneasily in their seats, Betty cut him off: "Willie!" she hissed. Fulbright desisted and the conversation shifted to other topics. Those who knew him realized that it was only a matter of time until the

6 News Summaries, Feb. 7, 1972, WHSpF, Box 38, Nixon Project.

7 Appointments calendar, Jan. 31, 1972, Williams Papers.

chairman of the SFRC loosed another broadside at the administration's foreign policy.

Sensing trouble ahead, Kissinger arranged to meet with Fulbright for two hours at Taylor House on Lafayette Square one evening during the last week in March.[8] The administration had had to react to the North Vietnamese offensive, he explained. The only way the United States could withdraw from Vietnam was with the Thieu government intact and the military situation stabilized. Fulbright said that he understood, but that he had to react as well. There were still plenty of hawks in the administration who believed that a military victory was possible, and plenty of doves who would be less understanding of Kissinger's position than was he.

On April 9 Fulbright appeared on the *Today* show once again. Clad in three-piece suit and regimental striped tie, he declared that the American bombing represented a major reescalation of the Vietnam War and that it signaled the bankruptcy of the policy of Vietnamization.[9] He attributed Hanoi's decision to launch the March offensive to the administration's "decision" to break off the Paris negotiations in mid-March. Having witnessed the rout of ARVN units on the nightly news throughout March, more than a few Americans were willing to believe the chairman of the SFRC.

The resumed bombing of the north on a massive scale maddened Fulbright because he feared that it portended a return to the strategy of "military victory" in Vietnam and, more important, that it would destroy détente with the Soviet Union. Following months of tedious negotiations, Kissinger had arranged for Nixon to go to Moscow and meet with Soviet premier Leonid Brezhnev in late May. The Kremlin denounced U.S. bombing in the harshest terms, and after four Soviet transports were damaged in Haiphong harbor in mid-April, it warned of "possible dangerous consequences."[10] For Fulbright this new outbreak of violence, at a time when the superpowers seemed to stand on the brink of an era of peace and reconciliation, was heartbreaking.

Indeed, Fulbright had come to care deeply about what the Soviet Union thought about him personally and the United States in general. He and Betty had developed a close personal relationship with Anatoly Dobrynin and his wife. Hardly a week went by that he did not meet with a group of Soviet journalists or academics.[11] During 1972 Fulbright was featured in *Tass* or *Isvestia* or appeared on Moscow television no fewer than a dozen times.

8 Ibid., Mar. 28, 1972, Williams Papers.

9 "New U.S. Bombing a Re-escalation, Fulbright Asserts," *Arkansas Gazette,* Apr. 10, 1972.

10 "Nixon Halts Bombing of Haiphong, Hanoi; Waits for Response," *Arkansas Gazette,* Apr. 18, 1972.

11 Appointments calendar, Mar. 6, 1972, Williams Papers.

Vladilen B. Vorontsov, a senior research scholar with the Far East Institute, published a laudatory biography of the Arkansan.[12]

Amid the endless rounds of hearings and meetings, Fulbright always found time to attend to his cultural duties. Shortly after Congress reconvened, he was an honored guest at a reception for the trustees of Amherst College held at Washington's Folger Shakespeare Library. He looked forward to his monthly board meetings at the Kennedy Center, and he continued to be an active member of the Smithsonian Board of Regents. In mid-February he spent three days in Panama visiting the Smithsonian's Tropical Research Institute. Although he had pretended not to know Jane Fonda when she called at his office, he and Betty were thrilled to be invited to a Roger Stevens reception for her father, Henry, at the Kennedy Center.[13] In March they met and were thoroughly charmed by Ingrid Bergman at another Stevens soirée.

"Reports from Vietnam are getting worse," Carl Marcy confided to Fulbright on May 2. "The President is going to find himself in a box – he must threaten to escalate the bombing (and do so if Hanoi doesn't come to an agreement) or, in the alternative, reach an agreement which may humiliate him."[14] Despite his several encounters with humiliation, Nixon had not accommodated himself to it. On May 8 the president decided to respond to General Abrams's warning that Hué and Kontum might soon fall unless Washington authorized decisive action. Ignoring Rogers and Laird's admonition that drastic measures could possibly push Congress over the edge and precipitate an end-the-war resolution with teeth in it, Nixon intensified the war against North Vietnam. "The bastards have never been bombed like they're going to be bombed this time," he told a staff member.[15] On May 8 Nixon announced to a startled nation the sharpest escalation of the war since 1968. The U.S. Navy had been instructed to mine Haiphong harbor and impose a blockade on all of North Vietnam, he told the American people. Meanwhile, air force and navy planes would bomb the enemy forces until they ceased their aggression.

The following day Fulbright met with members of the Democratic caucus, who passed by a vote of 29 to 14 his resolution "disapproving the escalation of the war in Vietnam." That was not enough, the Arkansan declared. Nixon had violated his pledge, given to him personally in the spring of 1969, to end

12 Ibid., Mar. 22, 1972, Williams Papers, and "Soviet Biography Praises Fulbright," *Pine Bluff Commercial,* June 18, 1971.
13 Appointments calendar, Jan. 26–27, 30, and Feb. 11, 1972, Williams Papers.
14 Marcy to JWF, May 2, 1972, Box 11, Apr.–June, Marcy Papers.
15 Quoted in George C. Herring, *America's Longest War: The United States and Vietnam, 1950–1975,* 2d ed. (New York, 1986), 247.

the war by negotiation and not to continue his predecessor's suicidal policies. If the Democratic majority had no confidence in the president, it must demonstrate the courage of its convictions. By a 2-to-1 margin the caucus approved the most recent end-the-war measure, an amendment sponsored by Clifford Case and Frank Church that would cut off funds for American troops in Vietnam after December 31, 1971.[16]

The mining of Haiphong harbor and the bombing escalation did not produce the public outcry that Rogers and Laird had feared. The American public had always considered bombing a more acceptable alternative than the use of ground forces, and many Americans felt that the North Vietnamese invasion justified Nixon's response. Moreover, the blows that Nixon rained down on the north seemed to have averted defeat in South Vietnam. The conventional military tactics employed by the North Vietnamese in the summer of 1972 depended heavily on vast quantities of fuel and ammunition, and the intensive bombing attacks, along with the blockade, made resupply extremely difficult. In South Vietnam itself, U.S. bombers flew round-the-clock missions, pummeling North Vietnamese supply lines and encampments. With the assistance of American airpower, the ARVN managed to stabilize the lines in front of Saigon and Hué, and it even mounted a small counteroffensive. Meanwhile, the build-down of American forces in Vietnam continued. "In 1965," explained an antiwar leader, "the American people knew there was a war, and we had to convince people it was wrong. In 1972, people know the war is wrong, but we have to convince them that there is a war."[17]

In mid-March the junior senator took a break from his war against various cold-war agencies for a week's vacation in Jamaica. He and Betty were the guests of Louis Reynolds, president of Reynolds Aluminum.[18] As usual, the sun and exercise rejuvenated Fulbright. Although his knees ached, he could still hit the golf ball accurately, and on a good day his score hovered around par. Not bad for a sixty-seven-year-old former football player, he bragged to Reynolds.

Tanned and rested, the junior senator from Arkansas returned to Washington to do battle with the United States Information Agency and its director, an eager young anticommunist named Frank Shakespeare. To the dismay of Shakespeare and his colleagues, a congressional reorganization act had placed the USIA under the jurisdiction of the SFRC rather than the much more con-

16 Marcy to JWF, May 9, 1972, Box 11, Apr.–June, Marcy Papers, and John W. Finney, "Democratic Caucus in the Senate Condemns the 'Escalation' in Vietnam by 29 to 14," *New York Times*, May 10, 1972.

17 Quoted in Charles DeBenedetti with Charles Chatfield, *An American Ordeal: The Antiwar Movement of the Vietnam Era* (Syracuse, 1990), 323.

18 Appointments calendar, Mar. 11, 1972, Williams Papers.

servative Appropriations Committee, which for years had routinely approved the agency's budget. Operating from 1776 Pennsylvania Avenue and a half-dozen other Washington buildings, the USIA, with a budget of $196 million, turned out a stream of books, magazines, pamphlets, films, radio broadcasts, and TV programs designed to sell foreigners, especially communists, on the American way of life.[19]

The USIA–SFRC relationship did not get off to an auspicious start when, during his maiden appearance, Shakespeare refused to provide the committee with his agency's country planning documents.[20] During the weeks that followed Fulbright and the staff of the SFRC revealed that the USIA had, among other things, published pamphlets espousing the benefits of private oil exploration that were given to Texaco–Gulf to distribute in Ecuador.[21] Infuriated by Fulbright's attack, a top Shakespeare aid, Bruce Herschensohn, blasted the Arkansan on a taped TV broadcast made by conservative Senator James Buckley (R–New York). His criticism of USIA was "naive and stupid," Herschensohn told the brother of the famous host of *Firing Line.* Given the fact that the SFRC was then considering USIA's $200 million request for fiscal 1973, his broadside was not well timed. Within the week Herschensohn, who had skillfully headed the agency's motion picture and television service, resigned, and Shakespeare publicly apologized to Fulbright.[22] Nixon was secretly delighted with the whole affair. "See that he gets a good job," the president directed Haldeman. Within weeks Herschensohn was working for the Committee to Reelect the President (CREEP).[23]

On the same program on which Herschensohn had derided Fulbright, Buckley had shown a USIA film entitled *Czechoslovakia 1968.* The skillfully produced piece – it won an Oscar for best documentary – was stridently anticommunist. It opened with footage of Nazi tanks rolling into Prague in 1938 and ended with scenes of Russian armor crushing the Czech uprising of 1968. Fulbright saw an opening and moved at once to exploit it. The USIA's release of the film to Buckley clearly violated its charter, Fulbright complained to Attorney General–designate Richard Kleindienst. "The Information Agency was created for the purpose of the dissemination abroad of information about the U.S., its people, and policies," he pointed out. "It was not

19 "Third Largest Propaganda Agency Alive and Active," *Jonesboro Sun,* Mar. 20, 1972.
20 UPI 94, Mar. 20, 1972.
21 John W. Finney, "U.S.I.A. Confirms Role in Unattributed Pamphlets," *New York Times,* Mar. 22, 1972.
22 "USIA Aide Raps Views of Fulbright," *Fort Smith Southwest Times Record,* Mar. 26, 1972; "Critic of Fulbright Quits USIA," *Washington Post,* Apr. 4, 1972; and Shakespeare to JWF, Mar. 29, 1972, Series 48:9, Box 33:6, SPF.
23 News Summaries, Apr. 4, 1972, WHSPF, Box 40, Nixon Project, and "Fulbright Critic Is Hired," *Arkansas Democrat,* Feb. 22, 1973.

created for dissemination of information in the U.S."[24] He then introduced legislation cutting $45.6 million from the USIA budget.

Although Congress and the American people were sick of the war in Southeast Asia, they were not ready to view communism as just another political ideology with which capitalism could forever peacefully coexist. Indeed, the frustrations of the war tended to sharpen the nation's deep-seated anticommunism. Predictably, the radical right and various East European émigré groups blasted Fulbright for his attacks on the USIA. Alexander Solzhenitsyn, who had just been awarded the Nobel Peace Prize, expressed his appreciation of the agency and its subsidiary, Radio Liberty.[25] Senator Buckley proceeded to show *Czechoslovakia 1968* on twelve TV stations throughout New York State. Perhaps most tellingly, two contenders for the 1972 Democratic presidential nomination, Gale McGee and Hubert Humphrey, announced their support for the organizations. On May 2 the Senate voted 57 to 15 to restore the cuts in the USIA budget made by the SFRC.[26] A triumphant Henry Jackson invited his Senate colleagues to a private viewing of *Czechoslovakia 1968* in the New Senate Office Building.[27] "Senate Gives Fulbright Another in a Series of Rebuffs," declared the *New York Times.*[28]

"In his moody, introspective way," John Finney wrote in the *New York Times,* "Senator J. William Fulbright . . . has an Achillean trait. When humiliated or scorned on the field of battle on the Senate floor, he, like the Greek hero on the fields of Troy, tends to sulk in his tent, discouraged with himself and the impervious ways of the Senate."[29] Indeed, rumors began to circulate in Washington that America's most distinguished neoisolationist was himself isolated and disconsolate to the point of considering retirement in 1974. During the spring of 1972, to his staff's surprise, he visited Burning Tree Country Club two and sometimes three times a week. Fulbright had always loved golf, but he had never allowed himself the luxury of playing very often.[30]

Even in his sixty-seventh year, however, Fulbright was still resilient; he responded positively to words of encouragement. Walter Pincus wrote consolingly:

> Perhaps some of the recent amendments you proposed went too far; perhaps there wasn't enough staff work done with other Sena-

24 JWF to Kleindienst, Mar. 28, 1972, Series 48:8, Box 33:3, SPF.
25 News Summaries, Apr. 10, 1972, WHSpF, Box 40, Nixon Project.
26 Spencer Rich, "Senate Votes Full Fund for USIA's Operations," *Washington Post,* May 2, 1972.
27 Jackson to Senators, undated, Series 48:9, Box 33:4, SPF.
28 John W. Finney, "Vote in Senate Gives Fulbright Another in a Series of Rebuffs," *New York Times,* May 26, 1972.
29 John W. Finney, "Fulbright: Trouble Getting the Right Time of Day," *New York Times,* June 4, 1972.
30 Appointments calendar, Apr. 13–16, 1972, Williams Papers.

> tors; perhaps the White House and others are specifically out to neutralize you. Whatever the cause and despite the setbacks and the inability of the media to understand the subtleties of the Senate . . . it's as important as ever that you and the committee continue to play the unhappy and unheralded role of shaping policy decisions through pressure and dissent.[31]

Most encouraging, there was an element within the White House that tacitly supported Fulbright's efforts to constrain the nation's most strident cold-war agencies.[32] That "element," of course, was Henry Kissinger. Seymour Hersh has noted that in 1972 the national security adviser began "to travel his own path inside the White House." He desperately wanted the Moscow summit to occur as scheduled. As he flew back and forth from Paris to Moscow during the spring of 1972, he labored to convince the Kremlin that Richard Nixon really did favor a policy of détente, and to convince Richard Nixon that détente was in his political interest.[33] In his frequent talks with Dobrynin and other Soviet officials and journalists, Fulbright proved to be an invaluable ally in that effort.

The last week in May Nixon and Kissinger journeyed to Moscow, where they met face to face with the leaders of the Soviet Union six times during five days of intense negotiations. The event dominated American newspapers and television, leaving little room for the Democrats and their election-year attacks on the administration. No less than five major bilateral agreements dealing with issues of trade and scientific cooperation were signed during the second, third, and fourth nights of the summit. The conclave culminated with the inking of the Strategic Arms Limitation Treaty. SALT I included two basic agreements: The first, in the form of an official treaty requiring a two-thirds vote of the Senate, would limit each side to two hundred antiballistic missiles for defense to be divided equally at two sites, one in the capital, and the other at an offensive missile site at least eight hundred miles away. The theory underlying the ABM pact was that, with such severe restrictions on its defense, each country would be deterred from launching a missile attack against the other lest their own population be wiped out. The second was a five-year executive Interim Agreement that put limits on land-based and submarine-launched missiles.[34]

Nixon and Kissinger favored SALT I for a variety of reasons. In the first place, it would enable the president to run in 1972 as the peace candidate. In the second, the administration had not budgeted for increased missile produc-

31 Pincus to JWF, June 7, 1972, Series 48:1, Box 10:3, SPF.

32 Rowland Evans and Robert Novak, "Détente Versus RFE," *Washington Post,* Mar. 29, 1972.

33 Seymour M. Hersh, *The Price of Power: Kissinger in the Nixon White House* (New York, 1983), 508, 509, 523.

34 "Nixon Makes Plea for Arms Accord," *New York Times,* June 16, 1972.

tion for the five-year life of the Interim Agreement anyway. Kissinger saw SALT as a major step toward his new world order. For their part, the Soviets were interested in reducing defense expenditures and in gaining access to the U.S. grain market.[35]

As soon as the official party returned to Washington, Nixon submitted both the SALT treaty and the Interim Agreement to Congress for its consideration. Following a meeting with the president at the White House,[36] Fulbright enthusiastically agreed to floor-manage the pacts. He wrote Tris Coffin:

> I think the agreements on missiles are most significant, as I believe they indicate a changed attitude on the part of the Russians, and, hopefully, the Americans. I personally think the Russians are fed up with spending so much money on useless arms and will be inclined to do what they can to implement the agreements. If the President means what he says . . . there could be quite a change in our approach.[37]

As had happened so often in the past, however, Fulbright's hopes would be crushed under the massive political weight of the military–industrial complex.

Indeed, Secretary of Defense Melvin Laird and the JCS had agreed to go along with SALT only in return for White House approval for the new Trident Submarine system and a 16 percent overall increase in the defense budget. In mid-June the Pentagon submitted an appropriation request bloated with funds for the immediate construction of not only the Trident but the B-1 bomber as well. If Congress should refuse to fund these systems, Laird announced, he would recommend to the president that he not sign the SALT agreements even if Congress should approve them.[38]

Fulbright was first incredulous, then furious. When Laird and JCS Chairman Admiral Thomas Moorer dutifully trooped up to the Hill to testify on SALT, Fulbright blistered them. The Pentagon was doing nothing less than blackmailing Congress, he charged. Are you trying to "sabotage the whole spirit" of SALT? Most certainly not, Laird replied. The new weapons systems would simply permit the United States to negotiate future accords from a position of strength.[39]

On August 4, 1972, the Senate approved the ABM portion of SALT by a vote of 88 to 2.[40] When Congress then turned its attention to the five-year Interim Agreement, the military–industrial complex's personal representative

35 Hersh, *Price of Power,* 529, 531.

36 Appointments calendar, June 2, 1972, Williams Papers.

37 JWF to Tris Coffin, June 7, 1972, Series 48:16, Box 42:3, SPF.

38 "Treaty Without New Arms Unacceptable, Laird Says," *Washington Evening Star,* June 20, 1972.

39 "Fulbright Says Laird Jeopardizing Accord," *Arkansas Gazette,* June 22, 1972.

40 "Senate Backs Defensive Half of Missile Pact," *Baltimore Sun,* Aug. 4, 1972.

to the Senate, Henry Jackson, dropped a bombshell. The second portion of SALT had imposed a five-year freeze on ICBMs and SLBMs (submarine-launched missiles). At that time the United States had an estimated 1,054 land-based missiles plus another 656 deployed aboard the Polaris submarine fleet. The Soviets possessed 1,607 land-based missile launchers and 740 SLBMs. Soviet superiority in number of missiles was offset by the United States' 3-to-2 advantage in MIRVed warheads.[41] Nonetheless, Jackson added an amendment to the Interim Agreement stipulating that in any future negotiations the president only sign agreements that provided equality in number of missiles. The first week in August, the White House announced that the Jackson amendment was "consistent" with administration policy.[42]

Led by Fulbright, the SFRC voted 11 to 0 to reject the Jackson amendment. "This [the Jackson amendment] means the President made a bum agreement," he told reporters. "How the President could agree to it is beyond my comprehension." It appeared that the junior senator from Washington was determined, he said, to perpetuate the arms race.[43] Huddling with Mansfield and the rest of the Senate leadership, the Arkansan announced that he would vote against the Interim Agreement if the Jackson amendment was part of it;[44] but in the end he could not bring himself to do so. In mid-September the Senate approved the Jackson amendment 56 to 35 and then endorsed the Interim Agreement by 88 to 2. Fulbright voted against the amendment but for the agreement.[45] In a fit of pique, Fulbright attempted to block funding for a $11.5 million federal pavilion at Spokane's Expo '74. "The only reason you guys support this bill," he told members of the SFRC, "is because it is sponsored by two powerful senators [Jackson and Magnuson] and they have gotten more than their share."[46]

In reality, the seemingly inconsistent stance taken by the Nixon administration over arms control in 1972 was carefully orchestrated by Nixon to obtain maximum political advantage. Indeed, it paralleled his policy of stepped up bombing coupled with troop withdrawals in Vietnam. "We must stay right on the tightrope," he told Alexander Haig, Kissinger's assistant. "Hold the

41 Hersh, *Price of Power,* 529.

42 The White House had not been enthusiastic about the Jackson amendment, but it had agreed reluctantly to endorse it in return for the Washingtonian's much-needed vote on the Trident sub, a project for which he had little enthusiasm. Rowland Evans and Robert Novak, "The Politics of Defense," *Washington Post,* Aug. 10, 1972.

43 "Jackson Arms Act Stand Rebuffed by Fulbright Panel," *Washington Evening Star,* Aug. 11, 1972.

44 Marcy to JWF, Sept. 6, 1972, Box 11, July–Sept., Marcy Papers.

45 "Senate Approves Pact with Soviet on Strategic Arms," *New York Times,* Sept. 18, 1972.

46 "Fulbright Trying to Block Expo 74 Fund," *Seattle Times,* Oct. 4, 1972.

hawks by continuing adequate defense – Hold the doves by pointing out that without SALT the arms budget would be much larger."[47]

The specter of the administration simultaneously negotiating an arms control agreement and coupling it with a demand for two major new arms systems once again deflated and disillusioned Fulbright, but he refused to blame the national security adviser. He and Kissinger had tried, Fulbright wrote a constituent, but the Pentagon and Nixon's ingrained Russophobia were too strong. Kissinger was sincere and no doubt influential with the president, he observed, but "the President's own experiences, especially his early ones in running against Jerry Voorhis and Helen Gahagan Douglas . . . created an attitude which I do not think Henry Kissinger . . . can change. In short, I believe the President is incapable of bringing himself to compromise with any communist regime."[48] With the Pentagon deluging the country with propaganda on the need to build the Trident and B-1, and American bombing of North Vietnam intensifying daily, Fulbright took a sudden and intense interest in the election of 1972.

47 Kissinger to Haig, minute, News Summaries, June 20, 1972, WHSpF, Box 40, Nixon Project.

48 JWF to Reuben Thomas, Dec. 30, 1972, Series 48:18, Box 64:7, SPF.

# 36

# *The invisible wars*

The Fulbrights' social calendar remained as full as ever during 1972: cocktails and dinner at the British embassy, black-tie Oxford–Cambridge dinner at the Statler Hilton, a White House reception for King Hussein. In June they cohosted a buffet for the board of governors of the IMF and World Bank at the Kennedy Center, following a concert by Isaac Stern and the Chamber Orchestra.[1] Their particular Georgetown dinner circuit continued to be geared toward journalist-celebrities and publishers: Scotty Reston, Marvin Kalb, Martin Agronsky, the Arthur Sulzbergers, Katherine Graham. Academic luminaries courted the Arkansan as never before. Whatever Peoria thought of him, J. William Fulbright was popular with America's intelligentsia. The Restons, Dillons, Schlesingers, and Sulzbergers could gossip about politics and power with the Fulbrights and not be embarrassed by reports that they had lowered themselves to social intercourse with mere politicians. Fulbright's standing with the eastern establishment was enhanced by his relationship with Henry Kissinger. Although some of their meetings were clandestine, others were deliberately public. Their lunches at Sans Souci, for example, were a frequent topic of conversation within the Beltway.[2]

For J. William Fulbright and Richard Nixon, Vietnam and the 1972 presidential election were inextricably intertwined. The president's diplomacy and policies toward Southeast Asia in the summer and fall of 1972 were keyed almost exclusively to securing victory over George McGovern and the Democrats. Fulbright, for his part, saw the election and McGovern's candidacy as a means to hasten the end of the war in Vietnam. Privately he was quite candid about the South Dakotan's chances for winning, but he believed that the nomination of a peace candidate would push Nixon toward an early and decisive end to the war.[3]

1 "Stern Amuses and Entertains," *Washington Star,* Sept. 27, 1972.
2 Appointments calendar, May 15, 1972, Williams Papers.
3 "Bumpers, Fulbright Back Vietnam Plank; End of War Seen," *Arkansas Gazette,* July 12, 1972.

Ironically, given his conservatism and his aversion to radical politics, it was Fulbright more than any other figure who molded and articulated the foreign policy program of the new Democratic Party. In the late summer of 1972 Random House published *The Crippled Giant.* Convinced that there was an extensive market for a sequel to *The Arrogance of Power,* the publishing house had approached Fulbright in 1971. After some deliberation, the chairman agreed to publish another critique of American foreign policy and society, and over the next year he and Seth Tillman had put together a manuscript based on material going back to 1967. Included in the synthesis were the *New Yorker* and *Progressive* articles, speeches at Yale and Dennison universities, and various statements Fulbright had made on the floor of the Senate.

Although the book was not a commercial success, it was widely read by the new leadership in the Democratic Party and did much to define their views on foreign policy. Indeed, Carl Marcy took great pains to see that McGovern and his advisers were supplied with galleys during the crucial weeks of July and August, when the campaign was writing its position papers.[4] *The Crippled Giant* was a thoroughgoing, systematic rejection of the cold warriorism of Democratic traditionalists like George Meany and Henry Jackson, and of the liberal activism of moderates such as Arthur Schlesinger. At the heart of Fulbright's critique was the argument that the United States had been using its power recklessly and irresponsibly – thus "fostering a world environment which is, to put it mildly, uncongenial to our society." This pattern of behavior, Fulbright believed, resulted from the Truman administration's oversell of the communist menace, the inability of American policy assumptions to change with the changing international situation, the development of a military–industrial complex with a vested interest in the continuation of the cold war, and the misdirected altruism of Americans committed to the notion that they had a mission to reshape the world in their own image. The result had been the globalization of United States commitments with a concomitant weakening of America's position abroad and a "material and spiritual drain" at home.[5] In a sense, Vietnam was the end product of these combined forces and the chief contributor to the nation's deteriorating position. By being more "selective" in its commitments and by disavowing ideological crusades, the United States could avoid future disasters like Vietnam. Increasingly, *The Crippled Giant* advised, the nation should emphasize its domestic priorities. "I am dubious about the proposition that we have a certain obligation as the richest nation in the world to help underdeveloped countries," he wrote Robert McCord, a columnist with the *Gazette.* "I believe the primary duty of this

4 Marcy to Purvis, June 8 and Aug. 7, 1972, Box 11, Folders Apr.–June and July–Sept., Marcy Papers.

5 Quoted in William C. Berman, *William Fulbright and the Vietnam War: The Dissent of a Political Realist* (Kent, Ohio, 1988), 162.

country at present is to get its economic house in order, and to set an example for other nations of prudent and wise government."[6]

From a historiographical perspective, Fulbright's interpretation was soft revisionism. He abjured the economic and systemic determinism of the New Left, instead viewing Russophobia and missionary globalism as aberrations that could be corrected. It should always be remembered that his perspective was that of a Fulbrighter abroad. He wanted to fashion a foreign policy that students and academics could be proud of when they were interacting with their enlightened counterparts in Europe, Asia, Africa, and Latin America. From a political perspective, *The Crippled Giant* articulated the foreign policy views of the McGovernite wing of the Democratic Party; but it was all for naught.

Disillusioned with the past and anesthetized by the present, the American people returned Richard Nixon to office by a record margin in November. Having identified himself as a forthright champion not only of minorities and the antiwar movement, but of the effort within the party to wrest control from the traditionalists and moderates, McGovern found it difficult to capture the vitally important center. Many longtime party stalwarts had been offended by the new Democratic rules, which they associated with McGovernism. In addition, on October 10 he had called for an American withdrawal from Vietnam in ninety days and the termination of all military aid to the Thieu regime, a proposal about which even Fulbright had expressed reservations.[7]

As Americans were preparing to celebrate Hanukkah, the birth of Christ, and the advent of 1973, the president once more ordered air force and navy planes into the skies over North Vietnam. Nixon was interested in more than a token show of force against the enemy. "I don't want any more of this crap about the fact that we couldn't hit this target or that one," he stormed at Admiral Thomas Moorer, chairman of the JCS. "This is your chance to use military power to win this war and if you don't I'll consider you responsible."[8] Over the next twelve days, the United States launched the most devastating attacks of the war, dropping more than thirty-six thousand tons of bombs, an amount exceeding the total for the entire period from 1969 through 1971.

The prevalent reaction to the Christmas bombing in the United States was outrage. Critics denounced Nixon as a "madman" and accused him of waging "war by tantrum." Nixon's popular approval rating dropped overnight to 39

6 JWF to McCord, Mar. 14, 1973, Series 78:3, Box 26:5, SPF.

7 The chairman did not want to do anything to tie Kissinger's hands: The national security adviser, as Fulbright knew, was then negotiating furiously in Paris to secure a peace agreement prior to the election. "Fulbright Backs Peace Proposal of McGovern," *Arkansas Gazette,* Oct. 12, 1972.

8 Quoted in George C. Herring, *America's Longest War: The United States and Vietnam, 1950–1975,* 2d ed. (New York, 1986), 253–4.

percent. On January 4, Senate Democrats met in caucus and passed a resolution calling for an immediate cutoff of funds for the war in Indochina, "subject only to the release of U.S. prisoners and the accounting of those missing in action."[9]

On December 23 Betty and Bill left to spend Christmas with the Teasdales in St. Louis. The Winnackers and Footes, with presents and grandchildren in tow, had already arrived. As usual the senator quickly became bored with the pleasures of domestic life. He and Betty stayed for only three days; then, a week following their return to Washington, they departed for ten days of sun and golf in San Juan and St. Martin's.[10]

Fulbright returned to Washington determined to force both Rogers and Kissinger to explain to the SFRC why the bombing had been resumed.[11] Before they could appear, Nixon suspended the aerial assault on the north and induced Hanoi to return to the negotiating table. Fulbright and, to an extent, Marcy were very nervous. If the committee began work on a fund cutoff bill, and Kissinger suddenly engineered a peace accord, the SFRC would be left with mud on its face. Nonetheless, the chairman and his chief of staff decided to press ahead; Nixon and Kissinger could use antiwar sentiment in Congress as a bargaining chip in their negotiations with Thieu. On January 2 the committee voted to start work on legislation to cut off funds for the war if Nixon had not negotiated peace by Inauguration Day. "The consensus of everyone present was that we did not wish to do anything to prejudice the negotiations starting next Monday," Fulbright told the press. "But if some settlement is not reached by the 20th, then it is our intention to employ legislative power to bring the war to a close."[12]

The negotiations resumed in Paris on January 8. By January 20 Kissinger and Le Duc Tho had hammered out an agreement that was acceptable to both sides. "Peace with honor" permitted American extrication from the war and secured the return of the POWs while leaving the Thieu government intact. At the same time North Vietnamese troops remained in the south and the People's Revolutionary Government (PRG) gained recognition as a legitimate political force. The major question over which the war had been fought – the political future of South Vietnam – was left to be resolved at a later date. The diplomats insisted that the future would be defined through the political process; but realists, including Saigon and Hanoi, recognized that the fate of their country would be decided by force.

9 Quoted in Berman, *Fulbright and the Vietnam War,* 166.
10 Appointments calendar, Dec. 26, 1972, and Jan. 4, 1973, Williams Papers.
11 Marcy to JWF, Dec. 27, 1972, Box 11, Sept.–Dec., Marcy Papers.
12 Richard Lyons, "Senate Unit Set to Act on Jan. 20," *Washington Post,* Jan. 3, 1973.

As part of an effort to persuade Thieu to accept what he had henceforth steadfastly rejected, Nixon secretly promised that if South Vietnam would go along with the accord, the United States would continue massive military aid and would "respond with full force" if North Vietnam violated the agreement, that is, if it attempted a military conquest of the south. At the same time, he made it clear that if Thieu did not acquiesce, Congress would not only cut off funds for continued American activity in Southeast Asia but would veto further aid, military and nonmilitary, to his government. Thieu stalled for a few days and then gave in. "I have done all that I can for my country," he resignedly told reporters.[13]

When Nixon announced the cease-fire agreement on the twenty-third, Fulbright at once called to congratulate him on his achievement. "It's later than I hoped, but it's good," he subsequently told reporters. When Nixon summoned twenty-five congressional leaders to the White House to brief them on the accords, the mood was one of relief and even euphoria. Nixon's announcement that he would not submit the agreement to the Senate for its advice and consent seemed to have no effect on most of those assembled. "I'm so relieved, I don't care what the agreement is called," Mike Mansfield told the press.[14] Fulbright was a bit less sanguine, remarking after the meeting that "it is inevitable that many difficulties will arise out of the liquidation of this long and costly and bitter struggle."[15]

Though he did not share the euphoria of many of his colleagues, Fulbright was in the mood for reconciliation. Tragically, Lyndon Johnson had died the day before Nixon announced the Vietnam cease-fire. The Arkansan was quick to pay homage to his colleague-turned-adversary:

> Lyndon Johnson had one of the most outstanding careers in American politics of any man in our history. . . . As a Senator and as a President he was responsible for some of the most significant legislation of our time. . . . I am saddened by his sudden death and by the fact that he did not live to witness the termination of the war. . . . He was my friend and colleague for many years, and it is one of my deepest regrets that our involvement in the war in Vietnam diverted President Johnson and our country.[16]

In mid-February, Fulbright extended an olive branch to the Nixon administration as well. The end of the war, he told Secretary of State Rogers, should pave the way for a new era of cooperation between the SFRC and the executive branch.[17] The affable Republican was willing enough to participate in

13 Quoted in Herring, *America's Longest War,* 255.
14 UPI 892, Jan. 24, 1973.
15 Quoted in Berman, *Fulbright and the Vietnam War,* 167.
16 "Vigorous and Dedicated Leader," *Arkansas Democrat,* Jan. 23, 1973.
17 Rogers to JWF, Feb. 16, 1973, Series 48:3, Box 18:3, SPF.

such a rapprochement, but his chief was not. It quickly became apparent that although he had won a landslide victory in the fall and was well on his way to extricating America from its ten-year ordeal in Southeast Asia, Richard Nixon, egged on by members of the White House staff, was in a bitter and vindictive mood. "When you go to the Capitol you must at all costs give no quarter whatever to the doves," Haldeman instructed Kissinger at Nixon's request. "You should flatly indicate . . . that the resolutions passed by the House and Senate caucuses . . . prolonged the war."[18] On February 1, White House counselor Charles Colson told television interviewer Elizabeth Drew that "a sellout brigade," which included Clark Clifford, William Fulbright, George McGovern, Frank Church, and Edward Kennedy, had kept the president from ending the war much earlier.[19] Throughout February, Nixon and his spokesmen emphasized again and again that they had not simply abandoned an ally as the doves had demanded, but had hammered out a peace accord that left in place a strong, independent Vietnam.

Fulbright may have wanted a rapprochement with the Nixon White House, but it was to be on his own terms. Now that the war was due to end, he decided, the administration had less reason than ever to upset the balance of power within the federal government, overcommit the United States overseas, and act in unconstitutional ways. Revelations relating to the break-in at the headquarters of the Democratic National Committee in the Watergate complex and the subsequent cover-up concerned the Arkansan, but not nearly as much as did Nixon's policy priorities and his arrogance toward Congress. The second Tuesday in February, Fulbright and Walter Lippmann spent two hours together over drinks.[20] Both agreed that the SFRC should play a role in implementing a lasting peace whether the administration wanted it to or not. The only lever available, as usual, was congressional control of the purse strings.

From November 1972 through January 1973 Moose and Lowenstein had traipsed back and forth between Washington and Hong Kong talking to Southeast Asia watchers situated there. On their way, they would usually stop off in Paris to be briefed, usually very superficially, by Ambassador David Bruce on the state of the peace talks. During one of their last trips, they had met with Philip Habib, a Bruce assistant who, in Moose's words, had "absolutely stonewalled" them. As they left, Moose asked to use the phone. The secretary ushered him into an office across the hall. Although he was outside the ambassador's complex, Moose was still then within the embassy's super-secure area. "I sat down at the desk to make my call," Moose remembered. "I

18 Haldeman to Kissinger, Jan. 25, 1973, WHSpF, Box 178, Nixon Project.
19 Quoted in Berman, *Fulbright and the Vietnam War,* 168.
20 Appointments calendar, Feb. 13, 1973, Williams Papers.

looked down and saw a Top Secret telegram. It had this astounding text."[21] The telegram indicated that, in a secret protocol to the Paris agreement, the Nixon administration had offered Hanoi $3.25 billion in postwar aid. As soon as the two SFRC investigators returned to Washington, they reported their find to Fulbright.

During a January press conference, Nixon had made some general comments about reconciliation and the willingness of his administration to help reconstruct all of Indochina after the war was completely over. He had said nothing about a specific pledge of dollar aid to Hanoi. Public opinion polls revealed that Americans would oppose such aid by 51 to 40 percent, and one influential member of the House remarked that any assistance given to North Vietnam would be over his "dead body." A week following the press conference, Fulbright wrote Nixon offering advice on how to administer the aid that no one was supposed to know about: "It would be good policy and good politics" to internationalize any aid program, he declared; not only would Hanoi be unable to characterize such aid as "reparations," but the United States would be protected from charges of imperialism.[22]

Fulbright's suggestion was greeted, of course, with an embarrassed silence. When the White House subsequently rebuffed the chairman's suggestion that the Paris accord at least be submitted to Congress for its perusal and discussion, he announced to reporters that he would not support funds for reconstructing North Vietnam unless they came out of the defense budget.[23] The administration had not even begun to consider the question, a White House spokesman declared uneasily.

While Fulbright was in Arkansas addressing the General Assembly in late February, three Oglala Sioux, members of the American Indian Movement, seized a Roman Catholic church and trading post near Wounded Knee, South Dakota. Russell Means, the militant head of the AIM, had selected Wounded Knee because of its notoriety. There on December 29, 1890, soldiers of the U.S. Cavalry had massacred at least 146 Sioux men, women, and children. Holding ten hostages at gunpoint and surrounded by a hundred heavily armed law officers, including FBI agents, Means and his cohorts demanded to see Senators J. William Fulbright and Edward Kennedy. They wanted the SFRC to hold hearings on the 371 treaties that allegedly had been violated by the U.S. government.[24]

21 Interview with Richard Moose, June 29, 1989, Washington, D.C., and Marilyn B. Young, *The Vietnam Wars, 1945–1990* (New York, 1991), 279.

22 JWF to Nixon, Feb. 5, 1973, Series 48:8, Box 31:4, SPF.

23 "Divert Military Funds to Aid Hanoi in Reconstruction, Fulbright Urges," *Arkansas Gazette,* Feb. 19, 1973.

24 "400 Indians Seize 10 Hostages, Ask to See Fulbright, Kennedy," *Arkansas Gazette,* Mar. 1, 1973.

In Little Rock Fulbright told reporters that although he was not too familiar with Indian problems, he would "do anything" to help resolve the conflict, including making a trip to South Dakota. It was "high time," he said, that government officials paid more attention to problems at home.[25]

After returning to Washington and consulting with Marcy, Justice Department officials, and Senators McGovern and James Abourezk (D–South Dakota), Fulbright decided to send Marcy instead. He wanted to "provide some semblance of a Committee presence" but not appear to accede to the Indians' demand that the SFRC assume jurisdiction. After Means and his supporters agreed to free the hostages, Marcy, McGovern, and Abourezk met twice with the militants, once on a hilltop and once in Wounded Knee itself. The three listened to complaints about the Bureau of Indian Affairs and discrimination in general. When Means argued that the Sioux and other tribes were sovereign nations and had been treated as such in innumerable negotiations between 1815 and 1871, Marcy pointed out that none of the treaties signed had ever been presented to the SFRC for its consideration and approval. He promised, however, that if anything could be done, Fulbright and the committee would act. At that point the Indians, angry and dissatisfied, surrendered to law enforcement authorities.[26]

Meanwhile, Moose and Lowenstein were winging their way to Phnom Penh again to investigate rumors of continued American military activity in Cambodia. The two were well known to, and thoroughly disliked by, American diplomatic and military personnel in the Cambodian capital. As they no doubt knew, it had been Moose who had written the resolution forbidding the deployment of U.S. combat troops in that country. The congressional prohibition was, to use Moose's phrase, "horsehide tough, bull strong, and pig tight." The administration had, however, secured an exception for a certain number of attaché and advisory personnel. Ever since passage of the Cambodian resolution, Lowenstein and his partner had traveled periodically to Cambodia to track down and count Americans.

When the SFRC investigators arrived the first week in April, their journalist friends told them that they suspected that American spotter planes were flying out of Phnom Penh airport, locating Khmer Rouge targets for U.S. fighter-bombers and B-52's. "Lowenstein and I would go out at odd moments and try to get into the far end of the airport and poke around," Moose remembered. "We could never quite do it."[27]

25 Ibid.
26 Marcy to SFRC, Mar. 2, 1973, Box 11, Jan.–Mar., Marcy Papers.
27 Moose interview.

The second Sunday morning they were there, the two investigators wandered over to the small office shared by the local *Washington Post* stringer and UPI correspondent to check on the baseball scores. When they arrived one of the correspondents was standing, listening intently to a small transistor radio.

"Dick, listen to this," she said.

"I heard unmistakably a flight of American air force planes identifying themselves: 'Blue Six, this is Fox Four, what is your location?' and so on. Finally one of them addressed the Embassy," Moose recalled. "Let's get over there while the planes are still in the air," Moose urged his partner.

Several days earlier the SFRC team had demanded and received blueprints for the American embassy building. Each area on each floor was identified according to function. They had visited the air attaché's office, but had found nothing out of the ordinary. It suddenly dawned on them as they raced across Phnom Penh that the air traffic control operation was housed in the lead-encased capsule that comprised the secure nucleus of every American embassy.

As Moose and Lowenstein parked the car beside the embassy, who should emerge but the air attaché. They had previously interviewed the man, and he had flatly denied that he or his staff were spotting for the air force. Moose confronted him: "I believe that you are controlling air strikes from within the embassy and that you're putting forward spotter planes out of the airport here. I have just heard the ground-to-air and air-to-air communications." The officer paled, hesitated, and then declared, "I'm not going to answer any more questions."

Moose and Lowenstein rushed back to the *Post*–UPI office and convinced the two reporters to hold up on the story until they could inform the SFRC. They readily agreed. When, subsequently, the embassy learned that the two journalists were the source of the story on the air strikes, they were expelled from Cambodia by the Lon Nol government.[28]

Lowenstein and Moose were not able to prepare a report for release until April 27, but even before he received confirmation that Ambassador Thomas Enders and his staff were violating the specific congressional ban on the use of combat troops in Cambodia, Fulbright had decided to make an issue of the post-cease-fire air offensive in that unfortunate country. The war in Vietnam might be over for all intents and purposes, and Henry Kissinger might be poised to establish a new world order based on détente, but, as Cambodia revealed, there was nothing to prevent Nixon or a future president from plunging the United States into another undeclared war such as Vietnam. Indeed, although the substance of American foreign policy seemed to be improving, the great issue of restoring a balance between Congress and the executive re-

[28] Ibid.

mained to be handled. Testifying on Capitol Hill on March 28, Assistant Secretary of State William Sullivan had been asked about Nixon's authority to bomb Cambodia. He had replied that two State Department lawyers were currently working on the problem, and then added that "for now, I'd say the justification is the reelection of President Nixon."[29]

Most observers in early 1973 predicted that Congress would never be able to stand up to the imperial presidency. Hamstrung by massive inefficiency and by rules that ensured delays, boredom, and interruption of business, run by crotchety and sometimes senile men sheltered by the seniority system and insensitive to the public will, so the argument ran, Congress could not hope to compete with the modern executive, especially in the person of Richard Nixon. That argument, however, did not take into account the burgeoning Watergate scandal.

By April 15, the political climate in Washington was beginning to change dramatically. Watergate was mushrooming into a major political and legal problem for the administration and a personal nightmare for Nixon. While Kissinger urged him to expand the bombing from Cambodia into North Vietnam to punish it for its alleged persistent violations of the Paris agreements, Nixon refused to act. To those who saw him, he seemed shell-shocked, and he spent endless hours with Haldeman, Ehrlichman, and White House counsel John Dean searching for some way to contain the crisis.

Fulbright sensed that Watergate was a window of opportunity. Appearing on *Face the Nation* on April 15, the chairman noted that the break-in by CREEP operatives had made it possible for Congress not only to discuss but to act against executive encroachments on its powers. The presidency and the president were no longer sacrosanct, able to operate above the law.[30]

On April 11 the SFRC opened hearings on Jacob Javits's war powers bill. The immediate backdrop for the debate that ensued was the continuing bombing campaign in Cambodia. On March 27 Fulbright addressed the Senate. "I noted on the back page of the press . . . a statement that United States Air Force planes had just completed the 19th consecutive daily B-52 bombing attack in Cambodia," he declared. Why and under what authority were these raids being conducted? There were no more Americans (the sixty-day withdrawal period provided for in the Paris accords had lapsed) in Vietnam to protect. Was there some secret commitment to Lon Nol? "Does the President assert – as the Kings of old – that as Commander in Chief he can order American forces anywhere for any purpose that suits him?"[31]

29 Quoted in Berman, *Fulbright and the Vietnam War,* 171.
30 Ibid., 172.
31 Statement by J. W. Fulbright, Mar. 27, 1973, Box 11, Jan.–Mar., Marcy Papers.

On April 29 Stuart Symington released the Lowenstein–Moose report on Cambodia. There was yet another secret, unauthorized war raging in Southeast Asia in which the United States was participating, they declared. The struggle in Cambodia did not involve Cambodians fighting North Vietnamese but rather Cambodians fighting Cambodians. It was a civil war, pure and simple. They went on to point out that until he and his comrades had overthrown Prince Sihanouk in 1970, Lon Nol and his generals had actively supported the NVA and VC. Declared Stuart Symington:

> At this late date in this long war in Indochina, it is indeed tragic to witness the beginning of another wasteful and immoral episode, one which has nothing to do with the security of the United States, one which finds us dropping bags of rice to some Cambodians and five hundred pound bombs on others.[32]

Throughout April and May, Fulbright was deluged with anguished letters from American servicemen flying missions over Cambodia – the so-called B-52 Letters. "It is hard to impart to you sir, the frustration of being on continuous temporary duty with no end in sight," wrote one B-52 gunner who was in his thirteenth month of combat missions against Cambodia and Laos. "I for one, sir, do not wish to die as a mercenary for a foreign dictator!" He commended Fulbright for his efforts "to have a legal end to this war declared."[33]

An airman from Blytheville, Arkansas, provided an exact chronology of the post-Paris bombing of Cambodia:

> On approximately the 15th of February, we ceased all bombing operations in all parts of Southeast Asia. We were told at that time that as soon as the North Vietnamese and Viet-Cong started a timely release of the P.O.W.'s our B-52's and personnel would begin to return to our home bases. On approximately the 17th of February we started bombing operations against the Republic of Laos. We were again told that as soon as a cease fire was accomplished in Laos, we would cease operations on Guam [home base for B-52's flying missions over Southeast Asia]. . . . In the latter part of February a cease fire was signed in Laos. We stopped bombing on the day the cease fire was signed in Laos for approximately 12 hours and then we started bombing in Cambodia. When we made inquiries as to the reason why . . . no one seemed to be able to give us a reason. We have been bombing for approximately 41 days now. . . .[34]

And yet, faced with irrefutable proof that Nixon had ordered the illegal and unconstitutional bombing of Cambodia, the Senate still hesitated. Neither

32 "Report on Air War in Cambodia," Apr. 29, 1973, Series 28:7, Box 27:1, SPF.
33 SSgt. Charles E. Shinn to JWF, Apr. 17, 1973, Series 48:18, Box 65:5, SPF.
34 SSgt. Robert E. Walker to JWF, Apr. 24, 1973, Series 48:17, Box 46:4, SPF.

house of Congress had yet voted an absolute fund cutoff for military action in the field, and that reluctance remained. John Finney noted in the *New York Times* that Congress did not want to be accused of "losing" Cambodia. Reports, even from impartial sources, indicated that without daily American bombing and strafing, Lon Nol's army would collapse and Cambodia would fall to the Khmer Rouge – the same Khmer Rouge that would slaughter 1.2 million people, the same Khmer Rouge rendered infamous by the Academy Award–winning *Killing Fields.*[35] Indeed, in 1971 following one of their trips to Cambodia, Moose and Lowenstein had reported that "there is considerable support for the government of Gen. Lon Nol" and that many Cambodians favored American air strikes to contain the NVA and control the Khmer Rouge.[36]

Far more important in restraining Congress than fear of contributing to the rise of the Khmer Rouge – most Americans were ignorant of the dynamics and goals of that organization in 1973 – was apprehension over Richard Nixon's political clout. Senators and congresspeople could not forget the unprecedented landslide the president had fashioned. Haldeman, Colson, and John Mitchell's mean-spirited declarations convinced many that a political purge was in the offing; but just as it seemed Congress would get cold feet again, Watergate heated up to warm them. As evidence mounted that the White House had been deeply involved in the "plumbers'" operation and that there was a conspiracy to cover up the Watergate break-in, Nixon went on television on April 30 to announce the resignations of H. R. Haldeman and John Ehrlichman and the firing of John Dean. Suddenly the president seemed eminently vulnerable. Doves and hawks alike began circling for the kill.

The first week in May the SFRC voted 13 to 3 to recommend a cutoff of funds for continued U.S. bombing raids in Cambodia.[37] Five days later the House passed a supplemental appropriations bill for the DOD that would deny money for continued operations in Cambodia.[38]

Sensing that at last the time was ripe, Frank Church informed the Senate on May 14 that he and Clifford Case had obtained thirty-eight cosponsors for their proposal to cut off funding for all American military forces involved "in hostilities in or over from off the shores of North Vietnam, South Vietnam, Laos, or Cambodia." Fulbright was not among the sponsors. The bill reached the floor of the Senate on June 14 – just as Henry Kissinger was concluding

35 "U.S. Will Continue Raids in Cambodia," *New York Times,* Mar. 28, 1973.

36 According to Moose, Fulbright was furious at the content of their report, especially after he told the chairman that it was based in part on interviews with twenty former Fulbrighters. The chairman at first attempted to bury the report, but then eventually released it. Moose interview, and "Fulbright Panel Aides Support Cambodia Help," *Washington Evening Star,* Feb. 2, 1971.

37 "2 Senate Panels Vote to Cut Off Bombing Funds," *Arkansas Gazette,* May 5, 1973.

38 *Congressional Record,* House, May 10, 1973, H509.

a follow-up round of talks on the peace agreement in Paris and just before Leonid Brezhnev flew into Washington for a summit with Richard Nixon. The resolution, attached to a State Department authorization measure, passed the Senate by a wide margin.

Competing with the end-the-war drive for Fulbright's attention was the political situation in Arkansas. In March, May, and then again in June he returned home to mend a few fences. Rumors were already circulating that Dale Bumpers, the immensely popular young governor, was going to challenge him for his Senate seat in 1974. Fulbright supporters from around the state reported to Lee Williams that voters were angry at the junior senator over Vietnam – even those who suspected that he had been right. Fulbright chose to address that problem not by backing off but by aggressively defending his position. During speaking engagements in Blytheville, Fort Smith, and Newport he touted his opposition to the war and to military spending. Misguided overseas adventures, he told an overflow crowd at the Quality Courts cocktail lounge in Blytheville, were the reason why farm subsidies had been cut and that eastern Arkansas could not get relief funds to help pay for recent flooding in the Delta. "I'll listen to you on agriculture," he told his constituents, "and you listen to me on Vietnam and other foreign policy questions."[39] His lack of enthusiasm for the Church–Case amendment had little to do, then, with a desire to ameliorate his opposition to the war for political purposes.

Frank Church later remarked that he would have welcomed Fulbright's cosponsorship, and expressed the view that the Arkansan had held back in order not "to trouble" Henry Kissinger.[40] There was some truth to Church's observation. Kissinger was engaged in intensive discussions with Le Duc Tho throughout the spring of 1972 on postwar aid, Cambodia, Laos, and the post-cease-fire political and military situation in South Vietnam. He continued to call Fulbright on a regular basis, reporting to him and asking for his cooperation. They lunched several times at the Metropolitan Club.[41] The reasons for Fulbright's failure to cosponsor and vote for Church–Case were multiple, however.

At times during the spring of 1973 J. William Fulbright suffered from bouts of intense cynicism about and disillusionment with public life. Watergate and the bombing of Cambodia and Laos coming in the wake of Richard Nixon's landslide victory were profoundly discouraging. Perhaps, he mused in the quiet of his office or on his screened-in porch overlooking Rock Creek Park, the Republic really had been perverted. Several times during the hearings on the Cambodian bombing he remarked that it did not matter what law Congress passed; Nixon and his henchmen would find "some specious legal

39 "Fulbright Uses 'Nam' as Weapon," *Blytheville Courier News,* May 5, 1973.
40 Quoted in Berman, *Fulbright and the Vietnam War,* 174–5.
41 Appointments calendar, Mar. 9, 1973, Williams Papers.

justification for doing exactly what it wishes to do."[42] Although he had once supported postwar aid to Vietnam, he could no longer do so, the Arkansan wrote Morris Rubin, editor of the *Progressive:*

> I realize that it may be narrow-minded, but I am so disillusioned with the Administration that I dislike giving them any kind of additional power over anything . . . because they misuse their power so crudely. This letter seems so negative, it may well be that the constant avalanche of revelations about the corruption in the government has distorted my judgment, and that I ought to get out of Washington for a while.[43]

On *Face the Nation* he declared that if Nixon "decided to bomb Burma tomorrow, I don't know how we could stop him from it."[44]

Betty convinced him that he needed to get away, not to Arkansas again as Lee had been urging, but really away. On Maundy Thursday the Fulbrights flew to West Palm Beach for golf and relaxation. They stayed through Easter and then returned to Washington by way of Augusta and the Masters Golf Tournament.[45] Fulbright arrived back in Washington refreshed, his determination to bring the imperial presidency to heel renewed.

By the first week in June the noose was beginning to close on the Nixon administration over Cambodia. White House aide William Timmons reported to the president that there were pending in Congress no fewer than five cutoff amendments, several of them attached to bills that would be very difficult to veto.[46]

In the midst of the brouhaha over Cambodia, Leonid Brezhnev arrived in Washington for his summit with the beleaguered Nixon. Fulbright was delighted – with Kissinger and the Russians, if not with the rest of the Nixon administration. Indeed, by 1973 the Arkansan's Russophilia had become part of his public persona. On the eve of the summit, he assembled the White House press corps and called for a thorough reappraisal of the military budget, arguing that by all accounts the Soviets were cutting back on their defense expenditures. Fulbright also arranged for a luncheon at Blair House for Brezhnev so that the Soviet leader could meet with twenty influential senators, including most members of the SFRC. During the course of their three-and-a-half-hour session, Brezhnev declared "the Cold War was, as far as we are concerned, over."[47]

On June 21 Kissinger, freshly arrived from Paris, met secretly with the

42 Quoted in Berman, *Fulbright and the Vietnam War,* 172.
43 JWF to Rubin, Mar. 30, 1973, Series 48:8, Box 31:4, SPF.
44 Quoted in Berman, *Fulbright and the Vietnam War,* 172.
45 Appointments calendar, Apr. 19–25, 1973, Williams Papers.
46 William Timmons to Nixon, June 15, 1973, WHSpF, Box 42, Nixon Project.
47 "Brezhnev Urges Senators to Help Work for Peace," *Arkansas Gazette,* June 20, 1973.

SFRC. Fulbright had arranged the conference following several private conversations with the NSC adviser. Kissinger told the senators that there was about a 50–50 chance for a comprehensive settlement of all outstanding issues relating to Indochina by early September, and he pled with them not to vote for an immediate fund cutoff.[48]

Nixon had hoped that the Brezhnev visit would divert public attention from the harrowing ordeal of Watergate and strengthen his hand in his confrontation with Congress over Cambodia. It did neither. On June 25 – the day Brezhnev left for Moscow – Sam Ervin resumed his Watergate hearings, which he had postponed for a week at the president's request. John Dean, Nixon's former counsel, took the stand and mesmerized the nation with his tale of intrigue, cover-up, and "blind ambition."

While Dean spilled his guts, to use a Nixonian phrase, and the SFRC considered Henry Kissinger's request, both houses passed a continuing resolution with an immediate fund cutoff attached. Nixon at once vetoed it, and an override measure failed in the House. At that point Fulbright stepped in and led the fight for a compromise on Cambodia, but the price he extracted from the administration was high.

On June 29 Fulbright rose on the floor of the Senate to inform his colleagues that the SFRC by a vote of 15 to 2 had approved an amendment to the general appropriations bill, then stalled in Congress, prohibiting the continuation of hostilities by U.S. forces anywhere in Indochina after August 15, 1973. The acceptance of the August 15 date "in no way" constituted recognition of the president's authority to be there in the first place, he declared. In return for this six-week extension, the administration had agreed not to resume hostilities after that date without the express approval of both houses of Congress. Was that not correct? he asked Hugh Scott, Senate minority leader. That was correct, Scott reluctantly declared.[49] Mike Mansfield, increasingly cut out of the decision-making process by the Kissinger–Fulbright relationship, led the fight against Fulbright's proposal. He denounced the compromise as a "capitulation and abdication of the Constitutional powers of the Senate."[50] His opposition was not enough. A reluctant and divided Senate voted 63 to 26 for the Fulbright compromise, and the House followed suit 236 to 169.[51] In effect the chairman had traded six more weeks of bombing in Cambodia for an explicit administration promise not to initiate further hostilities without congressional consent. Never during the history of the war in Indochina had any president conceded Congress the right to veto military action.

48 "Adm. Trying to Find Right Neg. in Cambodia," *Washington Post,* June 30, 1973.
49 *Congressional Record,* Senate June 29, 1973, 12560.
50 "Nixon Accepts a Cut-off," *New York Times,* July 1, 1973.
51 "Bombing to End by Aug. 15," *Washington Evening Star,* June 30, 1973.

Despite everything that the Americans could throw at them, the Khmer Rouge made steady progress during the next month and a half, chewing up Lon Nol's army at a rate of twelve hundred casualties a month. By the first week in August Phnom Penh was a city under siege. Every day American jets could be seen wheeling in the sky over the beleaguered city. Black clouds of smoke rose on the outskirts of town, and at night the undersides of the monsoon clouds glowed pink in the false dawn of exploding bombs. Nixon appealed to Congress to repudiate the Fulbright compromise, and warned that the fall of Cambodia to the Khmer Rouge would be its responsibility; but Congress would not relent. As Lon Nol's army went down the drain, hearings before the Armed Services Committee brought to light for the first time that the bombing of Cambodia had continued unabated past the 1970 invasion in direct contravention of Congress's expressed will. The military, moreover, had lied to cover up.[52] The Cambodian government would collapse in the spring of 1975, and the Khmer Rouge assume control of Phnom Penh on April 17.

Kissinger later argued that the congressionally mandated bombing halt denied him the leverage necessary to force Hanoi, and through it the Khmer Rouge, into accepting a cease-fire in Cambodia. Up to August 15, Communist China had proved willing to help engineer a halt to the fighting and had indicated a willingness to support a coalition government under Prince Sihanouk; but, according to Kissinger, Beijing seemed to lose interest after the August 15 cease-fire went into effect. The NSC adviser blamed Watergate for robbing Nixon of the will to resist Congress, and Congress for interfering in the diplomatic process and making possible the rise of Pol Pot and his gang of murderers.

The Nixon administration, however, had much earlier had the opportunity to facilitate the installation of a coalition government in Cambodia under Sihanouk and had chosen not to do so. The United States, seeing Cambodia as merely a pawn in the Vietnam War, encouraged the coup that overthrew Sihanouk and then supported Lon Nol, all as part of the Vietnamization strategy, which called for destruction of North Vietnamese sanctuaries in Cambodia. Although the Nixon administration was not responsible for the rise of the Khmer Rouge, its growth paralleled the policy of Vietnamization. Perhaps Congress did misunderstand the situation in Cambodia in the summer of 1973, but, as William Berman has argued, Nixon and Kissinger along with Hanoi bear the responsibility for destabilizing Cambodia. In the process, they chose to ignore the recommendation of seventy-five senators who, by voting

52 H. D. S. Greenway, "Cambodia: 'It Is Never Quiet Here,'" *Washington Post,* Aug. 4, 1973; John W. Finney, "Nixon Sees Peril in Bombing Halt; Warns Congress," *New York Times,* Aug. 4, 1973; and Seymour M. Hersh, "Senators Are Told U.S. Bombed Cambodia Secretly after Invasion in 1970," *New York Times,* Aug. 8, 1973.

for the Cooper–Church amendment on June 30, 1970, had urged that the United States stay out of that unfortunate country.[53]

The movement to undermine the imperial presidency's warmaking powers culminated with congressional passage of the War Powers Act in the fall of 1973. Ironically, J. William Fulbright was less than enthusiastic about the measure, which required the president to inform Congress within forty-eight hours of the deployment of American military forces abroad, and obligated him to withdraw them in sixty days in the absence of explicit congressional endorsement. In Fulbright's opinion, Jacob Javits's bill gave the president far too much latitude to involve the United States in foreign conflicts. America had learned once again during the long, painful Vietnam experience how difficult it was politically to compel the withdrawal of troops in the field once they were committed. In Fulbright's opinion the Constitution bound the president to ask for and secure a declaration of war, or at the very least congressional approval as provided in the National Commitments Resolution, before sending troops abroad.

Despite the sixty-day window, Nixon informed Minority Leader Gerald Ford (R–Michigan) that if the Javits bill reached him in any form, he would veto it. Meanwhile, each new day brought fresh revelations concerning Watergate, revelations that further undermined Richard Nixon's power. A thrill of excitement and anticipation shot through Congress and the nation when Alexander Butterfield informed the Ervin committee on July 16 that the president had employed a taping system inside the Oval Office and that the hundreds of hours Nixon, Haldeman, Ehrlichman, and Dean had discussed Watergate (and its cover-up) were recorded and available if the committee subpoenaed them.

When the war powers bill reached the floor of the Senate in mid-July, Fulbright offered several amendments designed to tighten it. The most important simply conformed to the Constitution, reiterating that the president had authority to commit troops to combat only when the nation was being threatened with invasion or its security directly imperiled. All his amendments were overwhelmingly defeated, as was that of Thomas Eagleton (D–Missouri), which would have included CIA covert activities in the bill's coverage, a step Fulbright strongly favored. On July 20 the Senate approved the war powers legislation by a wide margin and sent it to the House, which had already passed a similar measure. Fulbright not only voted for the Senate measure, but headed the Senate conferees who subsequently worked out a compromise with Representative Clement Zablocki (D–Pennsylvania) and his delegation. As he had promised, Richard Nixon vetoed the War Powers Act, but Watergate had so weakened him that he could only protest when on November 6, 1973, Congress voted to override. The following week the House and Senate

[53] Berman, *Fulbright and the Vietnam War,* 179.

endorsed an amendment to the Military Procurement Authorization Act banning the funding of any U.S. military action in any part of Indochina, and American involvement in the Second Indochina War effectively came to a halt.[54]

The end of American participation in the Vietnam War and the circumscription of presidential powers in the area of foreign policymaking brought little joy to J. William Fulbright. His long struggle had been, to his mind, to right a wrong, to correct an endless series of mistakes, to bring a halt to years of brutality and suffering. The country was exhausted, its confidence shaken, and Fulbright to an extent shared that malaise. There was little consolation in the thought that thousands more might have died and that democracy might have been seriously compromised in the United States had it not been for his efforts. America's great crusade in Southeast Asia had contained the seeds of its own destruction. The fact that he had perceived that fact early on and sounded the clarion call was of no comfort. Fulbright could not get the Gulf of Tonkin Resolution out of his mind; he could not forget that he had once embraced and been chief purveyor of the liberal activism that had been responsible for the horror that was Vietnam. Moreover, he realized that it was not just the ancient Greeks who killed messengers bearing bad tidings.

54 Young, *Vietnam Wars,* 285; "War Measure Approved," *Arkansas Democrat,* July 21, 1973; and Richard L. Madden, "Congress Leaders Confident on Bill to Curb President," *New York Times,* Oct. 5, 1973.

# 37

# *Dancing with Henry*

One of the major topics Leonid Brezhnev had addressed during his Blair House confab with Fulbright and his colleagues was the issue of Jewish emigration from the Soviet Union. He assured the assemblage that only a handful of Soviet Jews who had requested exit visas had not been granted them.[1] In reality, as the Israeli government, Soviet dissidents, and Senator Henry Jackson continually pointed out, the Kremlin continued not only to deny Soviet Jews the right to leave and go to Israel, but also persecuted them for attempting to do so.

In anticipation of the summit with Brezhnev, the Nixon administration had introduced in Congress a bill granting the Soviet Union most-favored-nation trading status in return for Moscow's agreeing to pay a specific sum settling a World War II Lend–Lease debt. However, to Nixon, Kissinger, and Fulbright's extreme annoyance, Jackson, along with seventy-six senatorial cosponsors, had attached an amendment to the bill requiring Brezhnev to grant the right of unrestricted immigration to Soviet Jews. Suddenly in the summer of 1973, the Middle East replaced Vietnam in Fulbright's mind as the rock upon which détente was most likely to crash.

The Jackson amendment made its appearance in the midst of yet another Arab–Israeli crisis. In the fall of 1970 Gamal Abdel Nasser had died. His successor, Anwar al-Sadat, shared Nasser's goal of ridding Egyptian land of Israeli forces and of helping the Palestinians obtain an equitable settlement to their claims, but without embracing his predecessor's dream of an Egyptian-led pan-Arab union. Sadat grew increasingly restive as he perceived the government of Golda Meir to be following a policy of creeping annexationism. Tel Aviv declared Jerusalem and the Golan Heights to be permanent acquisitions and established Jewish settlements in Jordan's West Bank, the Gaza Strip, and the Sinai Peninsula while the United States stood complacently by. Like Nasser before him, Sadat responded by turning to the Soviets for help.

As American policymakers watched with alarm, the Soviet Union engineered a massive military buildup in the Middle East. By 1971 the Kremlin's

[1] "Brezhnev Urges Senators to Help Work for Peace," *Arkansas Gazette,* June 20, 1973.

fleet and network of bases were large enough to challenge America's naval dominance in the Eastern Mediterranean. In response, the Nixon administration poured arms and money into Israel, giving Tel Aviv more aid than any previous American government. Nixon and Kissinger were committed to countering and containing Soviet power in the Middle East; but both the president and his national security adviser believed that American strategic interests were not served by a blindly pro-Israeli policy. Only if and when Israel could be persuaded to trade land for peace would the huge Arab world stop furnishing harbors for Soviet ships and land for Soviet bases.[2]

The early 1970s saw no weakening of the commitment of American Jewry to an Israel-right-or-wrong stance. By 1972 the Israeli Bond Organization, the United Jewish Appeal, and other organizations had raised and contributed to the Israeli government $4.2 billion, most of it in the form of tax-exempt bonds.[3] In the wake of the Vietnam debacle, many Americans identified with the state of Israel and its military successes. The "forgotten man," angered and shamed by his own armed services' build-down and disintegration in Southeast Asia, relished the sight of a well-trained, out-manned Israeli military beating up on disorganized Arabs, many of whose leaders were given to fits of extremist rhetoric. Consequently, Israeli aid bills were able regularly to command 75 to 80 votes in the United States Senate, and a corresponding number in the House.

The Israeli government continually declared itself to be an outpost of freedom and democracy defending Western interests against Soviet imperialism in the Middle East. Despite the fact that American Jewish leaders played increasingly prominent roles in the anti–Vietnam War movement, and that a substantial number of American Jews had voted against Richard Nixon in 1968, the military–industrial complex was avidly pro-Israel.[4] By 1973 the Middle East and the cold war had become inextricably intertwined.

Congress's most avid cold warrior and Zionist continued to be Henry "Scoop" Jackson. His amendment to the Soviet trade bill infuriated Fulbright. "Henry Jackson continues to have undue influence in maintaining the cold war, preventing détente with Russia, and increasing military expenditures," the Arkansan complained bitterly to Marriner Eccles. "It is much easier to inflame the emotions of members of Congress – and the public as well – by emphasizing the alleged brutality and intransigencies of any Communist country than it is to sell a restrained and reasonable policy."[5] Jackson, of course, believed Fulbright to be hopelessly naïve. The Soviet Union was run

2 News Summaries, Sept. 1969, WHSpF, Box 30, Nixon Project.
3 "American Jews Raise Billions as Charity to Israel," *Houston Chronicle,* May 13, 1973.
4 News Summaries, June 1969, WHSpF, Box 30, Nixon Project. In 1972 there was, however, a significant shift toward Nixon among Jewish voters.
5 JWF to Eccles, Oct. 19, 1973, Series 48:16, Box 42:3, SPF.

by a bunch of communist gangsters supported by an entrenched and corrupt *nomenklatura,* he insisted. As its appeals for trade concessions and American grain indicated, the Soviet economy was in long-term trouble. Détente and arms limitation would merely enable the Kremlin leadership to divert funds from the defense budget, patch up the civilian economy, and perpetuate totalitarianism in Russia and throughout the Soviet empire. Fulbright differed with Jackson not so much over the nature of Soviet society, but rather over the sources of oppression and aggression, and the best means to effect positive change there. He told Eccles:

> I do not minimize the significance of Russia's internal repression, but the question is how can one expect to influence it. It seems to me that over a period of time they are more likely to moderate their repressive policies as a result of détente than they are under the conditions created by continued pressure and competition in the building of armaments.[6]

In other words, it was the cold war that made the Kremlin autocratic and repressive rather than, as Jackson believed, the inherently expansionist tendencies of the totalitarian regime in Moscow being responsible for the cold war.

Fulbright's views on the Soviet Union and the cold war were intimately intertwined with his attitudes toward the Arab–Israeli conflict. If the Kremlin was truly committed to peaceful coexistence, including mutual disarmament, America's pro-Israeli policy was absurd. Israel was not an American strategic outpost bravely defending Western trade routes and petroleum deposits from the communists. It was rather a small, understandably insecure nation involved in a regional conflict. He thoroughly agreed with the Jewish psychoanalyst Erich Fromm, who wrote Fulbright in 1973:

> It seems to me that basically the political line of Jackson and of the Israelis is the same. . . . They both believe that only might and the decision of arms can regulate unsolved conflicts and they have no confidence in the spirit, in the warmth of the human heart to which one can appeal, in feelings of gratitude and respect which can be provoked by behavior leading to it. They both lack faith in life, in man, patience, and they both act like the false mother in Solomon's Judgment, who prefers to kill the child rather than to give up her claim.[7]

To Fulbright and Fromm it seemed that Jackson was willing to expose the world to the possibility of nuclear war rather than relinquish his demand for exceptional treatment (virtually all Soviet citizens were forbidden to emigrate) of the Jews in the Soviet Union and the restoration of liberty in that country.

6 Ibid.

7 Fromm to JWF, Nov. 19, 1973, and JWF to Fromm, Dec. 22, 1973, Series 48:15, Box 41:1, SPF.

Similarly, the Israelis were willing to risk national and international Armageddon rather than give up their obsession with the "secure" borders. "The Israelis' attitude is all the more tragic," Fromm observed, "because here is a people which claims to have a right to the land because of the religious tradition of the Jews and who violates one of the most fundamental principles announced by the Hebrew Prophets: 'Not with might and not with power, but with my spirit, says the Lord.'"[8]

Several times during April and May Fulbright met with Arab diplomats and representatives from the oil industry. Most of these interviews and luncheons were arranged by Seth Tillman, who by this time was taking an intense interest in the Middle East.[9] They warned the Arkansan that the Arab world was growing increasingly impatient with Israel's annexationist policies. If there was no willingness on Israel's part to negotiate, there was bound to be war; and if the United States continued its blind support of Tel Aviv, Saudi Arabia, the Gulf emirates, and Iraq would close off the oil spigot. They reminded Fulbright that Europe and Japan received 85 percent of their petroleum from the Middle East, and the United States 18 percent. Fulbright was at the same time alarmed by news that the United States had just concluded a $2 billion arms deal with the Shah of Iran, and that six hundred American servicemen were on their way to that country to service the Shah's new equipment. Could it be, he wondered, that Israel, Iran, and the United States were preparing to take control of the Middle East oil fields by force?

In mid-May, Fulbright called on the Senate once again for a comprehensive Middle East settlement based on a withdrawal by Israel to its pre-1967 borders in return for Arab recognition and international guarantees of its security. Continued Israeli intransigence and the establishment of an American-backed Iranian "protectorate" over the oil sheikdoms could only spell disaster, he warned. At the same time, he appealed to the Arab world to show restraint by holding down the price of oil. "The meat of the gazelle may be succulent indeed," he observed, quoting an old African proverb, "but the wise gazelle does not boast of it to lions."[10]

The chairman of the SFRC was now pursuing appeasement in another form, Scoop Jackson declared. Fulbright's solution "would make more precarious the situation of our friends in order to court and appease those Arab nations for whom blackmail and sanctuary for terrorists serve as foreign policy."[11]

Throughout the spring and summer of 1973 the two men waged a bitter verbal battle over America's Middle East policy in general and the Jackson

8 Fromm to JWF, Nov. 19, 1973, Series 48:15, Box 41:1, SPF.
9 Appointments calendar, Apr. 17 and 30, and May 16, 1973, Papers of Lee Williams.
10 *Congressional Record,* Senate, May 21, 1973, 16262–3.
11 "News from Senator Henry M. Jackson," May 21, 1973, Series 78:7, Box 33:3, SPF.

amendment in particular. In late July Fulbright told a meeting of the American Bankers Association that the Washington senator's campaign in behalf of Jewish rights in the Soviet Union would only perpetuate the cold war. "Learning to live together in peace is the most important issue for the Soviet Union and the United States," he declared, "too important to be compromised by meddling – even idealistic meddling – in each other's affairs." He accused Jackson of selective idealism. The United Nations Universal Declaration of Human Rights, which the Washington senator cited as justification for his amendment, established a person's right not only to leave a country but to return, Fulbright told the bankers. "Is the right of the Palestinians to return to their homes from which they were expelled any less fundamental than the right of Soviet Jews to make new homes in a new land?"

Not surprisingly, Fulbright's attacks on the Jackson amendment and his defense of Palestinian rights elicited cries of outrage from American Jews, whether maximalists or minimalists. Rabbi Arthur Hertzberg, president of the American Jewish Congress, accused the Arkansan of the "appeasement" of "totalitarian despotism and oppression." Harold Ostroff of the Workmen's Circle told reporters: "For a man who applauded the actions of Governor Faubus at Little Rock and who had remained mute about Wounded Knee, his own dismal record on civil and human rights hardly qualifies him to lecture the 77 senators and 185 House members who support the Jackson Amendment."[12]

Somewhat ironically Fulbright looked to the executive branch to counter congressional attitudes on the cold war and Middle East policy. Henry Kissinger, he believed, was his ace in the hole in his ongoing battle with Russophobes and Zionist maximalists, and consequently the chairman turned his full attention in August and September to securing the Harvard professor's confirmation as secretary of state.

The Kissinger–Rogers feud had continued unabated into the second Nixon administration. As the president put it to speechwriter William Safire, "It's really deep-seated. Henry thinks Bill isn't very deep, and Bill thinks Henry is power-crazy."[13] Kissinger had always wanted to be secretary of state, but Nixon would not make the move. He did not fully trust Kissinger; having him as national security adviser and Rogers as secretary of state allowed him some independence from, and gave him some leverage over, the ambitious academic. As his presidency disintegrated under the relentless blows of Watergate, however, Nixon became more and more psychologically dependent

12 "Sen. Jackson, National Jewish Leaders Reject Fulbright Israel, USSR Stands," *Detroit Jewish News,* July 20, 1973.

13 Quoted in Stephen E. Ambrose, *Nixon,* vol. II, *The Triumph of a Politician, 1962–1972* (New York, 1989), 509.

on Kissinger. In August Rogers resigned, and the president put forward his national security adviser's name.

By the time the SFRC opened hearings on Kissinger's nomination on September 7, investigative reporters had discovered that in May 1969, following William Beecher's page-one article in the *New York Times* accurately describing the secret B-52 bombings in Cambodia, the White House had ordered the FBI to tap the phones of seventeen staff members. The wiretaps had been instituted as part of an effort to plug leaks, and many of the victims worked for Kissinger. Clearly, he had participated in the decision to eavesdrop.[14] During a long lunch on July 30, Kissinger and Fulbright discussed the confirmation hearings and how best to handle the wiretap issue.[15] When Kissinger appeared before the SFRC on the seventh and Fulbright asked him about the wiretaps, the secretary of state–designate was prepared. His testimony implied that the idea had originated with Nixon and had had the full support of Attorney General Mitchell and J. Edgar Hoover; he had merely supplied the names of those with access to sensitive material.[16] At the committee's direction, Fulbright officially requested Attorney General Elliott Richardson to turn over copies of transcripts and other documents bearing on the decision to plant the bugs. Richardson refused, but agreed to allow two committee members – Sparkman and Case, as it turned out – to look at "summaries."[17]

The two senators were unable to uncover a "smoking gun," and the wiretap issue quickly faded into the background. Support for Kissinger's confirmation on the committee and in the Senate was wide and deep; it included Republican loyalists and Democratic liberals. After the SFRC voted 16 to 1 (McGovern dissented) to approve the nomination, the full Senate voted 78 to 7 on September 21 to confirm.[18] One of Kissinger's first acts as secretary was to have Fulbright to the State Department for lunch during which, as Fulbright subsequently told reporters, he promised continuous and thorough consultation with Congress.[19]

To constituents and friends who complained about his support of Kissinger, Fulbright responded that he was merely making the best of a bad situation. "So long as Nixon is in the White House," he wrote Harry Sions of Little, Brown, "do you really think we can get anything better? Compared to aides who appeared before the Ervin Committee, he is not so bad."[20] But, in fact, Fulbright was well satisfied by the ascension of Kissinger's star. There

14 Ibid., 448–9, and Seymour M. Hersh, *The Price of Power: Kissinger in the Nixon White House* (New York, 1983), 86–7.
15 Appointments calendar, July 30, 1973, Williams Papers.
16 "Excerpts from Kissinger's Testimony to Senators," *New York Times,* Sept. 8, 1973.
17 "Senators Ask to See Kissinger Tap File," *Washington Post,* Sept. 11, 1973.
18 "Kissinger Bid Advanced, 16–1," *Arkansas Gazette,* Sept. 19, 1973, and "Kissinger Wins OK," *Washington Star-News,* Sept. 21, 1973.
19 "Kissinger Seeking Views of Congress," *New York Times,* Sept. 28, 1973.
20 JWF to Harry Sions, Sept. 7, 1973, Series 48:4, Box 19:3, SPF.

were, he realized, important differences in their philosophies: Two weeks after Kissinger was nominated, both men spoke before a conference sponsored by the Center for the Study of Democratic Institutions. Fulbright declared that the pragmatic, balance-of-power approach utilized by the new secretary of state was "an improvement on the ideological crusade of the cold war," but he argued that there was a better way. Kissinger's system was too dependent on Kissinger. The national interest could best be served by stable institutions, not great men. "I remain, therefore, a Wilsonian," he told the conferees, "a seeker still of a world system of laws rather than of men, a believer still in the one great new idea of this century in the field of international relations, the idea of an international organization with permanent processes for the peaceful settlement of international disputes."[21] Fulbright may well have come full circle philosophically, but in the short run he was more than willing to support Kissingerian pragmatism, primarily because he believed the new secretary to be right on the issues and because he gave every evidence that he would consult with the SFRC and its chairman.[22]

Compared to détente, a balanced approach to the Arab–Israeli conflict, and improved congressional–executive relations, Kissinger's role in violating the constitutional rights of a few individuals paled in significance. One of the seventeen upon which the White House had spied was Richard Moose. In 1974 he and his wife, along with the Anthony Lakes, decided to file suit against Kissinger. When Moose went in to tell Fulbright of his intentions, the chairman blew up. "He didn't think it was a proper thing for a member of the Committee staff to do," Moose recalled. "He was very angry about it, and we had hard words." At one point Fulbright even decided to fire Moose if he persisted, and was restrained only after Javits and Symington intervened.[23]

Bermuda had for twenty-five years been one of Bill and Betty Fulbright's favorite vacation spots. They knew the island – its beaches, golf courses, and clubs – like an old friend. The semitropical setting, coupled with the English colonial flavor that still permeated the island's culture, made it irresistible to the former Rhodes scholar. The first week in September, before the Senate became overwhelmed with the press of business, the Fulbrights escaped Washington for a week at the Mid-Ocean Club.[24] As Bill and Betty vacationed, the Middle East pot prepared to boil over once again.

21 "Power Politics in Foreign Affairs," *Baltimore Sun,* Oct. 13, 1973.

22 In fact, fresh from a trip to Europe, Moose and Lowenstein reported to JWF in mid-October signs of "a new openness on the part of the Executive Branch people." Jim and Dick to JWF, Oct. 10, 1973, Series 48:1, Box 11:1, SPF.

23 Interview with Richard Moose, June 29, 1989, Washington, D.C.

24 Appointments calendar, Aug. 28–Sept. 5, 1973, Williams Papers.

By the fall of 1973 Anwar al-Sadat and other Arab leaders, convinced that they could gain nothing through peaceful diplomacy, decided to go to war. There was little or no chance the Egyptian, Syrian, and Jordanian armies could defeat Israel, they realized, but a resumption of hostilities would hopefully create sufficient havoc to force the great powers, especially the United States, to intervene and pressure Israel to compromise. In September Sadat announced that war was imminent, and both American and Israeli intelligence warned their governments that preparations were indeed underway. Nonetheless, the Arab armies were able to catch their opponents almost completely off guard.[25]

On October 6, 1973, the Jewish religious holiday of Yom Kippur and also a special day in the Muslim calendar, Egypt and Syria launched simultaneous attacks on Israeli forces in the Sinai and on the Golan Heights. Using top-of-the-line Russian missiles and other equipment, the attackers quickly overran front-line Israeli positions. Egyptian troops crossed the Suez Canal and dug in several miles beyond it.

The day following the outbreak of fighting, Fulbright appeared on *Face the Nation.* He called for the United Nations to intervene, militarily if necessary, to end the bloodshed and impose a peace settlement. "They should take action, they should meet the legitimate security requirements of Israel – and at the same time approach as closely as possible the principles of the resolution of '67," he told George Herman. Asked by Peter Lisagor if it would not be best if the United States and the Soviet Union simply agreed to stop supplying their client states in the Middle East, Fulbright assented but declared that that would never happen "because the Israelis control the policy in the Congress and the Senate."[26]

Reaction to Fulbright's remarks was intense. The office was flooded with calls and telegrams, some hailing the chairman as "truthful" and "courageous" and others denouncing him as "stupid" and "anti-Semitic." At a news conference in Little Rock, where he was meeting with his political advisers, Fulbright told reporters that he was "puzzled" as to why the American Jewish community was so upset about his proposals for an American guarantee of Israeli borders if that nation was willing to trade land for peace. They were, after all, in the "best interests of Israel."[27]

On October 10 the Soviets began replacing destroyed Arab armaments through an airlift and with accelerated surface shipments. American intelligence operatives reported to the White House that the new Soviet equipment

25 Leslie H. Gelb, "Why Did the Mideast Erupt Again? The Experts Offer Some Theories," *New York Times,* Oct. 9, 1973.

26 *Face the Nation,* Oct. 7, 1973, Series 48:15, Box 41:1, SPF.

27 "Fulbright Praised and Denounced for Remarks on Middle East War," *Arkansas Gazette,* Oct. 10, 1973.

sent Egypt included Scud surface-to-surface missiles, some of which were armed with tactical nuclear warheads.[28] Israel appealed frantically for more American arms to replace its losses. On October 12 Nixon ordered a massive airlift. Military planes flew directly to Israel to deliver tanks, ammunition, and planes. The equipment proved crucial to the Israeli counteroffensive launched on the fifteenth. Israeli troops drove into Syria, and a tank force crossed the Suez Canal and encircled an entire Egyptian army. By October 17 Israel appeared poised for another sweeping triumph.

On that same day in Kuwait, the Persian Gulf members of the Organization of Oil Exporting Countries (OPEC) met. They voted to raise the price for their petroleum by 400 percent; Arab delegates also voted to suspend oil shipments until the United Nations enforced Resolution 242. On the nineteenth, in response to the arms airlift and a request from Nixon to Congress for a $2.2 billion appropriation to pay for more jets for Israel, Saudi Arabia embargoed oil exports to the United States. Nevertheless, following a thirty-six-hour lobby phone blitz by the American Israel Public Affairs Committee, Congress passed the aid package.[29] Over the next few weeks gas prices rose dramatically throughout the Western world and Japan.

The effectiveness of the Arab oil boycott, together with mounting Egyptian and Syrian losses, forced the United States and Soviet Union into uneasy and temporary alliance. Moscow and Washington agreed to a cease-fire proposal, rushed it through the Security Council, and then pressured their respective client states into accepting it – or so they thought. After agreeing to a cease-fire on October 22, the Israelis fought on, widening their bridgehead in Egypt and improving their bargaining position for the forthcoming negotiations. On the twenty-fourth Brezhnev wrote Nixon proposing U.S.–Soviet intervention to impose a cease-fire. He warned that if the Israelis did not stop fighting at once and Washington procrastinated, the Soviet Union might have to act unilaterally.[30] Nixon and Kissinger responded by slowing arms shipments to Israel and at the same time placing American forces worldwide on nuclear alert. America, they hoped to indicate, was not going to tolerate Soviet intervention.

Although he perceived that the administration's views on the Middle East were essentially similar to his own, Fulbright was still apprehensive. He sensed that the administration was vulnerable to Jackson and his Russophobe supporters as well as to pro-Israeli sentiment. "I believe the President really supports the implementation of Resolution 242, but feels he must be cautious because of the enormous support in the Congress which had been generated by those primarily interested in supporting Israel," he wrote Samyr Souki,

28 Michael Getler, "A-Arms Believed In Egypt," *Washington Post,* Nov. 21, 1973.
29 "Fulbright and the Israeli Lobby," *Arkansas Democrat,* Oct. 26, 1973.
30 Drew Middleton, "Israelis Made Big Gains Between 2 Cease-Fires," *New York Times,* Oct. 25, 1973.

Beirut representative of the Middle East Business Services and Research Corp.[31] Although Kissinger kept him posted throughout the October crisis, including the decision to order a nuclear alert, Fulbright told reporters on the twenty-sixth that he doubted that the alert was justified. Brezhnev's note may have been couched in urgent terms, he said, "but from what I know it was not threatening." The crisis atmosphere may have been promoted by the Pentagon, he speculated, to justify increases in the military budget.[32]

Despite his potshots at the administration, Fulbright acted as a go-between for Kissinger and Anatoly Dobrynin throughout the last ten days of October, insisting to the Soviet ambassador that the United States was committed to a cease-fire, and downplaying the nuclear alert.[33] He repeatedly assured Dobrynin that Kissinger had not been part of an Israeli conspiracy to dupe Moscow and its Arab neighbors. When the Security Council voted to send a multinational peacekeeping force to the Middle East war zone, and the United States voted in the United Nations for a return to the October 22 truce lines, tensions eased.

Throughout the fall and winter of 1973, Fulbright and Kissinger continued to work hand in hand to defuse the Middle East situation and to hammer out a lasting peace, a peace that they believed to be absolutely crucial to the success of détente. As negotiations – indirect, of course – among the Israelis, Egyptians, and Syrians continued in Geneva, the Arabs kept the oil spigot turned off. In November, Nixon imposed emergency rationing, and certain congresspeople began to talk of the possibility of seizing the petroleum fields of the Middle East, by force if necessary. At the same time the administration, in response to the Israeli lobby and its chief representatives in Congress, threw its support behind a $2.2 billion special arms aid bill for Israel. Moreover, as Fulbright had predicted, the Pentagon took advantage of the Middle East crisis to ask for a $3.5 billion increase in its budget.[34] The Arkansan, again with wonderful irony, castigated the legislative branch for intervening in the policymaking process and handcuffing the nation's duly appointed diplomats. "Unfortunately, the Congress does not give Dr. Kissinger sufficient support, or, to put it another way, the Congress encourages the Israeli government to believe that there is no limit to our generosity, and that, therefore, there is no real, serious pressure upon the Israelis to give up any of their conquered lands," he wrote Thomas Stauffer of Harvard's Center for Middle Eastern Studies.[35]

31 JWF to Souki, Dec. 20, 1973, Series 48:15, Box 41:2, SPF.
32 "Kissinger Indignant at Hints Alert Used as 'Diversion,'" *Arkansas Gazette,* Oct. 26, 1973.
33 Appointments calendar, Oct. 25 and 31, 1973, Williams Papers, and "Report: Fulbright Cooled Off Soviets," *Fort Smith Southwest Times Record,* Oct. 28, 1973.
34 *Congressional Record,* Senate, Nov. 9, 1973, 20136.
35 JWF to Stauffer, Nov. 16, 1973, Series 48:15, Box 41:1, SPF.

If Kissinger was working both sides of the street and secretly catering to Jackson and the Israeli lobby, there is no evidence of it. When Jackson criticized Kissinger publicly over détente and his Middle East policy, the secretary of state cut off all contact with the Washington senator and flaunted his close ties to Fulbright. Jackson fumed to his friends that the administration was guilty of monstrous ingratitude; how could it abandon one of its staunchest supporters over Vietnam in favor of one of its bitterest critics?[36]

Privately and publicly Fulbright appealed to the oil-rich Arab states to end restrictions on production. "It is my belief that a significant relaxation in the present policies of the Arab States to restrict oil and gas exports would serve the long range interests of the Arab states, the world at large, and the interests of my own country," he wrote King Faisal in mid-November.[37] Using an American businessman named John McMullen as an intermediary, both Faisal and Sadat pleaded with Fulbright to come to the Middle East and mediate the dispute. The Saudi monarch told Fulbright that he realized the embargo was hurting everybody, including the Arabs.[38] Fulbright chose not go, but he did send Seth Tillman, who visited Cairo, Riyadh, Dhahran, Tel Aviv, and Beirut, talking with top government officials in each state.[39] All he needed to turn on the oil was an excuse, some small sign from the United States, Faisal advised Fulbright through Tillman. On December 12 Fulbright met with the oil ministers of Saudi Arabia and Algeria in Washington. "We are prepared to guarantee in a treaty the borders of Israel," they told him. "We would give an international guarantee if that were necessary."[40]

Fulbright responded to these appeals by mounting an offensive against the administration's $2.2 billion emergency military aid bill for Israel and reviving the peace plan he had proposed in 1970. During the last six weeks of 1973 the chairman of the Foreign Relations Committee repeatedly urged the United States, working through the United Nations, to sign a treaty guaranteeing Israel's 1967 boundaries.[41] From Beijing, where he was trying to shore up the new relationship with China, Kissinger endorsed the Fulbright plan;[42] but the political winds were set firmly against a U.S.-guaranteed land-

36 Rowland Evans and Robert Novak, "Allocating Oil 'the Military Way,'" *Washington Post,* Nov. 25, 1973.

37 Marcy to JWF, Nov. 15, 1973, Box 11, Folder Oct.–Dec., Marcy Papers.

38 JWF, Notes on telephone conversation with John J. McMullen, Dec. 30, 1973, Series 48:15, Box 41:2, SPF.

39 Tillman schedule, Nov. 21, 1973, Series 48:3, Box 18:3, SPF.

40 Informal Notes on Senator Fulbright Luncheon for Ministers Yamani and Abdesselam, Dec. 12, 1973, Box 11, Folder Sept.–Dec., Marcy Papers.

41 His new, revised plan would put U.N. peacekeeping forces in both the Sinai and Golan Heights, include a U.S. guarantee to protect Israel from aggression, and mandate direct negotiations on the issues of Palestinian repatriation and the future of Jerusalem. *Congressional Record,* Dec. 11, 1973, 22430.

42 "Fulbright Says Kissinger Wants Israelis to Give Up Some of Territory," *Arkansas Gazette,* Nov. 17, 1973.

for-peace deal. On the one hand, the American people were in no mood to become involved in another Vietnam-type conflict, and on the other they sympathized intensely with the Israelis in their struggle with the Arabs. From mid-October through mid-December, the percentage of Americans openly supporting the Israelis increased from 47 to 54 percent, whereas pro-Arab sentiment hovered around 7 percent.[43] A "balanced" Middle East policy, Fulbright was forced to conclude, was a goal as difficult to realize as disengagement from Vietnam. On December 21 the Senate passed the emergency authorization bill for Israel by a vote of 66 to 9.[44]

On the last day of 1973 Carl H. Marcy retired as chief of staff of the Senate Foreign Relations Committee. Although he was only sixty, Marcy had been with the SFRC since 1950 and had served as its staff director for eighteen years. He was tired of "playing amateur psychiatrist," as he told Pat Holt, who would succeed him. The terrible conflict in Vietnam was coming to a close, and the War Powers Act, together with similar legislation, had restored a semblance of balance between the executive and legislative branches in the field of foreign policy. It was time for him to devote his energies to writing and sailing. In addition, he sensed that Fulbright's attention was beginning to wander, that the monumental will that Marcy had so counted on was beginning to diminish. The Oregonian departed with little fanfare. There was a staff party with the Fulbrights and other committee members. The more knowledgeable members of the press corps recognized that his retirement marked the end of an era. He was, Smith Hempstone wrote in the *Washington Star-News,* one of the most powerful men in Washington – "Fulbright's Kissinger" he called him.[45] Unlike Kissinger, however, the chief of staff's power had stemmed in no small part from his anonymity. Having guarded it so carefully for so many years, Marcy found it impossible to discard in the end.

43 "Americans Support Israelis," *Washington Post,* Dec. 23, 1973.
44 Richard L. Madden, "Congress Passes Aid and Job Bills," *New York Times,* Dec. 21, 1973.
45 Smith Hempstone, "Fulbright's Kissinger," *Washington Star-News,* Dec. 28, 1973.

# 38

# *Broken fences*

Wrote Fulbright to John McMullen on the last day of 1973:

> I would like very much to go to the Middle East, but as I am a candidate for reelection next year, it is not easy for me to take such a trip until after the election. It is possible that I may have very serious opposition, to a great extent growing out of my views on the Middle East for, as you know, they are misunderstood by many of the people devoted to the cause of the present Israeli government.[1]

A year earlier, in December 1972, Fulbright's administrative assistant, political chief of staff, and fund-raiser par excellence, Lee Williams, had approached him about a decision on the 1974 race. "The primary subject of conversation among your constituents, who have visited and/or called," he had told his boss, "has been politics and specifically your intentions about running for re-election." There was something odd about this early and unsolicited interest, Williams had observed. "The feeling is almost unanimous among these people that Bumpers or his group are designedly encouraging this type of speculation in the hope that it will encourage you to think about not running."[2] Since Homer Adkins in 1944, J. William Fulbright had not faced a serious challenge for his Senate seat. Jim Johnson had pressed the incumbent in 1968, but Fulbright had still won without a runoff. Although Williams could not imagine that Bumpers would actually have the temerity to run against someone who had done so much for him, the administrative assistant knew that all things were possible in politics. His concern was justified.

In December 1969, Fulbright had received a letter from Dale Leon Bumpers, an obscure young lawyer from Charleston, Arkansas, who had said he was considering challenging Winthrop Rockefeller for the governorship.[3] Fulbright had welcomed him to the world of Arkansas politics, but withheld promises of support until the newcomer could prove his mettle. Orval Faubus was running again, and two more years of Rockefeller would be preferable to

1 JWF to Dr. John J. McMullen, Dec. 31, 1973, Series 48:15, Box 41:2, SPF.
2 Williams to JWF, Dec. 13, 1972, Williams Papers.
3 Quoted in Hal T. Smith, "J. William Fulbright and the Arkansas 1974 Senatorial Election," *Arkansas Historical Quarterly,* 44 (2), 107.

the reelection of a man who had become a universal symbol of Arkansas's shame.

Arkansas Democrats, however, especially black Democrats, had been waiting for an acceptable alternative to both Orval Faubus and Jim Johnson, and Bumpers had proved to be that person. Handsome, unassuming, a charismatic speaker, the Charleston lawyer was a tenacious and effective campaigner. To the astonishment of the state's political pundits, Bumpers had swamped Faubus in a Democratic primary runoff, winning 58 percent of the vote.[4] At the height of the Bumpers–Faubus campaign, Fulbright's political staff, especially Lee Williams, had begun urging the senator to throw his weight behind the newcomer. So had James O. Powell, editorial page editor of the *Arkansas Gazette,* and the paper's owner, Hugh Patterson. Fulbright had quickly come around, and Faubus would later conclude that this support had been crucial to his defeat.[5]

During the general election campaign that had ensued, two of Fulbright's Arkansas staffers, Jim McDougal and Ben Grinage, had gone to work for Bumpers on a full-time basis.[6] Fulbright had campaigned actively for Bumpers, telling reporters that the Democratic candidate would serve with "integrity and sobriety," a not-so-veiled reference to Rockefeller's notorious drinking habits.[7] Bumpers's surprising victory in the Democratic primary had thrown the Rockefeller camp into momentary confusion; they had been gearing up for Faubus but now had to face an opponent about whom they knew virtually nothing. Rockefeller had previously depended heavily on family money – by the time he left office, the New Yorker had "invested" some $35 million in the state – on Democrats for Rockefeller, and on the anti-Faubus vote, particularly among blacks. Although Arkansas Republicans tried to portray Bumpers as a vacuous, pleasant nonentity, nothing but "a smile, a shoeshine, and a speech," it was to no avail.[8] Bumpers's progressive program had left Rockefeller with little else but his money upon which to run. In November the challenger crushed Rockefeller, and Arkansas had become once again a predominantly Democratic state.[9]

Between 1969 and 1972, despite the winding down of the Vietnam War – or perhaps as a result of it – J. William Fulbright's prestige had clearly slipped in Arkansas. Popular perception of the junior senator as an Oxford-educated snob who rarely visited his home state, and who did so only grudg-

4 "Bumpers Swamps Faubus to Win Party Nomination," *Northwest Arkansas Times,* Sept. 9, 1970.
5 "Jobless Faubus Going Back to Ozarks," *Arkansas Democrat,* Sept. 10, 1970.
6 "2 Fulbright Staff Members at Work for Dale Bumpers," *Memphis Commercial Appeal,* Sept. 3, 1970.
7 "Democrats Ask Carruth to Rejoin Party," *Northwest Arkansas Times,* Oct. 30, 1970.
8 Quoted in Smith, "Fulbright and the 1974 Election," 108.
9 "Arkansas Democrat Leads Rockefeller," *New York Times,* Nov. 3, 1970.

ingly, had become widespread. In February 1970 an overflow crowd had attended the Arkansas Gridiron Club's annual political celebrity roast in the Old West Dinner Theater in Little Rock. In what had become an annual rite, the *Arkansas Democrat*'s Jon Kennedy impersonated Fulbright, dressing first in three-piece suit and singing "I am the Senate's big cheese if you please . . . I am the Senate's big cheese if you DON'T please," and then at election time changing into a checkered shirt and singing, "I'm just plain Bill, on Capitol Hill."[10] If even Arkansas's intelligentsia viewed Fulbright as an elitist, what could the forgotten man think? "I live in poverty Sir, with a wife and two children on $80 a week," a blue-collar constituent had written. "I only wish that I had the education to be your public relations man." If I were you, he had advised, "I would go on state wide TV. and talk to the people in such a way that every one could understand."[11]

In one sense, charges that Fulbright had neglected the state were unfair. He and his staff had continued to pay close attention to its vested interests. The junior senator had campaigned against a cut in the oil and gas depletion allowance, which had further endeared him to Witt Stephens and Charles Murphy.[12] His stance on the Middle East crisis, and particularly his efforts to persuade the Arabs to end their boycott, had pleased industrialists and agribusinessmen, all of whom had been grievously damaged by the energy crisis.[13] He had worked diligently and successfully to have Congress designate the Buffalo River as a national river, an achievement that had been important to the state's burgeoning tourist industry and to its small but active environmentalist community.[14] When Arkansas's massive poultry industry, spearheaded by Tyson Foods, had suffered a 30 percent increase in cost of production due to grain price increases, he had lobbied Secretary of Agriculture Earl Butz to increase price supports for cereals.[15] In an effort to gain the support of labor and blacks, Fulbright voted in 1973 for substantial increases in the minimum wage[16] and cosponsored a bill adding $44.5 million to the Neighborhood Youth Corps Project. The mission of the Youth Corps was to

10 "Spoofing Politics," *Arkansas Democrat,* Feb. 17, 1970. Kennedy subsequently wrote a column in which he declared that while Fulbright did not bear fools easily, he was warm and unpretentious in conversation, with a good sense of humor. Jon Kennedy, "Mimicking Once Again Our Own 'Oxford Snob,'" *Arkansas Democrat,* June 13, 1973.

11 Coleman Reynolds to JWF, July 6, 1970, Series 48:18, Box 61:3, SPF.

12 JWF to W. R. Stephens, Feb. 1, 1971, Series 48:18, Box 63:3, SPF.

13 John Bennett, "Bumpers–Fulbright Race Would Have Many Angles," *Memphis Commercial Appeal,* Dec. 23, 1973.

14 "Senate Approves Bill to Save Buffalo as Free-Flowing River," *Arkansas Democrat,* May 22, 1971.

15 "Sen. Fulbright Seeks Help for Broiler Industry," *Marion County News,* Dec. 21, 1972.

16 "Fulbright Votes for Wage Hike," *Northwest Arkansas Times,* Aug. 4, 1973.

provide transitional jobs for unemployed and underemployed Americans, a substantial number of whom lived in the Arkansas Delta.[17]

In fact, however, Fulbright was sick of cultivating constituents and extremely reluctant to return to the state. It was difficult for him to leave the stimulating world of embassy receptions, Smithsonian dinners, and tête-à-têtes with Henry Kissinger. He hated to be bored, and campaigning bored him. At the end of 1973 the chairman of the SFRC and originator of the Fulbright exchange program was sixty-eight years old and one of the most famous people in the world. It was not the prospect of visiting Delight and Smackover that so much discouraged him as it was having to sell himself all over again. His tolerance for the mild form of hypocrisy that all politics requires was at an all-time low. When Jim McDougal had written him in 1970 expressing concern at rumors of widespread disaffection and asking permission to conduct a poll, Fulbright had bristled:

> As you well know, during the early days of his term, a Senator is expected to be a statesman and is not expected to court the favor of his constituents with the same determination that he does during the last year of his term, so I am fully prepared to see my rating go down while I am trying to bring the war to a close.[18]

Fulbright's inattentiveness was just one of a number of factors contributing to his negative image with a growing number of Arkansans. Most would admit that the United States should never have gotten involved in the Vietnam War in the first place and that Fulbright had been right; but Arkansans were no less pleased to be reminded of the nation's mistakes and shortcomings than other Americans, and for many Fulbright was a living, breathing rebuke. Sid McMath, still popular and frequently mentioned as a possible challenger in 1974, repeatedly and pointedly criticized Fulbright's position on the war and on defense. Although the radical right was not as strong as it had been in 1952 or 1962, it was still active in Arkansas, and Fulbright continued to be one of its main targets. Citizens in northwest, south, and southeast Arkansas still read and were influenced by the ultraconservative *Tulsa World, Dallas Morning News,* and *Shreveport Times.* Thousands of Arkansans received *Life-Line,* the H. L. Hunt–subsidized Birchite bulletin; a September 1973 issue had accused Fulbright of having consorted with known communists and having openly aided Ho Chi Minh.[19] In brief, as much as a third of Arkansas's voting population was angry with Fulbright over Vietnam and intended to vote against him if it got a chance.

More significant as a political negative than Vietnam was the Middle East. Fulbright's attacks on the Jackson amendment and the "Zionist lobby," his

17 "Funds South by Fulbright for NYC Jobs," *Arkansas Gazette,* May 31, 1973.
18 JWF to McDougal, Mar. 14, 1970, Series 3:1, Box 3:2, SPF.
19 Melvin Munn, Life-Line Freedom Talk, Sept. 29, 1973, No. 72.

plan for an imposed peace based on Resolution 242, and his fraternization with prominent Arabs had the Arkansas and American Jewish communities up in arms. Dr. Elijah Palnick, Rabbi of Temple B'nai Israel in Little Rock, had denounced him for reviving "the anti-Semitic canards and propaganda of Joseph Goebbels or the Klan at its worst."[20] Paul Greenberg, in the wake of the Yom Kippur War, had run a series of editorials entitled "In Thrall to Fulbright," with subtitles such as "The Piety of J. William" and "Just Wild about Nikita." These had painted Fulbright as an appeaser and a racist, recalled his signing of the Southern Manifesto, and compared him none too subtly to America's most famous anti-Semite, Gerald L. K. Smith.[21]

If antipathy toward Fulbright's Middle East position had been limited to the tiny Jewish community in Arkansas, it would have been insignificant; but given the Vietnam debacle versus Israeli successes in the Yom Kippur War, a large number of gentiles continued to identify with Israel. In addition, in a state where Christian fundamentalism was especially strong, a large number of Protestants identified with the Israelis as the people of the Old Testament whose well-being it was incumbent upon them to look after. In November 1973 the Baptist Missionary Association of Arkansas, representing nearly three hundred congregations, had passed a resolution commending "our government's support of the nation of Israel in the current Middle East conflict."[22] In the aftermath of Vietnam, the fundamentalist aversion to Jews as "the killers of Jesus" seemed indeed to have abated.

Nor did the political scandals of the Nixon administration do the incumbent any good. Although Fulbright had not taken a leading role in the Watergate proceedings, he had denounced the break-in in no uncertain terms. In June 1973 he had told the Saline County Young Democrats' picnic that Nixon and Agnew should resign if they could not restore confidence in the government.[23] In October he had cosponsored the bill creating the office of special prosecutor.[24] Although polls taken in the fall had indicated that a majority of Arkansans favored impeachment of the president, a significant number did not; several "fairness" rallies were held in the predominantly Republican northwest part of the state.[25] Most significantly, however, Watergate had produced an irrational reaction against Congress and all political incumbents. A January 1974 *Washington Post* poll would show that only 21 percent of

20 Palnick to JWF, Oct. 8, 1973, Series 48:15, Box 41:1, SPF.

21 Paul Greenberg, "The Piety of J. William," *Pine Bluff Commercial,* Jan. 28, 1972; idem, "Just Wild about Nikita," *Pine Bluff Commercial,* Feb. 2, 1972; and idem, "Senator Fulbright's Remarks," *Pine Bluff Commercial,* Oct. 23, 1973.

22 Leon Carmichael to JWF, Nov. 7, 1973, Series 48:15, Box 40:1, SPF.

23 "Fulbright Says Restore Confidence or Resign," *Benton Courier,* June 7, 1973.

24 "Fulbright: Senate Plan Is Preferable," *Arkansas Democrat,* Oct. 28, 1973.

25 "Rally Pledges Support," *Arkansas Democrat,* Dec. 9, 1973; "Most Support Ouster," *Fort Smith Southwest Times Record,* Oct. 24, 1973; and Moose to Williams, Feb. 5, 1974, Williams Papers.

Americans felt Congress was doing a good job – a lower approval rating than Nixon was to receive on the eve of his departure from office.[26]

Lee Williams was aware of these and other negative factors, but the political outlook looked no bleaker than it had in 1962 when the state had seemed in thrall to the radical right and Orval Faubus had been taking soundings, or in 1968 with the Vietnam War at its height. "Your backers in the state believe if you do make an early decision to run and will try to spend all the spare time you can covering the state in the coming year," he had told his boss in late 1972, "you can essentially win re-election in 1973 instead of 1974."[27]

Fulbright initially refused to respond to these and other prods. To Williams and press secretary Hoyt Purvis's frustration, he would not even discuss his political future. At times, they believed he had decided not to run. Betty had suffered a second, more serious heart attack in 1972. Eight years of continual combat against the war in Vietnam, the Pentagon, and the imperial presidency had worn Fulbright out. Retirement was tempting; it would allow him to do what he claimed he liked to do best – read and converse. Almost on a weekly basis, Williams and Purvis would ask permission to begin raising money and commission polls in Arkansas; each time Fulbright said no. In March 1973 the two aides had attended a series of seminars conducted by the Senatorial Campaign Committee on the new politics. They had heard what they already knew to be true: that the old days of hands-on campaigning and reliance on a few deep pockets were over. In this new era of mass culture, successful candidates would have to emphasize television, hire political consultants, commission research, and utilize sophisticated computerized fund-raising techniques.[28] Clearly, time was of the essence. With some trepidation, they had arranged a dinner at Williams's house one evening in late March. The only participants would be the senator, Betty, the Williamses, and the Purvises.

One of the reasons Lee Williams was so valuable to Fulbright was that he was willing to talk to his boss about things he did not want to talk about and then weather the mild temper tantrums that ensued. He had come to learn that Fulbright, after expressing his frustration, nearly always listened to him. This was to be the case again. Following drinks, dinner, and the usual state-of-the-world discussion, the administrative assistant had gotten down to business. He did not want to be presumptuous, he had said, but Fulbright ought to run again. At the same time détente was gaining a full head of steam, Richard Nixon's presidency was beginning to unravel in a serious way. The country needed him and Kissinger to maintain some continuity in foreign policy, Williams had argued. There were as yet no serious contenders in the field,

26 "Close Look Reveals Why Congress Is Held in Low Esteem," *Washington Post,* Mar. 3, 1974.
27 Williams to JWF, Dec. 13, 1972, Williams Papers.
28 Williams to JWF, Apr. 16, 1973, Williams Papers.

and polls showed Fulbright's job approval rating to be 65 percent positive to 35 percent negative.[29] "You can win," he had told Fulbright, but emphasized that "you have to commit fully and completely." That meant going back to Arkansas and making repeated high-visibility appearances. It meant "turning him and Hoyt loose" to raise money, hire the necessary professionals, and lay the groundwork. After some discussion, Fulbright and his wife had given the green light.[30]

Although Fulbright had returned to Arkansas that March and again twice in the summer, he continually resisted Williams and Purvis's advice to be more image conscious. The new politics distressed him. "I don't want you selling me like a bar of soap," he had told Purvis.[31] It was going to be a long campaign, his aides had concluded.

In late August 1973, Fulbright had flown back to Arkansas to make an official announcement that he was going to run for a sixth term. Attending the annual fish fry at the John Gammon farm northeast of Marion, he'd told some two hundred onlookers that the only answer to the rampant inflation gripping the country was to slash the Pentagon budget. Gammon was a prosperous black farmer long prominent in state politics.[32] The spectacle of Fulbright lecturing the gathering – mostly black and all farmers, concerned primarily with the cost of feed and the state of race relations – on the evils of militarism and the need to preserve constitutional government had sent chills up the spines of the senator's entourage.[33]

Following Fulbright's October appearance on *Face the Nation* – in which he had declared, among other things, that Congress was completely dominated by the Zionist lobby – American Jewish leaders had begun actively soliciting candidates, Democratic or Republican, to oppose their nemesis in the 1974 election. They had approached former marine and Vietnam hawk Sid McMath, and Republicans Charles Bernard and John Paul Hammerschmidt, Arkansas's only GOP congressman. Another prospective challenger was former congressman David Pryor, who had narrowly lost to John McClellan in a runoff in 1972. He was young, popular, and an effective campaigner; but in deference to the support he had received from Fulbright, Pryor had ruled himself out.[34] As a result, American Zionists had pinned their hopes on Dale Bumpers.[35]

29 Mark Shields to Tony Isidore, John Marttila, et al., undated, Williams Papers.
30 Interview with Hoyt Purvis, Jan. 19, 1990, Fayetteville, Ark.
31 Ibid.
32 "Fulbright Eats Fried Fish, Attacks Inflation in U.S.," *Memphis Press Scimitar,* Aug. 20, 1973.
33 UPI 54, Aug. 25, 1973, Series 78:9, Box 71:1, SPF.
34 "Pryor Closes His Office, Rules Out a Race for Senator 'At This Time,'" *Arkansas Gazette,* Nov. 28, 1972.
35 "Jewish Leaders Seek '74 Opponents for Fulbright," *Arkansas Democrat,* Oct. 19, 1973.

The man who had come out of nowhere to beat Orval Faubus had proved to be a shrewd, effective administrator and, more important, had gotten on well with the Arkansas General Assembly. In 1971, a legislature tired of wrangling with Rockefeller had adopted under Bumpers most of the Rockefeller program, including a more progressive income tax. The governor had implemented new personnel policies making it easier for blacks to qualify for state jobs. Good fortune also appeared in the form of fiscal bounty: In 1970–1 total state revenues had been $565 million; in 1974 revenues had reached that level by mid-March.[36] Opinion polls taken in late 1973 showed that Bumpers had an incredible 91 percent job-approval rating with voters.[37]

As early as March 1972, Arkansas pollster and political scientist Jim Ranchino had expressed the opinion that Bumpers would challenge Fulbright. He reiterated that prediction a year-and-a half later. "Bumpers has nowhere else to go, and he is a politician – what do you expect of him!" he told the *Gazette*.[38] In 1973 the Bumpers organization, headed by public relations expert DeLoss Walker and Archie Schaffer, Bumpers's nephew, commissioned a poll. "We found not so much that I was very popular but that Senator Fulbright was very weak," Bumpers later remembered. "We discussed this among the inner sanctum people. We said Senator Fulbright is going to get beat. He would get beat by Sid McMath, who had not been in politics for years, in the second Congressional district."[39] Members of Bumpers's staff, especially Walker, urged him to go for it. So did other state officials and political figures, many of whom wanted to kick him upstairs: Bumpers had been elected as something of an independent, and much of the patronage he distributed went to those outside the Democratic establishment.[40]

Although the governor remained noncommittal, by mid-January 1974 speculation was rampant that he would indeed challenge Fulbright. At a news conference he specifically disagreed with the junior senator on a number of issues, most notably aid to Israel.[41] On January 22 Carl Whillock, a state Democratic activist, called Lee Williams and warned that the rumors were serious.[42] One of the principal factors constraining Bumpers was money. Fulbright seemed still to have his hand in all of the deep pockets – Darby,

36 "Fulbright Looks Down His Nose at a Charging White Horse," *Arkansas Democrat*, Mar. 17, 1974.

37 Shields to Isidore et al., undated, Williams Papers.

38 Jim Ranchino to Editor, *Arkansas Gazette*, Sept. 8, 1972.

39 Interview with Dale Bumpers, Apr. 19, 1992, Fayetteville, Ark.

40 Ernest Dumas, "That Big Decision by Dale Bumpers," *Arkansas Gazette*, Oct. 21, 1973.

41 "Governor Bumpers to Oppose Fulbright? New Speculation Says He Will," *Benton County Democrat*, Jan. 9, 1974, and Paul Greenberg, "Seeing Through the Fog," *Pine Bluff Commercial*, Jan. 13, 1974.

42 Notes on telephone conversation with Carl Whillock, Jan. 22, 1974, Williams Papers.

Pickens, Stephens. Indeed, it was that consideration that kept Sid McMath out of the race.[43] Somewhat surprisingly, it was McMath who offered to remedy the situation if Bumpers, a fellow ex-marine, would challenge Fulbright. In mid-January McMath journeyed to New York and talked to several prominent Zionists about funds for a campaign against their bête noire.[44]

In February, as rumors continued to fly, members of Fulbright's and Bumpers's entourages met at the Sam Peck Hotel in Little Rock for a "casual" get-together.[45] Williams urged Archie Schaffer and Brad Jesson, head of the state Democratic Party, to persuade the governor not to run. According to the Fulbright people, they were assured then, and continued to be assured, that Bumpers would not challenge their boss.

On March 11 Bumpers met reporters and a hundred would-be supporters in the conference room in the Capitol. According to the governor, he walked into the anticipation-filled room with two statements, one saying he would run and the other saying he would not. With his wife, Betty, seated a few feet from him, Bumpers declared that his hat was in the ring. After a loud whoop from the audience and a standing ovation, the governor was asked how his views differed from those of Fulbright. He replied enigmatically: "I think that's really a decision for the people to make. I've agreed with Sen. Fulbright more than I've disagreed with him."[46]

In reality the decision to challenge Fulbright in 1974 was not all that difficult for Bumpers to make. "Frankly I was not going to run for a third term," he later remembered. "That governor's office is a boneyard. It was a dead-end street." He had entered politics because he was bored with being a small-town lawyer; but his objective had always been Washington and not Little Rock. "As a matter of fact I always wanted to go to Congress; I never wanted to be governor," he recalled. Fulbright was ripe for the picking, and if he did not do it someone else would. "In this business being at the right place at the right time is everything."[47]

The people around Fulbright – Williams, Purvis, Parker Westbrook – were angry and distraught at Bumpers's decision. They felt betrayed and said so. There was nothing to do, however, but take up the cudgels. It was clear to all that it was going to be an uphill fight, the first the senator had had to wage since 1944.

43 He had told a reporter that he would have liked to challenge Fulbright, but the "important money people" would not consider anyone else. Quoted in Smith, "Fulbright and the 1974 Election," 109.

44 "McMath Denies Talking about Jewish Funding for Bumpers," *Jonesboro Sun*, Jan. 28, 1974.

45 "Bumpers–Fulbright Collision Might Ruin Some Beautiful Friendships," *Memphis Commercial Appeal*, Feb. 20, 1974.

46 "Bumpers Will Challenge Fulbright for U.S. Senate," *Arkansas Gazette*, Mar. 11, 1974.

47 Bumpers interview.

In January, Fulbright had named John Elrod to be his campaign manager. Elrod, a Rison lawyer and experienced political operator, had managed John McClellan's narrow, come-from-behind victory over David Pryor in 1972. Williams and company must have thought him to be the perfect ringmaster for a campaign pitting a hoary incumbent against a fresh-faced, appealing newcomer.[48] Unfortunately for the Fulbright campaign, Elrod fell ill soon after Bumpers announced, forcing the senator and his aides to cast about for a last-minute replacement. They chose James B. Blair, chief counsel for Tyson Foods, a young lawyer with a reputation as a courtroom wizard. A former child preacher, Blair had graduated from law school at twenty-one, entered private practice, and launched into a virtually unbroken string of legal triumphs. By 1974 he was making a fortune defending the colorful Don Tyson from corporate raiders and federal regulators. Like most lawyers, Blair had long been active in state politics and had established himself as a leader of the liberal wing of the Democratic Party. He had money, he had influence, but he was untested. Some said he was brash, intemperate, and suffered frequent lapses of judgment; but Williams and Fulbright decided to take a chance.

"I offer the carefully considered judgment that you face almost certain defeat in the May 28 primary," Steve Thomas reported to Fulbright on March 15. Thomas was then employed full-time by the Council for a Livable World, a nonprofit, Washington-based organization dedicated to advancing liberal causes and electing liberal candidates, to assess the prospects and conduct of Senate elections. The only way to salvage the situation, if it was salvageable, he advised the incumbent, was to abandon traditional campaigning techniques and concentrate on "sophisticated communications through the mass media." To this end he recommended hiring John Martilla and Associates of Boston, a professional political consulting firm. Martilla had been responsible for at least three come-from-behind Democratic congressional victories in 1972.[49] Fulbright and Williams not only hired Martilla but brought in Mark Shields, a political consultant whom Theodore White, in his *Making of the President, 1972,* had rated one of the two best in the country.[50] For the rest of the campaign, it was Shields who largely called the shots.

"We must face the hard truths of the survey research; Dale Bumpers is a more likable, personable, and winning public figure than Bill Fulbright," Shields told Blair, Williams, Purvis, Martilla, and the rest of the Fulbright team as soon as he arrived in Little Rock. "To try and compete with Bumpers on this turf would, I believe, be sheer folly and lead to certain defeat on May 28th." Bumpers would try to run a soft, nonideological campaign stressing

48 "Fulbright Opens Last Campaign," *Malvern Daily Record,* Jan. 3, 1974, and "Going Places," *Blytheville Courier,* Jan. 18, 1974.

49 Thomas to JWF, Mar. 15, 1974, Williams Papers.

50 "Fulbright Hires Campaign Advisor," *Northwest Arkansas Times,* Apr. 17, 1974.

the need for a change and a better tomorrow, he predicted. To be successful Fulbright would have to ensure that the campaign would focus on issues rather than personalities. He should run as THE SENATOR and stress how Arkansas had benefited from his seniority. As usual, the incumbent must emphasize his political independence: "Nobody owns Bill Fulbright. Nobody delivers Bill Fulbright."[51]

Although conservative by many standards, Fulbright had been able to run as a liberal in Arkansas; and, if anything, he had become more liberal during his last term. The *New Republic* awarded him favorable ratings in all categories except gun control, urban mass transit, and business regulation. Despite the fact that he continued to score poorly with labor, the Americans for Democratic Action had rated Fulbright the most liberal member of the Arkansas delegation, with a score of 55.[52] In addition, on ten selected issues involving medical care and Social Security, the National Council of Senior Citizens had given Fulbright a 78 percent score, the highest in the state's delegation.[53] Nevertheless, Bumpers's entry into the race forced Fulbright to run as a conservative.

In fact, Bumpers's liberalism enabled several important constituencies to vote their prejudices rather than their interests. Fulbright's voting record on issues important to the elderly was indeed strong, and Arkansas boasted the second highest median age of the voting population in the nation;[54] but with Bumpers committed to the same level of support on aging issues as Fulbright, the state's gray voters could vent their feelings over Vietnam and their general resentment at the political establishment. Eighteen percent of the voting population in Arkansas was black, and most lived in an arc running from northeast to east and across the south. In 1954 there had been fewer than fifty thousand registered black voters in the state, and they for the most part had been controlled by the landed gentry, whose members had been deeply committed to Fulbright. By 1975 approximately a hundred and twenty-five thousand would be registered, with the majority independent. The specter of Jim Johnson had driven African Americans into Fulbright's arms in 1968, but in 1974 they could afford to voice their anger over the junior senator's signing of the Southern Manifesto and his "no" vote on a variety of other civil rights bills.[55] Shields had targeted labor as a crucial battleground, but the continuing support of the AFL–CIO's J. Bill Becker notwithstanding, the rank and file could

51 Mark Shields to Tony Isidore et al., undated, Williams Papers.

52 "Rating the 92nd Congress," *New Republic,* Oct. 28, 1972; "Pryor Rated 100 by Labor; McClellan Zero," *Arkansas Gazette,* Dec. 13, 1972; and "Fulbright, Thornton 'Liberal,'" *Jonesboro Sun,* Jan. 22, 1974.

53 "Retired Give Fulbright Best Rating," *Arkansas Gazette,* Jan. 30, 1974.

54 Shields to Isidore et al., undated, Williams Papers.

55 "Will McClellan Face Formidable Opposition in 1972 and Is He Vulnerable?," undated, Williams Papers.

not forget Fulbright's consistent antilabor record during his first twenty-five years in office.

Driven to the political right, Fulbright had no choice but to cast down his bucket. Three days after Bumpers announced, the incumbent told a group of reporters that the state had definitely progressed under the leadership of Orval Faubus. The man from Greasy Creek had "served his state very well," Fulbright declared, claiming that he had supported Faubus in each of his six successful election bids.[56] Galling though it was, Fulbright forced himself to call on John McClellan at his Little Rock office. Although considered something of a dinosaur, McClellan was still able to command wide support from business, big farming, city halls, and courthouses. Fulbright acknowledged that the two had never traded endorsements before, but he confided to McClellan that he was in trouble and asked for his help. "Well, Bill, you've got my vote," McClellan replied with malicious double meaning.[57] Fulbright refused to recant his opposition to the Vietnam War – indeed, he continued to blame everything from inflation to the collapse of the infrastructure on it, and he hammered away at the defense budget – but he began to display a marked interest in the burgeoning Missing in Action (MIA) issue. In February he had endorsed a suggestion by the National League of Families that a delegation from the SFRC travel to Hanoi to persuade the government to allow American search teams into North Vietnam.[58] To Witt Stephens and Charles Murphy's delight, he had publicly defended the oil and gas industry from charges that it had been responsible for the energy crisis, and insisted that petroleum and gas prices be raised to stimulate exploration.[59] Fulbright's turn to the right attracted some strange bedfellows. Both Walter Carruth, onetime chairman of George Wallace's American Party in Arkansas, and anti-Semite Gerald L. K. Smith, ensconced in Eureka Springs adjacent to his Christ-only museum, endorsed Fulbright for reelection.[60]

The two areas in which Fulbright enjoyed a distinct advantage over Bumpers were fund-raising and national notoriety. The incumbent played both cards repeatedly. In mid-February Henry Kissinger had stopped off in Little Rock for a highly publicized consultation with Fulbright. The two had emerged from the lounge of the Central Flying Service to answer a broad range of questions on current foreign policy issues. Clearly, the idea was to leave the

56 "Fulbright Lauds Work of Faubus," *Fort Smith Southwest Times Record,* Mar. 14, 1974.

57 Interview with Clara Buchanan and Anna Thomas, June 7, 1989, Little Rock, Ark.

58 Moose to JWF, Feb. 6, 1974, Series 48:6, Box 27:6, SPF, and "Senator Eyes Trip to Hanoi," *Arkansas Democrat,* Apr. 1, 1974.

59 "Fulbright Says High Natural Gas, Fuel Prices Promote Exploration," *Arkansas Democrat,* Jan. 23, 1974.

60 Bennett, "Bumpers–Fulbright Race," and "Fulbright Endorses [*sic*] Gerald Smith," *Malvern Daily Record,* Mar. 21, 1974.

impression that Fulbright was crucial to the success of Kissingerian foreign policy. When one reporter suggested that the detour to see Fulbright had political implications, the secretary replied with a grin: "I am aware of the fact that he's running for re-election, but I am not in my job for my competence in domestic politics."[61] James Reston in the *New York Times* and Arthur Schlesinger, Jr., in the *Wall Street Journal* both wrote columns calling upon Arkansans to return their junior senator to Washington. "As Sam Ervin educated the country about the Constitution, Bill Fulbright educated us about the Indochina War . . . and he has made Congress matter in the conduct of our foreign affairs," Schlesinger wrote.[62]

Of Fulbright's 344 eventual campaign contributions, 146 were to come from out of state. Witt Stephens and Bill Darby headed up a series of "put" sessions – face-to-face meetings with the state's well-heeled in which those in attendance were challenged to contribute a certain amount in cash. The Council for a Livable World raised $25,000 directly and a great deal more indirectly, much of it on the East Coast. Arab-American organizations were solicited, and most responded. Senator James Abourezk sent a mass mailing to Arab Americans and those favoring a "balanced" approach to the Arab–Israeli conflict. Compared to the total amount eventually received, however, Arab-American contributions were insignificant.[63] By election eve Fulbright would manage to raise $428,711 to Bumpers's $151,000.

In a shrewd move, Bumpers limited contributions to less than a thousand dollars. He knew that his supporters typically could not give more, and it presented him with an issue to use against Fulbright. It was not that the governor did not have the opportunity to reap a harvest of large, out-of-state donations: Jewish Americans from all over the country pressed money on his campaign. One morning, he later recalled, he and his coworkers arrived at headquarters to discover a package with $17,000 in cash on the floor: A Jewish well-wisher had dropped it over the transom during the night. According to Bumpers, he returned that donation by registered mail. Immediately thereafter he had announced that he would not accept out-of-state donations at all, except from relatives and classmates.[64]

Throughout the last half of March and first part of April, Fulbright crisscrossed the state, mining the small towns of Arkansas, going bank to bank

61 "Kissinger Makes Stop at LR, Meets Fulbright at the Airport," *Arkansas Gazette*, Feb. 16, 1974.

62 Arthur Schlesinger, Jr., "The Future of Congress," *Wall Street Journal*, May 1, 1974, and James Reston, "Fulbright's Hardest Challenge," *New York Times*, Mar. 24, 1974.

63 "Bumpers' Donors Listed," *Arkansas Democrat*, May 13, 1974; "Fulbright Receives $428,711, 3-to-1 Margin Over Bumpers," *Arkansas Gazette*, May 14, 1974; John Martilla to Jim Blair, Mark Shields, Lee Williams, Apr. 11, 1974, Williams Papers; and Harry Kearns to Carl Marcy, Apr. 9, 1974, Williams Papers.

64 Bumpers interview.

and store to store. "Bill is out on the campaign-trail and going hard, coming into Little Rock only for clean shirts, new ideas, and a change of diet once in a while!" Betty wrote a relative.[65] The crowds, however, were disappointingly modest and their enthusiasm, reporters noted, clearly restrained; and most were Fulbright people already, not crucial undecided voters.[66] The junior senator had developed a tendency to ramble, sometimes taking ten to fifteen minutes to answer a single question, ignoring Betty's frantic signals from the back of the crowd to cut it short.[67]

To make matters worse, Fulbright frequently seemed out of touch with what was going on in the state, particularly among certain classes of voters. When the incumbent appeared before the Arkansas Education Association to seek its endorsement, York Williams, a black who operated a private school at Dermott, rose and complained that impoverished areas in East Arkansas had trouble obtaining local matching funds with which to apply for federal day-care center money. He did not find east Arkansas impoverished, Fulbright replied; rather, his recent travels in the region indicated that bumper crops put the delta "on the verge of becoming the most prosperous part of the state."[68] While the agribusinesspeople of east Arkansas were indeed prospering, mechanized farming had displaced thousands of tenants and sharecroppers, most of whom were reduced to welfare and intermittent day labor, and whose families still lived in tar-paper shacks and suffered from tuberculosis and malnutrition.

"Bumpers can smell a Wal-Mart three miles away," observed a political reporter for the *Gazette;* and, in fact, Wal-Marts and shopping centers were the focus of the indefatigable young governor's efforts because it was there that he could find uncommitted voters. He always introduced himself and then listened intently, departing with a "good luck to you," and never asking for votes directly. It was this technique that caused the Fulbright people to charge that Bumpers was running on "a smile and a shoeshine," a phrase they stole from Winthrop Rockefeller, who in turn had gotten it from Arthur Miller's Willy Loman. On the platform, the governor's style was distinctly Kennedyesque. He spoke intelligently but not condescendingly. He had a sense of timing and rhythm. Day in and day out he emphasized the same topics: The state had never been better off than under his administration; the country's problems were traceable to Washington and its entrenched politicians and bureaucrats; inflation was the country's number one problem; and the energy

65 Betty Fulbright to Dr. Richard C. Waugh, Apr. 26, 1974, Williams Papers.

66 Bill Lewis, "Race for U.S. Senate Nomination Attracting National Attention," *Arkansas Gazette,* May 26, 1974.

67 Purvis interview.

68 "Both Bumpers, Fulbright Back Education Plan," *Arkansas Gazette,* Apr. 13, 1974.

crisis was being caused by Big Oil, which was continuing to raise prices while realizing record profits.[69]

Although the candidates studiously avoided personal attacks and mudslinging, there was a certain bitterness to the campaign because of their overlapping constituencies. "I feel somewhat like the Civil War father, who had a son in Blue and a son in Gray," John Maberry wrote Bumpers. "Both you, and the Senator, are highly capable, honest men, and it's shameful that the State of Arkansas will lose . . . the services of one of you."[70] "It is a contest that has divided families, marriages, business partners and old friends," observed Robert Fisher in the *Democrat*. "Political wounds are being opened that may not heal until long after the May 28 balloting."[71] Little Rock lawyer Chris Barrier campaigned vigorously for Bumpers, while his wife, Emily, served as a volunteer in the Fulbright headquarters.[72]

On May 1, with four weeks to go in the campaign, Fulbright trailed Bumpers by twenty points in the polls. Up to that point there had been general agreement among Fulbright's advisers that their candidate had to avoid "frontal assaults" on his opponent; but when it became obvious that the campaign was going nowhere, signs of desperation began to appear. "Quite frankly, to win the election, the Bumpers image will have to be damaged," John Marttila told Lee Williams after the May 1 poll came out.[73] All the staff could come up with, however, was a concerted effort to shame Bumpers for his opportunism, his self-serving effort to deprive Arkansas of its most prestigious public servant.

By the second week in May Fulbright was issuing almost daily challenges to Bumpers to debate him in a series of televised public forums. The governor, who was enjoying all of the advantages of a front-runner, steadfastly refused. His job was to listen to the voters, he told reporters. Frustrated, Jim Blair lashed out at the governor at a Democratic rally in Fayetteville. "In 1970, I heard Dale Bumpers say that he would meet Governor Rockefeller in a debate anytime, anywhere," the six-foot-four evangelist-turned-corporate-lawyer declared. "Where's that fighting spirit now?" When it came Bumpers's turn to speak, he merely smiled and observed that courage was a relative thing.[74]

69 Mike Trimble, "Bumpers Campaigns Hard Against Fulbright," *Arkansas Gazette*, May 26, 1974.

70 Maberry to Bumpers, Mar. 12, 1974, Williams Papers.

71 Robert Fisher, "Governor Is Charting a Perilous Political Course," *Arkansas Democrat*, Apr. 28, 1974.

72 Ernest Dumas, "Bitterness Not Seen as Families, Partners Split Over Bumpers, Fulbright," *Arkansas Gazette*, Apr. 28, 1974.

73 Mark Shields to Hoyt Purvis et al., Apr. 20, 1974, and Martilla to Williams, May 1, 1974, Williams Papers.

74 "Fulbright Aide Gets Bumpers to Respond," *Arkansas Gazette*, May 12, 1974.

As the gap began to narrow, however – a poll taken on May 6 had showed Bumpers leading 52 percent to 40 percent – Bumpers's advisers decided that he would have to debate. He notified Fulbright, but insisted on delaying until the twenty-sixth, two days before the election. On that Sunday the two faced off on *Issues and Answers,* broadcast remote from KATV, Channel 7, in Little Rock. It was a public relations bust. Maddeningly polite, Bumpers spoke in generalities; so did Fulbright. The incumbent complained about the refusal of his opponent to focus on the issues, or to point out significant differences in their philosophies. To many, however, Fulbright appeared simply to be whining.[75]

During the last two weeks of the campaign, there appeared to be a substantial shift toward Fulbright. Indeed, Jim Blair produced a poll that showed the two Democratic aspirants in a dead-heat, 46 percent to 46 percent.[76] A cross section of the state's newspaper editors and county Democratic committee chairpersons predicted a narrow Fulbright victory.[77] Williams and Martilla smelled defeat, however.

The last days of the campaign degenerated into low comedy. The Fulbright campaign paid for the distribution of fifty thousand copies of an *Arkansas Sportsman* featuring an article accusing Bumpers of issuing a proclamation against hunting. As Blair, Williams, and company knew, in a state where children were released from school for several days each year for deer hunting season, such a charge was serious. The governor, it seems, had signed a proclamation declaring October 13 to be "Animal Liberation Day." An indignant Bumpers declared himself to be an avid hunter, and he lined up several noted gamesmen to testify in his behalf.[78]

On election eve, the Fulbright campaign bought thirty minutes of prime-time television to enable Bill and Betty to talk about their life in Washington and their service to Arkansas. The taping at KARK, Channel 4, went off without a hitch that afternoon; but halfway through the show's airing at 8:00 P.M., with Betty explaining Bill's opposition to the Vietnam War, images of Lawrence Welk, bubble machine and all, began appearing on the screen, superimposed over Betty. At one point, the incumbent's wife talked of war and peace to the background music of "Let Me Call You Sweetheart." Later, as she recalled that Secretary of State Kissinger had telephoned her husband just that week, Welk played "Have I Told You Lately That I Love You?" An enraged Blair called a press conference to charge political sabotage. So fearful became KARK executives at menacing phone calls that they locked the

75 "Fulbright–Bumpers TV Confrontation Brief, Subdued," *Pine Bluff Commercial,* May 27, 1974.

76 Jim Blair to Lee Williams, May 14, 1974, Williams Papers.

77 "Editors Predict Fulbright, Pryor," *Arkansas Democrat,* May 12, 1974.

78 "Antihunt Charge Backed by Fulbright, Paper Says," *Arkansas Democrat,* May 24, 1974, and "DB Surprised at Fulbright," *Blytheville Courier News,* May 17, 1974.

doors to the building. The station later claimed that a technician had simply failed to erase completely the videotape that was used for the Fulbright interview;[79] but the damage was done.

Even before the polls closed Fulbright campaign workers and supporters, hundreds of them, began gathering in the headquarters building, a converted Chinese restaurant in Little Rock. "For the past three hours I have felt the miracle was really coming off," Jim Blair told reporters shortly before eight. An hour later, his illusions were gone. A few minutes after eleven o'clock Bill and Betty approached the podium. With reporters from around the world straining to hear his words, the nation's longest-serving junior senator made a gracious concession speech. He congratulated Bumpers on a "fairly fought" campaign. To the disappointed, tearful throng, he said, "I urge you most sincerely to continue the struggle for peace and reason in all of our public affairs. Thank you," he said, "for having given me your trust for 30 years."[80]

Lawrence Welk may have had some impact on the 1974 senatorial election in Arkansas, but more than likely the challenger would have won anyway. On election day Bumpers outpolled the state's most famous citizen by 320,798 to 174,734. The 65 to 35 percent margin was almost exactly the same that had been predicted when Bumpers declared. The incumbent carried only four of Arkansas's seventy-five counties and even lost Fayetteville and Washington County. Fulbright came closest to matching Bumpers in the tier of counties bordering the Mississippi River.[81]

Fulbright's defeat was mourned and cheered around the nation and the world. Scoop Jackson's staff broke out a case of whiskey in celebration. As news of Fulbright's resounding defeat came across the wire services in Phnom Penh, members of the American embassy staff stood in their chairs and cheered wildly. Vice-President Gerald Ford, only recently appointed to replace the disgraced Spiro Agnew, walked off the eighteenth hole of the Kemper Open and observed to reporters that, after thirty years, Fulbright had simply lost touch with his constituents. Tass, the Soviet news agency, described the election as a victory for "American reaction, the military–industrial complex, and influential Zionist elements."[82]

James Reston, Tom Wicker, and Tom Braden wrote bittersweet eulogies. "The lesson to be learned is not that Fulbright should be younger, more handsome, better on TV," Braden wrote in the *Washington Post.* "The lesson is

79 "Welk Show Interferes with TV Talk by Mrs. Fulbright; Backers Angry," *Arkansas Gazette,* May 28, 1974.

80 Ernest Dumas, "Bumpers Shatters Fulbright; Pryor Takes Narrow Victory," *Arkansas Gazette,* May 29, 1974.

81 "Fulbright Beaten in Arkansas," *Arkansas Gazette,* May 28, 1974; and Dumas, "Bumpers Shatters Fulbright."

82 Purvis interview; interview with Richard Moose, June 29, 1989, Washington, D.C.; and "Lost Touch with Voters," *Arkansas Democrat,* May 30, 1974.

that we need to find a way to avoid the waste of our best-educated talent."[83] An editorial in the *Toronto Globe* lamented, "The voice of William Fulbright has been a courageous, and often lonely, countervailing force when the need has been greatest. . . . The choice may, in one sense, be a vindication of the lonely stands Mr. Fulbright has taken in the past."[84]

In the wake of Fulbright's crushing defeat, political analysts vied with each other to explain the outcome. Some emphasized Bumpers's personal popularity; others agreed with Gerald Ford that Arkansans were sick of thirty years of perceived neglect. Still others declared that it was a matter of chickens coming home to roost: Although civil rights were not an overt issue, blacks voted by a 4-to-1 margin for Bumpers. A number of commentators faulted poor leadership in the Fulbright camp, citing in particular John Elrod's illness. "The Fulbright crew floundered and missed his leadership," Robert Fisher declared in the *Democrat.*[85] The fact that Fulbright got much of his money from people living on the coasts allegedly aroused Arkansans' traditional resentment at "outside" meddling in their politics. "It was a victory for a local campaigner, with local backers, and local money against what some saw as an influx of out-of-state funds," John Dillin declared in the *Christian Science Monitor.*[86] Fatalists concluded that there was not a thing that Fulbright could have done to avoid defeat. Bumpers was the right challenger at the right time.

It may have been that J. William Fulbright could not have beaten Dale Bumpers in 1974; but John McClellan, a man with far less popular appeal than Fulbright, had held off a young, attractive liberal in 1972. Fulbright possessed an asset no other state politician could match: international prestige. People around the world who had never heard of Arkansas knew of and appreciated him. He was perceived to be everything Arkansas was presumed not to be: educated, cosmopolitan, self-confident, subtle, and influential. A generation of Arkansans, many of whom did not agree with his stands on specific issues, had taken great vicarious pleasure in his representation of the state. They had looked to Fulbright with the same pride and sense of renewed self-esteem as southerners had regarded Woodrow Wilson following his electrifying rise to national prominence. That pride had not completely evaporated by 1974. The big money in Arkansas had scared off Orval Faubus in 1962 and Sid McMath in 1968, and the Stephenses, Darbys, Murphys, and Pickenses were still with Fulbright in 1974; yet he lost 2 to 1.

The truth was that Fulbright was vulnerable not only because of his neglect of the state and his stands on Vietnam, Watergate, and the Middle East, but

83 Tom Braden, "A Place for the Fulbrights," *Washington Post,* June 8, 1974.
84 "A Canadian Viewpoint," *Northwest Arkansas Times,* June 18, 1974.
85 "Senate Campaign Made No Difference at All," *Arkansas Democrat,* June 2, 1974.
86 John Dillon, "How Fulbright Might Have Won," *Christian Science Monitor,* June 3, 1974.

also because his heart was not in the race. At sixty-eight, with American participation in Vietnam at an end and no Homer Adkins with whom to settle a score or Orval Faubus from whom to protect the nation, his ambition was at a low ebb. Lee Williams and Hoyt Purvis had sensed as much during that propitious dinner meeting in the spring of 1973. Had Bumpers smelled the iron determination, the total commitment that had been there previously, he might have waited four years and taken on John McClellan. Had the voters of Arkansas sensed that commitment, the polls might not have shown Fulbright to have been so massively vulnerable.[87] He would have very much liked another term in the Senate, but in the final analysis it just was not that important; and so he lost.

Betty and Bill returned to Washington to fill out his term. In the fall the SFRC held a much ballyhooed series of hearings on détente at which Fulbright and Kissinger were the stars. Staffers recalled that the chairman approached the proceedings with unparalleled intensity. There was the usual parade of expert witnesses – past and present policymakers, historians, political scientists, experts on human behavior – but no one was paying much attention. Richard Nixon had just resigned, and North Vietnam had begun its final assault on the south.

Arkansas's retiring junior senator was able to repay Henry Kissinger for his aid during the campaign. In the spring and summer of 1974 the SFRC conducted an official investigation into the secretary of state's role in ordering the wiretapping of White House aides and news correspondents.[88] In late July, Alexander Haig, who had served in the NSC under Kissinger, testified that the wiretaps were indeed Nixon's idea, and the SFRC subsequently gave the secretary of state a clean bill of health.[89] Addressing a throng of newspeople in the hallway outside the committee room, Fulbright declared the issue to be "a tempest in a teapot" and insinuated that enemies of détente, including Secretary of Defense James Schlesinger, had brought up the old charges against Kissinger in an effort to derail the Soviet–American rapprochement.[90]

After his defeat in May, Fulbright had told reporters that he and Betty planned to retire to Arkansas. That was not to be. Fulbright was disappointed at losing, but his wife was embittered. Although ultimately reconciled to de-

87 "Fulbright Attributes Loss to National Dissatisfaction," *Malvern Daily Record,* May 29, 1974.

88 Mary McGrory, "Fulbright Plays No Lame-duck Role," *Boston Globe,* June 22, 1974.

89 Marilyn Berger, "Haig Testimony Supports Kissinger," *Washington Post,* July 31, 1974.

90 Bernard Gwertzman, "Fulbright Sees Kissinger as Detente Foes' Target," *New York Times,* July 16, 1974.

feat, in the aftermath of the election she believed that the people of the state had betrayed her husband. Fulbright was angry, but not at his fellow Arkansans: He blamed and would continue to blame American Zionists for his defeat.[91] In November he was invited to come to Westminster College, the site of Winston Churchill's "iron curtain" speech, and deliver a major address on the state of the world. The principal threat to the international peace, he told the students, faculty, and assembled press corps, was the intransigence of the Israeli government and the slavish support it received from American Zionists. Unless and until Congress and the American people abandoned their attachment to a greater [*eretz*] Israel, détente would be tentative and the threat of a nuclear confrontation ever present.[92]

The Fulbrights did not return to Arkansas except for the perennial family reunions. They continued to live in the house on Belmont Road. The senator became a senior consultant for the prestigious Washington law firm of Hogan and Hartson. There were other opportunities: Louis Reynolds, president of Reynolds Aluminum, wanted to hire him to be the industry's representative to bauxite-producing nations around the world.[93] After some deliberation, Fulbright rejected Kissinger and Ford's offer to become ambassador to the Court of St. James: Betty's health had not improved during the course of the campaign and, perhaps more important, were he to work for the administration, he would have to tailor his opinions to conform to official policy. The more he thought about it the more unwilling he became to give up the independence that had become his trademark and most prized possession. During the campaign, while he sat on the steps of his motel at DeQueen, a group of reporters had asked him if he would ever consider a diplomatic appointment. "I'm not suited to play that kind of role under anyone," he told them. He remained to the end one of those "obdurately independent" Arkansans.[94]

91 Interview with J. William Fulbright, Oct. 11–18, 1988, Washington, D.C.
92 "The Clear and Present Danger," Statement by Senator J. W. Fulbright, Westminster College, Nov. 2, 1974.
93 Henry Mitchell, "A Farewell Dinner," *Washington Post,* July 31, 1974.
94 "'Not Applied,' Fulbright Says," *Arkansas Gazette,* Sept. 6, 1974.

# 39

# *Life after office*

After 1975 most Americans wanted to forget J. William Fulbright. He was a man shunned, a living, breathing reminder of the humiliation of Vietnam. It took years after the final marine helicopter lifted off the roof of the U.S. embassy in Saigon before the nation was ready to come to grips with the war, to heal the wounds it had inflicted. Fulbright was not destined to be part of that process. Americans were angry with themselves, angry with the political system, angry with the world, and angry particularly with Fulbright. For hawks he remained a symbol of betrayal, a reminder of the nation's lack of resolve, a key factor in America's decision not to make an all-out effort in Southeast Asia. For doves Fulbright continued to be a hero of a sort, but they still viewed him as a fixture of the "system" that had been discredited by Vietnam, and they could not forget that he had voted against every civil rights measure proposed in Congress between 1945 and 1970. At a huge commemorative anti–Vietnam War conference held in Toledo, Ohio, in 1990, Fulbright was barely mentioned. For those in the middle, Fulbright was an I-told-you-so emblem of their monumental error. The 1974 senatorial defeat had indeed cast the junior senator into the wilderness.

There was another reason for Fulbright's internal exile, however, a factor that undermined his standing even with liberal intellectuals: his ongoing support for a land-for-peace deal in the Middle East. Convinced that American Zionists had played a key role in his defeat at the hands of Dale Bumpers, Fulbright publicly and consistently cast his lot with the coalition of Arab states seeking a restoration of Palestinian rights. He became a registered lobbyist for the United Arab Emirates and an unofficial adviser to the Saudi government. He labored diligently if unsuccessfully to prevent the United States from retaliating against the Gulf states for various oil-price hikes implemented by OPEC. Angry over the oil-induced inflation that wracked the nation throughout the 1980s, mesmerized by acts of Arab terrorism, and identifying as never before with its gallant Israeli ally, Congress and the American people were in no mood for Fulbright and his advocacy of a balanced approach to the Middle East situation.

Still, Fulbright was not without influence in governmental circles, especially in the first few years after he left the Senate. The Ford and Carter administrations wanted to protect the nation's Middle Eastern oil supply and resolve the Arab–Israeli conflict. Fulbright's influence with the Arab states was indisputable. "Your statements have for years been the subject of admiration among Arabs," Abdul Majeed Shoman, chairman of the Arab Bank Unlimited, wrote the retiring senator in December 1974. "Yours has always been the same voice, often the only sane voice, in a world of corrupt information media, of irresponsible politicians seeking personal advancement at their country's expense."[1] In turn, Fulbright's status, especially with the Gulf states, gave him a degree of credibility with the State Department and White House. Shortly before Fulbright left the Senate, Secretary of State Kissinger spoke in his honor at a dinner given by the Board of Foreign Scholarships, praising him for among other things advocating "an evenhanded approach to settlement in the Middle East."[2]

As Fulbright contemplated the pleasures and frustrations of retirement, Kissinger faced an ominous situation in the Middle East. A temporary Soviet–American understanding in 1973 had produced a cease-fire in the Yom Kippur War, but the Arabs were angry and united as never before. Infuriated by America's support for Israel, OPEC had increased the price of crude by as much as 400 percent, and following the Yom Kippur War the Arab world had temporarily cut off the oil supply of those nations supporting Israel. During the winter of 1973–4 gasoline and heating-oil prices in the United States had gone up nearly 33 percent. As long lines formed at gas stations and the inflation rate increased, Americans railed at allegedly selfish sheiks. Kissinger, with President Ford's approval, continued his search for a formula that would establish peace between Israel and the Arab states. After arranging a disengagement of Israeli forces from the Egyptian and Syrian armies, the secretary of state was able to work out an interim agreement between Egypt and Israel in September 1975.

In the midst of the negotiating process Fulbright made an eighteen-day trip to the Middle East, during which he met with government officials and businessmen in Saudi Arabia, Qatar, Iraq, Lebanon, Syria, and Egypt.[3] Upon his return in early July he had a thirty-minute meeting with Ford at the White House and a longer session with Kissinger, during which he made a series of recommendations. The status quo in the Middle East was not "benign," Fulbright declared. "Time is working against us and against our interests." Egypt, Syria, Saudia Arabia, and Jordan were all governed by pragmatic men, he declared. "The Arabs have learned to be moderate, reasonable," he quoted King Khalid as saying. "Gone are the days of Nasser's period when

1 Abdul Majeed Shoman to JWF, Dec. 29, 1974, Box 4, Folder 1, Postsenatorial Papers of J. William Fulbright [hereinafter referred to as PsPF].
2 *Department of State Bulletin,* 72 (Jan. 20, 1975), 69–70.
3 "Fulbright, Ford Discuss Visit to Middle East," *Arkansas Gazette,* July 3, 1975.

the Arabs threatened to exterminate the Israelis." The United States must follow up the interim agreement then being negotiated with a comprehensive peace settlement including an Israeli withdrawal to the borders of 1967; establishment of a Palestinian state comprising the West Bank and Gaza, either separate or in association with Jordan; the permanent demilitarization of the Golan Heights and much or all of Sinai and the West Bank; the stationing of U.N. troops in demilitarized zones; and the guarantee of such a settlement by the great powers, including the Soviet Union. The Saudis, Fulbright reported, had offered the United States in return "assured access to its oil."[4] A month later Fulbright told Kissinger that "if we do not follow through quickly and forcefully on Golan and the West Bank," Anwar Sadat would be removed by means of a coup or assassination, and Yasir Arafat would become a prisoner of the radical wing of the PLO.[5]

By 1975 Fulbright had come to believe that a comprehensive solution to the Middle Eastern situation was the key to a new, more rational international order. In the first place, he argued, a land-for-peace deal guaranteed by the great powers was clearly in America's national interest. In a speech delivered at Kansas State University in February, Fulbright labored to make a distinction among vital, peripheral, and illusory national interests. The Middle East, involving as it did access to oil and avoidance of conflict with the Soviet Union, was clearly of vital interest to the United States. Of important but secondary concern to the country were such issues as the economic development of India, democracy in Latin America, and the survival and prosperity of Israel. In the last category were "matters of national prestige, imperial presumption, or the vanity of leaders who do not care to admit that they have made a mistake" – Vietnam being the prime example. A settlement of the Arab–Israeli conflict would do nothing less than preserve the international monetary system by preventing massive, destructive inflation in the West and Japan. It would, in addition, simultaneously eliminate a potential source of conflict between the United States and the Soviet Union and create a framework for great-power cooperation. The Soviet–American guarantee of a comprehensive peace settlement would create a mutuality of interest that would make war virtually unthinkable. Détente would advance the cause of peace in the Middle East and a settlement of the Arab–Israeli conflict would facilitate détente. Finally, Fulbright argued, a U.N.-brokered peace would at last elevate the international body to the primary role in international affairs it was intended to play.[6]

Ford and Kissinger listened attentively to Fulbright's recommendations, but politically little room for maneuver existed. That May some seventy-five

4 JWF to President Ford, June 27, 1975, Box 4, Folder 1, PsPF.

5 JWF to Kissinger, Aug. 19, 1975, Box 4, Folder 1, PsPF.

6 J. W. Fulbright, "Energy and the Middle East," *Vital Speeches,* 41 (Mar. 15, 1975), 331–5, and JWF to Nathaniel Kern, Mar. 3, 1975, Box 4, Folder 1, PsPF.

senators had signed an open letter to Ford in effect demanding that the United States continue its strong support of Israel. Among other things, they insisted that the administration supply its ally with the planes and tanks necessary to ensure its continued military domination of the region.[7] Fulbright was, as usual, pessimistic. Caught between "the Israelis in the Middle East and the Senate . . . between a rock and a hard place," Fulbright wrote James O. Powell of the *Arkansas Gazette*, the secretary was "going to have a very hard time bringing anything off."[8]

A number of foreign affairs commentators were certain that Kissinger never had any intention of pressing for a comprehensive settlement of the Middle Eastern situation along the lines of the Fulbright–Rogers plan. Despite Nixon's opening to China and the Soviet Union, anticommunism remained at a fever pitch in the United States, especially following the final humiliation in Vietnam. Defenders of Israel such as Henry Jackson continued to portray that country as America's last bastion against communism in the Middle East; any "compromising" of its strategic defenses would be disastrous, they argued. Kissinger allegedly never had any intention of challenging the powerful pro-Zionist, anticommunist coalition that dominated Congress and public opinion. According to Bernard Kalb, Fulbright was nothing more or less than Kissinger's dupe.[9]

Fulbright undermined his credibility as an impartial observer of the Arab–Israeli conflict by becoming a paid representative of various Middle Eastern governments. Hogan and Hartson, the huge Washington law firm he joined in early 1975, did a substantial amount of business in the Arab Middle East. In September the Institute of International Education retained Fulbright to secure a labor contract for them with Saudi Arabia,[10] and in January 1976 he registered with the Justice Department as the legal counsel of the United Arab Emirates.[11] Fulbright publicly advocated Arab investment in United States properties in order to correct the trade and monetary imbalance caused by ongoing American purchases of Middle Eastern oil. He personally persuaded at least one Kuwaiti businessman to invest in L'Enfant Plaza, Washington's newest and most luxurious real estate venture.[12] Late in 1976 he agreed to represent the PLO in its efforts to persuade the Ford administration to permit the establishment of a Palestinian information office in Washington.[13]

7 Stephen Isaacs, "75 Senators Back Israel in Letter to Ford," *Washington Post*, May 22, 1975.
8 JWF to Powell, Mar. 20, 1975, Box 4, Folder 1, PsPF.
9 "Fulbright Says He Doubted in 1940s Decision Right to Give Vote to Blacks," *Arkansas Gazette*, May 29, 1975.
10 JWF to James E. Akins, Sept. 25, 1975, Box 4, Folder 1, PsPF.
11 "Fulbright to Represent Arab Sheikdoms in U.S.," *New York Times*, Jan. 27, 1976.
12 JWF to Fawzi M. al-Saleh, Dec. 29, 1975, Box 4, Folder 1, PsPF.
13 JWF to Alfred L. Atherton, Jr., Nov. 9, 1976, Box 4, Folder 2, PsPF.

The ever-present conflict in Fulbright between a desire to wield influence and a contempt for conventional wisdom was to become even sharper after retirement. Indeed, he never missed an opportunity to rattle the chains of those with whom he had disagreed. Early in 1975 Fulbright was one of a number of luminaries attending a memorial service for Walter Lippmann at the Washington National Cathedral. After hailing the journalist as "one of those extraordinary men who appear in the world just often enough to keep alive the hope that reason, intelligence and empathy are not beyond man's reach," he declared that Americans should rely on Lippmann's writings "in much the same way the little red book of quotations from Chairman Mao serves the Chinese people."[14] Following the final defeat of South Vietnam, the former chairman of the Senate Foreign Relations Committee told reporters that he was no more upset by the loss of the war than by an Arkansas loss to Texas in football.[15] In addition, of course, he denounced the American Zionist lobby at every opportunity and heaped ridicule upon the American people for allowing themselves to be so easily manipulated.

His public scorn concealed, as usual, a deep private concern over the pervasiveness of the cold-war mentality. Fulbright expressed the hope to various confidants that the end of the Vietnam conflict would free America from the shackles of an obsessive anticommunism. America had not been "defeated" in Vietnam, but rather was the victim of poor leadership. There was no reason for a macho reaction, a drive by America to reassert its manliness. He agreed, however, with Erich Fromm that Watergate had distracted the nation, preventing it from learning the lessons of Vietnam. The pernicious coalition of extreme Zionists, anticommunists, and representatives of the military–industrial complex, with new hero Alexander Solzhenitsyn at their head, were conspiring to scuttle détente and keep the arms race alive.[16]

Fulbright may have been out of power and out of favor with the men and women on the street, but he was and would continue to be held in high esteem by academia and by foreign governments. In February he delivered the commencement address at George Washington University.[17] In mid-April he journeyed to Tokyo, where the Japanese government awarded him the Order of the Rising Sun for the exchange program and for his efforts to secure the return to Japan of Okinawa.[18] In October he and Betty flew to London and then entrained for Oxford, where he delivered the first R. B. McCallum Lecture. Former prime minister Harold Macmillan presided. Three months later

14 "Lippmann Memorial Held in Capital," *New York Times,* Jan. 9, 1975.
15 "Fulbright Not Upset by Loss," *Arkansas Gazette,* May 22, 1975.
16 JWF to Hugh Sidey, Aug. 21, 1975, Box 4, Folder 1, PsPF.
17 "Fulbright Says Jackson Caused Trade Collapse," *Arkansas Gazette,* Feb. 18, 1975.
18 "Order of Rising Sun for Fulbright," *New York Times,* Apr. 5, 1975.

President Anwar al-Sadat announced that Egypt was going to bestow the Order of the Republic on the Arkansan.

In November 1975 Fulbright published an article in the *Columbia Journalism Review* in which he bemoaned the American media's obsession with investigative journalism. "If once the press was excessively orthodox and unquestioning of Government policy," he asserted, "it has now become almost sweepingly iconoclastic." The media must show some restraint, he pleaded, or Americans would reject not only politicians but politics – with disastrous results. *Time* magazine commented that there was some truth to the former SFRC chair's criticism, but observed wryly that, given that no American had had more to do with discrediting the nation's leaders than J. William Fulbright, his critique was somewhat ironic.[19]

Late in 1975 Betty Fulbright underwent open heart surgery. She had suffered a major heart attack during the Democratic National Convention in 1972, and her health had grown steadily worse. The procedure served to arrest the congestive heart disease from which she suffered, but the operation constituted a major trauma that, together with the effects of her diabetes, left her greatly weakened. His wife's illness frustrated and depressed Fulbright. For years the two had looked forward to retirement when they would have the opportunity to travel together to their hearts' content; but Betty's infirmity made every overseas junket more and more of a chore.[20]

The prospect of James Earl Carter becoming president of the United States was not a pleasing one to Fulbright. Carter was a self-avowed outsider; he did not know how Washington worked and declared that he did not want to know. His foreign policy experience was nil. The Georgian's born-again Christianity put off Fulbright, as did his promise to base American foreign policy on respect for human rights. Fulbright did not exactly know what that meant, but it seemed to smack of the moralizing, missionary diplomacy that had gotten the nation mired in Vietnam. "In Carter's speeches," he later observed, "we always hear that it is up to us to establish order in the world. . . . Apparently he does not understand that other people have different views quite in particular about human right priorities."[21] Finally, he remained as attached to Kissinger as ever. The secretary of state continued to have Fulbright to lunch throughout 1975 and 1976. He might be ignored, but at least he was being consulted. Although he would not admit it, Fulbright probably voted for Gerald Ford in the 1976 presidential election.[22]

Upon surveying the new administration in early 1977, Fulbright decided that not all was lost. Zbigniew Brzezinski, the national security adviser, was a fire-breathing anticommunist émigré, but Secretary of State Cyrus Vance

19 "Truth Hurts," *Time,* Nov. 24, 1975, 78.
20 Interview with J. William Fulbright, Oct. 11–18, 1988, Washington, D.C.
21 Roman Berger, "Fulbright: A Parliamentary System," *Arkansas Gazette,* July 25, 1980.
22 See James Reston, "The Politics of Fear," *New York Times,* Apr. 4, 1979.

seemed to be a reasonable man. Somewhat ironically, Fulbright's favorite in the new foreign policy establishment was Carter's ambassador to the United Nations, Andrew Young. Upon learning of Young's sympathy for the plight of the Palestinians, Fulbright moved to establish a personal relationship and to use the former civil rights activist as a conduit to Carter for his plans for a settlement of the Middle Eastern problem. The principal Arab rulers were then both moderate and unified, Fulbright advised Carter and Young, but the situation could not hold for long. The new administration must move to take advantage of the brief window of opportunity that was presenting itself.[23]

By 1977 Fulbright was becoming obsessed with the existence of an extensive Zionist conspiracy that had as its goal the bending of the American political system to Israel's every whim. He had repeatedly warned against the influence of American Zionists, but his complaint was simply that they were an intelligent, wealthy, and influential minority who were very effectively exercising their constitutional rights.[24] In early 1977, however, Fulbright came into possession of an eyes-only memo, written in May 1974, from Herman Edelsberg to the Board of Governors of B'nai B'rith. In it Edelsberg had deplored the pro-Arab drift of American foreign policy under Kissinger and suggested that the organization do everything in its power to link the secretary of state with Watergate. Recognizing that an end to the cold war would dramatically reduce Israel's leverage with Washington, the Jewish activist urged B'nai B'rith to undermine directly and indirectly efforts to achieve détente. Most important, Edelsberg reported that "all the indications suggest that our actions in support of Governor Bumpers will result in the ousting of Mr. Fulbright from his key position in the Senate."[25] Perhaps, Fulbright concluded, American Zionists were more than just a misguided interest group.

Although the Carter administration resisted appeals from Fulbright and others to extend diplomatic recognition to the PLO, it did make some effort to correct the perceived pro-Israeli tilt in American foreign policy. Carter, Vance, and Brzezinski were all committed to maintaining the security of the state of Israel, but they were sensitive as well to the needs and desires of the four million Arabs displaced by the 1948–9 and 1967 wars. They were, in addition, acutely aware that the United States was dependent on Middle Eastern oil and that the petroleum-rich states of the region were willing to use oil as a weapon against Israel and its allies. A settlement of the Arab–Israeli conflict was manifestly in America's interests.

As his approval ratings dipped to an all-time low in late 1977 and early 1978, Carter decided to take the biggest risk of his presidency. He invited

23 JWF to Carter, Jan. 12, 1977, and JWF to Young, Jan. 13, 1977, Box 4, Folder 3, PsPF.
24 JWF to D. Edward Carbonaro, Apr. 23, 1976, Box 4, Folder 2, and JWF to Robert Burgess Stewart, Sept. 16, 1975, Box 4, Folder 1, PsPF.
25 JWF to Norman F. Dacey, Feb. 21, 1977, Box 4, Folder 3, PsPF.

Sadat and Israeli Prime Minister Menachem Begin to Camp David, the presidential retreat in Maryland, for nearly two weeks of discussions in September 1978. With the national and international media providing minute-by-minute coverage, the Egyptian and Israeli leaders, with Carter an active participant, signed two pacts: a "Framework for the Conclusion of a Peace Treaty between Egypt and Israel" and a "Framework for Peace in the Middle East." In the midst of the negotiations Fulbright published an article in *Newsweek* repeating his call for a land-for-peace trade and a great-power guarantee of Israeli boundaries.[26]

The Camp David accords did not produce the peace for which Carter so desperately longed. Begin was not going to tolerate the creation of a Palestinian state in the West Bank and Gaza. To do so, he believed, would be to expose the Israeli population to constant terrorist attacks. The most he was willing to do was to withdraw from the Sinai and include Palestinians living in the occupied territories in the Israeli political process. For their part, the other Arab states wanted nothing to do with the frameworks Sadat and Begin had hammered out. A separate peace between Egypt and Israel would make future attacks on Israel in behalf of the Palestinians almost impossible. Israel still controlled the West Bank, Gaza, and the Golan Heights. In early March 1979 Carter flew to the Middle East and persuaded Sadat and Begin to come to Washington later that month and sign the bilateral peace treaty. That agreement provided for gradual Israeli withdrawal from the Sinai, the establishment of diplomatic relations between the two countries, and multilateral negotiations on Palestinian rights in the West Bank and Gaza. Carter had achieved an important first step, but his dream of a general settlement to the bitter Arab–Israeli dispute remained unrealized.

The degree to which Fulbright's lobbying efforts affected the Carter administration's Middle East policy is impossible to discern. Probably it had little effect. The Arkansan had kept his distance from Carter and had few contacts with the administration. He certainly represented no significant constituency in the United States. Other voices were raised in behalf of a comprehensive land-for-peace settlement – most notably those of I. F. Stone, George Ball, and Nahum Goldman – but they were a tiny minority.[27] No doubt the oil embargo and subsequent price increases were the deciding factors with the administration. As usual, Fulbright had merely articulated the unpleasant realities of the situation.

Retirement brought a marked improvement in Fulbright's financial position, never weak under any conditions. After much debate and soul searching, the

26 "J. William Fulbright," *Newsweek*, Sept. 11, 1978, 43.
27 JWF to I. F. Stone, Feb. 21, 1978, Box 4, Folder 4, and Ball to JWF, Feb. 23, 1980, Box 6, Folder 5, PsPF.

family sold the *Northwest Arkansas Times* to the giant Canadian-based Thompson chain for some $8 million. Late in 1977 Stephens, Inc., asked Arkansas's most famous citizen to become chairman of the board. Fulbright refused but agreed to serve as a board member. He was handsomely compensated for his four meetings a year.[28] Finally, the connection with Hogan and Hartson brought in far more than he had earned as a U.S. senator.

Student and faculty exchange continued to be Fulbright's principal passion. He traveled extensively in Latin America and northern Europe in 1977 in behalf of the Fulbright program and the Institute for International Education. He lobbied multinational corporations to contribute to programs he argued were manifestly in their interest.[29] Early in 1988 he launched a campaign to amend the hated Jackson–Vanek amendment so that it would permit enlargement of the cultural exchange program with the Soviet Union. As part of the 1972 accords signed by Nixon and Brezhnev, the Soviet Union had agreed to remit to the United States $674 million in Lend–Lease payments. The Jackson–Vanek amendment, enacted two years later, had denied most-favored-nation status to the Soviet Union until and unless Congress was satisfied with its emigration policies. In response Moscow had canceled Lend–Lease remittances. Under Fulbright's proposal, payments – amounting to some $20 million a year – would be revived and devoted exclusively to Russian–American exchange. The Carter administration gave lukewarm support, and a modified version was introduced in Congress.[30] By that time, however, Soviet–American relations had deteriorated to such a point (primarily over the invasion of Afghanistan) that passage proved impossible.

The passing of the Fulbright–Marcy Senate Foreign Relations Committee was increasingly lamented by the national press. The *New York Times, Washington Post,* and various magazines were filled with articles deploring the weakness and lack of focus exhibited by post-Fulbright committees. Some blamed the "decline" of the SFRC on weak leadership. John Sparkman of Alabama had replaced Fulbright, and the media found him pitiably reluctant to confront the executive over foreign policy issues. Frank Church succeeded to the chairmanship in 1979; he was more than sufficiently confrontational, but he rarely carried a majority of the committee, much less a bipartisan ma-

28 "Fulbright Named Board Member of Stephens Firm," *Arkansas Gazette,* Aug. 22, 1977.

29 J. William Fulbright, "International Education: Focus for Corporate Support," *Harvard Business Review,* 53 (May–June 1977), 137–41.

30 J. W. Fulbright, "Lend Lease Debts to Pay for Educational Exchanges," *Just for the Press,* 1 (2) (Jan. 1978); JWF to J. K. Galbraith, Jan. 25, 1978, Marcy to S. Frederick Starr, May 1, 1978, JWF to Harold B. Scott, Feb. 7, 1978, and Marcy to JWF, Feb. 6, 1978, Box 3, Folder 6, PsPF.

jority, with him.[31] Reporters missed the drama of Fulbright's ongoing battle with the executive and the military–industrial complex, the strategic Marcy leaks, and the quotable quotes. In truth, none of Fulbright's successors were as skilled as he in controlling partisan passions or winning bipartisan support for various positions.[32]

The image of a diminished SFRC and congressional mismanagement of foreign policy matters was assiduously cultivated by the former chairman. In the spring of 1979, in an article in *Foreign Affairs,* Fulbright took Congress to task for seizing control of foreign affairs from the executive and then spending all its time pandering to constituents. The House and Senate, he declared, were not doing their part to educate the American people on the complexities of international relations; the void was being filled by special interests and professional anticommunists. "Products of the media age," he lamented, "the new breed of legislator . . . aims not to convey an idea but to project an image."[33] Polls, he declared, were the bane of modern political life. They had subverted the Burkean ideal, placing every politician at the momentary whim of the masses.[34] It should be noted, however, that while the visibility and prestige of the SFRC may have declined, other foreign policy power centers emerged in the Senate, and Congress proved more than willing to challenge the executive over foreign policy during the Carter and Reagan presidencies.

Although the Middle East was his primary preoccupation, Fulbright continued to pay close attention to Soviet–American relations. He was an unrelenting advocate of détente. The Carter administration received distinctly mixed grades from him in this crucial area. Its crusade in behalf of human rights was clearly counterproductive, Fulbright believed, but he fully supported the president's attempts to conclude a SALT II agreement.

The Soviet invasion of Afghanistan in 1979 tipped the balance within the Carter administration in favor of hard-liners, and as a result the president decided to cancel grain sales to the Soviets and forbid American athletes to participate in the Summer Olympic games scheduled for Moscow. Fulbright's response to Carter's tough line toward the Soviet Union's occupation of Afghanistan was remarkably restrained. Although he viewed the Soviet invasion as a mistake, it was, he wrote an Arkansas editor, an understandable response to the existence of an unstable and potentially hostile republic on one's fron-

31 See Richard Burt, "Senator Church Emulates Fulbright's Role on Panel," *New York Times,* Jan. 9, 1979, and idem, "Foreign Relations Committee's Influence at Lowest Point in 20 Years," *New York Times,* Nov. 23, 1977.

32 See Hugh Scott to Murray J. Gart, Aug. 2, 1978, Box 6, Folder 3, PsPF.

33 J. William Fulbright, "The Legislator as Educator," *Foreign Affairs,* 57 (Spring 1979), 719-32.

34 Robert G. Kaiser and Walter Pincus, "America Is Run by Amateurs," *Washington Post,* July 18, 1982.

tier.[35] Nevertheless, he approved of Carter's decision to cancel U.S. participation in the Olympics and remained silent on the grain sale. In part, Fulbright's restraint over the downturn in Soviet–American relations during the last days of the Carter administration had to do with his utter contempt for Ronald Reagan. He feared that Reagan would be elected, he wrote Sir Geoffrey Arthur during the 1980 campaign; the country's only hope was that the Republican candidate would prove to be "so shallow and uninformed that he very likely will be unable to conceal this during the course of the election and will be too much, even for the American electorate to accept."[36] Proven wrong, he remarked disgustedly in an interview with Walter Pincus that Reagan's Hollywood experience would lead him to a simple foreign policy formula: "'We're real good people and the Russians are bad and we must stand up and show we're tough.'"[37]

The Reagan presidency, accompanied as it was by the materialism and corruption of the 1980s, only served to sharpen Fulbright's contempt for popular culture and contemporary politics. His speeches once again focused on the pernicious influence of the military–industrial complex, the machinations of the CIA, and the corruption of American capitalism. The country was too "young and inexperienced" to govern itself, much less lead the international community. "Just because we've got a good piece of real estate and got rich quick," he told a Houston audience, "it doesn't mean we're wise."[38] America mistook an abundance of natural resources and subsequent wealth for wisdom.[39] By the latter part of the decade, Fulbright's set-pieces struck detached observers as a virtual parody of New Left textbooks, throwbacks to the 1970s. So disillusioned was the Arkansan that he took to advocating openly replacement of the reigning presidential system with a parliamentary arrangement. "I have come to the conclusion that our political system has out-lived its usefulness," he wrote Professor Alan Henrikson. "[W]e should have elections of members of Congress for five or six years, subject to votes of confidence, recreate effective parties, and allow the Congress to designate the Prime Minister and a ceremonial Head of State for a prescribed period."[40] This proposal became standard fare in speeches and interviews until Lee Williams, Fulbright's constant companion after 1980, observed to him diplomatically that Americans were rather attached to their Constitution.

In 1982 the University of Arkansas honored Fulbright by naming the College of Arts and Sciences for him. The Stephens family donated $1 million to

35 He also faulted Brzezinski's decision to play what he called the "China card." JWF to Perrin Jones, Feb. 11, 1980, Box 6, Folder 5, PsPF.
36 JWF to Arthur, June 10, 1980, Box 5, Folder 1, PsPF.
37 Kaiser and Pincus, "America Is Run by Amateurs."
38 Laurie Johnston, ed., "Notes on People," *New York Times,* Sept. 30, 1976.
39 Kaiser and Pincus, "America Is Run by Amateurs."
40 JWF to Henrikson, June 23, 1980, Box 6, Folder 5, PsPF.

the college as the first gift in a projected $30 million endowment fund. He and Betty were wined and dined in Fayetteville during a week of celebration in a massive ceremonial tribute. John Kenneth Galbraith delivered the principal address.[41] Although she was able to walk only haltingly and with the aid of a cane, Betty Fulbright seemed to enjoy the festivities immensely. The Footes and Winnackers attended, as did many former staffers. The outpouring of support finally broke down some of the resentment Betty had harbored toward the state since its rejection of her husband some eight years earlier.

The dedication was to be Betty Fulbright's last public hurrah. She remained bedridden for much of the last three years of her life and died in early October 1985 at the age of seventy-nine.[42] Following cremation, memorial services were held in Washington and Fayetteville. Not surprisingly, Betty's illness and death affected Fulbright profoundly. She had been his best friend and companion for fifty years – a devoted supporter, lively conversationalist, an independent voice. Friends and staffers remarked that he seemed lost and confused without Betty, increasingly afraid to travel, and incredibly negative.

Although he sharply curtailed his interviews and speeches after 1985 – he turned eighty that year – Fulbright was an unstinting opponent of Reagan's foreign policies. He denounced the massive arms buildup presided over by Secretary of Defense Caspar Weinberger as mindless catering to the military–industrial complex and anticommunist ideologues. Arkansas's elder statesman called upon NATO to reject the MX missile, and applauded Europe for defying the Reagan administration over the Soviet gas pipeline. The insurgency in El Salvador was indigenous – whether Marxist or not – and the United States ought to stop intervening there and in Nicaragua, he told interviewers.[43] To those of the administration's defenders who claimed that it was shrewdly trying to spend Soviet communism into oblivion, he replied that such an approach would only "result in a war or the impoverishment of both countries."[44] Appalled by Star Wars, Fulbright remarked to a reporter that the Strategic Defense Initiative (SDI) could only be the result of the president's overexposure to science fiction movies. In part the Arkansan's pessimism was due to age and to declining health – something he recognized. "All old men think things are worse than they were before," he observed laughingly to one interviewer.[45] There was another very good reason, however. From the early days of the Reagan administration, certain NSC staffers and the De-

41 Peggy Treiber, "Fulbright Lauded at Dinner as State's 'Greatest Man,'" *Arkansas Gazette,* July 10, 1982.

42 "Mrs. J. William Fulbright, 79, Dies; Was 'Good Campaigner' for Senator," *Arkansas Gazette,* Oct. 5, 1985.

43 "Fulbright Endorses Europe's Pipeline Defiance," *Times (London),* Oct. 7, 1982, and Hugh B. Patterson, Jr., "Fulbright in Little Rock," *Arkansas Gazette,* June 29, 1983.

44 E. Michael Myers, "Still in Dissent at 80," *Arkansas Gazette,* Mar. 17, 1985.

45 "Fulbright Little Changed Since Days as Senator," *New York Times,* June 9, 1985.

fense Department began portraying a nuclear conflict not as an unthinkable holocaust but as a winnable war. The United States, it seemed, could emerge victorious after suffering a mere twenty million deaths. Fulbright took such statements literally, and they frightened him.[46] With increasing despair but with occasional flashes of the old passion, he hammered away at the need for Americans and Russians to view each other as human beings and not as pawns on an ideological chess board.

The awards continued to pour in despite Fulbright's naysaying. In November 1986 alumni and friends gathered in Washington to celebrate the exchange program's fortieth anniversary and pay homage to its founder. Britain, Japan, and Germany held gala celebrations to commemorate the anniversary of their bilateral program and to honor Fulbright.[47] By 1986 a hundred and fifty-six thousand people had received scholarships and fellowships; many of them had become prime ministers, Members of Parliament, business leaders, journalists, and academics in Asian, European, and Latin American nations.[48] By the end of the decade the former chairman of the SFRC had been awarded fifty honorary degrees and turned down at least that many more.

The phenomenon that more than any other had dominated Fulbright's public life had been the cold war. For a generation he had both waged that war and bemoaned the distortions it was creating in America's domestic life and foreign policies. What he had envisioned was a peaceful economic, cultural, and political competition between communism and capitalism, with the ultimate triumph of capitalism – modernized and humanized – and democracy over communism and totalitarianism. Beginning in 1985 it seemed that his dream might be coming true.

Upon Konstantin Chernenko's death in March 1985, Mikhail Gorbachev became General Secretary of the Communist Party of the Soviet Union. Gorbachev represented a new generation of Soviet leaders – educated, nonideological technocrats who had shed the paranoia of Stalin's generation. In his mid-fifties, charismatic, cosmopolitan, Gorbachev was, like Peter the Great, fascinated by rather than fearful of Western technology and culture. He was determined to save socialism, the CPSU, and the Soviet Union by modernizing them. He understood that his country had fallen behind the United States, Japan, West Germany, and even some developing countries in technological innovation and economic output. The only way to reverse his country's dramatic and inevitable decline, Gorbachev reasoned, was through policies of

46 J. William Fulbright, "Fulbright on Peace and the Arms Race," *Arkansas Gazette*, Aug. 16, 1981; originally written for the *Miami Herald*.

47 Carol Matlack, "Tribute Paid Fulbright for Founding Program," *Arkansas Gazette*, Nov. 20, 1986, and "Fulbright Urges Expanding World Vision," *Arkansas Gazette*, Nov. 30, 1986.

48 "Fulbright Exchanges Enhance Our National Security," *Chronicle of Higher Education*, 33 (Dec. 10, 1986), 104.

*perestroika* (social and economic reform) and *glasnost'* (democracy and openness to the international community).

To create an opening to the West, Gorbachev took a number of unilateral steps. He stopped his country's nuclear testing program, halted the deployment of intermediate-range missiles in Eastern Europe, and called for on-site inspection to enforce future arms control agreements. In addition, Gorbachev concluded agreements with Japan and West Germany for the exchange of nonnuclear technology, and he replaced his hard-line foreign minister, Andrei Gromyko, with the pragmatic, sophisticated Edward Shevardnadze. During the summer of 1985 the new Soviet leader departed for a whirlwind tour of Europe, Latin America, and the United States.

Throughout his first five years in office Ronald Reagan had steadfastly refused to meet face to face with a Soviet chief of state. Perhaps because he sensed in Gorbachev the dawning of a new era – or perhaps because his wife Nancy's astrologer advised that the time was right – the president agreed to a summit in Geneva in November 1985. The meeting was only partially successful; but a year later, with very little prior publicity, Reagan and Gorbachev met in Reykjavik, Iceland. Both men discussed sweeping cuts in their nation's nuclear arsenals, and although once again their talks were inconclusive, the two leaders departed on a friendly note. The path to disarmament was still open. As the Gorbachev–Reagan relationship ripened, individuals on both sides of the iron curtain began tentatively to anticipate an end to the cold war.

The two leaders met again in Washington in 1987 and this time signed the first concrete arms reduction pact since the still-unratified SALT II. By this point Gorbachev had decided that SDI was probably both scientifically and politically unfeasible. He dropped his demand that Washington abandon the project, clearing the way for his and Reagan's signing of the Intermediate-Range Nuclear Forces (INF) Treaty, which called for the elimination of all intermediate range missiles in Europe and contained provisions for on-site inspection. The USSR and United States still controlled thirty thousand nuclear warheads aimed at each other, but the INF treaty was an important, concrete first step toward arms control.

In 1988 the Soviet Union pulled its troops out of Afghanistan and supported efforts to end civil wars in Africa and Southeast Asia. In June Reagan traveled to the heart of his "evil empire." In Moscow, in front of Lenin's Tomb, he embraced his friend, Mikhail. "They've changed," the U.S. president announced to reporters. Nancy Reagan's dream that her husband be remembered most for arms control and détente with the Soviet Union was well on its way to realization.

Not surprisingly, Fulbright was delighted with Gorbachev, *perestroika, glasnost'*, and Ronald Reagan's absolutely astounding turnabout. The eighty-two-year-old Arkansan hailed the 1987 summit as a sea change, the symbol of the dawning of a new era. Warhead numbers were irrelevant; the long-sought-after dialogue had at last begun. No more name calling; no more myths; no more Red Scares.[49] Suddenly, Fulbright's negativism began to evaporate; he accepted interviews again, overwhelming journalists as usual with blunt advice for the administration. The dismantling of the Berlin Wall and Soviet withdrawal from Eastern Europe were humiliating concessions by the new Soviet leadership that put it at great risk with communist hard-liners and nationalists, Fulbright observed. The Reagan administration must make immediate and massive cuts in its military budget – from $100 billion to $300 billion for starters – in order to disarm the hard-liners within the Kremlin.[50]

In the spring of 1989 Fulbright and Seth Tillman published *The Price of Empire,* an update of the world according to Fulbright. It was a paean to Gorbachev, who, by introducing elements of democracy and capitalism in the Soviet Union, had allegedly undercut ideologues and the military–industrial complex both in his country and the United States. The United States must refrain from gloating, the two longtime collaborators wrote, and concentrate on perfecting American democracy. Only after the United States had eliminated the last vestiges of racism, sexism, and poverty from its own society could it declare victory in the cold war. Above all, the United States must initiate a massive military build-down in order to protect both Gorbachev and Reagan's right flanks.[51] What Fulbright and Tillman did not recognize was that Gorbachev had set in motion events that he could not control – that the Soviet people, at least in the short run, would settle for nothing less than the breakup of the empire that Lenin and Stalin had so carefully and brutally crafted and the sweeping away of the old communist order within the Soviet Union. Nor did they anticipate the difficulty that future American leaders would have in building consensus for any foreign policy initiative given the absence of an overarching enemy.

The same year that Gorbachev and Reagan held their historic summit meetings, Fulbright began a casual relationship with Harriet Mayor, the fifty-three-year-old executive director of the Fulbright Alumni Association. Mayor, a divorced grandmother, had grown up on the East Coast and traveled extensively in Korea, Germany, France, and the Soviet Union. Her father had been in charge of overseas bureaus for *Time,* and her first husband, William Watts, was a career Foreign Service officer.[52] The friendship remained routine until

49 Maria Henson, "Fulbright Says Summit Shows New Attitude but Won't Tilt Power Balance," *Arkansas Gazette,* Dec. 6, 1987.

50 R. W. Apple, Jr., "Fulbright Out of Politics but Not Out of Opinions," *New York Times,* Feb. 13, 1989.

51 "Our New Opportunity to Beat Swords into Plowshares," *Chicago Tribune,* Apr. 19, 1989.

52 Jeffrey Stinson, "Fulbright Weds Association Head in Secret Today," *Arkansas Gazette,* Mar. 10, 1990.

Harriet, while bicycling in Washington in 1989, was struck and seriously injured by a milk truck. Fulbright visited her in the hospital with increasing frequency. A year later they were married in a small family wedding at Belmont Road. Fulbright was ecstatic. "I was afraid she wouldn't accept because I'm old and she's young," he remarked. "I like her company, if you know what I mean," he told reporters with a twinkle in his eye.[53]

To complete the amazing rebirth Fulbright experienced at the close of his eighth decade, William Jefferson Clinton, former mailroom boy and Fulbright protégé, was elected president in 1992. Fulbright was absolutely delighted. Actually, he had been quite pleased with George Bush, declaring him to be one of the most knowledgeable men ever to be in charge of American foreign policy;[54] but Clinton was an Arkansan, a Rhodes scholar, an educated, pragmatic, interested man who had opposed the war in Vietnam. The election of his protégé seemed a redemption to Fulbright, a repudiation of the true believers, a fitting response to those who had heaped aspersions on Arkansas through the years, a last laugh on Lyndon Johnson.[55] Although rumors concerning Fulbright's intervention in his behalf to keep him out of the draft had caused Clinton difficulty during the presidential campaign, the president took pains to acknowledge his debt to Fulbright and to embrace him publicly. In May 1993 at a gala ceremony in Washington, Clinton presented an overwhelmed Fulbright with the Medal of Freedom.[56] That summer Fulbright's amazing body finally failed him. The splendid physical and mental athlete suffered a massive stroke that left him wheelchair bound and both his speech and memory severely impaired. He died in his sleep at one o'clock in the morning on February 9, 1995. President Clinton delivered the eulogy at a moving ceremony in Washington's National Cathedral. That the ceremony ended with Aaron Copland's "Fanfare for the Common Man" was both fitting and ironic.

53 "Fulbright Plans Wedding," *Arkansas Gazette,* Feb. 23, 1989.

54 Jeffrey Stinson, "Fulbright Urges Restraint, Working within Guidelines," *Arkansas Gazette,* Jan. 18, 1991, and Keith Inman, "Fulbright Says Iraq Embargo Would Have Worked in Time," *Arkansas Gazette,* May 26, 1991.

55 George D. Moffett III, "The Other 'Bill' from Arkansas," *Christian Science Monitor,* Nov. 27, 1992.

56 Phil McCombs, "An 88-Candle Salute to Senator Fulbright," *Washington Post,* May 6, 1993.

# 40

# *Conclusion*

In their retirement years Bill and Betty Fulbright had become close friends with Monroe and Mary Donsker. The senator had met Donsker, who was chairman of the Board of Foreign Scholarships, when the two couples found themselves thrown together in Copenhagen for a Fulbright commission function. After walking out of a performance of an obscure opera, the four had explored the beautiful city for hours in the half light of the Scandinavian evening. Donsker, a physicist and child math prodigy, had a marvelous sense of humor and a fondness for teasing that appealed to Fulbright. Indeed, so close did they become that when Fulbright remarried some years after Betty's death, he took his friends along on his honeymoon in the Cotswolds.

A frequent topic of conversation between Donsker and Fulbright, as they consumed martinis at the former's New Hampshire home or at Belmont Road, was the lamentable difference between the natural and social sciences. In the mathematical sciences, both agreed, each generation learns with great exactitude what previous generations had discovered. Blessed with a marvelous system of notation, scientists were able to transmit knowledge through the ages completely and precisely, and as a result, to build on that knowledge with efficiency. There was in the process a minimum of waste and repetition. Would it were so for the social sciences, Fulbright often remarked. In politics and statecraft no one seemed to want to remember; they preferred instead to repeat the mistakes of the past and to give way to their passions and prejudices. If only political man could be as rational and efficient in his work as scientific man was in his, then the political world could achieve the same progressive trajectory as the natural.

For a time, Fulbright believed that the central problem in American foreign policy was a persistent irrationality, a natural tendency for a man whose public life was essentially a quest for rationality. He understood that no human being was capable of a pure state of sustained, undefiled reason, and he did not believe in the existence of a set of cosmic first principles that would produce the perfect society. Rather, Fulbright's rationality was that of a pragmatist. Like John Dewey and William James, Fulbright believed that if human beings were not innately enlightened, they were susceptible of being made so through education. They were capable of perceiving their self-interest and acting on it. He rejected the notion of absolutes, that the universe was run by natural, immutable laws and that all humanity had to do was discern them. What was true or good was what worked for a particular person at a particular time. Truth was not something absolute or final, but evolutionary and changing. Nothing should be taken on faith; the rational person or community must test every idea, construct, institution, and process to see whether it produced the greatest good for the greatest number. It was this rejection of rules and absolutes, this emphasis on questioning and testing, that no doubt made Fulbright so repugnant to the radical right. It also made his dramatic philosophical flip-flops somewhat more comprehensible.

If Fulbright had believed anything as a young man, he had believed in progress and the notion that an educated, rational person could make a difference in the quality of life in whatever sphere he or she chose to act. Given the time in which he lived and his family circumstances, that faith in progress and commitment to public service was not surprising. Bill Fulbright was the dutiful child of two people who had epitomized their age. Jay Fulbright had been a progressive-era businessman, hardheaded, pragmatic, efficient, and systematic, a man who was convinced that the communal good consisted of the collective achievements of its individual members. Roberta had shared his faith in rationality, order, and progress. After inheriting his business empire and, with some difficulty, defending it, she had ventured boldly into the public sphere, combating those bêtes noires of progressivism: corruption, bossism, and venality. She had followed national affairs with intense interest and spent hours debating various issues – the efficacy of scientific management, the proper role of government in a capitalist economy, the applicability of evolutionary concepts to social institutions – with her friends in the philosophy and economics departments in Fayetteville. Like so many other progressives, Roberta had believed intensely that society could be improved by an educated, enlightened elite working through the established democratic process. She had determined to be such a person, but quickly learned that the constraints of gender and situation limited her as an agent of change. As ambitious, activist, but thwarted parents have done throughout the ages, Roberta had looked to her children for ultimate fulfillment. If any in her family were to make a contribution to the public good, it would be Bill. The girls faced too many social obstacles, and Jack was an alarming mixture of passion and ignorance. Thus, first Jay and then Roberta had begun to teach Bill, to mold him and shape him into an agent of progress.

As Roberta had remarked on the eve of her trip to England to witness Bill's graduation, Oxford had always been for her a kind of Mecca. There her son would learn how the world operated and learn how to live like those who operated it. Despite its many distractions, the Oxford experience had advanced her agenda. Amid the dinner parties, theater trips, and outings to Paris, Bill had absorbed the tenets of nineteenth-century English liberalism, but done so under his young tutor, Robert McCallum, in a thoroughly modern way. Free trade, parliamentary democracy, republicanism were the forms within which progress could work itself out. For Western man in the first half of the twentieth century these were the processes and institutions that were most efficacious. Wilsonian internationalism, Fulbright had learned from McCallum, was just the logical extension of a system that combined freedom with responsibility. From his progressive parents and from his teachers and colleagues at Oxford, George Washington, and the University of Arkansas, Fulbright had acquired the belief that human beings would always act rationally if they just had enough information, if it were explained to them where their interests lay.

So it was that upon his election to Congress, he championed the internationalist cause and helped give birth to a new collective security organization. In economics he advocated multilateralism abroad and, when it did not encroach on the vested interests of his state, a mixed economy at home. During the 1960s, the junior senator from Arkansas would be converted to the notion that inequality was the product of socioeconomic disadvantages and that government had a responsibility to create conditions in which learning and achievement could take place. Thus did he come to support the War on Poverty; but he never endorsed the notion of equality of condition, and he remained wedded to the free-enterprise system. At the core of his ideal America was a meritocracy based on education and equality of opportunity. True to his emotional and intellectual roots, he created an academic exchange program intended to break down the barriers of ignorance, nationalism, and xenophobia. Out of this experience, he was convinced, would come educators and political figures determined to forge a world in which individuals, corporations, and nations could live out lives of enlightened self-interest.

The Fulbright philosophy was not particularly suited to coping with the problem of evil. Monroe Donsker remembered that in addition to the social and natural sciences, his and Fulbright's conversation occasionally touched the topic of religion. Fulbright seemed to believe in some sort of Supreme Being, and it was difficult for him to accept the notion that one day he would simply cease to exist. Nevertheless, Donsker recalled, Fulbright appeared not to have thought very much about the subject; indeed, according to the physicist, his friend's views on religion were at best "primitive." Ignorance, misjudgment, circumstance, and greed he could understand; calculated destructiveness and fanaticism he could not. Gratuitous violence and ideological fanaticism and their antidote, uncompensated self-sacrifice, were phenomena foreign to his nature. Guilt, salvation, and redemption were concepts with which he wanted nothing to do. Most of the world's tragedies, he believed, had been brought about by people claiming either to hear the voice of God or to have His ear, or both.

Inevitably, of course, Fulbright was forced to confront the "true believers," as he referred to rabid anticommunists, white supremacists, and religious zealots of various sorts. Thus did he do battle with McCarthyites, ultras, and extreme Zionists (products of Nazi fanaticism, they had become fanatics themselves); but members of the John Birch Society, the White Citizens Councils, and various fundamentalist groups lived in a world that baffled and repelled him. He was appalled by the church bombing in Birmingham in 1963, by the Kennedy assassination, and by the My Lai massacre, but he really did not know what to make of them. Wanton killing, racial violence, and ideological and religious zealotry were to him beyond the pale. His search for the roots of war and violence led him to gather a group of distinguished social scientists and psychologists, men and women who convinced him that man's inhumanity to man was attributable to a lack of socialization, to status envy, to genetically programmed aggression. These hearings were eminently satisfying to Fulbright because their implication was that aberrant behavior was correctable. Like the good progressive that he was, he believed that evil could be defined and controlled.

Fulbright's faith in progress and belief in the efficacy of social engineering created moral blind spots. Due to a combination of ignorance and political expediency, he attempted to sidestep one of the great issues of his day: the struggle of African Americans for equality and acceptance. Shocked though he was by the vituperation of the racist crowds in Little Rock and the killing of the four young girls in Birmingham, he insisted on seeing the problem as one of ignorance – on the part of both blacks and whites. For him racism and discrimination were irrational and counterproductive; because the vast majority of Americans were reasonable, these problems were correctable over time. Because he failed to give hatred and evil their due, he also proved incapable of recognizing the power of selflessness and self-sacrifice. Thus did he fail to apprehend the power of the second Reconstruction and the appeal of men like Martin Luther King. He was astounded at the effectiveness of nonviolent civil disobedience. The positions taken by the Israeli government and its American Zionist allies similarly mystified him. Why did they not trust the Palestinians and Arabs? Why they were not willing to accept a U.S.–U.N. guarantee of Israel's pre-1967 boundaries made no sense to him. He acknowledged that memories of the Holocaust contributed to Jewish insecurity, but he underestimated the impact that Hitler's calculated, systematic effort at mass extermination had on its survivors. For five years, Fulbright reviewed and critiqued every aspect of the Vietnam War in an effort to turn his countrymen against involvement. He then totally missed the significance of My Lai and its importance in eroding what was left of the Vietnam consensus.

If no moralist, J. William Fulbright was at times an idealist, as his dissent from the war and his attacks on American imperialism indicated. He certainly was of the opinion that the United States ought to act pragmatically to safeguard its economic and strategic well-being; but he also believed that America comprised above all a set of values and principles. If those values and principles were systematically violated, the nation itself would cease to exist. As a classicist and an Anglophile, Fulbright was devoted to republicanism. Representative democracy, individual liberty, free trade, and national as well as individual self-determination marked the political fulfillment of the West. These processes and theories had been tested by a particular culture in a specific time, and they worked; until and unless they were discredited, they must be preserved.

At the close of World War II and the dawn of the cold war, Fulbright perceived the central problem of U.S. foreign policy to be how to preserve Anglo–American civilization from destruction. Appalled by the bombing of Hiroshima and Nagasaki, he decided that the world was far too dangerous a place for the members of the Atlantic community simply to go their own way. As part of a universal effort to control the forces of nationalism and fascism, the Western democracies would have to surrender a portion of their national sovereignty within the context of an international collective security organization. Only in this way could aggression be nipped in the bud and eventually the socioeconomic roots of war be eliminated. Subsequently confronted with the reality that neither his country nor its wartime allies were willing to relinquish their freedom of action in a regional association of nations, much less an international one, Fulbright resigned himself to working toward the rehabilitation of Western Europe and the containment of Soviet and Chinese communism. Thus did he support not only the Marshall Plan – which, according to John Gaddis, represented the most perfect conflation of American ideals and self-interest in the postwar era – but military aid to Greece and Turkey, foreign aid in general, and limited intervention into foreign societies threatened by communism. He did not, however, buy into the globalist assumptions inherent in the Truman Doctrine, agreeing with George Kennan that America's response ought to be commensurate with the actual threat to its interests.

During the Eisenhower years Fulbright sensed a rigidity and moral absolutism in American policy that hindered America's drive for competitive coexistence with the Soviet Union; yet it was not so much rigid anticommunism for which the Arkansan attacked Dulles and Eisenhower, but their unimaginative and inflexible approach to combating America's enemies. Their emphasis on military aid and alliances, he charged, allowed the Soviet Union under Khrushchev to identify itself with anticolonialism and through pragmatic aid programs and support of indigenous nationalist movements to win the battle for the developing world.

Frightened by the resurgence of the radical right that began with the establishment of the John Birch Society in 1959, and mightily impressed by Nikita Khrushchev's conciliatory visit to the United States that same year, Fulbright moved beyond competitive coexistence and embraced the concept of détente. He was well pleased with the Kennedy administration's flexible response to the communist threat and, following the Berlin and Cuban missile crises, with its willingness to make a fresh start with the Soviet Union. Indeed, he greeted the signing of the nuclear test-ban treaty as nothing less than the dawning of a new age. Though he continued to be troubled by the structure of foreign aid and the vast sums spent on the military–industrial complex by Robert McNamara, the new chairman of the SFRC had every reason to believe that Kennedy's flexibility and the search for détente would continue under Lyndon Johnson. The "old myths and new realities" speech was designed to point the nation and the administration further down that road.

With the burgeoning of the military–industrial complex, the penetration of the military by the radical right, far-reaching covert operations by the CIA, and the onset of the Vietnam War, however, Fulbright decided that the United States was acting in ways that were counterproductive to its strategic and economic interests. The factors that underlay Fulbright's opposition to the war were indeed manifold. Some have argued that the Arkansan acted out of personal pique, miffed at President Johnson's decision not to make him secretary of state; but there was more to the Arkansan's dissent than resentment over thwarted ambition. At various times he blamed the war on the radical right and its hysterical fear of communism, on the burgeoning military–industrial complex, and on Lyndon Johnson's Texas heritage and Alamo mentality. In the end, however, Fulbright came to believe that the very liberal internationalist philosophy that he had espoused from 1944 through 1964 was equally culpable. In his view, the union of New Deal liberalism with militant anticommunism had spawned a foreign policy that was at the same time both altruistic and imperialist. Like Chester Bowles, Arthur Schlesinger, Jr., and John Kenneth Galbraith, Fulbright had accepted the need after World War II to embrace anticommunism and link it with a higher ideal. That heritage made his critique of contemporary American foreign policy all the more devastating. He was among the first cold-war activists to see that in harnessing their obsession with social justice to anticommunism, liberals had turned the cold war into a missionary crusade that blinded the nation to the political and cultural realities of Southeast Asia. It also made possible an unholy alliance between realpolitikers preoccupied with markets and bases, and emotionally committed to the domino theory, and idealists who wanted to spread the blessings of freedom, democracy, and a mixed economy to the less fortunate of the world.

By the summer of 1969 Fulbright concluded that, like Lyndon Johnson, Richard Nixon had become a prisoner of the radical right, the military–industrial complex, his own psyche, and other forces of which he was only dimly aware and could not control even if he wanted to. The country was frightened and exhausted, afraid to lose in Vietnam, but increasingly convinced that it could not win. The liberal internationalism of the Kennedy–Johnson years was dead, thoroughly discredited by events in Southeast Asia. The void in American foreign policy was being filled by the true believers, vested interests, and political opportunists who had a stake in the continuation of the war in Vietnam, the perpetuation of the cold war, and the maintenance and expansion of the network of bases and commitments that it had spawned. If Congress did not act, the nation would be dragged into one foreign adventure after another until, morally and financially bankrupt, it would disappear from the face of the earth like other empires before it.

With the activism of the Kennedy–Johnson years in disrepute, Fulbright reasoned, the best bet for checking the right-wing radicalism spawned by the cold war, and extricating America from Vietnam, was traditional conservatism. From the summer of 1969 until the Arkansan's departure from the Senate in 1975, the Constitution served as the principal rallying point in his campaign to end the war and contain the burgeoning American empire. Only that hallowed document, he perceived, offered sufficient political protection for those who were sure to be accused of endangering America's national security. Carefully, meticulously, Fulbright and his chief of staff, Carl Marcy, built support for the notion that first the Johnson and then the Nixon administrations were making international commitments and involving the country in future wars without its permission or even its knowledge, and in so doing were violating the basic law of the land. The movement that began with passage in 1969 of Fulbright's national commitments resolution was transformed into a relentless juggernaut by Cambodia, Kent State, and Watergate.

Fulbright's participation in the crusade against civil rights during the postwar period enabled him to communicate with disgruntled hawks when other members of the antiwar movement could not. In fact, the White House was not entirely wrong in believing that Fulbright's critique of liberal internationalism stemmed from his conservative, southern roots. As a southerner and a segregationist, not to mention the founder of the international exchange program that bore his name, Fulbright was especially jealous of the sanctity of indigenous cultures. Like so many other leaders of the New South, he never forgot that Arkansas and the entire region were onetime economic colonies of the North. Both his views on the South as an economic appendage of the North and his resentment at what he believed to be that region's efforts to impose its racial views on Dixie instilled in him an intense commitment to the principle of cultural and political self-determination. As an individual with a strong sense of class, kinship, and place, he believed it no less abhorrent that the United States should force its culture, political institutions, and economic theories on Vietnam than that the North should impose its mores on the South. In the end Fulbright's insights into the causes of the war, as well as his effectiveness as one of its opponents, stemmed in no small part from his experiences as a crusader in behalf of two apparently contradictory causes: internationalism and segregation.

It is difficult to categorize and label the Arkansan's foreign affairs philosophy. Fulbright, Seth Tillman, and Carl Marcy vehemently rejected the term "neoisolationist," a label that the Nixon administration sought to apply to them. They pointed out that the chairman of the SFRC remained a strong supporter of the United Nations, multilateral aid, and a multinational peace corps. He was against not international cooperation, but American unilateralism, they insisted. Fulbright readily admitted that he had repudiated liberal internationalism and the globalist foreign policy to which it had led; but like Gerald P. Nye, the famous isolationist of the Roosevelt era with whom he struck up a brief correspondence in 1969, he preferred the term "noninterventionist."

Above all, Fulbright considered himself a realist, and he perceived that the great goal of his labors was to restore American foreign policy to a rational basis. A self-proclaimed disciple of University of Chicago political scientist Hans Morgenthau, Fulbright in *The Price of Empire* and *The Arrogance of Power* advocated an Asian policy that resembled that espoused by Herbert Hoover in 1950 or even Alfred Thayer Mahan in 1895. The executive, he wrote, should abandon its efforts to "extend unilaterally its power in such a way as to promote its conception of 'world peace' generally, or the defense of 'free people' and seek to maintain such base facilities there as will protect the sea and air routes of the area from domination by hostile forces." Morgenthau and other realists thought him dangerously naïve concerning the threat posed by the Soviet Union and Communist China. Fulbright was convinced that the cold war was responsible for sustaining absolutism and paranoia in the Soviet Union rather than, as Henry Jackson and other cold warriors believed, that Russian imperialism was an inevitable by-product of communist totalitarianism.

Fulbright's stature as a prophet is debatable. From the very beginning of the cold war J. William Fulbright saw no reason why the Western democracies and the Soviet Union could not peacefully coexist. Like Mikhail Gorbachev, Fulbright never believed that communism and the Soviet empire would die a sudden death. Rather, he surmised that the Soviet Union would evolve economically and then perhaps politically. A new generation of leaders, untrammeled by history and ideology and anxious for popular support, would introduce a mixed economy, shift resources from military to nonmilitary production, and demythologize international relations. Perhaps the USSR and its satellites would never become multiparty democracies, but given the deep-seated nationalism, xenophobia, and political fragmentation of Eastern Europe, that might very well be for the best. He warned John F. Kennedy of the perils involved in the Bay of Pigs operation but subsequently recommended a course during the missile crisis that would surely have provoked nuclear war. On Vietnam, his opposition was largely an articulation of the views of disaffected scholars and diplomats; his contribution lay in his personal courage, his stature as a conservative, and his tactical skill. He made the Constitution and the issue of executive usurpation an umbrella under which hawks and doves, liberals and conservatives, idealists and cynics could gather.

There is no doubt that Fulbright transcended Arkansas and the U.S. Senate. In America, Western Europe, and Japan he came to epitomize the struggle of reason and restraint against excess. He was – as Cipriana Scelba, longtime head of the Italian Fulbright program, put it – what non-Americans wanted America to be. To their minds his sophistication, cosmopolitanism, and cultural humility stood in sharp contrast to the traits they associated with the bulk of Americans: parochialism, xenophobia, materialism, and cultural aggression. Most mistakenly wrote off his civil rights record to political expediency and focused instead on his foreign policy views. In the 1940s he endeared himself to Europeans by participating in the crusade to save them from Stalinism, in the 1950s by laboring to prevent a nuclear Armageddon, and in the 1960s and 1970s to save the world from America and America from itself. His attacks on colonialism, his advocacy of nonviolent change, and his paeans to neutrality won him plaudits in the developing world. All the while, the Fulbright program was endearing him to intelligentsia and cultural elites the world over.

Indeed, Fulbright was better known and respected abroad than in the United States. Part of the reason is that this man – a man who had so much to do with articulating the liberal–New Left critique of American foreign policy, who was as early as 1958 calling on his countrymen and -women to recognize the difference between Sino–Soviet imperialism and Marxism–Leninism as a socioeconomic principle – was a southerner, a segregationist, and an elitist. For a generation American academics, independent intellectuals, and social activists, the "New Class" of neoconservative nightmares, have viewed the anti–Vietnam War movement as exclusively their own. The anti-imperial onslaught against the military–industrial complex was, to their minds, their creation, an extension of the liberal tradition. Despite *The Arrogance of Power, The Price of Empire,* and *The Crippled Giant,* the nation's intelligentsia found it very difficult to give this quintessential conservative his due.

Whatever his errors and misperceptions, America was well served by J. William Fulbright, this rational man combating an irrational and immoral world. He was a voice, sometimes a lone voice, calling the nation to move ahead, to abandon old myths for new realities. His emotional and intellectual journey from cold-war activism to anti-imperialism comprised not so much a reflection as a counterpoint to some of the dominant trends in American foreign policy. When the isolationism of Taft and Hoover threatened America's efforts to save the world from the scourge of Stalinism, Fulbright denounced it. When in the name of anticommunism Lyndon Johnson and Richard Nixon intervened in Latin America and attempted to impose a Pax Americana on Asia, he invoked the neoisolationist theories he had once attacked. When Congress seemed dominated by nationalism and parochialism, he called for an activist presidency, one with maximum freedom to act in the international sphere. When he perceived the executive to have been taken over by militarists and imperialists, he campaigned for a restoration of congressional prerogatives. He insisted throughout his career that governmental agencies and departments not allow themselves to be used by vested interests, ideologues, and unscrupulous politicians to deceive and propagandize the American people. If Fulbright was not always right, he was generally beneficial to the Republic, a foreign affairs gyroscope dedicated to keeping the ship of state in trim.

# Index